FINANCIAL
MARKETS *and*
DEVELOPMENT

THE BROOKINGS INSTITUTION

THE WORLD BANK GROUP

This book is based on a conference entitled "Preventing Crises in Emerging Markets," held on March 26–27, 1999, in Palisades, New York. The conference was jointly sponsored by the World Bank Group and the Brookings Institution.

ALISON HARWOOD
ROBERT E. LITAN
MICHAEL POMERLEANO

Editors

FINANCIAL MARKETS *and* DEVELOPMENT

The Crisis in Emerging Markets

BROOKINGS INSTITUTION PRESS
Washington, D.C.

ABOUT BROOKINGS

The Brookings Institution is a private nonprofit organization devoted to research, education, and publication on important issues of domestic and foreign policy. Its principal purpose is to bring knowledge to bear on current and emerging policy problems. The Institution maintains a position of neutrality on issues of public policy. Interpretations or conclusions in Brookings publications should be understood to be solely those of the authors.

Copyright © 1999
THE BROOKINGS INSTITUTION
1775 Massachusetts Avenue, N.W., Washington, D.C. 20036
www.brookings.edu

Library of Congress Cataloging-in-Publication data

Financial markets and development : the crisis in emerging markets /
Alison Harwood, Robert E. Litan, and Michael Pomerleano, editors.
    p.   cm.
Based on a conference held on March 26–27, 1999, in Palisades, New York.
Includes bibliographical references and index.
    ISBN 0-8157-3497-2 (alk. paper)
    1. Financial crises—Asia—Congresses. 2. Capital market—Asia—Congresses.
3. Banks and banking—Asia—Congresses. 4. Financial crises—Developing
countries—Congresses. 5. Capital market—Developing countries—Congresses.
6. Banks and banking—Developing countries—Congresses.
I. Harwood, Alison. II. Litan, Robert E., 1950– III. Pomerleano, Michael.
IV. Title.
    HB3722 .F564 1999   99-006887
    332'.095—dc21   CIP

9 8 7 6 5 4 3 2 1

The paper used in this publication meets minimum requirements of the
American National Standard for Information Sciences—Permanence of Paper for
Printed Library Materials, ANSI Z39.48-1984.

Typeset in Adobe Garamond

Composition by R. Lynn Rivenbark
Macon, Georgia

Printed by Automated Graphic Systems
White Plains, Maryland

Contents

Foreword

THIS BOOK IS the product of a conference sponsored jointly by the World Bank and the Brookings Institution, with the participation of the International Monetary Fund, the Bank for International Settlements, and representatives from many investment and commercial banks.

The conference began by looking back at the causes of the Asian financial crisis—as well as at issues involving supervision, transparency, control, banking markets, and the capital markets themselves—and then moved to a discussion of how to avert such crises in the future.

Reflected in this volume is a rich agenda including broad treatment of the growth of the Asian markets, a look at how equity markets function in the region, a closer look at East Asian corporations, and corporate governance. The book then moves to supply-side issues: foreign investment in Asia, the future of emerging market investing, lessons learned from East Asia and Latin America, the role of the World Bank in this crisis, and, finally, a fascinating paper on prospects for the future.

The conference, and this book, was not designed to undertake a theoretical analysis of the crisis. Instead it offered a chance for practitioners, members of supervisory agencies, and persons from governments to come together to examine lessons learned and what we can do about it.

Many people contributed to the success of the conference and this volume, and we would like to acknowledge their support here, including all of the formal discussants and speakers at the conference shown in the following pages. Many others also participated as moderators or as informal discussants: Charles Adams, Walter Arnheim, Joyce Chang, Uri B. Dadush, Richard H. Frank, David Gill, Jack Glen, Luis Guisti, Guillermo Harteneck, Isaac Hunt Jr., Desmond Lachman, Kenneth G. Lay, Paulo Leme, Walter Molano, Claudia Morgenstern, John D. Rea, Walter Stern, Prasarn Trairatvorakul, Konstantinos Tsatsaronis, Philip Turner, Antoine W. van Agtmael, Douglas Alan Webb.

In addition, Charlene Mui at Brookings, Margaret Enis at the World Bank, and Perlita Peret at the International Finance Corporation provided valuable assistance throughout the planning and organizing of the conference. We also acknowledge the editorial and proofreading assistance of Elizabeth Forsyth and Carlotta Ribar.

Funding for the conference was generously supplied by the World Bank Group.

JAMES D. WOLFENSOHN
President, World Bank

MICHAEL H. ARMACOST
President, Brookings Institution

FINANCIAL
MARKETS *and*
DEVELOPMENT

ALISON HARWOOD
ROBERT E. LITAN
MICHAEL POMERLEANO

1

Introduction

FOR MANY INVESTORS, the 1990s has been the decade of the "emerging market" in both a positive and a negative sense. The good news is that this is the decade that set records for capital inflows into developing countries and transition economies, since dubbed the emerging markets. The bad news, of course, is that emerging markets were rocked twice with crisis, first following the devaluation of the Mexican peso in 1994–95 and then in 1997–98 following a series of financial crises in Southeast Asia and Russia. Only now, as this volume is appearing in the fall of 1999, does it look as though the countries most adversely affected by the latest crises are finally recovering from what, for most of them, has been the most significant economic downturn in the postwar era.

Emerging markets are important not only because their precipitous downfall sent a shudder through the economies of the rest of the world but also because they have most of the world's population and, over the next several decades, should account for most of the world's growth in economic output. As this occurs, financial flows and institutions within those markets, and between those markets and markets in the rest of the world, inevitably will become more important.

The time is ripe, therefore, for systematically and consistently monitoring the continued development of finance in emerging markets. Toward that end, the World Bank and the Brookings Institution have collaborated in producing this volume, which may become the first of an annual series on emerging market finance designed to be of interest to investors, analysts, and policymakers throughout the world.[1]

The papers in this volume were originally presented at a conference in Palisades, New York, before an audience consisting of representatives from all of these constituencies. The conference occurred only six months after the market instability in the fall of 1998, following the Russian default and devaluation, which in turn followed on the heels of the currency and economic crises in Asia during 1997 and 1998. It should not be surprising, therefore, that this initial conference and the papers in this volume concentrate so heavily on aspects of these crises.

We are acutely aware that much already has been written on this subject. But we believe that this conference and the papers presented at it were unique in focusing on the characteristics of the *financial and corporate systems* that arguably contributed to the severity of the crisis in each of the affected countries. Accordingly, virtually all of the chapters that follow deal with these subjects. To provide a broad perspective, the volume begins (following this introduction) in chapter 2 with an overview of the Asian crises provided by one of the world's leading international economists, Richard Cooper.

As Cooper explains, although the details differed from country to country—and those details matter—the common element among all of them was the rapid outflow of funds akin to a deposit run on a bank. The outflows triggered collapses in the values of each currency on world markets and, in turn, steep declines in real output in each of the affected countries. The crises were especially dramatic because each of the countries (with the exception of Russia) had been following sound macroeconomic policies by contemporary standards: government budgets were not unbalanced, while monetary policy was not generating disturbing rates of inflation.

So how could the series of crises have happened? To help answer this question, Cooper concentrates on the events in Thailand, where the sequence of events began, and uses the conditions in that country as a metaphor for explaining subsequent crises in other parts of the region. In brief, the problems in Thailand centered on excessive foreign currency bor-

---

1. Next year's volume is already being prepared, with papers to be presented at a conference in New York in the spring of 2000. In addition to the World Bank and the Brookings Institution, the International Monetary Fund will join as a cosponsor.

rowing by banks, which sought to arbitrage the low interest rates available on short-term foreign currency loans, using the funds to extend higher-interest loans in baht to domestic residents. All the while, Thailand was running a relatively large and growing current account deficit—the counterpart to the substantial capital flows into the country. Such a game can continue, Cooper points out, so long as foreigners continue to pour money into the country. When they stop—they need not actually withdraw their funds—sudden and sharp downward pressure is applied to the country's exchange rate.

In fact, investor sentiment about Thailand—not just among foreigners but within the domestic economy itself—began to change in 1996. Instead of recognizing that fact and allowing the exchange rate to decline, Thai leaders attempted to fight it by defending the currency: selling dollars as fast as investors offered baht in exchange.

We all know the end of the story. Eventually many of the borrowers whose debts depended on the stability of the baht, which events put seriously into question, rushed for the door, depleting the central bank's supply of foreign currency. The government had to obtain financing from the International Monetary Fund (IMF) to prevent a total collapse in trade. The financing came with conditions: not just tighter macroeconomic policies, but new, and some say more intrusive, requirements to change local banking supervision, abandon certain government projects, and change other domestic institutions that encouraged too much foreign currency borrowing in the first place.

Cooper describes how this sequence of events played out in other Asian countries. At the same time, he questions the simplistic view that the crises were "contagious." There is relatively little trade among the countries, and their firms do not generally compete with one another in foreign markets. If there was contagion, it was more likely to be financial in nature—as Morris Goldstein has described, when one currency dropped like a stone, it was a "wake up call" among investors that others could too.

But which investors? Cooper believes that domestic residents put more selling pressure on their currencies than did foreign investors. This is contrary to the view held among many observers in Asia, of course. More broadly, Cooper concludes that the Asian crises teach us that a healthy financial system is integral to the proper "fundamentals" of any modern economy. When finance goes wrong, so does the real economy. This is important because, Cooper argues, financial systems are intrinsically unstable. Savers often want liquidity, while borrowers want assured finance over long periods. Financial institutions and markets are supposed to bridge this gap in maturity preferences, but this process does not always occur smoothly. When it does not, financial crisis can be (and often is) the result.

What Went Wrong: A Financial View

A broad theme running through many of the chapters in this volume is that, if anything, the development of western economies has demonstrated that financial systems will not function properly unless they contain some basic elements of an appropriate market infrastructure. Banks must be supervised effectively to ensure that they do not take excessive risks and that they maintain the resources to pay back depositors. Markets will not allocate funds to worthy borrowers unless investors have accurate and timely information about them and use that information effectively. Corporations must follow appropriate rules of governance to ensure that managers, as agents for shareholders, act responsibly and do not waste resources. When these elements of a financial system are not in place, it is more than likely that eventually too much money will be sent to the wrong destinations and that economies will become vulnerable to a sudden collapse of confidence among firms and investors. That, of course, is exactly what happened in Southeast Asia and Russia. Each country that experienced a crisis of confidence had significant shortcomings in its banking and financial markets, as well as in its systems of corporate governance.

Three papers presented at the conference and contained as chapters in this volume focus in particular on flaws in the equity markets in the affected region. Campbell Harvey and Andrew Roper in chapter 3 provide a multifaceted quantitative assessment of capital markets in the region and report some surprising results.

Harvey and Roper document that Asian equity markets, in particular, grew rapidly in the 1990s. Total dollar market capitalization across the major Asian stock market exchanges in China, Indonesia, Korea, the Philippines, Malaysia, Taiwan (China), and Thailand increased more than threefold between 1990 and 1996, from roughly $300 billion to $1.1 trillion. Over the same period, total stock market capitalization of Latin America grew even faster, reaching $444 billion by 1996, more than five times its level in 1990.

The authors find that a significant proportion of the growth in market capitalization of Asian markets during the 1990s resulted from new capital mobilization (rather than growth in the value of existing equity). Unlike Latin America, where only about 100 initial public offerings (IPOs) found their way to the markets during the 1990–96 period, the number of IPOs in Southeast Asia jumped from roughly 1,600 to nearly 3,800. These new offerings totaled almost $120 billion in market value. Flows of this magnitude helped to sustain high investment rates throughout the region during the decade.

A considerable portion of the financing for Asian corporations came from international equity and debt markets. The latter proved far more important than the former. International equity placements totaled about $18 billion during the 1990–97 period, compared with more than $120 billion financed through international bond markets. Significantly, almost three-quarters of this amount, roughly $90 billion, was denominated in dollars.

Undoubtedly, the liberalization of Asian capital markets during the 1990s facilitated the flow of funds from international investors and contributed to the significant amount of new capital mobilization documented previously. The liberalization process was a gradual one, however.[2] Typically, governments would begin by relaxing restrictions on direct investment in specific industries, while raising the generic limits on foreign investment of all types. Still, until the various crises occurred, governments throughout East Asia maintained investment limits that were low enough to prevent foreign control of domestic industries. Asian governments especially were reluctant to relax foreign ownership limits in certain industries, notably finance and telecommunications.

The foreign investment limits undoubtedly helped to explain why Asian capital markets concentrated most of their funds among particular industries, indeed even more so than Latin American markets. As a result, equity returns on Asian exchanges tended to move together to a much greater

---

2. For example, Korea outlined a liberalization plan for financial markets as early as 1987. Initial foreign ownership limits were set at 10 percent of market capitalization, with a 3 percent limit for individual foreign investors. Between December 1991 and December 1997 the foreign ownership limit in Korea was raised on seven separate occasions; each time, it was ratcheted up by no more than 3 percent. Finally, in June 1998, Korean officials broke with the traditional policy of gradualism and increased foreign ownership levels from 26 to 55 percent. Under the new foreign investment limits, foreigners were permitted to own a controlling interest of domestic firms.

extent than would be expected in more diversified stock markets. More-over, although the returns varied across countries, they failed to exceed returns on less risky securities in more developed markets, while deteriorating well before the breakout of the crises in 1997–98.

One of the more disturbing findings reported in the paper by Harvey and Roper is that Asian corporate managers increasingly leveraged their companies despite their declining profitability. Why? The authors suggest that the managers "bet" their companies, hoping that added leverage could offset declining profit ratios. The bets, which were made by borrowing in foreign currency, assumed that exchange rates would remain stable. It turned out, of course, that these bets turned sour, aggravating each crisis as it hit. Harvey and Roper conclude that a real and significant failure in corporate governance throughout Asia permitted these bets to be made.

In chapter 4 Michael Pomerleano and Xin Zhang expand on and essentially confirm many of the findings of Harvey and Roper. The Pomerleano and Zhang study benchmarks the Asian economies against Latin American and industrial countries and explicitly links internal financial performance (reflected in corporate profitability) to the implied cost of capital. Among other things, the authors find that the real weighted average cost of capital, as well as nominal returns on investment, during the 1990s varied considerably across developing and developed countries, casting doubt on the view that capital markets are well integrated across national borders. More significant, their calculations, based on the best available data, reveal that the return on invested capital exceeded the opportunity cost of capital in only a few economies. This disturbing result suggests that there was much wasted investment in the region.[3]

The authors also examine the relationship between past and future stock prices in Asia, seeking to determine which types of stocks appealed most to investors. They find that in Asia so-called "glamour stocks" systematically outperformed value stocks (or those with low ratios of price to book value). Indeed, value stocks actually sold at a discount in Asia. Furthermore, with the exception of Korean stocks, market fundamentals—profitability, relative value, and ownership concentration—played virtually no role in the market during the Asian financial crises. Indeed, high levels of corporate leverage—widely considered a source of vulnerability in the crises—did not affect stock prices (again, excepting Republic of Korea).

---

3. The authors acknowledge that their results must be treated with caution, because many firms (especially financial firms that were highly leveraged) were not included in their database.

Pomerleano and Zhang conclude from their analytical work that emerging markets in Asia did not price risk adequately and thus did not exert effective financial discipline on corporations in the region. Why would Asian markets differ so markedly in this regard from those in western economies? The authors speculate that Asian markets lacked the high standards of transparency, including disclosure, research, and dissemination of relevant financial information, that are routinely found in the west. In the absence of transparency, speculation and volatility become much more dominant characteristics of markets. If this is right, then measures that bring Asian and other emerging markets up to western legal, regulatory, accounting, and information dissemination standards should help to insulate those markets in the future against a repeat of the 1997–98 crises.

Nonetheless, the authors also note that in several Latin American and Asian developing countries, the returns on invested capital are quite reasonable, although the cost of capital is surprisingly high in countries with high savings rates. They conclude that the cost of capital is high because of ineffective and costly intermediation of savings. One key challenge for developing countries in the future is to improve the process of financial intermediation so that investors and savers can be matched more efficiently and at lower cost.

Stijn Claessens, Simeon Djankov, and Larry H. P. Lang take yet another look at corporations in Asia in chapter 5, concentrating on the characteristics of ownership of Asian companies and their connections to the valuation of those firms. The authors find extensive family control of East Asian corporations. Ten families in Indonesia and the Philippines control more than *half* of the corporate sector. In Thailand, families control almost half of corporations, and in Hong Kong (China) and Korea, families control about one-third of corporations. This contrasts with Japan, where family control is insignificant.

Claessens, Djankov, and Lang argue that such heavy concentration of ownership strongly shaped the legal and regulatory institutions in East Asia—and not for the better, at least by western standards. Where families dominate, it is not surprising to find weak systems of corporate governance or close connections with banks and government sources of finance—the essence of what has been called "crony capitalism"—that many observers have asserted played an important role in contributing to the severity of the crises in the region.

In their empirical analysis, the authors find that family-controlled corporations are not valued as highly by the markets as firms where control is held more widely. Their analysis confirms earlier work, suggesting that large owners have a tendency to direct the gains earned by their corporations toward private uses rather than toward enhancing the future value of the corporation itself. This makes the protection of minority shareholders all the more important a subject of reform in Asian economies, a subject explored in depth by Kenneth Scott in chapter 10 and discussed in more detail below.

The Role of Foreign Investment

The Asian crisis has spawned many controversies. One of them is about the role played by foreign investment. Critics, many of them in the affected region, charge that foreign investors were too fickle, pouring too much money in too rapidly and then taking it out at an even faster pace. In our opening discussion, we briefly summarized Richard Cooper's views rejecting this simplistic view. But several of the chapters in the book, in part or in whole, explore the issue in greater depth.

Michael Barth and Xin Zhang concentrate their attention in chapter 6 on the behavior of foreign *portfolio* investors in particular—investors whose stake in the companies they buy is not sufficient to give them control or influence in the running of the corporations. The authors distinguish three types of foreign investors (mutual funds, pension funds, and hedge funds) and three means by which foreign institutions invest in local stock (through local markets, international placements of publicly traded depository receipts and private equity, and local private equity).

Barth and Zhang document that, in fact, equity flows were more resilient in the face of crisis than is generally understood. When account is taken of the decline in market values during the crises, there is no evidence that mutual funds withdrew funds from Asia in a major way. Furthermore, international placements and private equity investments were stable sources of finance during the Asian crises, and the evidence suggests that foreign investors did not destabilize Asian stock prices. The authors further document that foreign equity investors account for a very high share of the "free float"—shares traded in the open market—in Asian emerging markets, that foreign investors have investment horizons longer than those of domestic investors, and that they suffered significant losses during the crises. The paper infers that foreign investors in local markets appear to be motivated by economic fundamentals, not by "herd" behavior.

Barth and Zhang also find that mutual funds in particular have not been and are not likely to be a source of short-term volatility in emerging markets. Indeed, emerging market mutual funds experienced *inflows* throughout 1997, except for the month of December. The inflows continued into 1998, before turning into very small outflows at mid-year. Those emerging market funds that invest primarily in Asian economies outside Japan experienced steady but small outflows in 1997. These outflows began early in the year, well before the devaluation of the baht in July. In 1998, the outflows moderated considerably.

Actually, while portfolio equity was coming into Southeast Asia at the rate of about $10 billion a year in both 1997 and 1998, foreign direct investment (FDI) also was remarkably resilient during the crisis period. In contrast, there was a significant withdrawal of short-term loans by international banks (evidenced by a very large increase in the errors and omissions entered in the balance of payments data for the affected Asian countries), which clearly contributed to the severity of the crises.[4]

Barth and Zhang believe that portfolio equity will be needed in a big way to help the Asian countries out of their difficulties in the years ahead. For example, recapitalizing the banks and restructuring heavily indebted corporations in the region may require an injection of at least $200 billion in equity, or about ten times the total FDI and portfolio equity investment in these countries in 1998. In a situation of systemic distress in the domestic private sector, governments are the only other possible source of domestic equity. But the government has no special skill in corporate restructuring, so the case for increased equity investment by foreigners—whether FDI or portfolio equity—becomes even more compelling.

Ian Giddy in chapter 7 analyzes one particular way in which more and more foreign companies are attracting capital: rather than issuing stock in their own countries, they are issuing depository receipts, an instrument issued in a foreign country that is backed by securities in the home market. The most popular depository receipts are those issued in America by U.S. commercial banks.

Using data on American depository receipts (ADRs), Giddy finds that during the 1990–98 period returns on ADRs issued on behalf of Latin American firms were more highly correlated with returns earned in the U.S. market than was the case with Asian ADRs. At the same time, returns within each region were very highly correlated. These results lead Giddy to

4. World Bank. (1998).

conclude that capital markets continue to be significantly more integrated on a regional than on a global basis.

It is widely recognized in the wake of the crisis that portfolio equity and debt flows can be highly volatile in the short run. In chapter 8, Jarrod Wilcox agrees that emerging markets need foreign investment and should not introduce capital controls. At the same time, he finds that the particular mix of equity investors in the region—foreign and domestic—contributed to the severity of the crises and uses these findings to offer some interesting recommendations for moderating volatility in equity markets in the future.

In particular, Wilcox identifies five classes of investors: (1) *analysts* who earn returns by assessing and reacting to information; (2) *growth investors* who, like analysts, respond quickly to changes in information about company prospects; (3) *momentum investors* who buy what is going up and sell what is going down and thus often help to destabilize markets; (4) *index investors* who buy regardless of price or fundamentals of particular companies but instead purchase portfolios of stocks; and (5) *value investors* who respond quickly to price changes, but slowly to news about changes in fundamentals.

At bottom, Wilcox argues that there were too many momentum, growth, and index investors in Asia and too few analysts and value-oriented investors. This mix of investor types was ideal for funneling in too much money and then for having it exit too rapidly on the initial signs of market distress. It was especially disturbing, in his view, that had they wanted to make use of it, investors had sufficient information to know that prices of Asian equities were overpriced (we know this from the data set forth in the papers by Harvey and Roper and by Pomerleano and Zhang). Nonetheless, investors poured their money into the markets because they did not take either an analytical or a value-oriented approach.

Wilcox is not optimistic that this will change much in the future unless more timely and objective information is made available to enable analysts to do their jobs more effectively and thus perhaps give them more influence in the future; until more local investors, using value-oriented investment approaches, are cultivated; and until less emphasis is given to the current market indexes, perhaps by having the International Finance Corporation develop an alternative index that better reflects the fundamentals of value investing.

Foreign borrowing and lending have been much more controversial in the wake of the Asian crisis than equity flows. Indeed, many analysts and policymakers have urged countries to copy Chile's reserve requirement against short-term capital inflows as a way of discouraging excessively volatile capital movements. In chapter 9, Sebastian Edwards examines this idea, as part of a comparison of the currency crises of the 1980s and 1990s in Latin America with the more recent crises in Asia.

Edwards finds that the Chilean reserve requirements definitely altered the composition of capital inflows in Chile, moving them overwhelmingly toward longer-term loans. In this sense, the requirements "worked" as intended. Nonetheless, another announced purpose of the requirements was to reduce upward pressure on the exchange rate. Using a series of statistical tests, Edwards concludes that the requirements did not alter the Chilean exchange rate from what it otherwise would have been. In the same vein, Edwards also investigates whether the requirements enhanced the freedom of the Chilean monetary authorities to maintain higher interest rates to control inflation. Here, too, Edwards's statistical tests reject that view: the restrictions did not have a significant effect on interest rates in Chile.

From all this, Edwards joins several of the other authors in this volume in expressing skepticism toward the use of capital controls as a useful device for managing risk in increasingly global financial markets.

What to Do Now?

Clearly, if Asian firms borrowed excessively because they were not effectively disciplined by market forces, one key challenge must be to develop methods of corporate governance that might supply some of this discipline in the future. But this may be easier said than done. As Claessens and his colleagues show in chapter 5, families control a large portion of the corporate sector, which makes it difficult to rely on minority shareholders to supply the needed discipline.

Kenneth Scott attempts to resolve this difficulty in chapter 10. He observes three mechanisms of corporate governance that could protect the interests of minority shareholders: managerial reputation, shareholder voting for the board of directors, and conflict-of-interest rules.

Scott argues that reputation is a problematic constraining factor, although there are some encouraging signs, at least in Korea, that reputation may be beginning to be important.[5] Meanwhile, in the absence of an active market for corporate control, which certainly is true for the Asian countries, voting power itself has little relevance, at least until strong institutional investors come onto the scene.[6] And although some countries in Southeast Asia have required the presence of outside directors—Thailand requires a minimum of two, while Korea requires that 25 percent of the members of the board be independent and recently introduced a requirement for cumulative voting for board seats—Scott notes that strong cultural and institutional factors make it difficult for such outsiders to have much influence. Furthermore, boards in Korea, Indonesia, and Thailand meet relatively infrequently, and board committees are uncommon.[7]

Given these limitations, Scott believes that in Asian countries, where ownership is highly concentrated, the best source of protection for minority shareholders lies in rules concerning conflict of interest, especially transactions between a company and insiders (including representatives of dominant shareholders). These rules could either prohibit all self-dealing transactions or allow only those that pass a "fairness" test. Scott also suggests that by removing restrictions on voting and promoting investment by institutional investors, emerging market countries may also develop a market for control, which would help to provide more discipline against profligate corporate behavior. Scott's recommendations seem especially justified in light of the fact that many Asian corporations have strong incentives otherwise for self-dealing given their high degree of leverage and relatively poor profitability.

Rules cannot be effective, however, unless they are enforced. Scott finds variation among Asian countries in this regard. Malaysia has on paper a fairly good legal system and body of judicial decisions, in his view. Indonesia appears to lie at the other extreme, while Korea and Thailand

---

5. It should be noted that a shareholders' advocacy group in Korea has gathered support from minority shareholders to challenge the validity of self-dealing transactions benefiting corporate insiders of SK Telecom. The result was a settlement that has led to the cancellation of the transactions concerned. This suggests that in certain circumstances, reputational factors may be important, notwithstanding the difficulties and cost of using litigation to enforce shareholder rights.

6. In Asia, although some institutional investors are present, including some foreign portfolio investors, their impact has been limited by restrictions on their holdings in individual companies, by cross-ownership of companies in which they are invested, and by restrictions on the exercise of voting rights.

7. In many industrial countries, the law requires directors to comply with a *duty of care*—to act carefully in carrying out their functions—and a *duty of loyalty*. The duty of loyalty requires directors to use their powers only in the interests of the shareholders as a class and not for any other reason.

appear to be in-between. At the time Scott wrote his paper, Korea was in the process of allowing shareholder class action lawsuits against directors personally or external auditors if the company's financial statements or public offering documents contain false or misleading statements. The Korean bar is permitted to charge contingency fees, although it remains to be seen whether the courts will award significant damages that would provide incentives to take these actions.

Meanwhile, what should be done about the current overhang of debt in Asian markets? Sebastian Edwards offers one important suggestion in chapter 9: heavily indebted companies could engage in the type of debt-for-equity swap that was arranged during the Chilean debt crisis. Such an arrangement was accomplished in Chile through an intermediary, typically a commercial bank, and helped to reduce medium- and long-term foreign debt by 25 percent in just four years.

Looking Ahead

The volume concludes with several assessments of the future prospects for countries affected by the crisis and for emerging markets more broadly.

Michael Adler predicts in chapter 11 that the current account deficits in each of the crisis countries are likely to drop in the years immediately ahead, if not rise into surplus (as indeed several already have). The gradual improvement seen in Southeast Asia should be accompanied, however, by a deterioration in the current accounts and reserve levels of Latin American nations. In any event, reduced current account deficits will reduce country borrowing, as will the fear, among emerging market borrowers and policymakers, of "hot" money. Adler also believes that short- and long-term lending may be curtailed by regulations aimed at preventing a recurrence of "excessive" lending and that have already been, or are anticipated to be, adopted. Lending also will remain low until some of the fundamentals look considerably more positive. Adler is concerned that constrained borrowing and lending in the shorter term will harm the corporate and country recovery that is required to ensure much needed intermediate term financing.

Chapter 12 outlines the views of three experienced emerging market professionals about future prospects for the globalization and integration of financial markets, changes likely to manifest themselves in developing-country financial markets, and possible new private sector initiatives.

William Cline is much more optimistic about the future for emerging markets than is Michael Adler. Cline sees a resumption of the long-run favorable trends favoring many emerging markets before the crisis, after a few years of downturn and modest recovery. Indeed, given the aging of populations in the west, Cline sees increasing investment in emerging markets as a way of financing their retirement. Similarly, emerging market residents will find increasing needs to invest in industrial countries as a means of diversifying their portfolios. Cline warns that only a major global recession or depression would change these optimistic projections.

On the controversial questions surrounding reform of the "global financial architecture," Cline argues that much of the talk about investors being too heavily influenced by "moral hazard" is misplaced. In fact, not only did equity and bond investors in Asia lose substantial sums—on the order of $350 billion—but even multinational bank lenders lost as much as $60 billion. Cline warns about the undesirable precedent of placing rescheduling clauses into bond contracts, which he believes could discourage significant private investment in emerging markets in the future.

David Folkerts-Landau also expects global financial integration to continue. At the same time, he endorses what appears to be an emerging global consensus that national capital markets should not be prematurely opened before banking supervision is effective and well established. Folkerts-Landau argues further that supervisory rules need to be extended to the corporate sector as well. He also supports the use of capital controls in the midst of a crisis and approves of the intervention by the Hong Kong authorities in the local stock market to prevent a collapse of equity prices.

Folkerts-Landau also criticizes the IMF for failing in its surveillance role, stepping aside when too much capital poured into Asia. One reason for the IMF's failure, in his view, is that it has devoted only a fraction of its resources to surveillance.

Manuel Medina-Mora makes a case for deepening local markets, not just with foreign capital but also with domestic savings. To do this, he suggests the need to develop long-term domestic sovereign debt instruments, to improve risk management and control systems, to develop better mechanisms for hedging currency risks, to enhance transparency, and to develop ways for investors to differentiate different emerging markets from one another (to minimize "herding" effects when crises break out). Medina-Mora also suggests that emerging markets can better fund investments with local savings if they build a broader base of local institutional investors, especially pension funds.

Concluding Thoughts

The volume concludes in chapter 13 with a broad overview by Andrew Sheng, chairman of the Hong Kong Securities Commission, of the factors that led to the Asian financial crises and the challenges that policymakers, investors, and managers of financial institutions confront in the future. To put it simply, all three actors, in Sheng's view, failed to follow fundamental rules of risk management.

Governments failed to supervise their banks adequately and pegged their exchange rates for too long, putting at risk their scarce foreign exchange while encouraging firms and banks to borrow excessively in foreign currency and at short maturities. Investors ignored available information— even if it was sometimes late and not perfectly accurate—that more than amply warned of the risks of investing in Asian markets and of lending to borrowers in the region. And firms and banks in the region were just as guilty, attempting to leverage their way out of poor and often declining profitability.

In today's global marketplace, Sheng reminds us that risk management is *everyone's* business and responsibility. The challenge going forward for all concerned is to identify global, cross-border risks and then determine how best to measure and manage them so that local financial markets can better weather global storms.

Reference

World Bank. 1998. *Global Economic Prospects and the Developing Countries, 1998/99: Beyond Financial Crisis.* Washington, D.C.

RICHARD N. COOPER 2

The Asian Crises:
Causes and
Consequences

IT HAS BEEN OVER two years since Thailand unexpectedly withdrew its support from the foreign exchange market—on July 2, 1997—and the baht dropped dramatically in price relative to other currencies. Soon thereafter, Malaysia made the same move. Indonesia relaxed its support for the rupiah and then decided it could not even hold the relaxed version, effectively withdrawing from the foreign exchange market in October before exhausting its reserves. By late November it became clear that Korea was in difficulty, and the crisis emerged fully in December.

In August 1998, Russia, in a partly expected and partly extremely unexpected move, withdrew its support for the ruble and ceased payment on some of its government obligations. Brazil came under very strong pressure in October, but the break was postponed until January 1999 by the promise of a substantial international package of financial support in exchange for strong fiscal actions by Brazil.

Those are the main events. One reason for recounting them is that in the history of this period all these events will be smudged together and will undoubtedly be talked and written about as the financial crisis of 1997–98.

Those of us who lived through the events appreciate that in real time a month is a long time. Three months or six months are very long periods of time. I prefer to call these the "financial crises," plural, of 1997–98 because, although there are important similarities among them, there are also critically important differences. I consider the linkages among these various events an open question.

In the history of monetary affairs, these are very dramatic events. We had never before seen changes in what economists call real exchange rates—that is, exchange rates corrected for relative price differences—of the magnitude that we saw in the Asian countries in 1997. Large changes in exchange rates hitherto were associated with very high inflation rates, as in Argentina and Brazil in the 1980s. But the Asian countries all had modest rates of inflation. So if you correct for the inflation differentials, these were dramatic changes in real exchange rates.

The decline in output, particularly relative to the recent experience of the countries in question, was also dramatic. Comparisons have even been made with the Great Depression of the 1930s. Those comparisons are usually made by people who do not know the magnitude of the Great Depression in Germany and the United States. Nonetheless, in postwar experience the drop in output was extraordinary: this was Malaysia's first recession since 1985, Korea's first since 1980. Indonesia's last recession was in 1965. And Thailand had not had a recession in the past forty years. On the contrary, all had become accustomed to rapid economic growth. So these were unexpected events in the experience of the people directly affected. Few Thais remember the last economic disaster in Thailand, which goes back to World War II. The declines in output were not like the Great Depression. But by post–World War II standards they were deep recessions, especially in Indonesia, at minus 14 percent.

These events are the more surprising because the behavior of the Asian countries had been exemplary by the standards of the so-called Washington consensus. These countries had enjoyed rapid economic growth for many years. They were all fiscally well disciplined. All had moderate inflation rates that were low by standards of developing countries. So these countries were the darlings of the financial community around the world. We now understand that this was part of the problem. It made the turn of events after July 1997 all the more dramatic.

Fortunately, from a global perspective these countries are small. If you add up the Southeast Asian countries altogether, they are about the size of Spain, using gross domestic product (GDP) at market prices. That is the single most relevant measure of economic significance. One could look at exports, in which case they are smaller than Spain. South Korea alone is slightly smaller than the Southeast Asian countries altogether. Adding

Korea to the Southeast Asian countries achieves roughly the size of Italy. The financial disasters became economic disasters in the countries concerned. But fortunately from a global point of view, they were like a big recession in Italy, difficult but manageable.

Japan is altogether different. Japan is a very large economy, five times the size of these countries taken together. That is why we are worried about the softness of the Japanese economy, which is a major factor inhibiting recovery from the Asian financial crises.

I have been charged with indicating the causes of these crises. "Cause" is actually a complex concept. It involves implicitly getting into hypotheticals, what economists call counterfactuals. What would the world have been like if A, B, or C had not occurred? If A had not occurred, but D would have happened anyway, we cannot persuasively say that A caused D.

To pursue this analysis in a systematic way would take far too much time. But for concreteness, let me focus on Thailand, partly because that is where the dramatic events started. As I have said, important details differ from country to country. Focusing on Thailand will give some flavor of what happened and provide some similarities with other countries.

The banks of Thailand had borrowed exceptionally heavily in the world interbank market by June 1997, $69 billion as reported by the Bank for International Settlements, mostly in U.S. dollars and Japanese yen. Of this, $46 billion, or two-thirds, were under one year in maturity, sometimes under thirty days in maturity.[1] This compared with reported official foreign exchange reserves of $31 billion, of which, we now know, a substantial fraction had already been committed to the forward market. So short-term foreign currency indebtedness was very heavy.

Thailand had a large inflow of capital of all kinds in 1994 and 1995. It responded the way economists predict that countries should respond to large and sustained inflows of capital, with a rise in the current account deficit—the deficit of purchases of goods and services abroad—to 8 percent of GDP. This should have set off alarms. In mid-1996 the International Monetary Fund (IMF) warned the Thai government about the vulnerability of its large current account deficit, particularly given flat export growth. Export performance had been strikingly good through

1. Bank for International Settlements, "Statistical Annex: Historical Data," in *The Maturity, Sectoral, and Nationality Distribution of International Lending* (Basle: Bank for International Settlements, Monetary and Economic Department, International Finance Statistics, May 1998), tables 1 and 2, available under Regular Publications at http://www.bis.org/publ/index.htm [June 24, 1999].

1995, but took a turn for the worse in 1996. Thailand was in the process of reducing its current account deficit, but not, as it turned out, rapidly enough.

A country with a current account deficit can manage as long as capital inflows cover that deficit. But if people, residents as well as nonresidents, collectively decide to invest less financially in the country, a drop in the net capital inflow will put downward pressure on the country's foreign exchange rate. Foreigners do not have to withdraw their funds. They just have to cease investing at the same rate as they did before. That is what happened in Thailand.

Signs of a weakening Thai economy were already evident. Thailand had a real estate bust in early 1997. Net American equity investments in Thailand began to decline in 1996. Exposure to foreign banks did not grow after mid-1996. So there was already some downward pressure on the exchange market coming from those sources. Instead of recognizing it and accommodating it, the Thais chose to continue to support the dollar value of the baht by drawing down central bank foreign exchange reserves beginning in late 1996.

So the market effect of a change in market sentiment was obscured by the fact that the Thais were drawing down their reserves. And the Thai authorities were not exactly straightforward with the world or indeed with their own senior officials about how rapidly the reserves were being drawn down. They were being drawn down partly through commitments in the forward market, so the full drawdown did not show up on the balance sheet. It is said that only two Thai officials actually knew the true state of affairs, that reserves were virtually exhausted by June of 1997.

The question has been asked, where was the international community during all of this? We have an answer. In its annual article IV consultations in July 1996, one full year before the crisis broke, the IMF officially warned Thailand of the magnitude and the short maturity of its external debt, of the weakness of its bank supervision, of the dangerously large magnitude of its current account deficit, and of the relative inflexibility of its exchange rate policy. All of these warnings were conveyed to the Thai authorities. For whatever reason, the Thais chose to ignore the warnings. They who sow the wind may reap a whirlwind.

Most economists would agree, I think, that Thailand made several serious policy mistakes. But the international community, especially the banks, were implicit accomplices because they lent heavily without paying adequate attention to the evolving circumstances, although total bank loans ceased to rise after mid-1996.

I will not recount the story in other countries, although the details differ in important ways. The Asian countries all had substantial current account deficits, although the others were not as large relative to GDP as Thailand's. (Malaysia's deficit had been larger in 1996, but was on its way down.) They shared the characteristic of large external debt, tilted heavily toward short maturities, much of it in the interbank market, although in Indonesia much foreign bank lending was directly to Indonesian corporations.

All of these countries were supporting their exchange rates in one way or another. And all of them, with Malaysia being a partial exception, had poor banking regulation and supervision by Anglo-Saxon standards. In Thailand and Indonesia banking supervision was poor by any standard. Korea had quite tight supervision, but with different objectives from those governing banking regulation and supervision in the United States or in Britain and other countries that emulate British standards.

There has been a lot of talk about contagion, a metaphor drawn from infectious disease. That metaphor is perhaps apt if one thinks about Southeast Asia. The crisis broke in Thailand and spread very quickly to Malaysia, which, to avoid running out of reserves as Thailand had done, mistakenly announced that the central bank was withdrawing from the foreign exchange market altogether. The announcement precipitated a sharp depreciation of the currency. With slightly slower burn, the financial crisis moved to both Singapore, which weathered it, and Indonesia. But it was five to six months before it hit Korea seriously and more than a year later for Russia.

Although it has become the conventional wisdom, I have serious doubts about whether we can meaningfully speak of contagion in linking Korea and Russia directly to Southeast Asia. There are linkages, of course, but none is compelling. Korea had its own problems. Russia had its own problems. And Brazil had its own problems. Russia's behavior strongly affected Brazil, through frightened market reaction, but these remarks focus on Asia.

The forces of contagion can be divided into two categories. One is what I call the organic or economic effects, what the IMF calls spillover effects, the other concerns the response of financial markets. Organic effects arise from direct trade linkages—as a country's imports fall, the exports of its trading partners fall—and from the fact that country A may be in direct competition in third markets with country B, so that when its exchange rate depreciates demand for the exports of country B weakens.

If we leave aside Malaysia and Singapore, there is very little direct trade among these countries. Most of them are oriented toward the major markets of Japan, United States, and Europe.

There is some competition among them, to be sure. But not a lot of direct competition. Malaysia and Thailand are in somewhat closer competition than, say, those two and Indonesia or those three and Korea. It is difficult to explain what happened by looking at these organic economic linkages.

With respect to financial effects, Morris Goldstein has correctly observed that the Thai events were a wake-up call for investment managers around the world.[2] Here was an exemplary country, Thailand, and all of a sudden things went badly wrong. Investors around the world, in London, New York, Zurich, Hong Kong, asked, "If Thailand can go wrong, what about Korea, Indonesia, et cetera, et cetera?" So equity and bank portfolios in all emerging markets were probably reexamined.

Some people have made something of a possible liquidity squeeze. If some stocks in a mutual fund go bad but they become illiquid, the fund will have to sell its good stocks to meet redemptions, for example, the seizing up of Russian equities leads to sales of Chilean equities. That is a fertile field for research; I do not know how important it has been.

As time goes on, more data become available. They are still incomplete, so the full story cannot yet be told. But what we discover is a little surprising. In spite of all of the talk about reversals of capital flows into the Asian countries, the figures suggest that the actual runoff of bank loans was not consequential in the second half of 1997. True, and significantly, bank loans stopped flowing in. Banks loans to Thailand dropped $10.5 billion in the second half of 1997, significant but easily covered if reserves had been adequate.[3] Korea also experienced a runoff, no doubt contributing to the crisis. But the declines in bank loans to Malaysia and Indonesia were negligibly small. That is a big surprise.

We do not yet have comprehensive figures on equity funds. But net purchases or sales of equities by Americans again tell a surprising story. A selloff had already started in Thailand and Malaysia in late 1996, early 1997. But in the second half of 1997 there were net purchases in Thailand. The

2. Goldstein (1998).
3. Bank for International Settlements, "Statistical Annex," table 1.

picture for Malaysia was more mixed, but there was no great rush to the door. Net purchases of Korean equities occurred throughout the crisis, although the rate diminished in the fourth quarter. Perhaps Europeans, for which data are not yet available, were selling. And as I have said, even a drop in the rate of inflow can be important for a country with a current account deficit.

Foreign direct investment continued in all of these countries during this period, albeit at a somewhat reduced rate.

These preliminary figures are somewhat surprising. What was happening? Partly on anecdotal evidence, I believe the main pressure on foreign exchange rates in these countries, especially Southeast Asia, came from resident capital. It was not the withdrawal of foreign capital so much as the purchase of foreign exchange by residents that put such strong pressure on foreign exchange rates. Residents had directly or indirectly borrowed very heavily in foreign currencies—directly in the case of Indonesian corporations, indirectly in the case of Korea and Thailand through the banking system—on the implicit assumption that exchange rate policy would continue in the future as it had in the past.

That assumption turned out to be incorrect, and resident debtors had exposures directly proportional to the extent of currency depreciation. So residents rushed to the door, not to speculate, in the sense in which that term is used loosely in journalistic treatment, but to protect their asset positions by trying to cover their foreign currency liabilities.

Since the central banks were now out of the market, there was no strength on the other side. So currency values dropped precipitously, which in turn threw heavy foreign currency debtors into insolvency.

In his latest book George Soros offers a fascinating account both of Russian events in the summer of 1998 and of Southeast Asia.[4] Soros was personally taken to task by Prime Minister Mahathir of Malaysia for providing the ominous squeeze behind this whole crisis: not just trying to make money, which everyone takes for granted, but trying to bring down the mixed but successful economic system of Malaysia—an allegation of politically motivated short selling of Malaysia's currency, the ringgit.

Soros tells us in his book, and I see no reason to disbelieve him, that his fund was short on Indonesian rupiah in late 1996 and early 1997. But during the crisis in the fall of 1997 he covered his short positions, so he was a net purchaser of rupiah during the fourth quarter of 1997, thus providing

4. Soros (1998).

some support to the market. He avers that the rupiah was the only Southeast Asian currency he was in.

The whole dynamic of the situation suggests that most of the pressure was exerted by resident money responding to the revelation that a key market assumption, namely that tomorrow's exchange rate would be approximately the same as today's, turned out to be wrong.

Since generalizations from these episodes will be made for a long time to come, it is worth noting where the contagion did not hit. Singapore felt some pressure but held. Hong Kong (China) felt acute pressure from time to time, as France did in the 1992–93 European crisis, but held. China felt a diminution in foreign capital inflow and a flattening of export growth, leading to some decline in the growth rate, but held. Taiwan (China) held after deliberately devaluing its currency in October. India and other countries in South Asia held.

These countries have structural characteristics that are rather different from those of the countries that were subject to the crisis. Singapore, Taiwan, and China had current account surpluses; Hong Kong had a relatively small deficit; all four had very large foreign exchange reserves.

China, India, and Taiwan had relatively little short-term external debt. Hong Kong and Singapore had huge short-term interbank debt, but as international banking centers they also had huge short-term external claims. There are large gross figures on both sides of the balance sheet. And, unlike the other borrowers, the funds were not generally used for domestic loans. China and India had gone much less far in liberalizing international capital movements.

I said earlier that cause is a complex concept. I have described the symptoms and some proximate causes. But, of course, the deeper question is why did the Thais, the Indonesians, and the Koreans borrow at thirty-day maturities in dollars in order to make ten- or fifteen- or thirty-year investments in local currency? Why did bank regulation and supervision not prevent the tremendous transformations of both currency and maturity? Why were the ultimate borrowers willing to take such risks, if they were formally passed to them (as at least the currency risk often was)? Why did the regulators not step in and prevent that? A whole series of whys come to mind. I have given only a superficial explanation for the Thai crisis.

The usual response to the deeper questions typically turns to things like, pejoratively, the pervasiveness of crony capitalism or, more favorably, at least in some views of the world, the presence of active industrial policy. Banks made loans with the people's money under political guidance to firms whose owners supported the political elite. The Korean government for many years pursued an active role in steering the economy in certain directions, making decisions designed to achieve modernity, a path that was largely determined by emulation of Japan, driven by envy and resentment as much as by a desire to raise the living standards of Koreans. Corporations were encouraged to move into petrochemicals, into autos, into semiconductors, despite low rates of return in prospect as well as in practice. Banks were encouraged to make loans to targeted industries, and favored firms took on exceptionally high leverage. High domestic savings were augmented from abroad to make these heavy investments.

So uncritical lending was part of a pattern that was not merely tolerated but actively encouraged. And despite some rough edges here and there, it was fabulously successful, not only in generating rapid growth but also in achieving higher standards of living for ordinary people. But its fundamental weaknesses were revealed by the events of 1997.

What lessons can we draw? The first is aimed mainly at economists: the financial system is part of the "fundamentals" of any modern economy. Economists have an analytically useful construct of distinguishing between the real economy and the monetary economy. The real economy is the productive apparatus, the labor force, the plant and equipment, and the land used for producing goods and services that contribute to our standard of living. Money and the elaborate financial system play no direct role. This is a powerful analytical device. But economists fall too easily into the habit of thinking that the first is important and the second is not. This is a big mistake. Every modern economy requires a sophisticated financial system to support the real side of the economy. When things go badly wrong on the financial side, they necessarily spill over adversely into the real side of the economy. That is lesson number one.

The second lesson—really a reminder—is that financial systems are intrinsically unstable. It would take us too far afield to develop that thought in detail. Most ultimate lenders want liquid assets. They want something they can mobilize quickly if they have to. That is true of many purchasers of stocks and bonds as well as depositors; hence the importance of secondary markets in securities. Savers like their claims to be relatively liquid.

Most borrowers, in contrast, want to tie the funds up for some period of time. Apart from self-liquidating trade finance, they need at least three years if they are starting a new firm before there is likely to be positive cash flow and more or if they are building a plant with a life of fifteen or thirty years. So there is a maturity discrepancy between the preferences of lenders and the preferences of borrowers in every modern economy. The financial system bridges that by giving lenders the illusion, which is largely correct most of the time, preferably all of the time, that their assets are liquid and giving borrowers the illusion that they can use the money for fifteen years, say, subject to the conditions of the bond or loan contract. That is what financial systems do.

The financial system relies on something like the law of large numbers in order to play that juggling act successfully. It relies on the fact that not all of the lenders will want their money at the same time, that bank depositors will not run on the bank. Financial markets experience a tremendous loss of liquidity if everyone wants to sell their bonds or equities at the same time.

So we rely on a certain independence of decisionmaking among lenders and the fact that their needs come at different times. The financial intermediaries can play on that. It usually works. But as in sailing, every once in a while we run into really rough weather. And if the weather is too rough, it can end in disaster, even sinking the boat. So we have built up official regulations and a support apparatus in order to cover those rough periods. They are called the "regulatory system" for banks or securities markets, on the one hand, and a "lender of last resort," on the other. The lender of last resort's function is to liquefy good but illiquid assets in these rough periods. Since the financial system is intrinsically unstable, it needs that kind of support system to keep it going through rough periods.

The third lesson, which is especially important for developing countries, is that a well-functioning economy requires a high degree of public trust to mobilize private savings for the public good. Southeast Asians have long been high savers. But traditionally the savings went into gold leaf, silver coins, and jewelry for wives or daughters. This form of savings may be privately valuable, but it is not socially useful. It can be liquidated in a year of a bad crop or in other unfortunate circumstances. But it cannot be mobilized for productive investment.

The social contribution of modern financial systems is to mobilize the precautionary savings of households for uses that increase productivity in a way that gold jewelry does not. But such mobilization involves a great amount of trust on the part of the saving public. Instead of buying bracelets for their wives, they put their savings into an institution with a door, a teller counter, and (presumably) a vault, in exchange for a written or oral promise to pay on demand. They rely on the fact that they have been told that any time they want their money, they can get it back.

That trust has been grossly violated in experiences recently revealed. Public savings have been taken into financial institutions and lent in egregiously bad ways, in monuments to industrial modernity in Korea, in urban real estate in Thailand, in subsidies to the president's children in Indonesia, in operating subsidies to state-owned enterprises in China. China faces a huge potential problem if the public were to discover how its savings have been squandered. Fortunately, unlike the Japanese five years ago, Chinese leaders are not in denial about it. They know they must restructure the financial system.

Fourth, we discovered in 1997 not perhaps a clash of civilizations, but a clash of cultures played out in the financial world. Foreign lenders, based in London, New York, and other major financial centers, expect to be kept well informed about what is happening in the economies to which they lend and especially about what is happening to the borrowers. If, unexpectedly, borrowers are unable to repay on schedule, they expect orderly procedures for working out the situation, preferably procedures that maximize the likelihood they will be paid without loss. In short, they expect transparency and well-defined processes.

Asian borrowers have a different tradition, one that emphasizes personal connections and loyalties among the relevant parties, including political connections and loyalties. They operate on the assumption that problems can be worked out satisfactorily behind closed doors and that what foreign lenders or domestic depositors do not know will not hurt them. Indeed, timely and accurate information may unduly harm them. The Asian tradition—or something resembling it—was common in many European countries not long ago with discernible remnants even today.

It is difficult to pass definitive judgment on the respective merits of these two quite different traditions. One can find circumstances in which either is superior. But they do not mix well.

If foreign lenders in the first tradition suspect that serious problems are likely to arise with their borrowers in the second tradition, they do not expect to be told how serious the problems may be and what the likely solutions will be. They simply withdraw their funds as rapidly as they can, thus turning a financial problem or even a suspected financial problem into a financial rout.

Let us project ourselves forward to, say, the year 2005. Korea and Thailand and perhaps Malaysia will look back on this financial crisis of 1997, which resulted in a very painful recession in 1998, as adolescent growing pains. In each case the real side of the economy got out front of the financial system, and the resulting disconnect generated a financial crisis. But these countries will learn from this unpleasant experience more of what is needed in the way of a support system for the financial system. The United States had a financial crisis roughly once a decade from the 1830s to the 1930s, the last being a complete calamity. It took Americans a century—we are slow learners—to put in place the highly articulated and largely effective regulatory system that many within the financial system chafe under today. I do not mean to suggest that everything is exactly right. But such a system—put aside the details—is necessary. Even it did not save us from the savings and loan crisis.

It is a sad commentary on human affairs that we find great difficulty learning from the mistakes of others. We read about them with interest, even with curiosity. But we seem to have to make our own mistakes in order to learn from them.

Korea and Thailand made some serious mistakes. There is no doubt in my mind that they will learn from those mistakes and that in 2005 both economies will be the stronger for this episode. Indonesia is much more complicated because the crisis has been confounded with the legitimacy of the government itself. Resolution of the crisis has become tied up with constitution-making. Thus the final outcome is less predictable, although it is conceivable that the gains to Indonesians will ultimately exceed those of others affected by the crises.

References

Goldstein, Morris. 1998. *The Asian Financial Crisis: Causes, Cures, and Systemic Implications.* Policy Analyses in International Economics 55. Washington, D.C.: Institute for International Economics (June).

Soros, George. 1998. *The Crisis of Global Capitalism: Open Society Engandered.* New York: Public Affairs.

CAMPBELL R. HARVEY
ANDREW H. ROPER

3

The Asian Bet

T HE RECENT FINANCIAL CRISIS in Asia has dramatically changed the
world's perception of this region. Asian economies have gone from
"miraculous" to "problematic." As the wealth and relative incomes of these
economies have diminished, many observers have concluded that international and Asian capital markets have failed.

How else can we justify the violent swings observed in Asian equity
prices and exchange rates? If a well-functioning capital market serves to
allocate scarce capital efficiently from lenders to users, then the exodus of
international private capital from Asia may be interpreted as the failure of
international capital markets to expedite the flow of funds from lenders to
borrowers. However, the sudden withdrawal of funds from Asia need not
be interpreted as a signal of financial market failure. Moreover, if the risk
of investing in Asian markets has increased dramatically, capital flight by
risk-averse investors is exactly what one would expect as portfolios are
rebalanced.

Participants in international capital markets and local Asian capital markets have also been accused of ignoring risks inherent in investments in the

The authors have benefited from the comments of Michael Pomerleano and Emma Rasiel. They
also wish to thank Margaret Enis and Christian Lundblad for their help.

region. The critics argue that market participants ignored the deteriorating fundamentals of Asia's corporate sector and thus failed to take into account the growing risk of the region. They interpret the sudden collapse in equity prices following devaluation of the Thai baht in July 1997 as the bursting of Asia's asset price bubble. It is also possible to make the case that investors reacted rationally to a critical piece of new information. In effect, market discipline reasserted itself.

In this paper we assess the claim that capital markets failed to perform their primary duties during the 1990s. Our assessment is grounded in a quantitative and qualitative analysis of local Asian capital markets and the interaction of Asian corporations with international capital markets. Where possible, we compare the capital market performance and corporate performance within East Asia to that of Latin America.

Our results indicate that a significant proportion of the growth in market capitalization of Asian markets during the 1990s resulted from the mobilization of new capital. Asian capital markets and international capital markets provided the funds required to sustain the high investment rates that characterized the region. Furthermore, Asian capital markets provided investors with the liquidity commonly associated with developed capital markets.

During the 1990s, Asian capital markets also attempted to integrate themselves further into international capital markets. Financial market integration is arguably the most challenging issue that emerging markets face as they evolve into developed capital markets. We find that Asian governments pursued similar policies of gradual capital market reform including capital market liberalization during the 1990s. As a result of this process, foreign investors were able to participate directly in local equity markets. We show that foreign investors had a negligible impact on local stock market returns and volatility.

Despite their significant growth, new capital mobilization, and attempts at financial market liberalization, Asian stock markets remained heavily concentrated in terms of the market capitalization of individual firms and industry base. Financial firms and manufacturing firms dominated market indexes, accounting for a minimum of 60 percent of each index's market capitalization.[1] This lack of industrial diversification made Asian equity markets vulnerable to common industry-based shocks. Moreover, the high degree of concentration in the market capitalization of individual firms

---

1. The only exception being Malaysia.

contributed to a lack of cross-sectional variation in returns across firms in any given country. In general, individual corporations listed on Asian exchanges tended to move together to a much larger extent than would be expected in more diversified countries.

We argue that the overall returns of equity investments in Asia were not impressive relative to alternative investments in various other markets. Even dynamic trading strategies designed to capture price appreciation in these recently integrated markets failed to reward investors with returns that outperformed less risky investments. This analysis does not include the significant decline in share prices between January 1997 and the present.

We provide a micro-level analysis of participants in Asian financial markets by systematically evaluating the performance and financial risk of Asian corporations. We find that Asian corporate managers increasingly leveraged their companies despite their declining profitability. We also examine the characteristics of the debt. Here we study the cross-sectional characteristics of Eurobond-issuing Asian corporations. We find evidence suggesting that the typical Asian nonfinancial corporation that issued foreign-denominated debt experienced higher profitability than the average Asian firm. However, the typical Asian Eurobond issuer was much more highly leveraged than the average Asian nonfinancial corporation.

We refer to the higher leverage at a time of declining profitability as a "bet." The stakes were raised by managers tapping into foreign debt markets in an effort to bet that the exchange rate would remain stable. History proves that they lost both of these bets. We argue that the Asian crisis was greatly exacerbated by these bets. We also argue that corporate governance failed to control and manage risk.

The paper is organized as follows. The first section sets the stage and tone for our discussion. We summarize some of the more pertinent findings of the burgeoning literature on the Asian financial crisis, and we highlight key issues that have yet to be resolved. The second section documents the growth in Asian capital markets and attempts to determine how much of this growth constituted new capital mobilization. The third section summarizes Asia's attempts to integrate its local capital markets into world capital markets and the impact of this integration on Asian capital markets. The fourth section examines the degree of concentration in Asian equity markets. The fifth section records the performance of investments in the region. The sixth details the performance of Asian corporations and presents an analysis of the increasing financial risk of corporations in the region. The seventh explores common cross-sectional characteristics of

Asian Eurobond issuers and offers an overview of forthcoming research. The final section offers some concluding remarks.

Stylized Facts Describing East Asian Countries

Consider the following set of stylized facts that describe the Asian economic and financial experience in the 1990s. During most of the past two decades, Asia enjoyed consistently high economic growth, implemented gradual financial market liberalization, and maintained effectively pegged nominal exchange rates. These three forces encouraged high levels of private capital inflows that in turn supported increasing levels of investment. Although most of these private capital inflows resulted from long-term foreign direct investment, a nontrivial amount was portfolio inflows.

East Asia's large inflows of private capital brought about the appreciation of real exchange rates. This appreciation eventually affected the competitiveness of Asian exports. Export growth slowed in most countries, and profit margins tightened. Toward the end of the 1990s indicators of corporate performance worsened as investment returns failed to achieve the cost of capital in some cases.[2] Eventually, firms experienced cash flow shortages and were forced to reconsider their debt servicing obligations. Following the defaults on foreign loans by several Korean *chaebols* in early 1997, international investors refocused their attention on the region's fundamentals.

The speculative pressure placed on the Thai baht and its subsequent devaluation in July 1997 served as an announcement that investors had reevaluated the growth prospects of Asian corporations and decided that the expectations of the past needed to be revised given current conditions. The subsequent exodus of private foreign capital and attempts by monetary officials to restrain this capital flight placed Asia in a liquidity crisis of unprecedented size. Firms were unable to receive the funding they needed to service existing debts and in some cases to maintain operations and fill preexisting orders.[3]

Many authors blame the international financial community. Some researchers have gone so far as to argue that the crisis could have been avoided if the financial community had not over-reacted. Radelet and Sachs champion this view: "There were significant underlying problems

2. Corsetti, Pesenti, and Roubini (1998a).
3. Corsetti, Pesenti, and Roubini (1998a).

and weak fundamentals besetting the Asian economies . . . the imbalances were not severe enough to warrant a financial crisis of the magnitude that took place in the latter half of 1997." They argue that the worst of the crisis could have been largely avoided with relatively moderate adjustments and appropriate policy changes by the international community.[4]

Radelet and Sachs's condemnation of the international financial system is unequivocal. They argue that market participants ignored flaws in these economies and discounted the possibility of a regional crisis. These two criticisms suggest market failure. They also argue that these economies were prone to financial panic due to the lack of a lender of last resort and weak bankruptcy laws. They contend that individual investors fled the region, leaving viable investment opportunities behind and thus failed to expedite scarce capital from borrowers to lenders. This kind of investor herd mentality underestimates the rationality of investors. It is not clear that investors left valuable investments on the table in an attempt to withdraw their funds from the region. Provided that the risks of investment in the region had changed dramatically, it seems likely that investors should rationally rebalance their portfolios.

Another school of thought criticizes international financial investors for their lack of discipline prior to the financial crisis. Krugman and Corsetti, Pesenti, and Roubini assert that international investors placed too much emphasis on government guarantees.[5] Implicit and explicit government subsidization of private investment created large incentives for moral hazard. Excessive lending by local institutions in risky investment projects led to asset price inflation that in turn attracted foreign capital inflows. Corsetti, Pesenti, and Roubini summarize this vicious cycle in their argument that the Asian tigers collapsed under the excessive weight of the paper liabilities which had financed projects of doubtful profitability, covered losses, and led to unsustainable external imbalances.[6]

Krugman argues that these financial intermediaries were not solely responsible for the ills of Asia's asset price bubble: 'After all, private individuals and foreign institutional investors did buy stocks and even real estate in all the economies now in crisis. This suggests other kinds of market failure, notably 'herding' by investors."[7]

4. Radelet and Sachs (1998, p. 2).

5. Krugman (1998)(http://web.mit.edu/KRUGMAN/www/disinter.htm [accessed August 26, 1999]); Corsetti, Pesenti, and Roubini (1998b).

6. Corsetti, Pesenti, and Roubini (1998b, p. 29).

7. Krugman (1998).

Placing the blame for the crisis squarely on the shoulders of the financial community may be warranted. It appears on the surface as though most financial market participants largely ignored the possibility of a regional crisis. Examples of this ignorance are presented in Cline and Barnes, Radelet and Sachs, and Corsetti, Pesenti, and Roubini.[8] These authors present evidence of declining bond spreads, high sovereign credit ratings, and optimistic risk assessments by private corporations like Euromoney.

Some of this ignorance was to be expected given that the traditional signs of a currency crisis were not present in East Asia. By and large, East Asian governments followed strict fiscal discipline. They actively pursued policies of outward-oriented trade and financial market liberalization. Finally, the levels of government official debt did not appear to be unsustainable. In light of these revelations, financial markets and, in particular, foreign investors are easy scapegoats. However, there are other possible reasons for the regional collapse.

Although we have learned much from the research, the arguments rely on highly aggregated evidence. If we are to believe their assertions of capital market failure, we must believe either that self-interested investors withdrew their support from viable economic investments or that moral hazard provided risk-taking incentives for local Asian corporate managers that foreign investors willingly ignored.

Unfortunately, this literature only alludes to the financial market's failure ex post. Ideally we would like systematically to identify the sources of risk ex ante and verify whether or not financial markets correctly accounted for these risk factors. Moreover, we would like to be able to describe the financial market's relative discipline at the country level vis-à-vis each country's exposure to common sources of risk. This sort of approach must be based on a micro-level, firm by firm analysis.

Recently, several authors have attempted this sort of analysis. Pomerleano analyzes the performance of corporations across the region during the 1990s.[9] He employs firm-level data to construct indexes of corporate performance based on common accounting concepts like sales growth, profit margins, and real return on assets. He provides evidence that corporations sustained high investment rates through increased external financing. The study by Claessens, Djankov, and Lang is similar in

---

8. Cline and Barnes (1997); Radelet and Sachs (1998); and Corsetti, Pesenti, and Roubini (1998a).

9. Pomerleano (1998).

spirit.[10] It documents significant declines in corporate profitability ratios as well as increases in average corporate leverage ratios. In combination, both works provide new evidence suggesting that the causes of the Asian crisis may reside in firm-based decisions. These corporate-level decisions apparently placed the region in a very risky position.

Our paper explores a new micro-level analysis. First, we identify common sources of risk in terms of corporate performance, capital structure, and financial risk. This commonality helps to explain the high correlation between asset returns and corporate performance in East Asia. Second, we augment the analysis of Pomerleano and of Claessens, Djankov, and Lang by examining an additional common source of risk facing corporations: currency risk. We argue that deteriorating profit margins and high leverage ratios alone may not account for the magnitude of the crisis. Rather, the major factor contributing to the Asian crisis was the growing amount of U.S. dollar-denominated debt accruing to Asian corporations.

New Capital Mobilization in East Asia

East Asian capital markets experienced dramatic changes during the 1990s. Throughout the region, local equity and bond markets increased their market capitalization. In this section, we provide a quantitative review of the new capital mobilization within Asia during the 1990s. We also present evidence suggesting that the liquidity offered to investors in Asia rivaled that of any developed market in the world. In fact, in some cases Asian markets led the world in total value traded.

In addition to raising large amounts of new capital in their local capital markets, the region also tapped into international equity and bond markets. We examine two major sources of external finance available to Asian corporations, international equity offerings or depository receipts and international bond placements. To our knowledge, we are the first to use the Capital Data Bondware database. We examine not only the amount of international bonds floated each year but also the amount outstanding. Furthermore, we merge company-level data from World Scope in order to examine the cross-sectional attributes of Eurobond-issuing firms. Where possible, we comment on the extent to which Asia relied on internal versus external sources of funds.

---

10. Claessens, Djankov, and Lang (1999).

New Capital Mobilization within Domestic Markets

According to the International Finance Corporation's *Emerging Stock Markets Factbook 1998*, the total U.S. dollar market capitalization across the major Asian stock market exchanges in China, Indonesia, Korea, the Philippines, Malaysia, Taiwan (China), and Thailand increased more than threefold from roughly $297 billion to $1.105 trillion between 1990 and 1996.[11] Much of the growth in market capitalization in the region can be attributed to the outstanding growth on the Shanghai Stock Exchange and the Shenzhen Stock Exchange in China. Between 1991 and 1996 the combined U.S. dollar market capitalization of these two exchanges increased by a factor of fifty-five. In fact, China's stock market growth was the largest of any emerging market. Only four other countries—Argentina, Brazil, Malaysia, and the Philippines—managed this caliber of quadruple-digit growth rates, all of which were emerging stock markets. If we exclude China from our calculation, Asian stock markets doubled in size between 1990 and 1996. Although this figure seems impressive, it is substantially lower than the threefold increase mentioned previously.

Within each of the Asian countries we find a similar story for the growth in market capitalization of the local stock markets. Stock exchanges in Indonesia, Malaysia, the Philippines, Taiwan, and Thailand increased their market capitalization by factors of ten, five, twelve, two, and three, respectively. Korea was the only East Asian country that failed to double its stock market capitalization during the period. In fact, the Korean Stock Exchange recorded a gain in market capitalization of little more than 25 percent between 1990 and 1996. With the exception of Taiwan and Korea, the market capitalization of Asian stock markets exceeded the 270 percent growth rate that emerging markets as a group posted during the same period. Moreover, all Asian stock markets with the exception of Korea experienced growth rates of market capitalization in excess of the 170 percent increase in market capitalization posted by U.S. stock markets between 1990 and 1996. Overall, local Asian stock markets increased their market capitalization at a faster pace than most developed markets.

The growth rates of market capitalization that characterized the region allowed East Asian stock exchanges to remain the largest emerging stock markets in the world. As a region, the combined market capitalization of Asian equity markets accounted for 48 percent of the total stock market

---

11. International Finance Corporation (various issues).

capitalization in emerging markets in 1990. Asian equity markets maintained this market share up until 1996. As of 1990 Asian stock markets were roughly four times as large as the combined stock markets in Latin America. In fact, the market capitalization of both the Korean Stock Exchange and the Taiwan Stock Exchange was larger than the entire market capitalization across all Latin American stock exchanges in 1990.

However, Latin American stock markets grew much faster than stock markets in Asia. By 1996 the total stock market capitalization of Latin America stood at $444 billion and was more than five times as large as its level in 1990. As a result of their rapid growth, Latin American stock markets made progress in closing the size gap in market capitalization between the two regions. As of the end of 1996, Asian stock markets as a group were only twice as large as their Latin American counterparts. Were Latin American stock markets more efficient at rolling out new market capitalization, or were the phenomenal growth rates in market capitalization driven by share price appreciation?

Although these growth rates may seem impressive, they do not necessarily indicate the mobilization of new equity within these local stock markets. The total market capitalization of any individual stock exchange may increase as a result of either share price appreciation or new capital mobilization. To identify how much of the growth in Asia's market capitalization resulted from new capital mobilization, we examine the number of companies listed on each of the exchanges in Asia and the value of new shares issued by existing firms. We interpret an increase in the number of companies listed on each exchange as a proxy for the number of initial public offerings (IPOs) within the country.

The total number of listed companies on the exchanges in China, Indonesia, Korea, Malaysia, the Philippines, Taiwan, and Thailand increased from 1,642 to 3,766. The addition of more than 2,100 listed companies constituted a significant amount of new capital mobilization. Moreover, this figure may be a conservative estimate of the IPOs given that some new companies were listed and subsequently delisted between 1990 and 1996. Nevertheless, the number of IPOs introduced on Asian exchanges made up almost one-third of all IPOs in emerging markets.

The growth in the number of firms listed on Asian stock exchanges was influenced to a large extent by the introduction of the Shanghai Stock Exchange in December of 1990. Between 1991 and 1996, at least 540 firms successfully issued initial public equity offerings on the Shanghai and Shenzhen exchanges. In fact, the new equity offerings in

China accounted for roughly a quarter of the new equity offerings throughout Asia.

Notwithstanding China's tremendous success, the other stock exchanges in Asia also added new firms during the 1990s. For example, the Kuala Lumpur Stock Exchange in Malaysia listed at least 339 new firms between 1990 and 1996. Indonesia, Korea, the Philippines, Taiwan, and Thailand also managed to incorporate new companies on their local exchanges. Each of the local equity markets in these countries listed 128, 91, 62, 240, and 183 new firms, respectively, over the same period.

In contrast, only 108 IPOs found their way onto the Latin American exchanges between 1990 and 1996. In fact, the Santiago Stock Exchange and the Bolsa de Valores in Caracas were the only exchanges in Latin America that listed more firms on their exchanges in 1996 than in 1990. All other exchanges in the region experienced a decline in the number of firms listed during the same period. While 108 new firms began trading on organized exchanges in Latin America between 1990 and 1996, not all of these firms survived. In fact, the total number of firms listed across all Latin American exchanges increased by eleven between 1990 and 1996. In light of this evidence, we can safely conclude that the increase in market capitalization on the Latin American stock exchanges resulted primarily from share price appreciation. Asian exchanges, in contrast, increased their market capitalization in large part by floating new equity offerings.

Unfortunately, the IFC (International Finance Corporation) data do not allow us to study the size of the IPOs. However, we can study seasoned equity offerings for the subset of firms that make up the IFC's emerging market indexes using the emerging markets database. Although these indexes do not provide comprehensive coverage of a country's entire stock market, the firms selected encompass at least 60 percent of the market capitalization of the entire stock market at any given point in time. We must bear in mind, however, that the figures provided by the IFC on new share issuance serve as a conservative estimate of the total amount of new equity floated within the domestic stock market in any given year. In the section to follow we use seasoned equity offerings and new share offerings interchangeably.

The total U.S. dollar value of public share issuance for IFC constituent firms is presented in panel A of figure 3-1. More than two-thirds of the total value of new shares issued in China, Indonesia, Korea, Malaysia, the Philippines, Taiwan, and Thailand were issued in just three countries: Korea, Malaysia, and Taiwan. Korea alone accounted for just over a quarter of the

Figure 3-1. *New Capital Mobilization and Share Price Appreciation,*
1990–96

Panel A. Total Value of Public Offerings and Share Issuance by IFC Constituents
Millions of U.S. dollars

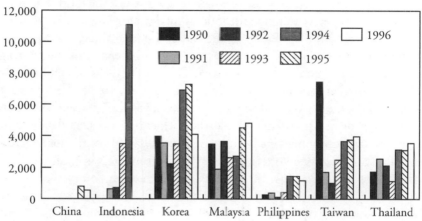

Panel B. Ratio of New Share Issuance to Change in Market Capitalization
Ratio

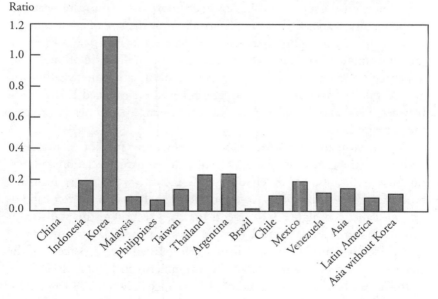

Source: Data from IFC's emerging markets database.

total value of new shares issued by these countries between 1990 and 1996. We should expect the total value of shares issued in Korea, Malaysia, and Taiwan to exceed that of other countries in the region because these markets are extremely large relative to the rest of the region.

In order to get a better sense of which markets issued the most shares relative to their size, we examine the ratio of total value of new shares to market capitalization. Between 1990 and 1996, the total value of new shares issued in Korea, Malaysia, and Taiwan averaged 3 percent of the existing market capitalization of these countries. The ratio of the total value of new shares to market capitalization in Thailand, however, averaged 3.9 percent during the same period. In Indonesia, this average was 7 percent. Based on the subset of firms available in the IFC's emerging markets database, it appears that equity markets in Indonesia and Thailand were more aggressive in issuing seasoned offerings than the larger markets in East Asia.

Asia issued more than three times more seasoned equity than Latin America during the period. The total value of seasoned equity offerings by IFC constituents in Asia between 1990 and 1996 was roughly $120 billion, while in Latin America the total issuance amounted to just over $32 billion. Of course, Asian equity markets are almost four times larger than equity markets in Latin America. Thus we should expect that within Asia new equity issues could be absorbed more easily into the relatively deeper equity markets. However, controlling for the size of these markets we find that Asian equity markets dominated Latin America not only in the total amount of new equity issuance, but also in the ratio of total value of new equity issuance to market capitalization. In Latin America, the ratio of total value of new equity to market capitalization averaged 1.41 percent between 1990 and 1996. In Asia, the ratio averaged 2.89 percent during the same period.

We can also use data from the IFC's emerging markets database to decompose the growth in market capitalization into appreciation and new capital mobilization. In order to examine these two effects, we form the ratio of total value of shares issued to the total change in market capitalization. Panel B of figure 3-1 presents the cross section of this statistic for various countries in Asia and Latin America. For the Asian countries presented in this figure, new share issuance accounted for 15 percent of the change in market capitalization of the region between 1990 and 1996.

In Korea, the total value of new share issuance between 1990 and 1996 exceeded the total change in market capitalization. During this same period the Korean IFC price index lost 50 percent of its value in U.S. dollar terms. This dramatic decline in share price reduced the overall market capitalization, and the ratio reported in figure 3-_ is greater than 1. Leaving out Korea from our average ratio across Asia, we find that seasoned equity offerings by IFC constituents accounted for 11 percent of the total change in market capitalization between 1990 and 1996.

Comparing Latin America to Asia we find that within Asia new capital mobilization played a larger role in explaining the growth in market capitalization. Only 8 percent of the growth in the market capitalization of Latin American stock markets could be attributed to new capital mobilization. In Asia, depending on the set of countries included, new capital mobilization accounted for between 11 and 15 percent of the growth in market capitalization of the region's equity markets.

Equity offerings on the local stock markets in East Asia were not the only means by which local companies could raise capital. Certain firms were able to tap into the local bond markets to raise capital. According to the International Federation of Stock Exchanges, the total market value of bonds listed on the exchanges in Indonesia, Korea, Malaysia, the Philippines, Taiwan, and Thailand exceeded \$105.8 billion in 1992. By the end of 1996, this figure had almost doubled to \$208.2 billion.[12] We make no attempt to ascertain how much of this increase in market value resulted from changes in interest rates. Furthermore, we only examine bonds that are listed on the major stock exchanges in each country.

The market value of bonds listed on major exchanges was not evenly distributed among the Asian countries. In fact, the market capitalization of bonds listed on the Korean Stock Exchange accounted for roughly three-fourths of the total market capitalization of bonds listed on exchanges throughout the region. The Taiwan Stock Exchange had the second largest market capitalization of bonds listed in all of East Asia. Between 1992 and 1996 the market value of bonds listed on the Taiwan exchange increased from \$20.8 billion to \$36.7 billion. Combined, bonds listed in Korea and Taiwan accounted for more than 95 percent of the total value of bonds listed on the major East Asian stock exchanges.

The rest of East Asia appears to have developed less mature local bond markets. Excluding Korea, the total value of bonds listed on the local exchanges in East Asia in any given year in the 1990s was less than the amount listed on the Buenos Aires Stock Exchange. In fact, excluding Korea, the total value of bonds listed on the Latin American exchanges

12. International Federation of Stock Exchanges (http://www.fibv.com).

averaged roughly twice the value of bonds listed in East Asian exchanges throughout the 1990s. So although East Asian equity markets are roughly four times the size of those in Latin America, the combined local equity and debt markets in East Asia are only twice the size of those in Latin America.

As a fraction of total liabilities, Asian corporations appear to have relied less heavily on bond financing than on equity financing during the early 1990s compared with other countries. In fact, the ratio of the market capitalization of bonds to equity was 28 percent in Asia in 1991 compared with 54 percent in the United States. The ratio of the market capitalization of bonds to equity was just over 25 percent in Latin America in 1991. Of course, one major source of financing that is conspicuously missing is the total amount of bank loans to Asian corporations. As such, our relative comparisons across regions consider only the ratio of bond finance to equity finance and not the ratio of debt finance to equity finance.

A closer examination reveals that Korea's extensive use of bond financing throughout the 1990s drove up the ratio of bond market capitalization to equity market capitalization for the region as a whole. In fact, Korea's average ratio of total market capitalization of bonds to total market capitalization of equity was roughly 90 percent between 1990 and 1996. At the end of 1996, Korean equity was highly leveraged with domestic bond issues alone! Excluding Korea from our calculations, the ratio of market capitalization of bonds to equity in Asia drops from 28 to 8 percent. Thus the ratio for Asia, excluding Korea, was roughly a third of that for Latin America and a fifth of that for the United States.

Comparing Asian bond markets to their Latin American counterparts, we find that, in general, the total market value of Latin American bonds was more evenly distributed across the region. Argentine bonds listed in Buenos Aires commanded the greatest share of the total market value of bonds listed on Latin American exchanges. Between 1992 and 1996, the market value of Argentine bonds made up roughly 50 percent of the entire market value of Latin American bonds. Mexican debt originally accounted for 55 percent of the Latin American total in 1992. However, between 1992 and 1994 the market value of bonds listed on the Bolsa de Valores in Mexico fell 50 percent. During the same period, the market value of bonds listed in Buenos Aires increased almost 300 percent. Despite the wide swings in the relative market valuations of bonds across countries, in general, the market capitalization of traded debt was more evenly distributed across Latin American markets than it was in Asia.

New Capital Mobilization outside Domestic Markets

The story is incomplete unless we examine Asia's use of external financing. In fact, during the 1990s, Asian corporations were extremely successful at raising capital in international equity and debt markets.

Throughout the 1990s, Asian corporations made extensive use of international equity markets to raise capital. Figure 3-2 provides a snapshot of the amount of international equity floated by East Asian countries during the early 1990s. Between 1992 and 1995, China, Indonesia, Korea, Malaysia, the Philippines, and Thailand raised more than $17.7 billion in equity in international capital markets. Over the same period, IFC constituents raised $62.7 billion. For every $3 raised in local equity markets, Asian firms raised approximately $1 in international equity markets.

The pace of international equity issuance by Asian countries increased throughout the 1990s. In 1992 twenty-five Asian firms raised a total of $1.9 billion in international equity markets. By 1995 the number of firms issuing international equity had increased to seventy, and the total amount issued rose to $7.2 billion. Moreover, the average amount that each firm issued increased throughout the 1990s. In 1992 Asian firms raised $76 million in each international equity issue. By 1995 this figure had increased to $104 million. Asian equity appeared to be well received by international investors.

The issuance record varies across Asian countries. Chinese firms were the most successful at raising funds in international equity markets. Between 1992 and 1995, seventy-six separate international equity issues by Chinese firms totaled $4.9 billion. In fact, more than a quarter of the total international equity issued in Asia came from Chinese equity issues. During the same period, only twenty-five Indonesian equity placements were recorded in international markets. Nevertheless, more than $3.6 billion of Indonesian equity found its way into international markets. Korean firms were also successful in their placements in international equity markets. Overall, forty-three placements were made between 1992 and 1995, bringing in a total of $3.2 billion. In contrast, Malaysia had only seven successful floats between 1992 and 1995. Combined, these international equity placements raised just over $1.6 billion dollars, roughly half the amount raised by Korea.

Comparing the international equity issuance record of Asia to that of Latin America, we find little difference at the aggregate level. Between 1992 and 1995, 209 Asian and 180 Latin American equity placements

Figure 3-2. *International Equity Offerings, 1992–95*

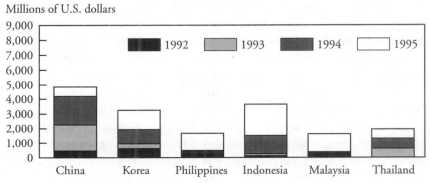

Panel A. East Asia

Millions of U.S. dollars

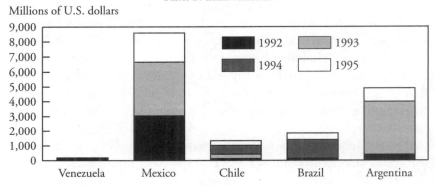

Panel B. Latin America

Millions of U.S. dollars

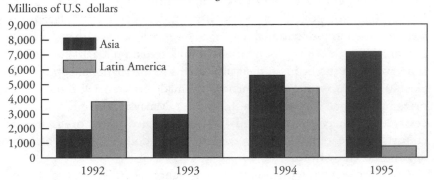

Panel C. Regional Totals

Millions of U.S. dollars

Source: Data taken from World Bank (various years).

were made in international equity markets. The total value of international equity placements during the same time period was $17.7 billion for Asia and $16.9 billion for Latin America. The average international equity placement raised $85 million in Asia and $94 million in Latin America. On the surface these two regions appear to have very similar issuance records.

However, at least one subtle but important distinction should be mentioned. Latin American firms tended to prefer publicly issued international equity to private placements. Of the 180 equity placements made by Latin American countries, 138 were public issues. Roughly three-quarters of the international equity issues were sold to the general public. In Asia, only 79 of the 209 international equity placements were public issues. Roughly two-thirds of the placements made by Asian companies were sold privately.

Unfortunately, the World Bank data do not allow us to distinguish between the various forms of international equity placement used by Asian firms. The Bank of New York's depository receipts database provides more detailed information on the classification of each of Asia's international equity offerings. Depository receipts allowed Asian firms to attract a broader base of investors as well as to improve their name recognition overseas. These receipts are negotiable certificates that usually represent a company's publicly traded equity or debt. They are created when a broker purchases the company's shares on the home stock market and delivers the shares to the depository's local custodian bank, which then instructs the depository bank to issue depository receipts.

Two common forms of depository receipts are American depository receipts (ADRs) and global depository receipts (GDRs). Both ADRs and GDRs are public issues. They are issued either as a sponsored Level I, that is, over the counter (OTC), or as a sponsored Level II, which allows the depository receipt to be traded on an exchange. In order to achieve Level II status, the issuing firm must comply with GAAP accounting principles and register with the U.S. Securities and Exchange Commission (SEC). Firms issuing under Level I status avoid having to comply with GAAP. Asian firms also participate in private placements under Rule 144a. Rule 144a allows these firms to place depository receipts with large international institutional investors while avoiding both SEC registration and GAAP regulations. Finally, depository receipts can be issued to non-U.S. institutional investors under Regulation "S."

The first Asian countries to tap into foreign markets using depository receipts were Singapore and Hong Kong (China). Both Neptune Orient

Lines (Singapore) and Applied International Holding (Hong Kong) issued over-the-counter ADRs in January 1989. Following these international offerings, companies from the Philippines and Korea decided to issue depository receipts in June 1990 and December 1990, respectively. The Korean ADR issue in 1990, Samsung Company, was the first Asian depository receipt to be filed under Rule 144a. The success of these four firms appeared to set a precedent.

Companies from Hong Kong enjoyed tremendous success in ADR issuance. Between 1990 and 1997, 101 firms based in Hong Kong issued depository receipts to international investors. This constitutes more than 37 percent of the total number of depository receipts issued from all of Asia. Nevertheless, the rest of Asia also enjoyed increasing success at depository receipt issuance throughout the 1990s. Several companies from China, Indonesia, Korea, Malaysia, the Philippines, Taiwan, and Thailand also managed to attract foreign investors by issuing ADRs and GDRs. We examine the record of each country in turn.

Between 1990 and 1997, forty-nine companies headquartered in Taiwan issued ADRs and GDRs to U.S. and international investors. Roughly 60 percent of these companies decided to issue under Rule 144a. This decision allowed companies to ignore SEC registration. Eleven of the remaining twenty companies issued under Regulation "S." The bulk of these companies issued depository receipts between 1995 and 1997. Of the forty-nine companies that raised capital through depository receipts, only one, Taiwan Manufacturing Semiconductor, issued ADRs under Level II. This issue was placed on the New York Stock Exchange (NYSE) in October 1997, three months after the onset of the Asian crisis. Overall, it appears as though Taiwanese companies preferred to avoid SEC registration in their bids for international capital.

Korean firms also enjoyed success in the depository receipts market. Twenty-six of the twenty-nine Korean firms that tapped into this market did so under Rule 144a. The remaining three firms issued Level II public ADRs on the NYSE in 1994 and 1995.

China holds the record for having the largest number of firms to issue Level II public ADRs on the NYSE. Between 1990 and 1997, ten Chinese firms tapped into the U.S. market using this form of depository receipt. Moreover, the Chinese firm Shanghai Petrochemical has the distinction of being the first firm in Asia excluding Japan to be listed on the NYSE under Level II rules. As early as July 1993, U.S. and international investors could trade ADR shares of Shanghai Petrochemical listed on the NYSE through

its custodial broker, the Bank of New York. Moreover, Shanghai Petrochemical was the first Chinese firm to issue depository receipts of any kind.
Although China waited until July 1993 to issue its first depository receipt,
twenty-eight firms had issued depository receipts by 1997, just one shy of
the number of firms from Korea, whose first issue occurred in 1990.
Clearly, Chinese firms drew considerable interest from international and
U.S. capital markets.

Companies from the Philippines and Thailand experienced limited success in the depository receipts market. Between 1990 and 1997 only nineteen firms from the Philippines and eleven firms from Thailand tapped into
international investors through ADRs and GDRs. Just over half of these
firms issued OTC Level I depository receipts. A third issued ADRs under
Rule 144a. Finally, one firm from the Philippines, the Philippine Long Distance Telephone Company, issued ADRs under Level II on the NYSE.

Indonesian and Malaysian companies issued the smallest number of
ADRs and GDRs. Only ten firms from Indonesia and eight firms from
Malaysia issued depository receipts between 1990 and 1997. Of these
eighteen firms, only three from Indonesia issued under Level II on the
NYSE. The remaining fifteen firms issued either OTC under Level I or
under Rule 144a.

Although ADRs and GDRs provided Asian firms with an attractive
means of raising international capital, it was not the only way these firms
could tap into international capital markets. Throughout the 1990s, the
international bond market served as an alternative source of foreign capital for Asian corporations. Between 1990 and 1997, East Asian firms managed to float more than $120 billion in the international bond market.[13]
Almost three-quarters of this amount, roughly $90 billion, was denomi-
nated in dollars. Although we do not have data on the total amount of
Asian international equity placements for this entire period, some comparison can be made. Recall that between 1992 and 1995, Asian corporations placed roughly $18 billion in international equity markets.
Comparing this figure to the amount placed in international bond markets, we find that for every $1.00 raised in international equity, Asian cor-
porations raised $2.50 in international bond offerings.

Korean and Chinese firms led in terms of the total market capitalization
of international bond floats. Combined, these two countries accounted for
65 percent of the total market capitalization of international bonds floated

13. All international bond data come from Capital Data Bondware database.

by East Asian issuers. Indonesia, Malaysia, the Philippines, and Thailand each managed to float between $9 billion and $11 billion over the same time period. Taiwanese companies floated just over $5 billion on the international bond market during the 1990s.

Korean firms led East Asia in terms of total market capitalization of international bonds issuance. Between 1990 and 1997, Korean firms managed to borrow $53.6 billion from the international bond markets; 65 percent of this total amount was denominated in U.S. dollars. Table 3-1 provides a snapshot of international bond activity. Like many other Asian countries, Korean firms tapped into the international bond market in increasing quantities through the 1990s. In 1990 the total Korean float amounted to roughly $1.5 billion. By 1993 the total float had increased to almost $4.3 billion. In 1997 Korean firms borrowed just over $11.4 billion from international investors in the international bond market. This increase in participation was common among East Asian corporations.

As Korean firms continued to issue debt in the international bond market, the total debt outstanding for the country increased. Ignoring the prepayment of loans, the total of international bonds outstanding increased dramatically during the 1990s. In 1990 the total amount of Korean-issued international bonds outstanding was $3.9 billion. As of 1993, this figure had increased to $10.3 billion. By 1996 the total amount of Korean-issued international bonds outstanding stood at $27.2 billion. More important, about 65 percent was denominated in dollars.

In order to appreciate the magnitude of this debt, we have constructed country-level leverage ratios. A firm's leverage ratio can be interpreted as providing some evidence of the financial risk borne by the equity holders of the firm. Our country-level leverage ratios provide some indication of the financial risk to investors interested in the country as a whole. We calculate country-level international bond leverage ratios for a given year as the total amount of international bonds outstanding at year's end divided by the market capitalization of the country's stock market. This ratio is only a proxy for a leverage ratio. First, the firms issuing international bonds may not belong to the national stock market. Second, East Asian governments implicitly or explicitly guaranteed many of these international bonds. Government backing may or may not remove the financial risk of highly leveraged firms. Nevertheless, our leverage ratios may be interpreted as providing a very "conservative" estimate of financial risk given that the total amount of international bond financing was conducted by a small subset of firms represented in the market capitalization of the entire national stock market.

Between 1990 and 1997 Korea's repeated use of the international market added to its overall foreign debt outstanding and increased its country-level leverage ratio. In 1990 Korea's country-level international bond leverage ratio was 3.5 percent. By 1993 this figure had increased to 7 percent. At the end of 1996, the ratio of total international bonds outstanding to equity market capitalization stood at 20 percent. The leverage ratio for dollar-denominated international bonds had grown to 13 percent by 1996.

Chinese firms were also very successful in their efforts to raise·capital in the international bond market (table 3-1). Between 1990 and 1997, China floated $15.8 billion on the international bond market. In contrast to Korea, just over half of this total float was denominated in U.S. dollars. However, like Korea, China's involvement in the international bond market increased throughout the 1990s. Between 1990 and 1994, a span of five years, Chinese firms raised a total of $6.4 billion in the international bond market. In contrast, in the short span of two years between 1996 and 1997, Chinese firms raised more than $8 billion.

The rapid increase in international bonds issued by Chinese firms contributed to the 150 percent increase in international bonds outstanding between 1990 and 1997. Despite this increase, China's country-level international bond leverage ratio was not significantly affected between 1992 and 1995. In fact, the leverage ratio actually decreased from its peak of 25 percent during 1992 to 8 percent in 1995. Although the decrease in the ratio of country-level international bond leverage can be interpreted as a reduction in financial risk, the greatest reduction in Chinese financial risk stemmed from the implicit government guarantees on its private foreign corporate debt.

Thai companies issued the third largest amount of international bond debt of any East Asian nation during the period 1990 to 1997 (table 3-1). During this period, Thailand floated just over $10.8 billion on the international bond market. More than 80 percent of this debt was denominated in U.S. dollars. By the end of 1997, Thailand had accumulated $12.9 billion of foreign debt outstanding from its activity in the international bond market. Almost 85 percent of this debt outstanding was denominated in U.S. dollars. Almost half came from international bond market activity in 1995 alone.

Table 3-1. *International Bond Floats and International Bonds Outstanding, 1985–97*

Millions of U.S. dollars

Country and indicator	1985 Bond floats	1985 Bonds outstanding	1990 Bond floats	1990 Bonds outstanding	1995 Bond floats	1995 Bonds outstanding	1996 Bond floats	1996 Bonds outstanding	1997 Bond floats	1997 Bonds outstanding
China										
U.S. dollar denominated	250	0	127	1,050	45	3,280	1,820	3,075	3,969	4,645
Total	759	84	127	4,435	1,433	9,006	3,183	9,699	4,738	11,454
Indonesia										
U.S. dollar denominated	0	525	200	875	2,358	1,986	4,751	4,144	4,406	8,809
Total	0	525	200	1,036	2,393	2,164	5,201	4,356	4,714	9,438
Korea, Republic of										
U.S. dollar denominated	930	365	1,050	2,110	6,575	12,405	10,209	17,720	7,896	27,099
Total	1,467	1,063	1,507	3,899	10,690	18,707	14,875	27,205	11,402	40,122
Malaysia										
U.S. dollar denominated	1,250	2,040	200	3,450	579	3,885	2,322	4,465	2,430	6,587
Total	2,004	2,274	200	5,236	579	5,768	2,527	6,136	3,506	8,463

Philippines										
U.S. dollar denominated	0	30	0	30	700	2,068	2,353	2,767	2,318	4,870
Total	0	30	0	30	817	2,144	2,722	2,962	2,487	5,434
Taiwan										
U.S. dollar denominated	0	165	0	340	688	2,004	1,375	2,692	2,778	4,067
Total	0	185	0	360	719	2,394	1,403	3,112	2,920	4,516
Thailand										
U.S. dollar denominated	700	145	0	1,045	1,620	5,053	3,957	6,673	1,250	10,605
Total	761	256	0	1,465	1,795	6,453	4,789	8,088	1,598	12,852
Latin America										
U.S. dollar denominated	0	2,935	1,014	4,027	5,027	36,681	25,690	37,435	35,242	54,967
Total	46	3,677	1,392	4,450	14,131	42,577	40,769	52,099	49,175	83,712
East Asia										
U.S. dollar denominated	3,130	3,270	1,577	8,900	12,566	30,681	26,967	41,537	25,047	66,683
Total	4,990	4,417	2,034	16,461	18,426	46,635	34,980	61,559	31,365	92,279

Source: Capital Data Bondware database.

Although Thailand's country-level ratio was never as high as Korea's or China's, it did increase dramatically over the course of the 1990s. Between 1993 and 1996 this leverage ratio more than tripled from 1 to 7 percent. Clearly, Thailand's activity in the international bond market was a factor in this dramatic increase. Moreover, Thailand carried a higher percentage of dollar-denominated debt than either Korea or China.

Indonesia, Malaysia, and the Philippines had similar experiences in the international bond markets. Each managed to float between $8.2 billion and $14.2 billion between 1990 and 1997 (table 3-1). All three of these countries experienced the greatest increases in their international bond floats between 1994 and 1996. Roughly 80 and 90 percent of both the Malaysian and the Philippine total floats, respectively, were denominated in dollars. Dollar-denominated floats in Indonesia contributed to 93 percent of the total amount. In the case of Indonesia, the country-level international bond leverage ratio declined significantly over the decade: from 13 percent in 1990 to 4.8 percent by the end of 1996. The reason for this decline is that the amount of Indonesian international bonds outstanding remained relatively small throughout the 1990s. In fact, between 1990 and 1997 the amount of Indonesian international bonds outstanding stayed below $10 billion. The Malaysian country-level international bond leverage ratio also decreased over the same time period. In 1990 Malaysia's ratio was 7 percent. By the end of 1996 it had dropped to 1.5 percent. The decline in the Malaysian leverage ratio can be understood in light of the outstanding performance of the Malaysian equity market during the 1990s. The buy and hold return on the IFC Malaysian index between 1990 and 1996 exceeded that of all other East Asian countries.

The ability of East Asian companies to tap into this international market can be judged vis-à-vis their Latin American counterparts. Figure 3-3 portrays the total international bond floats from emerging markets. Between 1990 and 1997, Latin American companies issued just over $104 billion in international bonds. The fact that Latin American firms surpassed their East Asian counterparts in total international bond issuance is astounding considering that the Latin American debt crisis remained a recent memory for most investors. The data concur with this assertion. Between 1982 and 1989, Latin America was able to raise only $4.3 billion in the international bond market. In fact, in 1983 and 1984, Latin America could not raise a single penny in these markets. Obviously, the Latin American debt crisis in 1982 had a noticeable impact on the ability of Latin American firms to raise

Figure 3-3. *Regional Shares of International Bonds, 1980–97*

Panel A. International Bond Floats

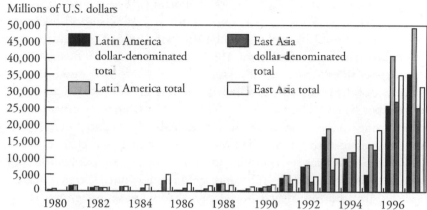

Millions of U.S. dollars

Panel B. International Bonds Outstanding

Millions of U.S. dollars

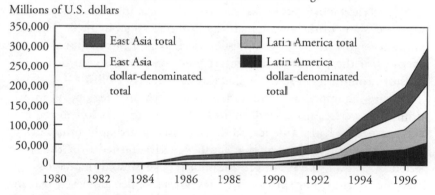

Source: Estimates from Capital Data Bondware database.

capital outside their national boundaries. During this same period, East Asian firms appeared unaffected by the crisis. They managed to borrow more than $16.6 billion in the international bond market between 1982 and 1989. Despite the East Asian advantage during the late 1980s and early 1990s, Latin American firms managed to convince investors of their financial strengths toward the end of the 1990s. Between 1990 and 1997 Latin America floated almost $150 billion in international bonds, almost $30 billion more than was issued out of East Asia.

New Capital Mobilization and Privatization

Perhaps the most conclusive evidence supporting the assertion that Asian capital markets were able to secure new funds for capital-starved organizations can be found by looking at the successful record of privatization throughout the region during the 1990s. In fact between 1992 and 1995, Asian governments sold stakes in state-owned enterprises amounting to 3 percent of the total market capitalization of their local stock markets on average per year. Of course, not all of the proceeds from these privatization efforts came from local investors. In fact, roughly 57 percent of the $18 billion in revenue during this period was paid for in foreign exchange.

The most popular forms of privatization in Asia were public offerings and new share issuance. In 1994 and 1995 Asian countries experimented with a third form of privatization designed to increase foreign participation: ADR issuance. The success of these privatization efforts resulted from successful marketing and public interest in these public offerings. The ability of local capital markets to absorb 3 percent a year in new issues provides some testimony of the overall maturity of these capital markets. The sustained foreign interest in the public offerings and international equity offerings of these state-owned enterprises serves as a signal of foreign investors' commitment to the region during the early 1990s.

Despite the impressive efforts made throughout the region, Asian privatization revenues from 1990 to 1996 paled in comparison to the revenues earned by Latin American countries. Asia earned only a third of the amount from privatizations that Latin America earned over the same period. Moreover, the Asian privatization process slowed dramatically in 1996. Across the region, privatization revenues dropped almost 50 percent from their levels in 1995 and more than 66 percent from the regional high in 1993. This decrease cannot be attributed to investors' loss of interest in privatization worldwide. Latin America experienced a 300 percent gain in privatization revenues between 1995 and 1996. The dramatic slowdown in the privatization process can be attributed to a combination of two factors: diminishing support for privatization programs among the Asian electorate and poor performance of public offerings due to flat performance in Asian equity markets overall.

More insight can be gained by looking at the privatization efforts of each country. China, Indonesia, and Malaysia led the Asian privatization effort in terms of gross privatization revenues. Malaysia's privatizations alone constituted roughly a third of the entire region's total revenues.

Between 1990 and 1995 the government earned more than $9.1 billion from the privatization of thirty separate firms. Most of this privatization program was planned in advance. In February of 1991, Malaysia released its Privatization Master Plan calling for the privatization of key industries, including the national electrical company, Tenaga Nacional, and the national automobile company, Perusahaan Otomobil Nacional. The public offering of Tenaga Nacional was the largest to date in Asia, generating the equivalent of $1.2 billion in local currency. This sale confirmed the government's commitment to privatization. Between 1993 and 1994 the Malaysian government sold 50 percent of its position in the national airline, Malaysia Airlines, and began to sell off its interests in various shipping concerns, agricultural and forestry firms, and petroleum firms. In 1995 the Malaysian government sold 21.3 percent of Petroras Gas to a combination of domestic and international investors, generating $1.1 billion. Nearly a third of this amount was in the form of hard foreign currency. The Privatization Master Plan had a significant impact on the Malaysian economy overall: between 1992 and 1995, the proceeds generated from privatization averaged 3 percent of annual gross domestic product (GDP). More important, the privatization effort demonstrated the ability of local capital markets to mobilize new equity. Roughly a quarter of the privatization earnings, a little over $2 billion, resulted from public offerings in local capital markets.

The Chinese government's privatization earnings between 1990 and 1996 amounted to just over $7.9 billion. As was the case in Malaysia, the bulk of these earnings were generated between 1992 and 1995. However, unlike Malaysia, China's successful privatization plan was implemented without an official government schedule. The most interesting aspect of the Chinese privatization experience is the method by which China managed to sell off its state-owned enterprises. All privatization efforts were brought about through equity issues floated on the Shanghai and Shenzhen exchanges. Beginning in 1991, the Chinese government began to sell off state-owned enterprises by issuing dollar-denominated B shares on the Shanghai Exchange and Hong Kong dollar-denominated B shares on the Shenzhen exchange. Between 1991 and 1995, 100 percent of China's $7.01 billion proceeds were paid for with foreign currency. By comparison, Malaysia earned only $1.24 billion in foreign currency on its $9.11 billion total privatization effort between 1990 and 1995. The largest privatization deal to date in China was the sale of 25 percent of the equity in Huang Power International in 1994. This deal was fully financed with an ADR float on the NYSE. In 1996 the China Securities Regulatory Commission stipulated that H share offerings would have to meet a minimum issue size, a minimum annual profit, and a three-year earnings record. These new regulations should strengthen the prospects for H share issues in the future.

Remarkably, Indonesia ranked third highest, among East Asian countries, in total privatization revenues between 1990 and 1996, despite the fact that the country's privatization program ranked second lowest in total number of companies privatized. Indonesia privatized only fifteen firms during this period. Nevertheless, the average size of each privatization in Indonesia was second only to that of Malaysia. The bulk of Indonesia's privatization proceeds stemmed from the privatization of its telecommunications industry. In 1994 PT Indonesian Satellite (INDOSAT) was put up for sale. The government sold 32 percent of INDOSAT for $1.16 billion. The deal was impressive not only because of its size but also because 78 percent of the proceeds came from the issuance of ADR shares on the New York Stock Exchange. Clearly, international investors were interested in Indonesia as late as 1994. In 1995 Indonesia returned to this market to help in its privatization of PT Telekomunikasi. Although the total sale of PT Telekomunikasi exceeded that of the INDOSAT privatization, this privatization relied to a lesser extent on the U.S. market: only 37.5 percent of the $1.68 billion deal was financed by ADR issuance. The pace of privatization decreased more than 50 percent between 1995 and 1996. During this time, Indonesia concluded only two sales. The combined earnings from the sale of PT Telekom and Bank Negara brought in just over $1 billion for the Indonesian government. It appears that the privatization slowdown in Indonesia was mainly caused by government in-fighting over the merits of privatization as well as disagreement over which firms should be privatized.

Following the Foreign Investment Act in June 1991, the Philippines embarked on its own privatization program. Between 1991 and 1995, the Philippine government placed eighty separate businesses onto the privatization docket. In fact, the Philippine government holds the regional record at fifty-one for number of privatization efforts in a single year. Despite the impressive number of firms put up for sale, the Philippine privatization program ranked fifth in cumulative privatization revenues in Asia. Malaysia, the leader in this category, with privatization revenues of $9.1 billion, earned almost three times as much as the Philippines. The Philippines generated lower revenues because its privatization efforts only included small firms. The average amount earned at each privatization amounted to only $41.7 million. Malaysia, in contrast, earned a little over $267 million on average from each of its privatization efforts. The Philippine privatization effort ran into a roadblock in 1996: the scheduled privatization of Manila Waterworks and Sewerage System was delayed, and the deal was not concluded until 1997. According to the World Bank, this delay was typical of all privatization efforts during the year. In aggregate the annual proceeds from privatization dropped almost 90 percent from $207 million in 1995 to $22 million in 1996.[14] It appears as though the pace of privatization had slowed significantly from its high in 1993.

Thailand's revenues from privatization paled in comparison to those of the rest of Asia. Between 1990 and 1995, the Thai government sold its interests in only six companies. The total proceeds generated from these sales amounted to $950.3 million. Although Thailand's total number of privatization sales was not impressive when compared to those of Indonesia and Malaysia, Thailand was extremely successful at using the capital markets to sell off its vested interests. In five out of six cases, the privatization sales took the form of public offerings. Moreover, 15 percent of the total revenue from these public offerings was sold to foreign investors. Most of the sales to foreigners resulted from the privatization of the Thailand petroleum industry, however. It is not obvious that foreigners were interested in the entire Thai economy.

In 1996 the sale of the Khanom Electricity Generating Company included a public offering for $240 million, making it the second largest privatization to date in Thailand. As a result, Thailand and China share the distinction of being the only two countries in Asia to experience an increase in privatization revenues from 1995 to 1996. Despite the successful sale of Khanom Electricity, we are unwilling to stipulate that the increase in privatization revenues from 1995 to 1996 signaled either increased government commitment or increased investor enthusiasm for privatization. In the case of Thailand, the privatization record is too sparse to draw any strong conclusion.

New Capital Mobilization and Secondary Market Liquidity

With the exception of Taiwan and Thailand, all East Asian countries experienced higher trading volume in the stocks that constituted their IFC indexes. The value of shares traded in Indonesia rose dramatically after the

---

14. International Federation of Stock Exchanges (http://www.fibv.com).

beginning of the 1990s. In January 1990, the historic twelve-month average value of shares traded per month amounted to roughly 350 billion Indonesian rupiah. By December 1996, this figure had increased more than tenfold to almost 3,700 billion rupiah.

The value of shares trading in the IFC Korea index increased more than 200 percent from January 1990 to November 1994 before settling at more than 4.5 trillion Korean won in December of 1996. The value of shares trading on the IFC Korea index increased approximately 33 percent between January 1990 and December 1996.

Malaysia and the Philippines both enjoyed large gains in the value of shares trading between 1990 and the end of 1996. The value of shares trading on the IFC Malaysia index increased roughly 140 and 180 percent, respectively.

The increase in value traded on the IFC country indexes indicates a broader trend in the overall stock markets. In fact, according to the International Federation of Stock Exchanges, the total U.S. dollar value of shares traded across the stock markets of China, Indonesia, Korea, Malaysia, the Philippines, Taiwan, and Thailand increased from just under $830 billion in 1990 to $1.179 trillion in 1996.[15] The results for each of the individual exchanges are similar to the statistics provided by the IFC for its country-level indexes. Combined, the Shanghai and Shenzhen exchanges in China registered the largest percentage increase in total value of stocks traded. From their inception in late 1990 and early 1991, the value traded on both exchanges increased from $820 million to $256 billion. Of course this increase coincided with the opening of the Chinese exchanges, so we would expect a significant growth in the total value traded. However, China is interesting because just four years after the opening of its exchanges, the total value of shares traded had ballooned to impressive heights. In 1996 the value of shares traded in China alone exceeded the entire value traded across all Latin American exchanges.

The Kuala Lumpur Stock Exchange in Malaysia experienced the second highest growth rate of value traded during the 1990s. Between 1990 and 1996, the U.S. dollar value traded increased by a factor of fifteen. During the same period, the value traded on the Philippine stock exchange grew by a factor of nineteen. Indonesia, Korea, and Thailand had less impressive growth rates. The U.S. dollar value of shares traded on those markets increased by factors of 7.0, 1.3, and 0.9, respectively. Taiwan is the single

15. International Federation of Stock Exchanges (http://www.fibv.com).

exception to the East Asian pattern of positive value growth. Between 1990 and 1996 the U.S. dollar value traded on the Taiwan Stock Exchange decreased 34 percent.

Asian markets as a whole experienced decreased liquidity during the 1990s. One proxy for the liquidity of a market is the turnover ratio. In 1990 the turnover ratio across the region was 219 percent a year. By 1996 this ratio had dropped significantly to 118 percent. The single most important reason for this loss in liquidity was the massive drop in the total value traded on the Taiwan Stock Exchange. Between 1990 and 1996, the turnover ratio for the Taiwan Stock Exchange decreased from 423 to 204 percent. Furthermore, both Indonesia and Thailand recorded drops in their turnover ratios. In contrast, China, Korea, and Malaysia witnessed an increase in liquidity on the stocks listed on their exchanges.

Despite the changes in turnover ratios across East Asia throughout the 1990s, the region stands out among the other emerging markets in terms of the liquidity offered to its equity market investors. Comparing across regions, we find that the turnover ratio in any given year in the 1990s was at least twice as high in Asia as it was in Latin America. In most years, markets were almost three times as liquid in Asia as they were in Latin America. Moreover, the region as a whole experienced a higher ratio of equity market turnover than the United States in every year after 1990. In fact Chinese and Taiwanese equities were the most heavily traded equities in the world.

Asian Capital Market Liberalization

All of the events and descriptions of East Asian capital markets presented thus far help to paint a clearer picture of the health and growth of these capital markets during the 1990s. We have deferred until now the issue of financial market integration. The opening of local equity markets and debt markets to foreign investors has the potential to be the most influential event in the evolution of any emerging market.

The process of capital market liberalization implemented in East Asia can be described as one of gradualism. In general, the first step taken was the relaxation of restrictions that limited which industries foreign investors could own. At the same time, many governments established foreign investment limits dictating the amount of a firm's market capitalization that could be owned by foreign investors. Throughout East Asia, governments set limits that were low enough to prevent foreign control of domestic industries. Moreover, Asian governments were reluctant to relax foreign ownership limits in certain industries, namely finance and telecommunications. Eventually, East Asia began to remove less obvious barriers to its capital markets. Restrictions governing the convertibility of foreign exchange, repatriation of capital gains, and the payment of dividends to foreigners were removed.

History of Liberalization Programs

Although this generalization serves as a guide to the liberalization of capital markets in Asia as a whole, each country began the process independently and set its own pace. The individuality of each country's liberalization program dictates the extent to which foreign investors may have affected each of the East Asian markets. Therefore, it is important that we consider this cross-sectional variation in national liberalization policies when we examine the claim that foreign investors contributed to the financial panic in the region. For this claim to be accurate, we would expect that the countries most affected by the crisis were the most liberalized. We evaluate this possibility by examining the major policy changes that took place in East Asia and by determining the impact of these policies on the underlying capital markets.

The opening of Thailand's capital markets to foreign investors began in the early 1980s. In 1983 the Board of Investment criteria were relaxed, permitting foreign ownership in export-oriented firms. Foreigners were prohibited from owning a majority of the shares in firms that produced goods for domestic consumption. In September 1987, Thailand introduced the Alien Board. All foreign trading by companies that had reached their foreign investment limits would be conducted on this specially created exchange. Bekaert and Harvey argue that this represents the effective opening of the Thai market.[16]

Although foreign investors were able to participate in the Thai market as early as 1987, they did so under strict rules governing the repatriation of profits, the conversion of foreign exchange, and the payment of dividends to foreigners by domestic companies. In fact, until January 1990, all domestic firms had to seek prior approval before they could pay dividends

16. Bekaert and Harvey (1999).

to foreign investors. In April 1991 several rules regarding the repatriation of profits and the conversion of foreign currency were finally relaxed. Thus, although foreign investors could participate in Thailand as early as 1987, they were treated as second-class citizens in their equity market investment activity.

Malaysia became the second East Asian nation to open its capital markets to foreign investors (see figure 3-4, panel A). The Malaysian case is interesting because the liberalization program put into effect in late 1988 was the antithesis of a policy that began in 1971. During the 1970s the Malaysian government actively pursued a policy to reduce the level of foreign ownership of Malaysian stocks from 55 percent of market capitalization in 1970 to 30 percent by 1990. The plan was effective. By 1990 foreigner investors owned an estimated market share that was less than 25 percent of Malaysia's market capitalization. In October 1988 the government budget called for complete reversal of these policy goals. The new policy goal was to attract foreign investors.

Bekaert and Harvey list December 1988 as the official liberalization date for Malaysia, but foreigners continued to face certain ownership restrictions throughout the region.[17] The Outline Perspective Plan passed by the Malaysian government in June 1991 encouraged foreign investment while maintaining a 30 percent cap on foreign ownership of any firm. Foreigners had to wait until the first part of 1993 for the 30 percent cap to be removed on manufacturing firms.

Barriers to foreign investors in the Indonesian capital markets date back at least to 1974 when the government passed the Foreign Investment Law mandating majority ownership by Indonesian nationals in all joint ventures with foreign citizens. The Indonesian government began to remove its discriminatory policies as early as 1987 (figure 3-4, panel B). In December of 1987, the government introduced measures that allowed foreigners to purchase shares in eight specified non–joint venture firms. During 1988 the pace of liberalization picked up.

In September 1989, the Indonesian finance minister raised the foreign ownership limit to 49 percent of market capitalization for all firms excluding financial companies. Bekaert and Harvey point to this action as the official liberalization for Indonesia.[18] In early 1992 the ceiling on foreign

---

17. Bekaert and Harvey (1999).
18. Bekaert and Harvey (1999).

Figure 3-4. *Capital Market Liberalization in Four Asian Countries, 1984–98*

Panel A. Case Study of Malaysia

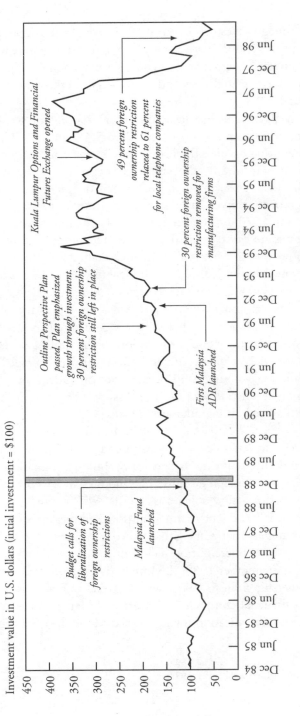

Investment value in U.S. dollars (initial investment = $100)

Panel B. Case Study of Indonesia

Investment value in U.S. dollars (initial investment = $100)

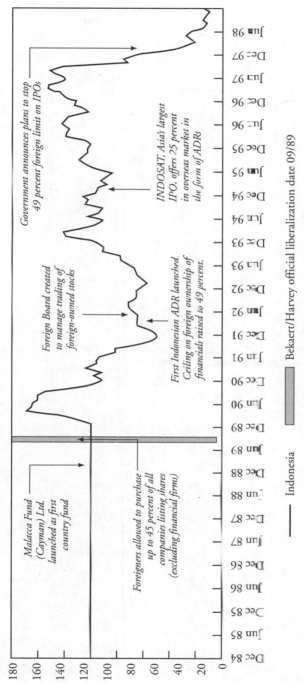

continued

Figure 3-4. *Capital Market Liberalization in Four Asian Countries, 1984–98 (continued)*

Panel C. Case Study of Taiwan

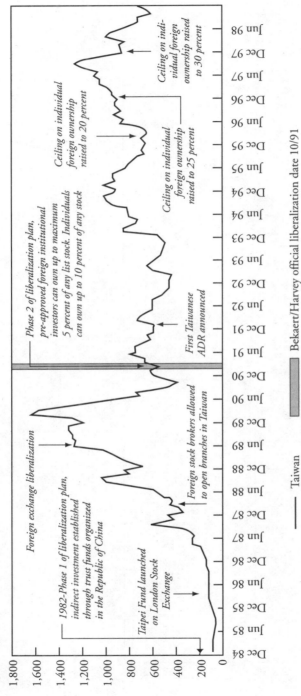

Panel D. Case Study of Korea

Investment value in U.S. dollars (intial investment = $100)

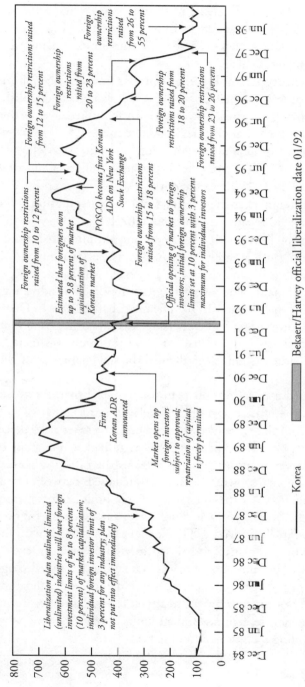

Source: Geert Bekaert and Campbell R. Harvey, "Chronology of Economic, Political, and Financial Events in Emerging Markets" (http://www.duke.edu/~charvey/Country_risk/couindex.htm).

ownership for Indonesian financial firms was raised to 49 percent. Soon after, in July 1992, Indonesia created the Foreign Board to manage the trading of foreign-owned stocks. These ownership limits remained in effect until the Asian financial crisis.

In Taiwan the government began to consider financial liberalization as early as 1982 (figure 3-4, panel C). The original plan was to establish trust funds in order to provide foreign investors with an indirect avenue through which they could participate in the Taiwanese market. Full implementation of the first phase of the liberalization program was delayed until August of 1983, at which point the International Trust Company was finally established. In 1986 Taiwan removed restrictions governing the convertibility of foreign exchange. Under the new regulations, foreign investors were able to repatriate profits more freely.

Phase two of the liberalization plan was not put into effect until early 1991. In January 1991 all approved foreign institutional investors were permitted to own up to a maximum of 10 percent of the market capitalization of any company. The ownership level for foreign individuals was raised twice between 1991 and 1996. The final change came in December 1996, when the level of foreign ownership was raised to 25 percent of a firm's market capitalization. In October 1997 this limit was increased to 30 percent. Once again gradualism defined the slow nature of the liberalization process.

Korea outlined a liberalization plan for financial markets as early as 1987; however, the official opening was delayed until January 1992 (figure 3-4, panel D). Initial foreign ownership limits were set at 10 percent of market capitalization with a 3 percent limit for individual foreign investors. Bekaert and Harvey consider January 1992 as the official liberalization date.[19] During the 1990s, ownership limits were raised. Between December 1991 and December 1997 the foreign ownership limit in Korea was raised on seven separate occasions; each time, it was ratcheted up by no more than 3 percent. Finally, in May 1998, Korean officials broke with the traditional policy of gradualism and raised foreign ownership levels from 26 to 55 percent. This move not only was dramatic in size but also signaled an overall shift of public opinion. Moreover, it demonstrates the desperate attempts by the Korean government to attract foreign currency during the crisis. Under the new foreign investment limits, foreigners were permitted to own a controlling interest of domestic firms.

---

19. Bekaert and Harvey (1999).

The Impact of Liberalization

The liberalization efforts throughout the region facilitated the flow of funds from international investors. At a rudimentary level, liberalization appears to be related to the crisis. As of December 1996, just six months before the Asian financial crisis, foreign investors were only allowed to own up to 25 percent of any firm's market capitalization in Taiwan. In contrast, foreign investors in Malaysia and the Philippines faced less prohibitive restrictions governing their ownership of domestic firms. As of December 1996, the foreign investor ownership limits for Indonesia and Malaysia were 49 and 30 percent, respectively. The economies that were most affected during the Asian crisis were those that pursued the most aggressive liberalization programs. Moreover, these economies were the first in the region to open their capital markets "effectively" to foreign investors.

On the surface it appears as though cross-sectional variation in official liberalization programs may in some way account for the cross-sectional variation in the severity of the Asian financial crisis. Did foreign portfolio investors and speculators therefore cause the crisis?

Several observers have argued that foreign speculation increases the volatility of local capital markets. Some have gone so far as to blame individual foreign speculators like George Sauris for the higher volatility of Asian markets during the crisis. Despite these accusations, the data suggest a different story. In fact, the volatility of the average annualized U.S. dollar stock market return during the five years following official liberalization decreased in all but one of the East Asian countries from its level in the five years proceeding liberalization (the only exception being Thailand).[20] For example, the average annualized volatility of U.S. dollar returns was 32 percent during the five years prior to Malaysia's official liberalization. In the five years following official liberalization, the average return volatility dropped to less than 22 percent. Similarly, in the Philippines, the average U.S. dollar return volatility five years before and five years after its official liberalization dropped from 42 to 27 percent. Thailand's unconditional U.S. dollar return volatility increased from an annualized 19 percent average over the five years prior to liberalization to 35 percent in the five years after liberalization.

These statistics do not provide sufficient evidence to make the claim that financial integration leads to lower volatility, however. Historical average

---

20. Liberalization date as defined by Bekaert and Harvey (1999).

Table 3-2. *Financial Market Characteristics before and after Capital Market Liberalization, by Country and Region*

Country or region	Number of companies in IFC index		Asset concentration		Market capitalization to GDP		Cross-sectional standard deviation	
	Five years before	Five years after	Five years before	Five years after	Five years before	Five years after	Five years before	Five years after
Country								
Indonesia	n.a.	57.375	n.a.	0.183	n.a.	0.087	n.a.	0.118
Korea	53.267	136.655	0.177	0.209	0.237	0.285	0.082	0.088
Malaysia	40.426	62.361	0.224	0.193	0.370	0.905	0.106	0.094
Philippines	21.017	37.328	0.335	0.257	0.093	0.322	0.135	0.122
Taiwan	44.917	79.852	0.205	0.161	0.491	0.503	0.111	0.085
Thailand	9.733	30.803	0.349	0.241	0.030	0.166	0.073	0.104
Mean	33.872	67.396	0.258	0.207	0.244	0.378	0.101	0.102
Latin America								
Mean	25.397	40.363	0.209	0.236	0.088	0.245	0.161	0.153
Percentage change (before / after)		0.589		0.127		0.157		−0.051
Pacific Rim								
Mean	33.872	67.396	0.258	0.207	0.244	0.378	0.101	0.102
Percentage change (before / after)		0.990		−0.197		0.134		0.005
Emerging Eurasia								
Mean	32.718	56.201	0.310	0.239	0.121	0.223	0.108	0.112
Percentage change (before / after)		0.718		−0.226		0.101		0.031

Source: Authors' calculations based on Bekaert and Harvey (1999).
n.a. Not available.

estimates of volatility cannot disentangle the impact of financial market liberalization from other dynamic changes that occurred simultaneously in these economies. Table 3-2 demonstrates that the number of companies included in the IFC country-level indexes increased and that the concentration ratio of individual firms in these indexes decreased after liberaliza-

Table 3-2. *Financial Market Characteristics before and after Capital Market Liberalization, by Country and Region (continued)*

Foreign exchange rate volatility		Institutional Investor's country credit rating		U.S. net equity level		U.S. bond flows	
Five years before	Five years after	Five years before	Five years after	Five years before	Five years after	Five years before	Five years after
n.a.	0.004	48.593	41.605	n.a.	0.022	2.650	155.049
0.008	0.006	65.580	69.813	0.014	0.025	−573.700	2,529.636
0.013	0.010	33.333	37.400	0.003	0.011	−177.533	−364.279
0.016	0.026	23.958	30.110	0.278	0.141	−341.500	−728.869
0.014	0.011	75.990	78.279	0.000	0.001	−539.650	−5,655.934
0.023	0.008	52.503	59.643	0.003	0.032	3.267	−153.639
0.015	0.011	46.876	52.808	0.071	0.039	−210.553	−703.006
0.081	0.098	36.616	41.023	0.014	0.047	−170.714	1,741.688
	0.220		12		2.399		1,912.402
0.015	0.011	46.876	52.808	0.071	0.039	−210.553	−703.006
	−0.273		13		−0.458		−492.453
0.023	0.023	41.51	42.82	−0.013	0.003	−79.000	−36.164
	0.013		3		−1.213		42.836

tion. Standard portfolio optimization theory suggests that we should expect a reduction in variance as additional firms are incorporated into the market. Furthermore, each market achieved higher risk ratings from Institutional Investor's country credit ratings. Higher perceived creditworthiness may coincide with lower levels of return volatility. Ideally, we would like to assess the impact of financial market liberalization on return volatility while controlling for these other contemporaneous effects.

Bekaert and Harvey offer the following type of analysis.[21] They use time-series data relating to fundamental market characteristics, economic characteristics, and market microstructure characteristics from twenty emerging markets as conditioning variables in an event study of the impact of financial market liberalization. We employ the results from their estimation and the average financial and economic characteristics of each Asian country five years before and five years after liberalization in order to evaluate the sources of the change in volatility of Asian markets (table 3-3).

The overall change in U.S. dollar return volatility in each of the five countries presented varies before and after liberalization. Korea and Taiwan experience an increase in volatility after controlling for changes in economic and financial characteristics (table 3-4). In contrast, U.S. dollar return volatility decreased after liberalization in Malaysia, the Philippines, and Thailand (table 3-4). Across all countries, changes in the economic environment that coincided with the official liberalization efforts led to increases in U.S. dollar return volatility (table 3-5). Most of this increase resulted from increases in the inflation rate after liberalization. As suggested, changes in key financial market characteristics led to decreases in U.S. dollar return volatility in all countries. After controlling for the changing economic and financial market characteristics, the remaining impact of financial market liberalization on U.S. dollar return volatility was less than 1 percent a year. These results suggest that increased foreign participation cannot be the sole culprit of increased volatility of returns in Asia. Thus we are hard pressed to believe that foreign investors alone accounted for the high level of market volatility during the Asian crisis.

Financial market integration may also affect the expected returns on investment. In completely segmented markets, investors must be compensated for bearing variance risk of the domestic market's portfolio return. Throughout East Asia this risk was quite high, especially during the 1990s. However, in integrated financial markets investors are compensated for covariance risk, where covariance is measured with respect to the global market portfolio. Given the low correlation of emerging markets with developed markets, we might expect that financial market integration would lead to lower expected returns for East Asian equity markets. Of course, this logic indicates that these markets might experience a price

21. Bekaert and Harvey (1999).

increase prior to liberalization, as market participants anticipate liberalization and drive down expected returns.

In order to assess the impact of liberalization on Asian stock market returns we investigate expected returns using a traditional framework, the international capital asset pricing model. Specifically, we attempt to explain the cross-sectional differences in returns before and after financial market liberalization using an international version of the Sharpe and Lintner capital asset pricing model.[22]

Table 3-6 and Figure 3-5 present the results of this exercise, revealing the before and after betas calculated for each of the East Asian U.S. dollar equity market returns. These betas are derived by regressing the monthly U.S. dollar-denominated returns of the IFC country-level indexes for five years prior to Bekaert and Harvey's identification of the official market liberalization (indicated in figure 3-4) in each Asian market on the corresponding five years of monthly return history of the Morgan Stanley world index.[23] Provided that the measure of official financial market integration offered by Bekaert and Harvey is relatively accurate, the regression employing the five-year history before integration should not be relevant. Nevertheless, it serves as an interesting reference point from which to judge the model after the impact of integration.

In four out of the five Asian countries presented, the beta decreases after integration. The point estimates of beta using the five-year period prior to liberalization are consistent with those presented in Harvey.[24] However, the coefficient of determination from each of the univariate regressions is less than 10 percent.

Overall, the model specification fails to describe accurately the cross-sectional variation of expected returns in East Asia. Prior to each country's financial market liberalization the security market line has the wrong slope. Although the estimated coefficient on beta turns positive after the Bekaert and Harvey liberalization date, it remains statistically insignificant.[25] These results do not necessarily indicate that Asian economies remain segmented. These simple tests rely only on unconditional moments and thus are unable to capture the significant time variation in expected returns that has been documented in studies by Harvey, by Bekaert, and by Ferson and Harvey.[26]

22. Sharpe (1964); Lintner (1965).
23. Bekaert and Harvey (1999).
24. Harvey (1995a).
25. Bekaert and Harvey (1999).
26. Harvey (1993); Bekaert (1995); Ferson and Harvey (1993).

Table 3-3. *Economic Fundamentals before and after Capital Market Liberalization, by Country and Region*

Country or region	GDP growth		GDP per capita growth		Trade sector to GDP		Inflation	
	Five years before	Five years after	Five years before	Five years after	Five years before	Five years after	Five years before	Five years after
Country								
Indonesia	5.268	6.941	3.104	5.578	0.447	0.529	7.042	8.329
Korea	9.563	7.121	8.500	6.033	0.646	0.627	6.871	5.443
Malaysia	4.353	8.738	1.696	5.671	1.153	1.624	1.556	3.620
Philippines	4.404	2.681	1.890	−0.220	0.563	0.727	9.333	9.958
Taiwan	7.638	5.490	7.638	5.490	0.835	0.759	2.208	3.785
Thailand	5.930	10.733	3.970	9.157	0.496	0.728	2.301	4.951
Mean	6.193	6.950	4.466	5.285	0.690	0.832	4.885	6.014
Latin America								
Mean	2.605	4.989	0.690	3.228	0.338	0.358	340.558	298.213
Percentage change (before / after)		0.024		0.025		0.020		−0.423
Pacific Rim								
Mean	6.193	6.950	4.466	5.285	0.690	0.832	5.149	6.651
Percentage change (before / after)		0.008		0.008		0.142		0.015
Emerging Eurasia								
Mean	4.413	4.694	1.790	2.321	0.544	0.520	18.149	22.570
Percentage change (before / after)		0.003		0.005		−0.024		0.044

Source: Authors' calculations based on Bekaert and Harvey (1999).
n.a. Not available.

Another potential problem with this analysis results from its implicit assumption that these markets switched from complete segmentation to complete integration. However, the evidence presented earlier suggests that the liberalization reforms in these economies followed a more gradual process. This sort of transition from closed to open capital markets captures the time-varying nature of integration suggested by Bekaert and

Table 3-3. *Economic Fundamentals before and after Capital Market Liberalization, by Country and Region (continued)*

Consumption to GDP		Private consumption to GDP		Public consumption to GDP		Gross fixed capital to GDP	
Five years before	Five years after	Five years before	Five years after	Five years before	Five years after	Five years before	Five years after
0.683	0.645	0.582	0.555	0.101	0.090	n.a.	n.a.
0.628	0.643	0.528	0.536	0.100	0.106	398.710	436.612
0.653	0.652	0.499	0.515	0.154	0.137	326.798	405.140
0.802	0.851	0.710	0.746	0.092	0.105	230.251	268.041
n.a.	n.a.	n.a.	n.a.	n.a.	n.a.	n.a.	n.a.
0.756	0.659	0.627	0.561	0.128	0.097	329.795	436.717
0.723	0.690	0.605	0.583	0.115	0.107	321.388	386.627
0.755	0.789	0.665	0.692	0.109	0.117	236.943	229.853
	0.034		0.027		0.008		−7.090
0.723	0.690	0.605	0.583	0.115	0.107	321.388	386.627
	−0.033		−0.022		−0.007		65.239
0.834	0.818	0.678	0.672	0.155	0.146	273.648	287.633
	−0.015		−0.006		−0.009		13.985

Harvey.[27] Moreover, much of the time variation in expected returns may result from factors that do not rely on financial market integration.

By itself, financial market integration implies an increase in excess returns on the order of 1.3 percent a month (table 3-5). This increase is

27. Bekaert and Harvey (1995).

Table 3-4. *Impact of Financial Market Liberalization on Local Stock Market Volatility*[a]

Country	Indonesia	Korea	Malaysia	Philippines	Taiwan	Thailand
Total	n.a.	−0.059	0.200	0.016	−0.003	0.139
Number of companies in IFC index	n.a.	−0.005	−0.002	−0.003	−0.003	−0.006
Asset concentration index	n.a.	0.008	−0.007	−0.019	−0.011	−0.025
Cross-sectional standard deviation to market capitalization	n.a.	0.001	−0.002	−0.003	−0.005	0.006
Inflation rate	0.022	−0.031	0.111	0.009	0.071	0.101
Foreign exchange rate volatility	n.a.	−0.003	−0.003	0.010	−0.003	−0.016
Exports plus imports to GDP	0.038	−0.009	0.222	0.077	−0.036	0.110
Institutional Investor's country credit rating	−0.003	0.001	0.002	0.005	0.001	0.003
Market capitalization	n.a.	−0.009	−0.098	−0.042	−0.002	−0.025
Cross-sectional standard deviation	n.a.	0.000	−0.008	−0.004	−0.000	0.006
Stock market effect	n.a.	−0.004	−0.119	−0.070	−0.021	−0.044
Macroeconomic development	n.a.	−0.041	0.333	0.100	0.033	0.197
Financial market liberalization	n.a.	0.007	0.007	0.007	0.007	0.007

Source: Authors' calculations based on results in Bekaert and Harvey (1999).

n.a. Not available.

a. Calculates the changes in volatility resulting from changes in financial and economic fundamentals as well as the isolated impact of financial market liberalization.

offset by a decrease in excess returns associated with changes in key financial market characteristics. On average, changes in the makeup of East Asian financial markets accounted for a reduction in monthly excess returns of 1.2 percent. Finally, increases in the East Asian credit ratings further reduced excess returns by another 0.5 percent a month. In all, the

Table 3-5. *Impact of Financial Market Liberalization on Local Stock Market Excess Returns*[a]

Country	Indonesia	Korea	Malaysia	Philippines	Taiwan	Thailand
Total	n.a.	0.026	0.023	0.008	0.013	0.030
Number of companies in IFC index	n.a.	−0.011	−0.005	−0.007	−0.007	−0.014
Asset concentration index	n.a.	0.001	−0.001	−0.003	−0.002	−0.004
Cross-sectional standard deviation to market capitalization	n.a.	0.004	−0.007	−0.008	−0.015	0.018
Inflation rate	n.a.	−0.001	0.001	0.001	0.003	−0.004
Foreign exchange rate volatility	n.a.	0.000	0.001	−0.002	0.001	0.003
Exports plus imports to GDP	n.a.	0.000	0.005	0.002	0.000	0.001
Institutional Investor's country credit rating	0.007	−0.003	−0.005	−0.011	−0.001	−0.006
Market capitalization	n.a.	n.a.	n.a.	n.a.	n.a.	n.a.
Cross-sectional standard deviation	n.a.	n.a.	n.a.	n.a.	n.a.	n.a.
Stock market effect	n.a.	−0.006	−0.013	−0.017	−0.024	0.000
Macroeconomic development	n.a.	−0.003	0.001	−0.009	0.002	−0.006
Financial market liberalization	n.a.	0.013	0.013	0.013	0.013	0.013

Source: Authors' calculations based on results in Bekaert and Harvey (1999).

n.a. Not available.

a. Calculates the changes in volatility resulting from changes in financial and economic fundamentals as well as the isolated impact of financial market liberalization.

net effect of financial market liberalization, financial market maturation, and economic transformation resulted in lower excess returns across the region. Thus we expect that the price appreciation associated with the pre-liberalization period can be attributed in part to changes in the makeup of the financial market.

Table 3-6. *Simple Tests of Financial Market Integration before and after Liberalization, by Country*

Country	Five years before		Five years after	
	Beta	Returns	Beta	Returns
Indonesia	n.a.	n.a.	0.366	2.465
Korea	0.535	13.371	0.414	–4.384
Malaysia	0.913	4.839	0.794	22.532
Phillipines	0.778	38.715	0.483	22.605
Taiwan	0.908	36.668	0.725	4.155
Thailand	–0.092	27.869	1.062	20.676
Slope coefficient on beta	–2.098	25.568	25.799	–5.187
Standard error	20.230	14.46641	18.204	12.48616
Security market line R^2	0.004		0.241	

Source: Returns are U.S. dollar-based log returns calculated from IFC country indexes. Betas are calculated with respect to the Morgan Stanley world index.

n.a. Not available five years prior to integration date.

Pre-Liberalization Investment Alternatives

Investors eager to invest in the East Asian markets did not necessarily have to wait for official government liberalization. Often foreign investors could gain exposure to these markets through country funds issued prior to the official liberalization. However, the diversification benefit of these country funds was ambiguous. Most were close-end funds that were not permitted to offer new shares as investors' interest in the fund grew. As a result, these funds traded at substantial premiums over the net asset value of the underlying stocks, and this premium eroded any potential gains to diversification that these funds offered.

East Asian countries benefited from allowing these country funds to trade shares in their local markets for at least two reasons, both of which are related to the asymmetry of information between domestic and foreign investors. First, country funds served as one of the few means by which investors could familiarize themselves with the volatility and returns of these emerging markets. Thus country funds introduced foreign investors to East Asian markets. Furthermore, country funds helped to increase the name recognition of East Asian firms among international investors. Increased familiarity with individual firms helped these firms to access international capital markets.

Figure 3-5. *Security Market Lines before and after Liberalization*

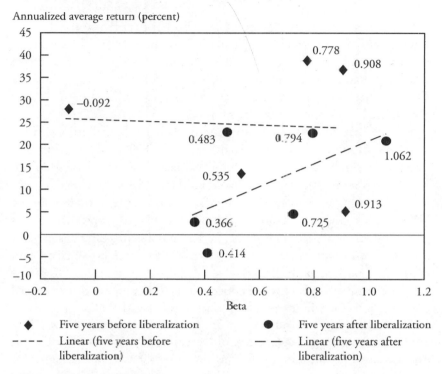

Annualized average return (percent)

Source: Authors' calculations.

Investors desiring to enter the Indonesian equity market could invest in close-end country funds up to eight months in advance of the market's official liberalization. The Malacca Fund (Cayman) began trading in January 1989. The JF Indonesia close-end country fund began trading on the London Stock Exchange (LSE) two months later, in March 1989. Prior to the official liberalization date, investors could choose between five different Indonesian country funds, sharing a combined market capitalization of $106 million.

Korean investors were able to select from several viable alternatives to direct foreign equity ownership prior to the market's gradual liberalization in the 1990s. Twenty-eight country funds were established between November 1981 and December 1991. The combined market capitalization of these funds was $1.56 billion as of December 1991. Seven of these funds traded as close-end funds on the LSE. The largest fund, Korean Fund, traded on the NYSE from its inception in August 1984.

Several open-end country funds focusing on Korea also emerged during the early 1980s and early 1990s. The majority of these funds were unlisted but were made available to the public. Both Korea Trust and Korean International Trust began issuing shares in November 1981. The advantage that these funds had over their close-end counterparts was their ability to issue new shares. Hence, in theory, these funds did not sell at a premium. The drawback of these open-end funds was their unlisted nature. Only experienced investors were able to find them.

Foreign investors were less fortunate in their pre-liberalization investment opportunities in Malaysia. As of December 1988, the official liberalization date, only three country funds existed. The first of these funds, Malaysian Ventures Berhad, established in March 1984, was closed to public investors. In December 1987, the Malaysia Fund began trading on the NYSE. This close-end country fund had a market capitalization of $98.3 million as of December 1991. Earlier in the same year, the small but open-end country fund, the Wardley GS Malaysia Fund, began trading on the Luxembourg Stock Exchange.

Eight country funds were introduced in the Philippines prior to official liberalization. One fund, JF Philippine Trust, began trading as early as 1974. Although the fund was an open-end fund, its small size, only $5.9 million under management as of December 1991, and unlisted status provided little justification for arguing that it served as a major channel for foreign investors interested in the Philippines. In 1989 and 1990, several Philippine country funds began trading on the major exchanges. In New York, the First Philippine Fund attracted $101.2 million in assets under management in December 1991. The combination of the First Philippine Investment Trust and JF Philippine Fund managed $97 million assets in December 1991 in active trading on the London Stock Exchange. Between these funds, which traded in New York and London, investors interested in the Philippine equity market had substantial opportunity for investment. Of course, each of these funds traded at substantial premiums due to their close-end status.

Investors interested in Taiwan could invest in the Formosa Fund as early as March 1986. This fund had many attractive qualities. The Formosa Fund traded on a major exchange (the LSE), it had substantial assets under management as of December 1991 ($133.7 million), and it was an open-end fund. U.S. investors unfamiliar with the Formosa Fund may have been introduced to Taiwan at the inception of the Taiwan Fund, in May 1986. This close-end fund traded on the NYSE. Two and a half years later a larger fund emerged that also traded on the NYSE, the ROC Taiwan Fund, which attracted more than $244 million in assets under management by December 1991. In total, investors could choose among seven separate Taiwan country funds prior to the market's official liberalization date.

The choices in Thailand were more limited. At the time of Thailand's official market liberalization, September 1987, only two country funds existed that focused on this market. The Bangkok Fund began trading on the LSE in July 1985. As of December 1991, this close-end fund had more than $163 million under management. In December 1996, the Thailand Fund issued shares to investors on the LSE. The open-end nature of this fund allowed investors to avoid the premiums charged in close-end funds. Nevertheless, it appeared as though many investors preferred the management of the older close-end Bangkok Fund. As of December 1991, the Bangkok Fund had more than three times the value of assets under management as did the Thailand Fund.

Asian Capital Market Concentration Measures

We have established that Asian capital markets experienced real growth during the 1990s. Both local equity markets and local bond markets increased their market capitalization to varying degrees through new capital mobilization. This growth is exactly what we would expect from maturing capital markets. In fact, in several countries the value of shares traded, turnover ratios, and market capitalization exceeded values found in key developed stock markets. However, despite their growth, local Asian equity markets possessed certain characteristics common to emerging stock markets. In particular, the market capitalization of local Asian equity markets remained highly concentrated among a small number of firms and within a few industries. Moreover, the ownership of Asian equity is highly concentrated in the hands of a small number of investors. In this section, we present several statistics regarding the degree of concentration along various dimensions.

Concentration of Asian Equity across Individual Firms

Within many emerging markets, the ten largest firms command a disproportionate share of the entire stock market capitalization. The IFC provides a concentration ratio designed to investigate this pattern. The IFC computes the ratio of the market capitalization for the top ten firms in their global (IFC-G) indexes to the entire market capitalization of the indexes. Figure 3-6 presents a sample of these data.

According to the IFC data, the top ten firms in their IFC-G indexes for Asian countries command between 14 and 52 percent of the market capitalization of the individual country-level indexes. The IFC-G China index has the lowest concentration ratio. Between 1992 and 1997 the top ten firms on the IFC-G China index constituted on average only 18 percent of the index's market capitalization. The most heavily concentrated index in Asia according to this ratio is the Philippine IFC-G index. Between 1992 and 1997, the top ten firms on the Philippine index controlled on average more than 45 percent of the index's market capitalization. The average of the IFC reported concentration ratios for Indonesia, Korea, Malaysia, Taiwan, and Thailand is 40, 32, 31, 31, and 36 percent, respectively.

Comparing the concentration ratio of the top ten firms of Asia to that of Latin America, we find that, on average, the IFC-G Asian indexes are less heavily concentrated than the Latin American indexes. For example, the lowest concentration ratio among the Latin American countries presented in figure 3-6 is Mexico, whose average concentration ratio between 1992 and 1997 was 35 percent. Four of the seven Asian countries reported had lower concentration ratios. Moreover, the highest concentration ratio in Asia was reported for the Philippine market. Three of the five Latin American markets reported higher concentration ratios.

Although the concentration ratio of the top ten firms provides some evidence of the degree of concentration in the market capitalization of a country, its focus on the top ten firms ignores concentration of the remaining firms. Ideally, we would like a measure of market capitalization that uses all of the available data. Using the market capitalization of all the constituents in the IFC-G indexes, we can construct a Herfindahl-type index. The modified Herfindahl index is:

$$\text{Sqrt} \{[N / (N-1)]^* \text{Sum}[W_i - (1 / N)]\}.$$

Through a convenient normalization of this sum, we can build an index of market capitalization that spans the unit interval. Under the simple scenario, whereby the IFC-G index consists of a single firm, its weight, W_i, equals 1, and the value of the index converges to 1. If each firm controls an equal fraction of the entire market capitalization, the modified Herfindahl index returns a value of 0.

Figure 3-7 presents the times series of the modified Herfindahl index for a cross section of emerging markets. In general, all Asian equity markets have index levels less than 0.25. The Philippines is the only country whose index level exceeds this, and it does so only until 1993. The Latin American countries appear to exhibit a lower degree of concentration relative to Asia. After 1992 their modified Herfindahl never exceeds 0.20.

Although this index may seem abstract, it helps us to compare the degree of market concentration across countries. For example, consider Korea, Malaysia, and Taiwan. According to the IFC all three countries had roughly the same average concentration ratio using the ratio of market capitalization of the top ten firms to the entire market capitalization, 31 percent. However, this concentration ratio considers only two groups, the top ten firms and the other firms. The modified Herfindahl index in figure 3-7 demonstrates that the pattern of concentration across these countries was far richer. In fact, the degree of concentration in Taiwan exceeds that of both Korea and Malaysia.

Consider also the case of Mexico. The IFC reported a concentration ratio based on the top ten firms for this country of 35 percent throughout the 1990s. By this standard, the Mexican markets appeared to be more heavily concentrated than markets in China, Korea, Malaysia, and Taiwan. However, using the modified Herfindahl index we find that Mexico is less concentrated by far than all four of these Asian markets. In fact, Mexico exhibits the lowest degree of concentration of any emerging market displayed in figure 3-7.

Industrial Concentration of Asian Equity Markets

Concentration based on market capitalization is only one way to measure concentration in emerging markets. For the most part, the capitalization of emerging stock markets tends to be heavily concentrated in a relatively few industries. Table 3-7 lists the relative market capitalization weights associated with eight industries for each of the East Asian equity markets.

The eight industries selected are conveniently picked from the eight industry aggregates specified by the IFC. We derive the time series of market capitalization weights from these industries using the individual market weights of the historical constituents of the IFC country-level indexes. Summing over the individual constituents according to their industry classification gives us the market capitalization of each industry.

Figure 3-6. *IFC-G Concentration Ratios Based on Top Ten Firms, 1992–97*

Percent

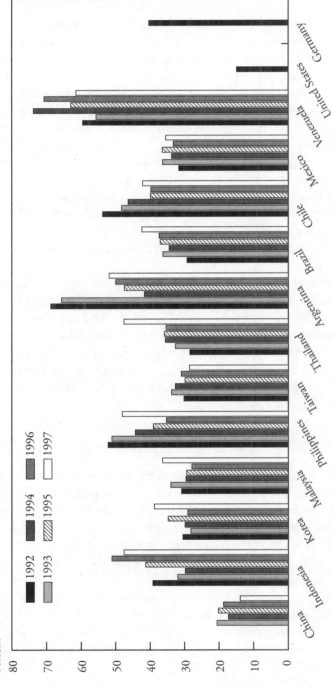

Source: Data from IFC (various years).

Figure 3-7. *Asset Concentration by Market Capitalization in Asia and Latin America*

Panel A. Asia

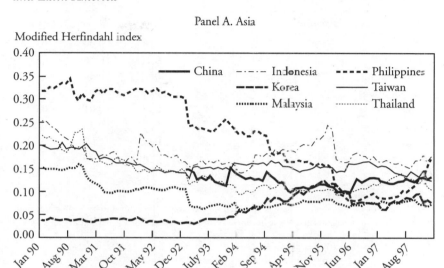

Panel B. Latin America

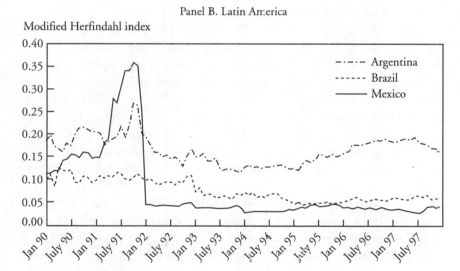

Source: Authors' calculations based on IFC's emerging markets database.

Table 3-7. *Industry Market Capitalization Weights
across East Asian Countries*[a]

Industry	Indonesia	Korea	Malaysia	Philippines	Taiwan	Thailand
Agriculture	0.03	0.00	0.09	0.00	0.00	0.02
Mining	0.01	0.00	0.00	0.16	0.06	0.04
Manufacturing	0.57	0.54	0.17	0.31	0.56	0.31
Transportation	0.10	0.17	0.19	0.22	0.01	0.09
Wholesale	0.02	0.06	0.01	0.00	0.01	0.02
Finance	0.15	0.23	0.24	0.29	0.36	0.50
Services	0.03	0.00	0.08	0.00	0.00	0.02
Government	0.00	0.00	0.00	0.00	0.00	0.00
Other	0.08	0.00	0.23	0.02	0.00	0.01

Source: International Finance Corporation.

a. All entries represent the time-series average from December 1984 to February 1998 of the market capitalization of stocks listed in the historical constituent indexes for a given country and a given industry divided by the total market.

The weights presented are the time-series average of the monthly weights from December 1984 to February 1998.

Our analysis suggests that the IFC indexes of East Asian countries were heavily tilted toward the manufacturing and finance sectors of these economies. This result is indicative of the underlying structure of these economies. However, industry concentration is low on the list of priorities for constructing IFC indexes. The primary goal of the IFC indexes is to cover at least 60 percent of the entire market of stocks existing in any given country. Therefore, we cannot be sure that the economies in these markets are as highly focused on these two industries as would be suggested by an analysis predicated solely on the market weights derived from the IFC indexes.

Varying degrees of industry concentration exist across individual countries in Asia. Indonesia's equity market, as measured by the IFC Indonesia index, is heavily tilted toward the manufacturing sector. Korea and Taiwan have similar industrial mixes. In each of these three markets, manufacturing firms make up more than 50 percent of the total market capitalization of the country's index (table 3-7). Financial firms have the second greatest weight in each of these countries.

Both Malaysia and the Philippines appear to have broader industrial mixes, with manufacturing, transportation, and finance each claiming shares close to or greater than 20 percent. Malaysian firms are not easily classified into these eight industrial groups. Roughly 23 percent of Malaysia's IFC market capitalization is placed into the "other" industry classification.

The firms representing Thailand are predominantly finance firms: on average, 50 percent of Thailand's market capitalization is made up of this category. Manufacturing firms place second in Thailand, constituting 31 percent of the market capitalization of the IFC Thailand index.

Table 3-7 analyzes the average East Asian industrial mix. Nevertheless, as individual industries grow and shrink over time, the industrial diversity of the entire market may be affected. One way to examine the industrial diversity of an entire market, and to compare this level of diversity across countries, is to examine a modified Herfindahl index coefficient of a country. Harvey and Divecha, Drach, and Stefek use the modified Herfindahl index to examine the diversity of a country's industry base at any given point in time.[28] We extend this analysis to an examination of the time path of the index for each country in East Asia.

The modified Herfindahl index is constructed by summing up the squared market weights of each of the nine specified industries and multiplying by a correction factor. If a country's index places an equal weight on each of the nine industries, the Herfindahl index value is 0. As a country's industrial base focuses toward one industry, the Herfindahl index approaches 1.

Malaysia has the most diverse industrial base of all East Asia. Once again, however, we are suspicious of this result because of the large proportion of market capitalization that the IFC does not classify. Ignoring Malaysia for the moment, we see that Korea, the Philippines, and Taiwan have experienced little time variation in their industrial mixes. The Taiwan index has the highest degree of industry concentration of the three countries. Examining Taiwan in detail reveals that the IFC index for this country consists heavily of manufacturing and finance stocks. From January 1990 to December 1996, these two industries made up a minimum of 82 percent of the IFC Taiwan index and averaged 89 percent of the index throughout the period.

The IFC Korea index has a broader industrial base than Taiwan's. The Herfindahl index averages 0.49 in Korea over the sample period and 0.57 in Taiwan. Examining Korea in more detail, we recall from table 3-7 that,

28. Harvey (1991); Divecha, Drach, and Stefek (1992).

on average, 17 percent of Korea's market capitalization is made up of transportation stocks. The relative market weights associated with transportation and finance in Korea switched in importance during the 1990s. Beginning in January 1990 transportation stocks made up 25 percent of the total market capitalization, whereas finance stocks constituted 32 percent of the total. By December 1996 these weights had reversed, with the transportation industry accounting for 31 percent and the finance industry making up 24 percent of the country's total market capitalization.

Indonesia and Thailand both experienced considerable variations during the 1990s in the value of their Herfindahl indexes. Indonesia has on average the highest degree of industry-based concentration of any East Asian equity market. This is not surprising given that the manufacturing sector within Indonesia averaged 57 percent of the country's entire market capitalization throughout the 1990s. From January 1990 to December 1996 the manufacturing sector constituted 60 percent. Financial stocks had the second largest capitalization, accounting for just over 15 percent of the market's total capitalization. Finally, the transportation industry made up a meager 5 percent of the market's capitalization on average during those years. The picture was completely different between January 1996 and December 1996. Both the manufacturing and finance sectors gave ground to transportation stocks. Between December 1995 and January 1996, the transportation industry increased its sector weight from 10 to 31 percent. From January to December 1996, this sector's weight averaged 31 percent of Indonesia's total market capitalization. Manufacturing remained in the lead, commanding 50 percent, while the finance industry took a back seat to the transport stocks with only a 9 percent share of the market's total capitalization.

Table 3-8 reexamines the liquidity within each market by focusing on turnover ratio within each of eight specified industrial groups. The individual elements within this table represent the time-series averages of each industry's turnover ratio. With the exception of Taiwan, across East Asia the liquidity within each industry is closely related to the liquidity of the market as a whole. On average, 3 percent of Indonesian manufacturing firms' market capitalization was traded each month during the 1990s. This represents the same proportion of value traded to market capitalization of the entire IFC Indonesia index.

Korea, Malaysia, the Philippines, and Thailand have similar characteristics. In each of these countries, the industry that commands the greatest weight in the index has a ratio of value traded to market capitalization sim-

Table 3-8. *Industry-Level Value Traded across East Asian Countries*[a]

Industry	Indonesia	Korea	Malaysia	Philippines	Taiwan	Thailand
Agriculture	0.06	0.00	0.01	0.00	0.61	0.04
Mining	0.06	0.00	0.07	0.03	0.16	0.06
Manufacturing	0.03[b]	0.08[b]	0.02	0.01[b]	0.27[b]	0.03[b]
Transportation	0.03	0.05	0.01[b]	0.02	0.10	0.02
Wholesale	0.06	0.13	0.02	0.00	0.19	0.02
Finance	0.04[b]	0.06[b]	0.02[b]	0.01[b]	0.09[b]	0.06[b]
Services	0.02	0.03	0.02	0.00	0.44	0.00
Government	0.00	0.00	0.00	0.00	0.00	0.00
Other	0.05	0.00	0.03	0.01	0.00	0.06
All industries	0.03	0.08	0.02	0.02	0.21	0.05

Source: Authors' calculations.

a. All entries represent the time-series average from December 1994 to February 1998 of the value traded for a given country and a given industry divided by the market capitalization of the same group of stocks.

b. Indicates the leading (second-place) industry group where industry groups are ranked by relative market capitalization.

ilar to the ratio of the overall market. In Taiwan, the agriculture and services industries exhibit the greatest degree of liquidity. On average, 61 percent of agricultural firms' capitalization changes hands each month. For service industries, this ratio is 44 percent. These numbers should be treated with caution because both of the industries constitute an infinitesimal proportion of Taiwan's equity market capitalization. More important, the finance industry, which commands on average 36 percent of Taiwan's total market capitalization, is rather illiquid compared with the country as a whole. On average only 9 percent of the finance industry's market capitalization is traded each month. Most of the liquidity reported for the overall market in Taiwan comes from the high ratio of value traded to market capitalization within the manufacturing industry, where roughly a quarter of the market capitalization changes hands each month. This is an impressive figure considering that manufacturing makes up more than half of Taiwan's market capitalization as measured by the IFC Taiwan index.

Although the stocks in some industries tend to be more liquid than other stocks, overall the high degree of liquidity of Asian stock markets is not driven by a small number of highly liquid stocks. Figure 3-8 presents the time series of a modified Herfindahl index constructed using the value traded of each firm in the IFC-G indexes. This modified index is designed

Figure 3-8. *Value Traded Concentration across Countries*

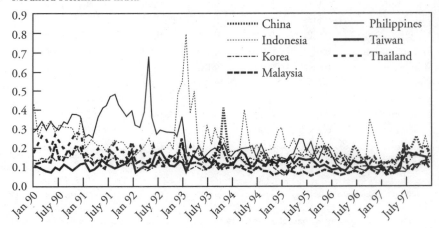

Panel A. Asia

Modified Herfindahl index

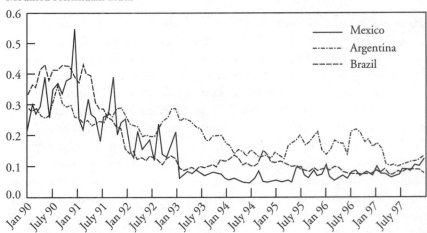

Panel B. Latin America

Modified Herfindahl index

Source: Authors' calculations.

to measure the concentration of liquidity across individual stocks. If the total value traded is highly influenced by the value traded of one particular stock, the index value converges to 1. Conversely, if the total value traded is distributed across all the stock in the index, the value of the modified Herfindahl index converges to 0.

The value traded in Asian stock markets is not heavily concentrated in certain key issues. In the two most heavily traded markets in Asia—China and Taiwan—the average value of our modified Herfindahl index was 0.15 and 0.11, respectively, between 1990 and 1996. The Korean and Malaysian stock markets' value traded concentration indexes averaged 0.11 over the same period. Both Indonesia and the Philippines recorded the highest levels of value traded concentration in Asia. The value traded concentration indexes for these two countries averaged 0.24 during the 1990s. During 1993 almost 100 percent of the value traded in the Indonesia IFC-G index resulted from the trading of one firm. The same degree of concentration occurred in 1992 in the Philippines.

The value traded in Asian equity markets tends to be less concentrated than that of Latin America. In fact, the value traded in China, Korea, Malaysia, and Taiwan is less heavily concentrated than in any market in Latin America. The average concentration index across all seven Asian markets averaged 0.16 during the 1990s. The average concentration index across Argentina, Brazil, and Mexico averaged 0.18 during the same time period.

The Effects of Asian Stock Market Concentration

Countries that exhibit a high degree of industry concentration and asset-based concentration may have very little cross-sectional variation in the returns of the firms within the country. Consider, for example, Thailand. Given that 50 percent of the Thai equity market capitalization is finance oriented, we might expect that interest rate movements affecting finance stocks would have a disproportionate impact on the Thai IFC index. In the case of Indonesia, Korea, and Taiwan, we might expect that shocks to the manufacturing sector would have a significant influence on their country-level indexes.

One measure of the degree to which stocks in country-level indexes move together can be constructed by forming the ratio of the number of stocks that experience a price appreciation over the past month to the total number of stocks in the index. We present a more general measure by changing the numerator to include the maximum of either the number of stocks moving up or down during the previous month.

For the region as a whole, 70 percent of the individual stocks exhibited price movements in the same direction each month. These common movements could be driven by industry-level shocks. In the market overview section of the IFC's *Monthly Emerging Stock Markets Review*, many of the Asian market movements are in fact rationalized by general industrywide shocks such as changes in U.S. interest rates or microchip prices. However, the general co-movement in stock prices could also be caused by a follow-the-leader type effect, where individual stocks on the market follow the lead of the larger stocks.

Taiwan exhibited the lowest degree of cross-sectional correlation as indicated by our measure. On average, about 55 percent of Taiwanese companies moved in the same direction each month. The Philippines and Thailand had similar levels of co-movement within their country-level indexes. Between 70 and 80 percent of the companies in each country moved in the same direction each month.

Stocks in Indonesia and Korea exhibited significant amounts of co-movement. Roughly 90 percent of the companies listed in the IFC Korea and Indonesia indexes moved in the same direction each month. The IFC index for Malaysia exhibited the highest degree of co-movement among its constituents. Throughout the 1990s, greater than 95 percent of the stocks that made up the IFC index for Malaysia moved in the same direction each month.

Performance of East Asian Capital Markets

The return performance of East Asian stock markets varied across countries. In some countries investors were rewarded with outstanding returns up until the crisis. However, in other markets the return performance failed to exceed less risky positions in more developed markets. Throughout Asia, the return performance of individual markets deteriorated well before the onslaught of the financial crisis.

Performance of a Buy and Hold Strategy

The buy and hold returns accruing to investors between January 1990 and December 1997 are presented in table 3-9. Only Malaysia and the Philippines outperformed the Morgan Stanley world index return over this period. During the same time frame, the U.S. Morgan Stanley index outperformed all of Asia. Moreover, Asian equity returns exhibited significantly higher volatility than U.S.-based returns.

If we include the performance of the Asian indexes subsequent to the events in 1997, their return performance is significantly degraded. The returns accruing to buy and hold strategies between January 1990 and December 1997 are negative for all of the Asian indexes. Investors lost a minimum of 18 percent in dollar terms over the period and a maximum of 84 percent. Including the crisis period increases the volatility of returns in each of the Asian indexes with the exception of Taiwan.

Between January 1997 and December 1997, all of the Asian economies experienced dramatic declines in share prices. Taiwan experienced the highest absolute dollar return. Investors in this market only lost 12 percent on their dollar-denominated portfolios. Investors in the rest of Asia were not as fortunate. Indonesia, Korea, Malaysia, the Philippines, and Thailand suffered tremendous market losses during the crisis. Each of these markets lost at least 65 percent of its market capitalization in dollar terms. Moreover, the return volatility more than doubled in Indonesia and Korea during the crisis.

Return Performance of a Dynamic Trading Strategy

The returns presented in table 3-9 represent naive buy and hold strategies. An investor more eager to participate in the region could choose a dynamic trading strategy to enhance the overall performance of his portfolio. One such strategy might capitalize on each economy's financial market liberalization. Consider, for example, the returns accruing to an investment of $100 placed into each market on that market's liberalization and liquidated three years after liberalization.

Figure 3-9, panel A, presents the dollar-denominated returns accruing to this investment strategy. In the six scenarios presented, only one—the Philippines liberalization investment strategy—rewarded the investor with significant returns. In fact, a $100 investment held in the Philippines stock market for the three years following its official liberalization experienced a total return of just over 150 percent. We should not be surprised by this return, however, given that the unconditional return for the Philippines between 1990 and 1996 was roughly 115 percent.

The remaining investment portfolios in figure 3-9 experienced varying degrees of success in terms of their buy and hold returns. The liberalization portfolios for Korea, Malaysia, Taiwan, and Thailand handed in buy and hold returns under 50 percent for the three years following liberalization.

Table 3-9. *Country-Level Performance throughout the 1990s*
Percent

Country	Pre-crisis, January 1990 to December 1996			Crisis, January 1997 to December 1997			Full sample, January 1990 to December 1997
	Buy and hold	*Averge annualized monthly return*	*Annualized standard deviation*	*Buy and hold*	*Average annualized monthly return*	*Annualized standard deviation*	*Buy and hold*
Indonesia	11.10	3.09	103.55	-76.19	-135.32	239.40	-71.29
Korea	-47.33	-9.52	95.47	-72.79	-118.38	199.69	-83.88
Malaysia	127.13	11.80	85.02	-70.20	-128.43	153.99	-37.12
Philippines	118.13	9.55	109.07	-65.07	-97.62	125.82	-17.82
Taiwan	-42.89	-4.26	151.92	-12.03	-8.64	113.85	-47.61
Thailand	29.56	3.12	111.48	-78.63	-160.80	183.33	-74.05
United States	184.14	13.96	39.76	25.47	29.33	55.94	280.99
World	78.55	7.60	46.20	14.82	15.04	49.64	107.52

Source: Authors' calculations.

Figure 3-9. *Performance of Liberalization Trading Strategies*

Panel A. Single-Country Liberalization Investment Strategy

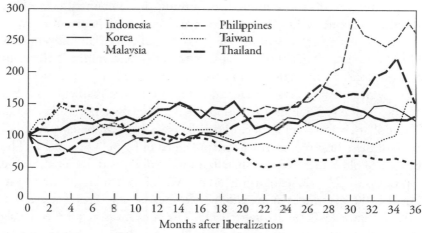

Panel B. Multicountry Liberalization Investment Strategy

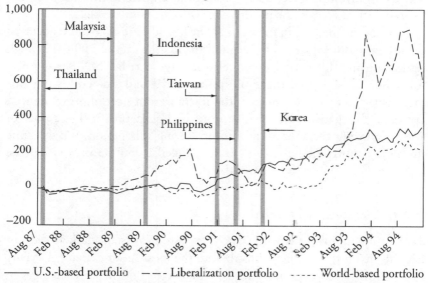

Source: Geert Bekaert and Campbell R. Harvey, "Chronology of Economic, Political, and Financial Events in Emerging Markets" (http://www.duke.edu/~charvey/Country_risk/couindex.htm) and IFC country-level indexes.

Investors attempting to capitalize on the Indonesia liberalization, in contrast, lost almost 50 percent of their initial investment in the three years following liberalization.[29]

Investors need not be limited to forming single-country portfolios. Another dynamic trading strategy designed to maximize an investor's exposure to the region consists of investing $100 into each Asian market on its liberalization and maintaining that investment. The combined returns to this portfolio of investments can be compared to a dollar-cost-averaging strategy of investing in $100 increments into the U.S. market over time. We define the regional East Asian portfolio as the liberalization portfolio. The dollar-cost-averaging portfolio is labeled the U.S.-based portfolio. Both of these investment returns are presented in figure 3-9, panel B. The buy and hold return for the liberalization portfolio is dominated by the return on the U.S.-based portfolio. The dynamic portfolio growth for an initial $100 investment in the U.S. portfolio exceeds 300 percent over the period August 1987 to December 1995. The same measure for the liberalization portfolio is almost 800 percent. Note that both of these strategies involve increasing the principal invested when a country liberalizes. The increasing investment occurs in the U.S. and liberalization portfolios at the same time. Hence, the portfolio growths are comparable.

Most of the increase in the value of the liberalization portfolio occurred between the third quarter of 1993 and the first quarter of 1994. The high returns during this period were fueled in large part by the dramatic performance of Malaysia, the Philippines, and Thailand. Following this incredible bout of performance, the liberalization portfolio experienced erratic and negative performance until its liquidation in December of 1995. Ignoring the substantial run-up during this period, the dynamic multiple-country liberalization strategy failed to outperform either the U.S. dynamic strategy or the world-based dynamic strategy.

Return Performance of ADRs

As mentioned, investors who wanted exposure to Asian markets did not need to invest their money directly into the local Asian exchanges. Many Asian firms issued depository receipts that traded on major exchanges in

29. Thailand experienced a significant run-up in the value of its index in months 34 through 36. This run-up allowed Thai investors to experience an overall buy and hold strategy for just over 50 percent of the three-year period following liberalization. However, ignoring this substantial short-term

the United States. Moreover, international investors may have preferred to invest in firms that complied with full SEC disclosure policies, rather than risking investment in firms on local exchanges where fundamental firm-level information may not have been as transparent.

In order to measure the performance of Asian ADRs, we form equally weighted portfolios of Asian-issued ADRs trading on either the NYSE or NASDAQ by country. The number of ADRs in each country's ADR index varies through time as the country's issuance record changes. Although this confuses the comparison of return performance across countries, these indexes do provide investors with the real-time investment performance of a portfolio designed to achieve maximum exposure to these markets.

Figure 3-10 displays the return performance for four Asian countries as well as two aggregated regional ADR indexes. We find that the ADR index for the Philippines outperformed all other ADR indexes during the 1990s. The buy and hold return of the ADR Philippine index exceeded 400 percent between 1990 and 1996. The ADR Indonesian index's buy and hold return for the same period was roughly 69 percent. The Taiwanese and Korean ADR indexes showed weak performance during this period. For Taiwan the buy and hold return was effectively zero, whereas the buy and hold return for Korea was negative 15 percent.

If we examine the regional ADR indexes, we find that the Asian ADR index outperformed its Latin American counterpart. The buy and hold return of the Asian ADR index exceeded 450 percent between 1990 and 1996. Over the same period, the buy and hold return of the Latin American index was roughly 120 percent. However, between June 1997 and June 1998, the Asian ADR index lost more than 60 percent of its value. Thus, over the broader time span from January 1990 to June 1998, the buy and hold returns on the ADR portfolios of Latin America and Asia were approximately equivalent.

Corporate Performance and Financial Risk

Our discussion of Asian capital markets to this point has relied on aggregated capital market price data. We have shown that Asian capital markets experienced significant growth via new capital mobilization. Furthermore,

---

run-up, the Thai investment would not have performed so well. In fact, an investment in the Thai index subsequent to liberalization earned under 10 percent over the first 34 months.

Figure 3-10. *ADR Index Performance across Countries and Regions, 1989–98*

Index level

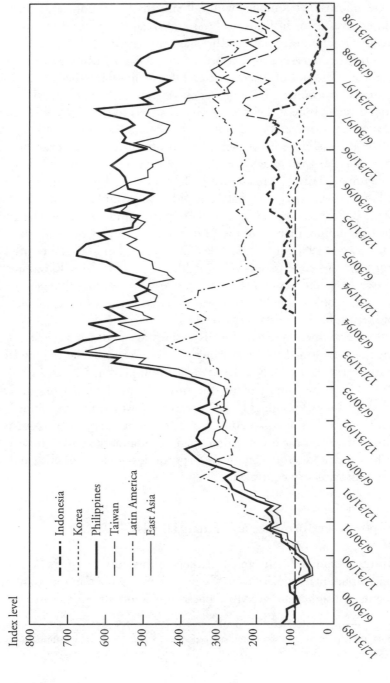

Source: Authors' calculations.

we have provided evidence suggesting that Asian firms solicited substantial amounts of new capital from international markets. Our analysis now shifts gears and investigates the issuer side of this new capital mobility.

In this section, we provide summary statistics describing the record of corporate performance in Asia as well as the financial risk of Asian corporations. Our approach is similar in spirit to that of Pomerleano and of Claessens, Djankov, and Lang.[30] However, although these authors present descriptive statistics relating to the average or median firm-level characteristic, we provide information on each characteristic's entire distribution across firms and across time. Thus our analysis allows us to analyze not only the average but also the entire shape of the distribution of each fundamental firm-level attribute.

Another important distinction between our analysis and that offered previously relates to our sample of firms. Pomerleano, for example, collects a sample of firms from each of the Asian countries using financial data from the Financial Times Information's Extel Card database.[31] He constrains his sample using the number of firms that have data available as of December 1992 and investigates the time series of the weighted average of certain characteristics of this group up to 1996.

One issue is that the constant sample approach ignores new firms that enter the database and assumes that the constant sample of firms remains the representative sample of firms throughout the period of investigation. However, new firms provide additional and valuable information as to the profitability and financial position of Asian corporations in general. Ideally, we would like to incorporate this information into the analysis of corporate performance. Moreover, the constant sample approach implicitly assumes that the sample firms maintain their relative position vis-à-vis the remaining firms in the economy. We can imagine a scenario whereby the firms chosen in 1992 were not the only firms that affected the economy in 1997. Furthermore, the average characteristics of these firms may or may not reflect the average characteristics of the rest of the firms. The deviation may be exaggerated as we move forward through time.

Our analysis examines the distribution of firm-level characteristics for all firms in the World Scope database. As new firms enter the World Scope database, we incorporate these firms into our analysis. Table 3-10 presents the details of our sample. Comparing our sample to that employed by

30. Pomerleano (1998); Claessens, Djankov, and Lang (1999).
31. Pomerleano (1998).

Table 3-10. *Number of Firms in Company-Level Analysis in Six Asian Countries, 1992–96*

Country and indicator	1992	1994	1996
Indonesia			
Return on equity	126	141	188
Return on invested capital	121	135	184
Total debt as a percentage of common equity	137	150	202
Interest expense on debt as a percentage of EBITDA[a]	132	144	194
Pomerleano sample	122	122	122
Korea			
Return on equity	107	176	225
Return on invested capital	103	178	228
Total debt as a percentage of common equity	123	213	25
Interest expense on debt as a percentage of EBITDA[a]	47	113	253
Pomerleano sample	44	44	44
Malaysia			
Return on equity	159	192	293
Return on invested capital	159	193	294
Total debt as a percentage of common equity	188	216	336
Interest expense on debt as a percentage of EBITDA[a]	186	214	335
Pomerleano sample	211	211	211
Philippines			
Return on equity	42	66	94
Return on invested capital	32	54	81
Total debt as a percentage of common equity	55	70	105
Interest expense on debt as a percentage of EBITDA[a]	42	57	90
Pomerleano sample	29	29	29
Taiwan			
Return on equity	24	43	182
Return on invested capital	23	42	183
Total debt as a percentage of common equity	27	105	201
Interest expense on debt as a percentage of EBITDA[a]	26	103	199
Pomerleano sample	16	16	16
Thailand			
Return on equity	157	346	377
Return on invested capital	157	350	385
Total debt as a percentage of common equity	261	366	417
Interest expense on debt as a percentage of EBITDA[a]	247	356	415
Pomerleano sample	173	173	173

Source: Authors' calculations based on firms in the Capital Data Bondware and World Scope databases; Pomerleano (1998).

a. EBITDA, earnings before interest and taxes plus depreciation and amortization.

Pomerleano, we find that in general our sample of firms is larger.[32] More-over, moving from 1992 to 1996 our sample incorporates more firms. Therefore, the marginal impact of any single firm on our reported statistics decreases as our sample increases. This may be particularly relevant to countries in which the sample size is "small." For example, as of 1992 our sample for Taiwan includes a maximum of twenty-seven firms. Pomerleano's sample size is sixteen. The marginal impact of any one firm in a sample this size is large. By including more firms into our sample, the number of firms grows to a minimum of 182 firms by 1996. Clearly, the marginal impact of any one firm on our sample statistics becomes minimal.

Measuring Asian Corporate Performance

Two of the more common ratios used to examine corporate performance are the rate of return on equity (ROE) and the return on invested capital (ROIC). World Scope calculates the return on equity, which is the ratio of net income to the average value of common equity. The ROE tells common shareholders how effectively their money is being employed. The ROIC measures a firm's earnings before interest and taxes as a percentage of the total amount of capital employed. ROIC indicates the efficiency of capital utilization. We discuss each of these indicators in this section.

Figure 3-11 depicts the distribution of Asian nonfinancial firms' ROE in 1992, 1994, and 1996. Throughout our sample of countries, the median ROE decreased over the course of the 1990s. For example, in Indonesia the median ROE dropped steadily, falling from 15.1 percent in 1992 to 12.5 percent in 1996. In Thailand this pattern is more pronounced. In 1992 the median ROE of all 107 firms in our sample was 19 percent. By 1996 the median ROE in Thailand had fallen to less than 8 percent. However, in Korea, Malaysia, the Philippines, and Taiwan the change in the median ROE between 1992 and 1996 was less dramatic.

From the data in figure 3-11 we also find that within certain countries the entire distribution of ROE across firms shifted to the left between 1992 and 1996. Consider the case of Thailand. The first, second, third, and fourth quartiles report a lower ROE in 1996 than in 1992. The same pattern holds across firms from Indonesia. Beginning in 1992, 25 percent of Indonesian firms sampled reported a return on equity less than 10 percent, 50 percent of firms reported an ROE around 15 percent, and for 75 percent

32. Pomerleano (1998).

Figure 3-11. *Summary Statistics of Changes in the Return on Common Equity (ROE) for a Cross Section of Firms, by Quartile Cutoff and Country, 1992, 1994, and 1996*

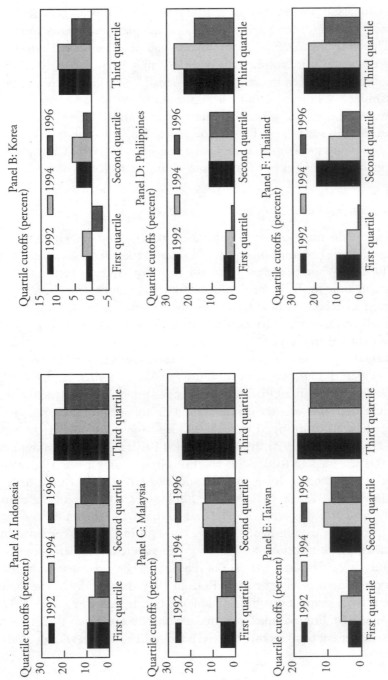

Source: The sample of firms for each country is described in table 3-10. For each sample period (1992, 1994, 1996), the first, second, and third quartile sample statistics are formed and reported. All firm-level data are taken from World Scope database.

of the firms the return to equity was around 24 percent. Four years later in
1996, the first quartile of firms recorded an ROE around 6 percent, the second quartile listed an ROE less than 13 percent, and the third quartile listed
an ROE around 20 percent. These data suggest that the entire sample distribution of the ROE across firms from Indonesia shifted left.

The return on invested capital provides another convenient indication
of a firm's performance. Figure 3-12 presents the distribution of ROIC for
our sample of firms across Asia. The changes in Asian ROIC during the
1990s parallel the changes in the ROE. For example, the distribution of
ROIC for both Indonesia and Thailand exhibits a significant shift to the
left between 1992 and 1996. This shift indicates that Indonesian and Thai
firms made less efficient use of their capital base as the 1990s progressed.
In fact, the median ROIC in Thailand fell from 12 percent in 1992 to
7 percent in 1996. This decrease in the ROIC is similar to that documented by Pomerleano.[33] The change in the ROIC in Korea, Malaysia,
the Philippines, and Taiwan was not as noticeable as it was in Indonesia
and Thailand.

In general indicators of corporate performance deteriorated throughout
emerging markets during the 1990s. Figure 3-13 details the median ROE
and ROIC for various emerging markets. Both the median ROE and the
median ROIC fell for most emerging markets presented between 1992 and
1996. The only country whose firms increased their profitability measures
was Mexico. Not only did Mexican firms increase their ROE and ROIC
between 1992 and 1996, they also had the highest level of these performance indicators across our sample of emerging markets. In the other
Latin American markets, the record of corporate performance was similar
to that of Asia. Both Brazilian and Chilean firms reported a lower ROE
and ROIC in 1996 than in 1992.

Measuring Financial Risk

A firm's leverage ratio—total book value of debt to book value of common
equity—can be interpreted as providing evidence of the amount of financial risk affecting stockholders. As stockholders are the residual claimants
to a firm's cash flow after debt is paid, high leverage ratios imply significant
financial risk. Another measure that attempts to ascertain the financial risk
borne by equity holders is the ratio of earnings before interest and taxes

---

33. Pomerleano (1998).

Figure 3-12. *Summary Statistics of Changes in the Return on Invested Capital (ROIC) for a Cross Section of Firms, by Quartile Cutoff and Country, 1992, 1994, and 1996*

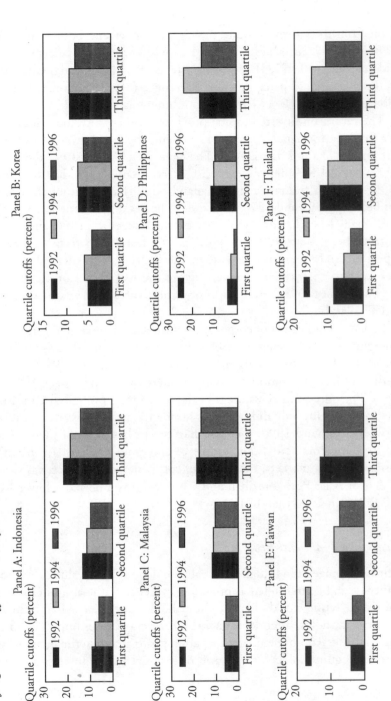

Source: The sample of firms for each country is described in table 3-10. For each sample period (1992, 1994, 1996), the first, second, and third quartile sample statistics are formed and reported. All firm-level data are taken from World Scope database.

Figure 3-13. *Changes in Medians of Various Corporate Performance Measures, 1992–96*

Panel A. Return on Equity

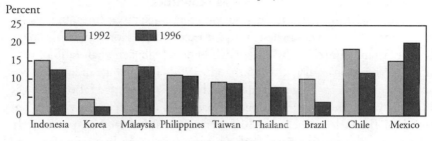

Panel B. Return on Invested Capital

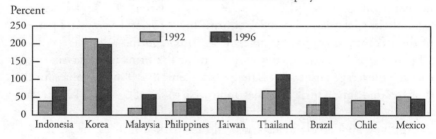

Panel C. Total Debt to Common Equity

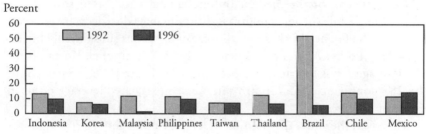

Panel D. Interest Payments to EBITDA[a]

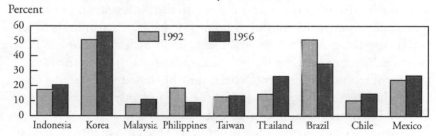

Source: World Scope database.
a. EBITDA, earnings before interest and taxes plus depreciation and amortization.

plus depreciation and amortization (EBITDA) to interest payments. Low ratios of EBITDA to interest payments indicate firms with high financial risk. In the analysis to follow, we examine these various indicators of financial risk through time and across Asian countries.

Figure 3-14 presents the distribution of leverage ratios through time for our sample of Asian countries. With the exception of Korea and Taiwan, all of the Asian countries represented exhibited a higher median ratio of total debt to common equity in 1996 than in 1992. The change in leverage was most noticeable in Thailand. In 1992 the median leverage ratio across the 261 firms in the World Scope database was 69 percent. By 1996 the median firm's leverage ratio had almost doubled to 114 percent. In Indonesia, the median firm doubled its leverage ratio between 1992 and 1996. Leverage for the median Indonesian firm increased from 39 to 78 percent. While the median firm in Korea managed to decrease its leverage ratio, the financial risk across all Korean firms was substantially higher than that of other Asian firms. In fact, only 25 percent of all Korean firms had leverage ratios less than 132 percent in 1992. By 1996, 75 percent of the 257 nonfinancial Korean firms in our sample shared leverage ratios in excess of 97 percent.

Moreover, the entire distribution of leverage ratios shifts to the right for most Asian countries. This shift indicates that most firms, and not just the median firm, increased their leverage ratios between 1992 and 1996. For example in Malaysia, 25 percent of firms in 1992 had leveraged 2 percent of their common equity, 50 percent of firms reported a leverage ratio of 19 percent or less, and finally 75 percent of the firms in Malaysia stated that their leverage ratio was less than 50 percent. By 1996 the values for the first, second, and third quartiles increased to 12, 58, and 112 percent, respectively. The distribution of leverage ratios for firms in Indonesia, the Philippines, and Thailand also showed this marked shift to the right.

The increase in the leverage ratio indicates that Asian equity holders faced the burden of growing financial risk to their investment. In order to appreciate this financial risk, we examine the ability of Asian firms to service their existing debt obligations. The ratio of interest paid to EBITDA indicates how much of the firm's cash flow is used to service the interest portion of its outstanding debt. Since equity holders are the residual owners of this cash flow, an increase in the ratio of interest payments to EBITDA indicates lower plowback and or dividends.

In figure 3-15 we present the distribution of the ratio of interest paid to EBITDA across firms for various countries in Asia. In Indonesia, Korea,

Malaysia, Taiwan, and Thailand the value of the median ratio increased between 1992 and 1996. Consider Thailand as an example. In Thailand the median ratio of interest paid to EBITDA increased from less than 15 to 26 percent in just four years. By the end of 1996, up to a quarter of the earnings of half of the firms in Thailand went to pay interest on their outstanding debt. For 25 percent of the firms in Thailand in 1996, between 25 and almost 50 percent of their earnings were dedicated to paying interest alone.

Although this may seem high, Thailand was not the most heavily indebted country in Asia. Korean leverage ratios were nearly double those of Thailand during the 1990s (figure 3-14). In fact, in 1996 roughly 25 percent of the firms in Korea dedicated between 50 and 75 percent of their earnings to pay off the interest on their debt.

Common Characteristics of Asian Eurobond Issuers

The previous section highlighted the increasing financial risk of Asian corporations. We found that throughout the region firms increasingly leveraged their firms' balance sheets. Furthermore, the amount of earnings dedicated to service the interest on this debt increased to very high levels. In Thailand, for example, corporations dedicated on average 25 percent of their cash flow to servicing the interest payments on their debt obligations. Moreover, in Thailand, the general profitability of corporations deteriorated during the second half of the 1990s.

Increasing leverage and decreasing profits are key determinants of default risk. In order to determine whether or not international capital markets contributed to this recipe for disaster, we examine the characteristics of Asian Eurobond-issuing firms. If international capital markets ignored Asia's increasing vulnerability and haphazardly issued capital, we would expect that Asian Eurobond issuers would have firm-level characteristics similar to the average firm-level characteristics of the entire region. However, if international capital markets rationed their capital investments, we would expect that only the most promising firms would receive funding from the Eurobond market.

In this section we explore average firm-level characteristics of Eurobond-issuing firms from Korea and Thailand. We compare these firms to the distribution of firms from the previous section in order to determine whether or not international capital markets provided capital on a systematic basis.

Figure 3-14. *Summary Statistics of Changes in the Debt to Common Equity (D/E) for a Cross Section of Firms, by Quartile Cutoff and Country, 1992, 1994, and 1996*

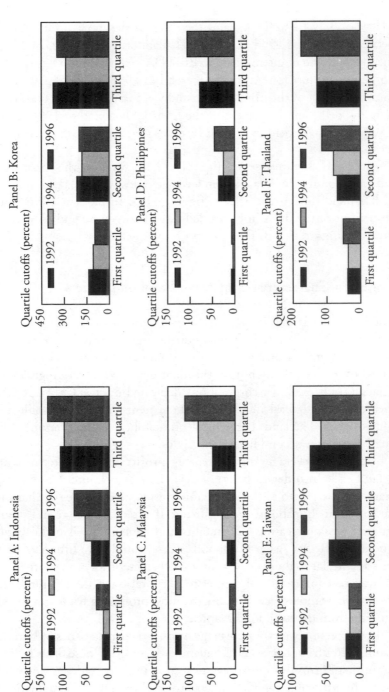

Source: The sample of firms for each country is described in table 3-10. For each sample period (1992, 1994, 1996), the first, second, and third quartile sample statistics are formed and reported. All firm-level data are taken from World Scope database.

Figure 3-15. *Summary Statistics of Changes in the Interest Payments to EBITDA (I/EBITDA) for a Cross Section of Firms, by Quartile Cutoff and Country, 1992, 1994, and 1996*

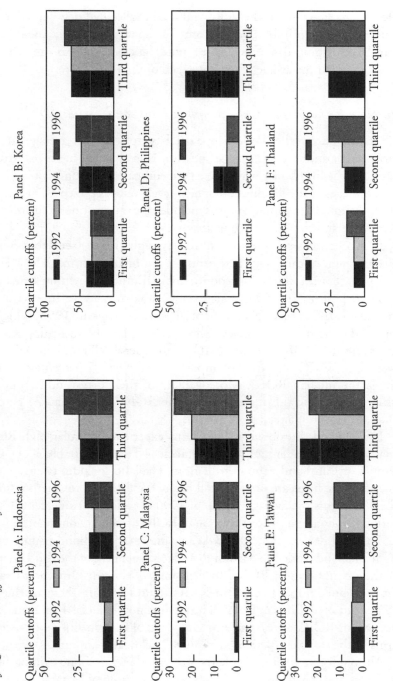

SOURCE: The sample of firms for each country is described in table 3-10. For each sample period (1992, 1994, 1996), the first, second, and third quartile sample statistics are formed and reported. All firm-level data are taken from World Scope database.

Our results suggest that the Eurobond market allocated new capital to the most highly profitable firms from Thailand. However, the typical Eurobond-issuing firm from Korea and Thailand was also more highly leveraged than the average firm from each of these countries.

Eurobonds and Firm-Level Attributes: Korea and Thailand

We use data from the World Scope database to construct average rates of profitability and leverage for the subset of Korean and Thai firms participating in the Eurobond market. We then compare Eurobond-issuing firm-level averages to the distribution of firm-level averages presented in the previous section. Our sample of firms includes the intersection of firms in the Bondware and the World Scope databases.

In Korea, our sample includes forty-eight firms (see table 3-11). Twenty-eight of the forty-eight firms are nonfinancial firms. The average ROIC across the thirty-four nonfinancial Eurobond-issuing firms was about 6 percent in 1996. This average was roughly in line with the median ROIC across all nonfinancial Korean firms in 1996, which is reported in figure 3-12. However, fifteen of the Eurobond-issuing Korean firms reported ROIC in excess of the median across all nonfinancials. The average of ROIC on this subsample was roughly 2.5 percentage points above the median ROIC. Moreover, six of the thirty-four Eurobond-issuing nonfinancial firms experienced an ROIC greater than 75 percent of all other nonfinancial Korean firms.

In Thailand, Eurobond-issuing firms experienced similar high ROIC relative to the broader sample of nonfinancial Thai firms (table 3-11). Our sample of Eurobond-issuing firms from Thailand includes twenty firms. Half of these firms are nonfinancial firms. We find that for the nonfinancial Thai firms the average ROIC in 1996 was almost 10 percent. Comparing this figure to the distribution of ROIC across all nonfinancial firms in Thailand presented in table 3-11, we find that Eurobond-issuing firms from Thailand tended to have an ROIC representative of the third quartile of the distribution of ROIC. In fact, four of the ten Eurobond-issuing firms in our sample handed in ROIC figures placing them in the top 25 percent of all firms in Korea. The median nonfinancial Thai firm experienced an ROIC of 6.7 percent. Only two of the ten Eurobond-issuing firms in the sample experienced an ROIC below this amount.

Although the previous evidence suggests that Eurobond-issuing firms in Korea and Thailand tended to be the most profitable, table 3-11 also

Table 3-11. *Cross-Sectional Characteristics of Eurobond-Issuing Firms in Korea and Thailand, 1996*

Country and company	Total debt as a percentage of common equity	Return on equity	Return on invested capital
Korea			
Nonfinancial firms (not real estate)			
Dacom Corporation	87.94	4.66	5.69
Daewoo Electronics Company	342.17	9.51	9.69
Daewoo Heavy Industries	175.83	1.15	4.25
Daewoo Telecom	163.44	3.77	7.33
Dong Ah Construction Industrial Company	298.48	−0.97	5.32
Hankook Tire Manufacturing Company	268.44	3.22	6.93
Hansol Paper Company	323.61	4.51	7.28
Hyundai Electronics Industries Company	574.64	n.a.	n.a.
Hyundai Engineering and Construction Company	573.15	1.90	6.33
Hyundai Motor Company	253.17	2.84	8.23
Jinro	1,723.66	n.a.	5.10
Kangwon Industries	303.57	−2.28	6.61
Kia Motors Corporation	353.63	−3.50	4.81
Kia Steel Company	2,293.88	−70.97	−3.02
Kolon Industries	241.47	4.03	n.a.
Kolon International Corporation	352.58	−0.90	7.36
Korea Electric Power Corporation	74.36	5.11	5.40
Korea Green Cross Corporation	117.33	6.16	7.19
LG Industrial Systems Company	323.94	3.89	8.37
LG Semicon Company	227.12	n.a.	n.a.
Medison Company	74.13	22.79	18.57
Miwon Company	1013.09	−31.90	1.71
Oriental Chemical Industries	115.19	14.42	11.15
Pohang Iron and Steel Company	95.66	9.78	7.94
Poongsan Corporation	406.63	−4.92	3.45
Samsung Company	386.20	4.09	5.27
Samsung Corporation	386.20	4.09	5.27
Samsung Electronics Company	296.12	1.90	3.78
Samwhan Corporation	216.25	2.73	6.55
SsangYong Cement Industrial Company	221.85	1.43	4.85
SsangYong Oil Refining Company	187.41	3.22	3.80
STC Corporation	595.59	−13.85	4.40
Tong Yang Cement Corporation	323.48	−3.12	4.35
Trigem Computer	145.83	5.90	10.52
Sample average	401.21	−0.36	6.27
Financial and real estate firms			
Boram Bank	133.95	−3.51	3.93
Cho Hung Bank	450.70	6.24	n.a.
Commercial Bank of Korea	388.14	6.90	n.a.

continued

Table 3-11. *Cross-Sectional Characteristics of Eurobond-Issuing Firms in Korea and Thailand, 1996 (continued)*

Country and company	Total debt as a percentage of common equity	Return on equity	Return on invested capital
Financial and real estate firms *(continued)*			
Hana Bank	315.44	10.46	n.a.
Housing and Commercial Bank	121.99	n.a.	n.a.
Kookmin Bank	515.43	17.39	n.a.
KorAm Bank	354.81	7.80	n.a.
Korea Exchange Bank	725.02	5.52	n.a.
Korea First Bank	535.61	−2.07	n.a.
Korea Long Term Credit Bank	1,253.06	9.31	6.79
Kwangju Bank	410.28	2.03	n.a.
Kyungki Bank	300.72	1.23	n.a.
Pusan Bank	557.05	10.23	n.a.
Shinhan Bank	364.33	7.62	n.a.
Sample average	459.04	6.09	5.36
Thailand			
Nonfinancial firms (not real estate)			
Banpu Public Company	163.13	18.47	8.37
Loxley Public Company	220.62	15.22	11.37
Precious Shipping Public Company	266.70	15.41	7.72
PTT Exploration and Production Public Company	85.53	9.21	8.03
Robinson Department Store Public Company	148.47	10.52	7.63
Srithai Superware Public Company	185.83	21.36	12.11
Thai Central Chemical Public Company	189.39	5.27	4.43
Tipco Asphalt Company	143.97	32.08	18.57
Total Access Communications Public Company	155.88	17.60	14.76
TPI Polene Public Company	323.84	7.65	4.75
Sample average	188.34	15.28	9.77
Financial and real estate firms			
Advance Agro Public Company	264.92	−16.79	−4.45
Cogeneration Public Company	120.01	n.a.	n.a.
Central Pattana Public Company	101.17	n.a.	n.a.
Hemaraj Land and Development Public Company	118.76	20.06	11.38
Juldis Develop Public Company	229.75	0.64	1.97
Land and Houses Public Company	139.41	12.08	6.73
MDX Public Company	82.33	−5.50	0.53
One Holding Public Company	273.15	−6.03	3.12
Property Perfect Public Company	220.02	10.48	3.45
Tanayong Public Company	125.93	3.21	1.75
Sample average	167.55	2.27	3.06

Source: Capital Data Bondware and World Scope databases.
n.a. Not available.

suggests that these firms were the most highly leveraged firms in these countries. In fact roughly 70 percent of the Eurobond-issuing firms from Korea recorded leverage ratios in 1996 greater than the median leverage of all nonfinancial firms from Korea. The average leverage ratio across the sample of nonfinancial Eurobond-issuing firms in 1996 was 401 percent. Comparing this to the distribution of leverage ratios from figure 3-14, we find that the average Eurobond-issuing nonfinancial Korean firm had a higher leverage ratio than 75 percent of the rest of the nonfinancial firms in the Korean economy.

Once again, Thailand's Eurobond-issuing nonfinancials displayed the same pattern of high leverage relative to the rest of the economy. Five out of the ten Eurobond-issuing firms from Thailand had leverage ratios greater than 75 percent of the rest of all nonfinancial firms in Thailand. In fact, the average leverage ratio across the sample of Eurobond-issuing firms was 182 percent in 1996. Only one Eurobond-issuing firm from Thailand reported a leverage ratio less than the median leverage ratio across all non-financial firms from Thailand.

Value at Risk: The Next Logical Step

The combination of the firm-level characteristics of Eurobond-issuing firms suggests that international capital markets allocated capital to the most profitable yet highly leveraged firms in Asia. This pattern of alloca-tion can be consistent with a rationally functioning capital market pro-vided that the markets correctly account for the financial risk of these firms. Assuming that this risk was priced into either bond yields or expected stock returns, it appears as though Asian corporate managers leveraged up their investments in an attempt to bet on the long-run per-formance of their firms.

We use the term "bet" for a number of reasons. First, corporate man-agers increased leverage in a period of declining corporate performance. Second, corporate managers increased the stake by using foreign currency-denominated debt. In this case, the "bet" covers both the firm's prospects as well as the direction of the country's exchange rate.

The substantial foreign exchange exposure is difficult to quantify with standard methods. For example, standard risk analysis would regress stock returns on changes in the foreign exchange rate. In many of our sample countries, the exchange rate was effectively fixed. The statistical measure of risk would suggest no significant exposure to changes in the exchange rate.

Current research by Harvey and Roper attempts to provide a systematic approach to measuring the risk inherent in funding projects with foreign currency-denominated debt.[34] Exposure is measured from the bottom up by looking at the firm's loan portfolio and the currency denomination and by simulating exchange rate scenarios. A value-at-risk exercise can then be conducted.

Value at risk (VaR) has become a popular measure in the banking sector for examining the impact of various scenarios on a bank's capital adequacy ratio. Although nonfinancial institutions do not have legal capital adequacy requirements, VaR can serve as a useful tool for measuring fluctuations in the financial risk of a firm brought about by changes in interest rate environments and exchange rates.

The VaR analysis in Harvey and Roper focuses on the VaR of dollar-denominated Eurobonds and foreign bank loans.[35] The first step of the exercise includes forming the Eurobond debt servicing obligations and international bank loan servicing obligations of Asian corporations on a firm by firm basis. They use Capital Data's Bondware and Loanware databases to collect information on the coupon, principal, issue date, maturity date, and currency of denomination for every Asian corporate debt obligation listed in the international marketplace. This paper is the first to use these databases to reconstruct a firm's foreign liabilities.

In order to determine the VaR of Asian firms, Harvey and Roper normalize the Eurobond and other debt service obligations of each company by their EBITDA.[36] This tells us that much of a firm's cash flow goes toward servicing total debt and the foreign currency-denominated component.

The idea of the VaR exercise is to fix a reference point prior to the crisis and to project into the future different scenarios for the exchange rate. Harvey and Roper compare the ratio of Eurobond debt servicing obligations to EBITDA across countries and firms in order to assess the value at risk of Asian corporations.[37] They are able to assess how much of a currency depreciation would wipe out all cash flows. Using the information about interfirm correlations, they estimate the impact of various levels of currency depreciation on the entire corporate sector. Indeed, the VaR analysis provides the basis for a type of emerging market early warning sys-

34. Harvey and Roper (1999).
35. Harvey and Roper (1999).
36. Harvey and Roper (1999).
37. Harvey and Roper (1999).

tem. This analysis contrasts with standard approaches that rely on historical movements in exchange rates.

Conclusions

Our quantitative and qualitative assessment of Asian capital markets reveals several common features across individual markets throughout the region. In general, a substantial part of growth in market capitalization associated with the markets during the 1990s resulted from new capital mobilization of equity and debt. Compared with local capital markets in Latin America, East Asia was more successful in the issuance of new shares, IPOs, and new bonds. Moreover, the degree of liquidity offered to investors in the secondary markets for these securities was higher than that in Latin America. In fact, the liquidity in China, Taiwan, and Malaysia rivals the liquidity offered in the United States.

We also find similar forms of concentration across East Asian stock exchanges throughout the 1990s. In general, the various stock exchanges tended to be heavily concentrated in certain industries. Moreover, the asset concentration of East Asian stock markets was higher than that of Latin America. The impact of asset concentration manifested itself in high correlation among individual stock returns. We show that most of the individual stocks in Asia moved up or down together throughout the 1990s. However, we also find that the concentration of value traded in secondary markets in Asia was more evenly distributed among firms than the levels found in Latin America.

Despite East Asia's success at new capital mobilization and its high degree of liquidity, the return performance for different types of portfolio investments in this region lagged behind that of the rest of the world. One exception to this record of poor performance was a dynamic trading strategy designed to capture the price appreciation associated with market liberalization. Another exception was the return to an investment in Philippine-issued ADRs that proved extremely profitable until 1996. In general, Asia's capital market liberalization programs had little impact on the volatility of local stock market returns. In fact, most of the changes in volatility and returns that occurred during the 1990s resulted from changes in the underlying economic and financial market fundamentals of each country.

Our firm-level analysis suggests that indicators of Asian corporate performance soured during the later half of the 1990s, while leverage ratios increased. Although any equity investment carries a certain degree of risk, this combination increased the financial risk of Asian corporations.

We also analyze the type of debt. In a case study of Korean and Thai firms that participated in the Eurobond market, we find a high ROIC compared with that of other firms in these markets. But these firms also had the highest preexisting levels of leverage.

It has been routine to assign blame for the Asian crisis. Foreign speculators and the structural characteristics of both local and international capital markets have taken a lot of flak. However, foreign speculators were not advising East Asian corporations to increase their leverage in a period of declining financial performance. Speculators did not advise corporations to issue foreign currency-denominated debt.

Our research focuses on a micro-level interpretation. Asian corporate managers "bet" their firms when they increased leverage in the face of lower corporate performance. They raised the stakes by issuing foreign currency-denominated debt. Here, they were betting that the exchange rates would remain fixed for an indefinite amount of time.

Although the causes of the Asian crisis are complex, our micro-level analysis suggests that individual firms greatly increased their risk exposure. Given the characteristics of the economy that guaranteed high correlation among these firms, this set the stage for the following possibility. A shock to the economy could have a greatly magnified and a potentially catastrophic effect because of the high risk exposure induced by corporate managers. Although Asian corporate managers did not initiate the crisis, deficiencies in their risk management practices greatly exacerbated it. The decline of many corporations can be tied directly to their failure to manage and control risk.

References

Bekaert, Geert. 1995. "Market Integration and Investment Barriers in Emerging Equity Markets." *The World Bank Economic Review* 9 (January): 75–107.

Bekaert, Geert, and Campbell R. Harvey. 1995. "Time-Varying World Market Integration." *Journal of Finance* 50 (June): 403–43.

———. 1999. "Foreign Speculators and Emerging Equity Markets." *Journal of Finance* (Forthcoming).

Claessens, Stijn, Simeon Djankov, and Larry H. P. Lang. 1999. "Who Controls East Asian Corporations?" Policy Research Working Paper 2054. Washington, D.C.: World Bank, Policy Research Department (February).

Cline, William R., and Kevin J. S. Barnes. 1997. "Spreads and Risks in Emerging Markets Lending." Research Paper 97-1. Institute of International Finance.

Corsetti, Giancarlo, Paolo Pesenti, and Nouriel Roubini. 1998a. "Paper Tigers? A Model of the Asian Crisis." Working Paper. New York University (December).

———. 1998b. "What Caused the Asian Currency and Financial Crisis? Part I: A Macroeconomic Overview." Working Paper. New York University (September).

Divecha, A., J. Drach, and D. Stefek. 1992. "Barriers of Portfolio Investments in Emerging Stock Markets." Working Paper. Washington. D.C.: World Bank.

Ferson, Wayne E., and Campbell R. Harvey. 1993. "The Risk and Predictability of International Equity Returns." *Review of Financial Studies* 6 (3): 527–66.

Harvey, Campbell R. 1991. "The World Price of Covariate Risk." *Journal of Finance* 46 (March): 111–57.

———. 1995a. "The Cross-Section of Volatility and Autocorrelation in Emerging Markets." *Finanzmarkt und Portfolio Management* 9: 12–34.

———. 1995b. "The Risk Exposure of Emerging Equity Markets." *World Bank Economic Review* 9 (January): 19–50.

Harvey, Campbell R., and Andrew H. Roper. 1999. "Estimating Emerging Market Financial Risk: An Application of Value at Risk." Unpublished Working Paper. Duke University, Finance Department.

International Finance Corporation. Various years. *Emerging Stock Markets Factbook.* Washington, D.C.

Krugman, Paul. 1998. "What Happened to Asia?" Unpublished manuscript. Massachusetts Institute of Technology, Economics Department (January).

Lintner, John. 1965. "The Valuation of Risk Assets and Selection of Risky Investments in Stock Portfolios and Capital Budgets." *Review of Economics and Statistics* 47 (February): 12–37.

Pomerleano, Michael. 1998. "East Asia Crisis and Corporate Finances: The Untold Story." *Emerging Markets Quarterly* 2 (Winter): 14–27.

Radelet, Steven, and Jeffrey Sachs. 1998. "The Onset of the East Asian Financial Crisis." NBER Working Paper 6680. National Bureau of Economic Research (August).

Sharpe, William F. 1964. "Capital Asset Prices: A Theory of Market Equilibrium under Conditions of Risk." *Journal of Finance* 19 (September): 425–42.

World Bank. Various years. *Emerging Markets Statistics Yearbook.* Washington, D.C.

MICHAEL POMERLEANO
XIN ZHANG

4

Corporate Fundamentals and the Behavior of Capital Markets in Asia

E QUITY MARKETS in the emerging economies of Asia have experienced enormous growth accompanied by episodes of volatility over the past two decades. The total market capitalization of Asia's emerging markets (China, Hong Kong [China], Indonesia, the Republic of Korea, Malaysia, the Philippines, Taiwan [China], Thailand, and Singapore) rose from $370 billion in 1988 to $1.7 trillion in 1996, an average increase of 45 percent a year. The past two decades have also been marked by episodes of volatility, however. The most recent episode, the crash of 1997, had a devastating effect on Asian capital markets, reducing the aggregate market capitalization of the four countries hardest hit by the crisis (Indonesia, Korea, Thailand, and Malaysia) from $637 billion in 1996 to $188 billion in 1997, a decline of 70 percent. Despite their growth and prospective role in capital formation, these markets are little understood, particularly as they concern the relationship of corporate fundamentals with underlying market dynamics.

Recent studies have examined Asian corporate financial fundamentals and documented declining profitability, accompanied by rapid growth of

The authors are indebted to Margaret Enis and Alex Lebedinsky for their dedicated and capable research assistance.

fixed assets financed by debt and excessive leverage.[1] These findings raise the question of whether Asian capital markets disciplined corporate decisionmaking before the crisis. A group of studies completed in the aftermath of the Asian crisis focuses on market herding behavior and whether foreign investors were responsible for the turmoil.[2] This points to a perceived gap in the current literature—the relation between corporate decisions and financial markets.

This paper is organized as follows. The first section introduces the methodology and data sources used. The second section explicitly links corporate decisions to capital market behavior by exploring whether the opportunity cost of capital influences the investment decisions of companies. The third section examines how investors interpret and react to corporate fundamentals and tries to determine whether Asian investors focus more on corporate growth rates or on underlying corporate profitability. From this evidence, we infer how the actions of investors influence corporate behavior. The final section concludes.

Methodology and Data Sources

In this paper we explore the effect that Asian capital markets have on corporate decisionmaking by explicitly linking internal financial performance (reflected in corporate profitability) to financing costs in the capital markets. We accomplish this by comparing corporate returns, as measured by return on invested capital, to the cost of mobilizing capital in the market, as measured by the after-tax weighted average cost of capital.[3] We then develop an analytical framework based on economic value added (EVA). We also apply a portfolio sorting technique to study how corporate fundamentals affect the movement of stock market prices. The portfolio sorting examines four areas: (a) the corporation's value relative to its stock price, as measured by the book-to-market and earnings-to-price ratios, (b) corpo-

1. See, for example, Pomerleano (1998).

2. Choe, Kho, and Stulz (1998); Brown, Goetzmann, and Park (1998); Froot, O'Connell, and Seasholes (1998).

3. Return on invested capital = {net income before preferred dividends + [(interest expense on debt − interest capitalized) * (1 − tax rate)]} / (last year's total capital + last year's short-term debt and current portion of long-term debt). Weighted average cost of capital = [cost of debt * (1 − tax rate)* (debt / capital) + cost of equity * (equity / capital)].

rate size as measured by market capitalization, (c) corporate assets and sales growth rates, and (d) corporate leverage, profitability, and ownership structure. The relationship between past and future stock prices in Asia is also examined.

The study uses two major data sources, the World Scope database (for annual balance sheet and income statement data) and the Financial Times security database (for monthly stock price data).

The study examines all of the major Asian emerging economies in Asia: China, Hong Kong, Indonesia, Republic of Korea, Malaysia, Philippines, Singapore, Taiwan, and Thailand. It includes firms for which both accounting data and stock price information are available. Financial firms are excluded because of their highly leveraged capital structure. The firms included represent a cross section of the local stock market and the country's overall economy (table 4-1).

Works by Pomerleano and by Claessens, Djankov, and Lang document the financial conditions of corporations before the crisis.[4] Using information from the World Scope database on corporate leverage and financial performance of Asian corporations, we validate earlier findings (tables 4-2 through 4-7). The data on corporate investment, funding, and profitability indicate rapid investment in fixed assets financed by excessive borrowing in some Asian countries.

Fixed assets grew at average rates of 16 percent in Malaysia, 20 percent in Thailand, 21 percent in Indonesia, and 20 percent in the Philippines between 1992 and 1996. As a result of this rapid expansion of fixed assets, debt-to-equity ratios increased in many economies in the region, causing a decline in the fixed-charge coverage ratio—an indication of capacity to repay and ability to service debts.[5] Similarly, returns on assets and invested capital also fell in some economies. Corporate performance was worst in the Republic of Korea and Thailand, the countries hit hardest by the subsequent crisis. Their figures far exceed those in other parts of the world. In Latin America, for example, fixed assets grew just 7–10 percent a year on average; in the United States, the average rate of growth was 10 percent a year.

---

4. Pomerleano (1998); Claessens, Djankov, and Lang (1998).

5. Debt-to-equity ratio: leverage = (current liabilities + long-term debt) / common equity. Fixed-charge coverage ratio: earnings before interest and taxes and depreciation / {interest expense on debt + [preferred dividends (cash)] / [1 − (tax rate / 100)]}.

Table 4-1. *Number of Companies in the Sample*

	Part 1		Part 2		
Region and economy	*Number of firms used to estimate cost of equity*	*Number of firms with both accounting and security price data used for portfolio sorting*	*Starting year for merged firms with accounting and price data*	*Percent of market capitalization of merged firms in local markets*	*Percent of sales of merged firms in local gross domestic product*
Asia					
China	11	86	1992	10	2
Hong Kong (China)	45	254	1987	29	78
India	78				
Indonesia	36	104	1990	49	14
Korea, Republic of	11	210	1987	39	90
Malaysia	104	294	1987	45	86
Philippines	6	62	1988	42	21
Singapore	52	160	1987	35	51
Taiwan (China)	10	180	1988	49	27
Thailand	16	195	1987	42	22
Latin America					
Argentina	5	n.a.	n.a.	n.a.	n.a.
Brazil	n.a.	n.a.	n.a.	n.a.	n.a.
Chile	33	n.a.	n.a.	n.a.	n.a.
Mexico	13	n.a.	n.a.	n.a.	n.a.
Industrial countries					
Australia	63	n.a.	n.a.	n.a.	n.a.
Canada	63	n.a.	n.a.	n.a.	n.a.
France	151	n.a.	n.a.	n.a.	n.a.
Germany	141	n.a.	n.a.	n.a.	n.a.
Japan	52	n.a.	n.a.	n.a.	n.a.
United Kingdom	143	n.a.	n.a.	n.a.	n.a.
United States	248	n.a.	n.a.	n.a.	n.a.

Source: Authors' calculations.
n.a. Not available.

Table 4-2. *Debt-to-Equity Ratios in Sample Companies, 1992–96*[a]
Percent

Economy	1992	1993	1994	1995	1996	Average
Asia						
China	274	153	106	112	101	149
Hong Kong (China)	101	82	84	103	93	93
India	213	169	168	162	173	177
Indonesia	120	107	108	121	159	123
Korea,						
Republic of	494	381	355	388	459	415
Malaysia	78	89	101	128	165	112
Philippines	106	101	85	98	113	101
Singapore	69	79	117	92	88	89
Taiwan (China)	66	71	71	74	82	73
Thailand	178	176	172	180	196	180
Latin America						
Argentina	50	67	73	84	84	72
Brazil	57	48	43	48	70	53
Chile	57	59	54	70	77	63
Mexico	87	58	79	110	78	82
Industrial countries						
Australia	116	120	100	101	102	108
Canada	173	157	150	157	151	158
France	316	305	273	235	264	289
Germany	228	241	233	269	220	238
Japan	483	467	451	456	442	460
United Kingdom	142	143	139	150	143	144
United States	204	174	179	195	193	189

Source: Authors' calculations.
a. Leverage = (current liabilities + long-term debt) / common equity.

Do Corporate Investment Decisions Reflect the Cost of Capital?

This section seeks to determine whether the cost of capital affected the allocation of investments in fixed capital assets in Asia. If market signals are effective, and reinforced by the deterrence of bankruptcy, we expect corporate management decisions to result in returns that exceed the cost of

Table 4-3. *Ratio of Total Liabilities to Equity in Sample Companies,*
1992–96

Percent

Economy	1992	1993	1994	1995	1996	Average
Asia						
China	223	153	108	113	103	140
Hong Kong (China)	101	82	87	97	97	93
India	216	171	170	164	176	179
Indonesia	123	111	111	129	140	123
Korea	540	423	396	429	509	459
Malaysia	83	114	115	136	173	124
Philippines	115	108	94	109	124	110
Singapore	73	122	120	94	94	101
Taiwan (China)	70	75	75	80	87	77
Thailand	184	185	180	187	204	188
Latin America						
Argentina	59	76	81	91	91	80
Brazil	75	62	58	62	88	69
Chile	64	66	62	79	88	72
Mexico	96	65	85	118	82	89
Industrial countries						
Australia	132	131	114	116	118	122
Canada	198	175	166	173	159	174
France	360	356	324	341	329	342
Germany	403	420	410	470	395	420
Japan	507	494	480	486	471	487
United Kingdom	172	171	168	172	170	171
United States	280	260	243	252	242	255

Source: Authors' calculations.

capital. Conversely, when incentives and the institutional framework are ineffective, the discipline transmitted through the financial markets is weak, and the informational content of the cost of debt and equity is all too often simply ignored. The absence of market incentives in emerging markets contributes to poor corporate investment allocation decisions and the attendant misallocation of resources. The legal structure to support bankruptcy is just now being introduced in parts of Asia, and the lack of credi-

Table 4-4. *Return on Assets in Sample Companies, 1992–96*
Percent

Economy	1992	1993	1994	1995	1996	Average
Asia						
China	12.4	13.7	8.1	7.3	5.5	9.4
Hong Kong (China)	8.7	10.6	9.1	6.7	7.3	8.5
India	10.1	11.3	12.2	10.6	9.0	10.6
Indonesia	13.0	9.6	10.2	12.7	9.4	11.0
Korea	4.5	4.6	5.8	6.3	4.2	5.1
Malaysia	8.5	10.1	8.4	8.7	9.0	8.9
Philippines	10.0	9.6	14.6	9.4	9.7	10.7
Singapore	6.7	7.3	5.8	6.4	6.4	6.5
Taiwan (China)	7.6	6.1	8.7	9.2	7.3	7.8
Thailand	9.5	8.2	7.5	7.3	6.0	7.7
Latin America						
Argentina	5.5	7.9	7.9	9.9	8.3	7.9
Brazil	23.8	89.6	33.8	2.7	4.7	30.9
Chile	11.7	10.0	10.4	10.6	9.0	10.4
Mexico	5.5	9.3	−0.1	12.8	13.6	8.23
Industrial countries						
Australia	4.1	5.7	6.0	7.3	6.1	5.8
Canada	3.6	2.7	5.7	5.3	6.1	4.7
France	4.4	3.3	3.6	3.5	3.2	3.6
Germany	3.0	1.9	3.2	3.4	3.6	3.0
Japan	2.2	1.8	1.9	2.2	2.2	2.1
United Kingdom	6.6	6.8	7.2	7.8	8.1	7.3
United States	3.3	5.1	6.8	7.2	7.4	6.0

Source: Authors' calculations.

ble bankruptcy regimes has allowed unprofitable companies to remain in business.

How efficiently is capital being used? The analysis introduces the weighted average cost of capital as a benchmark for the cost of capital. If the difference between weighted average cost of capital and return on invested capital is positive, wealth is created; if the difference is negative, wealth is destroyed. An analytical framework is then developed based on

Table 4-5. *Return on Invested Capital in Sample Companies, 1992–96*
Percent

Economy	1992	1993	1994	1995	1996	Average
Asia						
China	15.7	11.7	10.3	9.6	7.2	10.9
Hong Kong (China)	12.3	13.1	11.2	8.7	9.1	10.9
India	13.7	15.1	15.6	13.8	12.1	14.1
Indonesia	14.6	11.2	11.9	15.1	11.9	12.9
Korea	6.4	6.1	7.7	8.4	5.6	6.9
Malaysia	11.7	12.8	11.9	11.4	12.1	12.0
Philippines	13.1	12.4	18.4	11.8	12.6	13.7
Singapore	9.0	9.6	8.1	7.0	8.6	8.5
Taiwan (China)	8.6	6.8	10.1	10.8	8.6	9.0
Thailand	11.6	9.8	8.8	8.9	7.0	9.2
Latin America						
Argentina	6.7	10.7	10.6	11.7	9.8	9.9
Brazil	35.7	109.6	39.5	3.1	5.7	38.6
Chile	13.7	11.3	11.8	12.3	10.9	12.0
Mexico	9.4	6.2	−0.7	14.9	15.2	9.0
Industrial countries						
Australia	5.3	7.6	7.9	9.6	8.1	7.7
Canada	4.7	4.3	8.3	7.5	8.8	6.7
France	8.0	5.6	5.9	5.7	5.7	6.2
Germany	7.0	4.6	7.3	7.7	8.7	7.1
Japan	3.3	2.5	2.7	3.2	3.1	2.9
United Kingdom	9.8	11.5	11.3	12.4	13.3	11.4
United States	5.1	7.8	11.3	11.6	12.0	9.6

Source: Authors' calculations.

economic value added. Economic value analysis explicitly links internal financial performance (reflected in corporate profitability) to external financing costs in the capital markets. The analysis recognizes that equity has implied and debt has revealed opportunity costs, reflected in their market prices. To create value, a corporation must earn enough to cover the cost of its debt and exceed the opportunity cost of its equity. We determine whether corporations generate an economic return by comparing

Table 4-6. *Ratio of Capital Expenditures to Gross Fixed Assets in Sample Companies, 1992–96*
Percent

Economy	1992	1993	1994	1995	1996	Average
Asia
China	16.6	33.9	20.6	17.1	14.7	20.6
Hong Kong (China)	9.0	8.4	10.1	10.8	11.4	9.9
India	19.3	14.1	19.1	19.2	14.2	16.6
Indonesia	28.7	17.5	16.1	18.6	22.1	20.6
Korea	12.1	10.8	11.2	18.5	19.2	14.2
Malaysia	15.5	14.2	17.9	18.1	16.1	16.4
Philippines	16.0	15.1	18.9	25.2	22.5	19.5
Singapore	16.1	14.1	15.4	13.5	15.4	14.9
Taiwan (China)	9.4	9.2	10.1	11.7	14.1	10.9
Thailand	22.1	20.1	19.3	18.6	21.5	20.3
Latin America
Argentina	9.2	6.9	12.2	11.7	8.8	9.8
Brazil	4.9	6.0	6.0	4.8	6.0	5.5
Chile	8.2	9.9	9.8	9.5	9.2	9.3
Mexico	8.9	8.7	10.8	6.8	4.7	7.9
Industrial countries
Australia	9.6	9.5	10.4	12.0	12.2	10.7
Canada	8.2	8.1	8.3	10.0	9.8	8.9
France	12.4	10.7	10.6	10.7	9.9	10.8
Germany	12.0	9.9	9.6	9.8	10.4	10.3
Japan	10.6	8.7	7.9	7.6	7.8	8.5
United Kingdom	8.8	8.6	8.9	9.0	9.6	9.0
United States	9.8	9.8	10.2	10.6	10.6	10.2

Source: Authors' calculations.

corporate returns, as measured by return on invested capital, to the cost of mobilizing capital in the market, as measured by the after-tax weighted average cost of capital.[6]

6. Profitability changes over the economic cycle. Ideally the return on invested capital needs to be assessed across the cycle and compared with the costs of debt and equity to determine how sustainable corporate performance is.

Table 4-7. *Earnings before Interest and Taxes plus Depreciation and Amortization (EBITDA) Interest Expense on Debt, 1992–96*[a]

Economy	1992	1993	1994	1995	1996	Average
Asia						
China	7.4	6.9	19.0	8.6	8.0	10.0
Hong Kong (China)	24.4	18.2	11.9	8.7	12.8	15.2
India	3.8	4.7	5.5	6.8	5.5	5.3
Indonesia	6.5	7.3	8.2	7.5	6.2	7.1
Korea	4.5	2.4	7.6	3.3	2.6	4.1
Malaysia	217.4	82.3	79.0	62.9	37.0	95.7
Philippines	5.2	6.2	8.6	11.3	7.7	7.8
Singapore	353.3	82.6	48.3	48.9	83.1	123.3
Taiwan (China)	10.3	12.4	12.7	15.3	12.5	12.6
Thailand	11.3	7.9	6.7	6.1	4.6	7.3
Latin America						
Argentina	13.9	18.8	19.9	14.8	8.9	15.3
Brazil	3.7	3.2	4.5	9.4	4.5	5.1
Chile	14.9	9.9	11.2	11.0	10.2	11.4
Mexico	5.7	6.8	3.6	3.8	4.7	4.9
Industrial countries						
Australia	8.3	12.0	13.6	10.8	9.7	10.8
Canada	5.2	5.3	7.7	7.3	8.1	6.7
France	5.0	5.4	8.1	7.2	9.6	7.1
Germany	8.2	7.5	9.2	9.5	10.4	8.9
Japan	4.8	5.2	6.0	7.6	9.1	6.5
United Kingdom	8.7	10.4	13.9	12.9	12.6	11.7
United States	7.5	8.5	9.8	9.5	10.0	9.0

Source: Authors' calculations.

a. Interest expense on debt represents the service charge for the use of capital. If interest expense is reported net of interest income and interest income cannot be found, the net figure is shown. Interest expense includes (a) interest on short-term debt, long-term debt, and capitalized lease obligations and (b) amortization expense associated with the issuance of debt and similar charges. Capitalized interest charges are not included.

The methodology for calculating the equity costs for individual companies is presented in box 4-1. We select companies for which data are available for the period between 1992 and 1996 in order to estimate the growth of earnings and price-to-earnings ratios. We then calculate the aggregate

Box 4-1. *Calculating the Cost of Equity*

The relationship between equity prices and the implied growth of future nominal earnings is derived from the hypothesis that the current equity price, P_t, equals the discounted present value of future earnings, E_{t+j}, $(j \geq 1)$, with a discount factor r_t.

$$(1) \qquad P_t = \sum_{j=1}^{\infty} \left[\frac{1}{1 + r_t}\right]^j E_{t+j}$$

Assuming that future earnings grow at a constant rate, g_t, such that $E_{t+j+1} = (1 + g_t)E_{t+j}$, equation 1 becomes:

$$(2) \qquad P_t = E_t \sum_{j=1}^{\infty} \left[\frac{1 + g_t}{1 + r_t}\right]^j.$$

This implies the following relationship between the current price-to-earnings ratio (P/E), the discount factor, and the future earnings growth rate:

$$(3) \qquad \frac{P_t}{E_t} = \frac{(1 + g_t)}{(r_t - g_t)}.$$

Equation 3 is solved for the implied cost of equity:

$$(4) \qquad r = \frac{(1 + g_t)}{P/E}.$$

cost of equity at the economy level by removing outliers from the sample and weighing the individual equity costs by their market capitalization.

The methodology has some limitations. First, the cost of equity varies across industries and depends on a corporation's profile. Second, and perhaps more important, the cost of equity is based on prospective earnings growth, not past earnings.[7] We explored the possibility of using earnings

7. The static interpretation of the formula yields the opposite result: $\Delta r / \Delta g = [1 + (E / P)]$. In other words, the cost of capital increases when earnings growth increases.

Table 4-8. *Interest Rates, 1992–96*
Percent

Economy	1992	1993	1994	1995	1996
Asia					
China	8.64	10.98	10.98	12.06	10.08
Hong Kong (China)	6.50	6.50	9.88	9.00	7.26
India	18.92	16.25	14.75	15.46	15.96
Indonesia	24.03	17.25	14.50	18.00	17.68
South Korea	10.00	8.58	8.50	9.00	8.82
Malaysia	9.31	9.05	10.25	7.60	8.75
Philippines	19.48	14.68	15.06	14.68	14.84
Singapore	5.95	5.39	5.88	3.80	4.16
Taiwan (China)	6.93	6.50	7.60	7.47	6.92
Thailand	17.54	7.34	4.63	10.17	9.73
Latin America					
Argentina	n.a.	n.a.	10.06	17.85	10.51
Brazil	n.a.	n.a.	n.a.	n.a.	n.a.
Chile	23.92	24.30	20.34	18.16	17.37
Mexico	n.a.	22.04	20.38	58.59	36.89
Industrial countries					
Australia	11.06	9.72	9.55	11.12	11.00
Canada	7.48	5.94	6.88	8.65	6.06
France	10.00	8.90	7.89	8.12	6.77
Germany	13.59	12.85	11.48	10.94	10.02
Japan	6.15	4.41	4.13	3.40	2.66
United Kingdom	9.42	5.92	5.48	6.69	5.96
United States	6.25	6.00	7.14	8.83	8.27

Source: Authors' calculations.
n.a. Not available.

estimates, but such data are few and far between. Given these limitations, the estimates of the cost of equity should be seen as indicative of the order of magnitude rather than as a precise estimate.

First, we collected the cost of debt. We use multiple sources for the cost of domestic debt for the period 1993–98.[8] Table 4-8 presents the cost of

8. We encountered substantial difficulty in developing a comprehensive data set for the cost of bonds from one source and, therefore, abandoned efforts to use a consistent rating for the cost of debt. The cost of domestic currency–denominated corporate debt is estimated from three sources: lending

debt. Table 4-9 presents the nominal cost of equity, as well as the real cost of equity, adjusted for inflation. The estimates of the cost of equity should be seen as indicative of the order of magnitude, rather than as precise estimates. The nominal cost of equity was 21 percent in Indonesia, 17 percent in Thailand, 10 percent in Singapore, and 16 percent in Malaysia between 1992 and year-end 1996. The equivalent figure in Chile was 23 percent, while in the United States it was 19 percent. Important distinctions are notable in the real cost of equity, which ranged from a low of 3 percent in Taiwan to a high of 32 percent in Argentina.

Finally, we calculate the weighted average cost of capital from the weighted cost of equity (based on leverage) and the after-tax cost of debt (using the average tax calculated by World Scope; see figure 4-1). The real weighted average cost of capital for the period varies considerably across developing and developed countries, casting doubt on the immediacy of financial integration. Table 4-10 provides detailed results. We can explain some of the differences. For instance, we can ascribe the low cost of capital in Japan to low interest rates. Similarly, Argentina's high cost of capital is probably due to the crisis of the 1980s and early 1990s and the ensuing recapitalization. China's repression of the financial sector, and interest rate controls, leads to low cost of capital. Although outside our objectives in this paper, the differences in the cost of equity warrant further analysis.

The return on invested capital measures operating profit in relation to the total funds employed. The ratio is an indicator of the economic performance of the firm. The measure can be used to compare performance across firms or economies without regard to financing strategies (table 4-11). Real return on invested capital ranges from a high of almost 9 percent in Malaysia to a low of –12 percent in Mexico after adjusting for inflation. Comparison of the return on invested capital and weighted average cost of capital is instructive in determining a corporation's added economic value that exceeds the cost of capital. The return on invested capital minus weighted average cost of capital in Asian countries is negative with the exception of China and Taiwan. In Malaysia and Singapore, negative

rates are from World Bank (1998), International Monetary Fund (1999), and World Scope database, and estimated interest rates and Asian markets data are from *Asiamoney*. The information for the database is collated by *Asiamoney* mostly from prospectuses. The database covers Hong Kong, Taiwan, China-B shares, Korea, Indonesia, Philippines, Thailand, Malaysia, Singapore, India, Pakistan, Sri Lanka, and Bangladesh. It lists equities and fixed-income transactions from 1992 to the present with some exceptions. An alternative methodology would rely on the cost of external debt plus the cost of hedging the foreign exchange debt as measured by the historical swap costs.

Table 4-9. *Cost of Equity, 1992–96*

Percent

Economy	Cost of equity	Compounded average	Real cost of equity
Asia			
China	19.23	13.90	5.33
Hong Kong (China)	19.15	8.30	10.75
India	17.74	9.50	8.24
Indonesia	20.65	8.63	12.02
Korea, Republic of	18.78	5.33	13.45
Malaysia	15.52	4.16	11.36
Philippines	22.91	8.41	14.50
Singapore	10.01	2.15	7.86
Taiwan (China)	6.60	3.60	3.00
Thailand	17.33	4.82	12.51
Latin America			
Argentina	40.58	8.30	32.28
Chile	23.45	11.00	12.45
Mexico	24.60	19.73	4.87
Industrial countries			
Australia	10.57	2.38	8.19
Canada	24.00	1.45	22.55
France	8.08	1.98	6.10
Germany	10.71	3.11	7.60
Japan	8.13	0.74	7.39
United Kingdom	14.72	2.72	12.00
United States	19.08	2.86	16.22

Source: Authors' calculations.

economic value added is insignificant. Figure 4-2 presents the difference between return on invested capital and weighted average cost of capital (table 4-12 presents detailed data for the 1992–96 period).

Economic Value Added and Equity Valuation

Empirical studies testing the connection between economic value added and market value are inconclusive. Some authors suggest that higher than

Figure 4-1. *Real Weighted Cost of Capital, 1992–96*

Source: Authors' calculations.

Table 4-10. *Weighted Average Cost of Capital, 1992–96*
Percent

Economy	Compounded average cost of capital	Compounded average inflation	Real cost of equity
Asia			
China	16	13.90	2
Hong Kong (China)	16	8.30	8
India	16	9.50	6
Indonesia	16	8.63	7
Korea, Republic of	9	5.33	4
Malaysia	14	4.16	10
Philippines	21	8.41	12
Singapore	9	2.15	7
Taiwan (China)	9	3.60	5
Thailand	11	4.82	6
Latin America			
Argentina	32	8.30	24
Chile	22	11.00	11
Mexico	23	19.73	3
Industrial countries			
Australia	10	2.38	7
Canada	19	1.45	17
France	7	1.98	5
Germany	9	3.11	6
Japan	8	0.74	7
United Kingdom	13	2.72	11
United States	15	2.86	13

Source: Authors' calculations.

expected economic value added leads to higher market value and higher stock prices.[9] Others dismiss the importance of economic value added for share value.[10]

9. See Stewart (1990).
10. Bernstein and O'Byrne (1998).

Table 4-11. *Return on Invested Capital, 1992–96*
Percent

Economy	Compounded average return on invested capital	Compounded average inflation	Real return on invested capital
Asia			
China	18.60	13.90	4.70
Hong Kong (China)	11.30	8.30	3.00
India	13.40	9.50	3.90
Indonesia	12.90	8.63	4.27
Korea, Republic of	7.50	5.33	2.17
Malaysia	13.10	4.16	8.94
Philippines	14.90	8.41	6.49
Singapore	8.50	2.15	6.35
Taiwan (China)	9.30	3.60	5.70
Thailand	9.20	4.82	4.38
Latin America			
Argentina	10.90	8.30	2.60
Chile	11.10	11.00	0.10
Mexico	7.60	19.73	−12.13
Industrial countries			
Australia	8.80	2.38	6.42
Canada	8.60	1.45	7.15
France	7.30	1.98	5.32
Germany	9.40	3.11	6.29
Japan	3.60	0.74	2.86
United Kingdom	8.60	2.72	5.88
United States	11.50	2.86	8.64

Source: Authors' calculations.

An instructive exercise is to calculate the net present value (NPV) of the economic value of the companies based on their consolidated balance sheets. We then compare the resulting NPV with the market capitalization of the companies to determine the ratio of market capitalization to economic value added (table 4-13).

What can we conclude from the analysis? First, the nominal, as well as the real, cost of equity and the weighted average cost of capital vary

Figure 4-2. *Return on Invested Capital minus Weighted Average Cost of Capital, Compounded Average, 1992–96*

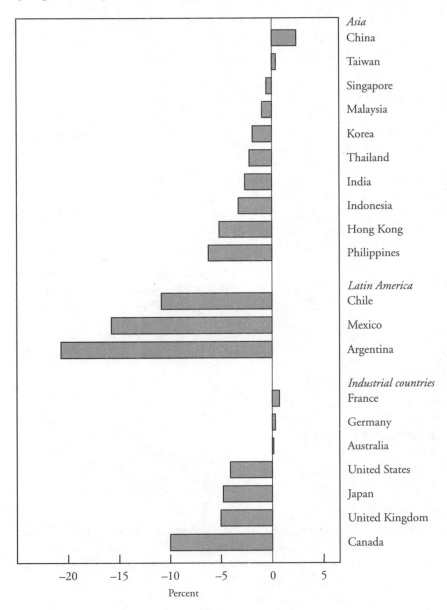

Source: Authors' calculations.

Table 4-12. *Return on Invested Capital Minus Weighted Average Cost of Capital, 1992–96*

Percent

Economy	1992	1993	1994	1995	1996	Compounded average
Asia						
China	−5.9	22.7	−6.7	12.2	−7.5	2.3
Hong Kong (China)	−4.0	−3.2	−5.3	−6.8	−5.9	−5.1
India	−5.0	−2.1	−0.5	−1.4	−3.3	−2.5
Indonesia	−2.5	−4.4	−2.5	−2.1	−3.8	−3.0
Korea, Republic of	−1.3	−1.6	0.6	−1.3	−4.2	−1.7
Malaysia	−0.4	−0.6	−0.5	−0.4	−2.0	−0.8
Philippines	−6.0	−8.6	1.0	−5.7	−8.6	−5.9
Singapore	−0.1	−0.4	1.0	−0.8	−1.1	−0.3
Taiwan (China)	1.3	−1.6	0.9	1.8	−1.4	0.2
Thailand	4.9	−2.2	−3.3	−3.7	−5.4	−2.0
Latin America						
Argentina	−22.7	−20.1	−19.7	−20.9	−21.4	−20.9
Chile	−10.4	−13.3	−10.3	−9.4	−11.5	−11.0
Mexico	n.a.	−14.7	−12.6	−23.6	−11.9	−15.8
Industrial countries						
Australia	−2.0	−1.0	−0.1	0.5	−1.1	−0.8
Canada	−11.6	−10.24	−9.7	−5.3	−8.8	−9.9
France	0.0	−0.0	1.4	1.0	0.2	0.5
Germany	−0.2	−0.6	0.5	1.5	−0.5	0.1
Japan	−3.8	−4.7	−4.4	−5.0	−4.8	−4.6
United Kingdom	−7.0	−5.3	−3.7	−3.8	−3.4	−4.7
United States	−6.5	−5.2	−3.5	−2.5	−1.7	−3.9

Source: Authors' calculations.

n.a. Not available.

Table 4-13. *Valuation of Economic Value Added:*
Market Capitalization to Net Present Value of Corporations, 1992–94
Percent, using weighted average cost of capital

Region and economy	1992	1993	1994
Asia			
China	n.a.	n.a.	n.a.
Hong Kong (China)	257	391	314
India	154	266	202
Indonesia	391	382	261
Korea, Rep. of	26	38	94
Malaysia	113	171	156
Philippines	n.a.	n.a.	n.a.
Singapore	65	97	108
Taiwan (China)	103	109	112
Thailand	101	140	128
Latin America			
Argentina	n.a.	n.a.	n.a.
Chile	n.m.	7,656	886
Mexico	n.a.	n.a.	n.a.
Industrial countries			
Australia	68	69	77
Canada	111	106	95
France	25	27	27
Germany	34	35	42
Japan	26	30	33
United Kingdom	99	86	79
United States	113	103	93

Source: Authors' calculations.
n.a. Not available.
n.m. Not meaningful.

considerably across countries. Second, estimated real returns on invested capital show marked differences across countries. Third, the calculations of an indicator of economic value added—the difference between return on invested capital and weighted average cost of capital—document that only a few countries exceed the opportunity cost of capital (see box 4-2). Fourth, the economic value added valuation methodology, with all its

Box 4-2. *Economic Value of Equities*

We reach the economic value of equities using the discounted cash
flow for all years (using the weighted average cost of capital as the discount rate) plus EBITDA (earnings before interest and taxes plus
depreciation and amortization) from the final year (discounted at
weighted average cost of capital), minus the outstanding debt from the
first year, and compare it to the market capitalization of the equities in
the first year to ascertain the premium or discount of share prices to
underlying economic value-added (EVA) value in various countries.
Although by no means rooted in robust theoretical foundations, the
methodology is nevertheless indicative of underlying economic value
and valuation of corporations in merger and acquisition activity.

Fixed Sample of Thirty-Six Companies in Indonesia with Data for 1992–96

Year	1992	1993	1994	1995	1996
Book capital	4,972,165	5,287,832	7,051,220	8,637,949	10,748,630
Net operating income post-tax (percent)	13.79	11.57	15.29	13.67	11.97
Weighted average cost of capital post-tax (percent)	20.17	18.55	18.00	18.96	18.76
Spread (percent)	−6.38	−6.98	−2.71	−5.29	−6.79
Economic value added loss (book capital * spread)	317,034	369,133	332,248	456,567	730,107
Total net present value of eco- nomic value added (discounted at weighted average cost of capital; U.S. dollars)	−1,409,208	n.a.	n.a.	n.a.	n.a.
EBITDA	1,132,699	1,304,695	1,655,460	1,945,014	2,246,626
EBITDA compound growth 18.7 percent (percent)	n.a.	15	27	17	16
Capitalized EBITDA (U.S. dollars)	7,423,106	n.a.	n.a.	n.a.	n.a.
1992 total debt (U.S. dollars)	2,756,770	n.a.	n.a.	n.a.	n.a.
Net present value of corporations (U.S. dollars)	1,480,596	n.a.	n.a.	n.a.	n.a.
Total market capitalization for corporations (U.S. dollars)	7,742,219	n.a.	n.a.	n.a.	n.a.
Total market capitalization to net present value of corporations (percent)	571	n.a.	n.a.	n.a.	n.a.

Source: Authors' calculations.
n.a. Not available.

limitations, is, however, indicative of pronounced overvaluations of equities in certain Asian countries, namely Hong Kong, India, and Indonesia. According to these calculations, Chilean equities were overvalued due to the high cost of capital. Similarly, European equities—in France, Germany, and the United Kingdom—were undervalued. European equities appreciated substantially subsequently during the 1992–98 bull market, and yet the distress of Asian equities is the topic of this conference![11]

How Do Corporate Fundamentals Affect Stock Market Movements?

In this section we examine how corporate fundamentals affect stock market movements in Asia. We begin by surveying the relevant literature. We then introduce the methodology (described in more detail in appendix A) and present our results. In the last part of the section, we draw conclusions.

Review of the Literature

Financial paradigms, such as Sharp's capital asset pricing model and Ross's arbitrage pricing theory, do not provide direct insight into the linkage between corporate fundamentals and stock price movements (or market returns).[12] Since risk associated with individual corporate fundamentals can be diversified in a large portfolio, the capital asset pricing model and arbitrage pricing theory argue that individual corporate fundamentals should not affect stock returns unless they are unexpected and cannot be diversified.

A separate line of research has tried to link stock prices to corporate fundamentals. This literature has focused on the existence of value premium— that is, the extent to which value stocks outperform glamour stocks (see box 4-3). Using U.S. stock market returns, Fama and French determine that corporate fundamentals—market capitalization and the corporate book-to-market ratio (B/M)—have significant explanatory power to account for stock returns.[13] Proponents of the efficient market hypothesis

---

11. Although the market rose in this period, according to the methods used in this paper, it seems to be undervalued with regard to economic value added.

12. Sharpe (1964); Ross (1976).

13. Fama and French (1992).

Box 4-3. *What Is Value Investing and What Are Value and Glamour Stocks?*

Value investing argues that buying cheap stocks beats buying expensive ones. According to this criterion, equities are classified into two groups based on fundamental characteristics: value stocks and glamour stocks. Value stocks have the following three attributes:

—Stocks with high relative value (or low market prices relative to corporate fundamentals). Value stocks in this category have relatively high ratios of book-to-market value (B/M), earnings-to-price (E/P), cash-flow-to-price (C/P), and dividend-to-price ratios (D/P).

—Stocks with poor historical corporate performance—that is low return on equity (ROE), low sales and asset growth rates, or high leverage levels.

—Stocks with historically low stock returns. Value stocks tend to be undervalued and, thus, have greater potential for higher returns—i.e., they offer "value" to investors. Glamour stocks have the opposite corporate fundamentals. They have demonstrated a strong record of corporate performance over time, and their market value is high relative to their fundamentals.

In industrial markets, value stocks traditionally produce higher investment returns than glamour stocks *over long periods of time*, and the difference is known as the value premium. In their 1992 and 1998 papers, the University of Chicago's Eugene Fama and Kenneth French demonstrated that small companies and those with high book-to-market ratios outperformed over the long term (from 1963 through 1990) in the United States. And for twelve major international markets for a shorter period—1975 through 1995—the average large-value stock beat the average large glamour stock by 7.6 percent.

interpret Fama and French's results as indicating that value premiums arise because value stocks are fundamentally risky.

Other researchers, such as Lakonishok, Shleifer, and Vishny, have questioned the interpretation of value premium.[14] They argue that market movements may not be related to fundamental risks in the marketplace.

14. Lakonishok, Shleifer, and Vishny (1994).

Value premiums reflect inherent irrationality and market overreaction. This irrationality causes investors to undervalue distressed (value) stocks and to overvalue well-performing (glamour) stocks.

Most of the existing studies look at industrial countries. There have been several limited attempts to examine the value hypothesis in emerging markets. Fama and French, Rouwenhorst, and Claessens, Dasgupta, and Glen all use the International Finance Corporation's emerging market database to analyze the relationship between stock returns and certain corporate-related variables, such as market beta, firm size, and book-to-market ratio in emerging markets.[15] They reach different conclusions. Fama and French and Rouwenhorst find a value premium that is similar to that in industrial countries (5.56–7.65 percent). Claessens, Dasgupta, and Glen, however, find that large firms (glamour stocks) tend to be associated with higher stock returns in eleven of the nineteen emerging economies in their sample. Data limitations in all of these studies restrict the coverage of corporate fundamentals to size, book-to-market ratio, and earnings-to-price ratio. These studies thus only offer limited insight into how corporate fundamentals are linked to market performance.

Methodology

Use of an extensive database and refined portfolio sorting procedures allows us to overcome some of the limitations of earlier studies. In addition to the corporate fundamentals covered in previous studies—size, B/M, and E/P—we include relative value, growth, leverage, profitability, and momentum. We construct stock portfolios with different corporate characteristics: relative value, size, growth, leverage, profitability, and momentum. Portfolio sorting is used to study the impact of these corporate fundamentals and stock market movements. We use B/M as an example to illustrate the portfolio sorting approach. In order to track the role of corporate fundamentals, indicators such as the B/M ratio of stocks in an economy are sorted at the end of each year. Three portfolios—high, medium, and low— are then formed according to their B/M ratios. The high portfolio includes the 33 percent of stocks with the highest B/M ratio (value stocks). The low portfolio includes the 33 percent of stocks with the lowest B/M ratio (glamour stocks). Investment returns of the two portfolios are then com-

15. Fama and French (1998); Rouwenhorst (1998); Claessens, Dasgupta, and Glen (1995).

pared. If the value portfolio outperforms the glamour portfolio, we conclude that a value premium exists and that market dynamics are similar to those in industrial economies. Using a similar methodology, we examine the role played by other fundamental attributes (size, growth prospects, corporate leverage, profitability) and the market momentum measure for all Asian countries. Appendix A describes the detailed sorting procedure.

Different corporate variables may be highly correlated. To understand the results from univariate sorting, we also explore bivariate sorting methods. For example, stocks with low B/M ratios may have large capitalizations. Stock returns on these stocks might thus reflect the impact of the corporation's size on the market. To untangle the effect of correlated corporate variables, we control for size by using a bivariate sorting technique. To isolate the impact of size from the effect of the B/M ratio, for example, we sort all stocks by firm size and form three portfolios based on large, medium, and small size. We then take the large-size portfolio and resort its stocks by B/M ratio, thereby creating three separate portfolios within the large-size group. The same sorting procedure is repeated for the medium- and small-size groups. We are then able to isolate the size-adjusted B/M effect. Similar procedures are used for adjustments using other variables such as leverage and growth. Appendix A describes the two-pass sorting procedure.

Using this methodology, we analyze all of the major emerging Asian economies from January 1987 to April 1997. We exclude the Asian financial crisis time frame so that the extreme price volatility during that period does not distort our results.

Results

The analysis provides evidence for value discounts: value firms systematically underperform glamour stocks. Figure 4-3 provides summary results. Detailed results are provided in appendix B. To test the robustness of the results, we weight the stocks in our portfolio by market capitalization to determine whether distortions from thinly traded stocks and outliers affect the results. The original findings are found to be robust. Next we discuss in detail the results linking each corporate fundamental to market movements.

RELATIVE VALUE AND MARKET PERFORMANCE. The relative value of a stock is measured by the ratio of some indicator of corporate fundamentals to market price. Relative value variables included here are the ratios of book

Figure 4-3. *Value Discounts: How Much Do Glamour Stocks Outperform Value Stocks in Asia, January 1987–April 1997?*

How much low B/M stocks
outperform high B/M stocks

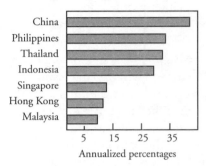

Annualized percentages

How much large-size stocks
outperform small-size stocks

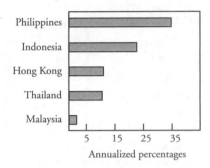

Annualized percentages

How much high-sales growth stocks
outperform low-sales growth stocks

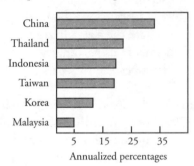

Annualized percentages

How much high-profitability stocks
outperform low-profitability stocks

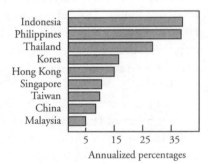

Annualized percentages

How much low-leverage stocks
outperform high-leverage stocks

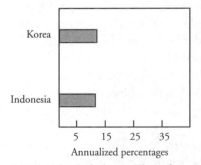

Annualized percentages

Momentum trading in Asia:
How much previous winners will
outperform previous losers in the future

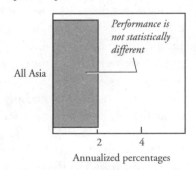

Annualized percentages

Source: Authors' calculations. The performance of value stocks and glamour stocks is *not* statistically different for countries not reported in the charts.

to market (B/M), earnings to price (E/P), cash flow to price (C/P), and dividends to price (D/P). Conventional investment strategy holds that stocks with high-value ratios have higher value to investors than do low-value stocks because they are relatively undervalued. Our findings in Asia reach the opposite conclusion. For the B/M portfolio high B/M stocks underperform low B/M stocks for all markets except Korea and Taiwan. The value discounts range from a high of 42 percent in China to a low of 9 percent in Taiwan. For Asia as a whole, the value discount is approximately 10 percent. Similar findings are obtained for E/P, C/P, and D/P portfolios.

FIRM SIZE AND MARKET PERFORMANCE. Most studies find a negative relationship between size and returns.[15] The explanation advanced is that small firms face higher default risk than large firms and tend to be more illiquid in secondary markets, so higher returns are required to compensate for risk. The alternative explanation offered by Lakonishok, Shleifer, and Vishny is that the market oversells small capitalization stocks when their prices drop and they become undervalued stocks.[17] The financial literature refers to this phenomenon as a "size premium." Our results, in Asian countries, find significant size discounts (large firms offer higher returns than small firms). The exceptions to the findings are China, Korea, Singapore, and Taiwan, whose results are not statistically significantly different from zero. Glamour (large-size) stocks outperform value (small-size) stocks in many Asian countries.

CORPORATE GROWTH AND MARKET PERFORMANCE. Findings on sales growth document a negative relationship between returns and historical sales growth rates in the United States.[18] The explanation offered is that low-growth stocks are undervalued by investors and therefore offer higher returns. Given that growth is one of the most important factors attracting investors to Asia, we examine a portfolio strategy based on three indicators of growth: sales growth, asset growth, and dividend growth. The findings on corporate growth in Asia are mostly contrary to what is found in the United States. They confirm the conventional wisdom that investors like growth (glamour) stocks in Asia. For all the three growth criteria, and for

16. Banz (1981); Fama and French (1992, 1998).
17. Lakonishok, Shleifer, and Vishny (1994).
18. Lakonishok, Shleifer, and Vishny (1994).

each of the Asian countries in our sample, we find that firms with a strong historical record of growth in sales, assets, and dividends outperform other firms in most countries. Hong Kong, the Philippines, and Singapore are the exceptions.

CORPORATE PROFITABILITY AND MARKET PERFORMANCE. Firms with high historical rates of return on capital employed outperform firms with relatively low rates in all economies except China, Malaysia, and Taiwan. The results highlight once again the fact that investors in Asia prefer glamour stocks (with good historical corporate performance).

CORPORATE LEVERAGE AND MARKET PERFORMANCE. Bhandari finds a positive relationship between leverage and average return using U.S. stock return data.[19] We find a negative relationship between returns and historical leverage ratios in Indonesia and Korea. Firms in these two economies, which have high debt-to-equity ratios, underperform firms with relatively low debt-to-equity ratios by 12 and 13 percent, respectively. In the traditional risk-return framework, this means that high-leverage firms are not considered risky in these two countries. The opposite results are found, however, in Malaysia and Thailand.

MOMENTUM TRADING. Consistent with Rouwenhorst's findings, we do not find significant profits from momentum trading.[20] The results do not support the hypothesis of a positive-feedback trading mechanism in Asian stock markets. Stocks with historically high returns do not produce higher returns in the future. These results hold for both semiannual and annual portfolio rebalancing.

CORPORATE FUNDAMENTALS AND MARKET DYNAMICS DURING THE ASIAN CRISIS. In order to shed light on market dynamics during the recent crisis, we extend our research by studying corporate fundamental profiles of losers and winners during the crisis. The portfolio sorting approach is used. Stocks are sorted according to their average returns during the crisis period (from April 1, 1997, to October 30, 1998) in order to create three portfolios. The winner portfolio includes the 33 percent of stocks with the highest returns. The loser portfolio includes the 33 percent

---

19. Bhandari (1988).
20. Rouwenhorst (1998).

of stocks with the lowest returns. A third portfolio includes the remaining stocks. We then compare the corporate fundamentals of the winners and losers by examining B / M, D / P, market capitalization, leverage, growth, profitability, historical returns, beta, and ownership concentration in 1996 (see table 4-14). Detailed results are found in appendix B.

Four results emerge from this analysis. First, corporate fundamentals were not relevant during the crisis. Winners and losers could not be distinguished based on corporate fundamentals. Second, "loser" stocks tended to have higher market capitalization and historical growth rates than "winner" stocks, suggesting that glamour stocks may have suffered more in the crisis than value stocks. Third, leverage, often cited as having precipitated the crisis, was not correlated with market performance. In fact, winners tended to have higher debt-to-equity ratios than losers. Finally, corporate ownership was not relevant during the crisis. Winners and losers could not be distinguished based on the level of ownership concentration.

What Accounts for the Fact That Stock Markets in Asia and Industrial Countries Behave So Differently?

Our results show that glamour stocks significantly outperform value stocks in Asia. The accepted paradigm of the risk-return trade-off states that higher returns simply compensate for higher risk—that is, the value premiums, size premiums, and leverage premiums in developed countries compensate for the assumption of high risk. We encounter difficulty applying this framework to Asia. For example, applying the paradigm in Asia, highly leveraged firms in Indonesia and Korea are regarded as *less risky* and small firms as *less risky*. Similarly, investors tend to regard low book-to-market stocks and large-size firms as *more risky*.

Why is it that the standard financial paradigm cannot explain stock market movements in Asia? We advance three possible interpretations, although there might be more, of the findings. The first interpretation is rooted in the arguments of Lakonishok, Shleifer, and Vishny and of Haugen; it represents a deviation from the standard risk-return paradigm.[21] It holds that Asian markets are dominated by "naïve" investors, who equate *quality companies* with *quality stocks*. Asian investors buy growth because they think they are getting quality; they also assume a trend in stock prices and overreact to good or bad news, extrapolating past sales growth, return

21. Lakonishok, Shleifer, and Vishny (1994); Haugen (1995).

Table 4-14. *Corporate Profiles of Winners and Losers in the Asian Financial Crisis*

Indicator	China	Hong Kong	Indonesia	Korea	Malaysia	Philippines	Singapore	Taiwan	Thailand
Book to market (percent)	0.75*	-0.05	-0.19	-1.42	-0.17	-0.36	-0.06	0.02	0.60
Market capitalization (millions of U.S. dollars)	-155,342*	-95,758	-220,090	-86,808	213,809	777,046	-136,409	-32,579	-7,020
Three-year sales growth (percent)	-0.86	4.34	-12.43	9.83	9.36	51.35*	2.51	-0.98	8.82
Return on equity (percent)	-3.69	-2.03	-1.94	-5.07	2.33	16.79*	-0.39	1.80	-2.49
Debt to equity (percent)	14.58	34.82*	3.32	-27.27	4.62	43.20	8.00	7.03	28.75
Past year's return (percent)	-43.09	16.01	12.52	8.45	3.75	66.12*	-7.91	3.71	-4.91
Beta	n.a.	0.05	-0.10	-0.06	-0.05	0.00	0.09	-0.04	-0.08
Ownership concentration (percent)	n.a.	2.08	-0.30	-2.13	1.36	-3.74	-2.47	-0.03	0.20

Source: Authors' calculations.

n.a. Not available.

* Statistically significant at the 5 percent confidence level in *t*-tests.

on assets, and leverage conditions far into the future. In the process, it appears that valuations get overstretched.

Another plausible explanation is that investors are rational and that the differences reflect a rational response to market realities. The differences are therefore attributable to the institutional setting and political economic reality. The fact that large firms outperform small firms in Asia offers a good example for this line of reasoning. In many Asian countries, competition policies were disregarded until recently, and large groups benefited from quasi-monopolies and easy access to capital through banks affiliated with those groups and to directed credit. Therefore, investors' appetite for the predictable safety of "blue chips" is understandable.[22]

We attempted to confirm the value discounts by using bivariate portfolio sorting methods. We did not find, however statistically significant results in the bivariate sorting. For example, once adjusted by firm size, the performance of portfolios with a high or low B / M ratio is not statistically significant. Such findings reflect the high correlation among accounting indicators. It also points to the importance for future studies in emerging stock markets to be cautious in interpreting the findings of univariate sorting methods.

Conclusions and Policy Implications

The findings lead to several observations. First, the evidence casts doubt on the economic allocative efficiency of emerging markets in Asia. The findings of the allocation of capital and portfolio sorting lead to the conclusion that Asian emerging markets price risk differently than developed markets. There is evidence that they do not price risk adequately. In markets that operate with high standards of transparency, including disclosure, research, and dissemination of information, participants have adequate information for making investment decisions. These financial markets are less prone to volatility because investors are able to interpret information and to discount risk realistically in a timely fashion ("efficient markets"). Emerging markets are by definition immature and therefore inefficient. In the context of limited transparency, the behavior of investors in emerging markets— the tendency to purchase leading companies—might be rational. However,

22. Foreign investors also prefer large stocks in Asia. See Kang and Stulz (1997).

this investment style is possibly speculative and leads to increased volatility. Supporting evidence is available in the lack of reference to the cost of capital in capital allocations. Therefore, efforts are warranted to improve transparency in emerging markets. Improvements should target measures designed to bring the microstructure in line with global legal, regulatory, accounting, and information dissemination standards.

Second, an interesting pattern emerges from this analysis. In several Latin American and Asian countries the return on invested capital is quite reasonable. However, the cost of capital is surprisingly punitive in countries with high savings rates. For instance, in Indonesia, the average nominal return on invested capital, at almost 13 percent, is superior to that in most countries in the sample, but the weighted average cost of capital, at 16 percent, is comparatively high. Similar results are evident for Chile and Argentina. The high cost of capital reflects in part poor intermediation of savings and leads to the conclusion that the challenge for developing countries is to improve the financial intermediation process, by improving the capacity of emerging markets, and thereby to reduce the cost of capital.

Third, is value investing dead in emerging markets? We should not foreclose on value investing in Asian markets. The findings on the superiority of glamour investing over a ten-year period need to be qualified with the caveat that the superiority of value investing prevails over long periods of time. The U.S. experience with glamour stocks is instructive in this regard. U.S. markets have abandoned the tenets of value investing by embracing low B/M, high P/E stocks on several occasions. For instance, over the past five years, the S&P/Barra growth index has returned 42 to 15 percent for Barra value on the valuations of high-tech growth stocks, such as the Internet. Similarly, in the late 1960s the so-called "nifty fifty" growth stocks soared beyond value stocks, but by 1970, most of these stocks had fallen to earth. Therefore, maybe what we are witnessing in Asia is a healthy reassessment of valuations. Longer time frames are needed before we can reach meaningful conclusions on the Asian markets!

Finally, although this paper has identified certain dynamics of emerging markets, more analytical work remains to be done on the links between corporate behavior and capital markets in Asia. For instance, future research should explore whether the markets priced leverage risks in a consistent manner in the United States and other developed markets.

Appendix A. Methods of Constructing Portfolios

This appendix presents the methods used to construct simple and size-adjusted portfolios.

Constructing Simple Portfolios

Stock indexes for a given country are constructed as follows. For each firm in the sample the following variables are computed as of December 31.

—*Value variables.* Book equity value to market equity value, earnings per share to price, dividend per share to price, cash flow per share to price.

—*Size variables.* Market capitalization and ownership concentration.

—*Growth variables.* Three-year average sales growth rate, dividend growth rate, and asset growth rate.

—*Profitability and efficiency variables.* Return on equity.

—*Leverage variables.* Debt-to-equity ratio.

—*Momentum trading variables.* Average returns of the previous twelve months during the first year.

Stocks are then sorted into groups based on the variables listed above. For each variable, three portfolios are created. The high portfolio includes the 33 percent of firms with the highest ratios for a given variable. The low portfolio includes the 33 percent of firms with the lowest ratios for a given variable.

Monthly returns are calculated for each of the three portfolios for the period of January to December. At the end of the next December, the same procedure is repeated, and the portfolio is rebalanced. In each of the portfolios, all stocks are weighted equally, and the returns to buying and holding for the coming year are computed. This procedure yields a time series of monthly returns for three portfolios (high, medium, and low) for each sorting category (B/M, C/P, E/P, and D/P, for example).

Constructing Size-Adjusted Portfolios

We obtain size-adjusted returns by using a two-pass sorting technique. For the ratio of book value to market price, for example, we first sort all stocks by firm size. We then take the portfolio of stocks of the largest companies and resort all stocks by book value to market, thereby creating three distinct portfolios within the large size group. At the end of the two-pass sorting (first by B/M and then by size), we have nine portfolios (see table 4A-1).

Table 4A-1. *Portfolio Sorting Procedure*

Size and firm's book-to-market ratio	Portfolio
Large size	
High	P1
Medium	P2
Low	P3
Medium	
High	P4
Medium	P5
Low	P6
Small	
High	P7
Medium	P8
Low	P9

Monthly returns are then calculated in each of the nine portfolios. At the end of the following December, the same procedure is repeated and the portfolio is rebalanced. In each of the portfolios constructed, we weight all stocks equally and compute the returns to the strategy of buying and holding for the coming year. To see how the problems associated with thinly traded stocks and outliers affect our results, we weight the stocks in our portfolio by their market capitalization. Thinly traded stocks are usually small stocks. The portfolio return is defined as follows:

Price index of value strategy (size adjusted) =
$$1/3 *[(P1 - P3) + (P4 - P6) + (P7 - P9)].$$

The size-adjusted value strategy represents the returns to a portfolio from purchasing high book-to-market stocks by selling low book-to-market stocks, controlling for size effect. We repeat the same procedure to study the impact of other factors, adjusting for the size effect.

Appendix B. Detailed Results

Table 4B-1. Mean Returns for Portfolios Constructed Based on Corporate Fundamentals, January 1998–April 1997[a]

Corporate fundamental[b]	China	Hong Kong	Indonesia	Korea	Malaysia	Philippines	Singapore	Taiwan	Thailand	All Asia
Panel 1. Relative value (book to market)										
High	-31.5300	-0.5700	-22.0190	6.5020	2.1530	-16.2053	-1.0931	-2.7580	-32.23793	-0.3703295
Low	9.9900	10.6000	10.6670	2.7550	12.5020	11.2184	12.1890	12.0720	1.161816	9.199581
High-low	-41.5200	-11.8400	-29.5330	3.7470	-10.1970	-33.6620	-13.2820	-8.5900	-32.412	-9.569
	[-2.04]	[-3.409]	[-4.087]	[0.173]	[-3.165]	[-2.479]	[3.443]	[-1.016]	[-4.808]	[-1.976]
Value weighted	-41.6400	-20.0793	-30.1682	-24.7595	-13.1602	-17.5407	-11.3267	-11.4007	-41.87	-19.79494
	[-2.171]	[-4.111]	[-3.481]	[-3.300]	[-3.222]	[-1.122]	[2.6972]	[-1.112]	[-5.011]	[-5.354]
Size-adjusted	-13.7405	-8.5567	-25.1802	-13.5464	-7.8339	-1.3862	-11.9663	-14.8845	-37.963	-12.01953
Return-on-equity adjusted	-18.7215	-5.8542	-21.9377	-7.2454	-12.1844	-5.8811	-6.3996	-5.0277	-28.874	-10.73018
Leverage-adjusted	-36.4190	-10.5832	-27.7098	-13.2691	-11.8565	-36.0873	-13.3260	-14.8265	-38.464	-15.91464
Sales-adjusted	-3.1728	-14.5341	-32.3886	-13.0126	-9.1515	6.4070	-10.6970	-6.1214	-34.4947	14.42756
Panel 2. Size (market capitalization)										
High	6.4974	12.7061	4.2437	-1.2044	8.8137	15.0118	8.9131	2.7211	-6.05061	5.067057
Low	-17.7293	4.7559	-15.0548	-5.1313	5.0768	-18.0332	2.1130	-3.9753	-7.012473	-0.8117562
High-low	24.2260	12.5380	23.8160	3.9260	3.7770	35.0070	6.8000	15.8130	11.947	5.878313
	[1.206]	[2.629]	[2.922]	[0.584]	[0.688]	[3.255]	[1.24]	[1.881]	[2.326]	[1.4530]
Value-weighted	23.0840	19.2474	26.4754	7.3403	6.8106	34.0802	9.4732	14.7290	16.48928	10.85377
	[1.0805]	[3.2923]	[2.9576]	[1.0037]	[1.1996]	[2.4801]	[-1.796]	[1.6561]	[2.4523]	[2.5528]
Book-to-market adjusted	15.1431	10.5498	8.8224	-5.0275	-0.7311	1.3100	3.8067	8.0882	0.269	1.483534
Return-on-equity adjusted	2.6813	5.7323	17.0527	-4.0180	2.4357	18.2356	2.6694	10.3623	3.863	1.930044
Leverage-adjusted	27.2645	12.6716	20.1246	-3.1157	3.0303	24.5487	6.9832	10.5752	14.338	1.893112
Sales-adjusted	9.6930	16.3640	17.3302	0.1302	-2.4877	5.3140	5.8337	8.3108	12.372	6.914011

continued

Table 4B-1. *Mean Returns for Portfolios Constructed Based on Corporate Fundamentals, January 1998–April 1997*[a] (Continued)

Corporate fundamental[b]	China	Hong Kong	Indonesia	Korea	Malaysia	Philippines	Singapore	Taiwan	Thailand	All Asia
Panel 3. Growth (three-year sales growth)										
High	20.8019	2.4461	6.0331	-3.7063	8.3438	-8.7875	2.5660	4.8594	-2.055936	2.389011
Low	-12.5152	4.7413	-11.9942	-15.5936	2.6897	-26.5534	0.0412	-10.7058	-16.26849	-2.365312
High-low	33.3170	-1.1330	20.0700	12.5720	6.4020	17.9210	2.5240	19.5050	22.82	4.754323
	[1.963]	[-0.312]	[2.622]	[2.029]	[2.3]	[1.6]	[0.775]	[2.646]	[3.77]	[3.3339]
Value-weighted high-low	38.8333	-1.5086	12.2109	-6.6404	6.3894	23.7808	17.4783	15.3299	35.96258	7.831326
	[2.1199]	[-0.286]	[0.9696]	[-0.705]	[1.7370]	[1.3364]	[-3.971]	[1.4328]	[4.1575]	[1.9675]
Panel 4. Profitability and efficiency (return on equity)										
High	-8.9772	15.7527	10.3256	-1.5142	13.7385	8.4723	11.1666	7.8463	-5.354841	9.636432
Low	-29.5561	0.0667	-27.2055	-18.0406	6.0009	-18.1033	-0.9518	-3.5360	-22.29653	-4.749838
High-low	9.1623	15.6860	38.1093	16.5263	6.0658	38.0790	12.1184	10.9567	29.04385	14.38627
	[0.6701]	[3.3912]	[4.6561]	[3.0321]	[1.1166]	[3.4862]	[3.2007]	[0.9553]	[4.7578]	[5.5546]
Value-weighted	-7.0307	16.8831	43.3700	26.8592	6.8229	24.5404	12.8246	14.5105	25.965	15.12385
	[-0.347]	[2.8493]	[4.0941]	[2.8336]	[1.2734]	[1.8423]	[-2.551]	[2.1153]	[3.0163]	[2.9450]

Panel 5. Leverage (debt-to-equity ratio)

High	-31.7050	6.1990	-17.4321	-15.1117	7.5282	-6.0707	3.5313	0.1793	-7.518903	1.154912
Low	-12.5614	9.7766	-4.9277	-1.8531	10.1263	0.7313	4.9676	9.1737	-11.72609	3.188587
High-low	-18.1065	-3.5777	-12.5045	-13.2586	-0.3791	-0.1979	-1.4364	-7.8283	8.350624	-2.033675
	[-1.571]	[-0.994]	[-2.223]	[-3.278]	[-0.068]	[-0.023]	[-0.571]	[-0.799]	[0.9770]	[-0.998]
Value-weighted	-25.6021	1.0361	-27.2738	-8.8795	1.4867	-13.8900	4.8516	-9.4083	11.98374	-4.265649
	[-1.462]	[0.2298]	[-3.654]	[-1.227]	[0.2503]	[-0.913]	[-1.343]	[-1.045]	[1.6926]	[-0.951]

Panel 6. Momentum trading (past returns)

High	-3.9963	14.5000	-19.1600	-6.1550	10.2209	8.4790	3.0611	8.2958	-10.327	
Low	6.6550	6.2390	-7.4500	-18.2277	9.4070	3.4600	0.6148	9.5841	-14.6506	
High-low	-10.6500	8.2617	-11.7100	12.0721	0.8135	5.0188	2.4460	-1.2882	4.33299	
	[-1.07]	[1.94]	[-1.36]	[1.68]	[0.1363]	[0.4835]	[0.568]	[-0.209]	[0.62]	

Source: Authors' calculations.

a. Figures in brackets are *t*-scores. Outliers are taken out at the 15 percent level for China and 10 percent level of all other countries. All returns are annualized and in dollar terms.

b. The high portfolio includes firms in the top 33 percent of mean returns for the sample period. The low portfolio includes firms in the bottom 33 percent. The high-low portfolio represents the difference between mean returns on the high and low portfolios. Value-weighted high-low is the return on the high-low portfolio weighted by market capitalization. Size-adjusted, return-on-investment-adjusted, leverage-adjusted, and sales-adjusted high-low portfolios represent mean returns (equally weighted) adjusted by the bivariate portfolio-sorting procedure.

Table 4B-2. Average Mean Returns on Stocks during the Asian Financial Crisis, January 1998–April 1997[a]

Corporate fundamental[b]	China	Hong Kong	Indonesia	Korea	Malaysia	Philippines	Singapore	Taiwan	Thailand
Panel 1. Relative value (book to market; percent)									
Winners	1.8969	2.6409	2.2192	6.3878	0.8881	1.6450	1.3184	0.8852	3.7742
Losers	1.1430	2.6912	2.4105	7.8072	1.0566	2.0014	1.3788	0.8670	3.1753
Difference	0.7539	−0.0503	−0.1913	−1.4193	−0.1685	−0.3565	−0.0604	0.0182	0.5989
	[3.0228]	[−0.142]	[−0.448]	[−1.577]	[−0.898]	[−0.535]	[−0.348]	[0.1911]	[1.1315]
Panel 2. Size (market capitalization; millions of U.S. dollars)									
Winners	117,672.5	337,353.5	414,032.0	204,704.6	568,434.4	1,134,620.0	282,445.5	762,183.9	206,772.9
Losers	273,014.6	433,111.7	634,122.8	291,512.8	354,625.7	357,574.8	418,854.8	794,763.4	213,792.7
Difference	−155,342.0	−95,758.0	−220,090.0	−86,808.0	213,808.7	777,045.6	−136,409.0	−32,579.0	−7,019.8
	[−2.105]	[−0.478]	[−0.695]	[−1.086]	[2.0097]	[1.2945]	[−1.049]	[−0.152]	[−0.078]
Panel 3. Growth (three-year sales growth; percent)									
Winners	14.3148	13.5132	3.9130	13.8764	36.8138	26.8270	13.4021	4.4660	15.8356
Losers	15.1787	9.1770	16.3435	4.0505	27.4521	−24.5269	10.8943	5.4438	7.0152
Difference	−0.8639	4.3362	−12.4305	9.8258	9.3617	51.3539	2.5077	−0.9779	8.8204
	[−0.060]	[0.7741]	[−1.168]	[0.8443]	[0.8942]	[3.1740]	[0.4481]	[−0.213]	[1.5556]
Panel 4. Profitability and efficiency (return on equity; percent)									
Winners	7.6650	7.9945	12.1501	−6.2450	13.5268	19.5909	7.1995	11.6686	4.2823
Losers	11.3599	10.0199	14.0930	−1.1735	11.1934	2.8046	7.5939	9.8728	6.7701
Difference	−3.6949	−2.0253	−1.9428	−5.0714	2.3334	16.7863	−0.3943	1.7958	−2.4877
	[−0.932]	[−0.454]	[−0.532]	[−1.102]	[0.5418]	[3.4438]	[−0.111]	[0.8445]	[−0.644]

Panel 5. Leverage (debt-to-equity ratio; percent)

Winners	70.6857	96.8251	94.4498	234.6569	75.3910	87.4839	54.7669	53.0846	132.0914
Losers	56.1009	62.0043	91.1335	261.9228	70.7713	44.2811	46.7634	46.0544	103.3371
Difference	14.5848	34.8208	3.3163	-27.2650	4.6197	43.2028	8.0035	7.0302	28.7544
	[1.0294]	[2.0032]	[0.1915]	[-0.791]	[0.3576]	[1.5578]	[0.7399]	[0.8715]	[1.5496]

Panel 6. Momentum trading (past returns; percent)

Winners	54.3650	36.9093	6.2216	-12.5344	19.1130	48.8830	-17.2273	29.0573	-32.2060
Losers	97.4521	20.8991	-6.2974	-20.9819	15.3625	-17.2344	-9.3170	25.3440	-27.3002
Difference	-43.0870	16.0101	12.5190	8.4475	3.7505	66.1173	7.9102	3.7133	-4.9058
	[-1.397]	[1.2040]	[0.7285]	[1.4383]	[0.5053]	[2.1055]	[-1.810]	[0.5875]	[-0.911]

Panel 7. Historical beta

Winners	n.a.	1.1935	0.6788	0.9929	1.2896	0.9620	1.0787	0.7890	0.9085
Losers	n.a.	1.1415	0.7818	1.0515	1.3347	0.9600	0.9890	0.8311	0.9870
Difference	n.a.	0.0519	-0.1030	-0.0586	-0.0452	0.0020	0.0897	-0.0421	-0.0785
		[0.6144]	[0.713]	[-0.686]	[-0.602]	[0.0146]	[1.0994]	[-0.669]	[-0.557]

Panel 8. Ownership concentration (percent)

Winners	n.a.	45.0683	47.9183	14.9972	31.2508	8.7878	38.8283	1.6264	11.2527
Losers	n.a.	42.9853	48.2151	17.1259	29.8935	12.5278	41.3021	1.6579	11.0540
Difference	n.a.	2.0830	-0.2969	-2.1286	1.3573	-3.7399	-2.4738	-0.0315	0.1986
		[0.9399]	[-0.078]	[-1.379]	[0.5974]	[-0.861]	[-0.768]	[-0.035]	[0.0732]

Source Authors' calculations.

n.a. Not available.

a. Figures in brackets are t-scores. Stock return outliers are taken out at the 10 percent level for all countries.

b. Stocks are sorted according to their average returns in the crisis period from April 1, 1997, to October 30, 1998. The winners' portfolio includes 33 percent of the stocks with the highest returns during the crisis. The losers' portfolio includes 33 percent of the stocks with the lowest returns. Difference represents the difference in corporate fundamentals between winners and losers.

References

Banz, Rolf W. 1981. "The Relationship between Return and Market Value of Common Stocks." *Journal of Financial Economics* 9 (March): 3–18.

Bernstein, Richard, and Stephen F. O'Byrne. 1998. "Debate: Can EVA™ Help You Pick Stocks?" Society of Quantitative Analysts (April).

Bhandari, Laxmi C. 1988. "Debt / Equity Ratio and Expected Common Stock Returns: Empirical Evidence." *Journal of Finance* 43 (June): 507–28.

Brown, Stephen J., William N. Goetzmann, and James Park. 1998. "Hedge Funds and the Asian Currency Crisis of 1997." NBER Working Paper 6427. Cambridge, Mass.: National Bureau of Economic Research (February).

Choe, Hyuk, Bong-Chan Kho, and Rene M. Stulz. 1998. "Do Foreign Investors Destabilize Stock Markets? The Korean Experience in 1997." NBER Working Paper 6661. Cambridge, Mass.: National Bureau of Economic Research (July).

Claessens, Stijn, Susmita Dasgupta, and Jack Glen. 1995. "The Cross-Section of Stock Returns: Evidence from Emerging Markets." Working Paper. Washington, D.C.: World Bank, Country Economics Department.

Claessens, Stijn, Simeon Djankov, and Larry H. P. Lang. 1998. "Corporate Growth, Financing, and Risks in the Decade before East Asia's Financial Crisis." Working Paper 2017. Washington, D.C.: World Bank (November).

———. 1999. "Who Controls East Asian Corporations?" Working Paper 2054. Washington, D.C.: World Bank (February).

Fama, Eugene F., and Kenneth R. French. 1992. "The Cross-Section of Expected Stock Returns." *Journal of Finance* 47 (June): 427–65.

———. 1998. "Value versus Growth: The International Evidence." *Journal of Finance* 53 (December): 1975–99.

Froot, Kenneth A., Paul G. J. O'Connell, and Mark S. Seasholes. 1998. "The Portfolio Flows of International Investors, I." NBER Working Paper 6687. Cambridge, Mass.: National Bureau of Economic Research (August).

Haugen, Robert A. 1995. *The New Finance: The Case against Efficient Markets.* Englewood Cliffs, N.J.: Prentice-Hall.

International Monetary Fund. 1999. *International Financial Statistics.* Washington, D.C. (January).

Kang, Jun-Koo, and Rene M. Stulz. 1997. "Why Is There a Home Bias? An Analysis of Foreign Portfolio Equity Ownership in Japan." *Journal of Financial Economics* 46 (October): 3–28.

Lakonishok, Josef, Andrei Shleifer, and Robert W. Vishny. 1994. "Contrarian Investment, Extrapolation, and Risk." *Journal of Finance* 49 (December): 1541–78.

Pomerleano, Michael. 1998. "The East Asia Crisis and Corporate Finances: The Untold Microeconomic Story." *Emerging Markets Quarterly* 2 (Winter): 14–27.

Ross, Stephen A. 1976. "The Arbitrage Theory of Capital Asset Pricing." *Journal of Economic Theory* 13 (December): 341–60.

Rouwenhorst, K. Greet. 1998. "International Momentum Strategies." *Journal of Finance* 53 (February): 267–84.

Sharpe, William F. 1964. "Capital Asset Prices: A Theory of Market Equilibrium under Conditions of Risk." *Journal of Finance* 19: 425–42.

Stewart, G. Bennet. 1990. *The Quest For Value: The EVA™ Management Guide*. New York: Harper Business.

World Bank. 1998. *World Development Indicators 1998*. CD-ROM. Washington, D.C.

STIJN CLAESSENS
SIMEON DJANKOV
LARRY H. P. LANG

5

Corporate Ownership and Valuation: Evidence from East Asia

EAST ASIAN CORPORATIONS have long been considered an exception to the notion of widely held ownership. Yet the degree to which ownership is concentrated in East Asian countries has not been documented on a systematic, cross-country basis. This is puzzling because East Asia provides a large diversity of economic development. In our sample, the richest country (Japan) has a per capita income that is forty times that of the poorest country (Indonesia). The differences in economic development and in legal and institutional structures across the East Asian countries provide us with a good opportunity to study the relation between the patterns of economic development and ownership.

We use the methodology of previous work—La Porta, Lopez-de-Silanes, and Shleifer; Claessens, Djankov, and Lang; and Claessens and others—to document the patterns of ownership and control in almost 3,000 publicly traded companies in Hong Kong (China), Indonesia, Japan, Korea (South), Malaysia, the Philippines, Singapore, Taiwan (China), and Thailand, differentiating companies by ultimate ownership: families and

The authors thank Andrei Shleifer and seminar participants for comments and helpful suggestions and Ying Lin for excellent research assistance. The paper draws on other work by Claessens, Djankov, Fan, and Lang.

individuals with large stakes, the state, widely held financial institutions, and widely held corporations.[1] Our study draws on this work to provide a more detailed and qualitative description of the findings.

The paper is organized as follows. The first section reviews the relevant literature. The second section discusses the construction of the data, develops the methodology for calculating ultimate control, and offers examples of ultimate control through pyramid structures. The third section details the basic findings and investigates differences in the concentration of control and the means of enhancing control. The fourth section studies the effects of ownership concentration and type of ownership on firm valuation and investigates valuation discounts of companies in East Asia. The fifth section revisits the issue of family control and draws implications for the evolution of legal frameworks in East Asian countries. The final section concludes.

Control Structures in East Asia

Although numerous scholars have examined the performance of East Asian corporations over the past four decades, the structure of control and its relationship to corporate performance remains largely unknown. Several studies on corporate governance in Japan point to the significance of *keiretsu* groups.[2] However, these studies focus on company performance while accounting for the influence of business groups and do not attempt to trace the ownership of each company to its ultimate owners or to identify those owners by type and control stake. Apart from some case studies of large business groups, the only cross-company study is by Lim, who details the control structures of the largest hundred corporations in Malaysia.[3]

Recent contributions go some way toward filling this gap in our knowledge. The study by La Porta and others documents the ownership structure of the ten largest nonfinancial corporations for a cross section of forty-nine countries, including nine East Asian countries.[4] The results show that

---

1. La Porta, Lopez-de-Silanes, and Shleifer (1999); Claessens, Djankov, and Lang (1999); Claessens and others (1999).
2. Nishiyama (1984); Prowse (1992); Hoshi, Kashyap, and Scharfstein (1991); Kaplan (1994).
3. Lim (1981).
4. La Porta and others (1997).

although ownership of East Asian corporations is highly concentrated, it is not significantly different from that in other countries at similar levels of economic and institutional development. Another study by La Porta, Lopez-de-Silanes, and Shleifer investigates in great detail the control structure of the twenty largest publicly traded corporations in twenty-seven rich countries, including Hong Kong, Japan, Korea, and Singapore.[5] It traces control to the ultimate owners of each company and distinguishes five types of owners. Ownership in the majority of Japanese and Korean corporations is found to be widely dispersed, corporations in Hong Kong are predominantly controlled by families, and about half of the sampled companies in Singapore are controlled by the state.

La Porta, Lopez-de-Silanes, and Shleifer also examine the means through which control is enhanced. They find that owners extend their resources through the use of pyramiding and management appointments as well as through frequent cross-ownership and the (less frequent) use of shares that have more votes. Another interesting pattern is also documented: control of East Asian corporations can be achieved with significantly less than an absolute majority because the probability of being a single controlling owner by holding only 20 percent (or more) is very high—above 80 percent across the four East Asian countries.

In Claessens and others and Claessens, Djankov, and Lang, we extend the previous research in several directions. First, we document differences in patterns and distribution of control across the East Asian countries, including less developed ones. Second, we describe within-country differences in the concentration and distribution of control. Third, we study the effect of ownership concentration on firm valuation and whether control rights have different effects on valuation than cash flow rights do. In particular, we investigate whether the valuation discount of firms differs for various levels of cash flow and voting rights. Finally, we study the extent to which corporate control is concentrated in the hands of particular families and the relation between institutional development and concentration of wealth. This paper builds on that work, providing policy lessons and interpreting the findings. In doing so, we offer a more general picture of the pattern and performance of ultimate ownership than was possible in the original work for East Asian firms.

---

5. La Porta, Lopez-de-Silanes, and Shleifer (1999).

Construction of the Data

Our starting point in the data collection is the World Scope database, which generally provides the names and holdings of large owners. World Scope has more than 8,000 publicly traded firms in the nine East Asian countries, but only 2,300 companies provide detailed information on ownership. We supplement the data with information from company handbooks and annual reports of the major stock exchanges, as well as with data on ownership.[6] We exclude 852 companies across the nine countries for which proxy ownership cannot be traced to a specific owner. In all cases, we collect the ownership structure as of December 1996 or the end of the 1996 fiscal year. We end up with 2,980 companies for which we have complete ownership information and can trace the ultimate owners.

Typically, we cover about three-quarters of total market capitalization even though the share of firms in our sample relative to the total number of listed firms is sometimes less than half (Korea, Malaysia, Taiwan, Thailand; see figure 5-1). This is because we always cover the 100 firms with the highest market capitalization.

We document the control pattern of companies by studying all ultimate shareholders who control more than 20 percent of the votes. The 20 percent cutoff is consistent with the previous literature. In the majority of cases, the principal shareholders are themselves corporate entities, not-for-profit foundations, or financial institutions. We then identify their owners, the owners of their owners, and so forth. We do not distinguish among individual family members and use the family group as a unit of analysis.

Our definition of ownership relies on voting rights, not on cash flow rights. This distinction can make an enormous difference in the analysis. Suppose, for example, that a family owns 15 percent of the stock of publicly traded firm A, which in turn has 31 percent of the stock of firm B. Since we look at control rights, we would say that the family controls 15 percent of firm B—the weakest link in the chain of voting rights. In contrast, we would say that the family owns about 5 percent of the cash flow rights of firm B—the product of the two ownership stakes along the chain. To make the distinction between cash flow and voting rights, we document deviations from one-share/one-vote rules, cross-holdings

6. For data sources, see Claessens, Djankov, and Lang (1999).

Figure 5-1. *Sample Coverage*

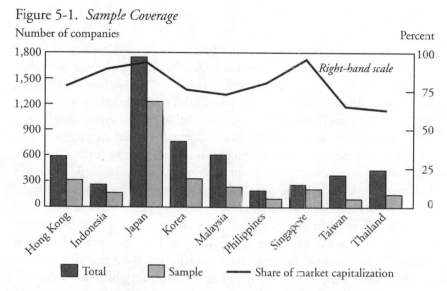

Number of companies

Percent

Source: World Scope database supplemented with information from company handbooks and annual reports of major stock exchanges.

among firms in the same business group, and pyramiding structures for each firm.

We divide corporations into firms that are widely held and firms that have ultimate owners. By our definition, a widely held corporation does not have any owners with control rights greater than 20 percent. Ultimate owners are further divided into four categories: families and individuals who have large stakes, the state, widely held financial institutions such as banks and insurance companies, and widely held corporations.

Our definition of ultimate control means that a firm can have more than one significant owner. If, for example, firm C has three owners—a family, the state, and a widely held corporation—each with 20 percent of voting rights, we say that this firm is one-third controlled by each type of owner. A different picture emerges if the owners do not have equal shares of voting rights. Take, for example, firm D, which has two owners—a family with 30 percent of the voting rights and a widely held financial institution with 10 percent of the voting rights. Firm D is defined to be 100 percent family controlled. To understand the variety of ownership structures that determine the ultimate control of companies, we illustrate using an example from our data.

The example is a simplified version of one presented in Claessens and others and is based on the Ayala group, the largest conglomerate in the Philippines (figure 5-2).[7] We identify forty-six companies whose ultimate owner is the Ayala family. First, we look at the ownership of the Ayala Corporation, the second largest company on the Manila Stock Exchange. The largest listed company (Ayala Land) and the fifth-largest listed company (Bank of the Philippine Islands) also belong to the Ayala conglomerate. The principal owners of the Ayala Corporation are the privately held Mermac (58 percent of total shares in Ayala Corporation) and the Mitsubishi Bank (20 percent). Each other owner of Ayala Corporation has less than 10 percent of the stock. We next trace the owners of the owners of Ayala Corporation. The Ayala family has 100 percent of the control of Mermac, while Meiji Life Insurance of Japan has 23 percent of the control of Mitsubishi Bank. There are no other significant owners of Mitsubishi Bank. We now can say that the ultimate owners of the Ayala Corporation are the Ayala family, with 58 percent of the control rights, and Meiji Life Insurance, with 20 percent of the voting rights.

Next we study the ultimate control structure of Globe Telecom, another member of the Ayala conglomerate. The two principal owners of Globe Telecom are the ITT corporation (32 percent) and the Ayala Corporation (40 percent). We have already established that the Ayala Corporation is controlled by the Ayala family and Meiji Life Insurance. We hence conclude that Globe Telecom has three ultimate owners: the Ayala family (40 percent), the ITT Corporation (32 percent), and Meiji Life Insurance (20 percent).

Finally, we investigate ultimate control for the Automated Electronics Company. Two of the ultimate owners are easily identified. The International Finance Corporation and Japan Asia (Japan) are both widely held corporations in their respective countries, and each controls 20 percent of Automated Electronics. Another 30 percent of Automated Electronics is owned by Assemblies, which in turn is owned almost entirely (90 percent) by IMicro Electronics, which in turn is majority owned (74 percent) by the Ayala Corporation. We thus determine that Automated Electronics has four ultimate owners: International Finance Corporation (United States) with 20 percent, Japan Asia (Japan) with 20 percent, Meiji Life Insurance (Japan) with 20 percent, and the Ayala family with 30 percent.

7. In Claessens and others (1999).

Ultimate Control: Descriptive Statistics

In this section we report simple statistics on the distribution of ultimate control among the five ownership groups identified in the previous section (figure 5-3). The numbers presented are unweighted averages. There are large differences across countries in the distribution of ultimate control. Less than one-tenth of Japanese companies (9.7 percent) are controlled by families, while almost four-fifths (79.8 percent) are widely held. In Korea and Taiwan, less then half are family controlled (48.4 and 48.2 percent, respectively); while in Thailand and Malaysia, approximately two-thirds are family controlled (61.6 and 67.2 percent, respectively).

Some of these differences likely arise from variations in company laws across countries and company-specific charters. For example, differences in the minimum percentage of shareholdings required to block major decisions or the minimum percentage required to entitle a shareholder to call an extraordinary meeting of shareholders are likely important in determining the minimum stake necessary for a shareholder to exercise effective control.

Other rules also affect the size of ownership needed to exercise effective control. In Korea, for example, restrictions on the voting rights of institutional investors in listed companies and high minimum percentages required to file class action suits imply that relatively low ownership stakes can result in effective control. An additional likely factor is the evolution of capital markets more generally. In Thailand and Indonesia, for example, formal stock markets were only established in 1975 and 1977, respectively, while the stock market in Japan has been in existence since 1878, and the Stock Exchange of Hong Kong has been in operation since 1891. This may influence the degree to which corporations are widely held. Furthermore, following World War II, the Occupational Forces deliberately sought to disperse ownership more widely in Japan. The role of widely held financial institutions is limited for all countries. This is not surprising because four of the nine countries (Hong Kong, Japan, Korea, Singapore) impose limits on the share of ownership that banks can have in other companies, while Indonesia prohibits such ownership altogether.[8]

A more complete picture of cross-country differences emerges once we weigh firms' ownership by market capitalization (figure 5-4). State ownership becomes much more pronounced, especially in Singapore, Malaysia,

8. Institute of International Bankers (1997).

Figure 5-2. *Ownership Structure of the Ayala Group, the Philippines*[a]

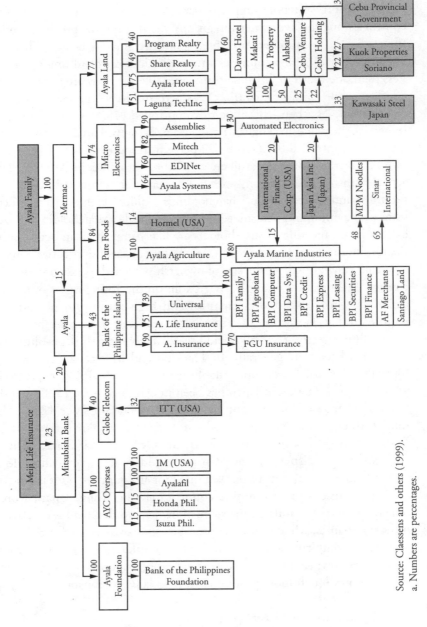

Source: Claessens and others (1999).
a. Numbers are percentages.

Figure 5-3. *Share of Control of Publicly Traded Companies Held by Different Classes of Owners*

Percent

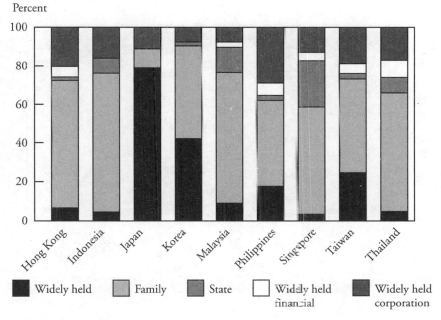

Widely held | Family | State | Widely held financial | Widely held corporation

Source: Authors' calculations.

Thailand, and Korea. The control of widely held financial institutions and corporations is diminished, as is control by families.

Several mechanisms are used to enhance corporate control even in the presence of small control stakes, in particular, multiple classes of voting rights, pyramid structures, and cross-holdings.

Deviations from one-share/one-vote through shares with different voting rights tend to be very small in the East Asian countries; it takes on average 19.23 percent of all shares to get 20 percent of voting rights (figure 5-5). This is consistent with other findings that companies around the world do not tend to issue shares with superior voting rights.[9]

Pyramid structures are defined as owning a majority of the stock of one corporation that, in turn, holds a majority of the stock of another—a process that can be repeated a number of times. In our sample, for more than two-fifths of companies ultimate control involves the use of a pyramid

9. Nenova (1999).

Figure 5-4. *Share of Control of Publicly Traded Companies Held by Different Classes of Owners, Weighted by Market Capitalization*

Percent

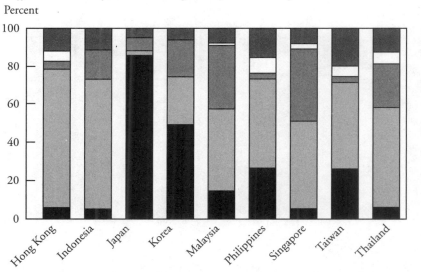

Source: Authors' calculations.

structure, with the number the largest in Indonesia and the smallest in Thailand (figure 5-5). Companies in Singapore also show a high incidence of pyramiding, while only a quarter of companies in Hong Kong that are not widely held are controlled through pyramid structures.

We do not find significant evidence of cross-holdings—where a company down the chain of control has some shares in another company in its chain of control—with the exception of Malaysia and Singapore. Korean companies are above the average for the nine East Asian countries on that indicator.

We also identify the share of firms where there is a single controlling owner. A second controlling owner is defined as somebody who has at least 10 percent of the voting rights. The idea is that if such a party exists, it may be more difficult for the first owner to control the firm. Figure 5-5 shows that in more than half of the sample companies that are not widely held the ultimate owners are alone. This share is highest in Japan and lowest in Thailand. The results for Thailand, combined with the infrequent use of

Figure 5-5. *Methods Used to Enhance Control of Firms Using These Methods*

Percent

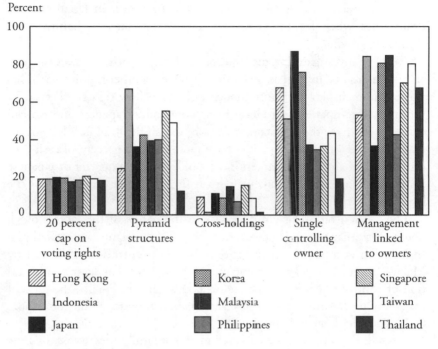

Source: Authors' calculations.

pyramids and cross-holdings, reflect the importance in Thailand of informal alliances among the small number of families controlling most of Thai companies.

Finally, we study the separation of control and management by investigating whether a member of the controlling family, or an employee of the controlling widely held financial institution or corporation, is the chief executive officer, chairman, honorary chairman, or vice chairman of the company. It is generally difficult to find out whether a manager is an employee of a controlling financial institution or corporation, although such information does exist in the stock exchange investment guides of several East Asian companies. It is easier to find family membership using family trees, even if the particular manager does not have the same last name.

The correspondence between control and management is high (figure 5-5): on average, two-thirds of companies that are not widely held have a controlling owner linked to a member of top management. Four-fifths or more of companies in Indonesia, Korea, Malaysia, and Taiwan have managers who are a member of the controlling owner. The correspondence between control and management is lower in Japan and the Philippines, where less than half of managers are related by family to the controlling owner.

We next investigate the distribution and degree of ultimate cash flow and voting rights, in level as well as relative to each other (figure 5-6). Thai corporations display the most concentrated cash flow rights, followed by Indonesian companies and Hong Kong companies. Japanese and Korean corporations have the least concentration of cash flow rights. Also important, a quarter of Thai companies have more than 40 percent of cash flow rights in the hands of the largest block holder, while a quarter of Japanese companies have only 2 percent of cash flow rights in the hands of the largest block holder.

The concentration of voting rights in the hands of the largest block holder is similar to the concentration of cash flow rights, with Thai and Indonesian companies having the highest concentration, followed by Malaysian and Hong Kong companies (figure 5-6). The least concentration of control rights is in Japan, Korea, and Taiwan. Finally, the ratio of cash flow to control rights is lowest in Japan, Indonesia, and Singapore and highest in Thailand and the Philippines.

Overall, the results suggest some remarkable similarities across the nine East Asian countries in the forms and means through which corporations are controlled. Although there are some differences, possibly related to the development of stock markets and legal and regulatory rules, most countries exhibit a similar pattern of family control through pyramid structures and management that is related by family to the ultimate owners. We next investigate the effects of these ownership structures on firm valuation.

Firm Valuation

Our study of firm valuation uses an industry-adjusted measure of the excess value of a firm, defined as the ratio of the firm's actual value to its imputed value. The actual value is measured by market capitalization, the market value of common equity, plus the book value of debt. To calculate the imputed value, we first construct an industry median market-to-sales ratio for each two-digit SIC (Standard Industrial Classification) code industry

Figure 5-6. *Cash Flow and Voting Rights (Mean)*

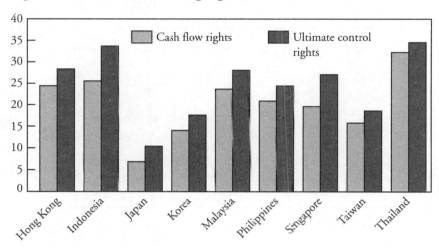

Source: Authors' calculations.

using only the single-segment firms in each country. The market-to-sales ratio is the market capitalization divided by firm sales. We then multiply the level of sales in each segment of a firm by its corresponding industry median market-to-sales ratio. The imputed value of the firm is obtained by summing the multiples across all of its segments.

Figure 5-7 provides the median statistics of the excess valuation measure. By construction the median of the variable is about 1. We find that a higher degree of cash flow rights is associated with somewhat higher median excess valuation. The relationship does appear to taper off, however, because the median values for the fourth quartile are only marginally higher than those for the third quartile.

The statistics for control rights suggest that there are some negative costs of block holder control because the median excess valuation is somewhat lower for higher level of control, but the relationship is not very strong. Since cash flow rights and control rights are correlated, it is not obvious what the net effect of increases in both cash flow and control rights on company valuation might be. We therefore also calculate the median valuation for different quartiles of the ratio of cash flow to control rights. We find that the median is lowest for the first quartile and increases monotonically with the ratio.

Figure 5-7. *Excess Valuation*

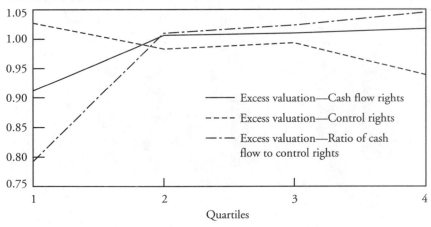

Ratio of excess valuation

Excess valuation—Cash flow rights
Excess valuation—Control rights
Excess valuation—Ratio of cash flow to control rights

Quartiles

Source: Authors' calculations.

As most East Asian corporations are family controlled, we study separately the effects of cash flow and control rights for corporations where families are the largest block holder of control rights. The number of corporations for which family is the largest block holder is 1,158, or about half of our sample. We find that the effects of family ownership concentration are very similar to those found for all classes of ownership combined (figure 5-8). As before, we find evidence of a positive impact of cash flow rights and of cash flow rights relative to voting rights, but a negative impact of voting rights. Because the slopes appear steeper than in the case of all ownership classes combined, especially for the cash flow rights relative to control rights variable, the valuation discount may be due to family control.

To investigate further whether the results of control ownership concentration for all classes are indeed due to family ownership only, we show the relationship between valuation and other types of control ownership. Figure 5-9 shows the relation between valuation of firms and ownership of cash flow and control by financial institutions. We find that cash flow ownership by financial institutions is positively associated with corporate valuation and that control rights are generally negatively associated with valuation. The relationship of valuation with the ratio of cash to voting rights is positive. More detailed analysis suggests that the negative effect of

Figure 5-8. *Excess Valuation for Family Ownership*

Ratio of excess valuation

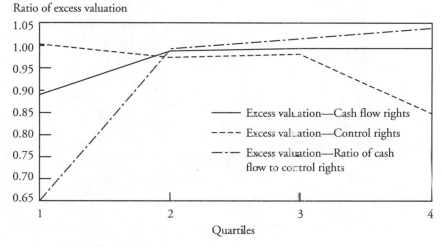

Source: Authors' calculations.

Figure 5-9. *Excess Valuation for Ownership by Financial Institutions*

Ratio of excess valuation

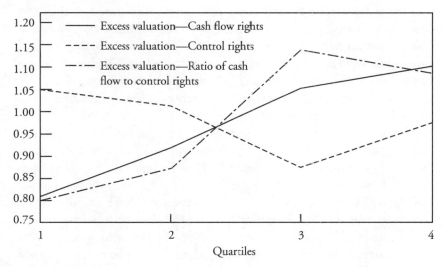

Source: Authors' calculations.

Figure 5-10. *Excess Valuation for Ownership by Widely Held Corporations*

Ratio of excess valuation

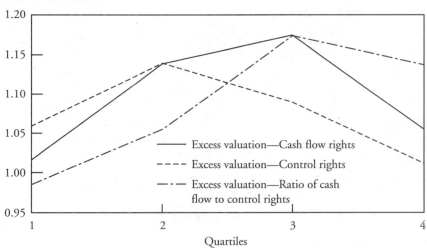

Quartiles

Source: Authors' calculations.

control by financial institutions arises from the role of financial institutions in Japan, as other work has also suggested.

Results for ownership by widely held corporations are less clear (figure 5-10). None of the relationships between cash, control, and the ratio of cash to control rights is monotonic. There is some evidence that low cash flow rights relative to control rights are associated with higher discounts, but the slope changes for high cash flow rights relative to voting rights. The results could be due to the ownership structure in some countries, particularly Japan and Korea, where cross-ownership is relatively large.

The association between state ownership and market valuation is similarly not obvious, regardless of whether cash flow or control rights or the ratio between the two is used (figure 5-11). Both increases in cash and control rights are associated with decreases in valuation up to the third or second quartile, respectively, but then valuation increases sharply for the fourth quartile for all three indicators. The fact that the valuation is highest for the fourth quartile of cash flow rights and control rights suggests that the state "chooses" its ownership and might have large stakes in relatively valuable enterprises.

Figure 5-11. *Excess Valuation for Ownership by the State*

Ratio of excess valuation

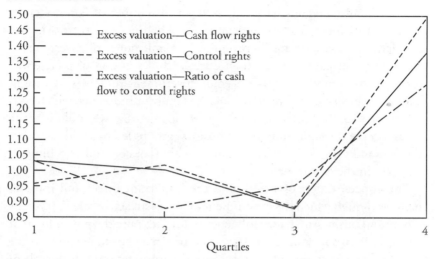

Quartiles

Source: Authors' calculations.

The Aggregate Effects of Extensive Family Control

So far we have investigated the incidence of ultimate control at the level of the individual firm. At the country level, a more meaningful unit of analysis, particularly if we are concerned with issues of market entry, access to financing, and government policy, is degree of control of the corporate sector by family groups. To capture this, we analyze the share of total market capitalization held by the top fifteen families.[10] At the extreme, about one-sixth of total market capitalization in Indonesia and the Philippines can be traced to the ultimate control of a single family (the Salims and the Ayalas, respectively). The top fifteen families in Indonesia and the Philippines control more than half of market capitalization in the corporate sector. The concentration of control is also high in Thailand and Hong Kong. A third of the corporate sector in Korea, Malaysia, and Singapore is controlled

10. To avoid discrepancies in the cross-country comparison due to different sample coverage, we have scaled down the control holdings of each family group by assuming that the firms missing from our sample are not controlled by any family group.

by the fifteen largest families. In contrast, family control is insignificant in Japan.

These results suggest that a relatively small number of families effectively control most East Asian economies. The question arises whether these families have a strong effect on the economic policy of governments. One direct mechanism for such an effect is the extension of preferential treatment to family members of senior government members. A case in point is the business empire of the Suharto family in Indonesia, which controls more than 400 listed and unlisted companies that we could identify in our sample through a number of business groups led by children, other relatives, and business partners, many of whom, besides Suharto himself, also serve in the government.

The concentration of wealth and the important direct and indirect channels though which the government may play an active role in business activity and businessmen may influence politicians raise the possibility that the legal systems in some East Asian countries may be endogenous to the forms and concentration of control over the corporate sector. If the role of a limited number of families in the corporate sector is large and the government is heavily involved in and influenced by business, the legal system is less likely to evolve in a manner that protects minority shareholders and more generally that promotes transparent and market-based activities. Although this argument has been frequently advanced by scholars in the wake of the East Asian financial crisis, little evidence has been collected to support it.

We can compare the concentration of corporate control in the hands of families to three indicators of judicial and legal development that are developed in La Porta and others.[11] The indexes we use are for the efficiency of the judicial system, the rule of law, and the degree of corruption; they run from one to ten, with ten being the best—that is, the most efficient judicial system, the strongest rule of law, and the least corruption. The correlations between the share of the fifteen largest families in total market capitalization, on the one hand, and the efficiency of the judicial system, the rule of law, and corruption, on the other, are very strong (figure 5-12). This suggests that the concentration of corporate control is a major determinant in the evolution of the legal system—that is, relationships exist between ownership structure of the whole corporate sector and the level of institutional development.

11. La Porta and others (1998).

Figure 5-12. *Ownership Concentration and Institutional Variables*

Ratings[a]

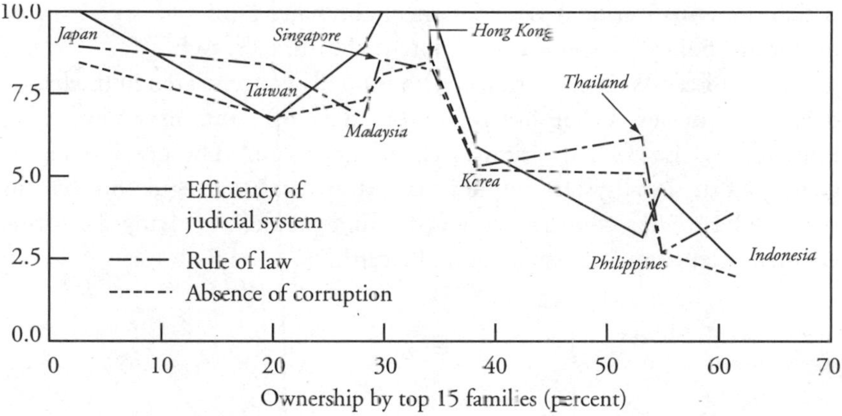

Source: Authors' calculations using indicators developed in La Porta and others (1998).
a. Ten is best; zero is worst.

Conclusions

This study presents a general picture of the pattern of ultimate ownership and its impact on company valuation, a task not accomplished in previous work.[12] We document large insider control for many East Asian corporations. This may have contributed to the weak performance and risky investment of many East Asian corporations. The finding that many firms in East Asia belong to the same group or are controlled by a single family warrants research on the performance of firms belonging to the same group or controlled by the same family and on the mechanisms for corporate governance used within such groups. The ownership structures and possible affiliation to a group may, for example, have affected the performance of firms during the 1997 financial crisis.

We study the relation between ultimate ownership and market valuation, differentiating voting from cash flow rights. We also find evidence that family control is an important factor behind the negative relation between control rights and market valuation. It is likely that the degree to which certain ownership structures are associated with valuation discounts depends on country-specific circumstances, including the quality of

12. Claessens and others (1999); Claessens, Djankov, and Lang (1999).

banking systems, the legal and judicial protection of individual shareholders, and the degree of financial disclosure required. The exact magnitude to which these institutional variables affect company valuation is an issue of important policy relevance and of potential future research.

In most East Asian countries, wealth is highly concentrated in the hands of a few families. Legal and regulatory developments may have been impeded by the concentration of corporate wealth. The possible endogeneity of the legal system implies that future legal and regulatory reform in some East Asian countries may not be independent of changes in ownership structure and concentration of wealth.

References

Claessens, Stijn, Simeon Djankov, Joseph P. H. Fan, and Larry H. P. Lang. 1999. "Expropriation of Minority Shareholders: Evidence from East Asia." Policy Research Working Paper 2088. Washington, D.C.: World Bank, Policy Research Department (March).

Claessens, Stijn, Simeon Djankov, and Larry H. P. Lang. 1999. "Who Controls East Asian Corporations?" Policy Research Working Paper 2054. Washington, D.C.: World Bank, Policy Research Department (February).

Hoshi, Takeo, Anil Kashyap, and David Scharfstein. 1991. "Corporate Structure, Liquidity, and Investment: Evidence from Japanese Industrial Groups." *Quarterly Journal of Economics* 106 (February): 33–60.

Institute of International Bankers. 1997. *Global Survey 1997: Regulatory and Market Developments.* New York.

Kaplan, Steven N. 1994. "Top Executive Rewards and Firm Performance: A Comparison of Japan and the United States." *Journal of Political Economy* 102 (June): 510–46.

La Porta, Rafael, Florencio Lopez-de-Silanes, and Andrei Shleifer. 1999. "Corporate Ownership around the World." *Journal of Finance* 54 (April): 471–517.

La Porta, Rafael, Florencio Lopez-de-Silanes, Andrei Shleifer, and Robert W. Vishny. 1997. "Legal Determinants of External Finance." *Journal of Finance* 52 (July): 1131–50.

———. 1998. "Law and Finance." *Journal of Political Economy* 106 (December): 1113–55.

Lim, Mah Hui. 1981. *Ownership and Control of the One Hundred Largest Corporations in Malaysia.* Oxford University Press.

Nenova, Tatiana. 1999. "The Value of a Corporate Vote and Private Benefits: Cross-Country Analysis." Working paper. Harvard University.

Nishiyama, Tadonori. 1984. "The Structure of Managerial Control: Who Owns and Controls Japanese Businesses." In *The Anatomy of Japanese Business*, edited by Kazuo Sato and Yasuo Hoshino. Armonk, N.Y.: M. E. Sharpe.

Prowse, Stephen D. 1992. "The Structure of Corporate Ownership in Japan." *Journal of Finance* 47 (July): 1121–40.

MICHAEL BARTH
XIN ZHANG

6

Foreign Equity Flows and the Asian Financial Crisis

IN THE AFTERMATH of the recent crisis in Asia, the role of foreign port-folio equity has come under scrutiny. The interest in the issue reflects both the importance of portfolio equity flows to emerging markets and their role in the debate on international financial infrastructure. The topic elicits strong and divergent viewpoints. One view holds that foreign capital flows are innately volatile and subject to abrupt reversals.[1] According to this view, capital flow reversals contributed substantially to the 1997 crisis. Proponents of this view often fail to differentiate among types of portfolio investment. Instead they tend to juxtapose this type of finance with the more stable foreign direct investment.

The opposing view is that reversals were less pronounced than was assumed and essentially took place in response to changed fundamentals,

The authors are indebted to Michael Pomerleano for his substantial assistance, Bill Shaw for use-ful comments, and Alexander Lebedinsky for dedicated and capable research assistance.

1. Radelet and Sachs (1998). The past two decades have witnessed a marked increase in interna-tional capital flows to developing countries. Total flows reached $337 billion in 1997, up threefold since the beginning of the decade, with the private sector component playing an increasingly dominant role. This number fell to $259 billion in 1998, mainly as a result of the Asian financial crisis. These numbers are World Bank estimates. International Monetary Fund (IMF) estimates are similar prior to 1998 but are much lower for 1998. For example, the total private flows by IMF estimates are only $70 billion, significantly lower than the World Bank estimates of $214 billion (see figure 6-1 for the main components of the capital flows during the 1990s).

Figure 6-1. *Capital Flows to Developing Countries, 1990–98*
Billions of U.S. dollars

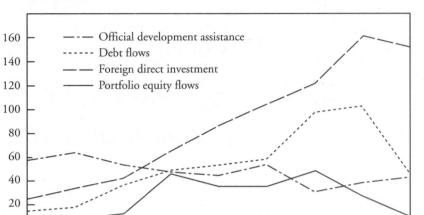

Source: World Bank data.

exacerbating but not causing the crisis. Proponents of this view tend to emphasize the long-term contributions made to the institutional capacity, depth, and breadth of emerging markets. Foreign expectations regarding the regulatory regime, disclosure practices, and operational infrastructure contribute to market efficiency, and proponents argue for improved corporate transparency and a sound macroeconomic environment.

Despite the importance of the topic, insufficient research has been conducted to frame the discussion. Reports produced by international financial institutions and others (Institute of International Finance, Institute for International Economics) provide descriptive overviews of aggregate equity flows to emerging markets but usually lack detailed analysis of different types of flows.[2] Moreover, they fail to explore nuances of the different classes of investors and thus leave underlying dynamics partially unanswered. Several academic papers focus on issues associated with foreign capital flows. Choe, Kho, and Stulz conclude that herding behavior by foreign investors was not significant during the crisis and that foreign investors did not destabilize the local stock market in the Republic of

2. Institute of International Finance (1999); Eichengreen (1999); World Bank (1999); International Monetary Fund (1998); Bank for International Settlements (1998).

Figure 6-2. *Foreign Equity Investments in Selected East Asian Economies, 1990–98*[a]

Billions of U.S. dollars

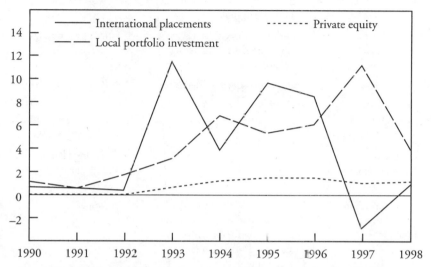

Source: World Bank, Jardine Fleming Securities, and *Asia Pacific Private Equity Bulletin.*
a. Data cover China, Indonesia, Korea, Malaysia, the Philippines, and Thailand.

Korea.[3] Froot, O'Connell, and Seasholes explore the behavior of international equity flows.[4] They report a strong correlation between monthly foreign flows and local market movements and provide evidence of trend chasing for international equity flows. A third study rejects the hypothesis that hedge fund capital flows were responsible for the crash of Asian currencies in late 1997.[5] That study focuses primarily on local portfolio investment and ignores the importance of private and international placements, which are becoming the dominant component of foreign equity flows (figure 6-2). Although this work expands our overall knowledge, it often lacks a panoramic view of foreign equity flows.

Thus there remains a gap in our understanding of what motivates foreign participation in emerging markets and the impact of portfolio investment on these markets. This paper aims to narrow that gap by reviewing foreign portfolio equity in Asian markets and differentiating among types

3. Choe, Kho, and Stulz (1998).
4. Froot, O'Connell, and Seasholes(1998).
5. Brown, Goetzmann, and Park (1998).

Table 6-1. *Sources of Data*

Type of data	Description	Source
Aggregate capital flows	Debt, equity, and foreign direct investment flows	World Bank
Foreign direct equity investment	Monthly and weekly net flows and turnovers for major Asian economies	Jardine Fleming Securities
GDRs/ADRs	Volume and source of depository receipts	Bank of New York
Private equity flows	Private equity flows in Asia	*Asia Pacific Private Equity Bulletin*
Trading activities of Jardine Fleming Securities clients		Jardine Fleming Securities
Individual offshore emerging market funds	1,191 funds, with $80 billion in total net assets. Funds include 865 equity funds, with total net assets of $44 billion (as of December 1997)	Lipper
Individual U.S. emerging market funds	375 funds, with $55 billion in total net assets. Funds include 332 equity funds, with total net assets of $52 billion (as of December 1997)	Lipper
Individual hedge funds data	1,227 funds, with $129 billion in total net assets (as of December 1997)	TASS hedge funds database
Aggregate flow and total net assets data on mutual funds with Asian exposure	U.S., U.K., Hong Kong, and Japanese mutual funds (and investment funds)	Jardine Fleming Securities, Hong Kong Investment Fund Association
Aggregate flow and total net assets data on pension funds with Asian exposure	U.S. and U.K. pension funds	Jardine Fleming Securities

of investors and investment instruments. We have developed a database that captures information on foreign portfolio flows into select Asian economies (see table 6-1). The data distinguish among foreign portfolio investment in local equity markets, international placements, and private equity investments, as well as among investors—that is, mutual funds, pension funds, and hedge funds. They cover asset allocations, destinations, indicators of performance and high-frequency trading, and foreign equity flows.

Specifically, we differentiate three types of investment: (1) local portfolio investment in Asian stock exchanges, (2) international placements—mainly American depository receipts (ADRs), global depository receipts (GDRs), and private placements—meaning investments in Asian equities in international markets, and (3) private equity. [5] We look at all three components because they have individual dynamics and collectively provide a comprehensive picture of foreign portfolio investment in Asian markets.[7]

Asia represents an interesting case study because foreign equity fueled the rapid growth of Asian markets in the decade before the crisis, presumably "abandoned" Asia in the wake of the financial turmoil that erupted in 1997, and is likely to be an essential factor in the restructuring of the corporate and banking sectors.

This paper examines the behavior and impact of the three types of foreign portfolio equity in Asia's markets (China, Indonesia, Korea, Malaysia, the Philippines, Taiwan [China], and Thailand).

It is organized as follows. The first section examines basic arguments and facts concerning the relationship between foreign investors and Asian markets. The second explores the behavior and impact of foreign investors during the crisis. The third takes a closer look at international placements and private equities. And the final section concludes.

The Relationship between Foreign Investors and Asian Markets: Basic Arguments and Facts

The concern over the destabilizing impact of foreign investors on Asia's emerging markets has often focused on the fact that foreign flows and local stock prices exhibit a strong positive correlation (figure 6-3). Some analysts note that panic engulfed the financial markets and that the ensuing capital reversals were a driving force in Asia's financial turmoil. The argument is deceptively simple and appealing. Huge foreign outflows put downward

6. Specifically, international placements include depository receipts (American and global), bought deals and block trades, initial public offerings, preference shares, rights issues, and issuance by funds.

7. The distinction between the components of foreign flows is not always clear-cut. For example, a portion of private equity may be counted as foreign direct investment, international placements, or both.

Figure 6-3. *Foreign Equity Flows to Local Markets and Local Market Indexes in Indonesia, Korea, Taiwan (China), and Thailand*

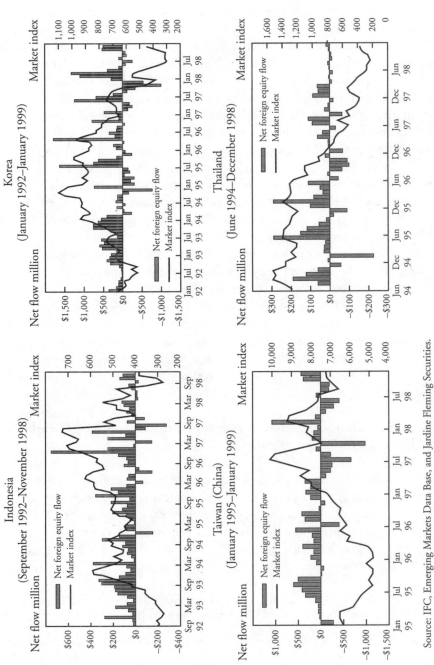

Source: IFC, Emerging Markets Data Base, and Jardine Fleming Securities.

price pressure on local stocks, sending stock prices spiraling downward. The downturn forced more investors to sell, causing the markets to plummet further. However, the correlation between foreign capital flows and stock prices could exist for any number of reasons. For instance, foreign and domestic investors alike could reassess prospects and simultaneously adjust to (lower) prices and lower foreign investment. This section presents facts on foreign presence in Asian markets and presents theoretical arguments and empirical findings on the impact of foreign equity flows.

Market Size and Foreign Presence

In isolation, financial theories alone cannot determine whether foreign investors affect the dynamics of Asian stock markets We start, therefore, by reviewing basic facts on market size, foreign presence, and foreign trading.

Asia's emerging equity markets have shown significant growth and volatility in recent years. Aggregate market capitalization in Indonesia, Korea, Malaysia, and Thailand—the four countries hit hardest by the crisis—was just $129 billion by the end of the 1980s (figure 6-4). Eight years later it had soared to $637 billion, an annual increase of 22 percent. By the end of 1997, market capitalization in these countries had fallen some 70 percent to about $188 billion dollars, a contraction of $448 billion.[8]

In the context of Asian markets, the total assets of foreign institutional investors are very large indeed. Pension funds in the United States and the United Kingdom alone had assets of $5.5 trillion at the end of 1996, while U.S. mutual funds had net assets of $1.7 trillion, and international hedge funds had estimated net assets of $90 billion.[9] Table 6-2 provides an overview of institutional investment with exposure in Asia. It consists of dedicated Asian funds (Asia-only funds) and funds that, in part, are invested in Asia.

8. Before the Asian crisis, the total capitalization of China, Indonesia, the Republic of Korea, Malaysia, the Philippines, Taiwan (China), and Thailand was $1.1 trillion, roughly twice the level in Latin America. By late 1997, the Asian crisis had reduced market capitalization to $713 billion, only slightly above that of Latin America. Asian market capitalization recovered modestly to $804 billion by the end of 1998.

9. Hedge funds data come from TASS database. Note that out of the 1,272 funds in the TASS database, 43 are in fact "emerging market funds" with estimated assets of about $4 billions, whose investments are regarded as risky by TASS.

Figure 6-4. *Growth of Asian Stock Market Capitalizations, 1988–98*
Billions of U.S. dollars

Source: IFC, Emerging Markets Data Base.
a. Latin America countries include Argentina, Brazil, Chile, Colombia, Mexico, and Venezuela.
b. Includes China, Indonesia, Korea, Malaysia, Philippines, Taiwan, and Thailand.
c. Includes Indonesia, Korea, Malaysia, and Thailand.

Foreign ownership as a percentage of total market capitalization is relatively modest (table 6-3; see also table 6-4).[10] Foreign investors account for 12 and 29 percent of market capitalizations in Korea and Indonesia, respectively. In part, foreign participation in the Asian market was, and to an extent is, restricted by regulatory constraints.[11] Other obstacles to foreign participation include government and family share ownership, crossholdings, and trading liquidity. The International Finance Corporation investable (IFC-I) index takes into account the restrictions on foreign ownership to determine the portion of stocks available to foreign investors and thus offers a good approximation of the ceiling on foreign participation.[12]

10. Foreign ownership of total market capitalization is estimated using actual ownership data in 1996 for Indonesia, Korea, the Philippines, and Thailand and the IFC-I index as an approximation for Malaysia.
11. Table 6-5 lists the restrictions on foreign investment in local Asian equity markets at year-end 1996. Before the Asian crisis, foreign-owned equity ownership was limited to 49 percent in Indonesia, 40 percent in the Philippines, and 20 percent in Korea.
12. The index calculates the capitalization of one of its constituents in the following way: if the government owns 35 percent of Bank ABC, and another IFC index constituent owns 25 percent, then

Table 6-2. *Total Net Assets of Institutional Investors, Year-End 1996*
Billions of U.S. dollars

Type of fund	All institutional investors	Institutional investors with Asian exposure
Mutual	1,726.1 (U.S)	85.1
Pension	5,501.2 (U.S. and U.K.)	4.5
Hedge	90.5 (global)	12.9

Source: For all institutional investors, data on U.S. mutual funds are from the Investment Company Institute; data on hedge funds are from the TASS hedge funds database; data on pension funds are the sum of U.K. funds and U.S. funds from Intersec Research. For institutional investors with Asian exposure, data on mutual funds for emerging funds with Asian exposure and Asia-only funds in the United States are from Lipper and for those in the United Kingdom and Hong Kong are from Jardine Fleming Securities; data on hedge funds are from TASS hedge funds database; and data on U.S. and U.K. pension fund investment in Asia are from Jardine Fleming Securities.

Figure 6-5 depicts the ratio of the IFC-I to local market capitalization. Notably, foreign investment rarely reached the caps. In Thailand, with a total market capitalization of $24 billion as of year-end 1997, a maximum of $5.1 billion was available for foreign investment (21 percent of the market). In Korea, for example, with a cap of about 20 percent, foreign ownership was 12 percent.

In Asian markets and elsewhere, share ownership is highly concentrated. Governments and local families control a significant proportion of closely held shares, which are not available for public ownership. The publicly outstanding shares are referred to as "free float."[13] Consequently, in the context of limited free float, foreign investors are a major presence. For instance, in Indonesia free float accounted for about 38 percent of market capitalization in 1997 and foreign investors accounted for 76 percent of the free float. The evidence clearly shows the importance of foreigners in local markets and the implications for building a strong base of domestic institutional investment.

---

40 percent of the shares outstanding nationally are available in the market. In this case, just 40 percent of Bank ABC's market capitalization would be included in the IFC-I index if the foreign ownership limit were higher than 40 percent.

13. We measure free float as the market capitalization of the shares not owned by the top fifteen families in each of the Asian countries as of December 1996. The data come from Claessens, Djankov, and Lang (1999) using mainly the World Scope database. They may overestimate the free float because they do not consider government ownership.

Table 6-3. *Foreign Ownership and Holding Period in Asian Equity Markets, 1997*
Percent unless otherwise noted

Indicator	Indonesia		Korea		Malaysia		Philippines		Thailand	
	Foreign	Domestic	Foreign	Domestic	Foreign	Domestic	Foreign	Domestic	Foreign	Domestic
Ownership of total market capitalization	29.0	71.0	12.0	88.0	50.0	50.0	38.0	62.0	21.0	79.0
Free float as a percentage of total market capitalization	38.0		62.0		72.0		45.0		47.0	
Ownership of free float	76.3	23.6	19.3	80.6	69.4	30.5	84.4	15.5	44.6	55.3
Foreign shares of trading	35.4	64.5	13.6	86.3	50.0	50.0	50.0	50.0	26.0	74.0
Holding period for free float (in years)	1.50	0.26	0.64	0.42	1.56	0.69	2.29	0.42	2.00	0.87

Source: World Bank, World Scope database, and Jardine Fleming Securities.

Table 6-4. *Restrictions on Foreign Investment on Asian Stock Markets as of Year-End 1996*

Economy	Restriction
China	Foreign institutions may purchase only 3-class shares without restrictions
Hong Kong (China)	Listed securities freely transferable; some restrictions apply to specific industries, however
Indonesia	Market closed to foreigners before 1987; considered open since September 1989, when 49 percent foreign ownership limit set for all companies
Korea, Republic of	Market gradually opened as limit on foreign stock holdings increased from 10 percent in 1992 to 12 percent in January 1995, 15 percent in July 1995, 18 percent in April 1996, and 20 percent in October 1996
Malaysia	No restrictions on foreign ownership for most stocks; some restrictions apply to banks and financial institutions, only 30 percent of which can be owned by foreigners
Philippines	Foreign ownership limited to 40 percent; media, retail, rural banking closed to foreigners; restrictions enforced through issuance of different classes
Singapore	No restrictions on foreign ownership except in media (40 percent), finance (20 percent), defense industries (15–25 percent); some restrictions self-imposed by companies
Taiwan (China)	Market closed to foreigners until 1991; initial limit of 10 percent ownership and $2.5 billion ceiling on total foreign investment; ownership limit raised to 12 percent in July 1995, 15 percent in September 1995, and 20 percent in March 1996; ceiling raised to $5 billion in August 1993 and $7.5 billion in March 1994 and eliminated in July 1995
Thailand	No restrictions on foreign ownership except in some industries (banking, finance, insurance), where foreign ownership limited to 25 percent

Source: International Society of Securities Administrators; International Finance Corporation.

Figure 6-5. *Regulatory Limitations on Foreign Participation, 1996*
Percent

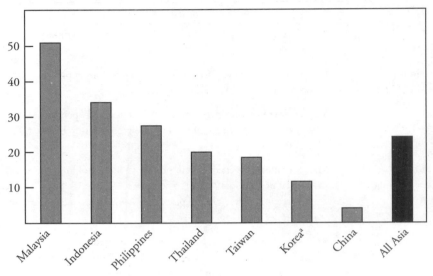

Source: IFC, Emerging Markets Data Base.
a. Assumed.

  The foreign share of trading (shares traded by foreign investors as a percentage of total local trading) provides useful information on local trading. The foreign share in trading is generally high in most Asian countries. For example, it was 50 percent in the Philippines and Malaysia and 35 percent in Indonesia during 1997. Note, however, that it has dropped steadily in Indonesia in the past few years (figure 6-6). The high foreign share in trading does not necessarily mean that foreigners trade more frequently than local investors. It reflects, rather, the fact that foreigners own the majority of the free float in many Asian countries. A more accurate indication of trading frequency is the holding period. It is noteworthy that the holding period is much longer for foreign investors. For example, foreigners held their part of the free float for eighteen months on average in 1997, while local investors in Indonesia only held theirs for three months (table 6-3). It follows that foreign investors are the proverbial "strong hands" that corporations covet. Figures 6-7 and 6-8 provide the free float holding period (measured in months) for foreign investors and local investors in Indonesia and Korea from 1992 to 1998.

Figure 6-6. *Foreign Shares in Trading in Indonesia and Republic of Korea, 1992–98*

Percent

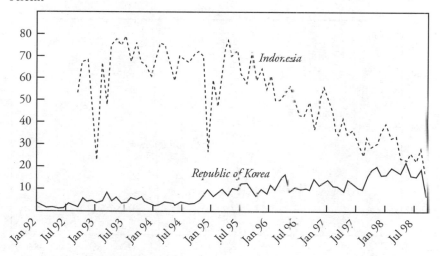

Source: Jardine Fleming Securities.

Figure 6-7. *Holding Period for Free Float in Indonesia, September 1992–November 1998*

Number of months

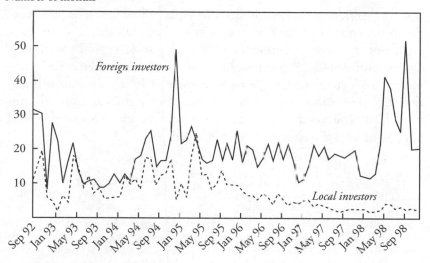

Source: Jardine Fleming Securities.

Figure 6-8. *Holding Period for Free Float in Korea,*
January 1992–January 1999
Number of months

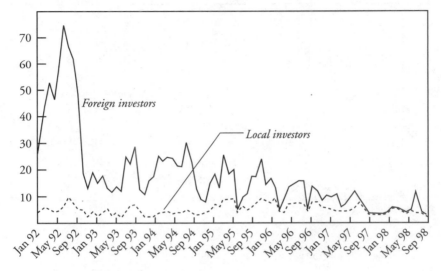

Source: Jardine Fleming Securities.

Why and How Foreign Equity Flows Lead Market Movements

Several theories have been advanced to explain how foreign equity flows
might strongly lead price movements in local equity markets.[14] The basic
argument that foreign outflows and inflows put downward and upward
price pressure on local stocks is buttressed by the "asymmetric size" argument, which suggests that the high presence of foreign investors implies
that their moves into and out of a market create significant price fluctuations. Critics point out that foreign investment represents a relatively small
portion of total investment in Asian markets.

14. This paper presents theories on why foreign equity investors can lead market movements in
Asia, mainly because our preliminary empirical results confirm such a leading role by foreign flows.
This is a basic discussion. Many other theories explain other possible ways foreigners can affect local
markets. For example, studies also show that foreign investors might have a destabilizing impact on
local markets even when they herd. If the foreigners are less informed than local investors, disadvanta-
geous foreign investors will tend to revise their market views more in response to news (Brennan and
Cao, 1997). This will lead foreign investors to act as positive feedback traders. In times of market crisis, the feedback trading behavior can significantly worsen the market situation.

Another school of thought suggests that even with a relatively small presence, foreign investors did affect the movement of Asian stock markets during the crisis. The arguments are in great part based on "asymmetric information" reasoning. A version of this argument, the "informed trader theory," argues that what happened in Asia was a market correction and that foreign investors helped to bring the market more in line with economic fundamentals: foreign investors were extremely astute and well-informed, and their purchases and sales revealed information about Asian economic fundamentals to less-informed investors. Less well-informed investors then traded in the same direction. The dynamics thus explain the positive correlation between foreign equity flows and stock returns.

A second "asymmetric information" argument holds that market movements in the crisis were not rational. It explains why foreign flows could have driven the Asian markets and led to divergence from underlying economic fundamentals.[15] A significant number of foreign "noise traders" sold in irrational ways. Arbitrage by informed rational investors failed to keep asset prices in line with fundamental values, because the unpredictability of the foreign noise traders' beliefs and actions created additional price risk in itself and deterred participation in the market. Informed domestic and foreign investors did not enter the market to counter the downtrend by buying stock, fearing that foreign "noise" traders would drive prices even lower. In this scenario, stock prices diverged significantly from fundamental values.

Behavior and Impact of Foreign Investors during the Crisis

Thus far we have established some basic facts on foreign presence in Asian markets, complemented by theoretical arguments regarding the impact of foreign investors. Next, we address the question of whether foreign investors are trend chasers or market leaders. Investors are defined as trend chasers if they purchase stocks in a market that performed well in a previous period and vice versa. They are defined as market leaders if their purchases and sales lead, respectively, to market surges and steep declines in the subsequent period. Investors can be both trend chasers and market leaders, which implies the existence of two-way causality. The existence of two-way causality between foreign equity flows and local market movements

15. See De Long and others (1990).

can exacerbate market moves and be destabilizing. Work in the dynamics of the markets during the Asian financial crisis is essentially limited to Korea. Using trading transaction data for individual stocks, Choe, Kho, and Stulz find no significant evidence of foreign investors' feedback trading in Korea.[16] Froot and others report evidence of trend chasing by international equity flows, but their work does not focus specifically on the Asian crisis.[17]

Our basic econometric analysis covers Indonesia, Korea, Taiwan, and Thailand.[18] It examines monthly and weekly foreign portfolio equity flows to the four markets between October 1992 and December 1998. These flows represent aggregate net investment (exclusive of ADRs and GDRs) by all foreign investors (both individual and institutional) in each local market. To assess whether foreign investors behaved in a trend-chasing manner, we regressed current foreign flows on past market returns in each of the four markets. To determine whether foreign investors "led" the markets, we regressed current market returns on past foreign flows.

The evidence shows that foreigners, as a group, were not trend chasers in the Asian markets. We find no evidence that fluctuations in foreign portfolio equity investment can be attributed to changes in past short-term market returns in Indonesia, Korea, Taiwan, and Thailand. In the regressions we find that coefficients of past returns are not significant at the 5 percent confidence level.[19] In other words, an increase in Asian stock market returns in the previous period is not significantly associated with increased foreign equity flows in the current period (results are reported in table 6-5).

We do find, however, that foreign investors led in Asian stock markets. In all four countries, past foreign equity flows are positively correlated with current returns.[20] An increase (or decrease) in foreign equity flows in the

---

16. Choe, Kho, and Stulz (1998).

17. Froot, O'Connell, and Seasholes (1998).

18. A more rigorous econometric treatment of the causality between flows and returns in Edwards and Zhang (1998) finds a two-way causality between U.S. equity mutual fund flows and U.S. stock market movements during market downturns. In this paper, we do not include structural factors in modeling flows and returns in the regressions. We believe that our simple approach can nonetheless shed light on this subject.

19. We tried different combinations of lagged returns in the regression and reached essentially the same results.

20. Monthly regressions do not show a leading role by foreign investors in Thailand and Taiwan. Weekly regressions do show a positive correlation, however. We have also tried different combinations of lagged flows in the regression and reached essentially the same results.

Table 6-5. *Did Foreign Investors Trend-Chase in Asian Equity Markets?*[a]

Independent variable	Indonesia (October 1992– November 1998)	Korea (January 1992– November 1998)	Taiwan (January 1995– November 1998)	Thailand (July 1994– November 1998)
Constant	−0.00001	−0.000224	0.000046	−0.024626
	(0.00039)	(0.00045)	(0.00019)	(0.02213)
$Return_{t-1}$	0.00096	0.002261	−0.000736	−0.037345
	(0.00411)	(0.00484)	(0.00254)	(17.4664)
$Return_{t-2}$	−0.004074	−0.010064	0.000977	−7.806316
	(0.00412)	(0.00497)	(0.00247)	(17.3553)
$Return_{t-3}$	−0.002195	−0.003432	−0.005416	−6.630172
	(0.00425)	(0.00497)	(0.00248)*	(17.3351)
$Return_{t-4}$	0.000115	−0.001136	−0.002591	−14.50776
	(0.00457)	(0.00503)	(0.00261)	(17.4365)
R^2	0.021538	0.067702	0.143513	0.030543

* Significant at the 5 percent level.
a. Regression equation:

$$Flow_t = \alpha + \beta_1 Return_{t-1} + \beta_2 Return_{t-2} + \beta_3 Return_{t-3} + \beta_4 Return_{t-4} + \epsilon_t.$$

Flow is the unexpected component of foreign equity flows to local markets (normalized by last month's market capitalization), and *Return* is the returns on local market index. Data are monthly. Market indexes are the Jakarta Composite Index (Indonesia), the KOSPI (Korea), the Taiwan Weighted Index (Taiwan), and the SET (Thailand). Numbers in parentheses are standard errors.

previous period is associated with higher (or lower) stock prices in the current period (table 6-6). However, the evidence that foreign investors led local market movements during the crisis should be interpreted with caution. It does not necessarily mean that foreigners destabilized Asian markets. We need to disentangle two possible explanations. The first explanation is premised on the assumption that foreign investors were "informed traders" who correctly predicted the downturn in Asian markets and decided to exit before the crisis. The alternative "noise traders" theory suggests that the irrational trading behavior of foreign investors helped to drive the market away from its fundamentals and contributed to the crisis. It is not clear which of these two explanations is correct. In addition, this evidence does not imply that all foreign investors are market leaders. For example, mutual funds, as are discussed later, seem to have been quite passive and are unlikely to have been market leaders during the Asian financial crisis.

Table 6-6. *Did Foreign Investors Lead in Asian Equity Markets?*[a]

Independent variable	Indonesia (October 1992– November 1998)	Korea (January 1992– November 1998)	Taiwan (February 3, 1995– December 11, 1998)	Thailand (July 29, 1994– December 11, 1998)
Constant	0.010519	–0.000201	–0.0000624	–0.005309
	(0.01233)	(0.01100)	(0.00261)	(0.00322)
Unexpected	6.681329	3.424083	–1.720547	17.88209
$Flow_{t-1}$	(3.89661)**	(2.73896)	(3.45330)	(5.29890)*
Unexpected	2.411424	–5.283967	6.299358	–2.823273
$Flow_{t-2}$	(4.03892)	(2.84986)**	(3.45536)**	(5.29975)
Unexpected	6.954321	–2.210203	6.131609	17.47276
$Flow_{t-3}$	(4.07069)**	(2.87247)	(3.47302)**	(5.32965)*
Unexpected	5.119215	–7.631897	0.860072	–4.414384
$Flow_{t-4}$	(4.11429)	(2.86992)*	(3.47246)	(5.48864)
R^2	0.11009	0.153455	0.033761	0.094491

* Significant at the 5 percent level.
** Significant at the 10 percent level.
a. Regression equation:

$$Return_t = \alpha + \beta_1 Flow_{t-1} + \beta_2 Flow_{t-2} + \beta_3 Flow_{t-3} + \beta_4 Flow_{t-4} + \epsilon_t.$$

Flow is the unexpected component of foreign equity flows to local markets (normalized by last month's market capitalization), and *Return* is the returns on local market index. Data are monthly (Indonesia and Korea) and weekly (Thailand and Taiwan). Market indexes are the Jakarta Composite Index (Indonesia), the KOSPI (Korea), the Taiwan Weighted Index (Taiwan), and the SET (Thailand). Numbers in parentheses are standard errors.

Foreign Investors' Main Objectives, Behavior, and Performance

This section examines the investment objectives, behavior, and performance of foreign equity investors in Asian emerging markets. It further explores the impact of foreign investors on local markets. Three key forces drove foreign participation in Asian equities: the desire to diversify portfolio risk, sound economic fundamentals and long-term growth prospects, and the presence of momentum investors with a short-term horizon. The following discussion briefly outlines these motivations.

GLOBAL PORTFOLIO DIVERSIFICATION. In the past decade diversification has become a standard technique of portfolio management. It has been perhaps the driving catalyst for institutional participation in emerging markets. The quest for diversification led U.S. equity mutual funds to increase their investments in emerging markets between 1992 and 1997.

Figure 6-9. *U.S. Mutual Fund Investment in International,*
Emerging, and Asian Markets, 1988–98

Percent

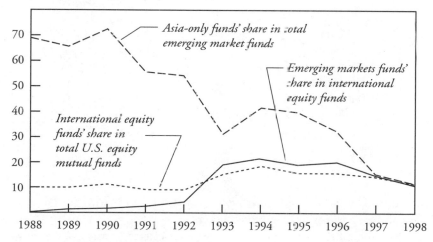

Source: Lipper; Investment Company Institute.

As shown in figure 6-9, evidence of geographical diversification is compelling. The share of international equity investment in total U.S. equity mutual funds rose from 6 percent in 1984 to a peak of almost 19 percent in 1994. Within the international equity investment segment, the share of emerging market investment rose steadily. The Lipper database indicates that about 20 percent of emerging market mutual funds had exposure in emerging markets before 1997, with an average of more than 45 percent of the assets, on average, invested in Asia. Data on U.S. and offshore mutual funds, as well as U.S. pension funds, show that the favorite Asian destinations were Hong Kong, Malaysia, and Singapore (the larger markets), followed by Thailand, Indonesia, and Korea.

Investment in emerging markets, driven primarily by diversification objectives, does not fluctuate significantly over the short term, nor does it typically disrupt markets. In fact, anecdotal evidence for pension plans with an emerging markets asset class suggests that their allocation typically has a five- to ten-year horizon, and some channeled additional funds during the market downturn to reach the target asset allocation. Similarly, closed-end funds in particular, and to a lesser extent open-end funds, have captive commitments to emerging markets. Mutual funds have a permanent presence in emerging markets despite potential turnover in the base of

Table 6-7. *Correlation between Monthly Asian and U.S. Market Returns: Crisis Period versus Non-Crisis Period*[a]

Period	Correlation
Crisis periods	
September 1987–September 1988	0.65
April 1997–April 1998	0.70
Non-Crisis periods	
Whole sample[b]	0.24
January 1985–October 1998 (entire period)	0.28

a. Asian stock market return is measured by IFC-G Asia index; U.S. stock market return is measured by S&P 500 Index return.

b. Without observations corresponding to crisis periods.

investors. Therefore, it can be argued that pension plans and mutual funds are stabilizing forces in emerging markets.

The value of diversification has been questioned recently. Wang shows that the diversification benefits of investing in emerging equity markets (in particular in Asian markets) are slim at best.[21] Tesar and Werner show that the risk premium in emerging market stocks has fallen as these markets have become more open.[22] According to these studies, diversification bestows few benefits because Asian economies have become more integrated and draw investments from international firms. Investment in multinational firms can be a proxy for Asian exposure. Further doubt about the benefits of international diversification is cast by the fact that the correlation between stock price movements, which is low and even negative under normal conditions, can become strongly positive during periods of turmoil, when the benefits of diversification are needed most (table 6-7).[23]

Recent concerns about the lack of benefit from diversifying into emerging markets may have profound implications for future capital flows. The

21. Patel, Sarkar, and Wang (1999).

22. Tesar and Werner (1998).

23. More generally, the evidence that the world's stock markets tend to become more correlated at times of high share-price volatility is overwhelming. It is not hard to explain the short-term synchronization. It reflects a reassessment of economic fundamentals in various markets, declining tolerance for risk on the part of investors in light of increased volatility, and asset reallocations to the newly cheaper assets. However, the evidence on the high short-term correlations needs to be qualified. Aside from occasional turbulence, there has not been a great increase in correlation between stock markets in different countries. However, as emerging countries have opened to international trade and foreign investment, their stock markets have rapidly become more correlated with those of developed countries.

effect may be to reduce the number of investors driven by longer-term diversification considerations. The relative increase in foreign flows driven by short-term considerations could potentially destabilize local markets.

ECONOMIC FUNDAMENTALS. A decade of uninterrupted, phenomenal economic growth until the 1997 crisis created high expectations for the future of Asia in the minds of investors. In order to gauge the relationship between economic fundamentals and foreign flows, we explore here foreign equity flows and corporate performance in six East Asian emerging economies. Annual net foreign equity flows prior to the crisis (1990–96) were regressed using panel data on equity market index returns, return on corporate equity (an accounting indicator of corporate profitability), and the growth rate of corporate sales over the preceding three-year relationship. We find that foreign equity flows are positively correlated, in a significant way, with sales growth and market returns (table 6-8), while the return on corporate equity is insignificant. The results suggest that foreign investors relied extensively on growth and market performance, expecting, of course, that this would translate into higher corporate profitability. Investors did not, however, pay sufficient attention to corporate fundamentals in a period in which corporations were rapidly leveraging and profitability was, in fact, declining.[24]

However, it should still be emphasized that investment behavior, driven primarily by economic fundamentals, tends to be long term and fairly stable. Since economic conditions do not generally change overnight (except in severe crises), investment shifts based essentially on the assessment of fundamentals are incremental and do not typically disrupt markets.

SHORT-TERM PARTICIPATION. The high contemporaneous correlation between monthly equity flows and equity price movements in the domestic market is also documented by many other studies.[25] Some investors went into the Asian markets with a short-term horizon seeking high returns. These investors exited quickly when the economies began to turn sour and the markets experienced large corrections Critics of this type of investor (which, notably, includes hedge funds) often point to a high correlation between monthly capital flows and Asian stock market returns. The correlations range from about 33 percent for Indonesia and Taiwan to almost 50 percent for Korea and Thailand.

24. See Pomerleano (1998) for details on Asian corporate performance.
25. For example, Froot, O'Connell, and Seasholes (1998).

Table 6-8. *What Drives Equity Flows (A Cross-Country Study)*[a]

Variable	Coefficient	t-statistic
ROCE	−61.14	−0.88
Sales growth	213.77	11.32
Return	14.39	6.31
R^2	0.30	...

Source: Based on yearly (1990–96) data from World Bank and World Scope for China, Indonesia, Korea, Malaysia, the Philippines, and Thailand.

a. Regression equation:

$$Flow_t = \alpha + \beta_1 Return_t + \beta_2 ROCE_t + \beta_3 Sales_t + \epsilon_t.$$

Flow is the equity flows to Asian countries; *ROCE* is the return on corporate equity. *Return* is the annual stock return on IFC-I country index. *Sales* is the average sales growth rate of the last three years. Regression is estimated by fixed-effects panel regression techniques.

Because of their short investment horizon and their leverage power, hedge funds came under close scrutiny as a possible root cause of the crisis. Largely because data on hedge fund activity are difficult to obtain, we were unable to ascertain their positions. However, the market power of hedge funds can be formidable. The convergence positions of Long-Term Capital Management, for example, were in the range of several hundred billion dollars and leveraged 100 to 1. Whether these flows actually had an adverse or a positive impact (due to bottom fishing) on the Asian markets is not clear. A recent report by the International Monetary Fund concludes that it is not clear that hedge funds acted differently from local and international banks in trading activities.[26] Relying on statistical models to estimate hedge fund flows, Brown, Goetzmann, and Park do not find significant statistical evidence that hedge funds affected local markets.[27]

Asset Allocations by Foreign Pension, Mutual, and Hedge Funds

In order to determine how foreign investors behaved during the 1997 Asian crisis, we look at investments by foreign pension funds, mutual funds, and hedge funds in four countries: Indonesia, Korea, Malaysia, and Thailand between 1994 and 1998.

26. International Monetary Fund (1998).
27. Brown, Goetzmann, and Park (1998).

Figure 6-10. *U.S. Mutual Funds' Investment in Asian Crisis Countries,*
1994–98
Millions of U.S. dollars

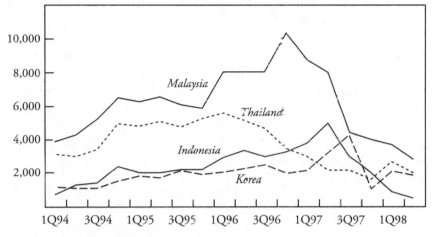

Source: Jardine Fleming Securities; Lipper.

INVESTMENTS BY PENSION FUNDS AND MUTUAL FUNDS. On the surface, mutual funds dropped significantly during the crisis (figure 6-10),
with U.S. pension funds basically following the same pattern. Much of the
decline, however, reflects a decrease in the value of invested funds rather
than the withdrawal of funds. For example, in Jardine Fleming's fund asset
allocation database, U.S. mutual fund assets in Malaysia were down about
50 percent from the third quarter of 1997 to the second quarter of 1998.
But U.S. mutual funds with Asian exposure suffered negative returns of at
least 40 percent during this same period. The decline was largely due to
value compression rather than to withdrawal of investment from Asian
markets.[28]

Data on U.S. mutual fund redemption and sales also indicate that
mutual funds maintained a large commitment in emerging market countries. In fact, the Investment Company Institute statistics on U.S. emerging market funds during the crisis period (July 1997 to March 1998) document negative flows in just one month (December 1997, when they fell
$249 million). Average monthly cash holdings between June 1996 and

28. We do not have pension fund performance data.

March 1997 of $1.4 billion were only slightly higher than the average holdings of $1.2 billion between January 1996 and March 1997. The lack of significant changes in redemptions and holdings of liquidity assets means that mutual funds maintained their presence in Asia during the early stage of the crisis.[29]

HEDGE FUNDS. Information on asset allocation by hedge funds is very difficult to obtain. Unlike mutual funds, hedge funds are not required to disclose their asset allocation publicly. Hedge funds shift their positions rapidly, and their positions are often heavily leveraged through derivative instruments. Asset allocations are thus not transparent. The data that are available (from the TASS hedge fund database) suggest that hedge funds substantially increased their activities, including investment in Asia, until early 1998 (figure 6-11).

How Did Foreign Investors Fare during the Crisis?

Our analysis shows that, as a group, foreign investors with Asian exposure (mutual funds and hedge funds) suffered significant losses in the crisis (table 6-9).[30] Mutual funds with Asian exposure experienced huge losses during and after the crisis. U.S. emerging market mutual funds (in the Lipper universe) enjoyed 12 percent average return annually from January 1992 to June 1997 (before the crisis). The value of their assets fell 40 percent during the ensuing market crash. U.S. emerging market funds focused on Asia had even worse returns (–75.8 percent). The IFC-Global Asia index fell 62 percent during the same period. These data indicate that some mutual fund investors performed worse than local market indexes and, no doubt, many local investors. This means that to the extent that these foreign investors pulled out of Asia, they did so later than did local investors. Sharpe ratio comparisons confirm these findings.[31]

29. Some emerging markets funds were not limited to Asia. It is therefore possible that investors withdrew from Asia and invested the proceeds in Latin America. However, we believe that the impact of such moves is limited by both the difficulty of shifting large positions from one continent to another as well as by the fact that most mutual funds do not, in fact, have the flexible mandate to do this.

30. Performance data on pension funds during the crisis were not available for gauging the impact of value compression on pension funds' presence in Asia.

31. Before the crisis, Sharpe ratios of U.S. and offshore emerging market mutual funds were lower than the S&P 500 index. Sharpe ratios of U.S. emerging market funds with Asian focus were worse than the IFC-G index. It appears that the mutual fund managers did not add much value to their investment.

Figure 6-11. *Hedge Funds with Asia Focus and Their Total Net Assets, 1988–98*[a]

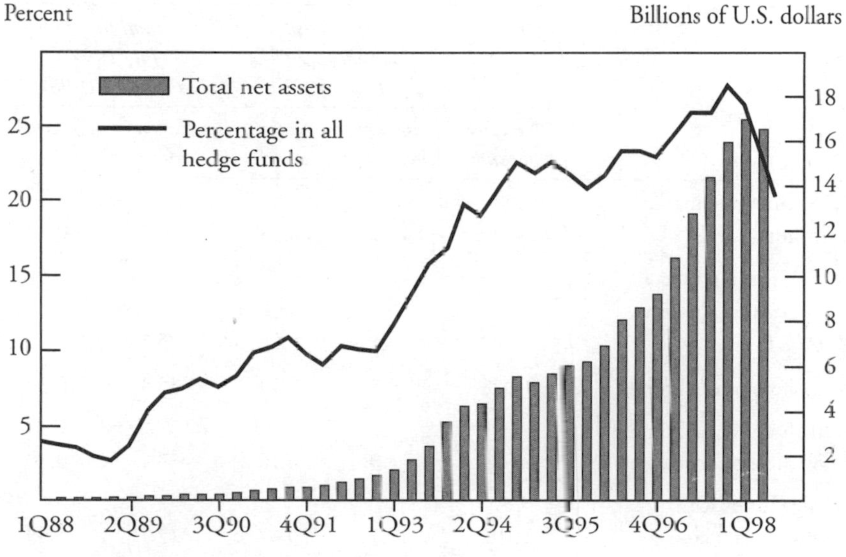

Percent   Billions of U.S. dollars

Source: TASS hedge funds database.

a. A fund can declare more than one geographical focus; that is, funds that invest in the United States can also invest in Africa.

We decompose the changes in assets of mutual funds into value compression and redemption components in figure 6-12. For the Asian emerging market mutual funds in the Lipper universe, value compression accounted for 54 percent of the change in asset value in 1997. Value compression was even more severe among U.K. mutual funds, where it accounted for nearly 80 percent of the total change in asset values in 1997. The findings dispel reports in the financial press that mutual funds pulled out of Asia during the crisis—value compressions accounted for most of the decline.

Hedge funds performed much better than mutual funds and local investors. In the TASS universe, hedge funds with an Asian geographic focus enjoyed annual returns of 8.2 percent during the crisis.

Who Lost out in the Asian Crisis?

What is the financial cost of the financial crisis, and who has borne that cost? Three types of asset losses were incurred as a result of the crash: equity

Table 6-9. *Returns by Mutual Funds and Hedge Funds,*
January 1992–October 1998

		Before crisis (January 1992– June 1997)		Around the crash (July 1997– February 1998)	
Type of funds	Number of funds	Average return[a]	Sharpe ratio[b]	Average return[a]	Sharpe ratio[b]
U.S. emerging market mutual funds	402	12.2	0.14	−40.2	−0.39
U.S. emerging market mutual funds with Asia focus	91	4.6	0.00	−75.8	−0.69
Off-shore mutual funds	1,078	9.5	0.14	−35.1	−0.39
Off-shore mutual funds with Asia focus	584	13.9	0.16	−53.1	−0.40
Hedge funds with non-Asia focus	1,102	19.1	0.67	17.7	0.49
Hedge funds with Asia focus	170	17.7	0.52	8.2	0.13
IFC-G Asian return	...	7.0	0.04	−61.7	−0.51
S&P 500[c]	...	14.2	0.30	27.0	0.37

Source: TASS hedge funds database; Lipper; IFC, Emerging Markets Data Base.

a. All returns are weighted by net asset value of individual funds

b. Sharpe ratio is defined as dividing the risk premium for a portfolio (mean return on the portfolio less mean U.S. Treasury bill rate) by the standard deviation of the portfolio returns.

c. S&P data run through May 1998.

market losses, bank loan defaults, and bond market defaults. Equity market losses represent the difference between the total equity market capitalization in the crisis countries before and after the crisis.[32] Foreign market losses during the crisis were about $166 billion, $107 billion of which was lost in Malaysia alone (table 6-10). A significant portion of the loss was due to foreign exchange rate movements in Asia. For example, currency depre-

32. The total market capitalization for the four crisis countries was $636.8 billion at year-end 1996 and $188.1 billion at year-end 1997—a decline of almost 70 percent. To estimate foreign losses, we use data on foreign market ownership for Indonesia, Korea, the Philippines, Thailand, and Taiwan, and we use the share of IFC-I index capitalization in total local market capitalization to approximate foreign ownership for China and Malaysia.

Figure 6-12. *Decomposing Changes in Asset Values in Asia, 1992–98*
Millions of U.S. dollars

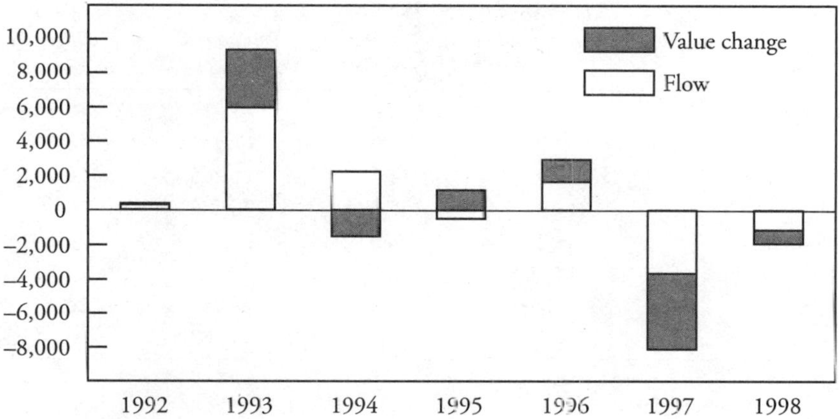

Source: Jardine Fleming Securities.

ciation accounted for 42 percent of foreign equity investors' loss in
Indonesia. An alternative calculation is based on the net assets of institutional investors with exposure in Asia; it amounts to about $83.5 billion
(table 6-11).[33] This calculation significantly underestimates the loss, however, because not all capital-source countries are included in our data sample. Moreover, even within the countries included in our sample, non-
institutional foreign investors are not included. Therefore it is fair to say
that losses were anywhere between $83.5 billion and $166 billion.

By comparison, foreign banks lost about $60 billion in East Asia and
Russia.[34] Other foreign creditors incurred losses of about $50 billion. The
losses of foreign equity investors thus vastly surpassed the losses of creditors.

International Placements and Private Equities

The relative importance of various types of investments varies across
economies (table 6-12). However, overall, international placements and
private equity investments accounted for more than half of the total foreign

33. Losses in our sample of mutual funds, pension funds, and hedge funds are at $32 billion. Our
data cover about 65 percent of mutual funds, 40 percent of pension funds, and 70 percent of hedge
funds investment in Asia.
34. Institute for International Finance (1999).

Table 6-10. *Estimated Losses by Foreign Investors in the Asian Crisis*

Country	Total crisis loss (millions of U.S. dollars)[a]	Foreign share (percent)	Foreign loss (millions of U.S. dollars)[a]	Percentage of loss due to exchange rate movements
China	−92,612	4.2	−3,890	−0.4
Indonesia	61,912	29.0	17,954	42.4
Korea, Republic of	96,936	11.6	11,245	30.1
Malaysia	213,571	50.0	106,786	16.4
Philippines	49,288	38.0	18,729	20.1
Taiwan (China)	−14,205	8.0	−1,136	19.7
Thailand	76,290	21.0	16,021	20.7
Total	391,180	. . .	165,709	. . .

Source: IFC, Emerging Markets Data Base.

a. Positive number means gain, and negative number means loss.

equity flows in Asian countries in our sample, specifically in six out of nine years between 1990 and 1998. This deserves special emphasis because, despite their importance, these types of investments have attracted scant attention.

For countries with relatively tight capital controls and less well-developed equity markets (such as China), international placements and private equities account for a higher proportion than does local portfolio investment. In economies with more open and mature capital markets (such as Malaysia and Thailand), local portfolio investment represents the largest form of foreign equity inflows. These differences partly reflect the level of development of domestic infrastructure, the regulatory capacity, and other aspects of the "enabling" environment. Ironically, economies that relied most heavily on international placements and private equities were hurt less by the crisis than economies that attracted more direct portfolio equity investment in their markets.

International Placements

International placements include depository receipts (ADRs and GDRs).[35] In table 6-12 we distinguish between listed and unlisted international

---

35. We used Euromoney's database. Euromoney's definition includes bought deals and block trades, initial public offerings, preference shares, rights issues, and issuance by funds.

Table 6-11. *Losses of Foreign Equity Investors in the Asian Crisis:*
Calculation from Investors' Perspective
Millions of U.S. dollars

Type of fund	Total loss for foreign equity investors in our sample	Total loss for the estimated whole universe
Mutual funds	20,652	31,772
Pension funds	9,939	49,695
Hedge funds	1,415	2,021
Total	32,006	83,489

Source: For all institutional investors, data on U.S. mutual funds are from the Investment Company Institute; data on hedge funds are from the TASS hedge funds database; data on pension funds are the sum of U.K. funds and U.S. funds from Intersec Research. For institutional investors with Asian exposure, data on mutual funds for emerging funds with Asian exposure and Asia-only funds in the United States are from Lipper and for those in the United Kingdom and Hong Kong are from Jardine Fleming Securities; data on hedge funds are from TASS hedge funds database; and data on U.S. and U.K. pension fund investment in Asia are from Jardine Fleming Securities.

placements. Listed international placements are mainly ADRs and GDRs that are publicly traded on stock exchanges. Unlisted international placements, such as 144As, are traded over the counter by "qualified institutional buyers."

Depository receipts have grown rapidly in recent years due to their advantages. Companies can tap larger pools of capital and broaden the shareholder base by issuing depository receipts, while investors can bypass the limitations of domestic trading and the local custodial infrastructure. However, a perceived disadvantage of (listed) depository receipts from the point of view of the issuers—the need to comply with U.S. generally accepted accounting principles and meet full Securities and Exchange Commission disclosure requirements—can be circumvented for unlisted depository receipts. For the Asian countries in our sample, the amount of capital raised through unlisted international placements is significantly higher than that raised through listed international placements. Out of the $18.5 billion of international placements from 1994 to 1996, the unlisted portion accounts for $14.2 billion.

International placements to Asian countries appear to have been more stable than direct portfolio equity investment. For example, in 1997, while all local Asian markets reported net portfolio outflows of $2.7 billion, new capital raised in international markets reached a record high of

Table 6-12. *Forms of Portfolio Equity Investments in Select East Asian Countries, Yearly Data, 1990–98*
Millions of U.S. dollars

Economy and form of investment	1990	1991	1992	1993	1994	1995	1996	1997	1998
China	0	653	1,194	4,241	4,679	3,714	4,378	8,919	1,220
International placements	0	12	689	1,874	2,602	892	2,078	9,103	1,052
Listed	0	0	334	720	1,134	206	537	1,484	234
Unlisted	0	12	355	1,154	1,468	686	1,541	7,619	818
Local portfolio investment	0	641	505	1,944	1,313	1,915	1,388	-646	101
Private equity	n.a.	n.a.	n.a.	423	764	907	912	462	67
Indonesia	586	110	119	2,510	3,795	5,046	3,230	472	250
International placements	586	110	119	345	1,322	1,473	1,234	935	n.a.
Listed	586	73	69	23	531	671	58	127	n.a.
Unlisted	0	36	50	322	791	802	1,175	808	n.a.
Local portfolio investment	0	0	0	2,107	2,350	3,400	1,865	-638	250
Private equity	n.a.	n.a.	n.a.	58	123	173	131	174	n.a.
Korea, Republic of	387	200	2,154	5,903	2,392	3,452	5,513	1,521	4,557
International placements	387	200	252	328	1,168	1,310	1,151	630	150
Listed	304	131	252	226	330	300	323	n.a.	n.a.
Unlisted	83	69	0	103	838	1,010	828	630	150
Local portfolio investment	n.a.	n.a.	1,902	5,391	1,025	1,803	3,968	456	3,574
Private equity	n.a.	n.a.	n.a.	184	200	339	394	435	833

Malaysia									
International placements	292	0	385	3,709	1,370	2,369	4,455	-408	604
Listed	0	0	385	0	0	569	600	424	162
Unlisted	0	0	134	0	0	0	44	n.a.	n.a.
Local portfolio investment	0	0	251	3,700	1,320	1,730	3,753	-913	430
Private equity	n.a.	n.a.	n.a.	9	50	70	102	81	12
Philippines									
International placements	32	98	333	1,464	1,596	2,025	1,341	102	697
Listed	32	98	333	126	949	749	1,001	265	375
Unlisted	8	98	195	82	0	0	142	n.a.	n.a.
Local portfolio investment	23	0	138	1,319	458	1,212	332	-192	319
Private equity	n.a.	n.a.	0	19	189	64	8	29	3
Thailand									
International placements	449	41	4	3,145	-513	2,175	1,583	-248	2,449
Listed	83	134	4	561	759	531	151	28	2,265
Unlisted	61	115	4	156	38	56	0	n.a.	n.a.
Local portfolio investment	21	19	0	2,556	-1,298	1,623	1,400	-336	167
Private equity	366	-93	n.a.	28	25	21	32	59	17
Total									
International placements	1,746	1,102	2,286	15,581	12,294	16,978	16,532	9,902	6,203
Listed	1,087	554	1,781	3,234	6,800	5,524	6,215	11,386	4,004
Unlisted	960	418	987	1,206	2,032	1,232	1,105	1,611	234
Local portfolio investment	127	136	794	2,028	4,767	4,292	5,110	9,775	3,770
Private equity	659	548	505	11,626	4,144	9,880	8,738	-2,725	951
	n.a.	0	0	721	1,351	1,574	1,579	1,240	1,247

Source: World Bank, Jardine Fleming Securities, and *Asia Pacific Private Equity Bulletin*.

n.a. Not available.

$11.4 billion in 1997.[36] Also 1998 continued to see significant foreign interest in Asian international placements, with unlisted international placements dominating. Out of the $11.4 billion worth of Asian paper issued in 1997, the unlisted portion accounted for $9.8 billion (in 1998 out of the $4 billion issued, it accounted for $3.8 billion).

The strong showing of Asian international placements in 1997 and 1998 has much to do with the China factor. China accounted for $9.1 billion of the total $11.4 billion issued in 1997 and for $1 billion out of the total $4 billion issued in 1998. The numbers for 1997 need to be interpreted with caution. Many placements may have been made in the first half of 1997 (prior to the crisis). However, 1998 continues the trend seen in 1997.

Aside from this, two other factors have supported the continued strong demand for Asian depository receipts. First, the majority of Asian international placements are placed directly with institutional investors, which continued to see investment opportunities in the wake of the crisis. Second, many of the companies issuing international placements are the most prominent firms in their home country. Evidence on the relative performance of firms that have access to depository receipt programs also comes from the Bank of New York's database. The Asian ADR index was down 9.8 percent from year-end 1996 to year-end 1997, whereas in the same period Asian market capitalization shrank 35.4 percent, suggesting that the stocks of depository receipt companies outperformed domestic markets.[37]

Investors perceive considerable advantages in depository receipts. Investors seeking to diversify their portfolios internationally can bypass domestic markets by purchasing ADRs and GDRs listed on international markets. The markets for depository receipts have adequate depth and liquidity to absorb the demand from U.S. mutual fund international investors. The total net assets of U.S. equity mutual funds invested internationally, which include emerging market, global, international, and regional funds, was $364.6 billion as of October 1998, while the volume of U.S.-listed ADR trading was $536 billion during 1998.[38]

The availability of depository receipts could affect domestic liquidity. Domowitz, Glen, and Madhavan show that, for the Mexican stocks available for foreign ownership, firms that listed their depository receipts on

36. A significant part of these placements took place in the first half of 1997.
37. The Bank of New York ADR index includes Japanese stocks, which might bring an upward bias to the estimates of Asia Ex-Japan ADR stock performance.
38. Investment Company Institute; Bank of New York.

U.S. exchanges saw a decrease in liquidity of their shares on their home exchange and an increase in the stock's at-home price volatility.[39] These findings are consistent with the migration of foreign investors to listed depository receipts, which could hinder the maturation of local stock markets. However, issuing new depository receipts can benefit the growth of domestic markets, for example by facilitating large issues. For instance, in Indonesia, the privatization of Telekom would not have been feasible without the participation of foreign investors. Telekom became one of the most frequently traded stocks on the Jakarta Stock Exchange. Further, the healthy competition from the depository receipt market encourages improvement in local stock markets, including harmonization with U.S. and European investing standards.

Private Equities

Private equity funds are typically structured as partnerships specializing in venture capital, leveraged buyouts, and corporate restructuring. The private equity fund mobilizes funds and selects and monitors investments, eventually exiting the investment and repaying the investors. The private equity industry has enjoyed a boom over the past fifteen years; this is reflected in the growth of the value of net assets from a modest $5 billion in 1980 to $150 billion in 1996. Data on developing countries are scant. Comprehensive information on Asian equity funds is available from Asia Pacific Private Equity Bulletin, a Hong Kong organization that tracks Asian private equity. Table 6-13 provides detailed information on private fundraising activity in Asian countries and offshore sources from 1993 to June 1998, including the funds established and the amount of dollars raised. The total amount of funds increased from $2.9 billion in 1993 to $9.4 billion in 1996, coinciding with the growing interest in Asian emerging markets during the period. For all but one of the years covered, more than fifty new funds were established. It is notable that the majority of funds were mobilized in Asian countries, with offshore funding accounting for some 20 percent of total funds.

The best approximation of the actual flow of private equity to a particular country is the amount of investment committed to the country by private equity funds. Table 6-14 provides investments committed to each Asian country by local and foreign equity investors from 1993 to June 1998.

39. Domowitz, Glen, and Madhavan (1998).

Table 6-13. *Asian Private Equity Fund-Raising Activities, 1993–98*
Millions of U.S. dollars

Economy	1993 Amount raised	1993 New funds established	1994 Amount raised	1994 New funds established	1995 Amount raised	1995 New funds established	1996 Amount raised	1996 New funds established	1997 Amount raised	1997 New funds established	1998[a] Amount raised	1998[a] New funds established
Taiwan	155	2	125	1	355	4	510	6	843	4	186	2
Indonesia	100	2	60	1	—		49	2	100	1		
Malaysia	14	1	133	4	170	1	231	8	12	1	12	2
Korea (South)	159	4	494	7	821	10[b]	494	5	330	3	60	2
China	1,617	21	1,723	17	860	7	763	7	230	3	40	2
Other[c]	816	22	2,800	22	3,967	48	4,677	33	4,863	44	3,683	28
Total												
From Asia origins	2,861	52	5,375	53	6,178	61	6,824	62	6,398	57	3,981	36
From offshore[d]	57	1	1,755	6	1,315	7	2,598	4	1,858	2	2,940	8
Grand total	2,918	53	7,130	59	7,493	68	9,421	66	8,256	59	6,921	44

Source: *Asia Pacific Private Equity Bulletin.*
— No fund-raising activity recorded that year.
a. Estimated values based on June data.
b. Estimated number of funds established.
c. Includes Hong Kong, Philippines, Vietnam, Myanmar, New Zealand, India, Australia, Japan, and Singapore.
d. Indicates capital based outside of Asia but seeking private equity investment opportunities in Asia.

Table 6-14. *Amount of Investment Committed by Local and Foreign Private Equity Investors in Asian Countries, 1993–98*
Millions of U.S. dollars

Economy	1993	1994	1995	1996	1997	1998[a]
China	423.11	764.45	906.95	911.80	462.05	67.20
Indonesia	57.77	122.62	172.72	130.85	174.10	n.a.
Korea,						
Republic of	184.20	199.60	338.90	393.60	435.20	832.60
Malaysia	9.31	50.07	69.70	102.28	80.64	12.00
Taiwan (China)	44.60	97.55	173.98	217.32	336.92	20.00
Thailand	28.00	25.00	21.10	32.10	59.36	16.60
Other[b]	859.69	1,056.81	1,150.85	1,320.98	1,185.26	998.16
Total	1,606.68	2,316.1	2,834.2	3,108.93	2,733.53	1,946.56

Source: *Asia Pacific Private Equity Bulletin.*
n.a. Not available.
a. Projected based on information in June 1998.
b. Includes Hong Kong, Philippines, Vietnam, Myanmar, New Zealand, India, Australia, Japan, and Singapore.

The average private equity committed to the select Asian countries detailed in table 6-12 was $1.3 billion annually from 1993 to 1996, or about one-tenth of the total foreign equity flows. In part, because of the long-term commitment, similar in nature to foreign direct investment, private equity flows were stable during the crisis. The total amount of committed private equity for the countries studied was $1.24 billion in 1997, only about $300 million below the level of committed equity in 1996. Similar evidence is reflected in fund mobilization activities. In the aftermath of the crisis, $6.9 billion was raised in 1998, with increased participation of offshore funds. The impact of the crisis on Asian private equity flows might be reflected in the motivations to invest. Prior to the crisis, infrastructure opportunities attracted private equity investment, but the recent surge in private equity appears to reflect opportunities associated with corporate restructuring.

Conclusions

The findings shed light on foreign investors' participation in emerging markets. The main messages conveyed in the paper are as follows:

—*The components of equity flows.* It is important to adopt a broad view of all the components of foreign portfolio equity flows. International placements and private equities, which are a significant part of foreign portfolio equity, respond to different factors and forces and have shown resiliency in the aftermath of the crisis. Their resiliency has important policy implications.

—*The motivations and asset allocations of foreign portfolio equity.* Three key forces drove foreign participation in Asian equities: geographic diversification, economic fundamentals (and, in particular, the expectation of high corporate growth), and short-term, opportunistic participation. Many foreign investors made long-term commitments to Asia; some had little alternative but to stay after the value of their investment had plummeted. Mutual fund assets dropped significantly during the crisis, but, taking into consideration the dramatic value compression of these assets, there is, in fact, no evidence that mutual funds withdrew from Asia in a significant way.

—*The losses of foreign investors during the crisis.* Equity investments fulfilled the role of equity as a traditional buffer. Foreign equity investors shouldered their part of the losses associated with the crisis, absorbing the currency devaluation and asset price decline. Mutual funds, in particular, suffered major losses in the crisis, performing worse than local indexes. Hedge funds, however, performed much better than the mutual funds and local investors.

—*Foreign presence in Asian equity markets.* International portfolio's investment share of Asian domestic markets was relatively modest in relation to total market capitalization. A different picture emerges of foreign holdings in relation to "free float." The numbers suggest high and possibly excessive foreign presence and influence on domestic markets. Foreign investors' share of total trading volume in Asian markets was higher than that of local investors, but not disproportionate to ownership. In fact, foreign investors have considerably longer holding periods, in line with the role of "strong hands" institutional investors. The data offer prima facie evidence, arguing strongly for development of a base of domestic institutional investors.

—*Momentum trading (trend chasing) and market leading.* In measuring the impact of foreign investors on local markets, we find no evidence of foreign momentum trading (trend chasing), but we do find evidence that foreign investors led the markets. The latter finding, however, can be subject to different interpretations. We cannot conclude that foreign investors destabilized these markets.

—*International diversification.* The virtues of international investment are being reassessed in the wake of the crisis. The poor performance of emerging markets has been disappointing. Coupled with the evidence of higher-than-expected correlations between developed and emerging markets in the recent downturns, investors are reappraising the wisdom of investing in emerging markets.

Policy Perspective

Foreign participation in corporate financial restructuring is inevitable given the staggering costs of recapitalization. In many Asian countries the prospective role of the banking sector has been profoundly diminished. Banks that "survived" either are unable to lend or are reluctant to do so. Although recapitalization of the banking and corporate sectors is essential to the resumption of long-term growth, it has to be accompanied by deleveraging of corporate balance sheets. A recent study by Jardine Fleming estimates the net debt-to-equity ratio for the top twenty listed companies in each of these countries to be 590 percent in Indonesia, 64 percent in the Philippines, and 230 percent in Thailand.[40] It estimates that reducing the debt-to-equity ratio of the top sixty listed companies in these countries to 60 percent would require $31.7 billion in asset sales, debt-for-equity swaps, debt forgiveness, and new capital. New equity mobilization is needed as part of the recapitalization.

The recapitalization of the banking sectors is the twin challenge.[41] Although governments can be expected to finance part of these costs, much of the funds needed are equity.

What are the prospects for portfolio equity flows? Against this murky background, which is hindering renewed commitments of foreign investors to Asia, there is a broader reassessment of the rationale for investing in emerging markets. In addition to massive losses, returns in the world's stock markets have become more highly correlated over time (particularly at times of high share price volatility). Many fund management

---

40. Jardine Fleming (1998).

41. The costs will depend on the volume of nonperforming loans, the recovery rate banks achieve on their bad debt, and domestic interest rates.

organizations have been discredited, investment banks have retrenched, and some market participants have withdrawn from emerging markets. Nonetheless, most observers agree that investment in emerging markets is likely to resume in the medium term, especially when growth resumes, the restructuring process accelerates, and a stronger sense emerges that risk is properly understood and priced. The reality is that emerging markets are an important part of the world economy that international investors simply cannot ignore. It is likely, however, that "top down" and "bottom up" investment analysis will become complementary, accompanied by a greater measure of selectivity.

What can the Asian countries and international organizations do to restore confidence, given that foreign participation is essential?

The Asian financial crisis and the economic turmoil in Russia and Brazil highlighted the need to reassess whether global financial arrangements can cope with today's circumstances. Although governments, international organizations, and academics have advanced ambitious blueprints and frameworks for overhauling the system, the growing consensus is that plans to undertake a major redesign of the global financial system, including the introduction of a global supervisor and a global central bank, are overly ambitious. Recent discussions of the architecture emphasize modest and realistic domestic agendas supported by international principles. For example, Eichengreen's recommendations, building on the G-22 principles, favor the implementation of domestic institutional reforms and international guidelines.[42] This involves better regulation and supervision, improved disclosure based on generally accepted auditing and accounting practices, stronger creditor rights, passage of investor protection laws, and adoption of fair and expeditious corporate bankruptcy procedures. These reforms can build on the work done by the Basle Committee on Banking Supervision (core principles of bank supervision), the International Organization of Securities Commissions (principles for regulating the securities markets), the International Bar Association (model bankruptcy), and the International Accounting Standards Committee (international accounting standards). In a practical program of "robust incrementalism," Eichengreen correctly emphasizes the importance of incentives to encourage effective implementation. Notably, in the area of access to foreign capital, where excessive risk has clearly been taken on, he

---

42. Eichengreen (1999).

suggests ways of making access conditional on compliance with international standards; he does not rule out flexible tax schemes to encourage long-term finance.

Asia's economic development was funded by channeling household savings from banks to corporations. It led to a highly leveraged financial structure, with high ratios of bank liabilities to gross domestic product. Excessive domestic bank debt was supplemented by excessive short-term foreign borrowings. With the benefit of hindsight, we now know that Asia depended too much on the banking sector and too little on capital markets, which led to deficient resource mobilization and allocation as well as systemic risk. Bond and equity markets in Asia lacked depth and breadth, risk-pricing discipline, regulatory and supervisory effectiveness, and the institutional capacity to be a reliable source of funds.[43] The lack of an equity buffer amplified the magnitude of the crisis, as leveraged corporations transmitted financial vulnerabilities to the real sector. In the longer term, a financial system should be developed in which equity plays a greater role. Capital markets can enhance effective resource mobilization and allocation through improved risk pricing and market signaling. Capital markets are also essential mechanisms for managing risk and conducting monetary policy, and they constitute a "delivery mechanism" for a host of other development objectives, such as pension reform, housing finance, corporate restructuring, and municipal finance. In the past year a second-generation agenda for developing capital markets has been articulated that incorporates key priorities, including the development of bond markets, domestic institutional investors, and strong self-regulatory organizations with the institutional capacity and incentives to oversee market development and regulate corporations.

Future Research Agenda

We have endeavored to present a panoramic overview of foreign equity flows. Clearly, a great deal of detailed analytical work needs to be done in order to deepen our understanding of emerging markets. In particular, the effects of depository receipts on domestic markets and the trading activities of international investors warrant research. Also, the increasing role of private equity merits substantial attention.

43. See chapter 4, Pomerleano and Zhang.

References

Asia Pacific Private Equity Bulletin. Various years. Asia Pacific Communications. Hong Kong.

Bank for International Settlements. 1998. *68th Annual Report.* Basle (June).

Brennan, Michael J., and H. Henry Cao. 1997. "International Portfolio Investment Flows." *Journal of Finance* 52 (December): 1851–80.

Brown, Stephen J., William N. Goetzmann, and James Park. 1998. "Hedge Funds and the Asian Currency Crisis of 1997." NBER Working Paper 6427. Cambridge, Mass.: National Bureau of Economic Research (February).

Choe, Hyuk, Bong-Chan Kho, and Rene M. Stulz. 1998. "Do Foreign Investors Destabilize Stock Markets? The Korean Experience in 1997." NBER Working Paper 6661. National Bureau of Economic Research (July).

Claessens, Stijn, Simeon Djankov, and Larry H. P. Lang. 1999. "Who Controls East Asian Corporations?" Working Paper 2054. Washington, D.C.: World Bank, Policy Research Department (February).

De Long, J. Bradford, Andrei Shleifer, Lawrence H. Summers, and Robert J. Waldmann. 1990. "Noise Trader Risk in Financial Markets." *Journal of Political Economy* 98 (August): 703–38.

Domowitz, Ian, Jack Glen, and Ananth Madhavan. 1998. "International Cross-Listing and Order Flow Migration: Evidence from an Emerging Market." *Journal of Finance* 53 (December): 2001–27.

Edwards, Franklin R., and Xin Zhang. 1998. "Mutual Funds and Stock and Bond Market Stability." *Journal of Financial Services Research* (June): 257–82.

Eichengreen, Barry. 1999. "Toward a New International Financial Architecture: A Practical Post-Asia Agenda." Washington, D.C.: Institute for International Economics (February).

Eichengreen, Barry, and Donald Mathieson. 1998. *Hedge Funds and Financial Market Dynamics.* Occasional Paper 166. Washington, D.C.: International Monetary Fund.

Froot, Kenneth A., Paul G. J. O'Connell, and Mark S. Seasholes. 1998. "The Portfolio Flows of International Investors, I." NBER Working Paper 6687. Cambridge, Mass.: National Bureau of Economic Research (August).

Institute of International Finance. 1999. "Report of the Working Group on Financial Crises in Emerging Market Economies." Washington, D.C. (January).

Jardine Fleming Research. 1998. "Deleveraging Asean-3." Hong Kong (August).

Patel, Sandeep, Asani Sarkar, and Zhenyu Wang. 1999. "Assessing the Impact of Short-Sale Constraints on the Gains from International Diversification." Working Paper. Columbia University.

Pomerleano, Michael. 1998. "The East Asia Crisis and Corporate Finances: The Untold Microeconomic Story." *Emerging Markets Quarterly* 2 (Winter): 14–27.

Radelet, Steven, and Jeffrey Sachs. 1998. "The Onset of the East Asian Financial Crisis." Working Paper. Harvard Institute for International Development (March).

Tesar, Linda L., and Ingrid M. Werner. 1998. "The Internationalization of Securities Markets since the 1987 Crash." In *Brookings-Wharton Papers on Financial Services: 1998,* edited by Robert E. Litan and Anthony M. Santomero, 281–349. Washington, D.C.: Brookings Institution.

World Bank. 1998. *Global Development Finance Report 1998.* Washington, D.C.

IAN H. GIDDY

7

Global Capital Markets: What Do They Mean?

THIS PAPER LOOKS at the integration of the global capital market, emphasizing equity market linkages between developed stock markets and emerging markets and taking a closer look at one mechanism for such linkages: American depository receipts.

The background to this paper is the crisis of capital flows, both inward and outward, experienced by developing countries following the financial market crisis that began in 1997 with the devaluation of the Thai baht. To some extent the surge in capital flows and their sudden reversal can be attributed to policy changes and institutional developments designed to ease international investors' access to the higher yields, capital gains, and diversification opportunities afforded by the emerging markets.

The Three Segments of the Global Capital Market

This paper is primarily concerned with the integration of global markets for equity. The path that equity markets have taken in becoming global differs from that of credit or debt markets in a fundamental way often overlooked by economists. Debt markets have evolved offshore, often driven there by banking regulations, credit allocation, and taxes. International equity investors and issuers have, in contrast, gravitated to well-developed domestic markets characterized by liquidity and high standards of trading, corporate governance, and disclosure. To clarify this, I distinguish between "bond" and "banking" channels. In direct financing (bonds), the saver is confronted directly with the credit risk of the issuer, while in financial intermediation (banks), a financial institution interjects itself between users and providers of funds.

The second categorization (domestic, foreign, and "Euro" or external) concerns the location, or *jurisdiction*, where funds are exchanged. Normally, saving-investment transfers take place in a nation's domestic financial market. However, most financial markets have links abroad: domestic investors purchase foreign securities, and domestic banks make loans to foreign residents. Similarly, foreign residents may issue securities or deposit funds with domestic banks. These are the traditional forms of international financial transactions.

Before the existence of the Euro-markets, all international finance was of this kind. The key feature of traditional foreign lending and borrowing is that all transactions are directly subject to the rules, usances, and institutional arrangements of the national markets involved.

Enter the Euro-markets, the forum for much of the development of the global capital market in the late twentieth century. During the past twenty-five years, market mechanisms have developed that remove international (and even national) borrowing and lending from the jurisdiction and influence of national authorities. This is done simply by locating the market for credit denominated in a particular currency *outside* the country of that currency. The markets for dollar-denominated loans, deposits, and bonds in Europe, for example, are not subject to U.S. banking or securities regulations. I refer to these markets as "Euro," or more properly "external," to indicate that they are distinct from the domestic or national financial systems. The essence of this classification criterion is the absence (or presence) and the nature of regulation. Differences in interest rates, practices, and terms that exist between domestic and external markets arise primarily from the extent to which regulatory constraints can be avoided.

Why No Euro-Equity Markets?

All the major stock exchanges are primarily local markets, deriving the great bulk of their turnover from intracountry trading. As markets grow and barriers fall, however, the national markets are gradually being integrated into a fledgling global stock market. There certainly is sufficient cross-border buying and selling to warrant calling this an international market for stocks. For the most part, however, international trading goes on in the same manner as domestic trading. For example, a Dutch mutual fund buys and sells General Motors stock on the New York Stock Exchange just as an American fund would do. To clear transactions more conveniently and avoid the costs of currency exchange and the inconvenience of time zone differences, it would be more desirable to have a single market for all the world's actively traded stock. London's International Stock Exchange is presently the closest thing to such an exchange.

An alternative vehicle for the internationalization of domestic stocks is multiple listings.[1] Shares of Sony, Nestlé, and IBM, for example, are listed and traded in New York, Tokyo, London, Paris, and several other exchanges. Such listing does make it easier for domestic residents to buy foreign stocks on their home exchanges, but it suffers from two disadvantages. First, it is costly. A Japanese firm wishing to list in the United States, for example, must satisfy the requirements of the Securities and Exchange Commission (SEC) as well as those of the exchange on which the stock is listed. Such requirements include recalculating all the published accounts according to U.S. generally accepted accounting principles (GAAP) and translating them into English. The second disadvantage is that some multiple listings have turned out to be cosmetic: the bulk of trading in a particular stock is likely to be concentrated in one or two markets, for the obvious reason that buyers and sellers gravitate to the market with good liquidity. Some argue that the value of multiple listings is moot.

So why not Euro-equities? This term refers to shares that are in part issued outside their home country and that resemble Eurobonds in that they are distributed worldwide through a multinational syndicate of banks to achieve better worldwide distribution. The international portion would not be subject to regulation by the SEC or any other national body, except the International Securities Dealers Association, a self-regulatory organization. Almost all such issues, however, have a domestic as well as an international tranche, so the issuing company saves little in the way of disclosure requirements or regulatory constraints. And beyond the initial issue, the stocks tend to find their way back to their home market. This is not surprising, for to be true equity they must carry the same rights as domestic stock and to ensure liquidity they must be fungible with domestic stock.

1. A stock is "listed" on a particular exchange when its shares are traded there, and listed foreign shares must be in full compliance with the requirements of domestic companies. In the United States, this means registration with the Securities and Exchange Commission.

Effectively, therefore, Euro-equities cannot be distinguished from domestic shares, and there is no distinct Euro secondary market for equities. They trade over the counter or on the issuing companies' domestic stock exchanges.

Role of Domestic Securities Markets

Most companies in emerging markets are listed only on their domestic exchange. This means that, to invest in them, individuals must employ a mutual fund or unit trust or purchase shares directly on the local exchange. The latter can be troublesome. If you want to buy shares of Samsung Electronics (Korea), you must first find a broker who has, or will find, a contact broker on the Korean Exchange in Seoul, exchange dollars for Korean won, decipher the Korean language and accounting standards, deal with dividends received in Korean won, and, when you decide to sell, convert the proceeds back to U.S. dollars.

Equity Market Integration: The Alternatives

Much of the disruption in the flow of capital to emerging markets has been attributed to bank lending and fixed-income investment. Excessive corporate leverage, debt issues that failed to match the timing or currency of the cash flows they were financing, and financial institutions that relied on guarantees and collateral rather than on sound business reasoning led to overlending and inflated asset prices. Sooner or later, these would lead to rapidly falling securities prices, loan defaults, and a pullback.

Equity investments, in contrast, are not guaranteed and demand fundamental analysis on the part of the investor. Since the failure to meet a dividend does not trigger a default, the growth of equity investments in the 1990s has been heralded as a more stable, long-term means than debt of financing growing countries. Price volatility, but not flow volatility, is to be expected in equities. This, however, was built on an idealized concept of the information and rights available to equity investors. In retrospect, financial contagion in equity markets has been far greater than can be accounted for by bilateral trade links or investment shares.

One reason for equity outflows and contagion lies in the fact that the overwhelming majority of international investment took place through the purchase of shares in domestic markets suffering from inadequate disclosure, trading rules, and corporate governance. The inability of foreign investors to rely on financial statements or a dispassionate community of analysts to differentiate between solid companies and firms whose profitability relies on the coattails of rapid economic growth can result in the problem of adverse selection. When one bubble is pricked, it acts as a wake-up call to euphoric investors who then abandon all companies in the region because they lack reliable information with which to distinguish good from bad.

This equity market contagion effect is likely to create a sharp contrast between the manifestation of equity market correlations under normal circumstances and those of heightened uncertainty about underlying economic valuation. This is expressed below as a hypothesis about extraregional and intraregional equity price correlations.

Role of Foreign Markets in Equity

One way in which informational problems and the concomitant liquidity and volatility issues can be mitigated is by arranging for the emerging market company's shares to be traded on a well-developed exchange with high standards of market practice and disclosure. As noted, when securities issued by nonresident companies are traded in a domestic market, they are termed "foreign" as opposed to domestic or offshore. As a rule, securities issued and traded in London, New York, Tokyo, or one of the other major markets are subject to rules governing accounting methods, disclosure, issuance procedures, and the like, as are domestic issuers. This may set a standard that investors can trust and hence yield more stable investor behavior.

The key feature is that foreign listings, particularly when used to raise new capital, demand different hurdles of disclosure and trading rules from shares owned and traded on many emerging market exchanges.

Foreign Listings and Depository Receipts

There are several ways in which a company from a developing country can attract foreign investors via another country's stock market rather than its own. The simplest is perhaps the depository receipt, which in principle requires no action on the part of the issuer. An ADR, or American depository receipt, is a negotiable instrument that represents ownership in securities of a non-U.S. company. ADRs enable investors to invest in non-U.S.

securities without having to worry about the complex details of cross-border transactions; they offer the same economic benefits enjoyed by the domestic shareholders of an ADR issuer. If used to trade existing shares, ADRs may offer benefits to non-U.S. companies, from broadening their potential base of shareholders to increasing their visibility in the U.S. market. Further, ADRs can help such companies raise capital in U.S. markets, allowing them to issue new securities in the United States.

Generally speaking, an ADR is issued by a U.S. commercial bank that functions as the depository.[2] The ADR is backed by a specific number of shares in the non-U.S. company (usually referred to as the "issuer" of the ADR). Each ADR, which comprises a specific number of American depository shares, or ADS's, is transferable on the books of the depository, which greatly simplifies and facilitates trading.[3] This study uses data on ADRs listed on the New York Stock Exchange, but they can be and are listed on other exchanges and may be quoted for trading on the National Association of Securities Dealers Automated Quotation system (NASDAQ), the NASD's over-the-counter market. They can also be privately placed and traded as Rule 144A securities. Finally, the concept of the ADR has been extended to other geographical markets, resulting in structures known as global depository receipts (GDRs), international depository receipts, and European depository receipts, which are generally traded or listed in one or more international markets.

Mechanics of Issuance and Cancellation

A broker-dealer can purchase existing ADRs in the United States or purchase underlying shares in an issuer's home market and have new ADRs created, or issued, by the depository bank. While the pool of available ADRs is constantly changing, the broker-dealer decides whether to purchase existing ADRs or have new ones issued, depending on factors such as availability, pricing, and market conditions in the United States and the issuer's home market. To create new ADRs, underlying shares are deposited with a custodian bank in the issuer's home market. The depository then

2. J. P. Morgan created the first ADR in 1927 to allow Americans to invest in the British retailer Selfridge's.

3. An ADR need not necessarily have a one-to-one correspondence with the underlying stock. ADRs are generally packaged to appeal to the American investor. Thus if shares of a particular foreign stock trade at the equivalent of $5 per share, the bank could package the ADR so that each ADR represents ten shares and trades at $50.

issues ADRs representing those shares. The process for canceling ADRs is similar to the process for issuing them, but the steps are reversed.

Types of International Equity Offerings

Within this framework, emerging market companies can offer equity to international investors through six different mechanisms:[4]

—Issuance on their domestic exchange, while seeking foreign participation in various ways such as by publishing reports in English and other languages. This requires no adaptation to international accounting and disclosure standards beyond what is required by the domestic exchange.

—Issuance on their domestic markets, while sponsoring depository receipts that are unlisted in a foreign market such as the United States when the issuer is not initially seeking to raise capital in the U.S. markets or does not wish to or cannot list its ADRs on an exchange or on NASDAQ. A Level I ADR program offers an easy and relatively inexpensive way for an issuer to gauge interest in its securities and begin building a presence in the U.S. securities markets. Requirements are minimal.[5]

—Issuance on their domestic markets and listing of the ADRs on a major exchange such as the New York Stock Exchange. ADR programs must comply with the full registration and reporting requirements of the SEC's Exchange Act, which entails the following: (1) a Form F-6 registration statement, to register the ADRs to be issued; (2) a Form 20-F registration statement, which contains detailed financial disclosure about the issuer, including financial statements and a reconciliation of those statements to U.S. GAAPs, to register the listing of the ADRs; (3) annual reports and any interim financial statements submitted on a regular, timely basis to the SEC.

—New issuance, through a public offering, of shares in the United States (for example) and a listing on a major exchange. This involves the same requirements as the previous form of ADRs. In addition, Form F-1

---

4. Although most new ADR programs are sponsored—that is, done with the collaboration of the company—many unsponsored programs (in which the ADRs are created and offered to investors without a company's active participation) still exist. In general, only sponsored ADRs can be listed on the major stock exchanges or be quoted under the NASDAQ system.

5. In the United States, the issuer seeks exemption from the SEC's traditional reporting requirements under Rule 12g3-2(b). With that exemption, the company agrees to send to the SEC summaries or copies of any public reporting documents required in its home market (including documents for regulatory agencies, stock exchanges, or direct shareholder communications). The depository, working with the issuer, also files the Form F-6 registration statement with the SEC in order to establish the program.

is required to register the equity securities underlying the ADRs that are offered publicly in the United States for the first time, including a prospectus to inform potential investors about the company and the risks inherent in its businesses, the offering price for the securities, and the plan for distributing the shares.

—New issuance, through a private placement of depository receipts, of shares in a major market. In the United States this would be done under Rule 144A, which permits the sale of unregistered foreign securities to qualified institutional investors.[6]

—A global offering employing GDRs, which allow issuers to raise capital in two or more markets simultaneously, thus broadening their base of shareholders. They can be settled outside the United States (using the two major European clearance and settlement facilities, Euroclear and Cedel, linked with the major U.S. clearance and settlement facility, the Depository Trust Company), and they can be traded in the Rule 144A private market. Under SEC Regulation S, securities offered or sold to investors outside the United States are not subject to SEC registration requirements.

Table 7-1 lays out some of the differences between the different forms of international listings. These forms not only offer a convenience but also set higher standards for disclosure and accounting, which means that one would expect greater liquidity (as measured by trading volume) for such shares, even after a crisis such as the recent one, than for the home market as a whole. This supposition is expressed as a hypothesis in the following section.

Hypotheses

The purpose of this paper is to consider the linkages among equity markets of certain developing countries before and after the financial market crisis in Asia began and to ascertain the role that depository receipts as a mechanism for global capital market integration may play. The hypotheses are as follows:

—In normal times, there is a stronger correlation between share prices in emerging markets and developed markets than among emerging markets.

---

6. Rule 144A facilitates the trading of privately placed securities by sophisticated institutional investors (also known as qualified institutional buyers, who must own or manage at least $100 million in securities). Such offerings do not require SEC review.

—In the event of a crisis, there is a spillover effect between emerging markets seen as suffering from similar problems or otherwise linked; hence the correlations among emerging markets tend to increase.

—Post-crisis correlations among emerging markets are stronger within regions than between regions.

—As measured by the relative influence of home-market and host-market factors, ADRs offer investors a good way to participate in emerging markets.

—As measured by pre- and post-crisis trading volume, ADRs offer international investors greater transparency and liquidity than do domestically traded shares and hence should be more stable at times of crisis.

Equity Market Linkages: The Evidence

The hypotheses are evaluated using data from the New York Stock Exchange and the emerging markets database of the International Finance Corporation (IFC). The data include month-end prices of stocks traded in several Latin American and Asian stock exchanges and the corresponding ADRs traded on the New York Stock Exchange. I also use the IFC's investable index, an index of emerging market stock prices that takes into account restrictions on foreign investors. To represent the U.S. market, I use the S&P 500 index. To assess trading volume, I use the value of shares traded for individual stocks and for the market as a whole.

Emerging Equity Market Correlations before and after the Asian Crisis

Tables 7-2 through 7-4 provide correlation matrixes measuring the linkages between the U.S. market and selected emerging markets of Latin America and Asia and among the emerging markets themselves for the period 1990–98. At the bottom of each table are some summary statistics.

First, the increasingly open character of most emerging markets and the strong interest from investors in developed countries suggests a stronger correlation between the emerging markets and the U.S. market than among the emerging markets themselves. For the whole period examined (table 7-2), the evidence is mixed. The average correlation between the S&P 500 index and fourteen emerging markets is only 8.06 percent. The S&P 500 correlation with Latin American markets,

Table 7-1. *Forms of International Equity Offerings*

Form	Use of existing shares to broaden shareholder base			Use of ADRs to raise capital	
	Level I	*Level II*	*Public offering, level III*	*Private placement, Rule 144a (ADR)*	*Global offering (GDR)*
Description	Unlisted program in the United States	Listed on a U.S. exchange	Shares offered and listed on a U.S. exchange	Private placement to qualified institutional buyers	Global offering of securities outside issuer's home market
Trading	Over the counter	Amex, NASDAQ, NYSE[a]	Amex, NASDAQ, NYSE[a]	U.S. private placement market	U.S. exchange and non-U.S. exchanges
SEC registration	Register under Form F-6	Register under Form F-6	Register under Forms F-1 and F-6	None	Varies depending on structure of the U.S. offering
U.S. reporting requirements	Exempt under Rule 12g3-2(b)	Form 20-Fb	Form 20-Fb	Exempt under Rule 12g3-2(b)	Varies depending on structure of the U.S. offering

Source: J. P. Morgan (http://adr.com).
a. Amex, American Exchange; NASDAQ, National Association of Securities Dealers Automated Quotations system; NYSE, New York Stock Exchange.

Table 7-2. *Correlations between Emerging Stock Markets and the United States and between One Another, 1990–98*

Economy	S&P 500	Argentina	Brazil	Chile	Colombia	Mexico	Peru	Venezuela	China	Indonesia	Korea	Malaysia	Philippines	Taiwan (China)	Thailand
S&P 500	1.000														
Argentina	0.651	1.000													
Brazil	0.766	0.849	1.000												
Chile	0.437	0.773	0.822	1.000											
Colombia	0.294	0.678	0.759	0.836	1.000										
Mexico	0.183	0.732	0.475	0.482	0.457	1.000									
Peru	0.507	0.677	0.880	0.727	0.500	-0.156	1.000								
Venezuela	0.171	0.503	0.287	0.181	0.054	0.435	0.454	1.000							
China	-0.710	-0.100	-0.350	-0.098	0.139	0.626	-0.453	0.181	1.000						
Indonesia	0.371	0.048	0.162	0.448	0.403	0.065	0.242	-0.072	0.425	1.000					
Korea	-0.745	-0.315	-0.228	0.444	0.311	0.128	-0.159	-0.304	0.497	0.739	1.000				
Malaysia	-0.116	0.346	0.404	0.670	0.546	0.294	0.200	-0.062	0.391	0.897	0.744	1.000			
Philippines	0.041	0.495	0.527	0.787	0.609	0.412	0.242	-0.093	0.299	0.755	0.754	0.941	1.000		
Taiwan (China)	0.465	0.609	0.802	0.655	0.637	0.201	0.712	0.244	-0.115	0.328	-0.025	0.383	0.434	1.000	
Thailand	-0.446	0.052	0.026	0.464	0.367	0.258	-0.197	-0.309	0.471	0.710	0.950	0.795	0.795	0.001	1.000
Average	0.0806														
Latin America					0.543										
Asia												0.564			

Table 7-3. *Correlations between Emerging Stock Markets and the United States and between One Another before the Crisis, 1990–96*

Economy	S&P 500	Argentina	Brazil	Chile	Colombia	Mexico	Peru	Venezuela	China	Indonesia	Korea	Malaysia	Philippines	Taiwan (China)	Thailand
S&P 500	1.000														
Argentina	0.637	1.000													
Brazil	0.818	0.773	1.000												
Chile	0.772	0.780	0.923	1.000											
Colombia	0.444	0.640	0.816	0.819	1.000										
Mexico	0.173	0.769	0.470	0.442	0.414	1.000									
Peru	0.786	0.438	0.850	0.838	0.376	-0.373	1.000								
Venezuela	-0.061	0.375	-0.052	-0.018	-0.301	0.354	-0.130	1.000							
China	-0.734	0.012	-0.566	-0.630	-0.159	0.731	-0.775	0.335	1.000						
Indonesia	0.693	0.362	0.727	0.612	0.629	0.086	0.767	-0.443	-0.448	1.000					
Korea	0.166	0.206	0.639	0.742	0.727	0.145	0.372	-0.498	-0.168	0.559	1.000				
Malaysia	0.842	0.689	0.922	0.855	0.792	0.423	0.785	-0.186	-0.463	0.842	0.601	1.000			
Philippines	0.780	0.745	0.933	0.894	0.886	0.494	0.774	-0.168	-0.382	0.769	0.664	0.962	1.000		
Taiwan (China)	0.435	0.378	0.696	0.622	0.571	0.112	0.582	-0.154	-0.317	0.607	0.519	0.631	0.654	1.000	
Thailand	0.583	0.621	0.825	0.837	0.839	0.497	0.419	-0.277	-0.088	0.717	0.887	0.876	0.905	0.523	1.000
Average	0.453														
Latin America					0.438										
Asia										0.510					

Table 7-4. *Correlations between Emerging Stock Markets and the United States and with One Another after the Crisis, 1996–98*

Economy	S&P 500	Argentina	Brazil	Chile	Colombia	Mexico	Peru	Venezuela	China	Indonesia	Korea	Malaysia	Philippines	Taiwan (China)	Thailand
S&P 500	1.000														
Argentina	-0.366	1.000													
Brazil	-0.455	0.946	1.000												
Chile	-0.661	0.894	0.913	1.000											
Colombia	-0.661	0.843	0.845	0.924	1.000										
Mexico	-0.176	0.909	0.827	0.718	0.777	1.000									
Peru	-0.613	0.872	0.934	0.937	0.920	0.743	1.000								
Venezuela	-0.504	0.876	0.827	0.890	0.924	0.861	0.818	1.000							
China	-0.726	0.801	0.801	0.945	0.871	0.610	0.844	0.847	1.000						
Indonesia	-0.839	0.534	0.628	0.823	0.679	0.249	0.712	0.569	0.821	1.000					
Korea	-0.705	0.563	0.618	0.810	0.649	0.256	0.659	0.585	0.846	0.934	1.000				
Malaysia	-0.822	0.489	0.581	0.757	0.600	0.185	0.656	0.467	0.759	0.972	0.903	1.000			
Philippines	-0.760	0.460	0.537	0.706	0.333	0.153	0.611	0.402	0.687	0.936	0.863	0.985	1.000		
Taiwan (China)	-0.606	0.855	0.866	0.921	0.782	0.625	0.805	0.791	0.926	0.791	0.835	0.767	0.720	1.000	
Thailand	-0.790	0.446	0.518	0.695	0.530	0.133	0.576	0.397	0.710	0.940	0.886	0.984	0.982	0.735	1.000
Average	-0.620														
Latin America								0.866							
Asia														0.865	

averaging 43.0 percent, is much greater than that with Asian markets (average negative 26.9 percent). This is evidence against a presumption of global lockstep integration.

The shaded areas in the correlation tables encompass regional linkages. The intraregional correlations are stronger than expected, averaging 54 percent for Latin America and 56 percent for Asia for the whole 1990–96 period.

Of course the 1990–96 period spans two very different economic environments. What of the hypothesis that the correlation pattern would shift after the onset of the 1997 Asian crisis? The evidence in table 7-3 and 7-4 indeed confirms the notion that the crisis resulted in much higher intraregional corrlations while diminishing those between the emerging markets and the U.S. market. For the pre-crisis 1990–96 period, the market's average correlations with one another are more or less in line with their linkages with the United States. After 1996, however, a sharp divergence occurs. Latin America's markets become highly correlated with one another (average correlation coefficients of 86.6 percent), as do Asia's (average 86.5 percent correlations). But all the markets demonstrate negative correlations with the United States. It is evident that in one respect, at least, the regional capital markets, not the global capital market, are integrated. In an atmosphere of crisis, their stock markets influence one another or are subject to the same influences.

Role of Depository Receipts before and after the Asian Crisis

In this paper I have argued that depository receipts both facilitate integration and may raise the standards of trading practice and disclosure. I looked at two kinds of evidence: price linkages and liquidity as measured by relative trading activity. The results are presented in appendix tables 7A-1 through 7A-8.

First, if ADRs do provide a good mechanism for foreign investors to participate in a domestic market, the ADR's price should be determined by the value of the underlying stocks and the home market rather than by the host market (the U.S. stock market). To test this, I regressed the ADR's price against the same company's domestic stock price, an index of home-market stock prices (the IFC's investable index), and a U.S. stock market index (again, the S&P 500). I did this for eight emerging markets that have ADRs with a reasonably long history of trading on the New York

Stock Exchange.[7] For each country I selected one actively traded ADR to include in the results shown here.

The regression results clearly show that ADR prices, as one would expect, are driven by the price at which the company's stock trades back home. In all cases the t-statistic shows the local price of the share to have a significant coefficient. The local market index and the S&P 500 index have a much smaller effect on the price. Thus the ADR does seem to be a good means of participating in the performance of a foreign stock.

Finally, I have argued that ADRs offer international investors greater transparency and liquidity than do domestically traded shares and hence should be more stable at times of crisis. In reality, the evidence does not support this conclusion. I measured the dollar value of trading in the United States (that is, in ADRs) and the value of trading in the same stock in its home market, both expressed as a percentage of the local market trading (based on shares in the IFC's investable index). The percentage change in this ratio from before to after the start of the crisis period in 1997 is taken as an indicator of the relative robustness of liquidity. In four cases (Chile, Colombia, Peru, and Indonesia) the ADR's trading volume increases or falls less than the local market's; in two cases (Argentina and Brazil) the local market seems more robust; and in two the difference is insignificant (Korea and the Philippines). More work needs be done to discover whether ADRs truly help a stock to retain liquidity amidst market turmoil.

Conclusions

This paper has analyzed five dimensions of the global capital market and its role in times of international financial market strain. On the fixed-income side, issuance and investment can take place in domestic markets, foreign markets, and external (or "Euro") markets. Since no external market of significance can exist for equities, they are issued and trade in their domestic markets or on a major exchange abroad. I have argued that domestic emerging markets and the companies that issue exclusively there may fall short of

7. The analysis was performed on thirty-six stocks, but many of them have a relatively short life. The ADR as a means of raising new capital for emerging market companies is a comparatively new phenomenon, with a large number of issues having been done shortly before the 1997 crisis; hence they do not yet have a sufficient history from which to draw conclusions.

ideal standards of transparency and corporate governance and hence are vulnerable to contagion in times of stress. The evidence bears this out.

I also have argued that ADRs and other variations of proxy markets can serve an important role in integrating capital markets in a robust way. Companies that choose to list on a major foreign stock exchange, even if they do so through ADRs rather than seek a full new-issuance listing, must comply with more stringent standards, scrutiny by analysts, and trading rules. This might offer investors as good a participation in emerging market companies as investing directly and perhaps offer more liquidity. The evidence supported the first hypothesis but was ambiguous on the liquidity effect.

Appendix A. American Depository Receipts for Selected Emerging Markets

Table 7A-1. *ADR Analysis for YPF, Argentina*

Type of analysis	Local shares	ADRs	Value	df	SS	MS	Coefficient	Standard error	t-statistic
Liquidity analysis[a]									
Before 1997	0.076	0.046							
After 1997	0.197	0.018							
Change	1.587	-0.622							
Regression analysis									
Regression statistics									
Multiple R			0.998						
R^2			0.997						
Adjusted R^2			0.996						
Standard error			0.321						
Number of observations			65						
Analysis of variance									
Regression				3	1,823.207	607.736			
Residual				61	6.276	0.103			
Total				64	1,829.484				
Independent variable analysis									
Intercept							-3.442	0.225	-15.297
Standard and Poor's 500 Index							0.006	0.000	24.866
Local index							0.001	0.000	2.277
Local price							0.842	0.020	42.604

a. Value of trading, percentage of local market.

Table 7A-2. ADR Analysis for Aracruz, Brazil

Type of analysis	Local shares	ADRs	Value	df	SS	MS	Coefficient	Standard error	t-statistic
Liquidity analysis[a]									
Before 1997	0.583	0.001							
After 1997	0.598	0.000							
Change	0.025	–0.707							
Regression analysis									
Regression statistics									
Multiple R			0.863						
R^2			0.746						
Adjusted R^2			0.735						
Standard error			2.209						
Number of observations			76						
Analysis of variance									
Regression				3	1,029.401	343.134			
Residual				72	351.187	4.878			
Total				75	1,380.588				
Independent variable analysis									
Intercept							3.484	1.522	2.289
Standard and Poor's 500 Index							–0.001	0.003	–0.257
Local index							0.064	0.006	11.633
Local price							–154.856	29.670	–5.219

a. Value of trading, percentage of local market.

Table 7A-3. *ADR Analysis for CTC, Chile*

Type of analysis	Local shares	ADRs	Value	df	SS	MS	Coefficient	Standard error	t-statistic
Liquidity analysis[a]									
Before 1997	0.421	0.015							
After 1997	0.208	0.025							
Change	−0.505	0.698							
Regression analysis									
Regression statistics									
Multiple R			0.916						
R^2			0.839						
Adjusted R^2			0.834						
Standard error			2.814						
Number of observations			101						
Analysis of variance									
Regression				3	4,012.1	1,337.373			
Residual				97	768.1	7.918			
Total				100	4,780.2				
Independent variable analysis									
Intercept							−1.131	1.186	−0.954
Standard and Poor's 500 Index							0.012	0.002	5.224
Local index							0.000	0.000	3.000
Local price							14.115	1.464	9.642

a. Value of trading, percentage of local market.

Table 7A-4. *ADR Analysis for Banco Ganadero, Colombia*

Type of analysis	Local shares	ADRs	Value	df	SS	MS	Coefficient	Standard error	t-statistic
Liquidity analysis[a]									
Before 1997	0.150	0.003							
After 1997	0.074	0.005							
Change	−0.507	0.764							
Regression analysis									
Regression statistics									
Multiple R			0.994						
R^2			0.987						
Adjusted R^2			0.986						
Standard error			0.891						
Number of observations			49						
Analysis of variance									
Regression				3	2,752.166	917.389			
Residual				45	35.746	0.794			
Total				48	2,787.912				
Independent variable analysis									
Intercept							−6.854	1.514	−4.526
Standard and Poor's 500 Index							0.007	0.002	4.584
Local index							0.006	0.002	2.379
Local price							82.085	5.217	15.734

a. Value of trading, percentage of local market.

Table 7A-5. *ADR Analysis for Bank Wiese, Peru*

Type of analysis	Local shares	ADRs	Value	df	SS	MS	Coefficient	Standard error	t-statistic
Liquidity analysis[a]									
Before 1997	0.023	0.002							
After 1997	0.014	0.002							
Change	−0.387	0.082							
Regression analysis									
Regression statistics									
Multiple R			0.956						
R^2			0.913						
Adjusted R^2			0.908						
Standard error			0.554						
Number of observations			51						
Analysis of variance									
Regression				3	152.085	50.695			
Residual				47	14.432	0.307			
Total				50	166.517				
Independent variable analysis									
Intercept							4.426	0.670	6.603
Standard and Poor's 500 Index							−0.005	0.000	−9.568
Local index							0.019	0.003	7.413
Local price							0.784	0.091	8.655

a. Value of trading, percentage of local market.

Table 7A-6. *ADR Analysis for Indosat, Indonesia*

Type of analysis	Local shares	ADRs	Value	df	SS	MS	Coefficient	Standard error	t-statistic
Liquidity analysis[a]									
Before 1997	0.057	0.004							
After 1997	0.028	0.002							
Change	−0.507	−0.374							
Regression analysis									
Regression statistics									
Multiple R			0.999						
R^2			0.997						
Adjusted R^2			0.997						
Standard error			0.523						
Number of observations			49						
Analysis of variance									
Regression				3	4,154.10	1,384.70			
Residual				45	12.32	0.27			
Total				48	4,166.42				
Independent variable analysis									
Intercept							−2.739	1.159	−2.365
Standard and Poor's 500 Index							0.002	0.001	2.921
Local index							0.004	0.004	1.182
Local price							9.986	0.256	39.035

a. Value of trading, percentage of local market.

Table 7A-7. ADR Analysis for Kepco, Korea

Type of analysis	Local shares	ADRs	Value	df	SS	MS	Coefficient	Standard error	t-statistic
Liquidity analysis[a]									
Before 1997	0.078	0.001							
After 1997	0.054	0.001							
Change	−0.306	−0.397							
Regression analysis									
Regression statistics									
Multiple R			0.965						
R^2			0.931						
Adjusted R^2			0.926						
Standard error			1.525						
Number of observations			51						
Analysis of variance									
Regression				3	1,465.44	488.48			
Residual				47	109.36	2.33			
Total				50	1,574.80				
Independent variable analysis									
Intercept							−1.158	3.321	−0.349
Standard and Poor's 500 Index							0.002	0.003	0.867
Local index							−0.010	0.025	−0.397
Local price							0.621	0.072	8.625

a. Value of trading, percentage of local market.

Table 7A-8. *ADR Analysis for PLDT, Philippines*

Type of analysis	Local shares	ADRs	Value	df	SS	MS	Coefficient	Standard error	t-statistic
Liquidity analysis[a]									
Before 1997	0.153	0.006							
After 1997	0.144	0.005							
Change	−0.062	−0.128							
Regression analysis									
Regression statistics									
Multiple R			0.974						
R^2			0.948						
Adjusted R^2			0.947						
Standard error			2.118						
Number of observations			107						
Analysis of variance									
Regression				3	8,455.50	2,818.50			
Residual				103	462.07	4.49			
Total				106	8,917.58				
Independent variable analysis									
Intercept							−7.027	0.704	−9.983
Standard and Poor's 500 Index							0.020	0.001	22.593
Local index							0.005	0.006	0.827
Local price							0.375	0.028	13.551

a. Value of trading, percentage of local market.

JARROD WILCOX **8**

An Investor's Perspective on the Asian Crisis

It was the best of times, it was the worst of times, it was the age of wisdom, it was the age of foolishness, it was the epoch of belief, it was the epoch of incredulity, it was the season of Light, it was the season of Darkness, it was the spring of hope, it was the winter of despair, we had everything before us, we had nothing before us.

CHARLES DICKENS[1]

OVER THE PAST *thirty* years, average living standards have increased very rapidly in East Asia. Over the past *two* years, Asian unemployment has increased, while stock prices and most currencies have declined dramatically. The Asian banking system is generally in shambles. What should we think about all this? Consider South America in the 1970s or, more generally, the United States during three enormous economic depressions in the nineteenth and twentieth centuries. Is this time so very different?

Policy debates around these issues have been vigorous in past months. This is a time of uncertainty regarding long-standing beliefs. One of the assertions put forward is that open capital markets in less-developed

---

1. Dickens (1859).

economies are too much of a good thing. Perhaps stock market and currency speculators are responsible for these economic crises. Perhaps interconnected global markets are simply too unstable for unfettered investment activity. Thus there is a natural interest in the following questions: (1) How were investment decisions in Asia made in the past? (2) How much could problems have been foreseen? (3) Did moral hazard arising from the expectation of an International Monetary Fund (IMF) bailout influence our decisions? and (4) What, if anything, have investors learned from the crisis that has resulted in changes to our investment strategies?

This paper seeks to answer those questions. Although it offers mainly anecdotal evidence and opinion, it does so in a manner that contributes a different and more precise structure to what seems an unfocused debate. My direct experience is with portfolio investing, not policy or economic research. As will be clear, this is an essay, not a scientific study. But investors like myself have a vested interest in being well informed, and global investors are often students of governmental policy as a result.

To better understand the situation, I start with two conceptual building blocks. First is that we will never conquer financial crises without a better common understanding of feedback phenomena. Second, policy analysts will not get very far in understanding the dynamics of markets as long as they insist on viewing investors as homogeneous. The alternative is to separate investors into different types with different dynamic impacts. The next two sections of the paper introduce these two ideas as they affect the impact of portfolio investors on the Asian crisis. Thereafter, I proceed to answer the four questions posed. I close with recommendations for policymakers. Overall, my main conclusion is that the Asian crisis would have occurred even without the actions of global investors because of preexisting instabilities in Asia. However, these market instabilities were aggravated by foreign investors, not so much because of hot money but because of the particular *investment styles* of investors operating in the Asian markets.

Feedback and Asian Financial Oscillations

A fundamental goal of emerging market development is to encourage sustainable economic growth while protecting against setbacks. However, we cannot prevent setbacks without preventing unsustainable run-ups. A supporting goal is to have a financial system that calms and controls rather than aggravates any economic oscillations or setbacks to stable, steady growth. To understand the possible role played by portfolio investors in accentuating instability, we must look at economic and financial systems in terms of feedback structures and relationships. To understand how to control oscillations, we must do more than analyze these systems merely in terms of equilibrium economics.

Basic Feedback Relationships

A feedback loop is a chain of causal events from decision A to B to C and then back to a later version of decision A. A *positive* feedback loop promotes continuing change in the same direction, either further growth or further decay. In contrast, a *negative* loop pulls deviations back from extremes toward equilibrium. If the loop is too strong and operates too slowly, it may overshoot equilibrium, causing oscillation.

Important economic feedback such as occurred in the Asian crisis involves interconnected positive and negative feedback loops. There is a long-term positive economic growth loop that may be disturbed by various negative feedbacks. Complicating the situation, there are also shorter-term positive feedbacks that can act to reinforce the negative loops and their oscillations. If we want to control the system better, the overall goal is (1) to alter the negative feedbacks so that their movement is damped rather than explosive and (2) to break up reinforcing short-term positive feedbacks.[2] The approach is to react quickly without accumulating errors, but to act in moderation.

The long-term compounding of financial and human capital is the basic positive feedback underlying economic growth. It involves higher income, savings, consumption, and eventually the perception of inadequate capacity and then more investment in more capacity. Negative feedbacks modify this process of positive-loop growth. These include external factors such as the negative environmental and social consequences of too-rapid economic growth. But most of the negative feedback potential is internal to the economic system. It arises as excessive capital begins to be deployed less productively, resulting in uneconomic capacity and slower growth. A new cycle of accelerated growth is promoted when the level of capital (relative to need) declines to the point where the capital is more efficiently utilized.

---

2. It is this phenomenon of positive feedback through panic contagion pushing negative feedback loops to extremes within the financial system that seems to have exercised George Soros.

The banking system, stock market, and currency markets can influence the impact of this negative feedback loop, either to calm or to accentuate its natural oscillations. Bankers can accentuate instability: for example, when faced with a broad-based level of prosperity, they can make more and more loans for further expansion of marginal projects. Of course, this reinforcement can operate in the opposite direction as well: faced with pessimism about project quality, bankers can tighten liquidity, with funding going to only the most desperately needed projects. Stock markets can accentuate the oscillations through styles of momentum investing or calm them through a more value-oriented approach.

Destabilizing Feedback Loops in Asia

At this point, it is worthwhile to list briefly some of the *preexisting* destabilizing factors confronting portfolio investors in Asia. As will be seen, speculators' hot money was not the only destabilizing factor.

Economic growth rates of emerging Asian countries exceeded sustainable levels in two basic ways. First, most of the growth was based on increasing inputs—capital, education, and work force participation.[3] When the reservoir of potential additional input began to be used up, growth had to slow. Second, a disproportionate share of incremental capacity was devoted to export industries. Excess capacity quickly developed as developed-country consumer households and governments became saturated with Asian-made consumer goods. The growth phase leading to these two basic imbalances was stimulated by at least three real economic shocks. These were the accelerated introduction of western-style capitalism, a long-term (not hot money) influx of foreign capital, and artificial cheapening of currency based on rigid links to the U.S. dollar during a period when the dollar declined sharply versus the yen.

Thus Asian economies during the pre-crisis period were already unstable and poised for the downward leg of a preexisting strong oscillation. The financial system, unfortunately, did nothing to calm either the upward or the downward legs of the boom and bust cycle. Before I consider the actions of portfolio investors, it should be noted that the banking system contributed very significantly to the oscillation. Banking problems included a lax regulatory environment that allowed poor-quality projects to

3. Krugman (1994).

be financed by favored elite groups, imprudent leveraging, and bank involvement in unhedged foreign currency borrowing.[4]

In sum, under this scenario of feedback relationships, there was ample cause in pre-crisis Asia to support a large boom and bust cycle, which was particularly aggravated by the immaturity of the banking system, even discounting the roles played by the stock and currency markets. Consequently, the meaningful portion of any long-term preventative medicine for future financial crises will be firmly grounded in policies affecting microeconomic structures and the banking system. However, portfolio investors also appeared to have played a destabilizing role, to which we now turn.

How Different Investors Affect Market Stability

How investment flows relate to or help cause periods of financial turmoil depends on the relative populations of different types of investors within the market.[5] Let me sketch the basic argument for this assertion.

Market pricing is embedded within negative feedback loops, defined earlier as the "pulling force" that brings excursions back from extremes toward equilibrium. But remember that negative feedback can, in its equilibrium-seeking nature, encourage oscillation, even extreme oscillation. For instance, if investors expect higher returns, then higher stock prices follow, which, after a delay, reduces future expected returns. There is always some time lag or delay in this loop. This may be months or years for some investors. This lag creates a potential for oscillation.

Harry Markowitz describes the primary objective of investors as maximizing the expected mean return, minus a risk tradeoff. The latter is measured as the expected variance of return times a risk aversion parameter. Let me use this description to build a picture of market pricing. Suppose, for example, that the only investment choices are stocks and cash. The optimal, desired portion of a portfolio invested in stocks can then be calculated as the excess return expected of stocks over cash divided by a risk tradeoff cost. The cost of risk, in turn, is the product of risk aversion strength and the expected stock variance.

4. See Pomerleano (1998).
5. The argument in this and the next sections is taken from results of computer simulations described in Wilcox (1999, chap. 4).

We see that the amplification of any change in expected return will be great if either the perceived risk is small or the aversion to that risk is small. We know, from the characteristics of negative feedback loops, that a more unstable system results from stronger reactions as investors become less concerned about risk (that is, become less risk-averse). Perhaps this is a good enough reason to shudder at any official or academic pronouncement that we are entering a "new era" of reduced risks.

One can follow a change in investors' expected return around the feedback loop to see its effect on prices. Even though the desired portion of the portfolio to be invested in stocks is linear in the difference between expected returns and the interest rate, the resulting impact on prices is highly nonlinear. If the expected return from stocks were to exceed interest costs by a margin that is sufficient to overcome the aversion to the perceived risk, then the fraction of wealth desired in stocks would approach unity (that is, become risk-indifferent). At that point, the equilibrium price of stocks must move toward infinity. Real-world externalities prevent this from happening. But during the delay—when investors adjust to the possibility of lower expected returns because of higher prices—stock prices may rise to extremely high levels. However, if expected returns for stocks are as low as those for cash, the desired stock holding is zero and the equilibrium price is zero. When expected returns are either very high or very low, small changes in expected return result in very large percentage changes in price. As a result, once expected returns and prices are driven to extremes, they become even more volatile.

Market-Amplified Cyclicality: Good Investors and Bad Investors

Conventional financial theory holds that stock, bond, and currency market investors are super-rational, differing only in their risk preferences. But this definition is based on a theoretical convenience that enables easy calculation of an equilibrium point. In reality, there are several investor types. Stock market equilibrium, or conditions approaching it, is attained when there is a balance in the transaction power exerted by these varying investor groups, not when everyone has the same expectation of return.

Investors, depending on their type, can be either fast or slow to recognize changes in economic fundamentals and prices that would affect their expected return. They consequently have different impacts on the stability of the negative feedback loop connecting price and expected return. Also, some destabilizing investors create additional short-term positive feedback on prices because their expectations of returns rise, rather than fall, when stock prices rise.

The occurrence of speculative booms and busts in stock and currency markets is simply a question of feedback stability. Feedback stability, in turn, depends on the relative predominance of the different investor types and the investment decisions they represent. Let us see how this works. For our purpose, the most important investor groups to consider are *analysts, growth investors, momentum investors, index investors,* and *value investors.*

ANALYSTS. In the fable "The Emperor's New Clothes," a small child is the only one willing to tell the emperor that he is naked. That child embodies the spirit of the analyst. Analysts depend on an informational infrastructure for their effectiveness. They earn a return simply by collecting and interpreting information, including current security prices, and then acting on this basis more quickly than the rest of the market. Analysts who do not balance price into their equations, including many fundamental analysts, do not qualify under this definition.

Analysts have no capability to make the system more unstable; rather their impact is the opposite. They should be considered as *good investors* because they reduce the time delays and the accumulation of errors in the basic negative feedback control loop that connects prices and expected returns. The aggregate ability to limit the accumulation of errors in pricing stocks and bonds is clearly weaker for Asian emerging markets, which have fewer information reporting requirements than the developed countries.

GROWTH INVESTORS. Growth investors are similar to analysts in that they respond quickly to changes in information on company sales and earnings prospects. Most who call themselves fundamental analysts act in support of growth investing. Growth investors differ from analysts in that they are very slow to respond to price changes. They continue reacting to improved fundamentals even when prices have already more than compensated. They are not especially destabilizing in themselves, but they add to system instability in the presence of momentum investors who may jump on the price trends thus created.

MOMENTUM INVESTORS. Momentum investors should be considered *bad investors* from the viewpoint of system stability. They exploit the fact that skillful analysts may not be able to deploy enough capital to move prices to the new equilibrium point signaled by new information. This attitude can be healthy, if in moderation. However, having no means themselves to judge when that point has been reached, momentum investors simply buy what has been going up and sell what has been going down, without knowing when to stop. By adding a short-term positive feedback loop to the underlying negative loop connecting price and expected return, they have the potential to profoundly destabilize the markets.

Whether momentum investors actually cause speculative bubbles and market crashes depends on three factors: (1) their relative frequency in the investor population; (2) whether they are opposed, and whether their overshoots are exploited, by value-oriented investors; and (3) whether shocks to the system are so large that they raise structural instability by driving prices to extremes.

This last point is very important and is well known to experienced speculators. The practical implication is that prices can move much further than is expected under normal circumstances. But momentum investors operate under the assumption that future returns are a linear function of past percentage price changes. Because this is not the case—because price volatility tends to explode toward infinity at either very high or very low levels of expected return—the impact of momentum investors is far more destabilizing under big shocks than under small ones.

INDEX INVESTORS.   Index investors simply buy regardless of price or fundamentals. They hope for a free ride on the work done by everyone else in the market to match prices correctly with fundamentals. However, if they invest in capitalization-weighted indexes, their desired fraction of assets to be held in a stock goes up in proportion to its price. This happens regardless of how high that price is or what the fundamentals are. In large numbers they are destabilizing because they validate whatever changes in prices are created by momentum investors.

VALUE INVESTORS.   The strongly destabilizing effects of momentum investors, reinforced by excessive proportions of growth and of capitalization-weighted index investors, would overcome price discipline in stock markets, except for the influence of value investors. These market participants are the inverse of growth investors. They can be defined as those investors very quick to respond to price changes but slow to react to news of changes in fundamentals. Obviously, this is not good in isolation because it biases away from accuracy. However, in the context of momentum investors, perhaps aggravated by a surplus of growth and index investors, value investors are *good investors* for system stability. They exploit the excesses created when prices move far from equilibrium. If there are enough value investors, prices will adjust to changes in fundamentals in a heavily damped manner, rather than continue to overshoot in an explosive fashion.

Implications for Policy

The implication of this second conceptual building block for analyzing policy is that the impact of investors on the Asian crisis should be analyzed in terms of separate investor types. In answering the questions noted earlier about investor behavior, I argue that the profile of the global investor population attracted to developing markets in East Asia has been tilted toward decision styles that promote instability. Immature Asian markets are made more unstable through a surplus of momentum, growth, and capitalization-weighted index investors and a dearth of analysts and value-oriented investors. Market evolution toward greater diversity of style and therefore greater stability may be either retarded or accelerated through policy decisions.

How Investment Decisions Were Made

This section focuses on the decisionmaking process of global investors, particularly U.S. investors.

The Influx of Global Investors

The sizable influx of global investors to Asia's emerging markets resulted primarily from the growth in institutional investors who had expectations of higher returns, based on past experience and plausible growth scenarios, and a desire to diversify their portfolios.

As is well known, institutional investors—mutual funds, pension funds, insurance companies—had been growing rapidly for decades and were better able than individuals to reach out and invest in international markets.[6]

---

6. For a useful summary of the growth of asset management and its impact, see Bank for International Settlements (1998, chap. 5).

Moreover, corporate pension funds were heavily influenced by an investment consultant industry that tends to encourage (as a means of livelihood) new fashions in investment management. International diversification was just one such innovation.

Beyond these, there were strong inducements to invest in international stocks. In the mid-1980s, the main driving force was the higher historical return of the Morgan Stanley EAFE index compared to that of the United States, albeit caused largely by the price appreciation of Japanese stocks.[7] At that time, only about 1 percent of U.S. pension funds were invested abroad. Five years later, the prospect of investing in the former nations of the Soviet Union that were joining the capitalist world was another alluring development.

Foreign diversification by U.S. investors grew rapidly even after the Japanese bubble was pierced in 1990 because of the comparatively low correlation of returns from foreign markets with returns from the United States. Thus international diversification became in vogue for global investors, particularly mutual funds, pension funds, and insurance companies.

Once institutional investors diversified into the EAFE, the next logical step was to move directly into Asia's emerging markets. Smaller Asian emerging markets, such as Thailand, were attractive because of their potential for high returns and their value to portfolios seeking to control risk through diversification. They also had a low correlation with the S&P 500, and few doubted their strong economic fundamentals and the likelihood of strong economic growth. Hindsight tells us how easy it was in 1993 for investors to believe that the growth and profits in Asian emerging markets would be enormous over the next several decades. But it required, as we know today, much harder thinking to understand that this view had already been more than adequately priced by the markets.

As institutional investment funds rolled into Asia, the inevitable result was to raise equity prices, which then, in turn, attracted even more investment, drawn in by ever-firming price trends. By late 1993, prices had risen to bubble proportions in a number of these countries.

Japanese prices in 1989, in the earlier bubble, reached some five times book equity; two times is a more plausible long-run equilibrium. Figure 7-1 draws from International Finance Corporation (IFC) data to show the price-to-book ratio equity valuation for five markets in the

7. EAFE: Europe, Australasia, and the Far East.

Figure 7-1. *Asian Equity Valuation in Five Asian Countries, 1993–99*
Price-to-book ratio

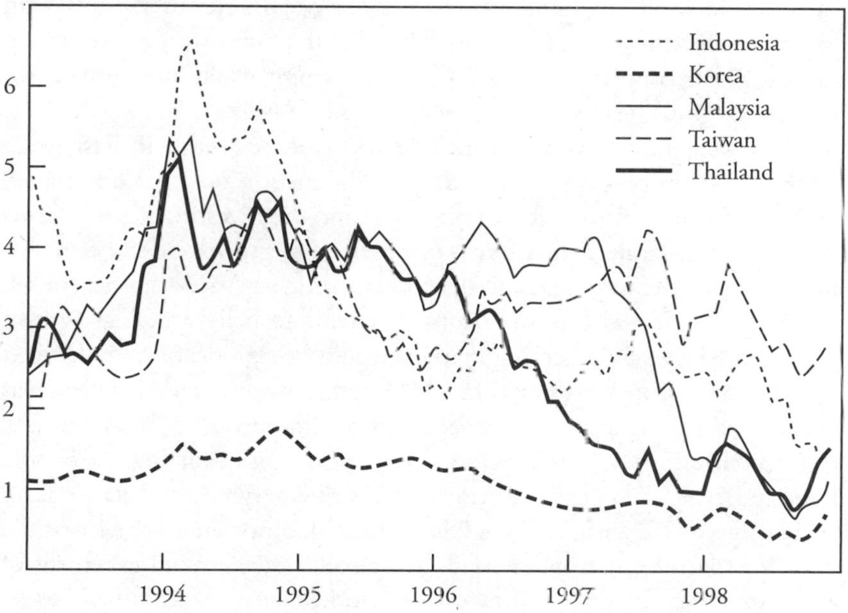

Source: International Finance Corporation.

region—Korea, Indonesia, Malaysia, Taiwan (China), and Thailand—between 1993 and 1999. Note that each country, except for Korea, had a price-to-book ratio at or above four in the 1994–95 period, with Indonesia spiking up over six in 1994.

Thailand, the proximate source of the crisis, had a peak valuation in early 1994 and continued to have a very high ratio until mid-1996. The only market to resist the sharp rise in price-to-book ratio values was Taiwan, giving at least some credence to the argument that capital controls can reduce the impact of hot money. I argue, however, that this is too simplistic an argument or, as some see it, a cure.

The Profile of the Global Investor in East Asia

As can be seen from the appendix, all types of institutional investors have been active in East Asia. But based on my personal observation and the size of foreign portfolio investment flowing into very high-priced countries, growth investors accounted for a disproportionate share of the investment.[8] In addition, while emerging markets may have had a surplus of inflows in general, problems were compounded because the funds were concentrated in East Asian countries that had passed the point where investment was needed and thus pushed prices to unsustainable levels.

My explanation of why growth investors were so sizable in East Asian markets rests in part on the workings of the institutions that dominated global investment flows. Money managers and the investment consultants who advise them need to attract customers, and growth-oriented investment funds for emerging markets, especially in East Asia, were easy to sell to customers. It was easy to encourage clients to believe that growth in profits in East Asian emerging markets would be significant over the next several decades. It was more difficult to communicate that this view was already more than adequately reflected in current prices.

Capitalization-weighted indexes also had a significant impact on the level and type of foreign investment in Asia's emerging markets. Indexes such as the EAFE and the IFC's Global Index Composite were used as the basis for specific Asian index funds and also for benchmarking returns of active investors. Investment drawn to the indexes meant that funds flowed to top-heavy East Asian markets, while some more deserving opportunities elsewhere in the world were perhaps overlooked.

Figure 7-2 clarifies another point: individual emerging markets are still not efficiently allocated in global portfolios. Surprisingly, an index annually equal-weighted by the countries in the IFC Global Index Composite has outperformed the capitalization-weighted IFC Composite by about 15 percent annually since the latter's inception.[9]

In sum, capitalization-weighted indexing in emerging markets has ill-served both investors and recipient markets. With the substantial presence of momentum investors in these markets, growth and capitalization-weighted index investing styles are inherently destabilizing, unless their excesses are offset by value investors. In my experience, however, strongly value-oriented investment approaches are atypical among global investors investing in emerging markets. Investment managers, guided to some

8. See, for example, the presentation by Howell in the sample of institutional presentations noted in the appendix.

9. Wilcox (1997, 1998).

Figure 7-2. *Equal-Weighted and Capitalization-Weighted Wealth Indexes in Emerging Markets, 1984–98*

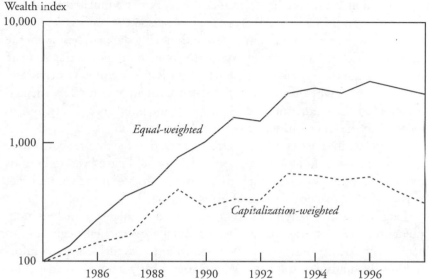

Source: International Finance Corporation.

extent by demand, have tended to emphasize growth, momentum, or capitalization-weighted indexing rather than value investing.

Could the Consequences Have Been Foreseen? And the Role of Moral Hazard

Economists and policy analysts alike have wondered whether the disastrous setback from the "Asian Miracle" could have been foreseen. There seems to be an urge (1) to believe that if more of the fundamentals had been known, the initial run-up would not have occurred, or at least that some problems should have been foreseen because the fundamentals cited often were rather optimistic, and (2) to place the blame on a failure to concentrate even *more* on growth fundamentals rather than on price. Should investors have looked more deeply into corporate credit quality, level, and the development of market infrastructure, among other areas? Yet that type of question misses the point that growth investors are heavily influenced by group optimism in an environment in which momentum investors keep things moving in a positive direction.

One implicit premise has been that the market is populated by homogeneous investors. Clearly, this is not the case, as some investors *did*, in fact, foresee that expected returns were low and moving down. These were the investors who underweighted Asian stocks in their portfolios. So the important question is not so much whether disaster could have been foreseen, but rather why there were so few balanced analysts and value-oriented investors in the market to guide us through the imbalances. I attempt to respond to this deficit in the recommendations section.

Of course, the answer to the question of whether the disaster could have been foreseen would have to be "yes." That it could have been foreseen is not very helpful, however, unless that answer translates into measures that change the relative populations of investor types.

I argue that sufficient information was already available to make a judgment that Asian stock markets were generally overpriced beginning in 1994. The pacing item was the willingness to use available pricing information. In hindsight, too few investors used clearly defined standards for pricing that would have led them to lower their expected returns on Asian investments.

What about the moral hazard question, specifically whether unwarranted portfolio investments were taken on because of a belief that the public sector, or quasi-public sector entities, would be lenders of last resort in the affected financial systems (that is, expecting an IMF bailout)? There is little doubt that moral hazard clearly was a factor in the banking system and with the IMF's lending arrangements. However, very few equity and currency investors of my acquaintance ever put much faith in the power of government to avoid catastrophe in the open securities markets. Asia's role model, Japan, which experienced a similar bubble and collapse some years earlier, has had great difficulty in governing its way out of its own financial difficulties in a way that protects its market values. Why then should a portfolio investor assume that this power exists in other Asian governments?

Consequently, based on personal experience and a sense of the investing culture, I do not believe that moral hazard contributed to the size and flow of portfolio investments made. Indeed, it may have been quite the opposite. Investors may have seen the potential for IMF lending and support as a potential source of risk—the risk that basic market forces of supply and demand might be hindered or crippled by official actions.

What Investors Have Learned from the Asian Experience

The Asian crisis has caused governments and global agencies to reexamine their assumptions about how to deal with emerging markets. Investors are another matter.

The global investor showed, first, disproportionate holdings in high-priced countries in Asia as opposed to emerging markets elsewhere; second, a clear predominance of growth and capitalization index styles of investing over value-oriented investing; and, third, momentum behavior (as evidenced in serious academic work on the Asian crisis). Many investors *have* learned that global investors contributed to some degree to the Asian market instability. (However, keep in mind that their activities merely accentuated a crisis already in the making in the real economy and especially in the banking system.) Has this investor learning translated into changes in investment policies or styles?

I think most observers would be disappointed if they looked for significant learning by *individual investors* from the Asian crisis. At the *institutional* level, slightly more change may be observed. Consider the case of Fidelity's Emerging Market Fund, referred to in the appendix. The portfolio manager was replaced by another manager who professed the belief that country weights in a portfolio should more closely track capitalization-weighted indexes. But overall, the learning ability of even individual institutions does not suggest that any lessons greatly affecting future stock market dynamics have been learned from the Asian crisis. Let me explain the reasoning behind this judgment.

The speculative bubble seen in East Asia in the mid-1990s was preceded by a very large and very similar bubble in the Japanese stock market in the late 1980s. The same kind of growth extrapolations were made for Japan that were later made for other East Asian countries. Sadly, I see little evidence that any generalized connection was made between the two. What global investors learned from the first episode was to be skeptical of *Japanese* growth. They did not learn to recognize the symptoms of a developing bubble in other Asian countries. Why should we expect greater learning this time?

The more recent and immediate consequence of Asian price decline was a movement of funds into Eastern Europe, where the growth stories were repeated. Eventually, as more emerging markets outside Asia were affected by the crisis, a feeling grew that perhaps all emerging markets were going through a down phase at the moment. This was dead wrong in Asia, which has gotten some rebound relief. Again, however, there seems to be little generalization that would enable investors to better avoid investing at speculative peaks. Otherwise how could we explain the participation of many of the same firms in the current excesses of the U.S. market?

On the one hand, it is not readily apparent that there is a growing appetite for diversification within emerging markets. I have heard the opposite—that now we have to be especially careful when selecting countries in which to invest. This is at first sight surprising because the need for diversification would seem to be the logical conclusion from the difficulty experienced by the market in anticipating the about-face in East Asia.

On the other hand, for those who decide to diversify, the implementation is usually faulty, because they move closer to a capitalization-weighted index. As figure 7-2 illustrates for emerging markets, capitalization-weighted indexes are far from optimal diversification. The valid choice is not between picking and choosing and indexing in capitalization-weighted fashion. It is between intelligent, diversified selection and passive investment in better-diversified indexes that do not contribute to instability.

If we look at populations of investor styles as they pertain to individual *markets*, I believe we will see something quite different and more encouraging. My reasoning is based on the gradual evolution in the market for Japanese securities. The proportion of value-oriented investors will increase in Thailand, Indonesia, and so on, as it seems to have done in Japan.[10] To repeat, we are likely to see almost no useful learning at the individual level. We see only little and painful adjustment by individual investment firms. But we will see, I believe, considerable system learning through changes in the relative populations (and capital weights) of different types of investment styles.

Conclusion and Policy Recommendations

The Asian crisis would have occurred with or without the actions of global portfolio investors, because of preexisting instabilities. However,

---

10. My evidence for the latter is that investing using simple value measures like price-to-book ratio used to earn incredible returns in Japan but now earns much smaller and more erratic returns. This is just what one would expect if the value-oriented ecological niche were becoming more fully populated.

the net effect of foreign investors probably aggravated the situation. The reason was not so much hot money, which I identify with momentum investing. Rather it was the market instability added to this hot money by a preponderance of growth-oriented investors and those influenced by capitalization-weighted indexes. Growth investors take too long to lower expected returns in the face of higher prices. Capitalization-weighted indexes, in common with momentum investors, actually increased allocations as prices went up.

The discussion of the feedback structure behind the financial instability observed in the Asian crisis does point to policy recommendations that could be considered. Is this a matter beyond investor purview? I think not. It is not only the client's money at stake; it is also the potentially disastrous impact of a financial crisis of this magnitude on the global financial system.

Emerging Market Governments—The Downside to Capital or Exchange Rate Controls

Clearly, emerging markets vary in their stage of development and thus in their needs. But generally speaking, the primary reason for opening their financial markets to foreign investment is to create a well-functioning market that more effectively allocates available capital. Foreign participation is likely to result in a more transparent system that weakens the impact of favoritism on the quality of decisionmaking and tends to provide impetus for further improvement in information reporting, transparency, and legal and accounting enhancements.

In this context, both exchange rate controls and capital controls have downsides that tend to outweigh any short-term beneficial effects. For example, in terms of the feedback system, exchange rate control is good for reducing hyperinflation but is counterproductive for trying to manage almost everything else. Once the tendency to borrow unhedged foreign currency has been curbed through a better-regulated banking system, currency devaluations can be implemented without undue pain and without a panic-driven overshoot of the market.

Capital controls can have some real, but short-term, beneficial effects in dampening the flow of hot money, that is, the money of momentum investors. However, they have negative long-term effects on resource allocation that are much greater than their proponents have reckoned. Although capital controls tend to limit the more obvious feedback problem implicit in the "hot money" complaint, they may well worsen the less obvious feedback that a closed market disastrously degrades the quality of allocation decisions when funds are plentiful.

There may be truth to the proposition that some currency speculators try to make money by talking down currencies in which they already have short positions. However, my observation is that such behavior is self-correcting in that its practitioners tend eventually to become the prey of smarter value investors.

With regard to promoting a healthier mix of investor types, the best aid to analysts is more timely and objective corporate and government information. Local governments interested in encouraging value investing should cultivate local investors as the value offset to less-informed global investors who are momentum players or are oriented toward purely growth or capitalization-weighted indexes. This involves reversing the instinctive desire to keep local capital at home. Give local investors complete freedom to move funds abroad, and they will diversify out of local markets that become too expensive. In turn, they will bring the funds back home when there are bargains to be had. In addition to encouraging more stability, this will help to reduce surges of foreign ownership when prices are unusually low.

Developed Governments and the International Monetary Fund

The role of the IMF in assuring the liquidity of governments that will reliably pay back temporary loans seems rather stretched when applied to many emerging markets. The policies and lessons derived in a developed country may not work well, without considerable refitting, in an emerging market at a very different point on the development scale. In very poor countries the need still is in getting the capital accumulation process started by helping them reach critical mass in terms of sustainable population growth, education, and funding. In countries with high savings rates and a record of sustained economic growth, the needs are very different.

Capital is no longer the bottleneck in much of East Asia. Consequently, sustainable capital growth is better promoted by encouraging a sound banking system, better operating capital markets, and perhaps some demonstration projects showing how to address environmental and social problems than by conducting large-scale lending.

Use of Supplemental Indexes

The International Finance Corporation should supplement the IFC indexes that are now based on capitalization weights with something else. The alternative should take the air out of momentum investors' sails and support value-oriented portfolios. Study should be given to indexes that capture shelf space as benchmarks for both passive and active investing.

For example, the Morgan Stanley EAFE index has experimented with a gross domestic product (GDP)–weighted version. It appears not to have caught on for two reasons: a once-a-year update and indifference by finance academics who believe that capitalization-weighted indexing is always optimal. The former could be overcome by monthly updates; the latter could be dealt with through careful study of the comparative records of capitalization-weighted versus other passive benchmarks in the emerging market universe, which is far less efficient than is the S&P 500. I would also propose an index with country weights set on *equity book value*, rather than GDP, as being quite feasible and more directly encouraging to value-oriented investment styles.

Cultivation of Analysts and Value-Oriented Investors

Analysts and value-oriented investors employ the types of investment styles that reduce the accumulation of errors and counter the destabilizing effects of momentum investors. Analysts can be cultivated by encouraging proper corporate and government reporting. Paradoxically local value orientation can be strengthened by allowing local investors the freedom to diversify outside the country.

Promotion of Diversification

So-called hot money is minimized when investors diversify adequately. Global institutions such as the IFC should conduct missionary research showing the value of better diversification, which is far from capitalization-weighted indexing in the case of emerging markets, and should implement the result with appropriate indexes.

Appendix
Samples of Investment Approaches by
Institutional Investors in Emerging Markets

This appendix presents informal but representative quotations from news articles, investor conferences, and the sparse findings of academics to illustrate the thinking of global investors in East Asian markets. Again, keep in mind that investors come in different styles, some dangerous, some benign, and some helpful.

A Popular Fund Marketed as a Growth Fund

Fidelity's Emerging Market Fund, once quite large, suffered poor results over several years, culminating in the replacement of its portfolio manager. It was heavily concentrated in Southeast Asia, astonishingly so in Malaysia; that is, it was more concentrated than even capitalization-weighted indexes on high-priced stocks with growth characteristics. The fund's 1997 annual report says:

> For the twelve-month period that ended on October 31, 1997, the fund was down 36.74 percent. For the same period, the Morgan Stanley Capital International Emerging Markets Free Index was down 8.48 percent. . . . There were two main factors that hurt the fund versus the index. First the fund was overweighted versus the index in Southeast Asia during a period when those markets underperformed dramatically. . . . For the past five years, the fund has been run by selecting investments on a stock-by-stock basis. . . . As a result, even though the fund owned stocks of companies whose earnings went up, their stock prices collapsed. . . . The second factor that hurt the fund was the significant redemptions from it during the year, which resulted in the fund selling heavily in markets that were often illiquid.[11]

The fund manager was clearly focused on growth rather than prices, which were about four times book value in Malaysia at the beginning of 1997. Even after the debacle, the blame was placed more on countrywide factors such as currency declines than on the practice of buying securities at high prices.

11. Fidelity Emerging Markets Fund (1997).

A Quantitative Approach

The Equity Research Group of Salomon Smith Barney regularly publishes country ratings based on a quantitative measurement of each market.[12] They label as *value* indicators price-to-book ratios, price-to-earnings ratios, and so on. (Price-to-earnings ratios, especially those based on changing forecast earnings, are more balanced than pure value. The latter is better represented by price-to-book ratios, because equity book value changes more slowly than earnings.) Their *growth* indicators include GDP growth rate and earnings growth rate forecasts. *Momentum* strategies are represented by recent stock price returns and by earnings estimate revision ratios. The weighting given these indicators has appeared to reflect a balance between different investment approaches. Their publication frequently provides statistics on how well the various components have done. Overall, this is a healthy antidote to the preponderance of emerging market growth-related material coming from Wall Street. Remember that, as I have defined it, a growth style can emphasize either good or bad news. What it does is pay little attention to price, thereby reinforcing the destabilizing momentum style.

A Popular Fund Marketed as Value Oriented

Templeton Emerging Markets Investment Trust (TEMIT) is a more subtle example of the power of the growth story. It highlights the fact that fund managers are in business. Their sales, intentionally or not, are often driven by the easier-to-understand growth story than by the benefits of diversification or the even harder-to-understand story of contrarian value investing.

The Templeton hallmark had been value-oriented investing. J. Mark Mobius, chief of TEMIT, is quoted as not wanting to invest in companies with a price-to-earnings ratio above fifteen.[13] Although one wonders how high prices are allowed to rise before the securities are sold, this philosophy does give credibility to the price-growth tradeoff. Mobius and the Templeton staff have also acted as analysts, making a considerable effort to get at the investment facts behind the superficial appearances.

Yet as we read press accounts, the feature communicated by the Templeton emerging market funds was growth—well-known growth that was very likely already factored into prices. To give a few examples:

12. Salomon Smith Barney, Equity Research Group (various issues).
13. "Mobius on Hong Kong: Templeton Manager Says HK Is Hot but Shanghai Is the Future," CNN, June 27, 1997.

Mobius is founding father to the current financial fad for emerging markets. And as many such markets are breaking into new all-time highs and as TEMIT shares have more than quadrupled since launch in 1989, Mobius is listened to with respect. . . . He claims that we are now seeing not only a transfer of technology from rich to poor countries but emerging countries are often leap-frogging the developed world. . . . China now has more TV sets—100 million—even more than the U.S. . . . Productivity is sky-rocketing in these countries, Mobius says.[14]

Mark Holowesko, the president and director of Global Equity Research for Templeton Worldwide: "In Indonesia [in 1970] 60 percent of the population were considered at the poverty level; in 1990, that number decreased to just 15 percent. . . . He said there will be enormous demands for electricity and water in countries like China and more consumption as a result of developing markets."[15]

According to Mark Mobius, "Because of technological advances in food, nutrition, health care, and information technology there's been a dramatic increase in productivity. . . . China is doubling the productivity per person every ten years. . . . The U.S. had to go through all these steps in its path toward industrialization. Now the emerging countries can just take the very best technology. . . . [Regarding the possibility of a crash:] You're bound to have mistakes. But the good news is that for every crash there's a boom.[16]

To be fair, Mobius often warned that people can get hurt in emerging markets. However, that message was lost in the simplistic implication that because Asian productivity had grown fast, it would continue to do so indefinitely. The subliminal message was that the long-term risk was not great. There was also an implicit appeal to momentum investors because of prior high returns in the glory days of emerging market investing up through 1993.

14. "Optimist in the Temple of Doom," *Evening Standard*, February 7, 1994, as cited in Templeton website.
15. "Templeton Stock Picker High on Asian Investment," *Oakville Beaver*, July 22, 1994, as cited in Templeton website.
16. "Let's Talk about the Fundamental Factors That Affect . . . ," *Asian Business*, August 21, 1996.

An Institutional Conference on Emerging Markets

This section presents examples of messages aimed at institutional investors taken from presentations that were typical of conferences on emerging markets. The conference was sponsored by the International Centre for Business Information and was held in Geneva on December 2–4, 1996, as the Asian markets were heading for a crash. The message given was more complex than that given to retail investors, but the end result was the same: a heavy stress on growth, with far less attention to price. There was also a strong thread of momentum thinking, whether phrased in terms of past returns, past economic success, or liquidity.

At the session "Malaysia: Growing towards the 21st Century," Lieven M. O. Debryne, MeesPierson Capital Management (Far East), presented statistical charts showing a decline in exports, stemming from a slowdown in the electronics industry, as well as competition from a depreciated yen. But this negative message was obscured by favorable references to the fact that imports were slowing down even faster, the exports slowdown appeared cyclical, and growth in lending to manufacturing had slowed. One exhibit heading over-accentuated the positive with the message "Significant Improvement in the Trade Balance since the Beginning of This Year." (Growth investor.)

Arnab Banerji, Foreign and Colonial Emerging Markets, in the session "Where Will the Smart Money Be Going in 1997 and Beyond?" illustrated the positive correlation of a measure of G-7 excess liquidity and subsequent increases in emerging market stock prices. He then projected that Asia, which had been half of emerging market portfolio investments of "funded schemes" in 1992, would rise to two-thirds in the year 2000. (Momentum investor.)

At the session "China Market: The International Forum on Emerging Markets Funds and Investment," C. Y. Ho, Credit Lyonnais Securities Asia, gave attention first to the "excitements" of huge consumption power, rapid coastal economic growth, cheap production cost, and extensive investment opportunities. He then compared these to the "disillusions" created by poor corporate management, state-owned enterprise dinosaurs, the problems in production and foreign competition, and so on. Although there was considerable skepticism, detailed information was almost entirely on fundamentals. Price multiples got far less attention, but at least were mentioned. (Growth investor and analyst.)

At the session entitled "The Outlook for Emerging Markets," the presenter—Michael J. Howell, CrossBorder Capital—noted fund flows and extrapolated results. His recommended emerging market allocations for 1997 were Southeast Asia, 42.5 percent; Northeast Asia, 17.0 percent; Southern Asia, 11.3 percent; Latin America, 19.0 percent; and Eastern Europe 1.3 percent. (Momentum investor.)

Finally, at the "Emerging Markets Funds and Investment Forum: Indonesia," in November 1996, Michael Roche, HSBC Asset Management Hong Kong, cited strong, consistent economic growth, recent strength of the rupiah, strong capital markets growth, and strong equity market returns. (Growth investor and momentum investor.)

Academic Papers

One recent National Bureau of Economic Research working paper by Froot, O'Connell, and Seasholes casts some light on the role of portfolio flows during and after both the Mexican and Asian crises.[17] The authors note that there is a very strong trend following momentum in portfolio flows. I ascribe great importance to this commonplace fact. Flows also led stock prices. There is sufficient ground for believing that momentum investing was taking place on a large scale.

Another working paper circulated by Choe, Kho, and Stulz examines the Korean experience in 1997.[18] The authors find a day-by-day pattern of foreigners buying more when stock prices had previously gone up—that is, predominately momentum investing by foreigners—that was more evident before the crisis than after. As one might expect given momentum investing, there is also strong evidence of "herding," with foreigners buying and selling as a group. However, the authors conclude that foreign buying was *not* destabilizing because price movements immediately after large foreign purchases did not trend in the same direction and actually tended to rebound slightly. I do not share this conclusion, because their evidence shows that the initial price movement was much larger than any rebound.

A Quantitative Value-Oriented Approach

It would be inappropriate to make this essay an advertisement for our approach at PanAgora Asset Management. However, I cite the strategy followed because it has been stabilizing in character. First, there is a strategic

17. Froot, O'Connell, and Seasholes (1998).
18. Choe, Kho, and Stulz (1998).

decision to emphasize countries with smaller market capitalization. This forces a lower price-to-book ratio and puts more money in countries with lower risk correlation. For years, the strategic allocation averages were equal-weighted by country. Today, with the addition of many tiny and illiquid stock markets to the emerging market universe, the strategic average allocation is tiered, but still far from capitalization-weighted. Around both of these longer-term strategic allocations already biased toward lower prices have been tactical allocations based on a balanced set of investment criteria. PanAgora underweighted the large-capitalization Asian countries prior to the crisis and was an emphatic buyer shortly after the worst breaks. No penalty was paid for this good citizenship, as returns have been far superior to those of any of the capitalization-weighted emerging market indexes.

References

Bank for International Settlements. 1998. *68th Annual Report*. Basle (June).

Choe, Hyuk, Bong-Chan Kho, and René M. Stulz. 1998. "Do Foreign Investors Destabilize Stock Markets? The Korean Experience in 1997." NBER Working Paper 6661. Cambridge, Mass.: National Bureau of Economic Research (July).

Dickens, Charles. 1859. *A Tale of Two Cities*. London: Chapman and Hall.

Fidelity Emerging Market Fund. 1997. *Emerging Market Fund Annual Report 1997*.

Froot, Kenneth A., Paul G. J. O'Connell, and Mark Seasholes. 1998. "The Portfolio Flows of International Investors, I." NBER Working Paper 6687. Cambridge, Mass.: National Bureau of Economic Research (August).

Krugman, Paul. 1994. "The Myth of Asia's Miracle." *Foreign Affairs* 73 (November/December): 62–78.

Pomerleano, Michael. 1998. "The East Asia Crisis and Corporate Finances: The Untold Microeconomic Story." *Emerging Markets Quarterly* (Winter): 14–27.

Salomon Smith Barney, Equity Research Group. Various issues. *Emerging Markets Equity Allocator*.

Wilcox, Jarrod W. 1997. "Better Emerging Market Portfolios." *Emerging Markets Quarterly* (Summer): 5–16.

———. 1998. "Investing at the Edge." *Journal of Portfolio Management* 24 (Spring): 9–21.

———. 1999. *Investing by the Numbers*. New Hope, Pa.: Frank J. Fabozzi Associates.

SEBASTIAN EDWARDS

9

On Crisis Prevention: Lessons from Mexico and East Asia

But now, ah now, to learn from crises.

WALT WHITMAN[1]

T HE EAST ASIAN CURRENCY CRISIS rocked the conventional wisdom.
All of a sudden the world seemed to be on its head. Yesterday's "miracle" countries became today's pariahs, and policies that were supposed to
be emulated by every emerging nation, and that were pushed with unrestricted enthusiasm by the multilateral institutions, became questionable.
The news is replete with stunning stories about bankruptcies, questionable
loans, dwindling international reserves, weak banks, and plunging currencies. Rescue packages had to be put together in haste, and the International
Monetary Fund had to coordinate bailout after bailout. Figures 9-1
through 9-3 present a picture of the East Asian crisis as seen from the perspective of exchange rates, interest rates, and stock markets.

To be sure, most observers were aware that Thai finance companies were
not completely healthy and that in Indonesia the succession from Suharto
was far from resolved. But the scope and depth of the crisis shocked even

The author is indebted to Rajesh Chakrabarti, Kyongchul Kim, and Alejandro Jara for assistance.
1. Walt Whitman, "Long, Too Long America."

269

Figure 9-1. *Exchange Rates versus U.S. Dollar during the Asian Currency Crisis, 1997–98*

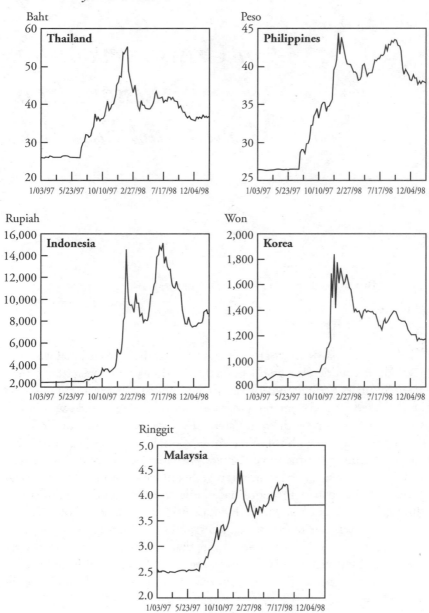

Source: Data Stream database.

Figure 9-2. *Interest Rates during the Asian Crisis, 1997–98*

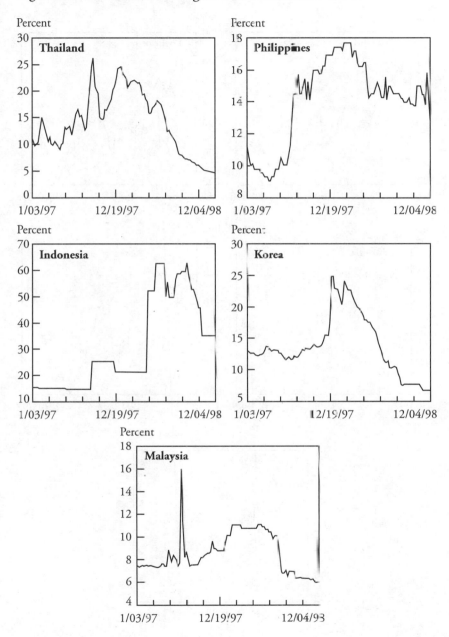

Source: Data Stream database.

Figure 9-3. *Stock Market Indexes during the Asian Crisis, 1997–98*

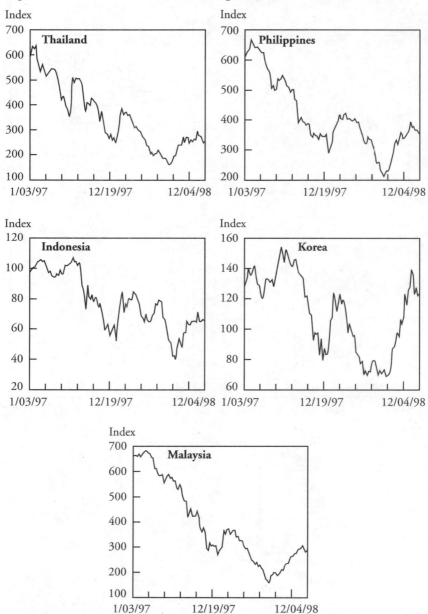

Source: Data Stream database.

veteran East Asian analysts. Business executives across the world asked themselves why their staff—or those highly regarded consultants, for that matter—did not warn them of the impeding collapse of the region.

By mid-1998 market participants were asking where the next crisis would erupt. Russia and Brazil, with large fiscal deficits and overvalued exchange rates, became obvious candidates and eventually joined the ranks of crisis nations. The Russian debacle was particularly traumatic, inflicting heavy losses on a number of large financial institutions. When the Russian moratorium was announced, investors scrambled for cover and safety. The demand for liquidity soared, yields on the U.S. long bond dropped to an all-time low, and interest rate spreads widened significantly, seriously straining financial markets in the United States and other industrial countries. The near collapse of Long-Term Capital Management, and its subsequent rescue by a group of investment houses coordinated by the Federal Reserve Bank of New York, clearly captured the remarkable degree of integration of world financial markets.

By early 1997 a "consensus view" on the causes of the Mexican crisis had developed in policy circles. A direct by-product of this "consensus" was the identification of a set of vulnerability indicators that were supposed to act as early signals of an impending balance of payments crisis. Surprisingly, however, East Asian analysts tended to ignore these Mexican lessons and, thus, underestimated the dangers of a serious collapse in the region. In the aftermath of the East Asian meltdown, there has been a renewed effort by private sector analysts, policy experts, journalists, and academics to understand the causes behind currency crises. These studies have reinforced, and in some cases amplified, the conclusions previously reached by analyses of the Mexican crisis and have concentrated on the role of large external imbalances, volatile capital flows, weak banking systems, loss of confidence, and overvalued exchange rates.[2]

The purpose of this paper is to provide a comparative analysis of the East Asian and Mexican crises and to draw broad lessons that would be helpful to the Latin American nations and other emerging economies.

---

2. On the Mexican crisis see, for example, Leiderman and Thorne (1995), Sachs, Tornell, and Velasco (1995), Calvo and Mendoza (1996), the papers in Edwards and Naim (1997), Edwards (1997), Cole and Kehoe (1996), and Frankel and Rose (1996). The view of Mexican authorities can be found in Gil Díaz and Carstens (1996, 1997). The financial community perspective is in Group of Thirty (1995). For the World Bank perspective, see Burki (1997); the IMF views are in Loser and Williams (1997). See also OECD (1995) and Birdsall, Gavin, and Hausmann (1997). On the East Asian crises, see Corsetti, Pesenti, and Roubini (1998), Radelet and Sachs (1998), Feldstein (1998), and Ito (1999).

Although much of the discussion concentrates on East Asia and Mexico, I also draw on the history of some previous crisis episodes. I argue that in spite of efforts to understand the anatomy of currency crises, there are still a large number of controversial and unresolved issues. More to the point, I argue that some of the lessons extracted from this crisis are based on a misreading of the historical record. As a result, some of the policy implications that have emerged from this debate are questionable, to say the least. In particular, I make two points. First, I argue that, in general, current account ratios have limited usefulness in determining a country's financial health. Although I fall short of taking the position that the current account is completely irrelevant, I do argue that a rigid interpretation of current account ratios may be highly misleading. Second, I argue that the rapidly growing popularity of controls on capital inflows as a device for reducing external vulnerability is rooted in a misreading of the recent history of external crises and, in particular, in a misunderstanding of some key Latin American experiences.

The paper is organized as follows. In the first section, I discuss what I call, for lack of a better term, the "consensus view" on the Mexican crisis and investigate the extent to which the lessons learned from this consensus view are applicable to the East Asian nations. I also discuss how the developments in East Asia during 1997–98 have, in turn, affected this "consensus view" on crisis prevention. In the second section, I discuss the relationship between current account deficits and currency crises. This is followed by a section devoted to a discussion of the effectiveness of capital controls. Finally, I deal with some unresolved issues and emphasize Latin American lessons, learned from the 1980s debt crisis, on corporate and financial restructuring. Appendix A discusses Mexico's experience with corporate restructuring during the 1980s. Appendix B contains an analysis of Chile's experience with debt-to-debt and debt-to-equity swaps during the early 1980s. Appendix C presents key data from East Asia and Latin America.

Lessons from Mexico and East Asia:
The Emergence of a "Consensus View"

The Mexican meltdown was followed by abundant postmortems and a few mea culpas. The International Monetary Fund (IMF) and the World Bank tried to explain their involvement in the episode, the financial sector

convened wise-men commissions, and the U.S. Senate investigated the
U.S. Treasury's role in unleashing the crisis. Grandiose phrases were
uttered, and everyone agreed that more vigilance was needed to avoid
major crises in the future. In retrospect it may be tempting to argue that
most of this was lip service and that international bureaucrats and Wall
Street professionals went on with their business, leaving the Mexican crisis behind as a bitter experience that affected that year's bonuses and somewhat bruised their reputations, but that would not be repeated in the fore-
seeable future. They were wrong. Merely thirty months later, the East
Asian "tigers" began to crumble in a way that, in more than one respect,
resembled the Mexican saga.

In spite of some differences of opinion, by late 1996 and early 1997
somewhat of a consensus had emerged on the main policy lessons from the
Mexican crisis. Although not every author subscribes to every one of them,
the following list constitutes what can be called the generally accepted consensus view from Mexico:[3]

—Pegged (or very rigid) exchange rates are dangerous; real exchange
rate overvaluation may be lethal.

—Very large current account deficits matter, even when they are
financed with private funds and when public finances are under control.

—Portfolio capital flows can be highly volatile. In particular, short-
term capital flows may be highly destabilizing. Issuing foreign currency–
denominated debt to defend the currency may prove to be extremely costly
in the eventuality that the exchange rate peg has to be abandoned. Moreover, central banks should avoid sterilizing international reserve losses in
the context of rigid exchange rates.

—Banks should be supervised closely; weak banks invite contagion. The
existence of weak banks reduces the authorities' ability to use interest rates
as a macroeconomics tool and is likely to amplify a currency crisis.

—Transparency in financial operations is important to build confidence
among investors. Timely and accurate information is of the essence.

Naturally, these lessons are related to one another and should not be
viewed in isolation; nor should they be considered as a rigid list of "necessary" or "sufficient" conditions for a crisis to erupt. The way to think about
them is as a set of factors that, according to a large number of analysts,
played a critical role in unleashing the Mexican events and should be
watched closely in other emerging countries. Not every analyst placed the

---

3. See the studies cited in footnote 2.

same emphasis on every one of these factors, and some observers even disagreed with some of them.

In the rest of this section, I elaborate briefly on each of these five Mexican lessons and discuss whether they are applicable to the East Asian nations. I also discuss the way in which this consensus view has evolved in light of the East Asian and subsequent crises of the 1990s (Russia and Brazil).

On the Dangers of Rigid Exchange Rates and Real Exchange Rate Overvaluation

The Mexican crisis brought to the core of the policy debate the merits of rigid nominal exchange rates, both in the short and long runs. In the late 1980s and early 1990s, and after a period of relative disfavor, rigid exchange rates made a comeback in academic and policy circles. A number of authors argued that fixed, or predetermined, nominal exchange rates provide an effective device for guiding a disinflation program and maintaining macroeconomic stability.[4] According to this view, a prerequisite for a successful exchange rate–based stabilization program is that the country in question have its public finances in order. Mexico did this as early as 1988, the year the exchange rate–based stabilization program known as the Pacto de Solidaridad was implemented in full force.[5]

A recurrent problem with exchange rate–based stabilization programs— and one that affected the countries of the South American cone during the early 1980s—is that inflation tends to have a considerable degree of inertia. That is, domestic prices and wages continue to increase even after the nominal exchange rate has been fixed. This, in turn, results in a decline in exports' competitiveness, because domestic costs rise at a faster pace than proceeds from exports. Eventually, as was the case in Mexico between 1988 and 1994, these perverse dynamics generate a serious degree of real exchange rate overvaluation, a slowdown in exports, and a very large current account deficit. Dornbusch has made this point forcefully within the context of the Mexican crisis:

> Exchange rate–based stabilization goes through three phases: The first one is very useful . . . [E]xchange rate stabilization helps bring

---

4. See Edwards (1993) for a discussion of the role of fixed exchange rates as nominal anchors.
5. See Aspe (1993).

under way a stabilization . . . In the second phase increasing real appreciation becomes apparent, it is increasingly recognized, but it is inconvenient to do something. . . . Finally, in the third phase, it is too late to do something. Real appreciation has come to a point where a major devaluation is necessary. But the politics will not allow that. Some more time is spent in denial, and then—sometime—enough bad news piles up to cause the crash.[6]

An additional complication is that under rigid exchange rates, negative external shock can result in a costly adjustment process. In principle, in a country with fixed exchange rates the authorities should react to a negative shock—a worsening of the terms of trade or a decline in capital inflows— by tightening monetary and fiscal policies until external balance is reestablished. A direct consequence of this is that economic activity declines significantly, and the rate of unemployment tends to increase sharply. Whether in the real world this process is allowed to play itself out depends largely on political economy factors. In their analysis of the Mexican crisis, Sachs, Tornell, and Velasco argue that it is "hard to find cases where governments have let the [adjustment process under fixed exchange rate] run its course."[7] This, according to them, reduces the degree of credibility of pegged exchange rate regimes and provides a good argument for adopting more flexible ones.

As may be seen in table 9-1, in spite of Mexico's negative experience with a rigid exchange rate regime, all five of the East Asian nations had a rigid—de facto, pegged, or quasi-pegged—exchange rate system with respect to the U.S. dollar. Whereas this system worked relatively well while the U.S. dollar was relatively weak in international currency markets, things turned to the worse when, starting in mid-1996, the dollar began to strengthen relative to the Japanese yen. Naturally, as the dollar appreciated relative to the yen, so did those currencies pegged to it. This strengthening of the East Asian currencies squeezed competitiveness of exports and fed back into larger current account imbalances.

The Mexican crisis reaffirmed the importance of avoiding overvalued exchange rates—that is, real exchange rates that are incompatible with maintaining sustainable external accounts. In the spring 1994 meetings of the Brookings Panel on Economic Activity, Rudiger Dornbusch argued

6. Dornbusch (1997, p. 131).
7. Sachs, Tornell, and Velasco (1995, p. 71).

Table 9-1. *Vulnerability and Crises in Mexico and Asia*

Country and year	Large current account?	Rigid nominal exchange rates?	Overvalued real exchange rates?	Weak banks?	Large portfolio flows?
Mexico, 1994	Yes, exceeded 6.5 percent of GDP (1992–94)	Yes	Yes	Yes, nonperforming loans high, weak supervision	Yes
Thailand, 1997	Yes, exceeded 8 percent of GDP (1995–96)	Yes	Yes	Yes, finance houses very weak	Yes, BIBF channeled short-term flows[a]
Malaysia, 1997	Yes, exceeded 6.5 percent (1995–96)	Yes	Yes	Yes, weak supervision	Yes
Korea, 1997	Moderate, averaged 4 percent of GDP (1996–97)	No	No	Yes, bad portfolio very large; concentrated on conglomerate sector	Yes
Indonesia, 1997	Moderate, averaged 3.5 percent of GDP (1995–96)	Yes, crawling band	Yes	Yes, financed conglomerate questionable projects	Yes
Philippines, 1997	Yes, exceeded 4 percent of GDP (1995–96)	Yes	Yes	Yes	Yes

Source: Constructed by the author.
a. BIBF is a government-run institution that helps to attract foreign capital.

that the Mexican peso was overvalued by at least 30 percent and that the authorities should rapidly find a way to solve the problem. In that same meeting, Stanley Fischer, soon to become the IMF's first deputy managing director, expressed his concerns regarding the external sustainability of the Mexican experiment. Internal U.S. government communications released to the U.S. Senate Banking Committee during 1995 also reflect a mounting concern among some U.S. officials. Several staff members of the Federal Reserve Bank of New York, for example, argued that a devaluation of the peso could not ruled out.[8] In their analysis of the Mexican crisis and its sequel during 1995, Sachs, Tornell, and Velasco emphasize the role of real exchange rate overvaluation; according to their computations, during the 1990–94 period the Mexican peso was overvalued, on average, by almost 29 percent.[9] Ades and Kaune, in a thorough analysis using a detailed empirical model that decomposes changes in fundamentals into permanent and temporary changes, indicates that by the fourth quarter of 1994 the Mexican peso was overvalued by 16 percent.[10]

After the Mexican debacle, academic and private sector analysts redoubled their efforts to understand the behavior of real exchange rates in emerging economies. Arguably, one of the most serious efforts was undertaken at Goldman Sachs, where a dynamic model based on modern time-series techniques was developed to evaluate the appropriateness of real exchange rates in twelve countries. The first version of this model, released in October of 1996, indicated that the real exchange rate was overvalued in Indonesia, the Philippines, and Thailand.[11] Subsequent releases of the model incorporated additional countries and suggested that the Korean won and the Malaysian ringgit were also overvalued. In mid-1997, Goldman Sachs introduced a refined version of its model; according to these new estimates, in June of 1997 the currencies of Indonesia, Korea, Malaysia, the Philippines, and Thailand were overvalued, as were the currencies of Hong Kong and Singapore. In contrast, the Taiwanese dollar was undervalued by approximately 7 percent. Although according to Goldman Sachs, in June 1997 the degree of overvaluation was rather modest in all five East Asian crisis countries, it had persisted for a number of

8. See D'Amato (1995).

9. Sachs, Tornell, and Velasco (1996, table 9).

10. Ades and Kaune (1996). In Edwards (1989) and Edwards and Santaella (1993), I document the connection between real exchange rate overvaluation and currency crises for more than seventy developing countries during the 1950–82 period.

11. See Goldman Sachs, Emerging Markets Economic Research Group (various years).

years: in Indonesia the real exchange rate had been overvalued since 1993, in Korea since 1988, in Malaysia since 1993, in the Philippines since 1992, and in Thailand since 1990.[12]

According to a study by Sachs, Tornell, and Velasco, by late 1994 the real exchange rate picture in the East Asian countries was mixed.[13] While the Philippines and Korea were experiencing overvaluation, Malaysia and Indonesia had undervalued real exchange rates, and the Thai baht appeared to be in equilibrium. In a recent study, Chinn uses a standard monetary model to estimate the appropriateness of nominal exchange rates in East Asia before the crisis.[14] According to his results, in the first quarter of 1997 Indonesia, Malaysia, and Thailand had overvalued exchange rates, while Korea and the Philippines were facing undervaluation.

Although in the aftermath of the Mexican crisis a broad consensus emerged on the perils of real exchange rate overvaluation, there was less of an agreement on what type of *nominal* exchange rate policy emerging countries should follow. Some authors argued that after a short initial period with a rigid exchange rate, a crawling peg should be adopted. This position was taken by Dornbusch, who argued, "Crawl now, or crash later," and by Bruno, who said, in general, "The choice of the exchange rate as the nominal anchor only relates to the initial phase of stabilization."[15] Sachs and others took a similar position: "The effectiveness of exchange rate pegging is probably higher in the early stages of an anti-inflation programme."[16] Goldstein maintained, "All things considered, moving toward greater flexibility of exchange rate at an early stage (before the overvaluation becomes too large) will be the preferred course of action."[17]

Others, however, have pointed out that most emerging markets are in a position to adopt a floating exchange rate.[18] For example, Wang and Shilling go as far as saying that one of Mexico's main lessons is that "exchange rates should be flexible and combined with an appropriate monetary and fiscal policy so that the current account deficit does not grow to unsustainable levels."[19] Another group—rather small in the months fol-

12. Goldman Sachs, Emerging Markets Economic Research Group (various years).
13. Sachs, Tornell, and Velasco (1996).
14. Chinn (1998).
15. Dornbusch (1997, p. 137); Bruno (1995, p. 282).
16. Sachs, Tornell, and Velasco (1995).
17. Goldstein (1998, p. 51).
18. Edwards and Savastano (1998) discuss Mexico's post-1995 experience with a floating exchange rate.
19. Wang and Shilling (1995, p. 54).

lowing the Mexican crisis, but growing rapidly since the East Asian debacle—maintains that the Argentine experience since 1991 suggests that, within the context of a currency board, overvaluation may be corrected through improvements in productivity.[20]

After the East Asian, Russian, and Brazilian crises, economists' views on nominal exchange rate regimes began to evolve quite rapidly. Fixed-but-adjustable regimes have been losing adepts, while the two extreme positions—complete fixity through a currency board or dollarization and floating rates are gaining popularity. From a policy standpoint, one of the more difficult issues is designing an "exit strategy" that would allow countries with a rigid exchange rate regime to move toward a more flexible one.[21]

Very Large Current Account Deficits Matter

In 1990 the international financial markets rediscovered Mexico, and large amounts of capital began flowing into the country. As a result, Mexico could finance significant current account deficits—in 1992–94 they averaged almost 7 percent of gross domestic product (GDP). When some analysts pointed out that these deficits were very large, Mexican authorities argued that, with the fiscal accounts under control, there was no reason to worry. The implicit notion was that current account deficits are a matter of concern only when they coexist with large fiscal imbalances. In 1993 the Bank of Mexico maintained that "The current account deficit has been determined exclusively by the private sector's decisions. . . . Because of the above and the solid position of public finances, the current account deficit should clearly not be a cause for undue concern."[22]

At the light of the Mexican crisis a large number of analysts maintained that this argument, sometimes referred to as Lawson's doctrine, is seriously flawed. In an address to the Board of Governors of the Inter-American Development Bank in 1995, Lawrence Summers, then U.S. deputy secretary of the Treasury, said, "Current account deficits cannot be assumed to be benign because the private sector generated them."[23] This position has also been taken by the IMF. In evaluating the role of the IMF during the Mexican crisis, the director of the Western Hemisphere Department and

20. Bartley (1997).
21. Eichengreen, Rose, and Wyplosz (1996); Eichengreen and Masson (1998).
22. Banco de México (1993, pp. 179–80).
23. Summers (1996).

the chief of the Mexico Division wrote, "Large current account deficits, regardless of the factors underlying them, are likely to be unsustainable."[24] Secretary Summers said, "Close attention should be paid to any current account deficit in excess of 5 percent of GDP, particularly if it is financed in a way that could lead to rapid reversals."

In the 1994 Brookings Panel Session on Mexico, Stanley Fischer supported the view that large current account deficits are dangerous. He argued that:

> The Mexican current account deficit is huge, and it is being financed largely by portfolio investment. Those investments can turn around very quickly and leave Mexico with no choice but to devalue . . . And as the European and especially the Swedish experiences show, there may be no interest rate high enough to prevent an outflow and a forced devaluation.[25]

The issue, of course, is that current account deficits are financed by the sale of domestic securities to foreigners. This means that the current account position a country can maintain over the medium run is determined by the pace at which foreigners want to accumulate that country's financial liabilities (bonds, certificates of deposit, bank debt, stocks, and so on). If foreigners lose confidence in the country, they will rapidly reallocate their portfolio, generating massive capital outflows and forcing the country to go through an adjustment process.

Immediately following the Mexican crisis the view that under most circumstances—and even if public finances are under control—current account deficits can rarely exceed 4 to 5 percent of GDP gained considerable popularity among private sector analysts. This view was clearly captured by Milesi-Ferreti and Razin: "What persistent level of current account deficits should be considered sustainable? Conventional wisdom is that current account deficits above 5 percent of GDP flash a red light, in particular if the deficit is financed with short-term debt."[26] And according to Ades and Kaune, the threshold number level that usually triggers concern among analysts is 4 percent of GDP.[27] A number of authors, however,

---

24. Loser and Williams (1997, p. 268).
25. Fischer (1994, p. 306).
26. Milesi-Ferreti and Razin (1996).
27. Ades and Kaune (1997).

argued that the fact that Mexico had a large current account deficit in 1990–94 should not be generalized to most—or not even the majority of—developing countries. This view was taken, for example, by Sachs, Tornell, and Velasco, who found that, contrary to popular accounts, high current account deficits do not explain the turmoil of 1995.[28]

In spite of these disagreements, the concern with large current account deficits was serious enough for a number of investment banks to attempt estimating a sustainable level of current account deficit for the major emerging economies. According to the Goldman Sachs model, in late 1996 Malaysia and Thailand were running current account deficits that exceeded—but not by much—their sustainable levels. In Indonesia, Korea, and the Philippines the actual current account deficits were below what was estimated to be sustainable.[29]

Whether "large" current account deficits were in fact a central cause of the East Asian debacle continues to be somewhat controversial. After analyzing the available evidence, in a recent comprehensive study, Corsetti, Pesenti, and Roubini analyze the period leading to the East Asian crisis and argue that there is some support for the position that large current account deficits were one of the principal factors behind the crisis.[30] According to them, "*As a group, the countries that came under attack in 1997 appear to have been those with large current account deficits throughout the 1990s*" (emphasis in the original). And then, they add in a rather guarded way, "Prima facie evidence suggests that current account problems may have played a role in the dynamics of the Asian meltdown."[31] Radelet and Sachs also argue that large current account deficits were an important factor behind the crisis.[32] And, commenting on the eruption of the crisis in Thailand, the Chase Manhattan Bank agrees that large current account deficits were a basic cause of the crises.[33]

There are some problems with this view, however. Perhaps the most important one is that, as may be seen from table 9-2, with the exceptions of Malaysia and Thailand the current account deficits were not very large. Take for instance the 1990–96 period: for the five crisis countries the

---

28. Sachs, Tornell, and Velasco (1996). A similar perspective was taken by Calvo and Mendoza (1996) and Frankel and Rose (1996).

29. Ades and Kaune (1997).

30. Corsetti, Pesenti, and Roubini (1998).

31. Corsetti, Pesenti, and Roubini (1998, pp. 7–8).

32. Radelet and Sachs (1998).

33. Chase Manhattan Bank (1997).

Table 9-2. *Current Account, Balance of Payments Definition, 1990–97*
Percentage of gross domestic product

Economy	1990	1991	1992	1993	1994	1995	1996	1997
Korea	−0.69	−2.83	−1.28	0.30	−1.02	−1.86	−4.75	−1.85
Indonesia	−2.82	−3.65	−2.17	−1.33	−1.58	−3.18	−3.37	−2.24
Malaysia	−2.03	−8.69	−3.74	−4.66	−6.24	−8.43	−4.89	−4.85
Philippines	−6.08	−2.28	−1.89	−5.55	−4.60	−2.67	−4.77	−5.23
Singapore	8.33	11.29	11.38	7.57	16.12	16.81	15.65	15.37
Thailand	−8.50	−7.71	−5.66	−5.08	−5.60	−8.06	−8.10	−1.90
China	3.09	3.27	1.33	−1.94	1.26	0.23	0.87	3.24
Taiwan (China)	4.74	4.39	1.69	1.6	1.66	1.61	3.45	2.35

Source: Corsetti, Pesenti, and Roubini (1998).

deficit exceeded the arbitrary 5 percent threshold in only twelve out of thirty-five possible times. The frequency of occurrence is even lower for the two years preceding the crisis: three out of ten possible times. Some authors have attempted to analyze the magnitude of these deficits using formal solvency criteria. However, as I argue later in this paper, even when solvency-based models are used, simple ratio analyses are bound to generate misleading results.

Short-Term Portfolio Capital Flows Can Be Highly Volatile

Perhaps one of the most difficult issues in designing a market-oriented reform program refers to the *sequencing* of policies. A key question in the sequencing debate has been whether the opening of the capital account should take place early in the process, or whether some form of impediments to capital mobility should be retained until the liberalization of trade has been consolidated and the domestic banking sector is strong enough.[34] Mexico lifted capital controls in late 1989, rather early in its reform process and before the banking sector was privatized. Between 1990 and December 1993 massive volumes of short-term capital moved into the country; foreigners' investments in the Mexican stock market swelled from less than $5 billion to more than $54 billion; during that same period, foreigners' holdings of Mexican government securities increased by almost $50 billion.

34. Edwards (1984).

After the assassination of PRI (Partido Revolucionario Institutional) presidential candidate Luis Donaldo Colosio in March 1994, there was a significant slowdown in capital inflows into Mexico. The authorities faced this situation by following a three-part strategy. The exchange rate was allowed to climb to the top of the band, interest rates on short-term peso-denominated securities were allowed to increase somewhat, and an expanding volume of dollar-linked securities—the infamous Tesobonos—were issued. Throughout the year the Bank of Mexico sterilized the losses of international reserves in an almost one-to-one fashion.[35] The increase in interest rates was timid, as the authorities feared that the policy could generate two undesirable effects: first, it would slow down the recovery in an election year, and second, and more important, a significant hike in interest rates would have a negative impact on an already weakened domestic banking sector.[36] As the year progressed, the issuing of Tesobonos became the principal element of Mexico's strategy. By the second half of the year, many wary foreign investors began to withdraw their funds from Mexico. Toward the end of the year, sensing a growing disequilibrium, domestic residents moved large volumes of funds out of the country. On December 19, with the level of international reserves dangerously low, Mexico broadened the band. A few days later it became apparent that the new band was not sustainable, and the peso was floated.

After the devaluation the large volume of Tesobonos came back to haunt Mexico and magnified the effects of the devaluation. As the value of the peso plunged, it became increasingly difficult for Mexico to pay its foreign obligations. During the first eight months of 1995 more than $15 billion of Tesobonos were maturing, and without access to new monies Mexico moved dangerously close to defaulting on its official debts. It was only after the U.S. Treasury and IMF massive assistance packages that an orderly workout could be achieved.

Between 1995 and 1997 almost every postmortem on Mexico emphasized the role of volatile capital flows in unleashing the crisis. Birdsall, Gavin, and Hausmann, for example, have argued, "The Mexican crisis illustrates the dangers of short-term debt."[37] A similar position was taken

---

35. For an account of the crisis from the Bank of Mexico's perspective, see Gil Díaz and Carstens (1997).

36. Edwards (1998a).

37. Birdsall, Gavin, and Hausmann (1997).

by Sachs and his associates and by Calvo and Mendoza.[38] Although the analytical stories behind these papers are somewhat different—some emphasize a self-fulfilling panic, while others concentrate on herd behavior—the bottom line in all of them is unmistakable: if investors' sentiments change, capital flows can be reversed suddenly, generating major dislocations and, even, a major crisis.

The initial reaction to the belief that capital flows were at the center of the crisis was somewhat guarded. Gavin, Hausmann, and Leiderman (1996) argued that, under some circumstances, it would make sense to implement policies aimed at slowing down capital inflows.[39] The cases of Chile and Colombia were mentioned as possible examples of how to manage large inflows of capital. Others argued that the way in which capital inflows are intermediated makes a big difference and that banks, through which most flows are channeled into the domestic economy, should be regulated closely. Not surprisingly, this was the view taken by the U.S. Treasury.

The most influential analyses on the role of capital inflows were written before the crisis. In a series of papers, Calvo, Leiderman, and Reinhart argued that very large capital inflows create three type of problems for policymakers.[40] First, capital inflows induce a real exchange rate appreciation; second, they may not be intermediated efficiently, generating a misallocation of resources; and third, sudden reversals in the flows may lead to a crisis. After contemplating a series of policy measures the authors concluded that a pragmatic approach to managing capital inflows would possibly work best: "There are grounds to support a policy intervention mix based on the imposition of a tax on short-term capital imports, on enhancing the flexibility of exchange rates, and on raising marginal reserve requirements on short-term bank deposits."[41]

Although the experiences of individual countries differed, short-term portfolio funds were substantial in most of East Asia during 1995–97. For example, and contrary to the cases of most emerging economies, Indonesia lifted capital controls very early on, allowing short-term capital to move in and out of the country with few impediments. Thailand, in contrast, established in 1993 a government-run institution (the BIBF) to help attract for-

---

38. Sachs, Tornell, and Velasco (1996); Calvo and Mendoza (1996).
39. Gavin, Hausmann, and Leiderman (1996).
40. Calvo, Leiderman, and Reinhart (1993, 1995).
41. Calvo, Leiderman, and Reinhart (1995, p. 380).

eign capital. Malaysia maintained some form of controls on short-term (port-folio) movements until 1996, at which point they were somewhat eased.

Korea was, at least on paper, an exception among the East Asian coun-tries. For a long time the Korean authorities were skeptical of lifting controls on short-term capital, arguing that their inherent volatility would generate major dislocation. This reluctance to allow a higher degree of capital mobil-ity was, in fact, a difficulty in Korea's negotiations to join the Organisation for Economic Co-operation and Development (OECD). In spite of its reluctance to open the stock market to foreign funds, Korea allowed its banks to borrow from international banks very heavily and at very short maturities. By the end of 1996, for example, Korean banks had borrowed $67 billion from OECD banks, of which $50 billion is estimated to have had a maturity of less than one year. What made things even worse was that by 1996 most of these monies were being used to shore up Korean con-glomerates whose extravagant investments had gone bad.[42]

According to the Bank for International Settlements, by the end of 1996 short-term (less than a year) lending by industrial countries' banks to the East Asian nations was reaching extremely high levels. In Korea, for ex-ample, short-term bank loans from the advanced nations exceeded two times the volume of (gross) international reserves. In Indonesia, short-term loans from foreign banks exceeded gross international reserves by more than one-third. In late 1997 total short-term debt exceeded total reserves in Malaysia by more than 60 percent. These figures are not very different from those for Mexico in 1994. Taiwan offers a sharp contrast; by early 1997, short-term debt to foreign banks was less than 20 percent of inter-national reserves.

It is difficult to find an evaluation of the East Asian crisis that does not ascribe a central role to large capital flows in the region's debacle. Most authors emphasize the fact that short-term capital is particularly volatile and that, in a world with high capital mobility, losses in confidence result in massive portfolio reallocation and large losses in reserves.[43] An impor-tant lesson from these crises is that international reserve management is key to preventing currency crises. Traditionally, analysts have measured the adequacy of a country's international reserves by comparing them to the annual volume of imports. This measure is, of course, irrelevant in a world

---

42. See Corsetti, Pesenti, and Roubini (1998); Sachs and Radelet (1998).
43. See Goldstein (1998); Chote (1998); Fischer (1998).

Table 9-3. *Ratio of M1 Money Supply to Foreign Reserves, 1990–97*

Economy	1990	1991	1992	1993	1994	1995	1996	1997
Korea	1.50	2.16	1.84	1.79	1.57	1.54	1.44	1.81
Indonesia	1.73	1.48	1.30	1.44	1.58	1.53	1.21	1.62
Malaysia	0.96	0.93	0.81	0.69	0.84	1.07	1.16	1.46
Philippines	1.14	1.21	1.05	1.13	1.01	1.19	0.89	1.24
Singapore	0.30	0.28	0.28	0.29	0.26	0.26	0.25	0.26
Thailand	0.57	0.50	0.48	0.48	0.47	0.43	0.44	0.52
Hong Kong	n.a.	0.45	0.46	0.45	0.40	0.35	0.35	0.23
Taiwan (China)	0.99	0.98	1.18	1.27	1.28	1.32	1.42	1.55
China	4.95	3.87	10.30	12.99	4.74	4.07	3.45	3.24

Source: Corsetti, Pesenti, and Roubini (1998).
n.a. Not available.

where capital can move freely. As Edwards, Calvo and Mendoza, and Radelet and Sachs, among others, argue, the appropriate way to measure reserves is in relation to the domestic stock of money (M1 or M2).[44] See table 9-3 for the evolution of the ratio of M1 to reserves in a number of East Asian countries.

Although large capital inflows were on almost everyone's list of causes of the Mexican crisis, by early 1997 there were no massive calls for imposing capital controls on inflows. Even though views differed, as in the case of other policies, the consensus seemed to recognize the importance of sequencing arguments: the capital account should be opened once some key reforms, such as fiscal stabilization, trade reform, and the implementation of modern supervision, had been attained. The Asian crisis changed all of that, and in its wake the calls for controlling capital mobility have rapidly increased. These proposals have come from academics, journalists, international civil servants, and financiers. Some, such as Krugman, have argued that countries that are affected by a crisis should contemplate imposing temporary controls on capital outflows.[45] This policy would allow the country in question to lower interest rates and restructure its economy in an orderly fashion. A more popular proposition, however, relates to imposing

44. Edwards (1989); Calvo and Mendoza (1996); Radelet and Sachs (1998).
45. Paul Krugman, "Saving Asia: It's Time to Get Radical," *Fortune,* September 7, 1998, pp. 74–80.

controls on capital inflows as a way to prevent currency crises. A growing number of authors have claimed that the example of Chile—where, between 1991 and 1995, capital inflows were subject to a one-year reserve requirement—shows that restrictions on capital inflows (and especially short-term flows) may reduce a country's degree of vulnerability.[46]

Banks and Other Financial Institutions Should Be Supervised Closely

What made the Mexican crisis so severe was that it went beyond the exchange rate sphere, engulfing the banking system. In 1991 the Mexican government began to privatize the nineteen banks that had been nationalized in 1982–83, during the debt crisis. The privatization process was completed in 1992, with every bank being sold at several times its book value. At the time this was hailed as a great success, even though it should have been a matter of concern. The new owners—mostly large industrial and commercial conglomerates but also (as was later learned) illegal cartels—knew very little about banking and decided not to inject new capital into the recently acquired banks.[47]

During the early 1990s Mexico's newly privatized banks were eager to get into new lines of business, including housing loans, consumer credit, and reversed mortgages. The abundance of foreign capital permitted a remarkable credit expansion during 1991–94, when bank loans increased in real terms at an annual rate in excess of 25 percent. The bad news was that at the same time the ratio of past due loans to total loans more than doubled, from 4 to 8 percent of bank's portfolio.

Mexico found that it was not easy to create effectively and rapidly a solid bank regulatory framework. The lack of trained personnel, including inspectors and accountants, slowed down the process, as did the rivalry between government institutions with overlapping responsibilities. When the peso crisis erupted in December 1994, the supervisory system was still seriously underdeveloped, and Mexico's financial sector was in a very weak position. Moreover, the type of policies that could have helped to avert the exchange rate crisis—the tightening of monetary and fiscal policy in 1994, for example—conceivably would have made the financial health of banks even weaker by increasing the number of bankruptcies.

---

46. Massad (1998); Ito (1999); Rodrik (1998).
47. Edwards (1998b).

According to Birdsall, Gavin, and Hausmann, the main policy lesson from Mexico is that "policymakers need to keep a vigilant eye on the banking system. In particular, they should 'lean against the wind' of lending booms, to ensure that bank lending does not grow too rapidly, and they should ensure that banks are robust enough to weather the shocks to which they will inevitably be exposed."[48] Similar points are made by Calvo, Leiderman, and Reinhart and by Hale, among others.[49] In 1995 then undersecretary of the treasury Lawrence Summers argued that to the extent that bank supervision is appropriate, there is no need for emerging countries to restrict capital mobility: "Countries should be very cautious about imposing capital controls with the objective of discouraging capital inflows . . . It is appropriate for supervisory authorities to think about reserve requirements and new regulations, and to be prepared to respond aggressively to changes in the pattern of capital inflows, through improvements in regulation and supervision."[50]

As in Mexico, the banking sector in every East Asian country was weak and poorly supervised. In Indonesia, for example, a number of banks—many of them owned by relatives and close associates of President Suharto—systematically financed questionable projects and, in a way that resembled Mexico's experience merely three years earlier, fueled a remarkable real estate bubble. The weakness of many of the East Asian banks was well known to international analysts. In May 1997, for example, Standard & Poor's lowered the ratings of the government-controlled Thai Finance Corporation (IFCT), and in June of that year financial analysts estimated that in Thailand nonperforming assets of the financial system were reaching 12 to 15 percent of loans (see table 9-4).

It was also well known that many Korean banks were having trouble getting paid by their clients. As some of the medium-size *chaebols* ran into financial difficulties, Korean banks rolled over their debts while increasing their short-term borrowing from international banks. The extent of supervision of Korea's banks was so weak that they were basically free to speculate in the international financial markets. In fact, throughout most of 1997 many of the Korean banks borrowed short term in yen in order to purchase Brazilian and other Latin American Brady bonds! As early as November 1996, Goldman Sachs expressed concern over the health of

48. Birdsall, Gavin, and Hausmann (1997, p. 289).
49. Calvo, Leiderman, and Reinhart (1995); Hale (1997).
50. Summers (1996, p. 55).

Table 9-4. *Nonperforming Loans as a Percentage of Total Lending, 1996*

Country	Share of total lending
Korea	8.0
Indonesia	13.0
Malaysia	10.0
Philippines	14.0
Singapore	4.0
Thailand	13.0
Hong Kong	3.0
China	14.0
Taiwan	4.0

Source: Bank for International Settlements (1997).

Korea's banks, giving them the next to worst rating in its vulnerability analysis. And according to Merrill Lynch, by late 1997 the Korean "banking system's equity capital has been effectively wiped out."[51]

In spite of these clear signs of weakness, many analysts dismissed the possibility of a major collapse in Korea. This perception was based on two factors. First, given the existence of implicit insurance and a long history of government intervention in the financial sector, it was believed that government would bail out the banks. Of course, what people missed was that in 1996 short-term external debt of Korean banks was already twice the country's stock of international reserves. Second, there was the notion that, because Korea had capital controls, the health of banks was not as important as in other countries. As I argue in greater detail later in this paper, this has become a generalized and dangerous myth among some policy analysts.

Starting in the second half of 1997, and largely as a result of the mounting difficulties in other countries in the region, international banks became increasingly reluctant to roll over their Korean loans. As the local banks could not come up with the required foreign exchange to repay their debts, they had to turn to the Bank of Korea. In a move that proved to be a fatal mistake, the Bank of Korea used up most of its (already low) international reserves in an effort to shore up domestic banks and avoid a major crisis. As reserves dwindled, more foreign creditors pulled out of the country, unleashing a perverse vicious circle.

51. Merrill Lynch (1997).

The East Asian crisis greatly strengthened the view that a weak banking sector can generate tremendous damage in an emerging economy in the process of liberalizing.[52] Everyone agrees on this one: bank supervision is of the essence. How supervision should be implemented in countries with weak institutions is another matter. In fact, as Mexico's experience shows, even when the authorities understand the importance of supervision, it may take a long time to have a new system in place.[53] There have been some new and specific proposals aimed at protecting the health of banks in countries with limited regulatory capacity. These range from imposing 100 percent reserves banking to having a majority presence of foreign-owned banks.[54] It is likely, however, that their implementation will be hampered by political economy factors.

Information and Transparency Are of the Essence

A postmortem of the Mexican crisis sponsored by the Council on Foreign Relations and undertaken by an independent task force chaired by John Whitehead concluded that in the period leading to the crisis full financial information was not forthcoming to all investors. A roundtable organized by the Group of Thirty under the telling title "Mexico: Why Didn't Wall Street Sound the Alarm?" reached a similar conclusion.

The IMF agreed with this conclusion and vowed to design a modern system of information gathering that would help to avoid unpleasant surprises in the future. A 1995 paper on Mexican lessons coauthored by the director of the IMF's Western Hemisphere Department and the chief of the IMF's Mexico Division argued that it was essential to establish "stricter requirements concerning the regular and timely submission of key economic and financial data to the fund and of standards for the publication of the kinds of economic data needed to enable markets to work more efficiently." To this effect the IMF established the Special Data Dissemination Standards (SDDS) program, whose purpose is to "enhance the availability of timely and comprehensive statistics and therefore contribute to the pursuit of sound macroeconomic policies; the SDDS is also expected to contribute to the improved functioning of financial markets."[55]

---

52. Ito (1999); Radelet and Sachs (1998); Corsetti, Pesenti, and Roubini (1998).
53. Finance Minister Aspe devoted almost a full chapter of his book on the Mexican reforms to discussing the importance of bank supervision (Aspe 1993, ch. 4).
54. Garber (1998).
55. From the SDDS website (http://dsbb.imf.org [July 2, 1999]).

In spite of these initiatives, the East Asian countries did little to improve the flow of information and availability of data cr to enhance the degree of transparency of government actions. Independent country-risk evaluators continued to make a point of the lack of transparency and heightened corruption in many East Asian nations. For example, when evaluating corruption, the *International Country Risk Guide* systematically gave poor marks to Indonesia, the Philippines, and Thailand and only marginally better marks to Korea and Malaysia.[56]

Most East Asian analysts were aware that the quality of available data was poor and that the degree of transparency was deplorable. In fact, little was known about the true quality of banks' portfolios or about the volume of loans granted to the dominant conglomerates. Moreover, there was virtually no reliable information on the off-balance-sheet position of the banking system—and in the case of Thailand, on that of the central bank—including the astonishingly large sales of dollars in the futures market. Worse yet, as in the case of Mexico, the rating agencies largely failed to anticipate the deepening weaknesses of the East Asian economies. For instance, Standard & Poor's did not change its rating on Thailand until August 1, 1997; Indonesia, in turn, was not downgraded until December 31, 1997! How to improve the dissemination of information continues to be a difficult issue that would-be international architects will have to tackle in the months to come.

Some Complications and the Multiplicative Nature of the Vulnerability Factors

The history of financial collapses indicates that, in addition to the financial factors discussed above, many emerging economies face two serious complications. The first is the presence of fiscal imbalances. In this case the government is forced either to print money or to attract—usually through very high domestic interest rates—foreign funds in order to close the gap between government revenues and expenditures. As the recent Brazilian crisis has shown, both alternatives, however, are short-term solutions and cannot be sustained in the longer run. At some point either international reserves will be depleted or the policy of high interest rates will backfire by slowing down the economy and igniting a series of bankruptcies. To the

56. *International Country Risk Guide Newsletter* (several issues).

extent that the public believes that this stance is not politically sustainable, it will move its funds out of the country, generating additional distress and eventually a crisis.

Many analysts had thought that fiscal imbalances were a required element in a currency crisis. Not at all. Once again, a careful reading of financial history suggests that there have been numerous currency collapses in countries that have had control over public sector finances. The Chilean crisis of 1982 and the Mexican meltdown of 1994 are the better known, but certainly not the only ones.[57]

The second complication is political. If the country faces political upheaval and social turmoil, international investors will become skittish and will withdraw from the market at the first signs of financial stress. This in turn—and especially in the presence of the vulnerability factors discussed above—is likely to unleash a series of events that could, sooner rather than later, end up in a major run against the currency. The stampede of foreign investors following the assassinations of Mexican presidential candidate Luis Donaldo Colosio and PRI's Secretary General Ruiz Massieu underscore this principle. In at least two East Asian countries—Indonesia and Korea—there were significant political uncertainties during 1997. Although under "normal" circumstances these problems would not have ignited a crisis, they proved to be decisive in an environment where many of the financial variables discussed above were showing weaknesses.

The relationship between vulnerability factors is highly complex and subject to numerous feedback mechanisms. Overvalued exchange rates, for example, slow down exports, encourage imports, and generate larger current account deficits. As a result, domestic interest rates have to rise in order to attract the foreign capital required to finance this deficit. Higher interest rates, in turn, hurt local companies and increase the ratio of non-performing bank loans. The banks, and sometimes the government, react to this picture by rolling over questionable loans, hiding their true financial situation, and issuing more dollar-denominated debt. As additional foreign funds pour in, the extent of overvaluation becomes more severe, and the vicious circle is reinforced.

Many country-risk models used by financial analysts ignore the highly complex ways in which these factors interact. Instead, these models compile lists of vulnerability indicators, adding them up in a mechanical fash-

---

57. On Chile, see Edwards and Edwards (1991); on other crises see Edwards and Santaella (1993).

ion. By neglecting the multiplicative nature of these factors, traditional approaches are bound, as in the case of East Asia, to miss many of the early distress signals. The problem is that, in spite of their sophisticated statistical models, financial analysts tend to ignore *history*—and, more specifically, *comparative history*—when evaluating a country's prospects and vulnerabilities. By concentrating almost exclusively on the country's immediate past (twenty-four to thirty-six months), standard statistical approaches, including value-at-risk analysis, neglect other countries' experiences, including events that have led to major crises. Moreover, most existing models used to evaluate country risk take a "linear" or "additive" view of the world and ignore the fact that "vulnerability factors" are multiplicative, feeding into each other and reinforcing themselves.

How Useful Are Current Account Ratios as External Sector Indicators?

During the past three decades there has been a considerable evolution in economists' views regarding the current account. In an important article, Corden distinguishes between the "old" and "new" views on the current account. According to the old view, "a country can run a current account deficit for a limited period. But no positive deficit is sustainable indefinitely."[58] The new view, in contrast, distinguishes between deficits that are the result of fiscal imbalances and those that respond to private sector decisions. According to the extreme version of this new view, "An increase in the current account deficit that results from a shift in private sector behavior—a rise in investment or a fall in savings—should not be a matter of concern at all."[59]

As mentioned in the preceding section, in the aftermath of the Mexican crisis many analysts argued that the new view was seriously flawed. While some, such as Bruno, argued that large deficits stemming from higher investment were not particularly dangerous, others maintained that any deficit in excess of a certain threshold—say, 4 percent of GDP—was a cause for concern.[60] Partially motivated by this debate, Milesi-Ferreti and Razin have developed a framework to analyze current

---

58. Corden (1994, p. 88).
59. Corden (1994, p. 92).
60. Bruno (1995).

account sustainability.[61] Their main point is that the "sustainable" level of the current account is the level that is consistent with solvency. This, in turn, means the level at which "the ratio of external debt to GDP is stabilized."[62]

The basic idea behind this type of sustainability analysis is captured by the following simple analysis. Solvency requires that the ratio of the (net) international demand for the country's liabilities (both debt and nondebt liabilities) stabilizes at a level compatible with foreigners' net demand for these claims on future income flows. Under standard portfolio theory, the net international demand for country j liabilities can be written as:

$$(9\text{-}1) \qquad \delta_j = \alpha_j (W - W_j) - (1 - \alpha_{jj}) W_j,$$

where α_j is the percentage of the world's wealth (W) that international investors are willing to hold in the form of country j's assets; W_j is country j's wealth (broadly defined), and α_{jj} is country j's allocation of its own assets. The asset allocation shares α_j and α_{jj} depend, as in standard portfolio analyses, on expected returns and perceived risk. Assuming that country j's wealth is a multiple λ of its (potential or full-employment) GDP and that country j's wealth is a fraction β_j of the world's wealth W, it is possible to write the (international) net demand for country j's assets as:[63]

$$(9\text{-}2) \qquad \delta_j = [\alpha_j \, \theta_j - (1 - \alpha_{jj})] \, \lambda_{jj} \, Y_j,$$

where Y_j is (potential) GDP, and $\theta_j = (1 - \beta_j) / \beta_j$.

Denoting $\{[\alpha_j \theta_j - (1 - \alpha_{jj})] \lambda_{jj}\} = \gamma *_j$, then

$$(9\text{-}3) \qquad \delta_j = \gamma *_j Y_j.$$

Equation 9-3 simply states that, in long-run equilibrium, the net international demand for country j's assets can be expressed as a proportion $\gamma *_j$ of the country's (potential or sustainable) GDP. The determinants of the factor of proportionality are given by equation 9-3 and, as expressed, include relative returns and perceived risk of country j and other countries.[64]

---

61. Milesi-Ferreti and Razin (1996).

62. Milesi-Ferreti and Razin (1998).

63. This expression will hold for every period t; I have omitted the subscript t in order to economize on notation.

64. The assumptions of constant λ and θ are, of course, highly simplifying.

In this framework, and under the simplifying assumption that international reserves do not change, the "sustainable" current account ratio is given by:[65]

$$(9-4) \qquad (C/Y)_j = (g_j + \pi^*_j) \{[\alpha_j \theta_j - (1 - \alpha_{jj})] \lambda_{jj}\},$$

where g_j is the country's sustainable rate of growth, and π^*_j is a valuation factor (approximately) equal to international inflation.[66] Notice that if $[\alpha_j \theta_j - (1 - \alpha_{jj})] < 0$, domestic residents' demand for foreign liabilities exceeds foreigners' demand for the country's liabilities. Under these circumstances the country has to run a current account surplus in order to maintain a stable ratio of (net external) liabilities to GDP. According to equation 9-4, there is no reason for the "sustainable" current account deficit to be the same across countries. In fact, that would only happen by sheer coincidence. The main message of equation 9-4 is that "sustainable" current account balances vary across countries and depend on whatever variables affect portfolio decisions and economic growth. In other words, the notion that no country can run a sustainable deficit in excess of 4 percent of GDP, 5 percent of GDP, or any other arbitrary number is nonsense.

Using a similar framework to the one developed above, Goldman Sachs has made a serious effort to estimate long-run sustainable current account deficits for a number of countries.[67] Using a twenty-five-country data set, Goldman Sachs estimates the ratio of external liabilities that foreigners are willing to hold—γ^*_j in the model sketched above—as well as each country's potential rate of growth. Table 9-5 contains the estimates of γ^*_j, while table 9-6 presents their estimates of long-run sustainable current account deficits. In addition to estimating these steady-state imbalances, Goldman Sachs calculates asymptotic convergence paths toward those long-run current accounts. These are presented in table 9-6 under the heading "short-run sustainable current account balances." Several interesting features emerge from these tables. First, there is a wide variety of estimated long-run "sustainable" deficits. Second, with the notable exception of China, whose estimated "sustainable" deficit is an improbable 11 percent of GDP,

65. As a result of this assumption, equation 9-3 overstates (slightly) the "sustainable" current account ratio.

66. Under the restrictive assumption that international inflation is equal to zero, this expression corresponds exactly to Goldman Sachs's equation 9-5. See Ades and Kaune (1997, p. 6).

67. Ades and Kaune (1997).

Table 9-5. *External World's Desired Holding of a Country's Liabilities*
Percentage of GDP

Country	Desired holding
Argentina	48.4
Bulgaria	42.8
China	129.2
Czech Republic	31.3
Hungary	31.3
Indonesia	53.9
Malaysia	53.9
Morocco	31.9
Peru	48.4
Poland	55.4
Russia	38.3
Thailand	64.6
Venezuela	38.3
Brazil	38.3
Chile	48.4
Colombia	38.3
Ecuador	31.3
India	47.2
Korea	55.4
Mexico	38.3
Panama	38.3
Philippines	57.1
Romania	38.3
South Africa	38.3
Turkey	38.3

Source: Goldman Sachs, Emerging Markets Economic Research Group (various years).

the estimated levels are very modest and range from 1.3 to 4.5 percent of GDP. Third, although the range for the short-run sustainable level is broader, still in very few countries it exceeds 4 percent of GDP. Fourth, the estimates of the ratio of each country's external liabilities that foreigners are willing to hold—γ^*_j in the model sketched above—exhibit more variability. Its range (excluding China) goes from 31.3 to 64.6 percent of GDP.

Although this type of analysis represents an improvement with respect to arbitrary current account thresholds, it is subject to some important limitations, including the fact that it is exceedingly difficult to obtain reli-

Table 9-6. *Sustainable Current Account Deficit*

Percentage of gross domestic product

Country	1997 current account deficit (expected)	Short-run, sustainable current account deficit	Long-run, steady-state sustainable current account deficit
Argentina	2.7	3.9	2.9
Brazil	4.5	2.9	1.9
Bulgaria	−2.6	0.4	2.4
Chile	3.7	4.2	2.9
China	−1.4	12.9	11.1
Colombia	4.8	2.6	1.9
Czech Republic	8.6	2.1	1.3
Ecuador	2.0	−0.5	1.3
Hungary	4.0	0.8	1.3
India	1.8	3.8	2.8
Indonesia	3.0	4.0	3.4
Korea	3.8	4.9	3.6
Malaysia	4.1	4.9	3.4
Mexico	1.7	2.1	1.9
Morocco	1.8	0.3	1.3
Panama	6.1	0.8	1.9
Peru	5.1	3.3	2.9
Philippines	4.2	4.5	3.8
Poland	3.8	4.7	3.6
Romania	0.5	2.3	1.9
Russia	−2.8	2.5	1.9
South Africa	1.8	3.0	1.9
Thailand	5.4	6.0	4.5
Turkey	1.2	2.1	1.9
Venezuela	−4.6	2.2	1.9

Source: Goldman Sachs, Emerging Markets Economic Research Group (various years).

able estimates for the key variables. In particular, there is very little evidence on equilibrium portfolio shares. Also, the underlying models used to calculate the long-term rate of growth tend to be very simplistic.

The most serious limitation of this framework, however, is that it does not take into account, in a satisfactory way, transitional issues arising from changes in portfolio allocations. These, however, can have a fundamental effect on the way in which the economy adjusts to changes in the external environment. For example, the speed at which a country absorbs surges in foreign demand for its liabilities has an effect on the sustainable path of the current account.[68]

The key point is that even small changes in foreign net demand for the country's liabilities may generate complex equilibrium adjustment paths for the current account. These current account movements are necessary for the new portfolio allocation to materialize and do not generate a dis-equilibrium—or unsustainable—balance. However, when this equilibrium path of the current account is contrasted with threshold levels obtained from models such as the one sketched above, analysts could (incorrectly) conclude that the country is facing a serious disequilibrium.

To illustrate this point, assume that equation 9-5 captures the way in which the current account responds to changes in portfolio allocations. In this equation γ^*_t is the new desired level (relative to GDP) of foreigners' (net) desired holdings of the country's liabilities; γ^*_{t-1} is the old desired level.

$$(9\text{-}5) \qquad (C/Y)_t = (g + \pi^*)\,\gamma^*_t + \beta\,(\gamma^*_t - \gamma^*_{t-1}) - \eta\,[(C/Y)_{t-1} - (g + \pi^*)\,\gamma^*_t]\,,$$

where, as before, $\gamma^* = \{[\alpha_j\,\theta_j - (1 - \alpha_{jj})]\,\lambda_{jj}\}$. According to this equation, short-term deviations of the current account from its long-run level can result from two forces. The first is a traditional stock adjustment term $(\gamma^*_t - \gamma^*_{t-1})$ that captures deviations between the demanded and the actual stock of assets. If $(\gamma^*_t > \gamma^*_{t-1})$, then the current account deficit exceeds its long-run value. β is the speed of adjustment, which depends on a number of factors, including the degree of capital mobility in the country in question and the maturity of its foreign debt. The second force, which is captured by $-\eta\,[(C/Y)_{t-1} - (g + \pi^*)\,\gamma^*_t]$ in equation 9-5, is a self-correcting term. This term plays the role of making sure that in this economy there is, at least, some form of "consumption smoothing." The importance of this self-correcting term depends on the value of η. If $\eta = 0$, the self-correcting term plays no role, and the dynamics of the current account are given by a more traditional stock adjustment equation. In the more general case, however, when both β and η are different from zero, the dynamics of the current account are richer, and discrepancies between γ^*_t and γ^*_{t-1} are resolved gradually through time.

68. Bacchetta and van Wincoop (1998).

As may be seen from equation 9-5, in the long-run steady state, when $\gamma^*_t = \gamma^*_{t-1}$ and $(CY)_{t-1} = (C/Y)$, the current account is at its sustainable level, $(g + \pi^*) \{[\alpha_j \theta_j - (1 - \alpha_{jj})] \lambda_{jj}\}$. The dynamic behavior for the net stock of the country's assets in the hands of foreigners, as a percentage of GDP, is given by equation 9-6:

$$(9\text{-}6) \qquad \gamma_t = [\gamma_{t-1} + (C/Y)_t] / (1 + g + \pi^*) .$$

The implications of incorporating the adjustment process can be illustrated with a simple example based on the Goldman Sachs computations presented above. According to the figures in table 9-5, by the end of 1996 there was a significant gap between foreigners' desired holdings of Mexican and Argentine liabilities: while the Mexican ratio stood at 38.3 percent of the county's GDP, the Argentine ratio was 48.4 percent. Assume that for some reason—a reduction in perceived Mexican country risk, for example—this gap is closed to half its initial level and that the demand for Mexican liabilities increases to 43 percent of Mexican GDP.

Figure 9-4 presents the estimated evolution of the sustainable current account path under the assumptions that Mexican growth remains at 5 percent and that world inflation is zero, both assumptions made by Goldman Sachs. In addition it is assumed that $\beta = 0.65$, $\eta = 0.45$, and the increase in γ^* is spread over three years.

The results from this simple exercise are quite interesting: first the initial level of the sustainable current account deficit is equal to 1.9 percent of GDP, exactly the level estimated by Goldman Sachs (see table 9-6). Second, the current account converges to 2.15 percent of GDP, as suggested by equation 9-5. Third, and more important for the analysis in this section, the dynamics of the current account are characterized by a sizable overshooting, with the "equilibrium path" deficit peaking at 3.5 percent of GDP. If, however, it is assumed that the increase in γ^* takes place in one period, the equilibrium deficit would peak at 5 percent, a figure more than twice as large as the new long-term sustainable level.

What makes this exercise particularly interesting is that these rather large overshootings are the result of very small changes in portfolio preferences. This strongly suggests that in a world where desired portfolio shares are constantly changing, the concept of a sustainable equilibrium current account path is very difficult to estimate. Moreover, this simple exercise indicates that relying on current account ratios—even ratios calculated using current "sustainability" frameworks—can be highly misleading. These dynamic features of current account adjustment may explain why so

Figure 9-4. *On the Equilibrium Path of the Current Account Deficit:*
A Simulation Exercise for Mexico

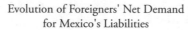

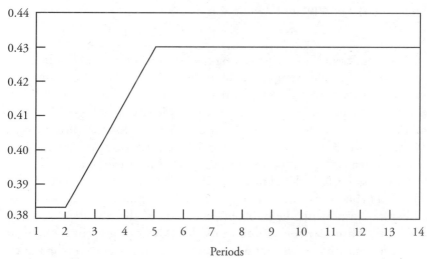

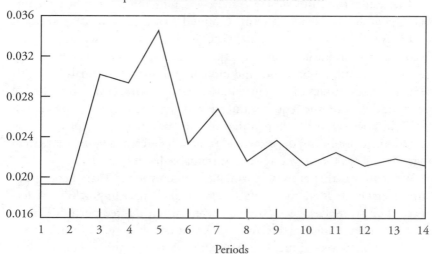

Source: Author's simulations.

many authors have failed to find a direct connection between current account deficits and currency crises.

The analysis presented above suggests two important dimensions of adjustment and crisis prevention. First, current account dynamics affect real exchange rate behavior. More specifically, current account overshooting is associated with a temporary appreciation of the real exchange rate. The actual magnitude of this appreciation depends on a number of variables, including the income demand elasticity for nontradables and the labor intensity of the nontradable sector. In order for this dynamic adjustment to be smooth, the country should have the ability to implement the required real exchange rate depreciation in the second phase of the process. This is likely to be easier under a flexible exchange rate regime than under a rigid one. Second, if foreigners' (net) demand for the country's liabilities declines—as is likely to be the case if there is some degree of contagion, for example—the required current account compression also overshoots. In the immediate run, the country will have to go through a very severe adjustment. This can be illustrated by the following simple example: assume that as a result of external events—a crisis in Brazil, say—the demand for Argentine liabilities declines from the level estimated by Goldman Sachs— 48.4 percent of GDP—to 40 percent of GDP. While the long-run equilibrium current account, as calculated by Goldman Sachs, would experience a very modest decline from 2.9 to 2.4 percent of GDP, in the short run the adjustment would be drastic. In fact, the simple model developed above suggests that after two years the deficit would have to be compressed to approximately 0.5 percent of GDP.[69]

The fact that the simple analysis of current account ratios can be misleading does not mean that the current account is a completely irrelevant variable. Indeed, within the spirit of the framework presented above, it is possible that the current account deficit is not compatible, even after considering a plausible dynamic path, with a stable ratio of liabilities to GDP. Moreover, if the economic structure of the country is overly rigid, the current account overshooting may generate serious dislocations that could, on their own, affect portfolio allocation and unleash a vicious circle.

---

69. This assumes that growth is not affected. If it declines, as is likely, the required compression would be even larger.

Do Controls on Capital Inflows Reduce Vulnerability?

In the aftermath of these crises a number of influential academics have argued that globalization has gone too far and that, in the words of Paul Krugman, "Sooner or later we will have to turn the clock at least part of the way back: to limit capital flows for countries that are unsuitable for either currency unions or free floating."[70] Discussions of the new international financial architecture have focused on two types of controls on cross-border capital movements: controls on (short-term) capital inflows, similar to those implemented in Chile between 1991 and 1998, and controls on capital outflows, of the type imposed in Malaysia in mid-1998. Although controls on outflows have remained rather unpopular among economists—a significant exception being Krugman—controls on inflows have rapidly grown in popularity.[71]

Some observers have argued that Chile's approach to capital movements has been effective in reducing a country's vulnerability to speculative spells and in reducing the real exchange rate "deprotection" effect of large capital inflows. It has also been argued that these restrictions have allowed Chile's monetary authorities to maintain greater control over monetary policy in the face of large capital inflows.[72] Joseph Stiglitz, the World Bank's chief economist, has been quoted by the *New York Times* as saying, "You want to look for policies that discourage 'hot money' but facilitate the flow of long-term loans, and there is evidence that now the Chilean approach, or some version of it, does this."[73] In this section I evaluate Chile's recent experience with capital controls on inflows. I argue that the evidence does not support the current enthusiasm for this policy and that the relative absence of contagion effect in Chile is due to its sturdy banking regulation and not to its capital controls policy.[74]

Chile's most recent experience with restrictions on capital inflows began in 1991 and lasted until September 1998. This policy took two basic forms: minimum-stay requirements for foreign direct investment flows and unremunerated reserve requirements on other forms of capital inflows.

---

70. Krugman (1999, p. 74).

71. Paul Krugman, "Saving Asia: It's Time to Get Radical," *Fortune,* September 7, 1998, pp. 74–80.

72. Massad (1998).

73. As quoted in the *New York Times,* February 1, 1998, Louis Uchitelle, "Ounces of Prevention for the Next Crisis," sec. 3, p. 9. This view has recently been endorsed by Ito (1999).

74. This discussion draws partially on Edwards (1998a).

Initially, 20 percent of capital entering the country had to be deposited at
the central bank for one year; during this period the deposit earned no
interest. The share of the deposit was increased to 30 percent in May of
1992, was reduced to 10 percent in July of 1998, and was reduced to zero
in September of 1998.

In evaluating Chile's recent experience with capital restrictions I focus
on three issues. First, is there evidence that capital controls have affected
the composition of capital flows? Second, is there evidence that the imposition of restrictions on capital mobility has affected the dynamic response
of the real exchange rate to capital flow shocks? The importance of this
question stems from the fact that the restrictions were deliberately imposed
to reduce the real exchange rate deprotection associated with the surge in
capital inflows.[75] In fact, as documented extensively earlier in this paper,
this real exchange rate deprotection effect of capital inflows is considered a
major force behind the East Asian crisis. I tackle this question by estimating a series of unrestricted vector autoregressions (VARs) on quarterly data
and analyzing the real exchange rate impulse response functions. And
third, is there evidence that the imposition of the unremunerated reserve
requirements affected in a significant way the relationship between Chile's
and international interest rates? More specifically, I inquire whether these
restrictions affected the time-series process of interest rate differentials (corrected by expected devaluation) in Chile. In general one would expect that
impediments to free capital mobility would affect both the speed at which
interest rate differentials decline as well as the level to which they converge.
I address this third question through the analysis estimation of a series of
univariate equations using a time-varying coefficients technique.

Chile's Controls and the Composition of Capital Inflows

In a recent study, Valdes-Prieto and Soto have calculated the tax equivalence of Chile's unremunerated reserve requirement on capital inflows and
have evaluated their effect on a number of variables including real exchange
rates.[76] These authors conclude that these restrictions were not (fully)
evaded and that for a 180-day loan their annual tax equivalence fluctuated
between 1.29 and 4.53 percent. The implicit tax equivalence of longer-
term funds has been proportional, since mid-1992, with loans with longer

75. Valdes-Prieto and Soto (1996).
76. Valdes-Prieto and Soto (1996).

maturities paying a lower implicit tax.[77] According to Valdes-Prieto and Soto, these capital restrictions altered the composition of capital inflows: they discouraged short-term capital inflows but had no significant effects on the aggregate volume of capital entering the country.[78]

Table 9-7 presents data on the composition of capital flows into Chile between 1988 and 1996. There was a marked change in the composition of capital inflows, with shorter (that is less than a year) flows declining steeply relative to longer-term capital. The fact that this change in composition happened immediately after the capital restrictions were imposed supports the view that the controls policy indeed affected the composition of inflows. These data also show that, with the exception of a brief decline in 1993, the total volume of capital inflows into the country continued to increase. In the rest of this section, I analyze the effect of (net) flows and capital controls on real exchange rates and on interest rate differentials.

One of the fundamental purposes—if not the main purpose—of Chile's restrictions on capital inflows has been to reduce their volume and, in that way, to ease their pressure on the real exchange rate. According to a recent paper coauthored by a former senior official in the Ministry of Finance, "Growing concerns about inflation and the exchange rate pressure of capital inflows have led policymakers to introduce specific capital controls."[79] Valdes-Prieto and Soto agree and argue that the imposition of these restrictions in mid-1991 responded to the authorities' attempt to balance two policy objectives: to reduce inflation and to maintain a competitive real exchange rate.[80] According to these authors, by implementing these unremunerated reserve requirements authorities hoped to reduce, or at least delay, the real exchange rate appreciation effects of these flows, while, at the same time, maintaining a higher differential between domestic and international interest rates (corrected by expected devaluations). This higher differential, in turn, was expected to help achieve the anti-inflationary objective. In this subsection, I evaluate the real exchange rate objective, while in the next I address the interest rate differential objective.

I use two approaches to evaluate the real exchange rate objective of Chile's capital controls policy. First, using quarterly data I estimate a series of VARs for two different subsamples—one with and one without capital controls—and evaluate the real exchange rate impulse response to capital

77. See also Cowan and de Gregorio (1998).
78. Valdes-Prieto and Soto (1996).
79. Cowan and de Gregorio (1998, p. 3).
80. Valdes-Prieto and Soto (1996).

inflow innovations. Under an effective policy one would expect that the real exchange rate response to a capital flow innovation would be less pronounced, especially in terms of its dynamics, in the period with controls. Second, I use the longer-period VARs (1987–96) estimates to evaluate the impulse response to a shock to the tax equivalence of the unremunerated reserve requirement.[81]

Figure 9-5 contains the impulse response functions for the log of the real exchange rate for the complete period (1981–96), a subperiod with no restrictions on capital inflows (1981–91:2), and a subperiod when the capital restrictions are in effect (1991:3–96). The same data definitions as in the preceding section are used. Figure 9-6 contains the real exchange rate response to an innovation to the (implicit) tax on capital inflows.[82] Two important facts emerge from these figures. First, the effect of the capital innovation on the (log) of the real exchange rate is extremely similar across periods. The maximum appreciation is almost the same in the period with restrictions as in the period with no restrictions on capital inflows. However, the (log of the) real exchange rate returns to equilibrium somewhat faster in the period with restrictions. This result is confirmed by the impulse response function in figure 9-6.[83] An innovation to restrictions on inflows results in a slight real depreciation. The effect, however, is short-lived and disappears after four quarters. The ordering of the variables is, as usual, important. In determining the ordering, one could be tempted to argue that capital controls are exogenous. This, however, could be misleading since in Chile, as in other emerging markets, the extent and coverage of controls have been adjusted in response to changes in the magnitude of capital flows. For this reason, alternative orderings, including one that was allowed to respond endogenously, are considered. Overall, the results under alternative orderings confirm the results in figure 9-6. The variance decomposition of the forecast errors of the (log of the) real exchange rate, not presented here due to space considerations (results are available on request), confirms that the restrictions on capital inflows have not been effective in affecting the real exchange rate behavior: the capital restrictions variable explains no more than 3 percent of the forecast error.

81. The tax equivalencies estimated by Valdes-Prieto and Soto (1996) were updated to the end of 1997.

82. Cardoso and Goldfajn (1997) analyze a series of impulse response functions to a capital controls innovation in Brazil.

83. As Cardoso and Goldfajn (1997) have argued, capital controls in Latin America are likely to be endogenous. Thus, care should be taken in establishing the vectors ordering in the VAR estimation.

Table 9-7. *Gross Capital Inflows to Chile, 1988–96*
Millions of U.S. dollars unless otherwise noted

| Year | Short-term loans | | Long-term loans | | Amount of total loans | Amount of deposits[a] |
	Amount	Percentage of total	Amount	Percentage of total		
1988	916,564	96.3	34,838	3.7	951,402	n.a.
1989	1,452,595	95.0	77,122	5.0	1,529,717	n.a.
1990	1,683,149	90.3	181,419	9.7	1,864,568	n.a.
1991	521,198	72.7	196,115	27.3	717,313	587
1992	225,197	28.9	554,072	71.1	779,269	11,424
1993	159,462	23.6	515,147	76.4	674,609	41,280
1994	161,575	16.5	819,699	83.5	981,274	87,039
1995	69,675	6.2	1,051,829	93.8	1,121,504	38,752
1996	67,254	3.2	2,042,456	96.8	2,109,710	172,320

Source: Banco Central de Chile (various years).
n.a. Not available.
a. Deposits in the Banco Central de Chile due to reserve requirements.

Figure 9-5. *Response of Real Exchange Rate to Capital Flow Controls in Chile*[a]

Real exchange rate (log)

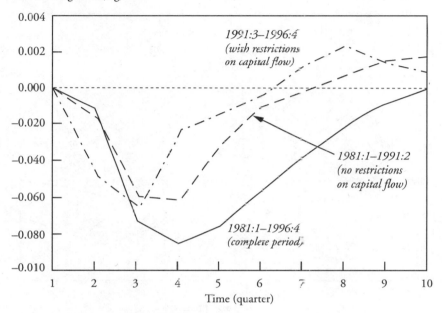

Source: Author's simulations.

a. Unrestricted vector autoregressions estimate within one standard deviation.

Although these results are subject to some limitations—the experience with capital restrictions is rather short, limiting the availability of data points—they do provide preliminary evidence that the impact of this policy on the real exchange rate has been very limited and short-lived. These results confirm previous findings by Valdes-Prieto and Soto, who, using a very different technique and a shorter sample to estimate a real exchange rate equation for Chile, conclude that "The unremunerated reserve requirement does not affect in any way the long-run level of the real exchange rate . . . [I]n addition . . . these reserve requirements have an insignificant effect on the real exchange rate in the short run."[84]

84. Valdes-Prieto and Soto (1996, p. 99).

Figure 9-6. *Response of Real Exchange Rate to Tax on Capital Control Inflows, 1988–96*[a]

Real exchange rate (log)

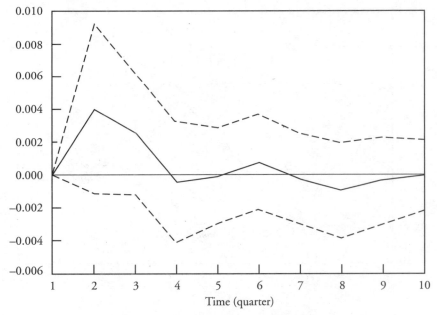

Time (quarter)

Source: Author's estimations.
a. Dashed lines show ±2 standard error bands.

Controls on Inflows and the Independence of Monetary Policy

Since the mid-1980s Chile's monetary authorities have used interest rate targeting as one of the main—if not the main—anti-inflationary tool.[85] More specifically, to reduce inflation the central bank has systematically attempted to maintain relatively high interest rates. This policy, however, became increasingly difficult to sustain during the late 1980s and 1990s when, as a result of Chile's improving stance in international financial markets, higher domestic rates started to attract increasingly large volumes of capital. A fundamental objective of the capital restrictions policy in effect

85. Fontaine (1996).

since 1991, then, has been to allow the country to maintain a higher interest rate. According to Cowan and de Gregorio, "Capital controls allowed policymakers to rely on the domestic interest rate as the main instrument for reducing inflation . . . [T]he reserve requirement has permitted maintaining the domestic interest rate above the international interest rate, without imposing excessive pressure on the exchange rate."[86] In this subsection I use monthly time series to investigate formally the way in which capital restrictions have, in fact, affected interest rate differentials and the ability to perform independent monetary policy in Chile.

In the absence of restrictions on capital mobility and under the assumption of risk neutrality and in the absence of country risk, the uncovered interest arbitrage condition will hold, and deviations from it will be white noise and unpredictable. The speed at which these deviations from interest arbitrage are eliminated is an empirical question, but in a well-functioning market it would be expected to happen very fast. The existence of restrictions on capital mobility and of country risk, however, alter this basic equation in a fundamental way. In this case there will be an equilibrium interest rate differential (δ):

(9-7) $$\delta_t = r_t - r^*_t - E\Delta e_t = k + R + u_t ,$$

where r_t is the domestic interest rate, r^*_t is the international interest rate for a security of the same maturity, $E\Delta e_t$ is the expected rate of devaluation, k is the tax equivalence of the capital restriction, R is the country-risk premium, and u_t is an i.i.d. random variable.[87] As in the case of free capital mobility, if at any moment in time the actual interest rate differential exceeds $k + R$, there will be incentives to arbitrageurs to move funds in or out of the country. This process will continue until the equilibrium interest rate differential is reestablished. The speed at which this process takes place will, in principle, depend on the degree of development of the domestic capital market as well as on the degree of capital mobility existing in the country in question. Countries with stiffer restrictions will experience slow corrections of deviations from the equilibrium interest rate differential.[88] Additionally, as equation 9-7 shows, the degree of capital restrictions (that is, k) will also affect the value toward which the interest rate differential will converge.

86. Cowan and de Gregorio (1998, p. 16).
87. An i.i.d. variable is identically, independently distributed.
88. Edwards and Khan (1985); Dooley (1995, 1997).

In a world with changing policies, k is not constant through time. In fact, the value of k has changed markedly in most Latin American countries during the last few years. With other things given, the imposition (or tightening) of capital restrictions is expected to have two effects on the behavior of the interest rate differential. First, it will increase the value toward which this differential converges; second, it will reduce the speed at which this convergence takes place. This means that, under stricter restrictions on capital mobility, the monetary authority gains greater control over domestic interest rates in two ways: first, it can maintain a higher interest rate differential—that is, the steady-state value of δ will be higher than what it would have been otherwise—and second, δ can deviate from its long-run equilibrium for longer periods of time. In this subsection, I construct and use quarterly and monthly data on interest rate differentials for Chile to investigate the way in which the imposition and tightening of capital restrictions affected their behavior.

A problem with equation 9-7 is that there are no long reliable series on expectations of devaluation. In order to address this problem, I have constructed a series of expected devaluations as the one-step-ahead forecasts obtained from an autoregressive moving average (ARMA) process for the actual rate of devaluation. After identifying the possible processes, several plausible representations are estimated. Finally, those that provide the better forecasts, measured according to standard criteria, are used. In the case of quarterly data, I use an ARMA(2,1), while for monthly data, I use an AR(1) to construct the expected devaluation series.

As a first step, unrestricted VARs estimated on quarterly data are used to estimate impulse response functions of interest rate differentials to a one standard deviation innovation of themselves. Figure 9-7 presents these impulses for two subsamples: 1986–91, when there were no capital restrictions, and 1991–96, when restrictions were in place. In both periods the deviation of δ from its equilibrium tends to disappear quite rapidly. This adjustment process seems to be somewhat faster in the period with no capital restrictions. As may be seen from the figure, during this early period δ essentially returns to trend after two quarters; for the later period, the adjustment is cyclical: after our quarters there is still a slight differential. This result is, in some ways, what one would expect: interest rate differentials are somewhat more sluggish in a period with capital restrictions than in a period with no controls. A potential problem with this interpretation, however, is that during part of the earlier period (1986–87) Chile was still facing a very severe foreign credit constraint and had very limited access to

Figure 9-7. *Response of Interest Rate Differential to an Innovation in Interest Rate Differential in Chile, 1981–96*[a]

Interest rate differential

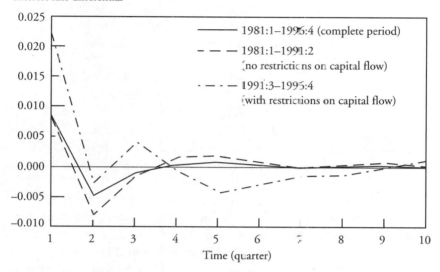

Time (quarter)

Source: Author's estimations.
a. Unrestricted vector autoregressions estimate within one standard deviation.

international capital markets. Unfortunately, due to the brevity of the experiments I am analyzing, the issue of "restrictions" versus "access" cannot be addressed in an adequate way using quarterly data. Monthly data, however, allow me to use additional information and to explore the behavior of interest rate differentials further.

In order to investigate the dynamic behavior of interest rates I estimate the following equation using a Kalman filter time-varying parameter technique:

$$(9\text{-}8) \qquad\qquad \delta_t = \alpha_t + \beta_t \, \delta_{t-1} + u_t \, ,$$

where α_t and β_t are time-varying parameters assumed to follow a random walk.[89] To the extent that β lies inside the unit circle, δ converges to $[\alpha / (1 - \beta)]$. In the absence of controls and with a zero country-risk premium, we expect $[\alpha / (1 - \beta)] \cong 0$, with interest rate differentials converging to zero. Moreover, in this case, we expect that β would be very

89. Hamilton (1994).

low, with interest rate differentials disappearing very rapidly. With country risk and capital restrictions, however, α will be different from zero, β will be rather high, and interest rate differentials will converge to a positive value. This means, then, that if the restrictions have been effective in increasing the authorities' ability to undertake independent monetary policy, we would expect that α, or β, or both would be higher in the period with capital controls.

The results obtained are presented in figure 9-8. As may be seen from panel A, the estimated coefficient for the intercept (α) declines throughout the period, capturing the fact that Chile's country risk was declining. Moreover, the estimated value of the coefficient of lagged interest rate differentials (β) indicates that it did not increase after the imposition of controls and, thus, that the speed at which interest rate differentials corrected themselves was not affected by this policy.

All in all, the results presented in this section suggest that the restrictions on capital inflows imposed in 1991 had, at best, a small and temporary effect on interest rate behavior in Chile. This means that, contrary to the authorities' goals, capital controls did not give significant control over monetary policy. These findings are consistent with the results reported by Calvo and Mendoza, who find that the decline in Chile's inflation has been largely unrelated to the authorities' attempts to target interest rates.[90] According to their VAR analysis, the main forces behind Chile's disinflation have been the real appreciation of the peso and (indirectly) a benign external environment, including positive terms of trade.

Open Issues and Some Concluding Remarks

One of the most important characteristics of the East Asian crisis is that a large number of corporations became insolvent literally overnight. In fact in almost every country there was a substantial net loss of wealth, which if not properly addressed could seriously undermine the working of the economy. Ideally, countries facing these problems will implement a scheme that would allow simultaneously for:

—Corporate restructuring and especially corporate recapitalization,

—Extinction of dollar-denominated debts issued by corporations, and

—Increased foreign direct investment.

90. Calvo and Mendoza (1998).

Figure 9-8. *Time-Varying Estimates of Interest Rate Differential Equation,
1986–96*

Coefficient value

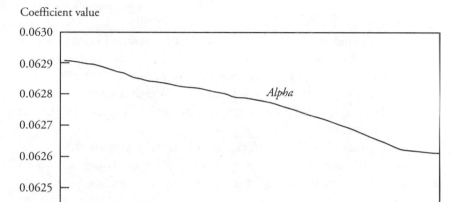

Coefficient value

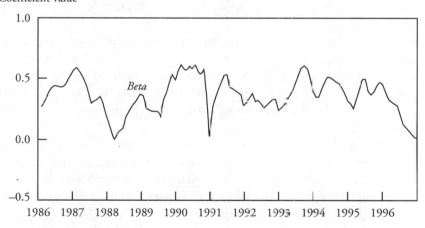

Source: Author's estimations.

In this section I discuss a debt-to-equity swap mechanism that, if properly managed, could indeed help to achieve these three objectives. A scheme similar to the one proposed here was used very successfully in Chile during the 1980s.[91]

91. This discussion is partially based on joint work with Juan Andres Fontaine. Greater details on this mechanism are provided in appendix B, which discusses Mexico's experience with restructuring during the 1980s.

Four entities usually participate in a successful debt-to-equity swap:

—The original holder of the emerging country debt. This would usually (but not always) be a foreign bank; for illustrative purposes I refer to it as the foreign bank.

—The original issuer of the debt, usually a corporation in the country in question, which I call the debtor.

—A foreign company eager to invest in this particular emerging country, if it can find an attractive deal. I call it the foreign investor.

—And a local firm (or project) that is an attractive investment target for the foreign investor. I call it the project.

A debt-to-equity swap is characterized by the following steps. One, the foreign investor buys from the international bank a note originally issued by the debtor. This transaction takes place in the secondary market and almost always involves a discount. That is, the foreign investor pays less than 100 cents to the dollar for the debt. If the discount is assumed to be d, then the foreign investor only pays $(1 - d)$ per nominal dollar of the debt. At this point, then, the international bank (or foreign supplier, for that matter) has unloaded an unwanted debt; this is now in the hands of the foreign investor.

Two, the foreign investor goes to the debtor country and locates the original debtor, or issuer of the note. The investor then offers the original debtor a discount f, if the latter prepays the debt fully in local currency (say, rupiah). Once this is done, the foreign investor has rupiahs in hand, and the original debtor has a better balance sheet position, since it has only paid $1 - f$ for each dollar retired.

Three, at this point the foreign investor uses the rupiah proceeds from the sale of the debt to the debtor to make an investment in "the project." This operation is considered to be foreign direct investment and, thus, is subject to all the legal provisions—for taxation, remittance of profits, and so on—governing foreign direct investment.

As a result of this debt-to-equity swap, the following has happened:

—The international bank has unloaded a debt it did not want to carry on its books.

—The original debtor has prepaid in rupiah and at a discount (f) a debt originally denominated in dollars.

—The foreign investor has participated in an investment project.

—The operation has taken place without the debtor country having to use any foreign exchange and, thus, without placing any pressure on the exchange rate.

The successful implementation of this type of scheme is likely to require some legal reform. What is clear, however, is that for it to work restrictions on foreign ownership should be lifted immediately in the debtor country.

Some comments on debt-to-equity swaps based on Chile's experience are in order:

—The difference between the discount given by the international bank to the foreign investor and the discount given by the foreign investor to the original debtor represents the financial incentive to the new investor to participate in the scheme.

—From a financial point of view, this discount differential plays a role similar to that of a subsidized exchange rate: it allows foreign investors to fund their investments on more favorable terms, that is, with lower disbursements. However, this mechanism does not imply any fiscal cost: the subsidy is paid by the original creditors, when they decide to sell their loans at a discount.

—Interested foreign investors have had to sign a contract with the government stipulating that they have the right to access the foreign exchange market to remit profits and capital, only after stipulated grace periods have expired. This restriction is needed to avoid a massive outflow of foreign exchange (or undue pressures on the exchange rate) by creditors interested in using debt-to-equity swaps as a means of speeding up amortizations of rescheduled debts.

—In Chile, care was taken to avoid the destabilizing effects on currency and financial markets of massive portfolio adjustments eventually triggered by the program. On the one hand, resident investors were not allowed to buy foreign exchange to participate in the program, except under a strict quota set by the Central Bank. Rights to participate in portions of the quota were auctioned off twice a month. On the other hand, an excessive appetite for the program by foreign investment, which could stress the local financial market (because debtors would crowd it in search of funding for the required prepayments), was regulated by the two market discounts referred to above. For example, the government could establish two quotas for participating in the program: one for local entities and one for foreigners. The size of these quotas should be adjusted periodically (say, every two weeks).

A debt-to-equity swap program along the lines proposed here was extremely successful in Chile. Starting in 1985, it helped to cut medium- and long-term foreign debt by 25 percent in just four years. As a result, highly indebted companies and banks were able to regain solvency and access to capital markets. Foreign investment helped to recapitalize companies and banks and brought depressed asset markets back to life. In time, direct investment, production, and employment surged. Although the program was only one element of a broader strategy aimed at relaunching the Chilean market-oriented model, there is ample consensus that it played a key role not only for its direct effects but also as a catalyst of a new area of creative solutions.

References

Ades, Alberto, and Federico Kaune. 1997. "A New Measure of Current Account Sustainability for Developing Countries." Goldman Sachs Emerging Markets Economic Research Group.

Aspe, Pedro. 1993. *Economic Transformation, the Mexican Way.* MIT Press.

Bacchetta, Philippe, and Eric van Wincoop. 1998 "Capital Flows to Emerging Markets: Liberalization, Overshooting, and Volatility." NBER Working Paper 6530. Cambridge, Mass.: National Bureau of Economic Research (April).

Banco Central de Chile. Various years. *Boletín Mensual.* Santiago.

Banco de México. 1993. *The Mexican Economy.* Mexico City.

Bank for International Settlements. 1997. *The Maturity, Sectoral, and Nationality Distribution of International Bank Lending.* Basle.

Bartley, L. Robert. 1997. "Peso Folklórico: Dancing away from Monetary Stability." In *Mexico 1994,* edited by Sebastian Edwards and Moises Naim. Washington, D.C.: Carnegie Endowment.

Birdsall, Nancy, Michael Gavin, and Ricardo Hausmann. 1997. "Getting the Lessons Right: A View from the Inter-American Development Bank." In *Mexico 1994,* edited by Sebastian Edwards and Moises Naim. Washington, D.C.: Carnegie Endowment.

Bruno, Michael. 1995. "Currency Crises and Collapses: Comment." *Brookings Papers on Economic Activity* 2: 278–85.

Burki, Shahid J. 1997. "A Fate Foretold: The World Bank and the Mexican Crisis." In *Mexico 1994,* edited by Sebastian Edwards and Moises Naim. Washington, D.C.: Carnegie Endowment.

Calvo, Guillermo A., Leonardo Leiderman, and Carmen Reinhart. 1993. "Capital Inflows and Real Exchange Rate Appreciation in Latin America: The Role of External Factors." IMF Staff Paper 40. Washington, D.C.: International Monetary Fund (March).

———. 1995. "Capital Inflows to Latin America with Reference to Asian Experience." In *Capital Controls, Exchange Rates, and Monetary Policy in the World Economy,* edited by Sebastian Edwards. Cambridge University Press.

Calvo, Guillermo A., and Enríque Mendoza. 1996. "Petty Crime and Cruel Punishment: Lessons from the Mexican Debacle." *American Economic Review* 86 (May): 170–75.

———. 1998. "Empirical Puzzles of Chilean Stabilization Policy." Mimeo. Duke University.

Cardoso, Eliana, and Ilan Goldfajn. 1997. "Capital Flows to Brazil: The Endogeneity of Capital Controls." IMF Working Paper WP/97/115. Washington, D.C.: International Monetary Fund.

Chase Manhattan Bank. 1997. "Emerging Markets after Thailand: Guilt by Association or Flattered by Comparison?" New York (October 1).

Chinn, Menzie. 1998. "Before the Fall: Were East Asian Currencies Overvalued?" NBER Working Paper 6491. National Bureau of Economic Research (March).

Chote, Robert. 1998. *Financial Crises and Asia.* CEPR Conference Report 6. London: Centre for Economic Policy Research.

Cole, Harold, and Timothy Kehoe. 1996. "A Self-Fulfilling Model of Mexico's 1994–1995 Debt Crisis." *Journal of International Economics* 41 (November): 309–30.

Corden, W. Max. 1994. *Economic Policy, Exchange Rates, and the International System.* Oxford University Press and University of Chicago Press.

Corsetti, Giancarlo, Paolo Pesenti, and Nouriel Roubini. 1998. "Paper Tigers? A Model of the Asian Crisis." Paper presented at the NBER-Bank of Portugal International Seminar on Macroeconomics, Lisbon, June 14–15.

Cowan, Kevin, and Jose de Gregorio. 1998. "Exchange Rate Policies and Capital Account Management." In *Managing Capital Flows and Exchange Rates: Perspectives from the Pacific Basin,* edited by Reuven Glick. Cambridge University Press.

D'Amato, Alfonse. 1995. "Report on the Mexican Economic Crisis." U.S. Senate document, Washington, D.C., June 29.

Dooley, Michael P. 1995. "A Survey of Academic Literature on Controls over International Capital Transactions." IMF Working Paper 95/127. Washington, D.C.: International Monetary Fund.

———. 1997. "A Model of Crises in Emerging Markets." NBER Working Paper 6300. Cambridge, Mass.: National Bureau of Economic Research.

Dornbusch, Rudiger. 1997. "The Folly, the Crash, and Beyond: Economic Policies and the Crisis." In *Mexico 1994,* edited by Sebastian Edwards and Moises Naim. Washington, D.C.: Carnegie Endowment.

———. 1998. "Capital Controls: An Idea Whose Time Is Past." In *Should the IMF Pursue Capital-Account Liberalization?* edited by Stanley Fischer and others. Essays in International Finance 207. Princeton University, International Finance Section (May).

Edwards, Sebastian. 1984. "The Order of Liberalization of the External Sector in Developing Countries." Princeton Essays in International Finance 156. Princeton University.

———. 1989. "Structural Adjustment Policies in Highly Indebted Countries." In *Developing Country Debt and Economic Performance,* vol. 2, edited by Jeffrey Sachs. University of Chicago Press.

———. 1993. "Exchange Rates as Nominal Anchors." *Weltwirtschaftliches Archiv* 129 (1): 1–32.

———. 1997. "The Mexican Peso Crisis? How Much Did We Know? When Did We Know It?" NBER Working Paper 6334. National Bureau of Economic Research.

———. 1998a. "Capital Flows, Real Exchange Rates, and Capital Controls: Some Latin American Experiences." NBER Working Paper 6800. National Bureau of Economic Research.

———. 1998b. "Capital Inflows into Latin America: A Stop-Go Story?" NBER Working Paper 6441. National Bureau of Economic Research.

Edwards, Sebastian, and Alejandra Edwards. 1991. *Monetarism and Liberalization: The Chilean Experience.* University of Chicago Press.

Edwards, Sebastian, and Moshin Khan. 1985. "Interest Rate Determination in Developing Countries: A Conceptual Framework." IMF Staff Paper 32. Washington, D.C.: International Monetary Fund (September).

Edwards, Sebastian, and Moises Naim, eds. 1997. *Mexico 1994*. Washington, D.C.: Carnegie Endowment.

Edwards, Sebastian, and Julio Santaella. 1993. "Devaluation Controversies in the Developing Countries: Lessons from the Bretton Woods Era." In *A Retrospective on the Bretton Woods System: Lessons for International Monetary Reform,* edited by Michael Bordo and Barry Eichengreen. University of Chicago Press.

Edwards, Sebastian, and Miguel Savastano. 1998. "The Morning After: The Mexican Peso in the Aftermath of the 1994 Currency Crisis." NBER Working Paper 6516. Cambridge, Mass.: National Bureau of Economic Research.

Eichengreen, Barry, and Paul Masson. 1998. "Exit Strategies: Policy Options for Countries Seeking Greater Exchange Rate Flexibility." IMF Occasional Paper 168. Washington, D.C.: International Monetary Fund.

Eichengreen, Barry, Andrew K. Rose, and Charles Wyplosz. 1996. "Contagious Currency Crises." NBER Working Paper 5681. National Bureau of Economic Research.

Feldstein, Martin. 1998. "Refocusing the IMF." *Foreign Affairs* 77 (March–April): 20–33.

Fischer, Stanley. 1994. "Comments on Dornbusch and Werner." *Brookings Papers on Economic Activity* 1: 304–09.

Fischer, Stanley. 1998. "The Asian Crisis: A View from the IMF." Address at the Midwater Conference of the Bankers' Association for Foreign Trade, Washington, D.C., January 22.

Fontaine, Juan A. 1996. *La construcción de un mercado de capitales: El caso de Chile.* Washington, D.C.: World Bank.

Frankel, Jeffrey A., and Andrew Rose. 1996. "Currency Crashes in Emerging Markets: An Empirical Treatment." *Journal of International Economics* 41 (November): 351–66.

Garber, Peter M. 1998. *Should the IMF Pursue Capital-Account Convertibility?* Princeton Essays in International Finance 207. Princeton University, International Finance Section (May).

Gavin, Michael, Ricardo Hausmann, and Leonardo Leiderman. 1996. "The Macro-economics of Capital Flows to Latin America: Experience and Policy Issues." In *Volatile Capital Flows,* edited by Ricardo Hausmann and Liliana Rojas-Suárez. Washington, D.C.: Inter-American Development Bank.

Gil Díaz, Francisco, and Agustín Carstens. 1996. "One Year of Solitude: Some Pilgrim Tales about the Mexican 1994–95 Crisis." *American Economic Review* 86 (May): 164–69.

———. 1997. "Pride and Prejudice: The Economics Profession and Mexico's Financial Crisis." In *Mexico 1994,* edited by Sebastian Edwards and Moises Naim. Washington, D.C.: Carnegie Endowment.

Goldman Sachs, Emerging Markets Economic Research Group. Various years. *Emerging Markets Biweekly.*

Goldstein, Morris. 1998. "The Asian Financial Crisis: Causes, Curses, and Systematic Implications." Policy Analyses in International Economics 55. Washington, D.C.: Institute for International Economics.

Group of Thirty. 1995. "Mexico: Why Didn't Wall Street Sound the Alarm?" New York.

Hale, David. 1997. "Rubin's Folly?" *International Economy* (September–October): 14–19.

Hamilton, James D. 1994. *Time-Series Analysis*. Princeton University Press.

International Monetary Fund. Various years. *International Financial Statistics*. Washington, D.C.

Ito, Takatoshi. 1999. "Capital Flows in Asia." NBER Working Paper 7134. Cambridge, Mass.: National Bureau of Economic Research.

J. P. Morgan. Various years. "Emerging Markets Outlook."

Krugman, Paul. 1999. "The Return of Depression Economics." *Foreign Affairs* 78 (January/February): 56–74.

Leiderman, Leonardo, and Alfredo Thorne. 1995. "Mexico's 1994 Crisis and Its Aftermath." Mimeo. Tel Aviv University (August).

Loser, Claudio M., and Ewart S. Williams. 1997. "The Mexican Crisis and Its Aftermath: An IMF Perspective." In *Mexico 1994,* edited by Sebastian Edwards and Moises Naim. Washington, D.C.: Carnegie Endowment.

Massad, Carlos. 1998. "The Liberalization of the Capital Account: Chile in the 1990s." In *Should the IMF Pursue Capital-Account Liberalization?* edited by Stanley Fischer and others. Essays in International Finance 207. Princeton University, International Finance Section (May).

Merrill Lynch. 1997. "South Korea." (December 23).

Milesi-Ferreti, Gian Maria, and Assaf Razin. 1996. "Sustainability of Persistent Current Account Deficits." NBER Working Paper 5467 National Bureau of Economic Research.

———. 1998. "Sharp Reduction in Current Account Deficits: An Empirical Analysis." *European Economic Review* 42 (May): 897–908.

OECD (Organisation for Economic Co-operation and Development). 1995. *OECD Economic Surveys: Mexico*. Geneva.

Radelet, Steven, and Jeffrey Sachs. 1998. "The Onset of the East Asian Financial Crisis." NBER Working Paper 6880. National Bureau of Economic Research.

Rodrik, Dani. 1998. "Who Needs Capital-Account Convertibility?" In *Should the IMF Pursue Capital-Account Liberalization?* edited by Stanley Fischer and others. Essays in International Finance 207. Princeton University, International Finance Section (May).

Sachs, Jeffrey, Aaron Tornell, and Andres Velasco. 1995. "Lessons from Mexico." Mimeo. Harvard University (March).

———. 1996. "Financial Crises in Emerging Markets: The Lessons of 1995." *Brookings Papers on Economic Activity* 1: 147–217.

Summers, Lawrence. 1996. "Commentary." In *Volatile Capital Flows,* edited by Ricardo Hausmann and Liliana Rojas-Suárez, pp. 53–57. Washington, D.C.: Inter-American Development Bank.

Valdes-Prieto, Salvador, and Marcelo Soto. 1996. "New Selective Capital Controls in Chile: Are They Effective?" Mimeo. Santiago: Catholic University of Chile.

Wang, Yan, and John D. Shilling. 1995. "Managing Capital Flows in East Asia." World Bank Discussion Paper. Washington, D.C.: World Bank.

Appendix 9A. Mexico's FICORCA

The recent East Asian crisis has shown that the restructuring of corporate debt is a fundamental ingredient in an early solution to a country's problems. Mexico and Chile provide two interesting historical precedents on government-led attempts at corporate restructuring.

In March 1983, six months into the debt crisis, the Mexican government created an institution to provide forward exchange coverage to Mexican debtors. This institution was known by its acronym, FICORCA, and its first chief executive was Mexico's current president Ernesto Zedillo Ponce de León.

For all practical purposes, FICORCA was a success story:

—Almost 1,350 corporations took part in the program.

—Almost $12 billion of foreign debt was covered.

FICORCA offered four basic programs that were distinguished by the debt covered and by the way in which the debtors financed their participation in the program. The table on the facing page summarizes the four programs. A scheme based on this experience could be helpful in East Asia. For East Asia the more appealing program would be one that offers complete coverage—both principal and interest—and is financed by a government loan.

Type of investment or payment	Only principal payments covered	Principal and accrued interest payments covered by program
Cash payment (in Mexican pesos)	Program took place through authorized banks, which acted as intermediaries only	Program took place through authorized banks, which acted as intermediaries only
	Firm with dollar-denominated debt bought dollars up-front at a subsidized exchange rate; subsidy ranged from 25 to 35 percent, depending on the terms of the restructured debt (six to eight years)	Debtor firm used pesos to buy, up-front, dollars at "official" exchange rate to cover principal and interest payments
	Foreign exchange for interest payments was bought in the free market	Debtor firm earned interest (LIBOR + 200 basis point spread) on undisbursed balance
	At the end of the grace period, the bank delivered to the creditor the U.S. dollars required to make the principal payments	Bank made payments to creditor according to agreed schedule
Loan obtained, in pesos, by original debtor in order to make payment	Debtor firm obtained credit in pesos from FICORCA at the "market" nominal interest rate	Debtor firm obtained credit in pesos from FICORCA at the "market" nominal interest rate
	Firm used proceeds from the loan to buy (from participating bank) dollars at a subsidized exchange rate; subsidy ranged from 25 to 35 percent, depending on the terms of the restructured debt	Firm used proceeds from loan to buy (from bank) dollars at "official rate"
		Debtor firm earned interest (LIBOR + 200 basis point spread) on undisbursed balance
	At the end of the grace period, the bank delivered to the creditor the U.S. dollars required to make the principal payments	Bank made payments to creditor according to agreed schedule

Appendix 9B. Applications of the Chilean Model

This appendix analyzes Chile's experience with debt-to-debt and debt-to-equity swaps during the early 1980s.

Debt-to-Debt Swaps to Hedge Foreign Exchange Risk

This section describes the way in which a Chilean-style debt-to-debt swap would work in a country in need of major corporate debt restructuring, such as Indonesia.

Let corporation A be a local (Indonesian) company with a foreign exchange–denominated loan with an international bank. The loan might originally have been a short-term or medium-term financial liability but, due to the crisis, is subject to the rescheduling negotiated between the government and creditor banks. Although this will benefit corporation A by lengthening the maturity of its liability, it has the disadvantage of keeping the company exposed to exchange risks. Corporation A, as many other foreign exchange debtors, no longer wants to hold such exposure. The following mechanism allows it to obtain longer maturities without additional exchange risk (see figure 9B-1).

THE MECHANISM. One, corporation A and its bank, the international bank, sign a new debt contract rescheduling its foreign exchange debt under the terms negotiated by the government (that is, eight-year maturity, three-year grace period).

Two, the central bank, or some other public agency, such as a debt restructuring facility, sells to corporation A an amount of foreign exchange equal to the principal of the rescheduled debt. The transaction is carried at the going market exchange rate.

Three, corporation A deposits with the central bank the purchased foreign exchange. The deposit has exactly the same terms (maturity and interest rates) as the rescheduled debt. Partial or total withdrawals are only allowed under the condition stated in step four.

Four, as a counterpart, corporation A gets a rupiah-denominated loan from the central bank. The maturity of this loan exactly matches that of the rescheduled debt, but it can be prepaid at any time without cost. Prepayments allow corporation A to withdraw the deposit described in step three. Such withdrawal can only be done in rupiah, at the going exchange rate.

Figure 9B-1. *Debt-to-Debt Swap to Hedge Foreign Risk*

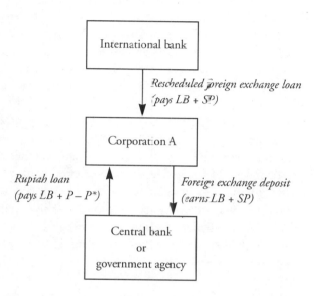

Five, interest rates of the rupiah loan are set so as to match the *real* interest rate charged on the rescheduled debt (its nominal rate, typically stated as LIBOR—London Interbank Offer Rate—plus a spread, minus the inflation rate of the correspondent currency). Two alternative formulas may be offered. First, the principal may be indexed to local inflation, and interest rates (R) are thus:

$$(1) \qquad R = LB + SP - P^*,$$

where LB is LIBOR of the currency of denomination of the loan, SP is the spread charged by banks on rescheduled debt, and P^* is the annual inflation (as measured by the consumer or wholesale price index) of such currency. Chile employed this option, using LIBOR and U.S. foreign currency inflation.

And second, the principal of the loan may not be indexed to local inflation, but then interest rates (I) are:

$$(2) \qquad I = LB + SP - P^* + P,$$

where P is the annual rate of local inflation. Interest payments are dated to match those of the rescheduled debt and the deposit.

Six, corporation A has to double its liabilities, holding on its books the foreign exchange–denominated rescheduled debt plus a local currency loan with the central bank of equal initial size. The former, though, will be matched with a deposit in the central bank of the same amount, term, currency, and rates. Since interest rates and exchange risks associated with this deposit get canceled out by those of the foreign exchange loan, corporation A faces no exchange risk and pays a net interest rate equivalent to that described in step five.

Seven, as a consequence of the simultaneous issuing of a foreign exchange deposit and the granting of a local currency loan, the central bank assumes the full exchange risks associated with any further depreciation. Conditions defined under step five allow the central bank to be compensated by local inflation, so it will stand to lose only if the local currency were to depreciate over and above local inflation. If the opposite happens, the central bank would benefit, as long as corporation A does not exert its option to prepay the loan and withdraw the deposit, thus reverting to the initial foreign exchange exposure.

RESULTS.   Corporation A has been allowed to convert a short- or medium-term liability, denominated in foreign currency and thus subjected to high perceived risk, into a source of long-term funds denominated in local currency and at a reasonable cost. The real cost of funds to corporation A would be equivalent to $LB + SP - P^*$. If LB is 6 percent, SP is 250 basis point spread, and P^* (U.S. inflation) is 2 percent, the real interest rate paid by corporation A would amount to 6.5 percent over a local currency–denominated loan. As a counterpart, the government, through the central bank or other designated agency, picks the full exchange risk associated with any future depreciation of the local currency over and above the local inflation rate. If the local currency were to appreciate in real terms, this would benefit the government, as long as corporation A does not exert its right to prepay and thus revert to the initial situation.

Debt-to-Equity Swap

This section provides a detailed explanation of Chilean-style debt-to-equity swaps.

Consider the case where a foreign investor is interested in investing in a troubled emerging economy, such as Indonesia, as long as asset prices are

Figure 9B-2. *Debt-to-Equity Swap to Compensate for Excessive Risk*[a]

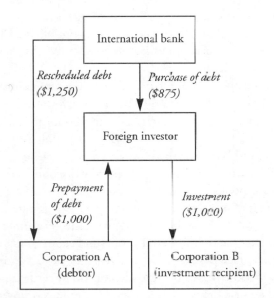

a. Investment to be made (K), \$1,000; discount accepted by lender (d), 30 percent; discount accepted by debtor (f), 20 percent; required disbursement (M), $M = 1,000 (0.7 / 0.8) = 875$.

perceived to be a "bargain." The following mechanism allows the foreign investor to be compensated for the excessive risk it perceives of investing in Indonesia, without generating an asset price destabilization or depression (see figure 9B-2). A similar mechanism was successfully applied in Chile after the 1982 debt crisis and is considered one of the key ingredients of Chile's subsequent impressive recovery.

THE MECHANISM. One, the foreign investor buys from a foreign bank a rescheduled Indonesian loan. If the original lender (the foreign bank) feels that the conditions of the loan do not fully compensate its credit risk, it is willing to sell the loan at a discount. In the case of banks the discount is typically equal to loan provisions. If d is the discount, the face value of every dollar loan could be bought at $(1 - d)$ dollars.

Two, the foreign investor approaches the issuer of that debt—say, corporation A—and negotiates a prepayment of the debt. Prepayment is in rupiah at the going market exchange rate. Corporation A is willing to pre-pay this obligation only if it is offered an attractive discount; that is, if for every dollar of original debt it is allowed to pay, say, $1 - f$ dollars. This assumes that the original debtor cannot, or is not allowed to, prepay in foreign exchange, because the whole debt-restructuring process would break down.

Three, with the proceeds of the prepayment the foreign investor buys or increases the capital of corporation B, its target investment. Given the discounts involved in the two previous steps, the amount of funds available to be invested is equal to $(1 - f) / (1 - d)$ for every dollar of original debt. Corporations A and B may be the same entity. In this case, the debt is converted into equity without prepayment, and the discount is included in the price of the corresponding capital increase.

Four, the foreign investor's investment is given foreign investment treatment. This means that through a contract with the government the foreign investment is given the right to remit profits and capital, after a given grace period. In Chile, grace periods were four years for profits and ten years for capital. These periods have to be made consistent with expected repayments of rescheduled debts so as to avoid a capital outflow. Remittance rights have to be completely secured, at the most favorable future exchange rate available at the corresponding date, thus isolating them from any future rescheduling, payment suspension, or capital controls.

Five, if the foreign investor wants to invest the equivalent of K dollars, through this mechanism it has to disburse only M dollars, where:

$$(3) \qquad M = K(1 - d) / (1 - f).$$

Therefore, if $d = 30$ percent and $f = 20$ percent (as seen in Chile), for every dollar of final investment, $0.875 = (0.7 / 0.8)$ dollars of disbursement are needed: an up-front 12.5 percent cut in capital costs.

Six, as indicated in step two, it is crucial to limit access to the program to investors with direct access to foreign exchange (like foreign investors). If local residents (including original debtors) could benefit from the discount d, they would massively demand foreign exchange and cause a steep depreciation of the currency. This would mean the breakdown of the debt rescheduling process. In order to avoid this outcome, Chile imposed exchange controls throughout the period under which this mechanism operated. However, local residents were allowed to operate in a similar, but limited, program; the central bank determined a maximum quota of restructuring available to local firms.

RESULTS. Through a debt-to-equity swap the foreign investor is able to fund investment projects at considerably lower capital costs. Conceptually this result is equivalent to the purchase of the corresponding assets at a discount (as would alternatively happen through asset price deflation or depreciation). The mechanism plays the role of a catalyst for foreign direct investment and foreign equity purchases, thus improving the business climate while fostering investment and employment. Local firms benefit from a debt reduction, prepaying foreign debts at a discount. Some companies (not necessarily foreign exchange debtors) may be sold partially or totally to foreign investors attracted by the capital cost advantage and thus see their market value bid up. The source of these benefits is the discount at which rescheduled debts are sold (d), so the bill is in the end paid by those creditors willing to take a loss and exit, rather than stay and share the (uncertain and risky) harvest of the (eventual) recovery.

Appendix 9C. Data Tables

Table 9C-1. *GDP Growth Rate, 1991–97*
Percent

Economy	1991	1992	1993	1994	1995	1996	1997
Korea	9.13	5.06	5.75	8.58	8.94	7.1	5.47
Indonesia	6.95	6.46	6.50	5.93	8.22	7.98	4.65
Malaysia	8.48	7.80	8.35	9.24	9.46	8.58	7.81
Philippines	−0.58	0.34	2.12	4.38	4.77	5.76	9.66
Singapore	7.27	6.29	10.44	10.05	8.75	7.32	7.55
Thailand	8.18	8.08	8.38	8.94	8.84	5.52	−0.43
China	9.19	14.24	12.09	12.66	10.55	9.54	8.80
Taiwan	7.55	6.76	6.32	6.54	6.03	5.67	6.81
Hong Kong (China)	4.97	6.21	6.15	5.51	3.85	5.03	5.29

Source: Corsetti, Pesenti, and Roubini (1998).

Table 9C-2. *Investment Rates in Asia, 1990–97*
Percentage of gross domestic product

Economy	1990	1991	1992	1993	1994	1995	1996	1997
Korea	36.93	38.90	36.58	35.08	36.05	37.05	38.42	34.97
Indonesia	36.15	35.50	35.87	29.48	31.06	31.93	30.80	31.60
Malaysia	31.34	37.25	33.45	37.81	40.42	43.50	41.54	42.84
Philippines	24.16	20.22	21.34	23.98	24.06	22.22	24.02	24.84
Singapore	35.87	34.21	35.97	37.69	32.69	33.12	35.07	37.40
Thailand	41.08	42.84	39.97	39.94	40.27	41.61	41.73	34.99
China	34.74	34.77	36.17	43.47	40.88	40.20	38.73	37.55
Taiwan	23.08	23.29	24.90	25.16	23.87	23.65	21.24	22.20
Hong Kong (China)	27.44	27.20	28.50	27.54	31.85	34.91	32.38	35.08

Source: Corsetti, Pesenti, and Roubini (1998).

Table 9C-3. *Stock Market Indexes in Asia, 1990–97*

Economy	1990	1991	1992	1993	1994	1995	1996	1997
Korea	396	610	678	866	1,027	882	651	376
Indonesia	417	247	274	588	469	513	637	401
Malaysia	505	556	643	1,275	971	995	1,237	594
Philippines	651	1,151	1,256	3,196	2,785	2,594	3,170	1,869
Singapore	1,154	1,490	1,524	2,425	2,239	2,266	2,216	1,529
Thailand	612	711	893	1,582	1,360	1,280	831	372
Hong Kong (China)	3,024	4,297	5,512	11,188	8,191	10,073	13,451	10,722
Taiwan (China)	4,350	4,600	3,377	6,070	7,111	5,158	6,933	8,187

Source: Corsetti, Pesenti, and Roubini (1998).

Table 9C-4. *Savings Rates in Asia, 1990–97*
Percentage of gross domestic product

Economy	1990	1991	1992	1993	1994	1995	1996	1997
Korea	35.69	35.74	34.88	34.91	34.60	35.14	33.60	33.06
Indonesia	31.75	31.10	33.41	28.66	29.52	27.65	27.50	27.98
Malaysia	29.07	23.24	30.06	27.70	35.81	34.65	37.81	39.34
Philippines	17.85	17.76	18.16	17.29	20.32	17.16	19.35	18.77
Singapore	45.32	46.56	48.35	46.17	50.82	51.05	51.33	51.30
Thailand	32.33	34.83	33.73	34.26	35.89	33.25	33.22	32.64
China	37.77	37.84	37.26	41.29	42.04	40.22	39.25	41.15
Taiwan (China)	30.50	30.26	28.93	28.68	26.99	26.70	25.92	25.43
Hong Kong (China)	35.85	33.78	28.93	28.68	26.99	26.70	25.92	25.43

Source: Corsetti, Pesenti, and Roubini (1998).

Table 9C-5. *Government Fiscal Balances in Asia, 1990–97*
Percentage of gross domestic product

Economy	1990	1991	1992	1993	1994	1995	1996	1997
Korea	−0.68	−1.63	−0.50	0.64	0.32	0.30	0.46	0.25
Indonesia	0.43	0.45	−0.44	0.64	1.03	2.44	1.26	0.00
Malaysia	−3.10	−2.10	−0.89	0.23	2.44	0.89	0.76	2.52
Philippines	−3.47	−2.10	−1.16	−1.46	1.04	0.57	0.28	0.06
Singapore	10.53	8.58	12.35	15.67	11.93	13.07	14.10	9.52
Thailand	4.59	4.79	2.90	2.13	1.89	2.94	0.97	−0.32
China	−0.79	−1.09	−0.97	−0.85	−1.22	−1.00	−0.82	−0.75
Taiwan (China)	1.85	−2.18	−5.34	−3.88	−1.73	−1.09	−1.34	−1.68

Source: Corsetti, Pesenti, and Roubini (1998).

Table 9C-6. *Inflation Rates in Asia, 1991–97*
Percent

Economy	1991	1992	1993	1994	1995	1996	1997
Korea	9.30	6.22	4.82	6.24	4.41	4.96	4.45
Indonesia	9.40	7.59	9.60	12.56	8.95	6.64	11.62
Malaysia	4.40	4.69	3.57	3.71	5.28	3.56	2.66
Philippines	18.70	8.93	7.58	9.06	8.11	8.41	5.01
Singapore	3.40	2.32	2.27	3.05	1.79	1.32	2.00
Thailand	5.70	4.07	3.36	5.19	5.69	5.85	5.61
China	3.50	6.30	14.60	24.20	16.90	8.30	2.80
Taiwan (China)	3.63	4.50	2.87	4.09	3.75	3.01	0.90
Hong Kong (China)	11.60	9.32	8.52	8.16	8.59	6.30	2.80

Source: International Monetary Fund (various years).

Table 9C-7. *Openness in Asia, 1990–97*
(Exports + imports) / 2 as a percentage of gross domestic product

Economy	1990	1991	1992	1993	1994	1995	1996	1997
Korea	30.04	29.38	29.38	29.04	30.47	33.59	34.36	38.48
Indonesia	26.30	27.18	28.23	25.26	25.94	26.98	26.13	28.22
Malaysia	75.23	86.52	76.64	87.72	92.15	97.42	91.50	93.55
Philippines	30.40	31.09	31.58	35.58	36.98	40.26	44.90	54.20
Thailand	37.76	39.24	38.98	39.69	40.99	44.88	42.19	46.69
Hong Kong (China)	129.93	135.28	140.37	137.18	138.92	151.67	142.28	132.68
Taiwan (China)	44.27	45.14	42.34	43.29	43.16	47.80	46.63	48.07

Source: Corsetti, Pesenti, and Roubini (1998).

Table 9C-8. *Real Exchange Rates in Asia, 1990–97*
Index (1990 = 100)

Economy	1990	1991	1992	1993	1994	1995	1996	1997
Korea	96.0	91.5	87.7	85.20	84.70	87.70	87.20	58.60
Indonesia	97.40	99.60	100.80	103.80	101.00	100.50	105.40	62.40
Malaysia	97.0	96.90	109.70	111.0	107.10	106.90	112.10	84.90
Philippines	92.40	103.10	107.10	97.40	111.70	109.60	116.40	90.90
Singapore	101.20	105.70	106.00	108.60	111.90	112.70	118.20	114.40
Thailand	102.20	99.0	99.70	101.90	98.30	101.70	107.60	72.40
Hong Kong (China)	99.70	103.90	108.50	116.0	114.50	116.0	125.80	138.40
Taiwan (China)	96.50	95.70	95.70	91.40	92.60	90.40	89.60	89.20

Source: J. P. Morgan (various years).

Table 9C-9. *Bank Lending to the Private Sector in Asia, 1991–97*
Percentage growth

Economy	1991	1992	1993	1994	1995	1996	1997
Korea	20.78	12.55	12.94	20.08	15.45	20.01	21.95
Indonesia	17.82	12.29	25.48	22.97	22.57	21.45	46.42
Malaysia	20.58	10.79	10.80	16.04	30.65	25.77	26.96
Philippines	7.33	24.66	40.74	26.52	45.39	48.72	28.79
Singapore	12.41	9.77	15.15	15.25	20.26	15.82	12.68
Thailand	20.45	20.52	24.03	30.26	23.76	14.63	19.80
China	19.76	20.84	43.52	24.58	24.23	24.68	20.96
Taiwan (China)	21.25	28.70	19.46	16.18	10.00	6.00	8.92
Hong Kong (China)	n.a.	10.17	20.15	19.94	10.99	15.75	20.10

Source: Corsetti, Pesenti, and Roubini (1998).
n.a. Not available.

Table 9C-10. *Real GDP Growth Rate in Latin America, 1995–98*
Percent

Country	1995	1996	1997	1998
Argentina	−4.6	4.3	8.4	4.6
Brazil	4.2	2.9	3.0	0.0
Chile	8.5	7.2	7.1	3.8
Colombia	5.3	2.0	3.1	1.5
Mexico	−6.2	5.1	7.0	4.7
Peru	7.0	2.5	7.2	1.0
Venezuela	3.4	−1.6	5.1	−1.5

Source: Goldman Sachs, Emerging Markets Economic Research Group (various years).

Table 9C-11. *Consumer Price Index Inflation in Latin America, 1995–98*
Percent

Country	1995	1996	1997	1998
Argentina	1.6	0.1	0.3	0.6
Brazil	15.2	10.0	4.8	1.0
Chile	8.2	6.6	6.0	4.5
Colombia	19.5	21.6	17.7	16.6
Mexico	52.0	27.7	15.7	18.6
Peru	10.3	11.8	6.5	6.0
Venezuela	56.6	103.2	37.6	29.9

Source: Goldman Sachs, Emerging Markets Economic Research Group (various years).

Table 9C-12. *Current Account Balance in Latin America, 1995–98*
Percentage of gross domestic product

Country	1995	1996	1997	1998
Argentina	−1.1	−1.6	−2.5	−3.8
Brazil	−2.6	−3.1	−4.2	−3.9
Chile	0.2	−5.4	−5.3	−7.2
Colombia	−5.4	−5.7	−6.0	−6.7
Mexico	−0.6	−0.5	−1.8	−3.6
Peru	−7.3	−6.0	−5.2	−6.3
Venezuela	3.0	13.1	6.7	−1.6

Source: Goldman Sachs, Emerging Markets Economic Research Group (various years).

Table 9C-13. *Total External Debt in Latin America, 1995–98*
Percentage of gross domestic product

Country	1995	1996	1997	1998
Argentina	26.6	27.7	35.0	37.3
Brazil	22.2	23.5	27.1	28.7
Chile	32.3	32.1	34.6	39.4
Colombia	31.0	32.8	30.4	34.4
Mexico	48.6	38.2	40.4	37.3
Peru	54.5	56.0	48.2	45.6
Venezuela	48.9	53.5	37.8	31.6

Source: Goldman Sachs, Emerging Markets Economic Research Group (various years).

KENNETH E. SCOTT # 10

Corporate Governance and East Asia: Korea, Indonesia, Malaysia, and Thailand

I N A BROADER PERSPECTIVE, of course, corporate governance is only one
element in the East Asian crisis of the last two years. An explanation of the
origins and development of the crisis in the region involves a complicated
interplay among numerous economic and social factors, as displayed in recent
reports by the World Bank and the International Monetary Fund.[1] But a pattern that runs through many accounts was the mounting volume of short-
term, foreign currency–denominated borrowings by large and already highly
leveraged domestic firms and banks, even as investor confidence, foreign currency reserves, and exchange rates drew near collapse. That behavior requires
some examination from the point of view of both the borrowers and the
lenders, and corporate governance has a part to play. Indeed, one study concludes that corporate governance was more important than macroeconomic
conditions or policy responses in determining the extent of exchange rate depreciation and stock market performance in 1997–98 across the emerging
market countries.[2] Likewise, these countries, through their recovery and
reform programs, are seeking to restore investor confidence and foreign capital inflows in part by changing their corporate governance institutions.

I would like to express appreciation for comments and source materials to Robert Litan, Michael
Pomerleano, and Douglas Webb.

1. World Bank (1998); International Monetary Fund (1999).
2. Johnson and others (1998, p. 49).

Obviously corporate governance is impinging on some much larger policy issues, such as whether the government is trying to direct the economy and capital investment along certain lines by directing bank loans or government guarantees to chosen industries or firms. If those ventures prove ill-advised, the next step often becomes a government bailout of the affected banks and corporations, to the benefit of their creditors and perhaps their stockholders as well (but not the taxpayers). The anticipation of bailouts in turn creates a misallocation of resources and perverse incentives for all concerned.[3] The institutions of corporate governance cannot by themselves prevent such government policies, but they are important if banks and corporations are to be run to maximize the value of the firm instead of to serve as arms of government ministries.

In its most comprehensive sense, corporate governance includes every force that bears on the decisionmaking of the firm. That would encompass not only the control rights of stockholders but also the contractual covenants and insolvency powers of debt holders, the commitments entered into with employees, customers, and suppliers, the regulations issued by government agencies, and the statutes enacted by parliamentary bodies. In addition, the firm's decisions are powerfully affected by competitive conditions in the various markets in which it operates. One could go still further to bring in the social and cultural norms of the society. All are relevant, but the analysis would become so diffuse that it risks becoming unhelpful as well as unbounded.

I go in the opposite direction and focus on a narrow and precise part of total corporate governance: the provision of external equity finance to the firm. This approach may require some justification. What is different or central about external equity finance? To go one step further, what is special about equity at all, as compared to debt finance for example?

For those who desire an explanation, or justification, for giving such prominence to external equity, the first section of the paper reviews what is unique, and crucial, about the position of external equity in the financial structure of the firm. In particular, I examine the distinctly different institutions that define and protect the status of minority shareholders in public and private firms, drawing in part on the experience of the highly developed economies. Those who agree with this approach, or who need no review of the argument, can go directly to the second section, which applies the analysis to the factual setting of the four East Asian countries.

3. Krugman (1998); Pomerleano (1998).

The final section concludes with some observations and recommendations as to the most important steps that might be taken to improve corporate governance, under the conditions prevailing in these countries.

External Equity

The special role of equity owners is that they are the residual risk-bearers of the firm. Their claim is only to whatever is left after all prior claims have been paid—lenders' principal or interest, employees' salaries, suppliers' bills, government taxes. Their investment in the firm is critical; it provides a degree of assurance that those fixed or prior claims will be paid in accordance with their terms and enables the firm to contract with others on more favorable terms for inputs to production. But the claim of shareholders not only comes last, but necessarily in no fixed amount, and shareholder funds are often invested in firm-specific assets that have less value in any other use.

If the equity owners are not the managers of the firm and their claims are highly imprecise, what gives them reason to believe that they will get much of anything? Why should the managers, who make decisions about the firm, not award themselves highly generous shares of the profits, beyond what their services could command on the labor market (while leaving the losses for the shareholders)? What keeps these managerial rents (which the economists often label agency costs) under some degree of control?

To begin, why do equity owners (whom I call shareholders, regardless of the particular legal form of the firm) have any basis to believe they will get a return on their investment, assuming they are not themselves the managers of the firm? As noted, their contract with the firm is highly incomplete, specifying neither a date for repayment of principal nor a rate of dividend pay-out. They "own" the residual equity but not the means of getting hold of it, and that residual itself is a function of what the controlling managers take for themselves.

One answer is that the managers have a stake in their own reputation, if they contemplate raising more equity in capital markets to support expansion of the firm. If they appropriate "too much" for themselves, obtaining additional equity may be difficult or possible only on onerous terms, so there is an implied contract that is self-enforcing. It is also vague—what is "too much" depends on the success of the firm, the behavior of other managers, and the expectations of shareholders going in. And it often has been observed that many large firms rely more on retained earnings than on new equity offerings. Reputation is no doubt a constraint, but an uncertain one.

A second answer is that, under most legal systems, shareholders have the power to elect a governing board, which in turn selects the managers who make the actual operating decisions, including decisions as to salaries and dividend payments. In theory, managers who reward themselves excessively or perform incompetently may be replaced by the shareholders. In practice, this will depend on whether the shareholders are able to take effective collective action, and that in turn depends on a host of considerations to which I shall return.

A third answer is that a set of legal rules may limit the ability of managers to act in ways that benefit themselves and harm shareholders. For example, provisions in U.S. corporate codes and court decisions impose on managers and directors a fiduciary "duty of loyalty" to act in the best interests of shareholders. This general duty finds application in many different contexts—executive compensation is one, but self-dealing transactions between a controlling insider and the firm is another, more far-reaching category. The consequence of the legal rule is to subject conflict-of-interest transactions by insiders to the possibility of outside review by a court; the value of that possibility likewise depends on a number of other factors, to which I shall return.

These answers to the pervasive problem of agency costs are not mutually exclusive but are potentially complementary. They are developed, and relied on, to different degrees in different countries. I shall not comment further on the reputational factor; it is hard to know how much importance to accord it, and in any event it is not very amenable to change by reform efforts. My focus, therefore, is on the role of shareholder voting power and conflict-of-interest law in corporate governance.

Let me develop further the significance of corporate governance by examining the significance of external equity finance in an economy. What are the alternatives for financing production? First, there could be greater reliance on debt, and, in theory, a firm could even be financed entirely by debt. Debt is by definition a fixed claim, and if the firm cannot meet its payment terms, the firm is insolvent. In an uncertain world, frequent recourse to bankruptcy and reorganization would impose a set of costs that are reduced by the inclusion of a layer of equity finance. What determines the optimal mix of debt and equity for a firm is the subject of a large amount of economic literature, both theoretical and empirical.[4] But observation verifies the conclusion that a significant amount of equity contributes to the efficiency of the firm.

The equity in a firm could be provided by the individuals or group who formed the company and are actively operating it. That would of course limit the amount to their financial resources and thereby ultimately limit the growth of the firm. But it would also limit the firm's choice of investment projects to the level of riskiness that is acceptable to the small group of owners. This would constitute another restriction on the growth of the firm.

There are three great advantages to having the equity provided by outside investors, who can hold investments in many companies and need not be active in their management. First, outside investors can diversify their investments and thereby eliminate some of the risk. Putting it the other way, the firm can raise equity capital from them at a lower cost. Second, outside investors can set their own level of risk by the way they form their portfolio; they are not concerned with limiting the riskiness of the individual firm's investment choices to conform to their own preferences. And third, the supply of equity capital is enlarged far beyond the resources of the founders.

The extent to which those advantages are realized is a function of the share of external equity in the capital structure of the firm. It may help to identify four contrasting possibilities. First, there may be broad public ownership of most of the firm's voting equity. That implies an active secondary trading market, in which the performance of the firm and its management is constantly being evaluated. But that also implies dispersed ownership among many small holders, who find it difficult to act in coordination. The advantages of their ability to hold diversified investment portfolios—an elimination of idiosyncratic risk for them, a lower cost of capital for the company—are attainable, but the reduction of agency costs is more problematic. This is where corporate governance in the sense of institutions facilitating the exercise of collective voting power becomes important.

Second, there may be a majority, or at least controlling, equity block holder, such as a founder and his family or associates, coupled with

---

4. Modigliani and Miller (1958) demonstrated that it does not matter in a formal model, which has given rise to a vast literature seeking to explain why in actual practice it does.

outsider ownership of the remainder of the shares. The outsiders can still diversify their holdings, but it is likely that the controlling insider is not well diversified. That means that the insider's risk tolerance determines the firm's investment policy; there is not the degree of separation (and value maximization) possible for the public firm. The result may be to lead the owner to diversify within the firm, whether doing so is economically efficient or not. The public investors cannot in practice use voting power, even ignoring all collective action problems, to discipline the controlling owner. That opens the door to a higher level of managerial rent-taking. The price at which the shares are purchased or traded will be discounted to reflect their vulnerability, resulting in a higher cost of capital to the firm. This is where corporate governance in the sense of legal rules bounding managerial rents becomes important.

Third, the firm might have no external equity. That would be true if it were 100 percent owned and operated by its founder. All of the advantages of external equity would be absent, but so would the disadvantages. There would be no agency costs, and no incentive problems, such as those between owner and manager. At a small scale of operations, the advantages are likely to dominate, but expansion to a larger scale becomes increasingly difficult.

Fourth, the firm might be owned by the government, in which case the taxpayer becomes the residual risk-bearer but has almost no ability to alter its operations. "Corporate governance" is at its most indirect and ineffectual, and the firm is very unlikely to be profit-maximizing. But the worst of all worlds is when the firm is privately owned, but the government in fact bears most of the equity risk, as when it explicitly or implicitly guarantees creditor claims on the firm. A "bailout" policy gives the owner the gains from good outcomes and the taxpayer the losses from bad outcomes, which in turn leads the owner to have the firm be thinly capitalized and take high risks. The price for such a one-sided bargain is likely to be a corrupt relationship between favored firms and government officials.

The first and second of these possibilities—the public firm and the founder firm—are the most germane to my present topic and are the ones I explore further. They play prominent roles in the East Asian economies and their current crises. What are the conditions for their effective functioning?

The institutions that support an efficient system of broad public ownership of firms in developed countries have been much studied in recent years. With dispersed shareholder ownership, how can management be monitored and controlled or replaced? How do owners remote from the firm know what is going on or exercise their dormant voting power?

The first requisite is to have reliable information about both firm performance and managerial rents. The professional participants in the secondary market seek such information to make trading and investment profits, but where do they find it and what is its quality? Disclosure rules bear on the first, and accounting rules bear on the second.

Disclosure is an amalgam of what companies find it in their own interest to disclose and what government bodies require them to disclose. There has been a long-standing debate over just how much the second adds to the first, but in the United States the disclosure regime of the Securities and Exchange Commission (SEC) has become quite extensive, at least insofar as it is directed at operating performance. It has never focused on disclosure of managerial rents, but nonetheless it does generate some relevant information.

Accounting and auditing standards help determine the value and reliability of the information and reports that companies issue. They vary significantly from country to country in the flexibility they give management to manipulate reported results. Since they are the product of a tug-of-war among management, accountants, and regulatory bodies, a lack of consistency is not surprising.

Given a certain quantity and quality of information, what can shareholders do with it? Individually, in a widely held firm, they have neither the capacity nor the incentive to do much. For monitoring to work, there must be some way to aggregate the fragmented voting power in the public firm. This occurs in developed countries like the United States, Germany, and Japan, but typically in markedly different ways.

In the United States, the aggregation of voting power takes place in the "market for corporate control" represented by the hostile takeover bid or proxy fight. The "raider" (never underestimate the power of a pejorative label) assembles for the occasion a new control block, which can oust a poorly performing incumbent management. Of course, this overstates the present reality. Management and its counsel, with help from courts and legislatures, have devised barriers to takeovers (such as poison pills and staggered boards) that have greatly reduced their prospects for success. Still, to the degree a threat remains, it constitutes a source of discipline on management to have regard for shareholder value.

In Germany, banks not only can own stock in public companies but also can vote the shares deposited with them by their account holders or owned by the investment funds they operate. The result is that a small group of banks vote a majority of the shares at the annual meetings of the largest corporations. Clearly, banks are in a position to monitor the incumbent managers, although somewhat awkwardly due to Germany's two-tier board structure, but on whose behalf? Shareholders in general or their own lending business with the firm? Still, management of the large public companies is not in a position of autonomy.

In Japan also, banks are thought to play an important monitoring role in their *keiretsu*—groups of firms bound together by stable cross-shareholding and often by customer-supplier relationships. The main bank has power, not from its own stockholding in the member firms (which may not exceed 5 percent), but from its position as a lender and as the delegated administrator on behalf of the group. Public shareholders outside the group may hold a substantial fraction of the stock but are traditionally completely passive.

The common element is that there has to be some mechanism (or mix of mechanisms) for recombining the otherwise meaningless voting power of shareholders in publicly held corporations. That mechanism is provided mainly through the market in the United States and through banks in Germany and Japan. None of those mechanisms seems particularly efficient. In the United States, the control market has been hobbled by the courts and legislatures. In Germany and Japan, the banks appear to have the voting strength, but their incentives to exercise it to maximize shareholder value are obscure at best. Each could easily improve its own system and borrow from the other; they are not mutually exclusive. But in none is management left completely unfettered and secure in its tenure, short of creditor intervention and bankruptcy.

When we turn to the founder-operated firm, that is precisely management's control position. Backed by ownership or control of a majority of the stock, outright or through pyramiding or a network of cross-shareholdings, or by control of a block sufficiently close to a majority to be difficult, if not impossible, to challenge in practice, the founder and his nominees cannot be ousted in the market. The voting rights of minority shares are largely irrelevant, unless and until the firm shifts to publicly held status. And a wide divergence between the dominant insider's control rights and his cash flow rights creates strong incentives to enhance the private benefits of control.

In consequence, the protection of the value of minority shares rests on legal rules. In the United States, management's fiduciary duty is usually broken into two parts: the duty of care and the duty of loyalty. The duty of care can be thought of as addressed to the issue of managerial competence and performance, and it provides minimal protection. The duty is typically phrased as requiring "ordinary" diligence, care, and skill. In practice it affords a ground for imposing liability for gross negligence, which is rarely adjudged. The market control mechanism, in contrast, offers in theory a way to replace management whenever its shortfall in performance is greater than the costs of takeover (including the bid premium). But in the privately controlled firm, the minority shareholder can do little about poor performance, either through legal recourse or through voting.

The duty of loyalty, however, is concerned with managerial rents and conflict-of-interest transactions, and its importance is easy to underestimate. It applies to public corporations as well as privately controlled ones. In the public corporation it would come under whatever discipline is exerted by the market as well as by banks or institutional investors. But in the privately controlled firm, the only discipline comes from the law; if the legal constraints are weak, the amount of insider expropriation from outside shareholders can be very great.

The duty of loyalty is a principle, in Anglo-American law, not a precise prescription. In general, it requires those in control of the firm's decisions to put the shareholders' interests above their own, when the two are in conflict. To quote a summary I wrote elsewhere:

> One can postulate a continuum of situations involving conflicts of interest between managers and owners, with the conflict becoming less sharp (and perhaps the legal rules less essential). At one extreme would be outright theft, embezzlement, and misappropriation; without effective legal sanctions in these cases, only the gullible would part with their money. A somewhat less transparent form of achieving the same end is the self-dealing transaction between the manager and his firm. By buying too low or selling too high, the controlling party transfers wealth from the firm to himself, but the picture can be confused by intricate transactions in non-standard assets or subject to varying degrees of price unfairness. Enforcement becomes more difficult, but still seems essential if agency costs are to have any bound. The appropriation of corporate opportunities, excessive compensation, and consumption of managerial perks can be still more judgmental, and probably the legal rules are less effective, but the order of magnitude is also less. And when one reaches

conflicts highly intertwined with the regular operation of the business, such as excessive diversification or self-retention by less competent managers, the fiduciary duty of loyalty probably offers little protection.[5]

Despite its limitations, the duty of loyalty or some equivalent seems to be a critical element in a country's corporate governance system. How well developed a set of rules there is to deal with managerial behavior in conflict-of-interest transactions has an important bearing on the risk borne by outside shareholders and the terms on which they are willing to invest.

Of course, a set of legal rules is not self-enforcing. There also has to be some mechanism for enforcement, so the existence of legal causes of action and of a fair and reliable judicial system is essential. Enforcement requires information, so here too disclosure and reporting obligations are a necessary predicate for action. Large-scale depredations may be hard to conceal, but a systematic reporting requirement for conflict-of-interest transactions would greatly facilitate enforcement.

Even in the founders-controlled firm, the number of outside shareholders and their limited stakes may make collective action to enforce legal duties difficult to undertake. In the United States, shareholder class actions or derivative suits are one response, in which an attorney seeking a contingent fee bears the brunt of organizing and pursuing the legal remedy. Without some form of representative action, the conflict-of-interest rules are likely to be paper tigers with little effect.

To this point I have made no mention of the role of the board of directors in corporate governance, for either the public or the founder firm. A managing board with outside members, in whatever exact form, may serve several functions. It may be, in technical legal terms, the origin of agency authority within the firm—the formal decisionmaker that empowers officers and employees to act for and bind the firm. It may be a consultative body enabling management to draw on experience and perspective beyond their own. But outside directors cannot typically be expected to exercise more than a modest constraint on the behavior of those who put and keep them in office. For a firm in financial trouble, the board may sometimes be a device for managerial replacement short of bankruptcy proceedings. But neither the power nor the incentives of outside directors make them in

5. Scott (1998).

general effective agents for minority shareholders, and imposing liability cannot fully compensate for the deficiency.

Application of the Analysis to Four East Asian Countries

In this section, I distill from the foregoing analysis some criteria for measuring and evaluating the state of corporate governance and possible reforms in different countries.

First, what is the proportion of external equity finance in the capital structure of firms for which reported data are available? What share of gross domestic product (GDP) do those firms represent? I argue that these are highly correlated with the status of corporate governance in a particular country. Of course, other factors play a role in determining the actual numbers—the tax treatment of returns to capital, the domestic savings rate, restrictions on foreign investment, exchange controls, and many other variables affecting the local economy. But the importance of external equity finance is an important indicator of the effectiveness of corporate governance. High ratios of bank debt to equity and low ratios of external to inside equity suggest corporate governance inadequacies.

A breakdown of GDP share between publicly held companies and privately controlled companies provides further insight. A large portion of GDP in public companies suggests the presence of institutions supporting the monitoring of management by shareholders, in some manner. Dominance of privately controlled companies suggests problems with those monitoring institutions.

Second, for publicly held firms, the search for possible improvements in corporate governance should focus on enhancing the disclosure of reliable information and reducing the costs of shareholder collective action, either through the market or by large block holders such as banks or other institutions. Each can be broken down into a number of more specific elements. As to financial information, we have the extent and scope of disclosure requirements, the level of accounting and auditing standards, the degree of enforcement, and so on. As to collective action, we have the presence of (or barriers to) takeover bids and proxy contests, restrictions on institutional holdings, the activism permitted to pension and mutual funds, and so on.

Third, for privately controlled firms, the focus should be on the effectiveness of legal rules constraining conflict-of-interest behavior by dominant insiders. Voting power and market institutions are not the primary concern, if control is firmly in the hands of the founding group and their friends and associates, who rely on personal bonds and other relationships instead. The size of the average fraction of truly outside ownership in such firms indicates the effectiveness of conflict law.

Improvements in conflict-bounding legal rules should be directed toward issues such as the scope of the rules, access to corporate information, reporting of conflict transactions (whether "material" or not), procedural barriers, and enforcement mechanisms that are viable for relatively small outside shareholders.

With the foregoing analysis as a framework, I now turn to the four East Asian countries: Korea, Indonesia, Malaysia, and Thailand. The discussion is preliminary and tentative, reflecting limited data and understanding, but it is intended to suggest areas where further inquiry would be useful. The recent study by Claessens, Djankov, and Lang constitutes a most valuable source of empirical data.[6]

Korea

The Korean economy is usually characterized as being dominated by the government-fostered *chaebol* system—a conglomerate group of firms, linked by indirect cross-shareholdings and a common founder-chairman in the core companies. The founder and his family on average own about 10 percent, and through cross-holdings control another 30 to 40 percent, of the group member firms in the top thirty *chaebol*.[7] The controlling shareholder is usually also the chief executive officer and chairman of the board, whose other members are executives he has selected.[8]

In 1996 there were 760 companies listed on the Korea Stock Exchange (KSE), with a market capitalization of $139 billion. A study of the control pattern of 345 companies (representing 76 percent of the total market capitalization) with the necessary data available shows that 14 percent were widely held and 68 percent were family controlled, if a holder with more than 10 percent is used as the dividing line; if a 30 percent holding is made the cutoff line, then 76 percent were widely held and 20 percent were family controlled.[9] When the size of the company is taken into account, the

6. Claessens, Djankov, and Lang (1999).
7. Lee (1996).
8. Choi (1999, p. 4).
9. Claessens, Djankov, and Lang (1999, p. 30).

proportion under family control rose as size declined; using the same 30 percent cutoff line, the number went from 10 percent of the top twenty firms to 80 percent of the fifty smallest firms in the sample.[10]

Korea, therefore, has both a significant publicly held sector and a large number of privately controlled firms in its public trading market, with the exact shares depending on where the control dividing line is drawn. One would expect some support for both in its legal institutions of corporate governance.

First, what is the position of small shareholders in the widely held firm? For all KSE firms in 1997, individuals owned 40 percent of the shares, financial institutions owned 22 percent, and other companies owned 23 percent.[11] Listing on the first tier of the KSE now requires that small shareholders (less than 1 percent) own at least 40 percent of total shares and that the principal owner or family own no more than 51 percent.[12]

Rahman has studied the accounting practices and disclosure rules in East Asian countries and compared them with selected international accounting standards (IAS's).[13] For Korea, he summarizes the findings for a sample of eleven of the largest banks and *chaebols* as follows:

> Our survey results show that none of the sample companies disclosed the amount of related party lending and borrowing. The financial statements of a little less than one-half of the sample companies made reference to existence of related party lending and borrowing but without disclosure of the amount. While all the sample companies reported foreign currency debt in the local currency, none disclosed the amount of foreign debt in the currency of repayment, and not a single corporation or bank follows IAS's in accounting and reporting for foreign currency translation gains and losses. Although a vast majority of the sample companies reported the amount of the issuance of derivative financial instruments, only a tiny portion complied with other disclosure requirements set by the relevant IAS's. Almost total non-compliance with IAS's was found in the case of segment information. While all the sample companies disclosed the amount of contingent liability, none disclosed any information on commitments for off-balance-sheet financing activities. Except in the

10. Claessens, Djankov, and Lang (1999, pp. 38, 40).
11. Choi (1999, p. 13).
12. Jeong and Mo (1997, p. 62)
13. Rahman (1998, p. 30).

case of a few items of disclosure, overall disclosures in the financial statements of almost all the sample banks lacked compliance with the specific disclosure requirements for bank set by IAS's.

Rahman examines those accounting standards most relevant to the financial crises, as they bore on disclosures of short-term foreign currency–denominated debt, contingent exposures, loan delinquencies, and the like. His conclusions do suggest, however, room for substantial improvement in financial statement disclosure in general. The Korean government has promised enhanced disclosure, through consolidated balance sheets for conglomerates and enforcement of accounting standards in line with generally accepted accounting principles. It remains to be seen how the promise will be fulfilled; in the past, disclosure laws have not been enforced.[14]

Likewise auditing, which for large companies and banks is usually performed by local member firms of the Big Five international accounting giants, is conducted throughout the region in accordance with local auditing standards and practices.[15] The differences from international standards are not described in the audit opinion, which would seem a minimum step forward. Korea has the institution of a shareholder-elected internal auditor (usually a retired executive), whose potential effectiveness is similar to that of an outside director; under normal conditions, management usually chooses both an internal auditor and an outside director. Under a 1998 law, the top thirty *chaebol* are to form auditor selection committees composed of internal auditors, outside directors, large creditors, and large non-control shareholders.[16]

As noted, there is a significant portion of publicly traded firms in Korea in which no controlling shareholder has a position impregnable to challenge in the market. But there was also, until recently, an effective set of barriers to hostile tender offers, ruling out discipline from a market for control. In 1998 legal amendments permitted even foreigners to purchase any percentage of shares without the restriction of board approval. In theory, a control market may now develop, but the U.S. experience suggests that management will be assiduous in finding ways to thwart it.

The other avenue for shareholder discipline through voting power lies in action by significant block holders, such as institutional investors. If

14. Kwon (1997, pp. 102–03).
15. Rahman (1998, p. 37).
16. Choi (1999, p. 9).

foreign owners are added to Korean financial institutions, they own 31 percent of total market shares, but that overstates their potential.[17] A number of insurance companies, securities companies, and banks are controlled by a *chaebol* and thus are neutralized as to any monitoring of their parent. Individually, their holding in a single company is restricted to a maximum of 20 percent for an investment trust company, 10 percent for a bank or insurance company, and 8 percent for a securities company.[18] The investment trust funds, with the most liberal limit, are the fastest growing institutional investor, going from 0 76 percent of total market share in 1986 to 6.26 percent in 1995.[19] However, their own shares are in turn held by a limited number of institutions, and they are required to shadow vote as directed by their fund holders. The mutual fund as a pooling of the voting power of numerous small investors did not exist in Korea, but it may now become possible, with the removal of the shadow voting requirement in 1998.[20] To this point, banks and other institutional investors have been passive and have not constituted a source of monitoring discipline on management.

The possibility of a proxy contest as another voice for small shareholder voting power should be mentioned, although only in passing. As in the United States, management is in control of the proxy solicitation machinery and the annual meeting agenda; it solicits "blanket" (discretionary) proxies to obtain a quorum. A proxy fight against an incumbent management owning a block of shares has poor prospects of success and has never been attempted.[21] The experience in the United States would suggest that a proxy contest is of value primarily as an adjunct to a hostile takeover bid.

Let me now turn to the position of a minority investor in an insider-controlled firm and the issue of conflict-of-interest law. The *chaebol* structure, a web of partially insider-owned firms with substantial outside shareholdings and cross-payment guarantees, is inherently riddled with potential self-dealing and abuse of control. I have insufficient information to characterize the content of Korean conflict-of-interest laws, beyond noting that the commercial code was amended at the end of 1998 to impose on directors an explicit fiduciary duty of loyalty to the company.

17. Choi (1999, p. 14).
18. Lim (1997, p. 146).
19. Lim (1997).
20. Choi (1999, p. 10).
21. Kwon (1997, p. 104).

The one broad attempt to survey shareholder and creditor protection law across forty-nine countries is by LaPorta and others.[22] They create an index for legal protection of shareholders by looking at a set of particular provisions: one share/one vote, voting by mail, share deposit to vote, cumulative voting, some avenue of challenge to directors' decisions, preemptive purchase rights, and shareholder percentage to call a special meeting (and mandatory dividends as a separate category). The middle six are equally weighted, and their presence is added to give a rating. For what it is worth, Korea gets a 2.0 (the United States has a 5.0), and the mean for all forty-nine countries is a 3.0.[23] Unfortunately for my purpose here, their index is both crude and largely directed to matters of shareholder voting, not conflict-of-interest standards.

There has been since 1982 a provision whereby a shareholder dissenting from a corporate decision to sell or merge the business can require the company to purchase his shares, at a price to be determined by negotiation, prior transaction prices, the SEC, or a court. This dissenters' appraisal remedy has been invoked rather frequently (almost 30 percent of the time) by the big investment trust companies.[24] Determining its value is another matter. As a remedy for minority shareholders in self-dealing acquisitions by those in control, it can be simple and effective. But in arm's-length transactions with outside companies, where the interests of managers and shareholders are mostly aligned, it just purports to give knowledgeable shareholders a free put option if there is a price decline compared to the sixty days prior to board action. The provision in Korea (as in the United States) makes no distinction between the two kinds of acquisitions.

The enforcement of shareholder rights is of course also an important consideration. We can begin for KSE-listed and KOSDAQ-registered firms with access to company information, such as accounting books and documents, which is limited to a shareholder owning at least 1 percent (0.5 percent for companies with more than 100 billion won in capital) of the stock, if he can prove the request is reasonable.[25] In other words, the shareholder can gain the information only by going to court.

Shareholders in KSE-listed companies can maintain derivative actions, if they own at least 0.01 percent of the stock.[26] I do not know if Korea has

22. La Porta and others (1998).
23. La Porta and others (1998, table 2, pp. 1130–31).
24. Lim (1997, p. 138).
25. Kwon (1997, pp. 103–04).
26. Choi (1999, p. 8).

had the misfortune to pick up from the United States all the arcane distinctions between class actions and derivative suits or all the procedural obstacles placed on the latter. For whatever reason, the derivative suit has rarely been used; the victory for the minority shareholders in the Korea First Bank case in 1997 is apparently a first.[27] Class actions are supposed to be authorized in 2000. For either to work well, the essential requirement is that there be attorneys who are prepared to bear the litigation costs on behalf of nominal shareholder plaintiffs in order to collect a substantial fee if successful. Otherwise, collective action problems and costs will usually continue to be insurmountable.

La Porta and others also rank on a scale of one to ten the systems of legal enforcement in their forty-nine-country study, using country-risk ratings produced by several commercial agencies for three variables pertinent here: efficiency of the judicial system, rule of law, and corruption. Korea received a 6.00, 5.35, and 5.30 compared to 10.00, 10.00, and 8.63 for the United States (or straight tens for New Zealand, the Netherlands, Switzerland, and the Scandinavian countries).

To sum up, Korea appears to have acquired at least the beginnings of the institutions necessary to support managerial monitoring and the operation of firms to maximize total shareholder value, which lead to reduced agency cost and lower cost of capital. It is considering requiring more outside directors and audit committees and has revised its financial accounting standards toward international norms.

Indonesia

I have too little current quantitative or qualitative information to justify firm conclusions about Indonesia. At the end of 1996 there were 253 companies listed on the Jakarta Stock Exchange (JSX), with a market capitalization of $91 billion. The Claessens, Djankov, and Lang study of a sample of 178 firms shows that, at the 10 percent cutoff line, less than 1 percent were widely held and 67 percent were family controlled, while at the 30 percent dividing line 25 percent were widely held and 59 percent family controlled. The top ten families controlled an incredible 58 percent of total market capitalization at the 20 percent line, through a complex web of interlinked conglomerates.[28] By the end of 1998, the number of

---

27. Choi (1999, p. 7).
28. Claessens, Djankov, and Lang (1999, pp 30, 36).

listed companies had grown to 288, but more than half were on a watch-list for possible delisting due to lack of profitability. From July 1997 to August 1998, the market capitalization of JSX stocks had fallen from $101 billion to $10 billion.[29] The category of the widely held public company in Indonesia appears to be rather insignificant. Hostile takeovers of a public company are permitted through a regulated tender offer.

Rahman's study of the accounting practices of a sample of seven large firms in Indonesia offers the following summary:

> More than half of the sample companies disclosed information on related party lending and borrowing. The amount of foreign currency debt was disclosed in both local and foreign currencies by a vast majority of the sample companies. Most of the sample companies did not comply with IAS's in the case of accounting and reporting for foreign currency gains and losses. Disclosure on foreign currency risk management policy was not found in any of the financial statements. The local currency as well as foreign currency amounts of derivative financial instruments were disclosed by a majority of the sample companies and some additional sample companies mentioned the existence of these instruments without specific disclosure of the amount. Most of the sample companies did not disclose any information on the interests and losses relating to derivative financial instruments, and terms, conditions, and accounting policies regarding such instruments. No one disclosed the extent of risk associated with the issuance of derivative financial instruments. Majority of the sample companies did not disclose segment information as per requirements of IAS's. A vast majority of the sample companies disclosed the nature and amount of contingent liabilities without disclosure of the amount of contingent liabilities [sic]. The amount of guarantees given was separately disclosed by a vast majority of the sample companies. As in the case of other countries in the region, no one disclosed any information on commitments in support of off-balance-sheet financing. The financial statements of none of the sample banks completely complied with the specific disclosure requirements for bank set by IAS's.[30]

29. Asia-Pacific Economic Cooperation (1999a).
30. Rahman (1998).

Indonesia has a two-tier board structure: a board of commissioners, who are elected at a shareholders meeting for up to a five-year term, is supposed to supervise the board of directors, who are executives elected by the shareholders for a five-year term to manage the company, subject to approval by a commissioner for certain actions. Under the 1996 Indonesian Company Law, commissioners and directors are required to "act in good faith and with a full sense of responsibility towards the company"; previously, they were not considered to be fiduciaries or to have an obligation to act in the best interests of a company's shareholders.[31]

A shareholder can bring a suit against a company if harmed by its "unfair and unreasonable" actions; a 10 percent shareholder can bring a derivative suit against a director or commissioner whose negligence caused losses to the company. There is also a dissenters' appraisal remedy for harm from mergers or purchases or sales of the business. The law lacks implementing regulations or judicial precedent, so it is difficult to say what will come of it.[32]

The Capital Markets Supervisory Agency (BAPEPAM) administers fairly extensive disclosure requirements but lacks enforcement authority. It also has rules permitting disinterested shareholders of Indonesian public companies to approve or disapprove "conflict of interest" transactions, as defined, between a company and its affiliates; the definition seems to exclude a transaction between the company and a controlling shareholder![33] The rules can be enforced by BAPEPAM and perhaps by shareholders.[34] It will be quite interesting to see how this provision develops over time, if it does. To this point, no minority shareholder oppression suits have ever been brought.[35]

The study by La Porta and others gives Indonesia a score of 2.00 on shareholder protection and ratings of 2.50, 3.98, and 2.15 on the legal enforcement variables (the lowest total of any country).[36] The judicial system is not highly regarded.[37] The picture is of a country in which external equity finance from small shareholders should be minimal. Any external

31. Perusahaan Perseroan (Persero) (1997, p. 239).
32. Perusahaan Perseroan (Persero) (1997, p. 240).
33. Asia-Pacific Economic Cooperation (1999a, app. 9).
34. Perusahaan Perseroan (Persero) (1997, p. 240).
35. Asia-Pacific Economic Cooperation (1999a, p. 29).
36. La Porta and others (1997, pp. 1130, 1143).
37. Asia-Pacific Economic Cooperation (1999a, p. 13).

equity is likely to be from large investors, who in effect rely on self-enforcing contractual rather than legal protections, and the financial structure of the firm is likely to use more debt and less equity.

Malaysia

In Malaysia at the end of 1996 there were 621 companies listed on the Kuala Lumpur Stock Exchange (KLSE), with a market capitalization of $139 billion. The Claessens, Djankov, and Lang study of a sample of 238 firms shows that 1 percent were widely held and 58 percent were family controlled at the 10 percent cutoff line; 41 percent were widely held and 46 percent were family controlled at a 30 percent cutoff.[38] By the end of 1997, the number of listed companies (main board and second board) was up to 708, but the market capitalization in ringgit was down by more than half.

Listed companies have to report financial information and substantial (more than 2 percent) shareholdings to the Securities Commission and KLSE. Most have two or three outside directors, who make up a majority of the audit committee.

Rahman was able to obtain a sample of fifteen of the twenty largest publicly traded corporations and banks, with the following findings as to their accounting practices in comparison to international standards:

> Although Malaysia officials adopted IAS's, the mixed findings on compliance with the required accounting and reporting practices suggest the absence of appropriate enforcement efforts in that country. A vast majority of the sample companies disclosed the amounts of intercompany receivables and payables, but there was negligible disclosure on lending and borrowing activities with the associates. Most of the sample companies did not disclose the amounts of foreign debt either in local currency or in the currency of repayment. All the sample companies mentioned the use of closing rate for translation of foreign currency transactions. However, the recognition and disclosure of the amount of foreign currency translation gains and losses by almost all the sample companies was not in compliance with International Accounting Standards. None of the sample companies disclosed the accounting policy on foreign currency risk manage-

---

38. Claessens, Djankov, and Lang (1999, p. 30).

ment. While more than a quarter of the sample companies disclosed the amount of derivative financial instruments, none disclosed the extent of risk associated with the issuance of derivative financial instruments and no sample company disclosed the other relevant information required by IAS's. Disclosures were made on various elements of segment information by about two-thirds of the sample companies. While most of the sample companies disclosed the amount of contingent liabilities, a lesser number separately disclosed the amount of guarantees given. There was no disclosure on commitments in support of off-balance-sheet debt financing. A high degree of compliance with IAS's was found in the case of some of the disclosure requirements in the financial statements of banks. However, some of the very important items of disclosure were not found in the financial statements of any one of the sample banks.[39]

Proxy contests are possible under Malaysian law, but with the usual advantages for incumbent management.[40] A shareholder group can call a special meeting only with 10 percent ownership. I do not have information on the extent of outside institutional shareholdings or the status of takeover contests, but institutional investors have generally been quite passive, and concentrated family ownership suggests low likelihood of any success in a hostile takeover.

Turning to the position of a minority outside shareholder in a controlled corporation, La Porta and others give Malaysia a 4.0 on protecting shareholder rights against director actions and scores of 9.0, 6.8, and 7.4 on the legal enforcement variables.[41]

Malaysia's corporate law is drawn from English sources and thus includes the common law concept of directors as fiduciaries; there are disclosure requirements for "material"-related party transactions.[42] Unfortunately, the shareholder approval requirement does not cover transactions with substantial owners.[43] Shareholders can bring both personal (contractual) and derivative actions, as well as a statutory remedy, for unfair or oppressive conduct of the company's affairs.[44] The derivative actions have

39. Rahman (1998).
40. Koh (1997, pp. 16–17).
41. La Porta and others (1998, pp. 1130, 1142).
42. Asia-Pacific Economic Cooperation (1999b, pp. 33–35).
43. Asia-Pacific Economic Cooperation (1999b, p. 44).
44. Koh (1997, p. 21).

familiar procedural burdens, so the statutory remedy would seem superior, and there are in fact a few decisions in favor of plaintiff shareholders in conflict-of-interest situations.[45] Fraud, misconduct, or oppression by management are also grounds for a court petition for a winding up of the company; the form of remedy would seem to make it unsuitable except as a threat to induce compromise or settlement. On the whole, therefore, the delineation of shareholder rights is superior to their means of enforcement.

Malaysia certainly seems far more advanced than Indonesia in dealing with the conflict-of-interest problem, at least on paper. One would like to examine empirically the actual practice.

Thailand

There were 454 companies listed on the Stock Exchange of Thailand (SET) at the end of 1996, with a market capitalization of $100 billion. A study by Claessens, Djankov, and Lang of a sample of 167 companies shows that 2 percent were widely held and 51 percent were family controlled at the 10 percent cutoff line; 25 percent were widely held and 55 percent were family controlled at the 30 percent cutoff.[46] At the end of 1997, the number of listed companies had fallen to 431, and their market capitalization (in baht) had dropped 56 percent.[47] SET requires listed companies to have at least two independent directors and an approved auditor.

Rahman, working with a full sample of the twenty largest corporations and banks in Thailand, describes accounting practices as follows:

> Of the total number of sample companies in Thailand, exactly one-half disclosed the amount of related party lending and borrowing. The amount of foreign debt in both local and foreign currencies was disclosed in most of the financial statements. In the case of recognition and reporting of foreign currency gains and losses, a vast majority of the sample companies did not comply with IAS's, and in the case of foreign currency risk management policy there was no disclosure by any one. While only a quarter of the sample companies disclosed the amount of derivative financial instruments in both local and foreign currencies, additional one-fifth mentioned the existence of such instruments but without any disclosure of the

45. Koh (1997, pp. 24–25).
46. Claessens, Djankov, and Lang (1999, p. 30).
47. Suwanmongkol (1998, p. 12).

amount. The amount of interest and losses relating to derivative financial instruments, and the terms, conditions, and accounting policies regarding such instruments, were disclosed by only one-fifth of the sample companies. None of the sample companies disclosed any information regarding the extent of risk associated with the issuance of derivative financial instruments. The disclosure of various elements of segment information, as per IAS's, was not found in the financial statements of a vast majority of the sample companies. A vast majority of the sample companies disclosed the nature and amount of contingent liabilities and guarantees. As in the case of other countries in the region, no one disclosed any information on commitments in support of off-balance-sheet financing. The financial statements of banks hardly complied with the specific disclosure requirements for bank set by IAS's.[48]

If an "indecent event" occurs in a company's financial reporting, shareholders owning 20 percent may request the Ministry of Commerce to appoint an inspector to investigate.[49]

The SEC Act of 1992 "protects" shareholder interests by requiring anyone acquiring 5 percent or more of equity securities of a listed company to file a report the next day; if the acquisition reaches 25 percent, then the acquirer must make a tender offer to purchase 100 percent.[50] Shareholders may call special meetings if they own 10 percent, but removal of a director requires the vote of three-fourths of the shareholders at the meeting. I have no empirical data on the incidence or success of hostile takeover bids for public corporations or on the position and role of domestic or foreign institutional investors. Proxy contests do not occur.

As to the status of a minority outside shareholder in a controlled corporation, the study by La Porta and others rates Thailand as a 2.0 on their shareholder rights protection scale and give it scores of 3.3, 6.3, and 5.2 on their enforcement variables.[51] Thai courts move at an exceedingly slow pace. A shareholder owning at least 5 percent may sue a director on behalf of the company for actions not "in good faith and with care to preserve the interests of the company."[52] A self-dealing transaction (loans excepted) is

48. Rahman (1998).
49. Asia-Pacific Economic Cooperation (1999c, p. 36).
50. Suwanmongkol (1998, p. 9).
51. La Porta and others (1998, pp. 1130, 1142).
52. Public Limited Companies Act B, E, 2535, sec. 85.

valid if approved by the board of directors, without reference to any standard of fairness, but it should be reported to SET and approved by shareholders.[53] A local author notes that, "Directors in Thailand do not have comprehensive fiduciary duties. . . . In reality, there have been very few civil or criminal cases relating to director liability in Thailand and even with the laws on the books, they have little meaning without use and enforcement."[54] In a country where even in the ten largest nonfinancial firms, the three largest shareholders own on average 44 percent, most outside shareholders are in family-controlled firms and depend on such legal provisions and incentives for protection of their interests.[55]

Conclusions

To summarize, using a 20 percent holding as the defining block, the portion of publicly traded companies that is widely held is 43 percent in Korea, 10 percent in Malaysia, 7 percent in Thailand, and 5 percent in Indonesia, compared to 80 percent in Japan. The portion that is family controlled is 48 percent in Korea, 62 percent in Thailand, 67 percent in Malaysia, and 72 percent in Indonesia, compared to 10 percent in Japan.[56] Corporate governance in the widely held firm is an important issue for Korea, but definitely a secondary concern for the other three or for the rest of Asia, for that matter.

A picture of the financial structure in East Asia is summarized in table 10-1, based on firms in the World Scope database, which contains 86 percent of world market capitalization. For each country, the table gives the number of firms in the sample, their percentage of total national market capitalization, and the percentage of those firms that are insider controlled (where the top five shareholders own more than 50 percent, which understates the actual extent of insider control). It also gives for the sample firms the amount of external equity (defined too broadly as all equity held outside the top five) and the composite debt-to-equity ratio.

If the percentage of equity that is external is taken as a rough indicator of the level of corporate governance in a country, as I have argued, the

53. Public Limited Companies Act B, E, 2535, sec. 87; Stock Exchange of Thailand (1998, pp. 53–66).

54. Viverito (1998, pp. 15–16).

55. Alba, Claessens, and Djankov (1998, p. 13).

56. Claessens, Djankov, and Lang (1999, p. 30).

Table 10-1. *Financial Structure of Four East Asian Countries, 1996*

Item	Korea	Indonesia	Malaysia	Thailand
Gross domestic product				
(billions of U.S. dollars)	484.5	227.4	99.3	181.4
Total national market capitalization				
(billions of U.S. dollars)	138.8	91.0	307.2	99.8
Number of firms in sample	272	148	418	276
Share of total national market				
capitalization (percent)	75	90	68	89
Insider controlled (percent)	12	81	50	44
External equity (percent)	70	34	49	61
Ratio of debt to equity (percent)	289	122	95	170

Source: World Scope database for year-end 1996, with expert assistance from Margaret Enis.

table reinforces the conclusion that at present corporate governance is most advanced in Korea and least advanced in Indonesia.

The percentage of firms that are insider controlled, even by a top 5/50 percent standard, also suggests that the position of a minority shareholder in a controlled firm is an issue that should be given priority at this time in at least three of these countries. My thesis has been that the minority outside shareholder in a controlled firm typically gets little protection from his voting power. This is of course a simplification; the world does not divide neatly into the two categories of widely held and insider owned and controlled. There are intermediate situations and complicating circumstances. But as a general proposition, improvement in the disclosure of and legal protections against conflict-of-interest transactions benefiting insiders would do the most to enlarge the pool of public investment capital—and lower its riskiness and cost—for most of Asia.

Although my information is incomplete, it seems that a great deal could be done to improve conflict-of-interest law in all four countries. Only Malaysia apparently follows the U.S.-U.K. approach of imposing a general fiduciary duty on those in control of the firm; the other countries rely on a scattering of specific requirements that leave a lot uncovered. But beyond the content, one must pay attention to the procedures for enforcement, both in the sense of various legal impediments to maintaining an action and in the sense of mechanisms to overcome the collective action problem that paralyzes small shareholders. Without procedures that are efficient (rather than deliberately costly) and incentives that capture a major part of the gain for the party bearing the expense and risk of initiating an action against corporate insiders, the rules on the statute books remain largely irrelevant. That may well be the current situation in all four countries.

The same collective action problem pervades the widely held company, but now voting power is not impotent if it can be mobilized. Mobilizing votes through takeover bids requires a set of supporting conditions, not only legal but also economic. The legal conditions in the United States are far from ideal, but they have not yet precluded all hostile takeovers, although not for want of management efforts in that direction. In most of Asia, the strength of concentrated power wielded by a small number of dominant families suggests that, if their holdings in individual firms were to drop to levels vulnerable to outside takeovers, they could erect legal barriers beyond those found in the United States—if they chose. And currently the economic conditions are also lacking, such as adequate and reliable disclosure, deep and well-functioning secondary trading markets, and ample sources of at least interim financing. They will not be developed quickly or by mere legislative enactment.

Mobilizing votes by coordination among a relatively small number of significant outside block holders is less difficult and seems easier to attain, again if not legally impeded. If they are to serve as general shareholder monitors, institutional investors must hold significant percentages and be independent of their portfolio companies. They must also have adequate incentive to take on the task on behalf of all equity holders, which raises empirical questions in both Germany and Japan. But this mode of corporate governance seems more likely in the short run, at least, for the Asian countries.

In conclusion and summary, then, if this analysis is accepted, I would translate it into the following set of priority recommendations for the countries concerned or for the programs of international financial institutions. A long list of measures and institutions play some role in corporate governance: independent directors, audit committees, proxy proposals, nominating committees, listing and delisting exchange requirements, insider trading rules, and so on for public companies; board or shareholder approval requirements for company transactions with directors, dissenters' appraisal remedies for mergers and acquisitions, preemptive subscription rights for shareholders, cumulative voting, and so on for privately controlled companies. (Both rest on a foundation of legal recognition and enforcement of a shareholder's status as an owner of the firm.) One strategy would be to press ahead on all fronts. These recommendations are for a strategy focusing on a limited number of the most salient issues.

Conflict-of-Interest Law

The potential for minority shareholders to be expropriated by conflict-of-interest transactions seems to be a major risk in all these economies, particularly given patterns of interlocking partial ownership of companies in a group. It can be addressed in two ways, which are not mutually exclusive. One is the imposition of a general "fiduciary duty of loyalty," developed in its particulars over time by lawsuits and courts. The other, which is probably more suitable for most non-common-law countries, is a set of more specific statutory rules.

SCOPE. The law should at a minimum cover transactions, direct and indirect, between the firm and those in control of it. In terms of persons covered, the important point is not formal status as an officer or director by itself, but the possession of control over decisions of the firm. That means the top management in truly public companies, but the dominant shareholders in others, whether or not they serve as directors also.

STANDARDS. One approach is to prohibit all self-dealing transactions. That might be desirable if it is anticipated that enforcement of the law will be problematic. Otherwise, a less stringent rule, such as a standard of "fairness," is probably preferable. Conflict-of-interest transactions can be mutually advantageous, like other contracts; it is just that the domination of one party gives no reason to presume that its interests will be served. A "fairness" standard implies a judgment by some outside party as to whether the terms resemble those that might have been arrived at in an actual arm's-length bargain.

ENFORCEMENT. Who is the outside party who determines whether that standard was observed? One finds a variety of answers in different legal codes.
 —"Disinterested" directors. Some statutes validate self-dealing transactions if they have been disclosed to and approved by directors on the board who do not have a personal stake in the matter. Unfortunately, "disinterested" does not mean "independent." If directors have been selected or

retained on the board by a controlling person who is a party to the transaction, their approval of the transaction should have little consequence.

—*Shareholders.* If shareholders (not counting those who are interested) approve the transaction with full disclosure of terms and gains, the question becomes the feasibility of collective action. In a private company with a small number of shareholders who hold substantial stakes, their approval should end the matter. But in a widely held public company, shareholder approval is likely to be a formality.

—*Courts.* The determination can be committed to a judge. How satisfactory a solution that will be depends primarily on two factors: the judicial system and litigation incentives. If the judicial system is independent and impartial, or is moving in that direction, this is probably the best answer, even given the subjective nature of the judgment being called for. But that rests on a further factor: whether the case will ever be presented. Only in a modest fraction of cases will an individual shareholder (or small group) find it economically sensible to bear the entire risks and costs of litigation for the prospect of a merely proportionate share of the recovery. For enforcement to be effective, there must be some mechanism for collective action, such as derivative suits and class action suits brought by attorneys in search of substantial fees if successful. This has proven a powerful enforcement mechanism in the United States, as is being demonstrated in an increasing variety of contexts. But it depends on its being acceptable under social norms and bar rules, which may require a process of explanation and adoption. Otherwise, conflict-of-interest rules may be of little value without some different avenue of enforcement.

—*Administrative agencies.* Enforcement could be committed to a government agency charged with the task. This is definitely second best to an effective bar, because agency incentives to act are weak and often vulnerable to political pressure. But if there is no better alternative, then it is the last line of defense.

Market Control

In the longer run, it is important to strengthen the prospects of managerial monitoring for public companies by facilitating the assembly of significant voting positions. Where it can be brought to bear, shareholder majorities can address not only conflict-of-interest expropriation but, even more significantly, the quality of managerial performance and the need for replacement. Only in Korea would such measures offer the possibility of immediate appreciable gains. To implement such an approach, several factors are worth stressing.

—*Information disclosure.* Trading markets are fundamentally markets in information. Obviously, the extent and reliability of corporate financial information reported to exchanges and shareholders help to determine the depth of capital markets, the liquidity of investors' positions, and the accuracy of pricing. If the required disclosure also addresses conflict-of-interest transactions, it facilitates enforcement of those rules as well.

—*The role of institutional investors.* Enhancing the growth and activism of institutional investors makes possible direct shareholder monitoring of management in public companies. As capital flows into pension funds, investment companies, insurance companies, and the like, with the growth of these economies, it is important that they not be restricted to ineffectual holdings and passive voting in portfolio companies. The same is true for banks, whose defaulted loans are bestowing on them large equity positions.

—*Takeovers.* The opportunity for hostile takeovers can be a powerful disciplinary force on the incumbent management of widely held firms and for that reason is fiercely resisted in the names of "stability" and "shareholder protection." I am not optimistic about the development of a market for corporate control in the short run because it requires large and liquid capital markets. If those funds are from foreign sources, it becomes easy to play on xenophobic fears as another line of defense. But looking forward, the threat of a hostile takeover is a mechanism worth fostering.

Education and Training

To the extent the institutions and concepts described above are unfamiliar, there is need for a program of explanation, consultation, and training. It would certainly not do simply to propound U.S. laws or institutions, which are themselves often inefficient in dealing with these matters. In particular, the United States has, as part of the process of contention among its own interest groups, added procedural obstacles to many of these devices, which no one would be well advised to emulate.

From the standpoint of international financial institutions, it would also be worthwhile to create and maintain a set of empirical indicators of status in dealing with corporate governance, beyond the valuable but simple beginning made in the 1998 study by La Porta and others. The actual incidence of various events, such as takeover attempts or conflict-of-interest lawsuits, adds a great deal of understanding of the reality that lies outside the pages of statutes.

References

Alba, Pedro, Stijn Claessens, and Simeon Djankov. 1998. "Thailand's Corporate Financing and Governance Structures: Impact on Firms' Competitiveness." Policy Research Paper 2003. Washington, D.C.: World Bank (November).

Asia-Pacific Economic Cooperation (with Asian Development Bank and the World Bank). 1999a. "Corporate Governance Country Assessment Report. Indonesia." Washington, D.C. (draft).

————. 1999b. "Corporate Governance Country Assessment Report. Malaysia." Washington, D.C. (draft).

————. 1999c. "Corporate Governance Country Assessment Report. Thailand." Washington, D.C. (draft).

Choi, J. 1999. *Global Corporate Governance in Korea.* Korea Stock Exchange. Seoul.

Claessens, Stijn, Simeon Djankov, and Larry H. P. Lang. 1999. "Who Controls East Asian Corporations?" Policy Research Paper 2054. Washington, D.C.: World Bank (February).

International Monetary Fund. 1999. *IMF-Supported Programs in Indonesia, Korea, and Thailand: A Preliminary Assessment.* Washington, D.C.

Jeong, Kap-Young, and Jongryn Mo. 1997. "The Political Economy of Corporate Governance Reform in Korea." *Global Economic Review* 26 (Autumn): 59–75.

Johnson, Simon. 1998. "Corporate Governance in the Asian Financial Crisis, 1997–98." Working Paper. School of Management, Massachusetts Institute of Technology.

Koh, P. 1997. *Principles, Practice, and Prospects of Corporate Governance: The Malaysian Legal Framework.* Singapore.

Krugman, Paul. 1998. "What Happened to Asia?" Massachusetts Institute of Technology. (http://web.mit.edu/krugman/www/DISINTER.html [July 1, 1998]).

Kwon, Jae-Yeol. 1997. "Strong Insiders, Weak Outsiders: A Critical Look at the Korean System of Corporate Governance." *Global Economic Review* 26 (Autumn): 97–111.

La Porta, Rafael, and others. 1997. "Legal Determinants of External Finance." *Journal of Finance* 52 (July): 1131–50.

————. 1998. "Law and Finance." *Journal of Political Economy* 106 (December): 1113–55.

Lee, Y. 1996. "Corporate Governance in Korea: The Structure and Issues." Working Paper. Korea Development Institute.

Lim, Ungki. 1997. "Institutional Shareholders' Dissenting Actions in the Korean Stock Market." *Global Economic Review* 26 (Autumn): 131–46.

Modigliani, Franco, and Merton H. Miller. 1958. "The Cost of Capital, Corporation Finance, and the Theory of Investment." *American Economic Review* 48 (June): 261–97.

Perusahaan Perseroan (Persero). 1997. "Public Offer Memorandum." Securities and Exchange Commission.

Pomerleano, Michael. 1998. "The East Asia Crisis and Corporate Finances: The Untold Microeconomic Story." *Emerging Markets Quarterly* 2 (Winter): 14–27.

Rahman, Matiur. 1998. *The Role of Accounting Disclosure in the East Asian Financial Crisis: Lessons Learned?* United Nations Conference on Trade and Development.

Scott, Kenneth. 1998. "The Role of Corporate Governance in South Korean Economic Reform." *Journal of Applied Corporate Finance* 10 (Winter): 8–15.

Stock Exchange of Thailand. 1998. *The Roles, Duties, and Responsibilities of the Directors of Listed Companies.* Bangkok.

Suwanmongkol, R. 1998. *The Thai Capital Market.* Bangkok: Securities and Exchange Commission.

Viverito, J. 1998. *Corporate Governance in the Kingdom of Thailand.* Bangkok: KMV (Thailand) Co. Ltd.

World Bank. 1998. *East Asia: The Road to Recovery.* Washington, D.C.

MICHAEL ADLER

11

Emerging Market Investing: Problems and Prospects

A s OF MID-FEBRUARY 1999, most emerging market activities on Wall Street are dead in the water. The industry is downsizing. Sell-side houses in the United States and Europe have for the past eight months been laying off personnel in emerging market research, sales, and both client-based and proprietary trading. New issues of emerging market sovereign and corporate bonds and new listings of American depository receipts (ADRs) have dried up. Portfolio managers report that their institutional clients are withdrawing from emerging market debt as an asset class and are at most maintaining, but not adding to, their positions in emerging market equity. Asset allocations this season have been minimal or even negative as some investors attempt to use rallies as an opportunity to unload.

For 1999 the Institute for International Finance (IIF) is expecting total private sector capital flows to emerging markets to fall from $327 billion in 1996 to no more than $140 billion this year.[1] In Latin America alone, the reduced supply of private capital is expected to produce a funding gap after reserve losses of between $15 billion and $30 billion, depending on growth rate assumptions and more if Brazil collapses. This gap will have to be covered, if at all, by governments and the multilateral agencies (see tables 11-1, 11-2, and 11-3).

---

1. See Institute for International Finance (1999a).

Table 11-1. *Sources and Uses of Funds in All Emerging Markets, 1995–99*
Billions of U.S. dollars

Use and source[a]	1995	1996	1997	1998 (estimated)	1999 (forecast)
Total uses of funds	−269.2	−331.9	−298.2	−201.4	−168.6
Current account deficit	−85.4	−95.7	−76.2	−40.3	−46.0
Resident lending abroad[b]	−89.5	−150.3	−179.4	−123.0	−100.0
Additions to reserves	−94.3	−85.9	−42.6	−38.1	−22.6
Total sources of funds	269.1	331.9	298.2	201.4	168.6
Private					
Direct investment	82.1	94.8	116.5	111.0	103.9
Equity portfolio	24.4	35.7	24.0	2.4	18.7
Commercial banks	99.4	121.0	24.8	−9.7	−8.2
Other private lenders	22.5	75.2	94.3	48.3	25.6
Official					
International agencies	20.5	7.0	27.2	36.7	14.2
Bilateral creditors	20.2	−2.2	11.4	12.8	14.4

Source: Institute for International Finance (1999a).

a. A positive use is a source; a negative source is a use.

b. Resident lending abroad includes reported net resident lending, monetary gold, and errors and omissions that proxy for capital flight.

Thus the wheel appears to have turned almost full circle. The efforts of the G-7 governments and the international agencies, beginning in the 1970s, to have private markets replace official sources of funding for emerging markets seem about to come to naught. The specter of a significant withdrawal of private investors from the emerging markets is with us for the first time in a decade.

The reasons for this withdrawal are quite clear. For several years now, emerging market portfolio investments have been underperforming, with low or even negative reward-to-risk ratios, depending on the sample period. The easy profits to be had from holding short-term local currency instruments in markets with high interest rates designed to protect pegged exchange rates have largely disappeared. Local stock markets and Brady or global bonds have proved volatile under the pressures of trade and capital account liberalization. And contagious crises have battered the portfolio returns of even the most sophisticated investors.

What comes next? This paper attempts to address the question as it pertains to the future of emerging market investment. The first section reviews

Table 11-2. *Sources and Uses of Funds in Five Asian Crisis Countries,*
1995–99

Billions of U.S. dollars

Use and source[a]	1995	1996	1997	1998 (estimated)	1999 (forecast)
Total uses of funds	−81.5	−100.6	−28.8	+0.5	+1.3
Current account deficit	−41.0	−54.6	−26.3	+58.5	+43.2
Resident lending abroad[b]	−26.5	−26.8	−35.0	−16.9	−14.9
Additions to reserves	−14.0	−19.3	+32.5	−41.1	−27.0
Total sources of funds	81.6	100.6	29.0	−0.5	−1.2
Private					
Direct investment	4.9	5.8	6.8	6.4	14.2
Equity portfolio	11.0	13.9	−3.2	2.1	4.5
Commercial banks	53.2	65.3	−25.6	−35.0	−18.8
Other private lenders	9.9	18.2	21.0	−1.7	−4.6
Official					
International agencies	−0.3	−2.0	22.1	21.6	−2.0
Bilateral creditors	2.9	−0.6	7.9	6.1	5.5

Source: Institute for International Finance (1999a).

a. A positive use is a source; a negative source is a use.

b. Resident lending abroad includes reported net resident lending, monetary gold, and errors and omissions that proxy for capital flight.

key data trends in emerging market investment. A key point is that debt market conditions are fundamental to any review of prospects for emerging market investing going forward. The second section looks at how regulators have understood and reacted to the crisis, the prospects for recovery, and emotional undercurrents of the debate about the crisis. It finds that most of the proposals now under consideration for addressing the crisis tend to reinforce the process of capital rationing now in progress. The third section reviews prospects for emerging market investment. It suggests that prospects are negative for long- and short-term debt, are moderate for equity, and are moderate to negative for foreign direct investment. The final section provides some conclusions and recommendations.

Key Data Trends and Their Future Implications

The data in tables 11-1, 11-2 and 11-3 suggest the presence of trends that, for reasons given in what follows, are likely to continue through 2001.

Table 11-3. *Sources and Uses of Funds in Latin America, 1995–99*
Billions of U.S. dollars

Use and source[a]	1995	1996	1997	1998 (estimated)	1999 (forecast)
Total uses of funds	−71.2	−92.6	−101.6	−100.3	−69.5
Current account deficit	−31.2	−34.0	−58.1	−83.1	−69.5
Resident lending abroad[b]	−16.9	−33.9	−29.2	−27.4	−9.9
Additions to reserves	−23.1	−24.7	−14.3	+10.2	+9.9
Total sources of funds	71.1	92.4	101.6	100.3	69.7
Private					
Direct investment	24.6	36.8	50.4	48.6	38.5
Equity portfolio	5.5	13.1	13.0	−3.2	5.1
Commercial banks	20.2	21.7	16.5	12.2	−3.4
Other private lenders	−5.2	32.4	26.4	30.0	13.9
Official					
International agencies	15.2	1.1	−1.5	7.6	11.0
Bilateral creditors	10.8	−12.7	−3.2	5.1	4.6

Source: Institute for International Finance (1999a).

a. A positive use is a source; a negative source is a use.

b. Resident lending abroad includes reported net resident lending, monetary gold, and errors and omissions that proxy for capital flight.

—First, emerging market current account deficits are likely to be much lower than they were in 1995–97: surpluses are appearing in Southeast Asia, and Latin America, led by Brazil, is going into recession. Emerging markets will have less need for external finance.

—Second, Asia's five crisis countries will add to reserves, but Latin America is likely to lose reserves unless these are replenished by official lending.

—Third, short-term borrowing and lending, evidenced by the withdrawal of the commercial banks, are likely to fall further, as will the short-maturity component of lending by other private creditors. Market conditions for long-term debt are unlikely to improve dramatically until emerging market policy mixes, financial systems, and their sovereign and corporate liability structures are all seen to be less vulnerable.

—Fourth, direct and portfolio equity investment, possibly fortified by bottom fishing in Asia, may recover but in Latin America not by enough fully to cover the current account deficit.

—Fifth, the exceptionally high official flows to support the crisis countries can be expected not to decline substantially and to rise if Brazil collapses.

—Sixth, resident lending abroad and capital flight, which have to be financed, are expected to remain at relatively high levels in all regions.

Of these trends, one can be most confident of those concerning debt. Tested theory makes two strong and related predictions, both of which seem borne out by recent events. First, lenders perceiving rising default risks raise required yields but end up rationing credit, as safe borrowers drop out of the loan pool at the higher rates and the remaining borrowers compensate for the high cost by adopting riskier projects with still higher default risks.[2] Second, anticipated borrower behavior increases the need for more frequent and intensive monitoring, which lenders accommodate by shortening the maturities of the credits they do extend.[3] In short, lending short term and rationing credit rather than raising interest rates still further are optimal for lenders in times of turmoil. If short-term transactions are in any way restricted, total lending will fall.

This is what we seem to be seeing in the data. Creditworthy borrowers greatly reduced their borrowing as rates peaked following August 1998. Some, including Argentina, Colombia, Mexico (Pemex), and Brazil (BNDES), maintained their access last autumn, but at minimal levels. Credit rationing is evident in the steep and ongoing decline of bank lending that is reflected also in tables 11-1, 11-2, and 11-3: it may lie, also, behind the greater reluctance of U.S. institutional investors to invest in emerging market debt. More generally, the theory makes clear that excessively short-term liability structures are as much a symptom as a cause of vulnerability to crisis and that high interest rates may be powerless to attract investor interest. Sovereigns like Mexico in 1994 and Brazil since 1997 and corporations throughout Southeast Asia undoubtedly borrowed on short-term or dollar-linked terms in large part because they had no alternative.[4] Unusually high interest rates are as likely to be signaling high default risks as good investment opportunities.

---

2. The possibility of backward-bending loan supply curves (as a function of yields) and the resulting capital rationing was established by Sachs (1984) and Folkerts-Landau (1985).

3. Lending short term is optimal for lenders facing asset-substitution problems, that is, borrowers likely to divert loan proceeds into risky uses so as to shift risks onto the lender, as pointed out in Jensen and Meckling (1976). It is also an implication of the repeated recontracting model of Bulow and Rogoff (1989a). If debt must be repeatedly renegotiated, its optimal maturity is very short.

4. Both the Mexican and Brazilian governments, however, tried to make a virtue of necessity. Both explained, at different times, that their refusal to borrow long term was a positive signal of their belief that local currency borrowing costs were only temporarily high and that interest rates would decline. Doubling up the risk was seen by officials as a way of encouraging market confidence. In retrospect, this reasoning seems quite wrong. High domestic interest rates combined with an increasingly short-term capital structure are more likely to be interpreted by the market as signs of risk and vulnerability than as reflections of a credible policy mix. See Kindleberger (1996, p. 8).

Historically, most of the funds supplied to emerging markets were in the form of debt. When countries are creditworthy and can borrow easily on good terms, other forms of capital flow including the repatriation of flight capital tend to be robust. Debt market conditions are therefore fundamental to any review of prospects for emerging market investing going forward. These depend, of course, on the policies that emerging markets undertake for themselves. In today's post-crises atmosphere, however, they also depend heavily on regulatory reactions in North America, Europe, and Japan.

Regulators' Views on and Responses to the Crisis

Regulators' understanding of the causes and regulatory implications of crises is evolving in response to ongoing, sometimes contradictory, economic analyses with conflicting policy implications. At the risk of oversimplifying, five, not mutually exclusive, explanations or perspectives seem to be influencing opinion.

First, crises can be viewed as a rapid, chaotic, and destructive version of an adjustment process that would have to happen in any case. To reduce excessive debt accumulation, countries have to engage in expenditure reduction (recession) and expenditure switching (by means of a devaluation that worsens the terms of trade and shifts resources to producing exports).[5] Crises do produce adjustment: witness the 1995–97 trade balance turnaround in Mexico and the trade surpluses now appearing in Southeast Asia. Because of market failures, however, the adjustment process perhaps overshoots in crises, producing too much poverty and delaying recovery. This possibility has led some perhaps confusingly to propose reversing traditional prescriptions: increasing rather than reducing fiscal deficits, for example, and lowering rather than raising interest rates. Such proposals may address the overshoot, but they leave the basic issue of the original debt overhang unresolved. The regulatory conundrum is how to allow the adjustment process, never pleasant for borrowers, perhaps to be more gradual but nonetheless to work as it should.

5. This is a thumbnail sketch of the much more complex theory set forth in H. G. Johnson (1956, 1958). However, it is not a misrepresentation. Note that the expenditure reduction and switching components of the adjustment both work to produce real wage erosion. Real currency depreciation makes citizens of the borrowing country worse off in real terms: it can be said to "cushion" the impact of debt reduction policies to the extent that it can facilitate a smooth transition to current account surpluses without massive unemployment by creating a market-based incentive for resources to flow to,

Second, financial safety nets in both borrowing and lending countries plus any real or implied bailout guarantees to investors by governments, lenders of last resort, or the International Monetary Fund (IMF) produce moral hazard.[6] The simple form of the moral hazard story follows directly from option theory. Guaranteed lenders have a perverse incentive to over-lend, and guaranteed borrowers to overborrow, as option values (that is, the values of the guarantees) rise with perceived risk. Traces of moral hazard can usually be found in the histories of almost all the severe financial crises that ever took place.[7]

The moral hazard account has become particularly influential partly because the United States/IMF support of Mexico in 1995 was seen to have bailed out private short-term investors and because, following the Russian episode, investors continued to believe that the G-7 would not let Russia fail and stayed in up to the day of the crash. Few regulators remain unaware of these propositions. True converts to the doctrine that financial system safety nets are the source of all the trouble take the view that they should all be dismantled. IMF rescue packages should stop; the IMF should be radically restructured; and deposit insurance schemes should be modified or removed. Progress toward these ideals, however, is likely to be slow. The financial safety nets installed by the advanced countries before and after World War II evolved democratically and continue to enjoy strong voter support. They are here to stay.

Four kinds of measures have been designed for dealing with moral hazard, short of eliminating safety nets. First is partial insurance exemplified by the Federal Deposit Insurance Corporation limit of $100,000 per account. Such limits are not fully credible when some banks are too big to fail. Second are the prudential regulations that attempt to restrict financial system exposures. These can most easily be applied to banks but seldom reach all big actors. Third is the possibility of private sector self-monitoring through requirements that banks hold tranches of each other's second-tier capital.[8] Schemes of this kind are still in their nascence in the United

---

and employment to rise in, the exporting sector. Currency depreciation cannot cause market failures in Johnson's account, which is why adjustment can be achieved without crisis.

6. Moral hazard, a term well known in the insurance industry, was brought into economics by Arrow (1963). Its role in crises is emphasized by influential conservative economists, including Calomiris (1993, 1998a) and McKinnon and Pill (1997), and is being acknowledged by regulators (see Fischer, 1999).

7. See Calomiris (1999).

8. Calomiris (1998b).

States and elsewhere. Fourth is the reduction of moral hazard incentives from penalizing those who make mistakes: managers are fired, and owners lose their equity. These approaches, to be sure, have not been completely successful at eliminating moral hazard incentives altogether, but they do appear to have reduced the frequency of financial crises at least in some of the advanced countries.

Rather than any wholesale dismantling of financial safety nets in response to the crises, emerging market investors should expect a tightening of the prudential regulations, in the industrial nations almost certainly and in the emerging markets more slowly. Short-term lending is likely to be a specific regulatory target for reasons elaborated below.

Third, another version of the moral hazard story stresses that government-directed and government-guaranteed lending over many years causes inefficiency, corruption, and debt-laden financial structures in firms and banks. Especially linked to Southeast Asia, this account applies also to much of Latin America until the early 1990s and perhaps even later. Holders of this view originally believed that borrowing countries should move rapidly toward U.S. standards of liberalization, transparency, and financial regulation.[9] Emerging market officials going forward are likely to continue to be pressured to improve the transparency and the supervision of their financial systems and to be cautioned as well that liberalization without these two might be dangerous.

A fourth body of opinion emphasizes that herding, contagion, and panic made recent crises unnecessarily deep.[10] These are the factors, along with bank failures and corporate bankruptcies, that cause the adjustment process to overshoot. From this perspective, crisis avoidance is imperative and requires the creation of an international lender of last resort, accompanied also by better bankruptcy protection for defaulting debtors, possibly including sovereigns, and by controls on capital inflows into and capital flight from vulnerable emerging market economies.

Finally, the fifth and by far the largest body of analysis focuses on the difficulty of maintaining credibly pegged exchange rates and on their vulnerability to exogenous shocks. This account weighs heavily the destabiliz-

9. This is a characterization of the so-called Washington consensus, vintage 1996 to June 1997. It has since been modified.

10. This is the story of bank runs that began with Diamond and Dybvig (1983). Chang and Velasco (1998) extend it to emerging market crises. Most emerging market financial crises have been associated with banking crises; see Kaminsky and Reinhart (1996) and Caprio and Klingebiel (1996, 1997).

ing impacts on East Asia of the devaluations of the renminbi in 1994 and
of the yen starting in 1995. The majority conclusion seems to be that
pegged rates should be abandoned in favor of floating rates except possibly
moving to a full currency board. Debate over this choice is heated, ongoing, and inconclusive.

Lessons Learned

Given the grain of truth in each of these points of departure, it is not surprising that no general consensus has emerged over what needs to be done.
Instead, what seems to be happening is more limited agreement on certain
aspects of the problem. Different this time around is the acknowledgment
that certain features of the financial safety nets in lending countries might
have helped to destabilize the borrowers. In the past, crises have always
been the borrowers' fault. My personal observation is that economists and
regulators seem to have extracted at least eleven main specific lessons. Some
of them are questions:

—Short-term lenders bring few benefits beyond trade and working capital financing. They do not provide technology, managerial expertise, or
reliable financing of current account deficits. In countries with high savings
rates, they encourage already excessive investment rates and make them
riskier. Their unreliability also forces countries to accumulate excessive
reserves.

—Short-term international lenders were not innocent bystanders.
Banks and short-term investors made huge bets on the "arbitrage"
(between local currency and offshore interest rates) in Mexico, Southeast
Asia, Russia, and Brazil. Some Japanese banks gambled their whole capital.
Then, sometimes belatedly, these investors rushed for the exit.

—Greater transparency need not eliminate the herding behavior of
short-term lenders. It seems clear in retrospect that they ignored early risk
warnings and signals or suppressed adverse information possibly because of
conflicts of interest. Strategists also tended to stay with currencies too long
because exiting too early would have cost them their jobs: so they stayed,
hoping to get out in time.

—Emerging market borrowers were not innocent bystanders either.
Their own financial safety nets and systems of government-sponsored and
guaranteed investing created massive inefficiencies and corruption in some
cases. These systems should be restructured and replaced with prudential

regulation to Bank for International Settlements (BIS) norms, enhanced credit analysis and risk management, and improved accounting practices and reporting.

—The countries that suffered most were the ones that liberalized their financial systems and capital flows but had simultaneously to raise interest rates to protect their currencies. This enhanced the arbitrage, attracted huge flows of hot money, and raised the risk of collapse.

—The combination of fixed exchange rates, free capital flows, and an imbalanced domestic policy mix that results in high interest rates is a recipe for disaster. One of the three must go.[11]

—Excessive sovereign foreign borrowing is not the only way for a country to get into debt-service difficulty. Private sector foreign borrowing can do it too, as no country can afford to let its financial system collapse. So can excessive domestic sovereign borrowing, due to rising fiscal deficits, as in Brazil. The huge costs of financial system bailouts are always paid by the taxpayer, sometimes letting borrowers and lenders off the hook.

—Financial system safety nets or the prospects of an IMF rescue do not create an equal degree of moral hazard for all types of emerging market lenders. The main beneficiaries are big banks deemed too big to fail and possibly also short-term investors financed by them. Equity investors are relatively unprotected. So also are most long-term, nonbank lenders, including bondholders, except to the extent that they need to be kept willing to buy new issues.[12] Unprotected by safety nets, foreign direct investors are expected to dollar average over the crisis-recovery cycle. Sovereign incentives are probably not greatly distorted simply because IMF conditionality is so burdensome.

—The IMF's resources are limited, and, therefore, the effects of an IMF support package on market confidence are uncertain. Often, it is a matter of too little, too late. In any event, IMF intervention cannot remove the

11. This is an implication of the theory of balance of payments crises; see Krugman (1979, 1996, 1999) and Obstfeld (1986). I do not deal here with the ongoing debate over optimal exchange rate regimes or the conditions for fixed exchange rates to survive; see Eichengreen (1996).

12. Sovereign bondholders have not been a focus of concern in recent crises. The United States/IMF assistance to Mexico in 1995 removed any fears of a sovereign default in that case. The Southeast Asians had no outstanding Brady bonds as they had not defaulted on their bank debt in the 1980s. The statement in the text refers to the flurry of IMF support for Bulgaria in 1996 when that country's risk of defaulting on its Brady bonds was perceived to have risen. At the time, the market interpreted the IMF's support for Bulgaria as reflecting an official belief that Brady bonds were too important to be allowed to go into default. It is unclear whether a similar opinion prevails today.

ultimate need for the over-indebted sector in an economy to reduce its level of debt and its prospective rate of borrowing. IMF assistance can at best smooth out the adjustment process and make it more gradual.

—Consequently, the IMF should try to avoid crisis management techniques that appear to aggravate a crisis. Should it require tight fiscal and monetary policies just as an economy is recessing that make the recession worse? What is the tradeoff between lowering interest rates to prevent private sector bankruptcies and the increased likelihood of capital flight? What is the prescription for restoring market confidence sooner rather than later?

—Coping with financial crises, or for that matter domestic bankruptcies, typically involves reducing the debt overhang. Domestically, creditors accept partial payment, sometimes in exchange for the acquisition of ownership, and managers are fired. Many emerging market economies need better bankruptcy codes. Can or should similar arrangements be made for defaulting sovereigns?

Against this background of lessons learned, I turn to the practical matter of reviewing the plans that are being made to deal with crises.

Proposals and Plans for Dealing with Crises

Given the absence of a political and financial global superstructure, it is hardly surprising that current plans for dealing with crises seem piecemeal. The results seem more like a scheme to fix some of the potholes than to repair the whole road. To create some order among diverse and what might appear to be unrelated proposals, they are organized below under three partly overlapping headings: prophylaxis, or crisis prevention; emergency procedures for dealing with ongoing crises; and recovery and post-crisis rehabilitation.

PROPHYLAXIS.

(a) *Emerging market borrowers.* Crisis prevention proposals for emerging market borrowers have macroeconomic and microeconomic aspects, addressed at reducing their domestic moral hazard incentives and vulnerability to external shocks. Among these proposals are the following:

—Maintain a credible mix of fiscal and monetary policy that is consistent with a country's exchange rate regime and its domestic and foreign debt service obligations. There is no point in adding to the mountain that has been written on this.

—Stabilize the local banking system by enforcing capital standards and risk control regulations that meet international norms, improving transparency, and passing regulations to reduce cronyism. World Bank teams have been working with client countries on this problem for some years, but progress on implementation may be slow.[13]

—Along with efforts to stabilize the local banking system, establish sovereign, corporate, and banking sector liability structures, the servicing burden of which is inversely correlated with economic conditions. For example, direct investment is safer than debt because dividends fall during recessions. Nonputable, fixed-rate, long-term debt is safer than short-term or variable-rate debt because its principal does not come due and its coupon does not rise along with interest rates during a crisis. Commodity producers should borrow under contracts that link coupons and principal to commodity prices. Local currency bond markets should be developed to facilitate fixed-rate, long-maturity, local currency debt: the costs of such borrowing are high when interest rates are high but fall compared to foreign currency–denominated debt in a crisis.[14] A guiding principle in this context should be the need to protect the sovereign's creditworthiness above all: history tells us that sovereign defaults are hard and take a long time to resolve. Of these latter proposals, few are anywhere near to being implemented except for the program of the International Finance Corporation (IFC) to encourage the establishment of local bond markets.

—Until the above changes are achieved, and especially in the absence of a credible domestic policy mix and a robust local banking system, consider the possibility of establishing controls on capital inflows and perhaps also outflows.

(b) *Emerging market lenders.* Lenders to emerging markets can also take macroeconomic and microeconomic prophylactic measures, including the following:

—Do not transmit major shocks. Arguably it was the 50 percent depreciation of the yen after it achieved its peak of 79 yen per U.S. dollar in April 1995 that destabilized Southeast Asia's pegs to the U.S. dollar. Calls

---

13. See Caprio and Honohan (1999).

14. The need for local currency bond markets is underscored by Michael Pettis, "Latin America Needs a Bond Market," *Wall Street Journal*, September 4, 1998, p. A11. The idea, however, is not an easy sell. Finance ministers are typically averse to the fiscal costs of long-term debt when interest rates are higher than they hope they eventually will be. The notion that long-term, fixed-rate, local currency debt operates as a hedge in times of crisis has little appeal when a crisis seems remote. See also footnote 4.

on Japan to put its economy in order continue to this day. Arguably, also, the U.S. current account deficit is not sustainable forever. When and if expectations of a turndown in the United States take hold, it is likely that a sharp drop in U.S. stocks will destabilize stock markets globally. Economic instability in the rich countries adversely affects the whole world. For emerging markets, exogenous shocks remain likely.

—Very carefully reduce the moral hazard effects of financial system safety nets in North America, Europe, and Japan on the behavior of lenders to emerging markets. Two specific proposals being considered partly address this concern. One is to change the BIS risk management standards that currently seem to discriminate in favor of short-term lending to emerging markets (long maturities are deemed riskier).[15] The second is for the major industrial nations to take the lead and require emerging market bond issues to contain collective action clauses under which rescheduling could be approved by a majority rather than, as now, a unanimous vote of bondholders. In addition, authorities are considering mandatory bail-in provisions, including haircuts and automatic extensions on defaulted loans. The two main proposals are quite likely to be implemented.

—Possibly also set up, if not exactly crisis insurance schemes, then at least lines of credit like Argentina's with interest rates fixed in advance of any crisis that can be called on when necessary. Although this might at first sight look like a primary candidate for private sector initiatives, actual prospects for success without official participation seem dim. Crises are hard to predict, and it is difficult for underwriters to vary commitment fees (read, insurance premiums) with the risk. When Mexico last year drew down its previously negotiated line of credit, it was widely noticed that market rates at that time exceeded committed rates by a wide margin that went uncompensated. Line-of-credit lenders might also fail to keep their commitment during an actual crisis. It is therefore unlikely that this proposal will progress significantly without what the IIF calls official sector mitigation of private sector risks, possibly along the lines of the Inter-American Development Bank's proposal effectively to guarantee contingent lines of credit offered by private sector firms.

15. The long-term efficacy of this regulatory change may be doubtful. Money is fungible, and the BIS's span of control does not reach to investment banks and other nonbank lenders that borrow from banks. If banks reduce short-term emerging market credit too much, that credit could in principle be replaced by others, although this might take time. Besides, the current rule as a technical matter correctly ranks the relative risk. It is not at all clear that the BIS should change it to accommodate G-7 policy preferences.

EMERGENCY PROCEDURES. Dissatisfaction with the IMF's reactions at the time to the Mexican and Southeast Asian crises has created much heated debate but little apparent convergence to a consensus. The five central questions are as follows:

—Should countries in crisis be required to target fiscal surpluses, as a condition of IMF support, when such a policy is likely only to make the crisis-related recession worse? Here the answers are perhaps no in Thailand or Indonesia if deficit reduction means reducing food subsidies and starving the poor, but probably yes in Brazil, where fiscal deficits are what is causing the crisis, even though the economy is recessing.

—Should the exchange rate be allowed to go to a float, or should there be a major effort to fix it even more rigidly?

—If the answer is the latter, can the necessary emergency lines of credit ever be large enough? In a crisis, money has to be found to cover balance of payments financing, lender of last resort outlays, the replacement of credit lost by firms, and the replenishment of their equity. These sums can be vast. The main example of a successful target zone defense, France in 1992, required the credible promise of unlimited Deutsche Bundesbank support. The IMF cannot offer unlimited credit, and the United States is politically constrained from doing so. In theory, only potentially infinite lines of credit will never be tapped. Should the IMF be reconstituted as a carefully circumscribed international lender of last resort?

—Should interest rates be raised to defend a currency under attack, precisely when firms need low rates and liberal credit to avoid going bankrupt? Britain raised short-term rates to 55 percent and Sweden raised them to 500 percent in 1992, both only briefly. Neither warded off devaluation. Brazil's ongoing experience confirms that high interest rates maintained too long themselves become noncredible, but that lowering rates might accelerate capital flight, as they appeared to do at one point in Indonesia and might do now in Brazil.

—Where market solutions are powerless in a panic, should standstill agreements on foreign-currency debt and emergency controls on capital flight be considered?

RECOVERY AND REHABILITATION. After the fall, how does one get the economy going again? At this stage, the real wage erosion and hardship that necessarily accompany an adjustment to a lower borrowing rate is occurring. Bank lending is at a standstill, with banks constrained by capital-depleting bad loans and a shortage of solvent borrowers. Foreign lenders and bondholders are nursing losses, making them reluctant to extend additional credit until their claims are addressed. And the firms and entrepreneurs that drove investment and growth before the crisis are, if not bankrupt, facing an equity constraint and are unable to raise capital.[16] Ultimately, the economy recovers if wage levels are flexible. Declining real wage levels lead to higher profitability with growing output and equity levels in firms and banks. However, as recent crises teach us, the recovery can take an extended period as equity levels are restored only slowly over time through rising retained earnings that are constrained by the need to resume service on past-due debt. The question arises: should formal programs be put in place to shorten the recovery period? There is a variety of somewhat inchoate proposals.

Most discussions have centered on restructuring banking systems to where they are once again capable of lending and making more flexible, equity-like investments to fund healthy firms. Strengthening banks by having the government take over their bad debt, as Mexico did, can be politically and fiscally problematic; however, there may be no other way out.

The key to recovery is to replenish otherwise healthy firms' equity levels as a basis for rejuvenating their operations. At the simplest level, this could mean rescuing the old entrepreneurs and managers (problematic if they are being held responsible for the crisis in the first place) or finding a new set, possibly foreign (problematic in the presence of xenophobia). Debt-for-equity swaps might seem able to solve the problem directly, but, on second thought, these would have to be made mandatory as there are few mechanisms in most emerging markets for forcing firms' owners to give up control even when they are bankrupt.

To avoid confronting these issues squarely, proposals typically aim at installing national bankruptcy codes that presumably would facilitate the transfer of assets from the bankrupt to the better funded, impose haircuts on creditors, and possibly also reverse current rules that prevent the transfer of assets to foreign creditors. Whose code should be used as a model is not a simple question to answer as European codes are typically harder on

16. The importance of equity constraints for explaining the magnification of emerging market crises is emphasized by Greenwald (1998), on the basis of a sequence of papers—for example, Greenwald and Stiglitz (1993)—written over the past fifteen years. The empirical evidence of the constraints' existence and how they work. now part of textbook corporate finance, began with Asquith and Mullins (1986).

defaulters than the U.S. code. There have even been proposals, attracted by the standstill, debt reduction, and collective action provisions in the U.S. procedure, for setting up a supranational bankruptcy court for defaulting sovereigns.[17] Progress on all these proposals will be slow as emerging market governments may seek to prevent national assets from being transferred to foreigners at fire-sale discounts.

When markets fail, official agencies may consider it their mandate to replace them. The World Bank (that is, the IFC) has engaged historically in emerging market development lending, in the process also accumulating equity positions in client firms. It has issued loan guarantees in two kinds of situations: project-based loans (where the aim was to have private funds replace its own but at below-market rates) and program-based loans (where it guaranteed select sovereign development loans). The proposal is now to extend World Bank guarantees to non-crisis sovereign borrowers that are willing to commit to certain policy and performance targets, but where market failures have denied them access to credit.[18] The plan raises two questions. Can World Bank sovereign analysts really differentiate credible commitments from those that are not? Perhaps. And does the guarantee add to moral hazard? The answer is that it depends on how unpleasant the World Bank can, or intends to, make it for private sector or sovereign borrowers that default on it.

Oddly enough, there is no plan to address the core problem, that is, the post-crisis shortage of equity capital. In principle, it could be just as easy to guarantee stock issues as bonds against the event of issuer default, and the task of selecting eligible clients would not be more difficult. Nonetheless, the mind boggles at the thought.

On an overall assessment, the inconsistencies among some of the proposals and the continuing disagreements especially over what policies to follow after a crisis reflect a deeper uncertainty. What should be done about creditors' outstanding claims following a default? Within the industrial countries, there is a clear conflict between the interests of exporters and governments that need lenders to lend more, so that the defaulting nations

17. Eichengreen and Portes (1995) make the case for sovereign bankruptcy-like procedures. Against private sector objections that bankruptcy rules for sovereigns would make default easier, cheaper, and more likely, they argue that domestic bankruptcy procedures also create moral hazard for private sector borrowers but that "nobody concludes from this that bankruptcy statutes should be revoked." Losses to lenders from moral hazard risk and formal debt reduction clauses should be balanced against their costs in a meltdown. Lenders, however, may prefer to take their chances.

18. See World Bank (1999, box 5.5).

can continue to import, and the interests of lenders whose incentive is to lend less until their claims are settled.[19]

It is quite unclear what the national interest is in this situation. Supporters of the sanctity of contracts, an important foundation of civil society, side with the lenders and bondholders. For those in both the borrowing and lending nations whose main goal is economic growth, in contrast, lenders' claims are an obstacle and an inconvenience: had they their choice, defaulted debt would be forgotten.[20] The obvious problem is that lending in that case would stop. This difficulty has existed for centuries: bankruptcy laws do not resolve it perfectly. Win-win solutions, where troubled borrowers can credibly commit to use additional loans only for growth that improves their ability to pay, remain elusive. Game theory suggests they are impossible.[21] Yet that is what has to happen. The search for solutions may continue, and in the meantime we must muddle through.

Emotional Undercurrents in the Ongoing Debate

A casual review of the two previous sections reveals that the preponderance of opinion and the majority of proposals involve tightening the regulatory environment to prevent excessive behavior. Emerging market investors have reason to expect that at least in the near future some of their opportunities and incentives will be curtailed.

Protections for long-term lenders are in the process of being diluted. The main target, however, is likely to be short-term emerging market lending, hopefully only over and above the trade balance component of current account financing. Suppressing hot money flows could turn into something of a crusade. Officials in the lending nations, especially in Europe, are by now fully sensitized to the potentially destabilizing impact of sudden

19. This is clear from the tension between the Paris Club and the private sector. From a bondholder's perspective, the Paris Club is a group of creditor governments that negotiates the restructuring of sovereign debt primarily to subsidize the creditors' export sectors.

20. Observers with compassion for borrowers' difficulties make the twofold point that, first, defaulted sovereign debt service often has to be resumed by the descendants of those who originally enjoyed the proceeds of the borrowing and. second, that the burden of repaying debt falls more heavily on ordinary taxpayers than on the rich whose capital flight contributed to the default. There is an obvious injustice on both counts, which accounts for the undertones of uneasiness sometimes evident in the ongoing debate.

21. As shown by Bulow and Rogoff (1989b). But see Yang (1999) for a ray of hope. Unfortunately, he has to concede that cooperative solutions do depend on the sovereign's ability to make a credible commitment, precisely the problem when there is an incentive to breach it.

reversals of yield-seeking, short-term capital flows. Further, they are acknowledging that their own financial safety nets may lie behind the possibility that their own investors took what were retrospectively excessive risks. There may be more to targeting short-term credit, however, than a simple desire to reduce the probability of having to bail out their own financial institutions: officials' consciences may be troubling them.

After all, the wave of emerging market capital account liberalizations in the last decade was undertaken, if not at the active instigation then at least with the tacit approval, of the industrial countries. Responsible officials of emerging economies that were following the liberalization path undoubtedly made forceful representations, in private, that they should have the right to defend their currencies with high interest rates, if need be, without having their treasuries massively raided. Official sensitivities might further have been pricked by statements from leading hedge fund managers that the kind of riskless arbitrage that was making them rich should not be allowed. Such declarations make it easier for regulators to pursue their objective under the well-worn slogan of doing battle with the speculators.

Another emotional undercurrent can be detected in the current climate. The main thrust of the opinions and proposals reviewed above is to reduce moral hazard. But "moral hazard" is a euphemism, a nice way of delivering a harsh judgment. The leaders of the world's largest financial institutions, otherwise men and women of great distinction, realize full well that they are being found responsible for excessive venality. The moral hazard–cum–adverse selection explanation of crises merely explains what happens when the embodied incentives are pursued too hard. Financial sector leaders consequently find themselves implicitly accused, at best of being foolish for getting caught by crises and at worst of betraying the spirit of the safety net and letting greed overwhelm their better judgment. This explains why recent private sector analyses of the crises seem somewhat defensive.

For example, private sector reviews of the moral hazard issue tend to make three basic points.[22] Grudgingly, they concede that an issue may exist but that, if it does, it is limited mainly to banks, to the extent that they continue to be guaranteed against failure, and to other investors only in the Mexican and Russian episodes. Otherwise, distortions in the behavior of other lender classes due to moral hazard are claimed to have been small as such lenders were not explicitly protected by safety nets and lost up to

22. Institute for International Finance (1999b).

$350 billion mostly on equity investments. Third, moral hazard in the future should be much less of a problem as investors will remember the losses they sustained in recent crises. One wonders whether this last point can be true. Investors have an incentive to try to recoup their losses and to use any moral hazard benefits they can get. In December one strategist recommended that clients buy Brazilian Brady bonds on the grounds that a successful IMF rescue would limit their downside risks. Is moral hazard really dead? Enough said.

Nonetheless, the private sector would be absolutely right to fear that excessive regulatory zeal could throw the baby out with the bathwater by either discouraging desirable kinds of investment or increasing inducements to panic. A notable feature of the crisis resolution proposals above is that they appear to include more provisions to penalize investors than to protect them. For instance, none deals with improving the availability of, and access to, sovereign collateral. On the one hand, this would appear crucial to the resumption of sufficient private sector long-term emerging market lending to replace the expected decline of short-term credit. On the other hand, several proposals appear to go too far in the wrong direction and have attracted, or are likely to attract, private sector opposition.

From the investors' perspective, any rule changes that reduce borrowers' expected costs of default and increase its probability or that increase investors' exposure to losses in the event of default have a negative effect on their willingness to invest. In this respect, several of the proposals seem flawed.

—Mandating compulsory haircuts or binding creditors into loan extensions during crises have obvious negative incentive effects; by increasing the penalties of getting caught, they also make mass rushes for the exit more likely. The recent G-7 initiative, which would result in recently issued sovereign Eurobonds being wrapped into future Paris Club debt restructuring agreements and put bondholders in the way of compulsory debt reduction, is an example of official failure to take these incentives adequately into account.[23]

—Requiring majority-vote bond-rescheduling clauses would make it easier and less costly for borrowers to suspend debt service, making lenders more reluctant even if they were instituted marketwide. Lenders would require

23. The issue here is comparability, the subject of recent G-7 communiqués regarding Russia's creditors and of recent Paris Club announcements about its negotiations with Pakistan. Paris Club traditions accord senior status to sovereign creditors. Comparability means that no other creditor can get a better outcome. Consequently, if Paris Club negotiations result in debt reduction for a borrower, all its other creditors must reduce their claims by at least the same fraction.

higher yields unless they came to regard such clauses as reflecting prudent liability management rather than as signaling a higher probability of default.

—An international bankruptcy court that made explicit provision for reducing principal and interest payments and reduced the freedom of individual lenders to act in their own self-interest would have the same effect. When sovereigns are involved, the ownership transfer features of domestic codes, including the firing of managers, are impossible to effect. A better solution might be to make access for borrowers to world financial markets conditional on having adequate domestic bankruptcy codes already in place. Foreign borrowing by sovereigns themselves should be reduced as much as possible.

—IMF "lending into arrears," which permits the IMF to continue lending to countries in default that are negotiating in good faith with private sector creditors, could have negative incentive effects unless the creditors took the view that such lending was desirable.

There is also the possibility of a private sector over-reaction, in response to the campaign against moral hazard and short-term lending, in the form of unwarranted cutbacks in emerging market trade financing. The *Financial Times* reported on December 10, 1998, that UBS, Europe's biggest bank, had cut its international loan book by half since the start of the year and that it was planning to withdraw altogether from global trade finance. The reason given for this move was that lending margins are too low to justify the risk, but when what is done is what the regulators seem to want done, can they have had no influence?

As this paper is being written, the market is awash with reports of bank after bank cutting back Brazil's lines of import-export finance. Again, this may be a rational response to perceptions of increased risk, but Brazil has never defaulted on its trade credit, and it has the reserves to enable it not to do so for the next nine to twelve months. Consequently, the possibility looms large that this too is an over-reaction to regulators' perceived desires. It appears that the BIS and national bank regulators will have to make exceptions for desirable forms of short-term lending if their campaign is not to inflict irreparable damage on world trade.

Prospects for Emerging Market Investors Revisited

Have we reached a post-crisis bottom? Should investors plunge to take advantage of a rapid post-crisis recovery? If so, what form should the investments take?

Table 11-4. *GDP Growth in Developing Countries, 1998–2001*

Percentage change

Region	1998 (estimated)	Forecast 1999	2000	2001
Developing countries	1.9	1.5	3.6	4.6
Sub-Saharan Africa	2.1	2.6	3.9	3.9
East Asia and Pacific	1.8	4.2	5.4	6.3
South Asia	4.8	3.7	4.3	5.2
Europe and Central Asia	−0.3	−1.4	2.5	3.6
Middle East and North Africa	1.5	0.6	2.5	3.3
Latin America and the Caribbean	2.1	−0.4	2.2	3.9
Memo item				
East Asia Crisis-5 (EA5)[a]	−7.7	0.1	3.1	4.4

Source: World Bank (1999).

a. Indonesia, Korea, Malaysia, the Philippines and Thailand.

The World Bank's forecasts of emerging markets' GDP growth rates for the next three years appear in table 11-4. According to these, the trough will form sometime in 1999. The GDP growth forecasts for 2000 and, especially, 2001 reflect optimism. The sharpest improvements are expected in South Asia and East Asia, with Latin America lagging but recovering nonetheless. The World Bank conditions these predictions on there being no deterioration along four dimensions of risk: no further destabilization from Japan in the form of either major recession or yen weakness; no collapse in Brazil and therefore no collapse of capital market financing to Latin America; no large stock or bond market corrections in the United States or Europe; and no further deterioration of the prices of commodities or of emerging market manufactured exports that could lead to anti-dumping challenges.

An informal survey of asset managers in January 1999 revealed an awareness of the possibilities for recovery but also caution rooted in an appreciation of the reality of the risks. None of the managers was expecting a return to the halcyon days of the early 1990s, and all were predicting a continuing contraction of excess capacity (read, employment opportunities) on Wall Street. None, for example, reported having clients avid to load up on Latin American stocks and bonds. Client interest, they said, was selective and measured. Emerging market debt, as an asset class, was out of favor and likely to remain so until the emerging markets "fixed up their economies." Asset managers reported, however, that institutional plan sponsors appeared willing to hold their positions in emerging market equity on a value-weighted basis. To the extent that these sentiments condition behavior, emerging market equity portfolio investment will be the first to recover.

The bulk of the analysis in this paper, which has focused on regulatory responses to crises, tends to support this view. Let me review the implications category by category.

Short-Term Debt: Prospects Negative

Short-term emerging market lending, particularly by banks, is the target of several BIS proposals and G-7 communiqués. The IIF is predicting an overall pullback in bank lending to emerging markets of $8.2 billion this year, but this may prove optimistic as no bottom is in sight. It is hard to see how the overall number can be so low when it is viewed in combination with the IIF's regional forecasts of bank credit retractions of $18.8 billion from Asia and the Pacific Islands and $3.4 billion from Latin America and the absence of any mention of regions scheduled to increase their bank borrowing.

Emerging nations' policymakers have also learned the dangers of attracting hot money and are likely to restrict its access as they impose prudential regulations on their financial systems. For short-term investors, increased uncertainty in the regulatory environment is compounded by the rise in currency risks following the shift to floating exchange rates in Mexico, Thailand, Indonesia, Korea, and now Brazil. Currency risks will rise further if more countries decide either to float or to install capital controls. The heyday of easy short-term arbitrage profits is over, never to return. The low-hanging fruit on most trees was picked some time ago, and what remains will require much more of a stretch. If the ongoing withdrawal of bank lending proves undiscriminating, emerging markets may have to seek trade and working capital credit from the market, in either local or foreign currency. No such trend is yet in place.[24]

---

24. Much as one might expect it, there is little evidence of a growing market for short-term, Euromarket, emerging market sovereign and corporate commercial-paper programs. Investment bankers report a few such issues by Mexican corporations, but no general issuer interest. Risk considerations

The rapid, ongoing contraction of international bank lending and, in particular, of emerging market trade financing is the single most important aspect of the current outlook. To all intents and purposes, it appears as if the G-7 banks, under pressure from regulators and perhaps also their stockholders to report less exposure to emerging markets, have redlined the entire emerging market bad neighborhood: mostly in Asia, but with Latin America not far behind. Much as this shift might seem benign from the perspective of systemic safety in the G-7, it is creating funding gaps, especially in Latin America, as the withdrawal of bank funding itself has to be financed.

How long will this last? At this point, the assessment becomes personal: probably longer than it should, even though sentiment toward the emerging markets can change quite rapidly. The reason is rooted in the organizational responses of large banks to real or perceived regulatory pressure: they seem more likely to abandon lines of business in their entirety than to undertake the large expense of stepping up their credit reviews, account by account. If correct, this reasoning suggests that at least some major banks will be ill-prepared for a rapid turnaround when it is next indicated.

The projected hiatus in the supply of short-term credit may be shortened, however, if emerging market governments construe it as a force impelling them toward meaningful reforms of their own financial systems. Of course, financial system reform is not the only factor at work. Brazil's system, for example, is stable and flexible enough to absorb all but the most major shocks, but the country nonetheless is being denied trade credit.

What it is that will bring about the restoration of short-term lending to emerging markets is not altogether clear. The general answer is lower default risk and improved commercial prospects in the borrowing economies combined with more focused regulatory reform, which encourages desirable forms of emerging market credit, in the industrial nations. And if the past is a guide, sentiment can change quickly once expectations shift.

Long-Term Debt: Prospects Negative

In what appears to be an attack of excessive regulatory zeal, protections for long-tenor lenders will effectively be reduced under several current

---

may explain the market's reluctance to replace the banks, and sovereigns in particular probably prefer to do their short-term issues in their local currency markets.

proposals, a counterproductive policy reaction in a period of credit rationing when optimal lending maturities are contracting. This, on balance, is likely both to raise borrowing costs and to make new issues harder to sell. Declining U.S. investor interest in emerging market debt is likely also to reduce liquidity and raise risk premiums in secondary market trading of Brady and global bonds. The thinner these markets, the less likely are spreads (over Treasuries and bid-ask) to fall. Relative value trading strategies are likely to continue to be riskier than they were prior to Russia's crisis. Already difficult market conditions cannot be helped if the United States raises interest rates. These factors lend support to the IIF's gloomy view that net private, nonbank lending to emerging markets will fall from $48 billion in 1998 to $26 billion in 1999.

This said, the foregoing should not be construed as a prediction that the market for emerging market bonds is in immediate danger of completely closing down as it did between the 1930s and the 1970s. The Russian moratorium caused spreads to rise globally but not equally for all borrowers. Argentina, Brazil, Colombia, and Mexico reopened previous bond issues or used a resettable floating-rate structure to raise money in the fourth quarter of 1998. Argentina and Mexico followed up with another $1 billion apiece of new bonds with warrants in February 1999. Malaysia sold $600 million of asset-backed bonds guaranteed by Japan's Ministry of International Trade and Industry in December. China and the Philippines issued $1 billion apiece in December and January.

Conditions are selectively improving for some Asian and Latin American sovereign borrowers, although they remain between 200 and 300 basis points worse than a year ago. Global bond market meltdown is therefore not yet an imminent prospect, but it could happen. Concerns focus mainly on Brazil's lack of market access. Brazil has about $52 billion of external fund requirements in 1999, including a current account deficit of $24 billion and amortizations of $28 billion. With $34 billion in estimated external financing from all sources, it is left with $18 billion of new financing requirements for which there appears to be no obvious current source other than reserves.[25] If Brazil's difficulties cascade, it may have to seek World Bank or other official guarantees: one hopes it will qualify for the new guarantee program.

25. This figure is probably an underestimate as the calculation makes no allowance for resident lending abroad or capital flight. Also omitted from consideration is Brazil's $300 billion of local currency government debt most of which is short term and matures within a year. A frequently debated

Portfolio Equity Investment: Prospects Moderate

The IIF projects $18.7 billion in net portfolios equity flows to all emerging markets in 1999. Although this amount is only 11 percent of emerging markets' total funds needs of $168.6 billion and is only one-half of the flows in 1996, it is almost eight times 1998's net flows of $2.4 billion. This recovery is likely to be led by Asia, where several stock markets, including South Korea (110 percent), Thailand (52 percent), the Philippines (74 percent), and Indonesia (94 percent), already registered strong fourth quarter gains in 1998 in U.S. dollar terms. However, Hong Kong (–6 percent) and China (–48 percent) were down for the year at year-end 1998.

At the moment, there is excitement throughout the region, with Indonesia lagging and the jury out on Malaysia until it relaxes more of its capital controls. Latin American markets, in contrast, remain down after 30 to 35 percent losses in 1998. Brazil's and Argentina's recessions are raising volatility, while Mexico continues to trade off the Dow. The IIF's forecast of $5.1 billion of net equity flows to Latin America this year may yet prove hard to meet.

Asset managers interviewed in late January confirmed that their clients were displaying more comfort with emerging market equity than with emerging market debt. Some noted that they observed a psychological shift to the view that emerging market equity is safer than debt. Clients had explained at meetings that equities represent net worth—tangible assets with residual value—while debt depends on sovereigns' nebulous credibility and is more prone to contagion. Firms pursue profit maximization, while sovereigns merely want to protect their ability to borrow again. Whatever the merits of such reasoning, the degree of comfort with the asset class bodes well for its future and is supportive of official forecasts.

---

question is what would happen if a collapse in public confidence regarding fiscal discipline made it impossible to refinance the domestic debt. There are two options. The nonmarket alternative would be a compulsory restructuring of the debt, as was attempted under the failed Collor plan of 1989. By making their assets less liquid, this would destabilize Brazil's banks, which own about 40 percent of the total, unless their liabilities were also restructured. Depositors might then run on the banks anyway for fear of having their bank accounts frozen. The more market-friendly alternative would be to monetize the debt by paying off maturing issues with noninterest-bearing cash. The resulting inflation tax would help to restore the government's fiscal position. Brazil has been down both these roads before, and neither is a positive prospect. There is little doubt, however, that Brazil's current market-oriented financial leaders would opt for inflation were they forced ineluctably to choose.

Foreign Direct Investment: Prospects Moderate to Down

Foreign direct investment (FDI) is an area of study unto itself and the subject of a large literature. It is hard to predict both because data appear with long lags and because the corporate expectations and forecasts that determine it are unobservable. Generally and roughly speaking, FDI is responsive to projected output: host-country GDP growth attracts FDI for supplying the local market, and donor-country growth generates FDI as multinationals diversify their sources.

On balance, FDI flows seem positively correlated with trade growth. Real devaluation overshoots, especially if accompanied by equity or liquidity constraints, bankruptcies, and other market failures that reduce host-country asset prices and make foreigners relatively wealthier and more liquid, tend to attract the kind of FDI called bottom fishing. Overall, FDI is usually thought to be much less volatile than financial market flows, although this impression is based on data that exclude hedging transactions, including accelerating subsidiaries' dividends and reducing their intracorporate debt, that multinationals undertake when risks rise.

Based on considerations such as these but presumably without a formal model, the IIF is forecasting emerging market FDI for 1999 at $104 billion, down from $111 billion last year but up from $95 billion in 1996. The percentage year-to-year variation in FDI flows is obviously much smaller than that of the other sources of emerging market funding. Because of this stability, FDI has become relatively the most important source of emerging markets' funds, rising from 29 percent of the total in 1996 to an expected 62 percent this year.

The global numbers conceal greater variability at the regional level. As contributors of FDI, North America and Europe are likely to rise relative to Japan, which is expected to continue cutting back on investments at home and abroad under the weight of its recession. Among the recipients, Southeast Asian economies, principally Korea as a result of the liberalization of its foreign investment restrictions, are likely to be the beneficiaries, if that is what they should be called, of increased bottom fishing FDI. FDI into China is likely to taper off going forward until the Chinese restabilize their financial system. Latin American prospects are also relatively dim because FDI will be depressed by the recessions in the major countries and offset only by privatizations. East European countries scheduled for accession to the European Union may receive rising FDI as they become more fully integrated. The uncertainties in Russia and Central Asia make any FDI forecasts for these regions impractical.

Conclusion

These are interesting times, although perhaps not yet times of exceptional opportunities for emerging market investors. The key to the intermediate-term outlook is how the world will resolve the question of short-term emerging market debt. The private sector is for the moment powerless to oppose official initiatives to reduce short-term emerging market lending and is likely to support them to the extent that they are compatible with the private sector's own incentives to ration credit.

However, given that short-maturity financial contracts are optimal when the risk of default is perceived to be high, a key question is whether the combination of credit rationing reinforced by regulation will constrain emerging market funding to the point where recoveries are delayed or aborted. The outcome is impossible to predict with any accuracy. The chances that a completely uncoordinated mixture of market and official reactions to crisis could precisely remove only the "excessive" component of short-term capital flows seems small, however excessive is defined.

In the end, the origin of all financial crises is excessive leverage, whether brought about by safety nets and other official inducements, insufficiently cautious credit analysis, or the materialization of an unlikely shock that leads to default. At the time of this writing, emerging market leverage, already reduced by the market's reactions to Southeast Asia, continues to decline under the pressure of Brazil's problems and possibly also those of Russia, its satellites, and China. It is hard to assess how long this process will go on: a stabilization of Brazil's outlook would help to end it. Given no major shocks from the industrial nations, the reduction of emerging market leverage should, perhaps sooner than later, help these markets to regain access to the debt market. This, when it happens, will lift all boats.

References

Arrow, Kenneth. 1963. *Social Choice and Individual Values.* Wiley and Sons.

Asquith, Paul, and David W. Mullins. 1986. "Equity Issues and Offering Dilution." *Journal of Financial Economics* 15 (January-February): 61–89.

Bulow, Jeremy, and Kenneth Rogoff. 1989a. "A Constant Recontracting Model of Sovereign Debt." *Journal of Political Economy* 97 (February): 155–78.

———. 1989b. "Sovereign Debt: Is to Forgive to Forget?" *American Economic Review* 79 (March): 43–50.

Calomiris, Charles W. 1993. "The Decline of Private Deposit Insurance in the United States: A Comment." *Carnegie-Rochester Conference Series on Public Policy* 38 (June): 129–42.

———. 1998a. "Blueprints for a New Global Financial Architecture." Testimony before the Joint Economic Committee of the U.S. Congress (October 7).

———. 1998b. "The IMF's Imprudent Role as Lender of Last Resort." *Cato Journal* 17 (Winter): 275–94.

———. 1999. "Victorian Perspectives on the Financial Fragility of the 1980s and 1990s." Columbia University Business School (in preparation).

Caprio, Gerard, and Patrick Honohan. 1999. "Beyond Capital Ideals: Restoring Banking Stability." Washington, D.C.: World Bank, Policy Research Department (in preparation).

Caprio, Gerard, and Daniela Klingebiel. 1996. "Bank Insolvencies: Cross-Country Experience." Policy Research Working Paper 1620. Washington, D.C.: World Bank, Policy Research Department (July).

———. 1997. "Bank Insolvency: Bad Luck, Bad Policy, or Bad Banking." In *Annual World Bank Conference on Development Economics 1996*, edited by Michael Bruno and Boris Pleskovic. Washington, D.C.: World Bank.

Chang, Roberto, and Andrés Velasco. 1998. "Financial Crises in Emerging Markets: A Canonical Model." NBER Working Paper 6606. Cambridge, Mass.: National Bureau of Economic Research (June).

Diamond, Douglas, and Philip Dybvig. 1983. "Bank Runs, Deposit Insurance, and Liquidity." *Journal of Political Economy* 91 (June): 401–19.

Eichengreen, Barry. 1996. "A More Perfect Union? The Logic of Economic Integration." Essays in International Finance 198. Princeton University (June).

Eichengreen, Barry, and Richard Portes. 1995. "Crisis? What Crisis? Orderly Workouts for Sovereign Debtors." London: Centre for Economic Policy Research.

Fischer, Stanley. 1999. "On the Need for an International Lender of Last Resort." Speech delivered to the joint luncheon of the AEA and the AFA, New York (January 3).

Folkerts-Landau, David. 1985. "The Changing Role of International Bank Lending in Development Finance." *IMF Staff Papers* 32 (June): 317–63.

Greenwald, Bruce. 1998. "International Adjustments in the Face of Imperfect Financial Markets." World Bank Annual Conference on Development Economics, Washington, D.C. (April 20–21).

Greenwald, Bruce, and Joseph E. Stiglitz. 1993. "Financial Market Imperfections and Business Cycles." *Quarterly Journal of Economics* 108 (February): 77–114.

Institute for International Finance. 1999a. "Capital Flows to Emerging Market Economies." Washington, D.C. (January 27).

———. 1999b. "Report of the Working Group on Financial Crises in Emerging Markets." Washington, D.C. (January).

Jensen, Michael C., and William H. Meckling. 1976. "Theory of the Firm: Managerial Behavior, Agency Costs, and Ownership Structure." *Journal of Financial Economics* 3 (October): 305–60.

Johnson, Harry G. 1956. "The Transfer Problem and Exchange Stability." *Journal of Political Economy* 64 (June): 212–25.

——. 1958. *International Trade and Economic Growth: Studies in Pure Theory.* London: George Allen and Unwin.

Kaminsky, Graciela, and Carmen M. Reinhart. 1996. "The Twin Crises: The Causes of Banking and Balance of Payments Problems." International Finance Discussion Papers 544. Board of Governors of the Federal Reserve System (March).

Kindleberger, Charles P. 1996. *Manias, Panics, and Crashes,* 3d ed. John Wiley and Sons.

Krugman, Paul. 1979. "A Model of Balance of Payments Crises." *Journal of Money, Credit, and Banking* 11 (August): 311–25.

——. 1996. "Are Currency Crises Self-Fulfilling?" In *NBER Macroeconomics Annual 1996,* edited by Ben S. Bernanke and Julio Rotemberg, 345–78. MIT Press.

——. 1999. "Balance Sheets, the Transfer Problem, and Financial Crises." Massachusetts Institute of Technology (http://web.mit.edu/krugman www/FLOOD.pdf [July 1, 1999]).

McKinnon, Ronald, and Huw Pill. 1997. "Credible Economic Liberalizations and Overborrowing." *American Economic Review* 87 (May): 189–93.

Obstfeld, Maurice. 1986. "Rational and Self-Fulfiling Balance of Payments Crises." *American Economic Review* 76 (March): 72–81.

Sachs, Jeffrey. 1984. "Theoretical Issues in International Borrowing." Princeton Studies in International Finance 54. Princeton University (July).

World Bank. 1999. *Global Development Finance 1999.* Washington, D.C. (in preparation).

Yang, Der-Yuan. 1999. "A Cooperative Perspective on Sovereign Debt: Past and Present." *Contemporary Economic Policy* 17 (January): 44–53.

12

Roundtable: Prospects for the Future

T HE ROUNDTABLE SESSION addressed prospects for the future in three
main areas and how new directions in those areas might influence the
ability to prevent, reduce, or better manage financial sector crises at the
global and national levels. The three areas assessed were (1) globalization
and integration of financial markets, (2) the process of developing financial
markets, and (3) private sector initiatives to promote financial market
development. Each of the three panelists was asked to comment on one of
the three areas.

William Cline, chief economist and deputy managing director of the
Institute for International Finance (IIF), commented on prospects for
globalization and integration of financial markets, addressing issues such as
whether financial markets will likely become more globalized and integrated and in what ways, whether financial architecture is changing and
how those changes might influence global financial markets, and how
changes in globalization and financial architecture will affect international
capital flows.

David Folkerts-Landau, managing director and global head of emerging
markets research at Deutsche Morgan Grenfell, commented on whether
changes might be made in the speed and process of financial sector development to help prevent and better manage crises. As is well understood

today, the process of financial market development is extremely comprehensive. Extensive and time-consuming technical infrastructure must be built (laws and regulations, trading and clearing systems, information systems) along with human resource capabilities—not just skills, but new attitudes, incentives, and behavior for regulators and market participants. Problems can occur during the transition or development process because the growth of market activity frequently outstrips development of important market infrastructure, skills, and attitudes.

Specific questions addressed were whether the liberalization process should be slowed to assure a better balance between market growth and development, whether regulatory models should be changed during the transition process to better reflect conditions in emerging markets (for example, whether emerging markets should regulate corporations and non-bank financial institutions to avoid the types of problems seen in Indonesia and Thailand and to compensate for the weak market discipline and corporate governance typically seen in emerging markets), and whether capital controls should be used to help prevent, reduce, or manage crises. Are controls needed if investors do not police themselves?

Finally, Manuel Medina-Mora, director general of the Grupo Financiero Banamex-ACCIVAL in Mexico, addressed initiatives that might be taken by the local private sector (issuers, investors, intermediaries) to help prevent and manage crises. (Earlier conference sessions had focused on market issuers, foreign investors, and regulators.) Mr. Medina-Mora commented on four areas:

—New instruments that might be introduced (such as bonds, derivatives, guarantees, special credit facilities) to help emerging market countries reduce or manage crises;

—The extent to which new institutional investors such as pension funds and insurance companies will help to improve financial market stability, by providing long-term, stable, local currency funding. These institutions are widely talked about as panaceas in these markets (providing more stable, sizable, and managed funds), but how long will it take before they are able to play an important role in financing and stabilization?

—Incentives that the private sector might take to help ensure that it has a vested interest in maintaining the quality as well as quantity and profitability of transactions;

—Initiatives that might be taken, and by whom, to encourage stronger relations between the private and public sectors? How and where can such relations be most helpful in preventing and better managing crises? Will improved relationships help to assure that the regulator and regulated understand one another and the market?

Globalization and Integration of Financial Markets
WILLIAM CLINE

I would like to make a few general remarks about globalization, about financial architecture and avoiding and resolving financial crises, and about medium-term prospects for capital flows to emerging markets. These are my personal views; they do not represent those of the Institute for International Finance, which just completed a study on the architectural issues.

On globalization, I think we can expect the long-term trend to continue and that events in 1997 and 1998 will be seen as a correction. The previous pace of flows was too rapid, in particular the pace of lending to East Asia. Net private capital flows to emerging markets rose from about $170 billion in 1994 to $325 billion in 1996. In 1998 they dropped back to $150 billion, consisting mainly of direct investment and portfolio equity. Net lending by banks was actually negative $10 billion in 1998 and will probably be the same in 1999. Bonds and other private sources of credit, about $100 billion in 1997, will likely be less than $25 billion in 1999. However, we may be nearing the turning point. Brazil could turn out to be the turning point.

In the longer term, avoiding integration with emerging market economies will be difficult. Industrial countries are going to enter a phase of acute aging and will need to finance their retired populations with returns on savings, creating a mutually beneficial relationship between the two regions and the exchange of capital. Finance and communication technology do not need to increase much to force emerging market finance to continue opening to globalization. That process seems to be moving hand-in-hand with the growing presence of international banks and financial institutions in these economies. In some sense, we are seeing today in global finance what we saw over the past two decades in trade integration, as a result of a rapid drop in transport costs and trade barriers.

It is also true that emerging market residents will need to invest in industrial countries. In 1996, when capital flows peaked, less than $100 billion of the $300 billion flowing into industrial countries covered current account deficits, more than $100 billion financed investment outflows by residents, and the rest built up reserves. There is a logic in the global portfolio diversification implicit in these flows. People in industrial countries need to develop the high-risk, high-return end of their portfolios. It is logical for them to seek emerging market assets and for emerging market residents who have plenty of risk at home to build up the low-risk, low-return end of their portfolios by investing in industrial countries.

We have seen a recent flirtation with capital controls, including from people such as Paul Krugman and Joseph Stiglitz, who lend a certain aura of respectability to this theme. Nonetheless, it is unlikely that we will see a massive shift toward capital controls. Even Malaysia seems to be back-pedaling fairly quickly from that position. And to a large extent, one could see capital restrictions not as a rigid control but as market-friendly disincentives to excessive short-term capital inflows, as used for example in Chile.

The caveat to this broad view of continued integration and globalization is that we could stumble into a global depression. There are some possibilities of that occurring, including a bubble in the United States, the seeming impossibility of eliminating stagnation in Japan, and the possible bias of Europe toward deflation, but I do not think a global depression is the base case.

Let me turn to issues of architecture, because the sustainability of globalization will depend on how well international financial systems can deal with avoiding and resolving financial crises. On avoiding crises, some progress has been made on transparency. The special data dissemination standards of the International Monetary Fund (IMF) represent an important advance. There is a push toward global best practices on accounting and regulation. The IIF study underscored the importance of developing an ongoing dialogue between private sector participants and authorities of emerging market economies, much along the lines of the Mexican teleconferences on a quarterly basis. Such dialogue could provide a vehicle for transparency and for feedback from the market to make it apparent to authorities when they are starting to lose their market credibility.

Contingent finance, or contingent credit lines, such as the Argentine and Mexican arrangements, also seem to hold some promise. These kinds of credit lines, which amounted to about $6 billion for Argentina, are likely to be more expensive than in the past because of the experience late last year with the Mexican drawdown of its credit line. But even so, these instruments can be a highly efficient form of crisis insurance. In addition, there is a process of sharpening risk-management techniques. There is growing recognition that the value-at-risk models need to be supplemented by a closer linkage of credit and market risk and a much more robust array of scenario analyses and stress tests.

On crisis resolution, it seems that we have been developing an ad hoc architecture through dealing with practical problems and gaining experience as a result. We have had six episodes of large crises and large financial support. There will likely be four wins and two losses. The four wins are Mexico in 1995, Korea and Thailand in 1997, and Brazil in 1998. The two losses are Russia in 1998 and Indonesia in 1997. Those two losses are driven by political collapse. The purpose of these programs is to restore market access promptly by restoring confidence. The overall objective is to avoid the long-term seizing up of the capital market through mandated reschedulings and debt reductions of the kind seen in the past. If we look at private capital flows to Mexico around 1995, we see a nice inverted head-and-shoulders curve with high flows, then negative flows, and then fairly high flows again fairly quickly. We probably will see that in Korea as well, although equity will be leading the return to higher flows rather than debt, because of the deleveraging process that is occurring in Korea.

Is this really desirable architecture? Is not this process susceptible to moral hazard in particular? Private investors have lost about $350 billion, potentially, from East Asia and Russia—perhaps $60 billion of losses, or potential losses, by the banks, $50 billion by other private creditors, and $240 billion in equity—so the lesson learned by the market is not that there is risk-free lending due to moral hazard created by public sector intervention. On the contrary, at the present time, if there is a distortion in this market, it is toward underlending and exorbitant spreads rather than overlending and razor-thin spreads. Similarly one can argue that the decline in spreads from 1995 to 1997 was not due to moral hazard from the Mexican bailout, but rather was part of the general excess market liquidity at the time, as best typified by the parallel decline in spreads on domestic high-yield bonds in the United States, which could not have been driven by moral hazard related to Mexico. I think all would agree, however, that there may have been geopolitical moral hazard in the case of Russia.

In addition, there is considerable discussion about inserting rescheduling clauses in bonds, as was discussed earlier in the conference. This raises a number of considerations, one of which is a time-inconsistency problem. If these rescheduling clauses are included in all bonds issued from now going forward, it will take some time for the amortization flow on the new bonds to begin to matter. Moreover, Eurobonds currently account for less than 20 percent of the outstanding stock of debt. There is also the question of whether an emerging market is made a pariah if it has to have a rescheduling clause in its bonds, but the U.S. government does not. Although official pronouncements recognize this difference, it will be a long time before rescheduling clauses are included in U.S. paper.

That being said, one has to recognize that bonds will be increasingly important in the future. But there is a chain of probabilities that will affect whether rescheduling clauses are important or desirable. There is a probability that debt rescheduling will be required, and that bond rescheduling will be crucial, as opposed to inessential, to the overall debt rescheduling process. Overall, it seems that there is a sufficiently small product from that chain of probabilities. Thus it seems practical, for some time to come, not to dwell too heavily on this issue. The IIF study argues that rescheduling clauses are fine if they are developed on a market basis. Rescheduling clauses can even be seen as a useful liability management technique, with some initial spread, but they certainly should not be mandated.

In sum, on architecture, it seems that we want a market-friendly, voluntary approach to crisis resolution. The private sector should be involved in the solution where necessary—perhaps by the Korea-type short-term debt conversion, by the Brazil-type agreement to maintain short-term credit lines, by mobilization of contingent credit lines such as the Mexico-Argentina variety, by an early reentry of equity, which is what we are seeing in Korea, or by multilateral mitigation of bank risk for private lending—but in any case by an array of approaches that lean toward the voluntary, rather than the mandatory, end of the spectrum. Certainly Russia presents the most efficient binding-in of creditors we have seen in the last two years, but no one would argue that the approach was desirable for Russia, let alone for the overall financial system.

There are some signs that give cause for concern. The Paris Club, in the name of comparability, is pushing the notion that Pakistan should reschedule its bonds. Again, the possible externalities to the rest of the system—the more important impact of, for instance, bond market actions in Brazil that might result from Pakistan's rescheduling—should be looked at very carefully. This decision should not be made on a rigid application of general principle. There is talk about a lender of last resort role for the IMF. There is talk about prequalified emergency lending. One of the key architectural changes has already been made. The IMF's quota has been increased from $200 billion to $300 billion. The IMF now has a supplemental reserve facility, which permits very large, very early disbursements that are much greater relative to quotas in the past. There is, under consideration, the notion of prequalification—if Mexico, for example, signs up to be prequalified and then is hit by a contagion effect, it could immediately receive large support without having to devise a new IMF program. Probably the most practical solution is to return to the earlier approach, which some countries such as Argentina now have, of having a precautionary IMF program that is in place and can be tapped as needed. But a rigid approach to prequalification raises all kinds of problems, not the least of which is political. How do you tell a country that it no longer qualifies and kick it out of the prequalified elite? That gets very difficult politically, and the IMF is certainly a political entity.

In sum, we have been strengthening the architecture, in practice, over the last four years. In a sense, this process has been broadly successful. But the most important element will be continued policy adjustments in the countries themselves.

This entire process is laying the groundwork for a resumption of flows to emerging markets. Let me conclude with a few words about that possible resumption. If credit flows are close to zero this year, and direct investment and portfolio equity bring total flows to, say, $100 billion or $125 billion, what can we expect in the medium term, say, 2000 or 2001? By a number of criteria, it would be unreasonable to expect credit flows—in other words, bank lending plus bonds and financing by other private creditors—to return to the $200 billion level of 1996, but I do think they could return to something like $100 billion a year by the year 2001 or thereabouts.

Two or three criteria tend to push in that direction. First, the debt burden for emerging market countries is not particularly high. The debt-to-export ratio has been flat, at 150 percent, for the past six years, which shows that the real problem in Korea, for example, was short-term debt, not the overall debt burden. Second, $100 billion in credit flows would be consistent with current accounts and capital flows along the following lines. If emerging market economies had $150 billion inflow for equity and $100 billion inflow for credit, their aggregate current account deficit would probably be about $150 billion or less. (By the way, that number never exceeded $100 billion in recent years for the emerging market economies. The rest of the inflows went to build up reserves and finance resident outflows.) A $150 billion current account deficit would only be 12 percent of exports of goods and services. That is a manageable level. Something like $100 billion of net credit inflows also would be consistent with a reasonable growth of the stock of debt, which in emerging markets is about $1.3 trillion in total, composed of about $600 billion of bank claims, $350 billion of Eurobonds, $200 billion of Brady bonds, and $130 billion of other private credits. If a country had $100 billion net increase in claims annually, that would constitute an 8 percent nominal growth in the stock of debt, which again would be perfectly consistent, it seems to me, with growth rates of nominal export bases.

What would be the division between bonds and bank credits in these kinds of flows? I am not sure that I have a firm basis for saying much about that, although presumably if there were a new campaign to force rescheduling of bonds, there would tend to be more bank credits than bonds.

The Development Process and Regulation
David Folkerts-Landau

Countries must recognize that we live in a very different world today. The financial environment has changed radically over the past five years. The degrees of freedom that countries have to make policy, macro as well as regulatory and supervisory, is significantly smaller today. In the past, through controls or various impediments, a country could move five or ten standard deviations from the equilibrium; today, remaining at one standard deviation from the equilibrium invites problems. It is my job, and that of many other participants at this conference, to identify countries that are away from a sustainable equilibrium and to pass that information on to leveraged market players. It is not difficult to list half a dozen countries that still have not internalized the lesson that this is a very dangerous environment that requires much more risk-averse policies than ever before.

From this point of view, I regard the discussion of whether globalization is here to stay as rather irrelevant. Financial markets are global. There is no major decision that we, at our bank, make that is not a global decision. We have a global equities division, a global fixed-income division. The top dozen financial institutions are all global in policy and activities. They think globally; they act globally.

Likewise, I also regard discussions of whether spreads are too small, too narrow, or too large as largely irrelevant. There simply is no model, no set of estimable equations, to determine whether spreads are too large or too small. The ability to reliably price financial assets, exchange rates, and interest rates does not exist. We, as economists, are paid to decide what constitutes equilibrium prices. Such judgments can change quickly, and the resulting movement in asset prices can be large, but this is the best the current financial market arrangements can do. Additional regulation is not going to produce better outcomes.

Ultimately, in some sense we must think in terms of aggregate, macro-level risk management. By that I mean looking at a country's total balance sheet and total exposure, including government and private sector positions, and ensuring that the overall position is maintained within manageable bounds. There is some evidence that, in Argentina for instance, this approach is guiding policy, that the government implicitly evaluates the risks associated with the country's overall balance sheet. The risk assessment cannot be done precisely, but it can be done enough to gain a sense of the vulnerabilities. We cannot think, as we did in the past, that the government's position alone reflects the country's total risk. We have learned that lesson painfully in places like Indonesia and Korea. Nor can we just look at private sector positions. We have to look at total exposure.

The answer to the question of whether to slow liberalization in light of these developments and new environment is no, but we need to be more conscious about the sequencing of liberalization measures. We understand the sequencing extremely well for the current account liberalization, but we do not understand it very well for the capital account. Some lessons have emerged from the past year and a half. One is that countries should not liberalize their capital account if their banking system cannot handle capital inflows and outflows equal to roughly 20 percent of the overall balance sheet. If that is the case, the capital account should be liberalized slowly only after the financial system has been strengthened.

The reason I hesitate in saying this is because one of the more fascinating things I have learned since leaving the IMF is how easy it is for global market participants to get around restrictions. Just because I say that countries should not move quickly to a complete capital account liberalization does not mean they should not try to liberalize very fast. This liberalization has to be done quickly because these rules can be circumvented. The financial restrictions on domestic banks holding domestic equity, for instance, can be circumvented by doing a total return swap with a hedge fund.

The IMF has done extraordinarily well in stressing the importance of sound financial systems, and there is no point repeating the arguments. Early and quick acceptance of the Basle core principles is one of the key steps that need to be taken if countries want to insulate themselves from the vagaries of the global market. This is fairly well-known territory.

In this regard, there is no doubt that the supervisory rules and regulations need to be extended to cover the corporate sector, as is done in the United States. If market discipline does not work well enough locally to discipline corporations, regulators need to review the corporation's balance sheet and impose restrictions on the balance sheet to help the system operate better. We should not just regulate the deposit-taking banking system and licensed banks. Financial technology is making the distinction between a bank and General Motors Acceptance Corporation smaller and smaller. The regulatory approach needs to be carried one step further, as it is increasingly done in some countries. Again, I hold out Argentina as a good example.

The other issue raised was whether to use capital controls during crises. The answer is yes. I can tell you that for leveraged investors who want to take large positions against a currency, or domestic currency instruments, the convertibility issue has loomed large and the ability to restrict the supply of domestic currency for the delivery of forward obligations is a real fear. Andrew Sheng once asked why the Hong Kong Monetary Authority should not use every available tool when it is up against highly sophisticated, leveraged players. And indeed, I think that is exactly the right question to ask. Why not use controls and direct market intervention to counteract a concerted attack on a currency, such as when Hong Kong authorities supported the equity market when hedge funds attacked the Hong Kong dollar, which drove up domestic interest rates, which in turn had a negative impact on the equity market. Equity market vulnerability had to be addressed and was addressed in an extremely efficient—and, as it turns out, highly profitable—way by the Hong Kong Monetary Authority. There are other examples of similar situations. The point is that there is no reason why a government should say, "We cannot do that because we believe in free markets." We all believe in free markets, but why not use the tools available?

Having said that, the main risk to emerging market financing in the coming years is to some extent the rewriting of history that is going on now. A view is developing that some Asian countries, and perhaps Russia too, had only small problems and that the crisis was due more to misbehavior on the part of financial market participants through herding, creating artificial liquidity problems, and the like. That is fundamentally wrong, in my view, because the Asian countries we are talking about—Thailand, Korea—did have fundamental problems. It is a wonder that these countries could live with those problems for so long without being attacked. The contagion happened very naturally, because the activities of fundamentally unsound financial institutions, such as Peregrine, spanned a number of countries. Peregrine single-handedly created an Asian junk bond market by using guaranteed Korean deposits to buy below-investment-grade Asian corporations such as the Indonesian Taxi Company. Once the problems with Thailand erupted, investors took a closer look, and a wholesale withdrawal followed. Problems spilled over into Russia, Brazil, and beyond. But fundamentally, these countries had major problems that were pushed to the fore by a rapid reexamination of their financial prospects by market participants.

Overall, this crisis cannot be viewed as having been caused by poorly behaving markets. This is an important point, not just a political one. If we allow history to be rewritten that way, it will detract from the kind of policies that need to be put in place. If we say, "Well, the crisis was just the market's fault," and support restrictions and regulations that, on the whole, are not socially optimal, we will then lead countries to become more complacent in designing their own policies again. That is a dangerous development.

I was not here for the discussion on restructuring covenants in Eurobonds and better burden sharing. All I suggest is that if we consider shifting a greater burden to private debtors, then we also consider restructuring the IMF's obligations to Russia. Russia's single most important debt burden is to the official sector and to the IMF. We should seriously question the IMF's seniority in getting repaid, particularly now in Russia. One of the worst ideas I have heard over the last ten to fifteen years is for the public sector to intervene in private contractual arrangements to achieve faster debt investment without a better burden sharing. The cost of that policy to emerging markets is a multiple of the gains that it would produce. The loss on the public sector's exposure to non-tied aid has been significantly smaller than the private losses.

I was asked to say a few words about the key lessons from the crisis. That is easy because there are very few of them, but those I see are powerful. The first one that strikes me, and it relates to the architecture issue, is that the IMF's basic surveillance role has failed. Countries with very high domestic savings rates were allowed to import significant volumes of capital, resulting in domestic credit expansion that is mind-boggling when looked at today. Yet we also saw high savings rates, so we never moved from the savings to the investment side and asked, "Are these good investments?"

Essentially, the IMF was mandated to separate out the losers, so to speak, and ring the alarm bells. That did not happen. I point this out because in all these discussions about architecture (which have produced very little except, as Bill Cline said, an increase in the IMF's quota and faster disbursement and faster access), the hard part is getting the surveillance right. It is easy to lend money when there is a crisis and have a policy discussion with countries, but getting the surveillance right is a priority. It is difficult to go to a country that is doing very well, as Korea was, and say, "Your banking system and the way you run your domestic credit markets are fundamentally unsound, and at the first external shock you are going to blow up." They laugh at you.

The current situation has not changed much. The IMF's ability to do surveillance is insufficient. Its ability to enforce its surveillance conclusions, even if they are negative (particularly if they are negative) and to do something about that is also missing. This is because the institution (as is true of the World Bank, but which I know less about) is very much geared to the world before globalization, where surveillance focused on individual countries rather than on global surveillance. It is an institution that is still organized along country lines, without sufficient emphasis on global surveillance. As a result, it misses the big crises. I believe the reason for this limited focus on surveillance is that the G-7 countries do not like surveillance either.

A word on implicit guarantees that were mentioned already: they are a cancer to the system, and they are something countries need to do without. Finally, let me conclude by saying that, as has been discussed, when you look over the flows of the last two years and divide them into various components and ask which was most volatile and most detrimental, it is interbank flows. Interbank flows grew extraordinarily after the Mexican crisis, and they came down at the first whiff of a crisis in Thailand. The reversal of international interbank flows had the single most important detrimental impact on liquidity, pushing the crisis forward. If there is a specific recommendation for regulation, interbank lending is a good candidate.

Private Sector Initiatives
Manuel Medina-Mora

Let me make some brief comments on local private sector initiatives in emerging markets from four perspectives—markets, institutional investors, corporations, and financial intermediaries. I look at what we can expect from them to prevent or more probably reduce or better manage crises in the future. I start with domestic financial markets. Why is it so important to develop domestic financial markets for local and international objectives?

If we do not deepen local financial markets, the liquidity we assume for risk management systems will not exist. Clearly, we need to make progress on both debt and equity markets in many respects, starting with trading and settlement procedures. We need to increase the percentage of capital requirements financed by domestic savings, because that will bring stability to domestic as well as global markets. Again, foreign investors could look at domestic emerging markets as another vehicle for investment.

Let me make five specific points on how we can deepen local markets. We need to (1) develop long-dated domestic sovereign debt instruments, or there will be no benchmark for corporate debt; (2) facilitate risk measurement mechanisms, or we cannot manage risks effectively; we can talk about risk management and risk control systems, but if there are no hedging instruments we are talking in theory; (3) develop hedging mechanisms, which are undeveloped in most domestic emerging markets; (4) enhance transparency, as has been discussed extensively in this conference; (5) develop a way to differentiate the quality of domestic markets, for they are not created equal—that is, create a benchmark system to measure and compare the domestic markets of different countries. If the buying side of the market follows such a benchmark, it will pressure our countries, our regulators, and market participants to keep the market up to competitive, comparative standards. All of these developments need, and call for, important structural reforms, and foreign investors and international organizations can help considerably in assuring that they are designed and implemented appropriately.

The second point concerns local institutional investors, which are very important in developing local markets. Latin America has had important successes in building pension funds—for instance, pension fund management companies in Chile in the 1980s and in Argentina and Mexico in the mid-1990s. For the first time, we have professional management of investments in Mexico, especially on the equity side. I remember asking a friend at the Federal Reserve whether he was concerned that there would be an adjustment in financial asset prices in the U.S. markets. He said that although 40 percent of the U.S. population directly or indirectly is involved in the stock market, most are investing through retirement accounts. That is very different from individuals investing in a few stocks in the short term. Pension funds and retirement funds take a long-term view, have a diversified portfolio, and are managed by professionals. They are likely the best way to channel domestic savings into the stock markets, especially in emerging market economies. Again, by building local institutional investors, we gain more stability, which is something we need to work on more. Moreover, local investors likely bring more pressure on domestic market discipline.

The third point concerns private sector incentives, again with a view to reducing the risk of crises and their impact on corporations. Clearly, emerging market issuers have more access to global financial markets, but even issuers that are well run face liquidity difficulties when a crisis arises. In this conference it was pointed out that Latin American corporations probably were not as troubled as Asian corporations, but when the crisis erupted, the borrowing window for any corporate name from Latin America, even some of our best corporate customers in Mexico, was closed and continued to be closed until very recently.

What is the solution? One can argue that in a country, as in any economic system, some sectors, or companies, are moving much more rapidly into globalization than are other sectors or companies. Earlier, a few people mentioned an idea that I would like to discuss and that is whether a corporate issuer from an emerging market can attempt to have a better credit rating than its country and become a better risk in the global markets than just an emerging market risk.

Let us think about that. Some of the actions the corporation would need to take to achieve that end are totally under its control: enhance transparency and improve corporate governance, for instance. Other areas are, of course, linked to the country.

Corporations can take two more actions to enhance their ability to handle crises and thereby raise their rating above that of their country. First, they can enhance their liquidity since liquidity is key to dealing with a crisis. Second, they can use structured financing, perhaps based on exports that earn hard currency, as some of the Latin American corporations are attempting now. At the same time, investors should start looking at the merits of each corporation, independent to some extent from those of the country in which it is based. This is a provocative idea, but something we have to think more about in the future. Somebody mentioned Cemex in the previous session. Cemex continues to be perceived as a Mexican company, although it sells more than half of its total sales abroad, but the tag of a Mexican company is still there when a crisis arises.

Let me finish with some comments about financial intermediaries and the banking and financial sector. It has been mentioned here, and I know that the Institute for International Finance has been looking at how to implement the Basle core principles in emerging markets and improve the operation, supervision, and regulation of banks. But that is not enough. We need to improve disclosure by domestic financial sector participants (which has been mentioned in this conference) because the health of the financial sector in an emerging market economy is key to understanding how well that economy is doing.

We need to work on government guarantees that were involved in some emerging market problems, which means, for instance, switching from unlimited depositor protection to a limited deposit safety net in our countries. We need to enhance market discipline over banks. Some Latin American countries are doing this already, but it has to be done gradually. Another related topic is that some foreign banks are not yet making money in our countries. They bring competition and better practices, which are welcome, but they are not lending as aggressively as the authorities would like because they are facing the same difficult environments that some local banks are facing. Their constrained lending highlights the need for emerging market countries to continue with institutional and legal reforms to improve the operating environment for the financial system. That is the case with Mexico.

Finally, can emerging market banks become more global? I argue that if their risk management systems and liquidity improve, they might lower the regulatory costs of the central bank. Domestic banks with direct access to external liquidity sources should have a different type of regulatory system from other domestic banks in those countries. Liquidity can be rebuilt, and this is the case with some Latin American banks, by structuring asset-backed financing linked to international flows and by applying to corporations the same concept of standby credit facilities that are now discussed with banks. I hope that we can evolve to a progressive or at least a two-tiered regulatory system for banks in some of the emerging market economies.

ANDREW SHENG

13

Conclusion: An Asian Perspective on the Asian Crisis

TRADITIONALLY, AT CONFERENCES on the Asian crisis, non-Asians begin by making a joke, and Asians begin by offering an apology. I will start with an apology. It is common with the Asian crisis to blame the victim, blame the investor, blame the policies, blame the International Monetary Fund or the World Bank, blame the international finance institutions, and finally blame the architecture.

Now, I am a Malaysian: blame capital controls. I work in Hong Kong: blame intervention. I worked in the World Bank: blame international finance institutions. I worked on the G-22 Working Party on Transparency and Accountability and participated in the big debate on whether there should be an Asian Monetary Fund. I am sorry for the Asian crisis. You can blame it all on me. Now let us get on with the work.

I now want to tell a little joke. Asians feel very much like a hospital patient where several distinguished doctors—Drs. Fischer, Krugman, Sachs, Stiglitz, and Summers—all stand around the patient and debate on the right diagnosis and prognosis. Finally, the patient whispers, "Excuse me. I think I have an infectious viral flu, and now you all have it."

Risk Management in One World

I would like to recast the theme of this conference in my own words: we are dealing with the issue of *risk management in one world*. Ten years ago I

413

started thinking about the issue of national risk management. I have since realized that with global financial markets, we need to think about one world because now we are living in an interdependent world. One reason why there were bubbles in Asia was the excess liquidity generated in the G-3 economies. Furthermore, the counterpart of Asia's current account deficits, as Professor Cooper has pointed out, was growing current account surpluses in other developing economies. It is no coincidence that the $80 billion current account surplus in Asia this year translates into an $80 billion deficit in Latin America. We live in one world where capital flight from Asia also helped to generate bubble-like effects in G-3 markets.

We need to understand that, as one world, we must deal with one risk management. The real point about the Asian crisis is that it was not, in fact, an Asian crisis. It was a global crisis. And that is the reason why, when participating in the very historic Manila Framework meeting in November 1997, I realized that we should reject an Asian solution and work toward a global solution. In hindsight, I did not realize that this would entail an enormous time-consuming due process of international negotiations that would delay quick solutions. But it was an eye-opening experience and also a reality: the present global financial architecture is not designed to react rapidly to a local financial crisis.

The fundamental problem with the Asian crisis or the global crisis was a failure of risk management. It was a failure of risk management on the part of investors: they did not understand the risk they were getting into when they entered emerging markets. It was a failure of policymakers and local banks: they did not appreciate the huge liquidity and currency risks they were assuming when they took in large capital flows. As David Folkerts-Landau rightly has pointed out, policymakers did not understand that in an open capital account, if they maintain a stable or fixed exchange rate, they have no interest rate room to maneuver. And, of course, lenders also made huge mistakes on many fronts, particularly in assessing credit risks.

Finance, Derivatives, and Assumptions

Many of you may be familiar with the cliché that the Chinese word for "crisis" is "risk plus opportunity." The more interesting analogy is that the Chinese word for "assumption" is "false certainty." If anything, one reason why nobody predicted the Asian crisis is that the assumptions made were wrong. All the things that we held to be true were wrong. The assumption that, for example, if a country has a stable exchange rate with limited capital flows, interest rate policy could still be implemented was wrong. The assumption that you had time—that you can buy time—because of inefficient intermediation processes was completely blown away with dynamic hedging. Derivative instruments totally removed this time gap because the duration of liabilities during a crisis can collapse to zero as everyone runs for total liquidity (often through capital flight) The Long-Term Capital Management model of risk management was a classic example. I understand that the model assumed four standard deviations of market movement, but the market moved fifteen standard deviations. The rest is history.

For example, the International Monetary Fund basically approached the Asian crisis through its standard two-gap (fiscal gap and balance of payments gap) Polak model of 1960s vintage. This model was essentially a flow model and did not include balance sheet stock items and therefore did not appreciate the implications of high interest rates on highly leveraged banking systems and the corporate sector. Thus everyone's key assumptions were called into question during the Asian crisis. That is something we need to understand.

We also need to understand that the world has changed in many important ways that we did not appreciate. We in Asia have been busy fighting fires. Asians did not comment very significantly on these issues because we ourselves could not fully understand what was happening. Slowly there is an emergence of understanding that I will try to articulate.

In simple fund manager's terms, Asian growth regressed to the mean. Such fast growth was statistically impossible to sustain. The old Rostovian model of developing economies taking off smoothly like a plane forgot to mention that sometimes planes crash. East Asian economies were suffering from the pains of growing globally It was the middle-income economies, the real tigers, that crashed because they did not fully appreciate the problems of globalization, which required them to play by the rules of globalization. They thought they could continue with an export-oriented manufacturing policy to produce growth by essentially channeling resources from a slightly repressed, protected financial system and toward the priority sectors. But in fact the system was redistributing the risks in a totally wrong manner.

I began to appreciate these problems when, as a fund manager responsible for Hong Kong's reserves, I had to understand derivatives. It struck me that finance is a derivative of the real economy and that the relationship with the derivative depends very much on the underlying asset. The relationship is delta. That delta relationship depends on the degree of leverage. If there are fundamental problems in the underlying asset (the real economy), there is instability or fragility in the financial sector. The interaction between the two is sometimes unstable in specific market conditions. And that specific market condition, as we all know, is the false assumption that information is perfect and that contracts are complete. In fact, the Asian financial crisis, or the global financial crisis, occurred because of asymmetric information—asymmetric, incomplete information and incomplete contracts. There was no adequate legal framework for the exit of corporations or banks or bonds in many emerging markets.

Asia needs to understand that it had fundamental problems of excess capacity in the real sector with fragile or probably not particularly well-managed banking systems. We tend to forget that banking systems are intended not only to allocate resources but also to help the real sector manage its risks. But the banking sectors did not manage their own risks well. Consequently, much of Asia lost a large part of the reserves they had built up through many years of successful exports and incurred huge losses in their banking systems.

Financial Markets as Networks

The second issue we need to think about is that, in the new economy of global markets, markets are networks and that local markets are like local area networks linked to the global network of finance. There are huge externalities in networks. But networks also have huge contagion or feedback impacts. That was the problem. Looking at the Asian financial system, one could use a simple engineering or even a derivative model analogy. The system was designed for two or three standard deviations of shocks. We had a fifteen-standard-deviation shock or power surge, and someone blew a fuse. It is as simple as that.

For example, under the Basle rules, a banking system must have an 8 percent capital adequacy ratio. If that banking system lends to a domestic corporate sector that has 30 percent of its liabilities in foreign exchange and the exchange rate drops 30 percent, other things being equal, the corporate sector will be bust and the banking system will be technically undercapitalized because of nonperforming loans.

Historically, we did not design local financial systems to absorb large global shocks. Now, clearly, that is the fault of local policymakers and regulators, but at the same time global fund managers and those responsible for the global architecture did not understand that global flows had large potential impacts on small illiquid emerging markets. To express this in simple hedging and derivatives terminology, we did not understand that during this period of financial innovation, domestic banking systems had assumed below-the-line derivative-type market and credit risks that were significantly larger than most bank supervisors or central banks appreciated. We did not understand this because information on the degree of leverage through derivatives was not transparent to all users, investors, borrowers, lenders, and policymakers.

Clearly markets, and networks generally, thrive on information and transparency. The lessons from Asia may be summarized as follows: bad accounts equal bad statistics equal bad policies equal bad risk management. All this adds up to financial crisis. Asia suffered because there was uneven adoption of international accounting standards, including poor implementation of accounting standards. Even the best managers were reading the accounts wrongly and making the wrong decisions. That is why the returns on equity turned out to be wrong. As usual in a crisis, there were crooks as well as people who genuinely made mistakes. Aristobulo de Juan, a former Spanish central banker who helped to resolve the Spanish banking crisis of the early 1980s, used to say how good bankers can become bad bankers under wrong incentives. Good corporate managers also can become bad corporate managers if they read the data wrongly. Asians made many of these mistakes.

Many people have not fully appreciated a fundamental mistake in the policy message. The language of advice to Asia needs to be turned around. The message is not: it is in the world's interest to have Asia or emerging markets open their banking systems. The message should be: it is in an emerging market's interest, and that of global risk management more generally, for an emerging market to open its local banking systems. The reason is simple. If a nation owns 100 percent of its banking system, it suffers 100 percent of the losses. Risk diversification involves swapping your asset with my asset, and by that swapping, our banks can diversify their risks in your financial system and your banks can diversify their risks in our financial system. Through this swapping, we reduce the risks to the system as a whole. If you put it in that context, emerging markets may see the suggested market liberalization not as a can-opening exercise by foreign banks but as a self-interested exercise in risk management.

Overall, we must appreciate that global markets have brought huge complexity to the financial world, and it is pointless to blame A or B or C or D. Globalization is much more complex than we have fully understood. We need to understand its implications much better, and, therefore, we need to move up the knowledge curve. For that we need transparency. The problem with the existing state of transparency—and frankly speaking this is the problem also of the United Nations System of National Accounts, which is only beginning to generate national and sectoral balance sheets for the public sector to record transactions in accrual terms—is that many financial systems have incurred economic loss but those losses still appear as paper profits.

That is one reason why the markets are not functioning efficiently. They are still responding to information based on outdated accounting, including national accounting, standards where there are no national balance sheets and no way to demonstrate that national economies are suffering from large economic losses and have huge (unrecognized) exposures. People assume that somehow economies can always grow out of their problems.

The real issue, as I see it from an investor's point of view, is whether investors understand the risks they are assuming, have mechanisms to manage the risks, and are diversifying their assets in a manner that is safe for them. Let me reiterate the false certainty of incorrect assumptions. Professor Sebastian Edwards's paper demonstrates how different countries have different maturity profiles. There is a common assumption that long-term foreign direct investment is "safer" than short-term capital flows.

We all know that during a crisis the duration of liabilities collapses toward zero. There are many derivatives you can use to hedge the liability side, and the asset side can be liquidated. And so all economies, if they do not manage their risks well, could suffer not only a liquidity crisis, but also a solvency crisis when interest rates rise. This is because all the assets are discounted at a much higher real interest rate, so all the asset values collapse and deflate, while all the liabilities are immediately realized.

These are some of the very complex issues that we have not fully understood. Furthermore, another lesson from the crisis is that not only do we need to have better information, we need to have more complete contracts. These include outdated bankruptcy laws. You cannot change the legislation or the rules of the game midway in a crisis. The trouble is that globally we still have local rules instead of global rules We have global markets, but national laws and regulations.

Transparency and Corporate Governance

To sum up, risk management is everybody's responsibility. So far, I have discussed risk management as an informational issue. But how you use that information is a question of governance and management. This leads to the political economy of global markets. We have discussed in this book the need for better corporate governance. Better corporate governance is essentially an issue of trust between principal and agent. At the sector level, it is a question of whether that sector has better governance than another sector. At the national level, we need to understand whether there can be better national governance. This is the political governance issue. To a large extent, one trouble in Asia was that there was too much delegated authority, if I may say so, without checks and balances at the corporate level, maybe even at the sector level, and, some would argue, at the market level as well.

One key problem in discussing the international architecture of globalization is the issue of no taxation without representation. The G-7, G-10 countries took it for granted that they had the right to write the rules for the rest of the world. All of a sudden they realized that emerging markets and others wanted to participate in the writing of new rules. How we divide that political governance issue is going to be a very difficult political cal economy problem that we have not yet totally resolved.

From a post-crisis perspective, we need to realize that large losses have already occurred and that distributing these losses is a political economy question that is impossible to decide simplistically. Therefore, we need global rules, global standards, global standards of accounting, global rules of regulation, global rules of asset valuation, global rules of national economic accounting, and global processes of risk management to help us understand that your risk diversification is my risk concentration and that my problems are your problems: we really are living in one world.

So how do we do this? Now that we are all moving toward a market-oriented point of view, as a regulator I believe that the essence of this issue is transparent information: making the market work better and getting the contracts right. This may boil down to what Securities and Exchange

Commission Chairman Arthur Levitt has put very well as the health warning for all investors: know your risks, know your counter-party, know your market, and know your contracts.

This is, of course, the ideal future. If we are to build global markets, we have to begin building domestic markets that have better risk management. Global market managers and fund managers must appreciate that the checks and balances in the system begin with a smart investor, a smart intermediary, and a smart policy framework that enables us to absorb the shocks that will definitely, in my view, come with global markets.

Global financial crisis is inevitable because it is part of the process of growing up. It is part of the pain of making mistakes at all levels. Without that pain, people will not learn how to adjust and how to manage risks. Given that we have now gone through a huge and painful process, we need to address the real sector problems, the financial sector problems, the need for better transparency, and the issues concerning leverage and derivatives that are still poorly understood.

Contributors

MICHAEL ADLER
Columbia University

MICHAEL BARTH
World Bank

STIJN CLAESSENS
World Bank

WILLIAM CLINE
Institute for International Finance

RICHARD N. COOPER
Harvard University

SIMEON DJANKOV
World Bank

SEBASTIAN EDWARDS
University of California, Los Angeles

DAVID FOLKERTS-LANDAU
Deutsche Morgan Grenfell

IAN H. GIDDY
New York University

CAMPBELL R. HARVEY
Duke University

ALISON HARWOOD
International Finance Corporation

LARRY H. P. LANG
*Chinese University of
Hong Kong*

ROBERT E. LITAN
Brookings Institution

MANUEL MEDINA-MORA
Banamex

MICHAEL POMERLEANO
World Bank

ANDREW H. ROPER
Duke University

ANDREW SHENG
*Securities and Futures
Commission, Hong Kong*

KENNETH E. SCOTT
Stanford University

JARROD WILCOX
PanAgora Asset Management

JAMES D. WOLFENSOHN
World Bank

XIN ZHANG
World Bank

a LANGE medical book

NINTH EDITION

REVIEW OF
Medical Microbiology
and Immunology

WARREN LEVINSON, MD, PhD

Professor of Microbiology
Department of Microbiology and Immunology
University of California, San Francisco
San Francisco, California

Lange Medical Books/McGraw-Hill
Medical Publishing Division

New York   Chicago   San Francisco   Lisbon   London   Madrid
Mexico City   Milan   New Delhi   San Juan   Seoul   Singapore
Sydney   Toronto

Review of Medical Microbiology & Immunology, Ninth Edition

Copyright © 2006 by **The McGraw-Hill Companies**, Inc. All rights reserved. Printed in the United States of America. Except as permitted under the United States Copyright Act of 1976, no part of this publication may be reproduced or distributed in any form or by any means, or stored in a data base or retrieval system, without the prior written permission of the publisher.

Previous editions copyright © 2004, 2002, 2000 by The McGraw-Hill Companies, Inc., and copyright © 1998, 1996, 1994, 1992, 1989 by Appleton & Lange.

1 2 3 4 5 6 7 8 9 0 DOC/DOC 0 9 8 7 6

ISBN: 0-07-146031-4
ISSN: 1042-8070

Cover illustration: A colorized computer graphic image of human immunodeficiency virus (HIV), the retrovirus that causes acquired immunodeficiency syndrome (AIDS). Note the red cylindrical nucleocapsid core characteristic of HIV.

This book was set in Adobe Garamond by Rainbow Graphics.
The editors were Jason Malley, Robert Pancotti, and Karen Davis.
The production supervisor was Catherine H. Saggese.
The text designer was Eve Siegel.
The cover designer was Pehrsson Design.
The index was prepared by Rainbow Graphics.
RR Donnelley was the printer and binder.

This book is printed on acid-free paper.

INTERNATIONAL EDITION ISBN: 0-07-110438-0
Exclusive rights by The McGraw-Hill Companies, Inc., for manufacture and export. This book cannot be re-exported from the country to which it is consigned by McGraw-Hill. The International Edition is not available in North America.

Contents

Preface

This book is a concise review of the medically important aspects of microbiology. It covers both the basic and clinical aspects of bacteriology, virology, mycology, parasitology, and immunology. Its two major aims are (1) to assist those who are preparing for the USMLE (National Boards) and (2) to provide students who are currently taking medical microbiology courses with a brief and up-to-date source of information.

This new edition presents current, medically important information in the rapidly changing fields of microbiology and immunology. It includes updated information on such topics as human immunodeficiency virus, hepatitis viruses, prions, and immunology. My goal is to provide the reader with an accurate source of clinically relevant information at a level appropriate for those beginning their medical education.

These aims are achieved by utilizing several different formats, which should make the book useful to students with varying study objectives and learning styles:

1. A narrative text for complete information.
2. Summaries of important microorganisms for rapid review of essentials.
3. Sample questions in the USMLE (National Board) style, with answers provided after each group of questions.
4. A USMLE (National Board) practice examination consisting of 80 microbiology and immunology questions. The questions are incorporated into a clinical case format and simulate the computer-based examination. Answers are provided at the end of each block of 40 questions.
5. Clinical case vignettes to provide both clinical information and practice for the USMLE.
6. A section titled "Pearls for the USMLE" that describes important epidemiological information helpful in answering questions on the USMLE.

The following features are included to promote a successful learning experience for students using this book:

1. The information is presented succinctly, with stress on making it clear, interesting, and up to date.
2. There is strong emphasis in the text on the clinical application of microbiology and immunology to infectious diseases.
3. In the clinical bacteriology and virology sections, the organisms are separated into major and minor pathogens. This allows the student to focus on the clinically most important microorganisms.
4. Key information is summarized in useful review tables. Important concepts are illustrated by figures using color.
5. Important facts called "Pearls" are listed at the end of each basic science chapter.
6. The 654 USMLE (National Board) practice questions cover the important aspects of each of the subdisciplines on the USMLE: Bacteriology, Virology, Mycology, Parasitology, and Immunology. A separate section containing *extended* matching questions is included. In view of the emphasis placed on clinical relevance in the USMLE, another section provides questions set in a clinical case context.
7. Brief summaries of medically important microorganisms are presented together in a separate section to facilitate rapid access to the information and to encourage comparison of one organism with another.
8. Fifty clinical cases are presented as unknowns for the reader to analyze in a brief, problem-solving format. These cases illustrate the importance of basic science information in clinical diagnosis.

After teaching both medical microbiology and clinical infectious disease for many years, I believe that students appreciate a book that presents the essential information in a readable, interesting, and varied format. I hope you find this book meets those criteria.

Warren Levinson, MD, PhD
San Francisco, California
January 2006

Acknowledgments

I am indebted to the editor of the first five editions, Yvonne Strong, to the editor of the sixth edition, Cara Lyn Coffey, to the editor of the seventh and ninth editions, Jennifer Bernstein, and to the editor of the eighth edition, Linda Conheady, all of whom ensured that the highest standards of grammar and style were met.

The invaluable assistance of my wife, Barbara, in making this book a reality is also gratefully acknowledged.

I dedicate this book to my father and mother, who instilled a love of scholarship, the joy of teaching, and the value of being organized.

Warren Levinson, MD, PhD

How to Use This Book

1. **TEXT:** A concise, complete description of medically important information for the professional student. Includes basic and clinical bacteriology (pages 1–191), basic and clinical virology (pages 192–333), mycology (fungi) (pages 334–349), parasitology (pages 350–390), and immunology (pages 391–476).

---

2. **SUMMARIES OF ORGANISMS:** A quick review for examinations describing the important characteristics of the organisms (pages 477–514).

---

3. **PEARLS FOR THE USMLE:** 8 tables containing important epidemiological information that will be useful for answering questions on the USMLE (pages 525–531).

---

4. **USMLE-TYPE QUESTIONS:** 654 practice questions that can be used to review for the USMLE and class examinations (pages 532–582).

---

5. **USMLE PRACTICE EXAM:** Two 40-question practice examinations in USMLE format (pages 583–594).

---

6. **PEARLS:** Summary points at the end of each basic science chapter.

---

7. **CLINICAL CASES:** 50 cases describing important infectious diseases with emphasis on diagnostic information (pages 515–524).

PART I
Basic Bacteriology

Bacteria Compared With Other Microorganisms

1

AGENTS

The agents of human infectious diseases belong to five major groups of organisms: bacteria, fungi, protozoa, helminths, and viruses. The bacteria belong to the prokaryote kingdom, the fungi (yeasts and molds) and protozoa are members of the kingdom of protists, and the helminths (worms) are classified in the animal kingdom (Table 1–1). The protists are distinguished from animals and plants by being either unicellular or relatively simple multicellular organisms. The helminths are complex multicellular organisms that are classified as metazoa within the animal kingdom. Taken together, the helminths and the protozoa are commonly called parasites. Viruses are quite distinct from other organisms. They are not cells but can replicate only within cells.

IMPORTANT FEATURES

Many of the essential characteristics of these organisms are described in Table 1–2. One salient feature is that bacteria, fungi, protozoa, and helminths are cellular, whereas viruses are not. This distinction is based primarily on three criteria.

(1) **Structure.** Cells have a nucleus or nucleoid (see below) containing DNA; this is surrounded by cytoplasm, within which proteins are synthesized and energy is generated. Viruses have an inner core of genetic material (either DNA or RNA) but no cytoplasm, so they depend on host cells to provide the machinery for protein synthesis and energy generation.

(2) **Method of replication.** Cells replicate either by binary fission or by mitosis, during which one parent cell divides to make two progeny cells while retaining its cellular structure. Prokaryotic cells, eg, bacteria, replicate by binary fission, whereas eukaryotic cells replicate by mitosis. In contrast, viruses disassemble, produce many copies of their nucleic acid and protein, and then reassemble into multiple progeny viruses. Furthermore, viruses must replicate within host cells because, as mentioned above, they lack protein-synthesizing and energy-generating systems. With the exception of rickettsiae and chlamydiae, which are bacteria that also require living host cells for growth, bacteria can replicate extracellularly.

Table 1–1. Biologic relationships of pathogenic microorganisms.

Kingdom	Pathogenic Microorganisms	Type of Cells
Animal	Helminths	Eukaryotic
Plant	None	Eukaryotic
Protist	Protozoa	Eukaryotic
	Fungi	Eukaryotic
Prokaryote	Bacteria	Prokaryotic
	Viruses	Noncellular

Table 1–2. Comparison of medically important organisms.

Characteristic	Viruses	Bacteria	Fungi	Protozoa and Helminths
Cells	No	Yes	Yes	Yes
Approximate diameter (μm)[1]	0.02–0.2	1–5	3–10 (yeasts)	15–25 (trophozoites)
Nucleic acid	Either DNA or RNA	Both DNA and RNA	Both DNA and RNA	Both DNA and RNA
Type of nucleus	None	Prokaryotic	Eukaryotic	Eukaryotic
Ribosomes	Absent	70S	80S	80S
Mitochondria	Absent	Absent	Present	Present
Nature of outer surface	Protein capsid and lipoprotein envelope	Rigid wall containing peptidoglycan	Rigid wall containing chitin	Flexible membrane
Motility	None	Some	None	Most
Method of replication	Not binary fission	Binary fission	Budding or mitosis[2]	Mitosis[3]

[1] For comparison, a human red blood cell has a diameter of 7 μm.

[2] Yeasts divide by budding, whereas molds divide by mitosis.

[3] Helminth cells divide by mitosis, but the organism reproduces itself by complex, sexual life cycles.

(3) **Nature of the nucleic acid.** Cells contain both DNA and RNA, whereas viruses contain either DNA or RNA but not both.

EUKARYOTES & PROKARYOTES

Cells have evolved into two fundamentally different types, **eukaryotic** and **prokaryotic,** which can be distinguished on the basis of their structure and the complexity of their organization. Fungi and protozoa are eukaryotic, whereas bacteria are prokaryotic.

(1) The eukaryotic cell has a true **nucleus** with multiple chromosomes surrounded by a nuclear membrane and uses a mitotic apparatus to ensure equal allocation of the chromosomes to progeny cells.

(2) The **nucleoid** of a prokaryotic cell consists of a single circular molecule of loosely organized DNA lacking a nuclear membrane and mitotic apparatus (Table 1–3).

In addition to the different types of nuclei, the two classes of cells are distinguished by several other characteristics.

Table 1–3. Characteristics of prokaryotic and eukaryotic cells.

Characteristic	Prokaryotic Bacterial Cells	Eukaryotic Human Cells
DNA within a nuclear membrane	No	Yes
Mitotic division	No	Yes
DNA associated with histones	No	Yes
Chromosome number	One	More than one
Membrane-bound organelles, such as mitochondria and lysosomes	No	Yes
Size of ribosome	70S	80S
Cell wall containing peptidoglycan	Yes	No

(1) Eukaryotic cells contain **organelles,** such as mitochondria and lysosomes, and larger (80S) ribosomes, whereas prokaryotes contain no organelles and smaller (70S) ribosomes.

(2) Most prokaryotes have a rigid external cell wall that contains **peptidoglycan,** a polymer of amino acids and sugars, as its unique structural component. Eukaryotes, on the other hand, do not contain peptidoglycan. Either they are bound by a flexible cell membrane or, in the case of fungi, they have a rigid cell wall with chitin, a homopolymer of *N*-acetylglucosamine, typically forming the framework.

(3) The eukaryotic cell membrane contains **sterols,** whereas no prokaryote, except the wall-less *Mycoplasma,* has sterols in its membranes.

Motility is another characteristic by which these organisms can be distinguished. Most protozoa and some bacteria are motile, whereas fungi and viruses are nonmotile. The protozoa are a heterogeneous group that possess three different organs of locomotion: flagella, cilia, and pseudopods. The motile bacteria move only by means of flagella.

TERMINOLOGY

Bacteria, fungi, protozoa, and helminths are named according to the binomial Linnean system that uses genus and species, but viruses are not so named. For example, regarding the name of the well-known bacteria *Escherichia coli, Escherichia* is the genus and *coli* is the species name. Similarly, the name of the yeast *Candida albicans* consists of *Candida* as the genus and *albicans* as the species. But viruses typically have a single name such as poliovirus, measles virus, or rabies virus. Some viruses have names with two words such as herpes simplex virus, but those do not represent genus and species.

PEARLS

- *The agents of human infectious diseases are* **bacteria, fungi (yeasts and molds), protozoa, helminths (worms),** *and* **viruses.**
- *Bacterial cells have a* **prokaryotic** *nucleus, whereas human, fungal, protozoan, and helminth cells have a* **eukaryotic** *nucleus. Viruses are not cells and do not have a nucleus.*
- *All cells contain both DNA and RNA, whereas viruses contain either DNA or RNA, not both.*
- *Bacterial and fungal cells are surrounded by a rigid cell wall, whereas human, protozoan, and helminth cells have a flexible cell membrane.*
- *The bacterial cell wall contains* **peptidoglycan,** *whereas the fungal cell wall contains chitin.*

PRACTICE QUESTIONS: USMLE & COURSE EXAMINATIONS

Questions on the topics discussed in this chapter can be found in the Basic Bacteriology section of Part XI: USMLE (National Board) Practice Questions starting on page 532. Also see Part XII: USMLE (National Board) Practice Examination starting on page 583.

Structure of Bacterial Cells

SHAPE & SIZE

Bacteria are classified by shape into three basic groups: **cocci**, **bacilli**, and **spirochetes** (Figure 2–1). The cocci are round, the bacilli are rods, and the spirochetes are spiral-shaped. Some bacteria are variable in shape and are said to be **pleomorphic** (many-shaped). The shape of a bacterium is determined by its rigid cell wall. The microscopic appearance of a bacterium is one of the most important criteria used in its identification.

In addition to their characteristic shapes, the arrangement of bacteria is important. For example, certain cocci occur in pairs (**diplococci**), some in chains (**streptococci**), and others in grapelike clusters (**staphylococci**). These arrangements are determined by the orientation and degree of attachment of the bacteria at the time of cell division. The arrangement of rods and spirochetes is less medically important and will not be described in this introductory chapter.

Bacteria range in size from about 0.2 to 5 µm (Figure 2–2). The smallest bacteria (*Mycoplasma*) are about the same size as the largest viruses (poxviruses) and are the smallest organisms capable of existing outside a host. The longest bacteria rods approach the size of some yeasts and human red blood cells (7 µm).

STRUCTURE

The structure of a typical bacterium is illustrated in Figure 2–3, and the important features of each component are presented in Table 2–1.

Cell Wall

The cell wall is the outermost component common to all bacteria (except *Mycoplasma* species, which are bounded by a cell membrane, not a cell wall). Some bacteria have surface features external to the cell wall, such as a capsule, flagella, and pili, which are less common components and are discussed below.

The cell wall is a multilayered structure located external to the cytoplasmic membrane. It is composed of an inner layer of **peptidoglycan** (see page 7) and an outer membrane that varies in thickness and chemical composition depending upon the bacterial type (Figure 2–4). The peptidoglycan provides structural support and maintains the characteristic shape of the cell.

A. CELL WALLS OF GRAM-POSITIVE AND GRAM-NEGATIVE BACTERIA

The structure, chemical composition, and thickness of the cell wall differ in gram-positive and gram-negative bacteria (Table 2–2 and Box).

(1) The peptidoglycan layer is much thicker in gram-positive than in gram-negative bacteria. Some gram-positive bacteria also have fibers of teichoic acid that protrude outside the peptidoglycan, whereas gram-negative bacteria do not.

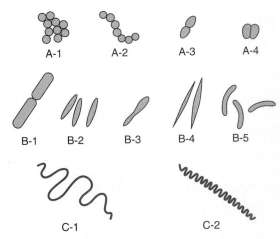

Figure 2–1. Bacterial morphology. **A:** Cocci: in clusters, eg, *Staphylococcus* (A-1); chains, eg, *Streptococcus* (A-2); in pairs with pointed ends, eg, *Streptococcus pneumoniae* (A-3); in pairs with kidney bean shape, eg, *Neisseria* (A-4). **B:** Rods (bacilli): with square ends, eg, *Bacillus* (B-1); with rounded ends, eg, *Salmonella* (B-2); club-shaped, eg, *Corynebacterium* (B-3); fusiform, eg, *Fusobacterium* (B-4); comma-shaped, eg, *Vibrio* (B-5). **C:** Spirochetes: relaxed coil, eg, *Borrelia* (C-1); tightly coiled, eg, *Treponema* (C-2). (Modified and reproduced, with permission, from Joklik WK et al: *Zinsser Microbiology,* 20th ed. Originally published by Appleton & Lange. Copyright © 1992 by The McGraw-Hill Companies, Inc.)

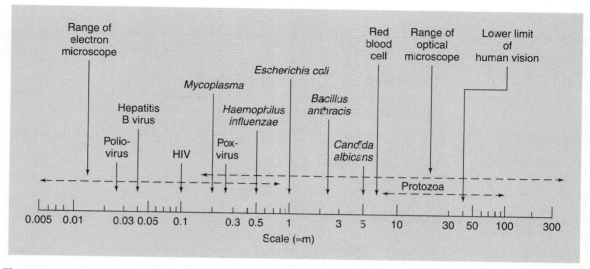

Figure 2–2. Sizes of representative bacteria, viruses, yeasts, protozoa, and human red cells. The bacteria range in size from *Mycoplasma,* the smallest, to *Bacillus anthracis,* one of the largest. The viruses range from poliovirus, one of the smallest, to poxviruses, the largest. Yeasts, such as *Candida albicans,* are generally larger than bacteria. Protozoa have many different forms and a broad size range. HIV, human immunodeficiency virus. (Modified and reproduced, with permission, from Joklik WK et al: *Zinsser Microbiology,* 20th ed. Originally published by Appleton & Lange. Copyright © 1992 by The McGraw-Hill Companies, Inc.)

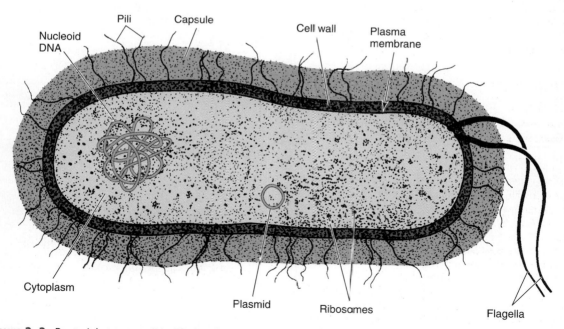

Figure 2–3. Bacterial structure. (Modified and reproduced, with permission, from Tortora G, Funk B, Case C: *Microbiology: An Introduction,* 5th ed. Benjamin/Cummings, 1995.)

Table 2–1. Bacterial structures.

Structure	Chemical Composition	Function
Essential components		
Cell wall		
Peptidoglycan	Sugar backbone with peptide side chains that are cross-linked	Gives rigid support, protects against osmotic pressure; is the site of action of penicillins and cephalosporins and is degraded by lysozyme.
Outer membrane of gram-negative bacteria	Lipid A	Toxic component of endotoxin.
	Polysaccharide	Major surface antigen used frequently in laboratory diagnosis.
Surface fibers of gram-positive bacteria	Teichoic acid	Major surface antigen but rarely used in laboratory diagnosis.
Cytoplasmic membrane	Lipoprotein bilayer without sterols	Site of oxidative and transport enzymes.
Ribosome	RNA and protein in 50S and 30S subunits	Protein synthesis; site of action of aminoglycosides, erythromycin, tetracyclines, and chloramphenicol.
Nucleoid	DNA	Genetic material.
Mesosome	Invagination of plasma membrane	Participates in cell division and secretion.
Periplasm	Space between plasma membrane and outer membrane	Contains many hydrolytic enzymes, including β-lactamases.
Nonessential components		
Capsule	Polysaccharide[1]	Protects against phagocytosis.
Pilus or fimbria	Glycoprotein	Two types: (1) mediates attachment to cell surfaces; (2) sex pilus mediates attachment of two bacteria during conjugation.
Flagellum	Protein	Motility.
Spore	Keratinlike coat, dipicolinic acid	Provides resistance to dehydration, heat, and chemicals.
Plasmid	DNA	Contains a variety of genes for antibiotic resistance and toxins.
Granule	Glycogen, lipids, polyphosphates	Site of nutrients in cytoplasm.
Glycocalyx	Polysaccharide	Mediates adherence to surfaces.

[1]Except in *Bacillus anthracis,* in which it is a polypeptide of D-glutamic acid.

(2) In contrast, the gram-negative organisms have a complex outer layer consisting of lipopolysaccharide, lipoprotein, and phospholipid. Lying between the outer-membrane layer and the cytoplasmic membrane in gram-negative bacteria is the **periplasmic space,** which is the site, in some species, of enzymes called β-lactamases that degrade penicillins and other β-lactam drugs.

The cell wall has several other important properties:

(1) In gram-negative organisms, it contains **endotoxin,** a lipopolysaccharide (see pages 9 and 45).

(2) Its polysaccharides and proteins are antigens that are useful in laboratory identification.

(3) Its **porin** proteins play a role in regulating the passage of small, hydrophilic molecules into the cell. Porin proteins in the outer membrane form a trimer

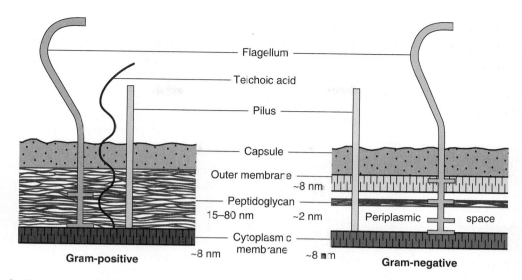

Figure 2–4. Cell walls of gram-positive and gram-negative bacteria. Note that the peptidoglycan in gram-positive bacteria is much thicker than in gram-negative bacteria. Note also that only gram-negative bacteria have an outer membrane containing endotoxin (lipopolysaccharide [LPS]) and have a periplasmic space where β-lactamases are found. Several important gram-positive bacteria, such as staphylococci and streptococci, have teichoic acids. (Reproduced, with permission, from Ingraham JL, Maaløe O, Neidhardt FC: *Growth of the Bacterial Cell.* Sinauer Associates, 1983.)

that acts, usually nonspecifically, as a channel to allow the entry of essential substances such as sugars, amino acids, vitamins, and metals, as well as many antimicrobial drugs such as penicillins.

B. Cell Walls of Acid-Fast Bacteria

Mycobacteria, eg, *Mycobacterium tuberculosis,* have an unusual cell wall, resulting in their inability to be Gram-stained. These bacteria are said to be **acid-fast,** because they resist decolorization with acid-alcohol after being stained with carbolfuchsin. This property is related to the high concentration in the cell wall of lipids called mycolic acids.

Table 2–2. Comparison of cell walls of gram-positive and gram-negative bacteria.

Component	Gram-Positive Cells	Gram-Negative Cells
Peptidoglycan	Thicker; multilayer	Thinner; single layer
Teichoic acids	Yes	No
Lipopolysaccharide (endotoxin)	No	Yes

In view of their importance, three components of the cell wall, ie, peptidoglycan, lipopolysaccharide, and teichoic acid, will be discussed in detail.

C. Peptidoglycan

Peptidoglycan is a complex, interwoven network that surrounds the entire cell and is composed of a single covalently linked macromolecule. It is found *only* in bacterial cell walls. It provides rigid support for the cell, is important in maintaining the characteristic shape of the cell, and allows the cell to withstand media of low osmotic pressure, such as water. A representative segment of the peptidoglycan layer is shown in Figure 2–5. The term "peptidoglycan" is derived from the peptides and the sugars (glycan) that make up the molecule. Synonyms for peptidoglycan are murein and mucopeptide.

Figure 2–5 illustrates the carbohydrate backbone, which is composed of alternating *N*-acetylmuramic acid and *N*-acetylglucosamine molecules. Attached to each of the muramic acid molecules is a tetrapeptide consisting of both D- and L-amino acids, the precise composition of which differs from one bacterium to another. Two of these amino acids are worthy of special mention: diaminopimelic acid, which is unique to bacterial cell walls, and D-alanine, which is involved in the cross-links between the tetrapeptides and in the action

---

GRAM STAIN

This staining procedure, developed in 1884 by the Danish physician Christian Gram, is the most important procedure in microbiology. It separates most bacteria into two groups: the gram-positive bacteria, which stain blue, and the gram-negative bacteria, which stain red. The Gram stain involves the following four-step procedure.

(**1**) The crystal violet dye stains all cells blue/purple.

(**2**) The iodine solution (a mordant) is added to form a crystal violet–iodine complex; all cells continue to appear blue.

(**3**) The organic solvent, such as acetone or ethanol, extracts the blue dye complex from the lipid-rich, thin-walled gram-negative bacteria to a greater degree than from the lipid-poor, thick-walled gram-positive bacteria. The gram-negative organisms appear colorless; the gram-positive bacteria remain blue.

(**4**) The red dye safranin stains the decolorized gram-negative cells red/pink; the gram-positive bacteria remain blue.

Note that if step #2 is omitted and Gram's iodine is not added, gram-negative bacteria stain *blue* rather than pink, presumably because the organic solvent removes the crystal violet–iodine complex but not the crystal violet alone. Gram-positive bacteria also stain *blue* when Gram's iodine is not added.

The Gram stain is useful in two ways:

(**1**) In the identification of many bacteria

(**2**) In influencing the choice of antibiotic, because, in general, gram-positive bacteria are more susceptible to penicillin G than are gram-negative bacteria.

However, not all bacteria can be seen in the Gram stain. Table 2–3 lists the medically important bacteria that cannot be seen and describes the reason why. The alternative microscopic approach to the Gram stain is also described.

---

of penicillin. Note that this tetrapeptide contains the rare D-isomers of amino acids; most proteins contain the L-isomer. The other important component in this network is the peptide cross-link between the two tetrapeptides. The cross-links vary among species; in *Staphylococcus aureus,* for example, five glycines link the terminal D-alanine to the penultimate L-lysine.

Because peptidoglycan is present in bacteria but not in human cells, it is a good target for antibacterial drugs. Several of these drugs, such as penicillins, cephalosporins, and vancomycin, inhibit the synthesis

of peptidoglycan by inhibiting the transpeptidase that makes the cross-links between the two adjacent tetrapeptides (see Chapter 10).

The enzyme **lysozyme,** which is present in human tears, mucus, and saliva, can cleave the peptidoglycan backbone by breaking its glycosyl bonds, thereby contributing to the natural resistance of the host to microbial infection. Lysozyme-treated bacteria may swell and rupture as a result of the entry of water into the cells, which have a high internal osmotic pressure. However, if the lysozyme-treated cells are in a solution with the

Table 2–3. Medically important bacteria that cannot be seen in the Gram stain.

Name	Reason	Alternative Microscopic Approach
Mycobacteria, including *M. tuberculosis*	Too much lipid in cell wall so dye cannot penetrate	Acid-fast stain
Treponema pallidum	Too thin to see	Dark-field microscopy or fluorescent antibody
Mycoplasma pneumoniae	No cell wall; very small	None
Legionella pneumoniae	Poor uptake of red counterstain	Prolong time of counterstain
Chlamydiae, including *C. trachomatis*	Intracellular; very small	Inclusion bodies in cytoplasm
Rickettsiae	Intracellular; very small	Giemsa or other tissue stains

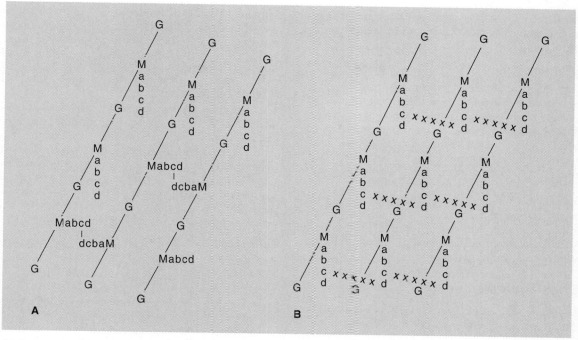

Figure 2–5. Peptidoglycan structure: *Escherichia coli* (**A**) has a different cross-link from that of *Staphylococcus aureus* (**B**). In *E. coli*, c is cross-linked directly to d, whereas in *S. aureus*, c and d are cross-linked by five glycines. However, in both organisms the terminal D-alanine is part of the linkage. M, muramic acid; G, glucosamine; a, L-alanine; b, D-glutamic acid; c, diaminopimelic acid (**A**) or L-lysine (**B**); d, D-alanine; x, pentaglycine bridge. (Modified and reproduced, with permission, from Joklik WK et al: *Zinsser Microbiology.* 20th ed. Originally published by Appleton & Lange. Copyright © 1992 by The McGraw-Hill Companies, Inc.)

same osmotic pressure as that of the bacterial interior, they will survive as spherical forms, called protoplasts, surrounded only by a cytoplasmic membrane.

D. Lipopolysaccharide (LPS)

The LPS of the outer membrane of the cell wall of gram-negative bacteria is **endotoxin**. It is responsible for many of the features of disease, such as fever and shock (especially hypotension), caused by these organisms. It is called endotoxin because it is an integral part of the cell wall, in contrast to exotoxins, which are freely released from the bacteria. The pathologic effects of endotoxin are similar irrespective of the organism from which it is derived.

The LPS is composed of three distinct units (Figure 2–6):

(1) A phospholipid called lipid A, which is responsible for the toxic effects

(2) A core polysaccharide of five sugars linked through ketodeoxyoctulonate (KDO) to lipid A

(3) An outer polysaccharide consisting of up to 25 repeating units of three to five sugars. This outer poly-

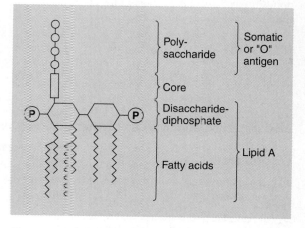

Figure 2–6. Endotoxin (LPS) structure. The O antigen polysaccharide is exposed on the exterior of the cell, whereas the lipid A faces the interior. (Modified and reproduced with permission, from Brooks GF et al: *Medical Microbiology,* 19th ed. Originally published by Appleton & Lange. Copyright © 1991 by The McGraw-Hill Companies, Inc.)

mer is the important somatic, or O, antigen of several gram-negative bacteria that is used to identify certain organisms in the clinical laboratory.

E. TEICHOIC ACID

These fibers of glycerol phosphate or ribitol phosphate are located in the outer layer of the gram-positive cell wall and extend from it. Some polymers of glycerol teichoic acid penetrate the peptidoglycan layer and are covalently linked to the lipid in the cytoplasmic membrane, in which case they are called **lipoteichoic acid;** others anchor to the muramic acid of the peptidoglycan.

The medical importance of teichoic acids lies in their ability to induce septic shock when caused by certain gram-positive bacteria; ie, they activate the same pathways as does endotoxin (LPS) in gram-negative bacteria. Teichoic acids also mediate the attachment of staphylococci to mucosal cells.

Cytoplasmic Membrane

Just inside the peptidoglycan layer of the cell wall lies the cytoplasmic membrane, which is composed of a phospholipid bilayer similar in microscopic appearance to that in eukaryotic cells. They are chemically similar, but eukaryotic membranes contain sterols, whereas prokaryotes generally do not. The only prokaryotes that have sterols in their membranes are members of the genus *Mycoplasma*. The membrane has four important functions: (1) active transport of molecules into the cell, (2) energy generation by oxidative phosphorylation, (3) synthesis of precursors of the cell wall, and (4) secretion of enzymes and toxins.

Mesosome

This invagination of the cytoplasmic membrane is important during cell division, when it functions as the origin of the transverse septum that divides the cell in half and as the binding site of the DNA that will become the genetic material of each daughter cell.

Cytoplasm

The cytoplasm has two distinct areas when seen in the electron microscope:

(1) An amorphous matrix that contains ribosomes, nutrient granules, metabolites, and plasmids

(2) An inner, nucleoid region composed of DNA.

A. RIBOSOMES

Bacterial ribosomes are the site of protein synthesis as in eukaryotic cells, but they differ from eukaryotic ribosomes in size and chemical composition. Bacterial ribosomes are 70S in size, with 50S and 30S subunits, whereas eukaryotic ribosomes are 80S in size, with 60S and 40S subunits. The differences in both the ribosomal RNAs and proteins constitute the basis of the selective action of several antibiotics that inhibit bacterial, but not human, protein synthesis (see Chapter 10).

B. GRANULES

The cytoplasm contains several different types of granules that serve as storage areas for nutrients and stain characteristically with certain dyes. For example, volutin is a reserve of high energy stored in the form of polymerized metaphosphate. It appears as a "metachromatic" granule, since it stains red with methylene blue dye instead of blue, as one would expect. Metachromatic granules are a characteristic feature of *Corynebacterium diphtheriae,* the cause of diphtheria.

C. NUCLEOID

The nucleoid is the area of the cytoplasm in which DNA is located. The DNA of prokaryotes is a single, circular molecule that has a molecular weight (MW) of approximately 2×10^9 and contains about 2000 genes. (By contrast, human DNA has approximately 100,000 genes.) Because the nucleoid contains no nuclear membrane, no nucleolus, no mitotic spindle, and no histones, there is little resemblance to the eukaryotic nucleus. One major difference between bacterial DNA and eukaryotic DNA is that bacterial DNA has no introns whereas eukaryotic DNA does.

D. PLASMIDS

Plasmids are extrachromosomal, double-stranded, circular DNA molecules that are capable of replicating independently of the bacterial chromosome. Although plasmids are usually extrachromosomal, they can be integrated into the bacterial chromosome. Plasmids occur in both gram-positive and gram-negative bacteria, and several different types of plasmids can exist in one cell.

(1) **Transmissible** plasmids can be transferred from cell to cell by conjugation (see Chapter 4 for a discussion of conjugation). They are large (MW 40–100 million), since they contain about a dozen genes responsible for synthesis of the sex pilus and for the enzymes required for transfer. They are usually present in a few (one to three) copies per cell.

(2) **Nontransmissible** plasmids are small (MW 3–20 million), since they do not contain the transfer genes; they are frequently present in many (10–60) copies per cell.

Plasmids carry the genes for the following functions and structures of medical importance:

(1) Antibiotic resistance, which is mediated by a variety of enzymes

(2) Resistance to heavy metals such as mercury (the active component of some antiseptics, such as Merthiolate and Mercurochrome) and silver, which is mediated by a reductase enzyme

(3) Resistance to ultraviolet light, which is mediated by DNA repair enzymes

(4) Pili (fimbriae), which mediate the adherence of bacteria to epithelial cells

(5) Exotoxins, including several enterotoxins.

Other plasmid-encoded products of interest are:

(1) Bacteriocins, which are toxins or enzymes that are produced by certain bacteria and are lethal for other bacteria

(2) Nitrogen fixation enzymes in *Rhizobium* in the root nodules of legumes

(3) Tumors caused by *Agrobacterium* in plants

(4) Several antibiotics produced by *Streptomyces*

(5) A variety of degradative enzymes that are produced by *Pseudomonas* and are capable of cleaning up environmental hazards such as oil spills and toxic chemical-waste sites.

E. TRANSPOSONS

Transposons are pieces of DNA that move readily from one site to another, either within or between the DNAs of bacteria, plasmids, and bacteriophages. In view of their unusual ability to move, they are nicknamed jumping genes. They can code for drug resistance enzymes, toxins, or a variety of metabolic enzymes, and they can either cause mutations in the gene into which they insert or alter the expression of nearby genes.

Transposons typically have four identifiable domains. On each end is a short DNA sequence of **inverted repeats,** which are involved in the integration of the transposon into the recipient DNA. The second domain is the gene for the transposase, which is the enzyme that mediates the excision and integration processes. The third region is the gene for the repressor that regulates the synthesis both of the transposase and of the gene product of the fourth domain, which, in many cases, is an enzyme mediating antibiotic resistance (Figure 2–7).

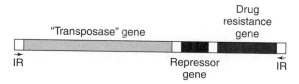

Figure 2–7. Transposon genes. This transposon is carrying a drug resistance gene. IR, inverted repeat.
(Modified and reproduced, with permission, from Fincham JR: *Genetics.* Jones and Bartlett, 1983.)

In contrast to plasmids or bacterial viruses, transposons are not capable of independent replication; they replicate as part of the recipient DNA. More than one transposon can be located in the DNA; for example, a plasmid can contain several transposons carrying drug resistance genes. **Insertion sequences** are a type of transposon that has fewer bases (800–1500 base pairs), since they do not code for their own integration enzymes. They can cause mutations at their site of integration and can be found in multiple copies at the ends of larger transposon units.

Specialized Structures Outside the Cell Wall

A. CAPSULE

The capsule is a gelatinous layer covering the entire bacterium. It is composed of polysaccharide, except in the anthrax bacillus, which has a capsule of polymerized D-glutamic acid. The sugar components of the polysaccharide vary from one species of bacteria to another and frequently determine the serologic type within a species. For example, there are 84 different serologic types of *Streptococcus pneumoniae*, which are distinguished by the antigenic differences of the sugars in the polysaccharide capsule.

The capsule is important for four reasons:

(1) It is a determinant of virulence of many bacteria, since it limits the ability of phagocytes to engulf the bacteria. Variants of encapsulated bacteria that have lost the ability to produce a capsule are usually nonpathogenic.

(2) Specific identification of an organism can be made by using antiserum against the capsular polysaccharide. In the presence of the homologous antibody, the capsule will swell greatly. This swelling phenomenon, which is used in the clinical laboratory to identify certain organisms, is called the **quellung reaction.**

(3) Capsular polysaccharides are used as the antigens in certain vaccines, for they are capable of eliciting protective antibodies. For example, the purified capsular polysaccharides of 23 types of *S. pneumoniae* are present in the current vaccine.

(4) The capsule may play a role in the adherence of bacteria to human tissues, which is an important initial step in causing infection.

B. FLAGELLA

Flagella are long, whiplike appendages that move the bacteria toward nutrients and other attractants, a process called **chemotaxis.** The long filament, which acts as a propeller, is composed of many subunits of a single protein, flagellin, arranged in several intertwined chains. The energy for movement, the **proton motive**

force, is provided by adenosine triphosphate (ATP), derived from the passage of ions across the membrane.

Flagellated bacteria have a characteristic number and location of flagella: some bacteria have one, and others have many; in some the flagella are located at one end, and in others they are all over the outer surface. Only certain bacteria have flagella; many rods do, but most cocci do not and are therefore nonmotile. Spirochetes move by using a flagellumlike structure called the **axial filament,** which wraps around the spiral-shaped cell to produce an undulating motion.

Flagella are medically important for two reasons:

(1) Some species of motile bacteria, eg, *Escherichia coli* and *Proteus* species, are common causes of urinary tract infections. Flagella may play a role in pathogenesis by propelling the bacteria up the urethra into the bladder.

(2) Some species of bacteria, eg, *Salmonella* species, are identified in the clinical laboratory by the use of specific antibodies against flagellar proteins.

C. PILI (FIMBRIAE)

Pili are hairlike filaments that extend from the cell surface. They are shorter and straighter than flagella and are composed of subunits of a protein, pilin, arranged in helical strands. They are found mainly on gram-negative organisms.

Pili have two important roles:

(1) They mediate the **attachment** of bacteria to specific receptors on the human cell surface, which is a necessary step in the initiation of infection for some organisms. Mutants of *Neisseria gonorrhoeae* that do not form pili are nonpathogens.

(2) A specialized kind of pilus, the sex pilus, forms the attachment between the male (donor) and the female (recipient) bacteria during conjugation (see Chapter 4).

D. GLYCOCALYX (SLIME LAYER)

The glycocalyx is a polysaccharide coating that is secreted by many bacteria. It covers surfaces like a film and allows the bacteria to **adhere firmly** to various structures, eg, skin, heart valves, and catheters. It also mediates adherence of certain bacteria, such as *Streptococcus mutans,* to the surface of teeth. This plays an important role in the formation of plaque, the precursor of dental caries.

Spores

These highly resistant structures are formed in response to adverse conditions by two genera of medically important gram-positive rods: the genus *Bacillus,* which includes the agent of anthrax, and the genus *Clostridium,* which includes the agents of tetanus and botulism. Spore formation (sporulation) occurs when nutrients, such as sources of carbon and nitrogen, are depleted (Figure 2–8). The spore forms inside the cell and contains bacterial DNA, a small amount of cytoplasm, cell membrane, peptidoglycan, very little water, and most importantly, a thick, keratinlike coat that is responsible for the remarkable resistance of the spore to heat, dehydration, radiation, and chemicals. This resistance may be mediated by **dipicolinic acid,** a calcium ion chelator found only in spores.

Once formed, the spore has no metabolic activity and can remain dormant for many years. Upon exposure to water and the appropriate nutrients, specific enzymes degrade the coat; water and nutrients enter; and germination into a potentially pathogenic bacterial cell occurs. Note that this differentiation process is *not* a means of reproduction, since one cell produces one spore that germinates into one cell.

The medical importance of spores lies in their **extraordinary resistance to heat** and chemicals. As a result of their resistance to heat, sterilization cannot be achieved by boiling. Steam-heating under pressure (autoclaving) at 121°C, usually for 30 minutes, is required to ensure the sterility of products for medical use. Spores are often not seen in clinical specimens recovered from patients infected by spore-forming organisms because the supply of nutrients is adequate.

Table 2–4 describes the medically important features of bacterial spores.

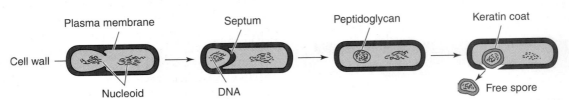

Figure 2–8. Bacterial spores. The spore contains the entire DNA genome of the bacterium surrounded by a thick, resistant coat. (Modified and reproduced, with permission, from Tortora G, Funk B, Case C: *Microbiology: An Introduction,* 5th ed. Benjamin/Cummings, 1995.)

Table 2–4. Important features of spores and their medical implications.

Important Features of Spores	Medical Implications
Highly resistant to heating; Spores are not killed by boiling (100°C) but are killed at 121°C.	Medical supplies must be heated to 121°C for at least 15 minutes to be sterilized.
Highly resistant to many chemicals, including most disinfectants. This is attributed to the thick keratinlike coat of the spore.	Only solutions designated as sporicidal will kill spores.
They can survive for many years, especially in the soil.	Wounds contaminated with soil can be infected with spores and cause diseases such as tetanus (C. tetani) and gas gangrene (C. perfringens).
They exhibit no measurable metabolic activity.	Antibiotics are ineffective against spores because antibiotics act by inhibiting certain metabolic pathways of bacteria. Also, spore coat is impermeable to antibiotics.
Spores form when nutrients are insufficient but then germinate to form bacteria when nutrients become available.	Spores are not often found at the site of infections because nutrients are not limiting. Bacteria rather than spores are usually seen in Gram-stained smears.
Spores are produced by members of only two genera of bacteria of medical importance, Bacillus and Clostridium, both of which are gram-positive rods.	Infections transmitted by spores are caused by species of either Bacillus or Clostridium.

PEARLS

Shape & Size

- Bacteria have three shapes: **cocci** (spheres), **bacilli** (rods), and **spirochetes** (spirals).
- Cocci are arranged in three patterns: pairs (diplococci), chains (streptococci), and clusters (staphylococci).
- The size of most bacteria ranges from 1 μm to 3 μm. **Mycoplasma,** the smallest bacteria (and therefore the **smallest cells**) are 0.2 μm. Some bacteria, such as Borrelia, are as long as 10 μm, ie, they are longer than a human red blood cell, which is 7 μm in diameter.

Bacterial Cell Wall

- All bacteria have a cell wall composed of **peptidoglycan** except Mycoplasma, which are surrounded only by a cell membrane.
- Gram-negative bacteria have a thin peptidoglycan covered by an outer lipid-containing membrane, whereas gram-positive bacteria have a thick peptidoglycan and no outer membrane. These differences explain why gram-negative bacteria lose the stain when exposed to a lipid solvent in the Gram stain process, whereas gram-positive bacteria retain the stain and remain purple.
- The outer membrane of gram-negative bacteria contains **endotoxin (lipopolysaccharide, LPS),** the main inducer of septic shock. Endotoxin consists of **lipid A,** which induces the fever and hypotension seen in septic shock, and a polysaccharide (**O antigen**), which is useful in laboratory identification.
- Between the peptidoglycan layer and the outer membrane of gram-negative bacteria lies the **periplasmic space,** which is the location of β**-lactamases,** the enzymes that degrade β-lactam antibiotics, such as penicillins and cephalosporins.
- Peptidoglycan is found only in bacterial cells. It is a network that covers the entire bacterium and gives the organism its shape. It is composed of a sugar backbone (**glycan**) and peptide side chains (**peptido.** The side chains are cross-linked by **transpeptidase,** the enzyme that is inhibited by penicillins and cephalosporins.

- The cell wall of mycobacteria, eg, Mycobacterium tuberculosis, has **more lipid** than either the gram-positive or gram-negative bacteria. As a result, the dyes used in the Gram stain do not penetrate into (do not stain) mycobacteria. The **acid-fast stain** does stain mycobacteria, and these bacteria are often called acid-fast bacilli (acid-fast rods).
- **Lysozymes** kill bacteria by cleaving the glycan backbone of peptidoglycan.
- The cytoplasmic membrane of bacteria consists of a phospholipid bilayer (without sterols) located just inside the peptidoglycan. It regulates active transport of nutrients into the cell and the secretion of toxins out of the cell.

Gram Stain

- **Gram stain** is the most important staining procedure. Gram-positive bacteria stain purple, whereas gram-negative bacteria stain pink. This difference is based on the ability of gram-positive bacteria to retain the crystal violet–iodine complex in the presence of a lipid solvent, *usually acetone-alcohol*. Gram-negative bacteria, because they have an outer lipid-containing membrane and thin peptidoglycan, lose the purple dye when treated with acetone-alcohol. They become colorless and then stain pink when exposed to a red dye such as safranin.
- Not all bacteria can be visualized using Gram stain. Some important human pathogens, such as the bacteria that cause tuberculosis and syphilis, cannot be seen using this stain.

Bacterial DNA

- The bacterial genome consists of a **single chromosome of circular DNA** located in the nucleoid.
- **Plasmids** are extrachromosomal pieces of circular DNA that encode both exotoxins and many enzymes that cause antibiotic resistance.

- **Transposons** are small pieces of DNA that move frequently between chromosomal DNA and plasmid DNA. They carry antibiotic-resistance genes.

Structures External to the Cell Wall

- **Capsules** are **antiphagocytic,** ie, they limit the ability of neutrophils to engulf the bacteria. Almost all capsules are composed of polysaccharide; the polypeptide capsule of anthrax bacillus is the only exception. Capsules are also the antigens in several vaccines, such as the pneumococcal vaccine. Antibodies against the capsule neutralize the antiphagocytic effect and allow the bacteria to be engulfed by neutrophils. **Opsonization** is the process by which antibodies enhance the phagocytosis of bacteria.
- **Pili** are filaments of protein that extend from the bacterial surface and mediate **attachment** of bacteria to the surface of human cells. A different kind of pilus, the sex pilus, functions in conjugation (see Chapter 4).
- The **glycocalyx** is a polysaccharide "slime layer" secreted by certain bacteria. It **attaches bacteria firmly** to the surface of human cells and to the surface of catheters, prosthetic heart valves, and prosthetic hip joints.

Bacterial Spores

- **Spores** are medically important because they are **highly heat resistant** and are not killed by many disinfectants. Boiling will not kill spores. They are formed by certain gram-positive rods, especially Bacillus and Clostridium species.
- Spores have a thick, keratin-like coat that allows them to survive for many years, especially in the soil. Spores are formed when nutrients are in short supply, but when nutrients are restored, spores germinate to form bacteria that can cause disease. Spores are metabolically inactive but contain DNA, ribosomes, and other essential components.

PRACTICE QUESTIONS: USMLE & COURSE EXAMINATIONS

Questions on the topics discussed in this chapter can be found in the Basic Bacteriology section of Part XI:

USMLE (National Board) Practice Questions starting on page 532. Also see Part XII: USMLE (National Board) Practice Examination starting on page 583.

Growth

GROWTH CYCLE

Bacteria reproduce by **binary fission**, a process by which one parent cell divides to form two progeny cells. Because one cell gives rise to two progeny cells, bacteria are said to undergo exponential growth (logarithmic growth). The concept of exponential growth can be illustrated by the following relationship:

$$\text{Number of cells} \quad 1 \quad 2 \quad 4 \quad 8 \quad 16$$
$$\text{Exponential} \quad 2^0 \quad 2^1 \quad 2^2 \quad 2^3 \quad 2^4$$

Thus, one bacterium will produce 16 bacteria after four generations.

The doubling (generation) time of bacteria ranges from as little as 20 minutes for *Escherichia coli* to more than 24 hours for *Mycobacterium tuberculosis*. The exponential growth and the short doubling time of some organisms result in rapid production of very large numbers of bacteria. For example, one *E. coli* organism will produce over 1000 progeny in about 3 hours and over 1 million in about 7 hours. The doubling time varies not only with the species but also with the amount of nutrients, the temperature, the pH, and other environmental factors.

The growth cycle of bacteria has four major phases. If a small number of bacteria are inoculated into a liquid nutrient medium and the bacteria are counted at frequent intervals, the typical phases of a standard growth curve can be demonstrated (Figure 3–1).

(1) The first is the **lag** phase, during which vigorous metabolic activity occurs but cells do not divide. This can last for a few minutes up to many hours.

(2) The **log** (logarithmic) phase is when rapid cell division occurs. β-Lactam drugs, such as penicillin, act during this phase because the drugs are effective when cells are making peptidoglycan, ie, when they are dividing.

(3) The **stationary** phase occurs when nutrient depletion or toxic products cause growth to slow until the number of new cells produced balances the number of cells that die, resulting in a steady state. Cells grown in a special apparatus called a "chemostat," into which fresh nutrients are added and from which waste prod-

ucts are removed continuously, can remain in the log phase and do not enter the stationary phase.

(4) The final phase is the **death** phase, which is marked by a decline in the number of viable bacteria.

AEROBIC & ANAEROBIC GROWTH

For most organisms, an adequate supply of oxygen enhances metabolism and growth. The oxygen acts as the hydrogen acceptor in the final steps of energy production catalyzed by the flavoproteins and cytochromes. Because the use of oxygen generates two toxic molecules, hydrogen peroxide (H_2O_2) and the free radical superoxide (O_2), bacteria require two enzymes to utilize oxygen. The first is **superoxide dismutase**, which catalyzes the reaction

$$2O_2^- + 2H^+ \rightarrow H_2O_2 + O_2$$

and the second is **catalase**, which catalyzes the reaction

$$2H_2O_2 \rightarrow 2H_2O + O_2$$

The response to oxygen is an important criterion for classifying bacteria and has great practical significance because specimens from patients must be incubated in the proper atmosphere for the bacteria to grow.

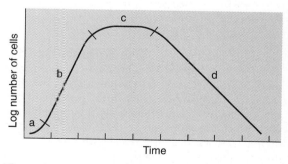

Figure 3–1. Growth curve of bacteria. a, lag phase; b, log phase; c, stationary phase; d, death phase. (Reproduced, with permission, from Joklik WK et al: *Zinsser Microbiology*, 20th ed. Originally published by Appleton & Lange. Copyright © 1992 by The McGraw-Hill Companies, Inc.)

(1) Some bacteria, such as *M. tuberculosis,* are **obligate aerobes;** ie, they require oxygen to grow because their ATP-generating system is dependent on oxygen as the hydrogen acceptor.

(2) Other bacteria, such as *E. coli,* are **facultative anaerobes (facultatives)**; they utilize oxygen to generate energy by respiration if it is present, but they can use the fermentation pathway to synthesize ATP in the absence of sufficient oxygen.

(3) The third group of bacteria consists of the **obligate anaerobes,** such as *Clostridium tetani,* which cannot grow in the presence of oxygen because they lack either superoxide dismutase or catalase, or both. Obligate anaerobes vary in their response to oxygen exposure; some can survive but are not able to grow, whereas others are killed rapidly.

FERMENTATION OF SUGARS

In the clinical laboratory, identification of several important human pathogens is based on the fermentation of certain sugars. For example, *Neisseria gonorrhoeae* and *Neisseria meningitidis* can be distinguished from each other on the basis of fermentation of either glucose or maltose (see page 116), and *Escherichia coli* can be differentiated from *Salmonella* and *Shigella* on the basis of fermentation of lactose (see page 129).

The term "fermentation" refers to the breakdown of a sugar (such as glucose or maltose) to pyruvic acid and then, usually, to lactic acid. (More specifically, it is the breakdown of a monosaccharide such as glucose, maltose, or galactose. Note that lactose is a disaccharide composed of glucose and galactose and therefore must be cleaved by β-galactosidase in *E. coli* before fermentation can occur.) Fermentation is also called the glycolytic (glyco = sugar, lytic = break down) cycle, and this is the process by which facultative bacteria generate ATP in the absence of oxygen.

If oxygen is present, the pyruvate produced by fermentation enters the Krebs cycle (oxidation cycle, tricarboxylic acid cycle) and is metabolized to two final products, CO_2 and H_2O. The Krebs cycle generates much more ATP than the glycolytic cycle; therefore, facultative bacteria grow faster in the presence of oxygen. Facultative and anaerobic bacteria ferment but aerobes, which can grow only in the presence of oxygen, do not. Aerobes, such as *Pseudomonas aeruginosa,* produce metabolites that enter the Krebs cycle by processes other than fermentation, such as the deamination of amino acids.

In fermentation tests performed in the clinical laboratory, the production of pyruvate and lactate turns the medium acid, which can be detected by a pH indicator that changes color upon changes in pH. For example, if a sugar is fermented in the presence of the indicator phenol red, the pH becomes acid and the medium turns yellow. If, however, the sugar is not fermented, no acid is produced and the phenol red remains red.

PEARLS

- *Bacteria reproduce by **binary fission,** whereas eukaryotic cells reproduce by mitosis.*

- *The bacterial growth cycle consists of four phases: the **lag** phase, during which nutrients are incorporated; the **log** phase, during which rapid cell division occurs; the **stationary** phase, during which as many cells are dying as are being formed; and the **death** phase, during which most of the cells are dying because nutrients have been exhausted.*

- *Some bacteria can grow in the presence of oxygen (aerobes and facultatives), but others die in the presence of oxygen (**anaerobes**). The use of oxygen by bacteria generates toxic products such as **superoxide** and **hydrogen peroxide.** Aerobes and facultatives have enzymes, such as **superoxide dismutase** and **catalase,** that detoxify these products, but anaerobes do not and are killed in the presence of oxygen.*

- *The fermentation of certain sugars is the basis of the laboratory identification of some important pathogens. Fermentation of sugars, such as glucose, results in the production of ATP and pyruvic acid or lactic acid. These acids lower the pH, and this can be detected by the change in color of indicator dyes.*

PRACTICE QUESTIONS: USMLE & COURSE EXAMINATIONS

Questions on the topics discussed in this chapter can be found in the Basic Bacteriology section of Part XI: USMLE (National Board) Practice Questions starting on page 532. Also see Part XII: USMLE (National Board) Practice Examination starting on page 583.

Genetics

The genetic material of a typical bacterium, *Escherichia coli*, consists of a single circular DNA molecule with a molecular weight of about 2×10^9 and composed of approximately 5×10^6 base pairs. This amount of genetic information can code for about 2000 proteins with an average molecular weight of 50,000. The DNA of the smallest free-living organism, the wall-less bacterium *Mycoplasma*, has a molecular weight of 5×10^8. The DNA of human cells contains about 3×10^9 base pairs and encodes about 100,000 proteins.

Note that bacteria are **haploid**; in other words, they have a single chromosome and therefore a single copy of each gene. Eukaryotic cells (such as human cells) are **diploid**, which means they have a pair of each chromosome and therefore have two copies of each gene. In diploid cells, one copy of a gene (allele) may be expressed as a protein, ie, be dominant, while another allele may not be expressed, ie, be recessive. In haploid cells, any gene that has mutated—and therefore is not expressed—results in a cell that has lost that trait.

MUTATIONS

A mutation is a change in the base sequence of DNA that usually results in insertion of a different amino acid into a protein and the appearance of an altered phenotype. Mutations result from three types of molecular changes:

(1) The first type is the **base substitution**. This occurs when one base is inserted in place of another. It takes place at the time of DNA replication, either because the DNA polymerase makes an error or because a mutagen alters the hydrogen bonding of the base being used as a template in such a manner that the wrong base is inserted. When the base substitution results in a codon that simply causes a different amino acid to be inserted, the mutation is called a **missense mutation**; when the base substitution generates a termination codon that stops protein synthesis prematurely, the mutation is called a **nonsense mutation**. Nonsense mutations almost always destroy protein function.

(2) The second type of mutation is the **frameshift mutation**. This occurs when one or more base pairs are added or deleted, which shifts the reading frame on the ribosome and results in incorporation of the wrong amino acids "downstream" from the mutation and in the production of an inactive protein.

(3) The third type of mutation occurs when **transposons** or **insertion sequences** are integrated into the DNA. These newly inserted pieces of DNA can cause profound changes in the genes into which they insert and in adjacent genes.

Mutations can be caused by chemicals, radiation, or viruses. Chemicals act in several different ways.

(1) Some, such as nitrous acid and alkylating agents, alter the existing base so that it forms a hydrogen bond preferentially with the wrong base; for example, adenine would no longer pair with thymine but with cytosine.

(2) Some chemicals, such as 5-bromouracil, are base analogues, since they resemble normal bases. Because the bromine atom has an atomic radius similar to that of a methyl group, 5-bromouracil can be inserted in place of thymine (5-methyluracil). However, 5-bromouracil has less hydrogen-bonding fidelity than does thymine, and so it binds to guanine with greater frequency. This results in a transition from an A-T base pair to a G-C base pair, thereby producing a mutation. The antiviral drug iododeoxyuridine acts as a base analogue of thymidine.

(3) Some chemicals, such as benzpyrene, which is found in tobacco smoke, bind to the existing DNA bases and cause frameshift mutations. These chemicals, which are frequently carcinogens as well as mutagens, intercalate between the adjacent bases, thereby distorting and offsetting the DNA sequence.

X-rays and ultraviolet light can cause mutations also.

(1) X-rays have high energy and can damage DNA in three ways: (a) by breaking the covalent bonds that hold the ribose phosphate chain together, (b) by producing free radicals that can attack the bases, and (c) by altering the electrons in the bases and thus changing their hydrogen bonding.

(2) Ultraviolet radiation, which has lower energy than x-rays, causes the cross-linking of the adjacent

pyrimidine bases to form dimers. This cross-linking, for example, of adjacent thymines to form a thymine dimer, results in inability of the DNA to replicate properly.

Certain viruses, such as the bacterial virus Mu (mutator bacteriophage), cause a high frequency of mutations when their DNA is inserted into the bacterial chromosome. Since the viral DNA can insert into many different sites, mutations in various genes can occur. These mutations are either frameshift mutations or deletions.

Conditional-lethal mutations are of medical interest because they may be useful in vaccines, eg, influenza vaccine. The word "conditional" indicates that the mutation is expressed only under certain conditions. The most important conditional-lethal mutations are the temperature-sensitive ones. Temperature-sensitive organisms can replicate at a relatively low, permissive temperature, eg, 32°C, but cannot grow at a higher, restrictive temperature, eg, 37°C. This behavior is due to a mutation that causes an amino acid change in an essential protein, allowing it to function normally at 32°C but not at 37°C because of an altered conformation at the higher temperature. An example of a condi-

tional-lethal mutant of medical importance is a strain of influenza virus currently used in an experimental vaccine. This vaccine contains a virus that cannot grow at 37°C and hence cannot infect the lungs and cause pneumonia, but it can grow at 32°C in the nose, where it can replicate and induce immunity.

TRANSFER OF DNA WITHIN BACTERIAL CELLS

Transposons transfer DNA from one site on the bacterial chromosome to another site or to a plasmid. They do so by synthesizing a copy of their DNA and inserting the copy at another site in the bacterial chromosome or the plasmid. The structure and function of transposons are described in Chapter 2, and their role in antimicrobial drug resistance is described in Chapter 11. The transfer of a transposon to a plasmid and the subsequent transfer of the plasmid to another bacterium by conjugation (see below) contributes significantly to the spread of antibiotic resistance.

Transfer of DNA within bacteria also occurs by **programmed rearrangements** (Figure 4–1). These gene re-

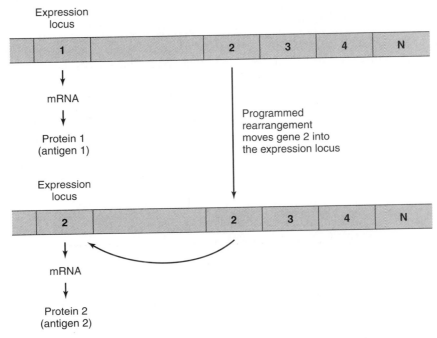

Figure 4–1. Programmed rearrangements. In the top part of the figure, the gene for protein 1 is in the expression locus and the mRNA for protein 1 is synthesized. At a later time, a copy of gene 2 is made and inserted into the expression locus. By moving only the copy of the gene, the cell always keeps the original DNA for use in the future. When the DNA of gene 2 is inserted, the DNA of gene 1 is excised and degraded.

arrangements account for many of the antigenic changes seen in *Neisseria gonorrhoeae* and in *Borrelia recurrentis,* the cause of relapsing fever. (They also occur in trypanosomes, which are discussed in Chapter 52.) A programmed rearrangement consists of the movement of a gene from a silent storage site where the gene is not expressed to an active site where transcription and translation occur. There are many silent genes that encode variants of the antigens, and the insertion of a new gene into the active site in a sequential, repeated programmed manner is the source of the consistent antigenic variation. These movements are not induced by an immune response but have the effect of allowing the organism to evade it.

TRANSFER OF DNA BETWEEN BACTERIAL CELLS

The transfer of genetic information from one cell to another can occur by three methods: conjugation, transduction, and transformation (Table 4–1). From a medical viewpoint, the most important consequence of DNA transfer is that antibiotic resistance genes are spread from one bacterium to another by these processes.

(1) **Conjugation** is the mating of two bacterial cells during which DNA is transferred from the donor to the recipient cell (Figure 4–2). The mating process is controlled by an F (**fertility**) **plasmid** (F factor), which carries the genes for the proteins required for conjugation. One of the most important proteins is pilin, which forms the **sex pilus** (conjugation tube). Mating begins when the pilus of the donor male bacterium carrying the F factor (F⁺) attaches to a receptor on the surface of the recipient female bacterium, which does not contain an F factor (F⁻). The cells are then drawn into direct contact by "reeling in" the pilus. After an enzymatic cleavage of the F factor DNA, one strand is transferred across the conjugal bridge into the recipient cell. The process is completed by synthesis of the complementary strand to form a double-stranded F factor plasmid in both the donor and recipient cells. The recipient is now an F⁺ male cell that is capable of transmitting the plasmid further. Note that in this instance only the F factor, and not the bacterial chromosome, has been transferred.

Some F⁺ cells have their F plasmid integrated into the bacterial DNA and thereby acquire the capability of transferring the chromosome into another cell. These cells are called **Hfr (high-frequency recombination)** cells (Figure 4–3). During this transfer, the single strand of DNA that enters the recipient F⁻ cell contains a piece of the F factor at the leading end followed by the bacterial chromosome and then by the remainder of the F factor. The time required for complete transfer of the bacterial DNA is approximately 100 minutes. Most matings result in the transfer of only a portion of the donor chromosome, because the attachment between the two cells can break. The donor cell genes that are transferred vary, since the F plasmid can integrate at several different sites in the bacterial DNA. The bacterial genes adjacent to the leading piece of the F factor are the first and therefore the most frequently transferred. The newly acquired DNA can recombine into the recipient's DNA and become a stable component of its genetic material.

(2) **Transduction** is the transfer of cell DNA by means of a bacterial virus (**bacteriophage, phage**) (Figure 4–4). During the growth of the virus within the cell, a piece of bacterial DNA is incorporated into the virus particle and is carried into the recipient cell at the time of infection. Within the recipient cell, the phage DNA can integrate into the cell DNA and the cell can acquire a new trait, a process called **lysogenic conversion** (see the end of Chapter 29). This process can change a nonpathogenic organism into a pathogenic one. Diphtheria toxin, botulinum toxin, cholera toxin, and erythrogenic

Table 4–1. Comparison of conjugation, transduction, and transformation.

Transfer Procedure	Process	Type of Cells Involved	Nature of DNA Transferred
Conjugation	DNA transferred from one bacterium to another	Prokaryotic	Chromosomal or plasmid
Transduction	DNA transferred by a virus from one cell to another	Prokaryotic	Any gene in generalized transduction; only certain genes in specialized transduction
Transformation	Purified DNA taken up by a cell	Prokaryotic or eukaryotic (eg, human)	Any DNA

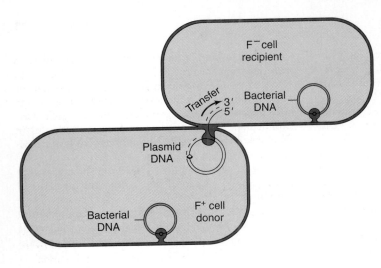

Figure 4–2. Conjugation. An F plasmid is being transferred from an F+ donor bacterium to an F- recipient. The transfer is at the contact site made by the sex pilus. The new plasmid in the recipient bacterium is composed of one parental strand (solid line) and one newly synthesized strand (dashed line). The previously existing plasmid in the donor bacterium now consists of one parental strand (solid line) and one newly synthesized strand (dashed line). Both plasmids are drawn with only a short region of newly synthesized DNA (dashed lines), but at the end of DNA synthesis, both the donor and the recipient contain a complete copy of the plasmid DNA. (Modified and reproduced, with permission, from Stanier RY, Doudoroff M, Adelberg EA: *The Microbial World,* 3rd ed. Copyright © 1970. With permission of Prentice-Hall, Inc., Englewood Cliffs, NJ.)

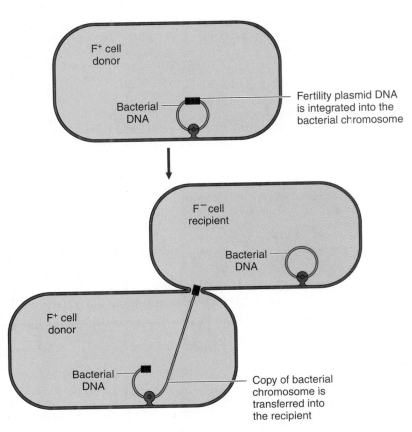

Figure 4–3. High-frequency recombination. In the top part of the figure, a fertility (F) plasmid has integrated into the bacterial chromosome. In the bottom part, the F plasmid mediates the transfer of the bacterial chromosome of the donor into the recipient bacteria.

toxin (*Streptococcus pyogenes*) are encoded by bacteriophages and can be transferred by transduction.

There are two types of transduction, generalized and specialized. The **generalized** type occurs when the virus carries a segment from any part of the bacterial chromosome. This occurs because the cell DNA is fragmented after phage infection and pieces of cell DNA the same size as the viral DNA are incorporated into the virus particle at a frequency of about 1 in every 1000 virus particles. The **specialized** type occurs when the bacterial virus DNA that has integrated into the cell DNA is excised and carries with it an adjacent part of the cell DNA. Since most lysogenic (temperate) phages integrate at specific sites in the bacterial DNA, the adjacent cellular genes that are transduced are usually specific to that virus.

(3) **Transformation** is the transfer of DNA itself from one cell to another. This occurs by either of the two following methods. In nature, dying bacteria may release their DNA, which may be taken up by recipient cells. There is little evidence that this natural process plays a significant role in disease. In the laboratory, an investigator may extract DNA from one type of bacteria and introduce it into genetically different bacteria. When purified DNA is injected into the nucleus of a eukaryotic cell, the process is called **transfection**. Transfection is frequently used in genetic engineering procedures.

The experimental use of transformation has revealed important information about DNA. In 1944, it was shown that DNA extracted from encapsulated smooth pneumococci could transform nonencapsulated rough pneumococci into encapsulated smooth organisms. This demonstration that the transforming principle was DNA marked the first evidence that DNA was the genetic material.

RECOMBINATION

Once the DNA is transferred from the donor to the recipient cell by one of the three processes just described, it can integrate into the host cell chromosome by recombination. There are two types of recombination:

(1) **Homologous recombination**, in which two pieces of DNA that have extensive homologous regions pair up and exchange pieces by the processes of breakage and reunion.

(2) **Nonhomologous recombination**, in which little, if any, homology is necessary.

Different genetic loci govern these two types, and so it is presumed that different enzymes are involved. Although it is known that a variety of endonucleases and ligases are involved, the precise sequence of events is unknown.

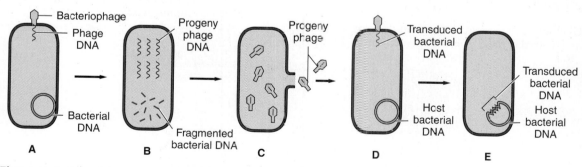

Figure 4–4. Transduction. **A:** A bacteriophage infects a bacterium, and phage DNA enters the cell. **B:** The phage DNA replicates, and the bacterial DNA fragments. **C:** The progeny phage assemble and are released; most contain phage DNA, and a few contain bacterial DNA. **D:** Another bacterium is infected by a phage containing bacterial DNA. **E:** The transduced bacterial DNA integrates into host DNA, and the host acquires a new trait. This host bacterium survives because no viral DNA is transduced; therefore, no viral replication can occur. Another type of transduction mechanism is depicted in Figure 29–8.

PEARLS

- *Bacteria have only one copy of their genome DNA, ie, they are **haploid**. In contrast, eukaryotic cells have two copies of their genome DNA, ie, they are diploid. Bacterial DNA is circular; human nuclear DNA is linear.*

- *The transfer of DNA within bacterial cells occurs by two processes: movement of transposons and programmed rearrangements. **Transposons** are small pieces of DNA that move readily from one site on the bacterial chromosome to another or from the bacterial chromosome to a plasmid. Medically, transposons are important because they commonly **carry antibiotic resistance genes.** The transfer of transposons on plasmids to other bacteria by conjugation contributes significantly to antibiotic resistance.*

- ***Programmed rearrangements** are the movement of genes from inactive (storage) sites into active sites where they are expressed as new proteins. Medically, this is important because bacteria can acquire new proteins (antigens) on their surface and evade the immune system. Two important organisms in which this occurs are Neisseria gonorrhoeae, the cause of gonorrhea, and Trypanosoma brucei, a protozoan that causes African sleeping sickness.*

- *The transfer of DNA between bacterial cells occurs mainly by two processes: conjugation and transduction. **Conjugation** is the process by which DNA, either plasmid or chromosomal, is transferred directly from one bacterium to another. For conjugation to occur, the donor bacterium must have a "fertility" plasmid (F plasmid) that encodes the proteins that mediate this process, the most important of which are the proteins that form the **sex pilus.** The DNA transferred by conjugation to the recipient bacterium is a new copy that allows the donor to keep a copy of the DNA. Plasmids carrying antibiotic resistance genes are commonly transferred by conjugation.*

- ***Transduction** is the process by which DNA, either plasmid or chromosomal, is transferred from one bacterium to another by a **virus.** The transferred DNA integrates into the chromosomal DNA of the recipient and new proteins, such as exotoxins, are made, a process called **lysogenic conversion.***

- ***Transformation** is the process by which DNA itself, either DNA released from dying cells or DNA purified in the laboratory, enters a recipient bacterium. Medically, this process appears to be less important than conjugation and transduction.*

PRACTICE QUESTIONS: USMLE & COURSE EXAMINATIONS

Questions on the topics discussed in this chapter can be found in the Basic Bacteriology section of Part XI: USMLE (National Board) Practice Questions starting on page 532. Also see Part XII: USMLE (National Board) Practice Examination starting on page 583.

Classification of Medically Important Bacteria

The current classification of bacteria is based primarily on morphologic and biochemical characteristics. A scheme that divides the medically important organisms by genus is shown in Table 5–1. For pedagogic purposes this classification scheme deviates from those derived from strict taxonomic principles in two ways:

(1) Only organisms that are described in this book in the section on medically important bacteria are included.

(2) Because there are so many gram-negative rods, they are divided into three categories: respiratory organisms, zoonotic organisms, and enteric and related organisms.

The initial criterion used in the classification is the nature of the cell wall; ie, is it rigid, flexible, or absent? Bacteria with rigid, thick walls can be subdivided into free-living bacteria, which are capable of growing on laboratory medium in the absence of human or other animal cells, and non-free-living bacteria, which are obligate intracellular parasites and therefore can grow only within human or other animal cells. The free-living organisms are further subdivided according to shape and staining reaction into a variety of gram-positive and gram-negative cocci and rods with different oxygen requirements and spore-forming abilities. Bacteria with flexible, thin walls (the spirochetes) and those without cell walls (the mycoplasmas) form separate units.

Using these criteria plus various biochemical reactions, many bacteria can be readily classified into separate genus and species. However, there have been several examples of these criteria placing bacteria into the same genus when DNA sequencing of their genome re-

veals they are significantly different and should be classified in a new or different genus. For example, an organism formerly known as *Pseudomonas cepacia* has been reclassified as *Burkholderia cepacia* because the base sequence of its DNA was found to be significantly different from the DNA of the members of the genus *Pseudomonas*.

PEARLS

- The classification of bacteria is based on various criteria, such as the nature of the cell wall, staining characteristics, ability to grow in the presence or absence of oxygen, and ability to form spores.
- The criterion currently used is the base sequence of the genome DNA. Several bacteria have been reclassified on the basis of this information.

PRACTICE QUESTIONS: USMLE & COURSE EXAMINATIONS

Questions on the topics discussed in this chapter can be found in the Basic Bacteriology section of Part XI: USMLE (National Board) Practice Questions starting on page 532. Also see Part XII: USMLE (National Board) Practice Examination starting on page 583.

Table 5–1. Classification of medically important bacteria.

Characteristics	Genus	Representative Diseases
I. Rigid, thick-walled cells		
A. Free-living (extracellular bacteria)		
1. Gram-positive		
a. Cocci	*Streptococcus*	Pneumonia, pharyngitis, cellulitis
	Staphylococcus	Abscess of skin and other organs
b. Spore-forming rods		
(1) Aerobic	*Bacillus*	Anthrax
(2) Anaerobic	*Clostridium*	Tetanus, gas gangrene, botulism
c. Non-spore-forming rods		
(1) Nonfilamentous	*Corynebacterium*	Diphtheria
	Listeria	Meningitis
(2) Filamentous	*Actinomyces*	Actinomycosis
	Nocardia	Nocardiosis
2. Gram-negative		
a. Cocci	*Neisseria*	Gonorrhea, meningitis
b. Rods		
(1) Facultative		
(a) Straight		
(i) Respiratory organisms	*Haemophilus*	Meningitis
	Bordetella	Whooping cough
	Legionella	Pneumonia
(ii) Zoonotic organisms	*Brucella*	Brucellosis
	Francisella	Tularemia
	Pasteurella	Cellulitis
	Yersinia	Plague
(iii) Enteric and related organisms	*Escherichia*	Urinary tract infection, diarrhea
	Enterobacter	Urinary tract infection
	Serratia	Pneumonia
	Klebsiella	Pneumonia, urinary tract infection
	Salmonella	Enterocolitis, typhoid fever
	Shigella	Enterocolitis
	Proteus	Urinary tract infection
(b) Curved	*Campylobacter*	Enterocolitis
	Helicobacter	Gastritis, peptic ulcer
	Vibrio	Cholera
(2) Aerobic	*Pseudomonas*	Pneumonia, urinary tract infection
(3) Anaerobic	*Bacteroides*	Peritonitis
3. Acid-fast	*Mycobacterium*	Tuberculosis, leprosy
B. Non-free-living (obligate intracellular parasites)	*Rickettsia*	Rocky Mountain spotted fever, typhus, Q fever
	Chlamydia	Urethritis, trachoma, psittacosis
II. Flexible, thin-walled cells	*Treponema*	Syphilis
(spirochetes)	*Borrelia*	Lyme disease
	Leptospira	Leptospirosis
III. Wall-less cells	*Mycoplasma*	Pneumonia

Normal Flora

Normal flora is the term used to describe the various bacteria and fungi that are **permanent residents** of certain body sites, especially the skin, oropharynx, colon, and vagina (Tables 6–1 and 6–2). The viruses and parasites, which are the two other major groups of microorganisms, are usually not considered members of the normal flora, although they can be present in asymptomatic individuals. The members of the normal flora vary in both number and kind from one site to another. Although the normal flora extensively populates many areas of the body, the internal organs usually are sterile. Areas such as the central nervous system, blood, lower bronchi and alveoli, liver, spleen, kidneys, and bladder are free of all but the occasional transient organism.

There is a distinction between the presence of these organisms and the **carrier state.** In a sense we all are carriers of microorganisms, but that is not the normal use of the term in the medical context. The term "carrier" implies that an individual harbors a potential pathogen and therefore can be a source of infection of others. It is most frequently used in reference to a person with an asymptomatic infection or to someone who has recovered from a disease but continues to carry the organism and may shed it for a long period.

There is also a distinction to be made between members of the normal flora, which are the permanent residents, and the **colonization** of the individual with a new organism. In a sense, we are all colonized by the

Table 6–1. Summary of the members of normal flora and their anatomic locations.

Members of the Normal Flora[1]	Anatomic Location
Bacteroides species	Colon, throat, vagina
Candida albicans	Mouth, colon, vagina
Clostridium species	Colon
Corynebacterium species (diphtheroids)	Nasopharynx, skin, vagina
Enterococcus faecalis	Colon
Escherichia coli and other coliforms	Colon, vagina, outer urethra
Gardnerella vaginalis	Vagina
Haemophilus species	Nasopharynx, conjunctiva
Lactobacillus species	Mouth, colon, vagina
Neisseria species	Mouth, nasopharynx
Propionibacterium acnes	Skin
Pseudomonas aeruginosa	Colon, skin
Staphylococcus aureus	Nose, skin
Staphylococcus epidermidis	Skin, nose, mouth, vagina, urethra
Viridans streptococci	Mouth, nasopharynx

[1]In alphabetical order.

Table 6–2. Medically important members of the normal flora.

Location	Important Organisms[1]	Less Important Organisms[2]
Skin	*Staphylococcus epidermidis*	*Staphylococcus aureus, Corynebacterium* (diphtheroids), various streptococci, *Pseudomonas aeruginosa,* anaerobes (eg, *Propionibacterium*), yeasts (eg, *Candida albicans*)
Nose	*Staphylococcus aureus*[3]	*S. epidermidis, Corynebacterium* (diphtheroids), various streptococci
Mouth	Viridans streptococci	Various streptococci, *Eikenella corrodens*
Dental plaque	*Streptococcus mutans*	*Prevotella intermedia, Porphyromonas gingivalis*
Gingival crevices	Various anaerobes, eg, *Bacteroides, Fusobacterium,* streptococci, *Actinomyces*	
Throat	Viridans streptococci	Various streptococci (including *Streptococcus pyogenes* and *Streptococcus pneumoniae*), *Neisseria* species, *Haemophilus influenzae, S. epidermidis*
Colon	*Bacteroides fragilis, Escherichia coli*	*Bifidobacterium, Eubacterium, Fusobacterium, Lactobacillus,* various aerobic gram-negative rods, *Enterococcus faecalis* and other streptococci, *Clostridium*
Vagina	*Lactobacillus, E. coli,*[3] group B streptococci[3]	Various streptococci, various gram-negative rods, *B. fragilis, Corynebacterium* (diphtheroids), *C. albicans*
Urethra		*S. epidermidis, Corynebacterium* (diphtheroids), various streptococci, various gram-negative rods, eg, *E. coli*[3]

[1]Organisms that are medically significant or present in large numbers.
[2]Organisms that are less medically significant or present in smaller numbers.
[3]These organisms are not part of the normal flora in this location but are important colonizers.

normal flora organisms, but the term "colonization" typically refers to the acquisition of a new organism. After the new organism colonizes (ie, attaches and grows, usually on a mucosal membrane), it may cause an infectious disease or it may be eliminated by our host defenses. Furthermore, the person colonized by a new organism can transmit that organism to others, ie, act as a reservoir of infection for others.

The members of the normal flora play a role both in the maintenance of health and in the causation of disease in three significant ways:

(1) They can cause disease, especially in immunocompromised and debilitated individuals. Although these organisms are nonpathogens in their usual anatomic location, they can be pathogens in other parts of the body.

(2) They constitute a protective host defense mechanism. The nonpathogenic resident bacteria occupy attachment sites on the skin and mucosa that can interfere with colonization by pathogenic bacteria. The ability of members of the normal flora to limit the growth of pathogens is called **colonization resistance.** If the

normal flora is suppressed, pathogens may grow and cause disease. For example, antibiotics can reduce the normal colonic flora that predisposes to pseudomembranous colitis caused by *Clostridium difficile.*

(3) They may serve a nutritional function. The intestinal bacteria produce several B vitamins and vitamin K. Poorly nourished people who are treated with oral antibiotics can have vitamin deficiencies as a result of the reduction in the normal flora. However, since germ-free animals are well nourished, the normal flora is not essential for proper nutrition.

NORMAL FLORA OF THE SKIN

The predominant organism is *Staphylococcus epidermidis,* which is a nonpathogen on the skin but can cause disease when it reaches certain sites such as artificial heart valves and prosthetic joints. It is found on the skin much more frequently than its pathogenic relative, *Staphylococcus aureus* (Table 6–2). There are about 10^3–10^4 organisms/cm^2 of skin. Most of them are located superficially in the stratum corneum, but some are found in the hair follicles and act as a reservoir to replenish the superficial flora after hand washing. Anaerobic organisms, such as *Propionibacterium* and *Peptococcus,* are situated in the deeper follicles in the dermis, where oxygen tension is low. *Propionibacterium acnes* is a common skin anaerobe that is implicated in the pathogenesis of acne.

The yeast, *Candida albicans,* is also a member of the normal flora of the skin. It can enter a person's bloodstream when needles pierce the skin (eg. in patients with intravenous catheters or in those who use intravenous drugs). It is an important cause of systemic infections in patients with reduced cell-mediated immunity.

NORMAL FLORA OF THE RESPIRATORY TRACT

A wide spectrum of organisms colonize the nose, throat, and mouth, but the lower bronchi and alveoli typically contain few, if any, organisms. The nose is colonized by a variety of streptococcal and staphylococcal species, the most significant of which is the pathogen *S. aureus.* Occasional outbreaks of disease due to this organism, particularly in the newborn nursery, can be traced to nasal, skin, or perianal carriage by personnel.

The throat contains a mixture of viridans streptococci, *Neisseria* species, and *S. epidermidis* (Table 6–2). These nonpathogens occupy attachment sites on the pharyngeal mucosa and inhibit the growth of the pathogens *Streptococcus pyogenes, Neisseria meningitidis,* and *S. aureus,* respectively.

In the mouth, viridans streptococci make up about half of the bacteria. *Streptococcus mutans,* a member of the viridans group, is of special interest since it is found in large numbers (10^{10}/g) in dental plaque, the precursor of caries. The plaque on the enamel surface is composed of gelatinous, high-molecular-weight glucans secreted by the bacteria. The entrapped bacteria produce a large amount of acid, which demineralizes the enamel and initiates caries. The viridans streptococci are also the leading cause of subacute bacterial (infective) endocarditis. These organisms can enter the bloodstream at the time of dental surgery and attach to damaged heart valves.

Eikenella corrodens, also part of the normal oral flora, causes skin and soft tissue infections associated with human bites and "clenched-fist" injuries, ie, injuries to the hand that occur during fist fights.

Anaerobic bacteria, such as species of *Bacteroides, Fusobacterium, Clostridium,* and *Peptostreptococcus,* are found in the gingival crevices, where the oxygen concentration is very low. If aspirated, these organisms can cause lung abscesses, especially in debilitated patients with poor dental hygiene. In addition, the gingival crevices are the natural habitat of *Actinomyces israelii,* an anaerobic actinomycete that can cause abscesses of the jaw, lungs, or abdomen.

NORMAL FLORA OF THE INTESTINAL TRACT

In normal fasting people, the stomach contains few organisms because of its low pH and its enzymes. The small intestine usually contains small numbers of streptococci, lactobacilli, and yeasts, particularly *C. albicans.* Larger numbers of these organisms are found in the terminal ileum.

The colon is the major location of bacteria in the body. Roughly 20% of the feces consists of bacteria, approximately 10^{11} organisms/g. The major bacteria found in the colon are listed in Table 6–3.

The normal flora of the intestinal tract plays a significant role in extraintestinal disease. For example, *Escherichia coli* is the leading cause of urinary tract infections and *Bacteroides fragilis* is an important cause of peritonitis associated with perforation of the intestinal wall following trauma, appendicitis, or diverticulitis. Other organisms include *Enterococcus faecalis,* which causes urinary tract infections and endocarditis, and *Pseudomonas aeruginosa,* which can cause various infections, particularly in hospitalized patients with decreased host defenses. *P. aeruginosa* is present in 10% of normal stools, as well as in soil and water.

Antibiotic therapy, for example, with clindamycin, can suppress the predominant normal flora, thereby allowing a rare organism such as the toxin-producing *Clostridium difficile* to overgrow and cause severe colitis. Administration of certain antibiotics, such as neomycin

Table 6–3. Major bacteria found in the colon.

Bacterium[1]	Number/g of Feces	Important Pathogen
Bacteroides, especially *B fragilis*	10^{10}–10^{11}	Yes
Bifidobacterium	10^{10}	No
Eubacterium	10^{10}	No
Coliforms	10^7–10^8	Yes
Enterococcus, especially *E. faecalis*	10^7–10^8	Yes
Lactobacillus	10^7	No
Clostridium, especially *C. perfringens*	10^6	Yes

[1]*Bacteroides, Bifidobacterium,* and *Eubacterium* (which make up more than 90% of the fecal flora) are anaerobes. Coliforms (*Escherichia coli, Enterobacter* species, and other gram-negative organisms) are the predominant facultative anaerobes.

orally, prior to gastrointestinal surgery to "sterilize" the gut leads to a significant reduction of the normal flora for several days, followed by a gradual return to normal levels.

NORMAL FLORA OF THE GENITOURINARY TRACT

The vaginal flora of adult women consists primarily of *Lactobacillus* species (Table 6–2). Lactobacilli are responsible for producing the acid that keeps the pH of the adult woman's vagina low. Before puberty and after menopause, when estrogen levels are low, lactobacilli are rare and the vaginal pH is high. Lactobacilli appear to prevent the growth of potential pathogens, since their suppression by antibiotics can lead to overgrowth by *C. albicans*. Overgrowth of this yeast can result in *Candida* vaginitis.

The vagina is located close to the anus and can be colonized by members of the fecal flora. For example, women who are prone to recurrent urinary tract infections harbor organisms such as *E. coli* and *Enterobacter* in the introitus. About 15–20% of women of childbearing age carry group B streptococci in the vagina. This organism is an important cause of sepsis and meningitis in the newborn and is acquired during passage through the birth canal. The vagina is colonized by *S. aureus* in approximately 5% of women, which predisposes them to toxic shock syndrome.

Urine in the bladder is sterile in the healthy person, but during passage through the outermost portions of the urethra it often becomes contaminated with *S. epidermidis,* coliforms, diphtheroids, and nonhemolytic streptococci. The area around the urethra of women and uncircumcised men contains secretions that carry *Mycobacterium smegmatis,* an acid-fast organism. The skin surrounding the genitourinary tract is the site of *Staphylococcus saprophyticus,* a cause of urinary tract infections in women.

PEARLS

- **Normal flora** are those microorganisms that are the **permanent residents** of the body that everyone has. Some people can be **colonized,** either transiently or for long periods, with certain organisms, but those are not considered members of the normal flora. **Carriers** (also called chronic carriers) are those individuals in whom pathogenic organisms are present in significant numbers and therefore are a source of infection for others.

- Normal flora organisms are either **bacteria** or **yeasts.** Viruses, protozoa, and helminths are not considered to be members of the normal flora (but humans can be carriers of some of these organisms).

- Normal flora organisms inhabit the body surfaces exposed to the environment, such as the **skin, oropharynx, intestinal tract, and vagina.** Members of the normal flora differ in number and kind at various anatomic sites.

- Members of the normal flora are **low-virulence** organisms. In their usual anatomic site, they are nonpathogenic. However, if they leave their usual anatomic site, especially in an immunocompromised individual, they can cause disease.

- **Colonization resistance** occurs when members of the normal flora occupy receptor sites on the skin and mucosal surfaces, thereby preventing pathogens from binding to those receptors.

Important Members of the Normal Flora

- **Skin.** The predominant member of the normal flora of the skin is **Staphylococcus epidermidis.** It is an important cause of infections of prosthetic heart valves and prosthetic joints. The yeast, **Candida albicans,** also found on the skin, can enter the bloodstream and cause disseminated infections such as endocarditis in intravenous drug users. **S. aureus** is also present on the skin, but its **main site is in the nose.** It causes abscesses in the skin and in many other organs.

- **Oropharynx.** The main members of the normal flora of the mouth and throat are the **viridans streptococci,** such as S. sanguis and S. mutans. Viridans streptococci are the most common cause of subacute endocarditis.

- **Gastrointestinal tract.** The stomach contains very few organisms because of the low pH. The colon contains the **largest number of normal flora** and the most diverse species, including both anaerobic and facultative bacteria. There are gram-positive rods and cocci as well as gram-negative rods and cocci. The members of the colonic normal flora are an important cause of disease outside of the colon. The two most important members of the colonic flora that cause disease are the anaerobe **Bacteroides fragilis** and the facultative **Escherichia coli.**

Enterococcus faecalis, *a facultative, is also a very important pathogen.*

- **Vagina. Lactobacilli** *are the predominant normal flora organisms in the vagina. They keep the pH of the vagina low, which inhibits the growth of organisms such as* C. albicans, *an important cause of vaginitis.*

- **Urethra.** *The outer third of the urethra contains a mixture of bacteria, primarily* S. epidermidis. *The female urethra can become colonized with fecal flora such as* E. coli, *which predisposes to urinary tract infections.*

PRACTICE QUESTIONS: USMLE & COURSE EXAMINATIONS

Questions on the topics discussed in this chapter can be found in the Basic Bacteriology section of Part XI:

USMLE (National Board) Practice Questions starting on page 532. Also see Part XII: USMLE (National Board) Practice Examination starting on page 583.

Pathogenesis

A microorganism is a **pathogen** if it is capable of causing disease; however, some organisms are highly pathogenic, that is, they often cause disease, whereas others cause disease rarely. **Opportunistic** pathogens are those that rarely if ever cause disease in immunocompetent people but can cause serious infection in immunocompromised patients. These opportunists are frequently members of the body's normal flora. The origin of the term "opportunistic" refers to the ability of the organism to take the opportunity offered by reduced host defenses to cause disease.

Virulence is a quantitative measure of pathogenicity and is measured by the number of organisms required to cause disease. The 50% lethal dose (LD_{50}) is the number of organisms needed to kill half the hosts, and the 50% infectious dose (ID_{50}) is the number needed to cause infection in half the hosts. The **infectious dose** of an organism required to cause disease varies greatly among the pathogenic bacteria. For example, *Shigella* and *Salmonella* both cause diarrhea by infecting the gastrointestinal tract, but the infectious dose of *Shigella* is less than 100 organisms, whereas the infectious dose of *Salmonella* is on the order of 100,000 organisms. The infectious dose of bacteria depends primarily on their **virulence factors**, for example, whether their pili allow them to adhere well to mucous membranes, whether they produce exotoxins or endotoxins, whether they possess a capsule to protect them from phagocytosis, and whether they can survive various nonspecific host defenses such as acid in the stomach.

There are two uses of the word **parasite**. Within the context of this chapter, the term refers to the parasitic relationship of the bacteria to the host cells; that is, the presence of the bacteria is **detrimental** to the host cells. Bacteria that are human pathogens can be thought of, therefore, as parasites. Some bacterial pathogens are **obligate intracellular parasites**, eg, *Chlamydia* and *Rickettsia*, because they can grow only within host cells. Many bacteria are facultative parasites because they can grow within cells, outside cells, or on bacteriologic media. The other use of the term "parasite" refers to the protozoa and the helminths, which are discussed in Part VI of this book.

WHY DO PEOPLE GET INFECTIOUS DISEASES?

People get infectious diseases when microorganisms overpower our host defenses, ie, when the balance between the organism and the host shifts in favor of the organism. The organism or its products are then present in sufficient amount to induce various symptoms, such as fever and inflammation, which we interpret as those of an infectious disease.

From the organism's perspective, the two critical determinants in overpowering the host are the **number of organisms** to which the host, or person, is exposed and the **virulence** of these organisms. Clearly, the greater the number of organisms, the greater is the likelihood of infection. It is important to realize, however, that a small number of highly virulent organisms can cause disease just as a large number of less virulent organisms can. The virulence of an organism is determined by its ability to produce various **virulence factors,** several of which are described above.

The production of specific virulence factors also determines what disease the bacteria cause. For example, a strain of *Escherichia coli* that produces one type of exotoxin causes watery (nonbloody) diarrhea, whereas a different strain of *E. coli* that produces another type of exotoxin causes bloody diarrhea. This chapter describes several important examples of specific diseases related to the production of various virulence factors.

From the host's perspective, the two main arms of our host defenses are innate immunity and acquired immunity, the latter of which includes both antibody-mediated and cell-mediated immunity. A reduction in the functioning of any component of our host defenses shifts the balance in favor of the organism and increases the chance that an infectious disease will occur. Some important causes of a reduction in our host defenses include genetic immunodeficiencies such as agammaglobulinemia; acquired immunodeficiencies such as AIDS; diabetes; and drug-induced immunosuppression in patients with organ transplants, with autoimmune diseases, and with cancer who are receiving chemotherapy.

An overview of our host defenses is presented in Chapters 8 and 57.

In many instances, a person acquires an organism but no infectious disease occurs because the host defenses were successful. Such **asymptomatic infections** are very common and are typically recognized by detecting antibody against the organism in the patient's serum.

TYPES OF BACTERIAL INFECTIONS

The term **infection** has more than one meaning. One meaning is that an organism has infected the person, that is, has entered the body of that person. For example, a person can be infected with an organism of low pathogenicity and not develop symptoms of disease. Another meaning of the term infection is to describe an infectious disease, such as when a person says, "I have an infection." In this instance, infection and disease are being used interchangeably, but it is important to realize that according to the first definition, the word infection does not have to be equated with disease. Usually the meaning will be apparent from the context.

Bacteria cause disease by two major mechanisms: (1) **toxin production** and (2) **invasion** and **inflammation.** Toxins fall into two general categories: **exotoxins** and **endotoxins.** Exotoxins are polypeptides released by the cell, whereas endotoxins are lipopolysaccharides, which form an integral part of the cell wall. Endotoxins occur only in gram-negative rods and cocci; are not actively released from the cell; and cause fever, shock, and other generalized symptoms. Both exotoxins and endotoxins by themselves can cause symptoms; the presence of the bacteria in the host is not required. Invasive bacteria, on the other hand, grow to large numbers locally and induce an inflammatory response consisting of erythema, edema, warmth, and pain. Invasion and inflammation are discussed below in the section entitled Determinants of Bacterial Pathogenesis.

Many, but not all, infections are **communicable,** ie, are spread from host to host. For example, tuberculosis is communicable, that is, it is spread from person to person via airborne droplets produced by coughing; but botulism is not because the exotoxin produced by the organism in the contaminated food affects only those eating that food. If a disease is highly communicable, the term "contagious" is applied.

An infection is **epidemic** if it occurs much more frequently than usual; it is **pandemic** if it has a worldwide distribution. An **endemic** infection is constantly present at a low level in a specific population. In addition to infections that result in overt symptoms, many are **inapparent** or **subclinical** and can be detected only by demonstrating a rise in antibody titer or by isolating the organism. Some infections result in a **latent** state, after which reactivation of the growth of the organism

and recurrence of symptoms may occur. Certain other infections lead to a **chronic carrier** state, in which the organisms continue to grow with or without producing symptoms in the host. Chronic carriers, eg, Typhoid Mary, are an important source of infection of others and hence are a public health hazard.

The determination of whether an organism recovered from a patient is actually the cause of the disease involves an awareness of two phenomena: normal flora and colonization. Members of the **normal flora** are permanent residents of the body and vary in type according to anatomic site (see Chapter 6). When an organism is obtained from a patient's specimen, the question of whether it is a member of the normal flora is important in interpreting the finding. **Colonization** refers to the presence of a new organism that is neither a member of the normal flora nor the cause of symptoms. It can be a difficult clinical dilemma to distinguish between a pathogen and a colonizer, especially in specimens obtained from the respiratory tract, such as throat cultures and sputum cultures.

STAGES OF BACTERIAL PATHOGENESIS

Most bacterial infections are acquired from an external source, and for those, the stages of infection are as described below. Some bacterial infections are caused by members of the normal flora and, as such, are not transmitted directly prior to the onset of infection.

A generalized sequence of the stages of infection is as follows

(1) Transmission from an external source into the portal of entry

(2) Evasion of primary host defenses such as skin or stomach acid

(3) Adherence to mucous membranes, usually by bacterial pili

(4) Colonization by growth of the bacteria at the site of adherence

(5) Disease symptoms caused by toxin production or invasion accompanied by inflammation

(6) Host responses, both nonspecific and specific (immunity), during steps 3, 4, and 5

(7) Progression or resolution of the disease.

DETERMINANTS OF BACTERIAL PATHOGENESIS

1. Transmission

An understanding of the mode of transmission of bacteria and other infectious agents is extremely important from a public health perspective, because interrupting the **chain of transmission** is an excellent way to prevent infectious diseases. The mode of transmission of many infectious diseases is "human-to-human," but infectious diseases are also transmitted from nonhuman sources such as soil, water, and animals. **Fomites** are inanimate objects, such as towels, that serve as a source of microorganisms that can cause infectious diseases. Table 7–1 describes some important examples of these modes of transmission.

Although some infections are caused by members of the normal flora, most are acquired by transmission from external sources. Pathogens exit the infected patient most frequently from the respiratory and gastrointestinal tracts; hence, transmission to the new host usually occurs via airborne respiratory droplets or fecal contamination of food and water. Organisms can also be transmitted by sexual contact, urine, skin contact, blood transfusions, contaminated needles, or biting insects. The transfer of blood, either by transfusion or by sharing needles during intravenous drug use, can transmit various bacterial and viral pathogens. The screening of donated blood for *Treponema pallidum,* HIV, human T-cell lymphotropic virus, hepatitis B virus, hepatitis C virus, and West Nile virus has greatly reduced the risk of infection by these organisms.

The major bacterial diseases **transmitted by ticks** in the United States are Lyme disease, Rocky Mountain spotted fever, ehrlichiosis, relapsing fever, and tularemia. Ticks of the genus *Ixodes* transmit three infectious diseases: Lyme disease; ehrlichiosis; and babesiosis, a protozoan disease.

Bacteria, viruses, and other microbes can also be transmitted from mother to offspring, a process called **vertical transmission.** The three modes by which organisms are transmitted vertically are across the placenta, within the birth canal during birth, and via breast milk. Table 7–2 describes some medically important organisms that are transmitted vertically. (**Horizontal transmission,** by contrast, is person-to-person transmission that is not from mother to offspring.)

There are four important portals of entry: respiratory tract, gastrointestinal tract, genital tract, and skin (Table 7–3). Important microorganisms and diseases transmitted by water are described in Table 7–4.

The important bacterial diseases transmitted by foods are listed in Table 7–5, and those transmitted by insects are listed in Table 7–6. The specific mode of transmission of each organism is described in the subsequent section devoted to that organism.

Animals are also an important source of organisms that infect humans. They can be either the source (**reservoir**) or the mode of transmission (**vector**) of certain organisms. Diseases for which animals are the

Table 7–1. Important modes of transmission.

Mode of Transmission	Clinical Example	Comment
I. Human to human		
A. Direct contact	Gonorrhea	Intimate contact: eg, sexual, or passage through birth canal
B. No direct contact	Dysentery	Fecal-oral: eg, excreted in human feces, then ingested in food or water
C. Transplacental	Congenital syphilis	Bacteria cross the placenta and infect the fetus
D. Blood-borne	Syphilis	Transfused blood or intravenous drug use can transmit bacteria and viruses. Screening of blood for transfusions has greatly reduced this risk
II. Nonhuman to human		
A. Soil source	Tetanus	Spores in soil enter wound in skin
B. Water source	Legionnaire's disease	Bacteria in water aerosol are inhaled into lungs
C. Animal source		
1. Directly	Cat-scratch fever	Bacteria enter in cat scratch
2. Via insect vector	Lyme disease	Bacteria enter in tick bite
3. Via animal excreta	*E. coli* hemolytic-uremic syndrome	Bacteria in cattle feces are ingested in undercooked hamburger
D. Fomite source	Staphylococcal skin infection	Bacteria on an object, eg, a towel, are transferred onto the skin

Table 7–2. Vertical transmission of some important pathogens.

Mode of Transmission	Pathogen	Type of Organism[1]	Disease in Fetus or Neonate
Transplacental	*Treponema pallidum*	B	Congenital syphilis
	Listeria monocytogenes[2]	B	Neonatal sepsis and meningitis
	Cytomegalovirus	V	Congenital abnormalities
	Parvovirus B19	V	Hydrops fetalis
	Toxoplasma gondii	P	Toxoplasmosis
Within birth canal/at time of birth	*Streptococcus agalactiae* (group B streptococcus)	B	Neonatal sepsis and meningitis
	Escherichia coli	B	Neonatal sepsis and meningitis
	Chlamydia trachomatis	B	Conjunctivitis or pneumonia
	Neisseria gonorrhoeae	B	Conjunctivitis
	Herpes simplex type-2	V	Skin, CNS, or disseminated infection (sepsis)
	Hepatitis B virus	V	Hepatitis B
	Human immunodeficiency virus[3]	V	Asymptomatic infection
	Candida albicans	F	Thrush
Breast milk	*Staphylococcus aureus*	B	Oral or skin infections
	Cytomegalovirus	V	Asymptomatic infection
	Human T-cell leukemia virus	V	Asymptomatic infection

CNS = central nervous system.
[1] B, bacterium; V, virus; F, fungus; P, protozoa.
[2] *Listeria monocytogenes* can also be transmitted at the time of birth.
[3] HIV is transmitted primarily at the time of birth but is also transmitted across the placenta and in breast milk.

reservoirs are called **zoonoses.** The important zoonotic diseases caused by bacteria are listed in Table 7–7.

2. Adherence to Cell Surfaces

Certain bacteria have specialized structures, eg, **pili,** or produce substances, eg, **capsules** or **glycocalyxes,** that allow them to adhere to the surface of human cells, thereby enhancing their ability to cause disease. These adherence mechanisms are essential for organisms that attach to mucous membranes; mutants that lack these mechanisms are often nonpathogenic. For example, the **pili** of *Neisseria gonorrhoeae* and *Escherichia coli* mediate the attachment of the organisms to the urinary tract epithelium, and the **glycocalyx** of *Staphylococcus epidermidis* and certain viridans streptococci allows the organisms to adhere strongly to the endothelium of heart valves. The various molecules that mediate adherence to cell surfaces are called **adhesins.**

The matrix formed by these adhesins forms a coating called a *biofilm*. Biofilms are important in pathogenesis because they protect the bacteria from antibodies and from antibiotics.

Foreign bodies, such as artificial heart valves and artificial joints, predispose to infections. Bacteria can adhere to these surfaces, but phagocytes adhere poorly owing to the absence of selectins and other binding proteins on the artificial surface (see Chapter 8).

Some strains of *E. coli* and *Salmonella* have surface proteins called **curli,** which mediate binding of the bacteria to endothelium and to extracellular proteins such as fibronectin. Curli also interact with serum proteins such as factor XII, a component of the coagulation cascade. Curli, therefore, are thought to play a role in the production of the thrombi seen in the disseminated intravascular coagulation (DIC) associated with sepsis caused by these bacteria. (See the discussion of endotoxin on page 45.)

Table 7–3. Portals of entry of some common pathogens.

Portal of Entry	Pathogen	Type of Organism[1]	Disease
Respiratory tract	Streptococcus pneumoniae	B	Pneumonia
	Neisseria meningitidis	B	Meningitis
	Haemophilus influenzae	B	Meningitis
	Mycobacterium tuberculosis	B	Tuberculosis
	Influenza virus	V	Influenza
	Rhinovirus	V	Common cold
	Epstein-Barr virus	V	Infectious mononucleosis
	Coccidioides immitis	F	Coccidioidomycosis
	Histoplasma capsulatum	F	Histoplasmosis
Gastrointestinal tract	Shigella dysenteriae	B	Dysentery
	Salmonella typhi	B	Typhoid fever
	Vibrio cholerae	B	Cholera
	Hepatitis A virus	V	Infectious hepatitis
	Poliovirus	V	Poliomyelitis
	Trichinella spiralis	H	Trichinosis
Skin	Clostridium tetani	B	Tetanus
	Rickettsia rickettsii	B	Rocky Mountain spotted fever
	Rabies virus	V	Rabies
	Trichophyton rubrum	F	Tinea pedis (athlete's foot)
	Plasmodium vivax	H	Malaria
Genital tract	Neisseria gonorrhoeae	B	Gonorrhea
	Treponema pallidum	B	Syphilis
	Chlamydia trachomatis	B	Urethritis
	Human papilloma virus	V	Genital warts
	Candida albicans	F	Vaginitis

[1]B, bacterium; V, virus; F, fungus; P, protozoa; H, helminth.

3. Invasion, Inflammation, & Intracellular Survival

One of the two main mechanisms by which bacteria cause disease is **invasion** of tissue followed by **inflammation.** (The inflammatory response is described in Chapter 8.) The other main mechanism, **toxin production,** is described in Section 4 of this chapter. A third mechanism, **immunopathogenesis,** is described in Section 5 of this chapter.

Several enzymes secreted by invasive bacteria play a role in pathogenesis. Among the most prominent are:

(1) **Collagenase** and **hyaluronidase,** which degrade collagen and hyaluronic acid, respectively, thereby allowing the bacteria to spread through subcutaneous tissue; they are especially important in cellulitis caused by *Streptococcus pyogenes.*

(2) **Coagulase,** which is produced by *Staphylococcus aureus* and accelerates the formation of a fibrin clot

Table 7-4. Transmission of important water-borne diseases.

Portal of Entry	Pathogen	Type of Organism[1]	Disease
Gastrointestinal tract			
1. Ingestion of drinking water	Salmonella species	B	Diarrhea
	Shigella species	B	Diarrhea
	Campylobacter jejuni	B	Diarrhea
	Norovirus[2]	V	Diarrhea
	Giardia lamblia	P	Diarrhea
	Cryptosporidium parvum	P	Diarrhea
2. Ingestion of water while swimming[3]	Leptospira interrogans	B	Leptospirosis
Respiratory tract			
Inhalation of water aerosol	Legionella pneumophila	B	Pneumonia (Legionnaire's disease)
Skin			
Penetration through skin	Pseudomonas aeruginosa	B	Hot-tub folliculitis
	Schistosoma mansoni	H	Schistosomiasis
Nose			
Penetration through cribriform plate into meninges and brain	Naegleria fowleri	P	Meningoencephalitis

[1]B, bacterium; V, virus, P, protozoa; H, helminth.

[2]Formerly called Norwalk-like viruses.

[3]All of the organisms that cause diarrhea by ingestion of drinking water also cause diarrhea by ingestion of water while swimming.

from its precursor, fibrinogen (this clot may protect the bacteria from phagocytosis by walling off the infected area and by coating the organisms with a layer of fibrin).

(3) **Immunoglobulin A (IgA) protease**, which degrades IgA, allowing the organism to adhere to mucous membranes, and is produced chiefly by *N. gonorrhoeae, Haemophilus influenzae,* and *Streptococcus pneumoniae.*

(4) **Leukocidins**, which can destroy both neutrophilic leukocytes and macrophages.

In addition to these enzymes, several virulence factors contribute to invasiveness by limiting the ability of the host defense mechanisms, especially phagocytosis, to operate effectively.

(1) The most important of these antiphagocytic factors is the **capsule** external to the cell wall of several important pathogens such as *S. pneumoniae* and *Neisseria meningitidis.* The polysaccharide capsule prevents the phagocyte from adhering to the bacteria; anticapsular antibodies allow more effective phagocytosis to occur (a process called **opsonization**) (see page 54). The vaccines against *S. pneumoniae, H. influenzae,* and *N. meningitidis*

contain capsular polysaccharides that induce protective anticapsular antibodies.

(2) A second group of antiphagocytic factors are the cell wall proteins of the gram-positive cocci, such as the M protein of the group A streptococci (*S. pyogenes*) and protein A of *S. aureus.* The M protein is antiphagocytic, and protein A binds to IgG and prevents the activation of complement. These virulence factors are summarized in Table 7–8.

Bacteria can cause two types of inflammation: **pyogenic** and **granulomatous**. In pyogenic (pus-producing) inflammation, neutrophils are the predominant cells. Some of the most important pyogenic bacteria are the gram-positive and gram-negative cocci listed in Table 7–3. In granulomatous inflammation, macrophages and T cells predominate. The most important organism in this category is *Mycobacterium tuberculosis.* No bacterial enzymes or toxins that induce granulomas have been identified. Rather, it appears that bacterial antigens stimulate the cell-mediated immune system, resulting in sensitized T-lymphocyte and macrophage activity. Phagocytosis by macrophages kills most of the bacteria, but some survive and grow within the macrophages in the granuloma.

Table 7–5. Bacterial diseases transmitted by foods.

Bacterium	Typical Food	Main Reservoir	Disease
I. Diarrheal diseases			
Gram-positive cocci			
Staphylococcus aureus	Custard-filled pastries; potato, egg, or tuna fish salad	Humans	Food poisoning, especially vomiting
Gram-positive rods			
Bacillus cereus	Reheated rice	Soil	Diarrhea
Clostridium perfringens	Cooked meat, stew, and gravy	Soil, animals, or humans	Diarrhea
Listeria monocytogenes	Unpasteurized milk products	Soil, animals, or plants	Diarrhea
Gram-negative rods			
Escherichia coli	Various foods and water	Humans	Diarrhea
E. coli O157:H7 strain	Undercooked meat	Cattle	Hemorrhagic colitis
Salmonella enteritidis	Poultry, meats, and eggs	Domestic animals, especially poultry	Diarrhea
Shigella species	Various foods and water	Humans	Diarrhea (dysentery)
Vibrio cholerae	Various foods, eg, seafood, and water	Humans	Diarrhea
Vibrio parahaemolyticus	Seafood	Warm salt water	Diarrhea
Campylobacter jejuni	Various foods	Domestic animals	Diarrhea
Yersinia enterocolitica	Various foods	Domestic animals	Diarrhea
II. Nondiarrheal diseases			
Gram-positive rods			
Clostridium botulinum	Improperly canned vegetables, smoked fish	Soil	Botulism
Listeria monocytogenes	Unpasteurized milk products	Cows	Sepsis in neonate or mother
Gram-negative rods			
Vibrio vulnificus	Seafood	Warm salt water	Sepsis
Brucella species	Meat, milk	Domestic animals	Brucellosis
Francisella tularensis	Meat	Rabbits	Tularemia
Mycobacteria			
Mycobacterium bovis	Milk	Cows	Intestinal tuberculosis

Intracellular survival is an important attribute of certain bacteria that enhances their ability to cause disease. These bacteria are called "intracellular" pathogens and commonly cause granulomatous lesions. The best-known of these bacteria belong to the genera *Mycobacterium, Legionella, Brucella,* and *Listeria.* The best-known fungus is *Histoplasma.* These organisms are not **obligate** intracellular parasites, which distinguishes them from *Chlamydia* and *Rickettsia.* They can be cul-

tured on microbiologic media in the laboratory and therefore are *not* obligate intracellular parasites. Rather, they prefer an intracellular location probably because they are protected there from antibody and neutrophils that function extracellularly.

These bacteria use several different mechanisms to allow them to survive and grow intracellularly. These include (1) inhibition of the fusion of the phagosome with the lysosome, which allows the organisms to avoid

Table 7–6. Bacterial diseases transmitted by insects.

Bacterium	Insect	Reservoir	Disease
Gram-negative rods			
Yersinia pestis	Rat fleas	Rodents, eg, rats, prairie dogs	Plague
Francisella tularensis	Ticks *(Dermacentor)*	Many animals, eg, rabbits	Tularemia
Spirochetes			
Borrelia burgdorferi	Ticks *(Ixodes)*	Mice	Lyme disease
Borrelia recurrentis	Lice	Humans	Relapsing fever
Rickettsias			
Rickettsia rickettsii	Ticks *(Dermacentor)*	Dogs, rodents, and ticks *(Dermacentor)*	Rocky Mountain spotted fever
Rickettsia prowazekii	Lice	Humans	Epidemic typhus
Ehrlichia chafeensis	Ticks *(Dermacentor)*	Dogs	Ehrlichiosis

the degradative enzymes in the lysosome; (2) inhibition of acidification of the phagosome, which reduces the activity of the lysosomal degradative enzymes; and (3) escape from the phagosome into the cytoplasm, where there are no degradative enzymes. Members of the genera *Mycobacterium* and *Legionella* are known to use the first and second mechanisms, whereas *Listeria* species use the third.

The invasion of cells by bacteria is dependent on the interaction of specific bacterial surface proteins called **invasins** and specific cellular receptors belonging to the integrin family of transmembrane adhesion proteins. The movement of bacteria into the cell is a function of actin microfilaments. Once inside the cell, these bacteria typically reside within cell vacuoles such as phagosomes. Some remain there, others migrate into the cytoplasm, and some move from the cytoplasm into adjacent cells through tunnels formed from actin. Infection of the surrounding cells in this manner allows the bacteria to evade host defenses. For example, *Listeria monocytogenes* aggregates actin filaments on its surface and is propelled in a "sling-shot" fashion, called **actin rockets,** from one host cell to another.

The "Yops" (*Yersinia* outer-membrane proteins) produced by several *Yersinia* species are important examples of bacterial virulence factors that act primarily after invasion of human cells by the organism. The most important effects of the Yops proteins are to inhibit phagocytosis by neutrophils and macrophages and to inhibit cytokine production, eg, tumor necrosis factor (TNF) production, by macrophages. For example, one of the Yops proteins of *Yersinia pestis* (Yop J) is a protease that cleaves signal transduction proteins required for the induction of TNF synthesis. This inhibits the activation of our host defenses and contributes to the ability of the organism to cause bubonic plague.

In 1999, a protein called DNA adenine methylase (Dam) was identified as a "master controller" of many virulence factors in several species of human pathogens. For example, in *E. coli* it controls the synthesis of the pili that attach the organism to the bladder epithelium. It was shown that mutant strains of *Salmonella* that fail to produce Dam become nonpathogenic. This suggests that these mutants may be useful as immunogens in live vaccines against many bacterial diseases.

The genes that encode many virulence factors in bacteria are clustered in **pathogenicity islands** on the bacterial chromosome. For example, in many bacteria, the genes encoding adhesins, invasins, and exotoxins are adjacent to each other. Nonpathogenic variants of these bacteria do not have these pathogenicity islands. It appears that these large regions of the bacterial genome were inherited as a block via conjugation or transduction. Pathogenicity islands are found in many gram-negative rods, such as *E. coli, Salmonella, Shigella, Pseudomonas,* and *Vibrio cholerae,* and in gram-positive cocci such as *S. pneumoniae.*

After bacteria have colonized and multiplied at the portal of entry, they may invade the bloodstream and spread to other parts of the body. Receptors for the bacteria on the surface of cells determine, in large part, the organs affected. For example, certain bacteria or viruses infect the brain because receptors for these microbes are located on the surface of brain neurons. The "blood-brain barrier," which limits the ability of certain drugs to penetrate the brain, is not thought to be a determinant of microbial infection of the brain. The concept of a "blood-brain barrier" primarily refers to the inability of hydrophilic (charged, ionized) drugs to enter the lipid-rich brain parenchyma, whereas lipophilic (lipid-soluble) drugs enter well.

Two important diseases, diphtheria and pseudo-

Table 7–7. Zoonotic diseases caused by bacteria.

Bacterium	Main Reservoir	Mode of Transmission	Disease
Gram-positive rods			
Bacillus anthracis	Domestic animals	Direct contact	Anthrax
Listeria monocytogenes	Domestic animals	Ingestion of unpasteurized milk products	Sepsis in neonate or mother
Erysipelothrix rhusiopathiae	Fish	Direct contact	Erysipeloid
Gram-negative rods			
Bartonella henselae	Cats	Skin scratch	Cat-scratch disease
Brucella species	Domestic animals	Ingestion of unpasteurized milk products; contact with animal tissues	Brucellosis
Campylobacter jejuni	Domestic animals	Ingestion of contaminated meat	Diarrhea
Escherichia coli O157:H7	Cattle	Fecal-oral	Hemorrhagic colitis
Francisella tularensis	Many animals, especially rabbits	Tick bite, direct contact	Tularemia
Pasteurella multocida	Cats	Cat bite	Cellulitis
Salmonella enteritidis	Poultry, eggs, and cattle	Fecal-oral	Diarrhea
Yersinia enterocolitica	Domestic animals	Fecal-oral	Diarrhea
Yersinia pestis	Rodents, especially rats and prairie dogs	Rat flea bite	Sepsis
Mycobacteria			
Mycobacterium bovis	Cows	Ingestion of unpasteurized milk products	Intestinal tuberculosis
Spirochetes			
Borrelia burgdorferi	Mice	Tick bite (*Ixodes*)	Lyme disease
Leptospira interrogans	Rats and dogs	Urine	Leptospirosis
Chlamydiae			
Chlamydia psittaci	Psittacine birds	Inhalation of aerosols	Psittacosis
Rickettsiae			
Rickettsia rickettsii	Rats and dogs	Tick bite (*Dermacentor*)	Rocky Mountain spotted fever
Coxiella burnetii	Sheep	Inhalation of aerosols of amniotic fluid	Q fever
Ehrlichia chafeensis	Dogs	Tick bite (*Dermacentor*)	Ehrlichiosis

membranous colitis, are characterized by inflammatory lesions called **pseudomembranes.** Pseudomembranes are thick, adherent, grayish or yellowish exudates on the mucosal surfaces of the throat in diphtheria and of the colon in pseudomembranous colitis. The term "pseudo" refers to the abnormal nature of these membranes in contrast to the normal anatomic membranes of the body such as the tympanic membrane and the placental membranes.

4. Toxin Production

The second major mechanism by which bacteria cause disease is the production of toxins. A comparison of the

Table 7–8. Surface virulence factors important for bacterial pathogenesis.

Organism	Virulence Factor	Used in Vaccine	Comments
Gram-positive cocci			
Streptococcus pneumoniae	Polysaccharide capsule	Yes	Determines serotype
Streptococcus pyogenes	M protein	No	Determines serotype[1]
Staphylococcus aureus	Protein A	No	Binds to Fc region of IgG, which prevents activation of complement
Gram-negative cocci			
Neisseria meningitidis	Polysaccharide capsule	Yes	Determines serotype
Gram-positive rods			
Bacillus anthracis	Polypeptide capsule	No	
Gram-negative rods			
Haemophilus influenzae	Polysaccharide capsule	Yes	Determines serotype
Klebsiella pneumoniae	Polysaccharide capsule	No	
Escherichia coli	Protein pili	No	Causes adherence
Salmonella typhi	Polysaccharide capsule	No	Not important for other salmonellae
Yersinia pestis	V and W proteins	No	

[1] Do not confuse the serotype with the grouping of streptococci, which is determined by the polysaccharide in the cell wall.

main features of **exotoxins** and **endotoxins** is shown in Table 7–9.

Exotoxins

Exotoxins are produced by several gram-positive and gram-negative bacteria, in contrast to endotoxins, which are present only in gram-negative bacteria. The essential characteristic of exotoxins is that they are **secreted** by the bacteria, whereas endotoxin is a component of the cell wall. Exotoxins are polypeptides whose genes are frequently located on plasmids or lysogenic bacterial viruses (bacteriophages). Some important exotoxins encoded by bacteriophage DNA are diphtheria toxin, cholera toxin, and botulinum toxin.

Exotoxins are among the **most toxic** substances known. For example, the fatal dose of tetanus toxin for a human is estimated to be less than 1 µg. Because some purified exotoxins can reproduce all aspects of the disease, we can conclude that certain bacteria play no other role in pathogenesis than to synthesize the exotoxin. Exotoxin polypeptides are good antigens and induce the synthesis of protective antibodies called antitoxins, some of which are useful in prevention or treatment of diseases such as botulism and tetanus. When treated with formaldehyde (or acid or heat), the exotoxin polypeptides are converted into **toxoids**, which are used in protective vaccines because they retain their antigenicity but have lost their toxicity.

Many exotoxins have an **A-B subunit** structure; the A (or active) subunit possesses the toxic activity, and the B (or binding) subunit is responsible for binding the exotoxin to specific receptors on the membrane of the human cell. Important exotoxins that have an A-B subunit structure include diphtheria toxin, tetanus toxin, botulinum toxin, cholera toxin, and the enterotoxin of *E. coli* (Figure 7–1).

The **A** subunit of several important exotoxins acts by **ADP-ribosylation**; ie, the A subunit is an enzyme that catalyzes the addition of adenosine diphosphate-ribose (ADP-ribose) to the target protein in the human cell. The addition of ADP-ribose to the target protein often inactivates it but can also hyperactivate it, either of which can cause the symptoms of disease. For example, diphtheria toxin and *Pseudomonas* exotoxin A ADP-ribosylate elongation factor-2, thereby inactivating it and resulting in the inhibition of protein synthesis. On the other hand, cholera toxin and *E. coli* toxin ADP-ribosylate G_s protein, thereby activating it. This causes an increase in adenylate cyclase activity, a consequent increase in the amount of cyclic adenosine monophosphate (AMP), and the production of watery diarrhea. Pertussis toxin is an interesting variation on the theme. It ADP-ribosylates G_i protein and inactivates it. Inactivation of the inhibitory G proteins turns on adenylate cyclase, causing an increase in the amount of cyclic AMP, which plays a role in causing the symptoms of whooping cough.

Table 7–9. Main features of exotoxins and endotoxins.

Property	Comparison of Properties	
	Exotoxin	**Endotoxin**
Source	Certain species of gram-positive and gram-negative bacteria	Cell wall of gram-negative bacteria
Secreted from cell	Yes	No
Chemistry	Polypeptide	Lipopolysaccharide
Location of genes	Plasmid or bacteriophage	Bacterial chromosome
Toxicity	High (fatal dose on the order of 1 μg)	Low (fatal dose on the order of hundreds of micrograms)
Clinical effects	Various effects (see text)	Fever, shock
Mode of action	Various modes (see text)	Includes TNF and interleukin-1
Antigenicity	Induces high-titer antibodies called antitoxins	Poorly antigenic
Vaccines	Toxoids used as vaccines	No toxoids formed and no vaccine available
Heat stability	Destroyed rapidly at 60 °C (except staphylococcal enterotoxin)	Stable at 100°C for 1 hour
Typical diseases	Tetanus, botulism, diphtheria	Meningococcemia, sepsis by gram-negative rods

TNF = tumor necrosis factor.

Some exotoxins are secreted by the bacterium into the extracellular space, but others are transferred by a **type III secretion system** (also called an injectosome) from the bacterium directly into the adjacent human cell. This secretion system is mediated by a needle-like projection ("molecular syringe") and by transport pumps in the bacterial cell membrane. Transfer via injectosome allows the toxin to avoid neutralizing antibody located in the extracellular space. The importance of the type III secretion system is illustrated by the finding that the strains of *Pseudomonas aeruginosa* that have this secretion system are significantly more virulent than those that do not. Other medically important gram-negative rods that

utilize injectosomes include *Shigella* species, *Salmonella* species, *Escherichia coli*, and *Yersinia pestis*.

The mechanisms of action of the important exotoxins produced by toxigenic bacteria are described below and summarized in Tables 7–10 to 7–12. The main location of symptoms of disease caused by bacterial exotoxins is described in Table 7–13.

A. GRAM-POSITIVE BACTERIA

The exotoxins produced by gram-positive bacteria have several different mechanisms of action and produce different clinical effects. Some important exotoxins in-

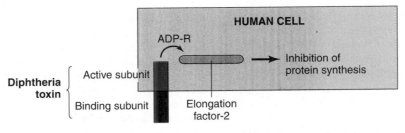

Figure 7–1. Mode of action of diphtheria toxin. The toxin binds to the cell surface via its binding subunit, and the active subunit enters the cell. The active subunit is an enzyme that catalyzes the addition of ADP-ribose (ADP-R) to elongation factor-2 (EF-2). This inactivates EF-2, and protein synthesis is inhibited.

Table 7–10. Important bacterial exotoxins.

Bacterium	Disease	Mode of Action	Toxoid Vaccine
Gram-positive rods			
Corynebacterium diphtheriae	Diphtheria	Inactivates EF-2 by ADP-ribosylation	Yes
Clostridium tetani	Tetanus	Blocks release of the inhibitory neurotransmitter glycine by proteolytic cleavage of releasing proteins	Yes
Clostridium botulinum	Botulism	Blocks release of acetylcholine by proteolytic cleavage of releasing proteins	Yes[1]
Clostridium difficile	Pseudomembranous colitis	Exotoxins A and B inactivate GTPases by glucosylation	No
Clostridium perfringens	Gas gangrene	Alpha toxin is a lecithinase. Enterotoxin is a superantigen	No
Bacillus anthracis	Anthrax	Edema factor is an adenylate cyclase. Lethal factor is a protease that cleaves MAP kinase, which is required for cell division	No
Gram-positive cocci			
Staphylococcus aureus	1. Toxic shock syndrome	Is a superantigen; binds to class II MHC protein and T-cell receptor; induces IL-1 and IL-2	No
	2. Food poisoning	Is a superantigen acting locally in the gastrointestinal tract	No
	3. Scalded skin syndrome	Is a protease that cleaves desmoglein in desmosomes	No
Streptococcus pyogenes	Scarlet fever	Is a superantigen; action similar to toxic shock syndrome toxin of S. aureus	No
Gram-negative rods			
Escherichia coli	1. Watery diarrhea	Labile toxin stimulates adenylate cyclase by ADP-ribosylation; stable toxin stimulates guanylate cyclase.	No
	2. Bloody diarrhea	Verotoxin is cytotoxic to enterocytes by degrading 28S ribosomal RNA	No
Vibrio cholerae	Cholera	Stimulates adenylate cyclase by ADP-ribosylation	No
Bordetella pertussis	Whooping cough	Stimulates adenylate cyclase by ADP-ribosylation; inhibits chemokine receptor	Yes[2]

[1]For high-risk individuals only.

[2]The acellular vaccine contains pertussis toxoid and four other proteins.

clude diphtheria toxin, which inhibits protein synthesis by inactivating elongation factor-2 (EF-2); tetanus toxin and botulinum toxin, which are neurotoxins that prevent the release of neurotransmitters; and toxic shock syndrome toxin, which acts as a superantigen causing the release of large amounts of cytokines from helper T cells and macrophages. The mechanisms of action and the clinical effects of exotoxins produced by gram-positive bacteria are described below.

(1) Diphtheria toxin, produced by *Corynebacterium diphtheriae*, inhibits protein synthesis by ADP-ribosylation of elongation factor-2 (EF-2) (Figure 7–1).[1]

The consequent death of the cells leads to two prominent symptoms of diphtheria: pseudomembrane formation in the throat and myocarditis.

---

[1] *Pseudomonas aeruginosa* exotoxin A has the same mode of action.

Table 7–11. Important mechanisms of action of bacterial exotoxins.

Mechanism of Action	Exotoxin
ADP-ribosylation	Diphtheria toxin, cholera toxin, *Escherichia coli* heat-labile toxin, pertussis toxin
Superantigen	Toxic shock syndrome toxin, staphylococcal enterotoxin, erythrogenic toxin
Protease	Tetanus toxin, botulinum toxin, lethal factor of anthrax toxin, scalded skin toxin
Lecithinase	*Clostridium perfringens* alpha toxin

The exotoxin activity depends on two functions mediated by different domains of the molecule. The toxin is synthesized as a single polypeptide (molecular weight 62,000) that is nontoxic because the active site of the enzyme is masked (Figure 7–2). A single proteolytic "nick" plus reduction of the sulfhydryl bonds yields two active polypeptides. Fragment A, a 22,000-molecular-weight peptide at the amino-terminal end of the exotoxin, is an enzyme that catalyzes the transfer of ADP-ribose from nicotinamide adenine dinucleotide (NAD) to EF-2, thereby inactivating it. The ADP-ribosylation of EF-2 freezes the translocation complex, and protein synthesis stops. The reaction is as follows:

$$EF\text{-}2 + NAD \rightarrow EF\text{-}2\text{–}ADP\text{-}ribose + Nicotinamide$$

Fragment B, a 40,000-molecular-weight peptide at the carboxy-terminal end, binds to receptors on the outer membrane of eukaryotic cells and mediates transport of fragment A into the cells.

To summarize, the exotoxin binds to cell membrane receptors via a region near its carboxyl end. The toxin is transported across the membrane, and the proteolytic nick and reduction of the disulfide bonds occur. This releases the active fragment A, which inactivates EF-2. The enzymatic activity is specific for EF-2; no other protein is ADP-ribosylated. The specificity is due to the presence in EF-2 of a unique amino acid, a modified histidine called diphthamide. The reaction occurs in all eukaryotic cells; there is no tissue or organ specificity. Prokaryotic and mitochondrial protein synthesis is not affected because a different, nonsusceptible elongation factor is involved. The enzyme activity is remarkably potent; a single molecule of fragment A will kill a cell within a few hours. Other organisms whose exotoxins act by ADP-ribosylation are *E. coli, V. cholerae,* and *Bordetella pertussis.*

The *tox* gene, which codes for the exotoxin, is carried by a temperate bacteriophage. As a result, only *C. diphtheriae* strains lysogenized by this phage cause diphtheria. (Nonlysogenized *C. diphtheriae* can be found in the throat of some healthy people.) Regulation of exotoxin synthesis is controlled by the interaction of iron in the medium with a *tox* gene repressor synthesized by the bacterium. As the concentration of iron increases, the iron-repressor complex inhibits the transcription of the *tox* gene.

(2) Tetanus toxin, produced by *Clostridium tetani,* is a **neurotoxin** that prevents release of the inhibitory neurotransmitter glycine. When the inhibitory neurons are nonfunctional, the excitatory neurons are unopposed, leading to muscle spasms and a spastic paralysis. Tetanus toxin (tetanospasmin) is composed of two polypeptide subunits encoded by plasmid DNA. The heavy chain of the polypeptide binds to gangliosides in the membrane of the neuron; the light chain is a protease that degrades the protein(s) responsible for the release of the inhibitory neurotransmitter. The toxin released at the site of the peripheral wound may travel either by retrograde axonal transport or in the bloodstream to the anterior horn and interstitial neurons of the spinal cord. Blockage of release of the inhibitory transmitter leads to convulsive contractions of the voluntary muscles best

Table 7–12. Exotoxins that increase intracellular cyclic AMP.

Bacterium	Exotoxin	Mode of Action
Vibrio cholerae	Cholera toxin	ADP-ribosylates G_s factor, which activates it, thereby stimulating adenylate cyclase
Escherichia coli	Labile toxin	Same as cholera toxin
Bordetella pertussis	Pertussis toxin	ADP-ribosylates G_i factor, which inactivates it, thereby stimulating adenylate cyclase
Bacillus anthracis	Edema factor of anthrax toxin	Is an adenylate cyclase

Table 7–13. Main location of symptoms of disease caused by bacterial exotoxins.

Main Location of Symptoms	Organism	Mode of Action of Exotoxin
Gastrointestinal tract		
1. Gram-positive cocci	*Staphylococcus aureus*	Enterotoxin is a superantigen
2. Gram-positive rods	*Clostridium difficile*	Inactivates GTPases in enterocytes
	Clostridium perfringens	Superantigen
	Bacillus cereus	Superantigen
3. Gram-negative rods	*Vibrio cholerae*	Stimulates adenylate cyclase
	Toxigenic *Escherichia coli*	Stimulates adenylate cyclase
	Escherichia coli O157	Inactivates protein synthesis
Nervous system		
1. Gram-positive rods	*Clostridium tetani*	Inhibits glycine release
	Clostridium botulinum	Inhibits acetylcholine release
Respiratory tract		
1. Gram-positive rods	*Corynebacterium diphtheriae*	Inactivates protein synthesis
2. Gram-negative rods	*Bordetella pertussis*	Stimulates adenylate cyclase; inhibits chemokine receptor
Skin, soft tissue, or muscle		
1. Gram-positive cocci	*Staphylococcus aureus* (scalded skin syndrome)	Protease cleaves desmosome in skin
	Streptococcus pyogenes (scarlet fever)	Erythrogenic toxin is a superantigen
2. Gram-positive rods	*Clostridium perfringens*	Lecithinase cleaves cell membranes
	Bacillus anthracis	Edema factor is an adenylate cyclase; lethal factor is a protease
Systemic		
1. Gram-positive cocci	*Staphylococcus aureus*	Toxic shock syndrome toxin is a superantigen

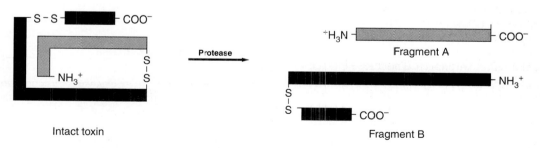

Figure 7–2. Diphtheria exotoxin. Intact extracellular toxin binds to a eukaryotic cell by its B region (dark fragment). After proteolytic cleavage and reduction of the disulfide bond, the A region (light fragment) containing the ribosylating enzyme is activated. (Modified and reproduced, with permission, from Pappenheimer AM Jr: Interaction of protein toxins with mammalian cell membranes. In *Microbiology—1979*. Schlessinger D [editor]. American Society for Microbiology, 1979.)

exemplified by spasm of the jaw and neck muscles ("lockjaw").

(3) Botulinum toxin, produced by *Clostridium botulinum,* is a **neurotoxin** that blocks the release of acetylcholine at the synapse, producing a flaccid paralysis. Approximately 1 µg is lethal for humans; it is one of the most toxic compounds known. The toxin is composed of two polypeptide subunits held together by disulfide bonds. One of the subunits binds to a receptor on the neuron; the other subunit is a protease that degrades the protein(s) responsible for the release of acetylcholine. There are six serotypes of botulinum toxin (A–F). Some serotypes are encoded on a plasmid, some on a temperate bacteriophage, and some on the bacterial chromosome.

(4) Two exotoxins are produced by *Clostridium difficile,* both of which are involved in the pathogenesis of pseudomembranous colitis. Exotoxin A is an enterotoxin that causes watery diarrhea. Exotoxin B is a **cytotoxin** that damages the colonic mucosa and causes pseudomembranes to form. Exotoxins A and B glucosylate signal transduction proteins called Rho GTPases, a process that inhibits these GTPases from performing their signal transduction function. Glucosylation by exotoxin B causes disaggregation of actin filaments in the cytoskeleton, leading to apoptosis and cell death.

(5) Multiple toxins are produced by *Clostridium perfringens* and other species of clostridia that cause gas gangrene. A total of 7 lethal factors and 5 enzymes have been characterized, but no species of *Clostridium* makes all 12 products. The best characterized is the **alpha toxin,** which is a **lecithinase** that hydrolyzes lecithin in the cell membrane, resulting in destruction of the membrane and widespread cell death. The other four enzymes are collagenase, protease, hyaluronidase, and deoxyribonuclease (DNase). The 7 lethal toxins are a heterogeneous group with hemolytic and necrotizing activity. Certain strains of *C. perfringens* produce an enterotoxin that causes watery diarrhea. This enterotoxin acts as a superantigen similar to the enterotoxin of *S. aureus* (see below).

(6) Three exotoxins are produced by *Bacillus anthracis,* the agent of anthrax: edema factor, lethal factor, and protective antigen. The three exotoxins associate with each other, but each component has a distinct function. Edema factor is an adenylate cyclase that raises the cyclic AMP concentration within the cell, resulting in loss of chloride ions and water and consequent edema formation in the tissue (Table 7–12). Lethal factor is a protease that cleaves a phosphokinase required for the signal transduction pathway that controls cell growth. Loss of the phosphokinase results in a failure of cell growth and consequent cell death. Protective antigen binds to a cell surface receptor and forms pores in the human cell membrane that allow edema factor and

lethal factor to enter the cell. The name protective antigen is based on the finding that antibody against this protein protects against disease. The antibody blocks the binding of protective antigen, thereby preventing edema factor and lethal factor from entering the cell.

(7) Toxic shock syndrome toxin (TSST) is a **superantigen** produced primarily by certain strains of *S. aureus* but also by certain strains of *S. pyogenes.* TSST binds directly to class II major histocompatibility (MHC) proteins on the surface of antigen-presenting cells (macrophages) without intracellular processing. This complex interacts with the β-chain of the T-cell receptor of many helper T cells (see the discussion of superantigens in Chapter 58). This causes the release of large amounts of interleukins, especially interleukin-1 and interleukin-2. These cytokines produce many of the signs and symptoms of toxic shock. TSST is also a T-cell "mitogen," ie, it induces T cells to multiply, which contributes to the overproduction of cytokines.

(8) Staphylococcal enterotoxin is also a superantigen but, because it is ingested, acts locally on the lymphoid cells lining the small intestine. The enterotoxin is produced by *S. aureus* in the contaminated food and causes food poisoning, usually within 1 to 6 hours after ingestion. The main symptoms are vomiting and watery diarrhea. The prominent vomiting seen in food poisoning is thought to be caused by cytokines released from the lymphoid cells stimulating the enteric nervous system, which activates the vomiting center in the brain.

(9) Exfoliatin is a protease produced by *S. aureus* that causes scalded skin syndrome. Exfoliatin cleaves desmoglein, a protein in the desmosomes of the skin, resulting in the detachment of the superficial layers of the skin. Exfoliatin is also called epidermolytic toxin.

(10) Erythrogenic toxin, produced by *S. pyogenes,* causes the rash characteristic of scarlet fever. Its mechanism of action is similar to that of TSST; ie, it acts as a superantigen (see above). The DNA that codes for the toxin resides on a temperate bacteriophage. Nonlysogenic bacteria do not cause scarlet fever, although they can cause pharyngitis.

B. GRAM-NEGATIVE BACTERIA

The exotoxins produced by gram-negative bacteria also have several different mechanisms of action and produce different clinical effects. Two very important exotoxins are the enterotoxins of *E. coli* and *V. cholerae* (cholera toxin), which induce an increase in the amount of cyclic AMP within the enterocyte, resulting in watery diarrhea (Table 7–12). The mechanisms of action and the clinical effects of exotoxins produced by gram-negative bacteria are described below.

(1) The **heat-labile enterotoxin** produced by *E. coli* causes **watery, nonbloody diarrhea** by stimulating

adenylate cyclase activity in cells in the small intestine (Figure 7–3). The resulting increase in the concentration of cyclic AMP causes excretion of the chloride ion, inhibition of sodium ion absorption, and significant fluid and electrolyte loss into the lumen of the gut. The heat-labile toxin, which is inactivated at 65°C for 30 minutes, is composed of two subunits, a B subunit, which binds to a ganglioside receptor in the cell membrane, and an A subunit, which enters the cell and mediates the transfer of ADP-ribose from NAD to a stimulatory coupling protein (G_s protein). This locks the G_s protein in the "on" position, thereby continually stimulating adenylate cyclase to synthesize cyclic AMP. This activates cyclic AMP–dependent protein kinase, an enzyme that phosphorylates ion transporters in the cell membrane, resulting in the loss of water and ions from the cell. The genes for the heat-labile toxin and for the heat-stable toxin (see below) are carried on plasmids.

In addition to the labile toxin, there is a **heat-stable toxin,** which is a polypeptide that is not inactivated by boiling for 30 minutes. The heat-stable toxin affects cyclic guanosine monophosphate (GMP) rather than cyclic AMP. It stimulates guanylate cyclase and thus increases the concentration of cyclic GMP, which inhibits the reabsorption of sodium ions and causes diarrhea.

(2) **Verotoxin** is an exotoxin produced by strains of *E. coli* with the O157:H7 serotype. These enterohemorrhagic strains cause **bloody diarrhea** and are the cause of outbreaks associated with eating undercooked hamburger in fast-food restaurants. The toxin is named for its cytotoxic effect on Vero (monkey) cells in culture. The toxin inactivates protein synthesis by removing adenine from a specific site on the 28S rRNA in the large

subunit of the human ribosome. The enterotoxin produced by *Shigella* (Shiga toxin) and the toxin ricin, which is produced by the *Ricinus* plant, have the same mode of action as does verotoxin. (Ricin coupled to monoclonal antibody to human tumor antigens has been used experimentally to kill human cancer cells.) Another name for verotoxin is Shiga-like toxin.

When verotoxin (Shiga-like toxin) enters the bloodstream, it can cause **hemolytic-uremic syndrome** (HUS). Verotoxin binds to receptors on the kidney and on the endothelium of small blood vessels. Inhibition of protein synthesis results in death of those cells, leading to renal failure and microangiopathic hemolytic anemia. Certain antibiotics, such as ciprofloxacin, can increase the amounts of verotoxin produced by *E. coli* O157, which predisposes to HUS.

(3) The enterotoxins produced by *V. cholerae,* the agent of cholera (see Chapter 18), and *Bacillus cereus,* a cause of diarrhea, act in a manner similar to that of the heat-labile toxin of *E. coli* (Figure 7–3).

(4) Pertussis toxin, produced by *B. pertussis,* the cause of whooping cough, is an exotoxin that catalyzes the transfer of ADP-ribose from NAD to an inhibitory G protein. Inactivation of this inhibitory regulator has two effects: one is in the stimulation of adenylate cyclase activity and a consequent increase in the amount of cyclic AMP within the affected cells (Table 7–12). This results in edema and other changes in the respiratory tract, leading to the cough of whooping cough. The second effect is the inhibition of the signal transduction pathway used by chemokine receptors. This causes the marked **lymphocytosis** seen in patients with pertussis. The toxin inhibits signal transduction by all chemokine receptors, resulting in an inability of lymphocytes to

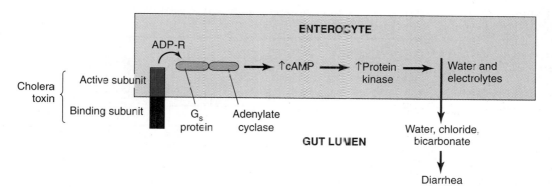

Figure 7–3. Mode of action of *Escherichia coli* and *Vibrio cholerae* enterotoxins. The enterotoxin, eg, cholera toxin, binds to the surface of the enterocyte via its binding subunit. The active subunit is an enzyme that catalyzes the addition of ADP-ribose (ADP-R) to the G_s regulatory protein. This activates adenylate cyclase to overproduce cyclic adenosine monophosphate (AMP). As a consequence, cyclic AMP-dependent protein kinase activity increases, and water and electrolytes leave the enterocyte, causing watery diarrhea.

migrate to and enter lymphoid tissue (spleen, lymph nodes). Because they do not enter tissue, there is an increase in their number in the blood (see the discussion of chemokines in Chapter 58).

Endotoxins

Endotoxins are integral parts of the cell walls of both gram-negative rods and cocci, in contrast to exotoxins, which are actively released from the cell (Table 7–9). In addition, several other features distinguish these substances. Endotoxins are **lipopolysaccharides (LPS)**, whereas exotoxins are polypeptides; the enzymes that produce the lipopolysaccharide are encoded by genes on the bacterial chromosome, rather than by plasmid or bacteriophage DNA, which usually encodes the exotoxins. The toxicity of endotoxins is low in comparison with that of exotoxins. All endotoxins produce the same generalized effects of **fever** and **shock,** although the endotoxins of some organisms are more effective than those of others (Figure 7–4). Endotoxins are weakly antigenic; they induce protective antibodies so poorly that multiple episodes of toxicity can occur. No toxoids have been produced from endotoxins, and endotoxins are not used as antigens in any available vaccine.

The findings of fever and hypotension are salient features of **septic shock.** Septic shock is one of the leading causes of death in intensive care units and has an estimated mortality rate of 30–50%. The endotoxins of gram-negative bacteria are the best-established causes of septic shock, but surface molecules of gram-positive bacteria (which do not have endotoxins) can also cause septic shock (see below).

Two features of septic shock are interesting:

(1) Septic shock is different from toxic shock. In septic shock, the bacteria are in the bloodstream, whereas in toxic shock, it is the toxin that is circulating in the blood. The clinical importance of this observation is that in septic shock, blood cultures are usually positive, whereas in toxic shock, they are usually negative.

(2) Septic shock can cause the death of a patient even though antibiotics have killed the bacteria in the patient's blood, ie, the blood cultures have become negative. This occurs because septic shock is mediated by cytokines, such as TNF and interleukin-1 (see below), that continue to act even though the bacteria that induced the cytokines are no longer present.

The structure of the LPS is shown in Figure 2–6. The toxic portion of the molecule is **lipid A,** which is composed of disaccharides with several fatty acids attached. β-Hydroxymyristic acid is always one of the fatty acids and is found only in lipid A. The other fatty acids differ according to species. The polysaccharide core in the middle of the molecule protrudes from the surface of the bacteria and has the same chemical composition within members of a genus. The repeat unit of sugars on the exterior differs in each species and frequently differs between strains of a single species. It is an important antigen of some gram-negative rods ("O" or somatic antigen) and is composed of three, four, or five sugars repeated up to 25 times. Because the number of permutations of this array is very large, many antigenic types exist. For example, more than 1500 antigenic types have been identified for *Salmonella.*

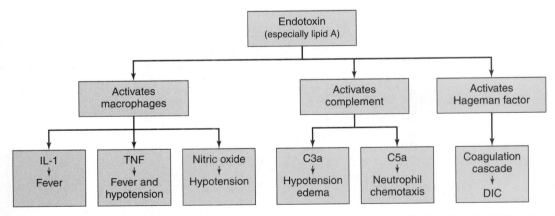

Figure 7–4. Mode of action of endotoxin. Endotoxin is the most important cause of septic shock, which is characterized primarily by fever, hypotension, and disseminated intravascular coagulation (DIC). Endotoxin causes these effects by activating three critical processes: (1) activating macrophages to produce interleukin-1 (IL-1), tumor necrosis factor (TNF), and nitric oxide; (2) activating complement to produce C3a and C5a; and (3) activating Hageman factor, an early component of the coagulation cascade.

The biologic effects of endotoxin (Table 7–14) include:

(1) **Fever** due to the release by macrophages of endogenous pyrogen (interleukin-1), which acts on the hypothalamic temperature-regulatory center

(2) **Hypotension**, shock, and impaired perfusion of essential organs owing to bradykinin-induced vasodilation, increased vascular permeability, and decreased peripheral resistance (nitric oxide, a potent vasodilator, also causes hypotension)

(3) **Disseminated intravascular coagulation (DIC)** due to activation of the coagulation system through Hageman factor (factor XII), resulting in thrombosis, a petechial or purpuric rash, and tissue ischemia, leading to failure of vital organs

(4) Activation of the alternative pathway of the complement cascade, resulting in inflammation and tissue damage

(5) Activation of macrophages, increasing their phagocytic ability, and activation of many clones of B lymphocytes, increasing antibody production. (Endotoxin is a polyclonal activator of B cells, but not T cells.)

Damage to the vascular endothelium plays a major role in both the hypotension and DIC seen in septic shock. Damage to the endothelium allows the leakage of plasma and red cells into the tissue, resulting in the loss of blood volume and consequent hypotension. Damaged endothelium also serves as a site of platelet aggregation and activation that leads to the thousands of endovascular clots manifesting as DIC.

The evidence that endotoxin causes these effects comes from the following two findings: (1) purified lipopolysaccharide, free of the organism, reproduces the effects; and (2) antiserum against endotoxin can mitigate or block these effects.

Clinically, the presence of DIC in the patient can be assessed by the D-dimer laboratory test. D-dimers are cleavage products of fibrin (fibrin split products) that are detected in the blood of patients with DIC.

Endotoxins do not cause these effects directly. Rather, they elicit the production of host factors such as interleukin-1 and TNF from macrophages.[2] TNF is the central mediator because purified recombinant TNF reproduces the effects of endotoxin and antibody against TNF blocks the effects of the endotoxin. Endotoxin also induces macrophage migration inhibitory factor, which also plays a role in the induction of septic shock.

Note that TNF in small amounts has beneficial effects, eg, causing an inflammatory response to the presence of a microbe, but in large amounts, it has detrimental effects, eg, causing septic shock and DIC. It is interesting that the activation of platelets, which results in clot formation and the walling-off of infections, is the same process that, when magnified, causes DIC and the necrosis of tumors. It is the ability of TNF to activate platelets that causes intravascular clotting and the consequent infarction and death of the tumor tissue. The symptoms of certain autoimmune diseases such as rheumatoid arthritis are also mediated by TNF; however, these symptoms are not induced by endotoxin but by other mechanisms, which are described in Chapter 66. Some of the important beneficial and harmful effects of TNF are listed in Table 7–15.

---

[2] Endotoxin (LPS) induces these factors by first binding to LPS-binding protein in the serum. This complex then binds to CD14, a receptor on the surface of the macrophage. CD14 interacts with a transmembrane protein called "toll-like receptor" that activates an intracellular signaling cascade leading to the activation of genes that encode various cytokines such as interleukin-1, TNF, and other factors.

Table 7–15. Beneficial and harmful effects of TNF.

Beneficial effects of small amounts of TNF
Inflammation, eg, vasodilation, increased vascular permeability
Adhesion of neutrophils to endothelium
Enhanced microbicidal activity of neutrophils
Activation and adhesion of platelets
Increased expression of class I and II MHC proteins
Harmful effects of large amounts of TNF
Septic shock, eg, hypotension and high fever
Disseminated intravascular coagulation
Inflammatory symptoms of some autoimmune diseases

TNF = tumor necrosis factor; MHC = major histocompatibility complex.

Table 7–14. Effects of endotoxin.

Clinical Findings[1]	Mediator or Mechanism
Fever	Interleukin-1
Hypotension (shock)	Bradykinin, nitric oxide
Inflammation	Alternative pathway of complement (C3a, C5a)
Coagulation (DIC)[2]	Activation of Hageman factor

[1]Tumor necrosis factor triggers many of these reactions.
[2]DIC, disseminated intravascular coagulation.

Endotoxins can cause a pyrogenic response in the patient if they are present in intravenous fluids. In the past, intravenous fluids were sterilized by autoclaving, which killed any organisms present but resulted in the release of endotoxins that were not heat-inactivated. For this reason, these fluids are now sterilized by filtration, which physically removes the organism without releasing its endotoxin. The contamination of intravenous fluids by endotoxin is detected by a test based on the observation that nanogram amounts of endotoxin can clot extracts of the horseshoe crab, *Limulus*.

Endotoxinlike pathophysiologic effects can occur in **gram-positive** bacteremic infections (eg, *S. aureus* and *S. pyogenes* infections) as well. Since endotoxin is absent in these organisms, a different cell wall component, namely, lipoteichoic acid, causes the release of TNF and interleukin-1 from macrophages.

Endotoxin-mediated septic shock is a leading cause of death, especially in hospitals. Attempts to treat septic shock with antibodies to lipid A and TNF have been unsuccessful, but in a study reported in 2001, treatment with protein C (drotrecogin-alfa, Zovant) reduced the mortality rate of patients with severe septic shock. Protein C is a normal human protein that functions as an anticoagulant by inhibiting thrombin formation. It also enhances fibrinolysis, which degrades clots once they are formed. Protein C appears to prevent DIC, thereby preventing the multiple organ failure so often seen in septic shock.

5. Immunopathogenesis

In certain diseases, such as rheumatic fever and acute glomerulonephritis, it is not the organism itself that causes the symptoms of disease but the immune response to the presence of the organism. For example, in rheumatic fever, antibodies are formed against the M protein of *S. pyogenes,* which cross-react with joint, heart, and brain tissue. Inflammation occurs, resulting in the arthritis, carditis, and chorea that are the characteristic findings in this disease.

BACTERIAL INFECTIONS ASSOCIATED WITH CANCER

The fact that certain viruses can cause cancer is well established, but the observation that some bacterial infections are associated with cancers is just emerging. Several documented examples include: (1) the association of *Helicobacter pylori* infection with gastric carcinoma and gastric mucosal-associated lymphoid tissue (MALT) lymphoma; (2) the association of *Campylobacter jejuni* infection with MALT lymphoma of the small intestine (also known as alpha-chain disease). Support

for the idea that these cancers are caused by bacteria comes from the observation that antibiotics can cause these cancers to regress if treated during an early stage.

DIFFERENT STRAINS OF BACTERIA CAN PRODUCE DIFFERENT DISEASES

Staphylococcus aureus causes inflammatory, pyogenic diseases such as endocarditis, osteomyelitis, and septic arthritis, as well as nonpyogenic, exotoxin-mediated diseases such as toxic shock syndrome, scalded skin syndrome, and food poisoning. How do bacteria that belong to the same genus and species cause such widely divergent diseases? The answer is that individual bacteria produce different virulence factors that endow those bacteria with the capability to cause different diseases. The different virulence factors are encoded on plasmids, on transposons, on the genome of lysogenic phages, and on pathogenicity islands. These transferable, extrachromosomal genetic elements may or may not be present in any single bacterium, which accounts for the ability to cause different diseases. Table 7–16 describes the different virulence factors for three of the most important bacterial pathogens: *S. aureus, Streptococcus pyogenes,* and *Escherichia coli.*

TYPICAL STAGES OF AN INFECTIOUS DISEASE

A typical acute infectious disease has four stages:

(1) The **incubation period,** which is the time between the acquisition of the organism (or toxin) and the beginning of symptoms (this time varies from hours to days to weeks, depending on the organism)

(2) The **prodrome period,** during which nonspecific symptoms such as fever, malaise, and loss of appetite occur

(3) The **specific-illness period,** during which the overt characteristic signs and symptoms of the disease occur

(4) The **recovery period,** during which the illness abates and the patient returns to the healthy state.

After the recovery period, some individuals become **chronic carriers** of the organisms and may shed them while remaining clinically well. Others may develop a **latent infection,** which can recur either in the same form as the primary infection or manifesting different signs and symptoms. Although many infections cause symptoms, many others are **subclinical;** ie, the individual remains asymptomatic although infected with the organism. In subclinical infections and after the recovery period is over, the presence of antibodies is often used to determine that an infection has occurred.

Table 7–16. Different strains of bacteria can cause different diseases.

Bacteria	Diseases	Virulence Factors	Mode of Action
Staphylococcus aureus			
1. Exotoxin mediated	Toxic shock syndrome	Toxic shock syndrome toxin	Superantigen
	Food poisoning (gastroenteritis)	Enterotoxin	Superantigen
	Scalded skin syndrome	Exfoliatin	Protease cleaves desmoglein
2. Pyogenic	Skin abscess, osteomyelitis, endocarditis	Enzymes causing inflammation and necrosis	Coagulase, hyaluronidase, leukocidin, lipase, nuclease
Streptococcus pyogenes			
1. Exotoxin mediated	Scarlet fever	Erythrogenic toxin	Superantigen
	Streptococcal toxic shock syndrome	Toxic shock syndrome toxin	Superantigen
2. Pyogenic (Suppurative)	Pharyngitis, cellulitis, necrotizing fasciitis	Enzymes causing inflammation and necrosis	Hyaluronidase (spreading factor)
3. Nonsuppurative (immunopathogenic)	Rheumatic fever	Certain M proteins on pilus	Antibody to M protein cross-reacts with cardiac, joint, and brain tissue
	Acute glomerulonephritis	Certain M proteins on pilus	Immune complexes deposit on glomeruli
Escherichia coli			
1. Exotoxin mediated	Watery, nonbloody diarrhea (traveler's diarrhea)	Labile toxin	Activation of adenylate cyclase increases cyclic AMP; no cell death
	Bloody diarrhea (associated with undercooked hamburger); O157:H7 strain	Shiga-like toxin (Verotoxin)	Cytotoxin inhibits protein synthesis; cell death occurs
2. Pyogenic	Urinary tract infection	Uropathic pili	Pili attach to Gal-Gal receptors on bladder epithelium
	Neonatal meningitis	K-1 capsule	Antiphagocytic

DID THE ORGANISM ISOLATED FROM THE PATIENT ACTUALLY CAUSE THE DISEASE?

Because people harbor microorganisms as members of the permanent normal flora and as transient passengers, this can be an interesting and sometimes confounding question. The answer depends on the situation. One type of situation relates to the problems of a disease for which no agent has been identified and a candidate organism has been isolated. This is the problem that Robert Koch faced in 1877 when he was among the first to try to determine the cause of an infectious disease, namely, anthrax in cattle and tuberculosis in humans. His approach led to the formulation of **Koch's postulates**, which are criteria that he proposed must be satisfied to confirm the causal role of an organism. These criteria are as follows:

(1) The organism must be isolated from every patient with the disease

(2) The organism must be isolated free from all other organisms and grown in pure culture in vitro

(3) The pure organism must cause the disease in a healthy, susceptible animal

(4) The organism must be recovered from the inoculated animal.

The second type of situation pertains to the practical, everyday problem of a specific diagnosis of a patient's illness. In this instance, the signs and symptoms of the illness usually suggest a constellation of possible causative agents. The recovery of an agent in *sufficient numbers* from the *appropriate specimen* is usually sufficient for an etiologic diagnosis. This approach can be illustrated with two examples: (1) in a patient with a sore throat, the presence of a few beta-hemolytic streptococci is insufficient for a microbiologic diagnosis, whereas the presence of many would be sufficient; and (2) in a patient with fever, alpha-hemolytic streptococci in the throat are considered part of the normal flora, whereas the same organisms in the blood are likely to be the cause of bacterial endocarditis.

In some infections, no organism is isolated from the patient and the diagnosis is made by detecting a rise in antibody titer to an organism. For this purpose, the titer (amount) of antibody in the second or late serum sample should be at least 4 times the titer (amount) of antibody in the first or early serum sample.

PEARLS

- The term **pathogen** refers to those microbes capable of causing disease, especially if they cause disease in immunocompetent people. The term **opportunistic pathogen** refers to microbes that are capable of causing disease only in immunocompromised people.

- **Virulence** is a measure of a microbe's ability to cause disease, ie, a highly virulent microbe requires fewer organisms to cause disease than a less virulent one. The **ID$_{50}$** is the number of organisms required to cause disease in 50% of the population. A low ID$_{50}$ indicates a highly virulent organism.

- The virulence of a microbe is determined by **virulence factors,** such as capsules, exotoxins, or endotoxins.

- Whether a person gets an infectious disease or not is determined by the balance between the number and virulence of the microbes and the competency of that person's host defenses.

- Many infections are **asymptomatic** or **inapparent** because our host defenses have eliminated the microorganism before it could multiply to sufficient numbers to cause the symptoms of disease.

- The term **infection** has two meanings: (1) the **presence of microbes** in the body and (2) the **symptoms of disease.** The presence of microbes in the body does not always result in symptoms of disease (see the previous bullet).

- Bacteria cause the symptoms of disease by two main mechanisms: **production of toxins** (both exotoxins and endotoxins) and **induction of inflammation.**

- Most bacterial infections are **communicable,** ie, capable of spreading from person to person, but some are not, eg, botulism and Legionella pneumonia.

- Three epidemiologic terms are often used to describe infections: **endemic** infections are those that occur at a persistent, usually low level in a certain geographic area, **epidemics** are those infections that occur at a much higher rate than usual, and **pandemics** are those infections that spread rapidly over large areas of the globe.

Determinants of Bacterial Pathogenesis

Transmission

- The modes of transmission of microbes include both **human-to-human** and **nonhuman-to-human** processes. Nonhuman sources include animals, soil, water, and food.

- Human-to-human transmission can occur either by **direct contact** or indirectly via a **vector** such as an insect, notably ticks or mosquitoes. Animal-to-human transmission can also occur either by direct contact with the animal or indirectly via a vector.

- The main "portals of entry" into the body are the **respiratory tract, the gastrointestinal tract, the skin,** and **the genital tract.**
- Human diseases for which animals are the reservoir are called **zoonoses.**

Adherence to Cell Surfaces

- **Pili** are the main mechanism by which bacteria adhere to human cells. They are fibers that extend from the surface of bacteria that **mediate attachment** to specific receptors on cells.
- **Glycocalyx** is a polysaccharide "slime layer" secreted by some strains of bacteria that **mediates strong adherence** to certain structures such as heart valves, prosthetic implants, and catheters.

Invasion, Inflammation, & Intracellular Survival

- Invasion of tissue is enhanced by enzymes secreted by bacteria. For example, **hyaluronidase** produced by Streptococcus pyogenes degrades hyaluronic acid in the subcutaneous tissue, allowing the organism to spread rapidly.
- **IgA protease** degrades secretory IgA, allowing bacteria to attach to mucous membranes.
- The **capsule** surrounding bacteria is **antiphagocytic,** ie, it retards the phagocyte from ingesting the organism. Mutant strains of many pathogens that do not produce capsules are nonpathogenic.
- **Inflammation** is an important host defense induced by the presence of bacteria in the body. There are two types of inflammation, **pyogenic and granulomatous,** and bacteria typically elicit one type or the other. **Pyogenic inflammation,** the host defense against pyogenic (pus-producing) bacteria such as S. pyogenes, consists of neutrophils (and antibody and complement). **Granulomatous inflammation,** the host defense against intracellular, granuloma-producing bacteria, such as Mycobacterium tuberculosis, consists of macrophages and CD4-positive T cells. The type of inflammatory lesion is an important diagnostic criterion.
- Bacteria can evade our host defenses by a process called **intracellular survival,** that is, bacteria that can live within cells are protected from attack by macrophages and neutrophils. Note that many of these bacteria, for example, M. tuberculosis, are not obligate intracellular parasites (which can grow only within cells), but rather have the ability to enter and survive inside cells.

Exotoxins

- **Exotoxins** are **polypeptides secreted** by certain bacteria that alter specific cell functions resulting in the symptoms of disease. They are produced by both gram-positive and gram-negative bacteria, whereas endotoxin is found only in gram-negative bacteria.
- Exotoxins are **antigenic** and induce antibodies called **antitoxins.** Exotoxins can be modified to form **toxoids,** which are antigenic but not toxic. Toxoids, such as tetanus toxoid, are used to immunize against disease.
- Many exotoxins have an **A-B subunit** structure in which the A subunit is the **active** (toxic) one and the B subunit is the one that **binds** to the cell membrane and mediates the entry of the A subunit into the cell.
- Exotoxins have different mechanisms of action and different targets within the cell and therefore cause a variety of diseases with characteristic symptoms. (See Tables 7–9 and 7–10.) Several exotoxins are enzymes that attach ADP-ribose to a cell component (**ADP-ribosylation**). Some exotoxins act by **proteolytic cleavage** of a cell component, whereas others act as **superantigens,** causing the overproduction of cytokines.

Endotoxins

- **Endotoxins** are **lipopolysaccharides (LPS)** located in the outer membrane only of gram-negative bacteria. They are not secreted by bacteria.
- **Lipid A** is the toxic component of LPS. It induces the **overproduction of cytokines,** such as tumor necrosis factor, interleukin-1, and nitric oxide, from macrophages, which causes the symptoms of septic shock, such as fever and hypotension. In addition, LPS activates the **complement cascade** (alternate pathway), resulting in increased vascular permeability, and the **coagulation cascade,** resulting in increased vascular permeability and **disseminated intravascular coagulation.**
- Endotoxins are poorly antigenic, do not induce antitoxins, and do not form toxoids.

Typical Stages of an Infectious Disease

- There are often four discrete stages. The **incubation period** is the time between the moment the person is exposed to the microbe (or toxin) and the appearance of symptoms. The **prodrome period** is the time during which nonspecific symptoms occur. The **spe-**

cific-illness period is the time during which the characteristic features of the disease occur. The *recovery period* is the time during which symptoms resolve and health is restored.

- After the recovery period, some people become

chronic carriers of the organism and in others *latent* infections develop.

- Some people have *subclinical* infections during which they remain asymptomatic. The presence of antibodies reveals that a prior infection has occurred.

PRACTICE QUESTIONS: USMLE & COURSE EXAMINATIONS

Questions on the topics discussed in this chapter can be found in the Basic Bacteriology section of Part XI:

USMLE (National Board) Practice Questions starting on page 532. Also see Part XII: USMLE (National Board) Practice Examination starting on page 583.

Host Defenses

Host defenses are composed of two complementary, frequently interacting systems: (1) **innate (nonspecific)** defenses, which protect against microorganisms in general, and (2) **acquired (specific)** immunity, which protects against a particular microorganism. Innate defenses can be classified into three major categories: (1) physical barriers, such as intact skin and mucous membranes; (2) phagocytic cells, such as neutrophils, macrophages, and natural killer cells; and (3) proteins, such as complement, lysozyme, and interferon. Figure 8–1 shows the role of several components of the nonspecific defenses in the early response to bacterial infection. Acquired defenses are mediated by antibodies and T lymphocytes. Chapter 57 describes these host defenses in more detail.

There are two main types of host defenses against bacteria, the **pyogenic** response and the **granulomatous** response. Certain bacteria, such as *Staphylococcus aureus* and *Streptococcus pyogenes,* are defended against by the pyogenic (pus-producing) response, which consists of antibody, complement, and neutrophils. These pyogenic bacteria are often called "extracellular pathogens" because they do not invade cells. Other bacteria, such as *Mycobacterium tuberculosis* and *Listeria monocytogenes,* are defended against by the granulomatous response, which consists of macrophages and CD4-positive (helper) T cells. These bacteria are often called "intracellular pathogens" because they can invade and survive within cells.

INNATE (NONSPECIFIC) IMMUNITY

Skin & Mucous Membranes

Intact skin is the first line of defense against many organisms. In addition to the physical barrier presented by skin, the fatty acids secreted by sebaceous glands in the skin have antibacterial and antifungal activity. The increased fatty acid production that occurs at puberty is thought to explain the increased resistance to ringworm fungal infections that occurs at that time. The low pH of the skin (between pH 3 and 5), which is due to these fatty acids, also has an antimicrobial effect. Although many organisms live on or in the skin as members of the normal flora, they are harmless as long as they do not enter the body.

A second important defense is the mucous membrane of the respiratory tract, which is lined with cilia and covered with mucus. The coordinated beating of the cilia drives the mucus up to the nose and mouth, where the trapped bacteria can be expelled. This mucociliary apparatus, the **ciliary elevator,** can be damaged by alcohol, cigarette smoke, and viruses; the damage predisposes the host to bacterial infections. Other protective mechanisms of the respiratory tract involve alveolar macrophages, lysozyme in tears and mucus, hairs in the nose, and the cough reflex, which prevents aspiration into the lungs.

Loss of the physical barrier provided by the skin and mucous membranes predisposes to infection. Table 8–1 describes the organisms that commonly cause infections associated with the loss of these protective barriers.

The nonspecific protection in the gastrointestinal tract includes hydrolytic enzymes in saliva, acid in the stomach, and various degradative enzymes and macrophages in the small intestine. The vagina of adult women is protected by the low pH generated by lactobacilli that are part of the normal flora.

Additional protection in the gastrointestinal tract and in the lower respiratory tract is provided by **defensins.** These are highly positively charged (cationic) peptides that create pores in the membranes of bacteria, which kills them. Neutrophils and Paneth cells in the intestinal crypts contain one type of defensin (α-defensins), whereas the respiratory tract produces different defensins called β-defensins. The mechanism by which defensins distinguish between bacterial membranes and human cell membranes is unknown.

The bacteria of the normal flora of the skin, nasopharynx, colon, and vagina occupy these ecologic niches, preventing pathogens from multiplying in these sites. The importance of the normal flora is appreciated in the occasional case when antimicrobial therapy suppresses these beneficial organisms, thereby allowing organisms such as *Clostridium difficile* and *Candida albicans* to cause diseases such as pseudomembranous colitis and vaginitis, respectively.

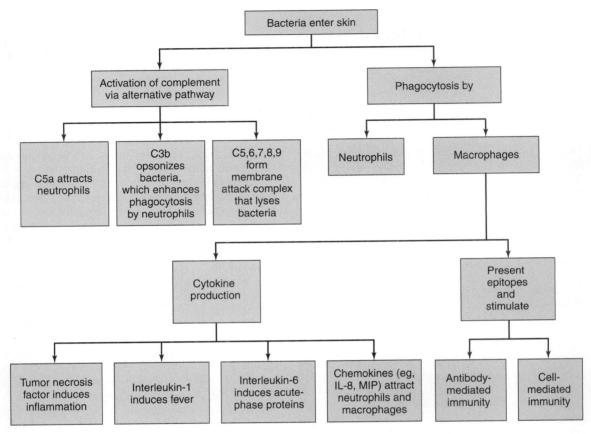

Figure 8–1. Early host responses to bacterial infection.

Table 8–1. Damage to skin and mucous membranes predisposes to infection caused by certain bacteria.

Predisposing Factor	Site of Infection	Bacteria Commonly Causing Infection Associated With Predisposing Factor
Intravenous catheters	Skin	*Staphylococcus epidermidis, Staphylococcus aureus*
Diabetes	Skin	*S. aureus*
Burns	Skin	*Pseudomonas aeruginosa*
Cystic fibrosis	Respiratory tract	*P. aeruginosa*[1]
Trauma to jaw	Gingival crevice	*Actinomyces israelii*
Dental extraction	Oropharynx	Viridans streptococci[2]
Oral mucositis secondary to cancer chemotherapy	Mouth but also entire GI tract	Viridans streptococci, *Capnocytophaga gingivalis*

[1]Bacteria less commonly involved include *Burkholderia cepacia* and *Stenotrophomonas maltophilia*.

[2]Viridans streptococci do not cause local infection after dental extraction but can enter the bloodstream and cause endocarditis.

Inflammatory Response & Phagocytosis

The presence of foreign bodies such as bacteria within the body provokes a protective inflammatory response (Figure 8–2). This response is characterized by the clinical findings of redness, swelling, warmth, and pain at the site of infection. These signs are due to increased blood flow, increased capillary permeability, and the escape of fluid and cells into the tissue spaces. The increased permeability is due to several chemical mediators, of which **histamine, prostaglandins,** and **leukotrienes** are the most important. Complement components, C3a and C5a, also contribute to increased vascular permeability. **Bradykinin** is an important mediator of pain.

Neutrophils and **macrophages,** both of which are phagocytes, are an important part of the inflammatory response. Neutrophils predominate in acute pyogenic infections, whereas macrophages are more prevalent in chronic or granulomatous infections. Macrophages perform two functions: they are phagocytic and they produce two important **"proinflammatory" cytokines, gamma interferon,** and **tumor necrosis factor (TNF).** The importance of the inflammatory response in limiting infection is emphasized by the ability of anti-inflammatory agents such as corticosteroids to lower resistance to infection.

Certain proteins, known collectively as the **"acute-phase response,"** are also produced early in inflammation, mainly by the liver. The best known of these are **C-reactive protein** and **mannose-binding protein,** which bind to the surface of bacteria and enhance the activation of the alternative pathway of complement (see Chapter 58). C-reactive protein was named for its ability to bind to a carbohydrate in the cell wall of *Streptococcus pneumoniae* (see page 113). **Lipopolysaccharide (endotoxin)-binding protein** is another important acute-phase protein that is produced in response to gram-negative bacteria. Interleukin-6 (IL-6) is the main inducer of the acute-phase response. Activated helper T cells are the principal source of IL-6, but many other types of cells produce it as well.

Neutrophils and macrophages are attracted to the site of infection by small polypeptides called **chemokines** (*chemo*tactic cyto*kines*). Chemokines are produced by tissue cells in the infected area, by local endothelial cells, and by resident neutrophils and macrophages. Interleukin-8 is a chemokine that attracts primarily neutrophils, whereas MCP-1, MIP, and RANTES are attractants for macrophages and monocytes (see Chapter 58).

As part of the inflammatory response, bacteria are engulfed (phagocytized) by polymorphonuclear neutrophils (PMNs) and macrophages. PMNs make up approximately 60% of the leukocytes in the blood, and their numbers increase significantly during infection

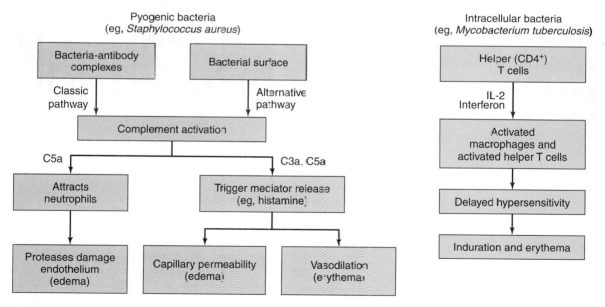

Figure 8–2. Inflammation. The inflammatory response can be caused by two different mechanisms. **Left:** Pyogenic bacteria, eg, *Staphylococcus aureus,* cause inflammation via antibody- and complement-mediated mechanisms. **Right:** Intracellular bacteria, eg, *Mycobacterium tuberculosis,* cause inflammation via cell-mediated mechanisms.

(leukocytosis). It should be noted, however, that in certain bacterial infections such as typhoid fever, a decrease in the number of leukocytes (leukopenia) is found. The increase in PMNs is caused by the production of granulocyte-stimulating factors (G-CSF and GM-CSF [see Chapter 58]) by macrophages soon after infection.

Note that although both PMNs and macrophages phagocytose bacteria, PMNs do not present antigen to helper T lymphocytes, whereas macrophages (and dendritic cells) do (see Chapter 58). Dendritic cells are the most important antigen-presenting cells. The phagocytic ability of dendritic cells is enhanced by the presence of receptors for mannose-binding protein.

The process of phagocytosis can be divided into three steps: migration, ingestion, and killing. Migration of PMNs to the site of the organisms is due to chemokines, such as interleukin-8, complement component C5a, and kallikrein, which—in addition to being chemotactic—is the enzyme that catalyzes the formation of bradykinin. Adhesion of PMNs to the endothelium at the site of infection is mediated first by the interaction of the PMNs with **selectin** proteins on the endothelium and then by the interaction of **integrin** proteins called "LFA proteins," located on the PMN surface, with ICAM proteins on the endothelial cell surface.[1]

ICAM proteins on the endothelium are increased by inflammatory mediators, such as IL-1 and TNF (see Chapter 58), which are produced by macrophages in response to the presence of bacteria. The increase in the level of ICAM proteins ensures that PMNs selectively adhere to the site of infection. Increased permeability of capillaries as a result of histamine, kinins, and prostaglandins[2] allows PMNs to migrate through the capillary wall to reach the bacteria. This migration is called **diapedesis** and takes several minutes to occur.

The bacteria are ingested by the invagination of the PMN cell membrane around the bacteria to form a vacuole (**phagosome**). This engulfment is enhanced by the binding of IgG antibodies (**opsonins**) to the surface of the bacteria, a process called **opsonization** (Figure 8–3). The C3b component of complement enhances opsonization. (The outer cell membranes of both PMNs and macrophages have receptors both for the Fc portion of IgG and for C3b.) Even in the absence of antibody, the C3b component of complement, which can be generated by the "alternative" pathway, can opsonize. This is particularly important for bacterial and fungal organisms whose polysaccharides activate the alternative pathway.

---

[1] LFA proteins and ICAM proteins mediate adhesion between many types of cells. These proteins are described in more detail in Chapter 58.
[2] The anti-inflammatory action of aspirin is the result of its ability to inhibit cyclooxygenase, thus reducing the synthesis of prostaglandins.

At the time of engulfment, a new metabolic pathway, known as the **respiratory burst,** is triggered; this results in the production of two microbicidal agents, the superoxide radical and hydrogen peroxide. These highly reactive compounds (often called "reactive oxygen intermediates") are synthesized by the following reactions:

$$O_2 + e^- \rightarrow O_2^-$$
$$2O_2^- + 2H^+ \rightarrow H_2O_2 + O_2$$

In the first reaction, molecular oxygen is reduced by an electron to form the superoxide radical, which is weakly bactericidal. In the next step, the enzyme superoxide dismutase catalyzes the formation of hydrogen peroxide from two superoxide radicals. Hydrogen peroxide is more toxic than superoxide but is not effective against catalase-producing organisms such as staphylococci.

Nitric oxide (NO) is another important microbicidal agent. It is a "reactive nitrogen intermediate" that is synthesized by an inducible enzyme called nitric oxide synthase in response to stimulators such as endotoxin. Overproduction of NO contributes to the hypotension seen in septic shock because it causes vasodilation of peripheral blood vessels.

The respiratory burst also results in the production of the microbicidal agent NO. NO contains a free radical that participates in oxidative killing of ingested microbes phagocytosed by neutrophils and macrophages. Nitric oxide synthase, the enzyme that produces NO, is induced in these cells following phagocytosis.

The killing of the organism within the phagosome is a two-step process that consists of degranulation followed by production of **hypochlorite** ions (see below), which are probably the most important microbicidal agents. In degranulation, the two types of granules in the cytoplasm of the neutrophil fuse with the phagosome, emptying their contents in the process. These granules are lysosomes that contain a variety of enzymes essential to the killing and degradation that occur within the phagolysosome.

(1) The larger lysosomal granules, which constitute about 15% of the total, contain the important enzyme myeloperoxidase, as well as lysozyme and several other degradative enzymes. (Myeloperoxidase, which is green, makes a major contribution to the color of pus.)

(2) The smaller granules, which make up the remaining 85%, contain lactoferrin and additional degradative enzymes such as proteases, nucleases, and lipases. Lysosomal granules can empty into the extracellular space as well as into the phagosome. Outside the cell, the degradative enzymes can attack structures too large to be phagocytized, such as fungal mycelia, as well as extracellular bacteria.

The actual killing of the microorganisms occurs by a variety of mechanisms, which fall into two categories:

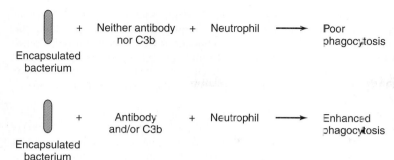

Figure 8–3. Opsonization. **Top:** An encapsulated bacterium is poorly phagocytized by a neutrophil in the absence of either IgG antibody or C3b. **Bottom:** In the presence of either IgG antibody or C3b or both, the bacterium is opsonized; ie, it is made more easily phagocytized by the neutrophil.

oxygen-dependent and oxygen-independent. The most important oxygen-dependent mechanism is the production of the bactericidal molecule **hypochlorite ion** according to the following reaction:

$$Cl^- + H_2O_2 \rightarrow ClO^- + H_2O$$

Myeloperoxidase catalyzes the reaction between chloride ion and H_2O_2, which was produced by the respiratory burst, to produce hypochlorite ion in the presence of myeloperoxidase. Hypochlorite by itself damages cell walls but can also react with H_2O_2 to produce singlet oxygen, which damages cells by reacting with double bonds in the fatty acids of membrane lipids.

Rare individuals are genetically deficient in myeloperoxidase, yet their defense systems can kill bacteria, albeit more slowly. In these persons, the respiratory burst that produces H_2O_2 and superoxide ion seems to be sufficient, but with two caveats: if an organism produces catalase, H_2O_2 will be ineffective, and if an organism produces superoxide dismutase, superoxide ion will be ineffective.

The oxygen-independent mechanisms are important under anaerobic conditions. These mechanisms involve lactoferrin, which chelates iron from the bacteria; lysozyme, which degrades peptidoglycan in the bacterial cell wall; cationic proteins, which damage bacterial membranes; and low pH.

Macrophages also migrate, engulf, and kill bacteria by using essentially the same processes as PMNs do, but there are several differences.

(1) Macrophages do not possess myeloperoxidase and so cannot make hypochlorite ion; however, they do produce H_2O_2 and superoxide by respiratory burst.

(2) Certain organisms such as the agents of tuberculosis, brucellosis, and toxoplasmosis are preferentially ingested by macrophages rather than PMNs and may remain viable and multiply within these cells; granulomas formed during these infections contain many of these macrophages.

(3) Macrophages secrete plasminogen activator, an enzyme that converts the proenzyme plasminogen to the active enzyme plasmin, which dissolves the fibrin clot.

The importance of phagocytosis as a host defense mechanism is emphasized by the following observations (Table 8–2).

(1) Repeated infections occur in children with genetic defects in the phagocytic process. Two examples of these defects are chronic granulomatous disease, in which the phagocyte cannot kill the ingested bacteria owing to a defect in NADPH oxidase and a resultant failure to generate H_2O_2; and Chédiak-Higashi syndrome, in which abnormal lysosomal granules that cannot fuse with the phagosome are formed, so that even though bacteria are ingested, they survive.

Table 8–2. Reduced phagocytosis predisposes to infection caused by certain bacteria.

Type of Reduction	Cause of Reduction	Bacteria Commonly Causing Infection Associated With the Type of Reduction
Decreased number of neutrophils	Cancer chemotherapy, total body irradiation	*Staphylococcus aureus, Pseudomonas aeruginosa*
Decreased function of neutrophils	Chronic granulomatous disease	*S. aureus*
Decreased function of spleen	Splenectomy, sickle cell anemia	*Streptococcus pneumoniae, Neisseria meningitidis, Haemophilus influenzae*

(2) Frequent infections occur in neutropenic patients, especially when the PMN count drops below 500/μL as a result of immunosuppressive drugs or irradiation. These infections are frequently caused by opportunistic organisms, ie, organisms that rarely cause disease in people with normal immune systems.

(3) Splenectomy removes an important source of both phagocytes and immunoglobulins, which predisposes to sepsis caused by three encapsulated pyogenic bacteria: *S. pneumoniae, Neisseria meningitidis,* and *Haemophilus influenzae. S. pneumoniae* causes approximately 50% of episodes of sepsis in splenectomized patients. Patients with sickle cell anemia and other hereditary anemias can auto-infarct their spleen, resulting in a loss of splenic function and a predisposition to sepsis caused by these bacteria.

(4) People who have diabetes mellitus, especially those who have poor glucose control or episodes of ketoacidosis, have an increased number of infections and more severe infections compared with people who do not have diabetes. The main host defense defect in these patients is reduced neutrophil function, especially when acidosis occurs.

Two specific diseases highly associated with diabetes are malignant otitis externa caused by *Pseudomonas aeruginosa* and mucormycosis caused by molds belonging to the genera *Mucor* and *Rhizopus.* In addition, there is an increased incidence and increased severity of community-acquired pneumonia caused by bacteria such as *S. pneumoniae* and *S. aureus* and of urinary tract infections caused by organisms such as *Escherichia coli* and *C. albicans.* Candidal vulvovaginitis is also more common in diabetics. Diabetics also have many foot infections, because atherosclerosis compromises the blood supply and necrosis of tissue occurs. Skin infections, such as ulcers and cellulitis, are common and can extend to the underlying bone, causing osteomyelitis. *S. aureus* and mixed facultative-anaerobic bacteria are the most common causes.

Fever

Infection causes a rise in the body temperature that is attributed to **endogenous pyrogen** (interleukin-1) released from macrophages. Fever may be a protective response, since a variety of bacteria and viruses grow more slowly at elevated temperatures.

ACQUIRED (SPECIFIC) IMMUNITY

Acquired immunity results either from exposure to the organism (active immunity) or from receipt of preformed antibody made in another host (passive immunity).

Passive acquired immunity is temporary protection against an organism and is acquired by receiving serum containing preformed antibodies from another person or animal. Passive immunization occurs normally in the form of immunoglobulins passed through the placenta (IgG) or breast milk (IgA) from mother to child. This protection is very important during the early days of life, when the child has a reduced capacity to mount an active response.

Passive immunity has the important advantage that its protective abilities are present immediately, whereas active immunity has a delay of a few days to a few weeks, depending on whether it is a primary or secondary response. However, passive immunity has the important disadvantage that the antibody concentration decreases fairly rapidly as the proteins are degraded, so that protection usually lasts for only a month or two. The administration of preformed antibodies can be lifesaving in certain diseases, such as botulism and tetanus, that are caused by powerful exotoxins. Serum globulins, given intravenously, are a prophylactic measure in patients with hypogammaglobulinemia or bone marrow transplants. In addition, they can mitigate the symptoms of certain diseases such as hepatitis caused by hepatitis A virus, but they appear to have little effect on bacterial diseases with an invasive form of pathogenesis.

Active acquired immunity is protection based on exposure to the organism in the form of overt disease; subclinical infection, ie, an infection without symptoms; or a vaccine. This protection has a slower onset but longer duration than passive immunity. The **primary response** usually takes 7 to 10 days for antibody to become detectable. An important advantage of active immunity is that an **anamnestic (secondary)** response occurs; ie, there is a rapid response (approximately 3 days) of large amounts of antibody to an antigen that the immune system has previously encountered. Active immunity is mediated by both antibodies (immunoglobulins) and T cells:

(1) Antibodies protect against organisms by a variety of mechanisms: neutralization of toxins, lysis of bacteria in the presence of complement, opsonization of bacteria to facilitate phagocytosis, and interference with adherence of bacteria and viruses to cell surfaces. If the level of IgG drops below 400 mg/dL (normal = 1000–1500), the risk of pyogenic infections caused by bacteria such as staphylococci increases.

Because antibodies, especially IgG, are detectable for days to weeks after infection, they are thought *not* to play a major role in combating the primary infection at the initial site of infection (usually the skin or mucous membrane) but rather to protect against hematogenous dissemination of the organism to distant sites in the body and against a second infection by that organism at some future time.

Table 8–3. Essential host defense mechanisms against bacteria.

Essential Host Defense Mechanism	Type of Bacteria or Toxin	Important Examples
Antibody-mediated (humoral immunity)	Encapsulated pyogenic bacteria	Streptococcus pneumoniae, Streptococcus pyogenes, Staphylococcus aureus, Neisseria meningitidis, Haemophilus influenzae, Pseudomonas aeruginosa
Antibody-mediated	Exotoxins	Corynebacterium diphtheriae, Clostridium tetani, Clostridium botulinum
Cell-mediated	Intracellular bacteria	Mycobacterium tuberculosis, atypical mycobacteria, Legionella pneumophila, Listeria monocytogenes

(2) T cells mediate a variety of reactions including cytotoxic destruction of virus-infected cells and bacteria, activation of macrophages, and delayed hypersensitivity. T cells also help B cells to produce antibody against many, but not all, antigens.

Table 8–3 describes the essential host defense mechanisms against bacteria. These mechanisms include both humoral immunity against pyogenic bacteria and exotoxins and cell-mediated immunity against several intracellular bacteria.

FAILURE OF HOST DEFENSES PREDISPOSES TO INFECTIONS

The frequency or severity of infections is increased when certain predisposing conditions exist. These predisposing conditions fall into two main categories: patients are immunocompromised or patients have foreign bodies such as indwelling catheters or prosthetic devices. Foreign bodies predispose because host defenses do not operate efficiently in their presence. Table 8–4 describes the predisposing conditions and the most

Table 8–4. Conditions that predispose to infections and the organisms that commonly cause these infections.

Predisposing Condition	Organisms Commonly Causing Infection
Immunocompromised state	
Low antibody	Pyogenic bacteria, eg, Staphylococcus aureus, Streptococcus pneumoniae
Low complement (C3b)	Pyogenic bacteria, eg, S. aureus, S. pneumoniae
Low complement (C6,7,8,9)	Neisseria meningitidis
Low neutrophil number	Pyogenic bacteria, eg, S. aureus, S. pneumoniae
Low neutrophil function as in CGD	S. aureus and Aspergillus fumigatus
Low CD4 cells as in AIDS	Various bacteria, eg, mycobacteria; various viruses, eg, CMV; and various fungi, eg, Candida
Presence of foreign bodies	
Urinary catheters	Escherichia coli
Intravenous catheters	Staphylococcus epidermidis, Candida albicans
Prosthetic heart valves	S. epidermidis, C. albicans
Prosthetic joints	S. epidermidis
Vascular grafts	S. epidermidis, S. aureus, Salmonella enterica

CGD = chronic granulomatous disease; CMV = cytomegalovirus.

common organisms causing infections when these predisposing conditions are present.

Certain diseases and anatomic abnormalities also predispose to infections. For example, patients with diabetes often have *S. aureus* infections, perhaps for two reasons: these patients have extensive atherosclerosis, which causes relative anoxia to tissue, and they appear to have a defect in neutrophil function. Patients with sickle cell anemia often have *Salmonella* osteomyelitis, probably because the abnormally shaped cells occlude the small capillaries in the bone. This traps the *Salmonella* within the bone, increasing the risk of osteomyelitis.

Patients with certain congenital cardiac defects or rheumatic valvular damage are predisposed to endocarditis caused by viridans streptococci. Neutrophils have difficulty in penetrating the vegetations formed on the valves in endocarditis. Patients with an aortic aneurysm are prone to vascular infections caused by *Salmonella* species.

PEARLS

- *Host defenses against bacterial infections include both **innate** and **adaptive (acquired)** defenses. Innate defenses are nonspecific, ie, they are effective against many different organisms. They include **physical barriers,** such as intact skin and mucous membranes; **cells,** such as neutrophils and macrophages; and **proteins,** such as complement and lysozyme. Adaptive (acquired) defenses are highly specific for the organism and include **antibodies** and **cells** such as CD4-positive helper T lymphocytes and CD8-positive cytotoxic T lymphocytes.*

Innate Immunity

- *Intact skin and mucous membranes provide a **physical barrier** to infection. Loss of skin integrity, eg, in a burn, predisposes to infection. The low pH of the skin, stomach, and vagina also protects against infection.*

- *The respiratory tract, a very important portal of entry for microbes, is protected by the ciliary elevator, **alveolar macrophages,** lysozyme, nose hairs, and the cough reflex.*

- *The normal flora of the skin and mucous membranes occupies receptors, which reduces the opportunity for pathogens to attach, a process called **colonization resistance. Suppression of the normal flora with antibiotics predisposes to infection** with certain organisms. Two important examples are the suppression of colon flora predisposing to pseudomembranous colitis caused by* Clostridium difficile *and the suppression of vaginal flora predisposing to vaginitis caused by* Candida albicans.*

- ***Inflammation,** ie, redness, swelling, warmth, and pain, is an important host defense. Redness, swelling, and warmth are the result of **increased blood flow** and **increased vascular permeability,** which has* the effect of bringing the cells and proteins of our host defenses to the site of infection. The increased blood flow and increased vascular permeability are caused by **mediators** such as **histamine, prostaglandins,** and **leukotrienes.***

- *The predominant phagocytic cells in inflammation are **neutrophils** and **macrophages.** Neutrophils are seen in the pyogenic inflammatory response to bacteria such as* Staphylococcus aureus *and* Streptococcus pyogenes, *whereas macrophages are seen in the granulomatous inflammatory response to bacteria such as* Mycobacterium tuberculosis.*

- *The **acute-phase response** consists of proteins, such as C-reactive protein, mannose-binding protein, and LPS-binding protein, that enhance the host response to bacteria. Interleukin-6 is the main inducer of this response.*

- *Neutrophils and macrophages are attracted to the site of infection by **chemokines,** which are small polypeptides produced by cells at the infected site. **Interleukin-8** and **C5a** are important chemokines for neutrophils.*

- *In response to most bacterial infections, there is an **increase in the number of neutrophils** in the blood. This increase is caused by the production of **granulocyte-stimulating factors** by macrophages.*

- *Both neutrophils and macrophages **phagocytose** bacteria, but macrophages (and similar cells called dendritic cells) also **present antigen** to CD4-positive (helper) T cells, whereas neutrophils do not. **Dendritic cells are probably the most important antigen-presenting cells** in the body.*

- *After neutrophils are attracted to the infected site by chemokines, they attach to the endothelium first using **selectins** on the endothelium, then by the inter-*

action of **integrins** (LFA proteins) on the neutrophils with ICAM proteins on the endothelium. The concentration of ICAM proteins is increased by cytokines released by activated macrophages, which results in neutrophils being attracted to the infected site.

- Neutrophils then migrate through the endothelium (**diapedesis**) and ingest the bacteria. **IgG and C3b are opsonins,** which enhance ingestion of the bacteria. There are receptors for the heavy chain of IgG and for C3b on the surface of the neutrophils.

- Killing of the bacteria within the neutrophil is caused by **hypochlorite, hydrogen peroxide,** and **superoxides. Lysosomes** contain various degradative enzymes and fuse with the phagosome to form a **phagolysosome** within which the killing occurs.

- Severe, recurrent **pyogenic infections** occur in those who have **inadequate neutrophils.** For example, people with defective neutrophils, people with fewer than 500 neutrophils/µL, and those who have had a splenectomy or who have diabetes mellitus are at increased risk for pyogenic infections.

Acquired Immunity

- **Passive immunity** refers to protection based on the transfer of preformed antibody from one person (or animal) to another person. Passive immunity provides **immediate but short-lived protection** (lasting a few months). Examples of passive immunity include administration of antitoxin, passage of IgG from mother to fetus across the placenta, and passage of IgA from mother to newborn in breast milk.

- **Active immunity** refers to protection based on the formation of both **antibodies and cell-mediated immunity after exposure** either to the microbe itself (with or without disease) or to the antigens of the microbe in a vaccine. Active immunity provides **long-term protection but is not effective** for days after exposure to the microbe. In the **primary response,** antibody appears in 7 to 10 days, whereas in the **secondary response,** antibody appears in approximately 3 days.

- The main **functions of antibodies** are to **neutralize bacterial toxins and viruses, opsonize bacteria, activate complement** to form a membrane-attack complex that can kill bacteria, and **interfere with attachment to mucosal surfaces.** IgG is the main opsonizing antibody, IgG and IgM activate complement, and IgA interferes with attachment to the mucosa.

- The main functions of **cell-mediated immunity** are to **protect against intracellular bacteria** and to **kill virus-infected cells.** Helper T cells (and macrophages) protect against intracellular bacteria, whereas cytotoxic T cells kill virus-infected cells.

Reduced Host Defenses

- **Reduced host defenses** result in an increase in the frequency and severity of infections. The main causes include various genetic immunodeficiencies, the presence of foreign bodies, and the presence of certain chronic diseases, such as diabetes mellitus and renal failure.

PRACTICE QUESTIONS: USMLE & COURSE EXAMINATION

Questions on the topics discussed in this chapter can be found in the Basic Bacteriology section of Part XI:

USMLE (National Board) Practice Questions starting on page 532. Also see Part XII: USMLE (National Board) Practice Examination starting on page 583.

Laboratory Diagnosis

The laboratory diagnosis of infectious diseases involves two main approaches: one is the **bacteriologic** approach in which the organism is identified by staining and culturing the organism, and the other is the **immunologic (serologic)** approach in which the organism is identified by detection of antibodies against the organism in the patient's serum.

In the bacteriologic approach to the diagnosis of infectious diseases, several important steps precede the actual laboratory work, namely, (1) choosing the appropriate specimen to examine, which requires an understanding of the pathogenesis of the infection; (2) obtaining the specimen properly to avoid contamination from the normal flora; (3) transporting the specimen promptly to the laboratory or storing it correctly; and (4) providing essential information to guide the laboratory personnel.

In general, there are three approaches to the bacteriologic laboratory work:

(1) *Observing* the organism in the microscope after staining

(2) *Obtaining* a pure culture of the organism by inoculating it onto a bacteriologic medium

(3) *Identifying* the organism by using biochemical reactions, growth on selective media, DNA probes, or specific antibody reactions. Which of these approaches are used and in what sequence depend on the type of specimen and organism. After the organism is grown in pure culture, its sensitivity to various antibiotics is determined by procedures described in Chapter 11.

A general approach to the diagnosis of a bacterial infection is described in Table 9–1. This approach emphasizes the importance of performing a Gram stain and obtaining a "pure culture" of the organism. However, sometimes the organism is not recovered by culturing, and other techniques must be used. Table 9–2 describes some approaches to making a diagnosis when the cultures are negative. One approach that is commonly used is serologic testing, which determines the presence of antibodies specific for the organism. In most cases, a 4-fold rise in antibody titer between the acute- and convalescent-phase serum samples is considered to be significant.

Obtaining a pure culture involves culturing the organism on bacteriologic agar. Initially, blood agar is used because it supports the growth of many bacteria and the type of hemolysis can be observed.

Blood agar contains red blood cells, but it should be noted that viruses and obligate intracellular bacteria, such as *Chlamydia* and *Rickettsia*, will not grow on blood agar. Red blood cells do not have a functioning nucleus and therefore are incapable of supporting the growth of either viruses or the obligate intracellular bacteria.

Blood agar contains inhibitors for certain bacteria, such as members of the *Neisseria* and *Haemophilus* genera, and the blood must be heated to inactivate these inhibitors. These bacteria therefore are grown on cooked blood agar or chocolate agar (so named because the heated blood turns a chocolate color). Other media contain either specific growth factors required for the bacteria to grow or contain antibiotics that inhibit normal flora, which allows the pathogenic bacteria to obtain sufficient nutrients to grow.

Certain other media called "selective, differential" media are often used. These media are selective because they contain compounds that selectively allow certain bacteria to grow and differential because they contain other compounds that allow one type of bacteria to be differentiated from another based on some biochemical reaction. Table 9–3 contains a list of various bacteriologic agars commonly used in the diagnostic laboratory and the function of these agars.

BACTERIOLOGIC METHODS

Blood Cultures

Blood cultures are performed most often when sepsis, endocarditis, osteomyelitis, meningitis, or pneumonia is suspected. The organisms most frequently isolated from blood cultures are two gram-positive cocci, *Staphylococcus aureus* and *Streptococcus pneumoniae,* and three gram-negative rods, *Escherichia coli, Klebsiella pneumoniae,* and *Pseudomonas aeruginosa.*

It is important to obtain at least three 10-mL blood samples in a 24-hour period, because the number of organisms can be small and their presence intermittent. The site for venipuncture must be cleansed with 2% iodine to prevent contamination by members of the

Table 9–1. General approach to the diagnosis of a bacterial infection.

1. Obtain a specimen from the infected site.

2. Stain the specimen using the appropriate procedure, eg, Gram stain or acid-fast stain. If bacteria are seen in the Gram-stain specimen, their shape (eg, cocci or rods), size, arrangement (eg, chains or clusters), and whether they are gram-positive or gram-negative should be observed. It is also important to determine whether only one or more than one type of bacteria is present. The microscopic appearance is *not* sufficient to speciate an organism, but it often allows an educated guess to be made regarding the genus of the organism and thereby guides empiric therapy.

3. Culture the specimen on the appropriate media, eg, blood agar plates. In most instances, the plates should be streaked in such a manner as to obtain isolated colonies, ie, a "pure culture." The plates should be incubated in the presence or absence of oxygen as appropriate.

4. Identify the organism using the appropriate tests, eg, sugar fermentation, DNA probes, antibody-based tests such as agglutination, or immunofluorescence. Note special features such as hemolysis and pigment formation.

5. Perform antibiotic susceptibility tests.

flora of the skin, usually *Staphylococcus epidermidis.* The blood obtained is added to 100 mL of a rich growth medium such as brain-heart infusion broth. Whether one or two bottles are inoculated varies among hospitals. If two bottles are used, one is kept under anaerobic conditions and the other is not. If one bottle is used, the low oxygen tension at the bottom of the bottle permits anaerobes to grow.

Blood cultures are checked for turbidity or for CO_2 production daily for 7 days or longer. If growth occurs, Gram stain, subculture, and antibiotic sensitivity tests are performed. If no growth is observed after 1 or 2 days, blind subculturing onto other media may reveal organisms. Cultures should be held for 14 days when infective endocarditis, fungemia, or infection by slow-growing bacteria, eg, *Brucella,* is suspected.

Throat Cultures

Throat cultures are used primarily to detect the presence of group A beta-hemolytic streptococci (*Streptococcus pyogenes*), an important and treatable cause of pharyngitis. They are also used when diphtheria, gonococcal pharyngitis, or thrush (*Candida*) is suspected.

When the specimen is being obtained, the swab should touch not only the posterior pharynx but both tonsils or tonsillar fossae as well. The material on the swab is inoculated onto a blood agar plate and streaked to obtain single colonies. If colonies of beta-hemolytic streptococci are found after 24 hours of incubation at 35°C, a bacitracin disk is used to determine whether the organism is likely to be a group A streptococcus. If growth is inhibited around the disk, it is a group A streptococcus; if not, it is a non–group A beta-hemolytic streptococcus.

Note that a Gram stain is typically *not* done on a throat swab because it is impossible to distinguish between the appearance of the normal flora streptococci and *S. pyogenes.*

Sputum Cultures

Sputum cultures are performed primarily when pneumonia or tuberculosis is suspected. The most frequent

Table 9–2. How to diagnose a bacterial infection when the culture is negative.

1. Detect antibody in the patient's serum. Detection of IgM antibody indicates a current infection. A 4-fold or greater rise in antibody titer between the acute serum sample and the convalescent serum sample also indicates a current infection. (A major drawback with the use of acute and convalescent serum samples is that the convalescent sample is usually taken 10–14 days after the acute sample. By this time, the patient has often recovered and the diagnosis becomes a retrospective one.) A single IgG antibody titer is difficult to interpret because it is unclear whether it represents a current or a previous infection. In certain diseases, a single titer of sufficient magnitude can be used as presumptive evidence of a current infection.

2. Detect antigen in the patient's specimen. Use known antibody to detect presence of antigens of the organisms, eg, fluorescent antibody to detect antigens in tissue, latex agglutination to detect capsular polysaccharide antigens in spinal fluid.

3. Detect nucleic acids in the patient's specimen. Use polymerase chain reaction (PCR) and DNA probes to detect the DNA or RNA of the organism.

Table 9–3. Commonly used bacteriologic agars and their function.

Name of Agar[1]	Bacteria Isolated on This Agar	Function or Properties of the Agar
Blood	Various bacteria	Detect hemolysis
Bordet-Gengou	*Bordetella pertussis*	Increased concentration of blood allows growth
Charcoal-yeast extract	*Legionella pneumophila*	Increased concentration of iron and cysteine allows growth
Chocolate	*Neisseria meningitidis* and *Neisseria gonorrhoeae* from sterile sites	Heating the blood inactivates inhibitors of growth
Chocolate agar plus X and V factors	*Haemophilus influenzae*	X and V factors are required for growth
Egg yolk	*Clostridium perfringens*	Lecithinase produced by the organism degrades egg yolk to produce insoluble precipitate
Eosin-methylene blue	Various enteric gram-negative rods	Selects against gram-positive bacteria and differentiates between lactose fermenters and non-fermenters
Löwenstein-Jensen	*Mycobacterium tuberculosis*	Selects against gram-positive bacteria in respiratory tract flora and contains lipids required for growth
MacConkey	Various enteric gram-negative rods	Selects against gram-positive bacteria and differentiates between lactose fermenters and nonfermenters
Tellurite	*Corynebacterium diphtheriae*	Tellurite metabolized to tellurium, which has black color
Thayer-Martin	*N. gonorrhoeae* from nonsterile sites	Chocolate agar with antibiotics to inhibit growth of normal flora
Triple sugar iron (TSI)	Various enteric gram-negative rods	Distinguishes lactose fermenters from nonfermenters and H_2S producers from nonproducers

[1] Names are listed in alphabetical order.

cause of community-acquired pneumonia is *S. pneumoniae,* whereas *S. aureus* and gram-negative rods, such as *K. pneumoniae* and *P. aeruginosa,* are common causes of hospital-acquired pneumonias.

It is important that the specimen for culture really be sputum, not saliva. Examination of a Gram-stained smear of the specimen frequently reveals whether the specimen is satisfactory. A reliable specimen has more than 25 leukocytes and fewer than 10 epithelial cells per 100 × field. An unreliable sample can be misleading and should be rejected by the laboratory. If the patient cannot cough and the need for a microbiologic diagnosis is strong, induction of sputum, transtracheal aspirate, bronchial lavage, or lung biopsy may be necessary. Because these procedures bypass the normal flora of the upper airway, they are more likely to provide an accurate microbiologic diagnosis. A preliminary assessment of the cause of the pneumonia can be made by Gram stain if large numbers of typical organisms are seen.

Culture of the sputum on blood agar frequently reveals characteristic colonies, and identification is made by various serologic or biochemical tests. Cultures of *Mycoplasma* are infrequently done; diagnosis is usually confirmed by a rise in antibody titer. If *Legionella* pneumonia is suspected, the organism can be cultured on charcoal-yeast agar, which contains the high concentrations of iron and sulfur required for growth.

If tuberculosis is suspected, an acid-fast stain should be done immediately and the sputum cultured on special media, which are incubated for at least 6 weeks. In diagnosing aspiration pneumonia and lung abscesses, anaerobic cultures are important.

Spinal Fluid Cultures

Spinal fluid cultures are performed primarily when meningitis is suspected. Spinal fluid specimens from cases of encephalitis, brain abscess, and subdural empyema usually show negative cultures. The most important causes of acute bacterial meningitis are three encapsulated organisms: *Neisseria meningitidis, S. pneumoniae,* and *Haemophilus influenzae.*

Because acute meningitis is a medical emergency, the specimen should be taken immediately to the laboratory. The Gram-stained smear of the sediment of the centrifuged sample guides the immediate empirical treatment. If organisms resembling *N. meningitidis, H. influenzae,* or *S. pneumoniae* are seen, the quellung test or immunofluorescence with specific antisera can identify the organism rapidly. Cultures are done on blood and on chocolate agar and incubated at 35°C in a 5% CO_2 atmosphere. Hematin and nicotinamide adenine dinucleotide (NAD) (factors X and V, respectively) are added to enhance the growth of *H. influenzae.*

In cases of subacute meningitis, *Mycobacterium tuberculosis* and the fungus *Cryptococcus neoformans* are the most common organisms isolated. Acid-fast stains of the spinal fluid should be performed, although *M. tuberculosis* may not be seen, because it can be present in small numbers. The fluid should be cultured and the cultures held for a minimum of 6 weeks. *C. neoformans,* a budding yeast with a prominent capsule, can be seen in spinal fluid when India ink is used.

Immunologic tests to detect the presence of capsular antigen in the spinal fluid can be used to identify *N. meningitidis, S. pneumoniae, H. influenzae,* group B streptococci, *E. coli,* and *C. neoformans.* The two tests most frequently used are latex particle agglutination and counter-immunoelectrophoresis.

Stool Cultures

Stool cultures are performed primarily for cases of enterocolitis. The most common bacterial pathogens causing diarrhea in the United States are *Shigella, Salmonella,* and *Campylobacter.*

A direct microscopic examination of the stool can be informative from two points of view: (1) a methylene blue stain that reveals many leukocytes indicates that an invasive organism rather than a toxigenic one is involved; and (2) a Gram stain may reveal large numbers of certain organisms, such as staphylococci, clostridia, or campylobacters. Gram stain of the stool is not usually done because the large numbers of bacteria in the normal flora of the colon make the interpretation difficult.

For culture of *Salmonella* and *Shigella,* a selective, differential medium such as MacConkey or eosin-methylene blue (EMB) agar is used. These media are selective because they allow gram-negative rods to grow but inhibit many gram-positive organisms. Their differential properties are based on the fact that *Salmonella* and *Shigella* do not ferment lactose, whereas many other enteric gram-negative rods do. If non-lactose-fermenting colonies are found, a triple sugar iron (TSI) agar slant is used to distinguish *Salmonella* from *Shigella.* Some species of *Proteus* resemble *Salmonella* on TSI agar but can be distinguished because they produce the enzyme urease, whereas *Salmonella* does not. The organism is further identified as either a *Salmonella* or a *Shigella* species by the use of specific antisera

to the organism's cell wall O antigen in an agglutination test. This is usually done in hospital laboratories, but precise identification of the species is performed in public health laboratories.

Campylobacter jejuni is cultured on antibiotic-containing media, eg, Skirrow's agar, at 42°C in an atmosphere containing 5% O_2 and 10% CO_2. It grows well under these conditions, unlike many other intestinal pathogens. Although the techniques are available, stool cultures are infrequently performed for organisms such as *Yersinia enterocolitica, Vibrio parahaemolyticus,* and enteropathic or toxigenic *E. coli.* Despite the presence of large numbers of anaerobes in feces, they are rarely pathogens in the intestinal tract, and anaerobic cultures of stool specimens are therefore unnecessary.

Urine Cultures

Urine cultures are performed primarily when pyelonephritis or cystitis is suspected. By far the most frequent cause of urinary tract infections is *E. coli.* Other common agents are *Enterobacter, Proteus,* and *Enterococcus faecalis.*

Urine in the bladder of a healthy person is sterile, but it acquires organisms of the normal flora as it passes through the distal portion of the urethra. To avoid these organisms, a midstream specimen, voided after washing the external orifice, is used for urine cultures. In special situations, suprapubic aspiration or catheterization may be required to obtain a specimen. Because urine is a good culture medium, it is essential that the cultures be done within 1 hour after collection or stored in a refrigerator at 4°C for no more than 18 hours.

It is commonly accepted that a bacterial count of at least 100,000/mL must be found to conclude that significant bacteriuria is present (in asymptomatic persons). There is evidence that as few as 100/mL are significant in symptomatic patients. For this determination to be made, quantitative or semiquantitative cultures must be performed. There are several techniques. (1) A calibrated loop that holds 0.001 mL of urine can be used to streak the culture. (2) Serial 10-fold dilutions can be made and samples from the dilutions streaked. (3) A screening procedure suitable for the physician's office involves an agar-covered "paddle" that is dipped into the urine. After the paddle is incubated, the density of the colonies is compared with standard charts to obtain an estimate of the concentration of bacteria.

Genital Tract Cultures

Genital tract cultures are performed primarily on specimens from individuals with an abnormal discharge or on specimens from asymptomatic contacts of a person with a sexually transmitted disease. One of the most important pathogens in the genital tract is *Neisseria gonorrhoeae*. The laboratory diagnosis of gonorrhea is made by microscopic examination of a Gram-stained smear and by culture of the organism.

Specimens are obtained by swabbing the urethral canal (for men), the cervix (for women), or the anal canal (for men and women). A urethral discharge from the penis is frequently used. Because *N. gonorrhoeae* is very delicate, the specimen should be inoculated directly onto a Thayer-Martin chocolate agar plate or onto a special transport medium (eg, Trans-grow).

Gram-negative diplococci found *intracellularly* within neutrophils on a smear of a urethral discharge from a man have over 90% probability of being *N. gonorrhoeae.* Because smears are less reliable when made from swabs of the endocervix and anal canal, cultures are necessary. The finding of only *extracellular* diplococci suggests that these neisseriae may be members of the normal flora and that the patient may have nongonococcal urethritis.

Nongonococcal urethritis and cervicitis are also extremely common infections. The most frequent cause is *Chlamydia trachomatis,* which cannot grow on artificial medium but must be grown in living cells. For this purpose, cultures of human cells or the yolk sacs of embryonated eggs are used. The finding of typical intracytoplasmic inclusions when using Giemsa stain or fluorescent antibody is diagnostic. Because of the difficulty of culturing *C. trachomatis,* non-bacteriologic methods, such as enzyme-linked immunosorbent assay (ELISA) to detect chlamydial antigens in exudates or urine or DNA probe assays to detect chlamydial nucleic acids, are now often used to diagnose sexually transmitted diseases caused by this organism.

Because *Treponema pallidum,* the agent of syphilis, cannot be cultured, diagnosis is made by microscopy and serology. The presence of motile spirochetes with typical morphologic features seen by darkfield microscopy of the fluid from a painless genital lesion is sufficient for the diagnosis. The serologic tests fall into two groups: the nontreponemal antibody tests such as the Venereal Disease Research Laboratory (VDRL) or rapid plasma reagin (RPR) test, and the treponemal antibody tests such as the fluorescent treponemal antibody-absorption (FTA-ABS) test. These tests are described on page 66.

Wound & Abscess Cultures

A great variety of organisms are involved in wound and abscess infections. The bacteria most frequently isolated differ according to anatomic site and predisposing factors. Abscesses of the brain, lungs, and abdomen are frequently caused by anaerobes such as *Bacteroides frag-*

ilis and gram-positive cocci such as *S. aureus* and *S. pyogenes.* Traumatic open-wound infections are caused primarily by members of the soil flora such as *Clostridium perfringens;* surgical-wound infections are usually due to *S. aureus.* Infections of dog or cat bites are commonly due to *Pasteurella multocida,* whereas human bites primarily involve the mouth anaerobes.

Because anaerobes are frequently involved in these types of infection, it is important to place the specimen in anaerobic collection tubes and transport it promptly to the laboratory. Because many of these infections are due to multiple organisms, including mixtures of anaerobes and nonanaerobes, it is important to culture the specimen on several different media under different atmospheric conditions. The Gram stain can provide valuable information regarding the range of organisms under consideration.

IMMUNOLOGIC METHODS

These methods are described in more detail in Chapter 64. However, it is of interest here to present information on how serologic reactions aid the microbiologic diagnosis. There are essentially two basic approaches: (1) using known antibody to identify the microorganism, and (2) using known antigens to detect antibodies in the patient's serum.

Identification of an Organism with Known Antiserum

A. CAPSULAR SWELLING (QUELLUNG) REACTION

Several bacteria can be identified directly in clinical specimens by this reaction, which is based on the microscopic observation that the capsule swells in the presence of homologous antiserum. Antisera against the following organisms are available: all serotypes of *S. pneumoniae* (Omniserum), *H. influenzae* type b, and *N. meningitidis* groups A and C.

B. SLIDE AGGLUTINATION TEST

Antisera can be used to identify *Salmonella* and *Shigella* by causing agglutination (clumping) of the unknown organism. Antisera directed against the cell wall O antigens of *Salmonella* and *Shigella* are commonly used in hospital laboratories. Antisera against the flagellar H antigens and the capsular Vi antigen of *Salmonella* are used in public health laboratories for epidemiologic purposes.

C. LATEX AGGLUTINATION TEST

Latex beads coated with specific antibody are agglutinated in the presence of the homologous bacteria or antigen. This test is used to determine the presence of the capsular antigen of *H. influenzae, N. meningitidis,* several species of streptococci, and the yeast *C. neoformans.*

D. COUNTER-IMMUNOELECTROPHORESIS TEST

In this test, the unknown bacterial antigen and a known specific antibody move toward each other in an electrical field. If they are homologous, a precipitate forms within the agar matrix. Because antibodies are positively charged at the pH of the test, only negatively charged antigens, usually capsular polysaccharides, can be assayed. The test can be used to detect the presence in the spinal fluid of the capsular antigens of *H. influenzae, N. meningitidis, S. pneumoniae,* and group B streptococci.

E. ENZYME-LINKED IMMUNOSORBENT ASSAY

In this test, a specific antibody to which an easily assayed enzyme has been linked is used to detect the presence of the homologous antigen. Because several techniques have been devised to implement this principle, the specific steps used cannot be detailed here (see Chapter 64). This test is useful in detecting a wide variety of bacterial, viral, and fungal infections.

F. FLUORESCENT-ANTIBODY TESTS

A variety of bacteria can be identified by exposure to known antibody labeled with fluorescent dye, which is detected visually in the ultraviolet microscope. Various methods can be used, such as the direct and indirect techniques (see Chapter 64).

Identification of Serum Antibodies with Known Antigens

A. SLIDE OR TUBE AGGLUTINATION TEST

In this test, serial 2-fold dilutions of a sample of the patient's serum are mixed with standard bacterial suspensions. The highest dilution of serum capable of agglutinating the bacteria is the titer of the antibody. As with most tests of a patient's antibody, at least a 4-fold rise in titer between the early and late samples must be demonstrated for a diagnosis to be made. This test is used primarily to aid in the diagnosis of typhoid fever, brucellosis, tularemia, plague, leptospirosis, and rickettsial diseases.

B. SEROLOGIC TESTS FOR SYPHILIS

The detection of antibody in the patient's serum is frequently used to diagnose syphilis, because *T. pallidum* does not grow on laboratory media. There are two kinds of tests.

(1) The nontreponemal tests use a cardiolipin-lecithin-cholesterol mixture as the antigen, not an antigen of the organism. Cardiolipin (diphosphatidylglycerol) is a lipid extracted from normal beef heart. Flocculation (clumping) of the cardiolipin occurs in the presence of antibody to *T. pallidum.* The VDRL and RPR tests are nontreponemal tests commonly used as screening procedures. They are not specific for syphilis but are inexpensive and easy to perform.

(2) The treponemal tests use *T. pallidum* as the antigen. The two most widely used treponemal tests are the FTA-ABS and the MHA-TP (microhemagglutination-*Treponema pallidum*) tests. In the FTA-ABS test, the patient's serum sample, which has been absorbed with treponemes other than *T. pallidum* to remove nonspecific antibodies, is reacted with nonviable *T. pallidum* on a slide. Fluorescein-labeled antibody against human immunoglobulin G (IgG) is then used to determine whether IgG antibody against *T. pallidum* is bound to the organism. In the MHA-TP test, the patient's serum sample is reacted with sheep erythrocytes coated with antigens of *T. pallidum.* If antibodies are present, hemagglutination occurs.

C. COLD AGGLUTININ TEST

Patients with *Mycoplasma pneumoniae* infections develop autoimmune antibodies that agglutinate human red blood cells in the cold (4°C) but not at 37°C. These antibodies occur in certain diseases other than *Mycoplasma* infections; thus, false-positive results can occur.

NUCLEIC ACID–BASED METHODS

There are three types of nucleic acid–based tests used in the diagnosis of bacterial diseases: nucleic acid amplification tests, nucleic acid probes, and nucleic acid sequence analysis. Nucleic acid–based tests are highly specific, quite sensitive (especially the amplification tests), and much faster than culturing the organism. These tests are especially useful for those bacteria that are difficult to culture such as *Chlamydia* and *Mycobacterium* species.

Nucleic acid amplification tests utilize the PCR (polymerase chain reaction) or other amplifying process to increase the number of bacteria-specific DNA or RNA molecules so the sensitivity of the test is significantly higher than that of unamplified tests. Many bacteria can be identified using these tests but they are especially useful in detecting *Chlamydia trachomatis* and *Neisseria gonorrhoeae* in urine samples in STD clinics.

Tests that use nucleic acid probes are designed to detect bacterial DNA or RNA directly (without amplification) using a labeled DNA or RNA probe that will hybridize specifically to the bacterial nucleic acid. These tests are simpler to perform than the amplification tests but are less sensitive.

Nucleic acid sequence analysis is used to identify bacteria based on the base sequence of the organism's ribosomal RNA. An organism that has never been cultured, *Tropheryma whippelii,* was identified using this approach.

PEARLS

- The **laboratory diagnosis** of infectious diseases includes **bacteriologic, immunologic (serologic), and molecular (nucleic acid–based) tests.**

Bacteriologic Tests

- Bacteriologic tests typically begin with **staining** the patient's specimen and **observing** the organism in the microscope. This is followed by **culturing** the organism, typically on blood agar, then **performing various tests** to identify the causative organism. Obtaining a **pure culture** of the bacteria is essential to accurate diagnosis.
- **Blood cultures** are useful in cases of **sepsis** and other diseases in which the organism is often found in the bloodstream, such as endocarditis, meningitis, pneumonia, and osteomyelitis.
- **Throat cultures** are most useful to diagnose **pharyngitis** caused by Streptococcus pyogenes (strep throat), but they are also used to diagnose diphtheria, gonococcal pharyngitis, and thrush caused by the yeast Candida albicans.
- **Sputum cultures** are used primarily to diagnose the cause of **pneumonia** but also are used in suspected cases of tuberculosis.
- **Spinal fluid cultures** are most useful in suspected cases of **meningitis.** These cultures are often negative in encephalitis, brain abscess, and subdural empyema.
- **Stool cultures** are useful primarily when the complaint is **bloody diarrhea** (dysentery, enterocolitis) rather than watery diarrhea, which is often caused by either enterotoxins or viruses.
- **Urine cultures** are used to determine the cause of either **pyelonephritis** or **cystitis.**
- **Genital tract cultures** are most often used to diagnose **gonorrhea** and chancroid. Chlamydia trachomatis is difficult to grow, so nonbacteriologic methods such as ELISA and DNA probes are now used more often than are cultures. The agent of syphilis has not been cultured, so the diagnosis is made serologically.
- **Wounds and abscesses** can be caused by a large variety of organisms. Cultures should be incubated both in the presence and in the absence of oxygen because **anaerobes** are often involved.

Immunologic (Serologic) Tests

- Immunologic (serologic) tests can determine whether **antibodies are present in the patient's serum** as well as detect the **antigens of the organism in tissues or body fluids.**
- In these tests, the antigens of the causative organism can be detected by using specific antibody often labeled with a dye such as fluorescein (fluorescent antibody tests). The presence of antibody in the patient's serum can be detected using antigens derived from the organism. In some tests, the patient's serum contains antibodies that react with an antigen that is not derived from the causative organism, such as the VDRL test in which beef heart cardiolipin reacts with antibodies in the serum of patients with syphilis.
- In many tests in which antibodies are detected in the patient's serum, an acute and convalescent serum sample is obtained and at least a **4-fold increase in titer** between the acute and convalescent samples must be found for a diagnosis to be made. The reason these criteria are used is that the presence of antibodies in a single sample could be from a prior infection, so a significant (4-fold or greater) increase in titer is used to indicate that this is a current infection. **IgM antibody** can also be used as an indicator of current infection.

PRACTICE QUESTIONS: USMLE & COURSE EXAMINATIONS

Questions on the topics discussed in this chapter can be found in the Basic Bacteriology section of Part XI: USMLE (National Board) Practice Questions starting on page 532. Also see Part XII: USMLE (National Board) Practice Examination starting on page 583.

Antimicrobial Drugs: Mechanism of Action

The most important concept underlying antimicrobial therapy is **selective toxicity**, ie, selective inhibition of the growth of the microorganism without damage to the host. Selective toxicity is achieved by exploiting the differences between the metabolism and structure of the microorganism and the corresponding features of human cells. For example, penicillins and cephalosporins are effective antibacterial agents because they prevent the synthesis of peptidoglycan, thereby inhibiting the growth of bacterial but not human cells.

There are four major sites in the bacterial cell that are sufficiently different from the human cell that they serve as the basis for the action of clinically effective drugs: cell wall, ribosomes, nucleic acids, and cell membrane (Table 10–1).

There are far more antibacterial drugs than antiviral drugs. This is a consequence of the difficulty of designing a drug that will selectively inhibit viral replication. Because viruses use many of the normal cellular functions of the host in their growth, it is not easy to develop a drug that specifically inhibits viral functions and does not damage the host cell.

Broad-spectrum antibiotics are active against several types of microorganisms, eg, tetracyclines are active against many gram-negative rods, chlamydiae, mycoplasmas, and rickettsiae. **Narrow-spectrum** antibiotics are active against one or very few types, eg, vancomycin is primarily used against certain gram-positive cocci, namely, staphylococci and enterococci.

■ BACTERICIDAL & BACTERIOSTATIC ACTIVITY

In some clinical situations, it is essential to use a bactericidal drug rather than a bacteriostatic one. A **bactericidal drug kills bacteria**, whereas a **bacteriostatic drug inhibits their growth but does not kill them.** The salient features of the behavior of bacteriostatic drugs are that (1) the bacteria can grow again when the drug is withdrawn, and (2) host defense mechanisms, such as

phagocytosis, are required to kill the bacteria. Bactericidal drugs are particularly useful in certain infections, eg, those that are immediately life-threatening; those in patients whose polymorphonuclear leukocyte count is below 500/μL; and endocarditis, in which phagocytosis is limited by the fibrinous network of the vegetations and bacteriostatic drugs do not effect a cure.

■ MECHANISMS OF ACTION

INHIBITION OF CELL WALL SYNTHESIS

1. Inhibition of Bacterial Cell Wall Synthesis

Penicillins

Penicillins (and cephalosporins) act by inhibiting transpeptidases, the enzymes that catalyze the final cross-linking step in the synthesis of peptidoglycan (see Figure 2–5). For example, in *Staphylococcus aureus,* transpeptidation occurs between the amino group on the end of the pentaglycine cross-link and the terminal carboxyl group of the D-alanine on the tetrapeptide side chain. Because the stereochemistry of penicillin is similar to that of a dipeptide, D-alanyl-D-alanine, penicillin can bind to the active site of the transpeptidase and inhibit its activity.

Two additional factors are involved in the action of penicillin.

(1) The first is that penicillin binds to a variety of receptors in the bacterial cell membrane and cell wall called **penicillin-binding proteins (PBPs)**. Some PBPs are transpeptidases; the function of others is unknown. Changes in PBPs are in part responsible for an organism's becoming resistant to penicillin.

(2) The second factor is that **autolytic enzymes** called murein hydrolases (murein is a synonym for peptidoglycan) are activated in penicillin-treated cells and degrade the peptidoglycan. Some bacteria, eg, strains of

Table 10–1. Mechanism of action of important antibacterial and antifungal drugs.

Mechanism of Action	Drugs
Inhibition of cell wall synthesis	
1. Antibacterial activity	
Inhibition of cross-linking (transpeptidation) of peptidoglycan	Penicillins, cephalosporins, imipenem, aztreonam, vancomycin
Inhibition of other steps in peptidoglycan synthesis	Cycloserine, bacitracin
2. Antifungal activity	
Inhibition of β-glucan synthesis	Caspofungin
Inhibition of protein synthesis	
Action on 50S ribosomal subunit	Chloramphenicol, erythromycin, clindamycin, linezolid
Action on 30S ribosomal subunit	Tetracyclines and aminoglycosides
Inhibition of nucleic acid synthesis	
Inhibition of nucleotide synthesis	Sulfonamides, trimethoprim
Inhibition of DNA synthesis	Quinolones
Inhibition of mRNA synthesis	Rifampin
Alteration of cell membrane function	
Antibacterial activity	Polymyxin, daptomycin
Antifungal activity	Amphotericin B, nystatin, ketoconazole
Other mechanisms of action	
1. Antibacterial activity	Isoniazid, metronidazole, ethambutol, pyrazinamide
2. Antifungal activity	Griseofulvin, pentamidine

S. aureus, are **tolerant** to the action of penicillin, because these autolytic enzymes are not activated. A tolerant organism is one that is inhibited but not killed by a drug that is usually bactericidal, such as penicillin (see page 85).

Penicillin-treated cells die by rupture as a result of the influx of water into the high-osmotic-pressure interior of the bacterial cell. If the osmotic pressure of the medium is raised about 3-fold, by the addition of sufficient KCl, for example, rupture will not occur and the organism can survive as a protoplast. Exposure of the bacterial cell to lysozyme, which is present in human tears, results in degradation of the peptidoglycan and osmotic rupture similar to that caused by penicillin.

Penicillin is bactericidal, but it **kills cells only when they are growing.** When cells are growing, new peptidoglycan is being synthesized and transpeptidation occurs. However, in nongrowing cells, no new cross-linkages are required and penicillin is inactive. Penicillins are therefore **more active during the log phase** of bacterial cell growth than during the stationary phase (see Chapter 3 for the bacterial cell growth cycle).

Penicillins (and cephalosporins) are called β-lactam drugs because of the importance of the β-lactam ring (Figure 10–1). An intact ring structure is essential for antibacterial activity; cleavage of the ring by penicillinases (**β-lactamases**) inactivates the drug. The most important naturally occurring compound is benzylpenicillin (penicillin G), which is composed of the 6-aminopenicillanic acid nucleus that all penicillins have, plus a benzyl side chain (see Figure 10–1). Penicillin G is available in three main forms:

(1) Aqueous penicillin G, which is metabolized most rapidly.

(2) Procaine penicillin G, in which penicillin G is conjugated to procaine. This form is metabolized more slowly and is less painful when injected intramuscularly because the procaine acts as an anesthetic.

(3) Benzathine penicillin G, in which penicillin G is conjugated to benzathine. This form is metabolized very slowly and is often called a "depot" preparation.

Benzylpenicillin is one of the most widely used and effective antibiotics. However, it has four disadvantages, three of which have been successfully overcome by chemical modification of the side chain. The three dis-

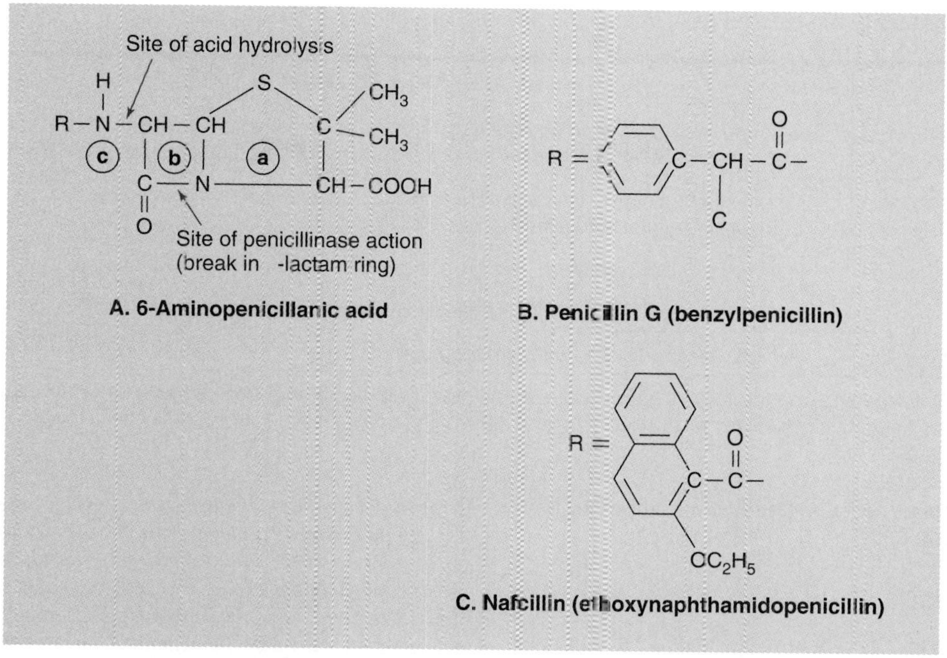

Figure 10–1. Penicillins. **A:** The 6-aminopenicillanic acid nucleus is composed of a thiazolidine ring (a), a β-lactam ring (b), and an amino group (c). The sites of inactivation by stomach acid and by penicillinase are indicated. **B:** The benzyl group, which forms benzylpenicillin (penicillin G) when attached at R. **C:** The large aromatic ring substituent that forms nafcillin, a β-lactamase-resistant penicillin, when attached at R. The large ring blocks the access of β-lactamase to the β-lactam ring.

advantages are (1) limited effectiveness against many gram-negative rods; (2) hydrolysis by gastric acids, so that it cannot be taken orally; and (3) inactivation by β-lactamases. The fourth disadvantage common to all penicillins that has *not* been overcome is hypersensitivity, especially anaphylaxis, in some recipients of the drug.

The effectiveness of penicillins against gram-negative rods has been increased by a series of chemical changes in the side chain (Table 10–2). It can be seen that ampicillin and amoxicillin have activity against several gram-negative rods that the earlier penicillins do not have. However, these drugs are not useful against *Pseudomonas aeruginosa* and *Klebsiella pneumoniae*. Hence, other penicillins were introduced. Generally speaking, as the activity against gram-negative bacteria increases, the activity against gram-positive bacteria decreases.

The second important disadvantage—acid hydrolysis in the stomach—also has been addressed by modification of the side chain. The site of acid hydrolysis is the amide bond between the side chain and penicillanic acid nucleus (see Figure 10–1). Minor modifications of the side chain in that region, such as addition of an oxygen (to produce penicillin V) or an amino group (to produce ampicillin), prevent hydrolysis and allow the drug to be taken orally.

The inactivation of penicillin G by β-lactamases is another important disadvantage, especially in the treatment of *S. aureus* infections. Access of the enzyme to the β-lactam ring is blocked by modification of the side chain with the addition of large aromatic rings containing bulky methyl or ethyl groups (methicillin, oxacillin, nafcillin etc; Figure 10–1). Another defense against β-lactamases is inhibitors such as clavulanic acid and sulbactam. These are structural analogues of penicillin that have little antibacterial activity but bind strongly to β-lactamases and thus protect the penicillin. Combinations, such as amoxicillin and clavulanic acid (Augmentin) are in clinical use. Some bacteria resistant to these combinations have been isolated from patient specimens.

Penicillins are usually nontoxic at clinically effective levels. The major disadvantage of these compounds is hypersensitivity, which is estimated to occur in 1–10% of patients. The hypersensitivity reactions include anaphylaxis, skin rashes, hemolytic anemia, nephritis, and drug fever. Anaphylaxis, the most serious complication,

Table 10–2. Activity of selected penicillins.

Drug	Major Organisms[1]
Penicillin G	Gram-positive cocci, gram-positive rods, *Neisseria*, spirochetes such as *Treponema pallidum*, and many anaerobes (except *Bacteroides fragilis*) but none of the gram-negative rods listed below
Ampicillin or amoxicillin	Certain gram-negative rods, such as *Haemophilus influenzae*, *Escherichia coli*, *Proteus*, *Salmonella*, and *Shigella* but not *Pseudomonas aeruginosa*
Carbenicillin or ticarcillin	*P. aeruginosa*, especially when used in synergistic combination with an aminoglycoside
Piperacillin	Similar to carbenicillin but with greater activity against *P. aeruginosa* and *Klebsiella pneumoniae*
Nafcillin or dicloxacillin	Penicillinase-producing *Staphylococcus aureus*

[1]The spectrum of activity is intentionally incomplete. It is simplified for the beginning student to illustrate the expanded coverage of gram-negative organisms with successive generations and does not cover all possible clinical uses.

occurs in 0.5% of patients. Death as a result of anaphylaxis occurs in 0.002% (1:50,000) of patients.

Cephalosporins

Cephalosporins are β-lactam drugs that act in the same manner as penicillins; ie, they are bactericidal agents that inhibit the cross-linking of peptidoglycan. The structures, however, are different: The cephalosporins have a six-membered ring adjacent to the β-lactam ring and are substituted in two places on the 7-aminocephalosporanic acid nucleus (Figure 10–2), whereas penicillins have a five-membered ring and are substituted in only one place.

The first-generation cephalosporins are active primarily against gram-positive cocci. Similar to the penicillins, new cephalosporins were synthesized with ex-

pansion of activity against gram-negative rods as the goal. These new cephalosporins have been categorized into second, third, and fourth generations, with each generation having expanded coverage against certain gram-negative rods. Cephalosporins are effective against a broad range of organisms, are generally well tolerated, and produce fewer hypersensitivity reactions than do the penicillins. Despite the structural similarity, a patient allergic to penicillin has only about a 10% chance of being hypersensitive to cephalosporins also. Most cephalosporins are the products of molds of the genus *Cephalosporium;* a few, such as cefoxitin, are made by the actinomycete *Streptomyces*.

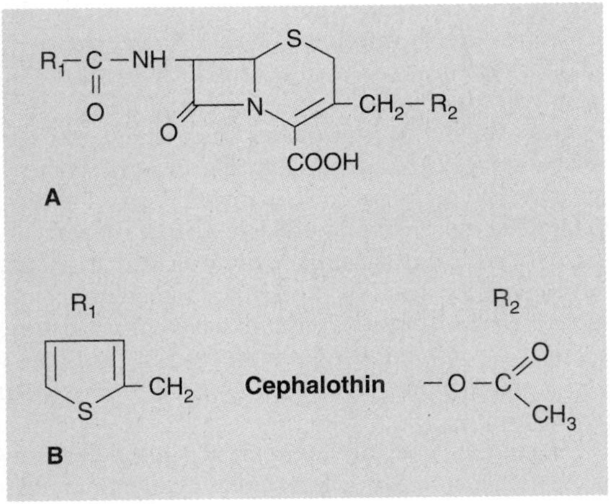

Carbapenems

Carbapenems are β-lactam drugs that are structurally different from penicillins and cephalosporins. For example, imipenem (*N*-formimidoylthienamycin), the currently used carbapenem, has a methylene group in the ring in place of the sulfur (Figure 10–3). Imipenem has the widest spectrum of activity of the β-lactam drugs. It has excellent bactericidal activity against many gram-positive, gram-negative, and anaerobic bacteria. It is effective against most gram-positive cocci, eg, streptococci and staphylococci; most gram-negative cocci, eg, *Neisseria;* many gram-negative rods, eg, *Pseudomonas, Haemophilus*, and members of the family Enterobacteriaceae such as *E. coli;* and various anaerobes, eg, *Bacteroides* and *Clostridium*. It is prescribed in combination with cilastatin, which is an inhibitor of dehydropeptidase, a kidney enzyme that inactivates imipenem. Imipenem is not inactivated by most β-lactamases.

Monobactams

Monobactams are also β-lactam drugs that are structurally different from penicillins and cephalosporins.

Figure 10–2. Cephalosporins. **A:** The 7-aminocephalosporanic acid nucleus. **B:** The two R groups in the drug cephalothin.

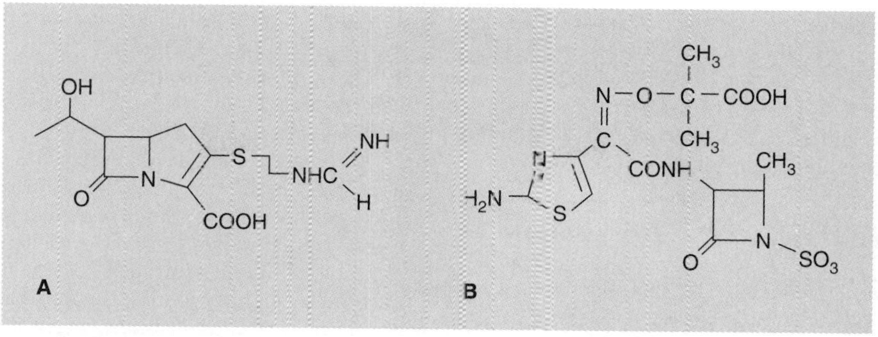

Figure 10–3. A: Imipenem. **B:** Aztreonam.

Monobactams are characterized by a β-lactam ring without an adjacent sulfur-containing ring structure; ie, they are monocyclic (Figure 10–3). Aztreonam, currently the most useful monobactam, has excellent activity against many gram-negative rods, such as Enterobacteriaceae and *Pseudomonas,* but is inactive against gram-positive and anaerobic bacteria. It is resistant to most β-lactamases. It is very useful in patients who are hypersensitive to penicillin, because there is no cross-reactivity.

Vancomycin

Vancomycin is a glycopeptide that **inhibits cell wall synthesis by blocking transpeptidation** but by a mechanism different from that of the β-lactam drugs. Vancomycin binds directly to the D-alanyl-D-alanine portion of the pentapeptide which blocks the transpeptidase from binding, whereas the β-lactam drugs bind to the transpeptidase itself. Vancomycin also inhibits a second enzyme, the bacterial transglycosylase, which also functions in synthesizing the peptidoglycan, but this appears to be less important than inhibition of the transpeptidase.

Vancomycin is a bactericidal agent **effective against certain gram-positive bacteria**. Its most important use is in the treatment of infections by *S. aureus* strains that are resistant to the penicillinase-resistant penicillins such as nafcillin. Note that vancomycin is not a β-lactam drug and, therefore, is not degraded by β-lactamase. Vancomycin is also used in the treatment of infections caused by *Staphylococcus epidermidis* and enterococci. Strains of *S. aureus, S. epidermidis,* and enterococci with partial or complete resistance to vancomycin have been recovered from patients.

Cycloserine & Bacitracin

Cycloserine is a structural analogue of D-alanine that inhibits the synthesis of the cell wall dipeptide D-alanyl-D-alanine. It is used as a second-line drug in the treatment of tuberculosis. Bacitracin is a cyclic polypeptide antibiotic that prevents the dephosphorylation of the phospholipid that carries the peptidoglycan subunit across the cell membrane. This blocks the regeneration of the lipid carrier and inhibits cell wall synthesis. Bacitracin is a bactericidal drug useful in the treatment of superficial skin infections but too toxic for systemic use.

2. Inhibition of Fungal Cell Wall Synthesis

Echinocandins, such as caspofungin (Cancidas) and micafungin (Mycamine) are lipopeptides that block fungal cell wall synthesis by inhibiting the enzyme that synthesizes β-glucan. β-Glucan is a polysaccharide composed of long chains of D-glucose that is an essential component of certain medically important fungal pathogens.

Caspofungin inhibits the growth of *Aspergillus* and *Candida* but not *Cryptococcus* or *Mucor.* Caspofungin is used for the treatment of disseminated candidiasis and for the treatment of invasive aspergillosis that does not respond to amphotericin B. Micafungin is approved for the treatment of esophageal candidiasis and the prophylaxis of invasive *Candida* infections in bone marrow transplant patients.

INHIBITION OF PROTEIN SYNTHESIS

Several drugs inhibit protein synthesis in bacteria without significantly interfering with protein synthesis in human cells. This selectivity is due to the differences between bacterial and human ribosomal proteins, RNAs, and associated enzymes. Bacteria have 70S[1] ribosomes with 50S and 30S subunits, whereas human cells have 80S ribosomes with 60S and 40S subunits.

---

[1] S stands for Svedberg units, a measure of sedimentation rate in a density gradient. The rate of sedimentation is proportionate to the mass of the particle.

Chloramphenicol, erythromycin, clindamycin, and linezolid act on the 50S subunit, whereas tetracyclines and aminoglycosides act on the 30S subunit. A summary of the modes of action of these drugs is presented in Table 10–3, and a summary of their clinically useful activity is presented in Table 10–4.

1. Drugs That Act on the 30S Subunit

Aminoglycosides

Aminoglycosides are bactericidal drugs especially useful against many gram-negative rods. Certain aminoglycosides are used against other organisms; eg, streptomycin is used in the multidrug therapy of tuberculosis, and gentamicin is used in combination with penicillin G against enterococci. Aminoglycosides are named for the amino sugar component of the molecule, which is connected by a glycosidic linkage to other sugar derivatives (Figure 10–4).

The two important modes of action of aminoglycosides have been documented best for streptomycin; other aminoglycosides probably act similarly. Both **inhibition of the initiation complex** and **misreading of messenger RNA** (mRNA) occur; the former is probably more important for the bactericidal activity of the drug. An initiation complex composed of a streptomycin-treated 30S subunit, a 50S subunit, and mRNA will not function—ie, no peptide bonds are formed, no polysomes are made, and a frozen "streptomycin monosome" results. Misreading of the triplet codon of mRNA so that the wrong amino acid is inserted into the protein also occurs in streptomycin-treated bacteria. The site of action on the 30S subunit includes both a ribosomal protein and the ribosomal RNA (rRNA). As

a result of inhibition of initiation and misreading, membrane damage occurs and the bacterium dies. (In 1993, another possible mode of action was described, namely, that aminoglycosides inhibit ribozyme-mediated self-splicing of rRNA.)

Aminoglycosides have certain limitations in their use: (1) They have a toxic effect both on the kidneys and on the auditory and vestibular portions of the eighth cranial nerve. To avoid toxicity, serum levels of the drug, blood urea nitrogen, and creatinine should be measured. (2) They are poorly absorbed from the gastrointestinal tract and cannot be given orally. (3) They penetrate the spinal fluid poorly and must be given intrathecally in the treatment of meningitis. (4) They are ineffective against anaerobes, because their transport into the bacterial cell requires oxygen.

Tetracyclines

Tetracyclines are a family of antibiotics with bacteriostatic activity against a variety of gram-positive and gram-negative bacteria, mycoplasmas, chlamydiae, and rickettsiae. They inhibit protein synthesis by binding to the 30S ribosomal subunit and by **blocking the aminoacyl transfer RNA (tRNA) from entering the acceptor site** on the ribosome. However, the selective action of tetracycline on bacteria is not at the level of the ribosome, because tetracycline in vitro will inhibit protein synthesis equally well in purified ribosomes from both bacterial and human cells. Its selectivity is based on its greatly increased uptake into susceptible bacterial cells compared with human cells.

Tetracyclines, as the name indicates, have four cyclic rings with different substituents at the three R groups (Figure 10–5). The various tetracyclines (eg, doxycy-

Table 10–3. Mode of action of antibiotics that inhibit protein synthesis.

Antibiotic	Ribosomal Subunit	Mode of Action	Bactericidal or Bacteriostatic
Aminoglycosides	30S	Blocks functioning of initiation complex and causes misreading of mRNA	Bactericidal
Tetracyclines	30S	Blocks tRNA binding to ribosome	Bacteriostatic
Chloramphenicol	50S	Blocks peptidyltransferase	Both[1]
Erythromycin	50S	Blocks translocation	Primarily bacteriostatic
Clindamycin	50S	Blocks peptide bond formation	Primarily bacteriostatic
Linezolid	50S	Blocks early step in ribosome formation	Both[1]
Telithromycin	50S	Same as other macrolides, eg, erythromycin	Both[1]
Streptogramins	50S	Causes premature release of peptide chain	Both[1]

[1] Can be either bactericidal or bacteriostatic, depending on the organism.

Table 10–4. Spectrum of activity of antibiotics that inhibit protein synthesis.

Antibiotic	Clinically Useful Activity	Comments
Aminoglycosides		
Streptomycin	Tuberculosis, tularemia, plague, brucellosis	Ototoxic and nephrotoxic.
Gentamicin and tobramycin	Many gram-negative rod infections including *Pseudomonas aeruginosa*	Most widely used aminoglycosides.
Amikacin	Same as gentamicin and tobramycin	Effective against some organisms resistant to gentamicin and tobramycin.
Neomycin	Preoperative bowel preparation	Too toxic to be used systemically; use orally since not absorbed.
Tetracyclines	Rickettsial and chlamydial infections, *Mycoplasma pneumoniae*	Not given during pregnancy or to young children.
Chloramphenicol	*Haemophilus influenzae* meningitis, typhoid fever, anaerobic infections (especially *Bacteroides fragilis*)	Bone marrow toxicity limits use to severe infections.
Erythromycin	Pneumonia caused by *Mycoplasma* and *Legionella*, infections by gram-positive cocci in penicillin-allergic patients	Generally well tolerated but some diarrhea.
Clindamycin	Anaerobes such as *Clostridium perfringens* and *Bacteroides fragilis*	Pseudomembranous colitis is a major side effect.
Linezolid	Vancomycin-resistant enterococci, methicillin-resistant *Staphylococcus aureus* and *Staphylococcus epidermidis,* and penicillin-resistant pneumococci	Generally well tolerated.
Telithromycin	Community-acquired pneumonia caused by various bacteria including multidrug-resistant *Streptococcus pneumoniae*	Many bacteria that are resistant to other macrolides are susceptible to telithromycin
Streptogramins	Bacteremia caused by vancomycin-resistant *Enterococcus faecium*	No cross-resistance between streptogramins and other drugs that inhibit protein synthesis

cline, minocycline, oxytetracycline) have similar antimicrobial activity but different pharmacologic properties. In general, tetracyclines have low toxicity but are associated with two important side effects. One is suppression of the normal flora of the intestinal tract, which can lead to diarrhea and overgrowth by drug-resistant bacteria and fungi. The other is brown staining of the teeth of fetuses and young children as a result of deposition of the drug in developing teeth; tetracyclines are avid calcium chelators. For this reason, tetracycline is contraindicated for use in pregnant women and in children younger than 8 years of age.

2. Drugs That Act on the 50S Subunit
Chloramphenicol

Chloramphenicol is active against a broad range of organisms, including gram-positive and gram-negative bac-

teria (including anaerobes). It is bacteriostatic against certain organisms, such as *Salmonella typhi*, but has bactericidal activity against the three important encapsulated organisms that cause meningitis: *Haemophilus influenzae, Streptococcus pneumoniae,* and *Neisseria meningitidis.*

Chloramphenicol inhibits protein synthesis by binding to the 50S ribosomal subunit and **blocking the action of peptidyltransferase;** this prevents the synthesis of new peptide bonds. It inhibits bacterial protein synthesis selectively, because it binds to the catalytic site of the transferase in the 50S bacterial ribosomal subunit but not to the transferase in the 60S human ribosomal subunit. Chloramphenicol inhibits protein synthesis in the mitochondria of human cells to some extent, since mitochondria have a 50S subunit (mitochondria are thought to have evolved from bacteria). This inhibition may be the cause of the dose-dependent toxicity of chloramphenicol to bone marrow (discussed below).

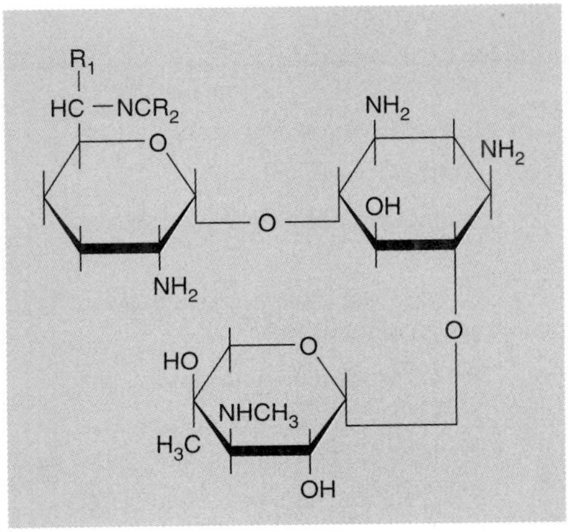

Figure 10–4. Aminoglycosides. Aminoglycosides consist of amino sugars joined by a glycosidic linkage. The structure of gentamicin is shown.

Chloramphenicol is a comparatively simple molecule with a nitrobenzene nucleus (Figure 10–6). Nitrobenzene itself is a bone marrow depressant; therefore, the nitrobenzene portion of the molecule may be involved in the hematologic problems reported with this drug. The most important side effect of chloramphenicol is bone marrow toxicity, of which there are two types. One is a dose-dependent suppression, which is more likely to occur in patients receiving high doses for long periods and which is reversible when administration of the drug is stopped. The other is aplastic anemia, which is caused by an idiosyncratic reaction to the drug. This reaction is not dose-dependent, can occur weeks after administration of the drug has been stopped, and is not reversible. Fortunately, this reaction is rare, occurring in about 1:30,000 patients.

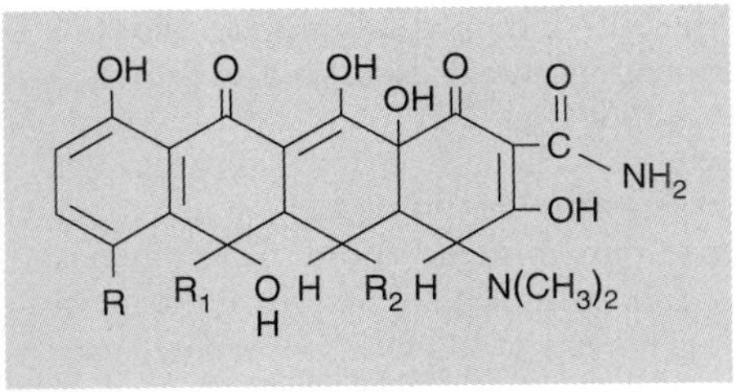

Figure 10–5. Tetracycline structure. The four-ring structure is depicted with its three R sites. Chlortetracycline, for example, has R = Cl, R_1 = CH_3, and R_2 = H.

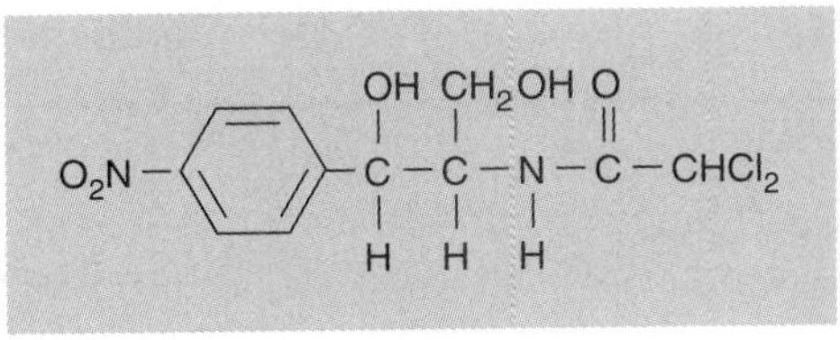

Figure 10–6. Chloramphenicol.

Erythromycin

Erythromycin is a bacteriostatic drug with a wide spectrum of activity. It is the treatment of choice for pneumonia caused by *Legionella* (a gram-negative rod) and *Mycoplasma* (a wall-less bacterium) and is also an effective alternative against a variety of infections caused by gram-positive cocci in penicillin-allergic patients. Erythromycin, azithromycin, and clarithromycin are members of a group of drugs called **macrolides,** named for their large ring structure (Figure 10–7).

Erythromycin binds to the 50S subunit and blocks protein synthesis by preventing the release of the uncharged tRNA from the donor site after the peptide bond is formed. It has a macrolide structure composed of a large 13-carbon ring to which two sugars are attached by glycosidic linkages (Figure 10–7). Erythromycin is one of the least toxic drugs, with only some gastrointestinal distress associated with oral use.

Two derivatives of erythromycin, azithromycin and clarithromycin, have the same mechanism of action as erythromycin but are effective against a broader range of organisms and have a longer half-life, which means they can be taken only once or twice a day.

Clindamycin

The most useful clinical activity of this bacteriostatic drug is against anaerobes, both gram-positive bacteria such as *Clostridium perfringens* and gram-negative bacteria such as *Bacteroides fragilis*.

Clindamycin binds to the 50S subunit and blocks peptide bond formation by an undetermined mechanism. Its specificity for bacteria arises from its inability to bind to the 60S subunit of human ribosomes.

The most important side effect of clindamycin is pseudomembranous colitis, which, in fact, can occur with virtually any antibiotic, whether taken orally or parenterally. The pathogenesis of this potentially severe complication is suppression of the normal flora of the bowel by the drug and overgrowth of a drug-resistant strain of *Clostridium difficile*. The organism secretes an exotoxin that produces the pseudomembrane in the colon and severe, often bloody diarrhea.

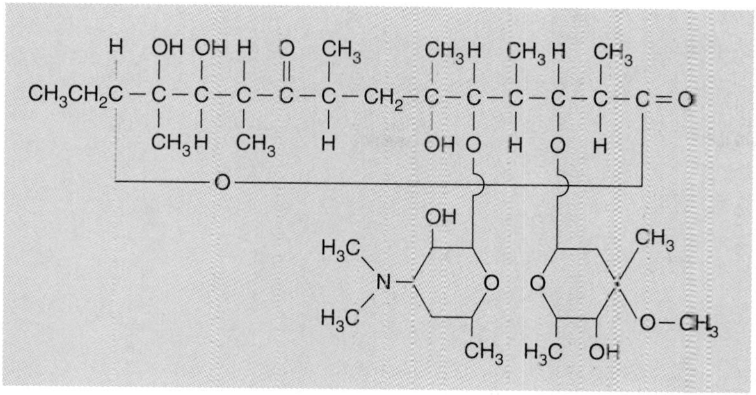

Figure 10–7. Erythromycin.

Linezolid

Linezolid is useful for the treatment of vancomycin-resistant enterococci, methicillin-resistant *S. aureus* and *S. epidermidis,* and penicillin-resistant pneumococci. It is bacteriostatic against enterococci and staphylococci but bactericidal against pneumococci.

Linezolid binds to the 23S ribosomal RNA in the 50S subunit and inhibits protein synthesis, but the precise mechanism is unknown. It appears to block some early step (initiation) in ribosome formation.

TELITHROMYCIN

Telithromycin (Ketek) is the first clinically useful member of the ketolide group of antibiotics. It is similar to the macrolides in general structure and mode of action but is sufficiently different chemically that organisms resistant to macrolides may be sensitive to telithromycin. It has a wide spectrum of activity against a variety of gram-positive and gram-negative bacteria (including macrolide-resistant pneumococci) and is used in the treatment of community-acquired pneumonia, bronchitis, and sinusitis.

STREPTOGRAMINS

A combination of two streptogramins, quinopristin and dalfopristin (Synercid), is used for the treatment of bloodstream infections caused by vancomycin-resistant *Enterococcus faecium* (but not vancomycin-resistant *Enterococcus faecalis*). It is also approved for use in skin infections caused by *Streptococcus pyogenes* and by methicillin-sensitive *Staphylococcus aureus.*

Streptogramins cause premature release of the growing peptide chain from the 50S ribosomal subunit. The structure and mode of action of streptogramins is different from all other drugs that inhibit protein synthesis and there is no cross-resistance between streptogramins and these other drugs.

INHIBITION OF NUCLEIC ACID SYNTHESIS

1. Inhibition of Precursor Synthesis

Sulfonamides

Either alone or in combination with trimethoprim, sulfonamides are useful in a variety of bacterial diseases such as urinary tract infections caused by *Escherichia coli,* otitis media caused by *S. pneumoniae* or *H. influenzae* in children, shigellosis, nocardiosis, and chancroid. In combination, they are also the drugs of choice for two protozoan diseases, toxoplasmosis and *Pneumocystis* pneumonia. The sulfonamides are a large family of bacteriostatic drugs that are produced by chemical synthesis. In 1935, the parent compound, sulfanilamide, became the first clinically effective antimicrobial agent.

The mode of action of sulfonamides is to block the synthesis of tetrahydrofolic acid, which is required as a methyl donor in the synthesis of the nucleic acid precursors adenine, guanine, and thymine. Sulfonamides are **structural analogues of *p*-aminobenzoic acid** (PABA). PABA condenses with a pteridine compound to form dihydropteroic acid, a precursor of tetrahydrofolic acid (Figure 10–8). Sulfonamides compete with PABA for the active site of the enzyme dihydropteroate synthetase. This competitive inhibition can be overcome by an excess of PABA.

The basis of the selective action of sulfonamides on bacteria is that many bacteria synthesize their folic acid from PABA-containing precursors, whereas human cells require preformed folic acid as an exogenous nutrient because they lack the enzymes to synthesize it. Human cells therefore bypass the step at which sulfonamides act. Bacteria that can use preformed folic acid are similarly resistant to sulfonamides.

The *p*-amino group on the sulfonamide is essential for its activity. Modifications are therefore made on the sulfonic acid side chain.

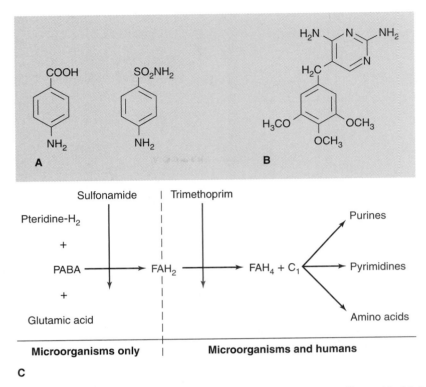

Figure 10–8. Sulfonamide and trimethoprim. **A:** Comparison of PABA (**left**) and sulfonamide (**right**). **B:** Trimethoprim. **C:** Inhibition of the folic acid pathway by sulfonamide and trimethoprim (FAH$_2$ = dihydrofolate; FAH$_4$ = tetrahydrofolate). (Modified and reproduced, with permission, from Corcoran JW, Hahn FE [editors]: *Mechanism of Action of Antimicrobial and Antitumor Agents.* Vol. 3 of: *Antibiotics.* Springer-Verlag, 1975.)

Sulfonamides are inexpensive and rarely cause side effects. However, drug-related fever, rashes, and bone marrow suppression can occur.

Trimethoprim

Trimethoprim also inhibits the production of tetrahydrofolic acid but by a mechanism different from that of the sulfonamides; ie, it inhibits the enzyme **dihydrofolate reductase** (Figure 10–8). Its specificity for bacteria is based on its much greater affinity for bacterial reductase than for the human enzyme.

Trimethoprim is used most frequently together with sulfamethoxazole. Note that both drugs act on the same pathway—but at different sites—to inhibit the synthesis of tetrahydrofolate. The advantages of the combination are that (1) bacterial mutants resistant to one drug will be inhibited by the other and that (2) the two drugs can act **synergistically,** ie, when used together, they cause significantly greater inhibition than the sum of the inhibition caused by each drug separately.

Trimethoprim-sulfamethoxazole is clinically useful in the treatment of urinary tract infections, *Pneumocystis* pneumonia, and shigellosis. It also is used for prophylaxis in granulopenic patients to prevent opportunistic infections.

2. Inhibition of DNA Synthesis

Quinolones

Quinolones are bactericidal drugs that block bacterial DNA synthesis by inhibiting **DNA gyrase (topoisomerase).** Fluoroquinolones, such as ciprofloxacin (Figure 10–9), norfloxacin, ofloxacin, and others, are active against a broad range of organisms that cause infections of the lower respiratory tract, intestinal tract, urinary tract, and skeletal and soft tissues. Fluoroquinolones should not be given to pregnant women and young children because they damage growing bone. Nalidixic acid, which is not a fluoroquinolone, is much less active and is used only for the treatment of urinary tract infections. Quinolones are not recommended for chil-

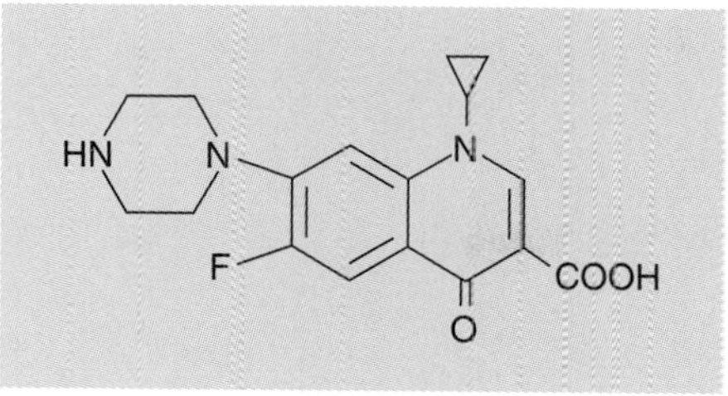

Figure 10–9. Ciprofloxacin. The triangle indicates a cyclopropyl group.

dren and pregnant women because they damage growing cartilage.

Flucytosine

Flucytosine (fluorocytosine, 5-FC) is an antifungal drug that inhibits DNA synthesis. It is a nucleoside analogue that is metabolized to fluorouracil, which inhibits thymidylate synthetase, thereby limiting the supply of thymidine. It is used in combination with amphotericin B in the treatment of disseminated cryptococcal or candidal infections, especially cryptococcal meningitis. It is not used alone because resistant mutants emerge very rapidly.

3. Inhibition of mRNA Synthesis

Rifampin is used primarily for the treatment of tuberculosis in combination with other drugs and for prophylaxis in close contacts of patients with meningitis caused by either *N. meningitidis* or *H. influenzae*. It is also used in combination with other drugs in the treatment of prosthetic-valve endocarditis caused by *S. epidermidis*. With the exception of the short-term prophylaxis of meningitis, rifampin is given in combination with other drugs because resistant mutants appear at a high rate when it is used alone.

The selective mode of action of rifampin is based on **blocking mRNA synthesis** by bacterial RNA polymerase without affecting the RNA polymerase of human cells. Rifampin is red, and the urine, saliva, and sweat of patients taking rifampin often turn orange; this is disturbing but harmless. Rifampin is excreted in high concentration in saliva, which accounts for its success in the prophylaxis of bacterial meningitis since the organisms are carried in the throat.

Rifabutin, a rifampin derivative with the same mode of action as rifampin, is useful in the prevention of disease caused by *Mycobacterium avium-intracellulare* in patients with severely reduced numbers of helper T cells, eg, AIDS patients.

ALTERATION OF CELL MEMBRANE FUNCTION

1. Alteration of Bacterial Cell Membranes

There are few antimicrobial compounds that act on the cell membrane, because the structural and chemical similarities of bacterial and human cell membranes make it difficult to provide sufficient selective toxicity.

Polymyxins are a family of polypeptide antibiotics of which the clinically most useful compound is polymyxin E (colistin). It is active against gram-negative rods, especially *P. aeruginosa*. Polymyxins are cyclic peptides composed of 10 amino acids, 6 of which are diaminobutyric acid. The positively charged free amino groups act like a cationic detergent to disrupt the phospholipid structure of the cell membrane.

Daptomycin is a cyclic lipopeptide that disrupts the cell membranes of gram-positive cocci such as *S. aureus, S. epidermidis, S. pyogenes, E. faecalis,* and *E. faecium,* including methicillin-resistant strains of *S. aureus,* and *S. epidermidis* and vancomycin-resistant strains of *E. faecalis* and *E. faecium*. It is approved for use in complicated skin and soft tissue infections caused by these bacteria.

2. Alteration of Fungal Cell Membranes

Amphotericin B, the most important antifungal drug, is used in the treatment of a variety of disseminated fungal diseases. It is classified as a polyene compound because it has a series of seven unsaturated double bonds in its macrolide ring structure (*poly* means many, and *-ene* is a suffix indicating the presence of double bonds; Figure 10–10). It disrupts the cell membrane of fungi because of its affinity for **ergosterol,** a component of fungal membranes but not of bacterial or human cell membranes. Fungi resistant to amphotericin B have rarely been recovered from patient specimens. Amphotericin B has significant renal toxicity; measurement of serum creatinine levels is used to monitor the dose. Nephrotoxicity is significantly reduced when the drug is administered in lipid vehicles such as liposomes, but these formulations are expensive. Fever, chills, nausea, and vomiting are common side effects.

Nystatin is another polyene antifungal agent, which, because of its toxicity, is used topically for infections caused by the yeast *Candida*.

Azoles are antifungal drugs that act by **inhibiting ergosterol synthesis.** They block cytochrome P-450-dependent demethylation of lanosterol, the precursor of ergosterol. Fluconazole, ketoconazole, voriconazole, and itraconazole are used to treat systemic fungal diseases; clotrimazole and miconazole are used only topi-

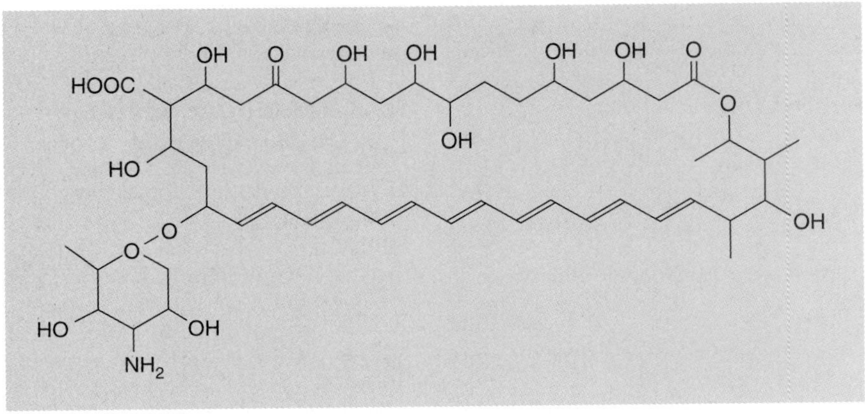

Figure 10–10. Amphotericin B.

cally because they are too toxic to be given systemically. The two nitrogen-containing azole rings of fluconazole can be seen in Figure 10–11.

Ketoconazole is useful in the treatment of blastomycosis, chronic mucocutaneous candidiasis, coccidioidomycosis, and skin infections caused by dermatophytes. Fluconazole is useful in the treatment of candidal and cryptococcal infections. Itraconazole is used to treat histoplasmosis and blastomycosis. Miconazole and clotrimazole, two other imidazoles, are useful for topical therapy of *Candida* infections and dermatophytoses. Fungi resistant to the azole drugs have rarely been recovered from patient specimens.

ADDITIONAL DRUG MECHANISMS

1. Antibacterial Activity

Isoniazid, or isonicotinic acid hydrazide (INH), is a bactericidal drug highly specific for *Mycobacterium tu-*

berculosis and other mycobacteria. It is used in combination with other drugs to treat tuberculosis and by itself to prevent tuberculosis in exposed persons. Because it penetrates human cells well, it is effective against the organisms residing within macrophages. The structure of isoniazid is shown in Figure 10–12.

INH **inhibits mycolic acid synthesis,** which explains why it is specific for mycobacteria and relatively nontoxic for humans. The drug inhibits a reductase required for the synthesis of the long-chain fatty acids called mycolic acids that are an essential constituent of mycobacterial cell walls. The active drug is probably a metabolite of INH formed by the action of catalase-peroxidase, because deletion of the gene for these enzymes results in resistance to the drug. Its main side effect is liver toxicity. It is given with pyridoxine to prevent neurologic complications.

Metronidazole (Flagyl) is bactericidal against anaerobic bacteria. (It is also effective against certain protozoa such as *Giardia* and *Trichomonas.*) This drug has two possible mechanisms of action, and it is unclear which is the more important. The first, which explains its specificity for anaerobes, is its ability to act as an **electron sink.** By accepting electrons, the drug deprives

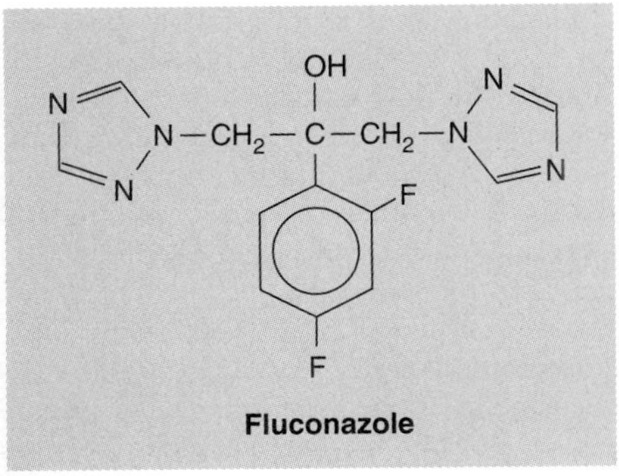

Fluconazole

Figure 10–11. Fluconazole.

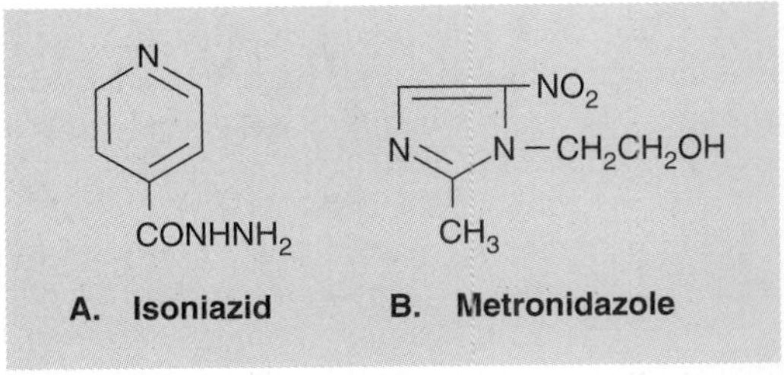

A. Isoniazid   **B. Metronidazole**

Figure 10–12. **A:** Isoniazid. **B:** Metronidazole.

the organism of required reducing power. In addition, when electrons are acquired, the drug ring is cleaved and a toxic intermediate is formed that damages DNA. The precise nature of the intermediate and its action is unknown. The structure of metronidazole is shown in Figure 10–12.

The second mode of action of metronidazole relates to its ability to inhibit DNA synthesis. The drug binds to DNA and causes strand breakage, which prevents its proper functioning as a template for DNA polymerase.

Ethambutol is a bacteriostatic drug active against *M. tuberculosis* and many of the atypical mycobacteria. It is thought to act by inhibiting the synthesis of arabinogalactan, which functions as a link between the mycolic acids and the peptidoglycan of the organism.

Pyrazinamide (PZA) is a bactericidal drug used in

Table 10–5. Chemoprophylactic use of drugs described in this chapter.

Drug	Use	Number of Chapter for Additional Information
Penicillin	1. Prevent recurrent pharyngitis in those who have had rheumatic fever	15
	2. Prevent syphilis in those exposed to *Treponema pallidum*	24
	3. Prevent pneumococcal sepsis in splenectomized young children	15
Ampicillin	1. Prevent neonatal sepsis and meningitis in children born of mothers carrying group B streptococci	15
	2. Prevent enterococcal endocarditis in those with damaged heart valves who are undergoing GI or GU tract surgery (used in combination with gentamicin)	15
Amoxicillin	Prevent endocarditis caused by viridans streptococci in those with damaged heart valves undergoing dental surgery	15
Cefazolin	Prevent staphylococcal surgical wound infections	15
Ceftriaxone	Prevent gonorrhea in those exposed to *Neisseria gonorrhoeae*	16
Ciprofloxacin	1. Prevent meningitis in those exposed to *Neisseria meningitidis*	16
	2. Prevent anthrax in those exposed to *Bacillus anthracis*	17
	3. Prevent infection n neutropenic patients	68
Rifampin	Prevent meningitis in those exposed to *N. meningitidis* and *Haemophilus influenzae*	16, 19
Isoniazid	Prevent progression of *Mycobacterium tuberculosis* in those recently infected who are asymptomatic[1]	21
Erythromycin	1. Prevent pertussis in those exposed to *Bordetella pertussis*	19
	2. Prevent gonococcal and chlamydial conjunctivitis in newborns	16, 25
Tetracycline	Prevent plague in those exposed to *Yersinia pestis*	20
Fluconazole	Prevent cryptococcal meningitis in AIDS patients	50
Clotrimazole	Prevent thrush in AIDS patients and in others with reduced cell-mediated immunity	50
Trimethoprim-sulfamethoxazole	1. Prevent *Pneumocystis* pneumonia in AIDS patients	52
	2. Prevent recurrent urinary tract infections	18
Pentamidine	Prevent *Pneumocystis* pneumonia in AIDS patients	52

GI = gastrointestinal, GU = genitourinary.

[1] Chemoprophylaxis with isoniazid is also viewed as treatment of asymptomatic individuals (see Chapter 21).

the treatment of tuberculosis but not in the treatment of most atypical mycobacterial infections. PZA is particularly effective against semidormant organisms in the lesion, which are not affected by INH or rifampin. PZA acts by inhibiting a fatty acid synthetase that prevents the synthesis of mycolic acid. It is converted to the active intermediate, pyrazinoic acid by an amidase in the mycobacteria.

2. Antifungal Activity

Griseofulvin is an antifungal drug that is useful in the treatment of hair and nail infections caused by dermatophytes. It binds to tubulin in microtubules and may act by preventing formation of the mitotic spindle.

Pentamidine is active against fungi and protozoa. It is widely used to prevent or treat pneumonia caused by *Pneumocystis carinii.* It inhibits DNA synthesis by an unknown mechanism.

CHEMOPROPHYLAXIS

In most instances, the antimicrobial agents described in this chapter are used for the *treatment* of infectious diseases. However, there are times when they are used to *prevent* diseases from occurring, a process called **chemoprophylaxis.**

Chemoprophylaxis is used in three circumstances: prior to surgery, in immunocompromised patients, and in people with normal immunity who have been exposed to certain pathogens. Table 10–5 describes the drugs and the situations in which they are used. For more information, see the chapters on the individual organisms.

Of particular importance is the prevention of endocarditis in patients undergoing dental, GI tract, or GU tract surgery who have a damaged heart valve or a prosthetic heart valve. Patients undergoing dental surgery are at risk for endocarditis caused by viridans streptococci and should be given amoxicillin perioperatively. Patients undergoing GI tract or GU tract surgery are at risk for endocarditis caused by enterococci and should be given ampicillin and gentamicin perioperatively. Note that other drug regimens for the chemoprophylaxis of endocarditis in these patients are also effective.

Prevention of infection in patients with prosthetic joints or vascular grafts undergoing dental, GI tract, or GU tract surgery is also important. Similar antibiotic regimens are employed. Chemoprophylaxis is not thought to be necessary in those with an implanted dialysis catheter, a cardiac pacemaker, or a ventriculoperitoneal shunt.

PROBIOTICS

In contrast to the chemical antibiotics previously described in this chapter, probiotics are live, nonpathogenic bacteria that may be effective in the treatment or prevention of certain human diseases. The suggested basis for the possible beneficial effect lies either in providing colonization resistance by which the nonpathogen excludes the pathogen from binding sites on the mucosa, in enhancing the immune response against the pathogen, or in reducing the inflammatory response against the pathogen. For example, the oral administration of live *Lactobacillus rhamnosus* strain GG significantly reduces the number of cases of nosocomial diarrhea in young children.

PEARLS

- *For an antibiotic to be clinically useful, it must exhibit **selective toxicity;** that is, it must inhibit bacterial processes significantly more than it inhibits human cell processes.*

- *There are four main targets of antibacterial drugs: **cell wall, ribosomes, cell membrane,** and **nucleic acids.** Humans are not affected by these drugs because we do not have a cell wall, and we have different ribosomes, nucleic acid enzymes, and sterols in our membranes.*

- ***Bactericidal** drugs kill bacteria, whereas **bacteriostatic** drugs inhibit the growth of the bacteria but*

do not kill. Bacteriostatic drugs depend on the phagocytes of the patient to kill the organism. If a patient has too few neutrophils, then bactericidal drugs should be used.

Inhibition of Cell Wall Synthesis

- ***Penicillins** and **cephalosporins** act by inhibiting **transpeptidases,** the enzymes that cross-link peptidoglycan. Transpeptidases are also referred to as **penicillin-binding proteins.** Several medically important bacteria, eg, Streptococcus pneumoniae, manifest resistance to penicillins based on* mutations in the genes encoding penicillin-binding proteins.

- Exposure to penicillins activates **autolytic enzymes** that degrade the bacteria. If these autolytic enzymes are not activated, eg, in certain strains of Staphylococcus aureus, the bacteria are not killed and the strain is said to be **tolerant.**

- Penicillins kill bacteria when they are growing, ie, when they are synthesizing new peptidoglycan. Penicillins are therefore **more active during the log phase** of bacterial growth than during the lag phase or the stationary phase.

- Penicillins and cephalosporins are **β-lactam drugs,** ie, an **intact β-lactam ring is required** for activity. **β-lactamases,** eg, penicillinases and cephalosporinases, cleave the β-lactam ring and inactivate the drug.

- **Modification of the side chain** adjacent to the β-lactam ring endows these drugs with **new properties,** such as expanded activity against gram-negative rods, ability to be taken orally, and protection against degradation by β-lactamases. For example, the original penicillin (benzyl penicillin, penicillin G) cannot be taken orally because stomach acid hydrolyzes the bond between the β-lactam ring and the side chain. But ampicillin and amoxicillin can be taken orally because they have a different side chain.

- **Hypersensitivity** to penicillins, especially **IgE-mediated anaphylaxis,** remains a significant problem.

- **Cephalosporins** are structurally similar to penicillins: both have a β-lactam ring. The first-generation cephalosporins are active primarily against gram-positive cocci and the second, third, and fourth generations have expanded coverage against gram-negative rods.

- Carbapenems, such as imipenem, and monobactams, such as aztreonam, are also β-lactam drugs but are structurally different from penicillins and cephalosporins.

- **Vancomycin** is a **glycopeptide,** ie, it is not a β-lactam drug, but its mode of action is very similar to that of penicillins and cephalosporins, ie, it **inhibits transpeptidases.**

- **Caspofungin** is a lipopeptide that inhibits fungal cell wall synthesis by blocking the synthesis of β-glucan, a polysaccharide component of the cell wall.

Inhibition of Protein Synthesis

- **Aminoglycosides** and **tetracyclines** act at the level of the 30S ribosomal subunit, whereas **chloramphenicol, erythromycins,** and **clindamycin** act at the level of the 50S ribosomal subunit.

- **Aminoglycosides** inhibit bacterial protein synthesis by binding to the 30S subunit, which **blocks the initiation complex.** No peptide bonds are formed and no polysomes are made. Aminoglycosides are a family of drugs that includes gentamicin, tobramycin, and streptomycin.

- **Tetracyclines** inhibit bacterial protein synthesis by **blocking the binding of aminoacyl t-RNA** to the 30S ribosomal subunit. The tetracyclines are a family of drugs; doxycycline is used most often.

- **Chloramphenicol** inhibits bacterial protein synthesis by **blocking peptidyl transferase,** the enzyme that adds the new amino acid to the growing polypeptide. Chloramphenicol can cause bone marrow suppression.

- **Erythromycin** inhibits bacterial protein synthesis by **blocking the release of the t-RNA** after it has delivered its amino acid to the growing polypeptide. Erythromycin is a member of the macrolide family of drugs that includes azithromycin and clarithromycin.

- **Clindamycin** binds to the same site on the ribosome as does erythromycin and is thought to act in the same manner. It is effective against many anaerobic bacteria. Clindamycin is one of the antibiotics that predisposes to pseudomembranous colitis caused by Clostridium difficile and is infrequently used.

Inhibition of Nucleic Acid Synthesis

- **Sulfonamides** and **trimethoprim** inhibit **nucleotide** synthesis, **quinolones** inhibit **DNA** synthesis, and **rifampin inhibits RNA** synthesis.

- **Sulfonamides** and **trimethoprim** inhibit the **synthesis of tetrahydrofolic acid,** the main donor of the methyl groups that are required to synthesize adenine, guanine, and thymine. **Sulfonamides** are structural analogues of para-aminobenzoic acid, which is a component of folic acid. **Trimethoprim** inhibits **dihydrofolate reductase,** the enzyme that reduces dihydrofolic acid to tetrahydrofolic acid. A combination of sulfamethoxazole and trimethoprim is often used because bacteria resistant to one drug will be inhibited by the other.

- *Quinolones* inhibit DNA synthesis in bacteria by **blocking DNA gyrase** (topoisomerase), the enzyme that unwinds DNA strands so that they can be replicated. Quinolones are a family of drugs that includes ciprofloxacin, ofloxacin, and levofloxacin.
- *Rifampin* inhibits RNA synthesis in bacteria by **blocking the RNA polymerase** that synthesizes mRNA. Rifampin is typically used in combination with other drugs because there is a **high rate of mutation of the RNA polymerase gene,** which results in rapid resistance to the drug.

Alteration of Cell Membrane Function

- *Antifungal* drugs predominate in this category. These drugs have selective toxicity because **fungal cell membranes contain ergosterol,** whereas human cell membranes have cholesterol. **Bacteria, with the exception of Mycoplasma,** do not have sterols in their membranes and therefore are resistant to these drugs.
- *Amphotericin B* disrupts fungal cell membranes by **binding at the site of ergosterol** in the membrane. It is used to treat the most serious systemic fungal diseases but has significant side effects, especially on the kidney.
- *Azoles* are antifungal drugs that **inhibit ergosterol synthesis.** The azole family includes drugs such as

ketoconazole, fluconazole, itraconazole, and clotrimazole. They are useful in the treatment of systemic as well as skin and mucous membrane infections.

Additional Drug Mechanisms

- *Isoniazid inhibits the synthesis of mycolic acid,* a long-chain fatty acid found in the cell wall of mycobacteria. Isoniazid is a **prodrug** that requires a bacterial **peroxidase (catalase) to activate isoniazid** to the metabolite that inhibits mycolic acid synthesis. Isoniazid is the most important drug used in the treatment of tuberculosis and other mycobacterial diseases.
- *Metronidazole* is **effective against anaerobic bacteria and certain protozoa** because it **acts as an electron sink,** taking away the electrons that the organisms need to survive. It also forms toxic intermediates that damage DNA.

Chemoprophylaxis

- Antimicrobial drugs are used to prevent infectious diseases as well as to treat them. Chemoprophylactic drugs are given primarily in three circumstances: to prevent surgical wound infections, to prevent opportunistic infections in immunocompromised patients, and to prevent infections in those known to be exposed to pathogens that cause serious infectious diseases.

PRACTICE QUESTIONS: USMLE & COURSE EXAMINATIONS

Questions on the topics discussed in this chapter can be found in the Basic Bacteriology section of Part XI:

USMLE (National Board) Practice Questions starting on page 532. Also see Part XII: USMLE (National Board) Practice Examination starting on page 583.

Antimicrobial Drugs: Resistance 11

There are four major mechanisms that mediate bacterial resistance to drugs (Table 11–1). (1) Bacteria produce enzymes that **inactivate the drug**; eg, β-lactamases can inactivate penicillins and cephalosporins by cleaving the β-lactam ring of the drug. (2) Bacteria **synthesize modified targets** against which the drug has no effect; eg, a mutant protein in the 30S ribosomal subunit can result in resistance to streptomycin, and a methylated 23S rRNA can result in resistance to erythromycin. (3) Bacteria **decrease their permeability** such that an effective intracellular concentration of the drug is not achieved; eg, changes in porins can reduce the amount of penicillin entering the bacterium. (4) Bacteria **actively export drugs** using a "multidrug resistance pump" (MDR pump, or "efflux" pump). The MDR pump imports protons and, in an exchange-type reaction, exports a variety of foreign molecules including certain antibiotics, such as quinolones.

Most drug resistance is due to a genetic change in the organism, either a chromosomal **mutation** or the acquisition of a **plasmid** or **transposon**. Nongenetic changes, which are of lesser importance, are discussed on page 89.

Hospital-acquired infections are significantly more likely to be caused by antibiotic-resistant organisms than are community-acquired infections. This is especially true for hospital infections caused by *Staphylococcus aureus* and enteric gram-negative rods such as *Escherichia coli* and *Pseudomonas aeruginosa*. Antibiotic-resistant organisms are common in the hospital setting because widespread antibiotic use in hospitals selects for these organisms. Furthermore, hospital strains are often resistant to multiple antibiotics. This resistance is usually due to the acquisition of plasmids carrying several genes that encode the enzymes that mediate resistance.

Table 11–2 describes certain medically important bacteria and the main drugs to which they are resistant. Note that although these bacteria are resistant to other drugs as well, for simplicity, only the most characteristic drugs are listed.

GENETIC BASIS OF RESISTANCE

Chromosome-Mediated Resistance

Chromosomal resistance is due to a mutation in the gene that codes for either the target of the drug or the transport system in the membrane that controls the uptake of the drug. The frequency of spontaneous mutations usually ranges from 10^{-7} to 10^{-9}, which is much

Table 11–1. Mechanisms of drug resistance.

Mechanism	Important Example	Drugs Commonly Affected
Inactivate drug	Cleavage by β-lactamase	β-Lactam drugs such as penicillins, cephalosporins
Modify drug target in bacteria	1. Mutation in penicillin-binding proteins	Penicillins
	2. Mutation in protein in 30S ribosomal subunit	Aminoglycosides, such as streptomycin
	3. Replace alanine with lactate in peptidoglycan	Vancomycin
	4. Mutation in DNA gyrase	Quinolones
	5. Mutation in RNA polymerase	Rifampin
	6. Mutation in catalase-peroxidase	Isoniazid
Reduce permeability of drug	Mutation in porin proteins	Penicillins, aminoglycosides, and others
Export of drug from bacteria	Multidrug-resistance pump	Tetracyclines, sulfonamides

lower than the frequency of acquisition of resistance plasmids. Therefore, chromosomal resistance is less of a clinical problem than is plasmid-mediated resistance.

The treatment of certain infections with two or more drugs is based on the following principle. If the frequency that a bacterium mutates to become resistant to antibiotic A is 10^{-7} (1 in 10 million) and the frequency that the same bacterium mutates to become resistant to antibiotic B is 10^{-8} (1 in 100 million), then the chance that the bacterium will become resistant to both antibiotics (assuming that the antibiotics act by different mechanisms) is the product of the two probabilities, or 10^{-15}. It is therefore highly unlikely that the bacterium will become resistant to *both* antibiotics. Stated another way, although an organism may be resistant to one antibiotic, it is likely that it will be effectively treated by the other antibiotic.

Plasmid-Mediated Resistance

Plasmid-mediated resistance is very important from a clinical point of view for three reasons:

(1) It occurs in many different species, especially gram-negative rods

(2) Plasmids frequently mediate resistance to multiple drugs

(3) Plasmids have a high rate of transfer from one cell to another, usually by conjugation.

Resistance plasmids (resistance factors, R factors) are extrachromosomal, circular, double-stranded DNA molecules that carry the genes for a variety of enzymes that can degrade antibiotics and modify membrane transport systems (Figure 11–1). Table 11–3 describes the most important mechanisms of resistance for several important drugs.

R factors may carry one antibiotic resistance gene or may carry two or more of these genes. The medical implications of a plasmid carrying more than one resistance gene is 2-fold: first and most obvious is that a bacterium containing that plasmid can be resistant to more than one class of antibiotics (eg, penicillins and aminoglycosides) and second, that the use of an antibiotic that selects for an organism resistant to one antibiotic will select for an organism that is resistant to all the antibiotics whose resistance genes are carried by the plasmid. For example, if an organism has the R plasmid depicted in Figure 11–1, then the use of penicillin will select for an

Table 11–2. Medically important bacteria that exhibit significant drug resistance.

Type of Bacteria	Clinically Significant Drug Resistance
Gram-positive cocci	
Staphylococcus aureus	Penicillin G, nafcillin
Streptococcus pneumoniae	Penicillin G
Enterococcus faecalis	Penicillin G, aminoglycosides, vancomycin
Gram-negative cocci	
Neisseria gonorrhoeae	Penicillin G
Gram-positive rods	
None	
Gram-negative rods	
Haemophilus influenzae	Ampicillin
Pseudomonas aeruginosa	β-Lactams,[1] aminoglycosides
Enterobacteriaceae[2]	β-Lactams,[1] aminoglycosides
Mycobacteria	
M. tuberculosis[3]	Isoniazid, rifampin
M. avium-intracellulare	Isoniazid, rifampin, and many others

[1]β-Lactams are penicillins and cephalosporins.
[2]The family Enterobacteriaceae includes bacteria such as *Escherichia coli, Enterobacter cloacae, Klebsiella pneumoniae,* and *Serratia marcescens.*
[3]Some strains of *M. tuberculosis* are resistant to more than two drugs.

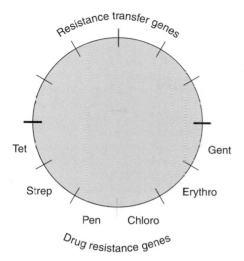

Figure 11–1. Resistance plasmid (R plasmid, R factor). Most resistance plasmids have two sets of genes: (1) resistance transfer genes that encode the sex pilus and other proteins that mediate transfer of the plasmid DNA during conjugation and (2) drug resistance genes that encode the proteins that mediate drug resistance. The bottom half of the figure depicts, from left to right, the genes that encode resistance to tetracycline, streptomycin, penicillin (β-lactamase), chloramphenicol, erythromycin, and gentamicin.

organism resistant not only to penicillin but also to tetracyclines, aminoglycosides (such as streptomycin and gentamicin), chloramphenicol, and erythromycin.

In addition to producing drug resistance, R factors have two very important properties: (1) They can replicate independently of the bacterial chromosome; therefore, a cell can contain many copies; and (2) they can be transferred not only to cells of the same species but also to other species and genera. Note that this conjugal

transfer is under the control of the genes of the R plasmid and not of the F (fertility) plasmid, which governs the transfer of the bacterial chromosome (see Chapter 4).

R factors exist in two broad size categories: large plasmids with molecular weights of about 60 million and small ones with molecular weights of about 10 million. The large plasmids are conjugative R factors, which contain the extra DNA to code for the conjugation process. The small R factors are not conjugative and contain only the resistance genes.

In addition to conveying antibiotic resistance, R factors impart two other traits: (1) resistance to metal ions (eg, they code for an enzyme that reduces mercuric ions to elemental mercury); and (2) resistance to certain bacterial viruses by coding for restriction endonucleases that degrade the DNA of the infecting bacteriophages.

Transposon-Mediated Resistance

Transposons are genes that are transferred either within or between larger pieces of DNA such as the bacterial chromosome and plasmids. A typical drug resistance transposon is composed of three genes flanked on both sides by shorter DNA sequences, usually a series of inverted repeated bases that mediate the interaction of the transposon with the larger DNA (see Figure 2–7). The three genes code for (1) transposase, the enzyme that catalyzes excision and reintegration of the transposon; (2) a repressor that regulates synthesis of the transposase; and (3) the drug resistance gene.

SPECIFIC MECHANISMS OF RESISTANCE

Penicillins & Cephalosporins. There are several mechanisms of resistance to these drugs. Cleavage by β-lactamases (penicillinases and cephalosporinases) is by far the most important (see Figure 10–1). β-Lactamases

Table 11–3. R-factor–mediated resistance mechanisms.

Drug	Mechanism of Resistance
Penicillins and cephalosporins	β-Lactamase cleavage of β-lactam ring
Aminoglycosides	Modification by acetylation, adenylylation, or phosphorylation
Chloramphenicol	Modification by acetylation
Erythromycin	Change in receptor by methylation of rRNA
Tetracycline	Reduced uptake or increased export
Sulfonamides	Active export out of the cell and reduced affinity of enzyme

produced by various organisms have different properties. For example, staphylococcal penicillinase is inducible by penicillin and is secreted into the medium. In contrast, some β-lactamases produced by several gram-negative rods are constitutively produced, are located in the periplasmic space near the peptidoglycan, and are not secreted into the medium. The β-lactamases produced by various gram-negative rods have different specificities; some are more active against cephalosporins, others against penicillins. Clavulanic acid and sulbactam are penicillin analogues that bind strongly to β-lactamases and inactivate them. Combinations of these inhibitors and penicillins, eg, clavulanic acid and amoxicillin (Augmentin), can overcome resistance mediated by many but not all β-lactamases.

Resistance to penicillins can also be due to changes in the **penicillin-binding proteins** in the bacterial cell membrane. These changes account for both the low-level and the high-level resistance exhibited by *Streptococcus pneumoniae* to penicillin G and for the resistance of *S. aureus* to nafcillin and other β-lactamase–resistant penicillins. The relative resistance of *Enterococcus faecalis* to penicillins may be due to altered penicillin-binding proteins. Low-level resistance of *Neisseria gonorrhoeae* to penicillin is attributed to **poor permeability** to the drug. High-level resistance is due to the presence of a plasmid coding for penicillinase.

Some isolates of *S. aureus* demonstrate yet another form of resistance, called **tolerance**, in which growth of the organism is inhibited by penicillin but the organism is not killed. This is attributed to a failure of activation of the autolytic enzymes, murein hydrolases, which degrade the peptidoglycan.

Vancomycin. Resistance to vancomycin is caused by a change in the peptide component of peptidoglycan from D-alanyl-D-alanine, which is the normal binding site for vancomycin, to D-alanine-D-lactate, to which the drug does not bind. Of the four gene loci mediating vancomycin resistance, VanA is the most important. It is carried by a transposon on a plasmid and provides high-level resistance to both vancomycin and teichoplanin. (Teichoplanin is used in Europe but is not approved in the United States.) The VanA locus encodes the enzymes that synthesize D-ala-D-lactate as well as several regulatory proteins.

Vancomycin-resistant strains of enterococci (VRE) have been recovered from clinical specimens. Rare isolates of *S. aureus* that exhibit resistance to vancomycin have also been recovered from patient specimens. Rare isolates of *S. pneumoniae* that exhibit tolerance to vancomycin have been recovered as well.

Aminoglycosides. Resistance to aminoglycosides occurs by three mechanisms: (1) modification of the drugs by plasmid-encoded phosphorylating, adenylylating, and acetylating enzymes (the most important mechanism); (2) chromosomal mutation, eg, a mutation in the gene that codes for the target protein in the 30S subunit of the bacterial ribosome; and (3) decreased permeability of the bacterium to the drug.

Tetracyclines. Resistance to tetracyclines is the result of failure of the drug to reach an inhibitory concentration inside the bacteria. This is due to plasmid-encoded processes that either reduce uptake of the drug or **enhance its transport** out of the cell.

Chloramphenicol. Resistance to chloramphenicol is due to a plasmid-encoded acetyltransferase that acetylates the drug, thus inactivating it.

Erythromycin. Resistance to erythromycin is due primarily to a plasmid-encoded enzyme that methylates the 23S rRNA, thereby blocking binding of the drug. An efflux pump that reduces the concentration of erythromycin within the bacterium causes low-level resistance to the drug.

Sulfonamides. Resistance to sulfonamides is mediated primarily by two mechanisms: (1) a plasmid-encoded transport system that **actively exports** the drug out of the cell; and (2) a chromosomal mutation in the gene coding for the target enzyme dihydropteroate synthetase, which reduces the binding affinity of the drug.

Trimethoprim. Resistance to trimethoprim is due primarily to mutations in the chromosomal gene that encodes dihydrofolate reductase, the enzyme that reduces dihydrofolate to tetrahydrofolate.

Quinolones. Resistance to quinolones is due primarily to chromosomal mutations that modify the bacterial DNA gyrase. Resistance can also be caused by changes in bacterial outer-membrane proteins that result in reduced uptake of drug into the bacteria.

Rifampin. Resistance to rifampin is due to a chromosomal mutation in the gene for the β subunit of the bacterial RNA polymerase, resulting in ineffective binding of the drug. Because resistance occurs at high frequency (10^{-5}), rifampin is not prescribed alone for the *treatment* of infections. It is used alone for the *prevention* of certain infections because it is administered for only a short time (see Table 10–5).

Isoniazid. Resistance of *Mycobacterium tuberculosis* to isoniazid is due to mutations in the organism's catalase-peroxidase gene. Catalase or peroxidase enzyme activity is required to synthesize the metabolite of isoniazid that actually inhibits the growth of *M. tuberculosis*.

Ethambutol. Resistance of *M. tuberculosis* to ethambutol is due to mutations in the gene that encodes arabinosyl transferase, the enzyme that synthesizes the arabinogalactan in the organism's cell wall.

Pyrazinamide. Resistance of *M. tuberculosis* to pyrazinamide (PZA) is due to mutations in the gene that encodes bacterial amidase, the enzyme that converts PZA to the active form of the drug, pyrazinoic acid.

NONGENETIC BASIS OF RESISTANCE

There are several nongenetic reasons for the failure of drugs to inhibit the growth of bacteria.

(1) Bacteria can be walled off within an abscess cavity that the drug cannot penetrate effectively. Surgical drainage is therefore a necessary adjunct to chemotherapy.

(2) Bacteria can be in a resting state, ie, not growing; they are therefore insensitive to cell wall inhibitors such as penicillins and cephalosporins. Similarly, *M. tuberculosis* can remain dormant in tissues for many years, during which time it is insensitive to drugs. If host defenses are lowered and the bacteria begin to multiply, they are again susceptible to the drugs, indicating that a genetic change did not occur.

(3) Under certain circumstances, organisms that would ordinarily be killed by penicillin can lose their cell walls, survive as **protoplasts,** and be insensitive to cell-wall–active drugs. Later, if such organisms resynthesize their cell walls, they are fully susceptible to these drugs.

(4) The presence of foreign bodies makes successful antibiotic treatment more difficult. This applies to foreign bodies such as surgical implants and catheters as well as materials that enter the body at the time of penetrating injuries, such as splinters and shrapnel.

(5) Several artifacts can make it appear that the organisms are resistant, eg, administration of the wrong drug or the wrong dose or failure of the drug to reach the appropriate site in the body. (A good example of the latter is the poor penetration into spinal fluid by several early-generation cephalosporins.) Failure of the patient to take the drug (noncompliance, nonadherence) is another artifact.

SELECTION OF RESISTANT BACTERIA BY OVERUSE & MISUSE OF ANTIBIOTICS

Serious outbreaks of diseases caused by gram-negative rods resistant to multiple antibiotics have occurred in many developing countries. In North America, many hospital-acquired infections are caused by multiple-resistant organisms. Three main points of overuse and misuse of antibiotics increase the likelihood of these problems by enhancing the selection of resistant mutants:

(1) Some physicians use multiple antibiotics when one would be sufficient, prescribe unnecessarily long courses of antibiotic therapy, use antibiotics in self-limited infections for which they are not needed, and overuse antibiotics for prophylaxis before and after surgery.

(2) In many countries, antibiotics are sold over the counter to the general public; this practice encourages the inappropriate and indiscriminate use of the drugs.

(3) Antibiotics are used in animal feed to prevent infections and promote growth. This selects for resistant organisms in the animals and may contribute to the pool of resistant organisms in humans.

ANTIBIOTIC SENSITIVITY TESTING

Minimal Inhibitory Concentration

For many infections, the results of sensitivity testing are important in the choice of antibiotic. These results are commonly reported as the **minimal inhibitory concentration (MIC),** which is defined as the lowest concentration of drug that inhibits the growth of the organism. The MIC is determined by inoculating the organism isolated from the patient into a series of tubes or cups containing 2-fold dilutions of the drug (Figure 11–2). After incubation at 35°C for 18 hours, the lowest concentration of drug that prevents visible growth of the organism is the MIC. This provides the physician with a precise concentration of drug to guide the choice of both the drug and the dose.

A second method of determining antibiotic sensitivity is the disk diffusion method, in which disks impregnated with various antibiotics are placed on the surface of an agar plate that has been inoculated with the organism isolated from the patient (Figure 11–3). After incubation at 35°C for 18 hours, during which time the antibiotic diffuses outward from the disk, the diameter of the zone of inhibition is determined. The size of the zone of inhibition is compared with standards to determine the sensitivity of the organism to the drug.

Minimal Bactericidal Concentration

For certain infections, such as endocarditis, it is important to know the concentration of drug that actually kills the organism rather than the concentration that merely inhibits growth. This concentration, called the **minimal bactericidal concentration (MBC),** is determined by taking a small sample (0.01 or 0.1 mL) from the tubes used for the MIC assay and spreading it over the surface of a drug-free blood agar plate (Figure 11–2). Any organisms that were inhibited but not killed now have a chance to grow, because the drug has been diluted significantly. After incubation at 35°C for 48 hours, the lowest concentration that has reduced the number of colonies by 99.9%, compared with the drug-free control, is the MBC. Bactericidal drugs usually have an MBC equal or very similar to the MIC, whereas bacteriostatic drugs usually have an MBC significantly higher than the MIC.

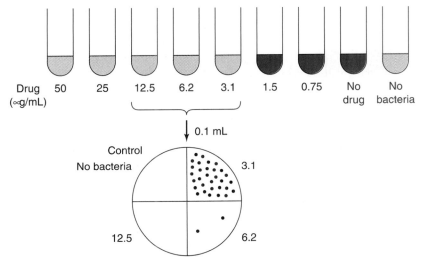

Figure 11–2. Determination of minimal inhibitory concentration (MIC) and minimal bactericidal concentration (MBC). In the top part of the figure, the patient's organism is added to tubes containing decreasing amounts of the antibiotic. After incubation at 37°C overnight, growth of the bacteria is observed visually. The lowest concentration of drug that inhibits growth, ie, 3.1 μg/mL, is the MIC. However, at this point, it is not known whether the bacteria have been killed or whether the drug has only inhibited their growth. To determine whether that concentration of drug is bactericidal, ie, to determine its MBC, an aliquot (0.1 mL) from the tubes is plated on an agar plate that does not contain any drug. The concentration of drug that inhibits at least 99.9% of the bacterial colonies, ie, 6.2 μg/mL, is the MBC.

Serum Bactericidal Activity

In the treatment of endocarditis, it can be useful to determine whether the drug is effective by assaying the ability of the drug in the patient's serum to kill the organism. This test, called the **serum bactericidal activity,** is performed in a manner similar to that of the MBC determination, except that it is a serum sample from the patient, rather than a standard drug solution, that is diluted in 2-fold steps. After a standard inoculum of the organism has been added and the mixture has been incubated at 35°C for 18 hours, a small sample is subcultured onto blood agar plates, and the serum dilution that kills 99.9% of the organisms is determined. Clinical experience has shown that a peak[1] serum bactericidal activity of 1:8 or 1:16 is adequate for successful therapy of endocarditis.

β-Lactamase Production

For severe infections caused by certain organisms, such as *S. aureus* and *Haemophilus influenzae,* it is important to

know as soon as possible whether the organism isolated from the patient is producing β-lactamase. For this purpose, rapid assays for the enzyme can be used that yield an answer in a few minutes, as opposed to an MIC test or a disk diffusion test, both of which take 18 hours.

A commonly used procedure is the chromogenic β-lactam method, in which a colored β-lactam drug is added to a suspension of the organisms. If β-lactamase is made, hydrolysis of the β-lactam ring causes the drug to turn a different color in 2–10 minutes. Disks impregnated with a chromogenic β-lactam can also be used.

USE OF ANTIBIOTIC COMBINATIONS

In most cases, the single best antimicrobial agent should be selected for use because this minimizes side effects. However, there are several instances in which two or more drugs are commonly given:

(1) To treat serious infections before the identity of the organism is known
(2) To achieve a synergistic inhibitory effect against certain organisms
(3) To prevent the emergence of resistant organisms. (If bacteria become resistant to one drug, the second drug will kill them, thereby preventing the emergence of resistant strains.)

---

[1] One variable in this test is whether the serum is drawn shortly after the drug has been administered (at the "peak concentration") or shortly before the next dose is due (at the "trough"). Another variable is the inoculum size.

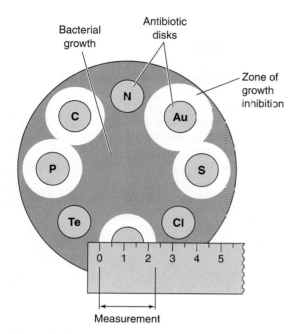

Figure 11–3. Antibiotic sensitivity testing. A zone of inhibition surrounds several antibiotic-containing disks. A zone of certain diameter or greater indicates that the organism is sensitive. Some resistant organisms will grow all the way up to the disk, eg, disk N. (Modified and reproduced, with permission, from Wistreich GA, Lechtman MD: *Laboratory Exercises in Microbiology,* 5th ed. Macmillan, 1984.)

Two drugs can interact in one of several ways (Figure 11–4). They are usually indifferent to each other, ie, additive only. Sometimes there is a **synergistic** interaction, in which the effect of the two drugs together is significantly greater than the sum of the effects of the two drugs acting separately. Rarely, the effect of the two drugs together is **antagonistic**, in which the result is significantly lower activity than the sum of the activities of the two drugs alone.

A synergistic effect can result from a variety of mechanisms. For example, the combination of a penicillin and an aminoglycoside such as gentamicin has a synergistic action against enterococci (*E. faecalis*), because penicillin damages the cell wall sufficiently to enhance the entry of aminoglycoside. When given alone, neither drug is effective. A second example is the combination of a sulfonamide with trimethoprim. In this instance, the two drugs act on the same metabolic pathway, such that if one drug does not inhibit folic acid synthesis sufficiently, the second drug provides effective inhibition by blocking a subsequent step in the pathway.

Although antagonism between two antibiotics is unusual, one example is clinically important. This involves the use of penicillin G combined with the bacteriostatic drug tetracycline in the treatment of meningitis caused by *S. pneumoniae.* Antagonism occurs because the tetracycline inhibits the growth of the organism, thereby preventing the bactericidal effect of penicillin G, which kills growing organisms only.

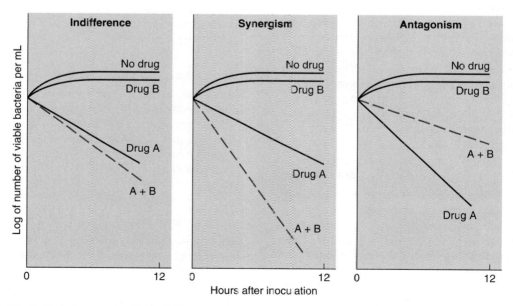

Figure 11–4. Drug interaction. The solid lines represent the response of bacteria to drug A alone, drug B alone, or no drug. The dotted lines represent the response to drug A and drug B together.

PEARLS

- The four main mechanisms of antibiotic resistance are: (1) **enzymatic degradation** of the drug, (2) **modification of the drug's target,** (3) **reduced permeability** of the drug, and (4) **active export** of the drug.
- Most drug resistance is the result of a genetic change in the organism, caused either by a chromosomal mutation or the acquisition of a plasmid or transposon.

Genetic Basis of Resistance

- **Chromosomal mutations** typically either **change the target of the drug** so that the drug does not bind or **change the membrane** so that the drug does not penetrate well into the cell. Chromosomal mutations occur at a low frequency (perhaps 1 in 10 million organisms), and often affect only one drug or one family of drugs.
- **Plasmids cause drug resistance by encoding enzymes** that degrade or modify drugs. Plasmid-mediated resistance occurs at a **higher frequency** than chromosomal mutations, often affecting **multiple drugs** or families of drugs.
- **Resistance plasmids** (R plasmids, R factors) usually carry two sets of genes. One set encodes the enzymes that degrade or modify drugs and the other encodes the proteins that **mediate conjugation,** the main process by which resistance genes are transferred from one bacterium to another.
- **Transposons** are small pieces of DNA that **move from one site on the bacterial chromosome to another** or from the bacterial chromosome to plasmid DNA. **Transposons often carry drug resistance genes.** Many R plasmids carry one or more transposons.

Specific Mechanisms of Resistance

- **Resistance to penicillins and cephalosporins** is mediated by three main mechanisms: (1) degradation by β-lactamases, (2) mutations in the genes for penicillin-binding proteins, and (3) reduced permeability. **Degradation by β-lactamases is the most important.**
- Resistance to vancomycin is caused by a change in the D-ala-D-ala part of the peptide in peptidoglycan to D-ala-D-lactate, resulting in an inability of vancomycin to bind.
- Resistance to aminoglycosides is mediated by three main mechanisms: modification of the drug by **phosphorylating, adenylylating, and acetylating enzymes,** mutations in the genes encoding one of the 30S ribosomal proteins, and reduced permeability.
- Resistance to **tetracyclines** is often caused by either reduced permeability or **active export** of the drug from the bacterium.
- Resistance to erythromycins is primarily caused by a plasmid-encoded enzyme that **methylates the 23S ribosomal RNA,** thereby blocking binding of the drug.
- Resistance to sulfonamides is due primarily to plasmid-encoded enzymes that **actively export** the drug from the bacterium.
- Resistance to quinolones is primarily caused by **mutations** in the gene encoding the bacterial DNA gyrase.
- Resistance to rifampin is primarily caused by **mutations** in the gene encoding the bacterial RNA polymerase.
- Resistance to isoniazid is due primarily to the **loss of the bacterial peroxidase (catalase)** that activates isoniazid to the metabolite that inhibits mycolic acid synthesis.

Nongenetic Basis of Resistance

- Nongenetic reasons why bacteria may not be inhibited by antibiotics are that drugs may not reach bacteria located in the center of an abscess and that certain drugs, such as penicillins, will not affect bacteria that are not growing. Also the presence of foreign bodies makes successful antibiotic treatment more difficult.

Antibiotic Sensitivity Testing

- The **minimal inhibitory concentration (MIC)** is the lowest concentration of drug that **inhibits the growth** of the bacteria isolated from the patient. In this test, it is not known whether the inhibited bacteria have been killed or just have stopped growing.

- The **minimal bactericidal concentration (MBC)** is the lowest concentration of drug that **kills** the bacteria isolated from the patient. In certain diseases, such as endocarditis, it is often necessary to use a concentration of drug that is bactericidal.

Use of Antibiotic Combinations

- Two or more antibiotics are used under certain circumstances, such as to treat life-threatening infections before the cause has been identified, to prevent the emergence of resistant bacteria during prolonged treatment regimens, and to achieve a synergistic (augmented) effect.
- A **synergistic effect** is one in which the effect of two drugs given together is much greater than the sum of the effect of the two drugs given individually. The best example of synergy is the marked killing effect of the combination of a penicillin and an aminoglycoside or enterococci compared to the minor effect of either drug given alone.

PRACTICE QUESTIONS: USMLE & COURSE EXAMINATIONS

Questions on the topics discussed in this chapter can be found in the Basic Bacteriology section of Part XI: USMLE (National Board) Practice Questions starting on page 532. Also see Part XII: USMLE (National Board) Practice Examination starting on page 583.

Bacterial Vaccines

Bacterial diseases can be prevented by the use of immunizations that induce either active or passive immunity. **Active** immunity is induced by vaccines prepared from bacteria or their products. This chapter will present a summary of the types of vaccines (Table 12–1); detailed information regarding each vaccine is located in the chapters on the specific organisms. **Passive** immunity is provided by the administration of preformed antibody in preparations called immune globulins. The immune globulins useful against bacterial diseases are described below. **Passive-active** immunity involves giving both immune globulins to provide immediate protection and a vaccine to provide long-term protection. This approach is described below in the section on tetanus antitoxin.

Active Immunity

Bacterial vaccines are composed of capsular polysaccharides, inactivated protein exotoxins (toxoids), killed bacteria, or live, attenuated bacteria. The available bacterial vaccines and their indications are as follows.

A. Capsular Polysaccharide Vaccines

(1) *Streptococcus pneumoniae* vaccine contains the capsular polysaccharides of the 23 most prevalent types. It is recommended for persons over 60 years of age and patients of any age with such chronic diseases as diabetes and cirrhosis or with compromised spleen function or splenectomy. A second vaccine containing the capsular polysaccharide of 7 pneumococcal serotypes coupled to a carrier protein (diphtheria toxoid) is available for the protection of young children who do not respond well to the unconjugated vaccine.

A potential problem regarding the use of the pneumococcal vaccine containing 7 serotypes is that of **serotype replacement.** Will the vaccine reduce the incidence of disease caused by the serotypes in the vaccine but not the overall incidence of pneumococcal disease because other serotypes that are not in the vaccine will now cause disease? This important question is being evaluated at this time.

(2) *Neisseria meningitidis* vaccine contains capsular polysaccharide of four important types (A, C, W-135, and Y). Two forms of the vaccine are available: one contains the polysaccharides conjugated to a carrier protein (diphtheria toxoid), and the other contains only the polysaccharides. It is given when there is a high risk of meningitis, eg, during an outbreak, when students enter college and are living in a dormitory, when military recruits enter boot camp, or for travelers to areas where meningitis is hyperendemic.

(3) *Haemophilus influenzae* vaccine contains the type b polysaccharide conjugated to diphtheria toxoid or other carrier protein. It is given to children between the ages of 2 and 15 months to prevent meningitis. The capsular polysaccharide alone is a poor immunogen in young children, but coupling it to a carrier protein greatly enhances its immunogenicity. A combined vaccine consisting of this vaccine plus the diphtheria, pertussis, and tetanus (DPT) vaccines is available.

(4) One of the vaccines against typhoid fever contains the capsular polysaccharide of *Salmonella typhi*. It is indicated for persons living or traveling in areas where there is a high risk of typhoid fever and for persons in close contact with either infected patients or chronic carriers.

B. Toxoid Vaccines

(1) *Corynebacterium diphtheriae* vaccine contains the toxoid (formaldehyde-treated exotoxin). Immunization against diphtheria is indicated for every child and is given in three doses at 2, 4, and 6 months of age, with boosters given 1 year later and at intervals thereafter.

(2) *Clostridium tetani* vaccine contains tetanus toxoid and is given to everyone both early in life and later as boosters for protection against tetanus.

(3) *Bordetella pertussis* vaccine contains pertussis toxoid but includes other proteins as well. It is, therefore, described in the next section.

C. Purified Protein Vaccines

(1) There are two types of *B. pertussis* vaccines: an acellular vaccine containing purified proteins and a vaccine containing whole killed bacteria. The acellular vaccine is now recommended in the United States. The principal antigen in the acellular vaccine is inactivated

Table 12–1. Current bacterial vaccines (2006).

Usage	Bacterium	Disease	Antigen
Common usage	Corynebacterium diphtheriae	Diphtheria	Toxoid
	Clostridium tetani	Tetanus	Toxoid
	Bordetella pertussis	Whooping cough	Acellular (purified proteins) or killed organisms
	Haemophilus influenzae	Meningitis	Capsular polysaccharide conjugated to carrier protein
	Streptococcus pneumoniae	Pneumonia	Capsular polysaccharide or capsular polysaccharide conjugated to carrier protein
Special situations	Neisseria meningitidis	Meningitis	Capsular polysaccharide or capsular polysaccharide conjugated to a carrier protein
	Salmonella typhi	Typhoid fever	Live organisms or capsular polysaccharide
	Vibrio cholerae	Cholera	Killed organisms
	Yersinia pestis	Plague	Killed organisms
	Bacillus anthracis	Anthrax	Partially purified proteins
	Mycobacterium bovis (BCG)	Tuberculosis	Live organisms
	Francisella tularensis	Tularemia	Live organisms
	Rickettsia prowazekii	Typhus	Killed organisms
	Coxiella burnetii	Q fever	Killed organisms
	Borrelia burgdorferi	Lyme disease[1]	Recombinant outer surface protein A

[1]The Lyme disease vaccine has been withdrawn and is no longer available in the United States.

pertussis toxin (pertussis toxoid), but other proteins, such as filamentous hemagglutinin and pertactin, are also required for full protection. Pertussis toxin for the vaccine is inactivated *genetically* by introducing two amino acid changes that eliminate its toxic (ADP-ribosylating) activity but retain its antigenicity. It is the first vaccine to contain a genetically inactivated toxoid. The vaccine is indicated for every child as a protection against whooping cough. It is usually given in combination with diphtheria and tetanus toxoids (DPT or DtaP vaccine).

(2) The vaccine against Lyme disease contains a purified outer surface protein (OspA) of *Borrelia burgdorferi* as the immunogen. OspA is made by recombinant DNA techniques. It is recommended for those who live in areas of endemic disease and whose occupation or recreation makes them likely to be exposed.

(3) *Bacillus anthracis* vaccine contains "protective antigen" purified from the organism. It is given to persons whose occupations place them at risk of exposure to the organism.

D. LIVE, ATTENUATED BACTERIAL VACCINES

(1) The vaccine against tuberculosis contains a live, attenuated strain of *Mycobacterium bovis* called BCG and is recommended for children at high risk for exposure to active tuberculosis in some countries.

(2) One of the vaccines against typhoid fever contains live, attenuated *Salmonella typhi*. It is indicated for persons living or traveling in areas where there is a high risk of typhoid fever and for persons in close contact with either infected patients or chronic carriers.

(3) The vaccine against tularemia contains live, attenuated *Francisella tularensis* organisms and is used primarily in people who are exposed in their occupation, such as laboratory personnel, veterinarians, and hunters.

E. KILLED BACTERIAL VACCINES

(1) *Vibrio cholerae* vaccine contains killed organisms and is given to persons traveling to areas where cholera is endemic.

(2) *Yersinia pestis* vaccine contains killed organisms and is indicated for persons at high risk for contracting plague.

(3) The vaccine against typhus contains killed *Rickettsia rickettsiae* organisms and is used primarily to immunize members of the armed forces.

(4) The vaccine against Q fever contains killed *Coxiella burnetii* organisms and is used to immunize those who are at high risk for being exposed to animals infected with the organism.

Passive Immunity

Antitoxins (immune globulins) can be used for either the treatment or prevention of certain bacterial diseases. The following preparations are available.

(1) **Tetanus** antitoxin is used in the treatment of tetanus and in its prevention (prophylaxis). In treatment, because the goal is to neutralize any unbound toxin to prevent the disease from getting worse, the antitoxin should be given promptly. In prevention, the antitoxin is given to inadequately immunized persons with contaminated ("dirty") wounds. The antitoxin is made in humans to avoid hypersensitivity reactions. In addition to the antitoxin, these people should receive tetanus toxoid. This is an example of **passive-active** immunity. The toxoid and the antitoxin should be given at different sites in the body to prevent the antitoxin from neutralizing the toxoid.

(2) **Botulinum** antitoxin is used in the treatment of botulism. Because the antitoxin can neutralize unbound toxin to prevent the disease from progressing, it should be given promptly. It contains antibodies against botulinum toxins A, B, and E, the most commonly occurring types. The antitoxin is made in horses, so hypersensitivity may be a problem.

(3) **Diphtheria** antitoxin is used in the treatment of diphtheria. The antitoxin can neutralize unbound toxin to prevent the disease from progressing; therefore, the antitoxin should be given promptly. The antitoxin is made in horses, so hypersensitivity may be a problem.

PEARLS

- *Immunity to certain bacterial diseases can be induced either by immunization with bacterial antigens (**active immunity**) or by administration of preformed antibodies (**passive immunity**).*

Active Immunity

- *Active immunity can be achieved by vaccines consisting of (1) **bacterial capsular polysaccharides, toxoids, whole bacteria** (either killed or live, attenuated) or (2) **purified proteins** isolated from bacteria.*

- ***Vaccines containing capsular polysaccharide** as the immunogen are directed against* Streptococcus pneumoniae, Haemophilus influenzae, Neisseria meningitidis, *and* Salmonella typhi. *The capsular polysaccharide in the pneumococcal vaccine, the meningococcal vaccine, and the* H. influenzae *vaccine is conjugated to a carrier protein to enhance the antibody response.*

- *Two vaccines contain **toxoids** as the immunogen, the vaccines against **diphtheria** and **tetanus**. A **toxoid is an inactivated toxin** that has lost its ability to cause disease but has retained its immunogenicity. (The pertussis vaccine also contains toxoid but contains other bacterial proteins as well and is described in the next section.)*

- *Two vaccines contain purified bacterial proteins as the immunogen. The most commonly used is the **acellular pertussis vaccine,** which in combination with diphtheria and tetanus toxoids is recommended for all children. The **vaccine against anthrax** also contains purified proteins but is recommended only for individuals who are likely to be exposed to the organism.*

- *The **BCG vaccine** against tuberculosis **contains live, attenuated** Mycobacterium bovis and is used in countries where the disease is endemic. One of the vaccines against typhoid fever contains live, attenuated* Salmonella typhi.

- *The vaccines against cholera, plague, typhus, and Q fever contain whole killed bacteria. These vaccines are used only to protect those likely to be exposed.*

Passive Immunity

- *Passive immunity in the form of **antitoxins** is available for the prevention and treatment of **tetanus, botulism,** and **diphtheria**. These three diseases are caused by exotoxins. **Antitoxins** (antibodies against the exotoxins) neutralize the exotoxins and prevent their toxic effects.*

Passive-Active Immunity

- *This involves providing both immediate (but short-term) protection in the form of antibodies and long-term protection in the form of active immunization. An excellent example of the use of passive-active immunity is the prevention of tetanus in an unim-munized person who has sustained a contaminated wound. Both tetanus antitoxin and tetanus toxoid should be given. They should be given at different sites so that the antibodies in the antitoxin do not neutralize the toxoid.*

PRACTICE QUESTIONS: USMLE & COURSE EXAMINATIONS

Questions on the topics discussed in this chapter can be found in the Basic Bacteriology section of Part XI: USMLE (National Board) Practice Questions starting on page 532. Also see Part XII: USMLE (National Board) Practice Examination starting on page 583.

Sterilization & Disinfection

Sterilization is the killing or removal of *all* microorganisms, including bacterial spores, which are highly resistant. Sterilization is usually carried out by autoclaving, which consists of exposure to steam at 121°C under a pressure of 15 lb/in² for 15 minutes. Surgical instruments that can be damaged by moist heat are usually sterilized by exposure to ethylene oxide gas, and most intravenous solutions are sterilized by filtration.

Disinfection is the killing of many, but not all, microorganisms. For adequate disinfection, pathogens must be killed, but some organisms and bacterial spores may survive. Disinfectants vary in their tissue-damaging properties from the corrosive phenol-containing compounds, which should be used only on inanimate objects, to less toxic materials such as ethanol and iodine, which can be used on skin surfaces. Chemicals used to kill microorganisms on the surface of skin and mucous membranes are called **antiseptics**.

■ RATE OF KILLING OF MICROORGANISMS

Death of microorganisms occurs at a certain rate dependent primarily upon two variables: the concentration of the killing agent and the length of time the agent is applied. The rate of killing is defined by the relationship

$$N \propto 1/CT$$

which shows that the number of survivors, N, is inversely proportionate to the concentration of the agent, C, and to the time of application of the agent, T. Collectively, CT is often referred to as the dose. Stated alternatively, the number of microorganisms killed is directly proportionate to CT. The relationship is usually stated in terms of survivors, because they are easily measured by colony formation. Death is defined as the inability to reproduce. In certain circumstances, the physical remains of dead bacteria can still cause problems (see page 48).

■ CHEMICAL AGENTS

Chemicals vary greatly in their ability to kill microorganisms. A quantitative measure of this variation is expressed as the **phenol coefficient**, which is the ratio of the concentration of phenol to the concentration of the agent required to cause the same amount of killing under the standard conditions of the test.

Chemical agents act primarily by one of three mechanisms: (1) disruption of the lipid-containing cell membrane, (2) modification of proteins, or (3) modification of DNA. Each of the following chemical agents has been classified into one of the three categories, but some of the chemicals act by more than one mechanism.

DISRUPTION OF CELL MEMBRANES

Alcohol

Ethanol is widely used to clean the skin before immunization or venipuncture. It acts mainly by disorganizing the lipid structure in membranes, but it denatures proteins as well. Ethanol requires the presence of water for maximal activity; ie, it is far more effective at 70% than at 100%. Seventy percent ethanol is often used as an antiseptic to clean the skin prior to venipuncture. However, because it is not as effective as iodine-containing compounds, the latter should be used prior to obtaining a blood culture and installing intravenous catheters.

Detergents

Detergents are "surface-active" agents composed of a long-chain, lipid-soluble, hydrophobic portion and a polar hydrophilic group, which can be a cation, an anion, or a nonionic group. These surfactants interact with the lipid in the cell membrane through their hydrophobic chain and with the surrounding water through their polar group and thus disrupt the membrane. Quaternary ammonium compounds, eg, benzalkonium chloride, are cationic detergents widely used for skin antisepsis.

Phenols

Phenol was the first disinfectant used in the operating room (by Lister in the 1860s), but it is rarely used as a disinfectant today because it is too caustic. Hexachlorophene, which is a biphenol with six chlorine atoms, is used in germicidal soaps, but concern over possible neurotoxicity has limited its use. Another phenol derivative is cresol (methylphenol), the active ingredient in Lysol. Phenols not only damage membranes but also denature proteins.

MODIFICATION OF PROTEINS

Chlorine

Chlorine is used as a disinfectant to purify the water supply and to treat swimming pools. It is also the active component of hypochlorite (bleach, Clorox), which is used as a disinfectant in the home and in hospitals. Chlorine is a powerful oxidizing agent that kills by cross-linking essential sulfhydryl groups in enzymes to form the inactive disulfide.

Iodine

Iodine is the most effective skin antiseptic used in medical practice and should be used prior to obtaining a blood culture and installing intravenous catheters because contamination with skin flora such as *Staphylococcus epidermidis* can be a problem. Iodine is supplied in two forms:

(1) Tincture of iodine (2% solution of iodine and potassium iodide in ethanol) is used to prepare the skin prior to blood culture. Because tincture of iodine can be irritating to the skin, it should be removed with alcohol.

(2) Iodophors are complexes of iodine with detergents that are frequently used to prepare the skin prior to surgery because they are less irritating than tincture of iodine. Iodine, like chlorine, is an oxidant that inactivates sulfhydryl-containing enzymes. It also binds specifically to tyrosine residues in proteins.

Heavy Metals

Mercury and silver have the greatest antibacterial activity of the heavy metals and are the most widely used in medicine. They act by binding to sulfhydryl groups, thereby blocking enzymatic activity. Thimerosal (Merthiolate) and merbromin (Mercurochrome), which contain mercury, are used as skin antiseptics. Silver nitrate drops are useful in preventing gonococcal ophthalmia neonatorum. Silver sulfadiazine is used to prevent infection of burn wounds.

Hydrogen Peroxide

Hydrogen peroxide is used as an antiseptic to clean wounds and to disinfect contact lenses. Its effectiveness is limited by the organism's ability to produce catalase, an enzyme that degrades H_2O_2. (The bubbles produced when peroxide is used on wounds are formed by oxygen arising from the breakdown of H_2O_2 by tissue catalase.) Hydrogen peroxide is an oxidizing agent that attacks sulfhydryl groups, thereby inhibiting enzymatic activity.

Formaldehyde & Glutaraldehyde

Formaldehyde, which is available as a 37% solution in water (Formalin), denatures proteins and nucleic acids. Both proteins and nucleic acids contain essential $-NH_2$ and $-OH$ groups, which are the main sites of alkylation by the hydroxymethyl group of formaldehyde. Glutaraldehyde, which has two reactive aldehyde groups, is 10 times more effective than formaldehyde and is less toxic. In hospitals, it is used to sterilize respiratory therapy equipment.

Ethylene Oxide

Ethylene oxide gas is used extensively in hospitals for the sterilization of heat-sensitive materials such as surgical instruments and plastics. It kills by alkylating both proteins and nucleic acids; ie, the hydroxyethyl group attacks the reactive hydrogen atoms on essential amino and hydroxyl groups.

Acids & Alkalis

Strong acids and alkalis kill by denaturing proteins. Although most bacteria are susceptible, it is important to note that *Mycobacterium tuberculosis* and other mycobacteria are relatively resistant to 2% NaOH, which is used in the clinical laboratory to liquefy sputum prior to culturing the organism. Weak acids, such as benzoic, propionic, and citric acids, are frequently used as food preservatives because they are bacteriostatic. The action of these acids is partially a function of the organic moiety, eg, benzoate, as well as the low pH.

MODIFICATION OF NUCLEIC ACIDS

A variety of dyes not only stain microorganisms but also inhibit their growth. One of these is crystal violet (gentian violet), which is used as a skin antiseptic. Its action is based on binding of the positively charged dye molecule to the negatively charged phosphate groups of the nucleic acids. Malachite green, a triphenylamine dye like crystal violet, is a component of Löwenstein-Jensen's medium, which is used to grow *M. tuberculosis*.

The dye inhibits the growth of unwanted organisms in the sputum during the 6-week incubation period.

■ PHYSICAL AGENTS

The physical agents act either by imparting energy in the form of heat or radiation or by removing organisms through filtration.

HEAT

Heat energy can be applied in three ways: in the form of moist heat (either boiling or autoclaving) or dry heat or by pasteurization. In general, heat kills by denaturing proteins, but membrane damage and enzymatic cleavage of DNA may also be involved. Moist heat sterilizes at a lower temperature than dry heat, because water aids in the disruption of noncovalent bonds, eg, hydrogen bonds, which hold protein chains together in their secondary and tertiary structures.

Moist-heat sterilization, usually **autoclaving**, is the most frequently used method of sterilization. Because bacterial **spores are resistant to boiling** (100°C at sea level), they must be exposed to a higher temperature; this cannot be achieved unless the pressure is increased. For this purpose, an autoclave chamber is used in which steam, at a pressure of 15 lb/in², reaches a temperature of 121°C and is held for 15–20 minutes. This kills even the highly heat-resistant spores of *Clostridium botulinum,* the cause of botulism, with a margin of safety.

Sterilization by dry heat, on the other hand, requires temperatures in the range of 180°C for 2 hours. This process is used primarily for glassware and is used less frequently than autoclaving.

Pasteurization, which is used primarily for milk, consists of heating the milk to 62°C for 30 minutes followed by rapid cooling. ("Flash" pasteurization at 72°C for 15 seconds is often used.) This is sufficient to kill the vegetative cells of the milk-borne pathogens, eg, *Mycobacterium bovis, Salmonella, Streptococcus, Listeria,* and *Brucella,* but not to sterilize the milk.

RADIATION

The two types of radiation used to kill microorganisms are **ultraviolet (UV) light and x-rays.** The greatest an-timicrobial activity of UV light occurs at 250–260 nm, which is the wavelength region of maximum absorption by the purine and pyrimidine bases of DNA. The most significant lesion caused by UV irradiation is the formation of thymine dimers, but addition of hydroxyl groups to the bases also occurs. As a result, DNA replication is inhibited and the organism cannot grow. Cells have repair mechanisms against UV-induced damage that involve either cleavage of dimers in the presence of visible light (photoreactivation) or excision of damaged bases, which is not dependent upon visible light (dark repair). Because UV radiation can damage the cornea and skin, the use of UV irradiation in medicine is limited. However, it is used in hospitals to kill airborne organisms, especially in operating rooms when they are not in use. Bacterial spores are quite resistant and require a dose up to 10 times greater than do the vegetative bacteria.

X-rays have higher energy and penetrating power than UV radiation and kill mainly by the production of free radicals, eg, production of hydroxyl radicals by the hydrolysis of water. These highly reactive radicals can break covalent bonds in DNA, thereby killing the organism. Sulfhydryl-containing compounds, such as the amino acid cysteine, can protect DNA from free-radical attack. Another mechanism is a direct hit on a covalent bond in DNA, resulting in chain breakage, but this is probably less important than the mechanism involving free radicals.

X-rays kill vegetative cells readily, but spores are remarkably resistant, probably because of their lower water content. X-rays are used in medicine for sterilization of heat-sensitive items, such as sutures and surgical gloves, and plastic items, such as syringes.

FILTRATION

Filtration is the preferred method of sterilizing certain solutions, eg, those with heat-sensitive components. In the past, solutions for intravenous use were autoclaved, but heat-resistant endotoxin in the cell walls of the dead gram-negative bacteria caused fever in recipients of the solutions. Therefore, solutions are now filtered to make them **pyrogen-free** prior to autoclaving.

The most commonly used filter is composed of nitrocellulose and has a pore size of 0.22 μm. This size will retain all bacteria and spores. Filters work by physically trapping particles larger than the pore size and by retaining somewhat smaller particles via electrostatic attraction of the particles to the filters.

PEARLS

- Sterilization is the **killing of all** forms of microbial life including bacterial spores. **Spores** are **resistant to boiling,** so sterilization of medical equipment is typically achieved at 121°C for 15 minutes in an autoclave. Sterilization of heat-sensitive materials is achieved by exposure to ethylene oxide, and liquids can be sterilized by filtration.

- **Disinfection** is **reducing the number of bacteria** to a level low enough that disease is unlikely to occur. Spores and some bacteria will survive. For example, disinfection of the water supply is achieved by treatment with chlorine. Disinfection of the skin prior to venipuncture is achieved by treatment with 70% ethanol. Disinfectants that are mild enough to use on skin and other tissues, such as 70% ethanol, are called **antiseptics.**

- The killing of microbes by either chemicals or radiation is proportional to the **dose,** which is defined as the product of the concentration multiplied by the time of exposure.

- Chemical agents kill bacteria by one of three actions: disruption of lipid in cell membranes, modification of proteins, or modification of DNA.

- Physical agents kill (or remove) bacteria by one of three processes: heat, radiation, or filtration.

- Heat is usually applied at temperatures above boiling (121°C) to kill spores, but heat-sensitive materials such as milk are exposed to temperatures below boiling (**pasteurization**) that kills the pathogens in milk but does not sterilize it.

- Radiation, such as **ultraviolet light** and x-radiation, is often used to sterilize heat-sensitive items. Ultraviolet light and x-radiation **kill by damaging DNA.**

- Filtration can sterilize liquids if the pore size of the filter is small enough to retain all bacteria and spores. Heat-sensitive liquids, eg, intravenous fluids, are often sterilized by filtration.

PRACTICE QUESTIONS: USMLE & COURSE EXAMINATIONS

Questions on the topics discussed in this chapter can be found in the Basic Bacteriology section of Part XI: USMLE (National Board) Practice Questions starting on page 532. Also see Part XII: USMLE (National Board) Practice Examination starting on page 583.

PART II
Clinical Bacteriology

Overview of the Major Pathogens & Introduction to Anaerobic Bacteria

14

OVERVIEW OF THE MAJOR PATHOGENS

The major bacterial pathogens are presented in Table 14–1 and described in Chapters 15–26. So that the reader may concentrate on the important pathogens, the bacteria that are less medically important are described in a separate chapter (see Chapter 27).

Table 14–1 is divided into organisms that are readily Gram-stained and those that are not. The readily stained organisms fall into four categories: gram-positive cocci, gram-negative cocci, gram-positive rods, and gram-negative rods. Because there are so many kinds of gram-negative rods, they have been divided into three groups:

(1) Organisms associated with the enteric tract
(2) Organisms associated with the respiratory tract
(3) Organisms from animal sources (zoonotic bacteria).

For ease of understanding, the organisms associated with the enteric tract are further subdivided into three groups: (1) pathogens both inside and outside the enteric tract, (2) pathogens inside the enteric tract, and (3) pathogens outside the enteric tract.

As is true of any classification dealing with biologic entities, this one is not entirely precise. For example,

Campylobacter causes enteric tract disease but frequently has an animal source. Nevertheless, despite some uncertainties, subdivision of the large number of gram-negative rods into these functional categories should be helpful to the reader.

The organisms that are not readily Gram-stained fall into six major categories: *Mycobacterium* species, which are acid-fast rods; *Mycoplasma* species, which have no cell wall and so do not stain with Gram stain; *Treponema* and *Leptospira* species, which are spirochetes too thin to be seen when stained with Gram stain; and *Chlamydia* and *Rickettsia* species, which stain well with Giemsa stain or other special stains but poorly with Gram stain. *Chlamydia* and *Rickettsia* species are obligate intracellular parasites, whereas members of the other four genera are not.

Table 14–2 presents the 10 most common "notifiable" bacterial diseases in the United States for 2003 as compiled by the Centers for Disease Control and Prevention. Note that only notifiable diseases are included and that certain common conditions such as streptococcal pharyngitis and impetigo are not included. Two sexually transmitted diseases, chlamydial infection and gonorrhea, are by far the most common diseases listed, followed by salmonellosis, syphilis, and shigellosis in the top five.

Table 14–1. Major bacterial pathogens.

Type of Organism	Genus
Readily Gram-stained	
Gram-positive cocci	*Staphylococcus, Streptococcus, Enterococcus*
Gram-negative cocci	*Neisseria*
Gram-positive rods	*Corynebacterium, Listeria, Bacillus, Clostridium, Actinomyces, Nocardia*
Gram-negative rods	
Enteric tract organisms	
Pathogenic inside and outside tract	*Escherichia, Salmonella*
Pathogenic primarily inside tract	*Shigella, Vibrio, Campylobacter, Helicobacter*
Pathogenic outside tract	*Klebsiella-Enterobacter-Serratia* group, *Pseudomonas, Proteus-Providencia-Morganella* group, *Bacteroides*
Respiratory tract organisms	*Haemophilus, Legionella, Bordetella*
Organisms from animal sources	*Brucella, Francisella, Pasteurella, Yersinia*
Not readily Gram-stained	
Not obligate intracellular parasites	*Mycobacterium, Mycoplasma, Treponema, Leptospira*
Obligate intracellular parasites	*Chlamydia, Rickettsia*

INTRODUCTION TO ANAEROBIC BACTERIA

Important Properties

Anaerobes are characterized by their ability to grow only in an atmosphere containing less than 20% oxygen; ie, they grow poorly if at all in room air. They are a heterogeneous group composed of a variety of bacteria, from those that can barely grow in 20% oxygen to those that can grow only in less than 0.02% oxygen. Table 14–3 describes the optimal oxygen requirements for several representative groups of organisms. The obligate aerobes, such as *Pseudomonas aeruginosa*, grow best in the 20% oxygen of room air and not at all under anaerobic conditions. Facultative anaerobes such as *Escherichia coli* can grow well under either circumstance. Aerotolerant organisms such as *Clostridium histolyticum* can grow to some extent in air but multiply much more rapidly in a lower oxygen concentration. Microaerophilic organisms such as *Campylobacter jejuni* require a reduced oxygen concentration (approximately 5%) to grow optimally. The obligate anaerobes such as *Bacteroides fragilis* and *Clostridium perfringens* require an almost total absence of oxygen. Many anaerobes use nitrogen rather than oxygen as the terminal electron acceptor.

The main reason why the growth of anaerobes is inhibited by oxygen is the reduced amount (or absence) of catalase and superoxide dismutase (SOD) in anaerobes. Catalase and SOD eliminate the toxic compounds hydrogen peroxide and superoxide, which are formed during production of energy by the organism (see Chapter 3). Another reason is the oxidation of es-

Table 14–2. The 10 most common notifiable bacterial diseases in the United States in 2003.[1]

Disease	Number of Cases
Chlamydial genital infections	877,478
Gonorrhea	335,104
Salmonellosis	43,657
Syphilis	34,270
Shigellosis	23,581
Lyme disease	21,273
Tuberculosis	14,874
Pertussis	11,647
Streptococcal disease, group A, invasive	5,872
Enterohemorrhagic *Escherichia coli* O157 infection	2,671

[1] The latest year for which complete data are available.

Table 14–3. Optimal oxygen requirements of representative bacteria.

Bacterial Type	Representative Organism	Growth Under Following Conditions	
		Aerobic	**Anaerobic**
Obligate aerobes	*Pseudomonas aeruginosa*	3 +	0
Facultative anaerobes	*Escherichia coli*	4 +	3 +
Aerotolerant organisms	*Clostridium histolyticum*	1 +	4 +
Microaerophiles	*Campylobacter jejuni*	0	1 +[1]
Obligate anaerobes	*Bacteroides fragilis*	0	4 +

[1]*C. jejuni* grows best (3 +) in 5% O_2 plus 10% CO_2. It is also called **capnophilic** in view of its need for CO_2 for optimal growth.

sential sulfhydryl groups in enzymes without sufficient reducing power to regenerate them.

In addition to oxygen concentration, the oxidation-reduction potential (E_h) of a tissue is an important determinant of the growth of anaerobes. Areas with low E_h, such as the periodontal pocket, dental plaque, and colon, support the growth of anaerobes well. Crushing injuries that result in devitalized tissue caused by impaired blood supply produce a low E_h, allowing anaerobes to grow and cause disease.

Anaerobes of Medical Interest

The anaerobes of medical interest are presented in Table 14–4. It can be seen that they include both rods and cocci and both gram-positive and gram-negative organisms. The rods are divided into the spore formers, eg, *Clostridium,* and the non–spore formers, eg, *Bacteroides.* In this book, three genera of anaerobes are described as major bacterial pathogens, namely, *Clostridium, Actinomyces,* and *Bacteroides. Streptococcus* is a genus of major pathogens consisting of both anaerobic and facultative organisms. The remaining anaerobes are less important and are discussed in Chapter 27.

Clinical Infections

Many of the medically important anaerobes are part of the normal human flora. As such, they are non-pathogens in their normal habitat and cause disease only when they leave those sites. The two prominent exceptions to this are *Clostridium botulinum* and *Clostridium tetani,* the agents of botulism and tetanus, respectively, which are soil organisms. *C. perfringens,* another important human pathogen, is found in the colon and in the soil.

Diseases caused by members of the anaerobic normal flora are characterized by abscesses, which are most frequently located in the brain, lungs, female genital tract, biliary tract, and other intra-abdominal sites. Most abscesses contain more than one organism, either multiple anaerobes or a mixture of anaerobes plus facultative anaerobes. It is thought that the facultative anaerobes consume sufficient oxygen to allow the anaerobes to flourish.

Three important findings on physical examination that arouse suspicion of an anaerobic infection are a foul-smelling discharge, gas in the tissue, and necrotic tissue. In addition, infections in the setting of pul-

Table 14–4. Anaerobic bacteria of medical interest.

Morphology	Gram Stain	Genus
Spore-forming rods	+	*Clostridium*
	−	None
Non-spore–forming rods	+	*Actinomyces, Bifidobacterium, Eubacterium, Lactobacillus, Propionibacterium*
	−	*Bacteroides, Fusobacterium*
Non-spore–forming cocci	+	*Peptococcus, Peptostreptococcus, Streptococcus*
	−	*Veillonella*

monary aspiration, bowel surgery, abortion, cancer, or human and animal bites frequently involve anaerobes.

Laboratory Diagnosis

Two aspects of microbiologic diagnosis of an anaerobic infection are important even before the specimen is cultured: (1) obtaining the appropriate specimen, and (2) rapidly transporting the specimen under anaerobic conditions to the laboratory. An appropriate specimen is one that does not contain members of the normal flora to confuse the interpretation. For example, such specimens as blood, pleural fluid, pus, and transtracheal aspirates are appropriate, but sputum and feces are not.

In the laboratory, the cultures are handled and incubated under anaerobic conditions. In addition to the usual diagnostic criteria of Gram stain, morphology, and biochemical reactions, the special technique of gas chromatography is important. In this procedure, organic acids such as formic, acetic, and propionic acids are measured.

Treatment

In general, surgical drainage of the abscess plus administration of antimicrobial drugs are indicated. Drugs commonly used to treat anaerobic infections are penicillin G, cefoxitin, chloramphenicol, clindamycin, and metronidazole. Note, however, that many isolates of the important pathogen *B. fragilis* produce β-lactamase and so are resistant to penicillin.

PRACTICE QUESTIONS: USMLE & COURSE EXAMINATIONS

Questions on the topics discussed in this chapter can be found in the Clinical Bacteriology section of Part XI: USMLE (National Board) Practice Questions starting on page 537. Also see Part XII: USMLE (National Board) Practice Examination starting on page 583.

Gram-Positive Cocci

There are two medically important genera of gram-positive cocci: *Staphylococcus* and *Streptococcus.* Two of the most important human pathogens, *Staphylococcus aureus* and *Streptococcus pyogenes,* are described in this chapter. Staphylococci and streptococci are nonmotile and do not form spores.

Both staphylococci and streptococci are gram-positive cocci, but they are distinguished by two main criteria.

(1) Microscopically, staphylococci appear in grapelike clusters, whereas streptococci are in chains.

(2) Biochemically, staphylococci produce catalase (ie, they degrade hydrogen peroxide), whereas streptococci do not.

STAPHYLOCOCCUS

Diseases

Staphylococcus aureus causes abscesses, various pyogenic infections (eg, endocarditis, septic arthritis, and osteomyelitis), food poisoning, and toxic shock syndrome. It is one of the most common causes of hospital-acquired pneumonia, septicemia, and surgical-wound infections. *Staphylococcus epidermidis* can cause endocarditis and prosthetic joint infections. *Staphylococcus saprophyticus* causes urinary tract infections. Kawasaki syndrome is a disease of unknown etiology that may be caused by certain strains of *S. aureus.*

Important Properties

Staphylococci are spherical gram-positive cocci arranged in irregular grapelike clusters. All staphylococci produce **catalase,** whereas no streptococci do (catalase degrades H_2O_2 into O_2 and H_2O). Catalase is an important virulence factor because H_2O_2 is microbicidal and its degradation limits the ability of neutrophils to kill.

Three species of staphylococci are human pathogens: *S. aureus, S. epidermidis,* and *S. saprophyticus* (Table 15–1). Of the three, *S. aureus* is by far the most important. *S. aureus* is distinguished from the others primarily by **coagulase** production. **Coagulase** is an enzyme that causes plasma to clot by activating prothrombin to form thrombin. Thrombin then catalyzes the activation of fibrinogen to form the fibrin clot. *S. epidermidis* and *S. saprophyticus* are often referred to as coagulase-negative staphylococci.

S. aureus produces a carotenoid pigment that imparts a golden color to its colonies. This pigment enhances the pathogenicity of the organism by inactivating the microbicidal effect of superoxides and other reactive oxygen species within neutrophils. *S. epidermidis* does not synthesize this pigment and produces white colonies. The virulence of *S. epidermidis* is significantly less than that of *S. aureus.* Two other characteristics further distinguish these species, namely, *S. aureus* usually ferments mannitol and hemolyzes red blood cells, whereas the others do not.

More than 90% of *S. aureus* strains contain plasmids that encode β-lactamase, the enzyme that degrades many, but not all, penicillins. Some strains of *S. aureus* are resistant to the β-lactamase-resistant penicillins, such as methicillin and nafcillin, by virtue of changes in the penicillin-binding protein in their cell membrane. These strains are commonly known as methicillin-resistant *S. aureus* (MRSA) or nafcillin-resistant *S. aureus* (NRSA). Rare strains called vancomycin-intermediate *S. aureus* (VISA), with reduced sensitivity to vancomycin, have emerged, as have strains fully resistant to vancomycin.

S. aureus has several important cell wall components and antigens.

(1) **Protein A** is the major protein in the cell wall. It is an important virulence factor because it binds to the Fc portion of IgG at the complement-binding site, thereby preventing the activation of complement. As a consequence, no C3b is produced, and the opsonization and phagocytosis of the organisms are greatly reduced. Protein A is used in certain tests in the clinical laboratory because it binds to IgG and forms a "coagglutinate" with antigen-antibody complexes. The coagulase-negative staphylococci do not produce protein A.

(2) Teichoic acids are polymers of ribitol phosphate. They mediate adherence of the staphylococci to mucosal cells and play a role in the induction of septic shock.

Table 15–1. Staphylococci of medical importance.

Species	Coagulase Production	Typical Hemolysis	Important Features[1]	Typical Disease
S. aureus	+	Beta	Protein A on surface	Abscess, food poisoning, toxic shock syndrome
S. epidermidis	–	None	Sensitive to novobiocin	Infection of prosthetic heart valves and hips; common member of skin flora
S. saprophyticus	–	None	Resistant to novobiocin	Urinary tract infection

[1]All staphylococci are catalase-positive.

(3) Polysaccharide capsule is also an important virulence factor. There are 12 serotypes, but types 5 and 8 cause 85% of infections. The capsule is poorly immunogenic, which has made producing an effective vaccine difficult.

(4) Surface receptors for specific staphylococcal bacteriophages permit the "phage typing" of strains for epidemiologic purposes. Teichoic acids make up part of these receptors.

(5) Most strains of *S. aureus* are coated with a small amount of polysaccharide capsule (microcapsule) that is antiphagocytic. There are 11 serotypes based on antigenicity of the capsular polysaccharide.

(6) The peptidoglycan of *S. aureus* has endotoxin-like properties; ie, it can stimulate macrophages to produce cytokines and can activate the complement and coagulation cascades. This explains the ability of *S. aureus* to cause the clinical findings of septic shock yet not possess endotoxin.

Transmission

Staphylococci are found primarily in the normal human flora. *S. epidermidis* is regularly present on normal **skin** and mucous membranes, and *S. saprophyticus* inhabits the skin surrounding the genitourinary tract. *S. aureus* is most often found in the **nose** and sometimes on the skin, especially in hospital staff and patients. *S. aureus* is also found in the vagina of approximately 5% of women, which predisposes them to toxic shock syndrome. Additional sources of staphylococcal infection are shedding from human lesions and fomites contaminated by these lesions.

Disease caused by *S. aureus* is favored by a heavily contaminated environment (eg, family members with boils) and a compromised immune system. Reduced humoral immunity, including low levels of antibody, complement, or neutrophils, especially predisposes to staphylococcal infections. Diabetes and intravenous drug use predispose to infections by *S. aureus*.

Pathogenesis

A. STAPHYLOCOCCUS AUREUS

S. aureus causes disease both by producing toxins and by inducing pyogenic inflammation. The typical lesion of *S. aureus* infection is an **abscess**. Abscesses undergo central necrosis and usually drain to the outside (eg, furuncles and boils), but organisms may disseminate via the bloodstream as well. **Foreign bodies,** such as sutures and intravenous catheters, are important predisposing factors to infection by *S. aureus*.

Several important toxins and enzymes are produced by *S. aureus*. The three clinically important exotoxins are enterotoxin, toxic shock syndrome toxin, and exfoliatin.

(1) En**terotoxin** causes food poisoning characterized by prominent vomiting and watery, nonbloody diarrhea. It acts as a superantigen within the gastrointestinal tract to stimulate the release of large amounts of interleukin-1 (IL-1) and interleukin-2 (IL-2) from macrophages and helper T cells, respectively. The prominent vomiting appears to be caused by cytokines released from the lymphoid cells, which stimulate the enteric nervous system to activate the vomiting center in the brain. Enterotoxin is fairly heat-resistant and therefore is usually not inactivated by brief cooking. It is resistant to stomach acid and to enzymes in the stomach and jejunum. There are six immunologic types of enterotoxin, types A–F.

(2) To**xic shock syndrome toxin** (TSST) causes toxic shock, especially in tampon-using menstruating women or in individuals with wound infections. Toxic shock also occurs in patients with nasal packing used to stop bleeding from the nose. TSST is produced locally by *S. aureus* in the vagina, nose, or other infected site. The toxin enters the bloodstream, causing a toxemia. Blood cultures typically do not grow *S. aureus*.

TSST is a superantigen and causes toxic shock by stimulating the release of large amounts of IL-1, IL-2, and tumor necrosis factor (TNF) (see the discussions of exotoxins in Chapter 7 and superantigens in Chapter 58). Approximately 5–25% of isolates of *S. aureus* carry the gene for TSST. Toxic shock occurs in people who do not have antibody against TSST.

(3) **Exfoliatin** causes "scalded skin" syndrome in young children. It is "epidermolytic" and acts as a protease that cleaves desmoglein in desmosomes, leading to the separation of the epidermis at the granular cell layer.

(4) Several toxins can kill leukocytes (leukocidins) and cause necrosis of tissues in vivo. Of these, the most important is **alpha toxin,** which causes marked necrosis of the skin and hemolysis. The cytotoxic effect of alpha toxin is attributed to the formation of holes in the cell membrane and the consequent loss of low-molecular-weight substances from the damaged cell. A second toxin, **P-V leukocidin,** also kills white blood cells by damaging cell membranes. The importance of P-V leukocidin as a virulence factor is indicated by the severe skin and soft tissue infection caused by methicillin-resistant *S. aureus* strains that produce this leukocidin.

(5) The enzymes include **coagulase,** fibrinolysin, hyaluronidase, proteases, nucleases, and lipases. Coagulase, by clotting plasma, serves to wall off the infected site, thereby retarding the migration of neutrophils into the site. Staphylokinase is a fibrinolysin that can lyse thrombi.

B. Staphylococcus epidermidis & Staphylococcus saprophyticus

Unlike *S. aureus,* these two coagulase-negative staphylococci do not produce exotoxins. Thus, they do not cause food poisoning or toxic shock syndrome. They do, however, cause pyogenic infections. For example, *S. epidermidis* is a prominent cause of pyogenic infections on prosthetic implants such as heart valves and hip joints.

Clinical Findings

The important clinical manifestations caused by *S. aureus* can be divided into two groups: pyogenic and toxin-mediated (Table 15–2). *S. aureus* is a major cause of skin, soft tissue, bone, joint, lung, heart, and kidney infections. In the following list, the first six are pyogenic in origin, whereas the last three are toxin-mediated.

A. Staphylococcus aureus: Pyogenic Diseases

(1) Skin infections are very common. These include impetigo, furuncles, carbuncles, paronychia, cellulitis, folliculitis, hydradenitis suppurativa, conjunctivitis, eyelid infections (blepharitis), and postpartum breast infections (mastitis). Severe necrotizing skin and soft tissue infections are caused by methicillin-resistant *S. aureus* strains that produce P-V leukocidin. These infections are typically community-acquired rather than hospital-acquired. People at risk for these infections include the homeless, intravenous drug users, and athletes who engage in close personal contact such as wrestlers and football players.

(2) Septicemia (sepsis) can originate from any localized lesion, especially wound infection, or as a result of intravenous drug abuse. Sepsis caused by *S. aureus* has clinical features similar to those of sepsis caused by certain gram-negative bacteria such as *Neisseria meningitidis* (see page 120).

Table 15–2. Important features of pathogenesis by staphylococci.

Organism	Type of Pathogenesis	Typical Disease	Predisposing Factor	Mode of Prevention
S. aureus	1. Toxigenic (superantigen)	Toxic shock syndrome	Vaginal or nasal tampons	Reduce time of tampon use
		Food poisoning	Improper food storage	Refrigerate food
	2. Pyogenic (abscess)			
	a. Local	Skin infection, eg, impetigo	Poor skin hygiene	Cleanliness
		Surgical-wound infections	Failure to follow aseptic procedures	Hand washing; reduce nasal carriage
	b. Disseminated	Sepsis, endocarditis[1]	IV drug use	Reduce IV drug use
S. epidermidis	Pyogenic	Infections of intravenous catheter sites and prosthetic devices	Failure to follow aseptic procedures or remove IV catheters promptly	Hand washing; remove IV catheters promptly
S. saprophyticus	Pyogenic	Urinary tract infection	Sexual activity	

IV = intravenous.

[1]For simplicity, many forms of disseminated diseases caused by *S. aureus,* eg, osteomyelitis, arthritis, were not included in the table.

(3) Endocarditis may occur on normal or prosthetic heart valves, especially right-sided endocarditis (tricuspid valve) in intravenous drug users. (Prosthetic valve endocarditis is often caused by *S. epidermidis*.)

(4) Osteomyelitis and arthritis may arise either by hematogenous spread from a distant infected focus or be introduced locally at a wound site. *S. aureus* is a very common cause of these diseases, especially in children.

(5) Postsurgical wound infections are an important cause of morbidity and mortality in hospitals. *S. aureus* is the most common cause.

(6) Pneumonia can occur in postoperative patients or following viral respiratory infection, especially influenza. Staphylococcal pneumonia often leads to empyema or lung abscess; in many hospitals it is the most common cause of nosocomial pneumonia.

(7) Abscesses can occur in any organ when the organism circulates in the bloodstream (bacteremia). These abscesses are often called "metastatic abscesses" because they occur by the spread of bacteria from the original site.

B. *Staphylococcus aureus*: Toxin-Mediated Diseases

(1) Food poisoning (gastroenteritis) is caused by ingestion of enterotoxin, which is preformed in foods and hence has a short incubation period (1–8 hours). In staphylococcal food poisoning, vomiting is typically more prominent than diarrhea.

(2) Toxic shock syndrome is characterized by fever; hypotension; a diffuse, macular, sunburn-like rash that goes on to desquamate; and involvement of three or more of the following organs: liver, kidney, gastrointestinal tract, central nervous system, muscle, or blood.

(3) Scalded skin syndrome is characterized by fever, large bullae, and an erythematous macular rash. Large areas of skin slough, serous fluid exudes, and electrolyte imbalance can occur. Hair and nails can be lost. Recovery usually occurs within 7–10 days. This syndrome occurs most often in young children.

C. *Staphylococcus aureus*: Kawasaki Syndrome

Kawasaki syndrome (KS) is a disease of unknown etiology that is discussed here because several of its features resemble toxic shock syndrome caused by the superantigens of *S. aureus* (and *S. pyogenes*). KS is a vasculitis involving small and medium-size arteries, especially the coronary arteries.

Clinically, KS is characterized by a high fever of at least 5 days' duration; bilateral nonpurulent conjunctivitis; lesions of the lips and oral mucosa (such as strawberry tongue, edema of the lips, and erythema of the oropharynx); a diffuse erythematous, maculopapular rash; erythema and edema of the hands and feet that often ends with desquamation; and cervical lymphadenopathy.

The most characteristic clinical finding of KS is cardiac involvement, especially myocarditis, arrhythmias, and regurgitation involving the mitral or aortic valves. The main cause of morbidity and mortality in KS is aneurysm of the coronary arteries.

KS is much more common in children of Asian ancestry, leading to speculation that certain major histocompatibility complex (MHC) alleles may predispose to the disease. It is a disease of children under 5 years of age, often occurring in mini-outbreaks. It occurs worldwide but is much more common in Japan.

There is no definitive diagnostic laboratory test for KS. Effective therapy consists of high-dose immune globulins (IVIG), which promptly reduces the fever and other symptoms and, most importantly, significantly reduces the occurrence of aneurysms.

D. *Staphylococcus epidermidis* & *Staphylococcus saprophyticus*

There are two coagulase-negative staphylococci of medical importance: *S. epidermidis* and *S. saprophyticus*. *S. epidermidis* infections are almost always hospital-acquired, whereas *S. saprophyticus* infections are almost always community-acquired.

S. epidermidis is part of the normal human flora on the skin and mucous membranes but can enter the bloodstream (bacteremia) and cause metastatic infections. It commonly infects intravenous catheters and prosthetic implants, eg, heart valves (endocarditis), vascular grafts, and joints (arthritis or osteomyelitis) (Table 15–2). *S. epidermidis* is also a major cause of sepsis in neonates and of peritonitis in patients with renal failure who are undergoing peritoneal dialysis through an indwelling catheter. It is the most common bacterium to cause cerebrospinal fluid shunt infections. Strains of *S. epidermidis* that produce a glycocalyx are more likely to adhere to prosthetic implant materials and therefore are more likely to infect these implants than strains that do not produce a glycocalyx. Hospital personnel are a major reservoir for antibiotic-resistant strains of *S. epidermidis*.

S. saprophyticus causes urinary tract infections, particularly in sexually active young women. Most women with this infection have had sexual intercourse within the previous 24 hours. This organism is second to *Escherichia coli* as a cause of community-acquired urinary tract infections in young women.

Laboratory Diagnosis

Smears from staphylococcal lesions reveal gram-positive cocci in grapelike clusters. Cultures of *S. aureus* typically yield golden-yellow colonies that are usually beta-hemolytic. *S. aureus* is **coagulase-positive.** Mannitol-salt agar is a commonly used screening device for *S. aureus.* Cultures of coagulase-negative staphylococci typically yield white colonies that are nonhemolytic. The two coagulase-negative staphylococci are distinguished by their reaction to the antibiotic novobiocin: *S. epidermidis* is sensitive, whereas *S. saprophyticus* is resistant. There are no generally useful serologic or skin tests. In toxic shock syndrome, isolation of *S. aureus* is not required to make a diagnosis as long as the clinical criteria are met.

For epidemiological purposes, *S. aureus* can be subdivided into subgroups based on the susceptibility of the clinical isolate to lysis by a variety of bacteriophages. A person carrying *S. aureus* of the same phage group as that which caused the outbreak may be the source of the infections.

Treatment

In the United States, 90% or more of *S. aureus* strains are resistant to penicillin G. Most of these strains produce **β-lactamase.** Such organisms can be treated with β-lactamase-resistant penicillins, eg, nafcillin or cloxacillin, some cephalosporins, or vancomycin. Treatment with a combination of a β-lactamase-sensitive penicillin, eg, amoxicillin, and a β-lactamase inhibitor, eg, clavulanic acid, is also useful.

Approximately 20% of *S. aureus* strains are methicillin-resistant or nafcillin-resistant by virtue of altered penicillin-binding proteins. These resistant strains of *S. aureus* are often abbreviated MRSA or NRSA, respectively. Such organisms can produce sizable outbreaks of disease, especially in hospitals. The drug of choice for these staphylococci is vancomycin, to which gentamicin is sometimes added. Community-acquired infections with MRSA also occur. Molecular analysis reveals that the community-acquired strains of MRSA are different from the hospital-associated strains.

Strains of *S. aureus* with intermediate resistance (so-called VISA strains) and with complete resistance to vancomycin have been isolated from patients. These strains are typically methicillin/nafcillin-resistant as well, which makes them very difficult to treat. A combination of two streptogramins, quinupristin-dalfopristin (Synercid), has been shown to be effective, but Synercid is available only as an investigational drug at this time. Streptogramins inhibit bacterial protein synthesis in a manner similar to macrolides but are bactericidal for *S. aureus.*

The treatment of toxic shock syndrome involves correction of the shock using fluids, pressor drugs, and inotropic drugs; administration of a β-lactamase-resistant penicillin such as nafcillin; and removal of the tampon or debridement of the infected site as needed. Pooled serum globulins, which contain antibodies against TSST, may be useful.

Mupirocin is very effective as a topical antibiotic in skin infections caused by *S. aureus.* It also has been used to reduce nasal carriage of the organism in hospital personnel and in patients with recurrent staphylococcal infections.

Some strains of staphylococci exhibit **tolerance;** ie, they can be inhibited by antibiotics but are not killed. (That is, the ratio of minimum bactericidal concentration [MBC] to minimum inhibitory concentration [MIC] is very high.) Tolerance may result from failure of the drugs to inactivate inhibitors of autolytic enzymes that degrade the organism. Tolerant organisms should be treated with drug combinations (see Chapter 10).

Drainage (spontaneous or surgical) is the cornerstone of abscess treatment. Previous infection provides only partial immunity to reinfection.

S. epidermidis is highly antibiotic resistant. Most strains produce β-lactamase and many are methicillin/nafcillin-resistant due to altered penicillin-binding proteins. The drug of choice is vancomycin, to which either rifampin or an aminoglycoside can be added. Removal of the catheter or other device is often necessary. *S. saprophyticus* urinary tract infections can be treated with a quinolone, such as norfloxacin, or with trimethoprim-sulfamethoxazole.

Prevention

There is no effective immunization with toxoids or bacterial vaccines. Cleanliness, frequent hand washing, and aseptic management of lesions help to control spread of *S. aureus.* Persistent colonization of the nose by *S. aureus* can be reduced by intranasal mupirocin or by oral antibiotics, such as ciprofloxacin or trimethoprim-sulfamethoxazole, but is difficult to eliminate completely. Shedders may have to be removed from high-risk areas, eg, operating rooms and newborn nurseries. Cefazolin is often used perioperatively to prevent staphylococcal surgical-wound infections.

STREPTOCOCCUS

Streptococci of medical importance are listed in Table 15–3. All but one of these streptococci are discussed in this section; *Streptococcus pneumoniae* is discussed separately at the end of this chapter because it is so important.

Diseases

Streptococci cause a wide variety of infections. *S. pyogenes* (group A streptococcus) is the leading bacterial

Table 15–3. Streptococci of medical importance.

Species	Lancefield Group	Typical Hemolysis	Diagnostic Features[1]
S. pyogenes	A	Beta	Bacitracin-sensitive.
S. agalactiae	B	Beta	Bacitracin-resistant; hippurate hydrolyzed.
E. faecalis	D	Alpha or beta or none	Growth in 6.5% NaCl.[3]
S. bovis[2]	D	Alpha or none	No growth in 6.5% NaCl.
S. pneumoniae	NA[4]	Alpha	Bile-soluble; inhibited by optochin.
Viridans group[5]	NA	Alpha	Not bile-soluble; not inhibited by optochin.

[1]All streptococci are catalase-negative.

[2]S. bovis is a nonenterococcal group D organism.

[3]Both E. faecalis and S. bovis grow on bile-esculin agar, whereas other streptococci do not. They hydrolyze the esculin, and this results in a characteristic black discoloration of the agar.

[4]NA, not applicable.

[5]Viridans group streptococci include several species, such as S. anguis, S. mutans, S. mitis, S. gordoni, S. salivarius, S. anginosus, S. milleri, and S. intermedius.

cause of pharyngitis and cellulitis. It is an important cause of impetigo, necrotizing fasciitis, and streptococcal toxic shock syndrome. It is also the inciting factor of two important immunologic diseases, namely, rheumatic fever and acute glomerulonephritis. *Streptococcus agalactiae* (group B streptococcus) is the leading cause of neonatal sepsis and meningitis. *Enterococcus faecalis* is an important cause of hospital-acquired urinary tract infections and endocarditis. Viridans group streptococci are the most common cause of endocarditis. *Streptococcus bovis* also causes endocarditis.

Important Properties

Streptococci are spherical gram-positive cocci arranged in chains or pairs. All streptococci are **catalase-negative**, whereas staphylococci are catalase-positive (Table 15–3).

One of the most important characteristics for identification of streptococci is the type of hemolysis.

(1) **Alpha-hemolytic** streptococci form a green zone around their colonies as a result of incomplete lysis of red blood cells in the agar.

(2) **Beta-hemolytic** streptococci form a clear zone around their colonies because complete lysis of the red cells occurs. Beta-hemolysis is due to the production of enzymes (hemolysins) called streptolysin O and streptolysin S (see the Pathogenesis section below).

(3) Some streptococci are nonhemolytic (gamma-hemolysis).

There are two important antigens of beta-hemolytic streptococci:

(1) **C carbohydrate** determines the *group* of beta-hemolytic streptococci. It is located in the cell wall, and its specificity is determined by an amino sugar.

(2) **M protein** is the most important virulence factor and determines the *type* of group A beta-hemolytic streptococci. It protrudes from the outer surface of the cell and interferes with ingestion by phagocytes; ie, it is antiphagocytic. Antibody to M protein provides type-specific immunity. There are approximately 80 serotypes based on the M protein, which explains why multiple infections with *S. pyogenes* can occur. Strains of *S. pyogenes* that produce certain M protein types are **rheumatogenic**, ie, cause primarily rheumatic fever, whereas strains of *S. pyogenes* that produce other M protein types are **nephritogenic**, ie, cause primarily acute glomerulonephritis. Although M protein is the main antiphagocytic component of *S. pyogenes,* the organism also has a polysaccharide capsule that plays a role in retarding phagocytosis.

Classification of Streptococci

A. BETA-HEMOLYTIC STREPTOCOCCI

These are arranged into groups A–U (known as Lancefield groups) on the basis of antigenic differences in C carbohydrate. In the clinical laboratory, the group is determined by precipitin tests with specific antisera or by immunofluorescence.

Group A streptococci (*S. pyogenes*) are one of the most important human pathogens. They are the most frequent bacterial cause of pharyngitis and a very common cause of skin infections. They adhere to pharyngeal epithelium via pili covered with lipoteichoic acid and M protein. Many strains have a hyaluronic acid capsule that is antiphagocytic. The growth of *S. pyogenes* is inhibited by the antibiotic bacitracin, an important diagnostic criterion.

Group B streptococci (*S. agalactiae*) colonize the genital tract of some women and can cause neonatal meningitis and sepsis. They are usually bacitracin-resistant. They hydrolyze (breakdown) hippurate, an important diagnostic criterion.

Group D streptococci include enterococci (eg, *Enterococcus faecalis* and *Enterococcus faecium*) and nonenterococci (eg, *S. bovis*). Enterococci are members of the normal flora of the colon and are noted for their ability to cause urinary, biliary, and cardiovascular infections. They are very hardy organisms; they can grow in hypertonic (6.5%) saline or in bile and are not killed by penicillin G. As a result, a synergistic combination of penicillin and an aminoglycoside (such as gentamicin) is required to kill enterococci. Vancomycin can also be used, but vancomycin-resistant enterococci (VRE) have emerged and become an important and much feared cause of life-threatening nosocomial infections. More strains of *E. faecium* are vancomycin-resistant than are strains of *E. faecalis.*

Nonenterococcal group D streptococci, such as *S. bovis,* can cause similar infections but are much less hardy organisms; for example, they are inhibited by 6.5% NaCl and killed by penicillin G. Note that the hemolytic reaction of group D streptococci is variable: most are alpha-hemolytic, but some are beta-hemolytic and others are nonhemolytic.

Groups C, E, F, G, H, and K–U streptococci infrequently cause human disease.

B. NON-BETA-HEMOLYTIC STREPTOCOCCI

Some produce no hemolysis; others produce alpha-hemolysis. The principal alpha-hemolytic organisms are *S. pneumoniae* and the viridans group of streptococci. The viridans streptococci (eg, *Streptococcus mitis, Streptococcus sanguis,* and *Streptococcus mutans*) are *not* bile-soluble and *not* inhibited by optochin—in contrast to *S. pneumoniae,* which is bile-soluble and inhibited by optochin. Viridans streptococci are part of the normal flora of the human pharynx and intermittently reach the bloodstream to cause infective endocarditis. *S. mutans* synthesizes polysaccharides (dextrans) that are found in dental plaque and lead to dental caries. *Streptococcus intermedius* and *Streptococcus anginosus* (also known as the *Streptococcus anginosus-milleri* group) are usually alpha-hemolytic or nonhemolytic, but some

isolates are beta-hemolytic. They are found primarily in the mouth and colon.

C. PEPTOSTREPTOCOCCI

These grow under anaerobic or microaerophilic conditions and produce variable hemolysis. Peptostreptococci are members of the normal flora of the gut, mouth, and the female genital tract and participate in mixed anaerobic infections. The term "mixed anaerobic infections" refers to the fact that these infections are caused by multiple bacteria, some of which are anaerobes and others are facultatives. For example, peptostreptococci and viridans streptococci, both members of the oral flora, are often found in brain abscesses following dental surgery. *Peptostreptococcus magnus* and *Peptostreptococcus anaerobius* are the species frequently isolated from clinical specimens.

Transmission

Most streptococci are part of the normal flora of the human throat, skin, and intestines but produce disease when they gain access to tissues or blood. Viridans streptococci and *S. pneumoniae* are found chiefly in the **oropharynx**; *S. pyogenes* is found on the **skin** and in the oropharynx in small numbers; *S. agalactiae* occurs in the **vagina** and colon; and both the enterococci and anaerobic streptococci are located in the **colon.**

Pathogenesis

Group A streptococci (*S. pyogenes*) cause disease by three mechanisms: (1) **pyogenic inflammation,** which is induced locally at the site of the organisms in tissue; (2) **exotoxin production,** which can cause widespread systemic symptoms in areas of the body where there are no organisms; and (3) **immunologic,** which occurs when antibody against a component of the organism cross-reacts with normal tissue or forms immune complexes that damage normal tissue (see the section on poststreptococcal diseases below). The immunologic reactions cause inflammation, eg, the inflamed joints of rheumatic fever, but there are no organisms in the lesions (Table 15–4).

The M protein of *S. pyogenes* is its most important antiphagocytic factor, but its capsule, composed of hyaluronic acid, is also antiphagocytic. Antibodies are not formed against the capsule because hyaluronic acid is a normal component of the body and humans are tolerant to it.

Group A streptococci produce three important **inflammation-related enzymes.**

(1) **Hyaluronidase** degrades hyaluronic acid, which is the ground substance of subcutaneous tissue. Hyaluronidase is known as **spreading factor** because it facili-

Table 15–4. Important features of pathogenesis by streptococci.

Organism	Type of Pathogenesis	Typical Disease	Main Site of Disease (D), Colonization (C), or Normal Flora (NF)

S. pyogenes (group A)	1. Pyogenic
	  a. Local
	
	  b. Disseminated
	2. Toxigenic
	
	3. Immune-mediated (post-streptococcal, nonsuppurative)
		Impetigo, cellulitis
		Pharyngitis
		Sepsis
		Scarlet fever
		Toxic shock
		Rheumatic fever
		Acute glomerulonephritis
			Skin (D)
			Throat (D)
			Bloodstream (D)
			Skin (D)
			Many organs (D)
			Heart, joints (D)
			Kidney (D)

S. agalactiae (group B)	Pyogenic	Neonatal sepsis and meningitis	Vagina (C) (& colon)
E. faecalis (group D)	Pyogenic	Urinary tract infection, endocarditis	Colon (NF)
S. bovis (group D)	Pyogenic	Endocarditis	Colon (NF)
S. pneumoniae	Pyogenic	Pneumonia, otitis media, meningitis	Oropharynx (C)
Viridans streptococci	Pyogenic	Endocarditis	Oropharynx (NF)

tates the rapid spread of *S. pyogenes* in skin infections (cellulitis).

(2) **Streptokinase** (fibrinolysin) activates plasminogen to form plasmin, which dissolves fibrin in clots, thrombi, and emboli. It can be used to lyse thrombi in the coronary arteries of heart attack patients.

(3) **DNase** (streptodornase) depolymerizes DNA in exudates or necrotic tissue. Antibody to DNase B develops during pyoderma; this can be used for diagnostic purposes. Streptokinase-streptodornase mixtures applied as a skin test give a positive reaction in most adults, indicating normal cell-mediated immunity.

In addition, group A streptococci produce five important **toxins and hemolysins.**

(1) **Erythrogenic toxin** causes the rash of scarlet fever. Its mechanism of action is similar to that of the toxic shock syndrome toxin (TSST) of *S. aureus;* ie, it acts as a superantigen (see *S. aureus,* above, and Chapter 58). It is produced only by certain strains of *S. pyogenes* lysogenized by a bacteriophage carrying the gene for the toxin. The injection of a skin test dose of erythrogenic toxin (Dick test) gives a positive result in persons lacking antitoxin (ie, susceptible persons).

(2) **Streptolysin O** is a hemolysin that is inactivated by oxidation (oxygen-labile). It causes beta-hemolysis only when colonies grow under the surface of a blood agar plate. It is antigenic, and antibody to it (ASO) develops after group A streptococcal infections. The titer of ASO antibody can be important in the diagnosis of rheumatic fever.

(3) **Streptolysin S** is a hemolysin that is not inactivated by oxygen (oxygen-stable). It is *not* antigenic but is responsible for beta-hemolysis when colonies grow on the surface of a blood agar plate.

(4) **Pyogenic exotoxin A** is the toxin responsible for most cases of streptococcal **toxic shock syndrome.** It has the same mode of action as does staphylococcal TSST; ie, it is a superantigen that causes the release of large amounts of cytokines from helper T cells and macrophages (see pages 44 and 410).

(5) **Exotoxin B** is a protease that rapidly destroys tissue and is produced in large amounts by the strains of *S. pyogenes* that cause necrotizing fasciitis.

Pathogenesis by group B streptococci (*S. agalactiae*) is based on the ability of the organism to induce an inflammatory response. However, unlike *S. pyogenes,* no cytotoxic enzymes or exotoxins have been described and there is no evidence for any immunologically induced disease. Group B streptococci have a polysaccharide capsule that is antiphagocytic, and anticapsular antibody is protective.

Clinical Findings

S. pyogenes causes three types of diseases: (1) **pyogenic** diseases such as pharyngitis and cellulitis, (2) **toxigenic** diseases such as scarlet fever and toxic shock syndrome, and (3) **immunologic** diseases such as rheumatic fever and acute glomerulonephritis. (See the section on Post-streptococcal Diseases, below.)

S. pyogenes (group A beta-hemolytic streptococcus)

is the most common bacterial cause of sore throat. **Pharyngitis** is characterized by inflammation, exudate, fever, leukocytosis, and tender cervical lymph nodes. If untreated, spontaneous recovery occurs in 10 days. However, it may extend to otitis, sinusitis, mastoiditis, and meningitis. If the infecting streptococci produce erythrogenic toxin and the host lacks antitoxin, scarlet fever may result. Rheumatic fever may occur, especially following pharyngitis. *S. pyogenes* also causes another toxin-mediated disease, streptococcal toxic shock syndrome, which has clinical findings similar to those of staphylococcal toxic shock syndrome (see page 107).

However, streptococcal TSS typically has a recognizable site of pyogenic inflammation and blood cultures are often positive, whereas staphylococcal TSS typically has neither a site of pyogenic inflammation nor positive blood cultures.

Group A streptococci can enter skin defects to produce **cellulitis**, erysipelas, necrotizing fasciitis (streptococcal gangrene), lymphangitis, or bacteremia. They can enter the uterus after delivery to produce endometritis and sepsis (puerperal fever). Streptococcal pyoderma (impetigo) is a superficial infection of abraded skin that forms pus or crusts. It is communicable among children, especially in hot, humid climates. Glomerulonephritis may occur, especially following skin infections.

Group B streptococci cause **neonatal sepsis** and **meningitis**. The main predisposing factor is prolonged (longer than 18 hours) rupture of the membranes in women who are colonized with the organism. Children born prior to 37 weeks' gestation have a greatly increased risk of disease. Also, children whose mothers who lack antibody to group B streptococci and who consequently are born without transplacentally acquired IgG have a high rate of neonatal sepsis caused by this organism. Group B streptococci are an important cause of neonatal pneumonia as well.

Although most group B streptococcal infections are in neonates, this organism also causes such infections as pneumonia, endocarditis, arthritis, and osteomyelitis in adults. Postpartum endometritis also occurs. Diabetes is the main predisposing factor for adult group B streptococcal infections.

Viridans streptococci (eg, *S. mutans, S. sanguis, S. salivarius,* and *S. mitis*) are the most common cause of infective **endocarditis**. They enter the bloodstream (bacteremia) from the oropharynx, typically after dental surgery. Signs of endocarditis are fever, heart murmur, anemia, and embolic events such as splinter hemorrhages, subconjunctival petechial hemorrhages, and Janeway lesions. It is 100% fatal unless effectively treated with antimicrobial agents. About 10% of endocarditis cases are caused by enterococci, but any organism causing bacteremia may settle on deformed valves.

At least three blood cultures are necessary to ensure recovery of the organism in more than 90% of cases.

Viridans streptococci, especially *S. anginosus, S. milleri,* and *S. intermedius,* also cause brain abscesses, often in combination with mouth anaerobes (a mixed aerobic-anaerobic infection). Dental surgery is an important predisposing factor to brain abscess because it provides a portal for the viridans streptococci and the anaerobes in the mouth to enter the bloodstream (bacteremia) and spread to the brain. Viridans streptococci are involved in mixed aerobic-anaerobic infections in other areas of the body as well, eg, abdominal abscesses.

Enterococci cause **urinary tract infections**, especially in hospitalized patients. Indwelling urinary catheters and urinary tract instrumentation are important predisposing factors. Enterococci also cause endocarditis, particularly in patients who have undergone gastrointestinal or urinary tract surgery or instrumentation. They also cause intra-abdominal and pelvic infections, typically in combination with anaerobes. *S. bovis,* a nonenterococcal group D streptococcus, causes **endocarditis**, especially in patients with carcinoma of the colon. This association is so strong that patients with *S. bovis* bacteremia or endocarditis should be investigated for the presence of colonic carcinoma.

In August 2005, it was reported that *Streptococcus suis* caused the death of 37 farmers in China. The illness is characterized by the sudden onset of hemorrhagic shock. This species is known to cause disease in pigs but only rarely in people prior to this outbreak. Spread of the bacteria from the index case to others has not occurred.

Peptostreptococci are one of the most common bacteria found in brain, lung, abdominal, and pelvic abscesses.

Poststreptococcal (Nonsuppurative) Diseases

These are disorders in which a local infection with group A streptococci is followed weeks later by inflammation in an organ that was *not* infected by the streptococci. The inflammation is caused by an **immunologic** response to streptococcal M proteins that cross-react with human tissues. Some strains of *S. pyogenes* bearing certain M proteins are nephritogenic and cause acute glomerulonephritis, and other strains bearing different M proteins are rheumatogenic and cause acute rheumatic fever.

A. ACUTE GLOMERULONEPHRITIS

Acute glomerulonephritis (AGN) typically occurs 2–3 weeks after skin infection by certain group A streptococcal types in children (eg, M protein type 49 causes AGN most frequently). AGN is more frequent after skin infections than after pharyngitis. The most striking clinical features are hypertension, edema of the face (especially periorbital edema) and ankles, and "smoky" urine (due to red cells in the urine). Most patients recover completely. Reinfection with streptococci rarely leads to recurrence of acute glomerulonephritis.

The disease is initiated by **antigen-antibody complexes on the glomerular basement membrane,** and soluble antigens from streptococcal membranes may be the inciting antigen. It can be prevented by early eradication of nephritogenic streptococci from skin colonization sites but *not* by administration of penicillin after onset of symptoms.

B. ACUTE RHEUMATIC FEVER

Approximately 2 weeks after a group A streptococcal infection—usually pharyngitis—rheumatic fever, characterized by fever, migratory polyarthritis, and carditis, may develop. The carditis damages myocardial and endocardial tissue, especially the mitral and aortic valves. Uncontrollable, spasmodic movements of the limbs or face (chorea) may also occur. ASO titers and the erythrocyte sedimentation rate are elevated. Note that group A streptococcal *skin* infections do not cause rheumatic fever.

Rheumatic fever is due to an **immunologic reaction between cross-reacting antibodies** to certain streptococcal M proteins **and antigens of joint, heart, and brain tissue.** It is an autoimmune disease, greatly exacerbated by recurrence of streptococcal infections. If streptococcal infections are treated within 8 days of onset, rheumatic fever is usually prevented. After a heart-damaging attack of rheumatic fever, reinfection must be prevented by long-term prophylaxis. In the United States, fewer than 0.5% of group A streptococcal infections lead to rheumatic fever, but in developing tropical countries, the rate is higher than 5%.

Laboratory Diagnosis

A. MICROBIOLOGIC

Gram-stained smears are useless in streptococcal pharyngitis because viridans streptococci are members of the normal flora and cannot be visually distinguished from the pathogenic *S. pyogenes.* However, stained smears from skin lesions or wounds that reveal streptococci are diagnostic. Cultures of swabs from the pharynx or lesion on blood agar plates show small, translucent beta-hemolytic colonies in 18–48 hours. If **inhibited by bacitracin** disk, they are likely to be group A streptococci. Group B streptococci are characterized by their ability to **hydrolyze hippurate** and by the production of a protein that causes enhanced hemolysis on sheep blood agar when combined with beta-hemolysin of *S. aureus* (CAMP test). Group D streptococci **hydrolyze esculin**

in the presence of bile; ie, they produce a black pigment on bile-esculin agar. The group D organisms are further subdivided: the enterococci **grow in hypertonic (6.5%) NaCl,** whereas the nonenterococci do not.

Although cultures remain the gold standard for the diagnosis of streptococcal pharyngitis, a problem exists because the results of culturing are not available for at least 18 hours and it is beneficial to know while the patient is in the office whether antibiotics should be prescribed. For this reason, rapid tests that provide a diagnosis in approximately 10 minutes were developed. The rapid test detects bacterial antigens in a throat swab specimen. In the test, specific antigens from the group A streptococci are extracted from the throat swab with certain enzymes and are reacted with antibody to these antigens bound to latex particles. Agglutination of the colored latex particles occurs if group A streptococci are present in the throat swab.

A rapid test is also available for the detection of group B streptococci in vaginal and rectal samples. It detects the DNA of the organism and results can be obtained in approximately 1 hour.

Viridans group streptococci form alpha-hemolytic colonies on blood agar and must be distinguished from *S. pneumoniae* (pneumococci), which is also alpha-hemolytic. Viridans group streptococci are resistant to lysis by bile and will grow in the presence of optochin, whereas pneumococci will not. The various viridans group streptococci are classified into species by using a variety of biochemical tests.

B. SEROLOGIC

ASO titers are high soon after group A streptococcal infections. In patients suspected of having rheumatic fever, an **elevated ASO titer** is typically used as evidence of previous infection because throat culture results are often negative at the time the patient presents with rheumatic fever. Titers of anti-DNase B are high in group A streptococcal skin infections and serve as an indicator of previous streptococcal infection in patients suspected of having AGN.

Treatment

All group A streptococci are susceptible to penicillin G, but neither rheumatic fever nor AGN patients benefit from penicillin treatment *after* onset. In mild group A streptococcal infections, oral penicillin V can be used. In penicillin-allergic patients, erythromycin or one of its long-acting derivatives, eg, azithromycin, can be used. However, erythromycin-resistant strains of *S. pyogenes* have emerged that may limit the effectiveness of the macrolide class of drugs in the treatment of streptococcal pharyngitis.

Endocarditis caused by most viridans streptococci is

curable by prolonged penicillin treatment. However, enterococcal endocarditis can be eradicated only by a penicillin or vancomycin combined with an aminoglycoside.

Enterococci resistant to multiple drugs, eg, penicillins, aminoglycosides, and vancomycin, have emerged. Vancomycin-resistant enterococci (VRE) are now an important cause of nosocomial infections; there is no reliable antibiotic therapy for these organisms. At present, two investigational drugs are being used to treat infections caused by VRE: linezolid (Zyvox) and quinupristin /dalfopristin (Synercid). Nonenterococcal group D streptococci, eg, *S. bovis,* are not highly resistant and can be treated with penicillin G.

The drug of choice for group B streptococcal infections is either penicillin G or ampicillin. Some strains may require higher doses of penicillin G or a combination of penicillin G and an aminoglycoside to eradicate the organism. Peptostreptococci can be treated with penicillin G.

Prevention

Rheumatic fever can be prevented by prompt treatment of group A streptococcal pharyngitis with penicillin. Prevention of streptococcal infections (usually with benzathine penicillin once each month for several years) in persons who have had rheumatic fever is important to prevent recurrence of the disease. There is no evidence that patients who have had AGN require similar penicillin prophylaxis.

In patients with damaged heart valves who undergo invasive dental procedures, endocarditis caused by viridans streptococci can be prevented by using amoxicillin perioperatively. In patients with damaged heart valves who undergo gastrointestinal or urinary tract procedures, endocarditis caused by enterococci can be prevented by using ampicillin and gentamicin perioperatively.

The incidence of neonatal sepsis caused by group B streptococci can be reduced by a two-pronged approach: (1) All pregnant women should be screened by doing vaginal and rectal cultures at 35–37 weeks. If cultures are positive, then penicillin G (or ampicillin) should be administered intravenously at the time of delivery. (2) If the patient has not had cultures done, then penicillin G (or ampicillin) should be administered intravenously at the time of delivery to women who experience prolonged (longer than 18 hours) rupture of membranes, whose labor begins before 37 weeks' gestation, or who have a fever at the time of labor. If the patient is allergic to penicillin, either cefazolin or vancomycin can be used. Oral ampicillin given to women who are vaginal carriers of group B streptococci does not eradicate the organism. Rapid screening tests for

group B streptococcal antigens in vaginal specimens can be insensitive, and neonates born of antigen-negative women have, nevertheless, had neonatal sepsis. Note, however, that as group B streptococcal infections have declined as a result of these prophylactic measures, neonatal infections caused by *E. coli* have increased.

There are no vaccines available against any of the streptococci except *S. pneumoniae* (see below).

STREPTOCOCCUS PNEUMONIAE

Diseases

Pneumococci cause pneumonia, bacteremia, meningitis, and infections of the upper respiratory tract such as otitis media and sinusitis. Pneumococci are the most common cause of community-acquired pneumonia, meningitis, sepsis in splenectomized individuals, otitis media, and sinusitis.

Important Properties

Pneumococci are gram-positive lancet-shaped cocci arranged in pairs (**diplococci**) or short chains. (The term "lancet-shaped" means that the diplococci are oval with somewhat pointed ends rather than being round.) On blood agar they produce alpha-hemolysis. In contrast to viridans streptococci, they are lysed by bile or deoxycholate and their growth is inhibited by optochin.

Pneumococci possess **polysaccharide capsules** of more than 85 antigenically distinct types. With type-specific antiserum, capsules swell (**quellung reaction**), and this can be used to identify the type. Capsules are virulence factors; ie, they interfere with phagocytosis and favor invasiveness. Specific antibody to the capsule opsonizes the organism, facilitates phagocytosis, and promotes resistance. Such antibody develops in humans as a result either of infection (asymptomatic or clinical) or of administration of polysaccharide vaccine. Capsular polysaccharide elicits primarily a B-cell (ie, T-independent) response.

Another important surface component of *S. pneumoniae* is a carbohydrate in the cell wall called **C-substance.** This carbohydrate is medically important, not for itself, but because it reacts with a normal serum protein made by the liver called **C-reactive protein** (CRP). CRP is an "acute-phase" protein that is elevated as much as a 1000-fold in acute inflammation. CRP is not an antibody (which are gamma globulins) but rather a beta-globulin. (Plasma contains alpha, beta, and gamma globulins.) Note that CRP is a nonspecific indicator of inflammation and is elevated in response to the presence of many organisms, not just *S. pneumoniae.* Clinically, CRP in human serum is measured in the laboratory by its reaction with the carbohydrate of *S. pneumoniae.* The medical importance of CRP is that an elevated CRP appears to be a better predictor of heart attack risk than an elevated cholesterol level.

Transmission

Humans are the natural hosts for pneumococci; there is no animal reservoir. Because a proportion (5–50%) of the healthy population harbor virulent organisms in the oropharynx, pneumococcal infections are not considered to be communicable. Resistance is high in healthy young people, and disease results most often when predisposing factors (see below) are present.

Pathogenesis

The most important virulence factor is the capsular polysaccharide, and anticapsular antibody is protective. Lipoteichoic acid, which activates complement and induces inflammatory cytokine production, contributes to the inflammatory response and to the septic shock syndrome that occurs in some immunocompromised patients. Pneumolysin, the hemolysin that causes alpha-hemolysis, may also contribute to pathogenesis. Pneumococci produce IgA protease that enhances the organism's ability to colonize the mucosa of the upper respiratory tract. Pneumococci multiply in tissues and cause inflammation. When they reach alveoli, there is outpouring of fluid and red and white blood cells, resulting in consolidation of the lung. During recovery, pneumococci are phagocytized, mononuclear cells ingest debris, and the consolidation resolves.

Factors that lower resistance and predispose persons to pneumococcal infection include (1) alcohol or drug intoxication or other cerebral impairment that can depress the cough reflex and increase aspiration of secretions; (2) abnormality of the respiratory tract (eg, viral infections), pooling of mucus, bronchial obstruction, and respiratory tract injury caused by irritants (which disturb the integrity and movement of the mucociliary blanket); (3) abnormal circulatory dynamics (eg, pulmonary congestion and heart failure); (4) **splenectomy;** and (5) certain chronic diseases such as sickle cell anemia and nephrosis. Trauma to the head that causes **leakage of spinal fluid** through the nose predisposes to pneumococcal meningitis.

Clinical Findings

Pneumonia often begins with a sudden chill, fever, cough, and pleuritic pain. Sputum is a red or brown "rusty" color. Bacteremia occurs in 15–25% of cases. Spontaneous recovery may begin in 5–10 days and is accompanied by development of anticapsular antibodies. Pneumococci are a prominent cause of otitis media, sinusitis, purulent bronchitis, pericarditis, bacterial meningitis, and sepsis, especially in immunocompromised patients.

Laboratory Diagnosis

In sputum, pneumococci are seen as lancet-shaped gram-positive diplococci in Gram-stained smears. They can also be detected by using the quellung reaction with multitype antiserum. On blood agar, pneumococci form small **alpha-hemolytic** colonies. The colonies are **bile-soluble**, ie, are lysed by bile, and growth is **inhibited by optochin**. Blood cultures are positive in 15–25% of pneumococcal infections. Culture of cerebrospinal fluid is usually positive in meningitis. Rapid diagnosis of pneumococcal meningitis can be made by detecting its capsular polysaccharide in spinal fluid using the latex agglutination test. A rapid test that detects urinary antigen (capsular polysaccharide) is also available for the diagnosis of pneumococcal pneumonia and bacteremia. Because of the increasing numbers of strains resistant to penicillin, antibiotic sensitivity tests must be done on organisms isolated from serious infections.

Treatment

Most pneumococci are susceptible to penicillins and erythromycin. In severe pneumococcal infections, penicillin G is the drug of choice, whereas in mild pneumococcal infections, oral penicillin V can be used. In penicillin-allergic patients, erythromycin or one of its long-acting derivatives, eg, azithromycin, can be used. In the United States, about 25% of isolates exhibit low-level resistance to penicillin, primarily as a result of changes in penicillin-binding proteins. An increasing percentage of isolates, about 15% currently, show high-level resistance, which is attributed to multiple changes in penicillin-binding proteins. They do *not* produce β-lactamase. Vancomycin is the drug of choice for the penicillin-resistant pneumococci. However, strains of pneumococci tolerant to vancomycin have emerged. (Tolerance to antibiotics is described on page 88.) Strains of pneumococci resistant to multiple drugs have also emerged.

Prevention

Despite the efficacy of antimicrobial drug treatment, the mortality rate is high in elderly (ie, persons older than 65 years), immunocompromised (especially splenectomized), or debilitated persons. Such persons should be immunized with the polyvalent (23-type) **polysaccharide vaccine.** The vaccine is safe and fairly effective and provides long-lasting (at least 5 years) protection. A booster dose is recommended for (1) people over the age of 65 who received the vaccine more than 5 years ago and who were less than 65 when they received the vaccine and (2) people between the ages of 2 and 64 who are asplenic, HIV-infected, receiving cancer chemotherapy, or receiving immunosuppressive drugs to prevent transplant rejection. Oral penicillin is given to young children with hypogammaglobulinemia or splenectomy because such children are prone to pneumococcal infections and respond poorly to the vaccine.

A different pneumococcal vaccine containing pneumococcal polysaccharide **coupled (conjugated) to a carrier protein (diphtheria toxoid)** is given to children under the age of 2 years. This "conjugate" vaccine is effective in young children in preventing both bacteremic infections, such as meningitis, and mucosal infections, such as otitis media. The vaccine contains the capsular polysaccharide of the seven most common pneumococcal serotypes. Immunization of *children* reduces the incidence of pneumococcal disease in *adults* because children are the main source of the organism for adults and immunization reduces the carrier rate in children.

A potential problem regarding the use of the pneumococcal vaccine containing 7 serotypes is that of **serotype replacement.** Will the vaccine reduce the incidence of disease caused by the serotypes in the vaccine but not the overall incidence of pneumococcal disease because other serotypes that are not in the vaccine will now cause disease? This important question is being evaluated at this time.

SUMMARIES OF ORGANISMS

Brief summaries of the organisms described in this chapter begin on page 477. Please consult these summaries for a rapid review of the essential material.

PRACTICE QUESTIONS: USMLE & COURSE EXAMINATIONS

Questions on the topics discussed in this chapter can be found in the Clinical Bacteriology section of Part XI: USMLE (National Board) Practice Questions starting on page 537. Also see Part XII: USMLE (National Board) Practice Examination starting on page 583.

Gram-Negative Cocci

NEISSERIA

Diseases

The genus *Neisseria* contains two important human pathogens: *Neisseria meningitidis* and *Neisseria gonorrhoeae*. *N. meningitidis* mainly causes meningitis and meningococcemia. It is the leading cause of death from infection in children in the United States. *N. gonorrhoeae* causes gonorrhea, the second most common notifiable bacterial disease in the United States (Tables 16–1 and 16–2). It also causes neonatal conjunctivitis (ophthalmia neonatorum) and pelvic inflammatory disease (PID).

Important Properties

Neisseriae are gram-negative cocci that resemble paired kidney beans.

(1) *N. meningitidis* (meningococcus) has a prominent **polysaccharide capsule** that enhances virulence by its antiphagocytic action and induces protective antibodies (Table 16–3). Meningococci are divided into at least 13 serologic groups on the basis of the antigenicity of their capsular polysaccharides.

(2) *N. gonorrhoeae* (gonococcus) has no polysaccharide capsule but has multiple serotypes based on the antigenicity of its pilus protein. There is **marked antigenic variation** in the gonococcal pili as a result of chromosomal rearrangement; more than 100 serotypes are known. Gonococci have three outer membrane proteins (proteins I, II, and III). Protein II plays a role in attachment of the organism to cells and varies antigenically as well.

Neisseriae are gram-negative bacteria and contain endotoxin in their outer membrane. The endotoxin of *N. meningitidis* is a lipo**poly**saccharide (LPS) similar to that found in many gram-negative rods, but the endotoxin of *N. gonorrhoeae* is a lipo**oligo**saccharide (LOS). Both LPS and LOS contain lipid A, but LOS lacks the long repeating sugar side chains of LPS.

The growth of both organisms is inhibited by toxic trace metals and fatty acids found in certain culture media, eg, blood agar plates. They are therefore cultured on "chocolate" agar containing blood heated to 80°C, which inactivates the inhibitors. Neisseriae are **oxidase-positive**; ie, they possess the enzyme cytochrome *c*. This is an important laboratory diagnostic test in which colonies exposed to phenylenediamine turn black as a result of oxidation of the reagent by the enzyme.

The genus *Neisseria* is one of several in the family Neisseriaceae. A separate genus contains the organism *Moraxella catarrhalis,* which is part of the normal throat flora but can cause such respiratory tract infections as sinusitis, otitis media, bronchitis, and pneumonia. *M. catarrhalis* and members of other genera, such as *Branhamella, Kingella,* and *Acinetobacter,* are described in Chapter 27. (*M. catarrhalis* is the new name for *Branhamella catarrhalis.*)

1. Neisseria meningitidis

Pathogenesis & Epidemiology

Humans are the only natural hosts for meningococci. The organisms are transmitted by **airborne droplets;** they colonize the membranes of the nasopharynx and become part of the transient flora of the upper respiratory tract. Carriers are usually asymptomatic. From the nasopharynx, the organism can enter the bloodstream and spread to specific sites, such as the meninges or joints, or be disseminated throughout the body (meningococcemia). About 5% of people become chronic carriers and serve as a source of infection for others. The carriage rate can be as high as 35% in people who live in close quarters, eg, military recruits; this explains the high frequency of outbreaks of meningitis in the armed forces prior to the use of the vaccine. The carriage rate is also high in close (family) contacts of patients. Outbreaks of meningococcal disease also have occurred in college students living in dormitories.

Two organisms cause more than 80% of cases of bacterial meningitis in persons over 2 months of age: *Streptococcus pneumoniae* and *N. meningitidis.* Of these organisms, meningococci, especially those in group A, are most likely to cause **epidemics of meningitis.** Overall, *N. meningitidis* ranks second to *S. pneumoniae* as a cause of meningitis but is the most common cause in persons between the ages of 2 and 18 years.

Meningococci have three important virulence factors:

(1) A **polysaccharide capsule** that enables the organism to resist phagocytosis by polymorphonuclear leukocytes (PMNs)

Table 16–1. Neisseriae of medical importance.[1]

Species	Portal of Entry	Polysaccharide Capsule	Maltose Fermentation	β-Lactamase Production	Available Vaccine
N. meningitidis (meningococcus)	Respiratory tract	+	+	None	+
N. gonorrhoeae (gonococcus)	Genital tract	−	−	Some	−

[1]All neisseriae are oxidase-positive.

(2) **Endotoxin (LPS)**, which causes fever, shock, and other pathophysiologic changes (in purified form, endotoxin can reproduce many of the clinical manifestations of meningococcemia)

(3) An immunoglobulin A (**IgA**) **protease** helps the bacteria attach to the membranes of the upper respiratory tract by cleaving secretory IgA.

Resistance to disease correlates with the presence of antibody to the capsular polysaccharide. Most carriers develop protective antibody titers within 2 weeks of colonization. Because immunity is group-specific, it is possible to have protective antibodies to one group of organisms yet be susceptible to infection by organisms of the other groups. Complement is an important feature of the host defenses, because people with complement deficiencies, particularly in the **late-acting complement components** (C6–C9), have an increased incidence of meningococcal bacteremia.

Clinical Findings

The two most important manifestations of disease are **meningococcemia** and **meningitis**. The most severe form of meningococcemia is the life-threatening **Waterhouse-Friderichsen syndrome**, which is characterized by high fever, shock, widespread purpura, disseminated intravascular coagulation, thrombocytopenia, and adrenal insufficiency. Bacteremia can result in the seeding of many organs, especially the meninges. The symptoms of meningococcal meningitis are those of a typical bacterial meningitis—namely, fever, headache, stiff neck, and an increased level of PMNs in spinal fluid.

Laboratory Diagnosis

The principal laboratory procedures are smear and culture of blood and spinal fluid samples. A presumptive diagnosis of meningococcal meningitis can be made if gram-negative cocci are seen in a smear of spinal fluid. The organism grows best on chocolate agar incubated at 37°C in a 5% CO_2 atmosphere. A presumptive diagnosis of *Neisseria* can be made if oxidase-positive colonies of gram-negative diplococci are found. The differentiation between *N. meningitidis* and *N. gonorrhoeae* is made on the basis of sugar fermentation: meningococci ferment maltose, whereas gonococci do not (both organisms ferment glucose). Immunofluorescence can also be used to identify these species. Tests for serum antibodies are not useful for clinical diagnosis. However, a procedure that can assist in the rapid diagnosis of meningococcal meningitis is the latex agglu-

Table 16–2. Important clinical features of neisseriae.

Organism	Type of Pathogenesis	Typical Disease	Treatment
N. meningitidis	Pyogenic	Meningitis, meningococcemia	Penicillin G
N. gonorrhoeae	Pyogenic		
	1. Local	Gonorrhea, eg, urethritis, cervicitis	Ceftriaxone[1] plus doxycycline[2]
	2. Ascending	Pelvic inflammatory disease	Cefoxitin plus doxycycline[1,2]
	3. Disseminated	Disseminated gonococcal infection	Ceftriaxone[1]
	4. Neonatal	Conjunctivitis (ophthalmia neonatorum)	Ceftriaxone[3]

[1]Other drugs can also be used. See treatment guidelines published by Centers for Disease Control and Prevention.
[2]Add doxycycline for possible coinfection with *Chlamydia trachomatis*.
[3]For prevention, use erythromycin ointment or silver nitrate drops.

Table 16–3. Properties of the polysaccharide capsule of the meningococcus.[1]

(1) Enhances virulence by its antiphagocytic action

(2) Is the antigen that defines the serologic groups

(3) Is the antigen detected in the spinal fluid of patients with meningitis

(4) Is the antigen in the vaccine

[1]The same four features apply to the capsule of the pneumococcus and *Haemophilus influenzae*.

tination test, which detects capsular polysaccharide in the spinal fluid.

Treatment

Penicillin G is the treatment of choice for meningococcal infections. Strains resistant to penicillin have rarely emerged, but sulfonamide resistance is common.

Prevention

Chemoprophylaxis and immunization are both used to prevent meningococcal disease. Either rifampin or ciprofloxacin can be used for prophylaxis in people who have had close contact with the index case. These drugs are preferred because they are efficiently secreted into the saliva, in contrast to penicillin G.

There are two forms of the meningococcal vaccine, both of which contain the capsular polysaccharide of groups A, C, Y, and W-135 as the immunogens. The conjugate vaccine (Menactra) contains the four polysaccharides conjugated to a carrier protein (diphtheria toxoid), whereas the unconjugated vaccine (Menomune) contains only the four polysaccharides (not conjugated to a carrier protein). The conjugate vaccine induces higher titers of antibodies in children than does the unconjugated vaccine. The two vaccines induce similar antibody titers in adults. Note that neither vaccine contains the group B polysaccharide because it is not immunogenic in humans.

The conjugate vaccine was licensed in 2005, so its long-term effectiveness is unknown. The unconjugated vaccine is effective in preventing epidemics of meningitis and in reducing the carrier rate, especially in military personnel. Travelers to areas where epidemics are occurring should receive the vaccine. College students living in dormitories are encouraged to receive the vaccine. No booster dose is recommended for either form of the vaccine. The conjugate vaccine is recommended for children at the age of 11–12, which will reduce the incidence of meningococcal disease in teenagers and young adults.

2. Neisseria gonorrhoeae

Pathogenesis & Epidemiology

Gonococci, like meningococci, cause disease only in humans. The organism is usually transmitted **sexually**; newborns can be infected during birth. Because the gonococcus is quite sensitive to dehydration and cool conditions, sexual transmission favors its survival. Gonorrhea is usually symptomatic in men but often asymptomatic in women. Genital tract infections are the most common source of the organism, but anorectal and pharyngeal infections are important sources as well.

Pili constitute one of the most important virulence factors, because they mediate attachment to mucosal cell surfaces and are antiphagocytic. Piliated gonococci are usually virulent, whereas nonpiliated strains are avirulent. Two virulence factors in the cell wall are **LOS** (a modified form of endotoxin) and the outer membrane proteins. Note that the endotoxin of gonococci is weaker than that of meningococci, so less severe disease occurs when gonococci enter the bloodstream than when meningococci do. The organism's **IgA protease** can hydrolyze secretory IgA, which could otherwise block attachment to the mucosa. Gonococci have no capsules.

The main host defenses against gonococci are antibodies (IgA and IgG), complement, and neutrophils. Antibody-mediated opsonization and killing within phagocytes occur, but repeated gonococcal infections are common primarily as a result of antigenic changes of pili and the outer membrane proteins.

Gonococci infect primarily the mucosal surfaces, eg, the urethra and vagina, but dissemination occurs. Certain strains of gonococci cause disseminated infections more frequently than others. The most important feature of these strains is their resistance to being killed by antibodies and complement. The mechanism of this "serum resistance" is uncertain, but the presence of a porin protein (porin A) in the cell wall, which inactivates the C3b component of complement, appears to play an important role.

The occurrence of a disseminated infection is a function not only of the strain of gonococcus but also of the effectiveness of the host defenses. Persons with a deficiency of the late-acting complement components (C6–C9) are at risk for disseminated infections, as are women during menses and pregnancy. Disseminated infections usually arise from asymptomatic infections, indicating that local inflammation may deter dissemination.

Clinical Findings

Gonococci cause both localized infections, usually in the genital tract, and disseminated infections with seeding of various organs. Gonococci reach these organs via the bloodstream (gonococcal bacteremia).

Gonorrhea in men is characterized primarily by urethritis accompanied by dysuria and a purulent discharge. Epididymitis can occur.

In women, infection is located primarily in the endocervix, causing a purulent vaginal discharge and intermenstrual bleeding (cervicitis). The most frequent complication in women is an ascending infection of the uterine tubes (**salpingitis, PID**), which can result in **sterility** or ectopic pregnancy as a result of scarring of the tubes.

Disseminated gonococcal infections (DGI) commonly manifest as arthritis, tenosynovitis, or pustules in the skin. Disseminated infection is the most common cause of septic arthritis in sexually active adults. The clinical diagnosis of DGI is often difficult to confirm using laboratory tests because the organism is not cultured in more than 50% of cases.

Other infected sites include the anorectal area, throat, and eyes. Anorectal infections occur chiefly in women and homosexual men. They are frequently asymptomatic, but a bloody or purulent discharge (proctitis) can occur. In the throat, pharyngitis occurs, but many patients are asymptomatic. In newborn infants, purulent conjunctivitis (ophthalmia neonatorum) is the result of gonococcal infection acquired from the mother during passage through the birth canal. The incidence of gonococcal ophthalmia has declined greatly in recent years because of the widespread use of prophylactic erythromycin eye ointment (or silver nitrate) applied shortly after birth. Gonococcal conjunctivitis also occurs in adults as a result of the transfer of organisms from the genitals to the eye.

Other sexually transmitted infections, eg, syphilis and nongonococcal urethritis caused by *Chlamydia trachomatis,* can coexist with gonorrhea; therefore, appropriate diagnostic and therapeutic measures must be taken.

Laboratory Diagnosis

The diagnosis of localized infections depends on Gram staining and culture of the discharge. In **men,** the finding of gram-negative diplococci **within PMNs** in a urethral discharge specimen is sufficient for diagnosis. In **women,** the use of the Gram stain alone can be difficult to interpret; therefore, cultures should be done. Gram stains on cervical specimens can be falsely positive because of the presence of gram-negative diplococci in the normal flora and can be falsely negative because of the inability to see small numbers of gonococci when using the oil immersion lens. Cultures must also be used in diagnosing suspected pharyngitis or anorectal infections.

Specimens from mucosal sites, such as the urethra and cervix, are cultured on Thayer-Martin medium, which is a chocolate agar containing antibiotics (van-comycin, colistin, trimethoprim, and nystatin) to suppress the normal flora. The finding of an oxidase-positive colony composed of gram-negative diplococci is sufficient to identify the isolate as a member of the genus *Neisseria.* Specific identification of the gonococcus can be made either by its fermentation of glucose (but not maltose) or by fluorescent-antibody staining. Note that specimens from sterile sites, such as blood or joint fluid, can be cultured on chocolate agar without antibiotics because there is no competing normal flora.

Two rapid tests that detect the presence of gonococcal nucleic acids in patient specimens are widely used as a screening test. These tests are highly sensitive and specific. In one type of test the gonococcal nucleic acids are amplified (amplification tests), and in the other type they are not amplified. The amplification tests can be used on urine samples, obviating the need for more invasive collection techniques. Serologic tests to determine the presence of antibody to gonococci are *not* useful for diagnosis.

Treatment

Ceftriaxone is the treatment of choice in uncomplicated gonococcal infections. Spectinomycin or ciprofloxacin should be used if the patient is allergic to penicillin. Because mixed infections with *C. trachomatis* are common, tetracycline should be prescribed also. A follow-up culture should be performed 1 week after completion of treatment to determine whether gonococci are still present.

Prior to the mid-1950s, all gonococci were highly sensitive to penicillin. Subsequently, isolates emerged with low-level resistance to penicillin and to other antibiotics such as tetracycline and chloramphenicol. This type of resistance is encoded by the bacterial chromosome and is due to reduced uptake of the drug or to altered binding sites rather than to enzymatic degradation of the drug. Then, in 1976, **penicillinase-producing (PPNG)** strains that exhibited high-level resistance were isolated from patients. Penicillinase is plasmid-encoded. PPNG strains are now common in many areas of the world, including several urban areas in the United States, where approximately 10% of isolates are resistant. Isolates resistant to fluoroquinolones, such as ciprofloxacin, have become a significant problem.

Prevention

The prevention of gonorrhea involves the use of condoms and the prompt treatment of symptomatic patients and their contacts. Cases of gonorrhea must be reported to the public health department to ensure proper follow-up. A major problem is the detection of asymptomatic carriers. Gonococcal conjunctivitis in newborns is prevented most often by the use of erythromycin ointment. Silver nitrate drops are used less frequently. No vaccine is available.

SUMMARIES OF ORGANISMS

Brief summaries of the organisms described in this chapter begin on page 479. Please consult these summaries for a rapid review of the essential material.

PRACTICE QUESTIONS: USMLE & COURSE EXAMINATIONS

Questions on the topics discussed in this chapter can be found in the Clinical Bacteriology section of Part XI: USMLE (National Board) Practice Questions starting on page 537. Also see Part XII: USMLE (National Board) Practice Examination starting on page 583.

Gram-Positive Rods

There are four medically important genera of gram-positive rods: *Bacillus, Clostridium, Corynebacterium,* and *Listeria. Bacillus* and *Clostridium* form spores, whereas *Corynebacterium* and *Listeria* do not. Members of the genus *Bacillus* are aerobic, whereas those of the genus *Clostridium* are anaerobic (Table 17–1).

These gram-positive rods can also be distinguished based on their appearance on Gram stain. *Bacillus* and *Clostridium* species are longer and more deeply staining than those of *Corynebacterium* and *Listeria* species. *Corynebacterium* species are club-shaped, ie, they are thinner on one end than the other. *Corynebacterium* and *Listeria* species characteristically appear as V- or L-shaped rods.

■ SPORE-FORMING GRAM-POSITIVE RODS

BACILLUS

There are two medically important *Bacillus* species: *Bacillus anthracis* and *Bacillus cereus*. Important features of pathogenesis by these two *Bacillus* species are described in Table 17–2.

1. Bacillus anthracis

Disease

B. anthracis causes anthrax, which is common in animals but rare in humans. Human disease occurs in three main forms: cutaneous, pulmonary (inhalation), and gastrointestinal. In 2001, an outbreak of both inhalation and cutaneous anthrax occurred in the United States. The outbreak was caused by sending spores of the organism through the mail. As of this writing, there were 18 cases, of whom 5 died.

Important Properties

B. anthracis is a large gram-positive rod with square ends, frequently found in chains. Its antiphagocytic capsule is composed of D-glutamate. (This is unique—capsules of other bacteria are polysaccharides.) It is nonmotile, whereas other members of the genus are motile. Anthrax toxin is encoded on one plasmid and the polyglutamate capsule is encoded on a different plasmid.

Transmission

Spores of the organism persist in soil for years. Humans are most often infected cutaneously at the time of trauma to the skin, which allows the **spores on animal products,** such as hides, bristles, and wool, to enter. Spores can also be inhaled into the respiratory tract. Pulmonary (inhalation) anthrax occurs when spores are inhaled into the lungs. Gastrointestinal anthrax occurs when contaminated meat is ingested.

Inhalation anthrax is not communicable from person-to-person, despite the severity of the infection. After being inhaled into the lung, the organism moves rapidly to the mediastinal lymph nodes, where it causes hemorrhagic mediastinitis. Because it leaves the lung so rapidly, it is not transmitted by the respiratory route to others.

Pathogenesis

Pathogenesis is based primarily on the production of two exotoxins, collectively known as anthrax toxin. The two exotoxins, **edema factor** and **lethal factor,** each consist of two proteins in an A-B subunit configuration. The B, or binding, subunit in each of the two exotoxins is **protective antigen.** The A, or active, subunit has enzymatic activity.

Edema factor, an exotoxin, is an **adenylate cyclase** that causes an increase in the intracellular concentration of cyclic AMP. This causes an outpouring of fluid from the cell into the extracellular space, which manifests as edema. (Note the similarity of action to that of cholera toxin.) Lethal factor is a protease that cleaves the phosphokinase that activates the mitogen-activated protein kinase (MAPK) signal transduction pathway. This pathway controls the growth of human cells, and cleavage of the phosphokinase inhibits cell growth. Protective antigen forms pores in the human cell membrane that allows edema factor and lethal factor to enter the cell. The

Table 17–1. Gram-positive rods of medical importance.

Genus	Anaerobic Growth	Spore Formation	Exotoxins Important in Pathogenesis
Bacillus	–	+	+
Clostridium	+	+	+
Corynebacterium	–	–	+
Listeria	–	–	–

name protective antigen refers to the fact that antibody against this protein protects against disease.

Clinical Findings

The typical lesion of cutaneous anthrax is a painless ulcer with a black eschar (crust, scab). Local edema is striking. The lesion is called a **malignant pustule**. Untreated cases progress to bacteremia and death.

Pulmonary (inhalation) anthrax, also known as "woolsorter's disease," begins with nonspecific respiratory tract symptoms resembling influenza, especially a dry cough and substernal pressure. This rapidly progresses to hemorrhagic mediastinitis, bloody pleural effusions, septic shock, and death. Although the lungs are infected, the classic features and x-ray picture of pneumonia are not present. Mediastinal widening seen on chest x-ray is an important diagnostic criterion. Hemorrhagic mediastinitis and hemorrhagic meningitis are severe life-threatening complications. The symptoms of gastrointestinal anthrax include vomiting, abdominal pain, and bloody diarrhea.

Laboratory Diagnosis

Smears show large, gram-positive rods in chains. Spores are usually not seen in smears of exudate because spores form when nutrients are insufficient, and nutrients are plentiful in infected tissue. Nonhemolytic colonies form on blood agar aerobically. In case of a bioterror attack, rapid diagnosis can be performed in special laboratories using polymerase chain reaction (PCR)-based assays. Another rapid diagnostic procedure is the direct fluorescent antibody test that detects antigens of the organism in the lesion. Serologic tests, such as an ELISA test for antibodies, require acute and convalescent serum samples and can only be used to make a diagnosis retrospectively.

Table 17–2. Important features of pathogenesis by *Bacillus* species.

Organism	Disease	Transmission/ Predisposing Factor	Action of Toxin	Prevention
B. anthracis	Anthrax	1. Cutaneous anthrax: spores in soil enter wound 2. Pulmonary anthrax: spores are inhaled into lung	Exotoxin has three components: Protective antigen binds to cells; edema factor is an adenylate cyclase; lethal factor is a protease that inhibits cell growth.	Vaccine contains protective antigen as the immunogen
B. cereus	Food poisoning	Spores germinate in reheated rice, then bacteria produce exotoxins, which are ingested	Two exotoxins (enterotoxins): 1. Similar to cholera toxin, it increases cyclic AMP 2. Similar to staphylococcal enterotoxin, it is a superantigen	No vaccine

Treatment

Ciprofloxacin is the drug of choice. Doxycycline is an alternative drug. No resistant strains have been isolated clinically.

Prevention

Ciprofloxacin or doxycycline was used as prophylaxis in those exposed during the outbreak in the United States in 2001. People at high risk can be immunized with cell-free vaccine containing purified protective antigen as immunogen. The vaccine is weakly immunogenic, and six doses of vaccine over an 18-month period are given. Annual boosters are also given to maintain protection. Incinerating animals that die of anthrax, rather than burying them, will prevent the soil from becoming contaminated with spores.

2. *Bacillus cereus*

Disease

B. cereus causes food poisoning.

Transmission

Spores on grains such as rice survive steaming and rapid frying. The spores germinate when rice is kept warm for many hours (eg, **reheated fried rice**). The portal of entry is the gastrointestinal tract.

Pathogenesis

B. cereus produces two enterotoxins. The mode of action of one of the enterotoxins is the same as that of cholera toxin; ie, it adds adenosine diphosphate-ribose, a process called ADP-ribosylation, to a G protein, which stimulates adenylate cyclase and leads to an increased concentration of cyclic adenosine monophosphate (AMP) within the enterocyte. The mode of action of the other enterotoxin resembles that of staphylococcal enterotoxin; ie, it is a superantigen.

Clinical Findings

There are two syndromes: (1) one has a short incubation period (4 hours) and consists primarily of nausea and vomiting, similar to staphylococcal food poisoning; (2) the other has a long incubation period (18 hours) and features watery, nonbloody diarrhea, resembling clostridial gastroenteritis.

Laboratory Diagnosis

This is not usually done.

Treatment

Only symptomatic treatment is given.

Prevention

No specific means of prevention. Rice should not be kept warm for long periods.

CLOSTRIDIUM

There are four medically important species: *Clostridium tetani*, *Clostridium botulinum*, *Clostridium perfringens* (which causes either gas gangrene or food poisoning), and *Clostridium difficile*. All clostridia are anaerobic, spore-forming, gram-positive rods. Important features of pathogenesis and prevention are described in Table 17–3.

Table 17–3. Important features of pathogenesis by *Clostridium* species.

Organism	Disease	Transmission/ Predisposing Factor	Action of Toxin	Prevention
C. tetani	Tetanus	Spores in soil enter wound	Blocks release of inhibitory transmitters, eg, glycine	Toxoid vaccine
C. botulinum	Botulism	Exotoxin in food is ingested	Blocks release of acetylcholine	Proper canning; cook food
C. perfringens	1. Gas gangrene	Spores in soil enter wound	Lecithinase	Debride wounds
	2. Food poisoning	Exotoxin in food is ingested	Superantigen	Cook food
C. difficile	Pseudomembranous colitis	Antibiotics suppress normal flora	Cytotoxin damages colon mucosa	Appropriate use of antibiotics

1. *Clostridium tetani*

Disease

C. tetani causes tetanus (lockjaw).

Transmission

Spores are widespread in soil. The portal of entry is usually a **wound** site, eg, where a nail penetrates the foot, but the spores also can be introduced during "skin-popping," a technique used by drug addicts to inject drugs into the skin. Germination of spores is favored by necrotic tissue and poor blood supply in the wound. Neonatal tetanus, in which the organism enters through a contaminated umbilicus or circumcision wound, is a major problem in some developing countries.

Pathogenesis

Tetanus toxin (tetanospasmin) is an exotoxin produced by vegetative cells at the wound site. This polypeptide toxin is carried intra-axonally (retrograde) to the central nervous system, where it binds to ganglioside receptors and blocks release of inhibitory mediators (eg, glycine) at spinal synapses. Tetanus toxin and botulinum toxin (see below) are among the most toxic substances known. They are proteases that cleave the proteins involved in mediator release.

Tetanus toxin has one antigenic type, unlike botulinum toxin, which has eight. There is therefore only one antigenic type of tetanus toxoid in the vaccine against tetanus.

Clinical Findings

Tetanus is characterized by strong muscle spasms (spastic paralysis, tetany). Specific clinical features include **lockjaw** (trismus) due to rigid contraction of the jaw muscles, which prevents the mouth from opening; a characteristic grimace known as **risus sardonicus**; and exaggerated reflexes. **Opisthotonos**, a pronounced arching of the back due to spasm of the strong extensor muscles of the back, is often seen. Respiratory failure ensues. A high mortality rate is associated with this disease. Note that in tetanus, **spastic paralysis** (strong muscle contractions) occurs, whereas in botulism, **flaccid paralysis** (weak or absent muscle contractions) occurs.

Laboratory Diagnosis

There is no microbiologic or serologic diagnosis. Organisms are rarely isolated from the wound site. *C. tetani* produces a **terminal spore**, ie, a spore at the end of the rod. This gives the organism the characteristic appearance of a "tennis racket."

Treatment

Tetanus immune globulin is used to neutralize the toxin. The role of antibiotics is uncertain. If antibiotics are used, either metronidazole or penicillin G can be given. An adequate airway must be maintained and respiratory support given. Benzodiazepines, eg, diazepam (Valium), should be given to prevent spasms.

Prevention

Tetanus is prevented by immunization with tetanus toxoid (formaldehyde-treated toxin) in childhood and every 10 years thereafter. Tetanus toxoid is usually given to children in combination with diphtheria toxoid and the acellular pertussis vaccine (DTaP).

When trauma occurs, the wound should be cleaned and debrided and tetanus toxoid booster should be given. If the wound is grossly contaminated, **tetanus immune globulin,** as well as the toxoid booster, should be given and penicillin administered. Tetanus immune globulin (tetanus antitoxin) is made in humans to avoid serum sickness reactions that occur when antitoxin made in horses is used. The administration of both immune globulins and tetanus toxoid (at different sites in the body) is an example of **passive-active immunity.**

2. *Clostridium botulinum*

Disease

C. botulinum causes botulism.

Transmission

Spores, widespread in soil, contaminate vegetables and meats. When these foods are canned or vacuum-packed without adequate sterilization, spores survive and germinate in the anaerobic environment. Toxin is produced within the canned food and **ingested preformed.** The highest-risk foods are (1) alkaline vegetables such as green beans, peppers, and mushrooms and (2) smoked fish. The toxin is relatively heat-labile; it is inactivated by boiling for several minutes. Thus, disease can be prevented by sufficient cooking.

Pathogenesis

Botulinum toxin is absorbed from the gut and carried via the blood to peripheral nerve synapses, where it **blocks release of acetylcholine.** It is a protease that cleaves the proteins involved in acetylcholine release. The toxin is a polypeptide encoded by a lysogenic phage. Along with tetanus toxin, it is among the most toxic substances known. There are eight immunologic types of toxin; types A, B, and E are the most common in human illness. Botox is a commercial preparation of exotoxin A used to remove wrinkles on the face. Minute amounts of the toxin are effective in the treatment of certain spasmodic muscle disorders such as torticollis, "writer's cramp," and blepharospasm.

Clinical Findings

Descending weakness and paralysis, including diplopia, dysphagia, and respiratory muscle failure, are seen. No fever is present. In contrast, Guillain-Barré syndrome is an ascending paralysis (see Chapter 66).

Two special clinical forms occur: (1) wound botulism, in which spores contaminate a wound, germinate, and produce toxin at the site; and (2) infant botulism, in which the organisms grow in the gut and produce toxins. Ingestion of honey containing the organism is implicated in transmission of infant botulism. Affected infants develop weakness or paralysis and may need respiratory support but usually recover spontaneously. In the United States, infant botulism accounts for about half of the cases of botulism, and wound botulism is associated with drug abuse, especially skin-popping with black tar heroin.

Laboratory Diagnosis

The organism is usually not cultured. Botulinum toxin is demonstrable in uneaten food and the patient's serum by mouse protection tests. Mice are inoculated with a sample of the clinical specimen and will die unless protected by antitoxin.

Treatment

Trivalent antitoxin (types A, B, and E) is given, along with respiratory support. The antitoxin is made in horses, and serum sickness occurs in about 15% of antiserum recipients.

Prevention

Proper sterilization of all canned and vacuum-packed foods is essential. Food must be adequately cooked to inactivate the toxin. Swollen cans must be discarded (clostridial proteolytic enzymes form gas, which swells cans).

3. Clostridium perfringens

C. perfringens causes two distinct diseases, gas gangrene and food poisoning, depending on the route of entry into the body.

Disease: Gas Gangrene

Gas gangrene (myonecrosis, necrotizing fasciitis) is one of the two diseases caused by *C. perfringens*. Gas gangrene is also caused by other histotoxic clostridia such as *Clostridium histolyticum, Clostridium septicum,* and *Clostridium novyi.*

Transmission

Spores are located in the soil; vegetative cells are members of the **normal flora of the colon and vagina.** Gas gangrene is associated with war wounds, automobile and motorcycle accidents, and septic abortions (endometritis).

Pathogenesis

Organisms grow in traumatized tissue (especially muscle) and produce a variety of toxins. The most important is **alpha toxin** (lecithinase), which damages cell membranes, including those of erythrocytes, resulting in hemolysis. Degradative enzymes produce gas in tissues.

Clinical Findings

Pain, edema, and cellulitis occur in the wound area. Crepitation indicates the presence of gas in tissues. Hemolysis and jaundice are common, as are blood-tinged exudates. Shock and death can ensue. Mortality rates are high.

Laboratory Diagnosis

Smears of tissue and exudate samples show large grampositive rods. Spores are not usually seen because they are formed primarily under nutritionally deficient conditions. The organisms are cultured anaerobically and then identified by sugar fermentation reactions and organic acid production. *C. perfringens* colonies exhibit a double zone of hemolysis on blood agar. Egg yolk agar is used to demonstrate the presence of the lecithinase. Serologic tests are not useful.

Treatment

Penicillin G is the antibiotic of choice. Wounds should be debrided.

Prevention

Wounds should be cleansed and debrided. Penicillin may be given for prophylaxis. There is no vaccine.

Disease: Food Poisoning

Food poisoning is the second disease caused by *C. perfringens.*

Transmission

Spores are located in **soil** and can contaminate **food.** The heat-resistant spores survive cooking and germinate. The organisms grow to large numbers in reheated foods, especially meat dishes.

Pathogenesis

C. perfringens is a member of the normal flora in the colon but not in the small bowel, where the enterotoxin acts to cause diarrhea. The mode of action of the enterotoxin is the same as that of the enterotoxin of *S. aureus;* ie, it acts as a superantigen.

Clinical Findings

The disease has an 8- to 16-hour incubation period and is characterized by watery diarrhea with cramps and little vomiting. It resolves in 24 hours.

Laboratory Diagnosis

This is not usually done. There is no assay for the toxin. Large numbers of the organisms can be isolated from uneaten food.

Treatment

Symptomatic treatment is given; no antimicrobial drugs are administered.

Prevention

There are no specific preventive measures. Food should be adequately cooked to kill the organism.

4. *Clostridium difficile*

Disease

C. difficile causes antibiotic-associated pseudomembranous colitis.

Transmission

The organism is carried in the **gastrointestinal tract** in approximately 3% of the general population and up to 30% of hospitalized patients. Most people are not colonized, which explains why most people who take antibiotics do not get pseudomembranous colitis. *C. difficile* is the most common nosocomial cause of diarrhea. It is transmitted by the fecal-oral route. The hands of hospital personnel are important intermediaries.

Pathogenesis

Antibiotics suppress drug-sensitive members of the normal flora, allowing *C. difficile* to multiply and produce exotoxins A and B. Both exotoxin A and exotoxin B are enzymes that glucosylate (add glucose to) a G protein called Rho GTPase. The main effect of exotoxin B in

particular is to cause depolymerization of actin, resulting in a loss of cytoskeletal integrity, apoptosis, and death of the enterocytes.

Clindamycin was the first antibiotic to be recognized as a cause of pseudomembranous colitis, but many antibiotics are known to cause this disease. At present, second- and third-generation cephalosporins are the most common causes because they are so frequently used. In addition to antibiotics, cancer chemotherapy also predisposes to pseudomembranous colitis. *C. difficile* rarely invades the intestinal mucosa.

Clinical Findings

C. difficile causes diarrhea associated with **pseudomembranes** (yellow-white plaques) on the colonic mucosa. (The term "pseudomembrane" is defined in Chapter 7 on page 38). The diarrhea is usually not bloody, and neutrophils are found in the stool in about half of the cases. Fever and abdominal cramping often occur. The pseudomembranes are visualized by sigmoidoscopy. Toxic megacolon can occur, and surgical resection of the colon may be necessary. Pseudomembranous colitis can be distinguished from the transient diarrhea that occurs as a side effect of many oral antibiotics by testing for the presence of the toxin in the stool.

Laboratory Diagnosis

The presence of exotoxins in a filtrate of the patient's stool specimen is the basis of the laboratory diagnosis. There are two types of tests usually used to detect the exotoxins. One is an enzyme-linked immunosorbent assay (ELISA) using known antibody to the exotoxins. The ELISA tests are rapid but are less sensitive than the cytotoxicity test. In the cytotoxicity test, human cells in culture are exposed to the exotoxin in the stool filtrate and the death of the cells is observed. This test is more sensitive and specific but requires 24–48 hours' incubation time. To distinguish between cytotoxicity caused by the exotoxins and cytotoxicity caused by a virus possibly present in the patient's stool, antibody against the exotoxins is used to neutralize the cytotoxic effect.

Treatment

The causative antibiotic should be withdrawn. Oral metronidazole or vancomycin should be given and fluids replaced. Metronidazole is preferred because using vancomycin may select for vancomycin-resistant enterococci. In many patients, treatment does not eradicate the carrier state and repeated episodes of colitis can occur.

Prevention

There are no preventive vaccines or drugs. Antibiotics should be prescribed only when necessary.

■ NON–SPORE-FORMING GRAM-POSITIVE RODS

There are two important pathogens in this group: *Corynebacterium diphtheriae* and *Listeria monocytogenes*. Important features of pathogenesis and prevention are described in Table 17–4.

CORYNEBACTERIUM DIPHTHERIAE

Disease

C. diphtheriae causes diphtheria. Other *Corynebacterium* species (diphtheroids) are implicated in opportunistic infections.

Important Properties

Corynebacteria are gram-positive rods that appear **club-shaped** (wider at one end) and are arranged in palisades or in **V**- or **L**-shaped formations. The rods have a beaded appearance. The beads consist of granules of highly polymerized polyphosphate, a storage mechanism for high-energy phosphate bonds. The granules stain **metachromatically;** ie, a dye that stains the rest of the cell blue will stain the granules red.

Transmission

Humans are the only natural host of *C. diphtheriae*. Both toxigenic and nontoxigenic organisms reside in the upper respiratory tract and are transmitted by **airborne droplets.** The organism can also infect the skin at the site of a preexisting skin lesion. This occurs primarily in the tropics but can occur worldwide in indigent persons with poor skin hygiene.

Pathogenesis

Although exotoxin production is essential for pathogenesis, invasiveness is also necessary because the organism must first establish and maintain itself in the throat. Diphtheria toxin inhibits protein synthesis by **ADP-ribosylation of elongation factor 2** (EF-2). The toxin affects all eukaryotic cells regardless of tissue type but has no effect on the analogous factor in prokaryotic cells.

The toxin is a single polypeptide with two functional domains. One domain mediates binding of the toxin to glycoprotein receptors on the cell membrane. The other domain possesses enzymatic activity that cleaves nicotinamide from nicotinamide adenine dinucleotide (NAD) and transfers the remaining ADP-ribose to EF-2, thereby inactivating it. Other organisms whose exotoxins act by ADP-ribosylation are described in Tables 7–9 and 7–10.

The DNA that codes for diphtheria toxin is part of the genetic material of a temperate bacteriophage. During the lysogenic phase of viral growth, the DNA of this virus integrates into the bacterial chromosome and the toxin is synthesized. *C. diphtheriae* cells that are not lysogenized by this phage do not produce exotoxin and are nonpathogenic.

The host response to *C. diphtheriae* consists of:

(1) Local inflammation in the throat, with a fibrinous exudate that forms the tough, adherent, gray **pseudomembrane** characteristic of the disease

(2) Antibody that can neutralize exotoxin activity by blocking the interaction of fragment B with the receptors, thereby preventing entry into the cell. The immune status of a person can be assessed by Schick's test. The test is performed by intradermal injection of 0.1 mL of purified standardized toxin. If the patient has no antitoxin, the toxin will cause inflammation at the site 4–7 days later. If no inflammation occurs, antitoxin is present and the patient is immune. The test is rarely performed in the United States except under special epidemiologic circumstances.

Clinical Findings

Although diphtheria is rare in the United States, physicians should be aware of its most prominent sign, the thick, gray, adherent **pseudomembrane** over the tonsils and throat. (The term "pseudomembrane" is defined in

Table 17–4. Important features of pathogenesis by *Corynebacterium diphtheriae* and *Listeria monocytogenes*.

Organism	Type of Pathogenesis	Typical Disease	Predisposing Factor	Mode of Prevention
C. diphtheriae	Toxigenic	Diphtheria	Failure to immunize	Toxoid vaccine
L. monocytogenes	Pyogenic	Meningitis; sepsis	Neonate; immunosuppression	No vaccine; pasteurize milk products

Chapter 7 on page 37.) The other aspects are nonspecific: fever, sore throat, and cervical adenopathy. There are three prominent complications:

(1) Extension of the membrane into the larynx and trachea, causing airway obstruction

(2) Myocarditis accompanied by arrhythmias and circulatory collapse

(3) Nerve weakness or paralysis, especially of the cranial nerves. Paralysis of the muscles of the soft palate and pharynx can lead to regurgitation of fluids through the nose. Peripheral neuritis affecting the muscles of the extremities also occurs.

Cutaneous diphtheria causes ulcerating skin lesions covered by a gray membrane. These lesions are often indolent and often do not invade surrounding tissue. Systemic symptoms rarely occur. In the United States, cutaneous diphtheria occurs primarily in the indigent.

Laboratory Diagnosis

Laboratory diagnosis involves both isolating the organism and demonstrating toxin production. It should be emphasized that the decision to treat with antitoxin is a clinical one and cannot wait for the laboratory results. A throat swab should be cultured on Löffler's medium, a **tellurite plate**, and a blood agar plate. The tellurite plate contains a tellurium salt that is reduced to elemental tellurium within the organism. The typical gray-black color of tellurium in the colony is a telltale diagnostic criterion. If C. diphtheriae is recovered from the cultures, either animal inoculation or an antibody-based gel diffusion precipitin test is performed to document toxin production. A PCR assay for the presence of the toxin gene in the organism isolated from the patient can also be used.

Smears of the throat swab should be stained with both Gram stain and methylene blue. Although the diagnosis of diphtheria cannot be made by examination of the smear, the finding of many tapered, pleomorphic gram-positive rods can be suggestive. The methylene blue stain is excellent for revealing the typical metachromatic granules.

Treatment

The treatment of choice is **antitoxin,** which should be given immediately on the basis of clinical impression because there is a delay in laboratory diagnostic procedures. The toxin binds rapidly and irreversibly to cells and, once bound, cannot be neutralized by antitoxin. The function of antitoxin is therefore to neutralize unbound toxin in the blood. Because the antiserum is made in horses, the patient must be tested for hypersensitivity and medications for the treatment of anaphylaxis must be available.

Treatment with penicillin G or an erythromycin is recommended also, but neither is a substitute for antitoxin. Antibiotics inhibit growth of the organism, reduce toxin production, and decrease the incidence of chronic carriers.

Prevention

Diphtheria is very rare in the United States because children are immunized with **diphtheria toxoid** (usually given as a combination of diphtheria toxoid, tetanus toxoid, and acellular pertussis vaccine, often abbreviated as DTaP). Diphtheria toxoid is prepared by treating the exotoxin with formaldehyde. This treatment inactivates the toxic effect but leaves the antigenicity intact. Immunization consists of three doses given at 2, 4, and 6 months of age, with boosters at 1 and 6 years of age. Because immunity wanes, a booster every 10 years is recommended. Immunization does not prevent nasopharyngeal carriage of the organism.

LISTERIA MONOCYTOGENES

Diseases

L. monocytogenes causes meningitis and sepsis in newborns, pregnant women, and immunosuppressed adults. It also causes outbreaks of febrile gastroenteritis.

Important Properties

L. monocytogenes is a small gram-positive rod arranged in V- or L-shaped formations similar to corynebacteria. The organism exhibits an unusual **tumbling** movement that distinguishes it from the corynebacteria, which are nonmotile. Colonies on a blood agar plate produce a narrow zone of beta-hemolysis that resembles the hemolysis of some streptococci.

Listeria grows well at cold temperatures, so storage of contaminated food in the refrigerator can increase the risk of gastroenteritis. This paradoxical growth in the cold is called "cold enhancement."

Pathogenesis

Listeria infections occur primarily in two clinical settings: (1) in the fetus or newborn as a result of transmission **across the placenta** or **during delivery;** and (2) in pregnant women and immunosuppressed adults, especially renal transplant patients. (Note that pregnant women have reduced cell-mediated immunity during the third trimester.)

The organism is distributed worldwide in animals, plants, and soil. From these reservoirs, it is transmitted to humans primarily by ingestion of unpasteurized milk products, undercooked meat, and raw vegetables.

Contact with domestic farm animals and their feces is also an important source. In the United States, listeriosis is primarily a food-borne disease associated with eating unpasteurized cheese and delicatessen meats.

The pathogenesis of *Listeria* depends on the organism's ability to invade and survive within cells. Invasion of cells is mediated by internalin made by *Listeria* and E-cadherin on the surface of human cells. The ability of *Listeria* to pass the placenta, enter the meninges, and invade the gastrointestinal tract depends on the interaction of internalin and E-cadherin on those tissues.

Upon entering the cell, the organism produces listeriolysin, which allows it to escape from the phagosome into the cytoplasm, thereby escaping destruction in the phagosome. Because *Listeria* preferentially grows intracellularly, cell-mediated immunity is a more important host defense than humoral immunity. Suppression of **cell-mediated immunity** predisposes to *Listeria* infections.

L. monocytogenes can move from cell to cell by means of **actin rockets,** a filament of actin that contracts and propels the bacteria through the membrane of one human cell and into another.

Clinical Findings

Infection during pregnancy can cause abortion, premature delivery, or sepsis during the peripartum period. Newborns infected at the time of delivery can have acute meningitis 1–4 weeks later. The bacteria reach the meninges via the bloodstream (bacteremia). The infected mother either is asymptomatic or has an influenzalike illness. *L. monocytogenes* infections in immunocompromised adults can be either sepsis or meningitis.

Gastroenteritis caused by *L. monocytogenes* is characterized by watery diarrhea, fever, headache, myalgias, and abdominal cramps but little vomiting. Outbreaks are usually caused by contaminated dairy products, but undercooked meats such as chicken and hot dogs have also been involved.

Laboratory Diagnosis

Laboratory diagnosis is made primarily by Gram stain and culture. The appearance of gram-positive rods resembling **diphtheroids** and the formation of small, gray colonies with a narrow zone of beta-hemolysis on a blood agar plate suggest the presence of *Listeria*. The isolation of *Listeria* is confirmed by the presence of motile organisms, which differentiate them from the nonmotile corynebacteria. Identification of the organism as *L. monocytogenes* is made by sugar fermentation tests.

Treatment

Treatment of invasive disease, such as meningitis and sepsis, consists of trimethoprim-sulfamethoxazole. Combinations, such as ampicillin and gentamicin or ampicillin and trimethoprim-sulfamethoxazole, can also be used. Resistant strains are rare. *Listeria* gastroenteritis typically does not require treatment.

Prevention

Prevention is difficult because there is no immunization. Limiting the exposure of pregnant women and immunosuppressed patients to potential sources such as farm animals, unpasteurized milk products, and raw vegetables is recommended. Trimethoprim-sulfamethoxazole given to immunocompromised patients to prevent *Pneumocystis* pneumonia also can prevent listeriosis.

SUMMARIES OF ORGANISMS

Brief summaries of the organisms described in this chapter begin on page 480. Please consult these summaries for a rapid review of the essential material.

PRACTICE QUESTIONS: USMLE & COURSE EXAMINATIONS

Questions on the topics discussed in this chapter can be found in the Clinical Bacteriology section of Part XI: USMLE (National Board) Practice Questions starting on page 537. Also see Part XII: USMLE (National Board) Practice Examination starting on page 583.

Gram-Negative Rods Related to the Enteric Tract

18

OVERVIEW

Gram-negative rods are a large group of diverse organisms. In this book, these bacteria are subdivided into three clinically relevant categories, each in a separate chapter, according to whether the organism is related primarily to the enteric or the respiratory tract or to animal sources (Table 18–1). Although this approach leads to some overlaps, it should be helpful because it allows general concepts to be emphasized.

Gram-negative rods related to the enteric tract include a large number of genera. These genera have therefore been divided into three groups depending on the major anatomic location of disease, namely, (1) pathogens both within and outside the enteric tract, (2) pathogens primarily within the enteric tract, and (3) pathogens outside the enteric tract (Table 18–1).

The frequency with which the organisms related to the enteric tract cause disease in the United States is shown in Table 18–2. *Salmonella, Shigella,* and *Campylobacter* are frequent pathogens in the gastrointestinal tract, whereas *Escherichia, Vibrio,* and *Yersinia* are less so. Enterotoxigenic strains of *Escherichia coli* are a common cause of diarrhea in developing countries but are less common in the United States. The medically important gram-negative rods that cause diarrhea are described in Table 18–3. Urinary tract infections are caused primarily by *E. coli;* the other organisms occur less commonly. The medically important gram-negative rods that cause urinary tract infections are described in Table 18–4.

Patients infected with such enteric pathogens as *Shigella, Salmonella, Campylobacter,* and *Yersinia* have a high incidence of certain autoimmune diseases such as Reiter's syndrome (see Chapter 66). In addition, infection with *Campylobacter jejuni* predisposes to Guillain-Barré syndrome.

Before describing the specific organisms, it is appropriate to describe the family Enterobacteriaceae, to which many of these gram-negative rods belong.

ENTEROBACTERIACEAE & RELATED ORGANISMS

The Enterobacteriaceae is a large family of gram-negative rods found primarily in the colon of humans and other animals, many as part of the normal flora. These organisms are the major facultative anaerobes in the large intestine but are present in relatively small numbers compared with anaerobes such as *Bacteroides.* Although the members of the Enterobacteriaceae are classified together taxonomically, they cause a variety of diseases with different pathogenetic mechanisms. The organisms and some of the diseases they cause are listed in Table 18–5.

Features common to all members of this heterogeneous family are their anatomic location and the following four metabolic processes: (1) they are all facultative anaerobes; (2) they all ferment glucose (fermentation of other sugars varies); (3) none have cytochrome oxidase (ie, they are oxidase-negative); and (4) they reduce nitrates to nitrites as part of their energy-generating processes.

These four reactions can be used to distinguish the Enterobacteriaceae from another medically significant group of organisms—the nonfermenting gram-negative rods, the most important of which is *Pseudomonas aeruginosa.*[1]

P. aeruginosa, a significant cause of urinary tract infection and sepsis in hospitalized patients, does not ferment glucose or reduce nitrates and is oxidase-positive. In contrast to the Enterobacteriaceae, it is a strict aerobe and derives its energy from oxidation, not fermentation.

Pathogenesis

All members of the Enterobacteriaceae, being gram-negative, contain endotoxin in their cell walls. In addi-

---

[1]The other less frequently isolated organisms in this group are members of the following genera: *Achromobacter, Acinetobacter, Alcaligenes, Eikenella, Flavobacterium, Kingella,* and *Moraxella;* see Chapter 27.

Table 18–1. Categories of gram-negative rods.

Chapter	Source of Site of Infection	Genus
18	Enteric tract	
	1. Both within and outside	*Escherichia, Salmonella*
	2. Primarily within	*Shigella, Vibrio, Campylobacter, Helicobacter*
	3. Outside only	*Klebsiella-Enterobacter-Serratia* group, *Proteus-Providencia-Morganella* group, *Pseudomonas, Bacteroides*
19	Respiratory tract	*Haemophilus, Legionella, Bordetella*
20	Animal sources	*Brucella, Francisella, Pasteurella, Yersinia*

tion, several exotoxins are produced; eg, *E. coli* and *Vibrio cholerae* secrete exotoxins, called enterotoxins, that activate adenylate cyclase within the cells of the small intestine, causing diarrhea (see Chapter 7).

Antigens

The antigens of several members of the Enterobacteriaceae, especially *Salmonella* and *Shigella,* are important; they are used for identification purposes both in the clinical laboratory and in epidemiologic investigations. The three surface antigens are as follows:

(1) The cell wall antigen (also known as the somatic, or O, antigen) is the outer polysaccharide portion of the lipopolysaccharide (see Figure 2–6). The O antigen, which is composed of repeating oligosaccharides consisting of three or four sugars repeated 15 or 20 times, is the basis for the serologic typing of many enteric rods. The number of different O antigens is very large; eg, there are approximately 1500 types of *Salmonella* and 150 types of *E. coli.*

(2) The H antigen is on the flagellar protein. Only flagellated organisms, such as *Escherichia* and *Salmonella,* have H antigens, whereas the nonmotile ones, such as *Klebsiella* and *Shigella,* do not. The H antigens of certain *Salmonella* species are unusual because the organisms can reversibly alternate between two types of H antigens called phase 1 and phase 2. The organisms

may use this change in antigenicity to evade the immune response.

(3) The capsular or K polysaccharide antigen is particularly prominent in heavily encapsulated organisms such as *Klebsiella.* The K antigen is identified by the quellung (capsular swelling) reaction in the presence of specific antisera and is used to serotype *E. coli* and *Salmonella typhi* for epidemiologic purposes. In *S. typhi,* the cause of typhoid fever, it is called the Vi (or virulence) antigen.

Laboratory Diagnosis

Specimens suspected of containing members of the Enterobacteriaceae and related organisms are usually inoculated onto two media, a blood agar plate and a selective differential medium such as MacConkey's agar or eosin–methylene blue (EMB) agar. The *differential* ability of these latter media is based on **lactose fermentation,** which is the most important metabolic criterion used in the identification of these organisms (Table 18–6). On these media, the non–lactose fermenters, eg, *Salmonella* and *Shigella,* form colorless colonies, whereas the lactose fermenters, eg, *E. coli,* form colored colonies. The *selective* effect of the media in suppressing unwanted gram-positive organisms is exerted by bile salts or bacteriostatic dyes in the agar.

An additional set of screening tests, consisting of triple sugar iron (TSI) agar and urea agar, is performed

Table 18–2. Frequency of diseases caused in the United States by gram-negative rods related to the enteric tract.

Site of Infection	Frequent Pathogens	Less-Frequent Pathogens
Enteric tract	*Salmonella, Shigella, Campylobacter*	*Escherichia, Vibrio, Yersinia*
Urinary tract	*Escherichia*	*Enterobacter, Klebsiella, Proteus, Pseudomonas*

Table 18–3. Gram-negative rods causing diarrhea.

Species	Fever	Leukocytes in Stool	Infective Dose	Typical Bacteriologic or Epidemiologic Findings
Enterotoxin-mediated				
1. Escherichia coli	−	−	?	Ferments lactose.
2. Vibrio cholerae	−	−	10^7	Comma-shaped bacteria.
Invasive-inflammatory				
1. Salmonella, eg, S. typhimurium	+	+	10^5	Does not ferment lactose.
2. Shigella, eg, S. dysenteriae	+	+	10^2	Does not ferment lactose.
3. Campylobacter jejuni	+	+	10^4	Comma- or S-shaped bacteria; growth at 42°C.
4. Escherichia coli (enteropathic strains)	+	+	?	
5. Escherichia coli O157:H7	+	+/−	?	Transmitted by undercooked hamburger; causes hemolytic-uremic syndrome.
Mechanism uncertain				
1. Vibrio parahaemolyticus[1]	+	+	?	Transmitted by seafood.
2. Yersinia enterocolitica[1]	+	+	10^8	Usually transmitted from pets, eg, puppies.

[1]Some strains produce enterotoxin, but its pathogenic role is not clear.

prior to the definitive identification procedures. The rationale for the use of these media and the reactions of several important organisms are presented in the Box (page 137) and in Table 18–7. The results of the screening process are often sufficient to identify the genus of an organism; however, an array of 20 or more biochemical tests is required to identify the species.

Another valuable piece of information used to identify some of these organisms is their motility, which is dependent on the presence of flagella. *Proteus* species are very motile and characteristically **swarm** over the blood agar plate, obscuring the colonies of other organisms. Motility is also an important diagnostic criterion in the differentiation of *Enterobacter cloacae*, which is motile, from *Klebsiella pneumoniae*, which is nonmotile.

If the results of the screening tests suggest the presence

Table 18–4. Gram-negative rods causing urinary tract infection[1] or sepsis.[2]

Species	Lactose Fermented	Features of the Organism
Escherichia coli	+	Colonies show metallic sheen on EMB agar.
Enterobacter cloacae	+	Causes nosocomial infections and often drug-resistant.
Klebsiella pneumoniae	+	Has large mucoid capsule and hence viscous colonies.
Serratia marcescens	−	Red pigment produced; causes nosocomial infections and often drug-resistant.
Proteus mirabilis	−	Motility causes "swarming" on agar; produces urease.
Pseudomonas aeruginosa	−	Blue-green pigment and fruity odor produced; causes nosocomial infections and often drug-resistant.

[1]Diagnosed by quantitative culture of urine.

[2]Diagnosed by culture of blood or pus.

EMB = eosin–methylene blue.

Table 18–5. Diseases caused by members of the Enterobacteriaceae.

Major Pathogen	Representative Diseases	Minor Related Genera
Escherichia	Urinary tract infection, traveler's diarrhea, neonatal meningitis	
Shigella	Dysentery	
Salmonella	Typhoid fever, enterocolitis	*Arizona, Citrobacter, Edwardsiella*
Klebsiella	Pneumonia, urinary tract infection	
Enterobacter	Pneumonia, urinary tract infection	*Hafnia*
Serratia	Pneumonia, urinary tract infection	
Proteus	Urinary tract infection	*Providencia, Morganella*
Yersinia	Plague, enterocolitis, mesenteric adenitis	

of a *Salmonella* or *Shigella* strain, an agglutination test can be used to identify the genus of the organism and to determine whether it is a member of group A, B, C, or D.

Coliforms & Public Health

Contamination of the public water supply system by sewage is detected by the presence of coliforms in the water. In a general sense, the term "coliform" includes not only *E. coli* but also other inhabitants of the colon such as *Enterobacter* and *Klebsiella*. However, because only *E. coli* is exclusively a large-intestine organism, whereas the others are found in the environment also, it is used as the indicator of fecal contamination. In water quality testing, *E. coli* is identified by its ability to ferment lactose with the production of acid and gas, its ability to grow at 44.5°C, and its characteristic colony type on EMB agar. An *E. coli* colony count above 4/dL in municipal drinking water is indicative of unacceptable fecal contamination. Because *E. coli* and the enteric pathogens are killed by chlorination of the drinking water, there is rarely a problem with meeting this standard. Disinfection of the public water supply is one

Table 18–6. Lactose fermentation by members of the Enterobacteriaceae and related organisms.

Lactose Fermentation	Organisms
Occurs	*Escherichia, Klebsiella, Enterobacter*
Does not occur	*Shigella, Salmonella, Proteus, Pseudomonas*
Occurs slowly	*Serratia, Vibrio*

of the most important advances of public health in the 20th century.

Antibiotic Therapy

The appropriate treatment for infections caused by members of the Enterobacteriaceae and related organisms must be individually tailored to the antibiotic sensitivity of the organism. Generally speaking, a wide range of antimicrobial agents are potentially effective, eg, some penicillins and cephalosporins, aminoglycosides, chloramphenicol, tetracyclines, quinolones, and sulfonamides. The specific choice usually depends upon the results of antibiotic sensitivity tests.

Note that many isolates of these enteric gram-negative rods are **highly antibiotic resistant** because of the production of β-lactamases and other drug-modifying enzymes. These organisms undergo conjugation frequently, at which time they acquire plasmids (R factors) that mediate multiple drug resistance.

■ PATHOGENS BOTH WITHIN & OUTSIDE THE ENTERIC TRACT

ESCHERICHIA

Diseases

E. coli is the most common cause of urinary tract infection and gram-negative rod sepsis. It is one of the two important causes of neonatal meningitis and the agent most frequently associated with "traveler's diarrhea," a watery diarrhea. Some strains of *E. coli* are enterohemorrhagic and cause bloody diarrhea.

Table 18–7. Triple sugar iron (TSI) agar reactions.

Reactions[1]				
Slant	**Butt**	**Gas**	**H$_2$S**	**Representative Genera**
Acid	Acid	+	−	*Escherichia, Enterobacter, Klebsiella*
Alkaline	Acid	−	−	*Shigella, Serratia*
Alkaline	Acid	+	+	*Salmonella, Proteus*
Alkaline	Alkaline	−	−	*Pseudomonas*[2]

[1]Acid production causes the phenol red indicator to turn yellow; the indicator is red under alkaline conditions. The presence of black FeS in the butt indicates H$_2$S production. Not every species within the various genera will give the above appearance on TSI agar. For example, some *Serratia* strains can ferment lactose slowly and give an acid reaction on the slant.

[2]*Pseudomonas*, although not a member of the Enterobacteriaceae, is included in this table because its reaction on TSI agar is a useful diagnostic criterion.

Important Properties

E. coli is the most abundant facultative anaerobe in the colon and feces. It is, however, greatly outnumbered by the obligate anaerobes such as *Bacteroides*.

E. coli **ferments lactose**, a property that distinguishes it from the two major intestinal pathogens, *Shigella* and *Salmonella*. It has three antigens that are used to identify the organism in epidemiologic investigations: the O, or cell wall, antigen; the H, or flagellar, antigen; and the K, or capsular, antigen. Because there are more than 150 O, 50 H, and 90 K antigens, the various combinations result in more than 1000 antigenic types of *E. coli*. Specific serotypes are associated

---

AGAR MEDIA FOR ENTERIC GRAM-NEGATIVE RODS

Triple Sugar Iron Agar

The important components of this medium are ferrous sulfate and the three sugars glucose, lactose, and sucrose. The glucose is present in one-tenth the concentration of the other two sugars. The medium in the tube has a solid, poorly oxygenated area on the bottom, called the butt, and an angled, well-oxygenated area on top, called the slant. The organism is inoculated into the butt and across the surface of the slant.

The interpretation of the test results is as follows: (1) If lactose (or sucrose) is fermented, a large amount of acid is produced, which turns the phenol red indicator yellow both in the butt and on the slant. Some organisms generate gases, which produce bubbles in the butt. (2) If lactose is not fermented but the small amount of glucose is, the oxygen-deficient butt will be yellow, but on the slant the acid will be oxidized to CO$_2$ and H$_2$O by the organism and the slant will be red (neutral or alkaline). (3) If neither lactose nor glucose is fermented, both the butt and the slant will be red. The slant can become a deeper red-purple (more alkaline) as a result of the production of ammonia from the oxidative deamination of amino acids. (4) If H$_2$S is produced, the black color of ferrous sulfide is seen.

The reactions of some of the important organisms are presented in Table 18–7. Because several organisms can give the same reaction, TSI agar is only a screening device.

Urea Agar

The important components of this medium are urea and the pH indicator phenol red. If the organism produces urease, the urea is hydrolyzed to NH$_3$ and CO$_2$. Ammonia turns the medium alkaline, and the color of the phenol red changes from light orange to reddish purple. The important organisms that are urease-positive are *Proteus* species and *Klebsiella pneumoniae*.

with certain diseases; eg, O55 and O111 cause outbreaks of neonatal diarrhea.

Pathogenesis

The reservoir of *E. coli* includes both humans and animals. The source of the *E. coli* that causes urinary tract infections is the patient's own colonic flora that colonizes the urogenital area. The source of the *E. coli* that causes neonatal meningitis is the mother's birth canal; the infection is acquired during birth. In contrast, the *E. coli* that causes traveler's diarrhea is acquired by ingestion of food or water contaminated with human feces. Note that the main reservoir of enterohemorrhagic *E. coli* O157 is cattle and the organism is acquired in undercooked meat.

E. coli has several clearly identified components that contribute to its ability to cause disease: pili, a capsule, endotoxin, and three exotoxins (enterotoxins), two that cause watery diarrhea and one that causes bloody diarrhea and hemolytic-uremic syndrome.

A. INTESTINAL TRACT INFECTION

The first step is the adherence of the organism to the cells of the jejunum and ileum by means of **pili** that protrude from the bacterial surface. Once attached, the bacteria synthesize **enterotoxins** (exotoxins that act in the enteric tract), which act on the cells of the jejunum and ileum to cause diarrhea. The toxins are strikingly cell-specific; the cells of the colon are not susceptible, probably because they lack receptors for the toxin. Enterotoxigenic strains of *E. coli* can produce either or both of two enterotoxins.

(1) The high-molecular-weight, heat-labile toxin (LT) acts by stimulating **adenylate cyclase.** Both LT and cholera toxin act by catalyzing the addition of adenosine diphosphate-ribose (a process called ADP-ribosylation) to the G protein that stimulates the cyclase. The resultant increase in intracellular cyclic adenosine monophosphate (AMP) concentration stimulates cyclic AMP–dependent protein kinase, which phosphorylates ion transporters in the membrane. The transporters export ions, which causes an outpouring of fluid, potassium, and chloride from the enterocytes into the lumen of the gut, resulting in watery diarrhea. Note that cholera toxin has the same mode of action.

(2) The other enterotoxin is a low-molecular-weight, heat-stable toxin (ST), which stimulates guanylate cyclase.

The enterotoxin-producing strains **do not cause inflammation,** do not invade the intestinal mucosa, and cause a watery, nonbloody diarrhea. However, certain strains of *E. coli* are enteropathic (enteroinvasive) and cause disease not by enterotoxin formation but by invasion of the epithelium of the large intestine, causing bloody diarrhea (dysentery) accompanied by inflammatory cells (neutrophils) in the stool.

Certain enterohemorrhagic strains of *E. coli,* ie, those with the O157:H7 serotype, also cause bloody diarrhea by producing an exotoxin called **verotoxin,** so called because it is toxic to Vero (monkey) cells in culture and presumably to the cells lining the colon. These toxins are also called **Shiga-like toxins** because they are very similar to those produced by *Shigella* species. Verotoxin acts by removing an adenine from the large (28S) ribosomal RNA, thereby stopping protein synthesis.

These O157:H7 strains are associated with outbreaks of bloody diarrhea following ingestion of undercooked hamburger, often at fast-food restaurants. The bacteria on the surface of the hamburger are killed by the cooking but those in the interior, which is undercooked, survive. Also, direct contact with animals, eg, visits to farms and petting zoos, have resulted in bloody diarrhea caused by O157:H7 strains.

Some patients with bloody diarrhea caused by O157:H7 strains also have a life-threatening complication called **hemolytic-uremic syndrome,** which occurs when verotoxin enters the bloodstream. This syndrome consists of hemolytic anemia, thrombocytopenia, and acute renal failure.

The hemolytic anemia and renal failure occur because there are receptors for verotoxin on the surface of the endothelium of small blood vessels and on the surface of kidney epithelium. Death of the endothelial cells of small blood vessels results in a microangiopathic hemolytic anemia in which the red cells passing through the damaged area become grossly distorted (schistocytes) and then lyse. Thrombocytopenia occurs because platelets adhere to the damaged endothelial surface. Death of the kidney epithelial cells leads to renal failure. Treatment of diarrhea caused by O157:H7 strains with antibiotics, such as ciprofloxacin, increases the risk of developing hemolytic-uremic syndrome by increasing the amount of verotoxin produced by the organism.

B. SYSTEMIC INFECTION

The other two structural components, the **capsule** and the **endotoxin,** play a more prominent role in the pathogenesis of systemic, rather than intestinal tract, disease. The capsular polysaccharide interferes with phagocytosis, thereby enhancing the organism's ability to cause infections in various organs. For example, *E. coli* strains that cause neonatal meningitis usually have a specific capsular type called the K1 antigen. The endotoxin of *E. coli* is the cell wall lipopolysaccharide, which causes several features of gram-negative sepsis such as fever, hypotension, and disseminated intravascular coagulation.

C. URINARY TRACT INFECTIONS

Certain O serotypes of *E. coli* preferentially cause urinary tract infections. These **uropathic** strains are characterized by pili with adhesin proteins that bind to specific receptors on the urinary tract epithelium. The binding site on these receptors consists of dimers of galactose (**Gal-Gal dimers**). The motility of *E. coli* may aid its ability to ascend the urethra into the bladder and ascend the ureter into the kidney.

Clinical Findings

E. coli causes a variety of diseases both within and outside the intestinal tract. It is the leading cause of community-acquired **urinary tract infections.** These occur primarily in women; this finding is attributed to three features that facilitate ascending infection into the bladder, namely, a short urethra, the proximity of the urethra to the anus, and colonization of the vagina by members of the fecal flora. It is also the most frequent cause of nosocomial (hospital-acquired) urinary tract infections, which occur equally frequently in both men and women and are associated with the use of indwelling urinary catheters. Urinary tract infections can be limited to the bladder or extend up the collecting system to the kidneys. If only the bladder is involved, the disease is called cystitis, whereas infection of the kidney is called pyelonephritis. The most prominent symptoms of cystitis are pain (dysuria) and frequency of urination; pyelonephritis is characterized by fever, chills, and flank pain.

E. coli is also a major cause, along with the group B streptococci, of **meningitis** and sepsis in neonates. Exposure of the newborn to *E. coli* and group B streptococci occurs during birth as a result of colonization of the vagina by these organisms in approximately 25% of pregnant women. *E. coli* is the organism isolated most frequently from patients with hospital-acquired sepsis, which arises primarily from urinary, biliary, or peritoneal infections. Peritonitis is usually a mixed infection caused by *E. coli* or other facultative enteric gram-negative rod plus anaerobic members of the colonic flora such as *Bacteroides* and *Fusobacterium*.

Diarrhea caused by **enterotoxigenic *E. coli*** is usually **watery,** nonbloody, self-limited, and of short duration (1–3 days). It is frequently associated with travel (traveler's diarrhea, or "turista").[2]

Infection with enterohemorrhagic *E. coli* (EHEC), on the other hand, results in a dysenterylike syndrome

characterized by **bloody diarrhea,** abdominal cramping, and fever similar to that caused by *Shigella*. The O157:H7 strains of *E. coli* also cause bloody diarrhea, which can be complicated by **hemolytic-uremic syndrome.** This syndrome is characterized by kidney failure, hemolytic anemia, and thrombocytopenia. It occurs particularly in children who have been treated with fluoroquinolones or other antibiotics for their diarrhea. For this reason, antibiotics should not be used to treat diarrhea caused by EHEC.

Laboratory Diagnosis

Specimens suspected of containing enteric gram-negative rods, such as *E. coli,* are grown initially on a blood agar plate and on a differential medium, such as EMB agar or MacConkey's agar. *E. coli,* which ferments lactose, forms pink colonies, whereas lactose-negative organisms are colorless. On EMB agar, *E. coli* colonies have a characteristic **green sheen.** Some of the important features that help distinguish *E. coli* from other lactose-fermenting gram-negative rods are as follows: (1) it produces indole from tryptophan, (2) it decarboxylates lysine, (3) it uses acetate as its only source of carbon, and (4) it is motile. *E. coli* O157:H7 does not ferment sorbitol, which serves as an important criterion that distinguishes it from other strains of *E. coli*. The isolation of enterotoxigenic or enteropathogenic *E. coli* from patients with diarrhea is not a routine diagnostic procedure.

Treatment

Treatment of *E. coli* infections depends on the site of disease and the resistance pattern of the specific isolate. For example, an uncomplicated lower urinary tract infection can be treated for just 1–3 days with oral trimethoprim-sulfamethoxazole or an oral penicillin, eg, ampicillin. However, *E. coli* sepsis requires treatment with parenteral antibiotics (eg, a third-generation cephalosporin, such as cefotaxime, with or without an aminoglycoside, such as gentamicin). For the treatment of neonatal meningitis, a combination of ampicillin and cefotaxime is usually given. Antibiotic therapy is usually *not* indicated in *E. coli* diarrheal diseases. However, administration of trimethoprim-sulfamethoxazole or loperamide (Imodium) may shorten the duration of symptoms. Rehydration is typically all that is necessary in this self-limited disease.

Prevention

There is no specific prevention for *E. coli* infections, such as active or passive immunization. However, various general measures can be taken to prevent certain in-

---

[2] Enterotoxigenic *E. coli* is the most common cause of traveler's diarrhea, but other bacteria (eg, *Salmonella*, *Shigella*, *Campylobacter*, and *Vibrio* species), viruses such as Norwalk virus, and protozoa such as *Giardia* and *Cryptosporidium* species are also involved.

fections caused by *E. coli* and other organisms. For example, the incidence of urinary tract infections can be lowered by the judicious use and prompt withdrawal of catheters and, in recurrent infections, by prolonged prophylaxis with urinary antiseptic drugs, eg, nitrofurantoin or trimethoprim-sulfamethoxazole. The use of cranberry juice to prevent recurrent urinary tract infections appears to be based on the ability of tannins in the juice to inhibit the binding of the pili of the uropathic strains of *E. coli* to the bladder epithelium rather than to acidification of the urine, which was the previous explanation. Some cases of sepsis can be prevented by prompt removal of or switching the site of intravenous lines. Traveler's diarrhea can sometimes be prevented by the prophylactic use of doxycycline, ciprofloxacin, trimethoprim-sulfamethoxazole, or Pepto-Bismol. Ingestion of uncooked foods and unpurified water should be avoided while traveling in certain countries.

SALMONELLA

Diseases

Salmonella species cause enterocolitis, enteric fevers such as typhoid fever, and septicemia with metastatic infections such as osteomyelitis. They are one of the most common causes of bacterial enterocolitis in the United States.

Important Properties

Salmonellae are gram-negative rods that **do not ferment lactose** but do produce H_2S—features that are used in their laboratory identification. Their antigens—cell wall O, flagellar H, and capsular Vi (virulence)—are important for taxonomic and epidemiologic purposes. The O antigens, which are the outer polysaccharides of the cell wall, are used to subdivide the salmonellae into groups A–I. There are two forms of the H antigens, phases 1 and 2. Only one of the two H proteins is synthesized at any one time, depending on which gene sequence is in the correct alignment for transcription into mRNA. The Vi antigens (capsular polysaccharides) are antiphagocytic and are an important virulence factor for *S. typhi,* the agent of typhoid fever. The Vi antigens are also used for the serotyping of *S. typhi* in the clinical laboratory.

There are three methods for naming the salmonellae. Ewing divides the genus into three species: *S. typhi, Salmonella choleraesuis,* and *Salmonella enteritidis.* In this scheme there is 1 serotype in each of the first two species and 1500 serotypes in the third. Kaufman and White assign different species names to each serotype; there are roughly 1500 different species, usually named for the city in which they were isolated. *Salmonella dublin* according to Kaufman and White would be *S. enteritidis* serotype *dublin* according to Ewing. The third approach to naming the salmonellae is based on relatedness determined by DNA hybridization analysis. In this scheme, *S. typhi* is not a distinct species but is classified as *Salmonella enterica* serotype (or serovar) *typhi.* All three of these naming systems are in current use.

Clinically, the *Salmonella* species are often thought of in two distinct categories, namely, the typhoidal species, ie, those that cause typhoid fever and the non-typhoidal species, ie, those that cause diarrhea (enterocolitis) and metastatic infections, such as osteomyelitis. The typhoidal species are *S. typhi* and *S. paratyphi.* The non-typhoidal species are the many strains of *S. enteritidis. S. choleraesuis* is the species most often involved in metastatic infections.

Pathogenesis & Epidemiology

The three types of *Salmonella* infections (enterocolitis, enteric fevers, and septicemia) have different pathogenic features.

(1) **Enterocolitis** is characterized by an invasion of the epithelial and subepithelial tissue of the small and large intestines. Strains that do not invade do not cause disease. The organisms penetrate both through and between the mucosal cells into the lamina propria, with resulting inflammation and diarrhea. A polymorphonuclear leukocyte response limits the infection to the gut and the adjacent mesenteric lymph nodes; bacteremia is infrequent in enterocolitis. In contrast to *Shigella* enterocolitis, in which the infectious dose is very small (on the order of 10 organisms), the dose of *Salmonella* required is much higher, at least 100,000 organisms. Various properties of salmonellae and shigellae are compared in Table 18–8. Gastric acid is an important host defense; gastrectomy or use of antacids lowers the infectious dose significantly.

(2) In **typhoid** and other enteric fevers, infection begins in the small intestine but few gastrointestinal symptoms occur. The organisms enter, multiply in the mononuclear phagocytes of Peyer's patches, and then spread to the phagocytes of the liver, gallbladder, and spleen. This leads to bacteremia, which is associated with the onset of fever and other symptoms, probably caused by endotoxin. Survival and growth of the organism within phagosomes in phagocytic cells are a striking feature of this disease, as is the predilection for invasion of the gallbladder, which can result in establishment of the **carrier state** and excretion of the bacteria in the feces for long periods.

(3) **Septicemia** accounts for only about 5–10% of *Salmonella* infections and occurs in one of two settings: a patient with an underlying chronic disease such as **sickle cell anemia** or cancer or a child with enterocolitis. The septic course is more indolent than that seen with many other gram-negative rods. Bacteremia results in the seeding of many organs, with **osteomyelitis**, pneu-

Table 18–8. Comparison of important features of *Salmonella* and *Shigella*.

Feature	*Shigella*	*Salmonella* except *S. typhi*	*Salmonella typhi*
Reservoir	Humans	Animals, especially poultry and eggs	Humans
Infectious dose (ID$_{50}$)	Low[1]	High	High
Diarrhea as a prominent feature	Yes	Yes	No
Invasion of bloodstream	No	Yes	Yes
Chronic carrier state	No	Infrequent	Yes
Lactose fermentation	No	No	No
H$_2$S production	No	Yes	Yes
Vaccine available	No	No	Yes

[1]An organism with a low ID$_{50}$ requires very few bacteria to cause disease.

monia, and meningitis as the most common sequelae. **Osteomyelitis in a child with sickle cell anemia** is an important example of this type of salmonella infection. Previously damaged tissues, such as infarcts and **aneurysms,** especially aortic aneurysms, are the most frequent sites of metastatic abscesses. *Salmonella* are also an important cause of vascular graft infections.

The epidemiology of *Salmonella* infections is related to the ingestion of food and water contaminated by human and animal wastes. *S. typhi,* the cause of typhoid fever, is **transmitted only by humans,** but all other species have a significant animal as well as human reservoir. Human sources are either persons who temporarily excrete the organism during or shortly after an attack of enterocolitis or chronic carriers who excrete the organism for years. The most frequent **animal source is poultry and eggs,** but meat products that are inadequately cooked have been implicated as well. Dogs and other pets, including turtles, snakes, lizards, and iguanas, are additional sources.

Clinical Findings

After an incubation period of 12–48 hours, enterocolitis begins with nausea and vomiting and then progresses to abdominal pain and diarrhea, which can vary from mild to severe, with or without blood. Usually the disease lasts a few days, is self-limited, causes nonbloody diarrhea, and does not require medical care except in the very young and very old. HIV-infected individuals, especially those with a low CD4 count, have a

much greater number of *Salmonella* infections, including more severe diarrhea and more serious metastatic infections than those who are not infected with HIV. *Salmonella typhimurium* is the most common species of *Salmonella* to cause enterocolitis in the United States, but almost every species has been involved.

In typhoid fever, caused by *S. typhi,* and in enteric fever, caused by organisms such as *S. paratyphi* A, B, and C (*S. paratyphi* B and C are also known as *Salmonella schottmuelleri* and *Salmonella hirschfeldii,* respectively), the onset of illness is slow, with fever and constipation rather than vomiting and diarrhea predominating. Diarrhea may occur early but usually disappears by the time the fever and bacteremia occur. After the first week, as the bacteremia becomes sustained, high fever, delirium, tender abdomen, and enlarged spleen occur. **Rose spots,** ie, rose-colored macules on the abdomen, are associated with typhoid fever but occur only rarely. Leukopenia and anemia are often seen. Liver function tests are often abnormal, indicating hepatic involvement.

The disease begins to resolve by the third week, but severe complications such as intestinal hemorrhage or perforation can occur. About 3% of typhoid fever patients become chronic carriers. The carrier rate is higher among women, especially those with previous gallbladder disease and gallstones.

Septicemia is most often caused by *S. choleraesuis.* The symptoms begin with fever but little or no enterocolitis and then proceed to focal symptoms associated with the affected organ, frequently bone, lung, or meninges.

Laboratory Diagnosis

In enterocolitis, the organism is most easily isolated from a stool sample. However, in the enteric fevers, a blood culture is the procedure most likely to reveal the organism during the first 2 weeks of illness. Bone marrow cultures are often positive. Stool cultures may also be positive, especially in chronic carriers in whom the organism is secreted in the bile into the intestinal tract.

Salmonellae form non-lactose-fermenting (colorless) colonies on MacConkey's or EMB agar. On TSI agar, an alkaline slant and an acid butt, frequently with both gas and H_2S (black color in the butt), are produced. *S. typhi* is the major exception; it does not form gas and produces only a small amount of H_2S. If the organism is urease-negative (*Proteus* organisms, which can produce a similar reaction on TSI agar, are urease-positive), the *Salmonella* isolate can be identified and grouped by the slide agglutination test into serogroup A, B, C, D, or E based on its O antigen. Definitive serotyping of the O, H, and Vi antigens is performed by special public health laboratories for epidemiologic purposes.

Salmonellosis is a notifiable disease, and an investigation to determine its source should be undertaken. In certain cases of enteric fever and sepsis, when the organism is difficult to recover, the diagnosis can be made serologically by detecting a rise in antibody titer in the patient's serum (Widal test).

Treatment

Enterocolitis caused by *Salmonella* is usually a self-limited disease that resolves without treatment. Fluid and electrolyte replacement may be required. Antibiotic treatment does not shorten the illness or reduce the symptoms; in fact, it may prolong excretion of the organisms, increase the frequency of the carrier state, and select mutants resistant to the antibiotic. Antimicrobial agents are indicated only for neonates or persons with chronic diseases who are at risk for septicemia and disseminated abscesses. Plasmid-mediated antibiotic resistance is common, and antibiotic sensitivity tests should be done. Drugs that retard intestinal motility (ie, that reduce diarrhea) appear to prolong the duration of symptoms and the fecal excretion of the organisms.

The treatment of choice for enteric fevers such as typhoid fever and septicemia with metastatic infection is either ceftriaxone or ciprofloxacin. Ampicillin or ciprofloxacin should be used in patients who are chronic carriers of *S. typhi*. Cholecystectomy may be necessary to abolish the chronic carrier state. Focal abscesses should be drained surgically when feasible.

Prevention

Salmonella infections are prevented mainly by public health and personal hygiene measures. Proper sewage treatment, a chlorinated water supply that is monitored for contamination by coliform bacteria, cultures of stool samples from food handlers to detect carriers, hand washing prior to food handling, pasteurization of milk, and proper cooking of poultry, eggs, and meat are all important.

Two vaccines are available, but they confer limited (50–80%) protection against *S. typhi*. One contains the Vi capsular polysaccharide of *S. typhi* (given intramuscularly) and the other contains a live, attenuated strain of *S. typhi* (given orally). The two vaccines are equally effective. The vaccine is recommended for those who will travel or reside in high-risk areas and for those whose occupation brings them in contact with the organism. A new conjugate vaccine against typhoid fever containing the capsular polysaccharide (Vi) antigen coupled to a carrier protein is safe and immunogenic in young children but is not available in the United States at this time.

■ PATHOGENS PRIMARILY WITHIN THE ENTERIC TRACT

SHIGELLA

Disease

Shigella species cause enterocolitis. Enterocolitis caused by *Shigella* is often called bacillary dysentery. The term "dysentery" refers to bloody diarrhea.

Important Properties

Shigellae are **non-lactose-fermenting**, gram-negative rods that can be distinguished from salmonellae by three criteria: they produce no gas from the fermentation of glucose, they **do not produce** H_2S, and they are **nonmotile**. All shigellae have O antigens (polysaccharide) in their cell walls, and these antigens are used to divide the genus into four groups: A, B, C, and D.

Pathogenesis & Epidemiology

Shigellae are the most effective pathogens among the enteric bacteria. They have a **very low** ID_{50}. Ingestion of as few as 100 organisms causes disease, whereas at least 10^5 *V. cholerae* or *Salmonella* organisms are required to produce symptoms. Various properties of shigellae and salmonellae are compared in Table 18–8.

Shigellosis is only a **human disease**, ie, there is no animal reservoir. The organism is transmitted by the fecal-oral route. The four F's—fingers, flies, food, and feces—are the principal factors in transmission. Food-borne outbreaks outnumber water-borne outbreaks by 2 to 1. Outbreaks occur in day-care nurseries and in mental hospitals, where **fecal-oral** transmission is likely to occur. Children younger than 10 years of age account for approximately half of *Shigella*-positive stool cultures. There is no prolonged carrier state with *Shigella* infections, unlike that seen with *S. typhi* infections.

Shigellae, which cause disease almost exclusively in the gastrointestinal tract, produce bloody diarrhea (dysentery) by invading the cells of the mucosa of the distal ileum and colon. Local inflammation accompanied by ulceration occurs, but the organisms rarely penetrate through the wall or enter the bloodstream, unlike salmonellae. Although some strains produce an enterotoxin (called Shiga toxin), invasion is the critical factor in pathogenesis. The evidence for this is that mutants that fail to produce enterotoxin but are invasive can still cause disease, whereas noninvasive mutants are nonpathogenic.

Clinical Findings

After an incubation period of 1–4 days, symptoms begin with fever and abdominal cramps, followed by diarrhea, which may be watery at first but later contains blood and mucus. The disease varies from mild to severe depending on two major factors: the species of *Shigella* and the age of the patient, with young children and elderly people being the most severely affected. *Shigella dysenteriae*, which causes the most severe disease, is usually seen in the United States only in travelers returning from abroad. *Shigella sonnei*, which causes mild disease, is isolated from approximately 75% of all individuals with shigellosis in the United States. The diarrhea frequently resolves in 2 or 3 days; in severe cases, antibiotics can shorten the course. Serum agglutinins appear after recovery but are not protective because the organism does not enter the blood. The role of intestinal IgA in protection is uncertain.

Laboratory Diagnosis

Shigellae form non-lactose-fermenting (colorless) colonies on MacConkey's or EMB agar. On TSI agar, they cause an alkaline slant and an acid butt, with no gas and no H_2S. Confirmation of the organism as *Shigella* and determination of its group are done by slide agglutination.

One important adjunct to laboratory diagnosis is a methylene blue stain of a fecal sample to determine whether neutrophils are present. If they are found, an invasive organism such as *Shigella, Salmonella,* or *Campylobacter* is involved rather than a toxin-producing organism such as *V. cholerae, E. coli,* or *Clostridium perfringens.* (Certain viruses and the parasite *Entamoeba histolytica* can also cause diarrhea without PMNs in the stool.)

Treatment

The main treatment for shigellosis is fluid and electrolyte replacement. In mild cases, no antibiotics are indicated. In severe cases, a fluoroquinolone (eg, ciprofloxacin) is the drug of choice, but the incidence of plasmids conveying multiple drug resistance is high enough that antibiotic sensitivity tests must be performed. Trimethoprim-sulfamethoxazole is an alternative choice. Antiperistaltic drugs are contraindicated in shigellosis, because they prolong the fever, diarrhea, and excretion of the organism.

Prevention

Prevention of shigellosis is dependent on interruption of fecal-oral transmission by proper sewage disposal, chlorination of water, and personal hygiene (hand washing by food handlers). There is no vaccine, and prophylactic antibiotics are not recommended.

VIBRIO

Diseases

Vibrio cholerae, the major pathogen in this genus, is the cause of cholera. *Vibrio parahaemolyticus* causes diarrhea associated with eating raw or improperly cooked seafood. *Vibrio vulnificus* causes cellulitis and sepsis. Important features of pathogenesis by *V. cholerae, C. jejuni,* and *Helicobacter pylori* are described in Table 18–9.

Important Properties

Vibrios are curved, **comma-shaped** gram-negative rods. *V. cholerae* is divided into two groups according to the nature of its O cell wall antigen. Members of the O1 group cause epidemic disease, whereas non-O1 organisms either cause sporadic disease or are nonpathogens. The O1 organisms have two biotypes, called El Tor and cholerae, and three serotypes, called Ogawa, Inaba, and Hikojima. (Biotypes are based on differences in biochemical reactions, whereas serotypes are based on antigenic differences.) These features are used to characterize isolates in epidemiologic investigations.

V. parahaemolyticus and *V. vulnificus* are **marine organisms;** they live primarily in the ocean, especially in warm saltwater. They are **halophilic;** ie, they require a high NaCl concentration to grow.

1. Vibrio cholerae

Pathogenesis & Epidemiology

V. cholerae is transmitted by **fecal contamination** of water and food, primarily from human sources. Human

Table 18–9. Important features of pathogenesis by curved gram-negative rods affecting the gastrointestinal tract.

Organism	Type of Pathogenesis	Typical Disease	Site of Infection	Main Approach to Therapy
Vibrio cholerae	Toxigenic	Watery diarrhea	Small intestine	Fluid replacement
Campylobacter jejuni	Inflammatory	Bloody diarrhea	Colon	Antibiotics[1]
Helicobacter pylori	Inflammatory	Gastritis; peptic ulcer	Stomach; duodenum	Antibiotics[1]

[1]See text for specific antibiotics.

carriers are frequently asymptomatic and include individuals who are either in the incubation period or convalescing. The main animal reservoirs are marine shellfish, such as shrimp and oysters. Ingestion of these without adequate cooking can transmit the disease.

A major epidemic of cholera, which spanned the 1960s and 1970s, began in Southeast Asia and spread over three continents to areas of Africa, Europe, and the rest of Asia. A pandemic of cholera began in Peru in 1991 and has spread to many countries in Central and South America. The organism isolated most frequently was the El Tor biotype of O1 *V. cholerae,* usually of the Ogawa serotype. The factors that predispose to epidemics are poor sanitation, malnutrition, overcrowding, and inadequate medical services. Quarantine measures failed to prevent the spread of the disease because there were many asymptomatic carriers.

The pathogenesis of cholera is dependent on colonization of the small intestine by the organism and secretion of enterotoxin. For colonization to occur, large numbers of bacteria (approximately 1 billion) must be ingested because the organism is particularly sensitive to stomach acid. Persons with little or no stomach acid, such as those taking antacids or those who have had gastrectomy, are much more susceptible. Adherence to the cells of the brush border of the gut, which is a requirement for colonization, is related to secretion of the bacterial enzyme mucinase, which dissolves the protective glycoprotein coating over the intestinal cells.

After adhering, the organism multiplies and secretes an **enterotoxin** called choleragen. This exotoxin can reproduce the symptoms of cholera even in the absence of the *Vibrio* organisms. Choleragen consists of an A (active) subunit and a B (binding) subunit. The B subunit, which is a pentamer composed of five identical proteins, binds to a ganglioside receptor on the surface of the enterocyte. The A subunit is inserted into the cytosol, where it catalyzes the addition of ADP-ribose to the G_s protein (G_s is the stimulatory G protein). This locks the G_s protein in the "on" position, which causes

the persistent stimulation of **adenylate cyclase.** The resulting overproduction of cyclic AMP activates cyclic AMP–dependent protein kinase, an enzyme that phosphorylates ion transporters in the cell membrane, resulting in the loss of water and ions from the cell. The watery efflux enters the lumen of the gut, resulting in a massive watery diarrhea without inflammatory cells. Morbidity and death are due to **dehydration** and **electrolyte imbalance.** However, if treatment is instituted promptly, the disease runs a self-limited course in up to 7 days.

The genes for cholera toxin and other virulence factors are carried on a single-stranded DNA bacteriophage called CTX. Lysogenic conversion of non-toxin-producing strains to toxin-producing ones can occur when the CTX phage transduces these genes. The pili that attach the organism to the gut mucosa are the receptors for the phage.

Non-O1 *V. cholerae* is an occasional cause of diarrhea associated with eating shellfish obtained from the coastal waters of the United States.

Clinical Findings

Watery diarrhea in large volumes is the hallmark of cholera. There are no red blood cells or white blood cells in the stool. **Rice-water stool** is the term often applied to the nonbloody effluent. There is no abdominal pain, and subsequent symptoms are referable to the marked dehydration. The loss of fluid and electrolytes leads to cardiac and renal failure. Acidosis and hypokalemia also occur as a result of loss of bicarbonate and potassium in the stool. The mortality rate without treatment is 40%.

Laboratory Diagnosis

The approach to laboratory diagnosis depends on the situation. During an epidemic, a clinical judgment is made and there is little need for the laboratory. In an area where the disease is endemic or for the detection of carriers, a variety of selective media[3] that are not in common use in the United States are used in the laboratory.

For diagnosis of sporadic cases in this country, a culture of the diarrhea stool containing *V. cholerae* will show colorless colonies on MacConkey's agar because lactose is fermented slowly. The organism is oxidase-positive, which distinguishes it from members of the Enterobacteriaceae. On TSI agar, an acid slant and an acid butt without gas or H_2S are seen because the organism ferments sucrose. A presumptive diagnosis of *V. cholerae* can be confirmed by agglutination of the organism by polyvalent O1 or non-O1 antiserum. A retrospective diagnosis can be made serologically by detecting a rise in antibody titer in acute- and convalescent-phase sera.

Treatment

Treatment consists of prompt, adequate replacement of water and electrolytes, either orally or intravenously. Antibiotics such as tetracycline are not necessary, but they do shorten the duration of symptoms and reduce the time of excretion of the organisms.

Prevention

Prevention is achieved mainly by public health measures that ensure a clean water and food supply. The vaccine, composed of killed organisms, has limited usefulness; it is only 50% effective in preventing disease for 3–6 months and does not interrupt transmission. A live vaccine is available in certain countries but not in the United States. Neither the killed nor the live vaccine is recommended for routine use in travelers. The use of tetracycline for prevention is effective in close contacts but cannot prevent the spread of a major epidemic. Prompt detection of carriers is important in limiting outbreaks.

2. Vibrio parahaemolyticus

V. parahaemolyticus is a marine organism transmitted by **ingestion of raw or undercooked seafood**, especially shellfish such as oysters. It is a major cause of diarrhea in Japan, where raw fish is eaten in large quantities, but is an infrequent pathogen in the United States, although several outbreaks have occurred aboard cruise ships in the Caribbean. Little is known about its pathogenesis, except that an enterotoxin similar to choleragen is secreted and limited invasion sometimes occurs.

The clinical picture caused by *V. parahaemolyticus* varies from mild to quite severe watery diarrhea, nausea

and vomiting, abdominal cramps, and fever. The illness is self-limited, lasting about 3 days. *V. parahaemolyticus* is distinguished from *V. cholerae* mainly on the basis of growth in NaCl: *V. parahaemolyticus* grows in 8% NaCl solution (as befits a marine organism), whereas *V. cholerae* does not. No specific treatment is indicated, because the disease is relatively mild and self-limited. Disease can be prevented by proper refrigeration and cooking of seafood.

3. Vibrio vulnificus

V. vulnificus is also a marine organism; ie, it is found in warm salt waters such as the Caribbean sea. It causes severe skin and soft tissue infections (**cellulitis**), **especially in shellfish handlers**, who often sustain skin wounds. It can also cause a rapidly fatal **septicemia in immunocompromised people who have eaten raw shellfish** containing the organism. Hemorrhagic bullae in the skin often occur in patients with sepsis caused by *V. vulnificus*. Chronic liver disease, eg, cirrhosis, predisposes to severe infections. The recommended treatment is doxycycline.

CAMPYLOBACTER

Diseases

Campylobacter jejuni is a frequent cause of enterocolitis, especially in children. Other *Campylobacter* species are rare causes of systemic infection, particularly bacteremia.

Important Properties

Campylobacters are curved, gram-negative rods that appear either **comma-** or **S-shaped**. They are **microaerophilic**, growing best in 5% oxygen rather than in the 20% present in the atmosphere. *C. jejuni* grows well at 42°C, whereas *Campylobacter intestinalis*[4] does not—an observation that is useful in microbiologic diagnosis.

Pathogenesis & Epidemiology

Domestic animals such as cattle, chickens, and dogs serve as a source of the organisms for humans. Transmission is usually **fecal-oral**. Food and water contaminated with animal feces is the major source of human infection. Foods, such as poultry, meat, and unpasteurized milk, are commonly involved. Puppies with diarrhea are a common source for children. Human-to-

---

[3] Media such as thiosulfate-citrate-bile salts agar or tellurite-taurocholate-gelatin are used.

[4] Also known as *Campylobacter fetus* subsp. *fetus*.

human transmission occurs but is less frequent than animal-to-human transmission. *C. jejuni* is a major cause of diarrhea in the United States; it was recovered in 4.6% of patients with diarrhea, compared with 2.3% and 1% for *Salmonella* and *Shigella,* respectively.

The pathogenesis of both the enterocolitis and the systemic diseases is unclear. The presence of watery diarrhea suggests an enterotoxin-mediated syndrome. An enterotoxin that acts in the same manner as cholera toxin is produced by some strains. Invasion often occurs, accompanied by blood in stools. Systemic infections, eg, bacteremia, occur most often in neonates or debilitated adults.

Clinical Findings

Enterocolitis, caused primarily by *C. jejuni,* begins as watery, foul-smelling diarrhea followed by bloody stools accompanied by fever and severe abdominal pain. Systemic infections, most commonly bacteremia, are caused by *C. intestinalis.* The symptoms of bacteremia, eg, fever and malaise, are associated with no specific physical findings.

Gastrointestinal infection with *C. jejuni* is associated with Guillain-Barré syndrome, the most common cause of acute neuromuscular paralysis. Guillain-Barré syndrome is an autoimmune disease attributed to the formation of antibodies against *C. jejuni* that cross-react with antigens on neurons (see Chapter 66). Infection with *Campylobacter* is also associated with two other autoimmune diseases: reactive arthritis and Reiter's syndrome. These are also described in Chapter 66.

Laboratory Diagnosis

If the patient has diarrhea, a stool specimen is cultured on a blood agar plate containing antibiotics[5] that inhibit most other fecal flora.

The plate is incubated at 42°C in a microaerophilic atmosphere containing 5% oxygen and 10% carbon dioxide, which favors the growth of *C. jejuni.* It is identified by failure to grow at 25°C, oxidase positivity, and sensitivity to nalidixic acid. Unlike *Shigella* and *Salmonella,* lactose fermentation is not used as a distinguishing feature. If bacteremia is suspected, a blood culture incubated under standard temperature and atmospheric conditions will reveal the growth of the characteristically comma- or S-shaped, motile, gram-negative rods. Identification of the organism as *C. intestinalis* is confirmed by its failure to grow at 42°C, its ability to grow at 25°C, and its resistance to nalidixic acid.

Treatment

Erythromycin or ciprofloxacin is used successfully in *C. jejuni* enterocolitis. The treatment of choice for *C. intestinalis* bacteremia is an aminoglycoside.

Prevention

There is no vaccine or other specific preventive measure. Proper sewage disposal and personal hygiene (hand washing) are important.

HELICOBACTER

Diseases

Helicobacter pylori causes gastritis and peptic ulcers. Infection with *H. pylori* is a risk factor for gastric carcinoma and is linked to mucosal-associated lymphoid tissue (MALT) lymphomas.

Important Properties

Helicobacters are curved gram-negative rods similar in appearance to campylobacters, but because they differ sufficiently in certain biochemical and flagellar characteristics, they are classified as a separate genus. In particular, helicobacters are strongly urease-positive, whereas campylobacters are urease-negative.

Pathogenesis & Epidemiology

H. pylori attaches to the mucus-secreting cells of the gastric mucosa. The production of large amounts of ammonia from urea by the organism's urease, coupled with an inflammatory response, leads to damage to the mucosa. Loss of the protective mucus coating predisposes to gastritis and peptic ulcer. The ammonia also neutralizes stomach acid, allowing the organism to survive. Epidemiologically, most patients with these diseases show *H. pylori* in biopsy specimens of the gastric epithelium.

The natural habitat of *H. pylori* is the human stomach, and it is probably acquired by ingestion. However, it has not been isolated from stool, food, water, or animals. Person-to-person transmission probably occurs, because there is clustering of infection within families. The rate of infection with *H. pylori* in developing countries is very high, a finding that is in accord with the high rate of gastric carcinoma in those countries.

Clinical Findings

Gastritis and peptic ulcer are characterized by recurrent pain in the upper abdomen, frequently accompanied by bleeding into the gastrointestinal tract. No bacteremia or disseminated disease occurs.

---

[5] For example, Skirrow's medium contains vancomycin, trimethoprim, cephalothin, polymyxin, and amphotericin B.

Laboratory Diagnosis

The organism can be seen on Gram-stained smears of biopsy specimens of the gastric mucosa. It can be cultured on the same media as campylobacters. In contrast to *C. jejuni*, *H. pylori* is urease-positive. Urease production is the basis for a noninvasive diagnostic test called the "urea breath" test. In this test, radiolabeled urea is ingested. If the organism is present, urease will cleave the ingested urea, radiolabeled CO_2 is evolved, and the radioactivity is detected in the breath.

A test for *Helicobacter* antigen in the stool can be used for diagnosis and for confirmation that treatment has eliminated the organism. The presence of IgG antibodies in the patient's serum can also be used as evidence of infection.

Treatment & Prevention

Treatment of duodenal ulcers with antibiotics, eg, amoxicillin and metronidazole, and bismuth salts (Pepto-Bismol) results in a greatly decreased recurrence rate. Tetracycline can be used instead of amoxicillin. There is no vaccine or other specific preventive measure.

■ PATHOGENS OUTSIDE THE ENTERIC TRACT

KLEBSIELLA-ENTEROBACTER-SERRATIA GROUP

Diseases

These organisms are usually opportunistic pathogens that cause nosocomial infections, especially pneumonia and urinary tract infections. *Klebsiella pneumoniae* is an important respiratory tract pathogen outside hospitals as well.

Important Properties

K. pneumoniae, Enterobacter cloacae, and *Serratia marcescens* are the species most often involved in human infections. They are frequently found in the **large intestine** but are also present in soil and water. These organisms have very similar properties and are usually distinguished on the basis of several biochemical reactions and motility. *K. pneumoniae* has a **very large capsule,** which gives its colonies a striking mucoid appearance. *S. marcescens* produces **red-pigmented colonies.**

Pathogenesis & Epidemiology

Of the three organisms, *K. pneumoniae* is most likely to be a primary, nonopportunistic pathogen; this property is related to its antiphagocytic capsule. Although this organism is a primary pathogen, patients with *K. pneumoniae* infections frequently have predisposing conditions such as advanced age, chronic respiratory disease, diabetes, or alcoholism. The organism is carried in the respiratory tract of about 10% of healthy people, who are prone to pneumonia if host defenses are lowered.

Enterobacter and *Serratia* infections are clearly related to hospitalization, especially to invasive procedures such as intravenous catheterization, respiratory intubation, and urinary tract manipulations. In addition, outbreaks of *Serratia* pneumonia have been associated with contamination of the water in respiratory therapy devices. Prior to the extensive use of these procedures, *S. marcescens* was a harmless organism most frequently isolated from environmental sources such as water.

As with many other gram-negative rods, the pathogenesis of septic shock caused by these organisms is related to the endotoxins in their cell walls.

Clinical Findings

Urinary tract infections and pneumonia are the usual clinical entities associated with these three bacteria, but bacteremia and secondary spread to other areas such as the meninges occur. It is difficult to distinguish infections caused by these organisms on clinical grounds, with the exception of pneumonia caused by *Klebsiella,* which produces a thick, bloody sputum ("currant-jelly" sputum) and can progress to necrosis and abscess formation.

There are two other species of *Klebsiella* that cause unusual human infections rarely seen in the United States. *Klebsiella ozaenae* is associated with atrophic rhinitis, and *Klebsiella rhinoscleromatis* causes a destructive granuloma of the nose and pharynx.

Laboratory Diagnosis

Organisms of this group produce lactose-fermenting (colored) colonies on differential agar such as MacConkey's or EMB, although *Serratia,* which is a late lactose fermenter, can produce a negative reaction. These organisms are differentiated by the use of biochemical tests.

Treatment

Because the antibiotic resistance of these organisms can vary greatly, the choice of drug depends on the results of sensitivity testing. Isolates from hospital-acquired infections are frequently resistant to multiple antibiotics.

An aminoglycoside, eg, gentamicin, and a cephalosporin, eg, cefotaxime, are used empirically until the results of testing are known. In severe *Enterobacter* infections, a combination of imipenem and gentamicin is often used.

Prevention

Some hospital-acquired infections caused by gram-negative rods can be prevented by such general measures as changing the site of intravenous catheters, removing urinary catheters when they are no longer needed, and taking proper care of respiratory therapy devices. There is no vaccine.

PROTEUS-PROVIDENCIA-MORGANELLA GROUP

Diseases

These organisms primarily cause urinary tract infections, both community- and hospital-acquired.

Important Properties

These gram-negative rods are distinguished from other members of the Enterobacteriaceae by their ability to produce the enzyme phenylalanine deaminase. In addition, they produce the enzyme **urease**, which cleaves urea to form NH_3 and CO_2. Certain species are very motile and produce a striking **swarming** effect on blood agar, characterized by expanding rings (waves) of organisms over the surface of the agar.

The cell wall O antigens of certain strains of *Proteus*, such as OX-2, OX-19, and OX-K, cross-react with antigens of several species of rickettsiae. These *Proteus* antigens can be used in laboratory tests to detect the presence of antibodies against certain rickettsiae in patients' serum. This test, called the Weil-Felix reaction after its originators, is being used less frequently as more specific procedures are developed.

In the past, there were four medically important species of *Proteus.* However, molecular studies of DNA relatedness showed that two of the four were significantly different. These species have been renamed: *Proteus morganii* is now *Morganella morganii,* and *Proteus rettgeri* is now *Providencia rettgeri.* In the clinical laboratory, these organisms are distinguished from *Proteus vulgaris* and *Proteus mirabilis* on the basis of several biochemical tests.

Pathogenesis & Epidemiology

The organisms are present in the human colon as well as in soil and water. Their tendency to cause urinary tract infections is probably due to their presence in the colon and to colonization of the urethra, especially in women. The vigorous motility of *Proteus* organisms may contribute to their ability to invade the urinary tract.

Production of the enzyme urease is an important feature of the pathogenesis of urinary tract infections by this group. Urease hydrolyzes the urea in urine to form ammonia, which raises the pH and encourages the formation of stones (calculi) called "struvite" composed of magnesium ammonium phosphate. Stones in the urinary tract obstruct urine flow, damage urinary epithelium, and serve as a nidus for recurrent infection by trapping bacteria within the stone. Because alkaline urine also favors growth of the organisms and more extensive renal damage, treatment involves keeping the urine at a low pH.

Clinical Findings

The signs and symptoms of urinary tract infections caused by these organisms cannot be distinguished from those caused by *E. coli* or other members of the Enterobacteriaceae. *Proteus* species can also cause pneumonia, wound infections, and septicemia. *P. mirabilis* is the species of *Proteus* that causes most community- and hospital-acquired infections, but *P. rettgeri* is emerging as an important agent of nosocomial infections.

Laboratory Diagnosis

These organisms usually are highly motile and produce a "swarming" overgrowth on blood agar, which can frustrate efforts to recover pure cultures of other organisms. Growth on blood agar containing phenylethyl alcohol inhibits swarming, thus allowing isolated colonies of *Proteus* and other organisms to be obtained. They produce non-lactose-fermenting (colorless) colonies on MacConkey's or EMB agar. *P. vulgaris* and *P. mirabilis* produce H_2S, which blackens the butt of TSI agar, whereas neither *M. morganii* nor *P. rettgeri* does. *P. mirabilis* is indole-negative, whereas the other three species are indole-positive, a distinction that can be used clinically to guide the choice of antibiotics. These four medically important species are urease-positive. Identification of these organisms in the clinical laboratory is based on a variety of biochemical reactions.

Treatment

Most strains are sensitive to aminoglycosides and trimethoprim-sulfamethoxazole, but because individual isolates can vary, antibiotic sensitivity tests should be performed. *P. mirabilis* is the species most frequently sensitive to ampicillin. The indole-positive species (*P. vulgaris, M. morganii,* and *P. rettgeri*) are more resistant to antibiotics than is *P. mirabilis,* which is indole-negative. The treatment of choice for the indole-positive species is a cephalosporin, eg, cefotaxime. *P. rettgeri* is frequently resistant to multiple antibiotics.

Prevention

There are no specific preventive measures, but many hospital-acquired urinary tract infections can be prevented by prompt removal of urinary catheters.

PSEUDOMONAS

Diseases

Pseudomonas aeruginosa causes infections (eg, sepsis, pneumonia, and urinary tract infections) primarily in patients with lowered host defenses. (*Pseudomonas aeruginosa* is also known as *Burkholderia aeruginosa*.) *Pseudomonas cepacia* (renamed *Burkholderia cepacia*) and *Pseudomonas maltophilia* (renamed *Xanthomonas maltophilia* and now called *Stenotrophomonas maltophilia*) also cause these infections, but much less frequently. *Pseudomonas pseudomallei,* the cause of melioidosis, is described in Chapter 27.

Important Properties

Pseudomonads are gram-negative rods that resemble the members of the Enterobacteriaceae but differ in that they are strict aerobes; ie, they derive their energy only by oxidation of sugars rather than by fermentation. Because they do not ferment glucose, they are called **non-fermenters,** in contrast to the members of the Enterobacteriaceae, which do ferment glucose. Oxidation involves electron transport by cytochrome c; ie, they are **oxidase-positive.**

Pseudomonads are able to grow in **water** containing only traces of nutrients, eg, tap water, and this favors their persistence in the hospital environment. *P. aeruginosa* and *P. cepacia* have a remarkable ability to withstand disinfectants; this accounts in part for their role in hospital-acquired infections. They have been found growing in hexachlorophene-containing soap solutions, in antiseptics, and in detergents.

P. aeruginosa produces two pigments useful in clinical and laboratory diagnosis: (1) **pyocyanin,** which can **color the pus in a wound blue;** and (2) pyoverdin (fluorescein), a yellow-green pigment that fluoresces under ultraviolet light, a property that can be used in the early detection of skin infection in burn patients. In the laboratory, these **pigments diffuse into the agar, imparting a blue-green color** that is useful in identification. *P. aeruginosa* is the only species of *Pseudomonas* that synthesizes pyocyanin.

Strains of *P. aeruginosa* isolated from cystic fibrosis patients have a prominent slime layer (glycocalyx), which gives their colonies a very mucoid appearance.

The slime layer mediates adherence of the organism to mucous membranes of the respiratory tract and prevents antibody from binding to the organism.

Pathogenesis & Epidemiology

P. aeruginosa is found chiefly in soil and water, although approximately 10% of people carry it in the normal flora of the colon. It is found on the skin in moist areas and can colonize the upper respiratory tract of hospitalized patients. Its ability to grow in simple aqueous solutions has resulted in contamination of respiratory therapy and anesthesia equipment, intravenous fluids, and even distilled water.

P. aeruginosa is primarily an opportunistic pathogen that causes infections in hospitalized patients, eg, those with extensive burns, in whom the skin host defenses are destroyed; in those with chronic respiratory disease (eg, cystic fibrosis), in whom the normal clearance mechanisms are impaired; in those who are immunosuppressed; in those with neutrophil counts of less than 500/μL; and in those with indwelling catheters. It causes 10–20% of hospital-acquired infections and, in many hospitals, is the most common cause of gram-negative nosocomial pneumonia.

Pathogenesis is based on multiple virulence factors: endotoxin, exotoxins, and enzymes. Its endotoxin, like that of other gram-negative bacteria, causes the symptoms of sepsis and septic shock. The best known of the exotoxins is exotoxin A, which causes tissue necrosis. It inhibits eukaryotic protein synthesis by the same mechanism as diphtheria exotoxin, namely, ADP-ribosylation of elongation factor 2. It also produces enzymes, such as elastase and proteases, which are histotoxic and facilitate invasion of the organism into the bloodstream. Pyocyanin damages the cilia and mucosal cells of the respiratory tract.

Strains of *P. aeruginosa* that have a "type III secretion system" are significantly more virulent than those that do not. This secretion system transfers the exotoxin from the bacterium directly into the adjacent human cell, which allows the toxin to avoid neutralizing antibody. Type III secretion systems are mediated by transport pumps in the bacterial cell membrane. Of the four exoenzymes known to be transported by this secretion system, Exo S is the one most clearly associated with virulence. Exo S has several modes of action, the most important of which is ADP-ribosylation of a Ras protein, leading to damage to the cytoskeleton.

Clinical Findings

P. aeruginosa can cause infections virtually anywhere in the body, but urinary tract infections, pneumonia (especially in **cystic fibrosis** patients), and wound infections (especially burns) predominate. From these sites, the organism can enter the blood, causing sepsis. The bacteria can spread to the skin, where they cause black, necrotic lesions called **ecthyma gangrenosum.** Patients with *P. aeruginosa* sepsis have a mortality rate of greater than 50%. It is an important cause of endocarditis in intravenous drug users.

Severe external otitis (malignant otitis externa) and other skin lesions (eg, folliculitis) occur in users of swimming pools and hot tubs in which the chlorination is inadequate. *P. aeruginosa* is the most common cause of osteochondritis of the foot in those who sustain puncture wounds through the soles of gym shoes. Corneal infections caused by *P. aeruginosa* are seen in contact lens users.

Laboratory Diagnosis

P. aeruginosa grows as non-lactose-fermenting (colorless) colonies on MacConkey's or EMB agar. It is **oxidase-positive.** A typical metallic sheen of the growth on TSI agar, coupled with the blue-green pigment on ordinary nutrient agar and a fruity aroma, is sufficient to make a presumptive diagnosis. The diagnosis is confirmed by biochemical reactions. Identification for epidemiologic purposes is done by bacteriophage or pyocin[6] typing.

Treatment

Because *P. aeruginosa* is **resistant to many antibiotics,** treatment must be tailored to the sensitivity of each isolate and monitored frequently; resistant strains can emerge during therapy. The treatment of choice is an antipseudomonal penicillin, eg, ticarcillin or piperacillin, plus an aminoglycoside, eg, gentamicin or amikacin. The drug of choice for infections caused by *B. cepacia* and *S. maltophilia* is trimethoprim-sulfamethoxazole.

Prevention

Prevention of *P. aeruginosa* infections involves keeping neutrophil counts above 500/μL, removing indwelling catheters promptly, taking special care of burned skin, and taking other similar measures to limit infection in patients with reduced host defenses.

BACTEROIDES & PREVOTELLA

Diseases

Members of the genus *Bacteroides* are the most common cause of serious anaerobic infections, eg, sepsis,

peritonitis, and abscesses. *Bacteroides fragilis* is the most frequent pathogen. *Prevotella melaninogenica* is also an important pathogen. *P. melaninogenica* was formerly known as *Bacteroides melaninogenicus,* and both names are still encountered.

Important Properties

Bacteroides and *Prevotella* organisms are anaerobic, non-spore-forming, gram-negative rods. Of the many species of *Bacteroides,* two are human pathogens: *B. fragilis,*[7] and *Bacteroides corrodens.*

Members of the *B. fragilis* group are the predominant organisms in the human colon, numbering approximately 10^{11}/g of feces, and are found in the vagina of approximately 60% of women. *P. melaninogenica* and *B. corrodens* occur primarily in the oral cavity.

Pathogenesis & Epidemiology

Because *Bacteroides* and *Prevotella* species are part of the normal flora, **infections** are endogenous, usually arising from a break in a mucosal surface, and are not communicable. These organisms cause a variety of infections, such as local abscesses at the site of a mucosal break, metastatic abscesses by hematogenous spread to distant organs, or lung abscesses by aspiration of oral flora.

Predisposing factors such as surgery, trauma, and chronic disease play an important role in pathogenesis. Local tissue necrosis, impaired blood supply, and growth of facultative anaerobes at the site contribute to anaerobic infections. The facultative anaerobes, such as *E. coli,* utilize the oxygen, thereby reducing it to a level that allows the anaerobic *Bacteroides* and *Prevotella* strains to grow. As a result, many anaerobic infections contain a mixed facultative and anaerobic flora. This has important implications for therapy; both the facultative anaerobes and the anaerobes should be treated.

The polysaccharide capsule of *B. fragilis* is an important virulence factor. Many of the symptoms of *Bacteroides* sepsis resemble those of sepsis caused by bacteria with endotoxin, but the lipopolysaccharide of *Bacteroides* is chemically different from the typical endotoxin. No exotoxins have been found.

Clinical Findings

The *B. fragilis* group of organisms is most frequently associated with intra-abdominal infections, either peri-

---

[6] A pyocin is a type of bacteriocin produced by *P. aeruginosa.* Different strains produce various pyocins, which can serve to distinguish the organisms.

[7] *B. fragilis* is divided into five subspecies, the most important of which is *B. fragilis* subsp. *fragilis.* The other four subspecies are *B. fragilis* subsp. *distasonis, ovatus, thetaiotamicron,* and *vulgatus.* It is proper, therefore, to speak of the *B. fragilis* group rather than simply *B. fragilis.*

tonitis or localized abscesses. Pelvic abscesses, necrotizing fasciitis, and bacteremia occur as well. Abscesses of the mouth, pharynx, brain, and lung are more commonly caused by *P. melaninogenica,* a member of the normal oral flora, but *B. fragilis* is found in about 25% of lung abscesses. In general, *B. fragilis* causes disease below the diaphragm, whereas *P. melaninogenica* causes disease above the diaphragm.

Laboratory Diagnosis

Bacteroides species can be isolated anaerobically on blood agar plates containing kanamycin and vancomycin to inhibit unwanted organisms. They are identified by biochemical reactions (eg, sugar fermentations) and by production of certain organic acids (eg, formic, acetic, and propionic acids), which are detected by gas chromatography. *P. melaninogenica* produces characteristic black colonies.

Treatment

Members of the *B. fragilis* group are resistant to penicillins, first-generation cephalosporins, and aminoglycosides, making them among the most antibiotic-resistant of the anaerobic bacteria. Penicillin resistance is the result of β-lactamase production. Metronidazole is the drug of choice, with cefoxitin, clindamycin, and chloramphenicol as alternatives. Aminoglycosides are

frequently combined to treat the facultative gram-negative rods in mixed infections. The drug of choice for *P. melaninogenica* infections is either metronidazole or clindamycin. β-Lactamase-producing strains of *P. melaninogenica* have been isolated from patients. Surgical drainage of abscesses usually accompanies antibiotic therapy, but lung abscesses often heal without drainage.

Prevention

Prevention of *Bacteroides* and *Prevotella* infections centers on perioperative administration of a cephalosporin, frequently cefoxitin, for abdominal or pelvic surgery. There is no vaccine.

SUMMARIES OF ORGANISMS

Brief summaries of the organisms described in this chapter begin on page 482. Please consult these summaries for a rapid review of the essential material.

PRACTICE QUESTIONS: USMLE & COURSE EXAMINATIONS

Questions on the topics discussed in this chapter can be found in the Clinical Bacteriology section of Part XI: USMLE (National Board) Practice Questions starting on page 537. Also see Part XII: USMLE (National Board) Practice Examination starting on page 583.

Gram-Negative Rods Related to the Respiratory Tract

19

There are three medically important gram-negative rods typically associated with the respiratory tract, namely, *Haemophilus influenzae*, *Bordetella pertussis*, and *Legionella pneumophila* (Table 19–1). *H. influenzae* and *B. pertussis* are found only in humans, whereas *L. pneumophila* is found primarily in environmental water sources.

HAEMOPHILUS

Diseases

H. influenzae used to be the leading cause of meningitis in young children, but the use of the highly effective "conjugate" vaccine has greatly reduced the incidence of meningitis caused by this organism. It is still an important cause of upper respiratory tract infections (otitis media, sinusitis, and epiglottitis) and sepsis in children. It also causes pneumonia in adults, particularly in those with chronic obstructive lung disease. *Haemophilus ducreyi*, the agent of chancroid, is discussed in Chapter 27.

Important Properties

H. influenzae is a small gram-negative rod (coccobacillus) with a polysaccharide capsule. It is one of the three important **encapsulated pyogens,** along with the pneumococcus and the meningococcus. Serologic typing is based on the antigenicity of the capsular polysaccharide. Of the six serotypes, **type b** causes most of the severe, invasive diseases, such as meningitis and sepsis. The type b capsule is composed of polyribitol phosphate. Unencapsulated and therefore untypeable strains can also cause disease, especially diseases of the upper respiratory tract such as sinusitis and otitis media, but are usually noninvasive. Growth of the organism on laboratory media requires the addition of two components, **heme (factor X)** and **NAD (factor V),** for adequate energy production.

Pathogenesis & Epidemiology

H. influenzae infects only humans; there is no animal reservoir. It enters the body through the **upper respiratory tract,** resulting in either asymptomatic colonization or infections such as otitis media, sinusitis, or pneumonia. The organism produces an IgA protease that degrades secretory IgA, thus facilitating attachment to the respiratory mucosa. After becoming established in the upper respiratory tract, the organism can enter the bloodstream (bacteremia) and spread to the meninges. Meningitis is caused primarily by the encapsulated strains (95% of which possess the type b capsule), but nonencapsulated strains are frequently involved in otitis media, sinusitis, and pneumonia. Pathogenesis involves the antiphagocytic capsule and endotoxin; no exotoxin is produced.

Most infections occur in children between the ages of 6 months and 6 years, with a peak in the age group from 6 months to 1 year. This age distribution is attributed to a decline in maternal IgG in the child coupled with the inability of the child to generate sufficient antibody against the polysaccharide capsular antigen until the age of approximately 2 years.

Clinical Findings

Meningitis caused by *H. influenzae* cannot be distinguished on clinical grounds from that caused by other bacterial pathogens, eg, pneumococci or meningococci. The rapid onset of fever, headache, and stiff neck along with drowsiness is typical. Sinusitis and otitis media cause pain in the affected area, opacification of the infected sinus, and redness with bulging of the tympanic membrane. *H. influenzae* is second only to the pneumococcus as a cause of these two infections.

Other serious infections caused by this organism include septic arthritis, cellulitis, and sepsis, the latter occurring especially in splenectomized patients. Rarely, **epiglottitis,** which can obstruct the airway, occurs. This life-threatening disease of young children is caused almost exclusively by *H. influenzae*. Pneumonia in elderly adults, especially those with chronic respiratory disease, can be caused by untypeable strains of *H. influenzae*.

Table 19–1. Gram-negative rods associated with the respiratory tract.

Species	Major Diseases	Laboratory Diagnosis	Factors X and V Required for Growth	Vaccine Available	Prophylaxis for Contacts
H. influenzae	Meningitis[1]; otitis media, sinusitis, pneumonia, epiglottitis	Culture; capsular polysaccharide in serum or spinal fluid	+	+	Rifampin
B. pertussis	Whooping cough (pertussis)	Fluorescent antibody on secretions; culture	–	+	Erythromycin
L. pneumophila	Pneumonia	Serology; urinary antigen; culture	–	–	None

[1]In countries where the *Haemophilus influenzae* b conjugate vaccine has been deployed, the vaccine has greatly reduced the incidence of meningitis caused by this organism.

Laboratory Diagnosis

Laboratory diagnosis depends on isolation of the organism on heated-blood ("chocolate") agar enriched with two growth factors required for bacterial respiration, namely, factor X (a heme compound) and factor V (NAD). The blood used in chocolate agar is heated to inactivate nonspecific inhibitors of *H. influenzae* growth.

An organism that grows only in the presence of both growth factors is presumptively identified as *H. influenzae;* other species of *Haemophilus,* such as *Haemophilus parainfluenzae,* do not require both factors. Definitive identification can be made with either biochemical tests or the capsular swelling (quellung) reaction. Additional means of identifying encapsulated strains include fluorescent-antibody staining of the organism and counterimmunoelectrophoresis or latex agglutination tests, which detect the capsular polysaccharide.

Treatment

The treatment of choice for meningitis or other serious systemic infections caused by *H. influenzae* is ceftriaxone. From 20% to 30% of *H. influenzae* type b isolates produce a β-lactamase that degrades penicillinase-sensitive β-lactams such as ampicillin but not ceftriaxone. It is important to institute antibiotic treatment promptly, because the incidence of neurologic sequelae, eg, subdural empyema, is high. Untreated *H. influenzae* meningitis has a fatality rate of approximately 90%. *H. influenzae* upper respiratory tract infections, such as otitis media and sinusitis, are treated with either amoxicillin-clavulanate or trimethoprim-sulfamethoxazole.

Prevention

The vaccine contains the capsular polysaccharide of *H. influenzae* type b **conjugated to diphtheria toxoid** or other carrier protein. Depending upon the carrier protein, it is given some time between the ages of 2 and 15 months. This vaccine is **much more effective** in young children than the unconjugated vaccine and has reduced the incidence of meningitis caused by this organism by approximately 90% in immunized children. Meningitis in close contacts of the patient can be prevented by rifampin. Rifampin is used because it is secreted in the saliva to a greater extent than ampicillin. Rifampin decreases respiratory carriage of the organism, thereby reducing transmission.

BORDETELLA

Disease

B. pertussis causes whooping cough (pertussis).

Important Properties

B. pertussis is a small, coccobacillary, encapsulated gram-negative rod.

Pathogenesis & Epidemiology

B. pertussis, a pathogen **only for humans,** is transmitted by **airborne droplets** produced during the severe coughing episodes. The organisms attach to the ciliated epithelium of the upper respiratory tract but do not invade the underlying tissue. Decreased cilia activity followed by death of the ciliated epithelial cells are important aspects of pathogenesis.

Pertussis is a highly contagious disease that occurs primarily in infants and young children and has a worldwide distribution. It occurs infrequently in the United States because use of the vaccine is widespread. However, an increase in the number of cases during the years 2000–2003 has led to the recommendation that an additional booster immunization be given (see Prevention).

Several factors play a role in the pathogenesis:

(1) Attachment of the organism to the cilia of the epithelial cells is mediated by a protein on the pili called filamentous hemagglutinin. Antibody against the filamentous hemagglutinin inhibits attachment and protects against disease.

(2) **Pertussis toxin** stimulates adenylate cyclase by catalyzing the addition of adenosine diphosphate-ribose, a process called ADP-ribosylation, to the inhibitory subunit of the G protein complex (G_i protein). This results in prolonged stimulation of adenylate cyclase and a consequent rise in cyclic adenosine monophosphate (AMP) and in cyclic AMP-dependent protein kinase activity. The toxin also has a domain that mediates its binding to receptors on the surface of respiratory tract epithelial cells.

Pertussis toxin also causes a striking **lymphocytosis** in the blood of patients with pertussis. The toxin inhibits signal transduction by chemokine receptors, resulting in a failure of lymphocytes to enter lymphoid tissue such as the spleen and lymph nodes. Because the lymphocytes do not enter lymphoid tissue, there is an increase in their number in the blood (see the discussion of chemokines in Chapter 58). The inhibition of signal transduction by chemokine receptors is also caused by ADP-ribosylation of the G_i protein.

(3) The organisms also synthesize and export adenylate cyclase. This enzyme, when taken up by phagocytic cells (eg, neutrophils) can inhibit their bactericidal activity. Bacterial mutants that lack cyclase activity are avirulent.

(4) Tracheal cytotoxin is a fragment of the bacterial peptidoglycan that damages ciliated cells of the respiratory tract. Tracheal cytotoxin appears to act in concert with endotoxin to induce nitric oxide, which kills the ciliated epithelial cells.

Clinical Findings

Whooping cough is an acute tracheobronchitis that begins with mild upper respiratory tract symptoms followed by a severe paroxysmal cough, which lasts from 1 to 4 weeks. The paroxysmal pattern is characterized by a series of hacking coughs, accompanied by production of copious amounts of mucus, that end with an inspiratory "whoop" as air rushes past the narrowed glottis. Despite the severity of the symptoms, the organism is restricted to the respiratory tract and blood cultures are negative. A pronounced leukocytosis with up to 70% lymphocytes is seen. Although central nervous system anoxia and exhaustion can occur as a result of the severe coughing, death is due mainly to pneumonia.

The classic picture of whooping cough described above occurs primarily in young children. In adults, *B. pertussis* infection often manifests as a paroxysmal cough of varying severity lasting weeks. The characteristic whoop is often absent, leading to difficulty in recognizing the cough as caused by this organism. In the correct clinical setting, adults with a cough lasting several weeks (often called the 100-day cough) should be evaluated for infection with *B. pertussis*.

Laboratory Diagnosis

The organism can be isolated from nasopharyngeal swabs taken during the paroxysmal stage. Bordet-Gengou[1] medium used for this purpose contains a high percentage of blood (20–30%) to inactivate inhibitors in the agar.

Identification of the isolated organism can be made by agglutination with specific antiserum or by fluorescent-antibody staining. However, the organism grows very slowly in culture, so direct fluorescent-antibody staining of the nasopharyngeal specimens is often used for diagnosis. Polymerase chain reaction–based tests are highly specific and sensitive and should be used if available.

Treatment

Erythromycin reduces the number of organisms in the throat and decreases the risk of secondary complications but has little influence on the course of the disease because the toxins have already damaged the respiratory mucosa. Supportive care, eg, oxygen therapy and suction of mucus, during the paroxysmal stage is important, especially in infants.

Prevention

There are two vaccines available: an acellular vaccine containing purified proteins from the organism and a killed vaccine containing inactivated *B. pertussis* organisms. The **acellular vaccine** consisting of five antigens purified from the organism is now recommended in the United States. The main immunogen in this vaccine is inactivated pertussis toxin (pertussis toxoid). The toxoid in the vaccine is pertussis toxin that has been inactivated genetically by introducing two amino acid changes that eliminates its ADP-ribosylating activity

---

[1] The French scientists who first isolated the organism in 1906.

but retains its antigenicity. It is the first vaccine to contain a genetically inactivated toxoid. The acellular vaccine has fewer side effects than the killed vaccine.

The pertussis vaccine is usually given combined with diphtheria and tetanus toxoids (DTaP) in three doses beginning at 2 months of age. A booster at 12–15 months of age and another at the time of entering school are recommended. Because outbreaks have occurred during the years 2000–2003, especially among teenagers, a booster for those between 10 and 18 years old is recommended. This vaccine, called Boostrix, contains diphtheria and tetanus toxoids also. A second vaccine called Adacel also contains diphtheria and tetanus toxoids and is approved for use not only in adolescents but in adults up to the age of 64. The killed vaccine is no longer recommended in the United States because it is suspected of causing various side effects, including postvaccine encephalopathy at a rate of about one case per million doses administered.

Erythromycin is useful in prevention of disease in exposed, unimmunized individuals. It should also be given to immunized children younger than 4 years who have been exposed because vaccine-induced immunity is not completely protective.

LEGIONELLA

Disease

L. pneumophila (and other legionellae) causes pneumonia, both in the community and in hospitalized immunocompromised patients. The genus is named after the famous outbreak of pneumonia among people attending the American Legion convention in Philadelphia in 1976 (legionnaires' disease).

Important Properties

Legionellae are gram-negative rods that **stain faintly with the standard Gram stain.** They do, however, have a gram-negative type of cell wall, and increasing the time of the safranin counterstain enhances visibility. Legionellae in lung biopsy sections do not stain by the standard hematoxylin-and-eosin (H&E) procedure; therefore, special methods, such as the Dieterle silver impregnation stain, are used to visualize the organisms.

During the 1976 outbreak, initial attempts to grow the organisms on ordinary culture media failed. This is because of the organism's requirement for a high concentration of iron and cysteine; culture media supplemented with these nutrients will support growth.

L. pneumophila causes approximately 90% of pneumonia attributed to legionellae. There are about 30 other Legionella species that cause pneumonia, but most of the remaining 10% of cases are caused by two species, Legionella micdadei and Legionella bozemanii.

Pathogenesis & Epidemiology

Legionellae are associated chiefly with **environmental water sources** such as air conditioners and water-cooling towers. Outbreaks of pneumonia in hospitals have been attributed to the presence of the organism in water taps, sinks, and showers. The portal of entry is the respiratory tract, and pathologic changes occur primarily in the lung. However, in severe cases, bacteremia occurs accompanied by damage to the vascular endothelium in multiple organs, especially the brain and kidneys. The major virulence factor of the organism is lipopolysaccharide (endotoxin). No exotoxins are produced.

The typical candidate for legionnaires' disease is an older man who smokes and consumes substantial amounts of alcohol. Patients with AIDS, cancer, or transplants (especially renal transplants) or patients being treated with corticosteroids are predisposed to Legionella pneumonia, which indicates that **cell-mediated immunity** is the most important defense mechanism. Despite airborne transmission of the organism, person-to-person spread does *not* occur, as shown by the failure of secondary cases to occur in close contacts of patients.

Clinical Findings

The clinical picture can vary from a mild influenzalike illness to a severe pneumonia accompanied by mental confusion, nonbloody diarrhea, proteinuria, and microscopic hematuria. Although cough is a prominent symptom, sputum is frequently scanty and nonpurulent. Hyponatremia (serum sodium $\leq$ 130 mEq/L) is an important laboratory finding that occurs more often in Legionella pneumonia than in pneumonia caused by other bacteria. Most cases resolve spontaneously in 7–10 days, but in older or immunocompromised patients, the infection can be fatal.

Legionellosis is an **atypical pneumonia**[2] and must be distinguished from other similar pneumonias such as Mycoplasma pneumonia, viral pneumonia, psittacosis, and Q fever.

Pontiac fever is a mild, flulike form of Legionella infection that does not result in pneumonia. The name "Pontiac" is derived from the city in Michigan that was the site of an outbreak in 1968.

Laboratory Diagnosis

Sputum Gram stains reveal many neutrophils but no bacteria. The organism **fails to grow on ordinary me-**

---

[2] A pneumonia is atypical when its causative agent cannot be isolated on ordinary laboratory media or when its clinical picture does not resemble that of typical pneumococcal pneumonia.

dia in a culture of sputum or blood, but it will grow on charcoal-yeast agar, a special medium supplemented with iron and cysteine. Diagnosis usually depends on a significant increase in antibody titer in convalescent-phase serum by the indirect immunofluorescence assay. Detection of *L. pneumophila* antigens in the urine is a rapid means of making a diagnosis. If tissue is available, it is possible to demonstrate *Legionella* antigens in infected lung tissue by using fluorescent-antibody staining. The cold-agglutinin titer does not rise in *Legionella* pneumonia, in contrast to pneumonia caused by *Mycoplasma*.

Treatment

Azithromycin or erythromycin (with or without rifampin) is the treatment of choice. Certain fluoroquinolones, such as levofloxacin and trovafloxacin, are also drugs of choice. These drugs are effective not only against *L. pneumophila* but also against *Mycoplasma pneumoniae* and *Streptococcus pneumoniae*. The organism frequently produces β-lactamase, and so penicillins and cephalosporins are less effective.

Prevention

Prevention involves reducing cigarette and alcohol consumption, eliminating aerosols from water sources, and reducing the incidence of *Legionella* in hospital water supplies by using high temperatures and hyperchlorination. There is no vaccine.

SUMMARIES OF ORGANISMS

Brief summaries of the organisms described in this chapter begin on page 486. Please consult these summaries for a rapid review of the essential material.

PRACTICE QUESTIONS: USMLE & COURSE EXAMINATIONS

Questions on the topics discussed in this chapter can be found in the Clinical Bacteriology section of Part XI: USMLE (National Board) Practice Questions starting on page 537. Also see Part XII: USMLE (National Board) Practice Examination starting on page 583.

Gram-Negative Rods Related to Animal Sources (Zoonotic Organisms)

Zoonoses are human diseases caused by organisms that are acquired from animals. There are bacterial, viral, fungal, and parasitic zoonoses. Some zoonotic organisms are acquired directly from the animal reservoir, whereas others are transmitted by vectors, such as mosquitoes, fleas, or ticks.

There are four medically important gram-negative rods that have significant animal reservoirs: *Brucella* species, *Francisella tularensis*, *Yersinia pestis*, and *Pasteurella multocida* (Table 20–1).

BRUCELLA

Disease

Brucella species cause brucellosis (undulant fever).

Important Properties

Brucellae are small gram-negative rods without a capsule. The three major human pathogens and their animal reservoirs are *Brucella melitensis* (goats and sheep), *Brucella abortus* (cattle), and *Brucella suis* (pigs).

Pathogenesis & Epidemiology

The organisms enter the body either by ingestion of **contaminated milk products** or **through the skin** by direct contact in an occupational setting such as an abattoir. They localize in the **reticuloendothelial system,** namely, the lymph nodes, liver, spleen, and bone marrow. Many organisms are killed by macrophages, but some survive within these cells, where they are protected from antibody. The host response is granulomatous, with lymphocytes and epithelioid giant cells, which can progress to form focal abscesses and caseation. The mechanism of pathogenesis of these organisms is not well defined, except that endotoxin is involved; ie, when the O antigen polysaccharides are lost from the external portion of the endotoxin, the organism loses its virulence. No exotoxins are produced.

Imported cheese made from unpasteurized goats' milk produced in either Mexico or the Mediterranean region has been a source of *B. melitensis* infection in the United States. The disease occurs worldwide but is rare in the United States because pasteurization of milk kills the organism.

Clinical Findings

After an incubation period of 1–3 weeks, nonspecific symptoms such as fever, chills, fatigue, malaise, anorexia, and weight loss occur. The onset can be acute or gradual. The undulating (rising-and-falling) fever pattern that gives the disease its name occurs in a minority of patients. Enlarged lymph nodes, liver, and spleen are frequently found. Pancytopenia occurs. *B. melitensis* infections tend to be more severe and prolonged, whereas those caused by *B. abortus* are more self-limited. Osteomyelitis is the most frequent complication. Secondary spread from person to person is rare.

Laboratory Diagnosis

Recovery of the organism requires the use of enriched culture media and incubation in 10% CO_2. The organisms can be presumptively identified by using a slide agglutination test with *Brucella* antiserum, and the species can be identified by biochemical tests. If organisms are not isolated, analysis of a serum sample from the patient for a rise in antibody titer to *Brucella* can be used to make a diagnosis. In the absence of an acute-phase serum specimen, a titer of at least 1:160 in the convalescent-phase serum sample is diagnostic.

Treatment

The treatment of choice is tetracycline plus rifampin. There is no significant resistance to these drugs.

Prevention

Prevention of brucellosis involves pasteurization of milk, immunization of animals, and slaughtering of infected animals. There is no human vaccine.

Table 20–1. Gram-negative rods associated with animal sources.

Species	Disease	Source of Human Infection	Mode of Transmission From Animal to Human	Diagnosis
Brucella species	Brucellosis	Pigs, cattle, goats, sheep	Dairy products; contact with animal tissues.	Serology or culture
Francisella tularensis	Tularemia	Rabbits, deer, ticks	Contact with animal tissues; ticks.	Serology
Yersinia pestis	Plague	Rodents	Flea bite.	Immunofluorescence or culture
Pasteurella multocida	Cellulitis	Cats, dogs	Cat or dog bite.	Wound culture

FRANCISELLA

Disease

Francisella tularensis causes tularemia.

Important Properties

F. tularensis is a small, pleomorphic gram-negative rod. It has a single serologic type. There are two biotypes, A and B, which are distinguished primarily on their virulence and epidemiology. Type A is more virulent and found primarily in the United States, whereas type B is less virulent and found primarily in Europe.

Pathogenesis & Epidemiology

F. tularensis is remarkable in the wide variety of animals that it infects and in the breadth of its distribution in the United States. It is enzootic (endemic in animals) in every state, but most human cases occur in the rural areas of Arkansas and Missouri. It has been isolated from more than 100 different species of **wild animals**, the most important of which are rabbits, deer, and a variety of rodents. The bacteria are transmitted among these animals by vectors such as **ticks**, mites, and lice, especially the *Dermacentor* ticks that feed on the blood of wild rabbits. The tick maintains the chain of transmission by passing the bacteria to its offspring by the transovarian route. In this process, the bacteria are passed through ovum, larva, and nymph stages to adult ticks capable of transmitting the infection.

Humans are accidental "dead-end" hosts who acquire the infection most often by being bitten by the vector or by having skin contact with the animal during removal of the hide. Rarely, the organism is ingested in infected meat, causing gastrointestinal tularemia, or is inhaled, causing pneumonia. There is no person-to-person spread. The main type of tularemia in the United States is tick-borne tularemia from a rabbit reservoir.

The organism enters through the skin, forming an ulcer at the site in most cases. It then localizes to the cells of the reticuloendothelial system, and granulomas are formed. Caseation necrosis and abscesses can also occur. Symptoms are caused primarily by endotoxin. No exotoxins have been identified.

Clinical Findings

Presentation can vary from sudden onset of an influenzalike syndrome to prolonged onset of a low-grade fever and adenopathy. Approximately 75% of cases are the "ulceroglandular" type, in which the site of entry ulcerates and the regional lymph nodes are swollen and painful. Other, less frequent forms of tularemia include glandular, oculoglandular, typhoidal, gastrointestinal, and pulmonary. Disease usually confers lifelong immunity.

Laboratory Diagnosis

Attempts to culture the organism in the laboratory are rarely undertaken, because there is a high risk to laboratory workers of infection by inhalation and the special cysteine-containing medium required for growth is not usually available. The most frequently used diagnostic method is the agglutination test with acute- and convalescent-phase serum samples. Fluorescent-antibody staining of infected tissue can be used if available.

Treatment

Streptomycin is the drug of choice. There is no significant antibiotic resistance.

Prevention

Prevention involves avoiding both being bitten by ticks and handling wild animals. There is a live, attenuated bacterial vaccine that is given only to persons, such as fur trappers, whose occupation brings them into close contact with wild animals. The vaccine is experimental and not available commercially but can be obtained from the US Army Medical Research Command, Fort Detrick, Maryland. This and the bacillus of Calmette-Guérin (BCG) vaccine for tuberculosis are the only two live bacterial vaccines for human use.

YERSINIA

Disease

Yersinia pestis is the cause of plague, also known as the black death, the scourge of the Middle Ages. It is also a contemporary disease, occurring in the western United States and in many other countries around the world. Two less important species, *Yersinia enterocolitica* and *Yersinia pseudotuberculosis,* are described in Chapter 27.

Important Properties

Y. pestis is a small gram-negative rod that exhibits bipolar staining; ie, it resembles a safety pin, with a central clear area. Freshly isolated organisms possess a capsule composed of a polysaccharide-protein complex. The capsule can be lost with passage in the laboratory; loss of the capsule is accompanied by a loss of virulence. It is one of the **most virulent** bacteria known and has a strikingly low ID_{50}; ie, 1–10 organisms are capable of causing disease.

Pathogenesis & Epidemiology

The plague bacillus has been endemic in the wild rodents of Europe and Asia for thousands of years but entered North America in the early 1900s, probably carried by a rat that jumped ship at a California port. It is now endemic in the wild rodents in the western United States, although 99% of cases of plague occur in Southeast Asia.

The enzootic (sylvatic) cycle consists of transmission among **wild rodents by fleas.** In the United States, prairie dogs are the main reservoir. Rodents are relatively resistant to disease; most are asymptomatic. Humans are accidental hosts, and cases of plague in this country occur as a result of being bitten by a flea that is part of the sylvatic cycle.

The urban cycle, which does not occur in the United States, consists of transmission of the bacteria among urban rats, with the **rat flea** as vector. This cycle predominates during times of poor sanitation, eg, wartime, when rats proliferate and come in contact with the fleas in the sylvatic cycle.

The events within the flea are fascinating as well as essential. The flea ingests the bacteria while taking a blood meal from a bacteremic rodent. The blood clots in the flea's stomach as a result of the action of the enzyme coagulase, which is made by the bacteria. The bacteria are trapped in the fibrin and proliferate to large numbers. The mass of organisms and fibrin block the proventriculus of the flea's intestinal tract, and during its next blood meal the flea regurgitates the organisms into the next animal. Because the proventriculus is blocked, the flea gets no nutrition, becomes hungrier, loses its natural host selectivity for rodents, and more readily bites a human.

The organisms inoculated at the time of the bite spread to the regional lymph nodes, which become swollen and tender. These swollen lymph nodes are the **buboes** that have led to the name **bubonic plague.** The organisms can reach high concentrations in the blood (bacteremia) and disseminate to form abscesses in many organs. The **endotoxin-related symptoms,** including disseminated intravascular coagulation and cutaneous hemorrhages, probably were the genesis of the term **black death.**

In addition to the sylvatic and urban cycles of transmission, respiratory droplet transmission of the organism from patients with pneumonic plague can occur.

The organism has several factors that contribute to its virulence: (1) the envelope capsular antigen, called F-1, which protects against phagocytosis; (2) endotoxin; (3) an exotoxin; and two proteins known as (4) V antigen and (5) W antigen. The V and W antigens allow the organism to survive and grow intracellularly, but their mode of action is unknown. The action of the exotoxin is unknown.

Other factors that contribute to the extraordinary pathogenicity of *Y. pestis* are a group of virulence factors collectively called **Yops (Yersinia outer proteins).** These are injected into the human cell via type III secretion systems and inhibit phagocytosis and cytokine production by macrophages and neutrophils. For example, one of the Yops proteins (YopJ) is a protease that cleaves two signal transduction pathway proteins required for the induction of tumor necrosis factor synthesis. This inhibits the activation of our host defenses and contributes to the ability of the organism to replicate rapidly within the infected individual.

Clinical Findings

Bubonic plague, which is the most frequent form, begins with pain and swelling of the lymph nodes draining the site of the flea bite and systemic symptoms such as high fever, myalgias, and prostration. The affected nodes enlarge and become exquisitely tender. These buboes are an early characteristic finding. Septic shock and pneumonia are the main life-threatening subsequent events. Pneumonic plague can arise either from inhalation of an aerosol or from septic emboli that reach the lungs. Untreated bubonic plague is fatal in approximately half of the cases, and untreated pneumonic plague is invariably fatal.

Laboratory Diagnosis

Smear and culture of blood or pus from the bubo is the best diagnostic procedure. Great care must be taken by the physician during aspiration of the pus and by laboratory workers doing the culture not to create an aerosol that might transmit the infection. Giemsa or Wayson stain reveals the typical safety-pin appearance of the organism better than does Gram stain. Fluorescent-antibody staining can be used to identify the organism in tissues. A rise in antibody titer to the envelope antigen can be useful retrospectively.

Treatment

The treatment of choice is a combination of streptomycin and tetracycline, although streptomycin alone can be used. There is no significant antibiotic resistance. In view of the rapid progression of the disease, treatment should not wait for the results of the bacteriologic culture. Incision and drainage of the buboes are not usually necessary.

Prevention

Prevention of plague involves controlling the spread of rats in urban areas, preventing rats from entering the country by ship or airplane, and avoiding both flea bites and contact with dead wild rodents. A patient with plague must be placed in strict isolation (quarantine) for 72 hours after antibiotic therapy is started. Only close contacts need receive prophylactic tetracycline, but all contacts should be observed for fever. Reporting a case of plague to the public health authorities is mandatory.

A vaccine consisting of formalin-killed organisms provides partial protection against bubonic but not pneumonic plague. This vaccine was used in the armed forces during the Vietnam war but is not recommended for tourists traveling to Southeast Asia.

PASTEURELLA

Disease

Pasteurella multocida causes wound infections associated with cat and dog bites.

Important Properties

P. multocida is a short, encapsulated gram-negative rod that exhibits bipolar staining.

Pathogenesis & Epidemiology

The organism is part of the normal flora in the mouths of many animals, particularly **domestic cats and dogs,** and is transmitted by **biting.** About 25% of animal bites become infected with the organism, with sutures acting as a predisposing factor to infection. Most bite infections are polymicrobial, with a variety of facultative anaerobes and anaerobic organisms present in addition to *P. multocida*. Pathogenesis is not well understood, except that the capsule is a virulence factor and endotoxin is present in the cell wall. No exotoxins are made.

Clinical Findings

A rapidly spreading cellulitis at the site of an animal bite is indicative of *P. multocida* infection. The incubation period is brief, usually less than 24 hours. Osteomyelitis can complicate cat bites in particular, because cats' sharp, pointed teeth can implant the organism under the periosteum.

Laboratory Diagnosis

The diagnosis is made by finding the organism in a culture of a sample from the wound site.

Treatment

Penicillin G is the treatment of choice. There is no significant antibiotic resistance.

Prevention

People who have been bitten by a cat should be given ampicillin to prevent *P. multocida* infection. Animal bites, especially cat bites, should not be sutured.

SUMMARIES OF ORGANISMS

Brief summaries of the organisms described in this chapter begin on page 487. Please consult these summaries for a rapid review of the essential material.

PRACTICE QUESTIONS: USMLE & COURSE EXAMINATIONS

Questions on the topics discussed in this chapter can be found in the Clinical Bacteriology section of Part XI: USMLE (National Board) Practice Questions starting on page 537. Also see Part XII: USMLE (National Board) Practice Examination starting on page 583.

Mycobacteria

Mycobacteria are aerobic, **acid-fast** bacilli (rods). They are neither gram-positive nor gram-negative; ie, they are stained poorly by the dyes used in Gram stain. They are virtually the only bacteria that are acid-fast. (One exception is *Nocardia asteroides,* the major cause of nocardiosis, which is also acid-fast.) The term "acid-fast" refers to an organism's ability to retain the carbol-fuchsin stain despite subsequent treatment with an ethanol-hydrochloric acid mixture. The high lipid content (approximately 60%) of their cell wall makes mycobacteria acid-fast.

The major pathogens are *Mycobacterium tuberculosis,* the cause of tuberculosis, and *Mycobacterium leprae,* the cause of leprosy. Atypical mycobacteria, such as *Mycobacterium avium-intracellulare* complex and *Mycobacterium kansasii,* can cause tuberculosislike disease but are less frequent pathogens. Rapidly growing mycobacteria, such as *Mycobacterium chelonei,* occasionally cause human disease in immunocompromised patients or those in whom prosthetic devices have been implanted (Table 21–1). The clinical features of three important mycobacteria are described in Table 21–2.

MYCOBACTERIUM TUBERCULOSIS

Disease

This organism causes tuberculosis. Worldwide, *M. tuberculosis* causes more deaths than any other single microbial agent. Approximately one-third of the world's population is infected with this organism. Each year, it is estimated that 3 million people die of tuberculosis and that 8 million new cases occur.

Important Properties

M. tuberculosis **grows slowly** (ie, it has a doubling time of 18 hours, in contrast to most bacteria, which can double in number in 1 hour or less). Because growth is so slow, cultures of clinical specimens must be held for 6–8 weeks before being recorded as negative. *M. tuberculosis* can be cultured on bacteriologic media, whereas *M. leprae* cannot. Media used for its growth (eg, Löwenstein-Jensen medium) contain complex nutrients (eg, egg yolk) and dyes (eg, malachite green). The dyes inhibit the unwanted normal flora present in sputum samples.

M. tuberculosis is an **obligate aerobe;** this explains its predilection for causing disease in highly oxygenated tissues such as the upper lobe of the lung and the kidney. Its cell wall contains several complex lipids: (1) long-chain (C_{78}–C_{90}) fatty acids called **mycolic acids,** which contribute to the organism's acid-fastness; (2) wax D, one of the active components in Freund's adjuvant, which is used to enhance the immune response to many antigens in experimental animals; and (3) phosphatides, which play a role in caseation necrosis.

Cord factor (trehalose dimycolate) is correlated with virulence of the organism. Virulent strains grow in a characteristic "serpentine" cordlike pattern, whereas avirulent strains do not. The organism also contains several proteins, which, when combined with waxes, elicit delayed hypersensitivity. These proteins are the antigens in the **PPD** (**purified protein derivative**) skin test (also known as the tuberculin skin test). A lipid located in the bacterial cell wall called phthiocercol dimycoserosate is required for pathogenesis in the lung.

M. tuberculosis is relatively resistant to acids and alkalis. NaOH is used to concentrate clinical specimens; it destroys unwanted bacteria, human cells, and mucus but not the organism. *M. tuberculosis* is resistant to dehydration and so survives in dried expectorated sputum; this property may be important in its transmission by aerosol.

Strains of *M. tuberculosis* resistant to the main antimycobacterial drug, isoniazid (**isonicotinic acid hydrazide, INH**), as well as strains resistant to multiple antibiotics (called **multidrug resistant,** or **MDR** strains), have become a worldwide problem. This resistance is attributed to one or more chromosomal mutations, because no plasmids have been found in this organism. One of these mutations is in a gene for mycolic acid synthesis, and another is in a gene for catalase-peroxidase, an enzyme required to activate INH within the bacterium.

Transmission & Epidemiology

M. tuberculosis is transmitted from person to person by respiratory aerosol, and its initial site of infection is the

Table 21–1. Medically important mycobacteria.

Species	Growth on Bacteriologic Media	Preferred Temperature in vivo (°C)	Source or Mode of Transmission
M. tuberculosis	Slow (weeks)	37	Respiratory droplets
M. bovis	Slow (weeks)	37	Milk from infected animals
M. leprae	None	32	Prolonged close contact
Atypical mycobacteria[1] M. kansasii	Slow (weeks)	37	Soil and water
M. marinum	Slow (weeks)	32	Water
M. avium-intracellulare complex	Slow (weeks)	37	Soil and water
M. fortuitum-chelonei complex	Rapid (days)	37	Soil and water

[1]Only representative examples are given.

lung. In the body, it resides chiefly within reticuloendothelial cells, eg, **macrophages. Humans are the natural reservoir** of *M. tuberculosis;* there is no animal reservoir. Most transmission occurs by aerosols generated by the coughing of "smear-positive" people, ie, those whose sputum contains detectable bacilli in the acid-fast stain. However, about 20% of people are infected by aerosols produced by the coughing of "smear-negative" people.

In the United States, tuberculosis is almost exclusively a human disease. In developing countries, *Mycobacterium bovis* also causes tuberculosis in humans. *M. bovis* is found in cow's milk, which, unless pasteurized, can cause gastrointestinal tuberculosis in humans. The disease tuberculosis occurs in only a small number of infected individuals. In the United States, most cases of tuberculosis are associated with reactivation in elderly, malnourished men. The risk of infection and disease is highest among socioeconomically disadvantaged people, who have poor housing and poor nutrition. These factors, rather than genetic ones, probably account for the high rate of infection among Native Americans, blacks, and Eskimos.

Pathogenesis

M. tuberculosis produces no exotoxins and does not contain endotoxin in its cell wall. In fact, no mycobacteria produce toxins. The organism preferentially infects macrophages and other reticuloendothelial cells. *M. tuberculosis* survives and multiplies within a cellular vacuole called a phagosome. The organism produces a protein called "exported repetitive protein" that prevents the phagosome from fusing with the lysosome, thereby allowing the organism to escape the degradative enzymes in the lysosome.

Lesions are dependent on the presence of the organism and the host response. There are two types of lesions:

(1) **Exudative lesions,** which consist of an acute inflammatory response and occur chiefly in the lungs at the initial site of infection

(2) **Granulomatous lesions,** which consist of a central area of giant cells containing tubercle bacilli surrounded by a zone of epithelioid cells. These giant cells, called **Langhans' giant cells,** are an important pathologic

Table 21–2. Clinical features of important mycobacteria.

Organism	Main Site of Infection	Skin Test in Common Use	Multiple Drug Therapy Used	Vaccine Available
M. tuberculosis	Lungs	Yes	Yes	Yes
M. avium-intracellulare	Lungs	No	Yes	No
M. leprae	Skin, nerves	No	Yes	No

finding in tuberculous lesions. A **tubercle** is a granuloma surrounded by fibrous tissue that has undergone central caseation necrosis. Tubercles heal by fibrosis and calcification.

The primary lesion of tuberculosis usually occurs in the lungs. The parenchymal exudative lesion and the draining lymph nodes together are called a **Ghon complex.** Primary lesions usually occur in the lower lobes, whereas reactivation lesions usually occur in the apices. Reactivation lesions also occur in other well-oxygenated sites such as the kidneys, brain, and bone. Reactivation is seen primarily in immunocompromised or debilitated patients.

Spread of the organism within the body occurs by two mechanisms:

(1) A tubercle can erode into a bronchus, empty its caseous contents, and thereby spread the organism to other parts of the lungs, to the gastrointestinal tract if swallowed, and to other persons if expectorated.

(2) It can disseminate via the bloodstream to many internal organs. Dissemination can occur at an early stage if cell-mediated immunity fails to contain the initial infection or at a late stage if a person becomes immunocompromised.

Immunity & Hypersensitivity

After recovery from the primary infection, resistance to the organism is mediated by **cellular immunity,** ie, by CD4-positive T cells and macrophages. Circulating antibodies also form, but they play no role in resistance and are not used for diagnostic purposes. Patients deficient in cellular immunity, such as AIDS patients, are at much higher risk for disseminated, life-threatening tuberculosis. Mutations in the γ-interferon receptor gene are another cause of defective cellular immunity that predisposes to severe tuberculosis. This emphasizes the importance of activation of macrophages by γ-interferon in the host defense against *M. tuberculosis.*

Prior infection can be detected by a positive **tuberculin skin test** result, which is due to a delayed hypersensitivity reaction. **PPD** is used as the antigen in the tuberculin skin test. The intermediate-strength preparation of PPD, which contains 5 tuberculin units, is usually used. The skin test is evaluated by measuring the diameter of the **induration** surrounding the skin test site. Note that induration (thickening), not simply erythema (reddening), must be observed.

The diameter required to judge the test as positive varies depending upon the status of the individual being tested. Induration of 15 mm or more is positive in a person who has no known risk factors. Induration of 10 mm or more is positive in a person with high-risk factors, such as a homeless person, intravenous drug

users, or nursing home residents. Induration of 5 mm or more is positive in a person who has deficient cell-mediated immunity, eg, AIDS patients, or has been in close contact with a person with active tuberculosis.

A positive skin test result indicates previous infection by the organism but not necessarily active disease. The tuberculin test becomes positive 4–6 weeks after infection. Immunization with BCG vaccine (see page 160) can cause a positive test, but the reactions are usually only 5–10 mm and tend to decrease with time. People with PPD reactions of 15 mm or more are assumed to be infected with *M. tuberculosis* even if they have received the BCG vaccine. A positive skin test reverts to negative in about 5–10% of people. Reversion to negative is more common in the United States nowadays than many years ago because now a person is less likely to be exposed to the organism and therefore less likely to receive a boost to the immune system.

The skin test itself does *not* induce a positive response in a person who has not been exposed to the organism. It can, however, "boost" a weak or negative response in a person who has been exposed to produce a positive reaction. The clinical implications of this "booster effect" are beyond the scope of this book.

Tuberculin reactivity is mediated by the cellular arm of the immune system; it can be transferred by CD4-positive T cells but not by serum. Infection with measles virus can suppress cell-mediated immunity, resulting in a loss of tuberculin skin test reactivity and, in some instances, reactivation of dormant organisms and clinical disease.

A gene called *Nramp* determines natural resistance to tuberculosis. People who have mutations in the *Nramp* gene have a much higher rate of clinical tuberculosis than those with a normal allele. The NRAMP protein is located in the membrane of the phagosome in macrophages and plays an important role in killing the organism within the phagosome.

Clinical Findings

Clinical findings are protean; many organs can be involved. Fever, fatigue, night sweats, and weight loss are common. Pulmonary tuberculosis causes cough and hemoptysis. Scrofula is mycobacterial cervical adenitis that presents as swollen nontender lymph nodes, usually unilaterally. Both *M. tuberculosis* and *Mycobacterium scrofulaceum* cause scrofula. Erythema nodosum, characterized by tender nodules along the extensor surfaces of the tibia and ulna, is a manifestation of primary infection seen in patients who are controlling the infection with a potent cell-mediated response. Miliary tuberculosis is characterized by multiple disseminated lesions that resemble millet seeds. Tuberculous meningitis and tuberculous osteomyelitis, especially vertebral osteomyelitis (Pott's disease), are important disseminated forms.

Gastrointestinal tuberculosis is characterized by abdominal pain and diarrhea accompanied by more generalized symptoms of fever and weight loss. Intestinal obstruction or hemorrhage may occur. The ileocecal region is the site most often involved. Tuberculosis of the GI tract can be caused by either *M. tuberculosis* when it is swallowed after being coughed up from a lung lesion or by *M. bovis* when it is ingested in unpasteurized milk products. **Oropharyngeal tuberculosis** typically presents as a painless ulcer accompanied by local adenopathy.

In **renal tuberculosis,** dysuria, hematuria, and flank pain occur. "Sterile pyuria" is a characteristic finding. The urine contains white blood cells, but cultures for the common urinary tract bacterial pathogens show no growth. However, mycobacterial cultures are often positive.

Note that most (approximately 90%) infections with *M. tuberculosis* are asymptomatic. Although there may be some differences in the virulence between strains of the organism, the most important determinant of whether overt disease occurs is the adequacy of the host's cell-mediated immune response. For example, AIDS patients have a very high rate of reactivation of prior asymptomatic infection and of rapid progression of the disease. In these patients, untreated disease caused by *M. tuberculosis* has a 50% mortality rate. Furthermore, administration of infliximab (Remicade), a monoclonal antibody that neutralizes tumor necrosis factor (TNF), has activated latent tuberculosis in some patients. Remicade is used in the treatment of rheumatoid arthritis (see Chapter 66).

Laboratory Diagnosis

Acid-fast staining of sputum or other specimens is the usual initial test. For rapid screening purposes, auramine stain, which can be visualized by fluorescence microscopy, can be used.

After digestion of the specimen by treatment with NaOH and concentration by centrifugation, the material is cultured on special media, such as Löwenstein-Jensen agar, for up to 8 weeks. It will *not* grow on a blood agar plate. In liquid BACTEC medium, radioactive metabolites are present and growth can be detected by the production of radioactive carbon dioxide in about 2 weeks. A liquid medium is preferred for isolation because the organism grows more rapidly and reliably than it does on agar. If growth in the culture occurs, the organism can be identified by biochemical tests. For example, *M. tuberculosis* produces **niacin,** whereas almost no other mycobacteria do. It also produces catalase. More rapid identification tests using DNA probes are also available.

Because drug resistance, especially to INH (see below), is a problem, susceptibility tests should be performed. However, the organism grows very slowly and susceptibility tests usually take several weeks, which is too long to guide the initial choice of drugs. The **luciferase assay,** which can detect drug-resistant organisms in a few days, is a distinct improvement. Luciferase is an enzyme isolated from fireflies that produces flashes of light in the presence of adenosine triphosphate (ATP). If the organism isolated from the patient is resistant, it will not be damaged by the drug; ie, it will make a normal amount of ATP, and the luciferase will produce the normal amount of light. If the organism is sensitive to the drug, less ATP will be made and less light produced.

Treatment & Resistance

Multidrug therapy is used to prevent the emergence of drug-resistant mutants during the long (6- to 9-month) duration of treatment. (Organisms that become resistant to one drug will be inhibited by the other.) **Isoniazid** (INH), a bactericidal drug, is the mainstay of treatment. Treatment for most patients with pulmonary tuberculosis is with three drugs: INH, rifampin, and pyrazinamide. INH and rifampin are given for 6 months, but pyrazinamide treatment is stopped after 2 months. In patients who are immunocompromised (eg, AIDS patients), who have disseminated disease, or who are likely to have INH-resistant organisms, a fourth drug, ethambutol, is added and all four drugs are given for 9–12 months. Although therapy is usually given for months, the patient's sputum becomes **noninfectious within 2–3 weeks.** The necessity for protracted therapy is attributed to (1) the intracellular location of the organism; (2) caseous material, which blocks penetration by the drug; (3) the slow growth of the organism; and (4) metabolically inactive "persisters" within the lesion. Because metabolically inactive organisms may not be killed by antitubercular drugs, treatment may not eradicate the infection and reactivation of the disease may occur in the future.

Treatment of latent (asymptomatic) infections consists of INH taken for 6 to 9 months. (This regimen used to be considered prophylactic because it reduced the risk of symptomatic infection appearing in the future.) This approach is most often used in asymptomatic patients whose PPD skin test recently converted to positive. The risk of symptomatic infection is greatest within the first 2 years after infection, so INH is particularly indicated for these "recent converters." INH is also used in children exposed to patients with symptomatic tuberculosis. Patients who receive INH should be evaluated for drug-induced hepatitis, especially those over the age of 35 years. Rifampin can be used in those exposed to INH-resistant strains. A combination of rifampin and pyrazinamide should not be used because it caused a high rate of severe liver injury.

Resistance to INH and other antituberculosis drugs is being seen with increasing frequency in the United States, especially in immigrants from Southeast Asia and Latin America. Strains of *M. tuberculosis* **resistant to multiple drugs** have emerged, primarily in AIDS patients. The most common pattern is resistance to both INH and rifampin, but some isolates are resistant to three or more drugs. The treatment of MDR organisms usually involves the use of four or five drugs, including ciprofloxacin, amikacin, ethionamide, and cycloserine. The precise recommendations depend on the resistance pattern of the isolate and are beyond the scope of this book.

Previous treatment for tuberculosis predisposes to the selection of these MDR organisms. **Noncompliance**, ie, the failure of patients to complete the full course of therapy, is a major factor in allowing the resistant organisms to survive. One approach to the problem of noncompliance is directly observed therapy (DOT), in which health care workers observe the patient taking the medication.

Prevention

The incidence of tuberculosis began to decrease markedly even before the advent of drug therapy in the 1940s. This is attributed to better housing and nutrition, which have improved host resistance. At present, prevention of the spread of the organism depends largely on the prompt identification and adequate treatment of patients who are coughing up the organism. The use of masks and other respiratory isolation procedures to prevent spread to medical personnel is also important.

An important component of prevention is the use of the PPD skin test to detect recent converters and to institute treatment for latent infections as described above. Groups that should be screened with the PPD skin test include people with HIV infection, close contacts of patients with active tuberculosis, low-income populations, alcoholics and intravenous drug users, prison inmates, and foreign-born individuals from countries with a high incidence of tuberculosis.

Because there are some problems associated with PPD skin tests, such as the measurement and the interpretation of results and the inconvenience of the patient having to return for the skin test to be read, a laboratory test to detect latent infections was developed. This test, called QuantiFERON-TB (QFT), measures the amount of γ-interferon released from the patient's lymphocytes after exposure to PPD in cell culture. QFT requires only a single blood specimen and determines the amount of γ-interferon by an ELISA test.

BCG vaccine can be used to induce partial resistance to tuberculosis. The vaccine contains a strain of live, attenuated *M. bovis* called bacillus Calmette-Guérin. The vaccine is effective in preventing the appearance of tuberculosis as a clinical disease, especially in children, although it does not prevent infection by *M. tuberculosis*. However, a major problem with the vaccine is its variable effectiveness, which can range from 0% to 70%. It is used primarily in areas of the world where the incidence of the disease is high. It is *not* usually used in the United States because of its variable effectiveness and because the incidence of the disease is low enough that it is not cost-effective.

The skin test reactivity induced by the vaccine given to children wanes with time, and the interpretation of the skin test reaction in adults is not altered by the vaccine. For example, skin test reactions of 10 mm or more should not be attributed to the vaccine unless it was administered recently. In the United States, use of the vaccine is limited to young children who are in close contact with individuals with active tuberculosis and to military personnel. BCG vaccine should not be given to immunocompromised people because the live BCG organisms can cause disseminated disease.

BCG vaccine is also used to treat bladder cancer. The vaccine is instilled into the bladder and serves to nonspecifically stimulate cell-mediated immunity, which can inhibit the growth of the carcinoma cells.

Pasteurization of milk and destruction of infected cattle are important in preventing intestinal tuberculosis.

ATYPICAL MYCOBACTERIA

Several species of mycobacteria are characterized as atypical, because they differ in certain respects from the prototype, *M. tuberculosis*. For example, atypical mycobacteria are widespread in the **environment** and are not pathogenic for guinea pigs, whereas *M. tuberculosis* is found only in humans and is highly pathogenic for guinea pigs.

The atypical mycobacteria are classified into four groups according to their rate of growth and whether they produce pigment under certain conditions (Table 21–3). Group I organisms produce a yellow-orange-pigmented colony only when exposed to light (**photochromogens**), whereas group II organisms produce the pigment chiefly in the dark (**scotochromogens**). Group III mycobacteria produce little or no yellow-orange pigment, irrespective of the presence or absence of light (**nonchromogens**). In contrast to the organisms in the previous three groups, which grow slowly, group IV organisms grow rapidly, producing colonies in fewer than 7 days.

Table 21–3. Runyon's classification of atypical mycobacteria.

| Group | Growth Rate | Pigment Formation In: | | Typical Species |
		Light	Dark	
I	Slow	+	−	*M. kansasii, M. marinum*
II	Slow	+	+	*M. scrofulaceum*
III	Slow	−	−	*M. avium-intracellulare* complex
IV	Rapid	−	−	*M. fortuitum-chelonei* complex

Group I (Photochromogens)

M. kansasii causes lung disease clinically resembling tuberculosis. Because it is antigenically similar to *M. tuberculosis,* patients are frequently tuberculin skin test–positive. Its habitat in the environment is unknown, but infections by this organism are localized to the midwestern states and Texas. It is susceptible to the standard antituberculosis drugs.

Mycobacterium marinum causes "swimming pool granuloma," also known as "fish tank granuloma." These granulomatous, ulcerating lesions occur in the skin at the site of abrasions incurred at swimming pools and aquariums. The natural habitat of the organism is both fresh and salt water. Treatment with a tetracycline such as minocycline is effective.

Group II (Scotochromogens)

M. scrofulaceum causes scrofula, a granulomatous cervical adenitis, usually in children. (*M. tuberculosis* also causes scrofula.) The organism enters through the oropharynx and infects the draining lymph nodes. Its natural habitat is environmental water sources, but it has also been isolated as a saprophyte from the human respiratory tract. Scrofula can often be cured by surgical excision of the affected lymph nodes.

Group III (Nonchromogens)

M. avium-intracellulare complex (MAI, MAC) is composed of two species, *M. avium* and *M. intracellulare,* that are very difficult to distinguish from each other by standard laboratory tests. They cause pulmonary disease clinically indistinguishable from tuberculosis, primarily in immunocompromised patients such as those with AIDS who have CD4 cell counts of less than 200/μL. MAI is the most common bacterial cause of disease in AIDS patients. The organisms are widespread in the environment, including water and soil, particularly in the southeastern United States. They are highly resistant to antituberculosis drugs, and as many as six drugs in combination are frequently required for adequate treatment. Current drugs of choice are clarithromycin plus one or more of the following: ethambutol, rifabutin, or ciprofloxacin. Clarithromycin is currently recommended for preventing disease in AIDS patients.

Group IV (Rapidly Growing Mycobacteria)

Mycobacterium fortuitum-chelonei complex is composed of two similar species, *M. fortuitum* and *M. chelonei.* They are saprophytes, found chiefly in soil and water, and rarely cause human disease. Infections occur chiefly in two populations: (1) immunocompromised patients and (2) individuals with prosthetic hip joints and indwelling catheters. Skin and soft tissue infections occur at the site of puncture wounds. They are often resistant to antituberculosis therapy, and therapy with multiple drugs in combination plus surgical excision may be required for effective treatment. Current drugs of choice are amikacin plus doxycycline.

Mycobacterium abscessus is another rapidly growing mycobacteria acquired from the environment. It causes chronic lung infections, as well as infections of the skin, bone, and joints. It is highly antibiotic-resistant.

Mycobacterium smegmatis is a rapidly growing mycobacterium that is not associated with human disease. It is part of the normal flora of smegma, the material that collects under the foreskin of the penis.

MYCOBACTERIUM LEPRAE

Disease

This organism causes leprosy.

Important Properties

M. leprae has **not been grown** in the laboratory, either on artificial media or in cell culture. It can be grown in the mouse footpad or in the armadillo.

Humans are the natural hosts, although the armadillo may also be a reservoir for human infection. The optimal temperature for growth (30°C) is lower than body temperature; it therefore grows preferentially in the skin and superficial nerves. It grows very slowly, with a doubling time of 14 days. This makes it the slowest-growing human bacterial pathogen. One consequence of this is that antibiotic therapy must be continued for a long time, usually several years.

Transmission

Infection is acquired by **prolonged contact with patients** with lepromatous leprosy, who discharge *M. leprae* in large numbers in nasal secretions and from skin lesions. In the United States, leprosy occurs primarily in Texas, Louisiana, California, and Hawaii. Most cases are found in immigrants from Mexico, the Philippines, southeast Asia, and India. The disease occurs worldwide, with most cases in the tropical areas of Asia and Africa. The armadillo is unlikely to be an important reservoir because it is not found in many areas of the world where leprosy is endemic.

Pathogenesis

The organism replicates intracellularly, typically within skin histiocytes, endothelial cells, and the Schwann cells of nerves. There are two distinct forms of leprosy—**tuberculoid** and **lepromatous**—with several intermediate forms between the two extremes (Table 21–4).

(1) In tuberculoid leprosy, the cell-mediated immune (CMI) response to the organism limits its growth, very few acid-fast bacilli are seen, and granulomas containing giant cells form.

The CMI response consists primarily of CD4-positive cells and a Th-1 profile of cytokines, namely, γ-interferon, interleukin-2, and interleukin-12. It is the CMI response that causes the nerve damage seen in tuberculoid leprosy.

The lepromin skin test result is positive. The lepromin skin test is similar to the tuberculin test (see above). An extract of *M. leprae* is injected intradermally, and induration is observed 48 hours later in those in whom a cell-mediated immune response against the organism exists.

(2) In lepromatous leprosy, the cell-mediated response to the organism is poor, the skin and mucous membrane lesions contain large numbers of organisms, foamy histiocytes rather than granulomas are found, and the lepromin skin test result is negative. Note that in lepromatous leprosy, only the cell-mediated response to *M. leprae* is defective; ie, the patient is anergic to *M. leprae*. The cell-mediated response to other organisms is unaffected, and the humoral response to *M. leprae* is intact. However, these antibodies are not protective. The T-cell response consists primarily of Th-2 cells.

Clinical Findings

The incubation period averages several years, and the onset of the disease is gradual. In tuberculoid leprosy, hypopigmented macular or plaque-like skin lesions, thickened superficial nerves, and significant anesthesia of the skin lesions occur. In lepromatous leprosy, multiple nodular skin lesions occur, resulting in the typical **leonine** (lionlike) **facies**. After the onset of therapy, patients with lepromatous leprosy often develop **erythema nodosum leprosum** (ENL), which is interpreted as a sign that cell-mediated immunity is being restored. ENL is characterized by painful nodules, especially along the extensor surfaces of the tibia and ulna; neuritis; and uveitis.

The disfiguring appearance of the disease results from several factors: (1) the skin anesthesia results in burns and other traumas, which often become infected; (2) resorption of bone leads to loss of features such as the nose and fingertips; and (3) infiltration of the skin

Table 21–4. Comparison of tuberculoid and lepromatous leprosy.

Feature	Tuberculoid Leprosy	Lepromatous Leprosy
Type of lesion	One or few lesions with little tissue destruction	Many lesions with marked tissue destruction
Number of acid-fast bacilli	Few	Many
Likelihood of transmitting leprosy	Low	High
Cell-mediated response to *M. leprae*	Present	Reduced or absent
Lepromin skin test	Positive	Negative

and nerves leads to thickening and folding of the skin. In most patients with a single skin lesion, the disease resolves spontaneously. Patients with forms of the disease intermediate between tuberculoid and lepromatous can progress to either extreme.

Laboratory Diagnosis

In lepromatous leprosy, the bacilli are easily demonstrated by performing an acid-fast stain of skin lesions or nasal scrapings. Lipid-laden macrophages called "foam cells" containing many acid-fast bacilli are seen in the skin. In the tuberculoid form, very few organisms are seen and the appearance of typical granulomas is sufficient for diagnosis. Cultures are negative because the organism does not grow on artificial media. No serologic tests are useful. False-positive results in the nonspecific serologic tests for syphilis, such as the VDRL and RPR tests, occur frequently in patients with lepromatous leprosy.

Treatment

The mainstay of therapy is **dapsone** (diaminodiphenyl-sulfone), but because sufficient resistance to the drug has emerged, combination therapy is now recom-mended, eg, dapsone, rifampin, and clofazimine for lepromatous leprosy and dapsone and rifampin for the tuberculoid form. Treatment is given for at least 2 years or until the lesions are free of organisms. Thalidomide is the treatment of choice for severe ENL reactions.

Prevention

Isolation of all lepromatous patients, coupled with chemoprophylaxis with dapsone for exposed children, is required. There is no vaccine.

SUMMARIES OF ORGANISMS

Brief summaries of the organisms described in this chapter begin on page 488. Please consult these summaries for a rapid review of the essential material.

PRACTICE QUESTIONS: USMLE & COURSE EXAMINATIONS

Questions on the topics discussed in this chapter can be found in the Clinical Bacteriology section of Part XI: USMLE (National Board) Practice Questions starting on page 537. Also see Part XII: USMLE (National Board) Practice Examination starting on page 583.

Actinomycetes

Actinomycetes are true bacteria (related to corynebacteria and mycobacteria), but they form **long, branching filaments** that resemble the hyphae of fungi. They are gram-positive, but some (such as *Nocardia asteroides*) are also weakly acid-fast (Table 22–1). There are two medically important organisms, *Actinomyces israelii* and *N. asteroides*.

ACTINOMYCES ISRAELII

Disease

Actinomyces israelii causes actinomycosis.

Important Properties & Pathogenesis

A. israelii is an **anaerobe** that forms part of the **normal flora of the oral cavity**. After local trauma such as a broken jaw or dental extraction, it may invade tissues, forming filaments surrounded by areas of inflammation. Hard, yellow granules (**sulfur granules**) composed of a mass of filaments are formed in pus.

Clinical Findings

Actinomycosis appears as a hard, nontender swelling that develops slowly and eventually drains pus through **sinus tracts.** In about 50% of cases, the initial lesion involves the face and neck; in the rest, the chest or abdomen is the site. Pelvic actinomycosis can occur in women who have retained an intrauterine device for a long period of time. *A. israelii* and *Arachnia* species are the most common causes of actinomycosis in humans. The disease is not communicable.

Laboratory Diagnosis

Diagnosis in the laboratory is made by (1) seeing gram-positive branching rods, especially in the presence of sulfur granules; and (2) seeing growth when pus or tissue specimens are cultured under anaerobic conditions. Organisms can be identified by immunofluorescence. There are no serologic tests.

Treatment & Prevention

Treatment consists of prolonged administration of penicillin G, coupled with surgical drainage. There is no significant resistance to penicillin G. No vaccine or prophylactic drug is available.

NOCARDIA ASTEROIDES

Disease

Nocardia asteroides causes nocardiosis.

Important Properties & Pathogenesis

Nocardia species are **aerobes** and are found in the environment, particularly in the **soil**. In immunocompromised individuals, they can produce lung infection and may disseminate. In tissues, *Nocardia* species are thin, branching filaments that are gram-positive on Gram stain. Many isolates of *N. asteroides* are **weakly acid-fast**; ie, the staining process uses a weaker solution of hydrochloric acid than that used in the stain for mycobacteria. If the regular-strength acid is used, they are not acid-fast.

Clinical Findings

N. asteroides and *Nocardia brasiliensis* are the most common causes of human nocardiosis. The disease begins as a pulmonary infection and may progress to form abscesses and sinus tracts. Unlike *A. israelii*, sulfur granules are not formed. In immunocompromised persons, the organism may spread to the brain, skin, or kidneys. The disease is not communicable.

Laboratory Diagnosis

Diagnosis in the laboratory involves (1) seeing branching rods or filaments that are gram-positive or weakly acid-fast and (2) seeing aerobic growth on bacteriologic media in a few days.

Table 22–1. Actinomycetes.

Species	Disease	Habitat	Growth in Media	Diagnosis	Treatment
A. israelii	Actinomycosis (abscess with draining sinuses)	Oral cavity	Strictly anaerobic	Gram-positive branching filaments; "sulfur granules" in pus; culture (anaerobic).	Penicillin G
N. asteroides	Nocardiosis (abscesses in brain and kidneys in immunodeficient patients, pneumonia)	Environment	Aerobic	Gram-positive filaments; often acid-fast; culture (aerobic).	Sulfonamides

Treatment & Prevention

Treatment is with trimethoprim-sulfamethoxazole. Surgical drainage may also be needed. Occasional drug resistance occurs. No vaccine or prophylactic drug is available.

SUMMARIES OF ORGANISMS

Brief summaries of the organisms described in this chapter begin on page 489. Please consult these summaries for a rapid review of the essential material.

PRACTICE QUESTIONS: USMLE & COURSE EXAMINATIONS

Questions on the topics discussed in this chapter can be found in the Clinical Bacteriology section of Part XI: USMLE (National Board) Practice Questions starting on page 537. Also see Part XII: USMLE (National Board) Practice Examination starting on page 583.

Mycoplasmas

Mycoplasmas are a group of very small, **wall-less** organisms, of which *Mycoplasma pneumoniae* is the major pathogen.

MYCOPLASMA PNEUMONIAE

Disease

M. pneumoniae causes "atypical" pneumonia.

Important Properties

Mycoplasmas are the **smallest free-living organisms;** many are as small as 0.3 μm in diameter. Their most striking feature is the absence of a cell wall.[1]

Consequently, mycoplasmas stain poorly with Gram stain, and antibiotics that inhibit cell wall synthesis, eg, penicillins and cephalosporins, are ineffective. Their outer surface is a flexible three-layer cell membrane; hence, these organisms can assume a variety of shapes. Theirs is the only bacterial membrane that contains **cholesterol,** a sterol usually found in eukaryotic cell membranes.

Mycoplasmas can be grown in the laboratory on artificial media, but they have complex nutritional requirements, including several lipids. They grow slowly and require at least 1 week to form a visible colony. The colony frequently has a characteristic "fried-egg" shape, with a raised center and a thinner outer edge.

Pathogenesis & Epidemiology

M. pneumoniae, a pathogen **only for humans,** is transmitted by **respiratory droplets.** In the lungs, the organism is rod-shaped, with a tapered tip that contains specific proteins that serve as the point of attachment to the respiratory epithelium. The respiratory mucosa is not invaded, but ciliary motion is inhibited and necrosis of the epithelium occurs. The mechanism by which *M. pneumoniae* causes inflammation is uncertain. It does produce hydrogen peroxide, which contributes to the damage to the respiratory tract cells.

M. pneumoniae has only one serotype and is antigenically distinct from other species of *Mycoplasma.* Immunity is incomplete, and second episodes of disease can occur. During *M. pneumoniae* infection, autoantibodies are produced against red cells (**cold agglutinins**) and brain, lung, and liver cells. These antibodies may be the source of the extrapulmonary manifestations of infection.

M. pneumoniae infections occur worldwide, with an increased incidence in the winter. This organism is the most frequent cause of pneumonia in young adults and is responsible for outbreaks in groups with close contacts such as families, military personnel, and college students. It is estimated that only 10% of infected individuals actually get pneumonia. *Mycoplasma* pneumonia accounts for about 5–10% of all community-acquired pneumonia.

Clinical Findings

Mycoplasma pneumonia is the most common type of atypical pneumonia. It was formerly called **primary atypical pneumonia.** (Other atypical pneumonias are legionnaires' disease, Q fever, psittacosis, and viral pneumonias such as influenza. The term "atypical" means that a causative bacterium cannot be isolated on routine media in the diagnostic laboratory or that the disease does not resemble pneumococcal pneumonia.) The onset of *Mycoplasma* pneumonia is gradual, usually beginning with a nonproductive cough, sore throat, or earache. Small amounts of whitish, nonbloody sputum are produced. Constitutional symptoms of fever, headache, malaise, and myalgias are pronounced. The paucity of findings on chest examination is in marked contrast to the prominence of the infiltrates seen on the patient's chest x-ray. The disease resolves spontaneously in 10–14 days.

Laboratory Diagnosis

Diagnosis is usually not made by culturing sputum samples; it takes at least 1 week for colonies to appear on special media. Culture on regular media reveals only normal flora.

Serologic testing is the mainstay of diagnosis. A

---

[1] Other types of bacteria, in the presence of penicillin, can exist in a wall-less state called an "L form" but can resynthesize their cell walls when penicillin is removed.

cold-agglutinin titer of 1:128 or higher is indicative of recent infection. Cold agglutinins are IgM autoantibodies against type O red blood cells that agglutinate these cells at 4°C but not at 37°C. However, only half of patients with *Mycoplasma* pneumonia will be positive for cold agglutinins. The test is nonspecific; false-positive results occur in influenza virus and adenovirus infections. The diagnosis of *M. pneumoniae* infection can be confirmed by a 4-fold or greater rise in specific antibody titer in the complement fixation test.

Treatment

The treatment of choice is either a macrolide, such as erythromycin or azithromycin, or a tetracycline, such as doxycycline. These drugs can shorten the duration of symptoms, although, as mentioned above, the disease resolves spontaneously. Penicillins and cephalosporins are **inactive** because the organism has no cell wall.

Prevention

There is no vaccine or other specific preventive measure.

OTHER MYCOPLASMAS

Mycoplasma hominis has been implicated as an infrequent cause of pelvic inflammatory disease. *Ureaplasma urealyticum* may cause approximately 20% of cases of nongonococcal urethritis. Ureaplasmas can be distinguished from mycoplasmas by their ability to produce the enzyme urease, which degrades urea to ammonia and carbon dioxide.

SUMMARIES OF ORGANISMS

Brief summaries of the organisms described in this chapter begin on page 490. Please consult these summaries for a rapid review of the essential material.

PRACTICE QUESTIONS: USMLE & COURSE EXAMINATIONS

Questions on the topics discussed in this chapter can be found in the Clinical Bacteriology section of Part XI: USMLE (National Board) Practice Questions starting on page 537. Also see Part XII: USMLE (National Board) Practice Examination starting on page 583.

Spirochetes

Three genera of spirochetes cause human infection: (1) *Treponema,* which causes syphilis and the nonvenereal treponematoses; (2) *Borrelia,* which causes Lyme disease and relapsing fever; and (3) *Leptospira,* which causes leptospirosis (Table 24–1).

Spirochetes are thin-walled, **flexible, spiral rods.** They are motile through the undulation of axial filaments that lie under the outer sheath. Treponemes and leptospirae are so thin that they are seen only by darkfield microscopy, silver impregnation, or immunofluorescence. Borreliae are larger, accept Giemsa and other blood stains, and can be seen in the standard light microscope.

TREPONEMA

1. Treponema pallidum

Disease

Treponema pallidum causes syphilis.

Important Properties

T. pallidum has **not been grown** on bacteriologic media or in cell culture. Nonpathogenic treponemes, which are part of the normal flora of human mucous membranes, can be cultured.

T. pallidum grows **very slowly.** The medical importance of that fact is that antibiotics must be present at an effective level for several weeks to kill the organisms and cure the disease (see Treatment section below). For example, benzathine penicillin is the form of penicillin used to treat primary and secondary syphilis because the penicillin is released very slowly from this depot preparation and bactericidal concentrations are present for weeks after administration of the antibiotic.

The antigens of *T. pallidum* induce specific antibodies, which can be detected by immunofluorescence or hemagglutination tests in the clinical laboratory. They also induce nonspecific antibodies (**reagin**),[1] which can be detected by the flocculation of lipids (cardiolipin) extracted from normal mammalian tissues, eg, beef heart.

Both specific antitreponemal antibody and nonspecific reagin are used in the serologic diagnosis of syphilis.

Transmission & Epidemiology

T. pallidum is transmitted from spirochete-containing lesions of skin or mucous membranes (eg, genitalia, mouth, and rectum) of an infected person to other persons by **intimate contact.** It can also be transmitted from pregnant women to their fetuses. Rarely, blood for transfusions collected during early syphilis is also infectious.

Syphilis occurs worldwide, and its incidence is increasing. It is one of the leading notifiable diseases in the United States. Many cases are believed to go unreported, which limits public health efforts. There has been a marked increase in incidence of the disease in homosexual men in recent years.

Pathogenesis & Clinical Findings

T. pallidum produces no important toxins or enzymes. The organism often infects the endothelium of small blood vessels, causing endarteritis. This occurs during all stages of syphilis but is particularly important in the pathogenesis of the brain and cardiovascular lesions seen in tertiary syphilis.

In **primary** syphilis, the spirochetes multiply at the site of inoculation and a local, nontender ulcer (**chancre**) usually forms in 2–10 weeks. The ulcer heals spontaneously, but spirochetes spread widely via the bloodstream (bacteremia) to many organs. One to three months later, the lesions of **secondary syphilis** may occur. These often appear as a maculopapular rash, notably on the **palms** and **soles,** or as moist papules on skin and mucous membranes. Moist lesions on the genitals are called **condylomata lata.** These lesions are rich in spirochetes and are highly infectious, but they also heal spontaneously. Patchy alopecia also occurs. Constitutional symptoms of secondary syphilis include low-grade fever, malaise, anorexia, weight loss, headache, myalgias, and generalized lymphadenopathy. There may be internal organ involvement (meningitis, nephritis, hepatitis, etc). These stages may be asymptomatic, and yet the disease may progress.

---

[1] Syphilitic reagin (IgM and IgG) should not be confused with the reagin (IgE) antibody involved in allergy.

Table 24–1. Spirochetes of medical importance.

Species	Disease	Mode of Transmission	Diagnosis	Morphology	Growth in Bacteriologic Media	Treatment
T. pallidum	Syphilis	Intimate (sexual) contact; across the placenta	Microscopy; serologic tests.	Thin, tight, spirals, seen by darkfield illumination, silver impregnation, or immunofluorescent stain.	–	Penicillin G
B. burgdorferi	Lyme disease	Tick bite	Clinical observations; microscopy.	Large, loosely coiled; stain with Giemsa stain.	+	Tetracycline or amoxicillin for acute; penicillin G for chronic
B. recurrentis	Relapsing fever	Louse bite	Clinical observations; microscopy.	Large, loosely coiled; stain with Giemsa stain.	+	Tetracycline
L. interrogans	Leptospirosis	Food or drink contaminated by urine of infected animals (rats, dogs, pigs, cows)	Serologic tests.	Thin, tight spirals, seen by darkfield illumination.	+	Penicillin G

About one-third of these early (primary and secondary) syphilis cases will "cure" themselves, without treatment. Another third remain **latent;** ie, no lesions appear, but positive serologic tests indicate continuing infection. The latent period can be divided into **early** and **late** stages. In the early latent period, which can last for a year or two after the secondary stage, the symptoms of secondary syphilis can reappear and patients can infect others. In the late latent period, which can last for many years, no symptoms occur and patients are not infectious. In the remaining one-third of people, the disease progresses to the **tertiary** stage. Tertiary syphilis may show granulomas (gummas), especially of skin and bones; central nervous system involvement (eg, tabes, paresis); or cardiovascular lesions (eg, aortitis, aneurysm of the ascending aorta). In tertiary lesions, treponemes are rarely seen.

T. pallidum also causes **congenital syphilis.** The organism is transmitted across the placenta, typically after the third month of pregnancy, and fetal infection can occur. Skin and bone lesions are common, as is hepatosplenomegaly. Unless the disease is treated promptly, stillbirth or multiple fetal abnormalities occur.

Immunity to syphilis is incomplete. Antibodies to the organism are produced but do not stop the progression of the disease. Patients with early syphilis who have been treated can contract syphilis again. Patients with late syphilis are relatively resistant to reinfection.

Laboratory Diagnosis

There are three important approaches.

A. MICROSCOPY

Spirochetes are demonstrated in the lesions of primary or secondary syphilis, such as chancres or condylomata lata, by **darkfield** microscopy or by direct fluorescent antibody (DFA) test. They are *not* seen on a Gram-stained smear. In biopsy specimens, such as those obtained from the gummas seen in tertiary syphilis, histologic stains such as silver stain or fluorescent antibody can be used.

B. NONSPECIFIC SEROLOGIC TESTS

These tests involve the use of **nontreponemal** antigens. Extracts of normal mammalian tissues (eg, **cardiolipin** from beef heart) react with antibodies in serum samples from patients with syphilis. These antibodies, which are a mixture of IgG and IgM, are called "reagin" antibodies (see above). Flocculation tests, eg, VDRL (Venereal Disease Research Laboratory) and RPR (rapid plasma reagin) tests, detect the presence of these antibodies. These tests are positive in most cases of primary syphilis and are almost always positive in secondary syphilis. The titer of these nonspecific antibodies **decreases with effective treatment**, in contrast to the specific antibodies, which are positive for life (see below).

False-positive reactions occur in infections such as leprosy, hepatitis B, and infectious mononucleosis and in various autoimmune diseases. Therefore, positive results have to be confirmed by specific tests (see below). Results of nonspecific tests usually **become negative after treatment** and should be used to determine the response to treatment. These tests can also be falsely negative as a result of the prozone phenomenon. In the prozone phenomenon, the titer of antibody is too high (antibody excess) and no flocculation will occur. On dilution of the serum, however, the test result becomes positive (see Chapter 64). These tests are inexpensive and easy to perform and therefore are used as a method of screening the population for infection. The nonspecific tests and the specific tests (see below) are described in more detail in Chapter 9.

The laboratory diagnosis of congenital syphilis is based on the finding that the infant has a higher titer of antibody in the VDRL test than has the mother. Furthermore, if a positive VDRL test result in the infant is a false-positive one because maternal antibody has crossed the placenta, the titer will decline with time. If the infant is truly infected, the titer will remain high. However, irrespective of the VDRL test results, any infant whose mother has syphilis should be treated.

C. SPECIFIC SEROLOGIC TESTS

These tests involve the use of treponemal antigens and therefore are more specific than those described above. In these tests, *T. pallidum* reacts in immunofluorescence (FTA-ABS)[2] or hemagglutination (TPHA, MHA-TP)[3] assays with specific treponemal antibodies in the patient's serum.

These antibodies arise within 2–3 weeks of infection; therefore, the test results are positive in most patients with primary syphilis. These **tests remain positive for life** after effective treatment and *cannot* be used to determine the response to treatment or reinfection. They are more expensive and more difficult to perform than the nonspecific tests and therefore are not used as screening procedures.

Treatment

Penicillin is effective in the treatment of all stages of syphilis. A single injection of benzathine penicillin G (2.4 million units) can eradicate *T. pallidum* and cure early (primary and secondary) syphilis. Note that benzathine penicillin is the form of penicillin used because the penicillin is released very slowly from this depot preparation. *T. pallidum* grows very slowly, which requires that the penicillin be present in bactericidal concentration for weeks. If the patient is allergic to penicillin, tetracycline or erythromycin can be used but must be given for prolonged periods to effect a cure. In neurosyphilis, high doses of aqueous penicillin G are administered. No resistance to penicillin has been observed.

More than half of patients with secondary syphilis who are treated with penicillin experience fever, chills, myalgias, and other influenzalike symptoms a few hours after receiving the antibiotic. This response, called the **Jarisch-Herxheimer reaction**, is attributed to the lysis of the treponemes and the release of endotoxinlike substances. Patients should be alerted to this possibility, advised that it may last for up to 24 hours, and told that symptomatic relief can be obtained with aspirin. The Jarisch-Herxheimer reaction also occurs after treatment of other spirochetal diseases such as Lyme disease, leptospirosis, and relapsing fever. Tumor necrosis factor (TNF) is an important mediator of this reaction because passive immunization with antibody against TNF can prevent its symptoms.

Prevention

Prevention depends on early diagnosis and adequate treatment, use of condoms, administration of antibiotic after suspected exposure, and serologic follow-up of infected individuals and their contacts. The presence of any sexually transmitted disease makes testing for syphilis mandatory, because several different infections are often transmitted simultaneously. There is no vaccine against syphilis.

2. Nonvenereal Treponematoses

These are infections caused by spirochetes that are virtually indistinguishable from *T. pallidum*. They are endemic in populations and are transmitted by direct contact. All of these infections result in positive (nontreponemal and treponemal) results on serologic tests for syphilis. None of these spirochetes have been grown on bacteriologic media. The diseases include bejel in Africa, yaws (caused by *T. pallidum* subspecies *pertenue*) in many humid tropical countries, and pinta (caused by *Treponema carateum*) in Central and South America. All can be cured by penicillin.

BORRELIA

Borrelia species are irregular, loosely coiled spirochetes that stain readily with Giemsa and other stains. They

---

[2] FTA-ABS is the fluorescent treponemal antibody-absorbed test. The patient's serum is absorbed with nonpathogenic treponemes to remove cross-reacting antibodies prior to reacting with *T. pallidum*.
[3] TPHA is the *T. pallidum* hemagglutination assay. MHA-TP is a hemagglutination assay done in a microtiter plate.

can be cultured in bacteriologic media containing serum or tissue extracts. They are transmitted by **arthropods.** They cause two major diseases, Lyme disease and relapsing fever.

1. *Borrelia burgdorferi*

Disease

Borrelia burgdorferi causes Lyme disease (named after a town in Connecticut). Lyme disease is also known as Lyme borreliosis.

Important Properties

B. burgdorferi is a flexible, motile spirochete that can be visualized by darkfield microscopy and by Giemsa and silver stains. It can be grown in certain bacteriologic media, but routine cultures obtained from patients (eg, blood, spinal fluid) are typically negative. In contrast, culture of the organism from the tick vector is usually positive.

Transmission & Epidemiology

B. burgdorferi is transmitted by tick bite. The tick *Ixodes scapularis* is the vector on the East Coast and in the Midwest; *Ixodes pacificus* is involved on the West Coast. The organism is found in a much higher percentage of *I. scapularis* (35–50%) than *I. pacificus* (approximately 2%) ticks. This explains the lower incidence of disease on the West Coast. The main reservoir of the organism consists of small mammals, especially the white-footed mouse, upon which the nymphs feed.[4]

Large mammals, especially deer, are an obligatory host in the tick's life cycle but are not an important reservoir of the organism.

The nymphal stage of the tick transmits the disease more often than the adult and larval stages do. Nymphs feed primarily in the summer, which accounts for the high incidence of disease at that time. The tick must feed for 24–48 hours to transmit an infectious dose. This implies that inspecting the skin after being exposed can prevent the disease. However, the nymphs are quite small and can easily be missed. There is no human-to-human spread.

The disease occurs worldwide. In the United States, three regions are primarily affected: the states along the North Atlantic seaboard; the northern Midwestern states, eg, Wisconsin; and the West Coast, especially California. In 1996, approximately 80% of the reported cases occurred in four states, New York, Connecticut, Pennsylvania, and New Jersey.

---

[4] In California, the woodrat is the main reservoir and a second tick, *Ixodes neotomae,* perpetuates the infection in the woodrat but does not transmit the infection to humans.

Lyme disease is the most common vector-borne disease in the United States. The major bacterial diseases transmitted by ticks in the United States are Lyme disease, Rocky Mountain spotted fever, ehrlichiosis, relapsing fever, and tularemia. *I. scapularis* ticks transmit three diseases: two bacterial diseases, Lyme disease and human granulocytic ehrlichiosis, and the protozoan disease, babesiosis.

Pathogenesis & Clinical Findings

Pathogenesis is associated with spread of the organism from the bite site through the surrounding skin followed by dissemination via the blood (bacteremia) to various organs, especially the heart, joints, and central nervous system. No exotoxins, enzymes, or other important virulence factors have been identified.

The clinical findings have been divided into three stages; however, this is a progressive disease, and the stages are not discrete. In stage 1, **erythema chronicum migrans** (also called **erythema migrans**), a spreading, nonpruritic, circular red rash with a clear center at the bite site, is the most common finding. Both the tick bite and the rash are painless. The rash can, but need not, be accompanied by nonspecific "flulike" symptoms such as fever, chills, fatigue, and headache. Secondary skin lesions frequently occur. Arthralgias, but not arthritis, are another common finding in the early stage. In approximately 25% of cases of Lyme disease, no rash is seen.

In stage 2, which occurs weeks to months later, cardiac and neurologic involvement predominates. Myocarditis, accompanied by various forms of heart block, occurs. Acute (aseptic) meningitis and cranial neuropathies, such as seventh-nerve palsy (Bell's palsy), are prominent during this stage. Peripheral neuropathies also occur. A latent phase lasting weeks to months typically ensues. In stage 3, arthritis, usually of the large joints, eg, knees, is a characteristic finding. Chronic progressive central nervous system disease also occurs.

Laboratory Diagnosis

Although the organism can be grown in the laboratory, cultures are rarely positive and hence are usually not performed. The diagnosis is typically made serologically by detecting either IgM antibody or a rising titer of IgG antibody with an enzyme-linked immunosorbent assay (ELISA) or an indirect immunofluorescence test. IgM is typically detectable 2 weeks after infection and peaks at 3–6 weeks. Serologic tests done before 2 weeks are likely to yield negative results. After 30 days postinfection, tests for IgG are more reliable.

Unfortunately, there are problems with the specificity and sensitivity of these tests because of the presence of cross-reacting antibodies against spirochetes in the normal flora. A positive test result should be confirmed with a Western blot analysis. In addition, patients treated early in the disease may not develop detectable antibodies. A PCR (polymerase chain reaction) test that detects the organism's DNA is also available.

Treatment & Prevention

The treatment of choice for stage 1 disease or other mild manifestations is either doxycycline or amoxicillin. For more severe forms or late-stage disease, penicillin G or ceftriaxone is more effective. There is no significant antibiotic resistance. Prevention centers on wearing protective clothing and using insect repellents. Examining the skin carefully for ticks is also very important, because the tick must feed for 24–48 hours to transmit an infective dose.

Should prophylactic antibiotics be given to people who have been bitten by a tick? The decision depends on two main factors, the percentage of infected ticks in the area and the length of time the tick has fed on the person. If the percentage of infected ticks is high and the length of time is more that 48 hours, it may be cost-effective to prescribe doxycycline prophylactically. Any person bitten by a tick should be advised to watch carefully for a rash or flulike symptoms for the next 3 weeks.

A vaccine containing a recombinant outer surface protein (OspA) of *B. burgdorferi* as the immunogen was available but has been withdrawn.

2. *Borrelia recurrentis & Borrelia hermsii*

Borrelia recurrentis, Borrelia hermsii, and several other borreliae cause relapsing fever. During infection, the **antigens** of these organisms **undergo variation.** As antibodies develop against one antigen, variants emerge and produce relapses of the illness. This can be repeated 3–10 times.

B. recurrentis is transmitted from person to person by the **human body louse.** Humans are the only hosts. *B. hermsii* and many other *Borrelia* species are transmitted to humans by soft **ticks** (*Ornithodoros*). Rodents and other small animals are the main reservoirs. These species of *Borrelia* are passed transovarially in the ticks, a phenomenon that plays an important role in maintaining the organism in nature.

During infection, the arthropod bite introduces spirochetes, which then multiply in many tissues, producing fever, chills, headaches, and multiple-organ dysfunction. Each attack is terminated as antibodies arise.

Diagnosis is usually made by seeing the large spirochetes in stained smears of peripheral blood. They can be cultured in special media. Serologic tests are rarely useful. Tetracycline may be beneficial early in the illness and may prevent relapses. Avoidance of arthropod vectors is the best means of prevention.

LEPTOSPIRA

Leptospiras are tightly coiled, fine spirochetes that are not stained with dyes but are seen by darkfield microscopy. They grow in bacteriologic media containing serum.

Leptospira interrogans is the cause of leptospirosis. It is divided into serogroups that occur in different animals and geographic locations. Each serogroup is subdivided into serovars by the response to agglutination tests.

Leptospiras infect various animals including **rats** and other rodents, domestic livestock, and household pets. In the United States, dogs are the most important reservoir. Animals excrete leptospiras in **urine,** which contaminates water and soil. Swimming in contaminated water or consuming contaminated food or drink can result in human infection. Outbreaks have occurred among participants in triathalon and adventure tours involving swimming in contaminated waters. Miners, farmers, and people who work in sewers are at high risk. In the United States, the urban poor have a high rate of infection as determined by the presence of antibodies. Person-to-person transmission is rare.

Human infection results when leptospiras are ingested or pass through mucous membranes or skin. They circulate in the blood and multiply in various organs, producing fever and dysfunction of the liver (jaundice), kidneys (uremia), lungs (hemorrhage), and central nervous system (aseptic meningitis). The illness is typically **biphasic,** with fever, chills, intense headache, and conjunctival suffusion (diffuse reddening of the conjunctivae) appearing early in the disease, followed by a short period of resolution of these symptoms as the organisms are cleared from the blood. The second, "immune," phase is most often characterized by the findings of aseptic meningitis and, in severe cases, liver damage (jaundice) and impaired kidney function. Serovar-specific immunity develops with infection.

Diagnosis is based on history of possible exposure, suggestive clinical signs, and a marked rise in IgM-antibody titer. Occasionally, leptospiras are isolated from blood and urine cultures.

The treatment of choice is penicillin G. There is no significant antibiotic resistance. Prevention primarily involves avoiding contact with the contaminated environment. Doxycycline is effective in preventing the disease in exposed persons.

OTHER SPIROCHETES

Anaerobic saprophytic spirochetes are prominent in the normal flora of the human mouth. Such spirochetes participate in mixed anaerobic infections, infected human bites, stasis ulcers, etc.

Spirillum minor causes one type of rat bite fever in humans. *Streptobacillus moniliformis,* a gram-negative rod, also causes rat bite fever. (See Chapter 27 for more information.)

SUMMARIES OF ORGANISMS

Brief summaries of the organisms described in this chapter begin on page 490. Please consult these summaries for a rapid review of the essential material.

PRACTICE QUESTIONS: USMLE & COURSE EXAMINATIONS

Questions on the topics discussed in this chapter can be found in the Clinical Bacteriology section of Part XI: USMLE (National Board) Practice Questions starting on page 537. Also see Part XII: USMLE (National Board) Practice Examination starting on page 583.

Chlamydiae

Chlamydiae are obligate intracellular organisms, that is, they can grow *only* within cells. They are the agents of common sexually transmitted diseases, such as urethritis and cervicitis, as well as other infections such as pneumonia, psittacosis, trachoma, and lymphogranuloma venereum.

Diseases

Chlamydia trachomatis causes eye, respiratory, and genital tract infections. *C. trachomatis* is the **most common cause of sexually transmitted disease** in the United States. *Chlamydia pneumoniae* (formerly called the TWAR strain) causes atypical pneumonia. *C. psittaci* causes psittacosis (Table 25–1).

C. pneumoniae and *C. psittaci* are sufficiently different molecularly from *C. trachomatis* that they have been reclassified into a new genus called *Chlamydophila*. Taxonomically, they are now *Chiamydophila pneumoniae* and *Chlamydophila psittaci*. However, from a medical perspective they are still known as *Chlamydia pneumoniae* and *Chlamydia psittaci*, and those are the names that will be used in this book.

Important Properties

Chlamydiae are **obligate intracellular** bacteria. They lack the ability to produce sufficient energy to grow independently and therefore can grow only inside host cells. They have a rigid cell wall but do not have a typical peptidoglycan layer. Their cell walls resemble those of gram-negative bacteria but lack muramic acid.

Chlamydiae have a replicative cycle different from that of all other bacteria. The cycle begins when the extracellular, metabolically inert, "sporelike" **elementary body** enters the cell and reorganizes into a larger, metabolically active **reticulate body** (Figure 25–1). The latter undergoes repeated binary fission to form daughter elementary bodies, which are released from the cell. Within cells, the site of replication appears as an inclusion body, which can be stained and visualized microscopically. These inclusions are useful in the identification of these organisms in the clinical laboratory.

All chlamydiae share a group-specific lipopolysac-charide antigen, which is detected by complement fixation tests. They also possess species-specific and immunotype-specific antigens (proteins), which are detected by immunofluorescence. *C. psittaci* and *C. pneumoniae* each have 1 immunotype, whereas *C. trachomatis* has at least 15.

Transmission & Epidemiology

C. trachomatis infects **only humans** and is usually transmitted by close personal contact, eg, **sexually** or by **passage through the birth canal**. Individuals with **asymptomatic genital tract infections** are an important reservoir of infection for others. In trachoma, *C. trachomatis* is transmitted by finger-to-eye or fomite-to-eye contact. *C. pneumoniae* infects only humans and is transmitted from person to person by aerosol. *C. psittaci* infects **birds** and many mammals. Humans are infected primarily by inhaling organisms in dry bird feces.

Sexually transmitted disease caused by *C. trachomatis* occurs worldwide, but trachoma is most frequently found in developing countries in dry, hot regions such as northern Africa.

Patients with a sexually transmitted disease are **coinfected** with both *C. trachomatis* and *Neisseria gonorrhoeae* in approximately 10–30% of cases.

Pathogenesis & Clinical Findings

Chlamydiae infect primarily **epithelial cells** of the mucous membranes or the lungs. They rarely cause invasive, disseminated infections. *C. psittaci* infects the lungs primarily. The infection may be asymptomatic (detected only by a rising antibody titer) or may produce high fever and pneumonia. Human psittacosis is not generally communicable. *C. pneumoniae* causes upper and lower respiratory tract infections, especially bronchitis and pneumonia, in young adults.

C. trachomatis exists in more than 15 immunotypes (A–L). Types A, B, and C cause **trachoma,** a chronic conjunctivitis endemic in Africa and Asia. Trachoma may recur over many years and may lead to blindness but causes no systemic illness. Types D–K cause **genital tract infections**, which are occasionally transmitted to

Table 25–1. Chlamydiae of medical importance.

Species	Disease	Natural Hosts	Mode of Transmission to Humans	Number of Immunologic Types	Diagnosis	Treatment
C. trachomatis	Urethritis, pneumonia, conjunctivitis, lymphogranuloma venereum, trachoma	Humans	Sexual contact; perinatal transmission	More than 15	Inclusions in epithelial cells seen with Giemsa stain or by immunofluorescence; also cell culture.	Tetracycline, erythromycin
C. pneumoniae	Atypical pneumonia	Humans	Respiratory droplets	1	Serologic test.	Tetracycline
C. psittaci	Psittacosis (pneumonia)	Birds	Inhalation of dried bird feces	1	Serologic test (cell culture rarely done).	Tetracycline

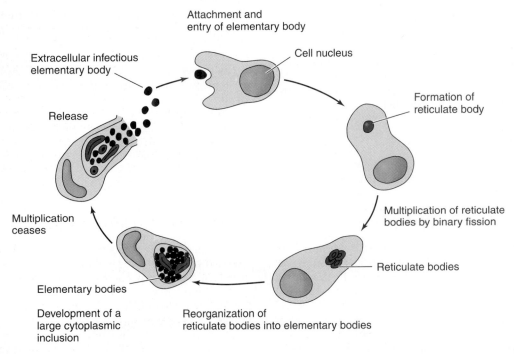

Figure 25–1. Life cycle of *Chlamydia*. The extracellular, inert elementary body enters an epithelial cell and changes into a reticulate body that divides many times by binary fission. The daughter reticulate bodies change into elementary bodies and are released from the epithelial cell. The cytoplasmic inclusion body, which is characteristic of chlamydial infections, consists of many daughter reticulate and elementary bodies. (Modified and reproduced, with permission, from Ryan K et al: *Sherris Medical Microbiology*, 3rd ed. Originally published by Appleton & Lange. Copyright © 1994 by The McGraw-Hill Companies, Inc.)

the eyes or the respiratory tract. In men, it is a common cause of nongonococcal urethritis, which may progress to epididymitis, prostatitis, or proctitis. In women, cervicitis develops and may progress to salpingitis and pelvic inflammatory disease (PID). Repeated episodes of salpingitis or PID can result in infertility or ectopic pregnancy.

Infants born to infected mothers often develop mucopurulent conjunctivitis (neonatal inclusion conjunctivitis) 7–12 days after delivery, and some develop chlamydial pneumonitis 2–12 weeks after birth. Chlamydial conjunctivitis also occurs in adults as a result of the transfer of organisms from the genitals to the eye. Patients with genital tract infections caused by *C. trachomatis* have a high incidence of **Reiter's syndrome,** which is characterized by urethritis, arthritis, and uveitis. Reiter's syndrome is an autoimmune disease caused by antibodies formed against *C. trachomatis* cross-reacting with antigens on the cells of the urethra, joints, and uveal tract (see Chapter 66).

C. trachomatis L1–L3 immunotypes cause **lymphogranuloma venereum,** a sexually transmitted disease with lesions on genitalia and in lymph nodes.

Infection by *C. trachomatis* leads to formation of antibodies and cell-mediated reactions but not to resistance to reinfection or elimination of organisms.

Laboratory Diagnosis

Chlamydiae form **cytoplasmic inclusions,** which can be seen with special stains (eg, Giemsa stain) or by immunofluorescence. The Gram stain is not useful. In exudates, the organism can be identified within epithelial cells by fluorescent antibody staining or hybridization with a DNA probe. Chlamydial antigens can also be detected in exudates or urine by ELISA (enzyme-linked immunosorbent assay). A polymerase chain reaction (PCR)-based test using the patient's urine can also be used to diagnose chlamydial sexually transmitted disease. Tests not involving culture are now more commonly used than culture-based tests.

Chlamydiae can be grown in cell cultures treated with cycloheximide, which inhibits host cell but not chlamydial protein synthesis, thereby enhancing chlamydial replication. In culture, *C. trachomatis* forms inclusions containing glycogen, whereas *C. psittaci* and *C. pneumoniae* form inclusions that do not contain glycogen. The glycogen-filled inclusions are visualized by staining with iodine. Exudates from the eyes, respiratory tract, or genital tract give positive cultures in about half of cases.

Serologic tests are used to diagnose infections by *C. psittaci* and *C. pneumoniae* but are rarely helpful in diagnosing disease caused by *C. trachomatis* because the frequency of infection is so high that many people already have antibodies.

Treatment

All chlamydiae are susceptible to tetracyclines, such as doxycyline, and macrolides, such as erythromycin and azithromycin. The drug of choice for *C. trachomatis* sexually transmitted diseases is azithromycin. Because the rate of coinfection with gonococci and *C. trachomatis* is high, any patient with a diagnosis of gonorrhea should also be treated for *C. trachomatis* with azithromycin.

The drug of choice for neonatal inclusion conjunctivitis is erythromycin. The drug of choice for *C. psittaci* and *C. pneumoniae* infections and for lymphogranuloma venereum is a tetracycline, such as doxycycline.

Prevention

There is no vaccine against any chlamydial disease. The best preventive measure against *C. trachomatis* sexually transmitted diseases is to limit transmission by prompt treatment of both the patient and the sexual partners, including persons who are asymptomatic. Sexual contacts should be traced, and those who had contact within 60 days should be treated. Several types of sexually transmitted diseases are often present simultaneously. Thus, diagnosis of one requires a search for other causative agents. Erythromycin given to newborn infants of infected mothers can prevent inclusion conjunctivitis and pneumonitis caused by *C. trachomatis*.

Psittacosis in humans is controlled by restricting the importation of psittacine birds, destroying sick birds, and adding tetracycline to bird feed. Domestic flocks of turkeys and ducks are tested for the presence of *C. psittaci*.

SUMMARIES OF ORGANISMS

Brief summaries of the organisms described in this chapter begin on page 491. Please consult these summaries for a rapid review of the essential material.

PRACTICE QUESTIONS: USMLE & COURSE EXAMINATIONS

Questions on the topics discussed in this chapter can be found in the Clinical Bacteriology section of Part XI: USMLE (National Board) Practice Questions starting on page 537. Also see Part XII: USMLE (National Board) Practice Examination starting on page 583.

Rickettsiae

Rickettsiae are obligate intracellular parasites. They are the agents of typhus, spotted fevers, and Q fever.

Diseases

In the United States, there are two rickettsial diseases of significance: Rocky Mountain spotted fever, caused by *Rickettsia rickettsii,* and Q fever, caused by *Coxiella burnetii.* Several other rickettsial diseases such as epidemic, endemic, and scrub typhus are important in developing countries. Rickettsialpox, caused by *Rickettsia akari,* is a rare disease found in certain densely populated cities in the United States. *Ehrlichia chaffeensis* is described in Chapter 27.

Important Properties

Rickettsiae are very short rods that are barely visible in the light microscope. Structurally, their cell wall resembles that of gram-negative rods, but they stain poorly with the standard Gram stain.

Rickettsiae are **obligate intracellular parasites,** because they are unable to produce sufficient energy to replicate extracellularly. Therefore, rickettsiae must be grown in cell culture, embryonated eggs, or experimental animals. Rickettsiae divide by binary fission within the host cell, in contrast to chlamydiae, which are also obligate intracellular parasites but replicate by a distinctive intracellular cycle.

Several rickettsiae, such as *Rickettsia prowazekii, Rickettsia tsutsugamushi,* and *R. rickettsii,* possess antigens that cross-react with antigens of the OX strains of *Proteus vulgaris.* The **Weil-Felix** test, which detects antirickettsial antibodies in a patient's serum by agglutination of the *Proteus* organisms, is based on this cross-reaction.

C. burnetii has a sporelike stage that is highly resistant to drying, which enhances its ability to cause infection. It also has a very low ID 50, estimated to be approximately one organism. *C. burnetii* exists in two phases that differ in their antigenicity and their virulence: phase I organisms are isolated from the patient, are virulent, and synthesize certain surface antigens, whereas phase II organisms are produced by repeated passage in culture, are nonvirulent, and have lost the ability to synthesize certain surface antigens. The clinical importance of phase variation is that patients with chronic Q fever have a much higher antibody titer to phase I antigens than those with acute Q fever.

Transmission

The most striking aspect of the life cycle of the rickettsiae is that they are maintained in nature in certain arthropods such as ticks, lice, fleas, and mites and, with one exception, are transmitted to humans by the **bite of the arthropod.** The rickettsiae circulate widely in the bloodstream (bacteremia), infecting primarily the endothelium of the blood vessel walls.

The exception to arthropod transmission is *C. burnetii,* the cause of Q fever, which is transmitted by aerosol and inhaled into the lungs. Virtually all rickettsial diseases are zoonoses (ie, they have an animal reservoir), with the prominent exception of **epidemic typhus, which occurs only in humans.** It occurs only in humans because the causative organism, *R. prowazekii,* is transmitted by the human body louse. A summary of the vectors and reservoirs for selected rickettsial diseases is presented in Table 26–1.

The incidence of the disease depends on the geographic distribution of the arthropod vector and on the risk of exposure, which is enhanced by such things as poor hygienic conditions and camping in wooded areas. These factors are discussed below with the individual diseases.

Pathogenesis

The typical lesion caused by the rickettsiae is a **vasculitis,** particularly in the endothelial lining of the vessel wall where the organism is found. Damage to the vessels of the skin results in the characteristic rash and in edema and hemorrhage caused by increased capillary permeability. The basis for pathogenesis by these organisms is unclear. There is some evidence that endotoxin is involved, which is in accord with the nature of some of the lesions such as fever and petechiae, but its role has not been confirmed. No exotoxins or cytolytic enzymes have been found.

Clinical Findings & Epidemiology

This section is limited to the two rickettsial diseases that are most common in the United States, ie, Rocky

Table 26–1. Summary of selected rickettsial diseases.

Disease	Organism	Arthropod Vector	Mammalian Reservoir	Important in the United States
Spotted fevers				
Rocky Mountain spotted fever	R. rickettsii	Ticks	Dogs, rodents	Yes (especially in southeastern states such as North Carolina)
Rickettsialpox	R. akari	Mites	Mice	No
Typhus group				
Epidemic	R. prowazekii	Lice	Humans	No
Endemic	R. typhi	Fleas	Rodents	No
Scrub	R. tsutsugamushi	Mites	Rodents	No
Others				
Q fever	C. burnetii	None	Cattle, sheep, goats	Yes

Mountain spotted fever and Q fever, and to the other major rickettsial disease, typhus.

A. ROCKY MOUNTAIN SPOTTED FEVER

This disease is characterized by the acute onset of non-specific symptoms, eg, fever, severe headache, myalgias, and prostration. The typical rash, which appears 2–6 days later, begins with macules that frequently progress to petechiae. The rash usually appears first on the hands and feet and then moves inward to the trunk. In addition to headache, other profound central nervous system changes such as delirium and coma can occur. Disseminated intravascular coagulation, edema, and circulatory collapse may ensue in severe cases. The diagnosis must be made on clinical grounds and therapy started promptly, because the laboratory diagnosis is delayed until a rise in antibody titer can be observed.

The name of the disease is misleading, because it occurs primarily along the **East Coast** of the United States (in the southeastern states of Virginia, North Carolina, and Georgia), where the dog tick, *Dermacentor variabilis,* is located. The name "Rocky Mountain spotted fever" is derived from the region in which the disease was first found.[1]

The **tick** is an important reservoir of *R. rickettsii* as well as the vector; the organism is passed by the transovarian route from tick to tick, and a lifetime infection results. Certain mammals, such as dogs and rodents, are also reservoirs of the organism. Humans are acci-

dental hosts and are not required for the perpetuation of the organism in nature; there is no person-to-person transmission. Most cases occur in children during spring and early summer, when the ticks are active. Rocky Mountain spotted fever accounts for 95% of the rickettsial disease in the United States; there are about 1000 cases per year. It can be fatal if untreated, but if it is diagnosed and treated, a prompt cure results.

B. Q FEVER[2]

Unlike the other rickettsial diseases, the main organ involved in Q fever is the lungs. It begins suddenly with fever, severe headache, cough, and other influenzalike symptoms. This is all that occurs in many patients, but pneumonia ensues in about half. Hepatitis is frequent enough that the combination of pneumonia and hepatitis should suggest Q fever. A rash is rare, unlike in the other rickettsial diseases. In general, Q fever is an acute disease and recovery is expected even in the absence of antibiotic therapy. Rarely, chronic Q fever characterized by life-threatening endocarditis occurs.

Q fever is the one rickettsial disease that is *not* transmitted to humans by the bite of an arthropod. The important reservoirs for human infection are cattle, sheep, and goats. The agent, *C. burnetii,* which causes an inapparent infection in these reservoir hosts, is found in high concentrations in the urine, feces, placental tissue, and amniotic fluid of the animals. It is transmitted to

---

[1] In the western United States, it is transmitted by the wood tick, *Dermacentor andersoni.*

[2] Q stands for "Query"; the cause of this disease was a question mark, ie, was unknown, when the disease was first described in Australia in 1937.

humans by **inhalation of aerosols** of these materials. The disease occurs worldwide, chiefly in individuals whose occupations expose them to livestock, such as shepherds, abattoir employees, and farm workers. Cows' milk is usually responsible for subclinical infections rather than disease in humans. Pasteurization of milk kills the organism.

C. TYPHUS

There are several forms of typhus, namely, louse-borne epidemic typhus caused by *R. prowazekii*, flea-borne endemic typhus caused by *Rickettsia typhi*, chigger-borne scrub typhus caused by *R. tsutsugamushi*, and several other quite rare forms. Cases of flea-borne endemic typhus, also called murine typhus, occur in small numbers in the southern regions of California and Texas. The following description is limited to epidemic typhus, the most important of the typhus group of diseases.

Typhus begins with the sudden onset of chills, fever, headache, and other influenzalike symptoms approximately 1–3 weeks after the louse bite occurs. Between the fifth and ninth days after the onset of symptoms, a maculopapular rash begins on the trunk and spreads peripherally. The rash becomes petechial and spreads over the entire body but spares the face, palms, and soles. Signs of severe meningoencephalitis, including delirium and coma, begin with the rash and continue into the second and third weeks. In untreated cases, death occurs from peripheral vascular collapse or from bacterial pneumonia.

Epidemic typhus is transmitted from person to person by the **human body louse**, *Pediculus*. When a bacteremic patient is bitten, the organism is ingested by the louse and multiplies in the gut epithelium. It is excreted in the feces of the louse during the act of biting the next person and autoinoculated by the person while scratching the bite. The infected louse dies after a few weeks, and there is no louse-to-louse transmission; therefore, human infection is an obligatory stage in the cycle. Epidemic typhus is associated with wars and poverty; at present it is found in developing countries in Africa and South America but not in the United States.

A recurrent form of epidemic typhus is called Brill-Zinsser disease. The signs and symptoms are similar to those of epidemic typhus but are less severe, of shorter duration, and rarely fatal. Recurrences can appear as long as 50 years later and can be precipitated by another intercurrent disease. In the United States, the disease is seen in older people who had epidemic typhus during World War II in Europe. Brill-Zinsser disease is epidemiologically interesting; persistently infected patients can serve as a source of the organism should a louse bite occur.

Laboratory Diagnosis

Laboratory diagnosis of rickettsial diseases is based on serologic analysis rather than isolation of the organism. Although rickettsiae can be grown in cell culture or embryonated eggs, this is a hazardous procedure that is not available in the standard clinical laboratory.

Of the serologic tests, the indirect immunofluorescence and ELISA tests are most often used. The Weil-Felix test is of historic interest but is no longer performed because its specificity and sensitivity are too low. The basis of the Weil-Felix test is described below.

A 4-fold or greater rise in titer between the acute and convalescent serum samples is the most common way the laboratory diagnosis is made. This is usually a retrospective diagnosis, because the convalescent sample is obtained 2 weeks after the acute sample. If the clinical picture is typical, a single acute-phase titer of 1:128 or greater is accepted as presumptive evidence. If the test is available, a diagnosis can be made during the acute phase of the disease by immunofluorescence assay on tissue obtained from the site of the petechial rash.

The Weil-Felix test is based on the cross-reaction of an antigen present in many rickettsiae with the O antigen polysaccharide found in *P. vulgaris* OX-2, OX-19, and OX-K. The test measures the presence of antirickettsial antibodies in the patient's serum by their ability to agglutinate *Proteus* bacteria. The specific rickettsial organism can be identified by the agglutination observed with one or another of these three different strains of *P. vulgaris*. However, as mentioned above, this test is no longer used in the United States.

Treatment

The treatment of choice for all rickettsial diseases is tetracycline, with chloramphenicol as the second choice.

Prevention

Prevention of many of these diseases is based on reducing exposure to the arthropod vector by wearing protective clothing and using insect repellent. Frequent examination of the skin for ticks is important in preventing Rocky Mountain spotted fever; the tick must be attached for several hours to transmit the disease. There is no vaccine against Rocky Mountain spotted fever.

Prevention of typhus is based on personal hygiene and "delousing" with DDT. A typhus vaccine containing formalin-killed *R. prowazekii* organisms is effective and useful in the military during wartime but is not available to civilians in the United States. Persons at high risk of contracting Q fever, such as veterinarians, shepherds, abattoir workers, and laboratory personnel exposed to *C. burnetii,* should receive the vaccine that consists of the killed organism.

SUMMARIES OF ORGANISMS

Brief summaries of the organisms described in this chapter begin on page 492. Please consult these summaries for a rapid review of the essential material.

PRACTICE QUESTIONS: USMLE & COURSE EXAMINATIONS

Questions on the topics discussed in this chapter can be found in the Clinical Bacteriology section of Part XI: USMLE (National Board) Practice Questions starting on page 537. Also see Part XII: USMLE (National Board) Practice Examination starting on page 583.

Minor Bacterial Pathogens

The bacterial pathogens of lesser medical importance are briefly described in this chapter. Experts may differ on their choice of which organisms to put in this category. Nevertheless, separating the minor from the major pathogens should allow the reader to focus on the more important pathogens while providing at least some information about the less important ones.

These organisms are presented in alphabetical order. Table 27–1 lists the organisms according to their appearance on Gram stain.

Achromobacter

Achromobacter species are gram-negative coccobacillary rods found chiefly in water supplies. They are opportunistic pathogens and are involved in sepsis, pneumonia, and urinary tract infections.

Acinetobacter

Acinetobacter species are gram-negative coccobacillary rods found commonly in soil and water, but they can be part of the normal flora. They are opportunistic pathogens that readily colonize patients with compromised host defenses. *Acinetobacter calcoaceticus,* the species usually involved in human infection, causes disease chiefly in a hospital setting usually associated with respiratory therapy equipment and indwelling catheters. Sepsis, pneumonia, and urinary tract infections are the most frequent manifestations. Previous names for this organism include *Herellea* and *Mima.*

Actinobacillus

Actinobacillus species are gram-negative coccobacillary rods. *Actinobacillus actinomycetemcomitans* is found as part of the normal flora in the upper respiratory tract. It is a rare opportunistic pathogen, causing endocarditis on damaged heart valves and sepsis.

Aeromonas

Aeromonas species are gram-negative rods found in water, soil, food, and animal and human feces. *Aeromonas hydrophila* causes wound infections, diarrhea, and sepsis, especially in immunocompromised patients.

Alcaligenes

Alcaligenes species are gram-negative coccobacillary rods found in soil and water and are associated with water-containing materials such as respirators in hospitals. *Alcaligenes faecalis* is an opportunistic pathogen, causing sepsis and pneumonia.

Arachnia

Arachnia species are anaerobic gram-positive rods that form long, branching filaments similar to those of *Actinomyces.* They are found primarily in the mouth (associated with dental plaque) and in the tonsillar crypts. *Arachnia propionica,* the major species, causes abscesses similar to those of *Actinomyces israelii,* including the presence of "sulfur granules" in the lesions.

Arcanobacterium

Arcanobacterium haemolyticum is a club-shaped gram-positive rod that closely resembles corynebacteria. It is a rare cause of pharyngitis and chronic skin ulcers. The pharyngitis can be accompanied by a rash resembling the rash of scarlet fever.

Arizona

Arizona species are gram-negative rods in the family Enterobacteriaceae; they ferment lactose slowly. *Arizona hinshawii* is found in the feces of chickens and other domestic animals and causes diseases similar to those caused by *Salmonella,* such as enterocolitis and enteric fevers. The organism is usually transmitted by contaminated food, eg, dried eggs.

Bartonella

Bartonella species are pleomorphic gram-negative rods. *Bartonella henselae* (formerly called *Rochalimaea henselae*) is the cause of **bacillary angiomatosis** and **cat-scratch fever.** The organism is a member of the oral flora of many cats. It is transmitted from cat to cat by fleas, but fleas are not thought to be involved in cat-to-human transmission. Cat scratches or bites, especially from kittens, are the main mode of transmission to humans.

Table 27–1. Minor bacterial pathogens.

Type of Bacterium	Genus or Species
Gram-positive cocci	*Micrococcus, Peptococcus, Peptostreptococcus, Sarcina*
Gram-positive rods	*Arachnia, Arcanobacterium, Bifidobacterium, Erysipelothrix, Eubacterium, Gardnerella, Lactobacillus, Mobiluncus, Propionibacterium, Rhodococcus*
Gram-negative cocci	*Veillonella*
Gram-negative rods	*Achromobacter, Acinetobacter, Actinobacillus, Aeromonas, Alcaligenes, Arizona, Bartonella, Calymmatobacterium, Capnocytophaga, Cardiobacterium, Chromobacterium, Chryseobacterium, Citrobacter, Corynebacterium jeikeium, Corynebacterium minutissimum, Edwardsiella, Eikenella, Erwinia, Fusobacterium, HACEK group, Haemophilus ducreyi, Hafnia, Kingella, Moraxella, Pleisomonas, Porphyromonas, Pseudomonas pseudomallei, Spirillum, Streptobacillus, Yersinia enterocolitica, Yersinia pseudotuberculosis*
Rickettsia	*Ehrlichia*
Unclassified	*Tropheryma*

Bacillary angiomatosis occurs in immunocompromised individuals, especially AIDS patients. It is characterized by proliferative, vascular lesions resembling Kaposi's sarcoma in the skin and visceral organs. Pathologic examination of tissue from the lesion will distinguish bacillary angiomatosis from Kaposi's sarcoma. The organism can be visualized in the biopsy tissue using the Warthin-Starry silver stain. An immunofluorescence assay can also be used. The organism can be cultured on artificial media but takes 5 days or longer to grow. This is not usually done. Treatment with doxycycline or erythromycin is effective. (Bacillary peliosis is similar to bacillary angiomatosis except that in peliosis the lesions occur primarily in the liver and spleen.)

In immunocompetent people, *B. henselae* causes **cat-scratch fever.** This disease is characterized by localized lymphadenopathy in a person who has had contact with a cat. The diagnosis is supported by characteristic histopathology on a lymph node biopsy specimen and an antibody titer of at least 1/64 in an indirect immunofluorescence assay for *Bartonella*. The Warthin-Starry silver stain reveals very few organisms. Cultures are not usually done. The disease is mild and self-limited, and no antibiotic therapy is recommended.

Bartonella quintana (formerly called *Rochalimaea quintana*) is the cause of trench fever and also is implicated as the cause of some cases of bacillary angiomatosis. Trench fever is transmitted by body lice, and humans are the reservoir for the organism. *Bartonella bacilliformis* causes two rare diseases: Oroya fever and verruga peruana, both of which are stages of Carrión's disease. The disease occurs only in certain areas of the Andes Mountains, and an animal reservoir is suspected.

Bifidobacterium

Bifidobacterium eriksonii is a gram-positive, filamentous, anaerobic rod found as part of the normal flora in the mouth and gastrointestinal tract. It occurs in mixed anaerobic infections.

Branhamella

Branhamella catarrhalis has been renamed *Moraxella catarrhalis* (see *Moraxella* below).

Calymmatobacterium

Calymmatobacterium granulomatis is a gram-negative rod that causes granuloma inguinale, a sexually transmitted disease characterized by genital ulceration and soft tissue and bone destruction. The diagnosis is made by visualizing the stained organisms (Donovan bodies) within large macrophages from the lesion. Tetracycline is the treatment of choice for this disease, which is rare in the United States but endemic in many developing countries.

Capnocytophaga

Capnocytophaga gingivalis is a gram-negative fusiform rod that is associated with periodontal disease, but it can also be an opportunistic pathogen, causing sepsis and mucositis in immunocompromised patients. *Capnocytophaga canimorsus* is a member of the oral flora of dogs and causes infections following dog bites. It also can cause sepsis in immunocompromised patients, especially those without a spleen.

Cardiobacterium

Cardiobacterium hominis is a gram-negative pleomorphic rod. It is a member of the normal flora of the human colon, but it can be an opportunistic pathogen, causing mainly endocarditis.

Chromobacterium

Chromobacterium violaceum is a gram-negative rod that produces a violet pigment. It is found in soil and water and can cause wound infections, especially in subtropical parts of the world.

Chryseobacterium

Chryseobacterium species are gram-negative rods found in soil and water. *Chryseobacterium meningosepticum,* the major pathogen in this genus, is an opportunistic pathogen, causing meningitis and sepsis especially in premature infants. In adults, it causes outbreaks of nosocomial pneumonia, especially in intubated patients. It is resistant to most antibiotics but is noteworthy as the only gram-negative bacterium that is susceptible to vancomycin. The genus *Chryseobacterium* was formerly called *Flavobacterium.*

Citrobacter

Citrobacter species are gram-negative rods (members of the Enterobacteriaceae) related to *Salmonella* and *Arizona.* They occur in the environment and in the human colon and can cause sepsis in immunocompromised patients.

Corynebacterium jeikeium

Corynebacterium jeikeium is a small gram-positive rod primarily found on the skin of hospitalized patients. It causes sepsis in immunocompromised patients, most often those who are neutropenic. Infections are often associated with indwelling catheters and prosthetic heart valves. The drug of choice is vancomycin. Hospital-acquired strains are resistant to many other antibiotics.

Corynebacterium minutissimum

Corynebacterium minutissimum is a small gram-positive rod that causes erythrasma. Erythrasma is characterized by pruritic, scaly, brownish macules on the skin of the genital region. The diagnosis is usually made by visualizing a coral-red fluorescence with a Wood's lamp rather than by culturing the organism. The drug of choice is oral erythromycin.

Edwardsiella

Edwardsiella species are gram-negative rods (members of the Enterobacteriaceae) resembling *Salmonella.* They can cause enterocolitis, sepsis, and wound infections.

Ehrlichia

Ehrlichia chaffeensis is a member of the rickettsia family and causes human monocytic ehrlichiosis (HME). This disease resembles Rocky Mountain spotted fever, except that the typical rash usually does not occur. High fever, severe headache, and myalgias are prominent symptoms. The organism is endemic in dogs and is transmitted to humans by ticks, especially the dog tick, *Dermacentor,* and the Lone Star tick, *Amblyomma. E. chaffeensis* primarily infects mononuclear leukocytes and forms characteristic **morulae** in the cytoplasm. (A morula is an inclusion body that resembles a mulberry. It consists of many *E. chaffeensis* cells.) Lymphopenia, thrombocytopenia, and elevated liver enzyme values are seen. In the United States, the disease occurs primarily in the southern states, especially Arkansas. The diagnosis is usually made serologically. Doxycycline is the treatment of choice.

Another form of ehrlichiosis, called human granulocytic ehrlichiosis (HGE), is caused by an organism closely resembling *Ehrlichia equi.* Either *Dermacentor* or *Ixodes* ticks are the vectors. In HGE, granulocytes rather than mononuclear cells are infected, but the disease is clinically indistinguishable from that caused by *E. chaffeensis.* The diagnostic approach and the treatment are the same for both forms of ehrlichiosis. *E. equi* has been reclassified and is now known as *Anaplasma phagocytophilum.*

Eikenella

Eikenella corrodens is a gram-negative rod that is a member of the normal flora in the human mouth and causes skin and bone infections associated with **human bites** and "clenched fist" injuries. It also causes sepsis and soft tissue infections of the head and neck, especially in immunocompromised patients and in drug abusers who lick needles prior to injection.

Erwinia

Erwinia species are gram-negative rods (members of the Enterobacteriaceae) found in soil and water and are rarely involved in human disease.

Erysipelothrix

Erysipelothrix rhusiopathiae is a gram-positive rod that causes erysipeloid, a skin infection that resembles erysipelas (caused by streptococci). Erysipeloid usually occurs on the hands of persons who handle meat and fish.

Eubacterium

Eubacterium species are gram-positive, anaerobic, non-spore-forming rods that are present in large numbers as part of the normal flora of the human colon. They rarely cause human disease.

Fusobacterium

Fusobacterium species are anaerobic gram-negative rods with pointed ends. They are part of the human normal flora of the mouth, colon, and female genital tract and are isolated from brain, pulmonary, intra-abdominal, and pelvic abscesses. They are frequently found in mixed infections with other anaerobes and facultative anaerobes. *Fusobacterium nucleatum* occurs, along with various spirochetes, in cases of Vincent's angina (trench mouth).

Gardnerella

Gardnerella vaginalis is a facultative gram-variable rod associated with **bacterial vaginosis,** characterized by a malodorous vaginal discharge and **clue cells,** which are vaginal epithelial cells covered with bacteria. The "whiff" test, which consists of treating the vaginal discharge with 10% KOH and smelling a pungent, "fishy" odor, is often positive. However, trichomoniasis, which can also cause a positive whiff test, must be ruled out before a diagnosis of bacterial vaginosis can be made. The drug of choice is metronidazole. *Mobiluncus* (see below), an anaerobic rod, is often found in this disease as well. Women with bacterial vaginosis have a higher incidence of preterm deliveries and, consequently, a higher incidence of morbidity and mortality occurs in their newborn children.

HACEK Group

This is a group of small gram-negative rods that have in common the following: slow growth in culture, the requirement for high CO_2 levels to grow in culture, and the ability to cause endocarditis. They are members of the human oropharyngeal flora and can enter the bloodstream from that site. The name "HACEK" is an acronym of the first letters of the genera of the following bacteria: *Haemophilus aphrophilus* and *Haemophilus paraphrophilus,* *Actinobacillus actinomycetemcomitans,* *Cardiobacterium hominis,* *Eikenella corrodens,* and *Kingella kingae.*

Haemophilus aegyptius

Haemophilus aegyptius (Koch-Weeks bacillus) is a small gram-negative rod that is an important cause of conjunctivitis in children. Certain strains of *H. aegyptius*

cause Brazilian purpuric fever, a life-threatening childhood infection characterized by purpura and shock. This organism is also known as *Haemophilus influenzae* biogroup *aegypticus.*

Haemophilus ducreyi

This small gram-negative rod causes the sexually transmitted disease **chancroid** (soft chancre), which is common in tropical countries but uncommon in the United States. The disease begins with penile lesions, which are painful; nonindurated (soft) ulcers; and local lymphadenitis (bubo). The diagnosis is made by isolating *H. ducreyi* from the ulcer or from pus aspirated from a lymph node. The organism requires heated (chocolate) blood agar supplemented with X factor (heme) but, unlike *H. influenzae,* does not require V factor (NAD). Chancroid can be treated with erythromycin, azithromycin, or ceftriaxone. Because many strains of *H. ducreyi* produce a plasmid-encoded penicillinase, penicillins cannot be used.

Hafnia

Hafnia species are gram-negative rods (members of the Enterobacteriaceae) found in soil and water and are rare opportunistic pathogens.

Kingella

K. kingae is a gram-negative rod in the normal flora of the human oropharynx. It is a rare cause of opportunistic infection and endocarditis.

Lactobacillus

Lactobacilli are gram-positive non-spore-forming rods found as members of the normal flora in the mouth, colon, and female genital tract. In the mouth, they may play a role in the production of dental caries. In the vagina, they are the main source of lactic acid, which keeps the pH low. Lactobacilli are rare causes of opportunistic infection.

Micrococcus

Micrococci are gram-positive cocci that are part of the normal flora of the skin. They are rare human pathogens.

Mobiluncus

Mobiluncus species are anaerobic gram-positive, curved rods that often stain gram-variable. They are associated with **bacterial vaginosis** in women. *Gardnerella* (see above), a facultative rod, is often found in this disease as well.

Moraxella

Moraxella species are gram-negative coccobacillary rods resembling neisseriae. *M. catarrhalis* is the major pathogen in this genus. It causes otitis media and sinusitis, primarily in children, as well as bronchitis and pneumonia in older people with chronic obstructive pulmonary disease. It is found only in humans and is transmitted by respiratory aerosol. Trimethoprim-sulfamethoxazole or amoxicillin-clavulanate can be used to treat these infections. Most clinical isolates produce β-lactamase. *Moraxella nonliquefaciens* is one of the two common causes of blepharitis (infection of the eyelid); *Staphylococcus aureus* is the other. The usual treatment is local application of antibiotic ointment, such as erythromycin.

Peptococcus

Peptococci are anaerobic gram-positive cocci, resembling staphylococci, found as members of the normal flora of the mouth and colon. They are also isolated from abscesses of various organs, usually from mixed anaerobic infections.

Peptostreptococcus

Peptostreptococci are anaerobic gram-positive cocci found as members of the normal flora of the mouth and colon. They are also isolated from abscesses of various organs, usually from mixed anaerobic infections.

Pleisomonas

Pleisomonas shigelloides is a gram-negative rod associated with water sources. It causes self-limited gastroenteritis, primarily in tropical areas, and can cause invasive disease in immunocompromised individuals.

Porphyromonas

Porphyromonas gingivalis and *Porphyromonas endodontalis* are anaerobic gram-negative rods found in the mouth. They cause periodontal infections, such as gingivitis and dental abscesses.

Propionibacterium

Propionibacteria are pleomorphic, anaerobic gram-positive rods found on the skin and in the gastrointestinal tract. *Propionibacterium acnes* is part of the normal flora of the skin and can cause catheter and shunt infections. It is involved in mixed infections associated with cat and dog bites and in head and neck abscesses.

P. acnes is also involved in the pathogenesis of acne, a condition that affects more than 85% of teenagers. The pathogenesis of acne involves impaction of the sebaceous gland followed by inflammation caused by the presence of *P. acnes*. The pustules of acne are composed of sebum, inflammatory cells such as neutrophils and lymphocytes, and the organism. Antibiotics, such as erythromycin, administered either topically or orally, are effective especially when coupled with other agents such as benzoyl peroxide or retinoids.

Pseudomonas pseudomallei

Pseudomonas pseudomallei is a gram-negative rod that causes melioidosis, a rare disease found primarily in Southeast Asia. The organism is found in soil and is transmitted most often when soil contaminates skin abrasions. This disease has been seen in the United States, because infections acquired by members of the armed forces during the Vietnam war have reactivated many years later. The acute disease is characterized by high fever and bloody, purulent sputum. Untreated cases can proceed to sepsis and death. In the chronic form, the disease can appear as pneumonia or lung abscess or may resemble tuberculosis. Diagnosis is made by culturing the organism from blood or sputum. The treatment of choice is ceftazidime, which is administered for several weeks. This organism is also known as *Burkholderia pseudomallei*.

Rhodococcus

Rhodococcus equi is a gram-positive bacterium whose shape varies from a coccus to a club-shaped rod. It is a rare cause of pneumonia and cavitary lung disease in patients whose cell-mediated immunity is compromised. The diagnosis is made by isolating the organism on laboratory agar and observing salmon-pink colonies that do not ferment most carbohydrates. The treatment of choice is a combination of rifampin and erythromycin. (*R. equi* used to be called *Corynebacterium equi*.)

Sarcina

Sarcina species are anaerobic gram-positive cocci grouped in clusters of four or eight. They are minor members of the normal flora of the colon and are rarely pathogens.

Spirillum

Spirillum minor is a gram-negative, spiral-shaped rod that causes rat-bite fever ("sodoku"). The disease is characterized by a reddish brown rash spreading from the bite, accompanied by fever and local lymphadenopathy. The diagnosis is made by a combination of microscopy and animal inoculation.

Streptobacillus

Streptobacillus moniliformis is a gram-negative rod that causes another type of rat-bite fever (see *Spirillum*, above).

Tropheryma

Tropheryma whippelii is the putative cause of Whipple's disease. Bacilli seen in duodenal lesions were identified as an actinomycete on the basis of amplification of the bacterial 16S ribosomal RNA and comparison with known related organisms. This identification is tentative because the organism has not been reproducibly grown in culture.

Veillonella

Veillonella parvula is an anaerobic gram-negative diplococcus that is part of the normal flora of the mouth, colon, and vagina. It is a rare opportunistic pathogen that causes abscesses of the sinuses, tonsils, and brain, usually in mixed anaerobic infections.

Yersinia enterocolitica & Yersinia pseudotuberculosis

Y. enterocolitica and *Y. pseudotuberculosis* are gram-negative, oval rods that are larger than *Yersinia pestis*. The virulence factors produced by *Y. pestis* are not made by these species. These organisms are transmitted to humans by contamination of food with the excreta of domestic animals such as dogs, cats, and cattle. *Yersinia* infections are relatively infrequent in the United States, but the number of documented cases has increased during the past few years, perhaps as a result of improved laboratory procedures.

Y. enterocolitica causes enterocolitis that is clinically indistinguishable from that caused by *Salmonella* or *Shigella*. Both *Y. enterocolitica* and *Y. pseudotuberculosis* can cause **mesenteric adenitis** that clinically resembles acute appendicitis. Mesenteric adenitis is the main finding in appendectomies in which a normal appendix is found. Rarely, these organisms are involved in bacteremia or abscesses of the liver or spleen, mainly in persons with underlying disease.

Yersinia infection is associated with two autoimmune diseases: reactive arthritis and Reiter's syndrome. Other enteric pathogens such as *Salmonella, Shigella,* and *Campylobacter* also trigger these diseases. Reactive arthritis and Reiter's syndrome are described further in Chapter 66, Tolerance & Autoimmune Disease.

Y. enterocolitica is usually isolated from stool specimens and forms a lactose-negative colony on MacConkey's agar. It grows better at 25°C than at 37°C; most biochemical test results are positive at 25°C and negative at 37°C. Incubation of a stool sample at 4°C for 1 week, a technique called "cold enrichment," increases the frequency of recovery of the organism. *Y. enterocolitica* can be distinguished from *Y. pseudotuberculosis* by biochemical reactions.

The laboratory is usually not involved in the diagnosis of *Y. pseudotuberculosis;* cultures are rarely performed in cases of mesenteric adenitis, and the organism is rarely recovered from stool specimens. Serologic tests are not available in most hospital clinical laboratories.

Enterocolitis and mesenteric adenitis caused by the organisms do not require treatment. In cases of bacteremia or abscess, either trimethoprim-sulfamethoxazole or ciprofloxacin is usually effective. There are no preventive measures except to guard against contamination of food by the excreta of domestic animals.

SUMMARIES OF ORGANISMS

Brief summaries of the organisms described in this chapter begin on page 492. Please consult these summaries for a rapid review of the essential material.

PRACTICE QUESTIONS: USMLE & COURSE EXAMINATIONS

Questions on the topics discussed in this chapter can be found in the Clinical Bacteriology section of Part XI: USMLE (National Board) Practice Questions starting on page 537. Also see Part XII: USMLE (National Board) Practice Examination starting on page 583.

PART III
Basic Virology

The other infectious agents described in this book, namely, bacteria, fungi, protozoa, and worms, are either single cells or composed of many cells. Cells are capable of independent replication, can synthesize their own energy and proteins, and can be seen in the light microscope. In contrast, viruses are not cells; they are not capable of independent replication, can synthesize neither their own energy nor their own proteins, and are too small to be seen in the light microscope.

Viruses are characterized by the following features:

(1) Viruses are particles composed of an internal core containing *either* DNA *or* RNA (but not both) covered by a protective protein coat. Some viruses have an outer lipoprotein membrane, called an envelope, external to the coat. Viruses do not have a nucleus, cytoplasm, mitochondria, or ribosomes. Cells, both prokaryotic and eukaryotic cells, have *both* DNA and RNA. Eukaryotic cells, such as fungal, protozoal, and human cells, have a nucleus, cytoplasm, mitochondria, and ribosomes. Prokaryotic cells, such as bacteria, are not divided into nucleus and cytoplasm and do not have mitochondria but do have ribosomes; therefore, they can synthesize their own proteins.

(2) Viruses must reproduce (replicate) within cells, because they cannot generate energy or synthesize proteins. Because they can reproduce only within cells, viruses are **obligate intracellular parasites.** (The only bacteria that are obligate intracellular parasites are chlamydiae and rickettsiae. They cannot synthesize sufficient energy to replicate independently.)

(3) Viruses replicate in a manner different from that of cells; ie, viruses do not undergo binary fission or mitosis. One virus can replicate to produce hundreds of progeny viruses, whereas one cell divides to produce only two daughter cells.

Table III–1 compares some of the attributes of viruses and cells.

Table III–1. Comparison of viruses and cells.

Property	Viruses	Cells
Type of nucleic acid	DNA or RNA but not both	DNA and RNA
Proteins	Few	Many
Lipoprotein membrane	Envelope present in some viruses	Cell membrane present in all cells
Ribosomes	Absent[1]	Present
Mitochondria	Absent	Present in eukaryotic cells
Enzymes	None or few	Many
Multiplication by binary fission or mitosis	No	Yes

[1]Arenaviruses have a few nonfunctional ribosomes.

Structure

SIZE & SHAPE

Viruses range from 20 to 300 nm in diameter; this corresponds roughly to a range of sizes from that of the largest protein to that of the smallest cell (see Figure 2–2). Their shapes are frequently referred to in colloquial terms, eg, spheres, rods, bullets, or bricks, but in reality they are complex structures of precise geometric symmetry (see below). The shape of virus particles is determined by the arrangement of the **repeating subunits** that form the protein coat (**capsid**) of the virus. The shapes and sizes of some important viruses are depicted in Figure 28–1.

VIRAL NUCLEIC ACIDS

The anatomy of two representative types of virus particles is shown in Figure 28–2. The viral nucleic acid (genome) is located internally and can be either single- or double-stranded DNA or single- or double-stranded RNA.[1]

Only viruses have genetic material composed of single-stranded DNA or of single-stranded or double-stranded RNA. The nucleic acid can be either linear or circular. The DNA is always a single molecule; the RNA can exist either as a single molecule or in several pieces. For example, both influenza virus and rotavirus have a segmented RNA genome. Almost all viruses contain only a single copy of their genome; ie, they are haploid. The exception is the retrovirus family, whose members have two copies of their RNA genome; ie, they are diploid.

VIRAL CAPSID & SYMMETRY

The nucleic acid is surrounded by a protein coat called a **capsid**, made up of subunits called capsomers. Each capsomer, consisting of one or several proteins, can be seen in the electron microscope as a spherical particle, sometimes with a central hole.

The structure composed of the nucleic acid genome and the capsid proteins is called the **nucleocapsid**. The arrangement of capsomers gives the virus structure its geometric symmetry. Viral nucleocapsids have two forms of symmetry: (1) **icosahedral**, in which the capsomers are arranged in 20 triangles that form a symmetric figure (an icosahedron) with the approximate outline of a sphere; and (2) **helical**, in which the capsomers are arranged in a hollow coil that appears rod-shaped. The helix can be either rigid or flexible. All human viruses that have a helical nucleocapsid are enclosed by an outer membrane called an **envelope**, ie, there are no naked helical viruses. Viruses that have an icosahedral nucleocapsid can be either enveloped or naked (Figure 28–2).

The advantage of building the virus particle from identical protein subunits is 2-fold: (1) it reduces the need for genetic information, and (2) it promotes self-assembly; ie, no enzyme or energy is required. In fact, functional virus particles have been assembled in the test tube by combining the purified nucleic acid with the purified proteins in the absence of cells, energy source, and enzymes.

VIRAL PROTEINS

Viral proteins serve several important functions. The outer capsid proteins **protect** the genetic material and **mediate the attachment** of the virus to specific receptors on the host cell surface. This interaction of the viral proteins with the cell receptor is the major determinant of species and organ **specificity**. Outer viral proteins are also **important antigens** that induce neutralizing antibody and activate cytotoxic T cells to kill virus-infected cells. These outer viral proteins not only induce antibodies but are also the target of antibodies, ie, antibodies bind to these viral proteins and prevent ("neutralize") the virus from entering the cell and replicating. The outer proteins induce these immune responses following both the natural infection and immunization (see below).

Some of the internal viral proteins are structural (eg, the capsid proteins of the enveloped viruses), whereas others are enzymes (eg, the polymerases that synthesize the viral mRNA). The internal viral proteins vary depending on the virus. Some viruses have a DNA or RNA polymerase attached to the genome; others do

---

[1] The nature of the nucleic acid of each virus is listed in Tables 31–1 and 31–2.

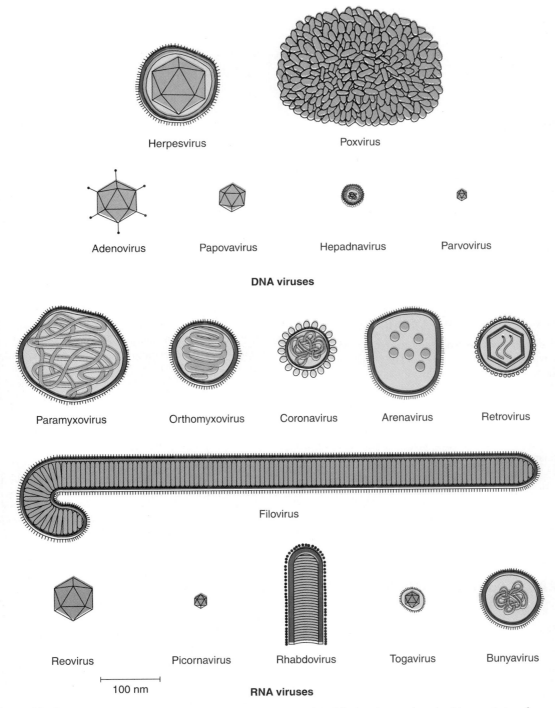

Figure 28–1. Shapes and sizes of medically important viruses. (Modified and reproduced, with permission, from Fenner F, White DO: *Medical Virology,* 4th ed. Academic Press, 1994.)

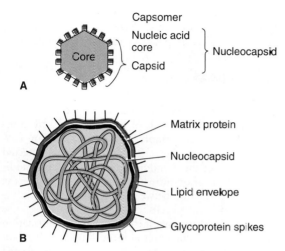

A

B

Figure 28–2. Cross-section of two types of virus particles. **A:** Nonenveloped virus with an icosahedral nucleocapsid. **B:** Enveloped virus with a helical nucleocapsid. (Modified and reproduced, with permission, from Brooks GF et al: *Medical Microbiology*, 20th ed. Originally published by Appleton & Lange. Copyright © 1995 by The McGraw-Hill Companies, Inc.)

not. If a virus has an envelope, then a matrix protein that mediates the interaction between the capsid proteins and the envelope proteins is present.

Some viruses produce proteins that act as "superantigens" similar in their action to the superantigens produced by bacteria, such as the toxic shock syndrome toxin of *Staphylococcus aureus* (see Chapters 15 and 58). Viruses known to produce superantigens include two members of the herpesvirus family, namely, Epstein-Barr virus and cytomegalovirus, and the retrovirus mouse mammary tumor virus. The current hypothesis offered to explain why these viruses produce a superantigen is that activation of CD4-positive T cells is required for replication of these viruses to occur.

VIRAL ENVELOPE

In addition to the capsid and internal proteins, there are two other types of proteins, both of which are associated with the envelope. The **envelope** is a **lipoprotein** membrane composed of lipid derived from the host cell membrane and protein that is virus-specific. Furthermore, there are frequently glycoproteins in the form of spike-like projections on the surface, which attach to host cell receptors during the entry of the virus into the cell. Another protein, the **matrix** protein, mediates the interaction between the capsid proteins and the envelope.

The viral envelope is acquired as the virus exits from

the cell in a process called "budding" (see Chapter 29). The envelope of most viruses is derived from the cell's outer membrane, with the notable exception of herpesviruses that derive their envelope from the cell's nuclear membrane.

In general, the presence of an envelope confers **instability** on the virus. Enveloped viruses are more sensitive to heat, drying, detergents, and lipid solvents such as alcohol and ether than are nonenveloped (nucleocapsid) viruses, which are composed only of nucleic acid and capsid proteins.

An interesting clinical correlate of this observation is that virtually all viruses that are transmitted by the fecal-oral route (those that have to survive in the environment) do *not* have an envelope, that is, they are naked nucleocapsid viruses. These include viruses such as hepatitis A virus, poliovirus, coxsackievirus, echovirus, Norwalk virus, and rotavirus. In contrast, enveloped viruses are most often transmitted by direct contact, such as by blood or by sexual transmission. Examples of these include human immunodeficiency virus, herpes simplex virus type 2, and hepatitis B and C viruses. Other enveloped viruses are transmitted directly by insect bite, eg, yellow fever virus and West Nile virus, or by animal bite, eg, rabies virus.

Many other enveloped viruses are transmitted from person to person in respiratory aerosol droplets, such as influenza virus, measles virus, rubella virus, respiratory syncytial virus, and varicella-zoster virus. If the droplets do not infect directly, they can dry out in the environment, and these enveloped viruses are rapidly inactivated. Note that rhinoviruses, which are transmitted by respiratory droplets, are naked nucleocapsid viruses and can survive in the environment for significant periods. They therefore can also be transmitted by hands that make contact with the virus on contaminated surfaces.

The surface proteins of the virus, whether they are the capsid proteins or the envelope glycoproteins, are the principal **antigens** against which the host mounts its immune response to viruses. They are also the determinants of type specificity (often called the **serotype**). For example, poliovirus types 1, 2, and 3 are distinguished by the antigenicity of their capsid proteins. It is important to know the number of serotypes of a virus, because vaccines should contain the prevalent serotypes. There is often little cross-protection between different serotypes. Viruses that have multiple serotypes, ie, have antigenic variants, have an enhanced ability to evade our host defenses because antibody against one serotype will not protect against another serotype.

ATYPICAL VIRUSLIKE AGENTS

There are four exceptions to the typical virus as described above:

(1) **Defective** viruses are composed of viral nucleic acid and proteins but cannot replicate without a "helper" virus, which provides the missing function. Defective viruses usually have a mutation or a deletion of part of their genetic material. During the growth of most human viruses, many more defective than infectious virus particles are produced. The ratio of defective to infectious particles can be as high as 100:1. Because these defective particles can interfere with the growth of the infectious particles, it has been hypothesized that the defective viruses may aid in recovery from an infection by limiting the ability of the infectious particles to grow.

(2) **Pseudovirions** contain host cell DNA instead of viral DNA within the capsid. They are formed during infection with certain viruses when the host cell DNA is fragmented and pieces of it are incorporated within the capsid protein. Pseudovirions can infect cells, but they do not replicate.

(3) **Viroids** consist solely of a single molecule of circular RNA without a protein coat or envelope. There is extensive homology between bases in the viroid RNA, leading to large double-stranded regions. The RNA is quite small (MW 1×10^5) and apparently does not code for any protein. Nevertheless, viroids replicate but the mechanism is unclear. They cause several plant diseases but are not implicated in any human disease.

(4) **Prions** are infectious particles that are composed **solely of protein;** ie, they contain no detectable nucleic acid. They are implicated as the cause of certain "slow" diseases called **transmissible spongiform encephalopathies,** which include such diseases as Creutzfeldt-Jakob disease in humans and scrapie in sheep (see Chapter 44). Because neither DNA nor RNA has been detected in prions, they are clearly different from viruses (Table 28–1). Furthermore, electron microscopy reveals filaments rather than virus particles. Prions are much **more resistant** to inactivation by ultraviolet light and heat than are viruses. They are remarkably resistant to formaldehyde and nucleases. However, they are inacti-

vated by hypochlorite, NaOH, and autoclaving. Hypochlorite is used to sterilize surgical instruments and other medical supplies that cannot be autoclaved.

Prions are composed of a single glycoprotein with a molecular weight of 27,000–30,000. With scrapie prions as the model, it was found that this protein is encoded by a single **cellular** gene. This gene is found in equal numbers in the cells of both infected and uninfected animals. Furthermore, the amount of prion protein mRNA is the same in uninfected as in infected cells. In view of these findings, **posttranslational** modifications of the prion protein are hypothesized to be the important distinction between the protein found in infected and uninfected cells.

There is evidence that a change in the conformation from the normal alpha-helical form (known as PrPC, or prion protein cellular) to the abnormal beta-pleated sheet form (known as PrPSC, or prion protein scrapie) is the important modification. The abnormal form then recruits additional normal forms to change their configuration, and the number of abnormal pathogenic particles increases. Although prions are composed only of proteins, specific cellular RNAs enhance the conversion of the normal alpha-helical form to the pathologic beta-pleated sheet form.

Evidence that recruitment is an essential step comes from "knockout" mice in which the gene for the prion protein is nonfunctional and no prion protein is made. These mice do not get scrapie despite the injection of the pathogenic scrapie prion protein.

The function of the normal prion protein is unclear. There is some evidence that it is one of the signal transduction proteins in neurons and that it is a copper-binding protein. "Knockout" mice in which the gene encoding the prion protein is inactive appear normal. The prion protein in normal cells is protease-sensitive, whereas the prion protein in infected cells is protease-resistant, probably because of the change in conformation.

Table 28–1. Comparison of prions and conventional viruses.

Feature	Prions	Conventional Viruses
Particle contains nucleic acid	No	Yes
Particle contains protein	Yes, encoded by cellular genes	Yes, encoded by viral genes
Inactivated rapidly by UV light or heat	No	Yes
Appearance in electron microscope	Filamentous rods (amyloid-like)	Icosahedral or helical symmetry
Infection induces antibody	No	Yes
Infection induces inflammation	No	Yes

The observation that the prion protein is the product of a normal cellular gene may explain why **no immune response** is formed against this protein; ie, tolerance occurs. Similarly, there is **no inflammatory response** in infected brain tissue. A vacuolated (**spongiform**) appearance is found, without inflammatory cells.

Prion proteins in infected brain tissue form rod-shaped particles that are morphologically and histochemically indistinguishable from **amyloid,** a substance found in the brain tissue of individuals with various central nervous system diseases (as well as diseases of other organs).

PEARLS

Virus Size & Structure

- Viruses range in size from that of large proteins (~ 20 nm) to that of the smallest cells (~ 300 nm). Most viruses appear as spheres or rods in the electron microscope.
- Viruses contain **either DNA or RNA, but not both.**
- All viruses have a **protein coat called a capsid** that covers the genome. The capsid is composed of repeating subunits called capsomers. In some viruses, the capsid is the outer surface, but in other viruses the capsid is covered with a lipoprotein **envelope** that becomes the outer surface. The structure composed of the nucleic acid genome and the capsid proteins is called the **nucleocapsid.**
- The repeating subunits of the capsid give the virus a symmetric appearance that is useful for classification purposes. Some viral nucleocapsids have **spherical (icosahedral) symmetry,** whereas others have **helical symmetry.**
- All human viruses that have a helical nucleocapsid are enveloped, ie, there are no naked helical viruses that infect humans. Viruses that have an icosahedral nucleocapsid can be either enveloped or naked.

Viral Nucleic Acids

- The genome of some viruses is **DNA,** whereas the genome of others is **RNA.** These DNA and RNA genomes can be either **single-stranded** or **double-stranded.**
- Some RNA viruses, such as influenza virus and rotavirus, have a **segmented genome,** ie, the genome is in several pieces.
- All viruses have one copy of their genome (haploid) except retroviruses, which have two copies (diploid).

Viral Proteins

- Viral surface proteins mediate **attachment to host cell receptors.** This interaction **determines the host specificity and organ specificity** of the virus.
- The surface proteins are the **targets of antibody,** ie, antibody bound to these surface proteins prevents the virus from attaching to the cell receptor. This "neutralizes" (inhibits) viral replication.
- Viruses also have internal proteins, some of which are **DNA or RNA polymerases.**
- The **matrix protein** mediates the interaction between the viral nucleocapsid proteins and the envelope proteins.
- Some viruses produce **antigenic variants** of their surface proteins that allow the viruses to evade our host defenses. Antibody against one antigenic variant (**serotype**) will not neutralize a different serotype. Some viruses have one serotype; others have multiple serotypes.

Viral Envelope

- The viral **envelope** consists of a membrane that contains lipid derived from the host cell and proteins encoded by the virus. Typically, the envelope is acquired as the virus exits from the cell in a process called **budding.**
- Viruses with an envelope are less stable, ie, they are more easily inactivated, than naked viruses (those without an envelope). In general, enveloped viruses are transmitted by direct contact via blood and body fluids, whereas naked viruses can survive longer in the environment and can be transmitted by indirect means such as the fecal-oral route.

Prions

- **Prions** are infectious particles composed **entirely of protein.** They have **no DNA or RNA.**
- They cause diseases such as Creutzfeldt-Jakob disease and kuru in humans and mad cow disease and

scrapie in animals. These diseases are called **transmissible spongiform encephalopathies.** The term **spongiform** refers to the sponge-like appearance of the brain seen in these diseases. The holes of the sponge are vacuoles resulting from dead neurons. These diseases are described in Chapter 44.

- Prion proteins are **encoded by a cellular gene.** When these proteins are in the **normal, alpha-helix configuration, they are nonpathogenic,** but when their configuration changes to a **beta-pleated sheet, they aggregate into filaments, which dis-**

rupts neuronal function and results in the symptoms of disease.

- Prions are **highly resistant to inactivation by ultraviolet light, heat,** and other inactivating agents. As a result, they have been inadvertently transmitted by human growth hormone and neurosurgical instruments.

- Because they are normal human proteins, they **do not elicit an inflammatory response or an antibody response** in humans.

PRACTICE QUESTIONS: USMLE & COURSE EXAMINATIONS

Questions on the topics discussed in this chapter can be found in the Basic Virology section of Part XI: USMLE (National Board) Practice Questions starting on page 545. Also see Part XII: USMLE (National Board) Practice Examination starting on page 583.

Replication

29

The viral replication cycle is described below in two different ways. The first approach is a growth curve, which shows the amount of virus produced at different times after infection. The second is a stepwise description of the specific events within the cell during virus growth.

VIRAL GROWTH CURVE

The growth curve depicted in Figure 29–1 shows that when one **virion** (one virus particle) infects a cell, it can replicate in approximately 10 hours to produce hundreds of virions within that cell. This remarkable amplification explains how viruses spread rapidly from cell to cell. Note that the time required for the growth cycle varies; it is minutes for some bacterial viruses and hours for some human viruses.

The first event shown in Figure 29–1 is quite striking: the virus disappears, as represented by the solid line dropping to the *x* axis. Although the virus particle, as such, is no longer present, the viral nucleic acid continues to function and begins to accumulate within the cell, as indicated by the dotted line. The time during which no virus is found inside the cell is known as the **eclipse period.** The eclipse period ends with the appearance of virus (solid line). The **latent period,** in contrast, is defined as the time from the onset of infection to the appearance of virus extracellularly. Note that infection begins with one virus particle and ends with several hundred virus particles having been produced; this type of reproduction is unique to viruses.

Alterations of cell morphology accompanied by marked derangement of cell function begin toward the end of the latent period. This **cytopathic effect** (CPE) culminates in the lysis and death of cells. CPE can be seen in the light microscope and, when observed, is an important initial step in the laboratory diagnosis of viral infection. Not all viruses cause CPE; some can replicate while causing little morphologic or functional change in the cell.

SPECIFIC EVENTS DURING THE GROWTH CYCLE

An overview of the events is described in Table 29–1 and presented in diagrammatic fashion in Figure 29–2. The infecting parental virus particle attaches to the cell membrane and then penetrates the host cell. The viral genome is "uncoated" by removing the capsid proteins, and the genome is free to function. Early mRNA and proteins are synthesized; the **early proteins are enzymes** used to replicate the viral genome. Late mRNA and proteins are then synthesized. These **late proteins are the structural, capsid proteins.** The progeny virions are assembled from the replicated genetic material and newly made capsid proteins and are then released from the cell.

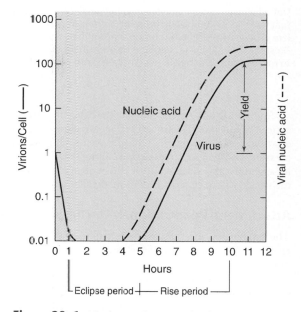

Figure 29–1. Viral growth curve. The figure shows that one infectious virus particle (virion) entering a cell at the time of infection results in more than 100 infectious virions 10 hours later, a remarkable increase. Note the eclipse period during which no infectious virus is detectable within the infected cells. In this growth curve, the amount of infecting virus is 1 virion/cell, ie, 1 infectious unit/cell. (Modified and reproduced, with permission, from Joklik WK et al: *Zinsser Microbiology,* 20th ed. Originally published by Appleton & Lange. Copyright © 1992 by The McGraw-Hill Companies, Inc.)

Table 29–1. Stages of the viral growth cycle.

Attachment and penetration by parental virion
↓
Uncoating of the viral genome
↓
Early[1] viral mRNA synthesis[2]
↓
Early viral protein synthesis
↓
Viral genome replication
↓
Late viral mRNA synthesis
↓
Late viral protein synthesis
↓
Progeny virion assembly
↓
Virion release from cell

[1]"Early" is defined as the period before genome replication. Not all viruses exhibit a distinction between early and late functions. In general, early proteins are enzymes, whereas late proteins are structural components of the virus.
[2]In some cases, the viral genome is functionally equivalent to mRNA; thus, early mRNA need not be synthesized.

Another, more general way to describe the growth cycle is as follows: (1) early events, ie, **attachment, penetration,** and **uncoating;** (2) middle events, ie, **gene expression** and **genome replication;** and (3) late events, ie, **assembly** and **release.** With this sequence in mind, each stage will be described in more detail.

Attachment, Penetration, & Uncoating

The proteins on the surface of the virion attach to specific receptor proteins on the cell surface through weak, noncovalent bonding. The **specificity** of attachment determines the **host range** of the virus. Some viruses have a narrow range, whereas others have quite a broad range. For example, poliovirus can enter the cells of only humans and other primates, whereas rabies virus can enter all mammalian cells. The organ specificity of viruses is governed by receptor interaction as well. Those cellular receptors that have been identified are surface proteins that serve various other functions. For example, herpes simplex virus type 1 attaches to the fibroblast growth factor receptor, rabies virus to the acetylcholine receptor, and human immunodeficiency virus (HIV) to the CD4 protein on helper T lymphocytes.

The virus particle penetrates by being engulfed in a pinocytotic vesicle, within which the process of uncoating begins. A low pH within the vesicle favors uncoating. Rupture of the vesicle or fusion of the outer layer of virus with the vesicle membrane deposits the inner core of the virus into the cytoplasm.

The receptors for viruses on the cell surface are proteins that have other functions in the life of the cell. Probably the best known is the CD4 protein that serves as one of the receptors for HIV but whose normal function is the binding of class 2 MHC proteins involved in the activation of helper T cells. A few other examples will serve to illustrate the point: rabies virus binds to the acetylcholine receptor, Epstein-Barr virus binds to a complement receptor, vaccinia virus binds to the receptor for epidermal growth factor, and rhinovirus binds to the integrin ICAM-1.

Certain bacterial viruses (bacteriophages) have a special mechanism for entering bacteria that has no counterpart in either human viruses or those of animals or plants. Some of the T group of bacteriophages infect *Escherichia coli* by attaching several tail fibers to the cell surface and then using lysozyme from the tail to degrade a portion of the cell wall. At this point, the tail sheath contracts, driving the tip of the core through the cell wall. The viral DNA then enters the cell through the tail core, while the capsid proteins remain outside.

It is appropriate at this point to describe the phenomenon of **infectious nucleic acid,** because it provides a transition between the concepts of host specificity described above and early genome functioning, which is discussed below. Note that we are discussing whether the purified genome is infectious. All viruses are "infectious" in a person or in cell culture, but not all purified genomes are infectious.

Infectious nucleic acid is purified viral DNA or RNA (without any protein) that can carry out the entire viral growth cycle and result in the production of complete virus particles. This is interesting from three points of view:

(1) The observation that purified nucleic acid is infectious is the definitive proof that nucleic acid, not protein, is the genetic material.

(2) Infectious nucleic acid can bypass the host range specificity provided by the viral protein–cell receptor interaction. For example, although intact poliovirus can grow only in primate cells, purified poliovirus RNA can enter nonprimate cells, go through its usual growth cycle, and produce normal poliovirus. The poliovirus produced in the nonprimate cells can infect only primate cells, because it now has its capsid proteins. These observations indicate that the internal functions of the nonprimate cells are capable of supporting viral growth once entry has occurred.

(3) Only certain viruses yield infectious nucleic acid. The reason for this is discussed below. Note that all viruses are infectious, but not all purified viral DNAs or RNAs (genomes) are infectious.

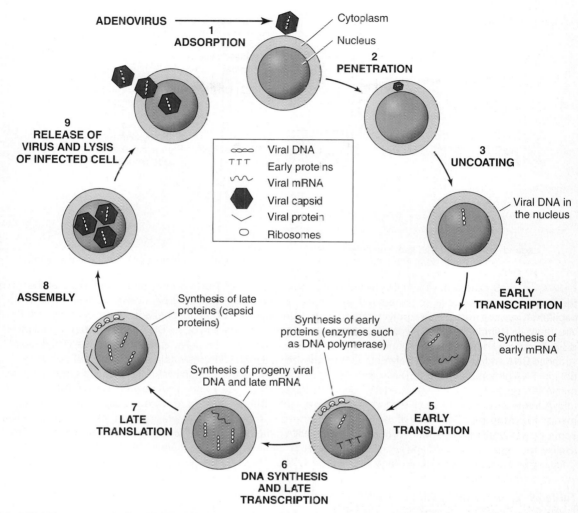

Figure 29–2. Viral growth cycle. The growth cycle of adenovirus, a nonenveloped DNA virus, is shown. (Modified and reproduced, with permission, from Jawetz E, Melnick JL, Adelberg EA: *Review of Medical Microbiology,* 16th ed. Originally published by Appleton & Lange. Copyright © 1994 by The McGraw-Hill Companies, Inc.)

Gene Expression & Genome Replication

The first step in viral gene expression is **mRNA synthesis.** It is at this point that viruses follow different pathways depending on the nature of their nucleic acid and the part of the cell in which they replicate (Figure 29–3).

DNA viruses, with one exception, **replicate in the nucleus** and use the host cell DNA-dependent RNA polymerase to synthesize their mRNA. The poxviruses are the exception because they replicate in the cytoplasm, where they do not have access to the host cell RNA polymerase. They therefore carry their own poly-

merase within the virus particle. **The genome of all DNA viruses consists of double-stranded DNA, except for the parvoviruses, which have a single-stranded DNA genome** (Table 29–2).

Most RNA viruses undergo their entire replicative cycle in the cytoplasm. The two principal exceptions are retroviruses and influenza viruses, both of which have an important replicative step in the nucleus. Retroviruses integrate a DNA copy of their genome into the host cell DNA, and influenza viruses synthesize their progeny genomes in the nucleus. In addition, the mRNA of hepatitis delta virus is also synthesized in the nucleus of hepatocytes.

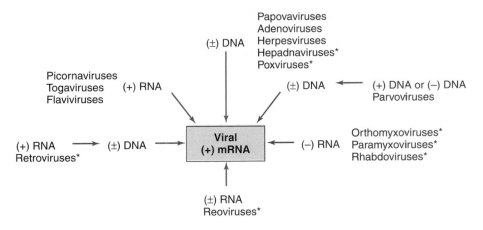

Legend: (+) = Strand with same polarity as mRNA   (±) = Double-stranded
       (−) = Strand complementary to mRNA   ＊ = These viruses contain a polymerase in the virion.

Figure 29–3. Synthesis of viral mRNA by medically important viruses. The following information starts at the top of the figure and moves clockwise. Viruses with a double-stranded DNA genome, eg, papovaviruses such as human papillomavirus, use host cell RNA polymerase to synthesize viral mRNA. Note that hepadnaviruses, eg, hepatitis B virus, contain a virion DNA polymerase that synthesizes the missing portion of the DNA genome but the viral mRNA is synthesized by host cell RNA polymerase. Parvoviruses use host cell DNA polymerase to synthesize viral double-stranded DNA and host cell RNA polymerase to synthesize viral mRNA. Viruses with a single-stranded, negative-polarity RNA genome, eg, orthomyxoviruses such as influenza virus, use a virion RNA polymerase to synthesize viral mRNA. Viruses with a double-stranded RNA genome, eg, reoviruses, use a virion RNA polymerase to synthesize viral mRNA. Some viruses with a single-stranded, positive-polarity RNA genome, eg, retroviruses, use a virion DNA polymerase to synthesize a DNA copy of the RNA genome but a host cell RNA polymerase to synthesize the viral mRNA. Some viruses with a single-stranded, positive-polarity RNA genome, eg, picornaviruses, use the virion genome RNA itself as their mRNA. (Modified and reproduced, with permission, from Ryan K et al: *Sherris Medical Microbiology*, 3rd ed. Originally published by Appleton & Lange. Copyright © 1994 by The McGraw-Hill Companies, Inc.)

Table 29–2. Important features of DNA viruses.

DNA Genome	Location of Replication	Virion Polymerase	Infectivity of Genome	Prototype Human Virus
Single strand	Nucleus	No[1,2]	Yes	Parvovirus B19
Double strand				
Circular	Nucleus	No[1]	Yes	Papillomavirus
Circular; partially single strand	Nucleus	Yes[3]	No	Hepatitis B virus
Linear	Nucleus	No[1]	Yes	Herpesvirus, adenovirus
Linear	Cytoplasm	Yes	No	Smallpox virus, vaccinia virus

[1]mRNA is synthesized by host cell RNA polymerase in the nucleus.
[2]Single-stranded genome DNA is converted to double-stranded DNA by host cell polymerase. A virus-encoded DNA polymerase then synthesizes progeny DNA.
[3]Hepatitis B virus uses a virion-encoded RNA-dependent DNA polymerase to synthesize its progeny DNA with full-length mRNA as the template. This enzyme is a type of "reverse transcriptase" but functions at a different stage in the replicative cycle than does the reverse transcriptase of retroviruses.
Note: All DNA viruses encode their own DNA polymerase that replicates the genome. They do not use the host cell DNA polymerase (with the minor exception of the parvoviruses as mentioned above).

The genome of all RNA viruses consists of single-stranded RNA, except for members of the reovirus family, which have a double-stranded RNA genome. Rotavirus is the important human pathogen in the reovirus family.

RNA viruses fall into four groups with quite different strategies for synthesizing mRNA (Table 29–3).

(1) The simplest strategy is illustrated by poliovirus, which has **single-stranded RNA** of **positive polarity**[1] as its genetic material. These viruses use their RNA genome directly as mRNA.

(2) The second group has **single-stranded RNA** of **negative polarity** as its genetic material. An mRNA must be transcribed by using the negative strand as a template. Because the cell does not have an RNA polymerase capable of using RNA as a template, the virus carries its own **RNA-dependent RNA polymerase**. There are two subcategories of negative-polarity RNA viruses: those that have a single piece of RNA, eg, measles virus (a paramyxovirus) or rabies virus (a rhabdovirus), and those that have multiple pieces of RNA, eg, influenza virus (a myxovirus).

Certain viruses, such as arenaviruses and some bunyaviruses, have a segmented RNA genome, most of which is negative stranded, but it has some positive RNA regions. RNA segments that contain both positive polarity and negative polarity regions are called "**ambisense**."

---

[1] Positive polarity is defined as an RNA with the same base sequence as the mRNA. RNA with negative polarity has a base sequence that is complementary to the mRNA. For example, if the mRNA sequence is an A-C-U-G, an RNA with negative polarity would be U-G-A-C and an RNA with positive polarity would be A-C-U-G.

(3) The third group has **double-stranded RNA** as its genetic material. Because the cell has no enzyme capable of transcribing this RNA into mRNA, the virus carries its own polymerase. Reovirus, the best-studied member of this group, has 10 segments of double-stranded RNA.

(4) The fourth group, exemplified by retroviruses, has single-stranded RNA of positive polarity that is transcribed into double-stranded DNA by the RNA-dependent DNA polymerase (**reverse transcriptase**) carried by the virus. This DNA copy is then transcribed into viral mRNA by the regular host cell RNA polymerase (polymerase II). Retroviruses are the only family of viruses that are **diploid**, ie, that have two copies of their genome RNA.

These differences explain why some viruses yield infectious nucleic acid and others do not. Viruses that do not require a polymerase in the virion can produce infectious DNA or RNA. By contrast, viruses such as the poxviruses, the negative-stranded RNA viruses, the double-stranded RNA viruses, and the retroviruses, which require a virion polymerase, cannot yield infectious nucleic acid. Several additional features of viral mRNA are described in the Box.

Note that two families of viruses utilize a reverse transcriptase (an RNA-dependent DNA polymerase) during their replicative cycle, but the purpose of the enzyme during the cycle is different. As described in Table 29–4, retroviruses, such as HIV, use their genome RNA as the template to synthesize a DNA intermediate early in the replicative cycle. However, hepadnaviruses, such as hepatitis B virus (HBV), use an RNA intermediate as the template to produce their DNA genome late in the replicative cycle.

Once the viral mRNA of either DNA or RNA

Table 29–3. Important features of RNA viruses.

RNA Genome	Polarity	Virion Polymerase	Source of mRNA	Infectivity of Genome	Prototype Human Virus
Single strand, nonsegmented	+	No	Genome	Yes	Poliovirus
Single strand					
Nonsegmented	–	Yes	Transcription	No	Measles virus, rabies virus
Segmented	–	Yes	Transcription	No	Influenza virus
Double strand, segmented	±	Yes	Transcription	No	Rotavirus
Single strand, diploid	+	Yes[1]	Transcription[2]	No[3]	HTLV, HIV[4]

[1]Retroviruses contain an RNA-dependent DNA polymerase.
[2]mRNA transcribed from DNA intermediate.
[3]Although the retroviral genome RNA is not infectious, the DNA intermediate is.
[4]HTLV, human T-cell leukemia virus; HIV, human immunodeficiency virus.

VIRAL mRNA

There are four interesting aspects of viral mRNA and its expression in eukaryotic cells. (1) Viral mRNAs have three attributes in common with cellular mRNAs: on the 5′ end there is a methylated GTP "cap," which is linked by an "inverted" (3′-to-5′) bond instead of the usual 5′-to-3′ bond; on the 3′ end there is a tail of 100–200 adenosine residues [poly(A)]; and the mRNA is generated by splicing from a larger transcript of the genome. In fact, these three modifications were first observed in studies on viral mRNAs and then extended to cellular mRNAs. (2) Some viruses use their genetic material to the fullest extent by making more than one type of mRNA from the same piece of DNA by "shifting the reading frame." This is done by starting transcription 1 or 2 bases downstream from the original initiation site. (3) With some DNA viruses, there is temporal control over the region of the genome that is transcribed into mRNA. During the beginning stages of the growth cycle, before DNA replication begins, only the early region of the genome is transcribed and, therefore, only certain early proteins are made. One of the early proteins is a repressor of the late genes; this prevents transcription until the appropriate time. (4) Three different processes are used to generate the monocistronic mRNAs that will code for a single protein from the polycistronic viral genome:

(1) Individual mRNAs are transcribed by starting at many specific initiation points along the genome, which is the same mechanism used by eukaryotic cells and by herpesviruses, adenoviruses, and the DNA and RNA tumor viruses

(2) In the reoviruses and influenza viruses, the genome is segmented into multiple pieces, each of which codes for a single mRNA

(3) In polioviruses, the entire RNA genome is translated into one long polypeptide, which is then cleaved into specific proteins by a protease.

---

viruses is synthesized, it is translated by host cell ribosomes into viral proteins, some of which are **early proteins,** ie, **enzymes** required for replication of the viral genome, and others of which are **late proteins,** ie, **structural proteins** of the progeny viruses. (The term "early" is defined as occurring before the replication of the genome, and "late" is defined as occurring after genome replication.) The most important of the early proteins for many RNA viruses is the polymerase that will synthesize many copies of viral genetic material for the progeny virus particles. No matter how a virus makes its mRNA, most viruses make a virus-encoded polymerase (a **replicase**) that replicates the genome, ie, that makes many copies of the parental genome that will become the genome of the progeny virions. Table 29–5 describes which viruses encode their own replicase and which viruses use host cell polymerases to replicate their genome.

Some viral mRNAs are translated into **precursor polypeptides that must be cleaved by proteases** to produce the functional structural proteins (Figure 29–4 and Table 29–6), whereas other viral mRNAs are translated directly into structural proteins. A striking example of the former occurs during the replication of picornaviruses (eg, poliovirus, rhinovirus, and hepatitis A virus), in which the genome RNA, acting as mRNA, is translated into a **single polypeptide,** which is then cleaved by a virus-coded protease into various proteins. This protease is one of the proteins in the single polypeptide, an interesting example of a protease acting upon its own polypeptide.

Another important family of viruses in which precursor polypeptides are synthesized is the retrovirus family. For example, the *gag* and *pol* genes of HIV are translated into precursor polypeptides, which are then cleaved by a virus-encoded protease. It is this protease that is inhibited by the drugs classified as **protease inhibitors.** Flaviviruses, such as hepatitis C virus and yel-

---

Table 29–4. Comparison of reverse transcriptase activity of HIV (retroviruses) and HBV (hepadnaviruses).

Type of Virus	RNA Template for Reverse Transcriptase	DNA Product of Reverse Transcriptase	Phase of Replication When Reverse Transcriptase Is Active
HIV (retrovirus)	Genome	Not genome	Early
HBV (hepadnavirus)	Not genome	Genome	Late

HBV = hepatitis B virus; HIV = human immunodeficiency virus.

Table 29–5. Origin of the genes that encode the polymerases that replicate the viral genome.

Type of Polymerase	Polymerase Encoded by	Medically Important Viruses
DNA	Cell	Parvovirus B19, human papilloma virus
DNA	Virus	Herpesviruses (HSV, VZV, CMV, EBV), adenovirus, hepatitis B virus, smallpox virus
RNA	Cell	HIV, HTLV
RNA	Virus	Poliovirus, HAV, HCV, influenza virus, measles virus, respiratory syncytial virus, rabies virus, rubella virus, rotavirus, Ebola virus, arenavirus, Hantavirus

CMV = cytomegalovirus; EBV = Epstein-Barr virus; HAV = hepatitis A virus; HCV = hepatitis C virus; HIV = human immunodeficiency virus; HSV = herpes simplex virus; HTLV = human T-cell leukemia virus; VZV = varicella-zoster virus.

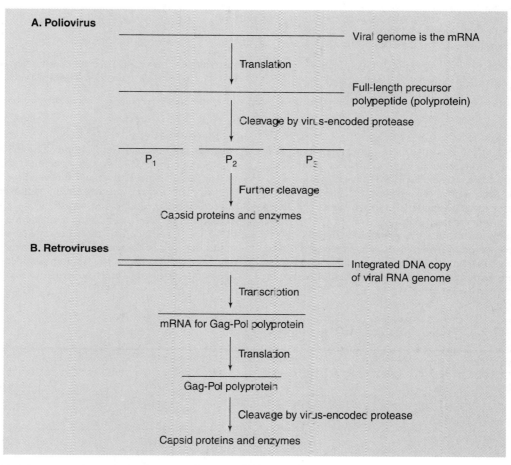

Figure 29–4. Synthesis of viral precursor polypeptides. **A:** Poliovirus mRNA is translated into a full-length precursor polypeptide, which is cleaved by the virus-encoded protease into the functional viral proteins. **B:** Retroviral mRNAs are translated into precursor polypeptides, which are then cleaved by the virus-encoded protease into the functional viral proteins. The cleavage of the Gag-Pol precursor polyprotein by the virion protease occurs in the immature virion after it has budded out from the cell membrane. The cleavage produces the capsid protein (p24), the matrix protein (p17), and enzymes such as the reverse transcriptase and the integrase. The cleavage of the Env polyprotein is carried out by a cellular protease, not by the virion protease. Inhibitors of the virion protease are effective drugs against human immunodeficiency virus.

Table 29–6. Virus-encoded proteases of medically important viruses.

Virus Family	Nature of Polyprotein	Site of Proteolytic Cleavage	Medically Important Viruses
Picornavirus	Single polypeptide formed by translation of entire genome RNA	Cytoplasm	Poliovirus, rhinovirus, hepatitis A virus, coxsackievirus
Flavivirus	Single polypeptide formed by translation of entire genome RNA	Cytoplasm	Hepatitis C virus, yellow fever virus, dengue virus
Togavirus	More than one polypeptide formed by translation of subgenomic mRNAs	Cytoplasm	Eastern and western equine encephalitis viruses, rubella virus
Coronaviruses	More than one polypeptide formed by translation of genome RNA	Cytoplasm	Coronavirus
Retroviruses	More than one polypeptide formed by translation of subgenomic mRNAs	Budding virion	Human immunodeficiency virus, human T-cell leukemia virus

low fever virus, also synthesize precursor polypeptides that must be cleaved to form functional proteins. In contrast, other viruses, such as influenza virus and rotavirus, have segmented genomes, and each segment encodes a specific functional polypeptide rather than a precursor polypeptide.

Replication of the viral genome is governed by the principle of **complementarity,** which requires that a strand with a complementary base sequence be synthesized; this strand then serves as the template for the synthesis of the actual viral genome. The following examples from Table 29–7 should make this clear: (1) poliovirus makes a negative-strand intermediate, which is the template for the positive-strand genome; (2) influenza, measles, and rabies viruses make a positive-strand intermediate, which is the template for the negative-strand genome; (3) rotavirus makes a positive strand that acts both as mRNA and as the template for the negative strand in the double-stranded genome RNA; (4) retroviruses use the negative strand of the

Table 29–7. Complementarity in viral genome replication.

Prototype Virus	Parental Genome[1]	Intermediate Form	Progeny Genome
Poliovirus	+ ssRNA	− ssRNA	+ ssRNA
Influenza virus, measles virus, rabies virus	− ssRNA	+ ssRNA	− ssRNA
Rotavirus	dsRNA	+ ssRNA	dsRNA
Retrovirus	+ ssRNA	dsDNA	+ ssRNA
Parvovirus B19	ssDNA	dsDNA	ssDNA
Hepatitis B virus	dsDNA	+ ssRNA	dsDNA
Papovavirus, adenovirus, herpesvirus, poxvirus	dsDNA	dsDNA	dsDNA

[1]Code: ss, single-stranded; ds, double-stranded; +, positive polarity; −, negative polarity.

DNA intermediate to make positive-strand progeny RNA; (5) hepatitis B virus uses its mRNA as a template to make progeny double-stranded DNA; and (6) the other double-stranded DNA viruses replicate their DNA by the same semiconservative process by which cell DNA is synthesized.

As the replication of the viral genome proceeds, the structural capsid proteins to be used in the progeny virus particles are synthesized. In some cases, the newly replicated viral genomes can serve as templates for the late mRNA to make these capsid proteins.

Assembly & Release

The progeny particles are assembled by packaging the viral nucleic acid within the capsid proteins. Little is known about the precise steps in the assembly process. Surprisingly, certain viruses can be assembled in the test tube by using only purified RNA and purified protein. This indicates that the specificity of the interaction resides within the RNA and protein and that the action of enzymes and expenditure of energy are not required.

Virus particles are released from the cell by either of two processes. One is rupture of the cell membrane and release of the mature particles; this usually occurs with unenveloped viruses. The other, which occurs with enveloped viruses, is release of viruses by **budding** through the outer cell membrane (Figure 29–5). (An exception is the **herpesvirus** family, whose members acquire their envelopes from the **nuclear membrane** rather than from the outer cell membrane.) The budding process begins when virus-specific proteins enter the cell membrane at

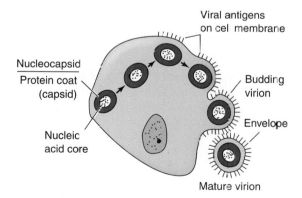

Figure 29–5. Budding. Most enveloped viruses derive their lipoprotein envelope from the cell membrane. The matrix protein mediates the interaction between the viral nucleocapsid and the viral envelope. (Reproduced, with permission, from Mims CA: *The Pathogenesis of Infectious Disease,* 3rd ed. Academic Press, 1987.)

specific sites. The viral nucleocapsid then interacts with the specific membrane site mediated by the **matrix protein**. The cell membrane evaginates at that site, and an enveloped particle buds off from the membrane. Budding frequently does not damage the cell, and in certain instances the cell survives while producing large numbers of budding virus particles.

LYSOGENY

The typical replicative cycle described above occurs most of the time when viruses infect cells. However, some viruses can use an alternative pathway, called the **lysogenic cycle**, in which the viral DNA becomes integrated into the host cell chromosome and no progeny virus particles are produced at that time (Figure 29–6). The viral nucleic acid continues to function in the integrated state in a variety of ways. One of the most important functions from a medical point of view is the synthesis of several exotoxins in bacteria, such as **diphtheria**, **botulinum**, **cholera**, and **erythrogenic toxins**, encoded by the genes of the integrated bacteriophage (**prophage**). **Lysogenic conversion** is the term applied to the new properties that a bacterium acquires as a result of expression of the **integrated prophage genes** (Figure 29–7).

The lysogenic or "temperate" cycle is described for lambda bacteriophage, because it is the best-understood model system (Figure 29–8). Several aspects of infections by tumor viruses and herpesviruses are similar to the events in the lysogenic cycle of lambda phage.

Infection by lambda phage in *E. coli* begins with injection of the linear, double-stranded DNA genome through the phage tail into the cell. The linear DNA becomes a circle as the single-stranded regions on the 5' end and the 3' end pair their complementary bases. A ligating enzyme makes a covalent bond in each strand to close the circle. Circularization is important because it is the circular form that integrates into host cell DNA.

The choice between the pathway leading to lysogeny and that leading to full replication is made as early protein synthesis begins. Simply put, the choice depends on the balance between two proteins, the **repressor** produced by the *c-I* gene and the **antagonizer of the repressor** produced by the *cro* gene (Figure 29–9). If the repressor predominates, transcription of other early genes is shut off and lysogeny ensues. Transcription is inhibited by binding of the repressor to the two operator sites that control early protein synthesis. If the *cro* gene product prevents the synthesis of sufficient repressor, replication and lysis of the cell result. One correlate of the lysogenic state is that the repressor can also prevent the replication of additional lambda phages that infect subsequently. This is called "immu-

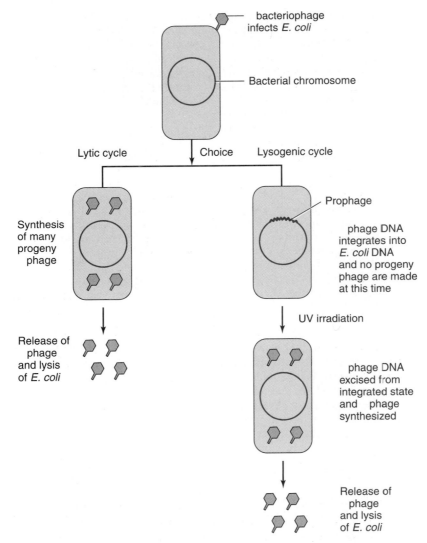

Figure 29–6. Comparison of the lytic and lysogenic cycles of bacteriophage (phage) replication. In the lytic cycle, replication of the phage is completed without interruption. In the lysogenic cycle, replication of the phage is interrupted and the phage DNA integrates into the bacterial DNA. The integrated DNA is called a prophage and can remain in the integrated state for long periods. If the bacteria are exposed to certain activators such as UV light, the prophage DNA is excised from the bacterial DNA and the phage enters the lytic cycle, which ends with the production of progeny phage.

nity" and is specifically directed against lambda phage because the repressor binds only to the operator sites in lambda DNA; other phages are not affected.

The next important step in the lysogenic cycle is the **integration** of the viral DNA into the cell DNA. This occurs by the matching of a specific attachment site on the lambda DNA to a homologous site on the *E. coli* DNA and the integration (breakage and rejoining) of the two DNAs mediated by a phage-encoded recombination enzyme. The integrated viral DNA is called a **prophage.** Most lysogenic phages integrate at one or a few specific sites, but some, such as the Mu (or mutator) phage, can integrate their DNA at many sites, and other phages, such as the P1 phage, never actually inte-

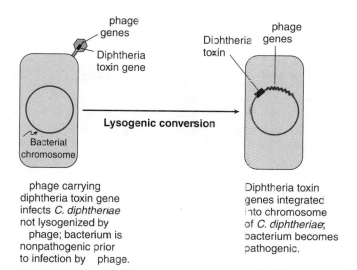

phage
genes

Diphtheria
toxin gene

Bacterial
chromosome

Lysogenic conversion

Diphtheria
toxin

phage
genes

phage carrying
diphtheria toxin gene
infects *C. diphtheriae*
not lysogenized by
phage; bacterium is
nonpathogenic prior
to infection by phage.

Diphtheria toxin
genes integrated
into chromosome
of *C. diphtheriae*;
bacterium becomes
pathogenic.

Figure 29–7. Lysogenic conversion. In the left-hand panel, transduction of the diphtheria toxin gene by beta bacteriophage results in lysogenic conversion of the non-lysogenized, nonpathogenic *Corynebacterium diphtheriae*. In the right-hand panel, the recipient lysogenized bacterium can now produce diphtheria toxin and can cause the disease diphtheria. Note that no progeny phages are made within the lysogenized bacterium because the diphtheria toxin gene has replaced some of the beta phage genes required for replication. The beta phage therefore cannot replicate. The lysogenized bacterium is not killed by the phage and can multiply, produce diphtheria toxin, and cause disease.

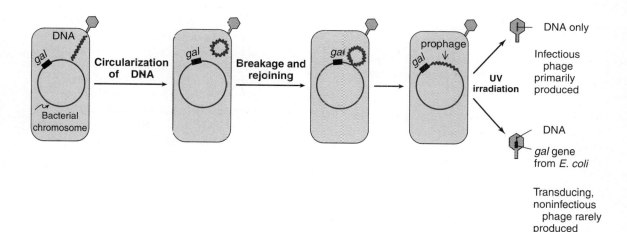

DNA

gal

Bacterial
chromosome

Circularization
of DNA

gal

Breakage and
rejoining

gal

prophage

gal

UV
irradiation

DNA only

Infectious
phage
primarily
produced

DNA

gal gene
from *E. coli*

Transducing,
noninfectious
phage rarely
produced

Figure 29–8. Lysogeny. The linear lambda phage DNA is injected into the bacterium, circularizes, and then integrates into the bacterial DNA. When integrated, the phage DNA is called a prophage. When the prophage is induced to enter the replicative cycle, aberrant excision of the phage DNA can occur; ie, part of the phage DNA and part of the bacterial DNA including the adjacent *gal* gene are excised. The *gal* gene can now be transduced to another bacterium. Transduction is also described in Figure 4–4. (Reproduced, with permission, from Jawetz E et al: *Review of Medical Microbiology*, 17th ed. Originally published by Appleton & Lange. Copyright © 1986 by The McGraw-Hill Companies, Inc.)

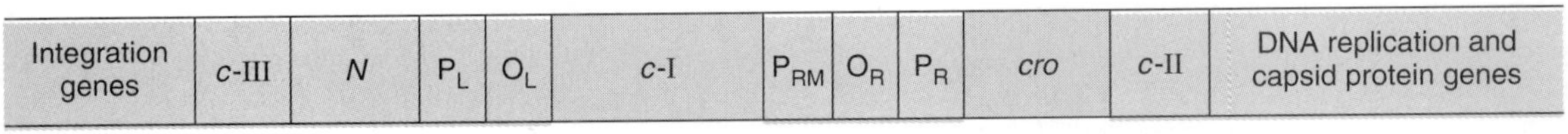

Integration genes	c-III	N	P_L	O_L	c-I	P_RM	O_R	P_R	cro	c-II	DNA replication and capsid protein genes

Figure 29–9. Control of lysogeny. Shortly after infection, transcription of the *N* and *cro* genes begins. The *N* protein is an antiterminator that allows transcription of *c*-II and *c*-III and the genes to the right of *c*-II and to the left of *c*-III. The *c*-II protein enhances the production of the *c*-I repressor protein. *c*-I has two important functions: (1) It inhibits transcription at P_RO_R and P_LO_L, thereby preventing phage replication; and (2) it is a positive regulator of its own synthesis by binding to P_{RM}. The crucial decision point in lysogeny is the binding of either *c*-I repressor or the *cro* protein to the O_R site. If *c*-I repressor occupies O_R, lysogeny ensues; if *cro* protein occupies O_R, viral replication occurs. *N*, antiterminator gene; *c*-I, repressor gene; *c*-II and *c*-III, genes that influence the production of *c*-I; P_LO_L, left promoter and operator; P_RO_R, right promoter and operator; P_{RM}, promoter for repressor maintenance; *cro*, gene that antagonizes the *c*-I repressor.

grate but remain in a "temperate" state extrachromosomally, similar to a plasmid.

Because the integrated viral DNA is replicated along with the cell DNA, each daughter cell inherits a copy. However, the prophage is not permanently integrated. It can be induced to resume its replicative cycle by the action of UV light and certain chemicals that damage DNA. UV light induces the synthesis of a protease, which cleaves the repressor. Early genes then function, including the genes coding for the enzymes that excise the prophage from the cell DNA. The virus then completes its replicative cycle, leading to the production of progeny virus and lysis of the cell.

PEARLS

Viral Growth Curve

- *One virion infects a cell and hundreds of progeny virions are produced within hours. This is a remarkable amplification and explains the rapid spread of virus from cell to cell.*
- *The **eclipse period** is the time when no virus particles are detected within the infected cell. It occurs soon after the cell is infected.*
- *Cytopathic effect (CPE) is the term used to describe the damage, both morphologic and functional, inflicted on the cell by the virus. In the clinical laboratory, the presence of a virus in the patient's specimen is often detected by seeing a CPE in cell culture.*

Viral Growth Cycle

- ***Attachment:** The interaction of proteins on the surface of the virus with specific receptor proteins on the surface of the cell is one of the main determinants of both the **species specificity** and the **organ specificity** of the virus.*
- ***Infectious nucleic acid** is viral genome DNA or RNA, purified free of all proteins, that can undergo the* entire replicative cycle within a cell and produce infectious progeny viruses. Infectious nucleic acid, because it has no associated protein, can enter and replicate within cells that the intact virion cannot.
- ***Polarity of Viral Genome RNA:** Genome RNA that has the same base sequence as the mRNA is, by definition, positive-polarity RNA. Most positive-polarity genomes are translated into viral proteins without the need for a polymerase in the virion. The exception is the retroviruses, which use reverse transcriptase in the virion to transcribe the genome RNA into DNA. Genome RNA that has a base sequence complementary to mRNA has, by definition, negative polarity. A virus with a negative-polarity RNA genome must have an RNA polymerase in the virion to synthesize its mRNA.*
- ***Viral Gene Expression:** All viruses require virus-specific messenger RNA to synthesize virus-specific proteins.*
- ***RNA Viruses:** Some RNA viruses, such as poliovirus, have a positive-polarity RNA genome that serves as the mRNA, ie, the genome is the mRNA. Other viruses, such as influenza virus, have a negative-polarity*

RNA genome and have an RNA polymerase in the virion that synthesizes the viral mRNA. Rotavirus has a double-stranded RNA genome and has an RNA polymerase in the virion that synthesizes the viral mRNA. Retroviruses, such as HIV, have a positive-polarity RNA genome and have a DNA polymerase in the virion that synthesizes a DNA copy of the RNA genome. This DNA is the template used by the host cell RNA polymerase to synthesize the viral mRNA.

- **DNA Viruses:** Most DNA viruses, such as herpesviruses, adenoviruses, and papillomaviruses, have a double-stranded DNA genome and use the host cell RNA polymerase to synthesize the viral mRNA. Poxviruses have a double-stranded DNA genome but have an RNA polymerase in the virion that synthesizes the viral mRNA. Poxviruses have an RNA polymerase in the virion because they replicate in the cytoplasm and do not have access to the host cell RNA polymerase in the nucleus.

- **Viral Replication:** All DNA viruses replicate in the nucleus, except poxviruses, which replicate in the cytoplasm. All RNA viruses replicate in the cytoplasm, except retroviruses, influenza virus, and hepatitis D virus, which require an intranuclear step in their replication. Many viruses encode a replicase, which is a DNA or RNA polymerase that synthesizes the many copies of the progeny viral genomes.

- **Viral Genome:** The genome of all DNA viruses is double-stranded except for that of parvoviruses, which is single-stranded. The genome of all RNA viruses is single-stranded except for that of reoviruses, eg, rotavirus, which is double-stranded.

- **Viral Proteins:** Early proteins are typically enzymes used in the synthesis of viral components, whereas late proteins are typically structural proteins of the progeny viruses. Some viruses, such as poliovirus and retroviruses, translate their mRNA into precursor polyproteins, which must be cleaved by proteases to produce functional proteins.

- **Assembly and Release:** All enveloped viruses acquire their envelope by budding through the external cell membrane as they exit the cell, except herpesviruses, which acquire their envelope by budding through the nuclear membrane. The matrix protein mediates the interaction of the nucleocapsid with the envelope.

- **Lysogeny** is the process by which viral DNA becomes integrated into host cell DNA, replication stops, and no progeny virus is made. Later, if DNA is damaged by, for example, UV light, viral DNA is excised from the host cell DNA and progeny viruses are made. The integrated viral DNA is called a **prophage.** Bacterial cells carrying a prophage can acquire new traits, such as the ability to produce exotoxins such as diphtheria toxin. **Transduction** is the process by which viruses carry genes from one cell to another. **Lysogenic conversion** is the term used to indicate that the cell has acquired a new trait as a result of the integrated prophage.

PRACTICE QUESTIONS: USMLE & COURSE EXAMINATIONS

Questions on the topics discussed in this chapter can be found in the Basic Virology section of Part XI: USMLE (National Board) Practice Questions starting on page 545. Also see Part XII: USMLE (National Board) Practice Examination starting on page 583.

Genetics & Gene Therapy

30

The study of viral genetics falls into two general areas: (1) mutations and their effect on replication and pathogenesis, and (2) the interaction of two genetically distinct viruses that infect the same cell. In addition, viruses serve as **vectors** in gene therapy and in recombinant vaccines, two areas that hold great promise for the treatment of genetic diseases and the prevention of infectious diseases.

MUTATIONS

Mutations in viral DNA and RNA occur by the same processes of base substitution, deletion, and frameshift as those described for bacteria in Chapter 4. Probably the most important practical use of mutations is in the production of vaccines containing live, attenuated virus. These attenuated mutants have lost their pathogenicity but have retained their antigenicity—they therefore induce immunity without causing disease.

There are two other kinds of mutants of interest. The first are antigenic variants such as those that occur frequently with influenza viruses, which have an altered surface protein and are therefore no longer inhibited by a person's preexisting antibody. The variant can thus cause disease, whereas the original strain cannot. The second are drug-resistant mutants, which are insensitive to an antiviral drug because the target of the drug, usually a viral enzyme, has been modified.

Conditional-lethal mutations are extremely valuable in determining the function of viral genes. These mutations function normally under permissive conditions but fail to replicate or to express the mutant gene under restrictive conditions. For example, temperature-sensitive conditional-lethal mutants express their phenotype normally at a low (permissive) temperature, but at a higher (restrictive) temperature the mutant gene product is inactive. To give a specific example, temperature-sensitive mutants of Rous sarcoma virus can transform cells to malignancy at the permissive temperature of 37°C. When the transformed cells are grown at the restrictive temperature of 41°C, their phenotype reverts to normal appearance and behavior. The malignant phenotype is regained when the permissive temperature is restored.

Note that temperature-sensitive mutants have now entered clinical practice. Temperature-sensitive mutants of influenza virus are now being used to make a vaccine, because this virus will grow in the cooler, upper airways where it causes few symptoms and induces antibodies, but it will not grow in the warmer, lower airways where it can cause pneumonia.

Some deletion mutants have the unusual property of being **defective interfering particles.** They are defective because they cannot replicate unless the deleted function is supplied by a "helper" virus. They also interfere with the growth of normal virus if they infect first and preempt the required cellular functions. Defective interfering particles may play a role in recovery from viral infection; they interfere with the production of progeny virus, thereby limiting the spread of the virus to other cells.

INTERACTIONS

When two genetically distinct viruses infect a cell, three different phenomena can ensue.

(1) **Recombination** is the exchange of genes between two chromosomes that is based on crossing over within regions of significant base sequence homology. Recombination can be readily demonstrated for viruses with double-stranded DNA as the genetic material and has been used to determine their genetic map. However, recombination by RNA viruses occurs at a very low frequency, if at all. **Reassortment** is the term used when viruses with segmented genomes, such as influenza virus, exchange segments. This usually results in a much higher frequency of gene exchange than does recombination. Reassortment of influenza virus RNA segments is involved in the major antigenic changes in the virus that are the basis for recurrent influenza epidemics.

(2) **Complementation** can occur when either one or both of the two viruses that infect the cell have a mutation that results in a nonfunctional protein (Figure 30–1). The nonmutated virus "complements" the mutated one by making a functional protein that serves for both viruses. Complementation is an important method by which a helper virus permits replication of a defective virus. One clinically important example of

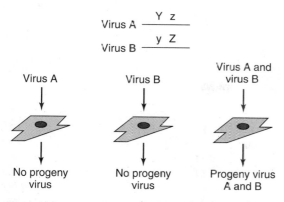

Figure 30–1. Complementation. If *either* virus A *or* virus B infects a cell, no virus is produced because each has a mutated gene. If *both* virus A and virus B infect a cell, the protein product of gene Y of virus A will complement virus B, the protein product of gene Z of virus B will complement virus A, and progeny of both virus A and virus B will be produced. Note that no recombination has occurred and that the virus A progeny will contain the mutated z gene and the virus B progeny will contain the mutant y gene. Y, Z, functional genes; y, z, mutated, nonfunctional genes.

complementation is hepatitis B virus providing its surface antigen to hepatitis delta virus, which is defective in its ability to produce its own outer protein.

This phenomenon is the basis for the complementation test, which can be used to determine how many genes exist in a viral genome. It is performed by determining whether mutant virus A can complement mutant virus B. If it can, the two mutations are in separate genes because they make different, complementary proteins. If it cannot, the two mutations are in the same gene and both proteins are nonfunctional. By performing many of these paired tests with different mutants, it is possible to determine functional domains of complementation groups that correspond to genes. Appropriate controls are needed to obviate the effects of recombination.

(3) In **phenotypic mixing,** the genome of virus type A can be coated with the surface proteins of virus type B (Figure 30–2). This phenotypically mixed virus can infect cells as determined by its type B protein coat. However, the progeny virus from this infection has a type A coat; it is encoded solely by its type A genetic material. An interesting example of phenotypic mixing is that of **pseudotypes,** which consist of the nucleocapsid of one virus and the envelope of another. Pseudotypes

composed of the nucleocapsid of vesicular stomatitis virus (a rhabdovirus) and the envelope of human immunodeficiency virus (HIV, a retrovirus) are currently being used to study the immune response to HIV.

GENE THERAPY & RECOMBINANT VACCINES

Viruses are being used as genetic vectors in two novel ways: (1) to deliver new, functional genes to patients with genetic diseases (gene therapy); and (2) to produce new viral vaccines that contain recombinant viruses carrying the genes of several different viruses, thereby inducing immunity to several diseases with one immunization.

Gene Therapy

Retroviruses are currently being used as vectors of the gene encoding adenine deaminase (ADA) in patients with immunodeficiencies resulting from a defective ADA gene. Retroviruses are excellent vectors because a DNA copy of their RNA genome is stably integrated into the host cell DNA and the integrated genes are expressed efficiently. Retroviral vectors are constructed by removing the genes encoding several viral proteins from the virus and replacing them with the human gene of interest, eg, the ADA gene. Virus particles containing the human gene are produced within "helper cells" that contain the deleted viral genes and therefore can supply, by complementation, the missing viral proteins necessary for the virus to replicate. The retroviruses produced by the helper cells can infect the patient's cells and introduce the human gene into the cells, but the viruses cannot replicate because they lack several viral genes. This inability of these viruses to replicate is an important advantage in human gene therapy.

Recombinant Vaccines

Recombinant viral vaccines contain viruses that have been genetically engineered to carry the genes of other viruses. Viruses with large genomes, eg, vaccinia virus, are excellent candidates for this purpose. To construct the recombinant virus, any vaccinia virus gene that is not essential for viral replication is deleted, and the gene from the other virus that encodes the antigen that elicits neutralizing antibody is introduced. For example, the gene for the surface antigen of hepatitis B virus has been introduced into vaccinia virus and is expressed in infected cells. Recombinant vaccines are not yet clinically available, but vaccines of this type promise to greatly improve the efficiency of our immunization programs.

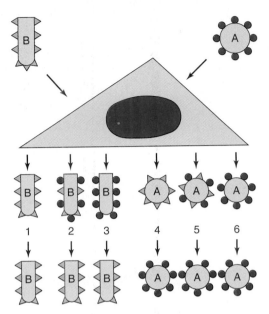

Figure 30–2. Phenotypic mixing. A retrovirus (A) and a rhabdovirus (B) infect the same cell. The progeny viruses include phenotypically mixed particles (2, 3, 4, and 5) and normal progeny virions (1 and 6). Assume that virus A can infect human cells but not chicken cells (a property determined by the circular surface proteins) and that virus B can infect chicken cells but not human cells (a property determined by the triangular surface proteins). However, both virus A and virus B can infect a mouse cell. As shown in the figure, six types of progeny viruses can arise when both virus A and virus B infect a mouse cell. Progeny virus #1 is not phenotypically mixed and can infect chicken cells but not human cells because it has the triangular surface proteins. If progeny virus #1 infects chicken cells, the progeny virus from that infection is determined by the B genome and will be identical to the parental B virus. Progeny virus #2 is phenotypically mixed and can infect both chicken cells and human cells because it has both the triangular and the circular surface proteins. Note that when progeny virus #2 infects either chicken cells or human cells, the progeny of that infection is determined by the B genome and will be identical to the parental B virus. Progeny virus #3 is phenotypically mixed and can infect human cells but not chicken cells because it has the circular surface proteins. Note that when progeny virus #3 infects human cells, the progeny of that infection is determined by the B genome and will be identical to the parental B virus. The reader should use the interpretation of progeny viruses 1, 2, and 3 to understand the properties of progeny viruses 4, 5, and 6. (Modified and reproduced, with permission, from Boettiger D. Animal virus pseudotypes. *Prog Med Virol* 1979;25:37.)

 PEARLS

- *Mutations in the viral genome can produce antigenic variants and drug-resistant variants. Mutations can also produce **attenuated** (weakened) variants that cannot cause disease but retain their antigenicity and are useful in vaccines.*

- *Temperature-sensitive mutants can replicate at a low (permissive) temperature but not at a high (restrictive) temperature. Temperature-sensitive mutants of influenza virus are used in one of the vaccines against this disease.*

- ***Reassortment** (exchange) of segments of the genome RNA of influenza virus is important in the pathogenesis of the worldwide epidemics caused by this virus.*

- ***Complementation** occurs when one virus produces a protein that can be used by another virus. A medically important example is hepatitis D virus that uses the surface antigen of hepatitis B virus as its outer coat protein.*

- ***Phenotypic mixing** occurs when two different viruses infect the same cell and progeny viruses contain proteins of both parental viruses. This can endow the progeny viruses with the ability to infect cells of species that ordinarily parental virus could not.*

PRACTICE QUESTIONS: USMLE & COURSE EXAMINATIONS

Questions on the topics discussed in this chapter can be found in the Basic Virology section of Part XI: USMLE (National Board) Practice Questions starting on page 545. Also see Part XII: USMLE (National Board) Practice Examination starting on page 583.

Classification of Medically Important Viruses

31

The classification of viruses is based on chemical and morphologic criteria. The two major components of the virus used in classification are (1) the nucleic acid (its molecular weight and structure); and (2) the capsid (its size and symmetry and whether it is enveloped). A classification scheme based on these factors is presented in Tables 31–1 and 31–2 for DNA and RNA viruses, respectively. This scheme was simplified from the complete classification to emphasize organisms of medical importance. Only the virus families are listed; subfamilies are described in the chapter on the specific virus.

DNA VIRUSES

The families of DNA viruses are described in Table 31–1. The three **naked** (ie, nonenveloped) icosahedral virus families—the parvoviruses, papovaviruses, and adenoviruses—are presented in order of increasing particle size, as are the three **enveloped** families. The hepadnavirus family, which includes hepatitis B virus, and the herpesviruses are enveloped icosahedral viruses. The largest viruses, the poxviruses, have a complex internal symmetry.

Parvoviruses

These are very small (22 nm in diameter), naked icosahedral viruses with single-stranded linear DNA. There are two types of parvoviruses: defective and nondefective. The defective parvoviruses, eg, adeno-associated virus, require a helper virus for replication. The DNA of defective parvoviruses is unusual because plus-strand DNA and minus-strand DNA are carried in separate particles. The nondefective parvoviruses are best illustrated by B19 virus, which is associated with aplastic crises in sickle cell anemia patients and with erythema infectiosum, an innocuous childhood disease characterized by a "slapped-cheeks" rash.

Papovaviruses

These are naked icosahedral viruses (55 nm in diameter) with double-stranded circular supercoiled DNA. The name "papova" is an acronym of *pa*pilloma, *po*lyoma, and simian *va*cuolating viruses. Three human papovaviruses are JC virus, isolated from patients with progressive multifocal leukoencephalopathy; BK virus, isolated from the urine of immunosuppressed kidney transplant patients; and human papillomavirus. Polyomavirus and simian vacuolating virus 40 (SV40 virus) are papovaviruses of mice and monkeys, respectively, that induce malignant tumors in a variety of species.

Adenoviruses

These are naked icosahedral viruses (75 nm in diameter) with double-stranded linear DNA. They cause pharyngitis, upper and lower respiratory tract disease, and a variety of other less common infections. There are at least 40 antigenic types, some of which cause sarcomas in animals but no tumors in humans.

Hepadnaviruses

These are double-shelled viruses (42 nm in diameter) with an icosahedral capsid covered by an envelope. The DNA is a double-stranded circle that is unusual because the complete strand is not a covalently closed circle and the other strand is missing approximately 25% of its length. Hepatitis B virus is the human pathogen in this family.

Herpesviruses

These are enveloped viruses (100 nm in diameter) with an icosahedral nucleocapsid and double-stranded linear DNA. They are noted for causing latent infections. The five important human pathogens are herpes simplex virus types 1 and 2, varicella-zoster virus, cytomega-

Table 31–1. Classification of DNA viruses.

Virus Family	Envelope Present	Capsid Symmetry	Particle Size (nm)	DNA MW (×10⁶)	DNA Structure[1]	Medically Important Viruses
Parvovirus	No	Icosahedral	22	2	SS, linear	B19 virus
Papovavirus	No	Icosahedral	55	3–5	DS, circular, supercoiled	Papillomavirus
Adenovirus	No	Icosahedral	75	23	DS, linear	Adenovirus
Hepadnavirus	Yes	Icosahedral	42	1.5	DS, incomplete circular	Hepatitis B virus
Herpesvirus	Yes	Icosahedral	100[2]	100–150	DS, linear	Herpes simplex virus, varicella-zoster virus, cytomegalovirus, Epstein-Barr virus
Poxvirus	Yes	Complex	250 × 400	125–185	DS, linear	Smallpox virus, vaccinia virus

[1]SS, single-stranded; DS, double-stranded.
[2]The herpesvirus nucleocapsid is 100 nm, but the envelope varies in size. The entire virus can be as large as 200 nm in diameter.

lovirus, and Epstein-Barr virus (the cause of infectious mononucleosis).

Poxviruses

These are the largest viruses, with a bricklike shape, an envelope with an unusual appearance, and a complex capsid symmetry. They are named for the skin lesions, or "pocks," that they cause. Smallpox virus and vaccinia virus are the two important members. The latter virus is used in the smallpox vaccine.

RNA VIRUSES

The 14 families of RNA viruses are described in Table 31–2. The three **naked icosahedral** virus families are listed first and are followed by the three **enveloped icosahedral** viruses. The remaining eight families are **enveloped helical** viruses; the first five have single-stranded linear RNA as their genome, whereas the last three have single-stranded circular RNA.

Picornaviruses

These are the smallest (28 nm in diameter) RNA viruses. They have single-stranded, linear, nonsegmented, positive-polarity RNA within a naked icosahedral capsid. The name "picorna" is derived from *pico* (small), *RNA*-containing. There are two groups of hu-

man pathogens: (1) enteroviruses such as poliovirus, coxsackievirus, echovirus, and hepatitis A virus; and (2) rhinoviruses.

Caliciviruses

These are naked viruses (38 nm in diameter) with an icosahedral capsid. They have single-stranded, linear, nonsegmented, positive-polarity RNA. There are two human pathogens: Norwalk virus and hepatitis E virus.

Reoviruses

These are naked viruses (75 nm in diameter) with two icosahedral capsid coats. They have 10 segments of double-stranded linear RNA. The name is an acronym of *r*espiratory *e*nteric *o*rphan, because they were originally found in the respiratory and enteric tracts and were not associated with any human disease. The main human pathogen is rotavirus, which causes diarrhea mainly in infants.

Flaviviruses

These are enveloped viruses with an icosahedral capsid and single-stranded, linear, nonsegmented, positive-polarity RNA. The flaviviruses include hepatitis C virus, yellow fever virus, dengue virus, West Nile virus, and St. Louis and Japanese encephalitis viruses.

Table 31–2. Classification of RNA viruses.

Virus Family	Envelope Present	Capsid Symmetry	Particle Size (nm)	RNA MW (×10⁶)	RNA Structure[1]	Medically Important Viruses
Picornavirus	No	Icosahedral	28	2.5	SS linear, nonsegmented, positive polarity	Poliovirus, rhinovirus, hepatitis A virus
Calicivirus	No	Icosahedral	38	2.7	SS linear, nonsegmented, positive polarity	Norwalk virus, hepatitis E virus
Reovirus	No	Icosahedral	75	15	DS linear, 10 segments	Rotavirus
Flavivirus	Yes	Icosahedral	45	4	SS linear, nonsegmented, positive polarity	Yellow fever virus, dengue virus, West Nile virus, hepatitis C virus
Togavirus	Yes	Icosahedral	60	4	SS linear, nonsegmented, positive polarity	Rubella virus
Retrovirus	Yes	Icosahedral	100	7[2]	SS linear, 2 segments, positive polarity	HIV, human T-cell leukemia virus
Orthomyxovirus	Yes	Helical	80–120	4	SS linear, 8 segments, negative polarity	Influenza virus
Paramyxovirus	Yes	Helical	150	6	SS linear, nonsegmented, negative polarity	Measles virus, mumps virus, respiratory syncytial virus
Rhabdovirus	Yes	Helical	75 × 180	4	SS linear, nonsegmented, negative polarity	Rabies virus
Filovirus	Yes	Helical	80[3]	4	SS linear, nonsegmented, negative polarity	Ebola virus, Marburg virus
Coronavirus	Yes	Helical	100	10	SS linear, nonsegmented, positive polarity	Coronavirus
Arenavirus	Yes	Helical	80–130	5	SS circular, 2 segments with cohesive ends, negative polarity	Lymphocytic choriomeningitis virus
Bunyavirus	Yes	Helical	100	5	SS circular, 3 segments with cohesive ends, negative polarity	California encephalitis virus, hantavirus
Deltavirus	Yes	Uncertain[4]	37	0.5	SS circular, closed circle, negative polarity	Hepatitis delta virus

[1]SS, single-stranded; DS, double-stranded.
[2]Retrovirus RNA contains 2 identical molecules of MW 3.5 × 10⁶.
[3]Particles are 80 nm wide but can be thousands of nanometers long.
[4]The nucleocapsid appears spherical but its symmetry is unknown.

Togaviruses

These are enveloped viruses with an icosahedral capsid and single-stranded, linear, nonsegmented, positive-polarity RNA. There are two major groups of human pathogens: the alphaviruses and rubiviruses. The alphavirus group includes eastern and western encephalitis viruses; the rubivirus group consists only of rubella virus.

Retroviruses

These are enveloped viruses with an icosahedral capsid and two identical strands of single-stranded, linear, positive-polarity RNA. The term "retro" pertains to the reverse transcription of the RNA genome into DNA. There are two medically important groups: (1) the oncovirus group, which contains the sarcoma and leukemia viruses, eg, human T-cell leukemia virus (HTLV); and (2) the lentivirus ("slow virus") group, which includes human immunodeficiency virus (HIV) and certain animal pathogens, eg, visna virus. A third group, spumaviruses, is described in Chapter 46.

Orthomyxoviruses

These viruses (myxoviruses) are enveloped, with a helical nucleocapsid and eight segments of linear, single-stranded, negative-polarity RNA. The term "myxo" refers to the affinity of these viruses for mucins, and "ortho" is added to distinguish them from the paramyxoviruses. Influenza virus is the main human pathogen.

Paramyxoviruses

These are enveloped viruses with a helical nucleocapsid and single-stranded, linear, nonsegmented, negative-polarity RNA. The important human pathogens are measles, mumps, parainfluenza, and respiratory syncytial viruses.

Rhabdoviruses

These are bullet-shaped enveloped viruses with a helical nucleocapsid and a single-stranded, linear, nonsegmented, negative-polarity RNA. The term "rhabdo" refers to the bullet shape. Rabies virus is the only important human pathogen.

Filoviruses

These are enveloped viruses with a helical nucleocapsid and single-stranded, linear, nonsegmented, negative-polarity RNA. They are highly pleomorphic, long filaments that are 80 nm in diameter but can be thousands of nanometers long. The term "filo" means "thread" and refers to the long filaments. The two human pathogens are Ebola virus and Marburg virus.

Coronaviruses

These are enveloped viruses with a helical nucleocapsid and a single-stranded, linear, nonsegmented, positive-polarity RNA. The term "corona" refers to the prominent halo of spikes protruding from the envelope. Coronaviruses cause respiratory tract infections, such as the common cold and SARS (severe acute respiratory syndrome) in humans.

Arenaviruses

These are enveloped viruses with a helical nucleocapsid and a single-stranded, circular, negative-polarity RNA in two segments. (A part of both segments is positive-polarity RNA, and the term "ambisense RNA" is used to describe this unusual genome.) The term "arena" means "sand" and refers to granules on the virion surface that are nonfunctional ribosomes. Two human pathogens are lymphocytic choriomeningitis virus and Lassa fever virus.

Bunyaviruses

These are enveloped viruses with a helical nucleocapsid and a single-stranded, circular, negative-polarity RNA in three segments. Some bunyaviruses contain ambisense RNA in their genome. (See arenaviruses above.) The term "bunya" refers to the prototype, Bunyamwera virus, which is named for the place in Africa where it was isolated. These viruses cause encephalitis and various fevers such as Korean hemorrhagic fever. Hantaviruses, such as Sin Nombre virus (see Chapter 46), are members of this family.

Deltavirus

Hepatitis delta virus (HDV) is the only member of this genus. It is an enveloped virus with an RNA genome that is a single-stranded, negative-polarity, covalently closed circle. The symmetry of the nucleocapsid is uncertain. It is a defective virus because it cannot replicate unless hepatitis B virus (HBV) is present within the same cell. HBV is required because it encodes hepatitis B surface antigen (HBsAg), which serves as the outer protein coat of HDV. The RNA genome of HDV encodes only one protein, the internal core protein called delta antigen.

PEARLS

- *The classification of viruses is based primarily on the nature of the genome and whether the virus has an envelope.*
- *Poxviruses, herpesviruses, and hepadnaviruses are DNA viruses with an envelope, whereas adenoviruses, papovaviruses, and parvoviruses are DNA viruses without an envelope, ie, they are naked nucleocapsid viruses. Parvoviruses have single-stranded DNA, whereas all the other families of DNA viruses have double-stranded DNA. The DNA of hepadnaviruses (hepatitis B virus) is mostly double-stranded but has a single-stranded region.*

- *Picornaviruses, caliciviruses, and reoviruses are RNA viruses without an envelope, whereas all the other families of RNA viruses have an envelope. Reoviruses have double-stranded RNA; all the other families of RNA viruses have single-stranded RNA. Reoviruses and influenza viruses have segmented RNA; all the other families of RNA viruses have nonsegmented RNA. Picornaviruses, caliciviruses, flaviviruses, togaviruses, retroviruses, and coronaviruses have positive-polarity RNA, whereas all the other families have negative-polarity RNA.*

PRACTICE QUESTIONS: USMLE & COURSE EXAMINATIONS

Questions on the topics discussed in this chapter can be found in the Basic Virology section of Part XI: USMLE (National Board) Practice Questions starting on page 545. Also see Part XII: USMLE (National Board) Practice Examination starting on page 583.

Pathogenesis

The ability of viruses to cause disease can be viewed on two distinct levels: (1) the changes that occur within individual cells and (2) the process that takes place in the infected patient.

THE INFECTED CELL

There are four main effects of virus infection on the cell: (1) death, (2) fusion of cells to form multinucleated cells, (3) malignant transformation, and (4) no apparent morphologic or functional change.

Death of the cell is probably due to inhibition of macromolecular synthesis. Inhibition of host cell protein synthesis frequently occurs first and is probably the most important effect. Inhibition of DNA and RNA synthesis may be a secondary effect. It is important to note that synthesis of **cellular** proteins is inhibited but **viral** protein synthesis still occurs. For example, poliovirus inactivates an initiation factor (IF) required for cellular mRNA to be translated into cellular proteins, but poliovirus mRNA has a special ribosome-initiating site that allows it to bypass the IF so that viral proteins can be synthesized.

Infected cells frequently contain **inclusion bodies,** which are discrete areas containing viral proteins or viral particles. They have a characteristic intranuclear or intracytoplasmic location and appearance depending on the virus. One of the best examples of inclusion bodies that can assist in clinical diagnosis is that of **Negri bodies,** which are eosinophilic cytoplasmic inclusions found in rabies virus–infected brain neurons. Another important example is the **owl's eye inclusion** seen in the nucleus of cytomegalovirus-infected cells. Electron micrographs of inclusion bodies can also aid in the diagnosis when virus particles of typical morphology are visualized.

Fusion of virus-infected cells produces **multinucleated giant cells,** which characteristically form after infection with **herpesviruses** and **paramyxoviruses.** Fusion occurs as a result of cell membrane changes, which are probably caused by the insertion of viral proteins into the membrane. The clinical diagnosis of herpesvirus skin infections is aided by the finding of multinucleated giant cells with eosinophilic intranuclear inclusions in skin scrapings.

A hallmark of viral infection of the cell is the **cytopathic effect** (CPE). This change in the appearance of the infected cell usually begins with a rounding and darkening of the cell and culminates in either lysis (disintegration) or giant cell formation. Detection of virus in a clinical specimen frequently is based on the appearance of CPE in cell culture. In addition, CPE is the basis for the plaque assay, an important method for quantifying the amount of virus in a sample.

Infection with certain viruses causes **malignant transformation,** which is characterized by unrestrained growth, prolonged survival, and morphologic changes such as focal areas of rounded, piled-up cells. These changes are described in more detail in Chapter 43.

Infection of the cell accompanied by virus production can occur **without** morphologic or gross functional changes. This observation highlights the wide variations in the nature of the interaction between the virus and the cell, ranging from rapid destruction of the cell to a symbiotic relationship in which the cell survives and multiplies despite the replication of the virus.

THE INFECTED PATIENT

Pathogenesis in the infected patient involves (1) transmission of the virus and its entry into the host; (2) replication of the virus and damage to cells; (3) spread of the virus to other cells and organs; (4) the immune response, both as a host defense and as a contributing cause of certain diseases; and (5) persistence of the virus in some instances.

The stages of a typical viral infection are the same as those described for a bacterial infection in Chapter 7, namely, an **incubation period** during which the patient is asymptomatic, a **prodromal period** during which nonspecific symptoms occur, a **specific-illness period** during which the characteristic symptoms and signs occur, and a **recovery period** during which the illness wanes and the patient regains good health. In some patients, the infection persists and a chronic carrier state or a latent infection occurs (see below).

Transmission & Portal of Entry

Viruses are transmitted to the individual by many different routes, and their portals of entry are varied

(Table 32–1). For example, person-to-person spread occurs by transfer of respiratory secretions, saliva, blood, or semen and by fecal contamination of water or food. The transfer of blood, either by transfusion or by sharing needles during intravenous drug use, can transmit various viruses (and bacteria). The screening of donated blood for human immunodeficiency virus, human T-cell lymphotropic virus, hepatitis B virus, hepatitis C virus, and West Nile virus (as well as *Treponema pallidum*) has greatly reduced the risk of infection by these pathogens.

Transmission can occur also between mother and offspring in utero across the placenta, at the time of delivery, or during breast feeding (Table 32–2). (Transmission between mother and offspring is called **vertical transmission.** Person-to-person transmission that is not from mother to offspring is called **horizontal transmission.**)

Animal-to-human transmission can take place either directly from the bite of a reservoir host as in rabies or indirectly through the bite of an insect vector, such as a mosquito, which transfers the virus from an animal reservoir to the person. The zoonotic diseases caused by viruses are described in Table 32–3. In addition, activation of a latent, nonreplicating virus to form an active, replicating virus can occur within the individual, with no transmission from an external source.

Table 32–1. Main portal of entry of important viral pathogens.

Portal of Entry	Virus	Disease
Respiratory tract[1]	Influenza virus	Influenza
	Rhinovirus	Common cold
	Respiratory syncytial virus	Bronchiolitis
	Epstein-Barr virus	Infectious mononucleosis
	Varicella-zoster virus	Chickenpox
	Herpes simplex virus type 1	Herpes labialis
	Cytomegalovirus	Mononucleosis syndrome
	Measles virus	Measles
	Mumps virus	Mumps
	Rubella virus	Rubella
	Hantavirus	Pneumonia
	Adenovirus	Pneumonia
Gastrointestinal tract[2]	Hepatitis A virus	Hepatitis A
	Poliovirus	Poliomyelitis
	Rotavirus	Diarrhea
Skin	Rabies virus[3]	Rabies
	Yellow fever virus[3]	Yellow fever
	Dengue virus[3]	Dengue
	Human papillomavirus	Papillomas (warts)
Genital tract	Human papillomavirus	Papillomas (warts)
	Hepatitis B virus	Hepatitis B
	Human immunodeficiency virus	AIDS
	Herpes simplex virus type 2	Herpes genitalis and neonatal herpes
Blood	Hepatitis B virus	Hepatitis B
	Hepatitis C virus	Hepatitis C
	Hepatitis D virus	Hepatitis D
	Human T-cell lymphotropic virus	Leukemia
	Human immunodeficiency virus	AIDS
	Cytomegalovirus	Mononucleosis syndrome or pneumonia
Transplacental	Cytomegalovirus	Congenital abnormalities
	Rubella	Congenital abnormalities

[1]Transmission of these viruses is typically by respiratory aerosols or saliva.
[2]Transmission of these viruses is typically by the fecal-oral route in contaminated food or water.
[3]Transmission of these viruses is typically by the bite of an infected animal.

Table 32–2. Viruses that commonly cause perinatal infections.

Type of Transmission	Virus
Transplacental[1]	Cytomegalovirus
	Parvovirus B19 virus
	Rubella virus
At time of birth[2]	Hepatitis B virus
	Hepatitis C virus
	Herpes simplex virus type-2
	Human immunodeficiency virus[3]
	Human papillomavirus
Breast feeding	Cytomegalovirus
	Human T-cell lymphotropic virus

[1]Note that there are important bacteria, namely, *Treponema pallidum* and *Listeria monocytogenes,* and an important protozoan, namely, *Toxoplasma gondii,* that are also transmitted transplacentally.
[2]Note that there are important bacteria, namely, *Neisseria gonorrhoeae, Chlamydia trachomatis,* and group B streptococcus, that are also transmitted at the time of birth.
[3]HIV is also transmitted transplacentally and in breast milk.

Localized or Disseminated Infections

Viral infections are either **localized** to the portal of entry or spread **systemically** through the body. The best example of the localized infection is the common cold, which involves only the upper respiratory tract. Influenza is localized primarily to the upper and lower respiratory tracts. One of the best-understood systemic viral infections is paralytic poliomyelitis (Figure 32–1). After poliovirus is ingested, it infects and multiplies within the cells of the small intestine and then spreads to the mesenteric lymph nodes, where it multiplies again. It then enters the bloodstream and is transmitted to certain internal organs, where it multiplies again. The virus reenters the bloodstream and is transmitted to the central nervous system, where damage to the anterior horn cells occurs, resulting in the characteristic muscle paralysis. It is during this obligatory viremia that circulating IgG antibodies induced by the polio vaccine can prevent the virus from infecting the central nervous system. Viral replication in the gastrointestinal tract results in the presence of poliovirus in the feces, thus perpetuating its transmission to others.

Some of the molecular determinants of pathogenesis have been determined by using reovirus infection in mice as a model system. This virus has three different outer capsid proteins, each of which has a distinct function in determining the course of the infection. One of the proteins binds to specific receptors on the cell surface and thereby determines tissue tropism. A second

Table 32–3. Medically important viruses that have an animal reservoir.

Virus	Animal Reservoir	Mode of Transmission	Disease
Rabies virus	In United States, skunks, raccoons, and bats; in developing countries, dogs	Usually bite of infected animal; also aerosol of bat saliva	Rabies
Hantavirus[1]	Deer mice	Aerosol of dried excreta	Hantavirus pulmonary syndrome (pneumonia)
Yellow fever virus	Monkeys	Bite of *Aedes* mosquito	Yellow fever
Dengue virus	Monkeys	Bite of *Aedes* mosquito	Dengue
Encephalitis viruses[2]	Wild birds, eg, sparrows	Bite of various mosquitoes	Encephalitis
SARS[3] coronavirus	Civet cat	Aerosol droplets	SARS
Avian influenza virus (H5N1)	Chickens and other fowl	Aerosol droplets	Influenza

[1] Sin Nombre virus is the most important hantavirus in the United States.
[2] Important encephalitis viruses in the United States include eastern and western equine encephalitis viruses, West Nile virus, and St. Louis encephalitis virus.
[3] SARS, severe acute respiratory syndrome.

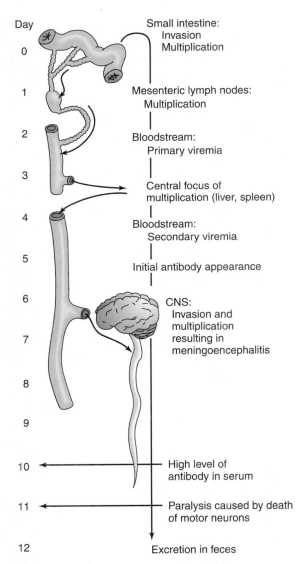

Day	
0	Small intestine: Invasion Multiplication
1	Mesenteric lymph nodes: Multiplication
2	Bloodstream: Primary viremia
3	Central focus of multiplication (liver, spleen)
4	Bloodstream: Secondary viremia
5	Initial antibody appearance
6	CNS: Invasion and multiplication
7	resulting in meningoencephalitis
8	
9	
10	High level of antibody in serum
11	Paralysis caused by death of motor neurons
12	Excretion in feces

Figure 32–1. Systemic viral infection by poliovirus, resulting in paralytic poliomyelitis. (Modified and reproduced, with permission, from Brooks GF et al: *Medical Microbiology*, 20th ed. Originally published by Appleton & Lange. Copyright © 1995 by The McGraw-Hill Companies, Inc.)

protein conveys resistance to proteolytic enzymes in the gastrointestinal tract and acts as the antigen that stimulates the cellular immune response. The third protein inhibits cellular RNA and protein synthesis, leading to death of the cell. Alternatively, this third protein can play a role in the initiation of persistent viral infection.

Pathogenesis & Immunopathogenesis

The signs and symptoms of most viral diseases undoubtedly are the result of cell killing by virus-induced inhibition of macromolecular synthesis. Death of the virus-infected cells results in a loss of function and in the symptoms of disease. For example, when poliovirus kills motor neurons, paralysis of the muscles innervated by those neurons results. Also, the hemorrhages caused by Ebola virus are due to the damage to the vascular endothelial cells caused by the envelope glycoprotein of the virus.

However, there are some diseases that are not caused by the virus damaging or killing the infected cell. For example, rotavirus-induced diarrhea is caused primarily by stimulation of the enteric nervous system. It is thought that the rotavirus-infected enterocytes produce cytokines that stimulate the enteric neurons, resulting in excess fluid and electrolyte secretion into the bowel lumen.

There are other diseases in which cell killing by **immunologic attack** plays an important role in pathogenesis. Both cytotoxic T cells and antibodies play a role in immunopathogenesis.

(1) The best-studied system is lymphocytic choriomeningitis (LCM) in mice; LCM occurs in humans also but is quite rare. When LCM virus is inoculated into the brain of an adult mouse, virus replication occurs and death follows. However, when LCM virus is inoculated into the brain of an immunosuppressed adult mouse or a newborn mouse, the animal remains well despite extensive virus replication. When immune lymphocytes are inoculated into these infected, healthy mice, death ensues. It appears that death of the cells is caused by immune attack by cytotoxic T cells on the new viral antigens in the cell membrane rather than by virus-induced inhibition of cell functions.

(2) Cytotoxic T cells are involved in the pathogenesis of hepatitis caused by hepatitis A, B, and C viruses. These viruses do not cause a cytopathic effect, and the damage to the hepatocytes is the result of the recognition of viral antigens on the hepatocyte surface by cytotoxic T cells. The rash of measles is similarly caused by these cells attacking the infected vascular endothelium in the skin.

(3) Immune-mediated pathogenesis also occurs when virus-antibody-complement complexes form and are deposited in various tissues. This occurs in hepatitis B virus infection, in which immune complexes play a role in producing the arthritis characteristic of the early stage of hepatitis B. Immune complexes also cause the arthritis seen in parvovirus B19 and rubella virus infections. The pathogenesis of pneumonia caused by respiratory syncytial virus in infants is attributed to immune complexes formed by maternal IgG and viral antigens.

Virulence

Strains of viruses differ greatly in their ability to cause disease. For example, there are strains of poliovirus that have mutated sufficiently such that they have lost the ability to cause polio in immunocompetent individuals; ie, they are **attenuated.** These strains are used in vaccines. The viral genes that control the virulence of the virus are poorly characterized, and the process of virulence is poorly understood.

Evasion of Host Defenses

Viruses have several ways by which they evade our host defenses. These processes are often called **immune evasion.** Some viruses encode the receptors for various mediators of immunity such as interleukin-1 (IL-1) and tumor necrosis factor (TNF). For example, vaccinia virus encodes a protein that binds to IL-1 and fibroma virus encodes a protein that binds to TNF. When released from virus-infected cells, these proteins bind to the immune mediators and block their ability to interact with receptors on their intended targets, our immune cells that mediate host defenses against the viral infection. By reducing our host defenses, the virulence of the virus is enhanced. These virus-encoded proteins that block host immune mediators are often called **cytokine decoys.**

In addition, some viruses (eg, HIV, cytomegalovirus) can reduce the expression of class I MHC proteins, thereby reducing the ability of cytotoxic T cells to kill the virus-infected cells, and others (eg, herpes simplex virus) inhibit complement. Several viruses (HIV, Epstein-Barr virus, and adenovirus) synthesize RNAs that block the phosphorylation of an initiation factor (eIF-2), which reduces the ability of interferon to block viral replication (see Chapter 33). Measles virus blocks synthesis of IL-12, thereby reducing an effective Th-1 response. Ebola virus synthesizes two proteins, one of which blocks the induction of interferon, while the other blocks its action. Collectively, these viral virulence factors are called **virokines.**

A third important way by which viruses evade our host defenses is by having multiple antigenic types (also known as multiple serotypes). The clinical importance of a virus having multiple serotypes is that a patient can be infected with one serotype, recover, and have antibodies that protect from infection by that serotype in the future; however, that person can be infected by another serotype of that virus. The classic example of a virus with multiple serotypes is rhinovirus, which has more than 100 serotypes. This is the reason why the "common cold" caused by rhinoviruses is so common. Influenza virus also has multiple serotypes, and the severe worldwide epidemics of influenza are attributed to the emergence of new antigenic types. HIV and hepatitis C virus have multiple serotypes, which contributes to the difficulty in obtaining a vaccine against these viruses. Note that only some viruses have multiple serotypes. Many important human pathogens (such as measles virus, rubella virus, varicella-zoster virus, and rabies virus) have only one serotype, and some have only a few serotypes (eg, poliovirus has three serotypes).

Persistent Viral Infections

In most viral infections, the virus does not remain in the body for a significant period after clinical recovery. However, in certain instances, the virus persists for long periods either intact or in the form of a subviral component, eg, the genome. The mechanisms that may play a role in the persistence of viruses include (1) integration of a DNA provirus into host cell DNA, as occurs with retroviruses; (2) immune tolerance, because neutralizing antibodies are not formed; (3) formation of virus-antibody complexes, which remain infectious; (4) location within an immunologically sheltered "sanctuary," eg, the brain; (5) rapid antigenic variation; (6) spread from cell to cell without an extracellular phase, so that virus is not exposed to antibody; and (7) immunosuppression, as in AIDS.

There are three types of persistent viral infections of clinical importance. They are distinguished primarily by whether virus is usually produced by the infected cells and by the timing of the appearance both of the virus and of the symptoms of disease.

A. Chronic-Carrier Infections

Some patients who have been infected with certain viruses continue to produce significant amounts of the virus for long periods. This **carrier state** can follow an asymptomatic infection as well as the actual disease and can itself either be asymptomatic or result in chronic illness. Important clinical examples are chronic hepatitis, which occurs in hepatitis B and hepatitis C virus carriers, and neonatal rubella virus and cytomegalovirus infections, in which carriers can produce virus for years.

B. Latent Infections

In these infections, best illustrated by the herpesvirus group, the patient recovers from the initial infection and virus production stops. Subsequently, the symptoms may recur, accompanied by the production of virus. In herpes simplex virus infections, the virus enters the latent state in the cells of the sensory ganglia. The molecular nature of the latent state is unknown. Herpes simplex virus type 1, which causes infections primarily of the eyes and face, is latent in the trigeminal ganglion, whereas herpes simplex virus type 2, which causes infections primarily of the genitals, is latent in the lumbar and sacral ganglia. Varicella-zoster virus, another member of the herpesvirus family, causes varicella (chickenpox) as its initial manifestation and then remains latent, primarily in the trigeminal or thoracic ganglion cells. It can recur in the form of the painful vesicles of zoster (shingles), usually on the face or trunk.

C. SLOW VIRUS INFECTIONS

The term "slow" refers to the **prolonged period** between the initial infection and the onset of disease, which is usually measured in years. In instances in which the cause has been identified, the virus has been shown to have a normal, not prolonged, growth cycle.

It is not, therefore, that virus growth is slow; rather, the incubation period and the progression of the disease are prolonged. Two of these diseases are caused by conventional viruses, namely, subacute sclerosing panencephalitis, which follows several years after measles virus infections, and progressive multifocal leukoencephalopathy (PML), which is caused by JC virus, a papovavirus. PML occurs primarily in patients who have lymphomas or are immunosuppressed. Other slow infections in humans, eg, Creutzfeldt-Jakob disease and kuru, may be caused by unconventional agents called **prions** (see Chapter 28). Slow virus infections are described in Chapter 44.

PEARLS

The Infected Cell

- Death of infected cells is probably caused by inhibition of cellular protein synthesis. Translation of viral mRNA into viral proteins preempts the ribosomes preventing synthesis of cellular proteins.

- **Inclusion bodies** are aggregates of virions in specific locations in the cell that are useful for laboratory diagnosis. Two important examples are **Negri bodies** in the cytoplasm of rabies virus–infected cells and **owl's eye inclusions** in the nucleus of cytomegalovirus-infected cells.

- Multinucleated giant cells form when cells are infected with certain viruses, notably herpesviruses and paramyxoviruses such as respiratory syncytial virus.

- **Cytopathic effect** (CPE) is a visual or functional change in infected cells typically associated with the death of cells.

- Malignant transformation occurs when cells are infected with oncogenic viruses. Transformed cells are capable of unrestrained growth.

- Some virus-infected cells appear visually and functionally normal, yet are producing large numbers of progeny viruses.

The Infected Patient

- Viral infection in the person typically has four stages: incubation period, prodromal period, specific-illness period, and recovery period.

- The main portals of entry are the respiratory, gastrointestinal, and genital tracts, but through the skin, across the placenta, and via blood are important as well.

- Transmission from mother to offspring is called **vertical transmission;** all other modes of transmission, eg, fecal-oral, respiratory aerosol, and insect bite, are **horizontal transmission.** Transmission can be from human to human or from animal to human.

- Most serious viral infection are systemic, ie, the virus travels from the portal of entry via the blood to various organs. However, some are localized to the portal of entry, such as the common cold, which involves only the upper respiratory tract.

Pathogenesis

- The symptoms of viral diseases are usually caused by **death of the infected cells and a consequent loss of function.** For example, poliovirus kills neurons, resulting in paralysis.

- **Immunopathogenesis** is the process by which the symptoms of viral diseases are caused by the immune system rather than by the killing of cells directly by the virus. One type of immunopathogenesis is the **killing of virus-infected cell by the attack of cytotoxic T cells** that recognize viral antigens on the cell surface. Damage to the liver caused by hepatitis viruses occurs by this mechanism. Another is the **formation of virus-antibody complexes that are deposited in tissues.** Arthritis associated with parvovirus B19 or rubella virus infection occurs by this mechanism.

- Virulence of viruses differs markedly from one virus to another and among different strains of the same virus. The genetic basis for these differences is not well understood. Strains with weakened (attenuated) virulence are often used in vaccines.

- Viruses can evade host defenses by producing **multiple antigens,** thereby avoiding inactivation by antibodies, and by **reducing the synthesis of class I MHC proteins,** thereby decreasing the ability of a cell to present viral antigens and blunting the ability of cytotoxic T cells to kill the virus-infected cells. Viruses also produce receptors for immune mediators, such as IL-1 and TNF, thereby preventing the ability of these mediators to activate antiviral processes.

Persistent Viral Infections

- **Carrier state** refers to people who produce virus for long periods of time and can serve as a source of infection for others. The carrier state that is frequently associated with hepatitis C virus infection is a medically important example.

- **Latent infections** are those infections that are not producing virus at the present time but can be reactivated at a subsequent time. The latent infections that are frequently associated with herpes simplex virus infection are a medically important example.

- **Slow virus infections** refer to those diseases with a long incubation period, often measured in years. Some, such as progressive multifocal leukoencephalopathy, are caused by viruses, whereas others, such as Creutzfeldt-Jakob disease, are caused by prions. The brain is often the main site of these diseases.

PRACTICE QUESTIONS: USMLE & COURSE EXAMINATIONS

Questions on the topics discussed in this chapter can be found in the Basic Virology section of Part XI: USMLE (National Board) Practice Questions starting on page 545. Also see Part XII: USMLE (National Board) Practice Examination starting on page 583.

Host Defenses

Host defenses against viruses fall into two major categories: (1) **nonspecific,** of which the most important are interferons and natural killer cells; and (2) **specific,** including both humoral and cell-mediated immunity. Interferons are an early, first-line defense, whereas humoral immunity and cell-mediated immunity are effective only later because it takes several days to induce an immune response.

A description of how viruses evade our host defenses appears in Chapter 32 (see page 218).

NONSPECIFIC DEFENSES

1. Interferons

Interferons are a heterogeneous group of glycoproteins produced by human and other animal cells after viral infection (or after exposure to other inducers). They inhibit the growth of viruses by **blocking the translation of viral proteins.** Interferons are divided into three groups based on the cell of origin, namely, leukocyte, fibroblast, and lymphocyte. They are also known as alpha, beta, and gamma interferons, respectively. Alpha and beta interferons are induced by viruses, whereas gamma (T cell, immune) interferon is induced by antigens and is one of the effectors of cell-mediated immunity (see Chapter 58). Interferons are cytokines that inhibit the growth of certain cancer cells, bacteria, and protozoa, but the focus here will be on their inhibitory effect on viral growth. The following discussion of alpha and beta interferons focuses on two aspects of their antiviral effect: induction and action (Figure 33–1).

Induction of Alpha & Beta Interferons

The strong inducers of these interferons are **viruses** and **double-stranded RNAs.** Induction is not specific for a particular virus; many DNA and RNA viruses of humans, other animals, plants, and bacteria are competent, although they differ in effectiveness. The finding that double-stranded RNA, but not single-stranded RNA or DNA, is a good inducer has led to the hypothesis that a double-stranded RNA is synthesized as part of the replicative cycle of all inducing viruses. The double-stranded RNA poly (rI-rC) is one of the strongest

inducers and was under consideration as an antiviral agent, but toxic side effects prevented its clinical use. The weak inducers of microbiologic interest include a variety of intracellular bacteria and protozoa, as well as certain bacterial substances such as endotoxin.

This extensive list of inducers makes it clear that **induction** of these interferons is **not specific.** Similarly, their inhibitory **action** is **not specific** for any particular virus. However, they are typically **specific** in regard to the **host species** in which they act; ie, interferons produced by human cells are active in human cells but are much less effective in cells of other species. It is clear, therefore, that other animals cannot be used as a source of interferons for human therapy. Rather, the genes for human interferons have been cloned and material for medical trials is now produced by genetic engineering techniques.

Action of Alpha & Beta Interferons

Interferons inhibit the intracellular replication of a **wide variety** of both DNA and RNA viruses but have little effect on the metabolism of normal cells; ie, they exhibit a remarkable degree of **selective inhibition.**

They act by inducing the synthesis of three cell-encoded proteins that **inhibit the translation of viral mRNA** without affecting the translation of cellular mRNA. The three proteins are (1) a 2,5-oligonucleotide synthetase that synthesizes an adenine trinucleotide [2,5-oligo(A)]; (2) a **ribonuclease** that is activated by 2,5-oligo(A) and that degrades viral but not cellular mRNAs; and (3) a protein kinase that phosphorylates an initiation factor for protein synthesis (eIF-2), thereby inactivating it. The endonuclease selectively degrades viral mRNAs by recognizing a nucleotide sequence on viral mRNAs that is not present on cellular mRNAs.

Interferons have **no direct effect** on extracellular virus particles. Interferons do not enter the cell but act by binding to a receptor on the cell surface that signals the cell to synthesize the ribonuclease and the other antiviral proteins.

Because interferons are produced within a few hours of the initiation of viral replication, they may act in the

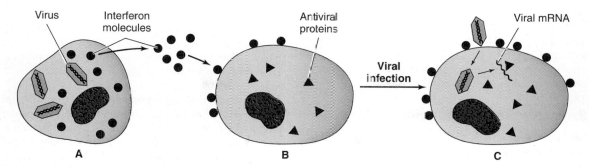

Figure 33–1. Induction and action of interferon. **A:** Virus infection induces the synthesis of interferon, which then leaves the infected cell. **B:** Interferon binds to the surface receptor of an uninfected cell and induces the synthesis of three new cell-encoded enzymes (antiviral proteins). **C:** A new virion enters the cell, but the translation of viral mRNA is inhibited by the interferon-induced antiviral proteins. One of these antiviral proteins is a ribonuclease that degrades viral, but not cellular, mRNA. (Modified and reproduced, with permission, from Tortora G, Funk B, Case C: *Microbiology: An Introduction*, 5th ed. Benjamin/Cummings, 1995.)

early phase of viral diseases to limit the spread of virus. In contrast, antibody begins to appear in the blood several days after infection.

Alpha interferon has been approved for use in patients with condyloma acuminatum and chronic active hepatitis caused by hepatitis C virus. Gamma interferon reduces recurrent infections in patients with chronic granulomatous disease (see Chapter 68). Interferons are also used clinically in patients with cancers such as Kaposi's sarcoma and hairy cell leukemia.

2. Natural Killer Cells

Natural killer (NK) cells are an important part of the innate defenses against virus-infected cells. They are called "natural" killer cells because they are active without the necessity of being exposed to the virus previously and because they are not specific for any virus. NK cells are a type of T lymphocyte but do not have an antigen receptor. They recognize virus-infected cells by the absence of class I MHC proteins on the surface of the virus-infected cell. They kill virus-infected cells by secreting perforins and granzymes, which cause apoptosis of the infected cells. (See page 407 for more information.)

3. Phagocytosis

Macrophages, particularly fixed macrophages of the reticuloendothelial system and alveolar macrophages, are the important cell types in limiting virus infection. In contrast, polymorphonuclear leukocytes are the predominant cellular defense in bacterial infections.

4. α-Defensins

α-Defensins are a family of positively charged peptides with antiviral activity. (They also have antibacterial activity. See Chapter 8.) They interfere with human immunodeficiency virus (HIV) binding to the CXCR4 receptor and block entry of the virus into the cell. The production of α-defensins may explain why some HIV-infected individuals are long-term "non-progressors."

5. Apolipoprotein B RNA-Editing Enzyme (APOBEC3G)

APOBEC3G is an important member of the innate host defenses against retroviral infection, especially against HIV. APOBEC3G is an enzyme that causes hypermutation in retroviral DNA by deaminating cytosines in both mRNA and retroviral DNA, thereby inactivating these molecules and reducing infectivity. HIV defends itself against this innate host defense by producing Vif (viral infectivity protein), which counteracts APOBEC3G, thereby preventing hypermutation from occurring.

6. Fever

Elevated body temperature may play a role in host defenses, but its importance is uncertain. Fever may act in two ways. (1) The higher body temperature may directly inactivate the virus particles, particularly enveloped viruses, which are more heat-sensitive than nonenveloped viruses. (2) Replication of some viruses is reduced at higher temperatures; therefore, fever may inhibit replication.

7. Mucociliary Clearance

The mucociliary clearance mechanism of the respiratory tract may protect the host. Its damage, eg, from smoking, results in an increased frequency of viral respiratory tract infections, especially influenza.

8. Factors That Modify Host Defenses

Several factors influence host defenses in a nonspecific or multifactorial way.

(1) Age is a significant variable in the outcome of viral infections. In general, infections are more severe in neonates and in the elderly than in older children and young adults. For example, influenza is typically more severe in older people than in younger adults, and herpes simplex virus infections are more severe in neonates than in adults.

(2) Increased corticosteroid levels predispose to more severe infections with some viruses, such as varicella-zoster virus; the use of topical cortisone in herpetic keratitis can exacerbate eye damage. It is not clear how these effects are mediated, because corticosteroids can cause a variety of pertinent effects, namely, lysis of lymphocytes, decreased recruitment of monocytes, inhibition of interferon production, and stabilization of lysosomes.

(3) Malnutrition leads to more severe viral infections; eg, there is a much higher death rate from measles in developing countries than in developed ones. Poor nutrition causes decreased immunoglobulin production and phagocyte activity as well as reduced skin and mucous membrane integrity.

SPECIFIC DEFENSES

There is evidence for natural resistance to some viruses in certain species, which is probably based on the absence of receptors on the cells of the resistant species. For example, some people are resistant to HIV infection because they lack one of the chemokine receptors that mediate entry of the virus into the cell. However, by far the most important type of defense is **acquired immunity**, either actively acquired by exposure to the virus or passively acquired by the transfer of immune serum. Active immunity can be elicited by contracting the actual disease, by having an inapparent infection, or by being vaccinated.

1. Active Immunity

Active immunity, in the form of both antibodies and cytotoxic T cells, is very important in the prevention of viral diseases. The first exposure to a virus, whether it causes an inapparent infection or symptomatic disease, stimulates the production of antibodies and the activation of cytotoxic T cells. The role that antibodies and cytotoxic T cells play in the recovery from this first infection is uncertain and may vary from virus to virus, but it is clear that they play an essential role in protecting against disease when exposed to the same virus at some time in the future.

The duration of protection varies; disseminated viral infections such as measles and mumps confer lifelong immunity against recurrences, but localized infections such as the common cold usually impart only a brief immunity of several months. IgA confers protection against viruses that enter through the respiratory and gastrointestinal mucosa, and IgM and IgG protect against viruses that enter or are spread through the blood. The lifelong protection against systemic viral infections such as the childhood diseases measles, mumps, rubella, and chickenpox (varicella) is a function of the anamnestic (secondary) response of IgG. For certain respiratory viruses such as parainfluenza and respiratory syncytial viruses, the IgA titer in respiratory secretions correlates with protection, whereas the IgG titer does not. Unfortunately, protection by IgA against most respiratory tract viruses usually lasts less than 5 years.

The role of active immunity in recovery from a viral infection is uncertain. Because recovery usually precedes the appearance of detectable humoral antibody, immunoglobulins may not be important. Also, children with agammaglobulinemia recover from measles infections normally and can be immunized against measles successfully, indicating that cell-mediated immunity plays an important role. This is supported by the observation that children with congenital T-cell deficiency are vulnerable to severe infections with measles virus and herpesviruses. T cells are important in recovery from many but not all viral illnesses.

The protection offered by active immunity can be affected by the phenomenon of **original antigenic sin**. This term refers to the observation that when a person is exposed to a virus that cross-reacts with another virus to which that individual was previously exposed, more antibody may be produced against the original virus than against the current one. It appears that the immunologic memory cells can respond to the original antigenic exposure to a greater extent than to the subsequent one. This was observed in people with antibodies to the A_1 type of influenza virus, who, when exposed to the A_2 type, produced large amounts of antibody to A_1 but very little antibody to the A_2 virus. It is also the underlying cause of severe hemorrhagic dengue fever (see Chapter 42). This phenomenon has two practical consequences as well: (1) Attempts to vaccinate people against the different influenza virus strains may be less effective than expected, and (2) epidemiologic studies based on measurement of antibody titers may yield misleading results.

How does antibody inhibit viruses? There are two main mechanisms. The first is **neutralization** of the infectivity of the virus by antibody binding to the proteins on the outer surface of the virus. This binding has two effects: (1) It can prevent the interaction of the virus with cell receptors, and (2) it can cross-link the viral proteins and stabilize the virus so that uncoating does not occur. The virus therefore cannot replicate. Furthermore, antibody-coated virus is more rapidly phagocytized than normal virus, a process similar to the opsonizing effect of antibody on bacteria. Antibody does not degrade the virus particle; fully infectious virus can be recovered by dissociating the virus-antibody complex. Incomplete, also called "blocking," antibody can interfere with neutralization and form immune complexes, which are important in the pathogenesis of certain diseases. Some viruses, such as herpesviruses, can spread from cell to cell across intercellular bridges, eluding the neutralizing effect of antibody.

Antibodies that interfere with the adherence (adsorption and penetration) of viruses to cell surfaces are called neutralizing antibodies. Note that neutralizing antibody is directed against the surface proteins of the virus, typically the proteins involved with the interaction of the virus with receptors on the surface of the host cell. Antibodies formed against internal components of the virus, eg, the core antigen of hepatitis B virus, do not neutralize the infectivity of the virus.

The second main mechanism is the **lysis of virus-infected cells** in the presence of antibody and complement. Antibody binds to new virus-specific antigens on the cell surface and then binds complement, which enzymatically degrades the cell membrane. Because the cell is killed before the full yield of virus is produced, the spread of virus is significantly reduced.

Lysis of virus-infected cells is also caused by **cytotoxic T lymphocytes.** These CD8-positive T cells recognize viral antigen only when it is presented in association with class I MHC proteins (see Chapter 58). They kill virus-infected cells by three methods: (1) by releasing **perforins,** which make holes in the cell membrane of the infected cells; (2) by releasing proteolytic enzymes called **granzymes** into the infected cell, which degrade the cell contents; and (3) by activating the **FAS protein,** which causes programmed cell death (**apoptosis**).

Not all virus infections induce antibodies. **Tolerance** to viral antigens can occur when the virus infection develops in a fetus or newborn infant. The model system in which tolerance has been demonstrated is lymphocytic choriomeningitis (LCM) infection in mice. If LCM virus is inoculated into a newborn mouse, the virus replicates widely but no antibodies are formed during the lifetime of the animal. The virus is recognized as "self," because it was present at the time of maturation of the immune system. If LCM virus is

given to an adult mouse, antibodies are formed normally. There is no example of total tolerance to a virus in humans: even in congenital rubella syndrome, in which the virus infects the fetus, some antibody against rubella virus is made. However, virus production and shedding can go on for months or years.

Suppression of the cell-mediated response can occur during infection by certain viruses. The best-known example is the loss of tuberculin skin test reactivity during measles infection. Infection by cytomegalovirus or HIV can also cause suppression. Some viruses can "downregulate" (reduce) the amount of class I and class II MHC protein made by cells, which may be a mechanism by which these viruses suppress cell-mediated immunity.

2. Passive Immunity

Transfer of human serum containing the appropriate antibodies provides prompt short-term immunity for individuals exposed to certain viruses. The term "passive" refers to the administration of **preformed antibodies.** Two types of immune globulin preparations are used for this purpose. One has a high titer of antibody against a specific virus, and the other is a pooled sample from plasma donors that contains a heterogeneous mixture of antibodies with lower titers. The immune globulins are prepared by alcohol fractionation, which removes any viruses in the serum. The three most frequently used high-titer preparations are used after exposure to hepatitis B, rabies, and varicella-zoster viruses. Low-titer immune globulin is used mainly to prevent hepatitis A in people traveling to areas where this infection is hyperendemic.

Two specialized examples of passive immunity include the transfer of IgG from mother to fetus across the placenta and the transfer of IgA from mother to newborn in colostrum.

3. Herd Immunity

"Herd immunity" (also known as "community immunity") is the protection of an individual from infection by virtue of the other members of the population (the herd) being **incapable of transmitting the virus** to that individual. Herd immunity can be achieved by immunizing a population with a vaccine that interrupts transmission, such as the live, attenuated polio vaccine, but not with a vaccine that does not interrupt transmission, such as the killed polio vaccine (even though it protects the immunized individual against disease). Note that herd immunity occurs with the live polio vaccine primarily because it induces secretory IgA in the gut, which inhibits infection by virulent virus, thereby preventing its transmission to others. In addition, the live virus in the vaccine can replicate in the immunized person and spread to other members of the population, thereby increasing the number of people protected. However, the important feature as far as herd immunity is concerned is the induction of IgA, which prevents transmission.

Herd immunity can be achieved by natural infection as well as vaccines. For example, if a viral disease, such as measles, occurred in approximately 90% of a group and if those who recovered from the disease had sufficient immunity to prevent them from becoming infected and serving as a source of virus for others, then the remaining 10% of the group are protected by herd immunity.

PEARLS

Interferons

- *Interferons inhibit virus replication by blocking the production of viral proteins, primarily by **degrading viral mRNA.** They **induce the synthesis of a ribonuclease** that specifically cleaves viral mRNA but not cell mRNA.*
- *Viruses and double-stranded RNA are the most potent inducers of interferons. Many viruses induce interferons, and many viruses are inhibited by interferons, ie, neither the induction of interferons nor its action is specific.*
- *Interferons act by binding to a receptor on the cell surface that signals the cell to synthesize the ribonuclease and the other antiviral proteins. Interferons do not enter the cell and have no effect on extracellular viruses.*
- *Alpha and beta interferons have a stronger antiviral action than gamma interferon. The latter acts primarily as an interleukin that activates macrophages.*

Other Nonspecific Defenses

- *Natural killer (NK) cells are lymphocytes that **destroy cells infected by many different viruses, ie, they are nonspecific.** NK cells do not have an antigen receptor on their surface, unlike T and B lymphocytes. Rather, NK cells **recognize and destroy cells that do not display class I MHC proteins on the surface.** They kill cells by the same mechanisms as do cytotoxic T cells, ie, by secreting perforins and granzymes.*
- *Phagocytosis by macrophages and the clearance of mucus by the cilia of the respiratory tract are also*

important defenses. Damage to these defenses predisposes to viral infection.
- *Increased corticosteroid levels suppress various host defenses and predispose to severe viral infections, especially disseminated herpesvirus infections. Malnutrition predisposes to severe measles infections in developing countries. The very young and the very old have more severe viral infections.*

Specific Defenses

- *Active immunity to viral infection is effected by both antibodies and cytotoxic T cells. It can be elicited either by exposure to the virus or by immunization with a viral vaccine.*
- *Passive immunity consists of antibodies preformed in another person or animal.*
- *The duration of active immunity is much longer than that of passive immunity. Active immunity is measured in years, whereas passive immunity lasts a few weeks to a few months.*
- *Passive immunity is effective immediately, whereas it takes active immunity 7–10 days in the primary response (or 3–5 days in the secondary response) to stimulate detectable amounts of antibody.*
- *Herd immunity is the protection of an individual that results from immunity in many other members of the population (the herd) that interrupts transmission of the virus to the individual. Herd immunity can be achieved either by immunization or by natural infection of a sufficiently high percentage of the population.*

PRACTICE QUESTIONS: USMLE & COURSE EXAMINATIONS

Questions on the topics discussed in this chapter can be found in the Basic Virology section of Part XI: USMLE

(National Board) Practice Questions starting on page 545. Also see Part XII: USMLE (National Board) Practice Examination starting on page 583.

Laboratory Diagnosis

34

There are five approaches to the diagnosis of viral diseases by the use of clinical specimens: (1) identification of the virus in cell culture, (2) microscopic identification directly in the specimen, (3) serologic procedures to detect a rise in antibody titer or the presence of IgM antibody, (4) detection of viral antigens in blood or body fluids, and (5) detection of viral nucleic acids in blood or the patient's cells.

IDENTIFICATION IN CELL CULTURE

The growth of viruses requires cell cultures, because viruses replicate only in living cells, not on cell-free media the way most bacteria can. Because many viruses are inactivated at room temperature, it is important to inoculate the specimen into the cell culture as soon as possible; brief transport or storage at 4°C is acceptable.

Virus growth in cell culture frequently produces a characteristic **cytopathic effect** (CPE) that can provide a **presumptive identification.** CPE is a change in the appearance of the virus-infected cells. This change can be in such features as size, shape, and the fusion of cells to form multinucleated giant cells (syncytia). CPE is usually a manifestation of virus-infected cells that are dying or dead. The time taken for the CPE to appear and the type of cell in which the virus produces the CPE are important clues in the presumptive identification.

If the virus does not produce a CPE, its presence can be detected by several other techniques:

(1) **Hemadsorption,** ie, attachment of erythrocytes to the surface of virus-infected cells. This technique is limited to viruses with a hemagglutinin protein on their envelope, such as mumps, parainfluenza, and influenza viruses.

(2) **Interference** with the formation of a CPE by a second virus. For example, rubella virus, which does not cause a CPE, can be detected by interference with the formation of a CPE by certain enteroviruses such as echovirus or coxsackievirus.

(3) A decrease in acid production by infected, dying cells. This can be detected visually by a color change in the phenol red (a pH indicator) in the culture medium.

The indicator remains red (alkaline) in the presence of virus-infected cells but turns yellow in the presence of metabolizing normal cells as a result of the acid produced. This technique can be used to detect certain enteroviruses.

A **definitive identification** of the virus grown in cell culture is made by using known antibody in one of several tests. Complement fixation, hemagglutination inhibition, and neutralization of the CPE are the most frequently used tests. Other procedures such as fluorescent antibody, radioimmunoassay, enzyme-linked immunosorbent assay (ELISA), and immunoelectron microscopy are also used in special instances. A brief description of these tests follows. They are described in more detail in the section on immunology.

Complement Fixation

If the antigen (the unknown virus in the culture fluid) and the known antibody are homologous, complement will be fixed (bound) to the antigen-antibody complex. This makes it unavailable to lyse the "indicator" system, which is composed of sensitized red blood cells.

Hemagglutination Inhibition

If the virus and antibody are homologous, the virus is blocked from attaching to the erythrocytes and no hemagglutination occurs. Only viruses that agglutinate red blood cells can be identified by this method.

Neutralization

If the virus and antibody are homologous, the antibody bound to the surface of the virus blocks its entry into the cell. This neutralizes viral infectivity, because it prevents viral replication and subsequent CPE formation or animal infection.

Fluorescent-Antibody Assay

If the virus-infected cells and the fluorescein-tagged antibody are homologous, the typical apple-green color of fluorescein is seen in the cells by ultraviolet (UV) microscopy.

Radioimmunoassay

If the virus and the antibody are homologous, there is less antibody remaining to bind to the known radio-labeled virus.

Enzyme-Linked Immunosorbent Assay

In the ELISA test to identify a virus, known antibody is bound to a surface. If the virus is present in the patient's specimen, it will bind to the antibody. A sample of the antibody linked to an enzyme is added, which will attach to the bound virus. The substrate of the enzyme is added and the amount of the bound enzyme is determined.

Immunoelectron Microscopy

If the antibody is homologous to the virus, aggregates of virus-antibody complexes are seen in the electron microscope.

MICROSCOPIC IDENTIFICATION

Viruses can be detected and identified by direct microscopic examination of clinical specimens such as biopsy material or skin lesions. Three different procedures can be used. (1) Light microscopy can reveal characteristic inclusion bodies or multinucleated giant cells. The Tzanck smear, which shows herpesvirus-induced multinucleated giant cells in vesicular skin lesions, is a good example. (2) UV microscopy is used for fluorescent-antibody staining of the virus in infected cells. (3) Electron microscopy detects virus particles, which can be characterized by their size and morphology.

SEROLOGIC PROCEDURES

In the third approach, a rise in the titer[1] of antibody to the virus can be used to diagnose current infection.

A serum sample is obtained as soon as a viral etiol-

---

[1] Titer is a measure of the concentration of antibodies in the patient's serum. It is defined as the highest dilution of serum that gives a positive reaction in the test. See Chapter 64 for a discussion of titer and various serologic tests.

ogy is suspected (**acute-phase**), and a second sample is obtained **10–14 days later** (**convalescent-phase**). If the antibody titer in the convalescent-phase serum sample is at least **4-fold higher** than the titer in the acute-phase serum sample, the patient is considered to be infected. For example, if the titer in the acute-phase serum sample is 1/4 and the titer in the convalescent-phase serum sample is 1/16 or greater, the patient has had a significant rise in antibody titer and has been recently infected. If, however, the titer in the convalescent-phase serum sample is 1/8, this is not a significant rise and should not be interpreted as a sign of recent infection.

It is important to realize that an antibody titer on a single sample does not distinguish between a previous infection and a current one. The antibody titer can be determined by many of the immunologic tests mentioned above. These serologic diagnoses are usually made retrospectively, because the disease has frequently run its course by the time the results are obtained.

In certain viral diseases, the presence of IgM antibody is used to diagnose current infection. For example, the presence of IgM antibody to core antigen indicates infection by hepatitis B virus.

Other nonspecific serologic tests are available. For example, the heterophil antibody test (Monospot) can be used to diagnose infectious mononucleosis (see Chapter 37).

DETECTION OF VIRAL ANTIGENS

Viral antigens can be detected in the patient's blood or body fluids by various tests but most often by an ELISA. Tests for the p24 antigen of human immunodeficiency virus (HIV) and the surface antigen of hepatitis B virus are common examples of this approach.

DETECTION OF VIRAL NUCLEIC ACIDS

Viral nucleic acids, ie, either the viral genome or viral mRNA, can be detected in the patient's blood or tissues with complementary DNA or RNA (cDNA or cRNA) as a probe. If only small amounts of viral nucleic acids are present in the patient, the polymerase chain reaction can be used to amplify the viral nucleic acids. Assays for the RNA of HIV in the patient's blood (viral load) are commonly used to monitor the course of the disease and to evaluate the patient's prognosis.

Identification in Cell Culture

- *The presence of a virus in a patient's specimen can be detected by seeing a "cytopathic effect" (CPE) in cell culture. CPE is not specific, ie, many viruses cause it. A specific identification of the virus usually involves an antibody-based test such as fluorescent antibody, complement fixation, or ELISA.*

Microscopic Identification

- ***Inclusion bodies,*** *formed by aggregates of many virus particles, can be seen in either the nucleus or cytoplasm of infected cells. They are not specific. Two important examples are the nuclear inclusions formed by certain herpesviruses and the cytoplasmic inclusions formed by rabies virus (Negri bodies).*
- ***Multinucleated giant cells*** *are formed by several viruses, notably certain herpesviruses, respiratory syncytial virus, and measles virus.*
- *Fluorescent-antibody staining of cells obtained from the patient or of cells infected in culture can provide a rapid, specific diagnosis.*
- *Electron microscopy is not often used in clinical diagnosis but is useful in the diagnosis of certain viruses, such as Ebola virus, that have a characteristic appearance and are dangerous to grow in culture.*

Serologic Procedures

- *The **presence of IgM** can be used to **diagnose current infection.***
- ***The presence of IgG cannot be used to diagnose current infection*** *because the antibody may be due to an infection in the past. In view of this, an acute and convalescent serum sample should be analyzed. An antibody titer that is 4-fold or greater in the convalescent serum sample compared to the acute sample can be used to make a diagnosis.*

Detection of Viral Antigens & Nucleic Acids

- *The presence of viral proteins, such as p24 of HIV and hepatitis B surface antigen, is commonly used in diagnosis.*
- *The presence of viral DNA or RNA is increasingly becoming the "gold standard" in viral diagnosis. Labeled probes are highly specific and results are rapidly obtained. Small amounts of viral nucleic acids can be amplified using reverse transcriptase to produce amounts detectable by the probes. An important example is the "viral load" assay of HIV RNA.*

PRACTICE QUESTIONS: USMLE & COURSE EXAMINATIONS

Questions on the topics discussed in this chapter can be found in the Basic Virology section of Part XI: USMLE (National Board) Practice Questions starting on page 545. Also see Part XII: USMLE (National Board) Practice Examination starting on page 583.

Antiviral Drugs

Compared with the number of drugs available to treat bacterial infections, the number of antiviral drugs is **very small**. The major reason for this difference is the **difficulty in obtaining selective toxicity** against viruses; their replication is intimately involved with the normal synthetic processes of the cell. Despite the difficulty, several virus-specific replication steps have been identified that are the site of action of effective antiviral drugs (Table 35–1).

Another limitation of antiviral drugs is that they are relatively ineffective because many cycles of viral replication occur during the incubation period when the patient is well. By the time the patient has a recognizable systemic viral disease, the virus has spread throughout the body and it is too late to interdict it. Furthermore, some viruses, eg, herpesviruses, become latent within cells, and no current antiviral drug can eradicate them.

Another potential limiting factor is the emergence of drug-resistant viral mutants. At present, this is not of major clinical significance. Mutants of herpesvirus resistant to acyclovir have been recovered from patients, but they do not interfere with recovery.

INHIBITION OF EARLY EVENTS

Amantadine (α-adamantanamine, Symmetrel) is a three-ring compound (Figure 35–1) that blocks the replication of influenza A virus. It prevents replication by **inhibiting uncoating of the virus** by blocking the "ion channel" activity of the matrix protein in the virion. Absorption and penetration occur normally, but transcription by the virion RNA polymerase does not because uncoating cannot occur. This drug specifically inhibits influenza A virus; influenza B and C viruses are not affected.

Despite its efficacy in preventing influenza, it is not widely used in the United States because the vaccine is preferred for the high-risk population. The main side effects of amantadine are central nervous system alterations such as dizziness, ataxia, and insomnia. Rimantadine (Flumadine) is a derivative of amantadine and has the same mode of action but fewer side effects.

Enfuvirtide (Fuzeon) is a synthetic peptide that binds to gp41 on the surface of the virion, thereby blocking the entry of human immunodeficiency virus (HIV) into the cell. It is the first of a new class of anti-HIV drugs known as "fusion inhibitors," ie, they prevent the fusion of the viral envelope with the cell membrane.

INHIBITION OF VIRAL NUCLEIC ACID SYNTHESIS

Inhibitors of Herpesviruses

A. NUCLEOSIDE INHIBITORS

These drugs are analogues of nucleosides that inhibit the DNA polymerase of one or more members of the herpesvirus family. For example, acyclovir inhibits the DNA polymerase herpes simplex virus types 1 and 2 (HSV-1 and -2) and varicella-zoster virus but not cytomegalovirus (CMV).

1. Acyclovir—Acyclovir (acycloguanosine, Zovirax) is a guanosine analogue that has a three-carbon fragment in place of the normal sugar, ribose, that has five carbons (Figure 35–1). The term "acyclo" refers to the fact that the three-carbon fragment does not have a sugar ring structure (*a* = without, *cyclo* = ring).

Acyclovir is active primarily against HSV-1 and -2 and varicella-zoster virus (VZV). It is relatively nontoxic, because it is activated preferentially within virus-infected cells. This is due to the **virus-encoded thymidine kinase**, which phosphorylates acyclovir much more effectively than does the cellular thymidine kinase. Because only HSV-1, HSV-2, and VZV encode a kinase that efficiently phosphorylates acyclovir, the drug is active primarily against these viruses. It has no activity against CMV. Once the drug is phosphorylated to acyclovir monophosphate by the viral thymidine kinase, cellular kinases synthesize acyclovir triphosphate, which inhibits viral DNA polymerase much more effectively than it inhibits cellular DNA polymerase. Acyclovir causes **chain termination** because it lacks a hydroxyl group in the 3′ position.

To recap, the selective action of acyclovir is based on two features of the drug. (1) Acyclovir is phosphorylated to acyclovir monophosphate much more effectively by herpesvirus-encoded thymidine kinase than by

Table 35–1. Potential sites for antiviral chemotherapy.

Site of Action	Effective Drugs
Early events (entry or uncoating of the virus)	Amantadine, rimantadine, enfuvirtide
Nucleic acid synthesis by viral DNA and RNA polymerases	Acyclovir, ganciclovir, valacyclovir, penciclovir, famciclovir, cidofovir, vidarabine, iododeoxyuridine, trifluridine, foscarnet, zidovudine (azidothymidine), didanosine (dideoxyinosine), zalcitabine (dideoxycytidine), stavudine (d4T), lamivudine (3TC), abacavir, nevirapine, delavirdine, efavirenz, ribavirin, adefovir, entecavir
Cleavage of precursor polypeptides	Saquinavir, indinavir, ritonavir, nelfinavir, amprenavir, atazanavir
Protein synthesis directed by viral mRNA	Interferon, fomivirsen, methisazone
Action of viral regulatory proteins	None
Assembly of the virus, including the matrix protein	None
Release of the virus	Zanamivir, oseltamivir

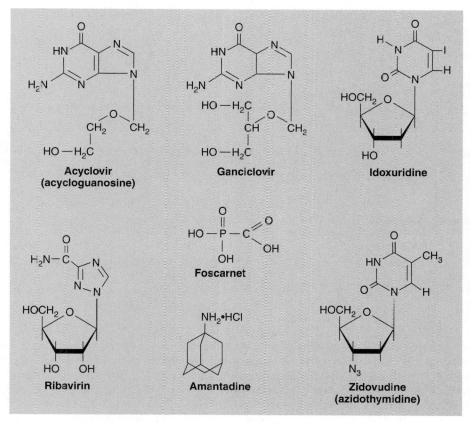

Figure 35–1. Structures of some medically important antiviral drugs.

cellular thymidine kinase. It is therefore preferentially activated in herpesvirus-infected cells and much less so in uninfected cells, which accounts for its relatively few side effects. (2) Acyclovir triphosphate inhibits herpesvirus-encoded DNA polymerase much more effectively than it does cellular DNA polymerase. It therefore inhibits viral DNA synthesis to a much greater extent than cellular DNA synthesis (Figure 35–2).

Topical acyclovir is effective in the treatment of primary genital herpes and reduces the frequency of recurrences while it is being taken. However, it has **no effect on latency** or on the rate of recurrences after treatment is stopped. Acyclovir is the treatment of choice for HSV-1 encephalitis and is effective in preventing systemic infection by HSV-1 or VZV in immunocompromised patients. It is not effective treatment for HSV-1 recurrent lesions in immunocompetent hosts. Acyclovir-resistant mutants have been isolated from HSV-1- and VZV-infected patients. Acyclovir is well-tolerated and causes few side effects—even in patients who have taken it orally for many years to suppress genital herpes. Intravenous acyclovir may cause renal or central nervous system toxicity.

Derivatives of acyclovir with various properties are now available. Valacyclovir (Valtrex) achieves a high plasma concentration when taken orally and is used in herpes genitalis and in herpes zoster. Penciclovir cream (Denavir) is used in the treatment of recurrent orolabial herpes simplex. Famciclovir (Famvir) when taken orally is converted to penciclovir and is used to treat herpes zoster and in herpes simplex infections.

2. Ganciclovir—Ganciclovir (dihydroxypropoxymethylguanine, DHPG, Cytovene) is a nucleoside analogue of guanosine with a four-carbon fragment in place of the normal sugar, ribose (Figure 35–1). It is structurally similar to acyclovir but is more active against CMV than is acyclovir. Ganciclovir is activated by a CMV-encoded phosphokinase in a process similar to that by which HSV activates acyclovir.

Ganciclovir is effective in the treatment of retinitis caused by CMV in AIDS patients and may be useful in other disseminated infections, such as colitis and esophagitis, caused by this virus. The main side effects of ganciclovir are leukopenia and thrombocytopenia as a result of bone marrow suppression. Valganciclovir, which can be taken orally, is also effective against CMV retinitis.

3. Cidofovir—Cidofovir (hydroxyphosphonylmethoxypropylcytosine, HPMPC, Vistide) is a nucleoside analogue of cytosine that lacks a ribose ring. It is useful in

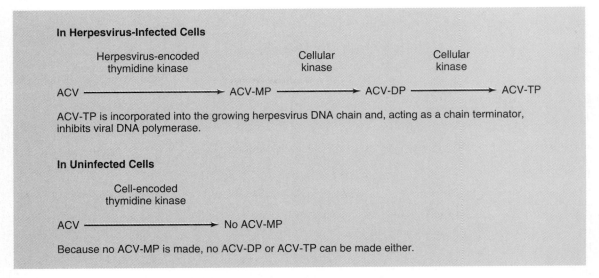

Figure 35–2. Acyclovir (ACV) is phosphorylated to ACV-MP very effectively by herpesvirus-encoded thymidine kinase but very poorly by cell-encoded thymidine kinase. The thymidine kinases encoded by herpes simplex virus (HSV)-1, HSV-2, and varicella-zoster virus (VZV) are particularly active on ACV; the thymidine kinases encoded by cytomegalovirus and Epstein-Barr virus are not. This accounts for the selective action of ACV in cells infected by HSV-1, HSV-2, and VZV. The fact that ACV-TP is not made in uninfected cells explains why ACV has so few side effects, ie, why DNA synthesis is not inhibited in uninfected cells. ACV-MP, ACV monophosphate; ACV-DP, ACV diphosphate; ACV-TP, ACV triphosphate.

the treatment of retinitis caused by CMV and in severe human papillomavirus infections. It may be useful in the treatment of severe molluscum contagiosum in immunocompromised patients. Kidney damage is the main side effect.

4. Vidarabine—Vidarabine (adenine arabinoside, ara-A) is a nucleoside analogue with arabinose in place of the normal sugar, ribose. On entering the cell, the drug is phosphorylated by cellular kinases to the triphosphate, which inhibits the herpesvirus-encoded DNA polymerase more effectively than the cellular DNA polymerase. Vidarabine is effective against HSV-1 infections such as encephalitis and keratitis but is less effective and more toxic than acyclovir.

5. Iododeoxyuridine—Iododeoxyuridine (idoxuridine, IDU, IUDR) is a nucleoside analogue in which the methyl group of thymidine is replaced by an iodine atom (Figure 35–1). The drug is phosphorylated to the triphosphate by cellular kinases and incorporated into DNA. Because IDU has a high frequency of mismatched pairing to guanine, it causes the formation of faulty progeny DNA and mRNA. However, because IDU is incorporated into normal cell DNA as well as viral DNA, it is too toxic to be used systemically. It is clinically useful in the topical treatment of keratoconjunctivitis caused by herpes simplex virus, but in the United States, trifluorothymidine (see below) is the drug of choice.

6. Trifluorothymidine—Trifluorothymidine (trifluridine, Viroptic) is a nucleoside analogue in which the methyl group of thymidine contains three fluorine atoms instead of three hydrogen atoms. Its mechanism of action is probably similar to that of IDU. Like IDU, it is too toxic for systemic use but is clinically useful in the topical treatment of keratoconjunctivitis caused by herpes simplex virus.

B. NON-NUCLEOSIDE INHIBITORS

These drugs inhibit the DNA polymerase of herpesviruses by mechanisms distinct from the nucleoside analogues described above. Foscarnet is the only approved drug in this class at this time.

1. Foscarnet—Foscarnet (trisodium phosphonoformate, Foscavir), unlike the previous drugs which are nucleoside analogues, is a pyrophosphate analogue. It binds to DNA polymerase at the pyrophosphate cleavage site and prevents removal of the phosphates from nucleoside triphosphates (dNTP). This inhibits the addition of the next dNTP and, as a consequence, the extension of the DNA strand. Foscarnet inhibits the DNA polymerases of all herpesviruses, especially HSV and CMV. Unlike acyclovir, it does not require activation by thymidine kinase. Foscarnet also inhibits the reverse transcriptase of HIV. It is useful in the treatment of retinitis caused by CMV, but ganciclovir is the treatment of first choice for this disease. Foscarnet is also used to treat patients infected with acyclovir-resistant mutants of HSV-1 and VZV.

Inhibitors of Retroviruses

A. NUCLEOSIDE INHIBITORS

The selective toxicity of azidothymidine, dideoxyinosine, dideoxycytidine, d4T, and 3TC is based on their ability to **inhibit DNA synthesis by the reverse transcriptase** of HIV to a much greater extent than they inhibit DNA synthesis by the DNA polymerase in human cells. The effect of these drugs on the replication of HIV is depicted in Figure 45–3.

1. Azidothymidine—Azidothymidine (zidovudine, Retrovir, AZT) is a nucleoside analogue that causes **chain termination** during DNA synthesis; it has an azido group in place of the hydroxyl group on the ribose (Figure 35–1). It is particularly effective against DNA synthesis by the reverse transcriptase of HIV and inhibits growth of the virus in cell culture. It is currently the drug of choice in patients with AIDS. The main side effects of AZT are bone marrow suppression and myopathy.

2. Dideoxyinosine—Dideoxyinosine (didanosine, Videx, ddI) is a nucleoside analogue that causes chain termination during DNA synthesis; it is missing hydroxyl groups on the ribose. The administered drug ddI is metabolized to ddATP, which is the active compound. It is effective against DNA synthesis by the reverse transcriptase of HIV and is used to treat patients with AIDS who are intolerant of or resistant to AZT. The main side effects of ddI are pancreatitis and peripheral neuropathy.

3. Dideoxycytidine—Dideoxycytidine (zalcitabine, Hivid, ddC) is a nucleoside analogue that causes chain termination during DNA synthesis; it is missing hydroxyl groups on the ribose. The administered drug ddC is metabolized to ddCTP, which is the active compound. It is effective against DNA synthesis by the reverse transcriptase of HIV and is used to treat patients who are intolerant of or resistant to AZT. The main side effects of ddC are the same as those of ddI but occur less often.

4. Stavudine—Stavudine (d4T, Zerit) is a nucleoside analogue that causes chain termination during DNA synthesis. It inhibits DNA synthesis by the reverse transcriptase of HIV and is used to treat patients with advanced AIDS who are intolerant of or resistant to other approved therapies. The molecular name of stavudine is didehydrodideoxythymidine. The main side effect is peripheral neuropathy.

5. Lamivudine—Lamivudine (3TC, Epivir) is a nucleoside analogue that causes chain termination during DNA synthesis by the reverse transcriptase of HIV. When used in combination with AZT, it is very effective both in reducing the viral load and in elevating the CD4 cell count. The molecular name of lamivudine is dideoxythiacytidine. Lamivudine is also used in the treatment of chronic hepatitis B. It is one of the best-tolerated of the nucleoside inhibitors, but side effects such as neutropenia, pancreatitis, and peripheral neuropathy do occur.

6. Abacavir—Abacavir (Ziagen) is a nucleoside analogue of guanosine that causes chain termination during DNA synthesis. It is available through the "expanded access" program to those who have failed currently available drug regimens. Abacavir is used in combination with either a protease inhibitor or AZT plus lamivudine.

7. Tenofovir—Tenofovir (Viread) is an acyclic nucleoside phosphonate that is an analogue of adenosine monophosphate. It is a reverse transcriptase inhibitor that acts by chain termination. It is approved for use in patients who have developed resistance to other reverse transcriptase inhibitors and in those who are starting treatment for the first time. It should be used in combination with other anti-HIV drugs.

B. Non-Nucleoside Inhibitors

Unlike the drugs described above, the drugs in this group are not nucleoside analogues and do not cause chain termination. The non-nucleoside reverse transcriptase inhibitors (NNRTI) act by binding near the active site of the reverse transcriptase and inducing a conformational change that inhibits the synthesis of viral DNA. NNRTIs should not be used as monotherapy because resistant mutants emerge rapidly. Strains of HIV resistant to one NNRTI are usually resistant to others as well. NNRTIs are typically used in combination with one or two nucleoside analogues.

1. Nevirapine—Nevirapine (Viramune) is usually used in combination with zidovudine and didanosine. There is no cross-resistance with the nucleoside inhibitors of reverse transcriptase described above. The main side effect of nevirapine is a severe skin rash (Stevens-Johnson syndrome). Nevirapine is a member of a class of drugs called the dipyridodiazepinones; its precise name is beyond the scope of this book.

2. Delavirdine—Delavirdine (Rescriptor) is effective in combination with either zidovudine or zidovudine plus didanosine. Delavirdine is a member of a class of drugs called bisheteroarylpiperazines; its precise name is beyond the scope of this book.

3. Efavirenz—Efavirenz (Sustiva) in combination with zidovudine plus lamivudine was more effective and better tolerated than the combination of indinavir, zidovudine, and lamivudine. The most common side effects are referable to the central nervous system, such as dizziness, insomnia, and headaches. Efavirenz is a member of a class of drugs called benzoxazin-2-ones; its precise name is beyond the scope of this book.

Inhibitors of Other Viruses

A. Ribavirin

Ribavirin (Virazole) is a nucleoside analogue in which a triazole-carboxamide moiety is substituted in place of the normal purine precursor aminoimidazole-carboxamide (Figure 35–1). The drug inhibits the synthesis of guanine nucleotides, which are essential for both DNA and RNA viruses. It also inhibits the 5' capping of viral mRNA. Ribavirin aerosol is used clinically to treat pneumonitis caused by respiratory syncytial virus in infants and to treat severe influenza B infections.

B. Adefovir

Adefovir (Hepsera) is a nucleotide analogue of adenosine monophosphate that inhibits the DNA polymerase of hepatitis B virus. It is used for the treatment of chronic active hepatitis caused by this virus.

C. Entecavir

Entecavir (Baraclude) is a guanosine analogue that inhibits the DNA polymerase of hepatitis B virus (HBV). It has no activity against the DNA polymerase (reverse transcriptase) of HIV. It is approved for the treatment of adults with chronic HBV infection.

INHIBITION OF CLEAVAGE OF PRECURSOR POLYPEPTIDES

Several drugs, such as saquinavir (Invirase, Fortovase), indinavir (Crixivan), ritonavir (Norvir), amprenavir (Agenerase), and nelfinavir (Viracept), are inhibitors of the protease encoded by HIV (Figure 35–3). The protease cleaves the *gag* and *pol* precursor polypeptides to produce several nucleocapsid proteins, eg, p24, and enzymatic proteins, eg, reverse transcriptase, required for viral replication. These inhibitors contain peptide bonds that bind to the active site of the viral protease, thereby preventing the protease from cleaving the viral precursor. These drugs inhibit production of infectious virions but do not affect the proviral DNA and therefore do not cure the infection. The effect of protease inhibitors on the replication of HIV is depicted in Figure 45–3.

Monotherapy with protease inhibitors should not be used because resistant mutants emerge rapidly. These drugs are prescribed in combination with reverse transcriptase inhibitors, either nucleoside analogues such as zidovudine and lamivudine or non-nucleoside inhibitors such as nevirapine.

The side effects of protease inhibitors include nausea, diarrhea, and abnormal fat accumulation in the back of the neck that can result in a "buffalo hump" appearance. These abnormal fat deposits can be disfiguring and cause patients to stop taking the drug. The fat deposits are a type of lipodystrophy; the metabolic

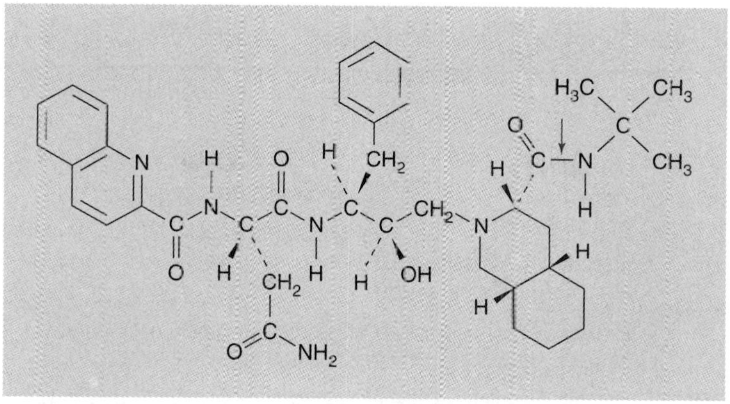

Figure 35–3. Structure of the protease inhibitor saquinavir. Note the presence of several peptide bonds, which interact with the active site of the protease. An arrow indicates one of the peptide bonds.

process by which this occurs is unknown. Indinavir can cause kidney stones; thus, extra water should be consumed to reduce the likelihood of stone formation. Ritonavir can cause circumoral paresthesias.

INHIBITION OF VIRAL PROTEIN SYNTHESIS

A. INTERFERON

The mode of action of interferon is described in Chapter 33. Recombinant alpha interferon is effective in the treatment of some patients with chronic hepatitis B and chronic hepatitis C infections. It also causes regression of condylomata acuminata lesions caused by human papillomavirus and the lesions of Kaposi's sarcoma caused by human herpesvirus-8.

Pegylated interferon (Peg-intron), which is interferon alpha conjugated to polyethylene glycol, is available for the treatment of chronic hepatitis C. The advantage of pegylated interferon is that it has a longer half-life than unconjugated interferon alpha and can be administered once a week instead of three times a week.

B. FOMIVIRSEN

Fomivirsen (Vitravene) is an antisense DNA that blocks the replication of CMV. Antisense DNA is a single-stranded DNA whose base sequence is the complement of the viral mRNA. Antisense DNA binds to the mRNA within the infected cell and prevents it from being translated into viral protein. Fomivirsen is approved for the intraocular treatment of CMV retinitis. It is the first and, at present, the only antisense molecule to be approved for the treatment of human disease.

C. METHISAZONE

Methisazone (N-methylisatin-β-thiosemicarbazone) specifically inhibits the protein synthesis of poxviruses, such as smallpox and vaccinia viruses, by blocking the translation of late mRNA. The drug can be used to treat certain rare, severe side effects of the smallpox vaccine, eg, disseminated vaccinia. However, it is rarely (if ever) used, because the smallpox vaccine is no longer administered except to military personnel.

INHIBITION OF RELEASE OF VIRUS

Zanamivir (Relenza) and oseltamivir (Tamiflu) inhibit the neuraminidase of influenza virus. This enzyme is located on the surface of influenza virus and is required for the release of the virus from infected cells. Inhibition of release of influenza virus limits the infection by reducing the spread of virus from one cell to another. These drugs are effective against both influenza A and B viruses, in contrast to amantadine, which is effective only against influenza A virus. These drugs are effective against strains of influenza virus resistant to amantadine.

CHEMOPROPHYLAXIS

In most instances, the antiviral agents described in this chapter are used to *treat* infectious diseases. However, there are times when they are used to *prevent* diseases from occurring, a process called **chemoprophylaxis**. Table 35–2 describes the drugs used for this purpose and the situations in which they are used. For more information, see the chapters on the individual viruses.

Table 35–2. Chemoprophylactic use of drugs described in this chapter.

Drug	Use	Number of Chapter for Additional Information
Amantadine	Prevention of influenza during outbreaks caused by influenza A virus	39
Acyclovir	Prevention of disseminated HSV or VZV disease in immunocompromised patients	37
Ganciclovir	Prevention of disseminated CMV disease in immunocompromised patients, especially retinitis in AIDS patients	37
Azidothymidine or nevirapine	Prevention of HIV infection of neonate	45
Azidothymidine, lamivudine, and indinavir	Prevention of HIV infection in needle-stick injuries	45

PEARLS

- ***Selective toxicity*** *is the ability of a drug to inhibit viral replication without significantly damaging the host cell. It is difficult to achieve a high degree of selective toxicity with antiviral drugs because the virus can only replicate within cells and uses many cellular functions during replication.*

Inhibitors of Early Events

- *Amantadine inhibits the uncoating of influenza A virus by blocking "ion channel" activity of the viral matrix protein. The drug has no effect on influenza B or C viruses.*

Inhibitors of Herpesviruses: Nucleoside Inhibitors

- ***Acyclovir inhibits the DNA polymerase*** *of herpes simplex virus (HSV) type-1, HSV-2, and varicella-zoster virus (VZV).* ***Acyclovir must be activated within the infected cell by a virus-encoded thymidine kinase*** *that phosphorylates the drug. Acyclovir is not phosphorylated in uninfected cells and cellular DNA synthesis is not inhibited. Selective toxicity is high and there are very few adverse effects.*

- ***Acyclovir is a chain-terminating drug*** *because it lacks a hydroxyl group in the 3′ position. It does not*

have a ribose ring, ie, it is "acyclo," meaning without a ring. The absence of this hydroxyl group means the next nucleoside triphosphate cannot be added and the replicating DNA chain is terminated.

- ***Acyclovir inhibits viral replication but has no effect on the latency*** *of HSV-1, HSV-2, and VZV.*

- *Ganciclovir action is very similar to that of acyclovir, but it is effective against cytomegalovirus (CMV), whereas acyclovir is not.*

Inhibitors of Herpesviruses: Non-Nucleoside Inhibitors

- ***Foscarnet inhibits the DNA polymerase*** *of all herpesviruses but is clinically useful against HSV and CMV. It also* ***inhibits the DNA polymerase of the retrovirus HIV.*** *It is a* ***pyrophosphate analogue*** *that inhibits the cleavage of pyrophosphate from the nucleoside triphosphate that has been added to the growing DNA chain.*

Inhibitors of Retroviruses: Nucleoside Inhibitors

- ***Azidothymidine (zidovudine, AZT) inhibits the DNA polymerase*** *(reverse transcriptase)* ***of HIV.*** *It is a* ***chain-terminating drug*** *because it has an azide group in place of the hydroxyl group in the 3′ posi-*

tion. Unlike acyclovir, it does not require a viral-encoded kinase to be phosphorylated. Cellular kinases phosphorylate the drug, so it is active in uninfected cells and significant adverse effects can occur.

- Other drugs that have a similar mode of action include didanosine, zalcitabine, stavudine, lamivudine, abacavir, and tenofovir.

Inhibitors of Retroviruses: Non-Nucleoside Inhibitors

- **Nevirapine, delavirdine, and efavirenz inhibit the DNA polymerase (reverse transcriptase) of HIV** but are not nucleoside analogues.

Inhibitors of Other Viruses

- Ribavirin is a guanosine analogue that can inhibit nucleic acid synthesis of several DNA and RNA viruses.

Protease Inhibitors

- **Indinavir and other similar drugs inhibit the virus-encoded protease of HIV.** Inhibition of the protease prevents cleavage of precursor polypeptides, which prevents formation of the structural proteins of the virus. Synthesis of infectious virus is inhibited, but the viral DNA integrated into the host cell DNA is unaffected.

Inhibitors of Viral Protein Synthesis

- **Interferons inhibit virus replication by blocking the production of viral proteins,** primarily by degrading **viral mRNA.** They **induce the synthesis of a ribonuclease** that specifically cleaves viral mRNA but not cell mRNA. (See Chapter 33 for more information.)
- Fomivirsen is an antisense DNA that binds to the mRNA of CMV, which prevents the mRNA from being translated into viral proteins.

Inhibitors of Release of Virus

- **Zanamir and oseltamivir inhibit the neuraminidase of both influenza A and B viruses. This inhibits the release of progeny virus,** which reduces spread of virus to neighboring cells.

PRACTICE QUESTIONS: USMLE & COURSE EXAMINATIONS

Questions on the topics discussed in this chapter can be found in the Basic Virology section of Part XI: USMLE (National Board) Practice Questions starting on page 545. Also see Part XII: USMLE (National Board) Practice Examination starting on page 583.

Viral Vaccines

Because few drugs are useful against viral infections, prevention of infection by the use of vaccines is very important. Prevention of viral diseases can be achieved by the use of vaccines that induce active immunity or by the administration of preformed antibody that provides passive immunity.

ACTIVE IMMUNITY

There are two types of vaccines that induce **active im-munity**: those that contain **live virus** whose pathogenicity has been **attenuated**[1] and those that contain **killed virus.** Some vaccines, such as the hepatitis B vaccine, contain purified viral proteins and are often called **subunit** vaccines. The features of subunit vaccines resemble those of killed vaccines because no viral replication occurs in these vaccines. The attributes of live and killed vaccines are listed in Table 36–1.

In general, live vaccines are preferred to vaccines containing killed virus because their protection is **greater** and **longer-lasting.** With live vaccines, the virus multiplies in the host, producing a prolonged antigenic stimulus, and both IgA and IgG are elicited when the vaccine is administered by the natural route of infection, eg, when polio vaccine is given orally. Killed vaccines, which are usually given intramuscularly, do not stimulate a major IgA response. Killed vaccines typically do not stimulate a cytotoxic T-cell response, because the virus in the vaccine does not replicate. In the absence of replication, no viral epitopes are presented in association with class I MHC proteins and the cytotoxic T-cell response is not activated (see Chapter 58). Although live vaccines stimulate a long-lasting response, booster doses are now recommended with measles and polio vaccines.

One unique form of a live, attenuated viral vaccine is the influenza vaccine that contains a **temperature-sensitive** mutant of the virus as the immunogen. The temperature-sensitive mutant will replicate in the cooler air passages of the nose, where it induces IgA-

based immunity, whereas it will not replicate in the warmer lung tissue and therefore will not cause disease.

There are three concerns about the use of live vaccines:

(1) They are composed of attenuated viral mutants, which can **revert to virulence** either during vaccine production or in the immunized person. Reversion to virulence during production can be detected by quality control testing, but there is no test to predict whether reversion will occur in the immunized individual. Of the commonly used live vaccines, only polio vaccine has had problems regarding revertants; measles, mumps, rubella, and varicella vaccines have not.

Even if the virus in the live vaccine does not revert, it can still cause disease because, although attenuated (weakened), it can still be pathogenic in a host with reduced immunity. For this reason, live viral vaccines should *not* be given to immunocompromised people or to pregnant women because the fetus may become infected.

(2) The live vaccine can be **excreted** by the immunized person. This is a double-edged sword. It is advantageous if the spread of the virus successfully immunizes others, as occurs with the live polio vaccine. However, it could be a problem if, eg, a virulent poliovirus revertant spreads to a susceptible person. Rare cases of paralytic polio occur in the United States each year by this route of infection.

(3) A second virus could **contaminate** the vaccine if it was present in the cell cultures used to prepare the vaccine. This concern exists for both live and killed vaccines, although, clearly, the live vaccine presents a greater problem, because the process that inactivates the virus in the killed vaccine could inactivate the contaminant as well. It is interesting, therefore, that the most striking incidence of contamination of a vaccine occurred with the *killed* polio vaccine. In 1960, it was reported that live simian vacuolating virus 40 (SV40 virus), an inapparent "passenger" virus in monkey kidney cells, had contaminated some lots of polio vaccine and was resistant to the formaldehyde used to inactivate the poliovirus. There was great concern when it was found that SV40 virus causes sarcomas in a variety of rodents. Fortunately, it has not caused cancer in the

---

[1] An attenuated virus is one that is unable to cause disease but retains its antigenicity and can induce protection.

Table 36–1. Characteristics of live and killed viral vaccines.

Characteristic	Live Vaccine	Killed Vaccine
Duration of immunity	Longer	Shorter
Effectiveness of protection	Greater	Lower
Immunoglobulins produced	IgA[1] and IgG	IgG
Cell-mediated immunity produced	Yes	Weakly or none
Interruption of transmission of virulent virus	More effective	Less effective
Reversion to virulence	Possible	No
Stability at room temperature	Low	High
Excretion of vaccine virus and transmission to nonimmune contacts	Possible	No

[1]If the vaccine is given by the natural route.

individuals inoculated with the contaminated polio vaccine.

Certain viral vaccines, namely, influenza, measles, mumps, and yellow fever vaccines, are grown in chick embryos. These vaccines should *not* be given to those who have had an **anaphylactic reaction to eggs.** People with allergies to chicken feathers can be immunized.

In addition to the disadvantages of the killed vaccines already mentioned—namely, that they induce a **shorter duration** of protection, are **less protective,** and **induce fewer IgA antibodies**—there is the potential problem that the inactivation process might be inadequate. Although this is rare, it happened in the early days of the manufacture of the killed polio vaccine. However, killed vaccines do have two advantages: they **cannot revert to virulence** and they are **more heat-stable;** they therefore can be used more easily in tropical climates.

Most viral vaccines are usually given before a known exposure; ie, they are administered **preexposure.** However, there are two vaccines, the vaccines against rabies and hepatitis B, that are also effective when given **post-exposure,** because the incubation period of these diseases is long enough that the vaccine-induced immunity can prevent the disease. Thus, the rabies vaccine is most often used in people after they have received a bite from a potentially rabid animal and the hepatitis B vaccine is used in people who have sustained a needle-stick injury.

The prospect for the future is that some of the disadvantages of current vaccines will be bypassed by the use of purified viral antigens produced from genes cloned in either bacteria or yeasts. The advantages of antigens produced by the cloning process are that they contain no viral nucleic acid and so cannot replicate or revert to virulence; they have no contaminating viruses from cell culture; and they can be produced in large amounts. A disadvantage of these cloned vaccines is that they are unlikely to stimulate a cytotoxic T-cell response because no viral replication occurs.

Another prospect for the future is the use of "DNA vaccines." These vaccines contain purified DNA encoding the appropriate viral proteins genetically engineered into a viral vector or plasmid. Immunization with this composite DNA elicits both antibody and cytotoxic T cells and protects against disease in experimental animals.

Certain live viral vaccines, such as the vaccines containing vaccinia virus, adenovirus, and poliovirus, are being used experimentally to immunize against other viruses such as HIV. This is done by splicing the HIV gene into the live viral genome and then infecting the experimental animal with the constructed virus. The advantage of this procedure is that a cytotoxic T-cell response is elicited (because the virus is replicating), whereas if the purified antigen alone were used to immunize the animal, an antibody response but not a cytotoxic T-cell response would be elicited.

The viral vaccines currently in use are described in Table 36–2.

PASSIVE IMMUNITY

Passive immunity is provided by the administration of preformed antibody in preparations called immune globulins. The immune globulins useful in the prevention of viral diseases are described below. **Passive-active** immunity is induced by giving both immune globulins

Table 36–2. Current viral vaccines (2006).

Usage	Vaccine	Live Virus, Killed Virus, or Subunit of Virus
Common	Measles	Live
	Mumps	Live
	Rubella	Live
	Varicella (chickenpox)	Live
	Polio	Live and killed[1]
	Influenza	Live and killed (purified subunits)[2]
	Hepatitis A	Killed
	Hepatitis B	Subunit[3]
	Rabies	Killed
Special situations	Yellow fever[4]	Live
	Japanese encephalitis[4]	Killed
	Adenovirus[5]	Live
	Smallpox[5]	Live

[1]Only the killed vaccine is recommended for routine immunizations in the United States.
[2]The live vaccine contains a temperature-sensitive mutant of influenza virus. The killed vaccine contains two purified protein subunits (hemagglutinin and neuraminidase) obtained after the virus is chemically inactivated.
[3]Recombinant vaccine contains HBV surface antigen only.
[4]Used when traveling in endemic areas.
[5]Used for military personnel and certain medical personnel such as "first responders" and emergency room staff.

to provide immediate protection and a vaccine to provide long-term protection. This approach is described below in the sections on rabies and hepatitis B.

The following preparations are available.

(1) **Rabies** immune globulin (RIG) is used in the prevention of rabies in people who may have been exposed to the virus. It is administered by injecting as much RIG as possible into the tissue at the bite site and the remainder is given intramuscularly. The preparation contains a high titer of antibody made by hyperimmunizing human volunteers with rabies vaccine. RIG is obtained from humans to avoid hypersensitivity reactions. In addition to RIG, the vaccine containing killed rabies virus made in human diploid cells should be given. RIG and the vaccine should be given at different sites. This is an example of passive-active immunization.

(2) **Hepatitis B** immune globulin (HBIG) is used in the prevention of hepatitis B in people who may have been exposed to the virus either by needle-stick or as a neonate born of a mother who is a carrier of HBV. The preparation contains a high titer of antibody to hepatitis

B virus and is obtained from humans to avoid hypersensitivity reactions. HBIG is often used in conjunction with hepatitis B vaccine, an example of passive-active immunization.

(3) **Varicella-zoster** immune globulin (VZIG) is used in the prevention of disseminated zoster in people who may have been exposed to the virus and who are immunocompromised. The preparation contains a high titer of antibody to varicella-zoster virus and is obtained from humans to avoid hypersensitivity reactions.

(4) **Vaccinia** immune globulins (VIG) can be used to treat some of the complications of the smallpox vaccination.

(5) Immune globulins (IGs) are useful in the prevention (or mitigation) of **hepatitis A** or **measles** in people who may have been exposed to these viruses. IGs are commonly used prior to traveling to areas of the world where hepatitis A virus is endemic. IGs contain pooled serum obtained from a large number of human volunteers who have not been hyperimmunized. The effectiveness of IG is based on antibody being present in many members of the pool.

HERD IMMUNITY

Herd immunity (also known as community immunity) occurs when a sufficiently large percentage of the population (the "herd") is immunized so that an unimmunized individual is protected (see Chapter 33). For herd immunity to occur, the vaccine must prevent transmission of the virus as well as prevent disease. For example, the live, at-tenuated polio vaccine can provide good herd immunity because it induces intestinal IgA, which prevents poliovirus from replicating in the gastrointestinal tract and being transmitted to others. However, the killed polio vaccine does not induce herd immunity because secretory IgA is not produced, and immunized individuals (although protected from poliomyelitis) can still serve as a source of poliovirus for others.

PEARLS

Active Immunity

- *Active immunity can be elicited by vaccines containing killed viruses, purified protein subunits, or live, attenuated (weakened) viruses.*

- *In general, **live viral vaccines are preferable to killed vaccines** for three reasons: (1) they induce a higher titer of antibody and hence longer-lasting protection; (2) they induce a broader range of antibody, eg, both IgA and IgG, not just IgG; (3) they activate cytotoxic T cells, which kill virus-infected cells.*

- *There are some potential **problems with live viral vaccines, the most important of which is reversion to virulence.** Transmission of the vaccine virus to others who may be immunocompromised is another concern. Also there may be a second, unwanted virus in the vaccine that was present in the cells used to make the vaccine virus. This second virus may cause adverse effects.*

- ***Live viral vaccines should not be given to immunocompromised individuals or to pregnant women.***

- *Vaccines grown in chick embryos, especially influenza vaccine, should not be given to those who have had an anaphylactic reaction to eggs.*

Passive Immunity

- ***Passive immunity is immunity acquired by an individual by the transfer of preformed antibodies** made in either other humans or in animals. These antibody preparations are often called **immune globulins.*** *Passive immunity also occurs naturally when IgG is transferred from the mother to the fetus across the placenta and when IgA is transferred from the mother to the newborn in colostrum.*

- ***The main advantage of passive immunity** is that it provides immediate protection.* *The main disadvantage is that it does not provide long-term protection, ie, it is active only for a few weeks to a few months.*

- *Immune globulin preparations against rabies virus, hepatitis A virus, hepatitis B virus, and varicella-zoster virus are in common use.*

- ***Passive-active immunity consists of administering both immune globulins and a viral vaccine.*** *This provides both immediate as well as long-term protection. For example, protection against rabies in an unimmunized person who has been bitten by a potentially rabid animal consists of both rabies immune globulins and the rabies vaccine.*

- ***Herd immunity** is the protection of an individual that results from immunity in many other members of the population (the herd) that interrupts transmission of the virus to the individual. Herd immunity can be achieved either by active immunization or by natural infection of a sufficiently high percentage of the population. Herd immunity is unlikely to be achieved by passive immunity because, although antibodies can protect the individual against spread of virus through the bloodstream, they are unlikely to prevent viral replication at the portal of entry and consequent transmission to others.*

PRACTICE QUESTIONS: USMLE & COURSE EXAMINATIONS

Questions on the topics discussed in this chapter can be found in the Basic Virology section of Part XI: USMLE (National Board) Practice Questions starting on page 545. Also see Part XII: USMLE (National Board) Practice Examination starting on page 583.

PART IV
Clinical Virology

Most of the clinically important viral pathogens can be categorized into groups according to their structural characteristics, ie, DNA enveloped viruses, DNA nonenveloped[1] viruses, RNA enveloped viruses, and RNA nonenveloped viruses (see Chapters 37–40 and Table IV–1).

However, some viruses, eg, arboviruses, tumor viruses, and slow viruses (see Chapters 41–45), are described best in terms of their biologic features. Several clinically less prominent viruses, eg, parvoviruses and coronaviruses, are described in Chapter 46. An overview of the viruses in the four structural categories follows.

DNA ENVELOPED VIRUSES

Herpesviruses

These viruses are noted for their ability to cause latent infections. This family includes (1) herpes simplex virus types 1 and 2, which cause painful vesicles on the face and genitals, respectively; (2) varicella-zoster virus, which causes varicella (chickenpox) typically in children and, when it recurs, zoster (shingles); (3) cytomegalovirus, an important cause of congenital malformations; (4) Epstein-Barr virus, which causes infectious mononucleosis; and (5) human herpesvirus 8, which causes Kaposi's sarcoma. (See Chapter 37.)

Hepatitis B Virus

This virus is one of the important causes of viral hepatitis. In contrast to hepatitis A virus (an RNA nucleocapsid virus), hepatitis B virus causes a more severe form of hepatitis, results more frequently in a chronic carrier state, and is implicated in the induction of hepa-

tocellular carcinoma, the most common cancer worldwide. (See Chapter 41.)

Poxviruses

Poxviruses are the largest and most complex of the viruses. The disease smallpox has been eradicated by effective use of the vaccine. Molluscum contagiosum virus is the only poxvirus that causes human disease in the United States at this time. (See Chapter 37.)

DNA NONENVELOPED VIRUSES

Adenoviruses

These viruses are best known for causing upper and lower respiratory tract infections, including pharyngitis and pneumonia. (See Chapter 38.)

Papillomaviruses

These viruses cause papillomas on the skin and mucous membranes of many areas of the body. Some types are implicated as a cause of cancer, eg, carcinoma of the cervix. (See Chapter 38.)

Parvovirus B19

This virus causes "slapped cheeks" syndrome, hydrops fetalis, and severe anemia, especially in those with hereditary anemias such as sickle cell anemia. (See Chapter 38.)

RNA ENVELOPED VIRUSES

Respiratory Viruses

(1) Influenza A and B viruses. Influenza A virus is the major cause of recurrent epidemics of influenza.

---

[1] Nonenveloped viruses are also called naked nucleocapsid viruses.

Table IV–1. Major viral pathogens.

Structure	Viruses
DNA enveloped viruses	Herpesviruses (herpes simplex virus types 1 and 2, varicella-zoster virus, cytomegalovirus, Epstein-Barr virus, human herpesvirus 8), hepatitis 3 virus, smallpox virus
DNA nucleocapsid viruses	Adenovirus, papillomaviruses, parvovirus E19
RNA enveloped viruses	Influenza virus, parainfluenza virus, respiratory syncytial virus, measles virus, mumps virus, rubella virus, rabies virus, human T-cell lymphotropic virus, human immunodeficiency virus, hepatitis C virus
RNA nucleocapsid viruses	Enteroviruses (poliovirus, coxsackievirus, echovirus, hepatitis A virus), rhinovirus, rotavirus, Norwalk virus

(2) Parainfluenza viruses. These viruses are the leading cause of croup in young children and an important cause of common colds in adults.

(3) Respiratory syncytial virus. This virus is the leading cause of bronchiolitis and pneumonia in infants. (See Chapter 39.)

Measles, Mumps, and Rubella Viruses

These viruses are well known for the complications associated with the diseases they cause (eg, rubella virus infection in a pregnant woman can cause congenital malformations). The incidence of these three diseases has been markedly reduced in the United States as a result of immunization. (See Chapter 39.)

Rabies Virus

This virus causes almost invariably fatal encephalitis following the bite of a rabid animal. In the United States, wild animals such as skunks, foxes, raccoons, and bats are the major sources, but human infection is rare. (See Chapter 39.)

Hepatitis C Virus

This virus causes hepatitis C, the most prevalent form of viral hepatitis in the United States. It causes a very high rate of chronic carriers and predisposes to chronic hepatitis and hepatic carcinoma.

Human T-Cell Lymphotropic Virus

This virus causes T-cell leukemia in humans. It also causes an autoimmune disease called tropical spastic paraparesis. (See Chapter 43.)

Human Immunodeficiency Virus

Human immunodeficiency virus (HIV) causes acquired immunodeficiency syndrome (AIDS). (See Chapter 45.)

RNA NONENVELOPED VIRUSES

Enteroviruses

These viruses infect the enteric tract and are transmitted by the fecal-oral route. Poliovirus rarely causes disease in the United States because of the vaccine but remains an important cause of aseptic meningitis and paralysis in developing countries. Of more importance in the United States are coxsackieviruses, which cause aseptic meningitis, myocarditis, and pleurodynia; and echoviruses, which cause aseptic meningitis. (See Chapter 40.)

Rhinoviruses

These viruses are the most common cause of the common cold. They have a large number of antigenic types, which may account for their ability to cause disease so frequently. (See Chapter 40.)

Reoviruses (Rotavirus)

These viruses possess an unusual genome composed of double-stranded RNA in 10 segments. "Reo" is an acronym for *r*espiratory *e*nteric *o*rphan. They were initially called "orphan" viruses because they were not associated with any specific disease. However, one of the reoviruses, rotavirus, is an important cause of viral gastroenteritis in young children. (See Chapter 40.)

Hepatitis A Virus

This virus is an important cause of hepatitis. It is an enterovirus but is described in this book in conjunction with hepatitis B virus. It is structurally different from hepatitis B virus, a DNA enveloped virus. Furthermore, it is epidemiologically distinct; ie, it primarily affects children, is transmitted by the fecal-oral route, and rarely causes a prolonged carrier state. (See Chapter 41.)

Table IV–2. The 10 most common notifiable viral diseases in the United States in 2003.[1]

Disease	Number of Cases
AIDS	44,232
Chickenpox (varicella)	20,948
Hepatitis A	7,653
Hepatitis B	7,526
Encephalitis, West Nile	2,866
Hepatitis C	1,102
Mumps	231
Encephalitis, California serogroup	108
Measles	56
Hantavirus pulmonary syndrome	26

[1] The latest year for which complete data are available.

Norwalk Virus (Norovirus)

Norwalk virus (also known as norovirus) is a common cause of gastroenteritis, especially in adults. It is a well-known cause of outbreaks of vomiting and diarrhea on cruise ships (see Chapter 40).

OTHER CATEGORIES

Chapter 42 describes the large and varied group of arboviruses, which have the common feature of being transmitted by an arthropod. Chapter 43 covers tumor viruses, and Chapter 44 covers the "slow" viruses, which cause degenerative central nervous system diseases primarily. Chapter 45 describes HIV, the cause of AIDS. The less common viral pathogens are described in Chapter 46.

Table IV–2 lists the frequency of the 10 most common notifiable viral diseases in the United States for 2003 (the latest year for which complete data are available). AIDS is the most frequent and chickenpox (varicella) is in second place. In previous years, chickenpox was the most common notifiable disease, but the widespread use of the vaccine has greatly reduced the number of cases. Hepatitis A, hepatitis B, and hepatitis C are in third, fourth, and fifth places, respectively. Note that the common cold, which is probably the most frequent disease, is not listed because it is not a notifiable disease.

DNA Enveloped Viruses

37

■ HERPESVIRUSES

The herpesvirus family contains six important human pathogens: herpes simplex virus types 1 and 2, varicella-zoster virus, cytomegalovirus, Epstein-Barr virus, and human herpesvirus 8 (the cause of Kaposi's sarcoma).

All herpesviruses are structurally similar. Each has an **icosahedral** core surrounded by a lipoprotein **envelope.** The genome is linear double-stranded DNA. The virion does not contain a polymerase. They are large (120–200 nm in diameter), second in size only to poxviruses. They replicate in the nucleus, form intranuclear inclusions, and are the only viruses that obtain their envelopes by budding from the nuclear membrane.

Herpesviruses are noted for their ability to cause **latent infections.** In these infections, the acute disease is followed by an asymptomatic period during which the virus remains in a quiescent (latent) state. When the patient is exposed to an inciting agent or immunosuppression occurs, reactivation of virus replication and disease can occur. With some herpesviruses, eg, herpes simplex virus, the symptoms of the subsequent episodes are similar to those of the initial one; however, with others, eg, varicella-zoster virus, they are different (Table 37–1).

Three of the herpesviruses, herpes simplex virus types 1 and 2 and varicella-zoster virus, cause a **vesicular rash,** both in primary infections and in reactivations. Primary infections are usually more severe than reactivations. The other two herpesviruses, cytomegalovirus and Epstein-Barr virus, do not cause a vesicular rash.

The herpesvirus family can be subdivided into three categories based on the type of cell most often infected and the site of latency. The alpha herpesviruses, consisting of herpes simplex viruses 1 and 2, and varicella-zoster virus infect epithelial cells primarily and cause latent infection in neurons. The beta herpesviruses, consisting of cytomegaloviruses and human herpesvirus 6, infect and become latent in a variety of tissues. The gamma herpesviruses, consisting of Epstein-Barr virus

and human herpesvirus 8 (Kaposi's sarcoma–associated virus), infect and become latent primarily in lymphoid cells. Table 37–2 describes some important clinical features of the common herpesviruses.

Certain herpesviruses are suspected of causing cancer in humans; eg, Epstein-Barr virus is associated with Burkitt's lymphoma and nasopharyngeal carcinoma, and human herpesvirus 8 is associated with Kaposi's sarcoma. Several herpesviruses cause cancer in animals, eg, leukemia in monkeys and lymphomatosis in chickens (see Tumor Viruses, Chapter 43).

HERPES SIMPLEX VIRUSES (HSV)

Herpes simplex virus type 1 (HSV-1) and type 2 (HSV-2) are distinguished by two main criteria: antigenicity and location of lesions. Lesions caused by HSV-1 are, in general, above the waist, whereas those caused by HSV-2 are below the waist. Table 37–3 describes some important differences between the diseases caused by HSV-1 and HSV-2.

Diseases

HSV-1 causes acute gingivostomatitis, recurrent herpes labialis (cold sores), keratoconjunctivitis, and encephalitis. HSV-2 causes genital herpes, neonatal herpes, and aseptic meningitis.

Important Properties

HSV-1 and HSV-2 are structurally and morphologically indistinguishable. They can, however, be differentiated by the restriction endonuclease patterns of their genome DNA and by type-specific monoclonal antisera. Humans are the natural hosts of both HSV-1 and HSV-2.

Summary of Replicative Cycle

HSV-1 attaches to the cell surface at the site of the receptor for fibroblast growth factor. After entry into the cell, the virion is uncoated and the genome DNA enters the nucleus. Within the nucleus, the incoming genome DNA changes its configuration from linear to circular. Early virus messenger RNA (mRNA) is tran-

Table 37–1. Important features of common herpesvirus infections.

Virus	Primary Infection	Usual Site of Latency	Recurrent Infection	Route of Transmission
HSV-1	Gingivostomatitis[1]	Cranial sensory ganglia	Herpes labialis,[2] encephalitis, keratitis	Via respiratory secretions and saliva
HSV-2	Herpes genitalis, perinatal disseminated disease	Lumbar or sacral sensory ganglia	Herpes genitalis	Sexual contact, perinatal infection
VZV	Varicella	Cranial or thoracic sensory ganglia	Zoster[2]	Via respiratory secretions
EBV	Infectious mononucleosis[1]	B lymphocytes	None[3]	Via respiratory secretions and saliva
CMV	Congenital infection (in utero), mononucleosis	Uncertain[4]	Asymptomatic shedding[2]	Intrauterine infection, transfusions, sexual contact, via secretions (eg, saliva and urine)
HHV-8[5]	Uncertain[6]	Uncertain	Kaposi's sarcoma	Sexual or organ transplantation

[1]Primary infection is often asymptomatic.
[2]In immunocompromised patients, dissemination is common.
[3]The relationship of EBV infection to "chronic fatigue syndrome" and B-cell neoplasms is unclear.
[4]CMV may be latent within circulating lymphoid cells or epithelial cells.
[5]Also known as Kaposi's sarcoma–associated herpesvirus.
[6]A mononucleosis-like syndrome has been described. KS itself also can result from a primary infection.

scribed by host cell RNA polymerase and then translated into early, nonstructural proteins in the cytoplasm. Two of these early proteins, thymidine kinase and DNA polymerase, are important because they are sufficiently different from the corresponding cellular enzymes to be involved in the action of antiviral drugs, eg, acyclovir.

Early protein synthesis by HSV can be subdivided into two categories: "immediate early" and "early." "Immediate early" proteins are those whose mRNA synthesis is activated by a protein brought in by the incoming parental virion; ie, no new viral protein synthesis is required for the production of the five "immediate early" proteins. The "early" proteins, on the other hand, do

Table 37–2. Clinical features of herpesviruses.

Virus	Giant Cells Produced	Fetal or Neonatal Disease Important	Important Laboratory Diagnostic Technique	Antiviral Therapy Commonly Used
HSV-1	Yes	No	Culture	Acyclovir[1]
HSV-2	Yes	Yes	Culture	Acyclovir
VZV	Yes	No	Culture	Acyclovir[2]
CMV	Yes	Yes	Culture	Ganciclovir[3]
EBV	No	No	Heterophil	None
HHV-8	No	No	DNA probes	Alpha interferon

[1] Not used in recurrent herpes labialis.
[2] Not used in varicella in immunocompetent children.
[3] Used in CMV retinitis and other severe forms of disease.

Table 37–3. Comparison of diseases caused by HSV-1 and HSV-2.

Site	Disease Caused by HSV-1	Disease Caused by HSV-2
Skin	Vesicular lesions above the waist	Vesicular lesions below the waist (especially genitals)
Mouth	Gingivostomatitis	Rare
Eye	Keratoconjunctivitis	Rare
Central nervous system	Encephalitis (temporal lobe)	Meningitis
Neonate	Rare	Skin lesions and disseminated infection
Dissemination to viscera in immunocompromised patients	Yes	Rare

require the synthesis of new viral regulatory proteins to activate the transcription of their mRNAs.

The viral DNA polymerase replicates the genome DNA, at which time early protein synthesis is shut off and late protein synthesis begins. These late structural proteins are transported to the nucleus, where virion assembly occurs. The virion obtains its envelope by budding through the nuclear membrane and exits the cell via tubules or vacuoles that communicate with the exterior. In latently infected cells, multiple copies of HSV-1 DNA are found in the cytoplasm of infected neurons. Only a few genes are transcribed, and none are translated into protein.

Transmission & Epidemiology

HSV-1 is transmitted primarily in **saliva,** whereas HSV-2 is transmitted by **sexual contact.** As a result, HSV-1 infections occur mainly on the face, whereas HSV-2 lesions occur in the genital area. However, oral-genital sexual practices can result in HSV-1 infections of the genitals and HSV-2 lesions in the oral cavity (this occurs in about 10–20% of cases). Although transmission occurs most often when active lesions are present, asymptomatic shedding of both HSV-1 and HSV-2 does occur and plays an important role in transmission.

The number of HSV-2 infections has markedly increased in recent years, whereas that of HSV-1 infections has not. Roughly 80% of people in the United States are infected with HSV-1, and 40% have recurrent herpes labialis. Most primary infections by HSV-1 occur in childhood, as evidenced by the early appearance of antibody. In contrast, antibody to HSV-2 does not appear until the age of sexual activity.

Pathogenesis & Immunity

The virus replicates in the skin or mucous membrane at the initial site of infection, then migrates up the neu-

ron and becomes **latent in the sensory ganglion cells.** In general, HSV-1 becomes latent in the **trigeminal ganglia,** whereas HSV-2 becomes latent in the **lumbar and sacral ganglia.** During latency, most—if not all—viral DNA is located in the cytoplasm rather than integrated into nuclear DNA. The virus can be reactivated from the latent state by a variety of inducers, eg, sunlight, hormonal changes, trauma, stress, and fever, at which time it migrates down the neuron and replicates in the skin, causing lesions.

The typical skin lesion is a **vesicle** that contains serous fluid filled with virus particles and cell debris. When the vesicle ruptures, virus is liberated and can be transmitted to other individuals. **Multinucleated giant cells** are typically found at the base of herpesvirus lesions.

Immunity is type-specific, but some cross-protection exists. However, immunity is incomplete, and both reinfection and reactivation occur in the presence of circulating IgG. **Cell-mediated immunity** is important in limiting herpesviruses, because its suppression often results in reactivation, spread, and severe disease.

Clinical Findings

HSV-1 causes several forms of primary and recurrent disease:

(1) **Gingivostomatitis** occurs primarily in children and is characterized by fever, irritability, and vesicular lesions in the mouth. The primary disease is more severe and lasts longer than recurrences. The lesions heal spontaneously in 2–3 weeks. Many children have asymptomatic primary infections.

(2) **Herpes labialis** (fever blisters or cold sores) is the milder, recurrent form and is characterized by crops of vesicles, usually at the mucocutaneous junction of the lips or nose. Recurrences frequently reappear at the same site.

(3) **Keratoconjunctivitis** is characterized by corneal ulcers and lesions of the conjunctival epithelium. Recurrences can lead to scarring and blindness.

(4) **Encephalitis** caused by HSV-1 is characterized by a necrotic lesion in one temporal lobe. Fever, headache, vomiting, seizures, and altered mental status are typical clinical features. The onset may be acute or protracted over several days. The disease occurs as a result of either a primary infection or a recurrence. MRI imaging often reveals the lesion. Examination of the spinal fluid typically shows a moderate increase of lymphocytes, a moderate elevation in the amount of protein, and a normal amount of glucose. HSV-1 encephalitis has a high mortality rate and causes severe neurologic sequelae in those who survive.

(5) **Herpetic whitlow** is a pustular lesion of the skin of the finger or hand. It can occur in medical personnel as a result of contact with patient's lesions.

(6) Disseminated infections, such as esophagitis and pneumonia, occur in immunocompromised patients with depressed T-cell function.

HSV-2 causes several diseases, both primary and recurrent:

(1) **Genital herpes** is characterized by painful vesicular lesions of the male and female genitals and anal area. The lesions are more severe and protracted in primary disease than in recurrences. Primary infections are associated with fever and inguinal adenopathy. Asymptomatic infections occur in both men (in the prostate or urethra) and women (in the cervix) and can be a source of infection of other individuals. Many infections are asymptomatic; ie, many people have antibody to HSV-2 but have no history of disease.

(2) **Neonatal herpes** originates chiefly from contact with vesicular lesions within the birth canal. In some cases, although there are no visible lesions, HSV-2 is being shed (asymptomatic shedding) and can infect the child during birth. Neonatal herpes varies from severe disease (eg, disseminated lesions or encephalitis) to milder local lesions (skin, eye, mouth) to asymptomatic infection. Neonatal disease may be prevented by performing cesarean section on women with either active lesions or positive viral cultures. Both HSV-1 and HSV-2 can cause severe neonatal infections that are acquired after birth from carriers handling the child. Despite their association with neonatal infections, neither HSV-1 nor HSV-2 causes congenital abnormalities to any significant degree.

Serious neonatal infection is more likely to occur when the mother is experiencing a primary herpes infection than a recurrent infection for two reasons: (1) the amount of virus produced during a primary infection is greater than during a secondary infection, and (2) mothers who have been previously infected can pass IgG across the placenta, which can protect the neonate from serious disseminated infection.

(3) Aseptic meningitis caused by HSV-2 is usually a mild, self-limited disease with few sequelae.

Laboratory Diagnosis

The most important diagnostic procedure is isolation of the virus from the lesion by growth in cell culture. The typical cytopathic effect occurs in 1–3 days, after which the virus is identified by fluorescent-antibody staining of the infected cells or by detecting virus-specific glycoproteins in enzyme-linked immunosorbent assays (ELISAs). A rapid diagnosis from skin lesions can be made by using the **Tzanck smear,** in which cells from the base of the vesicle are stained with Giemsa stain. The presence of multinucleated giant cells suggests herpesvirus infection. A rapid diagnosis of encephalitis can be made by detecting HSV-1 DNA in the spinal fluid using a PCR assay, but virus is rarely recovered from the spinal fluid. The diagnosis of neonatal herpes infection typically involves the use of viral cultures or PCR assay.

Serologic tests such as the neutralization test can be used in the diagnosis of primary infections because a significant rise in antibody titer is readily observed. However, they are of no use in the diagnosis of recurrent infections because many adults already have circulating antibodies and recurrences rarely cause a rise in antibody titer.

Treatment

Acyclovir (acycloguanosine, Zovirax) is the treatment of choice for encephalitis and systemic disease caused by HSV-1. It is also useful for the treatment for primary and recurrent genital herpes; it **shortens the duration** of the lesions and **reduces the extent of shedding** of the virus. Acyclovir is also used to treat neonatal infections caused by HSV-2. Mutants of HSV-1 resistant to acyclovir have been isolated from patients; foscarnet can be used in these cases. For HSV-1 eye infections, other nucleoside analogues, eg, trifluridine (Viroptic), are used topically. Penciclovir (a derivative of acyclovir) or docosanol (a long-chain saturated alcohol) can be used to treat recurrences of orolabial HSV-1 infections in immunocompetent adults. Valacyclovir (Valtrex) and famciclovir (Famvir) are used in the treatment of genital herpes and in the suppression of recurrences. Note that no drug treatment of the primary infection prevents recurrences; drugs have **no effect on the latent state,** but prophylactic, long-term administration of acyclovir, valacyclovir, or famciclovir can suppress clinical recurrences.

Prevention

Prevention involves avoiding contact with the vesicular lesion or ulcer. Cesarean section is recommended for women who are at term and who have genital lesions or positive viral cultures.

VARICELLA-ZOSTER VIRUS (VZV)

Disease

Varicella (chickenpox) is the primary disease; zoster (shingles) is the recurrent form.

Important Properties

VZV is structurally and morphologically identical to other herpesviruses but is antigenically different. It has a single serotype. The same virus causes both varicella and zoster. Humans are the natural hosts.

Summary of Replicative Cycle

The cycle is similar to that of HSV (see page 251).

Transmission & Epidemiology

The virus is transmitted by **respiratory droplets** and by direct contact with the lesions. Varicella is a highly contagious disease of childhood; more than 90% of people in the United States have antibody by age 10 years. Varicella occurs worldwide. Prior to 2001, there were more cases of chickenpox than any other notifiable disease, but the widespread use of the vaccine has significantly reduced the number of cases.

There is infectious VZV in zoster vesicles. This virus can be transmitted, usually by direct contact, to children and can cause varicella. The appearance of either varicella or zoster in a hospital is a major infection control problem because the virus can be transmitted to immunocompromised patients and cause life-threatening disseminated infection.

Pathogenesis & Immunity

VZV infects the mucosa of the upper respiratory tract, then spreads via the blood to the skin, where the typical **vesicular rash** occurs. **Multinucleated giant cells** with intranuclear inclusions are seen in the base of the lesions. After the host has recovered, the virus becomes **latent,** probably in the **dorsal root ganglia.** During latency, most—if not all—viral DNA is located in the cytoplasm rather than integrated into nuclear DNA. Later in life, frequently at times of reduced cell-mediated immunity or local trauma, the virus is activated and causes the vesicular skin lesions and **nerve pain** of zoster.

Immunity following varicella is lifelong: a person gets varicella only once, but zoster can occur despite this immunity to varicella. Zoster usually occurs only once. The frequency of zoster increases with advancing age, perhaps as a consequence of waning immunity.

Clinical Findings

A. Varicella

After an incubation period of 14–21 days, brief prodromal symptoms of fever and malaise occur. A papulovesicular rash then appears in crops on the trunk and spreads to the head and extremities. The rash evolves from papules to vesicles, pustules, and, finally, crusts. Itching (pruritus) is a prominent symptom, especially when vesicles are present. Varicella is mild in children but more severe in adults. Varicella pneumonia and encephalitis are the major rare complications, occurring more often in adults. **Reye's syndrome,** characterized by encephalopathy and liver degeneration, is associated with VZV and influenza B virus infection, especially in children given aspirin. Its pathogenesis is unknown.

B. Zoster

The occurrence of painful vesicles along the course of a sensory nerve of the head or trunk is the usual picture. The pain can last for weeks, and postzoster neuralgia can be debilitating. In immunocompromised patients, life-threatening disseminated infections such as pneumonia can occur.

Laboratory Diagnosis

Although most diagnoses are made clinically, laboratory tests are available. A presumptive diagnosis can be made by using the Tzanck smear. Multinucleated giant cells are seen in VZV as well as HSV lesions. The definitive diagnosis is made by isolation of the virus in cell culture and identification with specific antiserum. A rise in antibody titer can be used to diagnose varicella but is less useful in the diagnosis of zoster, since antibody is already present.

Treatment

No antiviral therapy is necessary for chickenpox or zoster in immunocompetent children. Immunocompetent adults with either moderate or severe cases of chickenpox or zoster often are treated with acyclovir because it can reduce the duration and severity of symptoms. Immunocompromised children and adults with chickenpox, zoster, or disseminated disease should be treated with acyclovir. Disease caused by acyclovir-resistant strains of VZV can be treated with foscarnet. Two drugs similar to acyclovir, famciclovir (Famvir) and valacyclovir (Valtrex), can be used in patients with zoster to accelerate healing of the lesions, but none of these drugs can cure the latent state and none have any effect on postzoster neuralgia.

Prevention

The main mode of prevention is the vaccine that contains **live, attenuated** VZV (Varivax), which was approved by the FDA in 1995. The vaccine is very effective in preventing varicella in children and zoster in adults. The vaccine does not eliminate the virus, which remains in the latent state. One dose is recommended for children 1–12 years of age. Teenagers and adults who have not had the disease should receive two doses. Because it is a live vaccine, it should not be given to immunocompromised people or to pregnant women.

Acyclovir is useful in preventing varicella and disseminated zoster in immunocompromised people exposed to the virus. **Varicella-zoster immune globulin** (VZIG), which contains a high titer of antibody to the virus, is also used for such prophylaxis.

CYTOMEGALOVIRUS (CMV)

Diseases

CMV causes cytomegalic inclusion disease (especially congenital abnormalities) in neonates. It is the **most common cause of congenital abnormalities** in the United States. It also causes pneumonia and other diseases in immunocompromised patients and heterophil-negative mononucleosis in immunocompetent individuals.

Important Properties

CMV is structurally and morphologically identical to other herpesviruses but is antigenically different. It has a single serotype. Humans are the natural hosts; animal CMV strains do not infect humans. Giant cells are formed, hence the name "cytomegalo."

Summary of Replicative Cycle

The cycle is similar to that of HSV (see page 251). One unique feature of CMV replication is that some of its "immediate early proteins" are translated from mRNAs brought into the infected cell by the parental virion rather than being translated from mRNAs synthesized in the newly infected cell.

Transmission & Epidemiology

CMV is transmitted by a **variety of modes.** Early in life it is transmitted across the placenta, within the birth canal, and quite commonly in breast milk. In young children, its most common mode of transmission is via saliva. Later in life it is transmitted sexually; it is present in both semen and cervical secretions. It can also be transmitted during blood transfusions and organ transplants. CMV infection occurs worldwide, and more than 80% of adults have antibody against this virus.

Pathogenesis & Immunity

Infection of the fetus can cause **cytomegalic inclusion disease,** characterized by multinucleated giant cells with prominent intranuclear inclusions. Many organs are affected, and widespread congenital abnormalities result. Infection of the fetus occurs mainly when a **primary infection** occurs in the pregnant woman, ie, when she has no antibodies that will neutralize the virus before it can infect the fetus. The fetus usually will not be infected if the pregnant woman has antibodies against the virus. Congenital abnormalities are **more common when a fetus is infected during the first trimester** than later in gestation, because the first trimester is when development of organs occurs and the death of any precursor cells can result in congenital defects.

Infections of children and adults are usually asymptomatic, except in immunocompromised individuals. CMV enters a **latent** state in leukocytes and can be reactivated when cell-mediated immunity is decreased. CMV can also persist in kidneys for years. Reactivation of CMV from the latent state in cervical cells can result in infection of the newborn during passage through the birth canal.

CMV has a specific mechanism of "immune evasion" that allows it to maintain the latent state for long periods. In CMV-infected cells, assembly of the MHC class I–viral peptide complex is unstable, so viral antigens are not displayed on the cell surface and killing by cytotoxic T cells does not occur.

CMV infection causes an immunosuppressive effect by inhibiting T cells. Host defenses against CMV infection include both circulating antibody and cell-mediated immunity. Cellular immunity is more important, because its suppression can lead to systemic disease.

Clinical Findings

Approximately 20% of infants infected with CMV during gestation show clinically apparent manifestations of cytomegalic inclusion disease such as microcephaly, seizures, deafness, jaundice, and purpura. Hepatosplenomegaly is very common. Cytomegalic inclusion disease is one of the leading causes of mental retardation in the United States. Infected infants can continue to excrete CMV, especially in the urine, for several years.

In immunocompetent adults, CMV can cause **heterophil-negative mononucleosis,** which is characterized by fever, lethargy, and the presence of abnormal lymphocytes in peripheral blood smears. Systemic CMV infections, especially pneumonitis and hepatitis, occur in a high proportion of immunosuppressed patients, eg, those with renal and bone marrow transplants. In AIDS patients, CMV commonly infects the intestinal tract and causes intractable diarrhea. CMV also causes retinitis in AIDS patients, which can lead to blindness.

Laboratory Diagnosis

The preferred approach involves culturing in special tubes called **shell vials** coupled with the use of immunofluorescent antibody, which can make a diagnosis in 72 hours. If available, polymerase chain reaction (PCR)-based assays that detect viral nucleic acids are also useful. Other diagnostic methods include fluorescent-antibody and histologic staining of inclusion bodies in giant cells in urine and in tissue. The inclusion bodies are intranuclear and have an oval **owl's-eye** shape. A 4-fold or greater rise in antibody titer is also diagnostic. PCR-based assays for CMV DNA or RNA in tissue or body fluids, such as spinal fluid, and amniotic fluid are also very useful.

CMV antigenemia can be measured by detecting pp65 within blood leukocytes using an immunofluorescence assay. pp65 is a protein located in the nucleocapsid of CMV and can be identified within infected leukocytes using fluorescein-labeled monoclonal antibody specific for pp65.

Treatment

Ganciclovir (Cytovene) is moderately effective in the treatment of CMV retinitis and pneumonia in patients with AIDS. Valganciclovir, which can be taken orally, is also effective against CMV retinitis. Foscarnet (Foscavir) is also effective but causes more side effects. Unlike HSV and VZV, CMV is largely resistant to acyclovir. Cidofovir (Vistide) is also useful in the treatment of CMV retinitis. Fomivirsen (Vitravene) is an antisense DNA approved for the intraocular treatment of CMV retinitis. It is the first and, at present, the only antisense molecule to be approved for the treatment of human disease.

Prevention

There is no vaccine. Ganciclovir can suppress progressive retinitis in AIDS patients. Infants with cytomegalic inclusion disease who are shedding virus in their urine should be kept isolated from other infants. Blood for transfusion to newborns should be CMV antibody-negative. If possible, only organs from CMV antibody-negative donors should be transplanted to antibody-negative recipients. A high-titer immune globulin preparation (CytoGam) is used to prevent disseminated CMV infections in organ transplant patients.

EPSTEIN-BARR VIRUS (EBV)

Diseases

EBV causes infectious mononucleosis. It is associated with Burkitt's lymphoma, other B-cell lymphomas, and nasopharyngeal carcinoma. EBV is also associated with hairy leukoplakia, a whitish, nonmalignant lesion on the tongue seen especially in AIDS patients.

Important Properties

EBV is structurally and morphologically identical to other herpesviruses but is antigenically different. The most important antigen is the **viral capsid antigen** (VCA), because it is used most often in diagnostic tests. The early antigens (EA), which are produced prior to viral DNA synthesis, and nuclear antigen (EBNA), which is located in the nucleus bound to chromosomes, are sometimes diagnostically helpful as well. Two other antigens, lymphocyte-determined membrane antigen and viral membrane antigen, have been detected also. Neutralizing activity is directed against the viral membrane antigen.

Humans are the natural hosts. EBV infects mainly lymphoid cells, primarily **B lymphocytes.** In latently infected cells, multiple copies of EBV DNA are found in the cytoplasm of infected B lymphocytes. Some, but not all, genes are transcribed, and only a subset of those are translated into protein.

Summary of Replicative Cycle

The cycle is similar to that of HSV (see page 251). EBV enters B lymphocytes at the site of the receptor for the C3 component of complement.

Transmission & Epidemiology

EBV is transmitted primarily by the exchange of **saliva,** eg, during kissing. The saliva of people with a reactivation of a latent infection as well as people with an active infection can serve as a source of the virus. In contrast to CMV, blood transmission of EBV is very rare.

EBV infection is one of the most common infections worldwide; more than 90% of adults in the United States have antibody. Infection in the first few years of life is usually asymptomatic. Early infection tends to occur in individuals in lower socioeconomic groups. The frequency of clinically apparent infectious mononucleosis, however, is highest in those who are exposed to the virus later in life, eg, college students.

Pathogenesis & Immunity

The infection first occurs in the oropharynx and then spreads to the blood, where it infects B lymphocytes. Cytotoxic T lymphocytes react against the infected B cells. The T cells are the "atypical lymphs" seen in the blood smear. EBV remains **latent within B lymphocytes.** A few copies of EBV DNA are integrated into the cell genome; many copies of circular EBV DNA are found in the cytoplasm.

The immune response to EBV infection consists first of IgM antibody to the VCA. IgG antibody to the VCA follows and persists for life. The IgM response is therefore useful for diagnosing acute infection, whereas the IgG response is best for revealing prior infection. Lifetime immunity against second episodes of infectious mononucleosis is based on antibody to the viral membrane antigen.

In addition to the EBV-specific antibodies, nonspecific **heterophil antibodies** are found. The term "heterophil" refers to antibodies that are detected by tests using antigens different from the antigens that induced them. The heterophil antibodies formed in infectious mononucleosis agglutinate sheep or horse red blood cells in the laboratory. (Cross-reacting Forssman antibodies in human serum are removed by adsorption with guinea pig kidney extract prior to agglutination.) Note that these antibodies do not react with any component of EBV. It seems likely that EBV infection modifies a cell membrane constituent such that it becomes antigenic and induces the heterophil antibody. Heterophil antibodies usually disappear within 6 months after recovery. These antibodies are not specific for EBV infection and are also seen in individuals with hepatitis B and serum sickness.

Clinical Findings

Infectious mononucleosis is characterized primarily by fever, sore throat, lymphadenopathy, and splenomegaly. Anorexia and lethargy are prominent. Hepatitis is frequent; encephalitis occurs in some patients. Spontaneous recovery usually occurs in 2–3 weeks. Splenic rupture, associated with contact sports such as football, is a feared but rare complication of the splenomegaly.

In addition to infectious mononucleosis, EBV causes two other diseases. One is a severe, often fatal, progressive form of infectious mononucleosis that occurs in children with an inherited immunodeficiency called X-linked lymphoproliferative syndrome. The mutated gene encodes a signal transduction protein required for both T-cell and NK-cell function. The mortality rate is 75% by age 10. Bone marrow or cord blood transplants may cure the underlying immunodeficiency. The other disease is hairy leukoplakia, a whitish lesion on the tongue of AIDS patients.

Laboratory Diagnosis

The diagnosis of infectious mononucleosis in the clinical laboratory is based primarily on two approaches:

(1) In the **hematologic** approach, absolute lymphocytosis occurs and as many as 30% abnormal lymphocytes are seen on a smear. These **atypical lymphs** are large and have a lobulated nucleus and a vacuolated, basophilic cytoplasm. They are cytotoxic T cells that are reacting against the EBV-infected B cells.

(2) In the **immunologic** approach, there are two types of serologic tests. (a) The **heterophil antibody** test is useful for the early diagnosis of infectious mononucleosis because it is usually positive by week 2 of illness. However, because the antibody titer declines after recovery, it is not useful for detection of prior infection. The Monospot test is often used to detect the heterophil antibody; it is more sensitive, more specific, and less expensive than the tube agglutination test. (b) The **EBV-specific antibody tests** are used primarily in diagnostically difficult cases. The IgM VCA antibody response can be used to detect early illness; the IgG VCA antibody response can be used to detect prior infection. In certain instances, antibodies to EA and EBNA can be useful diagnostically.

Although EBV can be isolated from clinical samples such as saliva by morphologic transformation of cord blood lymphocytes, it is a technically difficult procedure and is not readily available. No virus is synthesized in the cord lymphocytes; its presence is detected by fluorescent-antibody staining of the nuclear antigen.

Treatment

No antiviral therapy is necessary for uncomplicated infectious mononucleosis. Acyclovir has little activity against EBV, but administration of high doses may be useful in life-threatening EBV infections.

Prevention

There is no EBV vaccine.

Association With Cancer

EBV infection is associated with cancers of lymphoid origin: **Burkitt's lymphoma** in African children, other B-cell lymphomas, nasopharyngeal carcinoma in the Chinese population, and thymic carcinoma in the United States. The initial evidence of an association of EBV infection with Burkitt's lymphoma was the production of EBV by the lymphoma cells in culture. In fact, this was how EBV was discovered by Epstein and Barr in 1964. Additional evidence includes the finding of EBV DNA and EBNA in the tumor cells. EBV DNA and antigens are found in nasopharyngeal and thymic carcinoma cells also. EBV can induce malignant transformation in B lymphocytes in vitro. The role of EBV in carcinogenesis is unclear.

HUMAN HERPESVIRUS 8 (KAPOSI'S SARCOMA–ASSOCIATED HERPESVIRUS)

In 1994, it was reported that a new herpesvirus, now known as HHV-8, or Kaposi's sarcoma–associated herpesvirus (KSHV), may be the cause of Kaposi's sarcoma (KS), the most common cancer in patients with AIDS. The idea that a virus other than HIV is the cause of KS arose from epidemiologic data that showed that KS was common in patients who acquired HIV sexually but rare in patients who acquired HIV via blood transfusion. A second virus transmitted sexually appeared likely to be the cause.

The initial evidence that HHV-8 was involved was the finding that most KS cells taken from AIDS patients contain the DNA of this virus, but tissues taken from AIDS patients without KS had very little viral DNA. The DNA of this virus was also found in KS cells that arose in non–HIV-infected patients. On DNA analysis, HHV-8 resembles the lymphotropic herpesviruses, eg, Epstein-Barr virus and herpesvirus saimiri, more than it does the neurotropic herpesviruses, such as herpes simplex virus and varicella-zoster virus.

Additional support was provided by serologic studies showing that most HIV-infected patients with KS had antibodies to HHV-8, whereas considerably fewer HIV-infected patients without KS had antibodies to the virus and very few patients with other sexually transmitted diseases, but who were not HIV-infected, had these antibodies. The current estimate of HHV-8 infection in the general population ranges from about 3% in the United States and England to about 50% in East Africa.

HHV-8 causes malignant transformation by a mechanism similar to that of other DNA viruses (such as human papillomavirus), namely, inactivation of a tumor suppressor gene. A protein encoded by HHV-8 called nuclear antigen inactivates the RB (retinoblastoma) tumor suppressor protein, which causes the cells to grow in an uncontrolled manner.

Transmission of HHV-8 is primarily sexually, but it is also transmitted in transplanted organs such as kidneys and appears to be the cause of transplantation-associated KS. The DNA of HHV-8 is found in the cells of transplantation-associated KS but not in the cells of other transplantation-associated cancers.

KS in AIDS patients is a malignancy of vascular endothelial cells that contains many spindle-shaped cells and erythrocytes. The lesions are dark purple, flat to nodular, and often appear at multiple sites such as the skin, oral cavity, and soles (but not the palms). Internally, lesions occur commonly in the gastrointestinal tract and the lungs. The extravasated red cells give the lesions their purplish color. HHV-8 also infects B cells, inducing them to proliferate and produce a type of lymphoma called primary effusion lymphoma.

Laboratory diagnosis of KS is often made by biopsy of the skin lesions. HHV-8 DNA and RNA are present in most spindle cells, but that analysis is not usually done. Virus is not grown in culture.

The type of treatment depends upon the site and number of the lesions. Surgical excision, radiation, and systemic drugs, such as alpha interferon or vinblastine, can be used. There is no specific antiviral therapy and no vaccine against HHV-8.

POXVIRUSES

The poxvirus family includes three viruses of medical importance: smallpox virus, vaccinia virus, and molluscum contagiosum virus (MCV). Poxviruses are the largest and most complex viruses.

SMALLPOX VIRUS

Disease

Smallpox virus, also called variola virus, is the agent of smallpox, the only disease that has been eradicated from the face of the Earth. **Eradication is due to the vaccine.** There is concern regarding the use of smallpox virus as an agent of bioterrorism. Pox viruses of animal origin, such as cowpox and monkey pox, are described in Chapter 46.

Important Properties

Poxviruses are brick-shaped particles containing linear double-stranded DNA, a disk-shaped core within a double membrane, and a lipoprotein envelope. The virion contains a DNA-dependent RNA polymerase. This enzyme is required because the virus replicates in the cytoplasm and does not have access to the cellular RNA polymerase, which is located in the nucleus.

Smallpox virus has a single, stable serotype, which is the key to the success of the vaccine. If the antigenicity varied as it does in influenza virus, eradication would not have succeeded. Smallpox virus infects only humans; there is no animal reservoir.

Summary of Replicative Cycle

Vaccinia virus, a poxvirus virtually nonpathogenic for humans, is used for studies on poxvirus replication and as a vector in certain gene therapy experiments. After penetration of the cell and uncoating, the virion DNA-dependent RNA polymerase synthesizes early mRNA, which is translated into early, nonstructural proteins, mainly enzymes required for subsequent steps in viral replication. The viral DNA then is replicated, after which late, structural proteins are synthesized that will form the progeny virions. The virions are assembled and acquire their envelopes by budding from the cell membrane as they are released from the cell. Note that all steps in replication occur in the cytoplasm, which is unusual for a DNA virus.

Transmission & Epidemiology

Smallpox virus is transmitted via respiratory aerosol or by direct contact with virus either in the skin lesions or on fomites such as bedding.

Prior to the 1960s, smallpox was widespread throughout large areas of Africa, Asia, and South America, and millions of people were affected. In 1967, the World Health Organization embarked on a vaccination campaign that led to the eradication of smallpox. The last naturally occurring case was in Somalia in 1977.

Pathogenesis & Immunity

Smallpox begins when the virus infects the upper respiratory tract and local lymph nodes and then enters the blood (primary viremia). Internal organs are infected; then the virus reenters the blood (secondary viremia) and spreads to the skin. These events occur during the incubation period, when the patient is still well. The rash is the result of virus replication in the skin, followed by damage caused by cytotoxic T cells attacking virus-infected cells.

Immunity following smallpox disease is lifelong; immunity following vaccination lasts about 10 years.

Clinical Findings

After an incubation period of 7–14 days, there is a sudden onset of prodromal symptoms such as fever and malaise. This is followed by the rash, which is worse on the face and extremities than on the trunk (ie, it has a centrifugal distribution). The rash evolves through stages from macules to papules, vesicles, pustules, and, finally, crusts in 2–3 weeks.

Laboratory Diagnosis

In the past when the disease occurred, the diagnosis was made either by growing the virus in cell culture or chick embryos or by detecting viral antigens in vesicular fluid by immunofluorescence.

Prevention

The disease was eradicated by global use of the **vaccine**, which contains live, attenuated **vaccinia virus**. The success of the vaccine is dependent upon five critical factors: (1) smallpox virus has a single, stable serotype; (2) there is no animal reservoir, and humans are the only hosts; (3) the antibody response is prompt; therefore, exposed persons can be protected; (4) the disease is easily recognized clinically; therefore, exposed persons can be immunized promptly; and (5) there is no carrier state or subclinical infection.

The vaccine is inoculated intradermally, where virus replication occurs. The formation of a vesicle is indicative of a "take" (success). Although the vaccine was relatively safe, it became apparent in the 1970s that the incidence of side effects such as encephalitis, generalized vaccinia, and vaccinia gangrenosa exceeded the incidence of smallpox. Routine vaccination of civilians was discontinued, and it is no longer a prerequisite for international travel. Military personnel are still vaccinated.

In response to the possibility of a bioterrorism attack using smallpox virus, the U.S. federal government has instituted a program to vaccinate "first responders" so that they can give emergency medical care without fear of contracting the disease. To protect the unimmunized general population, the concept of "ring vaccination" will be used. This is based on the knowledge that **an exposed individual can be immunized as long as 4 days after exposure and be protected.** Therefore, if an attack occurs, people known to be exposed will be immunized as well as the direct contacts of those people and then the contacts of the contacts, in an expanding ring. Several military personnel and civilians have experienced myocarditis following vaccination and, as of this writing, caution has been urged regarding expanding this program to the general population.

Vaccinia immune globulins (VIG), containing high-titer antibodies against vaccinia virus, can be used to treat most of the complications of vaccination. In the past, methisazone was used to treat the complications of vaccination and could be useful again. Rifampin inhibits viral DNA-dependent RNA polymerase but was not used clinically against smallpox.

MOLLUSCUM CONTAGIOSUM VIRUS

Molluscum contagiosum virus (MCV) is a member of the poxvirus family but is quite distinct from smallpox and vaccinia viruses. It causes small, pink, papular, wartlike benign tumors of the skin or mucous membranes. The lesions have a characteristic cup-shaped crater with a white core. Note that these lesions are different from warts, which are caused by papillomavirus, a member of the papovavirus family.

MCV is transmitted by close personal contact, including sexually. The disease is quite common in children, and the lesions can be widespread in patients with reduced cellular immunity. In immunocompetent patients, the lesions are self-limited but may last for months. The diagnosis is typically made clinically; the virus is not isolated in the clinical laboratory, and antibody titers are not helpful. Removal of the lesions by curettage or with liquid nitrogen is often effective. There is no established antiviral therapy, but cidofovir may be useful in the treatment of the extensive lesions that occur in immunocompromised patients. There is no vaccine.

■ HEPATITIS B VIRUS

Hepatitis B virus, a DNA-enveloped virus, is described in Chapter 41 with the other hepatitis viruses.

SUMMARIES OF ORGANISMS

Brief summaries of the organisms described in this chapter begin on page 493. Please consult these summaries for a rapid review of the essential material.

PRACTICE QUESTIONS: USMLE & COURSE EXAMINATIONS

Questions on the topics discussed in this chapter can be found in the Clinical Virology section of Part XI: USMLE (National Board) Practice Questions starting on page 549. Also see Part XII: USMLE (National Board) Practice Examination starting on page 583.

DNA Nonenveloped Viruses

ADENOVIRUSES

Diseases

Adenoviruses cause a variety of upper and lower respiratory tract diseases such as pharyngitis, conjunctivitis, the common cold, and pneumonia. Keratoconjunctivitis, hemorrhagic cystitis, and gastroenteritis also occur. Some adenoviruses cause sarcomas in rodents. Table 38–1 describes some of the important clinical features of adenoviruses and compares them with features of the other two medically important viruses in this chapter, human papillomavirus (HPV) and parvovirus B19.

Important Properties

Adenoviruses are **nonenveloped** viruses with double-stranded linear DNA and an **icosahedral** nucleocapsid. They are the only viruses with a **fiber** protruding from each of the 12 vertices of the capsid. The fiber is the organ of attachment and is a hemagglutinin. When purified free of virions, the fiber is toxic to human cells.

There are 41 known antigenic types; the fiber protein is the main type-specific antigen. All adenoviruses have a common group-specific antigen located on the hexon protein.

Certain serotypes of human adenoviruses (especially 12, 18, and 31) cause **sarcomas** at the site of injection in laboratory rodents such as newborn hamsters. There is no evidence that adenoviruses cause tumors in humans.

Summary of Replicative Cycle

After attachment to the cell surface via its fiber, the virus penetrates and uncoats, and the viral DNA moves to the nucleus. Host cell DNA-dependent RNA polymerase transcribes the early genes, and splicing enzymes remove the RNA representing the introns, resulting in functional mRNA. (Note that introns and exons, which are common in eukaryotic DNA, were first described for adenovirus DNA.) Early mRNA is translated into nonstructural proteins in the cytoplasm. After viral DNA replication in the nucleus, late mRNA is transcribed and then translated into structural virion proteins. Viral assembly occurs in the nucleus, and the virus is released by lysis of the cell, not by budding.

Transmission & Epidemiology

Adenoviruses are transmitted by several mechanisms: **aerosol** droplet, the **fecal-oral** route, and **direct inoculation** of conjunctivas by tonometers or fingers. The fecal-oral route is the most common mode of transmission among young children and their families. Many species of animals are infected by strains of adenovirus, but these strains are not pathogenic for humans.

Adenovirus infections are endemic worldwide, but outbreaks occur among military recruits, apparently as a result of the close living conditions that facilitate transmission. Certain serotypes are associated with specific syndromes; eg, types 3, 4, 7, and 21 cause respiratory disease, especially in military recruits; types 8 and 19 cause epidemic keratoconjunctivitis; types 11 and 21 cause hemorrhagic cystitis; and types 40 and 41 cause infantile gastroenteritis.

Pathogenesis & Immunity

Adenoviruses infect the mucosal epithelium of several organs, eg, the **respiratory tract** (both upper and lower), the **gastrointestinal tract,** and the **conjunctivas.** Immunity based on neutralizing antibody is type-specific and lifelong.

In addition to acute infection leading to death of the cells, adenoviruses cause a latent infection, particularly in the adenoidal and tonsillar tissues of the throat. In fact, these viruses were named for the adenoids, from which they were first isolated in 1953.

Clinical Findings

In the upper respiratory tract, adenoviruses cause such infections as pharyngitis, pharyngoconjunctival fever, and acute respiratory disease, characterized by fever, sore throat, coryza (runny nose), and conjunctivitis. In the lower respiratory tract, they cause bronchitis and atypical pneumonia. Hematuria and dysuria are prominent in hemorrhagic cystitis. Gastroenteritis with nonbloody diarrhea occurs mainly in children younger than 2 years of age. Most adenovirus infections resolve spontaneously. Approximately half of all adenovirus infections are asymptomatic.

Table 38–1. Clinical features of DNA nonenveloped viruses.

Virus	Mode of Transmission	Types Cause Different Diseases	Certain Types Cause Cancer	Vaccine Available
Adenovirus	Respiratory; fecal-oral	Yes	Yes, in animals but not humans	Yes, but used only in military
Human papillomavirus	Sexual; skin contact	Yes	Yes, in humans	No
Parvovirus B19	Respiratory; transplacental	No	No	No

Laboratory Diagnosis

The most frequent methods of diagnosis are isolation of the virus in cell culture and detection of a 4-fold or greater rise in antibody titer. Complement fixation and hemagglutination inhibition are the most important serologic tests.

Treatment

There is no antiviral therapy.

Prevention

Three live, nonattenuated vaccines against serotypes 4, 7, and 21 are available but are used only by the military. Each of the three vaccines is monovalent; ie, each contains only one serotype. The viruses are administered separately because they interfere with each other when given together. The vaccines are delivered in an enteric-coated capsule, which protects the live virus from inactivation by stomach acid. The virus infects the gastrointestinal tract, where it causes an asymptomatic infection and induces immunity to respiratory disease. This vaccine is not available for civilian use.

Epidemic keratoconjunctivitis is an iatrogenic disease, preventable by strict asepsis and hand washing by health care personnel who examine eyes.

PAPILLOMAVIRUSES

Diseases

Human papillomavirus (HPV) causes papillomas, which are benign tumors of squamous cells, eg, warts on the skin. Some HPVs, eg, HPV-16, are implicated as the cause of carcinomas, especially **carcinoma of the cervix**.

Important Properties

Papillomaviruses are nonenveloped viruses with double-stranded circular DNA and an icosahedral nucleocapsid. They are members of the papovavirus family. They are similar to polyomavirus and SV40 virus (see Chapter 43) but are larger, have a larger genome, and are antigenically distinct. Two of the early genes, E6 and E7, are implicated in carcinogenesis. They encode proteins that inactivate proteins encoded by tumor suppressor genes in human cells, eg, the p53 gene and the retinoblastoma (RB) gene, respectively. Inactivation of the p53 and RB proteins is an important step in the process by which a normal cell becomes a cancer cell.

There are at least 100 types of papillomaviruses, classified primarily on the basis of DNA restriction fragment analysis. There is a pronounced **predilection of certain types to infect certain tissues**. For example, skin warts are caused primarily by HPV-1 through HPV-4, whereas genital warts are usually caused by HPV-6 and HPV-11. Approximately 30 types of HPV infect the genital tract.

Summary of Replicative Cycle

Little is known of the specifics of viral replication, because the virus grows poorly, if at all, in cell culture. In human tissue, infectious virus particles are found in the terminally differentiated squamous cells rather than in the basal cells. In malignant cells, viral DNA is integrated into host cell DNA in the vicinity of cellular proto-oncogenes, and E6 and E7 are overexpressed. However, in latently infected, nonmalignant cells, the viral DNA is episomal and E6 and E7 are not overexpressed. This difference occurs because another early gene, E2, controls E6 and E7 expression. The E2 gene is functional when the viral DNA is episomal but is inactivated when it is integrated.

Transmission & Epidemiology

Papillomaviruses are transmitted primarily by skin-to-skin contact and by genital contact. Genital warts are among the **most common sexually transmitted diseases**. Skin warts are more common in children and young adults and tend to regress in older adults. Many species of animals are infected with their own types of papillomaviruses, but these viruses are not an important source of human infection.

Pathogenesis & Immunity

Papillomaviruses infect squamous epithelial cells and induce within those cells a characteristic cytoplasmic vacuole. These vacuolated cells, called **koilocytes**, are the hallmark of infection by these viruses. Most warts are benign and do not progress to malignancy. However, HPV infection is associated with carcinoma of the uterine cervix and penis. The proteins encoded by viral genes E6 and E7 interfere with the growth-inhibitory activity of the proteins encoded by the p53 and RB tumor suppressor genes and thereby contribute to oncogenesis by these viruses. The E6 and E7 proteins of HPV type 16 bind more strongly to p53 and RB proteins than the E6 and E7 proteins of HPV types not implicated in carcinomas, a finding that explains why type 16 causes carcinomas more frequently than the other types.

Both cell-mediated immunity and antibody are induced by viral infection and are involved in the spontaneous regression of warts. Immunosuppressed patients, eg, AIDS patients, have more extensive warts, and women infected with HIV have a very high rate of carcinoma of the cervix.

Clinical Findings

Papillomas of various organs are the predominant finding. These papillomas are caused by specific HPV types. For example, skin and plantar warts are caused primarily by HPV-1 through HPV-4, whereas genital warts (**condylomata acuminata**) are caused primarily by HPV-6 and HPV-11. Carcinoma of the uterine cervix, the penis, and the anus, as well as premalignant lesions called intraepithelial neoplasia, are associated with infection by HPV-16 and HPV-18. Occult premalignant lesions of the cervix and penis can be revealed by applying acetic acid to the tissue.

Laboratory Diagnosis

Infections are usually diagnosed clinically. The presence of koilocytes in the lesions indicates HPV infection. DNA hybridization tests to detect the presence of viral DNA are commercially available. Diagnostic tests based on detection of antibodies in a patient's serum or on isolation of the virus from a patient's tissue are not used.

Treatment & Prevention

The usual treatment for genital warts is podophyllin; alpha interferon is also effective and is better at preventing recurrences than are non-antiviral treatments. Liquid nitrogen is commonly used for skin warts. Plantar warts can be removed surgically or treated with salicylic acid topically. Cidofovir may be useful in the treatment of severe HPV infections.

There is no vaccine against HPV. However, an experimental vaccine consisting of the L1 capsid protein of HPV types 16 and 18 significantly reduced the incidence of both HPV infections and HPV-induced cervical intraepithelial neoplasia. The role of cesarean section in preventing transmission of HPV from a mother with genital warts to her newborn is uncertain.

PARVOVIRUSES

Diseases

Parvovirus B19 causes erythema infectiosum (slapped cheek syndrome, fifth disease), aplastic anemia (especially in patients with sickle cell anemia), and fetal infections, including hydrops fetalis.

Important Properties

Parvovirus B19 is a very small (22-nm) nonenveloped virus with a **single-stranded DNA genome.** The genome is negative-strand DNA, but there is no virion polymerase. The capsid has icosahedral symmetry. There is one serotype.

Summary of Replicative Cycle

After adsorption to host cell receptors, the virion penetrates and moves to the nucleus, where replication occurs. The single-stranded genome DNA has "hairpin" loops at both of its ends that provide double-stranded areas for the cellular DNA polymerase to initiate the synthesis of the progeny genomes. The viral mRNA is synthesized by cellular RNA polymerase from the double-stranded DNA intermediate. The progeny virions are assembled in the nucleus. B19 virus replicates only when a cell is in S phase, which explains why the virus replicates in red cell precursors but not in mature red cells.

Transmission & Epidemiology

B19 virus is transmitted primarily by the respiratory route; transplacental transmission also occurs. Blood donated for transfusions also can transmit the virus. B19 virus infection occurs worldwide, and about half the people in the United States older than 18 years of age have antibodies to the virus. Humans are the natural reservoir; animals are not a source of human infection.

Pathogenesis & Immunity

B19 virus infects primarily two types of cells: **red blood cell precursors** (erythroblasts) in the bone marrow, which accounts for the aplastic anemia, and endothelial cells in the blood vessels, which accounts, in part, for the rash associated with erythema infectiosum. Immune complexes composed of virus and IgM or IgG also contribute to the pathogenesis of the rash and to the arthritis that is seen in some adults infected with B19 virus. Infection provides lifelong immunity against reinfection.

Hydrops fetalis manifests as massive edema of the fetus. This is secondary to congestive heart failure precipitated by severe anemia caused by the death of parvovirus B19–infected erythroblasts in the fetus.

Clinical Findings

There are four main clinical presentations.

A. Erythema Infectiosum (Slapped Cheek Syndrome, Fifth Disease)

This is a mild disease, primarily of childhood, characterized by a bright red rash that is most prominent on the cheeks, accompanied by low-grade fever, runny nose (coryza), and sore throat. A "lacy," less intense, erythematous rash appears on the body. The symptoms resolve in about 1 week.

The disease in children is also called fifth disease. The four other macular or maculopapular rash diseases of childhood are measles, rubella, scarlet fever, and roseola.

B. Aplastic Anemia

Children with chronic anemia, such as sickle cell anemia, thalassemia, and spherocytosis, can have transient but severe aplastic anemia (aplastic crisis) when infected with B19 virus. People with normal red blood cells do not have clinically apparent anemia, although their red blood cell precursors are infected.

C. Fetal Infections

If a woman is infected with B19 virus during the first or second trimester of pregnancy, the virus may cross the placenta and infect the fetus. Infection during the first trimester is associated with fetal death, whereas infection during the second trimester leads to **hydrops fetalis.** Third-trimester infections do not result in important clinical findings. B19 virus is not a common cause of congenital abnormalities probably because the fetus dies when infected early in pregnancy.

D. Arthritis

Parvovirus B19 infection in adults, especially women, can cause arthritis mainly involving the small joints of the hands and feet bilaterally. It resembles rheumatoid arthritis. Other viral infections that cause an immune-complex-related arthritis include hepatitis B and rubella.

E. Chronic B19 Infection

People with immunodeficiencies, especially HIV-infected, chemotherapy, or transplant patients, can have chronic anemia, leukopenia, or thrombocytopenia as a result of chronic B19 infection.

Laboratory Diagnosis

Fifth disease and aplastic anemia are usually diagnosed by detecting IgM antibodies. B19 virus can be isolated from throat swabs, but this is not usually done. In immunocompromised patients, antibodies may not be detectable; therefore, viral DNA in the blood can be assayed by polymerase chain reaction (PCR) methods. Fetal infection can be determined by PCR analysis of amniotic fluid.

Treatment & Prevention

There is no specific treatment of B19 infection. Pooled immune globulins may have a beneficial effect on chronic B19 infection in patients with immunodeficiencies. There is no vaccine or chemoprophylaxis.

SUMMARIES OF ORGANISMS

Brief summaries of the organisms described in this chapter begin on page 495. Please consult these summaries for a rapid review of the essential material.

PRACTICE QUESTIONS: USMLE & COURSE EXAMINATIONS

Questions on the topics discussed in this chapter can be found in the Clinical Virology section of Part XI: USMLE (National Board) Practice Questions starting on page 549. Also see Part XII: USMLE (National Board) Practice Examination starting on page 583.

RNA Enveloped Viruses

39

■ ORTHOMYXOVIRUSES

INFLUENZA VIRUSES

Influenza viruses are the only members of the orthomyxovirus family. The orthomyxoviruses differ from the paramyxoviruses primarily in that the former have a segmented RNA genome (usually eight pieces), whereas the RNA genome of the latter consists of a single piece.[1] The term "myxo" refers to the observation that these viruses interact with mucins (glycoproteins on the surface of cells).

In addition, the orthomyxoviruses are smaller (110 nm in diameter) than the paramyxoviruses (150 nm in diameter). See Table 39–1 for additional differences.

Table 39–2 shows a comparison of influenza A virus with several other viruses that infect the respiratory tract. Table 39–3 describes some of the important clinical features of influenza virus and compares them with the clinical features of the other medically important viruses in this chapter.

Disease

Influenza A virus causes worldwide epidemics (pandemics) of influenza; influenza B virus causes major outbreaks of influenza; and influenza C virus causes mild respiratory tract infections but does not cause outbreaks of influenza. The pandemics caused by influenza A virus occur approximately every 10–20 years, but major outbreaks caused by this virus occur virtually every year in various countries. In the 1918 influenza pandemic, more Americans died than in World War I, World War II, the Korean war, and the Vietnam war combined. Influenza B virus does not cause pandemics, and the major outbreaks caused by this virus do not occur as often as those caused by influenza A virus.

Important Properties

Influenza virus is composed of a **segmented** single-stranded RNA genome, a helical nucleocapsid, and an outer lipoprotein envelope. The virion contains an RNA-dependent **RNA polymerase,** which transcribes the **negative-polarity** genome into mRNA. The genome is therefore not infectious. The envelope is covered with two different types of spikes, a **hemagglutinin** and a **neuraminidase.**[2]

The function of the hemagglutinin is to bind to the cell surface receptor (neuraminic acid, sialic acid) to initiate infection. In the clinical laboratory, the hemagglutinin agglutinates red blood cells, which is the basis of a diagnostic test called the hemagglutination inhibition test. The hemagglutinin is also the target of neutralizing antibody.

The neuraminidase cleaves neuraminic acid (sialic acid) to release progeny virus from the infected cell. The hemagglutinin functions at the beginning of infection, whereas the neuraminidase functions at the end. Neuraminidase also degrades the protective layer of mucus in the respiratory tract. This enhances the ability of the virus to infect the respiratory epithelium.

Influenza viruses, especially influenza A virus, show **changes in the antigenicity** of their hemagglutinin and neuraminidase proteins; this property contributes to their capacity to cause devastating **worldwide epidemics.** There are two types of antigenic changes: (1) **antigenic shifts,** which are major changes based on the reassortment of segments of the genome RNA and (2) **antigenic drifts,** which are minor changes based on mutations in the genome RNA. Note that in reassortment, entire segments of RNA are exchanged, each one of which codes for a single protein, eg, the hemagglutinin (Figure 39–1).

Influenza viruses have both **group-specific** and **type-specific** antigens.

---

[1] The total molecular weight of influenza virus RNA is approximately $2–4 \times 10^6$, whereas the molecular weight of paramyxovirus RNA is higher, approximately $5–8 \times 10^6$.

[2] Paramyxoviruses also have a hemagglutinin and a neuraminidase, but the two proteins are located on the same spike.

Table 39–1. Properties of orthomyxoviruses and paramyxoviruses.

Property	Orthomyxoviruses	Paramyxoviruses
Viruses	Influenza A, B, and C viruses	Measles, mumps, respiratory syncytial, and parainfluenza viruses
Genome	Segmented (eight pieces) single-stranded RNA of negative polarity	Nonsegmented single-stranded RNA of negative polarity
Virion RNA polymerase	Yes	Yes
Capsid	Helical	Helical
Envelope	Yes	Yes
Size	Smaller (110 nm)	Larger (150 nm)
Surface spikes	Hemagglutinin and neuraminidase on different spikes	Hemagglutinin and neuraminidase on the same spike[1]
Giant cell formation	No	Yes

[1]Individual viruses differ in detail. See Table 39–4.

(1) The internal ribonucleoprotein is the group-specific antigen that distinguishes influenza A, B, and C viruses.

(2) The hemagglutinin and the neuraminidase are the type-specific antigens located on the surface. Antibody against the hemagglutinin neutralizes the infectivity of the virus (and prevents disease), whereas antibody against the group-specific antigen (which is located internally) does not. Antibody against the neuraminidase does not neutralize infectivity but does reduce disease, perhaps by decreasing the amount of virus released from the infected cell and thus reducing spread.

Many species of animals (eg, aquatic birds, chickens, swine, and horses) have their own influenza A viruses. These **animal viruses are the source of the RNA segments** that encode the antigenic shift variants that cause epidemics among humans. For example, if an avian and a human influenza A virus infect the same cell (eg, in a farmer's respiratory tract), reassortment could occur and a new variant of the human A virus, bearing the avian virus hemagglutinin, may appear.

There is evidence that aquatic birds (waterfowl) are a common source of these new genes and that the reassortment event leading to new human strains occurs in pigs. Because influenza B virus is only a human virus, there is no animal source of new RNA segments. Influenza B virus therefore does not undergo antigenic shifts. It does, however, undergo enough antigenic drift that the current strain must be included in the new version of the influenza vaccine produced each year.

A/Philippines/82 (H3N2) illustrates the nomenclature of influenza viruses. "A" refers to the group antigen. Next are the location and year the virus was isolated. H3N2 is the designation of the hemagglutinin (H) and neuraminidase (N) types. The H1N1 and H3N2 strains of influenza A virus are the most common at this time and are the strains included in the current vaccine. The H2N2 strain caused a pandemic in 1968.

In 1997, the H5N1 strain that causes **avian influenza**, primarily in chickens, caused an aggressive form of human influenza with high mortality in Hong Kong. In the winter of 2003–2004, an outbreak of avian influenza caused by H5N1 strain killed thousands of chickens in several Asian countries. Millions of chickens were killed in an effort to stop the spread of the disease. In this outbreak of H5N1 influenza, 122 people have been infected, of whom 62 have died, a 50% mortality rate (as of November 2005). Note that these 122 people were infected directly from chickens. The spread of the H5N1 strain from person to person occurs rarely but remains a major concern because it could increase dramatically if reassortment with the human-adapted strains occurs. In 2005, the H5N1 virus spread from Asia to Siberia and into eastern Europe, where it killed thousands of birds but has not caused human disease.

As of this writing (November 2005), there have been no cases of human influenza caused by an H5N1 virus in the United States. However, there have been two cases of human influenza caused by an H7N2 strain of avian influenza virus. In 2005, the RNA of the virus that caused the 1918 pandemic was sequenced and found to resemble avian influenza strains.

Table 39–2. Features of viruses that infect the respiratory tract.[1]

Virus	Disease	Number of Serotypes	Lifelong Immunity to Disease	Vaccine Available	Viral Latency	Treatment
RNA viruses						
Influenza virus	Influenza	Many	No	+	–	Amantadine rimantidine, oseltamivir, zanamivir
Parainfluenza virus	Croup	Many	No	–	–	None
Respiratory syncytial virus	Bronchiolitis	One	Incomplete	–	–	Ribavirin
Rubella virus	Rubella	One	Yes	+	–	None
Measles virus	Measles	One	Yes	+	–	None
Mumps virus	Parotitis, meningitis	One	Yes	+	–	None
Rhinovirus	Common cold	Many	No	–	–	None
Coronavirus	Common cold, SARS[2]	Three	No	–	–	None
Coxsackievirus	Herpangina, pleurodynia, myocarditis	Many	No	–	–	None
DNA viruses						
Herpes simplex virus type 1	Gingivostomatitis	One	No	–	+	Acyclovir in immunodeficient patients
Epstein-Barr virus	Infectious mononucleosis	One	Yes	–	+	None
Varicella-zoster virus	Chickenpox, shingles	One	Yes[3]	–	+	Acyclovir in immunodeficient patients
Adenovirus	Pharyngitis, pneumonia	Many	No	+[4]	+	None

[1]Influenza virus, parainfluenza virus, respiratory syncytial virus, rubella virus, measles virus, mumps virus, and coronavirus are enveloped RNA viruses and are described in this chapter.
[2]SARS is severe acute respiratory syndrome.
[3]Lifelong immunity to varicella (chickenpox) but not to zoster (shingles).
[4]For military recruits only.

The virulence of the H5N1 strain is significantly greater than the H1N1 and H3N2 strains that have been causing disease in humans for many years. This is attributed to two features of the H5N1 strain, namely, relative resistance to interferon and increased induction of cytokines, especially TNF. The increase in cytokines is thought to mediate the pathogenesis of the pneumonia and acute respiratory distress syndrome (ARDS) seen in H5N1 infection.

The H5N1 strain is sensitive to the neuraminidase inhibitors, oseltamivir (Tamiflu) and zanamivir (Relenza) but not to amantadine and rimantidine, the drugs that inhibit entry (see Treatment section below). Tamiflu is the drug of choice for both treatment and prevention. There is no human vaccine against the H5N1 strain, but there is one available for use in avian species.

Summary of Replicative Cycle

The virus adsorbs to the cell when the viral hemagglutinin interacts with sialic acid receptors on the cell sur-

Table 39–3. Clinical features of certain RNA enveloped viruses.

Virus	Rash Occurs	Giant Cells Formed	Type of Vaccine	Immune Globulins Commonly Used
Influenza	No	No	Killed	No
Respiratory syncytial	No	Yes	None	No
Measles	Yes	Yes	Live	No
Rubella	Yes	No	Live	No
Rabies	No	No	Killed	Yes

face. (The hemagglutinin on the virion surface is cleaved by extracellular proteases to generate a modified hemagglutinin that actually mediates attachment to the cell surface.) The virus then enters the cell in vesicles and uncoats within an endosome. Uncoating is facilitated by the low pH within the endosome.

The virion RNA polymerase transcribes the eight genome segments into eight mRNAs in the nucleus. Synthesis of the eight mRNAs occurs in the nucleus because a methylated guanosine "cap" is required. The cap is obtained from cellular nuclear RNAs in a process called "cap snatching." Most of the mRNAs move to the cytoplasm, where they are translated into viral proteins. Some of the viral mRNAs remain in the nucleus, where they serve as the template for the synthesis of the negative-strand RNA genomes for the progeny virions. Replication of the progeny genomes is performed by a different subunit of the viral RNA polymerase (acting as a replicase) from the subunit that functioned earlier as a transcriptase that synthesized the mRNAs. Two newly synthesized proteins, NP protein and matrix protein, bind to the progeny RNA genome in the nucleus and that complex is transported to the cytoplasm.

The helical ribonucleoprotein assembles in the cytoplasm, matrix protein mediates the interaction of the nucleocapsid with the envelope, and the virion is released from the cell by budding from the outer cell membrane at the site where the hemagglutinin and neuraminidase are located. The neuraminidase acts to release the virus by cleaving neuraminic acid on the cell surface at the site of the budding progeny virions. Influenza virus, hepatitis delta virus, and retroviruses are the **only RNA viruses** that have an important stage of their replication take place in the **nucleus**.

Transmission & Epidemiology

The virus is transmitted by **airborne respiratory droplets**. The ability of influenza A virus to cause epidemics is dependent on antigenic changes in the hemagglutinin and neuraminidase. As mentioned previously, influenza A virus undergoes both major antigenic shifts as well as minor antigenic drifts. Antigenic shift variants appear less frequently, about every 10 or 11 years, whereas drift variants appear virtually every year. Epidemics and pandemics (worldwide epidemics) occur when the antigenicity of the virus has changed sufficiently that the preexisting immunity of many people is no longer effective. The antigenicity of influenza B virus also varies but not as dramatically or as often.

Influenza occurs primarily in the winter months, when it and bacterial pneumonia secondary to influenza cause a significant number of deaths, especially in older people. In the southern hemisphere, eg, in Australia and New Zealand, influenza occurs primarily in the winter months of June through August.

Pathogenesis & Immunity

After the virus has been inhaled, the neuraminidase degrades the protective mucus layer, allowing the virus to gain access to the cells of the upper and lower respiratory tract. The infection is limited primarily to this area because the proteases that cleave the hemagglutinin are located in the respiratory tract. Despite systemic symptoms, viremia rarely occurs. The systemic symptoms, such as severe myalgias, are due to cytokines circulating in the blood. There is necrosis of the superficial layers of the respiratory epithelium. Influenza virus pneumonia, which can complicate influenza, is interstitial in location.

Immunity depends mainly upon secretory IgA in the respiratory tract. IgG is also produced but is less protective. Cytotoxic T cells also play a protective role.

Clinical Findings

After an incubation period of 24–48 hours, fever, myalgias, headache, sore throat, and cough develop suddenly. Severe myalgias (muscle pains) coupled with respiratory tract symptoms are typical of influenza. Vomiting and diarrhea are rare. The symptoms usually

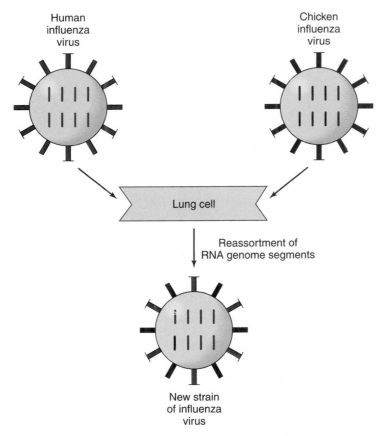

Figure 39–1. Antigenic shift in influenza virus. A human strain of influenza virus containing the gene encoding one antigenic type of hemagglutinin (colored orange) infects the same lung cell as a chicken strain of influenza virus containing the gene encoding a different antigenic type of hemagglutinin (colored black). Reassortment of the genome RNA segments that encode the hemagglutinin occurs, and a new strain of influenza virus is produced containing the chicken type of hemagglutinin (colored black).

resolve spontaneously in 4–7 days, but influenzal or bacterial pneumonia may complicate the course. One of the well-known complications of influenza is pneumonia caused by *Staphylococcus aureus*.

Reye's syndrome, characterized by encephalopathy and liver degeneration, is a rare, life-threatening complication in children following some viral infections, particularly influenza B and chickenpox. Aspirin given to reduce fever in viral infections has been implicated in the pathogenesis of Reye's syndrome.

Laboratory Diagnosis

Although most diagnoses of influenza are made on clinical grounds, laboratory tests are available. Virus can be detected in such specimens as nasal or throat washings,

nasal or throat swabs, and sputum by various techniques, such as direct fluorescent antibody, polymerase chain reaction (PCR), or cell culture–based tests. Several rapid tests suitable for a physician's office laboratory are also available. Two tests (FLU OIA and QUICKVUE Influenza Test) are based on detection of viral antigen using monoclonal antibodies, and a third test (ZSTATFLU) is based on detection of viral neuraminidase using a colored substrate of the enzyme. The rationale for using the rapid tests is that treatment with the neuraminidase inhibitors should be instituted within 48 hours of the onset of symptoms.

Influenza can also be diagnosed by the detection of antibodies in the patient's serum. A rise in antibody titer of at least 4-fold in paired serum samples taken early in the illness and 10 days later is sufficient for diagnosis. Either the hemagglutination inhibition or complement fixation (CF) test can be used to assay the antibody titer.

Treatment

Amantadine (Symmetrel) is used for both the treatment and prevention of influenza A. Its main indication is in the prevention of influenza in a confined, elderly, unimmunized population, such as in a retirement home, where influenza can be life-threatening. Note that amantadine is effective only against influenza A, not against influenza B. A derivative of amantadine, **rimantadine** (Flumadine), can also be used for treatment and prevention of influenza A and has fewer side effects than amantadine. Strains of influenza virus resistant to amantadine and rimantadine have been isolated from patients. Note that the vaccine is still preferred over these drugs in the prevention of influenza.

Zanamivir (Relenza) and oseltamivir (Tamiflu) are also used for the treatment of influenza. They belong to a new class of drugs called neuraminidase inhibitors that act by inhibiting the release of virus from infected cells. This limits the infection by reducing the spread of virus from one cell to another. These drugs are effective against both influenza A and B viruses in contrast to amantadine, which is effective only against influenza A viruses. Relenza is delivered by inhalant directly into the respiratory tract, whereas Tamiflu is taken orally. Clinical studies showed they reduce the duration of symptoms by 1–2 days. Strains of influenza virus resistant to zanamivir and oseltamivir are uncommon.

Prevention

The main mode of prevention is the **vaccine,** which consists of influenza A and B viruses, typically two A strains and one B strain. The two A strains are recent H1N1 and H3N2 isolates. The vaccine is usually reformulated each year to contain the current antigenic strains. Both the killed and the live vaccines (see below) contain two A strains and one B strain of influenza virus.

There are two types of influenza vaccines available in the United States. The vaccine that has been utilized for many years is a killed vaccine containing purified protein subunits of the virus (hemagglutinin and neuraminidase). The virus is inactivated with formaldehyde, then treated with a lipid solvent that disaggregates the virions. This type of vaccine is available in two versions; one is called a "split virus" vaccine and the other a "purified subunit" vaccine. These vaccines are administered intramuscularly.

The new vaccine that was approved in 2003 is a live vaccine containing temperature-sensitive mutants of in-fluenza A and B viruses. These temperature-sensitive mutants can replicate in the cooler (33°C) nasal mucosa where they induce IgA, but not in the warmer (37°C) lower respiratory tract. The live virus in the vaccine therefore immunizes but does not cause disease. This vaccine is administered by spraying into the nose ("nasal mist").

Note that the killed vaccine is not a good immunogen, because little IgA is made and the titer of IgG is relatively low. Protection lasts only 6 months. Yearly boosters are recommended and should be given shortly before the flu season, eg, in October. These boosters also provide an opportunity to immunize against the latest antigenic changes. The vaccine should be given to people older than 50 years of age, children 6 to 23 months of age, and to those with chronic diseases, particularly respiratory and cardiovascular conditions. It should also be given to health care personnel who are likely to transmit the virus to those at high risk. In 1994, the vaccination recommendations were expanded to include all persons who want to reduce their risk of acquiring influenza.

One side effect of the influenza vaccine used in the 1970s containing the swine influenza strain (Asw/New Jersey) was an increased risk of Guillain-Barré syndrome, which is characterized by an ascending paralysis. Analysis of the side effects of the influenza vaccines in use during the last 10 years has shown no increased risk of Guillain-Barré syndrome.

In addition to the vaccine, influenza can be prevented by using three of the drugs (amantadine, rimantadine, and oseltamivir) described in the treatment section above. These drugs are particularly useful in elderly people who have not been immunized and who may have been exposed. Note that these drugs should not be thought of as a substitute for the vaccine. Immunization is the most reliable mode of prevention.

■ PARAMYXOVIRUSES

The paramyxovirus family contains four important human pathogens: measles virus, mumps virus, respiratory syncytial virus (RSV), and parainfluenza viruses. They differ from orthomyxoviruses in that their **genomes are not segmented,** they have a larger diameter, and their surface spikes are different (Table 39–1).

Paramyxoviruses are composed of **one piece** of single-stranded RNA, a helical nucleocapsid, and an outer lipoprotein envelope. The virion contains an RNA-dependent **RNA polymerase,** which transcribes the **negative-polarity** genome into mRNA. The genome is therefore not infectious. The envelope is covered with spikes, which contain hemagglutinin, neuraminidase, or a fusion protein that causes cell fusion and, in some cases, hemolysis (Table 39–4).

MEASLES VIRUS

Disease

This virus causes measles.

Important Properties

The genome RNA and nucleocapsid of measles virus are those of a typical paramyxovirus (see above). The virion has two types of envelope spikes, one with hemagglutinating activity and the other with cell-fusing and hemolytic activities (Table 39–4). It has a single serotype, and the hemagglutinin is the antigen against which neutralizing antibody is directed. Humans are the natural host.

Summary of Replicative Cycle

After adsorption to the cell surface via its hemagglutinin, the virus penetrates and uncoats, and the virion RNA polymerase transcribes the negative-strand genome into mRNA. Multiple mRNAs are synthesized, each of which is translated into the specific viral proteins; no polyprotein analogous to that synthesized by poliovirus is made. The helical nucleocapsid is assembled, the matrix protein mediates the interaction with the envelope, and the virus is released by budding from the cell membrane.

Transmission & Epidemiology

Measles virus is transmitted via **respiratory droplets** produced by coughing and sneezing both during the prodromal period and for a few days after the rash appears. Measles occurs worldwide, usually in outbreaks every 2–3 years, when the number of susceptible children reaches a high level. The attack rate is one of the highest of viral diseases; most children contract the clinical disease on exposure. When this virus is introduced into a population that has not experienced measles, such as the inhabitants of the Hawaiian Islands in the 1800s, devastating epidemics occur. In malnourished children, especially those in developing countries, measles is a much more serious disease than in well-nourished children. Vitamin A deficiency is especially important in this regard, and supplementation of this vitamin greatly reduces the severity of measles. Patients with deficient cell-mediated immunity, eg, AIDS patients, have a severe, life-threatening disease when they contract measles.

Pathogenesis & Immunity

After infecting the cells lining the upper respiratory tract, the virus enters the blood and infects reticuloendothelial cells, where it replicates again. It then spreads via the blood to the skin. The **rash** is caused primarily by cytotoxic T cells attacking the measles virus–infected vascular endothelial cells in the skin. Antibody-mediated vasculitis may also play a role. Shortly after the rash appears, the virus can no longer be recovered and the patient can no longer spread the virus to others. **Multinucleated giant cells,** which form as a result of the fusion protein in the spikes, are characteristic of the lesions.

Lifelong immunity occurs in individuals who have had the disease. Although IgG antibody may play a role in neutralizing the virus during the viremic stage, cell-mediated immunity is more important. The importance of cell-mediated immunity is illustrated by the fact that agammaglobulinemic children have a normal course of disease, are subsequently immune, and are protected by immunization. Maternal antibody passes the placenta, and infants are protected during the first 6 months of life.

Table 39–4. Envelope spikes of paramyxoviruses.

Virus	Hemagglutinin	Neuraminidase	Fusion Protein[1]
Measles virus	+	−	+
Mumps virus[2]	+	+	+
Respiratory syncytial virus	−	−	+
Parainfluenza virus[2]	+	+	+

[1]The measles and mumps fusion proteins are hemolysins also.
[2]In mumps and parainfluenza viruses, the hemagglutinin and neuraminidase are on the same spike and the fusion protein is on a different spike.

Infection with measles virus can **transiently depress cell-mediated immunity** against other intracellular microorganisms, such as *Mycobacterium tuberculosis,* leading to a loss of PPD skin test reactivity, reactivation of dormant organisms, and clinical disease. The proposed mechanism for this unusual finding is that when measles virus binds to its receptor (called CD46) on the surface of human macrophages, the production of IL-12, which is necessary for cell-mediated immunity to occur, is suppressed.

Clinical Findings

After an incubation period of 10–14 days, a prodromal phase characterized by fever, conjunctivitis (causing photophobia), running nose, and coughing occurs. **Koplik's spots** are bright red lesions with a white, central dot that are located on the buccal mucosa and are virtually diagnostic. A few days later, a maculopapular rash appears on the face and proceeds gradually down the body to the lower extremities, including the palms and soles. The rash develops a brownish hue several days later.

The complications of measles can be quite severe. Encephalitis occurs at a rate of 1 per 1000 cases of measles. The mortality rate of encephalitis is 10%, and there are permanent sequelae, such as deafness and mental retardation, in 40% of cases. In addition, both primary measles (giant-cell) pneumonia and secondary bacterial pneumonia occur. Bacterial otitis media is quite common. Subacute sclerosing panencephalitis (SSPE) is a rare, fatal disease of the central nervous system that occurs several years after measles (see Chapter 44).

Measles in a pregnant woman leads to an increased risk of stillbirth rather than congenital abnormalities. Measles virus infection of the fetus is more severe than rubella virus infection, so the former typically causes fetal death, whereas the latter causes congenital abnormalities.

Atypical measles occurs in some people who were given the killed vaccine and were subsequently infected with measles virus. It is characterized by an atypical rash without Koplik's spots. Because the killed vaccine has not been used for many years, atypical measles occurs only in adults and is infrequent.

Laboratory Diagnosis

Most diagnoses are made on clinical grounds, but the virus can be isolated in cell culture; a rise in antibody titer of greater than 4-fold can be used to diagnose difficult cases.

Treatment

There is no antiviral therapy available.

Prevention

Prevention rests on immunization with the **live, attenuated vaccine.** The vaccine is effective and causes few side effects. It is given subcutaneously to children at 15 months of age, usually in combination with rubella and mumps vaccines. The vaccine should not be given to children prior to **15 months of age, because maternal antibody in the child can neutralize the virus** and reduce the immune response. Because immunity can wane, a **booster dose** is recommended. The vaccine contains live virus, so it should not be given to immunocompromised persons or pregnant women. The vaccine has decreased the number of cases of measles greatly in the United States; there were only 138 reported cases of measles in 1997. However, outbreaks still occur among unimmunized individuals, eg, children in inner cities and in developing countries.

The killed vaccine should not be used. Immune globulin can be used to modify the disease if given to unimmunized individuals early in the incubation period. This is especially necessary if the unimmunized individuals are immunocompromised.

MUMPS VIRUS

Disease

This virus causes mumps.

Important Properties

The genome RNA and nucleocapsid are those of a typical paramyxovirus. The virion has two types of envelope spikes, one with both hemagglutinin and neuraminidase activities and the other with cell-fusing and hemolytic activities (Table 39–4).

The virus has a single serotype. Neutralizing antibody is directed against the hemagglutinin. The internal nucleocapsid protein is the S (soluble) antigen detected in the complement fixation test used for diagnosis. Humans are the natural host.

Summary of Replicative Cycle

Replication is similar to that of measles virus (see page 272).

Transmission & Epidemiology

Mumps virus is transmitted via respiratory droplets. Mumps occurs worldwide, with a peak incidence in the winter. About 30% of children have a subclinical (inapparent) infection, which confers immunity. There were only 683 reported cases of mumps in the United States in 1997, a finding attributed to the widespread use of the vaccine.

Pathogenesis & Immunity

The virus infects the upper respiratory tract and then spreads through the blood to infect the parotid glands, testes, ovaries, pancreas, and, in some cases, meninges. Alternatively, the virus may ascend from the buccal mucosa up Stensen's duct to the parotid gland.

Lifelong immunity occurs in persons who have had the disease. There is a popular misconception that unilateral mumps can be followed by mumps on the other side. Mumps occurs only once; subsequent cases of parotitis can be caused by other viruses such as parainfluenza viruses, by bacteria, and by duct stones. Maternal antibody passes the placenta and provides protection during the first 6 months of life.

Clinical Findings

After an incubation period of 18–21 days, a prodromal stage of fever, malaise, and anorexia is followed by tender swelling of the parotid glands, either unilateral or bilateral. There is a characteristic increase in parotid pain when drinking citrus juices. The disease is typically benign and resolves spontaneously within 1 week.

Two complications are of significance. One is orchitis in postpubertal males, which, if bilateral, can result in sterility. Postpubertal males have a fibrous tunica albuginea, which resists expansion, thereby causing pressure necrosis of the spermatocytes. Unilateral orchitis, although quite painful, does not lead to sterility. The other complication is meningitis, which is usually benign, self-limited, and without sequelae. Mumps virus, coxsackievirus, and echovirus are the three most frequent causes of viral (aseptic) meningitis. The widespread use of the vaccine in the United States has led to a marked decrease in the incidence of mumps meningitis.

Laboratory Diagnosis

The diagnosis of mumps is usually made clinically, but laboratory tests are available for confirmation. The virus can be isolated in cell culture from saliva, spinal fluid, or urine. In addition, a 4-fold rise in antibody titer in either the hemagglutination inhibition or the CF test is diagnostic. A single CF test that assays both the S and the V (viral) antigens can also be used. Because antibody to S antigen appears early and is short-lived, it indicates current infection. If only V antibody is found, the patient has had mumps in the past.

A mumps skin test based on delayed hypersensitivity can be used to detect previous infection, but serologic tests are preferred. The mumps skin test is widely used to determine whether a patient's cell-mediated immunity is competent.

Treatment

There is no antiviral therapy for mumps.

Prevention

Prevention consists of immunization with the live, attenuated vaccine. The vaccine is effective and long-lasting (at least 10 years) and causes few side effects. It is given subcutaneously to children at 15 months of age, usually in combination with measles and rubella vaccines. Because it is a live vaccine, it should not be given to immunocompromised persons or pregnant women. Immune globulin is not useful for preventing or mitigating mumps orchitis.

RESPIRATORY SYNCYTIAL VIRUS

Diseases

Respiratory syncytial virus (RSV) is the most important cause of pneumonia and bronchiolitis in infants. It is also an important cause of otitis media in children and of pneumonia in the elderly and in patients with chronic cardiopulmonary diseases.

Important Properties

The genome RNA and nucleocapsid are those of a typical paramyxovirus (Table 39–1). Its surface spikes are fusion proteins, not hemagglutinins or neuraminidases (Table 39–4). The fusion protein causes cells to fuse, forming multinucleated giant cells (syncytia), which give rise to the name of the virus.

Humans are the natural hosts of RSV. For many years, RSV was thought to have one serotype; however, two serotypes, designated subgroup A and subgroup B, have been detected by monoclonal antibody tests. Antibody against the fusion protein neutralizes infectivity.

Summary of Replicative Cycle

Replication is similar to that of measles virus (see page 272).

Transmission & Epidemiology

Transmission occurs via respiratory droplets and by direct contact of contaminated hands with the nose or mouth. RSV causes outbreaks of respiratory infections every winter, in contrast to many other "cold" viruses, which reenter the community every few years. It occurs worldwide, and virtually everyone has been infected by the age of 3 years. RSV also causes outbreaks of respiratory infections in hospitalized infants; these outbreaks can be controlled by hand washing and use of gloves, which interrupt transmission by hospital personnel.

Pathogenesis & Immunity

RSV infection in **infants is more severe** and more often involves the lower respiratory tract than in older children and adults. The infection is localized to the respiratory tract; viremia does not occur.

The severe disease in infants may have an **immunopathogenic** mechanism. Maternal antibody passed to the infant may react with the virus, form immune complexes, and damage the respiratory tract cells. Trials with a killed vaccine resulted in more severe disease, an unexpected finding that supports such a mechanism.

Most individuals have multiple infections caused by RSV, indicating that immunity is incomplete. The reason for this is unknown, but it is not due to antigenic variation of the virus. IgA respiratory antibody reduces the frequency of RSV infection as a person ages.

Clinical Findings

In infants, RSV is an important cause of lower respiratory tract diseases such as bronchiolitis and pneumonia. RSV is also an important cause of otitis media in young children. In older children and young, healthy adults, RSV causes upper respiratory tract infections that resemble the common cold. However, in the elderly (people over 65 years of age) and in adults with chronic cardiopulmonary diseases, RSV causes severe lower respiratory tract disease, including pneumonia.

Laboratory Diagnosis

The presence of the virus can be detected rapidly by immunofluorescence on smears of respiratory epithelium or by isolation in cell culture. The cytopathic effect in cell culture is characterized by the formation of multinucleated giant cells. A rise in antibody titer of at least 4-fold is also diagnostic. A reverse transcriptase polymerase chain reaction (RRT-PCR) test is also available.

Treatment

Aerosolized ribavirin (Virazole) is recommended for severely ill hospitalized infants, but there is uncertainty regarding its effectiveness. A combination of ribavirin and hyperimmune globulins against RSV may be more effective.

Prevention

There is no vaccine. Previous attempts to protect with a killed vaccine resulted in an increase in severity of symptoms. Passive immunization with a monoclonal antibody directed against the fusion protein of RSV (palivizumab, Synagis) can be used for prophylaxis in premature or immunocompromised infants. Hyperimmune globulins (RespiGam) are also available for prophylaxis in these infants and in children with chronic lung disease. Nosocomial outbreaks can be limited by hand washing and use of gloves.

PARAINFLUENZA VIRUSES

Diseases

These viruses cause croup (acute laryngotracheobronchitis), laryngitis, bronchiolitis, and pneumonia in children and a disease resembling the common cold in adults.

Important Properties

The genome RNA and nucleocapsid are those of a typical paramyxovirus (Table 39–1). The surface spikes consist of hemagglutinin (H), neuraminidase (N), and fusion (F) proteins (Table 39–4). The fusion protein mediates the formation of multinucleated giant cells. The H and N proteins are on the same spike; the F protein is on a separate spike. Both humans and animals are infected by parainfluenza viruses, but the animal strains do not infect humans. There are four types, which are distinguished by antigenicity, cytopathic effect, and pathogenicity (see below). Antibody to either the H or the F protein neutralizes infectivity.

Summary of Replicative Cycle

Replication is similar to that of measles virus (see page 272).

Transmission & Epidemiology

These viruses are transmitted via **respiratory droplets.** They cause disease worldwide, primarily in the winter months.

Pathogenesis & Immunity

These viruses cause upper and lower respiratory tract disease without viremia. A large proportion of infections are subclinical. Parainfluenza viruses 1 and 2 are **major causes of croup.** Parainfluenza virus 3 is the most common parainfluenza virus isolated from children with lower respiratory tract infection in the United States. Parainfluenza virus 4 rarely causes disease, except for the common cold.

Clinical Findings

Parainfluenza viruses are best known as the main cause of croup in children younger than 5 years of age. Croup is characterized by a harsh cough and hoarseness. In addition to croup, these viruses cause a variety of respiratory diseases such as the common cold, pharyngitis, laryngitis, otitis media, bronchitis, and pneumonia.

Laboratory Diagnosis

Most infections are diagnosed clinically. The diagnosis can be made in the laboratory either by isolating the virus in cell culture or by observing a 4-fold or greater rise in antibody titer.

Treatment & Prevention

There is neither antiviral therapy nor a vaccine available.

■ CORONAVIRUSES

CORONAVIRUS

Diseases

Coronaviruses are an important cause of the common cold, probably second only to rhinoviruses in frequency. In 2002, a new disease, an atypical pneumonia called SARS (severe acute respiratory syndrome) emerged.

Important Properties

Coronaviruses have a nonsegmented, single-stranded, positive-polarity RNA genome. They are enveloped viruses with a helical nucleocapsid. There is no virion polymerase. In the electron microscope, prominent club-shaped spikes in the form of a "corona" (halo) can be seen. There are two serotypes called 229E and OC43. The genome sequence of the coronavirus that caused the SARS (CoV-SARS) outbreak is different from the existing human strains. The genome sequence of different isolates of CoV-SARS is very similar, so the antigenicity of the virus is likely to be quite stable. The receptor for the SARS coronavirus on the surface of cells is angiotensin-converting enzyme-2.

Summary of Replicative Cycle

The virus adsorbs to cells via its surface spikes (hemagglutinin), after which it enters the cytoplasm, where it is uncoated. The positive-strand genome is translated into two large polypeptides, which are self-cleaved by the virus-encoded protease. Two of these peptides aggregate to form the RNA polymerase (transcriptase) that replicates the genome. In addition, mRNAs are synthesized, then translated into the structural proteins. The virus is assembled and obtains its envelope from the endoplasmic reticulum, not from the plasma membrane. Replication occurs in the cytoplasm.

Transmission & Epidemiology

Coronaviruses are transmitted by the respiratory aerosol. Infection occurs worldwide and occurs early in life, as evidenced by finding antibody in more than half of children. Outbreaks occur primarily in the winter on a 2- to 3-year cycle.

SARS originated in China in November 2002 and spread rapidly to other countries. As of this writing, there have been 8300 cases and 785 deaths, a fatality rate of approximately 9%. Human-to-human transmission occurs, and some patients with SARS are thought to be "super-spreaders", but this remains to be confirmed. Early in the outbreak, many hospital personnel were affected, but respiratory infection control procedures have greatly reduced the spread within hospitals.

There are many animal coronaviruses, and they are suspected of being the source of the CoV-SARS. The horseshoe bat appears to be the natural reservoir for CoV-SARS, with the civet cat serving as an intermediate host.

Pathogenesis & Immunity

Coronavirus infection is typically limited to the mucosal cells of the respiratory tract. Approximately 50% of infections are asymptomatic, and it is unclear what role they play in the spread of infection. Immunity following infection appears to be brief and reinfection can occur.

Pneumonia caused by SARS coronavirus is characterized by diffuse edema resulting in hypoxia. The binding of the virus to angiotensin-converting enzyme-2 on the surface of respiratory tract epithelium may contribute to the dysregulation of fluid balance and edema in the alveolar space.

Clinical Findings

The common cold caused by coronavirus is characterized by coryza (rhinorrhea, runny nose), scratchy sore throat, and low-grade fever. This illness typically lasts several days and has no long-term sequelae.

SARS is a severe atypical pneumonia characterized by a fever of at least 38°C, nonproductive cough, dyspnea, and hypoxia. Chills, rigors, malaise, and headache commonly occur, but sore throat and rhinorrhea are uncommon. Chest x-ray reveals interstitial "ground-glass" infiltrates that do not cavitate. Leukopenia and thrombocytopenia are seen. The incubation period for SARS ranges from 2 to 10 days, with a mean of 5 days.

Laboratory Diagnosis

The diagnosis of the "common cold" is primarily a clinical one. If SARS is suspected, antibody-based and PCR-based tests can be used.

Treatment & Prevention

There is no antiviral therapy or vaccine available. A combination of ribavirin and steroids has been tried in the treatment of life-threatening cases of SARS, but their efficacy is uncertain.

■ TOGAVIRUSES

RUBELLA VIRUS

Diseases

This virus causes rubella (German measles) and congenital rubella syndrome. Congenital rubella syndrome is characterized by **congenital malformations.**

Important Properties

Rubella virus is a member of the togavirus family. It is composed of one piece of single-stranded RNA, an **icosahedral** nucleocapsid, and a lipoprotein **envelope.** However, unlike the paramyxoviruses, such as measles and mumps viruses, it has a **positive-strand** RNA and therefore has no virion polymerase. Its surface spikes contain hemagglutinin. The virus has a single antigenic type. Antibody against hemagglutinin neutralizes infectivity. Humans are the natural host.

Summary of Replicative Cycle

Because knowledge of rubella virus replication is incomplete, the following cycle is based on the replication of other togaviruses. After penetration of the cell and uncoating, the plus-strand RNA genome is translated into several nonstructural and structural proteins. Note the difference between togaviruses and poliovirus, which also has a plus-strand RNA genome but translates its RNA into a single large polyprotein, which is subsequently cleaved. One of the nonstructural rubella proteins is an RNA-dependent RNA polymerase, which replicates the genome first by making a minus-strand template and then, from that, plus-strand progeny. Both replication and assembly occur in the cyto-

plasm, and the envelope is acquired from the outer membrane as the virion exits the cell.

Transmission & Epidemiology

The virus is transmitted via **respiratory droplets** and from mother to fetus **transplacentally.** The disease occurs worldwide. In areas where the vaccine is not used, epidemics occur every 6–9 years.

In 2005, the Centers for Disease Control and Prevention (CDC) declared rubella eliminated from the United States. The few cases that occurred in the United States were acquired outside and imported into this country. Elimination was made possible by the widespread use of the vaccine. As a result, cytomegalovirus is a much more common cause of congenital malformations in the United States than is rubella virus.

Pathogenesis & Immunity

Initial replication of the virus occurs in the nasopharynx and local lymph nodes. From there it spreads via the blood to the internal organs and skin. The origin of the rash is unclear; it may be due to antigen-antibody-mediated vasculitis.

Natural infection leads to **lifelong immunity.** Second cases of rubella do not occur; similar rashes are caused by other viruses, such as coxsackieviruses and echoviruses. Antibody crosses the placenta and protects the newborn.

Clinical Findings

A. RUBELLA

Rubella is a milder, shorter disease than measles. After an incubation period of 14–21 days, a brief prodromal period with fever and malaise is followed by a maculopapular rash, which starts on the face and progresses downward to involve the extremities. Posterior auricular lymphadenopathy is characteristic. The rash typically lasts 3 days. When rubella occurs in adults, especially women, polyarthritis caused by immune complexes often occurs.

B. CONGENITAL RUBELLA SYNDROME

The significance of rubella virus is not as a cause of mild childhood disease but as a **teratogen.** When a nonimmune pregnant woman is **infected during the first trimester,** especially the first month, significant congenital malformations can occur as a result of maternal viremia and fetal infection. The increased rate of abnormalities during the early weeks of pregnancy is attributed to the very sensitive organ development that occurs at that time. The malformations are widespread and involve primarily the heart (eg, patent ductus arteriosus), the eyes (eg, cataracts), and the brain (eg, deafness and mental retardation).

In addition, some children infected in utero can **continue to excrete** rubella virus for months following birth, which is a significant public health hazard because the virus can be transmitted to pregnant women. Some congenital shedders are asymptomatic and without malformations and hence can be diagnosed only if the virus is isolated. Congenitally infected infants also have significant IgM titers and persistent IgG titers long after maternal antibody has disappeared.

Laboratory Diagnosis

Rubella virus can be grown in cell culture, but it produces little cytopathic effect (CPE). It is therefore usually identified by its ability to interfere with echovirus CPE. If rubella virus is present in the patient's specimen and has grown in the cell culture, no CPE will appear when the culture is superinfected with an echovirus. The diagnosis can also be made by observing a 4-fold or greater rise in antibody titer between acute-phase and convalescent-phase sera in the hemagglutination inhibition test or ELISA or by observing the presence of IgM antibody in a single acute-phase serum sample.

In a pregnant woman exposed to rubella virus, the presence of **IgM antibody indicates recent infection,** whereas a 1:8 or greater titer of IgG antibody indicates immunity and consequent protection of the fetus. If recent infection has occurred, an **amniocentesis** can reveal whether there is rubella virus in the amniotic fluid, which indicates definite fetal infection.

Treatment

There is no antiviral therapy.

Prevention

Prevention involves immunization with the **live, attenuated vaccine.** The vaccine is effective and long-lasting (at least 10 years) and causes few side effects, except for transient arthralgias in some women. It is given subcutaneously to children at 15 months of age (usually in combination with measles and mumps vaccine) and to unimmunized young adult women if they are not pregnant and will use contraception for the next 3 months. There is no evidence that the vaccine virus causes malformations. Because it is a live vaccine, it should not be given to immunocompromised patients or to pregnant women.

The vaccine has caused a significant reduction in the incidence of both rubella and congenital rubella syndrome. It induces some respiratory IgA, thereby interrupting the spread of virulent virus by nasal carriage.

Immune serum globulins (IG) can be given to pregnant women in the first trimester who have been exposed to a known case of rubella and for whom termination of the pregnancy is not an option. The main problems with giving IG are that there are instances in which it fails to prevent fetal infection and that it may confuse the interpretation of serologic tests. If termination of the pregnancy is an option, it is recommended to attempt to determine whether the mother and fetus have been infected as described in the Laboratory Diagnosis section above.

To protect pregnant women from exposure to rubella virus, many hospitals require their personnel to demonstrate immunity, either by serologic testing or by proof of immunization.

OTHER TOGAVIRUSES

Several other medically important togaviruses are described in the chapter on arboviruses (see Chapter 42).

■ RHABDOVIRUSES

RABIES VIRUS

Disease

This virus causes rabies.

Important Properties

Rabies virus is the only medically important member of the rhabdovirus family. It has a **single-stranded RNA** enclosed within a **bullet-shaped** capsid surrounded by a lipoprotein **envelope.** Because the genome RNA has **negative polarity,** the virion contains an RNA-dependent **RNA polymerase.** Rabies virus has a single antigenic type. The antigenicity resides in the envelope glycoprotein spikes.

Rabies virus has a **broad host range:** it can infect all mammals, but only certain mammals are important sources of infection for humans (see below).

Summary of Replicative Cycle

Rabies virus attaches to the **acetylcholine receptor** on the cell surface. After entry into the cell, the virion RNA polymerase synthesizes five mRNAs that code for viral proteins. After replication of the genome viral RNA by a virus-encoded RNA polymerase, progeny RNA is assembled with virion proteins to form the nucleocapsid, and the envelope is acquired as the virion buds through the cell membrane.

Transmission & Epidemiology

The virus is transmitted by the **bite** of a rabid animal that manifests aggressive, biting behavior induced by the viral encephalitis. In the United States, transmission is usually from the bite of **wild animals** such as skunks, raccoons, and bats; dogs and cats are frequently immunized and therefore are rarely sources of human infection. In recent years, **bats** have been the source of most cases of human rabies in the United States. Rodents and rabbits do not transmit rabies.

Human rabies has also occurred in the United States in people who have not been bitten, so-called "nonbite" exposures. The most important example of this type of transmission is exposure to aerosols of bat secretions containing rabies virus. Another rare example is transmission in transplants of corneas taken from patients who died of undiagnosed rabies.

In the United States, fewer than 10 cases of rabies occur each year (mostly imported), whereas in developing countries there are hundreds of cases, mostly due to rabid dogs. Worldwide, approximately 50,000 people die of rabies each year.

The country of origin and the reservoir host of a strain of rabies virus can often be identified by determining the base sequence of the genome RNA. For example, a person developed clinical rabies in the United States, but sequencing of the genome RNA revealed that the virus was the Mexican strain. It was later discovered that the man had been bitten by a dog while in Mexico several months earlier.

Pathogenesis & Immunity

The virus multiplies locally at the bite site, infects the sensory neurons, and **moves by axonal transport to the central nervous system.** During its transport within the nerve, the virus is sheltered from the immune system and little, if any, immune response occurs. The virus multiplies in the central nervous system and then travels down the peripheral nerves to the salivary glands and other organs. From the salivary glands, it enters the saliva to be transmitted by the bite. There is no viremic stage.

Within the central nervous system, **encephalitis** develops, with the death of neurons and demyelination. Infected neurons contain an eosinophilic cytoplasmic inclusion called a **Negri body,** which is important in laboratory diagnosis of rabies. Because so few individuals have survived rabies, there is no information regarding immunity to disease upon being bitten again.

Clinical Findings

The incubation period varies, according to the location of the bite, from as short as 2 weeks to 16 weeks or longer. It is shorter when bites are sustained on the head rather than on the leg, because the virus has a shorter distance to travel to reach the central nervous system.

Clinically, the patient exhibits a prodrome of nonspecific symptoms such as fever, anorexia, and changes in sensation at the bite site. Within a few days, signs such as confusion, lethargy, and increased salivation develop. Most notable is the painful spasm of the throat muscles on swallowing. This results in **hydrophobia,** an aversion to swallowing water because it is so painful. Within several days, the disease progresses to seizures, paralysis, and coma. Death almost invariably ensues, but with the advent of life support systems a few individuals have survived.

Laboratory Diagnosis

Rapid diagnosis of rabies infection in the animal is usually made by examination of brain tissue by using either fluorescent antibody to rabies virus or histologic staining of Negri bodies in the cytoplasm of hippocampal neurons. The virus can be isolated from the animal brain by growth in cell culture, but this takes too long to be useful in the decision of whether to give the vaccine.

Rabies in humans can be diagnosed by fluorescent-antibody staining of a biopsy specimen, usually taken from the skin of the neck at the hairline; by isolation of the virus from sources such as saliva, spinal fluid, and brain tissue; or by a rise in titer of antibody to the virus. Negri bodies can be demonstrated in corneal scrapings and in autopsy specimens of the brain.

Treatment

There is no antiviral therapy for a patient with rabies. Only supportive treatment is available.

Prevention

There are two approaches to prevention of rabies in humans: **preexposure** and **postexposure.** Preexposure immunization with rabies vaccine should be given to individuals in high-risk groups, such as veterinarians, zookeepers, and travelers to areas of hyperendemic infection, eg, Peace Corps members. Preexposure immunization consists of three doses given on days 0, 7, and 21 or 28. Booster doses are given as needed to maintain an antibody titer of 1:5.

The rabies vaccine is the *only* vaccine that is routinely used postexposure, ie, after the person has been exposed to the virus via animal bite. The long incubation period of the disease allows the virus in the vaccine sufficient time to induce protective immunity.

In the United States, the **rabies vaccine** contains inactivated virus grown in human diploid cells. (Vaccine grown in monkey lung cells or chick embryo cells is also available.) In other countries, the duck embryo vaccine or various nerve tissue vaccines are available as well. Duck embryo vaccine has low immunogenicity, and the nerve tissue vaccines can cause an allergic encephalomyelitis as a result of a cross-reaction with human myelin; for these reasons, the human diploid cell vaccine (HDCV) is preferred.

Postexposure immunization involves the use of both the **vaccine and human rabies immune globulin** (RIG, obtained from hyperimmunized persons) plus immediate cleaning of the wound. This is an example of passive-active immunization. Tetanus immunization should also be considered.

The decision to give postexposure immunization depends on a variety of factors, such as (1) the type of animal (all wild-animal attacks demand immunization); (2) whether an attack by a domestic animal was provoked, whether the animal was immunized adequately, and whether the animal is available to be observed; and (3) whether rabies is endemic in the area. The advice of local public health officials should be sought. Hospital personnel exposed to a patient with rabies need not be immunized unless a significant exposure has occurred, eg, a traumatic wound to the health care worker.

If the decision is to immunize, both HDCV and RIG are recommended. Five doses of HDCV are given (on days 0, 3, 7, 14, and 28), but RIG is given only once with the first dose of HDCV (at a different site). HDCV and RIG are given at different sites to prevent neutralization of the virus in the vaccine by the antibody in the RIG. As much as possible of the RIG is given into the bite site, and the remainder is given intramuscularly. If the animal has been captured, it should be observed for 10 days and euthanized if symptoms develop. The brain of the animal should be examined by immunofluorescence.

The vaccine for immunization of dogs and cats consists of inactivated rabies virus. The first immunization is usually given at 3 months of age, with booster doses given either annually or at 3-year intervals.

■ RETROVIRUSES

HUMAN T-CELL LYMPHOTROPIC VIRUS

There are two important human retroviruses: human T-cell lymphotropic virus, which is described here, and human immunodeficiency virus (HIV), which is described in Chapter 45.

Disease

Human T-cell lymphotropic virus-1 (HTLV) causes two distinctly different diseases: a cancer called adult T-cell leukemia/lymphoma and a neurologic disease called HTLV-associated myelopathy (also known as tropical spastic paraparesis or chronic progressive myelopathy). HTLV-2 also appears to cause these diseases, but the association is less clearly documented. (All information in this section refers to HTLV-1 unless otherwise stated.)

Important Properties

HTLV and HIV are the two medically important members of the retrovirus family. Both are enveloped viruses with reverse transcriptase in the virion and two copies of a single-stranded, positive-polarity RNA genome. However, HTLV does not kill T cells, whereas HIV does. In fact, HTLV does just the opposite; it causes malignant transformation that "immortalizes" the infected T cells and allows them to proliferate in an uncontrolled manner.

The genes in the HTLV genome whose functions have been clearly identified are the three structural genes common to all retroviruses, namely, *gag*, *pol*, and *env*, plus two regulatory genes, *tax* and *rex*. In general, HTLV genes and proteins are similar to those of HIV in size and function, but the genes differ in base sequence and therefore the proteins differ in amino acid sequence (and antigenicity). For example, p24 is the major nucleocapsid protein in both HTLV and HIV, but they differ antigenically. The virions of both HTLV and HIV contain a reverse transcriptase, integrase, and protease. The envelope proteins of HTLV are gp46 and gp21, whereas those of HIV are gp120 and gp41.

The proteins encoded by the *tax* and *rex* genes play the same functional roles as those encoded by the HIV regulatory genes, *tat* and *rev*. The Tax protein is a transcriptional activator, and the Rex protein governs the processing of viral mRNA and its export from the nucleus to the cytoplasm. Tax protein is required for malignant transformation of T cells.

In contrast to other oncogenic retroviruses, such as Rous sarcoma virus in chickens (see page 308), HTLV does not possess an oncogene in its genome and does not integrate its proviral DNA at a specific site near a cellular oncogene in the T-cell DNA; ie, it does not cause insertional mutagenesis. Rather, it is the activation of transcription of both cellular and viral mRNA synthesis by the Tax protein that initiates oncogenesis. The Tax protein activates the synthesis of IL-2 (which is T-cell growth factor) and of the IL-2 receptor. IL-2 promotes rapid T-cell growth and eventually malignant transformation of the T cell.

The stability of the genes of HTLV is much greater

than that of HIV. As a consequence, HTLV does not show the high degree of variability of the antigenicity of the envelope proteins that occurs in HIV.

Summary of Replicative Cycle

The replication of HTLV is thought to follow a typical retroviral cycle, but specific information has been difficult to obtain because the virus grows poorly in cell culture. HTLV primarily infects CD4-positive T lymphocytes. The cellular receptor for the virus is unknown. Within the cytoplasm, reverse transcriptase synthesizes a DNA copy of the genome, which migrates to the nucleus and integrates into cell DNA. Viral mRNA is made by host cell RNA polymerase and transcription is upregulated by Tax protein, as mentioned above. The Rex protein controls the synthesis of the *gag/pol* mRNA, the *env* mRNA, and their subsequent transport to the cytoplasm, where they are translated into structural viral proteins. Full-length RNA destined to become progeny genome RNA is also synthesized and transported to the cytoplasm. The virion nucleocapsid is assembled in the cytoplasm and budding occurs at the outer cell membrane. Cleavage of precursor polypeptides into functional structural proteins is mediated by the virus-encoded protease.

Transmission & Epidemiology

HTLV is transmitted primarily by intravenous drug use, sexual contact, or breast feeding. Transplacental transmission has been rarely documented. Transmission by blood transfusion has greatly decreased in the United States with the advent of screening donated blood for antibodies to HTLV and discarding those that are positive. Transmission by processed blood products, such as immune serum globulins, has not occurred. Transmission is thought to occur primarily by the transfer of infected cells rather than free, extracellular virus. For example, whole blood, but not plasma, is a major source and infected lymphocytes in semen are the main source of sexually transmitted virus.

HTLV infection is endemic in certain geographic areas, namely, the Caribbean region including southern Florida, eastern South America, western Africa, and southern Japan. The rate of seropositive adults is as high as 20% in some of these areas, but infection can occur anywhere because infected individuals migrate from these areas of endemic infection. At least half the people in the United States who are infected with HTLV are infected with HTLV-2, usually acquired via intravenous drug use.

Pathogenesis & Immunity

HTLV causes two distinct diseases, each with a different type of pathogenesis. One disease is adult T-cell leukemia/lymphoma (ATL) in which HTLV infection of CD4-positive T lymphocytes induces malignant transformation. As described above, HTLV-encoded Tax protein enhances synthesis of IL-2 (T-cell growth factor) and IL-2 receptor, which initiates the uncontrolled growth characteristic of a cancer cell. All the malignant T cells contain the same integrated proviral DNA, indicating that the malignancy is monoclonal, ie, it arose from a single HTLV-infected cell. HTLV remains latent within the malignant T cells; ie, HTLV is typically not produced by the malignant cells.

The other disease is HTLV-associated myelopathy (HAM), also known as tropical spastic paraparesis or chronic progressive myelopathy. HAM is a demyelinating disease of the brain and spinal cord, especially of the motor neurons in the spinal cord. HAM is caused either by an autoimmune cross-reaction in which the immune response against HTLV damages the neurons or by cytotoxic T cells that kill HTLV-infected neurons.

Clinical Findings

ATL is characterized by lymphadenopathy, hepatosplenomegaly, lytic bone lesions, and skin lesions. These features are caused by proliferating T cells infiltrating these organs. In the blood, the malignant T cells have a distinct "flower-shaped" nucleus. Hypercalcemia due to increased osteoclast activity within the bone lesions is seen. Patients with ATL often have reduced cell-mediated immunity, and opportunistic infections with fungi and viruses are common.

The clinical features of HAM include gait disturbance, weakness of the lower limbs, and low back pain. Loss of bowel and bladder control may occur. Loss of motor function is much greater than sensory loss. T cells with a "flower-shaped" nucleus can be found in the spinal fluid. Magnetic resonance imaging of the brain shows nonspecific findings. Progression of symptoms occurs slowly over a period of years. HAM occurs primarily in women of middle age. The disease resembles multiple sclerosis except that HAM does not exhibit the remissions characteristic of multiple sclerosis.

Both ATL and HAM are relatively rare diseases. The vast majority of people infected with HTLV develop asymptomatic infections, usually detected by the presence of antibody. Only a small subset of those infected develop either ATL or HAM.

Laboratory Diagnosis

Infection with HTLV is determined by detecting antibodies against the virus in the patient's serum using the ELISA test. The Western blot assay is used to confirm a positive ELISA result. PCR assay can detect the presence of HTLV RNA or DNA within infected cells. The laboratory tests used to screen donated blood contain only HTLV-1 antigens, but because there is cross-reactivity between HTLV-1 and HTLV-2, the presence of antibodies against both viruses is usually detected. However, some HTLV-2 antibodies are missed in these routine screening tests. Isolation of HTLV in cell culture from the patient's specimens is not done.

ATL is diagnosed by finding malignant T cells in the lesions. The diagnosis of HAM is supported by the presence of HTLV antibody in the spinal fluid or finding HTLV nucleic acids in cells in the spinal fluid.

Treatment & Prevention

There is no specific antiviral treatment for HTLV infection, and no antiviral drug will cure latent infections by HTLV. ATL is treated with anti-cancer chemotherapy regimens. Antiviral drugs have not been effective in the treatment of HAM. Corticosteroids and danazol have produced improvement in some patients.

There is no vaccine against HTLV. Preventive measures include screening donated blood for the presence of antibodies, using condoms to prevent sexual transmission, and encouraging women with HTLV antibodies to refrain from breast feeding.

SUMMARIES OF ORGANISMS

Brief summaries of the organisms described in this chapter begin on page 496. Please consult these summaries for a rapid review of the essential material.

PRACTICE QUESTIONS: USMLE & COURSE EXAMINATIONS

Questions on the topics discussed in this chapter can be found in the Clinical Virology section of Part XI: USMLE (National Board) Practice Questions starting on page 549. Also see Part XII: USMLE (National Board) Practice Examination starting on page 583.

RNA Nonenveloped Viruses

40

■ PICORNAVIRUSES

Picornaviruses are small (20–30 nm) **nonenveloped** viruses composed of an **icosahedral nucleocapsid** and a **single-stranded** RNA genome. The genome RNA has positive polarity; ie, on entering the cell, it functions as the viral mRNA. The genome RNA is unusual because it has a protein on the 5′ end that serves as a primer for transcription by RNA polymerase. Picornaviruses replicate in the cytoplasm of cells. They are not inactivated by lipid solvents, such as ether, because they do not have an envelope.

The picornavirus family includes two groups of medical importance: the **enteroviruses** and the **rhinoviruses.** Among the major enteroviruses are poliovirus, coxsackieviruses, echoviruses, and hepatitis A virus (which is described in Chapter 41). Enteroviruses infect primarily the enteric tract, whereas rhinoviruses are found in the nose and throat (rhino = nose).

Important features of viruses that commonly infect the intestinal tract are summarized in Table 40–1. Enteroviruses replicate optimally at 37°C, whereas rhinoviruses grow better at 33°C, in accordance with the lower temperature of the nose. Enteroviruses are stable under acid conditions (pH 3–5), which enables them to survive exposure to gastric acid, whereas rhinoviruses are acid-labile. This explains why rhinovirus infections are restricted to the nose and throat.

ENTEROVIRUSES

1. Poliovirus

Disease

This virus causes poliomyelitis.

Important Properties

The host range is limited to primates, ie, humans and nonhuman **primates** such as apes and monkeys. This limitation is due to the binding of the viral capsid protein to a receptor found only on primate cell membranes. However, note that purified viral RNA (without the capsid protein) can enter and replicate in many nonprimate cells—the RNA can bypass the cell membrane receptor; ie, it is "infectious RNA."

There are **three serologic (antigenic) types** based on different antigenic determinants on the outer capsid proteins. Because there is little cross-reaction, protection from disease requires the presence of antibody against each of the three types.

Summary of Replicative Cycle

The virion interacts with specific cell receptors on the cell membrane and then enters the cell. The capsid proteins are then removed. After uncoating, the genome RNA functions as mRNA and is translated into **one very large polypeptide** called noncapsid viral protein 00. This polypeptide is cleaved by a virus-encoded protease in multiple steps to form both the capsid proteins of the progeny virions and several noncapsid proteins, including the RNA polymerase that synthesizes the progeny RNA genomes. Replication of the genome occurs by synthesis of a complementary negative strand, which then serves as the template for the positive strands. Some of these positive strands function as mRNA to make more viral proteins, and the remainder become progeny virion genome RNA. Assembly of the progeny virions occurs by coating of the genome RNA with capsid proteins. Virions accumulate in the cell cytoplasm and are released upon death of the cell. They do not bud from the cell membrane.

Transmission & Epidemiology

Poliovirus is transmitted by the **fecal-oral** route. It replicates in the oropharynx and intestinal tract. Humans are the only natural hosts.

As a result of the success of the vaccine, poliomyelitis caused by naturally occurring "wild-type" virus has been **eradicated** from the United States and, indeed, **from the entire Western hemisphere.** The rare cases in the United States occur mainly in (1) people exposed to virulent revertants of the attenuated virus in the live vaccine and (2) unimmunized people exposed to "wild-type" poliovirus while traveling abroad. Before the vaccine was available, epidemics occurred in the summer and fall.

Poliomyelitis used to be a feared disease worldwide,

Table 40–1. Features of viruses commonly infecting the intestinal tract.

Virus	Nucleic Acid	Disease	Number of Serotypes	Lifelong Immunity to Disease	Vaccine Available	Antiviral Therapy
Poliovirus	RNA	Poliomyelitis	3	Yes (type-specific)	+	−
Echoviruses	RNA	Meningitis, etc	Many	No	−	−
Coxsackieviruses	RNA	Meningitis, carditis, etc	Many	No	−	−
Hepatitis A virus (enterovirus 72)	RNA	Hepatitis	1	Yes	+	−
Rotavirus	RNA	Diarrhea	Several[1]	No	−[2]	−
Norwalk virus (Norovirus)	RNA	Diarrhea	Unknown	No	−	−
Adenovirus	DNA	Diarrhea	41; of which 2 cause diarrhea	Unknown	−	−

[1]Exact number uncertain.
[2]Rotavirus vaccine was released but was withdrawn because of side effects (see text).

but the World Health Organization anticipates that by the year 2005 or soon thereafter, it will be eradicated. The widespread use of the live vaccine (see below) made this remarkable feat possible. Thus far, smallpox is the only infectious disease that has been eradicated, a consequence of the worldwide use of the smallpox vaccine.

Pathogenesis & Immunity

After replicating in the oropharynx and small intestine, especially in lymphoid tissue, the virus spreads through the bloodstream to the central nervous system. It can also spread retrograde along nerve axons.

In the central nervous system, poliovirus preferentially replicates in the **motor neurons** located in the **anterior horn** of the spinal cord. Death of these cells results in paralysis of the muscles innervated by those neurons. Paralysis is not due to virus infection of muscle cells. The virus also affects the brain stem, leading to "bulbar" poliomyelitis (with respiratory paralysis), but rarely damages the cerebral cortex.

In infected individuals, the immune response consists of both intestinal IgA and humoral IgG to the specific serotype. Infection provides lifelong type-specific immunity.

Clinical Findings

The range of responses to poliovirus infection includes (1) inapparent, asymptomatic infection; (2) abortive poliomyelitis; (3) nonparalytic poliomyelitis; and (4)

paralytic poliomyelitis. Asymptomatic infection is quite common. Roughly 1% of infections are clinically apparent. The incubation period is usually 10–14 days.

The most common clinical form is abortive poliomyelitis, which is a mild, febrile illness characterized by headache, sore throat, nausea, and vomiting. Most patients recover spontaneously. Nonparalytic poliomyelitis manifests as aseptic meningitis with fever, headache, and a stiff neck. This also usually resolves spontaneously. In paralytic poliomyelitis, flaccid paralysis is the predominant finding, but brain stem involvement can lead to life-threatening respiratory paralysis. Painful muscle spasms also occur. The motor nerve damage is permanent, but some recovery of muscle function occurs as other nerve cells take over. In paralytic polio, both the meninges and the brain parenchyma (meningoencephalitis) are often involved. If the spinal cord is also involved, the term meningomyeloencephalitis is often used.

A post-polio syndrome that occurs many years after the acute illness has been described. Marked deterioration of the residual function of the affected muscles occurs many years after the acute phase. The cause of this deterioration is unknown.

No permanent carrier state occurs following infection by poliovirus, but virus excretion in the feces can occur for several months.

Laboratory Diagnosis

The diagnosis is made either by isolation of the virus or by a rise in antibody titer. Virus can be recovered from the throat, stool, or spinal fluid by inoculation of cell cultures. The virus causes a cytopathic effect (CPE) and can be identified by neutralization of the CPE with specific antisera.

Treatment

There is no antiviral therapy. Treatment is limited to symptomatic relief and respiratory support, if needed. Physiotherapy for the affected muscles is important.

Prevention

Poliomyelitis can be prevented by both the **killed** vaccine (Salk vaccine, inactivated vaccine, IPV) and the **live, attenuated** vaccine (Sabin vaccine, oral vaccine, OPV) (Table 40–2). Both vaccines induce humoral antibodies, which neutralize virus entering the blood and hence prevent central nervous system infection and disease. Both the killed and the live vaccines contain all three serotypes. At present, the **inactivated vaccine** is preferred for reasons that are described below.

The current version of the inactivated vaccine is called **enhanced polio vaccine, or eIPV**. It has a higher seroconversion rate and induces a higher titer of antibody than the previous IPV. eIPV also induces some mucosal immunity IgA, making it capable of interrupting transmission, but the amount of secretory IgA induced by eIPV is significantly less than the amount induced by OPV. OPV is therefore preferred for eradication efforts. The only version of polio vaccine currently produced in the United States is eIPV. In certain countries where polio remains endemic (eg, India), a monovalent oral polio vaccine is used because the rate of seroconversion is higher with the monovalent vaccine than with the trivalent one.

In the past, the live vaccine was preferred in the United States for two main reasons. (1) It interrupts fecal-oral transmission by inducing secretory IgA in the gastrointestinal tract. (2) It is given orally and so is more readily accepted than the killed vaccine, which must be injected.

The live vaccine has four disadvantages: (1) Rarely, **reversion** of the attenuated virus to virulence will occur, and disease may ensue (especially for the type 3 virus): (2) it can cause disease in immunodeficient persons and therefore should not be given to them; (3) infection of the gastrointestinal tract by other enteroviruses can limit replication of the vaccine virus and reduce protection; and (4) it must be kept refrigerated to prevent heat inactivation of the live virus.

The duration of immunity is thought to be longer with the live than with the killed vaccine, but a booster dose is recommended with both.

The currently approved vaccine schedule consists of four doses of inactivated vaccine administered at 2 months, 4 months, 6–18 months, and upon entry to school at 4–6 years. One booster (lifetime) is recommended for adults who travel to endemic areas. The use of the inactivated vaccine should prevent some of the approximately 10 cases per year of vaccine-associated

Table 40–2. Important features of poliovirus vaccines.

Attribute	Killed (Salk)	Live (Sabin)
Prevents disease	Yes	Yes
Interrupts transmission	No	Yes
Induces humoral IgG	Yes	Yes
Induces intestinal IgA	No	Yes
Affords secondary protection by spread to others	No	Yes
Interferes with replication of virulent virus in gut	No	Yes
Reverts to virulence	No	Yes (rarely)
Coinfection with other enteroviruses may impair immunization	No	Yes
Can cause disease in the immunocompromised	No	Yes
Route of administration	Injection	Oral
Requires refrigeration	No	Yes
Duration of immunity	Shorter	Longer

paralytic polio that arise from reversion of the attenuated virus in the vaccine. In the past, some lots of poliovirus vaccines were contaminated with a papovavirus, SV40 virus, which causes sarcomas in rodents. SV40 virus was a "passenger" virus in the monkey kidney cells used to grow the poliovirus for the vaccine. Fortunately, no increase in cancer occurred in persons inoculated with the SV40 virus–containing polio vaccine. However, there is some evidence that SV40 DNA can be found in certain human cancers such as non-Hodgkin's lymphoma; the role of SV40 as a cause of cancer in persons immunized with early versions of the polio vaccine is unresolved. At present, cell cultures used for vaccine purposes are carefully screened to exclude the presence of adventitious viruses.

Passive immunization with immune serum globulin is available for protection of unimmunized individuals known to have been exposed. Passive immunization of newborns as a result of passage of maternal IgG antibodies across the placenta also occurs.

Quarantine of patients with disease is not effective, because fecal excretion of the virus occurs in infected individuals prior to the onset of symptoms and in those who remain asymptomatic.

2. Coxsackieviruses

Coxsackieviruses are named for the town of Coxsackie, NY, where they were first isolated.

Diseases

Coxsackieviruses cause a variety of diseases. Group A viruses cause, for example, herpangina, acute hemorrhagic conjunctivitis, and hand-foot-and-mouth disease, whereas group B viruses cause pleurodynia, myocarditis, and pericarditis. Both types cause nonspecific upper respiratory tract disease (common cold), febrile rashes, and aseptic meningitis.

Important Properties

Group classification is based on pathogenicity in mice. Group A viruses cause widespread myositis and flaccid paralysis, which is rapidly fatal, whereas group B viruses cause generalized, less severe lesions of the heart, pancreas, and central nervous system and focal myositis. At least 24 serotypes of coxsackievirus A and 6 serotypes of coxsackievirus B are recognized.

The size and structure of the virion and the nature of the genome RNA are similar to those of poliovirus. Unlike poliovirus, they can infect mammals other than primates.

Summary of Replicative Cycle

Replication is similar to that of poliovirus.

Transmission & Epidemiology

Coxsackieviruses are transmitted primarily by the **fecal-oral** route, but respiratory **aerosols** also play a role. They replicate in the oropharynx and the intestinal tract. Humans are the only natural hosts. Coxsackievirus infections occur worldwide, primarily in the summer and fall.

Pathogenesis & Immunity

Group A viruses have a predilection for skin and mucous membranes, whereas group B viruses cause disease in various organs such as the heart, pleura, pancreas, and liver. Both group A and B viruses can affect the meninges and the motor neurons (anterior horn cells) to cause paralysis. From their original site of replication in the oropharynx and gastrointestinal tract, they disseminate via the bloodstream.

Immunity following infection is provided by type-specific IgG antibody.

Clinical Findings

A. GROUP A–SPECIFIC DISEASES

Herpangina is characterized by fever, sore throat, and tender vesicles in the oropharynx. Hand-foot-and-mouth disease is characterized by a vesicular rash on the hands and feet and ulcerations in the mouth, mainly in children.

B. GROUP B–SPECIFIC DISEASES

Pleurodynia (Bornholm disease, epidemic myalgia, "devil's grip") is characterized by fever and severe pleuritic-type chest pain. **Myocarditis** and pericarditis are characterized by fever, chest pain, and signs of congestive failure. Dilated cardiomyopathy with global hypokinesia of the myocardium is a feared sequel that often requires cardiac transplantation to sustain life. **Diabetes** in mice can be caused by pancreatic damage as a result of infection with coxsackievirus B4. This virus is suspected to have a similar role in juvenile diabetes in humans.

C. DISEASES CAUSED BY BOTH GROUPS

Both groups of viruses can cause **aseptic meningitis,** mild paresis, and acute flaccid paralysis similar to poliomyelitis. Upper respiratory infections and minor febrile illnesses with or without rash can occur also.

Laboratory Diagnosis

The diagnosis is made either by isolating the virus in cell culture or suckling mice or by observing a rise in titer of neutralizing antibodies.

Treatment & Prevention

There is neither antiviral drug therapy nor a vaccine available against these viruses. No passive immunization is recommended.

3. Echoviruses

The prefix ECHO is an acronym for *enteric cytopathic human orphan*. Although called "orphans" because they were not initially associated with any disease, they are now known to cause a variety of diseases such as aseptic meningitis, upper respiratory tract infection, febrile illness with and without rash, infantile diarrhea, and hemorrhagic conjunctivitis.

The structure of echoviruses is similar to that of other enteroviruses. More than 30 serotypes have been isolated. In contrast to coxsackieviruses, they are not pathogenic for mice. Unlike polioviruses, they do not cause disease in monkeys. They are transmitted by the **fecal-oral** route and occur worldwide. Pathogenesis is similar to that of the other enteroviruses.

Along with coxsackieviruses, echoviruses are one of the **leading causes of aseptic (viral) meningitis.** The diagnosis is made by isolation of the virus in cell culture. Serologic tests are of little value, because there are a large number of serotypes and no common antigen. There is no antiviral therapy or vaccine available.

4. Other Enteroviruses

In view of the difficulty in classifying many enteroviruses, all new isolates have been given a simple numerical designation since 1969.

Enterovirus 70 is the main cause of acute hemorrhagic conjunctivitis, characterized by petechial hemorrhages on the bulbar conjunctivas. Complete recovery usually occurs, and there is no therapy.

Enterovirus 71 is one of the leading causes of viral central nervous system disease, including meningitis, encephalitis, and paralysis. It also causes diarrhea, pulmonary hemorrhages, hand-foot-and-mouth disease, and herpangina. Enterovirus 72 is hepatitis A virus, which is described in Chapter 41.

RHINOVIRUSES

Disease

These viruses are the main cause of the common cold.

Important Properties

There are **more than 100 serologic types**. They **replicate better at 33°C** than at 37°C, which explains why they affect primarily the nose and conjunctiva rather than the lower respiratory tract. Because they are **acid-labile**, they are killed by gastric acid when swallowed. This explains why they do not infect the gastrointestinal tract, unlike the enteroviruses. The host range is limited to humans and chimpanzees.

Summary of Replicative Cycle

Replication is similar to that of poliovirus. The cell surface receptor for rhinoviruses is ICAM-1, an adhesion protein located on the surface of many types of cells.

Transmission & Epidemiology

There are **two modes** of transmission for these viruses. In the past, it was accepted that they were transmitted directly from person to person via aerosols of respiratory droplets. However, now it appears that an indirect mode, in which respiratory droplets are deposited on the hands or on a surface such as a table and then transported by fingers to the nose or eyes, is also important.

The common cold is reputed to be the most common human infection, although data are difficult to obtain because it is not a well-defined or notifiable disease. Millions of days of work and school are lost each year as a result of "colds." Rhinoviruses occur worldwide, causing disease particularly in the fall and winter. The reason for this seasonal variation is unclear. Low temperatures per se do not predispose to the common cold, but the crowding that occurs at schools, for example, may enhance transmission during fall and winter. The frequency of colds is high in childhood and tapers off during adulthood, presumably because of the acquisition of immunity.

A few serotypes of rhinoviruses are prevalent during one season, only to be replaced by other serotypes during the following season. It appears that the population builds up immunity to the prevalent serotypes but remains susceptible to the others.

Pathogenesis & Immunity

The portal of entry is the upper respiratory tract, and the infection is limited to that region. Rhinoviruses rarely cause lower respiratory tract disease, probably because they grow poorly at 37°C.

Immunity is serotype-specific and is a function of nasal secretory IgA rather than humoral antibody.

Clinical Findings

After an incubation period of 2–4 days, sneezing, nasal discharge, sore throat, cough, and headache are common. A chilly sensation may occur, but there are few other systemic symptoms. The illness lasts about 1 week. Note that other viruses such as coronaviruses, adenoviruses, influenza C virus, and coxsackieviruses also cause the common cold syndrome.

Laboratory Diagnosis

Diagnosis can be made by isolation of the virus from nasal secretions in cell culture, but this is rarely attempted. Serologic tests are not done.

Treatment & Prevention

No specific antiviral therapy is available. Vaccines appear impractical because of the large number of serotypes. Paper tissues impregnated with a combination of citric acid (which inactivates rhinoviruses) and sodium lauryl sulfate (a detergent that inactivates enveloped viruses such as influenza virus and respiratory syncytial virus) limit transmission when used to remove viruses from fingers contaminated with respiratory secretions. High doses of vitamin C have little ability to prevent rhinovirus-induced colds. Lozenges containing zinc gluconate are available for the treatment of the common cold, but their efficacy remains unproved.

■ CALICIVIRUSES

Caliciviruses are small, nonenveloped viruses with single-stranded RNA of positive polarity. Although they share those features with picornaviruses, caliciviruses are distinguished from picornaviruses by having a larger genome and having distinctive spikes on the surface. There are two human pathogens in the Calicivirus family: Norwalk virus and hepatitis E virus. Hepatitis E virus is described in Chapter 41.

NORWALK VIRUS (NOROVIRUS)

Disease

Norwalk virus (also known as Norovirus) is one of the most common causes of viral gastroenteritis in adults worldwide. It is named for an outbreak of gastroenteritis in a school in Norwalk, Ohio, in 1969.

Important Properties

Norwalk virus has a nonsegmented, single-stranded, positive-polarity RNA genome. It is a nonenveloped virus with an icosahedral nucleocapsid. There is no virion polymerase. In the electron microscope, 10 prominent spikes and 32 cup-shaped depressions can be seen. The number of serotypes is uncertain.

Summary of Replicative Cycle

Norwalk virus has not been grown efficiently in cell culture, so its replicative cycle has been difficult to study. It is presumed to replicate in a manner similar to that of picornaviruses.

Transmission & Epidemiology

Norwalk virus is transmitted by the fecal-oral route, often involving the ingestion of contaminated seafood and water. Outbreaks typically occur in group settings such as cruise ships (especially in the Caribbean region), schools, camps, hospitals, and nursing homes. Person-to-person transmission also occurs, especially in group settings. There are many animal caliciviruses, but there is no evidence that they cause human infection.

Infection is enhanced by several features of the virus: low infectious dose, excretion of virus in the stool for several weeks after recovery, and resistance to inactivation by chlorination and by drying in the environment.

Pathogenesis & Immunity

Norwalk virus infection is typically limited to the mucosal cells of the intestinal tract. Watery diarrhea without red cells or white cells occurs. Many asymptomatic infections occur, as determined by the detection of antibodies. Immunity following infection appears to be brief and reinfection can occur.

Clinical Findings

Disease is characterized by sudden onset of vomiting and diarrhea accompanied by low-grade fever and abdominal cramping. Both the emesis and stool do not contain blood. The illness typically lasts several days and there are no long-term sequelae, except in certain immunocompromised patients in whom a prolonged infection can occur. In some outbreaks, certain patients manifest signs of central nervous system involvement such as headache, meningismus, photophobia, and obtundation.

Laboratory Diagnosis

The diagnosis is primarily a clinical one. A polymerase chain reaction (PCR)-based test can be used but is not often done.

Treatment & Prevention

There is no antiviral therapy or vaccine available. Dehydration and electrolyte imbalance caused by the vomiting and diarrhea may require intravenous fluids. Personal hygiene, such as hand washing, and public health measures, such as proper sewage disposal, are likely to be helpful.

■ REOVIRUSES

REO is an acronym for *r*espiratory *e*nteric *o*rphan; when the virus was discovered, it was isolated from the respiratory and enteric tracts and was not associated with any disease. Rotaviruses are the most important human pathogens in the reovirus family.

ROTAVIRUS

Disease

Rotavirus is the most common cause of viral gastroenteritis in young children.

Important Properties

Reoviruses, including rotavirus, are composed of a **segmented,**[1] **double-stranded RNA genome** surrounded by a double-layered icosahedral capsid without an envelope.

The virion contains an **RNA-dependent RNA polymerase.** A virion polymerase is required because human cells do not have an RNA polymerase that can synthesize mRNA from a double-stranded RNA template.

Many domestic animals are infected with their own strains of rotaviruses, but these are not a source of human disease. There are at least six serotypes of human rotavirus. The viral hemagglutinin is the type-specific antigen.

Summary of Replicative Cycle

Reoviruses attach to the cell surface at the site of the β-adrenergic receptor. After entry of the virion into the cell, the RNA-dependent RNA polymerase synthesizes mRNA from each of the 10 or 11 segments within the cytoplasm. The 10 or 11 mRNAs are translated into the corresponding number of structural and nonstructural proteins. One of these, an RNA polymerase, synthesizes minus strands that will become part of the genome of the progeny virus. Capsid proteins form an incomplete capsid around the minus strands, and then the plus strands of the progeny genome segments are synthesized. The virus is released from the cytoplasm by lysis of the cell, not by budding.

Transmission & Epidemiology

Rotavirus is transmitted by the **fecal-oral** route. Infection occurs worldwide, and by age 6 years most children have antibodies to at least one serotype.

Pathogenesis & Immunity

Rotavirus replicates in the mucosal cells of the small intestine, resulting in the excess secretion of fluids and electrolytes into the bowel lumen. The consequent loss of salt, glucose, and water leads to diarrhea. No inflammation occurs, and the diarrhea is nonbloody. It is thought that this watery diarrhea is caused primarily by stimulation of the enteric nervous system.

The virulence of certain reoviruses in mice has been localized to the proteins encoded by several specific genome segments. For example, one gene governs tissue tropism, whereas another controls the inhibition of cell RNA and protein synthesis.

Immunity to rotavirus infection is unclear. It is likely that intestinal IgA directed against specific serotypes protects against reinfection and that colostrum IgA protects newborns up to the age of 6 months.

Clinical Findings

Rotavirus infection is characterized by nausea, vomiting, and watery, nonbloody diarrhea. **Gastroenteritis** is most serious in **young children,** in whom dehydration and electrolyte imbalance are a major concern. Adults usually have minor symptoms.

Laboratory Diagnosis

Although the diagnosis of most cases of viral gastroenteritis does not involve the laboratory, a diagnosis can be made by **detection of rotavirus in the stool** by using radioimmunoassay or ELISA. This approach is feasible because there are large numbers of virus particles in the stool. The original demonstration of rotavirus in the stool was done by immunoelectron microscopy, in which antibody aggregated the virions, allowing them to be visualized in the electron microscope. This technique is not feasible for routine clinical use. In addition to antigen detection, the diagnosis can be made by observation of a 4-fold or greater rise in antibody titer. Although the virus can be cultured, this procedure is not routinely done.

Treatment & Prevention

There is no antiviral therapy and there is no vaccine. A previously approved vaccine (Rotashield) was withdrawn when a high rate of intussusception occurred in vaccine recipients. Hygienic measures such as proper sewage disposal and hand washing are helpful.

---

[1] Rotaviruses have 11 segments; other reoviruses have 10.

SUMMARIES OF ORGANISMS

Brief summaries of the organisms described in this chapter begin on page 498. Please consult these summaries for a rapid review of the essential material.

PRACTICE QUESTIONS: USMLE & COURSE EXAMINATIONS

Questions on the topics discussed in this chapter can be found in the Clinical Virology section of Part XI: USMLE (National Board) Practice Questions starting on page 549. Also see Part XII: USMLE (National Board) Practice Examination starting on page 583.

Hepatitis Viruses

Many viruses cause hepatitis. Of these, five medically important viruses are commonly described as "hepatitis viruses" because their main site of infection is the liver. These five are hepatitis A virus (HAV); hepatitis B virus (HBV); hepatitis C virus (HCV); hepatitis D virus (HDV, delta virus); and hepatitis E virus (HEV) (Tables 41–1 and 41–2). Other viruses, such as Epstein-Barr virus (the cause of infectious mononucleosis), cytomegalovirus, and yellow fever virus, infect the liver but also infect other sites in the body and therefore are not exclusively hepatitis viruses. They are discussed elsewhere.

HEPATITIS A VIRUS

Disease

HAV causes hepatitis A.

Important Properties

HAV is a typical **enterovirus** classified in the picornavirus family. It has a single-stranded RNA genome and a nonenveloped icosahedral nucleocapsid and replicates in the cytoplasm of the cell. It is also known as enterovirus 72. It has one serotype, and there is no antigenic relationship to HBV or other hepatitis viruses.

Summary of Replicative Cycle

HAV has a replicative cycle similar to that of other enteroviruses (the replicative cycle of poliovirus is discussed in Chapter 40).

Transmission & Epidemiology

HAV is transmitted by the **fecal-oral** route. Humans are the reservoir for HAV. Virus appears in the feces roughly 2 weeks before the appearance of symptoms, so quarantine of patients is ineffective. **Children are the most frequently infected** group, and outbreaks occur in special living situations such as summer camps and boarding schools. Common-source outbreaks arise from fecally contaminated water or food such as oysters grown in polluted water and eaten raw. Unlike HBV,

HAV is **rarely transmitted via the blood**, because the level of viremia is low and chronic infection does not occur. About 50–75% of adults in the United States have been infected, as evidenced by IgG antibody.

Pathogenesis & Immunity

The pathogenesis of HAV infection is not completely understood. The virus probably replicates in the gastrointestinal tract and spreads to the liver via the blood. Hepatocytes are infected, but the mechanism by which cell damage occurs is unclear. HAV infection of cultured cells produces no cytopathic effect. It is likely that attack by cytotoxic T cells causes the damage to the hepatocytes. The infection is cleared, the damage is repaired, and no chronic infection ensues. Hepatitis caused by the different viruses cannot be distinguished pathologically.

The immune response consists initially of IgM antibody, which is detectable at the time jaundice appears. It is therefore important in the laboratory diagnosis of hepatitis A. The appearance of IgM is followed 1–3 weeks later by the production of IgG antibody, which provides lifelong protection.

Clinical Findings

The clinical manifestations of hepatitis are virtually the same, regardless of which hepatitis virus is the cause (Table 41–3). Fever, anorexia, nausea, vomiting, and jaundice are typical. Dark urine, pale feces, and elevated transaminase levels are seen. Most cases resolve spontaneously in 2–4 weeks. Hepatitis A has a short incubation period (3–4 weeks), in contrast to that of hepatitis B, which is 10–12 weeks. Most HAV infections are asymptomatic and are detected solely by the presence of IgG antibody. No chronic hepatitis or chronic carrier state occurs, and there is no predisposition to hepatocellular carcinoma.

Laboratory Diagnosis

The detection of **IgM antibody** is the most important test. A 4-fold rise in IgG antibody titer can also be used. Isolation of the virus in cell culture is possible but not available in the clinical laboratory.

Table 41–1. Glossary of hepatitis viruses and their serologic markers.

Abbreviation	Name and Description
HAV	Hepatitis A virus (enterovirus 72), a picornavirus (nonenveloped RNA virus).
IgM HAVAb	IgM antibody to HAV; best test to detect acute hepatitis A.
HBV	Hepatitis B virus, a hepadnavirus (enveloped, partially double-stranded DNA virus); also known as Dane particle.
HBsAg	Antigen found on surface of HBV, also found on noninfectious particles in patient's blood; positive during acute disease; continued presence indicates carrier state.
HBsAb	Antibody to HBsAg; provides immunity to hepatitis B.
HBcAg	Antigen associated with core of HBV.
HBcAb	Antibody to HBcAg; positive during window phase. IgM HBcAb is an indicator of recent disease.
HBeAg	A second, different antigenic determinant in the HBV core. Important indicator of transmissibility.
HBeAb	Antibody to e antigen; indicates low transmissibility.
Non-A, non-B	Hepatitis viruses that are neither HAV nor HBV.
HCV	Enveloped RNA virus; one of the non-A, non-B viruses.
HDV	Small RNA virus with HBsAg envelope; defective virus that replicates only in HBV-infected cells.
HEV	Nonenveloped RNA virus; one of the non-A, non-B viruses.

Treatment & Prevention

No antiviral therapy is available. **Active immunization** with a vaccine containing inactivated HAV is available. The virus is grown in human cell culture and inactivated with formalin. Two doses, an initial dose followed by a booster 6–12 months later, should be given. No subsequent booster dose is recommended. The vaccine is recommended for travelers to developing countries, for children ages 2 to 18 years, and for men who have sex with men. Because many adults have antibodies to HAV, it may be cost-effective to determine whether antibodies are present before giving the vaccine. A combination vaccine that immunizes against both HAV and HBV called Twinrix is available. Twinrix contains the same immunogens as the individual HAV and HBV vaccines. **Passive immunization** with immune serum globulin prior to infection or within 14 days after exposure can prevent or mitigate the disease. Observation of proper hygiene, eg, sewage disposal and hand washing after bowel movements, is of prime importance.

Table 41–2. Important properties of hepatitis viruses.

Virus	Genome	Replication Defective	DNA Polymerase in Virion	HBsAg in Envelope	Virus Family
HAV	ssRNA	No	No	No	Picornavirus
HBV	dsDNA[1]	No	Yes	Yes	Hepadnavirus
HCV	ssRNA	No	No	No	Flavivirus
HDV	ssRNA[2]	Yes	No	Yes	Deltavirus
HEV	ssRNA	No	No	No	Calicivirus

[1]Interrupted, circular dsDNA.
[2]Circular, negative-stranded ssRNA.

Table 41–3. Clinical features of hepatitis viruses.

Virus	Mode of Transmission	Chronic Carriers	Laboratory Test Usually Used for Diagnosis	Vaccine Available	Immune Globulins Useful
HAV	Fecal-oral	No	IgM HAV	Yes	Yes
HBV	Blood, sexual, at birth	Yes	HBsAg, HBsAb, IgM HBcAb	Yes	Yes
HCV	Blood, sexual[1]	Yes	HCV Ab	No	No
HDV	Blood, sexual[1]	Yes	Ab to delta Ag	No	No
HEV	Fecal-oral	No	None	No	No

[1]Sexual transmission seems likely but is poorly documented.

HEPATITIS B VIRUS

Disease

HBV causes hepatitis B.

Important Properties

HBV is a member of the hepadnavirus family. It is a 42-nm **enveloped** virion,[1] with an icosahedral nucleocapsid core containing a **partially double-stranded circular** DNA genome (Figure 41–1 and Table 41–2).

The envelope contains a protein called the **surface** antigen (HBsAg), which is important for laboratory diagnosis and immunization.[2]

Within the core is a **DNA-dependent DNA polymerase.** The genome contains four genes (four open reading frames) that encode the following proteins: surface (envelope) protein, core (nucleocapsid) protein, DNA polymerase, and X protein, an activator of viral RNA transcription. The DNA polymerase has both RNA-dependent (reverse transcriptase) and DNA-dependent activity.

Electron microscopy of a patient's serum reveals three different types of particles: a few 42-nm virions and

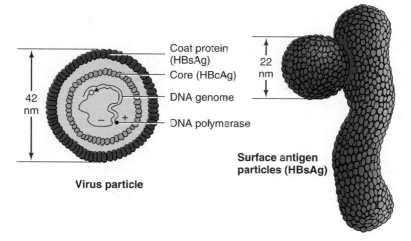

Figure 41–1. Hepatitis B virus. **Left:** Cross-section of the HBV virion. **Right:** The 22-nm spheres and filaments composed only of hepatitis B surface antigen. Because there is no viral DNA in the spheres and filaments, they are not infectious. (Modified and reproduced, with permission from Ryan K et al: *Sherris Medical Microbiology,* 3rd ed. Originally published by Appleton & Lange. Copyright © 1994 by The McGraw-Hill Companies, Inc.)

[1] Also known as a Dane particle (named for the scientist who first published electron micrographs of the virion).
[2] HBsAg was known as Australia antigen, because it was first found in the serum of an Australian aborigine.

many 22-nm **spheres** and long **filaments** 22 nm wide, which are composed of surface antigen. HBV is the only human virus that produces these spheres and filaments in such large numbers in the patient's blood. The ratio of filaments and small spheres to virions is 1000:1.

In addition to HBsAg, there are two other important antigens: the **core antigen** (HBcAg) and the **e antigen** (HBeAg), both of which are located in the core (nucleocapsid) protein but are antigenically different. HBeAg is an important indicator of **transmissibility** because the e antigen is located on the core protein, which means the infectious particle must be present in the patient's blood.

For vaccine purposes, HBV has one serotype based on HBsAg. However, for epidemiologic purposes, there are four serologic subtypes of HBsAg based on a group-specific antigen, "a," and two sets of mutually exclusive epitopes, d or y and w or r. This leads to four serotypes—adw, adr, ayw, and ayr—which are useful in epidemiologic studies because they are concentrated in certain geographic areas.

The specificity of HBV for liver cells is based on two properties: virus-specific receptors located on the hepatocyte cell membrane (facilitate entry) and transcription factors found only in the hepatocyte that enhance viral mRNA synthesis (act post-entry).

Humans are the only natural hosts of HBV. There is no animal reservoir.

Summary of Replicative Cycle

After entry of the virion into the cell and its uncoating, the virion DNA polymerase synthesizes the missing portion of DNA and a double-stranded closed-circular DNA is formed in the nucleus. This DNA serves as a template for mRNA synthesis by cellular RNA polymerase. After the individual mRNAs are made, a full-length positive-strand transcript is made, which is the template for the minus strand of the progeny DNA. The minus strand then serves as the template for the plus strand of the genome DNA. This **RNA-dependent DNA synthesis** takes place within the newly assembled virion core in the cytoplasm. The RNA-dependent DNA synthesis that produces the genome and the DNA-dependent DNA synthesis that fills in the missing portion of DNA soon after infection of the next cell are carried out by the same enzyme; ie, the HBV genome encodes only one polymerase.

Hepadnaviruses are the *only* viruses that produce genome DNA by reverse transcription with mRNA as the template. (Note that this type of RNA-dependent DNA synthesis is similar to but different from the process in retroviruses, in which the genome RNA is transcribed into a DNA intermediate.) Some of the progeny DNA integrates into the host cell genome, and this seems likely

to be the DNA that maintains the carrier state. Progeny HBV with its HBsAg-containing envelope is released from the cell by budding through the cell membrane.

Transmission & Epidemiology

The three main modes of transmission are via blood, during sexual intercourse, and perinatally from mother to newborn. The observation that needle-stick injuries can transmit the virus indicates that only very small amounts of blood are necessary. HBV infection is especially prevalent in addicts who use intravenous drugs. Screening of blood for the presence of HBsAg has greatly decreased the number of transfusion-associated cases of hepatitis B.[3]

However, because blood transfusion is a modern procedure, there must be another, natural route of transmission. It is likely that **sexual** transmission and transmission from **mother to child** during birth or breast feeding are the natural routes. Note that enveloped viruses, such as HBV, are more sensitive to the environment than nonenveloped viruses and hence are more efficiently transmitted by intimate contact, eg, sexual contact. Nonenveloped viruses, such as HAV, are quite stable and are transmitted well via the environment, eg, fecal-oral transmission.

Hepatitis B is found worldwide but is particularly prevalent in Asia. Globally, more than 300 million people are chronically infected with HBV and about 75% of them are Asian. There is a high incidence of **hepatocellular carcinoma (hepatoma)** in many Asian countries, a finding that indicates that HBV may be a human tumor virus (see Chapter 43). Immunization against HBV in Taiwan has significantly reduced the incidence of hepatoma in children. It appears that the HBV vaccine is the **first vaccine to prevent a human cancer.**

Pathogenesis & Immunity

After entering the blood, the virus infects hepatocytes, and viral antigens are displayed on the surface of the cells. Cytotoxic T cells mediate an immune attack against the viral antigens, and inflammation and necrosis occur. **Immune attack** against viral antigens on infected hepatocytes is mediated by cytotoxic T cells. The pathogenesis of hepatitis B is probably the result of this cell-mediated immune injury, because HBV itself does not cause a cytopathic effect. Antigen-antibody complexes cause some of the early symptoms, eg, arthral-

---

[3] In the United States, donated blood is screened for HBsAg and antibodies to HBcAg, HCV, HIV-1, HIV-2, and HTLV-1. Two other tests are also performed: a VDRL test for syphilis and a transaminase assay, which, if elevated, indicates liver damage and is a surrogate marker of viral infection.

gias, arthritis, and urticaria, and some of the complications in chronic hepatitis, eg, immune-complex glomerulonephritis, cryoglobulinemia, and vasculitis.

About 5% of patients with HBV infection become chronic carriers; in contrast, there is no prolonged carrier state in patients with HAV infection. A chronic carrier is someone who has **HBsAg persisting in their blood for at least 6 months.** The chronic carrier state is attributed to a persistent infection of the hepatocytes, which results in the prolonged presence of HBV and HBsAg in the blood. The main determinant of whether a person clears the infection or becomes a chronic carrier is the adequacy of the cytotoxic T-cell response. HBV DNA exists primarily as an episome in the cytoplasm of persistently infected cells; a small number of copies of HBV DNA are integrated into cell DNA.

A high rate of **hepatocellular carcinoma occurs in chronic carriers.** The HBV genome has no oncogene, and hepatocellular carcinoma appears to be the result of persistent cellular regeneration that attempts to replace the dead hepatocytes. Alternatively, malignant transformation could be the result of insertional mutagenesis, which could occur when the HBV genome integrates into the hepatocyte DNA. Integration of the HBV DNA could activate a cellular oncogene, leading to a loss of growth control.

Chronic carriage is more likely to occur when infection occurs in a newborn than in an adult, probably because a newborn's immune system is less competent than an adult's. Approximately 90% of infected neonates become chronic carriers. Chronic carriage resulting from neonatal infection is associated with a high risk of hepatocellular carcinoma.

Lifelong immunity occurs after the natural infection and is mediated by humoral antibody against HBsAg. Antibody against HBsAg (HBsAb) is protective because it binds to surface antigen on the virion and prevents it from interacting with receptors on the hepatocyte. (HBsAb is said to neutralize the infectivity of HBV.) Note that antibody against the core antigen (HBcAb) is *not* protective because the core antigen is inside the virion and the antibody cannot interact with it.

Clinical Findings

Many HBV infections are asymptomatic and are detected only by the presence of antibody to HBsAg. The mean incubation period for hepatitis B is 10–12 weeks, which is much longer than that of hepatitis A (3–4 weeks). The clinical appearance of acute hepatitis B is similar to that of hepatitis A. However, with hepatitis B, symptoms tend to be more severe, and life-threatening hepatitis can occur. Most chronic carriers are asymptomatic, but some have chronic active hepatitis, which can lead to cirrhosis and death.

Patients coinfected with both HBV and HIV may have increased hepatic damage if human immunodeficiency virus (HIV) is treated prior to treating HBV. This occurs because the "immune reconstitution" that results when HIV is treated successfully leads to increased damage to the hepatocytes by the restored, competent cytotoxic T cells. For this reason, it is suggested that HBV be treated prior to treating HIV.

Laboratory Diagnosis

The most important laboratory test for the detection of early HBV infection is the immunoassay for **HBsAg.** HBsAg appears during the incubation period and is detectable in most patients during the prodrome and acute disease (Figure 41–2). It falls to undetectable levels during convalescence in most cases; its **prolonged presence** (at least 6 months) indicates the carrier state and the risk of chronic hepatitis and hepatic carcinoma. As described in Table 41–4, HBsAb is not detectable in the chronic carrier state. Note that HBsAb is, in fact, being made but is not detectable in the laboratory tests because it is bound to the large amount of HBsAg present in the blood. HBsAb is also being made during the acute disease but is similarly undetectable because it is bound in immune complexes.

Note that there is a period of several weeks when HBsAg has disappeared but HBsAb is not yet detectable. This is the **window phase.** At this time, the HBcAb is always positive and can be used to make the diagnosis. HBcAb is present in those with acute infection and chronic infection, as well as in those who have recovered from acute infection. Therefore, it cannot be used to distinguish between acute and chronic infection. The IgM form of HBcAb is present during acute infection and disappears approximately 6 months after infection. The test for HBcAg is not readily available. Table 41–4 describes the serologic test results that characterize the four important stages of HBV infection.

HBeAg arises during the incubation period and is present during the prodrome and early acute disease and in certain chronic carriers. Its presence indicates a **high likelihood of transmissibility,** and, conversely, the finding of HBeAb indicates a lower likelihood, but transmission can still occur. DNA polymerase activity is detectable during the incubation period and early in the disease, but the assay is not available in most clinical laboratories. The detection of viral DNA in the serum is strong evidence that infectious virions are present.

Treatment & Prevention

Alpha interferon (Intron-A) is clinically useful for the treatment of chronic hepatitis B infections. Some nu-

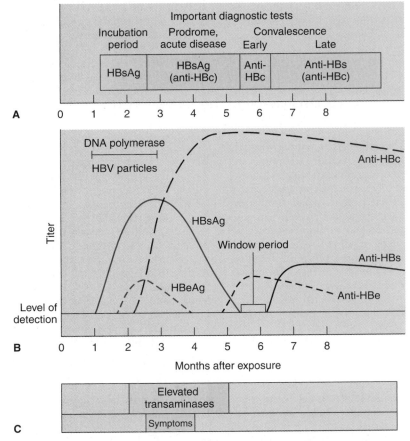

Figure 41–2. A: Important diagnostic tests during various stages of hepatitis B. **B:** Serologic findings in a patient with acute hepatitis B. **C:** Duration of increased liver enzyme activity and of symptoms in a patient with acute hepatitis B. (Modified and reproduced, with permission, from Hollinger FB, Dienstag JL: Hepatitis viruses. Chapter 81 in: *Manual of Clinical Microbiology*, 4th ed. Lennette EH et al [editors]. American Society for Microbiology, 1985.)

cleoside analogues, such as lamivudine (Epivir-HBV), that inhibit the reverse transcriptase of HIV also are effective against the DNA polymerase of HBV. Adefovir (Hepsera) is a nucleotide analogue of adenosine monophosphate that also inhibits the DNA polymerase of HBV. These drugs reduce hepatic inflammation and lower the levels of HBV in patients with chronic active hepatitis. Neither interferon nor the nucleoside analogues cure the HBV infection. In most patients when the drug is stopped, HBV replication resumes.

Table 41–4. Serologic test results in four stages of HBV infection.

Test	Acute Disease	Window Phase	Complete Recovery	Chronic Carrier State
HBsAg	Positive	Negative	Negative	Positive
HBsAb	Negative	Negative	Positive	Negative
HBcAb	Positive[1]	Positive	Positive	Positive

[1]IgM is found in the acute stage; IgG is found in subsequent stages.

Note: People immunized with HBV vaccine have HBsAb but not HBcAb because the immunogen in the vaccine is purified HBsAg.

Prevention involves the use of either the **vaccine** or **hyperimmune globulin** or both.

(1) The vaccine, eg, Recombivax, contains HBsAg produced in yeasts by recombinant DNA techniques. The vaccine is highly effective in preventing hepatitis B and has few side effects. It is indicated for people who are frequently exposed to blood or blood products, such as certain health care personnel (eg, medical students, surgeons, and dentists), patients receiving multiple transfusions or dialysis, patients with frequent sexually transmitted disease, and abusers of illicit intravenous drugs. Travelers who plan a long stay in areas of endemic infection, such as many countries in Asia and Africa, should receive the vaccine. The U.S. Public Health Service recommends that all newborns and adolescents receive the vaccine. At present, booster doses after the initial three-dose regimen are not recommended. Widespread immunization with the HBV vaccine in Taiwan has significantly reduced the incidence of hepatocellular carcinoma in children.

(2) Hepatitis B immune globulin (HBIG) contains a high titer of HBsAb because it is prepared from sera of patients who have recovered from hepatitis B. It is used to provide immediate, passive protection to individuals known to be exposed to HBsAg-positive blood, eg, after an accidental needle stick.

Precise recommendations for use of the vaccine and HBIG are beyond the scope of this book. However, the recommendation regarding one common concern of medical students, the needle-stick injury from a patient with HBsAg-positive blood, is that both the vaccine and HBIG be given (at separate sites). This is true even if the patient's blood is HBeAb positive. Both the vaccine and HBIG should also be given to a newborn whose mother is HBsAg-positive. These are good examples of **passive-active** immunization, in which both immediate and long-term protection are provided.

All blood for transfusion should be screened for HBsAg. No one with a history of hepatitis (of any type) should donate blood, because non-A, non-B viruses may be present.

NON-A, NON-B HEPATITIS VIRUSES

The term "non-A, non-B hepatitis" was coined to describe the cases of hepatitis for which existing serologic tests had ruled out all known viral causes. The term is not often used because the main cause of non-A, non-B hepatitis, namely, HCV, has been identified. In addition, HDV and HEV have been described. Cross-protection experiments indicate additional hepatitis viruses exist.

HEPATITIS C VIRUS

Disease

HCV causes hepatitis C.

Important Properties

HCV is a member of the flavivirus family. It is an enveloped virion containing a genome of single-stranded, positive-polarity RNA. It has no virion polymerase.

HCV has at least six genotypes and multiple subgenotypes based on differences in the genes that encode one of its two envelope glycoproteins. This genetic variation results in a "hypervariable" region in the envelope glycoprotein. The genetic variability is due to the high mutation rate in the envelope gene coupled with the absence of a proofreading function in the virion-encoded RNA polymerase. As a result, multiple subspecies (quasi-species) often occur in the blood of an infected individual at the same time. Genotypes 1a and 1b are the most common in the United States.

Summary of Replicative Cycle

The replication of HCV is uncertain because it has not been grown in cell culture. Other flaviviruses replicate in the cytoplasm and translate their genome RNA into large polyproteins, from which functional viral proteins are cleaved by a virion-encoded protease. It is likely that HCV replication follows this model.

The replication of HCV in the liver is enhanced by a liver-specific micro-RNA. This micro-RNA acts by increasing the synthesis of HCV mRNA. (Micro-RNAs are known to enhance cellular mRNA synthesis in many tissues.)

Transmission & Epidemiology

Humans are the reservoir for HCV. It is transmitted primarily via **blood**. At present, injection drug use accounts for almost all new HCV infections. Transmission via blood transfusion rarely occurs because donated blood containing antibody to HCV is discarded. Transmission via needle-stick injury occurs, but the risk is lower than for HBV. Sexual transmission and transmission from mother to child occur but are inefficient modes.

HCV is the **most prevalent blood-borne pathogen** in the United States. (In the nationally reported incidence data, HCV ranks below HIV and HBV as a blood-borne pathogen, but it is estimated that HCV is more prevalent.) Approximately 4 million people in the United States (1–2% of the population) are chronically infected with HCV. Unlike yellow fever virus, another flavivirus that infects the liver and is transmitted by mosquitoes, there is no evidence for an insect vector for HCV.

In the United States, about 1% of blood donors have antibody to HCV. People who share needles when taking intravenous drugs are very commonly infected. Commercially prepared immune globulin preparations are generally very safe, but several instances of the transmission of HCV have occurred. This is the only example of an infectious disease transmitted by immune globulins.

Pathogenesis & Immunity

HCV infects hepatocytes primarily, but there is no evidence for a virus-induced cytopathic effect on the liver cells. Rather, death of the hepatocytes is probably caused by immune attack by cytotoxic T cells. HCV infection strongly predisposes to hepatocellular carcinoma, but there is no evidence for an oncogene in the viral genome or for insertion of a copy of the viral genome into the DNA of the cancer cells.

Alcoholism greatly enhances the rate of hepatocellular carcinoma in HCV-infected individuals. This supports the idea that the cancer is caused by prolonged liver damage and the consequent rapid growth rate of hepatocytes as the cells attempt to regenerate rather than by a direct oncogenic effect of HCV. Added support for this idea is the observation that patients with cirrhosis of any origin, not just alcoholic cirrhosis, have an increased risk of hepatocellular carcinoma. (A report in 1998 that the core protein of HCV causes hepatocellular carcinoma in mice may lead to a greater understanding of oncogenesis by HCV.)

Antibodies against HCV are made, but approximately 75% of patients are chronically infected and continue to produce virus for at least 1 year. (Note that the rate of **chronic carriage of HCV is much higher** than the rate of chronic carriage of HBV.) Chronic active hepatitis and cirrhosis occur in approximately 10% of these patients. For patients who clear the infection, it is not known whether reinfection can occur or whether there is lifelong immunity.

Clinical Findings

Clinically, the acute infection with HCV is milder than infection with HBV. Fever, anorexia, nausea, vomiting, and jaundice are common. Dark urine, pale feces, and elevated transaminase levels are seen.

Hepatitis C resembles hepatitis B as far as the ensuing chronic liver disease, cirrhosis, and the predisposition to hepatocellular carcinoma are concerned. Note that a chronic carrier state occurs more often with HCV infection than with HBV. Liver biopsy is often done in patients with chronic infection to evaluate the extent of liver damage and to guide treatment decisions. Many infections with HCV, including both acute and chronic infections, are asymptomatic and are detected only by the presence of antibody. The mean incubation period is 8 weeks. Cirrhosis resulting from chronic HCV infection is the most common indication for liver transplantation.

HCV infection also leads to significant autoimmune reactions, including vasculitis, arthralgias, purpura, and membranoproliferative glomerulonephritis. HCV is the main cause of essential mixed cryoglobulinemia. The cryoprecipitates often are composed of HCV antigens and antibodies.

Laboratory Diagnosis

HCV infection is diagnosed by detecting antibodies to HCV in an ELISA. The antigen in the assay is a recombinant protein formed from three immunologically stable HCV proteins and does not include the highly variable envelope proteins. The test does not distinguish between IgM and IgG and does not distinguish between an acute, chronic, or resolved infection. Because false-positive results can occur in the ELISA, a RIBA (recombinant immunoblot assay) should be performed as a confirmatory test. If the results of RIBA are positive, a PCR-based test that detects the presence of viral RNA in the serum should be performed to determine whether active disease exists. Isolation of the virus from patient specimens is not done. A chronic infection is characterized by elevated transaminase levels, a positive RIBA, and detectable viral RNA for at least 6 months.

Treatment & Prevention

Treatment of acute hepatitis C with alpha interferon significantly decreases the number of patients that become chronic carriers. A combination of alpha interferon and ribavirin (Rebetron) is the treatment of choice for chronic hepatitis C, but it is expensive and has side effects that can limit its use. This treatment reduces viral replication and lowers aminotransferase levels but does not eliminate the carrier state. If side effects limit the use of the combination therapy, alpha interferon alone can be used but is less effective; ribavirin alone has no effect on HCV replication. Pegylated interferon (Peg-intron), which is alpha interferon conjugated to polyethylene glycol, is available for the treatment of chronic hepatitis C. The advantage of pegylated interferon is that it has a longer half-life than unconjugated alpha interferon and can be administered once a week instead of three times a week. Treatment with a combination of pegylated interferon and ribavirin resulted in sustained eradication of HCV in approximately half of the patients.

Blood found to contain antibody is discarded, a procedure that has prevented virtually all cases of transfusion-acquired HCV infection since 1994, when screening began. There is no vaccine, and hyperimmune globulins are not available. Pooled immune serum globulins are not useful for postexposure prophylaxis. There is no effective regimen for prophylaxis following needle-stick injury; only monitoring is recommended.

Patients with chronic HCV infection should be advised to reduce or eliminate their consumption of alcoholic beverages to reduce the risk of hepatocellular carcinoma and cirrhosis. Patients with chronic HCV infection and cirrhosis should be monitored with alpha-fetoprotein tests and liver sonograms to detect carcinoma at an early stage. Patients in liver failure due to HCV infection can receive a liver transplant, but reinfection of the graft with HCV occurs.

Patients coinfected with HCV and HIV should be prescribed "HAART" (highly active anti-retroviral therapy) with caution because recovery of cell-mediated immunity (immune reconstitution) can result in an exacerbation of hepatitis. Consideration should be given to treat the HCV infection prior to starting HAART.

HEPATITIS D VIRUS (DELTA VIRUS)

Disease

Hepatitis D virus (HDV) causes hepatitis D (hepatitis delta).

Important Properties & Replicative Cycle

HDV is unusual in that it is a **defective** virus; ie, it cannot replicate by itself because it does not have the genes for its envelope protein. HDV can replicate only in cells also infected with HBV, because HDV uses the surface antigen of HBV (HBsAg) as its envelope protein. HBV is therefore the helper virus for HDV (Figure 41–3).

HDV is an enveloped virus with an RNA genome that is a single-stranded, negative-polarity, covalently

closed circle. The RNA genome of HDV is very small and encodes only one protein, the internal core protein called **delta antigen.** HDV genome RNA has no sequence homology to HBV genome DNA. HDV has no virion polymerase; the genome RNA is replicated and transcribed by the host cell RNA polymerase. HDV genome RNA is a "ribozyme"; ie, it has the ability to self-cleave and self-ligate, properties that are employed during replication of the genome. HDV replicates in the nucleus, but the specifics of the replicative cycle are complex and beyond the scope of this book.

HDV has one serotype because HBsAg has only one serotype. There is no evidence for the existence of an animal reservoir for HDV.

Transmission & Epidemiology

HDV is transmitted by the same means as is HBV, ie, sexually, by blood, and perinatally. In the United States, most HDV infections occur in intravenous drug users who share needles. HDV infections occur worldwide with a similar distribution to that of HBV infections.

Pathogenesis & Immunity

It seems likely that the pathogenesis of hepatitis caused by HDV and HBV is the same; ie, the virus-infected hepatocytes are damaged by cytotoxic T cells. There is some evidence that delta antigen is cytopathic for hepatocytes.

IgG antibody against delta antigen is not detected for long periods after infection; it is therefore uncertain whether long-term immunity to HDV exists.

Clinical Findings

Because HDV can replicate only in cells also infected with HBV, hepatitis delta can occur only in a person infected with HBV. A person can either be infected with both HDV and HBV at the same time, ie, be "coinfected," or be previously infected with HBV and then "superinfected" with HDV.

Hepatitis in patients coinfected with HDV and HBV is more severe than in those infected with HBV alone, but the incidence of chronic hepatitis is about the same in patients infected with HBV alone. However, hepatitis in chronic carriers of HBV who become superinfected with HDV is much more severe, and the incidence of fulminant, life-threatening hepatitis, chronic hepatitis, and liver failure is significantly higher.

Laboratory Diagnosis

The diagnosis of HDV infection in the laboratory is made by detecting either delta antigen or IgM antibody to delta antigen in the patient's serum.

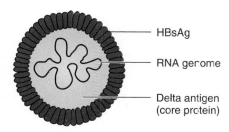

Figure 41–3. Hepatitis D virus. Note that hepatitis B surface antigen forms the outer envelope and the genome consists of circular RNA. (Modified and reproduced, with permission, from Ryan K et al: *Sherris Medical Microbiology,* 3rd ed. Originally published by Appleton & Lange. Copyright © 1994 by The McGraw-Hill Companies, Inc.)

HBsAg

RNA genome

Delta antigen
(core protein)

Treatment & Prevention

Alpha interferon can mitigate some of the effects of the chronic hepatitis caused by HDV but does not eradicate the chronic carrier state. There is no specific antiviral therapy against HDV. There is no vaccine against HDV, but a person immunized against HBV will not be infected by HDV because HDV cannot replicate unless HBV infection also occurs.

HEPATITIS E VIRUS

HEV is a major cause of enterically transmitted hepatitis. It is a common cause of water-borne epidemics of hepatitis in Asia, Africa, India, and Mexico but is uncommon in the United States. HEV is a nonenveloped, single-stranded RNA virus tentatively classified as a member of the calicivirus family. Clinically the disease resembles hepatitis A, with the exception of a high mortality rate in pregnant women. Chronic liver disease does not occur, and there is no prolonged carrier state.

The test for HEV antibody is not readily available; the diagnosis is therefore typically made by excluding HAV and other causes. There is no antiviral treatment and no vaccine.

HEPATITIS G VIRUS

In 1996, hepatitis G virus (HGV) was isolated from patients with posttransfusion hepatitis. HGV is a member of the flavivirus family, as is HCV. However, unlike HCV, which is clearly the cause of both acute hepatitis and chronic active hepatitis and predisposes to hepatocellular carcinoma, HGV has not been documented to cause any of these clinical findings. The role of HGV in the causation of liver disease has yet to be established, but it can cause a chronic infection lasting for decades. Approximately 60% to 70% of those infected clear the virus and develop antibodies.

HGV is transmitted via sexual intercourse and blood. It is carried in the blood of millions of people worldwide. In the United States, it is found in the blood of approximately 2% of random blood donors, 15% of those infected with HCV, and 35% of those infected with HIV. Patients coinfected with HIV and HGV have a lower mortality rate and have less HIV in their blood than those infected with HIV alone. It is hypothesized that HGV may interfere with the replication of HIV. (HGV is also known as GB virus C.)

SUMMARIES OF ORGANISMS

Brief summaries of the organisms described in this chapter begin on page 499. Please consult these summaries for a rapid review of the essential material.

PRACTICE QUESTIONS: USMLE & COURSE EXAMINATIONS

Questions on the topics discussed in this chapter can be found in the Clinical Virology section of Part XI: USMLE (National Board) Practice Questions starting on page 549. Also see Part XII: USMLE (National Board) Practice Examination starting on page 583.

Arboviruses

Arbovirus is an acronym for *ar*thropod-*bo*rne virus and highlights the fact that these viruses are transmitted by **arthropods,** primarily mosquitoes and ticks. It is a collective name for a large group of diverse viruses, more than 400 at last count. In general, they are named either for the diseases they cause, eg, yellow fever virus, or for the place where they were first isolated, eg, St. Louis encephalitis virus.

A new group of viruses called **roboviruses** has recently emerged. The term "robo" refers to the fact that these viruses are *rodent-bo*rne, that is, they are transmitted directly from rodents to humans without an arthropod vector. Transmission occurs when dried rodent excrement is inhaled into the human lung, as when sweeping the floor of a cabin. Two roboviruses cause a respiratory distress syndrome that is often fatal: Sin Nombre virus (a hantavirus) and Whitewater Arroyo virus (an arenavirus). These viruses are described in Chapter 46.

IMPORTANT PROPERTIES

Most arboviruses are classified in three families,[1] namely, togaviruses, flaviviruses, and bunyaviruses (Table 42–1).

(1) Togaviruses[2] are characterized by an icosahedral nucleocapsid surrounded by an envelope and a single-stranded, positive-polarity RNA genome. They are 70 nm in diameter, in contrast to the flaviviruses, which are 40–50 nm in diameter (see below). Togaviruses are divided into two families, alphaviruses and rubiviruses. Only alphaviruses are considered here. The only rubivirus is rubella virus, which is discussed in Chapter 39.

(2) Flaviviruses[3] are similar to togaviruses in that they also have an icosahedral nucleocapsid surrounded by an envelope and a single-stranded, positive-polarity RNA genome, but the flaviviruses are only 40–50 nm in diameter, whereas the togaviruses have a diameter of 70 nm.

(3) Bunyaviruses[4] have a helical nucleocapsid surrounded by an envelope and a genome consisting of three segments of negative-polarity RNA that are hydrogen-bonded together.

TRANSMISSION

The life cycle of the arboviruses is based on the ability of these viruses to multiply in *both* the vertebrate host and the bloodsucking vector. For effective transmission to occur, the virus must be present in the bloodstream of the vertebrate host (viremia) in sufficiently high titer to be taken up in the small volume of blood ingested during an insect bite. After ingestion, the virus replicates in the gut of the arthropod and then spreads to other organs, including the salivary glands. Only the female of the species serves as the vector of the virus, because only she requires a blood meal in order for progeny to be produced. An obligatory length of time, called the **extrinsic incubation period,**[5] must pass before the virus has replicated sufficiently for the saliva of the vector to contain enough virus to transmit an infectious dose. For most viruses, the extrinsic incubation period ranges from 7 to 14 days.

In addition to transmission through vertebrates, some arboviruses are transmitted by vertical "transovarian" passage from the mother tick to her offspring. Vertical transmission has important survival value for the virus if a vertebrate host is unavailable.

Humans are involved in the transmission cycle of arboviruses in two different ways. Usually, humans are **dead-end hosts,** because the concentration of virus in human blood is too low and the duration of viremia too brief for the next bite to transmit the virus. However, in some diseases, eg, yellow fever and dengue, humans have a high-level viremia and act as reservoirs of the virus.

---

[1] A few arboviruses belong to two other families. For example, Colorado tick virus is a reovirus; Kern Canyon virus and vesicular stomatitis virus are rhabdoviruses.
[2] Toga means cloak.
[3] Flavi means yellow, as in yellow fever.

[4] "Bunya" is short for Bunyamwera, the town in Africa where the prototype virus was located.
[5] The intrinsic incubation period is the interval between the time of the bite and the appearance of symptoms in the human host.

Table 42–1. Classification of the major arboviruses.

Family	Genus	Viruses of Medical Interest in the Americas
Togavirus	Alphavirus[1]	Eastern equine encephalitis virus, western equine encephalitis virus
Flavivirus	Flavivirus[2]	St. Louis encephalitis virus, yellow fever virus, dengue virus, West Nile virus
Bunyavirus	Bunyavirus[3]	California encephalitis virus
Reovirus	Orbivirus	Colorado tick fever virus

[1]Alphaviruses of other regions include Chikungunya, Mayaro, O'Nyong-Nyong, Ross River, and Semliki Forest viruses.
[2]Flaviviruses of other regions include Japanese encephalitis, Kyasanur Forest, Murray Valley encephalitis, Omsk hemorrhagic fever, Powassan encephalitis viruses, and West Nile viruses.
[3]Bunyaviruses of other regions include the Bunyamwera complex of viruses and Oropouche virus.

Infection by arboviruses usually does not result in disease either in the arthropod vector or in the vertebrate animal that serves as the natural host. Disease occurs primarily when the virus infects dead-end hosts. For example, yellow fever virus cycles harmlessly among the jungle monkeys in South America, but when the virus infects a human, yellow fever can occur.

The arboviral diseases occur primarily in the **tropics** but are also found in temperate zones such as the United States and as far north as Alaska and Siberia. They have a tendency to cause sudden outbreaks of disease, generally at the interface between human communities and jungle or forest areas.

CLINICAL FINDINGS & EPIDEMIOLOGY

The diseases caused by arboviruses range in severity from mild to rapidly fatal. The clinical picture usually fits one of three categories: (1) **encephalitis;** (2) **hemorrhagic fever;** or (3) fever with myalgias, arthralgias, and nonhemorrhagic rash. The pathogenesis of these diseases involves not only the cytocidal effect of the virus but also, in some, a prominent immunopathologic component. After recovery from the disease, immunity is usually lifelong.

■ ARBOVIRUSES THAT CAUSE DISEASE IN THE UNITED STATES

EASTERN EQUINE ENCEPHALITIS VIRUS

Of the four encephalitis viruses listed in Table 42–2, eastern equine encephalitis (EEE) virus causes the **most severe** disease and is associated with the highest fatality

Table 42–2. Epidemiology of important arbovirus diseases in the United States.

Disease[1]	Vector	Animal Reservoir	Geographic Distribution	Approximate Incidence Per Year[2]
EEE	Mosquito	Wild birds[3]	Atlantic and Gulf states	0–4
WEE	Mosquito	Wild birds[3]	West of Mississippi	5–20[4]
SLE	Mosquito	Wild birds	Widespread in southern, central, and western states	10–30[4]
CE	Mosquito	Small mammals	North-central states	40–80
CTF	Tick	Small mammals	Rocky Mountains	100–300

[1]Venezuelan equine encephalitis virus causes disease in the United States too rarely to be included.
[2]Human cases.
[3]Horses are dead-end hosts, not reservoirs.
[4]Hundreds of cases during an outbreak.

rate (approximately 50%). In its natural habitat, the virus is transmitted primarily by the swamp **mosquito**, *Culiseta*, among the small wild birds of the Atlantic and Gulf Coast states. Species of *Aedes* mosquitoes are suspected of carrying the virus from its **wild-bird reservoir** to the principal **dead-end hosts, horses** and **humans.** The number of cases of human encephalitis caused by EEE virus in the United States usually ranges from zero to four per year, but outbreaks involving hundreds of cases also occur. Subclinical infections greatly exceed the number of overt cases.

The encephalitis is characterized by the sudden onset of severe headache, nausea, vomiting, and fever. Changes in mental status, such as confusion and stupor, ensue. A rapidly progressive downhill course with nuchal rigidity, seizures, and coma occurs. If the patient survives, the central nervous system sequelae are usually severe. Immunity following the infection is lifelong.

The diagnosis is made by either isolating the virus or demonstrating a rise in antibody titer. Clinicians should have a high index of suspicion in the summer months in the appropriate geographic areas. The disease does not occur in the winter because mosquitoes are not active. It is not known how the virus survives the winter—in birds, mosquitoes, or perhaps some other animal.

No antiviral therapy is available. A killed vaccine is available to protect horses but not humans. The disease is too rare for production of a human vaccine to be economically feasible.

WESTERN EQUINE ENCEPHALITIS VIRUS

Western equine encephalitis (WEE) virus causes disease more frequently than does EEE virus, but the illness is less severe. Inapparent infections outnumber the apparent by at least 100:1. The number of cases in the United States usually ranges between 5 and 20 per year, and the fatality rate is roughly 2%.

The virus is transmitted primarily by *Culex* **mosquitoes** among the **wild-bird** population of the western states, especially in areas with irrigated farmland.

The clinical picture of WEE virus infection is similar to but less severe than that caused by EEE virus. Sequelae are less common. The diagnosis is made by isolating the virus or observing a rise in antibody titer. There is no antiviral therapy. There is a killed vaccine for horses but not for humans.

ST. LOUIS ENCEPHALITIS VIRUS

St. Louis encephalitis (SLE) virus causes disease over a wider geographic area than do EEE and WEE virus. It is found in the southern, central, and western states

and causes 10–30 cases of encephalitis per year in the United States.

The virus is transmitted by several species of *Culex* **mosquitoes** that vary depending upon location. Again, small **wild birds**, especially English sparrows, are the reservoir and humans are dead-end hosts. Although EEE and WEE viruses are predominantly rural, SLE virus occurs in **urban areas** because these mosquitoes prefer to breed in stagnant wastewater.

SLE virus causes moderately severe encephalitis with a fatality rate that approaches 10%. Most infections are inapparent. Sequelae are uncommon.

The diagnosis is usually made serologically, because the virus is difficult to isolate. No antiviral therapy or vaccine is available.

CALIFORNIA ENCEPHALITIS VIRUS

California encephalitis (CE) virus was first isolated from mosquitoes in California in 1952, but its name is something of a misnomer because most human disease occurs in the north-central states. The strain of the 11 CE viruses that causes encephalitis most frequently is called La Crosse for the city in Wisconsin where it was isolated. CE virus is the only one of the four major encephalitis viruses in the United States that is a member of the **bunyavirus** family.

La Crosse virus, as it is often called, is the most common arboviral cause of encephalitis in the United States. It is transmitted by the **mosquito** *Aedes triseriatus* among forest **rodents.** The virus is passed transovarially in mosquitoes and thus survives the winter when mosquitoes are not active.

The clinical picture can be mild, resembling enteroviral meningitis, or severe, resembling herpes encephalitis. Death rarely occurs. Diagnosis is usually made serologically rather than by isolation of the virus. No antiviral therapy or vaccine is available.

COLORADO TICK FEVER VIRUS

Of the five diseases described in Table 42–2, Colorado tick fever (CTF) is the most easily distinguished from the others, both biologically and clinically. CTF virus is a **reovirus** transmitted by the wood **tick** *Dermacentor andersoni* among the small **rodents,** eg, chipmunks and squirrels, of the Rocky Mountains. There are approximately 100–300 cases per year in the United States.

The disease occurs primarily in people hiking or camping in the Rocky Mountains and is characterized by fever, headache, retro-orbital pain, and severe myalgia. The diagnosis is made either by isolating the virus from the blood or by detecting a rise in antibody titer. No antiviral therapy or vaccine is available. Prevention involves wearing protective clothing and inspecting the skin for ticks.

WEST NILE VIRUS

West Nile virus (WNV) caused an outbreak of encephalitis in New York City and environs in July, August, and September 1999. This is the first time WNV caused disease in the United States. In this outbreak, there were 27 confirmed cases and 23 probable cases, including 5 deaths. Many birds, especially crows, died as well. No human cases occurred after area-wide spraying of mosquito-control compounds and the onset of cooler weather.

In the summer of the year 2000, there were 18 cases and 1 death, and by July 2001, the virus had spread to many states along the East Coast (from New Hampshire to Florida) and as far west as Louisiana. In the year 2001, there were 48 human cases of West Nile encephalitis and 5 deaths. In 2002, there was a marked increase in the number of cases. There were more than 4000 cases, 274 people died, and the virus had spread as far west as Colorado. This is the highest number of deaths ever caused by a mosquito-borne encephalitis in the United States. In 2003, there were 7700 cases, of whom 166 died, and the virus had spread to California. It is not known how WNV entered the United States, but either an infected traveler or an infected mosquito brought by an airplane seems likely to be involved.

WNV is a flavivirus that is classified in the same antigenic group as SLE virus. It is endemic in Africa but has caused encephalitis in areas of Europe and Asia as well. Wild birds are the main reservoir of this virus, which is transmitted by mosquitoes, especially *Culex* species. Humans are dead-end hosts.

The clinical picture includes fever, confusion, and striking muscle weakness similar to that of Guillain-Barré syndrome in previously healthy people over the age of 60 years. Less than 1% of those infected have symptomatic disease.

The laboratory diagnosis can be made by either isolation of the virus from brain tissue, blood, or spinal fluid or by detection of antibodies in spinal fluid or blood. PCR-based assays are also available. No antiviral therapy or vaccine is available. In an attempt to prevent blood-borne transmission, blood banks are screening donated blood for the presence of WNV using nucleic acid probes specific for the virus.

■ IMPORTANT ARBOVIRUSES THAT CAUSE DISEASE OUTSIDE THE UNITED STATES

Although yellow fever and dengue are not endemic in the United States, extensive travel by Americans to tropical areas means that imported cases occur. It is reasonable, therefore, that physicians in the United States be acquainted with these two diseases. Both yellow fever virus and dengue virus are classified as flaviviruses. Table 42–3 describes the epidemiology of the important arboviral diseases that occur primarily outside the United States. Japanese encephalitis virus, also a flavivirus and an important cause of epidemic encephalitis in Asia, is described in Chapter 46.

YELLOW FEVER VIRUS

As the name implies, yellow fever is characterized by jaundice and fever. It is a severe, life-threatening disease that begins with the sudden onset of fever, headache, myalgias, and photophobia. After this prodrome, the symptoms progress to involve the liver, kidneys, and heart. Prostration and shock occur, accompanied by upper gastrointestinal tract hemorrhage with hematemesis ("black vomit"). Diagnosis in the laboratory can be made either by isolating the virus or by detecting a rise in antibody titer. No antiviral therapy is available, and the mortality rate is high. If the patient recovers, no chronic infection ensues and lifelong immunity is conferred.

Table 42–3. Epidemiology of important arboviral diseases outside the United States.

Disease	Vector	Animal Reservoir	Geographic Distribution	Vaccine Available
Yellow fever				Yes
a) Urban	*Aedes* mosquito	Humans	Tropical Africa and South America	
b) Jungle	*Haemagogus* mosquito	Monkeys	Tropical Africa and South America	
Dengue	*Aedes* mosquito	Humans; probably monkeys also	Tropical areas, especially Caribbean	No

Yellow fever occurs primarily in the tropical areas of Africa and South America. In the epidemiology of yellow fever, **two distinct cycles** exist in nature, with different reservoirs and vectors.

(1) Jungle yellow fever is a disease of **monkeys** in tropical Africa and South America; it is transmitted primarily by the treetop **mosquitoes** of the *Haemagogus* species. Monkeys are the permanent reservoir, whereas humans are accidental hosts. Humans (eg, tree cutters) are infected when they enter the jungle occupationally.

(2) In contrast, urban yellow fever is a disease of **humans** that is transmitted by the **mosquito** *Aedes aegypti,* which breeds in stagnant water. In the urban form of the disease, humans are the reservoir. For effective transmission to occur, the virus must replicate in the mosquito during the 12- to 14-day extrinsic incubation period. After the infected mosquito bites the person, the intrinsic incubation period is 3–6 days.

Prevention of yellow fever involves mosquito control and immunization with the **vaccine** containing live, attenuated yellow fever virus. Travelers to and residents of endemic areas should be immunized. Protection lasts up to 10 years, and boosters are required every 10 years for travelers entering certain countries. Epidemics still occur in parts of tropical Africa and South America. Because it is a live vaccine, it should not be given to immunocompromised people or to pregnant women.

DENGUE VIRUS

Although dengue is **not endemic** in the United States, some tourists to the Caribbean and other tropical areas return with this disease. In recent years, there were 100–200 cases per year in the United States, mostly in the southern and eastern states. No indigenous transmission occurred within the United States. It is estimated that about 20 million people are infected with dengue virus each year worldwide. Dengue is the most common arboviral disease in the world.

Classic dengue (**breakbone fever**) begins suddenly with an influenzalike syndrome consisting of fever, malaise, cough, and headache. Severe pains in muscles and joints (breakbone) occur. Enlarged lymph nodes, a maculopapular rash, and leukopenia are common. After a week or so, the symptoms regress but weakness may persist. Although unpleasant, this typical form of dengue is rarely fatal and has few sequelae.

In contrast, **dengue hemorrhagic fever** is a much more severe disease, with a fatality rate that approaches 10%. The initial picture is the same as classic dengue, but then shock and hemorrhage, especially into the gastrointestinal tract and skin, develop. Dengue hemorrhagic fever occurs particularly in southern Asia,

whereas the classic form is found in tropical areas worldwide.

Hemorrhagic shock syndrome is due to the production of large amounts of **cross-reacting antibody** at the time of a second dengue infection. The pathogenesis is as follows: The patient recovers from classic dengue caused by one of the four serotypes, and antibody against that serotype is produced. When the patient is infected with another serotype of dengue virus, an anamnestic, heterotypic response occurs, and large amounts of cross-reacting antibody to the first serotype are produced. There are two hypotheses about what happens next. One is that immune complexes composed of virus and antibody are formed that activate complement, causing increased vascular permeability and thrombocytopenia. The other is that the antibodies increase the entry of virus into monocytes and macrophages with the consequent liberation of a large amount of cytokines. In either scenario, shock and hemorrhage result.

Dengue virus is transmitted by the *A. aegypti* **mosquito**, which is also the vector of yellow fever virus. Humans are the reservoir for dengue virus, but a jungle cycle involving monkeys as the reservoir and other *Aedes* species as vectors is suspected.

The diagnosis can be made in the laboratory either by isolation of the virus in cell culture or by serologic tests that demonstrate the presence of IgM antibody or a 4-fold or greater rise in antibody titer in acute and convalescent sera.

No antiviral therapy or vaccine for dengue is available. Outbreaks are controlled by using insecticides and draining stagnant water that serves as the breeding place for the mosquitoes. Personal protection includes using mosquito repellent and wearing clothing that covers the entire body.

SUMMARIES OF ORGANISMS

Brief summaries of the organisms described in this chapter begin on page 500. Please consult these summaries for a rapid review of the essential material.

PRACTICE QUESTIONS FOR THE UNITED STATES MEDICAL LICENSING EXAMINATION (USMLE) & COURSE EXAMINATIONS

Questions on the topics discussed in this chapter can be found in the Clinical Virology section of Part XI: USMLE (National Board) Practice Questions starting on page 549. Also see Part XII: USMLE (National Board) Practice Examination starting on page 583.

Tumor Viruses

OVERVIEW

Viruses can cause benign or malignant tumors in many species of animals, eg, frogs, fishes, birds, and mammals. Despite the common occurrence of tumor viruses in animals, only a few viruses are associated with **human** tumors, and evidence that they are truly the causative agents exists for very few.

Tumor viruses have no characteristic size, shape, or chemical composition. Some are large, and some are small; some are enveloped, and others are naked (ie, nonenveloped); some have DNA as their genetic material, and others have RNA. The factor that unites all of them is their common ability to cause tumors.

Tumor viruses are at the forefront of cancer research for two main reasons:

(1) They are more rapid, reliable, and efficient tumor producers than either chemicals or radiation. For example, many of these viruses can cause tumors in all susceptible animals in 1 or 2 weeks and can produce malignant transformation in cultured cells in just a few days.

(2) They have a small number of genes compared with a human cell (only three, four, or five for many retroviruses), and hence their role in the production of cancer can be readily analyzed and understood. To date, the genomes of many tumor viruses have been cloned and sequenced and the number of genes and their functions have been determined; all of this has provided important information.

MALIGNANT TRANSFORMATION OF CELLS

The term "malignant transformation" refers to changes in the growth properties, shape, and other features of the tumor cell (Table 43–1). Malignant transformation can be induced by tumor viruses not only in animals but also in cultured cells. In culture, the following changes occur when cells become malignantly transformed.

Altered Morphology

Malignant cells lose their characteristic differentiated shape and appear rounded and more refractile when seen in a microscope. The rounding is due to the disaggregation of actin filaments, and the reduced adherence of the cell to the surface of the culture dish is the result of changes in the surface charge of the cell.

Altered Growth Control

(1) Malignant cells grow in a disorganized, piled-up pattern in contrast to normal cells, which have an organized, flat appearance. The term applied to this change in growth pattern in malignant cells is **loss of contact inhibition.** Contact inhibition is a property of normal cells that refers to their ability to stop their growth and movement upon contact with another cell. Malignant cells have lost this ability and consequently move on top of one another, continue to grow to large numbers, and form a random array of cells.

(2) Malignant cells are able to grow in vitro at a much lower concentration of serum than are normal cells.

(3) Malignant cells grow well in suspension, whereas normal cells grow well only when they are attached to a surface, eg, a culture dish.

(4) Malignant cells are easily cloned; ie, they can grow into a colony of cells starting with a single cell, whereas normal cells cannot do this effectively.

(5) Infection of a cell by a tumor virus "immortalizes" that cell by enabling it to continue growing long past the time when its normal counterpart would have died. Normal cells in culture have a lifetime of about 50 generations, but malignantly transformed cells grow indefinitely.

Altered Cellular Properties

(1) DNA synthesis is induced. If cells resting in the G_1 phase are infected with a tumor virus, they will promptly enter the S phase, ie, synthesize DNA and go on to divide.

(2) The karyotype becomes altered; ie, there are changes in the number and shape of the chromosomes as a result of deletions, duplications, and translocations.

(3) Antigens different from those in normal cells appear. These new antigens can be either virus-encoded proteins, preexisting cellular proteins that have been

Table 43–1. Features of malignant transformation.

Feature	Description
Altered morphology	Loss of differentiated shape
	Rounded as a result of disaggregation of actin filaments and decreased adhesion to surface
	More refractle
Altered growth control	Loss of contact inhibition of growth
	Loss of contact inhibition of movement
	Reduced requirement for serum growth factors
	Increased ability to be cloned from a single cell
	Increased ability to grow in suspension
	Increased ability to continue growing ("immortalization")
Altered cellular properties	Induction of DNA synthesis
	Chromosomal changes
	Appearance of new antigens
	Increased agglutination by lectins
Altered biochemical properties	Reduced level of cyclic AMP
	Enhanced secretion of plasminogen activator
	Increased anaerobic glycolysis
	Loss of fibronectin
	Changes in glycoproteins and glycolipids

modified, or previously repressed cellular proteins that are now being synthesized. Some new antigens are on the cell surface and elicit either circulating antibodies or a cell-mediated response that can kill the tumor cell. These new antigens are the recognition sites for immune surveillance against tumor cells.

(4) Agglutination by lectins is enhanced. Lectins are plant glycoproteins that bind specifically to certain sugars on the cell membrane surface, eg, wheat germ agglutinin. The increased agglutination of malignant cells may be due to the clustering of existing receptor sites rather than to the synthesis of new ones.

Altered Biochemical Properties

(1) Levels of cyclic adenosine monophosphate (AMP) are reduced in malignant cells. Addition of cyclic AMP will cause malignant cells to revert to the appearance and growth properties of normal cells.

(2) Malignant cells secrete more plasminogen activator than do normal cells. This activator is a protease that

converts plasminogen to plasmin, the enzyme that dissolves the fibrin clot.

(3) Increased anaerobic glycolysis leads to increased lactic acid production (Warburg effect). The mechanism for this change is unknown.

(4) There is a loss of high-molecular-weight glycoprotein called fibronectin. The effect of this loss is unknown.

(5) There are changes in the sugar components of glycoproteins and glycolipids in the membranes of malignant cells.

ROLE OF TUMOR VIRUSES IN MALIGNANT TRANSFORMATION

Malignant transformation is a permanent change in the behavior of the cell. Must the viral genetic material be present and functioning at all times, or can it alter some cell component and not be required subsequently? The answer to this question was obtained by using a temperature-sensitive mutant of Rous sarcoma virus. This mutant has an altered transforming gene that is functional at the low, permissive temperature (35°C) but not at the high, restrictive temperature (39°C). When chicken cells were infected at 35°C they transformed as expected, but when incubated at 39°C they regained their normal morphology and behavior within a few hours. Days or weeks later, when these cells were returned to 35°C, they recovered their transformed phenotype. Thus, continued production of some functional virus-encoded protein is required for the maintenance of the transformed state.

Although malignant transformation is a permanent change, revertants to normality do appear, albeit rarely. In the revertants studied, the viral genetic material remains integrated in cellular DNA, but changes in the quality and quantity of the virus-specific RNA occur.

PROVIRUSES & ONCOGENES

The two major concepts of the way viral tumorigenesis occurs are expressed in the terms **provirus** and **oncogene.** These contrasting ideas address the fundamental question of the source of the genes for malignancy.

(1) In the provirus model, the genes enter the cell at the time of infection by the tumor virus.

(2) In the oncogene model, the genes for malignancy are already present in all cells of the body by virtue of being present in the initial sperm and egg. These oncogenes encode proteins that encourage cell growth, eg, fibroblast growth factor. In the oncogene model, carcinogens such as chemicals, radiation, and tumor viruses activate cellular oncogenes to overproduce these growth factors. This initiates inappropriate cell growth and malignant transformation.

Both proviruses and oncogenes may play a role in malignant transformation. Evidence for the provirus mode consists of finding copies of viral DNA integrated into cell DNA only in cells that have been infected with the tumor virus. The corresponding uninfected cells have no copies of the viral DNA.

The first direct evidence that oncogenes exist in normal cells was based on results of experiments in which a DNA copy of the *onc* gene of the chicken retrovirus Rous sarcoma virus was used as a probe. DNA in normal embryonic cells hybridized to the probe, indicating that the cells contain a gene homologous to the viral gene. It is hypothesized that the **cellular oncogenes** (proto-oncogenes) may be the precursors of viral oncogenes. Although cellular oncogenes and viral oncogenes are similar, they are not identical. They differ in base sequence at various points; and cellular oncogenes have exons and introns, whereas viral oncogenes do not. It seems likely that viral oncogenes were acquired by incorporation of cellular oncogenes into retroviruses lacking these genes. Retroviruses can be thought of as **transducing agents,** carrying oncogenes from one cell to another.

Since this initial observation, **more than 20 cellular oncogenes** have been identified by using either the Rous sarcoma virus DNA probe or probes made from other viral oncogenes. Many cells contain several different cellular oncogenes. In addition, the same cellular oncogenes have been found in species as diverse as fruit flies, rodents, and humans. Such conservation through evolution suggests a normal physiologic function for these genes. Some are known to be expressed during normal embryonic development.

A marked **diversity** of viral oncogene function has been found. Some encode a **protein kinase** that specifically phosphorylates the amino acid tyrosine,[1] in contrast to the commonly found protein kinase of cells, which preferentially phosphorylates serine.

Other oncogenes have a base sequence almost identical to that of the gene for certain cellular **growth factors,** eg, epidermal growth factor. Several proteins encoded by oncogenes have their effect at the cell membrane (eg, the *ras* oncogene encodes a G protein), whereas some act in the nucleus by binding to DNA (eg, the *myc* oncogene encodes a transcription factor). These observations suggest that growth control is a multistep process and that carcinogenesis can be induced by affecting one or more of several steps.

On the basis of the known categories of oncogenes, the following model of growth control can be constructed. After a **growth factor** binds to its **receptor** on the cell membrane, membrane-associated **G proteins** and **tyrosine kinases** are activated. These, in turn, interact with **cytoplasmic proteins** or produce **second messengers,** which are transported to the nucleus and interact with nuclear factors. DNA synthesis is activated, and cell division occurs. Overproduction or inappropriate expression of any of the above factors **in boldface type** can result in malignant transformation. Not all tumor viruses of the retrovirus family contain *onc* genes. How do these viruses cause malignant transformation? It appears that the DNA copy of the viral RNA integrates near a cellular oncogene, causing a marked increase in its expression. **Overexpression** of the cellular oncogene may play a key role in malignant transformation by these viruses.

Although it has been demonstrated that viral oncogenes can cause malignant transformation, it has not been directly shown that cellular oncogenes can do so. However, as described in Table 43–2, the following evidence suggests that they do:

---

[1] The cellular protein(s) phosphorylated by this kinase are unknown.

Table 43–2. Evidence that cellular oncogenes (c-*onc*) can cause tumors.

Evidence	Description
Mutation of c-*onc* gene	DNA isolated from tumor cells can transform normal cells. This DNA has a c-*onc* gene with a mutation consisting of a single base change.
Translocation of c-*onc* gene	Movement of c-*onc* gene to a new site on a different chromosome results in malignancy accompanied by increased expression of the gene.
Amplification of c-*onc* gene	The number of copies of c-*onc* genes is increased, resulting in enhanced expression of their mRNA and proteins.
Insertion of retrovirus near c-*onc* gene	Proviral DNA inserts near c-*onc* gene, which alters its expression and causes tumors.
Overexpression of c-*onc* gene by modification in the laboratory	Addition of an active promoter site enhances expression of the c-*onc* gene, and malignant transformation occurs.

(1) DNA containing cellular oncogenes isolated from certain tumor cells can transform normal cells in culture. When the base sequence of these "transforming" cellular oncogenes was analyzed, it was found to have a **single base change** from the normal cellular oncogene; ie, it had **mutated.** In several tumor cell isolates, the altered sites in the gene are the same.

(2) In certain tumors, characteristic **translocations of** chromosomal segments can be seen. In Burkitt's lymphoma cells, a translocation occurs that moves a cellular oncogene (c-*myc*) from its normal site on chromosome 8 to a new site adjacent to an immunoglobulin heavy-chain gene on chromosome 14. This shift enhances expression of the c-*myc* gene.

(3) Some tumors have multiple copies of the cellular oncogenes, either on the same chromosome or on multiple tiny chromosomes. The **amplification** of these genes results in overexpression of their mRNA and proteins.

(4) **Insertion** of the DNA copy of the retroviral RNA (proviral DNA) near a cellular oncogene stimulates expression of the c-*onc* gene.

(5) Certain cellular oncogenes isolated from normal cells can cause malignant transformation if they have been modified to be **overexpressed** within the recipient cell.

In summary, two different mechanisms—**mutation** and **increased expression**—appear to be able to activate the quiescent "proto-oncogene" into a functioning oncogene capable of transforming a cell. Cellular oncogenes provide a rationale for carcinogenesis by chemicals and radiation; eg, a chemical carcinogen might act by enhancing the expression of a cellular oncogene. Furthermore, DNA isolated from cells treated with a chemical carcinogen can malignantly transform other normal cells. The resulting tumor cells contain cellular oncogenes from the chemically treated cells, and these genes are expressed with high efficiency.

There is another mechanism of carcinogenesis involving cellular genes, namely, mutation of a **tumor suppressor gene.** A well-documented example is the retinoblastoma susceptibility gene, which normally acts as a suppressor of retinoblastoma formation. When both alleles of this **antioncogene** are mutated (made nonfunctional), retinoblastoma occurs. Human papillomavirus and SV40 virus produce a protein that binds to and inactivates the protein encoded by the retinoblastoma gene. Human papillomavirus also produces a protein that inactivates the protein encoded by the p53 gene, another tumor suppressor gene in human cells. The p53 gene encodes a transcription factor that activates the synthesis of a second protein, which blocks the cyclin-dependent kinases required for cell division to occur. The p53 protein also promotes apoptosis of cells that have sustained DNA damage or contain activated cellular oncogenes. Apoptosis-induced death of these cells has a "tumor-suppressive" effect by killing those cells destined to become cancerous.

Inactivation of tumor suppressor genes appears likely to be an important general mechanism of viral oncogenesis. Tumor suppressor genes are involved in the formation of other cancers as well, eg, breast and colon carcinomas and various sarcomas. For example, in many colon carcinomas, two genes are inactivated, the p53 gene and the DCC (*d*eleted in *c*olon *c*arcinoma) gene. **More than half of human cancers have a mutated p53 gene in the DNA of malignant cells.**

OUTCOME OF TUMOR VIRUS INFECTION

The outcome of tumor virus infection is dependent on the virus and the type of cell. Some tumor viruses go through their entire replicative cycle with the production of progeny virus, whereas others undergo an interrupted cycle, analogous to lysogeny, in which the **proviral DNA is integrated** into cellular DNA and limited expression of proviral genes occurs. Therefore, malignant transformation does not require that progeny virus be produced. Rather, all that is required is the expression of one or, at most, a few viral genes. Note, however, that some tumor viruses transform by inserting their proviral DNA in a manner that activates a cellular oncogene.

In most cases, the DNA tumor viruses such as the papovaviruses transform only cells in which they do not replicate. These cells are called "nonpermissive" because they do not permit viral replication. Cells of the species from which the DNA tumor virus was initially isolated are "permissive"; ie, the virus replicates and usually kills the cells, and no tumors are formed. For example, SV40 virus replicates in the cells of the African green monkey (its species of origin) and causes a cytopathic effect but no tumors. However, in rodent cells the virus does not replicate, expresses only its early genes, and causes malignant transformation. In the "nonproductive" transformed cell, the viral DNA is integrated into the host chromosome and remains there through subsequent cell divisions. The underlying concept applicable to both DNA and RNA tumor viruses is that **only viral gene expression,** not replication of the viral genome or production of progeny virus, is required for transformation.

The essential step required for a DNA tumor virus, eg, SV40 virus, to cause malignant transformation is expression of the **"early" genes** of the virus (Table 43–3). (The early genes are those expressed prior to the replication of the viral genetic material.) These required early genes produce a set of early proteins called **T antigens.**[2]

The large T antigen, which is both necessary and sufficient to induce transformation, binds to SV40 virus DNA at the site of initiation of viral DNA synthesis. This is compatible with the finding that the large T antigen is required for the initiation of cellular DNA synthesis in the virus-infected cell. Biochemically, large T antigen has protein kinase and adenosine triphosphate (ATPase) activity. Almost all the large T antigen is located in the cell nucleus, but some of it is in the outer cell membrane. In that location, it can be detected as a transplantation antigen called **tumor-specific transplantation antigen** (TSTA). TSTA is the antigen that induces the immune response against the transplantation of virally transformed cells. Relatively little is known about the SV40 virus small T antigen, except that if it is not synthesized the efficiency of transformation decreases. In polyomavirus-infected cells, the middle T antigen plays the same role as the SV40 virus large T antigen.

In RNA tumor virus–infected cells, this required gene has one of several different functions, depending on the retrovirus. The oncogene of Rous sarcoma virus and several other viruses codes for a protein kinase that phosphorylates tyrosine. Some viruses have a gene for a factor that regulates cell growth (eg, epidermal growth

---

[2] In SV40 virus–infected cells, two T antigens, large (MW 100,000) and small (MW 17,000), are produced, whereas in polyomavirus-infected cells, three T antigens, large (MW 90,000), middle (MW 60,000), and small (MW 22,000), are made. Other tumor viruses such as adenoviruses also induce T antigens, which are immunologically distinct from those of the two papovaviruses.

Table 43–3. Viral oncogenes.

Characteristic	DNA Virus	RNA Virus
Prototype virus	SV40 virus	Rous sarcoma virus
Name of gene	Early-region A gene	*src* gene
Name of protein	T antigen	Src protein
Function of protein	Protein kinase, ATPase activity, binding to DNA, and stimulation of DNA synthesis	Protein kinase that phosphorylates tyrosine[1]
Location of protein	Primarily nuclear, but some in plasma membrane	Plasma membrane
Required for viral replication	Yes	No
Required for cell transformation	Yes	Yes
Gene has cellular homologue	No	Yes

[1]Some retroviruses have *onc* genes that code for other proteins such as platelet-derived growth factor and epidermal growth factor.

factor or platelet-derived growth factor), and still others have a gene that codes for a protein that binds to DNA. The conclusion is that normal growth control is a multistep process that can be affected at any one of several levels. The addition of a viral oncogene perturbs the growth control process, and a tumor cell results.

The viral genetic material remains stably integrated in host cell DNA by a process similar to lysogeny. In the lysogenic cycle, bacteriophage DNA becomes stably integrated into the bacterial genome. The linear DNA genome of the temperate phage, lambda, forms a double-stranded circle within the infected cell and then covalently integrates into bacterial DNA (Table 43–4). A repressor is synthesized that prevents transcription of most of the other lambda genes. Similarly, the double-stranded circular DNA of the DNA tumor virus covalently integrates into eukaryotic-cell DNA, and only early genes are transcribed. Thus far, no repressor has been identified in any DNA tumor virus–infected cell. With RNA tumor viruses (retroviruses), the single-stranded linear RNA genome is transcribed into a double-stranded linear DNA that integrates into cellular DNA. In summary, despite the differences in their genomes and in the nature of the host cells, these viruses go through the common pathway of a double-stranded DNA intermediate followed by covalent integration into cellular DNA and subsequent expression of certain genes.

Just as a lysogenic bacteriophage can be induced to enter the replicative cycle by ultraviolet radiation and certain chemicals, tumor viruses can be induced by several mechanisms. Induction is one of the approaches used to determine whether tumor viruses are present in human cancer cells; eg, human T-cell lymphotropic virus was discovered by inducing the virus from leukemic cells with iododeoxyuridine.

Three techniques have been used to induce tumor viruses to replicate in the transformed cells.

(1) The most frequently used method is the addition of nucleoside analogues, eg, iododeoxyuridine. The mechanism of induction by these analogues is uncertain.

(2) The second method involves fusion with "helper" cells; ie, the transformed, nonpermissive cell is fused with a permissive cell, in which the virus undergoes a normal replicative cycle. Within the heterokaryon (a cell with two or more nuclei that is formed by the fusion of two different cell types), the tumor virus is induced and infectious virus is produced. The mechanism of induction is unknown.

(3) In the third method, helper viruses provide a missing function to complement the integrated tumor virus. Infection with the helper virus results in the production of both the integrated tumor virus and the helper virus.

The process of rescuing tumor viruses from cells revealed the existence of **endogenous** viruses. Treatment of *normal, uninfected* embryonic cells with nucleoside analogues resulted in the production of retroviruses. Retroviral DNA is integrated within the chromosomal DNA of all cells and serves as the template for viral replication. This proviral DNA probably arose by retrovirus infection of the germ cells of some prehistoric ancestor.

Endogenous retroviruses, which have been rescued from the cells of many species (including humans), differ depending upon the species of origin. Endogenous viruses are xenotropic (*xeno* means foreign; *tropism* means to be attracted to); ie, they infect cells of other species more efficiently than they infect the cells of the species of origin. Entry of the endogenous virus into the cell of origin is limited as a result of defective viral envelope–cell receptor interaction. Although they are retroviruses, most endogenous viruses are not tumor viruses; ie, only a few cause leukemia.

TRANSMISSION OF TUMOR VIRUSES

Tumor virus transmission in experimental animals can occur by two processes, vertical and horizontal. **Vertical transmission** indicates movement of the virus from mother to newborn offspring, whereas **horizontal transmission** describes the passage of virus between an-

---

Table 43–4. Lysogeny as a model for the integration of tumor viruses.

Type of Virus	Name	Genome[1]	Integration	Limited Transcription of Viral Genes
Temperate phage	Lambda phage	Linear dsDNA	+	+
DNA tumor virus	SV40 virus	Circular dsDNA	+	+
RNA tumor virus	Rous sarcoma virus	Linear ssRNA	+	+[2]

[1]Abbreviations: ds, double-stranded; ss, single-stranded.
[2]Limited transcription in some cells or under certain conditions but full transcription with viral replication in others.

imals that do not have a mother-offspring relationship. Vertical transmission occurs by three methods: (1) the viral genetic material is in the sperm or the egg; (2) the virus is passed across the placenta; and (3) the virus is transmitted in the breast milk.

When vertical transmission occurs, exposure to the virus early in life can result in tolerance to viral antigens and, as a consequence, the immune system will not eliminate the virus. Large amounts of virus are produced, and a high frequency of cancer occurs. In contrast, when horizontal transmission occurs, the immunocompetent animal produces antibody against the virus and the frequency of cancer is low. If an immunocompetent animal is experimentally made immunodeficient, the frequency of cancer increases greatly.

Horizontal transmission probably does not occur in humans; those in close contact with cancer patients, eg, family members and medical personnel, do not have an increased frequency of cancer. There have been "outbreaks" of leukemia in several children at the same school, but these have been interpreted statistically to be random, rare events that happen to coincide.

EVIDENCE FOR HUMAN TUMOR VIRUSES

At present, only two viruses, human T-cell lymphotropic virus and human papillomavirus, are considered to be human tumor viruses. However, several other candidate viruses are implicated by epidemiologic correlation, by serologic relationship, or by recovery of virus from tumor cells.

Human T-Cell Lymphotropic Virus

There are two human T-cell lymphotropic virus (HTLV) isolates so far, HTLV-1 and HTLV-2, both of which are associated with leukemias and lymphomas. HTLV-1 was isolated in 1980 from the cells of a patient with a cutaneous T-cell lymphoma. It was induced from the tumor cells by exposure to iododeoxyuridine. Its RNA and proteins are different from those of all other retroviruses. In addition to cancer, HTLV is the cause of tropical spastic paraparesis, an autoimmune disease in which progressive weakness of the legs occurs. (Additional information regarding HTLV can be found in Chapter 39.)

HTLV-1 may cause cancer by a mechanism different from that of other retroviruses. It has **no viral oncogene.** Rather, it has two special genes (in addition to the standard retroviral genes *gag, pol,* and *env*) called *tax* and *rex* that play a role in oncogenesis by regulating mRNA transcription and translation. The Tax protein has two activities: (1) it acts on the viral long terminal repeat (LTR) sequences to stimulate viral mRNA synthesis, and (2) it induces NF-kB, which stimulates the production of interleukin-2 (IL-2) and the IL-2 receptor. The increase in levels of IL-2 and its receptor stimulates the T cells to continue growing, thus increasing the likelihood that the cells will become malignant. The Rex protein determines which viral mRNAs can exit the nucleus and enter the cytoplasm to be translated.

HTLV-1 is not an endogenous virus; ie, proviral DNA corresponding to its RNA genome is not found in normal human cell DNA. It is an **exogenously acquired** virus, because its proviral DNA is found only in the DNA of the malignant lymphoma cells. It infects CD4-positive T cells preferentially and will induce malignant transformation in these cells in vitro. Some (but not all) patients with T-cell lymphomas have antibodies against the virus, indicating that it may not be the cause of all T-cell lymphomas. Antibodies against the virus are not found in the general population, indicating that infection is not widespread.

Transmission occurs primarily by sexual contact and by exchange of contaminated blood, eg, in transfusions and intravenous drug users. In the United States, blood for transfusions is screened for antibodies to HTLV-1 and HTLV-2 and discarded if positive. In recent years, HTLV-1 and HTLV-2 were found in equal frequency in donated blood. Serologic tests for HTLV do not cross-react with human immunodeficiency virus (HIV).

At about the same time that HTLV-1 was found, a similar virus was isolated from malignant T cells in Japan. In that country, a clustering of cases in the rural areas of the west coast of Kyushu was found. Antibodies in the sera of leukemic individuals and in the sera of 25% of the normal population of Kyushu react with the Japanese isolate and with HTLV-1. (Only a small fraction of infected individuals contract leukemia, indicating that HTLV infection alone is insufficient to cause cancer.) In addition, HTLV-1 is endemic in some areas of Africa and on several Caribbean islands, as shown by the high frequency of antibodies. The number of people with positive antibody titers in the United States is quite small, except in certain parts of the southeastern states.

HTLV-2 has 60% genetic homology with HTLV-1. Like HTLV-1, it is transmitted primarily by blood and semen and infects CD4-positive cells. Routine serologic tests do not distinguish between HTLV-1 and HTLV-2; therefore, other techniques, eg, polymerase chain reaction, are required.

Human Papillomavirus

Human papillomavirus (HPV) is one of the two viruses definitely known to cause tumors in humans. Papillomas (warts) are benign but can progress to form carci-nomas, especially in an immunocompromised person. HPV primarily infects keratinizing or mucosal squamous epithelium. (Additional information regarding HPV can be found in Chapter 38.)

Papillomaviruses are members of the family of papovaviruses, an acronym of *papilloma, polyoma,* and *va*cuolating (eg, SV40 virus) viruses. They are DNA nucleocapsid viruses with double-stranded, circular, supercoiled DNA and an icosahedral nucleocapsid. The papillomaviruses have a somewhat larger genome and diameter than do polyomavirus and SV40 virus.[3]

Carcinogenesis by HPV involves two proteins encoded by HPV genes E6 and E7 that interfere with the activity of the proteins encoded by two tumor suppressor genes, p53 and Rb (retinoblastoma), found in normal cells.

There are at least 100 different types of HPV, many of which cause distinct clinical entities. For example, HPV-1 through HPV-4 cause plantar warts on the soles of the feet, whereas HPV-6 and HPV-11 cause anogenital warts (condylomata acuminata) and laryngeal papillomas. Certain types of HPV, especially types 16 and 18, are implicated as the cause of carcinoma of the cervix. Approximately 90% of anogenital cancers contain the DNA of these HPV types. In most of these tumor cells, the viral DNA is integrated into the cellular DNA and the E6 and E7 proteins are produced.

Epstein-Barr Virus

Epstein-Barr virus (EBV) is a herpesvirus that was isolated from the cells of an East African individual with **Burkitt's lymphoma.** EBV, the cause of infectious mononucleosis, transforms B lymphocytes in culture and causes lymphomas in marmoset monkeys. It is also associated with **nasopharyngeal carcinoma,** a tumor that occurs primarily in China, and with thymic carcinoma and B-cell lymphoma in the United States. However, cells from Burkitt's lymphoma patients in the United States show no evidence of EBV infection. (Additional information regarding EBV can be found in Chapter 37.)

Cells isolated from East African individuals with Burkitt's lymphoma contain EBV DNA and EBV nuclear antigen. Only a small fraction of the many copies of EBV DNA is integrated; most viral DNA is in the form of closed circles in the cytoplasm.

The difficulty in proving that EBV is a human tumor virus is that infection by the virus is widespread but the tumor is rare. The current hypothesis is that EBV infection induces B cells to proliferate, thus increasing the likelihood that a second event (such as activation of a cellular oncogene) will occur. In Burkitt's lymphoma cells, a cellular oncogene, c-*myc,* which is normally located on chromosome 8, is **translocated** to chromosome 14 at the site of immunoglobulin heavy-chain genes. This translocation brings the c-*myc* gene in juxtaposition to an active promoter, and large amounts of c-*myc* RNA are synthesized. It is known that the c-*myc* oncogene encodes a transcription factor, but the role of this factor in oncogenesis is uncertain.

Hepatitis B Virus

Hepatitis B virus (HBV) infection is significantly more common in patients with primary hepatocellular carcinoma (**hepatoma**) than in control subjects. This relationship is striking in areas of Africa and Asia where the incidence of both HBV infection and hepatoma is high. Chronic HBV infection commonly causes cirrhosis of the liver; these two events are the main predisposing factors to hepatoma. Part of the HBV genome is integrated into cellular DNA in malignant cells. However, no HBV gene has been definitely implicated in oncogenesis. The integration of HBV DNA may cause insertional mutagenesis, resulting in the activation of a cellular oncogene. (Additional information regarding HBV can be found in Chapter 41.)

Hepatitis C Virus

Chronic infection with hepatitis C virus (HCV), like HBV, also predisposes to hepatocellular carcinoma. HCV is an RNA virus that has no oncogene and forms no DNA intermediate during replication. It does cause chronic hepatitis, which seems likely to be the main predisposing event. (Additional information regarding HCV can be found in Chapter 41.)

Human Herpesvirus 8

HHV-8, also known as Kaposi's sarcoma–associated herpesvirus (KSHV), may cause Kaposi's sarcoma. The DNA of the virus has been detected in the sarcoma cells, but the role of the virus in oncogenesis remains to be determined. (Additional information regarding HHV-8 can be found in Chapter 37.)

DO ANIMAL TUMOR VIRUSES CAUSE CANCER IN HUMANS?

There is no evidence that animal tumor viruses cause tumors in humans. In fact, the only available information suggests that they do not, because (1) people who were inoculated with poliovirus vaccine contaminated with SV40 virus have no greater incidence of cancers

---

[3] Papillomaviruses are 55 nm in diameter with a DNA molecular weight of 5×10^6, in contrast to the others, which have a diameter of 45 nm and a DNA molecular weight of 3×10^6.

than do uninoculated controls, (2) soldiers inoculated with yellow fever vaccine contaminated with avian leukemia virus do not have a high incidence of tumors, and (3) members of families whose cats have died of leukemia caused by feline leukemia virus show no increase in the occurrence of leukemia over control families. Note, however, that some human tumor cells, namely, non-Hodgkin's lymphoma, contain SV40 DNA, but the relationship of that DNA to malignant transformation is uncertain.

ANIMAL TUMOR VIRUSES

1. DNA Tumor Viruses

The important DNA tumor viruses are listed in Table 43–5.

Papovaviruses

The two best-characterized oncogenic papovaviruses are **polyomavirus** and **SV40 virus.** Polyomavirus (*poly* means many; *oma* means tumor) causes a wide variety of histologically different tumors when inoculated into newborn rodents. Its natural host is the mouse. SV40 virus, which was isolated from normal rhesus monkey kidney cells, causes sarcomas in newborn hamsters.

Polyomavirus and SV40 virus share many chemical and biologic features, eg, double-stranded, circular, supercoiled DNA of molecular weight 3×10^6 and a 45-nm icosahedral nucleocapsid. However, the sequence of their DNA and the antigenicity of their proteins are quite distinct. Both undergo a lytic (permissive) cycle in the cells of their natural hosts, with the production of progeny virus. However, when they infect the cells of a heterologous species, the nonpermissive cycle ensues, no virus is produced, and the cell is malignantly transformed.[4]

---

[4] The ability of polyomaviruses to transform mouse cells is an exception to the generalization that cells of the natural host do not become malignant. Polyomavirus not only causes a cytopathic effect in most mouse cells but also can induce a rare transformed cell.

In the transformed cell, the viral DNA integrates into the cell DNA and only early proteins are synthesized. Some of these proteins, eg, the T antigens described on page 310, are required for induction and maintenance of the transformed state.

JC virus, a human papovavirus, is the cause of progressive multifocal leukoencephalopathy (see Chapter 44). It also causes brain tumors in monkeys and hamsters. There is no evidence that it causes human cancer.

Adenoviruses

Some human adenoviruses, especially serotypes 12, 18, and 31, induce sarcomas in newborn hamsters and transform rodent cells in culture. There is no evidence that these viruses cause tumors in humans, and no adenoviral DNA has been detected in the DNA of any human tumor cells.

Adenoviruses undergo both a permissive cycle in some cells and a nonpermissive, transforming cycle in others. The linear genome DNA (MW 23×10^6) circularizes within the infected cell, but—in contrast to the papovaviruses, whose entire genome integrates—only a small region (10%) of the adenovirus genome does so; yet transformation still occurs. This region codes for several proteins, one of which is the T (tumor) antigen. Adenovirus T antigen is required for transformation and is antigenically distinct from the polyomavirus and SV40 virus T antigens.

Herpesviruses

Several animal herpesviruses are known to cause tumors. Four species of herpesviruses cause **lymphomas** in nonhuman primates. Herpesviruses saimiri and ateles induce T-cell lymphomas in New World monkeys, and herpesviruses pan and papio transform B lymphocytes in chimpanzees and baboons, respectively.

A herpesvirus of chickens causes Marek's disease, a contagious, rapidly fatal neurolymphomatosis. Immunization of chickens with a live, attenuated vaccine has resulted in a considerable decrease in the number of cases. A herpesvirus is implicated as the cause of kidney carcinomas in frogs.

Table 43–5. Varieties of tumor viruses.

Nucleic Acid	Virus
DNA	Papovaviruses, eg, polyomavirus, SV40 virus; papillomaviruses; adenoviruses, especially types 12, 18, and 31; herpesviruses, eg, herpesvirus saimiri; poxviruses, eg, fibroma-myxoma virus.
RNA	Avian sarcoma viruses, eg, Rous sarcoma virus; avian leukemia viruses; murine sarcoma viruses; murine leukemia viruses; mouse mammary tumor virus; feline sarcoma virus; feline leukemia virus; simian sarcoma virus; human T-cell lymphotropic virus.

Poxviruses

Two poxviruses cause tumors in animals; these are the fibroma-myxoma virus, which causes fibromas or myxomas in rabbits and other animals, and Yaba monkey tumor virus, which causes benign histiocytomas in animals and human volunteers. Little is known about either of these viruses.

2. RNA Tumor Viruses (Retroviruses)

RNA tumor viruses have been isolated from a large number of species: snakes, birds, and mammals including nonhuman primates. The important RNA tumor viruses are listed in Table 43–5. They are important because of their ubiquity, their ability to cause tumors in the host of origin, their small number of genes, and the relationship of their genes to cellular oncogenes (see page 308).

These viruses belong to the retrovirus family (the prefix "retro" means reverse), so named because a **reverse transcriptase** is located in the virion. This enzyme transcribes the genome RNA into double-stranded proviral DNA and is essential to their replication. The viral genome consists of two identical molecules of positive-strand RNA. Each molecule has a molecular weight of approximately 2×10^6 (these are the only viruses that are diploid, ie, have two copies of their genome in the virion). The two molecules are hydrogen-bonded together by complementary bases located near the 5′ end of both RNA molecules. Also bound near the 5′ end of each RNA is a transfer RNA (tRNA) that serves as the primer[5] for the transcription of the RNA into DNA.

The icosahedral capsid is surrounded by an envelope with glycoprotein spikes. Some internal capsid proteins are group-specific antigens, which are common to retroviruses within a species. There are three important morphologic types of retroviruses, labeled B, C, and D, depending primarily on the location of the capsid or core. Most of the retroviruses are C-type particles, but mouse mammary tumor virus is a B-type particle, and HIV, the cause of AIDS, is a D-type particle.

The gene sequence of the RNA of a typical avian sarcoma virus is *gag, pol, env,* and *src*. The nontransforming retroviruses have three genes; they are missing *src*. The *gag* region codes for the group-specific antigens, the *pol* gene codes for the reverse transcriptase, the *env* gene codes for the two envelope spike proteins, and the *src* gene codes for the protein kinase. In other oncogenic retroviruses, such as HTLV-1, there is a fifth coding region (the *tax* gene) near the 3′ end, which encodes a protein that enhances viral transcription.

The sequences at the 5′ and 3′ ends function in the integration of the proviral DNA and in the transcription of mRNA from the integrated proviral DNA by host cell RNA polymerase II. At each end is a sequence[6] called an LTR that is composed of several regions, one of which, near the 5′ end, is the binding site for the primer tRNA.

After infection of the cell by a retrovirus, the following events occur. Using the genome RNA as the template, the reverse transcriptase (RNA-dependent DNA polymerase) synthesizes double-stranded proviral DNA. The DNA then integrates into cellular DNA. Integration of the proviral DNA is an obligatory step, but there is no specific site of integration. Insertion of the viral LTR can enhance the transcription of adjacent host cell genes. If this host gene is a cellular oncogene, malignant transformation may result. This explains how retroviruses without viral oncogenes can cause transformation.

SUMMARIES OF ORGANISMS

Brief summaries of the organisms described in this chapter begin on page 501. Please consult these summaries for a rapid review of the essential material.

PRACTICE QUESTIONS: USMLE & COURSE EXAMINATIONS

Questions on the topics discussed in this chapter can be found in the Clinical Virology section of Part XI: USMLE (National Board) Practice Questions starting on page 549. Also see Part XII: USMLE (National Board) Practice Examination starting on page 583.

---

[5] The purpose of the primer tRNA is to act as the point of attachment for the first deoxynucleotide at the start of DNA synthesis. The primers are normal-cell tRNAs that are characteristic for each retrovirus.

---

[6] The length of the sequence varies from 250 to 1200 bases, depending on the virus.

Slow Viruses & Prions

"Slow" infectious diseases are caused by a heterogeneous group of agents containing both conventional viruses and unconventional agents that are not viruses, eg, prions. **Prions** are **protein-containing particles** with **no detectable nucleic acid** that are highly resistant to inactivation by heat, formaldehyde, and ultraviolet light at doses that will inactivate viruses. Note that prions are resistant to the temperatures usually employed in cooking, a fact that may be important in their suspected ability to be transmitted by food (see variant Creutzfeldt-Jakob disease [CJD] below). Prions are, however, inactivated by protein- and lipid-disrupting agents such as phenol, ether, NaOH, and hypochlorite (see Chapter 28).

The prion protein is encoded by a normal cellular gene and is thought to function in a signal transduction pathway in neurons. The normal prion protein (known as PrPC, or prion protein cellular) has a significant amount of alpha-helical conformation. When the alpha-helical conformation changes to a beta-pleated sheet (known as PrPSC, or prion protein scrapie), these abnormal forms aggregate into filaments, which disrupt neuron function and cause cell death. Prions, therefore, "reproduce" by the abnormal beta-pleated sheet form recruiting normal alpha-helical forms to change their conformation. Note that the normal alpha-helical form and the abnormal beta-pleated sheet form have the same amino acid sequence. It is only their conformation that differs. A specific cellular RNA enhances this conformational change. Prions are described in more detail in Chapter 28.

In humans, the "slow" agents cause **central nervous system** diseases characterized by a long incubation period, a gradual onset, and a progressive, invariably fatal course. There is no antimicrobial therapy for these diseases. Note that the term "slow" refers to the disease, not to the rate of replication of those viruses that cause these "slow" diseases. The replication rate of these viruses is similar to that of most other viruses.

The human prion-mediated diseases, eg, kuru and CJD, are called **transmissible spongiform encephalopathies (TSE)**. The term "spongiform" refers to the spongy, Swiss cheese–like holes seen in the brain parenchyma that are caused by death of the neurons.

No virus particles are seen in the brain of people with these diseases.

The term "encephalopathy" refers to a pathologic process in the brain without signs of inflammation. In contrast, "encephalitis" refers to an inflammatory brain process in which either neutrophils or lymphocytes are present. In TSEs, there are no inflammatory changes in the brain.

The transmissibility of the agent of kuru and CJD ("prions") was initially established by inoculation of material from the brains of infected patients into the brains of primates followed by serial transfer to the brains of other primates.

Note, however, that both kuru and variant CJD (and bovine spongiform encephalopathy [BSE]—"mad cow" disease) are acquired by ingestion. In this route, the prion protein must survive digestion in the intestinal tract and then penetrate the gut mucosa. The prion protein is then amplified within follicle dendritic cells in lymphatic tissue, such as Peyer's patches. Prions then spread to the spleen, carried by migrating dendritic cells. From the spleen, prions spread to the central nervous system probably via the sympathetic nerves.

It is also possible that prions reach the brain within lymphocytes, as there is a documented case of CJD that was acquired by transfused blood. In addition, CJD has been transmitted **iatrogenically,** ie, in a medical context, via corneal transplants, dura mater grafts, implanted brain electrodes, and growth hormone extracts made from human pituitary glands.

There is evidence that quinacrine and other acridine analogues inhibit the formation of the pathologic PrPC form in cell culture. These drugs are currently being tested in animal models for their ability to treat or prevent prion diseases.

Prion-caused diseases can be classified into three categories: some are clearly **transmissible (infectious)** such as kuru, some are clearly **hereditary (genetic)** such as fatal familial insomnia, and others are **sporadic** (neither infectious nor hereditary) such as most cases of CJD. The sporadic cases seem likely to be due to spontaneous somatic mutations in the affected individual.

SLOW DISEASES CAUSED BY CONVENTIONAL VIRUSES

Progressive Multifocal Leukoencephalopathy

Progressive multifocal leukoencephalopathy (PML) is a fatal demyelinating disease of the white matter and involves multiple areas of the brain. The clinical picture includes visual field defects, mental status changes, and weakness. The disease rapidly progresses to blindness, dementia, and coma, and most patients die within 6 months. It occurs primarily in individuals with compromised cell-mediated immunity, especially AIDS patients and those who are receiving cancer chemotherapy and immunosuppressive drugs following organ transplantation. Some patients undergoing treatment for multiple sclerosis with the monoclonal antibody natalizumab developed PML (see Chapter 62 for a description of monoclonal antibodies in clinical use). Table 44–1 describes some important features of slow viral diseases in humans caused by conventional viruses.

PML is caused by JC virus, a papovavirus antigenically distinct from other human papovaviruses such as human papillomavirus. JC virus infects and kills oligodendroglia and causes syncytia in astrocytes. Antibodies to JC virus are found in approximately 75% of normal human sera, indicating that infection is widespread. Disease occurs when latent JC virus is activated in an immunocompromised patient. The virus persists in the kidney and is excreted in the urine. The diagnosis is typically made by polymerase chain reaction assay of a brain biopsy specimen or spinal fluid. There is no effective antiviral treatment, but cidofovir may be beneficial.

Subacute Sclerosing Panencephalitis

Subacute sclerosing panencephalitis (SSPE) is a slowly progressive disease characterized by inflammatory lesions in many areas of the brain. It is a rare disease of children who were infected by **measles virus** several years earlier. SSPE begins with mild changes in personality and ends with dementia and death.

SSPE is a persistent infection by a variant of measles virus that cannot complete its replication. The evidence for this is as follows:

(1) Inclusion bodies containing helical nucleocapsids, which react with antibody to measles virus, are seen in the affected neurons.

(2) A virus very similar to measles virus can be induced from these cells by cocultivation with permissive cells in culture. The induced virus has a different matrix protein; this protein is important in viral assembly.

(3) Patients have high titers of measles antibody in the blood and spinal fluid.

(4) SSPE has virtually disappeared in the United States since the onset of widespread immunization with measles vaccine.

A progressive panencephalitis can also occur in patients with congenital rubella.

Acquired Immunodeficiency Syndrome (AIDS)

AIDS is caused by human immunodeficiency virus (HIV), a member of the lentivirus group of retroviruses. AIDS is a disease with a long latent period and a progressive course and can involve the central nervous system. See Chapter 45 for more information.

SLOW DISEASES CAUSED BY PRIONS

There are five human transmissible spongiform encephalopathies caused by prions: kuru, CJD, variant CJD, Gerstmann-Sträussler-Scheinker syndrome (GSS), and fatal familial insomnia. Table 44–2 describes some important features of slow viral diseases in humans caused by prions.

Table 44–1. Important features of slow viral diseases caused by conventional viruses.

Disease	Virus	Virus Family	Important Characteristic
Progressive multifocal leukoencephalopathy	JC virus	Papovavirus	Infection widespread; disease only in immunocompromised
Subacute sclerosing panencephalitis	Measles virus	Paramyxovirus	Disease in young children with defective virus in brain
Acquired immunodeficiency syndrome (AIDS)	Human immunodeficiency virus (HIV)	Retrovirus	HIV infects CD4-positive cells, eg, brain macrophages

Table 44–2. Important features of slow viral diseases caused by prions.

Disease	Pathogenesis	Important Feature
Kuru	Transmissible/infectious	Caused by ingesting or handling brain tissue. Occurred in New Guinea tribespeople.
Creutzfeldt-Jakob disease	1. Transmissible/infectious	Iatrogenic transmission by corneal transplant, brain electrodes, and growth hormone
	2. Hereditary/genetic	Mutation in germ cells
	3. Sporadic	No relationship to any known cause; possible new mutation in somatic cells; most common form
Variant Creutzfeldt-Jakob disease	Transmissible/infectious	Probably acquired by eating meat or nervous tissue from animals with "mad cow" disease
Gerstmann-Sträussler-Scheinker syndrome	Hereditary/genetic	Mutation in germ cells
Fatal familial insomnia	Hereditary/genetic	Mutation in germ cells

Kuru

This fatal disease is characterized by progressive tremors and ataxia but not dementia. It occurs *only* among the **Fore tribes in New Guinea.** It was transmitted during a ritual in which the skulls of the dead were opened and the brains eaten. It is suspected that transmission occurred through cuts in the skin during preparation rather than by eating the brain, because the women who prepared the brains were affected more frequently than the men who ate them. Since the practice was stopped, kuru has almost disappeared. The agents of kuru and CJD (see below) have been transmitted serially in primates.

Creutzfeldt-Jakob Disease

Pathologic examination of the brains of patients with CJD and kuru reveals a spongiform (sponge or Swiss-cheese) appearance similar to that associated with scrapie in sheep (see below). The spongiform changes are the result of neuronal vacuolation and neuronal loss rather than demyelination. No inflammatory cells are seen in the brains. Prions cause scrapie and have been found in the brains of CJD patients.

In contrast to kuru, CJD is **found sporadically worldwide** and affects both sexes. The incidence of CJD is approximately 1 case per 1 million population, and there is no increased risk associated with dietary habits, occupation, or animal exposure. Vegetarians and meat eaters have the same rate. The rate of CJD is the same in countries whose animals have scrapie and those whose animals do not. There is no evidence for person-to-person or transplacental transmission.

There is no increased risk for medical caregivers; therefore, gowns and masks are unnecessary. The standard precautions for obtaining infectious specimens should be observed. It has been transmitted **iatrogenically,** eg, in a corneal transplant, via intracerebral electrodes, in hormones extracted from human pituitaries, and in grafts of cadaveric dura mater. There is only one confirmed case of CJD being transmitted by blood transfusion, and intravenous drug use does not increase the risk. Proper sterilization of CJD agent–contaminated material consists of either autoclaving or treating with sodium hypochlorite.

The main clinical findings of CJD are dementia (including behavioral changes, memory loss, and confusion) and myoclonic jerking. Additional findings include ataxia, aphasia, visual loss, and hemiparesis. The symptoms typically appear gradually and progress inexorably. In the terminal stage, the patient becomes mute and akinetic, then comatose. About 80% of those affected die within 1 year. Most cases occur in people who are 50–70 years of age.

A presumptive diagnosis of CJD can be made pathologically by detecting spongiform changes in a brain biopsy specimen. Neuronal loss and gliosis are seen. Amyloid plaques are also seen in some cases of CJD. In variant CJD, "florid" plaques composed of flower-like amyloid plaques surrounded by a halo of vacuoles are seen. Brain imaging and the electroencephalogram may show characteristic changes. There is no evidence of inflammation, ie, no neutrophils or lymphocytes are seen. The blood count and routine spinal fluid test results are normal. The finding of a normal brain protein called 14-3-3 in the spinal fluid supports the diagnosis.

The specific diagnosis of CJD is typically made by immunohistochemistry in which labeled anti-prion antibodies are used to stain the patient's brain specimen. Because we do not make antibodies to prion proteins, there are no serologic diagnostic tests. No antibodies are made in humans because humans are tolerant to our prion proteins. (The antibodies used in the immunohistochemical lab tests are made in other animals in which the human prions are immunogenic.) Unlike viruses, prions cannot be grown in culture, so there are no culture-based diagnostic tests.

Tonsillar tissue obtained from patients with variant CJD was positive for prion protein using monoclonal antibody–based assays. The use of tonsillar or other similar lymphoid tissue may obviate the need for a brain biopsy. Pathologic prion proteins have also been detected in the olfactory epithelium of patients with CJD.

There is no treatment for CJD, and there is no drug or vaccine available for prevention.

Although most cases of CJD are sporadic, about 10% are hereditary. The hereditary (familial) form is inherited as an autosomal dominant trait. In these patients, 12 different point mutations and several insertion mutations in the prion protein gene have been found. One of these, a point mutation in codon 102, is the same mutation found in patients with **GSS syndrome**, another slow central nervous system disease of humans. The main clinical features of GSS are cerebellar ataxia and spastic paraparesis. The hereditary forms of these diseases may be prevented by the detection of carriers and genetic counseling.

The origin of these spongiform encephalopathies is three-fold: **infectious, hereditary,** and **sporadic.** The infectious forms are kuru and probably variant CJD (see below). Transmission of the infectious agent was documented by serial passage of brain material from a person with CJD to chimpanzees. The hereditary form is best illustrated by GSS syndrome described above and by a disease called fatal familial insomnia. The term "sporadic" refers to the appearance of the disease in the absence of either an infectious or a hereditary cause.

Fatal familial insomnia is a very rare disease characterized by progressive insomnia, dysautonomia (dysfunction of the autonomic nervous system) resulting in various symptoms, dementia, and death. A specific mutation in the prion protein is found in patients with this disease.

SLOW DISEASES OF ANIMALS

The "slow" transmissible diseases of animals that are important models for human diseases. Scrapie and visna are diseases of sheep, and BSE ("mad cow" disease) is a disease of cattle that appears to have arisen from the ingestion of sheep tissue by the cattle. Chronic wasting disease occurs in deer and elk. Visna is caused by a virus, whereas the other three are prion-mediated diseases.

Scrapie

Scrapie is a disease of sheep, characterized by tremors, ataxia, and itching, in which the sheep scrape off their wool against fence posts. It has an incubation period of many months. Spongiform degeneration without inflammation is seen in the brain tissue of affected animals. It has been transmitted to mice and other animals via a brain extract that contained no recognizable virus particles. Studies of mice revealed that the infectivity is associated with a 27,000-molecular-weight protein known as a prion (see page 196).

Visna

Visna is a disease of sheep that is characterized by pneumonia and demyelinating lesions in the brain. It is caused by visna virus, a member of the lentivirus subgroup of retroviruses. As such, it has a single-stranded, diploid RNA genome and an RNA-dependent DNA polymerase in the virion. It is thought that integration of the DNA provirus into the host cell DNA may be important in the persistence of the virus within the host and, consequently, in its long incubation period and prolonged, progressive course.

Bovine Spongiform Encephalopathy

BSE is also known as "mad cow" disease. The cattle become aggressive, ataxic, and eventually die. Cattle acquire BSE by eating feed supplemented with organs, eg, brains, obtained from sheep infected with scrapie prions. (It is also possible that BSE arose in cattle by a mutation in the gene encoding the prion protein.)

BSE is endemic in Great Britain. Supplementation of feed with sheep organs was banned in Great Britain in 1988 and thousands of cattle were destroyed, two measures that have led to a marked decline in the number of new cases of BSE. BSE has been found in cattle in other European countries such as France, Germany, Italy, and Spain, and there is significant concern in those countries that variant CJD may emerge in humans. Two cases of BSE in cattle in the United States have been reported.

In 1996, several cases of CJD occurred in Great Britain that are attributed to the ingestion of beef. These cases are a new variant of CJD (vCJD, also called nvCJD) because they occurred in much younger people than usual and had certain clinical and pathologic findings different from those found in the typical form of the disease. None of those affected had consumed cattle or sheep brains, but brain material may have been admixed into processed meats such as sausages.

Only people whose native prion protein is homozygous for methionine at amino acid 129 contract vCJD. People whose native prion protein is homozygous for valine at amino acid 129 or who are heterozygotic do not contract vCJD. These findings indicate that prion proteins with methionine are more easily folded into the pathologic beta-pleated sheet form.

The prions isolated from the "variant CJD" cases in humans chemically resemble the prions isolated from "mad cow" disease more than they resemble other prions, which is evidence to support the hypothesis that variant CJD originated by eating beef. There is no evidence that eating lamb is associated with variant CJD. As of June 2002, vCJD has killed more than 120 people in Europe, 117 of whom live in Great Britain. No cases of variant CJD have occurred in North America.

It is unknown how many people harbor the pathogenic prion in a latent (asymptomatic) form. The possibility that there may be people who are asymptomatic carriers of the vCJD prion and who could be a source for infection of others, eg, via blood transfusions, has led blood banks in the United States to eliminate from the donor pool people who have lived in Great Britain for more than 6 months.

Chronic Wasting Disease

Chronic wasting disease (CWD) of deer and elk is a prion-mediated disease that exists in the United States.

Because vCJD is strongly suspected to be transmitted by ingesting meat, there is concern regarding the consequences of eating deer and elk meat (venison). In 2002, it was reported that neurodegenerative diseases occurred in three men who ate venison in the 1990s. One of these diseases was confirmed as CJD. Whether there is a causal relationship is unclear and surveillance continues.

SUMMARIES OF ORGANISMS

Brief summaries of the organisms described in this chapter begin on page 501. Please consult these summaries for a rapid review of the essential material.

PRACTICE QUESTIONS: USMLE & COURSE EXAMINATIONS

Questions on the topics discussed in this chapter can be found in the Clinical Virology section of Part XI: USMLE (National Board) Practice Questions starting on page 549. Also see Part XII: USMLE (National Board) Practice Examination starting on page 583.

Human Immunodeficiency Virus

Disease

Human immunodeficiency virus (HIV)[1] is the cause of acquired immunodeficiency syndrome (AIDS).

Both HIV-1 and HIV-2 cause AIDS, but HIV-1 is found worldwide, whereas HIV-2 is found primarily in West Africa. This chapter refers to HIV-1 unless otherwise noted.

Important Properties

HIV is one of the two important human T-cell lymphotropic retroviruses (human T-cell leukemia virus is the other). HIV preferentially infects and **kills helper (CD4) T lymphocytes**, resulting in the loss of cell-mediated immunity and a high probability that the host will develop **opportunistic infections**. Other cells (eg, macrophages and monocytes) that have CD4 proteins on their surfaces can be infected also.

HIV belongs to the lentivirus subgroup of retroviruses, which cause "slow" infections with long incubation periods (see Chapter 44). HIV has a bar-shaped (type D) core surrounded by an envelope containing virus-specific glycoproteins (gp120 and gp41) (Figure 45–1). The genome of HIV consists of two identical molecules of single-stranded, positive-polarity RNA and is said to be **diploid**. The HIV genome is the most complex of the known retroviruses (Figure 45–2). In addition to the three typical retroviral genes *gag, pol,* and *env,* which encode the structural proteins, the genome RNA has six regulatory genes (Table 45–1). Two of these regulatory genes, *tat* and *rev,* are required for replication, and the other four, *nef, vif, vpr,* and *vpu,* are not required for replication and are termed "accessory" genes.

The *gag* gene encodes the internal "core" proteins, the most important of which is p24, an antigen used in serologic tests. The *pol* gene encodes several proteins, including the virion "reverse transcriptase," which synthesizes DNA by using the genome RNA as a template, an integrase that integrates the viral DNA into the cel-

lular DNA, and a protease that cleaves the various viral precursor proteins. The *env* gene encodes gp160, a precursor glycoprotein that is cleaved to form the two envelope (surface) glycoproteins, gp120 and gp41.

On the basis of differences in the base sequence of the gene that encodes gp120, HIV has been subdivided into subtypes (**clades**) A through I. The B clade is the most common subtype in North America. Subtype B preferentially infects mononuclear cells and appears to be passed readily during anal sex, whereas subtype E preferentially infects female genital tract cells and appears to be passed readily during vaginal sex.

Three enzymes are located within the nucleocapsid of the virion: reverse transcriptase, integrase, and protease. Reverse transcriptase is the RNA-dependent DNA polymerase that is the source of the family name retroviruses. This enzyme transcribes the RNA genome into the proviral DNA. Reverse transcriptase is a bifunctional enzyme; it also has ribonuclease H activity. Ribonuclease H degrades RNA when it is in the form of an RNA-DNA hybrid molecule. The degradation of the viral RNA genome is an essential step in the synthesis of the double-stranded proviral DNA. Integrase, another important enzyme within the virion, mediates the integration of the proviral DNA into the host cell DNA. The viral protease cleaves the precursor polyproteins into functional viral polypeptides.

One essential regulatory gene is the ***tat*** (transactivation of transcription)[2] gene, which encodes a protein that enhances viral (and perhaps cellular) gene transcription.

The Tat protein and another HIV-encoded regulatory protein called Nef repress the synthesis of class I MHC proteins, thereby reducing the ability of cytotoxic T cells to kill HIV-infected cells. The other essential regulatory gene, *rev,* controls the passage of late mRNA from the nucleus into the cytoplasm. The function of the four accessory genes is described in Table 45–1.

---

[1] Formerly known as human T-lymphotropic virus type 3 (HTLV-III), lymphadenopathy-associated virus (LAV), and AIDS-related virus (ARV).

[2] Transactivation refers to activation of transcription of genes distant from the gene, ie, other genes on the same proviral DNA or on cellular DNA. One site of action of the Tat protein is the long terminal repeat at the 5′ end of the viral genome.

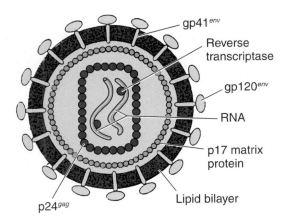

Figure 45–1. Cross-section of HIV. In the interior, two molecules of viral RNA are shown associated with reverse transcriptase. Surrounding those structures is a rectangular nucleocapsid composed of p24 proteins. On the exterior are the two envelope proteins, gp120 and gp41, which are embedded in the lipid bilayer derived from the cell membrane. (Modified and reproduced, with permission, from Greene WC: *N Engl J Med* 1993;328:330.)

The accessory protein Vif (*viral infectivity*) enhances HIV infectivity by inhibiting the action of APOBEC3G, an enzyme that causes hypermutation in retroviral DNA. APOBEC3G is "apolipoprotein B RNA-editing enzyme" that deaminates cytosines in both mRNA and retroviral DNA, thereby inactivating these molecules and reducing infectivity. APOBEC3G is considered to be an important member of the innate host defenses against retroviral infection. HIV defends itself against this innate host defense by producing Vif,

which counteracts APOBEC3G, thereby preventing hypermutation from occurring.

There are several important antigens of HIV.

(1) gp120 and gp41 are the **type-specific envelope glycoproteins.** gp120 protrudes from the surface and interacts with the CD4 receptor (and a second protein, a chemokine receptor) on the cell surface. gp41 is embedded in the envelope and mediates the fusion of the viral envelope with the cell membrane at the time of infection. The gene that encodes gp120 mutates rapidly, resulting in many **antigenic variants.** The most immunogenic region of gp120 is called the V3 loop; it is one of the sites that varies antigenically to a significant degree. Antibody against gp120 neutralizes the infectivity of HIV, but the rapid appearance of gp120 variants will make production of an effective vaccine difficult. The high mutation rate may be due to lack of an editing function in the reverse transcriptase.

(2) The group-specific antigen, p24, is located in the core and is not known to vary. Antibodies against p24 do not neutralize HIV infectivity but serve as important serologic markers of infection.

The natural host range of HIV is limited to humans, although certain primates can be infected in the laboratory. HIV is **not an endogenous virus** of humans; ie, no HIV sequences are found in normal human cell DNA. The origin of HIV and how it entered the human population remains uncertain. There is evidence that chimpanzees living in West Africa were the source of HIV-1.

Viruses similar to HIV have been isolated. Examples are listed below.

(1) Human immunodeficiency virus type 2 (HIV-2) was isolated from AIDS patients in West Africa in 1986. The proteins of HIV-2 are only about 40% identical to those of the original HIV isolates. HIV-2 remains local-

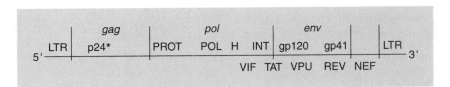

Figure 45–2. The genome of HIV. Above the line are the three genes for the main structural proteins: (1) *gag* encodes the internal group-specific antigens, eg, p24; (2) *pol* encodes the polymerase protein (reverse transcriptase), which has four enzymatic activities: protease (PROT), polymerase (POL), RNase H (H), and integrase (INT); (3) *env* encodes the two envelope glycoproteins, gp120 and gp41. Below the line are five regulatory genes: viral infectivity factor (VIF), transactivating protein (TAT), viral protein U (VPU), regulator of expression of virion protein (REV), and negative regulatory factor (NEF). At both ends are long terminal repeats (LTR), which are transcription initiation sites. Within the 5′ LTR is the binding site for the TAT protein, called the transactivation response element (TAR). TAT enhances the initiation and elongation of viral mRNA transcription.

* p24 and other smaller proteins such as p17 and p7 are encoded by the *gag* gene.

Table 45–1. Genes and proteins of human immunodeficiency virus.

Gene	Proteins Encoded by Gene	Function of Proteins
I. Structural Genes Found in All Retroviruses		
gag	p24, p7	Nucleocapsid
	p17	Matrix
pol	Reverse transcriptase[1]	Transcribes RNA genome into DNA
	Protease	Cleaves precursor polypeptides
	Integrase	Integrates viral DNA into host cell DNA
env	gp120	Attachment to CD4 protein
	gp41	Fusion with host cell
II. Regulatory Genes Found in Human Immunodeficiency Virus That Are Required for Replication		
tat	Tat	Activation of transcription of viral genes
rev	Rev	Transport of late mRNAs from nucleus to cytoplasm
III. Regulatory Genes Found in Human Immunodeficiency Virus That Are *Not* Required for Replication (Accessory Genes)		
nef	Nef	Decreases CD4 proteins and class I MHC proteins on surface of infected cells; induces death of uninfected cytotoxic T cells; important for pathogenesis by SIV[2]
vif	Vif	Enhances infectivity by inhibiting the action of APOBEC3G, an enzyme that causes hypermutation in retroviral DNA
vpr	Vpr	Transports viral core from cytoplasm into nucleus in nondividing cells
vpu	Vpu	Enhances virion release from cell

[1]Reverse transcriptase also contains ribonuclease H activity, which degrades the genome RNA to allow the second strand of DNA to be made.
[2]Mutants of the *nef* gene of simian immunodeficiency virus (SIV) do not cause AIDS in monkeys.

ized primarily to West Africa and is much less transmissible than HIV-1.

(2) Simian immunodeficiency virus (SIV) was isolated from monkeys with an AIDS-like illness. Antibodies in some African women cross-react with SIV. The proteins of SIV resemble those of HIV-2 more closely than they resemble those of the original HIV isolates.

(3) Human T-cell lymphotropic virus (HTLV)-4 infects T cells but does not kill them and is not associated with any disease.

Summary of Replicative Cycle

In general, the replication of HIV follows the typical retroviral cycle (Figure 45–3). The initial step in the entry of HIV into the cell is the binding of the virion gp120 envelope protein to the CD4 protein on the cell surface. The virion gp120 protein then interacts with a second protein on the cell surface, one of the

chemokine receptors. Next, the virion gp41 protein mediates fusion of the viral envelope with the cell membrane, and the virion enters the cell.

Chemokine receptors, such as CXCR4 and CCR5 proteins, are required for the entry of HIV into CD4-positive cells. The T-cell-tropic strains of HIV bind to CXCR4, whereas the macrophage-tropic strains bind to CCR5. Mutations in the gene encoding CCR5 endow the individual with protection from infection with HIV. People who are homozygotes are completely resistant to infection, and heterozygotes progress to disease more slowly. Approximately 1% of people of Western European ancestry have homozygous mutations in this gene and about 10–15% are heterozygotes.

After uncoating, the virion RNA-dependent DNA polymerase transcribes the genome RNA into double-stranded DNA, which integrates into the host cell DNA. The viral DNA can integrate at different sites in the host cell DNA, and multiple copies of viral DNA

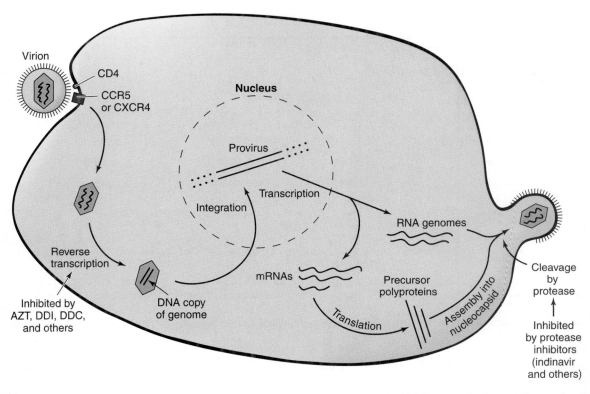

Figure 45–3. Replicative cycle of HIV. The sites of action of the important antiviral drugs are indicated. The mode of action of the reverse transcriptase inhibitors and the protease inhibitors is described in Chapter 35. (Modified and reproduced, with permission, from Ryan K et al: *Sherris Medical Microbiology,* 3rd ed. Originally published by Appleton & Lange. Copyright © 1994 by The McGraw-Hill Companies.)

can integrate. Integration is mediated by a virus-encoded endonuclease (integrase). Viral mRNA is transcribed from the proviral DNA by host cell RNA polymerase and translated into several large polyproteins. The Gag and Pol polyproteins are cleaved by the viral-encoded protease, whereas the Env polyprotein is cleaved by a cellular protease. The Gag polyprotein is cleaved to form the main core protein (p24), the matrix protein (p17), and several smaller proteins. The Pol polyprotein is cleaved to form the reverse transcriptase, integrase, and protease. The immature virion containing the precursor polyproteins forms in the cytoplasm, and cleavage by the viral protease occurs as the immature virion buds from the cell membrane. It is this cleavage process that results in the mature, infectious virion.

Transmission & Epidemiology

Transmission of HIV occurs primarily by sexual contact and by transfer of infected blood. Perinatal trans-

mission from infected mother to neonate also occurs, either across the placenta, at birth, or via breast milk. It is estimated that more than 50% of neonatal infections occur at the time of delivery and that the remainder is split roughly equally between transplacental transmission and transmission via breast feeding.

Infection occurs by the transfer of either HIV-infected cells or free HIV (ie, HIV that is not cell-associated). Although small amounts of virus have been found in other fluids, eg, saliva and tears, there is no evidence that they play a role in infection. In general, transmission of HIV follows the pattern of hepatitis B virus, except that HIV infection is much less efficiently transferred; ie, the dose of HIV required to cause infection is much higher than that of HBV. People with sexually transmitted diseases, especially those with ulcerative lesions such as syphilis, chancroid, and herpes genitalis, have a significantly higher risk of both transmitting and acquiring HIV.

Transmission of HIV via blood transfusion has been greatly reduced by screening donated blood for the presence of antibody to HIV. However, there is a "window" period early in infection when the blood of an infected person can contain HIV but antibodies are not detectable. Blood banks now test for the presence of p24 antigen in an effort to detect blood that contains HIV.

Between 1981, when AIDS was first reported, and 2001, approximately 1.3 million people in the United States have been infected with HIV. During this time, there were approximately 816,000 cases of AIDS and 467,000 deaths. In 2004, there were 23,000 deaths caused by AIDS. It is estimated there are approximately 900,000 people living with HIV infection in the United States and it is further estimated that about one quarter of those infected are unaware of their infection. The number of adults and children newly infected with HIV in 2004 is estimated to be approximately 44,000. The number of children with AIDS who acquired HIV by perinatal transmission declined from a high of 954 in 1992 to 101 in 2001 and has continued to remain low. The prevalence of AIDS in the United States in 2003 was about 490,000 individuals.

Worldwide, it is estimated that approximately 40 million people are infected, two-thirds of whom live in sub-Saharan Africa. Three regions, Africa, Asia, and Latin America, have the highest rates of new infections. AIDS is the fourth leading cause of death worldwide. (Ischemic heart disease, cerebrovascular disease, and acute lower respiratory disease are ranked first, second, and third, respectively.)

In the United States and Europe during the 1980s, HIV infection and AIDS occurred primarily in men who have sex with men (especially those with multiple partners), intravenous drug users, and hemophiliacs. Heterosexual transmission was rare in these regions in the 1980s but is now rising significantly. Heterosexual transmission is the predominant mode of infection in African countries.

Very few health care personnel have been infected despite prolonged exposure and needle-stick injuries, supporting the view that the infectious dose of HIV is high. The risk of being infected after percutaneous exposure to HIV-infected blood is estimated to be about 0.3%. In 1990, it was reported that a dentist may have infected five of his patients. It is thought that transmission of HIV from health care personnel to patients is exceedingly rare.

Pathogenesis & Immunity

HIV infects helper T cells and kills them, resulting in **suppression of cell-mediated immunity**. This predisposes the host to various opportunistic infections and certain cancers such as Kaposi's sarcoma and lymphoma. However, HIV does not directly cause these tumors because HIV genes are not found in these cancer cells. The initial infection of the genital tract occurs in dendritic cells that line the mucosa (Langerhans' cells), after which the local CD4-positive helper T cells become infected. HIV is first found in the blood 4–11 days after infection.

HIV also infects brain monocytes and macrophages, producing multinucleated giant cells and significant central nervous system symptoms. The fusion of HIV-infected cells in the brain and elsewhere mediated by gp41 is one of the main pathologic findings. The cells recruited into the syncytia ultimately die. The death of HIV-infected cells is also the result of immunologic attack by cytotoxic CD8 lymphocytes. Effectiveness of the cytotoxic T cells may be limited by the ability of the viral Tat and Nef proteins to reduce class I MHC protein synthesis (see below).

Another mechanism hypothesized to explain the death of helper T cells is that HIV acts as a "superantigen," which indiscriminately activates many helper T cells and leads to their demise. The finding that one member of the retrovirus family, mouse mammary tumor virus, can act as a superantigen lends support to this theory. Superantigens are described in Chapter 58.

Persistent noncytopathic infection of T lymphocytes also occurs. Persistently infected cells continue to produce HIV, which may help sustain the infection in vivo. A person infected with HIV is considered to be infected for life. This seems likely to be the result of integration of viral DNA into the DNA of infected cells. Although the use of powerful antiviral drugs (see Treatment section below) can significantly reduce the amount of HIV being produced, latent infection in CD4-positive cells and in immature thymocytes serve as a continuing source of virus.

In 1995, it was reported that a group of HIV-infected individuals has lived for many years without opportunistic infections and without a reduction in the number of their helper T (CD4) cells. The strain of HIV isolated from these individuals has mutations in the *nef* gene, indicating the importance of this gene in pathogenesis. The Nef protein decreases class I MHC protein synthesis, and the inability of the mutant virus to produce functional Nef protein allows the cytotoxic T cells to retain their activity.

Another explanation why some HIV-infected individuals are long-term "nonprogressors" may lie in their ability to produce large amounts of α-defensins. α-Defensins are a family of positively charged peptides with antibacterial activity. In 2002, they were shown to also have antiviral activity. They interfere with HIV binding to the CXCR4 receptor and block entry of the virus into the cell.

In addition to the detrimental effects on T cells, abnormalities of B cells occur. Polyclonal activation of B cells is seen, with resultant high immunoglobulin levels. Autoimmune diseases, such as thrombocytopenia, occur.

The main immune response to HIV infection consists of cytotoxic CD8-positive lymphocytes. These cells respond to the initial infection and control it for many years. Mutants of HIV, especially in the *env* gene encoding gp120, arise, but new clones of cytotoxic T cells proliferate and control the mutant strain. It is the ultimate failure of these cytotoxic T cells that results in the clinical picture of AIDS. Cytotoxic T cells lose their effectiveness because so many CD4 helper T cells have died; thus, the supply of lymphokines, such as IL-2, required to activate the cytotoxic T cells is no longer sufficient.

There is evidence that "escape" mutants of HIV are able to proliferate unchecked because the patient has no clone of cytotoxic T cells capable of responding to the mutant strain. Furthermore, mutations in any of the genes encoding class I MHC proteins result in a more rapid progression to clinical AIDS. The mutant class I MHC proteins cannot present HIV epitopes, which results in cytotoxic T cells being incapable of recognizing and destroying HIV-infected cells.

Antibodies against various HIV proteins, such as p24, gp120, and gp41, are produced, but they neutralize the virus poorly in vivo and appear to have little effect on the course of the disease.

HIV has three main mechanisms by which it evades the immune system: (1) integration of viral DNA into host cell DNA, resulting in a persistent infection; (2) a high rate of mutation of the *env* gene; and (3) the production of the Tat and Nef proteins that downregulate class I MHC proteins required for cytotoxic T cells to recognize and kill HIV-infected cells. The ability of HIV to infect and kill CD4-positive helper T cells further enhances its capacity to avoid destruction by the immune system.

Clinical Findings

The clinical picture of HIV infection can be divided into three stages: an early, acute stage; a middle, latent stage; and a late, immunodeficiency stage (Figure 45–4). In the acute stage, which usually begins 2–4 weeks after infection, a mononucleosis-like picture of fever, lethargy, sore throat, and generalized lymphadenopathy occurs. A maculopapular rash on the trunk, arms, and legs (but sparing the palms and soles) is also seen. Leukopenia occurs, but the number of CD4 cells is usually normal. A high-level viremia typically occurs, and the infection is readily transmissible during this acute stage. This acute stage typically resolves spontaneously in about 2 weeks. Resolution of the acute stage is usually accompanied by a lower level of viremia and a rise in the number of CD8-positive (cytotoxic) T cells directed against HIV.

Antibodies to HIV typically appear 10–14 days after infection, and most will have seroconverted by 3–4 weeks after infection. Note that the inability to detect antibodies prior to that time can result in "false-nega-

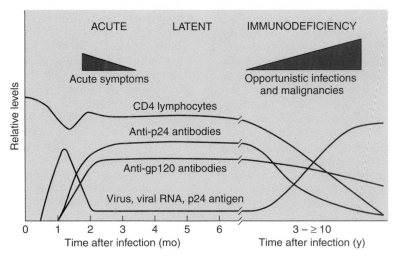

Figure 45–4. Time course of HIV infection. The three main stages of HIV infection—acute, latent, and immunodeficiency—are shown in conjunction with several important laboratory findings. Note that the levels of virus and viral RNA (viral load) are high early in the infection, become low for several years, and then rise during the immunodeficiency stage. The level of CD4 lymphocytes remains more or less normal for many years but then falls. This results in the immunodeficiency stage, which is characterized by opportunistic infections and malignancies. (Modified and reproduced, with permission, from Feinberg M: *Curr Opin Infect Dis* 1992;5:214.)

tive" serologic tests; ie, the person is infected, but antibodies are not detectable at the time of the test. This has important implications because HIV can be transmitted to others during this period. Of those who become seropositive during the acute infection, approximately 87% are symptomatic; ie, about 13% experience an asymptomatic initial infection.

After the initial viremia, a viral **set point** occurs, which can differ from one person to another. The set point represents the amount of virus produced, ie, the **viral load**, and tends to remain "set," or constant, for years. The higher the set point at the end of the initial infection, the more likely the individual is to progress to symptomatic AIDS. It is estimated that an infected person can produce up to 10 billion new virions each day. This viral load can be estimated by using an assay for viral RNA in the patient's plasma. (The assay detects the RNA in free virions in the plasma, not cell-associated virions.)

The amount of viral RNA serves to guide treatment decisions and the prognosis. For example, if a drug regimen fails to reduce the viral load, the drugs should be changed. As far as the prognosis is concerned, a patient with more than 10,000 copies of viral RNA/mL of plasma is significantly more likely to progress to AIDS than a patient with fewer than 10,000 copies.

The number of CD4-positive T cells is another important measure that guides the management of infected patients. It is used to determine whether a patient needs chemoprophylaxis against opportunistic organisms, to determine whether a patient needs anti-HIV therapy, and to determine the response to this therapy.

In the middle stage, a long latent period, measured in years, usually ensues. In untreated patients, the latent period usually lasts for 7–11 years. The patient is asymptomatic during this period. Although the patient is asymptomatic and viremia is low or absent, a large amount of HIV is being produced by lymph node cells but remains sequestered within the lymph nodes. This indicates that during this period of clinical latency, the virus itself does not enter a latent state.

A syndrome called AIDS-related complex (ARC) can occur during the latent period. The most frequent manifestations are persistent fevers, fatigue, weight loss, and lymphadenopathy. ARC often progresses to AIDS.

The late stage of HIV infection is AIDS, manifested by a decline in the number of CD4 cells to below 400/μL and an increase in the frequency and severity of opportunistic infections. Table 45–2 describes some of the common opportunistic infections and their causative organism seen in HIV-infected patients during the late, immunocompromised stage of the infection.

The two most characteristic manifestations of AIDS are *Pneumocystis* pneumonia and Kaposi's sarcoma.

However, many other opportunistic infections occur with some frequency. These include viral infections such as disseminated herpes simplex, herpes zoster, and cytomegalovirus infections and progressive multifocal leukoencephalopathy; fungal infections such as thrush (caused by *Candida albicans*), cryptococcal meningitis, and disseminated histoplasmosis; protozoal infections such as toxoplasmosis and cryptosporidiosis; and disseminated bacterial infections such as those caused by *Mycobacterium avium-intracellulare* and *Mycobacterium tuberculosis*. Many AIDS patients have severe neurologic problems, eg, dementia and neuropathy, which can be caused by either HIV infection of the brain or by many of these opportunistic organisms.

In 1992, patients with AIDS who had no evidence of infection by HIV-1 or HIV-2 were reported. At present, it is unknown whether another virus can cause AIDS.

Laboratory Diagnosis

The presumptive diagnosis of HIV infection is made by the detection of antibodies by **ELISA**. Because there are some false-positive results with this test, the definitive diagnosis is made by **Western blot** analysis, in which the viral proteins are displayed by acrylamide gel electrophoresis, transferred to nitrocellulose paper (the blot), and reacted with the patient's serum. If antibodies are present, they will bind to the viral proteins (predominantly to the gp41 or p24 protein). Enzymatically labeled antibody to human IgG is then added. A color reaction reveals the presence of the HIV antibody in the infected patient's serum.

OraQuick is a rapid screening immunoassay for HIV antibody that uses a blood sample obtained by fingerprick. Results are available in 20 minutes. Positive results require confirmation by a Western blot test.

HIV can be grown in culture from clinical specimens, but this procedure is available only at a few medical centers. The polymerase chain reaction (PCR) is a very sensitive and specific technique that can be used to detect HIV DNA within infected cells. Some individuals who do not have detectable antibodies have been shown by this test to be infected. As already mentioned, the amount of viral RNA in the plasma (ie, the viral load) can also be determined using PCR-based assays.

During the first month after infection, antibody tests may be negative. In view of this, the diagnosis of acute HIV infection may not be able to be made using serologic tests. The presence of HIV can be detected during that period by either viral culture, p24 antigen test, or PCR assay. Approximately 10–20 days after infection, an increase in HIV RNA can be detected by PCR assay and by 30 days after infection, an increase in p24 antigen can be seen in patients whose antibody test results are negative.

Table 45–2. Common opportunistic infections in AIDS patients.

Site of Infection	Disease or Symptom	Causative Organism
Lung	1. Pneumonia 2. Tuberculosis	*Pneumocystis carinii,* cytomegalovirus *Mycobacterium tuberculosis*
Mouth	1. Thrush 2. Hairy leukoplakia 3. Ulcerations	*Candida albicans* Epstein-Barr virus Herpes simplex virus-1, *Histoplasma capsulatum*
Esophagus	1. Thrush 2. Esophagitis	*Candida albicans* Cytomegalovirus, herpes simplex virus-1
Intestinal tract	Diarrhea	*Salmonella* sp., *Shigella* sp, cytomegalovirus, *Cryptosporidium parvum, Giardia lamblia*
Central nervous system	1. Meningitis 2. Brain abscess 3. Progressive multifocal leukoencephalopathy	*Cryptococcus neoformans* *Toxoplasma gondii* JC virus
Eye	Retinitis	Cytomegalovirus
Skin	1. Kaposi's sarcoma 2. Zoster 3. Subcutaneous nodules	Human herpesvirus 8 Varicella-zoster virus *Cryptococcus neoformans*
Reticuloendothelial system	Lymphadenopathy or splenomegaly	*Mycobacterium avium* complex, Epstein-Barr virus

Treatment

The current treatment of choice for advanced disease is a regimen consisting of two nucleoside inhibitors (zidovudine and lamivudine) and a protease inhibitor (indinavir). This combination is known as **HAART,** which is an acronym for "highly active antiretroviral therapy." It is very effective in prolonging life, improving quality of life, and reducing viral load but does not cure the chronic HIV infection, ie, replication of HIV within CD4-positive cells continues indefinitely. Discontinuation of HAART almost always results in viremia, a return of the viral load to its pretreatment set point, and a fall in the CD4 count.

Another highly effective regimen, especially in children, is the combination of zidovudine, lamivudine, and the non-nucleoside reverse transcriptase inhibitor, efavirenz. Adding the protease inhibitor, nelfinavir, to this three-drug combination enhanced the potency and duration of the antiviral effect in children.

Zidovudine (ZDV, azidothymidine, AZT, Retrovir) inhibits HIV replication by interfering with proviral DNA synthesis. However, it cannot cure an infected cell of an already integrated copy of proviral DNA. Strains of HIV resistant to ZDV have been isolated from patients receiving long-term ZDV therapy. Severe hematologic side effects can limit its use. ZDV can be combined with didanosine or zalcitabine to lower the dose of each and thereby reduce the incidence and severity of side effects.

Didanosine (dideoxyinosine, ddI, Videx) is recommended for patients who are intolerant of ZDV or whose disease has progressed while they were taking ZDV. Its mechanism of action is similar to that of ZDV. Three other drugs, zalcitabine (dideoxycytidine, ddC, Hivid), stavudine (d4T, Zerit), and lamivudine (3TC, Epivir), are also used in similar situations.

In addition to the nucleoside inhibitors mentioned above, there are non-nucleoside reverse transcriptase inhibitors (NNRTI) that are effective against HIV. Nevirapine (Viramune), delavirdine (Rescriptor), and efavirenz (Sustiva) are the currently approved drugs in this class. The combination of nevirapine, ZDV, and didanosine lowers viral RNA levels and raises CD4 counts significantly more than the two-drug regimen of ZDV and didanosine. NNRTIs should not be used as monotherapy because resistant mutants emerge rapidly.

Protease inhibitors, such as saquinavir (Invirase), ritonavir (Norvir), nelfinavir (Viracept), and indinavir (Crixivan), when combined with nucleoside analogues, such as ZDV, are very effective in inhibiting viral replication and increasing CD4 cell counts. Mutants of HIV resistant to protease inhibitors can be a significant clinical problem. Resistance to one protease inhibitor conveys resistance to all; however, the combination of two protease inhibitors, namely, ritonavir and lopinavir (Kaletra), is effective against both mutant and non-mutant strains of HIV. Mutants of HIV resistant to protease inhibitors and to reverse transcriptase inhibitors have also been recovered from patients.

A major side effect of protease inhibitors is abnormal fat deposition in specific areas of the body, such as the back of the neck. The fat deposits in the back of the neck are said to give the person a "buffalo hump" appearance. These abnormal fat deposits are a type of lipodystrophy; the metabolic process by which this occurs is unknown.

Treatment for acute HIV infection with two reverse transcriptase inhibitors and a protease inhibitor is recommended. With this regimen, the viral load drops below the level of detection, CD4 cell counts rise, and CD8 activity increases. The long-term effect of this approach on rate of progression to AIDS has yet to be determined.

Pregnant women should be treated with two nucleosides and a protease inhibitor. ZDV or nevirapine alone reduced transmission from mother to fetus. ZDV appears not to cause malformations in the fetus, although rare instances of mitochondrial dysfunction and death have been reported. The reader is urged to consult the current information regarding the use of these drugs in pregnancy. A full discussion is beyond the scope of this book.

In 2003, the U.S. Food and Drug Administration approved the use of enfuvirtide (Fuzeon), the first of a new class of anti-HIV drugs known as **fusion inhibitors**, ie, they prevent the fusion of the viral envelope with the cell membrane. Enfuvirtide is a synthetic peptide that binds to gp41 on the viral envelope, thereby blocking the entry of HIV into the cell. It must be administered by injection and is quite expensive.

Drug-resistant mutants of HIV have emerged that significantly affect the ability of both reverse transcriptase inhibitors and protease inhibitors to sustain their clinical efficacy. Approximately 10% of newly infected patients are infected with a strain of HIV resistant to at least one antiretroviral drug. Laboratory tests to detect mutant strains include both genotypic and phenotypic analysis. Genotyping reveals the presence of specific mutations in either the reverse transcriptase (RT) or protease (PR) genes. Phenotyping determines the ability of the virus to grow in cell culture in the presence of the drug. One method of phenotyping recovers the RT and PR genes from the patient's virus and splices them into a test strain of HIV, which is then used to infect cells in culture.

"**Immune reconstitution syndrome**" may occur in HIV-infected patients who are treated with a HAART regimen and who are coinfected with other microbes such as hepatitis B virus, hepatitis C virus, *Mycobacterium avium* complex, *Cryptococcus neoformans*, and *Toxoplasma gondii*. In this syndrome, an exacerbation of clinical symptoms occurs because the antiretroviral drugs en-

hance the ability to mount an inflammatory response. HIV-infected patients with a low CD4 count have a reduced capacity to produce inflammation, but HAART restores the inflammatory response and, as a result, symptoms become more pronounced. To avoid immune reconstitution syndrome, the coinfection should be treated prior to instituting HAART whenever possible.

Prevention

No vaccine for human use is available. A vaccine containing recombinant gp120 protects nonhuman primates against challenge by HIV and by HIV-infected cells. The success of a vaccine containing a live, attenuated mutant of SIV in protecting monkeys against challenge by a large dose of SIV may encourage a similar effort with a mutant of HIV in humans.

Prevention consists of taking measures to avoid exposure to the virus, eg, using condoms, not sharing needles, and discarding donated blood that is contaminated with HIV. Postexposure prophylaxis, such as that given after a needle-stick injury, consists of zidovudine, lamivudine, and a protease inhibitor, such as indinavir. Two steps can be taken to reduce the number of cases of HIV infection in children: ZDV or nevirapine should be given perinatally to HIV-infected mothers and neonates, and HIV-infected mothers should not breast-feed. In addition, the risk of neonatal HIV infection is lower if delivery is accomplished by cesarean section rather than by vaginal delivery. Circumcision reduces HIV infection.

Several drugs are commonly taken by patients in the advanced stages of AIDS to prevent certain opportunistic infections. Some examples are trimethoprim-sulfamethoxazole to prevent *Pneumocystis* pneumonia, fluconazole to prevent recurrences of cryptococcal meningitis, ganciclovir to prevent recurrences of retinitis caused by cytomegalovirus, and oral preparations of antifungal drugs, such as clotrimazole, to prevent thrush caused by *Candida albicans*.

SUMMARIES OF ORGANISMS

Brief summaries of the organisms described in this chapter begin on page 502. Please consult these summaries for a rapid review of the essential material.

PRACTICE QUESTIONS: USMLE & COURSE EXAMINATIONS

Questions on the topics discussed in this chapter can be found in the Clinical Virology section of Part XI: USMLE (National Board) Practice Questions starting on page 549. Also see Part XII: USMLE (National Board) Practice Examination starting on page 583.

Minor Viral Pathogens

These viruses are presented in alphabetical order. They are listed in Table 46–1 in terms of their nucleic acid and presence of an envelope.

Astroviruses

Astroviruses are nonenveloped RNA viruses similar in size to polioviruses. They have a characteristic five- or six-pointed morphology. These viruses cause watery diarrhea, especially in children. Most adults have antibodies against astroviruses, suggesting that infection occurs commonly. No antiviral drugs or preventive measures are available.

Cache Valley Virus

This virus was first isolated in Utah in 1956 but is found throughout the western hemisphere. It is a bunyavirus transmitted by *Aedes, Anopheles,* or *Culiseta* mosquitoes from domestic livestock to people. It is a rare cause of encephalitis in humans. There is no treatment or vaccine for Cache Valley virus infections.

Ebola Virus

Ebola virus is named for the river in Zaire that was the site of an outbreak of **hemorrhagic fever** in 1976. The disease begins with fever, headache, vomiting, and diarrhea. Later, bleeding into the gastrointestinal tract occurs, followed by shock and disseminated intravascular coagulation. The hemorrhages are caused by severe thrombocytopenia. The mortality rate associated with this virus approaches 100%. Most cases arise by secondary transmission from contact with the patient's blood or secretions, eg, in hospital staff. Reuse of needles and syringes is also implicated in the spread within hospitals. Although greatly feared, Ebola hemorrhagic fever is quite rare. As of this writing, approximately 1000 cases have occurred since its appearance in 1976.

Ebola virus is a member of the filovirus family. The natural reservoir of this virus is unknown. Monkeys can be infected but, because they become sick, are unlikely to be the reservoir. Bats are suspected of being the reservoir but this has not been established. The high mortality rate of Ebola virus is attributed to several viral virulence factors: its glycoprotein kills endothelial cells, resulting in hemorrhage, and two other proteins inhibit the induction and action of interferon. Lymphocytes are killed and the antibody response is ineffective.

Diagnosis is made by isolating the virus or by detecting a rise in antibody titer. (Extreme care must be taken when handling specimens in the laboratory.) No antiviral therapy is available. Prevention centers on limiting secondary spread by proper handling of patient's secretions and blood. There is no vaccine.

Hantaviruses

Hantaviruses are members of the bunyavirus family. The prototype virus is Hantaan virus, the cause of Korean hemorrhagic fever (KHF). KHF is characterized by headache, petechial hemorrhages, shock, and renal failure. It occurs in Asia and Europe but not North America and has a mortality rate of about 10%. Hantaviruses are part of a heterogeneous group of viruses called roboviruses, which stands for "*rodent-bo*rne" viruses. Roboviruses are transmitted from rodents directly (without an arthropod vector), whereas arboviruses are "*ar*thropod-*bo*rne."

In 1993, an outbreak of a new disease, characterized by influenza-like symptoms followed rapidly by acute respiratory failure, occurred in the western United States, centered in New Mexico and Arizona. This disease, now called hantavirus pulmonary syndrome, is caused by a hantavirus (Sin Nombre virus) endemic in deer mice (*Peromyscus*) and is acquired by inhalation of aerosols of the rodent's urine and feces. It is not transmitted from person to person. Very few people have antibody to the virus, indicating that asymptomatic infections are not common. The diagnosis is made by detecting viral RNA in lung tissue with the polymerase chain reaction (PCR) assay, by performing immunohistochemistry on lung tissue, or by detecting IgM antibody in serum. The mortality rate of hantavirus pulmonary syndrome is very high, approximately 38%. As of June 2003, a total of 339 cases of hantavirus pulmonary syndrome have been reported in the United States. Most cases occurred in the states west of the

Table 46–1. Minor viral pathogens.

Characteristics	Representative Viruses
DNA enveloped viruses	Herpes B virus, human herpesvirus 6, poxviruses of animal origin (cowpox virus, monkeypox virus)
DNA nonenveloped viruses	None
RNA enveloped viruses	Cache Valley virus, Ebola virus, hantaviruses, Hendra virus, human metapneumovirus, Japanese encephalitis virus, Lassa fever virus, lymphocytic choriomeningitis virus, Nipah virus, Marburg virus, spumaviruses, Tacaribe complex of viruses (eg, Junin and Machupo viruses), Whitewater Arroyo virus
RNA nonenveloped viruses	Astroviruses, encephalomyocarditis virus

Mississippi, particularly in New Mexico, Arizona, California, and Colorado, in that order.

There is no effective drug; ribavirin has been used but appears to be ineffective. There is no vaccine for any hantavirus.

Hendra Virus

This virus was first recognized as a human pathogen in 1994, when it caused severe respiratory disease in Hendra, Australia. It is a paramyxovirus resembling measles virus and was previously called equine morbillivirus. The human infections were acquired by contact with infected horses, but fruit bats appear to be the natural reservoir. There is no treatment or vaccine for Hendra virus infections.

Herpes B Virus

This virus (monkey B virus or herpesvirus simiae) causes a rare, often fatal encephalitis in persons in close contact with monkeys or their tissues, eg, zookeepers or cell culture technicians. The virus causes a latent infection in monkeys that is similar to herpes simplex virus (HSV)-1 infection in humans.

Herpes B virus and HSV-1 cross-react antigenically, but antibody to HSV-1 does not protect from herpes B encephalitis. The presence of HSV-1 antibody can, however, confuse serologic diagnosis by making the interpretation of a rise in antibody titer difficult. The diagnosis can therefore be made only by recovering the virus. Acyclovir may be beneficial. Prevention consists of using protective clothing and masks to prevent exposure to the virus. Immune globulin containing antibody to herpes B virus should be given after a monkey bite.

Human Herpesvirus 6

This herpesvirus is the cause of exanthem subitum (roseola infantum), a common disease in infants that is characterized by a high fever and a transient rash. The virus is found worldwide, and up to 80% of people are seropositive. The virus is lymphotropic and infects both T and B cells. It remains latent within these cells but can be reactivated in immunocompromised patients and cause pneumonia. Many virologic and clinical features of HHV-6 are similar to those of cytomegalovirus, another member of the herpesvirus family.

Human Metapneumovirus

This paramyxovirus was first reported in 2001 as a cause of severe bronchiolitis and pneumonia in young children in the Netherlands. It is similar to respiratory syncytial virus (also a paramyxovirus) in the range of respiratory tract disease it causes. Serologic studies showed that most children have been infected by 5 years of age and that this virus has been present in the human population for at least 50 years.

Japanese Encephalitis Virus

This virus is the most common cause of **epidemic encephalitis**. The disease is characterized by fever, headache, nuchal rigidity, altered states of consciousness, tremors, incoordination, and convulsions. The mortality rate is high, and neurologic sequelae are severe and can be detected in most survivors. The disease occurs throughout Asia but is most prevalent in Southeast Asia. The rare cases seen in the United States have occurred in travelers returning from that continent. American military personnel in Asia have been affected.

Japanese encephalitis virus is a member of the flavivirus family. It is transmitted to humans by certain species of *Culex* mosquitoes endemic to Asian rice fields. There are two main reservoir hosts—birds and pigs. The diagnosis can be made by isolating the virus, by detecting IgM antibody in serum or spinal fluid, or by staining brain tissue with fluorescent antibody. There is no antiviral therapy. Prevention consists of an inactivated vaccine and pesticides to control the mosquito vector. Immunization is recommended for individuals living in areas of endemic infection for several months or longer.

Lassa Fever Virus

Lassa fever virus was first seen in 1969 in the Nigerian town of that name. It causes a severe, often fatal **hemorrhagic fever** characterized by multiple-organ involvement. The disease begins slowly with fever, headache, vomiting, and diarrhea and progresses to involve the lungs, heart, kidneys, and brain. A petechial rash and gastrointestinal tract hemorrhage ensue, followed by death from vascular collapse.

Lassa fever virus is a member of the arenavirus family, which includes other infrequent human pathogens such as lymphocytic choriomeningitis virus and certain members of the Tacaribe group. Arenaviruses ("arena" means sand) are united by their unusual appearance in the electron microscope. Their most striking feature is the "sandlike" particles on their surface, which are ribosomes. The function, if any, of these ribosomes is unknown. Arenaviruses are enveloped viruses with surface spikes, a helical nucleocapsid, and single-stranded RNA with negative polarity.

The natural host for Lassa fever virus is the small rodent *Mastomys,* which undergoes a chronic, lifelong infection. The virus is transmitted to humans by contamination of food or water with animal urine. Secondary transmission among hospital personnel occurs also. Asymptomatic infection is widespread in areas of endemic infection.

The diagnosis is made either by isolating the virus or by detecting a rise in antibody titer. Ribavirin reduces the mortality rate if given early, and hyperimmune serum, obtained from persons who have recovered from the disease, has been beneficial in some cases. No vaccine is available, and prevention centers on proper infection control practices and rodent control.

Lymphocytic Choriomeningitis Virus

Lymphocytic choriomeningitis virus is a member of the arenavirus family. It is a rare cause of aseptic meningitis and cannot be distinguished clinically from the more frequent viral causes, eg, echovirus, coxsackievirus, or mumps virus. The usual picture consists of fever, headache, vomiting, stiff neck, and changes in mental status. Spinal fluid shows an increased number of cells, mostly lymphocytes, with an elevated protein level and a normal or low sugar level.

The virus is endemic in the mouse population, in which chronic infection occurs. Animals infected transplacentally become healthy lifelong carriers. The virus is transmitted to humans via food or water contaminated by mouse urine or feces. There is no human-to-human spread: ie, humans are accidental dead-end hosts. Diagnosis is made by isolating the virus from the spinal fluid or by detecting an increase in antibody titer. No antiviral therapy or vaccine is available.

This disease is the prototype used to illustrate **immunopathogenesis** and immune-complex disease. If immunocompetent adult mice are inoculated, meningitis and death ensue. If, however, newborn mice or x-irradiated immunodeficient adults are inoculated, no meningitis occurs despite extensive viral replication. If sensitized T cells are transplanted to the immunodeficient adults, meningitis and death occur. The immunodeficient adult mice, who are apparently well, slowly develop immune-complex glomerulonephritis. It appears that the mice are partially tolerant to the virus in that their cell-mediated immunity is inactive, but sufficient antibody is produced to cause immune complex disease.

Marburg Virus

Marburg virus and Ebola virus are similar in that they both cause **hemorrhagic fever** and are members of the filovirus family; however, they are antigenically distinct. Marburg virus was first recognized as a cause of human disease in 1967 in Marburg, Germany. The common feature of the infected individuals was their exposure to African green monkeys that had recently arrived from Uganda. As with Ebola virus, the natural reservoir of Marburg virus is unknown.

The clinical picture of this hemorrhagic fever is as described for Ebola virus (see page 330). In 2005, an outbreak of hemorrhagic fever caused by Marburg virus killed hundreds of people in Angola. No cases of disease caused by either Ebola or Marburg virus have occurred in the United States.

The diagnosis is made by isolating the virus or detecting a rise in antibody titer. No antiviral therapy or vaccine is available. As with Ebola virus, secondary cases among medical personnel have occurred; therefore, stringent infection control practices must be instituted to prevent nosocomial spread.

Nipah Virus

Nipah virus is a paramyxovirus that caused encephalitis in Malaysia and Singapore in 1998 and 1999. People who had contact with pigs were particularly at risk for encephalitis caused by this previously unrecognized virus. There is no treatment or vaccine for Nipah virus infections.

Poxviruses of Animal Origin

Four poxviruses cause disease in animals and also cause poxlike lesions in humans on rare occasions. They are transmitted by contact with the infected animals, usually in an occupational setting.

Cowpox virus causes vesicular lesions on the udders of cows and can cause similar lesions on the skin of persons who milk cows. Pseudocowpox virus causes a similar picture but is antigenically distinct. Orf virus is the cause of contagious pustular dermatitis in sheep and of vesicular lesions on the hands of sheepshearers.

Monkeypox virus is different from the other three; it causes a human disease that resembles smallpox. It occurs almost exclusively in Central Africa. In 2003, an outbreak of monkeypox occurred in Wisconsin, Illinois, and Indiana. In this outbreak, the source of the virus was animals imported from Africa. It appears that the virus from the imported animals infected local prairie dogs, which then were the source of the human infection. None of those affected died. In Africa, monkeypox has a death rate of between 1% and 10%, in contrast to 50% for smallpox. There is no effective antiviral treatment. The vaccine against smallpox appears to have some protective effect against monkeypox.

Any new case of smallpoxlike disease must be precisely diagnosed to ensure that it is not due to smallpox virus. There has not been a case of smallpox in the world since 1977,[1] and smallpox immunization has been allowed to lapse.

For these reasons, it is important to ensure that new cases of smallpoxlike disease are due to monkeypox virus. Monkeypox virus can be distinguished from smallpox virus in the laboratory both antigenically and by the distinctive lesions it causes on the chorioallantoic membrane of chicken eggs.

Spumaviruses

Spumaviruses are a subfamily of retroviruses that cause a foamy appearance in cultured cells. They can present a problem in the production of viral vaccines if they contaminate the cell cultures used to make the vaccine. There are no known human pathogens.

---

[1] With the exception of two laboratory-acquired cases in 1978.

Tacaribe Complex of Viruses

The Tacaribe[2] complex contains several human pathogens, all of which cause hemorrhagic fever.

The best known are Sabia virus in Brazil, Junin virus in Argentina, and Machupo virus in Bolivia. Hemorrhagic fevers, as the name implies, are characterized by fever and bleeding into the gastrointestinal tract, skin, and other organs. The bleeding is due to thrombocytopenia. Death occurs in up to 20% of cases, and outbreaks can involve thousands of people. Agricultural workers are particularly at risk.

Similar to other arenaviruses such as Lassa fever virus and lymphocytic choriomeningitis virus, these viruses are endemic in the rodent population and are transmitted to humans by accidental contamination of food and water by rodent excreta. The diagnosis can be made either by isolating the virus or by detecting a rise in antibody titer. In a laboratory-acquired Sabia virus infection, ribavirin was an effective treatment. No vaccine is available.

Whitewater Arroyo Virus

This virus is the cause of a hemorrhagic fever/acute respiratory distress syndrome in the western part of the United States. It is a member of the arenavirus family, as is Lassa fever virus, a cause of hemorrhagic fever in Africa (see page 332). Wood rats are the reservoir of this virus, and it is transmitted by inhalation of dried rat excrement. This mode of transmission is the same as that of the hantavirus, Sin Nombre virus (see page 330). There is no established antiviral therapy and there is no vaccine.

SUMMARIES OF ORGANISMS

Brief summaries of the organisms described in this chapter begin on page 502. Please consult these summaries for a rapid review of the essential material.

PRACTICE QUESTIONS: USMLE & COURSE EXAMINATIONS

Questions on the topics discussed in this chapter can be found in the Clinical Virology section of Part XI: USMLE (National Board) Practice Questions starting on page 549. Also see Part XII: USMLE (National Board) Practice Examination starting on page 583.

---

[2] Tacaribe virus was isolated from bats in Trinidad in 1956. It does not cause human disease.

PART V
Mycology

Basic Mycology

STRUCTURE & GROWTH

Because fungi (yeasts and molds) are **eukaryotic** organisms whereas bacteria are prokaryotic, they differ in several fundamental respects (Table 47–1). Two fungal cell structures are important medically:

(1) The fungal cell wall consists primarily of chitin (not peptidoglycan as in bacteria); thus, fungi are insensitive to antibiotics, such as penicillin, that inhibit peptidoglycan synthesis.

Chitin is a polysaccharide composed of long chains of *N*-acetylglucosamine. The fungal cell wall contains other polysaccharides as well, the most important of which is β-glucan, a long polymer of D-glucose. The medical importance of β-glucan is that it is the site of action of the antifungal drug caspofungin.

(2) The fungal cell membrane contains ergosterol, in contrast to the human cell membrane, which contains cholesterol. The selective action of amphotericin B and azole drugs, such as fluconazole and ketoconazole, on fungi is based on this difference in membrane sterols.

There are two types of fungi: yeasts and molds. **Yeasts** grow as **single cells** that reproduce by asexual budding. **Molds** grow as **long filaments** (**hyphae**) and form a mat (**mycelium**). Some hyphae form transverse walls (**septate hyphae**), whereas others do not (**nonseptate hyphae**). Nonseptate hyphae are multinucleated (coencytic).

Several medically important fungi are thermally **dimorphic;** ie, they form different structures at different temperatures. They exist as molds in the environment at ambient temperature and as yeasts (or other structures) in human tissues at body temperature.

Most fungi are obligate aerobes; some are facultative anaerobes; but none are obligate anaerobes. All fungi require a preformed organic source of carbon—hence their frequent association with decaying matter. The natural habitat of most fungi is, therefore, the **environment.** An important exception is *Candida albicans,* which is part of the normal human flora.

Some fungi reproduce sexually by mating and forming sexual spores, eg, **zygospores, ascospores,** and **basidiospores.** Zygospores are single large spores with thick walls; ascospores are formed in a sac called ascus; and basidiospores are formed externally on the tip of a pedestal called a basidium. The classification of these fungi is based on their sexual spores. Fungi that do not form sexual spores are termed "imperfect" and are classified as **Fungi Imperfecti.**

Most fungi of medical interest propagate asexually by forming **conidia** (asexual spores) from the sides or ends of specialized structures (Figure 47–1). The shape, color, and arrangement of conidia aid in the identification of fungi. Some important conidia are (1) **arthrospores,**[1] which arise by fragmentation of the ends of hyphae and are the mode of transmission of *Coccidioides immitis;* (2) **chlamydospores,** which are rounded, thick-walled, and quite resistant (the terminal chlamydospores of *C. albicans* aid in its identification); (3) **blastospores,** which are formed by the budding process by which yeasts reproduce asexually (some yeasts, eg, *C. albicans,* can form multiple buds that do not detach, thus producing sausagelike chains called **pseudohyphae,** which can be used for identification); and (4) **sporangiospores,** which

---

[1] The term "spores" can be replaced by "conidia," eg, arthroconidia.

Table 47–1. Comparison of fungi and bacteria.

Feature	Fungi	Bacteria
Diameter	Approximately 4 μm (*Candida*)	Approximately 1 μm (*Staphylococcus*)
Nucleus	Eukaryotic	Prokaryotic
Cytoplasm	Mitochondria and endoplasmic reticulum present	Mitochondria and endoplasmic reticulum absent
Cell membrane	Sterols present *(ergosterol)*	Sterols absent (except *Mycoplasma*)
Cell wall content	Chitin	Peptidoglycan
Spores	Sexual and asexual spores for reproduction	Endospores for survival, not for reproduction
Thermal dimorphism	Yes (some)	No
Metabolism	Require organic carbon; no obligate anaerobes	Many do not require organic carbon; many obligate anaerobes

are formed within a sac (sporangium) on a stalk by molds such as *Rhizopus* and *Mucor*.

Although this book focuses on the fungi that are human pathogens, it should be remembered that fungi are used in the production of important foods, eg, bread, cheese, wine, and beer. Fungi are also responsible for the spoilage of certain foods. Because molds can grow in a drier, more acidic, and higher-osmotic-pressure environment than bacteria, they tend to be involved in the spoilage of fruits, grains, vegetables, and jams.

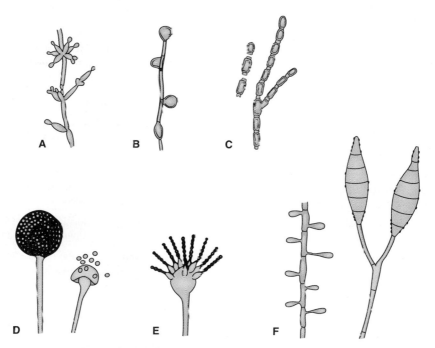

Figure 47–1. Asexual spores. **A:** Blastoconidia and pseudohyphae (*Candida*). **B:** Chlamydospores (*Candida*). **C:** Arthrospores (*Coccidioides*). **D:** Sporangia and sporangiospores (*Mucor*). **E:** Microconidia (*Aspergillus*). **F:** Microconidia and macroconidia (*Microsporum*). (Modified and reproduced, with permission, from Conant NF et al: *Manual of Clinical Mycology*, 3rd ed. Saunders, 1971.)

PATHOGENESIS

The response to infection with many fungi is the formation of **granulomas.** Granulomas are produced in the major systemic fungal diseases, eg, coccidioidomycosis, histoplasmosis, and blastomycosis, as well as several others. The cell-mediated immune response is involved in granuloma formation. Acute suppuration, characterized by the presence of neutrophils in the exudate, also occurs in certain fungal diseases such as aspergillosis and sporotrichosis. Fungi do not have endotoxin in their cell walls and do not produce bacterial-type exotoxins.

Activation of the cell-mediated immune system results in a **delayed hypersensitivity skin test** response to certain fungal antigens injected intradermally. A positive skin test indicates exposure to the fungal antigen. It does *not* imply current infection, because the exposure may have occurred in the past. A negative skin test makes the diagnosis unlikely unless the patient is immunocompromised. Because most people carry *Candida* as part of the normal flora, skin testing with *Candida* antigens can be used to determine whether cell-mediated immunity is normal.

The transmission and geographic locations of some important fungi are described in Table 47–2.

Intact skin is an effective host defense against certain fungi (eg, *Candida,* dermatophytes), but if the skin is damaged, organisms can become established. Fatty acids in the skin inhibit dermatophyte growth, and hormone-associated skin changes at puberty limit ring-worm of the scalp caused by *Trichophyton.* The normal flora of the skin and mucous membranes suppress fungi. When the normal flora is inhibited, eg, by antibiotics, overgrowth of fungi such as *C. albicans* can occur.

In the respiratory tract, the important host defenses are the mucous membranes of the nasopharynx, which trap inhaled fungal spores, and alveolar macrophages. Circulating IgG and IgM are produced in response to fungal infection, but their role in protection from disease is uncertain. The cell-mediated immune response is protective; its suppression can lead to reactivation and dissemination of asymptomatic fungal infections and to disease caused by opportunistic fungi.

FUNGAL TOXINS & ALLERGIES

In addition to mycotic infections, there are two other kinds of fungal disease: (1) **mycotoxicoses,** caused by ingested toxins, and (2) **allergies** to fungal spores. The best-known mycotoxicosis occurs after eating *Amanita* mushrooms. These fungi produce five toxins, two of which—amanitin and phalloidin—are among the most potent hepatotoxins. The toxicity of amanitin is based on its ability to inhibit cellular RNA polymerase, which prevents mRNA synthesis. Another mycotoxicosis, ergotism, is caused by the mold *Claviceps purpura,* which infects grains and produces alkaloids (eg, ergotamine and lysergic acid diethylamide [LSD]) that cause pronounced vascular and neurologic effects.

Other ingested toxins, **aflatoxins,** are coumarin de-

Table 47–2. Transmission and geographic location of some important fungi.

Genus	Habitat	Form of Organism Transmitted	Portal of Entry	Endemic Geographic Location
Coccidioides	Soil	Arthrospores	Inhalation into lungs	Southwestern United States and Latin America
Histoplasma	Soil (associated with bird feces)	Microconidia	Inhalation into lungs	Mississippi and Ohio River valleys in United States; many other countries
Blastomyces	Soil	Microconidia	Inhalation into lungs	States east of Mississippi River in United States; Africa
Paracoccidioides	Soil	Uncertain	Inhalation into lungs	Latin America
Cryptococcus	Soil (associated with pigeon feces)	Yeast	Inhalation into lungs	Worldwide
Aspergillus	Soil and vegetation	Conidia	Inhalation into lungs	Worldwide
Candida	Human body	Yeast	Normal flora of skin, mouth, gastrointestinal tract, and vagina	Worldwide

rivatives produced by *Aspergillus flavus* that cause liver damage and tumors in animals and are suspected of causing hepatic carcinoma in humans. Aflatoxins are ingested with spoiled grains and peanuts and are metabolized by the liver to the epoxide, a potent carcinogen. Aflatoxin B1 induces a mutation in the p53 tumor suppressor gene, leading to a loss of p53 protein and a consequent loss of growth control in the hepatocyte.

Allergies to fungal spores, particularly those of *Aspergillus*, are manifested primarily by an asthmatic reaction (rapid bronchoconstriction mediated by IgE), eosinophilia, and a "wheal and flare" skin test reaction. These clinical findings are caused by an immediate hypersensitivity response to the fungal spores.

LABORATORY DIAGNOSIS

There are four approaches to the laboratory diagnosis of fungal diseases: (1) direct microscopic examination, (2) culture of the organism, (3) DNA probe tests, and (4) serologic tests. Direct microscopic examination of clinical specimens such as sputum, lung biopsy material, and skin scrapings depends on finding characteristic asexual spores, hyphae, or yeasts in the light microscope. The specimen is either treated with 10% KOH to dissolve tissue material, leaving the alkali-resistant fungi intact, or stained with special fungal stains. Some examples of diagnostically important findings made by direct examination are (1) the spherules of *C. immitis* and (2) the wide capsule of *Cryptococcus neoformans* seen in India ink preparations of spinal fluid. Calcofluor white is a fluorescent dye that binds to fungal cell walls and is useful in the identification of fungi in tissue specimens. Methenamine-silver stain is also useful in the microscopic diagnosis of fungi in tissue.

Fungi are frequently cultured on Sabouraud's agar, which facilitates the appearance of the slow-growing fungi by inhibiting the growth of bacteria in the specimen. Inhibition of bacterial growth is due to the low pH of the medium and to the chloramphenicol and cy-cloheximide that are frequently added. The appearance of the mycelium and the nature of the asexual spores are frequently sufficient to identify the organism.

Tests involving DNA probes can identify colonies growing in culture at an earlier stage of growth than can tests based on visual detection of the colonies. As a result, the diagnosis can be made more rapidly. At present, DNA probe tests are available for *Coccidioides*, *Histoplasma*, *Blastomyces*, and *Cryptococcus*.

Tests for the presence of antibodies in the patient's serum or spinal fluid are useful in diagnosing systemic mycoses but less so in diagnosing other fungal infections. As is the case for bacterial and viral serologic testing, a significant rise in the antibody titer must be observed to confirm a diagnosis. The complement fixation test is most frequently used in suspected cases of coccidioidomycosis, histoplasmosis, and blastomycosis. In cryptococcal meningitis, the presence of the polysaccharide capsular antigens of *C. neoformans* in the spinal fluid can be detected by the latex agglutination test.

ANTIFUNGAL THERAPY

The drugs used to treat bacterial diseases have no effect on fungal diseases. For example, penicillins and aminoglycosides inhibit the growth of many bacteria but do not affect the growth of fungi. This difference is explained by the presence of certain structures in bacteria, eg, peptidoglycan and 70S ribosomes, that are absent in fungi.

The most effective antifungal drugs, amphotericin B and the various azoles, exploit the presence of **ergosterol** in fungal cell membranes that is not found in bacterial or human cell membranes. Another antifungal drug, caspofungin (Cancidas), inhibits the synthesis of β-glucan, which is found in fungal membranes but not present in either bacterial or human cell membranes. The mode of action of these drugs is described in Chapter 10. There is no clinically significant resistance to antifungal drugs.

PEARLS

Structure & Growth

• *Fungi are eukaryotic organisms that exist in two basic forms: **yeasts and molds.** Yeasts are single cells, whereas molds consist of long filaments of cells called hyphae. Yeasts reproduce by **budding,** a process in which the daughter cells are unequal in*

size, whereas molds reproduce by cell division (daughter cells are equal in size).

• *Some fungi are **dimorphic,** ie, they can exist either as yeasts or molds, depending on the temperature. At room temperature, eg, 25 °C, dimorphic fungi are molds, whereas at body temperature they are yeasts (or some other form such as a spherule).*

- *The fungal cell wall is made of **chitin;** the bacterial cell wall is made of peptidoglycan. Therefore, antibiotics that inhibit peptidoglycan synthesis such as penicillins, cephalosporins, and vancomycin are not effective against fungi.*
- *The fungal cell membrane contains **ergosterol,** whereas the bacterial cell membrane does not contain ergosterol. Therefore, antibiotics that inhibit ergosterol synthesis (such as the azole drugs) are not effective against bacteria. Similarly, amphotericin B that binds to fungal cell membranes at the site of ergosterol is not effective against bacteria.*

Pathogenesis

- *Infection with certain systemic fungi, such as Histoplasma and Coccidioides, elicits a **granulomatous host defense response** (composed of macrophages and helper T cells). Infection with other fungi, notably Aspergillus, Mucor, and Sporothrix, elicits a **pyogenic response** (composed of neutrophils).*
- *Infection with the systemic fungi, such as Histoplasma and Coccidioides, can be detected by using **skin tests.** An antigen extracted from the organism injected intradermally elicits a **delayed hypersensitivity reaction** manifested as **induration** (thickening) of the skin. Note that a positive skin test only indicates that infection has occurred, but it is not known whether that infection occurred in the past or at the present time. Therefore, a positive skin test does not indicate that the disease the patient has now is caused by that organism. Note also that a false-negative skin test can occur in patients with reduced cell-mediated immunity, such as those with a low CD4 count. To determine whether the patient can mount a delayed hypersensitivity response, a control skin test with a common antigen, such as Candida albicans, can be used.*
- *Reduced cell-mediated immunity predisposes to disseminated disease caused by the systemic fungi, such as Histoplasma and Coccidioides, whereas a reduced number of neutrophils predisposes to disseminated disease caused by fungi such as Aspergillus and Mucor.*

Fungal Toxins & Allergies

- *Ingestion of Amanita mushrooms causes **liver necrosis** due to the presence of two fungal toxins, amanitin and phylloidin. **Amanitin** inhibits the RNA polymerase that synthesizes cellular mRNA.*
- *Ingestion of peanuts and grains contaminated with Aspergillus flavus causes **liver cancer** due to the presence of **aflatoxin.** Aflatoxin epoxide induces a mutation in the p53 gene that results in a loss of the p53 tumor suppressor protein.*
- *Inhalation of the spores of Aspergillus fumigatus can cause **allergic bronchopulmonary aspergillosis.** This is an IgE-mediated immediate hypersensitivity response.*

Laboratory Diagnosis

- *Microscopic examination of a **KOH preparation** can reveal the presence of fungal structures. The purpose of the KOH is to dissolve the human cells, allowing visualization of the fungi.*
- ***Sabouraud's agar** is often used to grow fungi because its low pH inhibits the growth of bacteria, allowing the slower-growing fungi to emerge.*
- *DNA probes can be used to identify fungi growing in culture at a much earlier stage, ie, when the colony size is much smaller.*
- *Tests for the presence of fungal antigens and for the presence of antibodies to fungal antigens are often used. Two commonly used tests are those for cryptococcal antigen in spinal fluid and for Coccidioides antibodies in the patient's serum.*

Antifungal Therapy

- *The selective toxicity of antifungal drugs is based on the presence of **ergosterol** in fungal cell membranes, in contrast to the cholesterol found in human cell membranes and the absence of sterols in bacterial cell membranes.*
- *Amphotericin B binds to fungal cell membranes at the site of ergosterol and disrupts the integrity of the membranes.*
- *Azole drugs, such as itraconazole, fluconazole, and ketoconazole, inhibit the synthesis of ergosterol.*

PRACTICE QUESTIONS: USMLE & COURSE EXAMINATIONS

Questions on the topics discussed in this chapter can be found in the Mycology section of Part XI: USMLE (National Board) Practice Questions starting on page 556. Also see Part XII: USMLE (National Board) Practice Examination starting on page 583.

Cutaneous & Subcutaneous Mycoses

Medical mycoses can be divided into four categories: (1) **cutaneous**, (2) **subcutaneous**, (3) **systemic**, and (4) **opportunistic**. Some features of the important fungal diseases are described in Table 48–1. Cutaneous and subcutaneous mycoses are discussed below; systemic and opportunistic mycoses are discussed in later chapters.

CUTANEOUS MYCOSES

Dermatophytoses

Dermatophytoses are caused by fungi (**dermatophytes**) that infect only superficial keratinized structures (skin, hair, and nails), not deeper tissues. The most important dermatophytes are classified in three genera: *Epidermophyton, Trichophyton,* and *Microsporum.* They are spread from infected persons by direct contact. *Microsporum* is also spread from animals such as dogs and cats. This indicates that to prevent reinfection, the animal must be treated also.

Dermatophytoses (tinea, ringworm) are chronic infections often located in the warm, humid areas of the body, eg, athlete's foot and jock itch.[1] Typical ringworm lesions have an inflamed circular border containing papules and vesicles surrounding a clear area of relatively normal skin. Broken hairs and thickened broken nails are often seen. *Trichophyton tonsurans* is the most common cause of outbreaks of tinea capitis in children and is the main cause of endothrix (inside the hair) infections. *Trichophyton rubrum* is also a very common cause of tinea capitis. *Trichophyton schoenleinii* is the cause of favus, a form of tinea capitis in which crusts are seen on the scalp.

In some infected persons, hypersensitivity causes **dermatophytid ("id")** reactions, eg, vesicles on the fingers. Id lesions are a response to circulating fungal antigens; the lesions do not contain hyphae. Patients with tinea infections show positive skin tests with fungal extracts, eg, trichophytin.

Scrapings of skin or nail placed in 10% KOH on a glass slide show hyphae under microscopy. Cultures on Sabouraud's agar at room temperature develop typical hyphae and conidia. Tinea capitis lesions caused by *Microsporum* species can be detected by seeing fluorescence when the lesions are exposed to ultraviolet light from a Wood's lamp. Treatment involves local antifungal creams (undecylenic acid, miconazole, tolnaftate, etc) or oral griseofulvin. Prevention centers on keeping skin dry and cool.

Tinea Versicolor

Tinea versicolor (pityriasis versicolor), a superficial skin infection of cosmetic importance only, is caused by *Malassezia furfur.* The lesions are usually noticed as hypopigmented areas, especially on tanned skin in the summer. There may be slight scaling or itching, but usually the infection is asymptomatic. It occurs more frequently in hot, humid weather. The lesions contain both budding yeast cells and hyphae. Diagnosis is usually made by observing this mixture in KOH preparations of skin scrapings. Culture is not usually done. The treatment of choice is topical miconazole, but the lesions have a tendency to recur and a permanent cure is difficult to achieve.

Tinea Nigra

Tinea nigra is an infection of the keratinized layers of the skin. It appears as a brownish spot caused by the melaninlike pigment in the hyphae. The causative organism, *Cladosporium werneckii,* is found in the soil and transmitted during injury. In the United States, the disease is seen in the southern states. Diagnosis is made by microscopic examination and culture of skin scrapings. The infection is treated with a topical keratolytic agent, eg, salicylic acid.

SUBCUTANEOUS MYCOSES

These are caused by fungi that grow in soil and on vegetation and are introduced into subcutaneous tissue through **trauma**.

Sporotrichosis

Sporothrix schenckii is a **dimorphic** fungus that lives on vegetation. When introduced into the skin, typically by

---

[1] These infections are also known as tinea pedis and tinea cruris, respectively.

Table 48–1. Features of important fungal diseases.

Type	Anatomic Location	Representative Disease	Genus of Causative Organism(s)	Seriousness of Illness
Cutaneous	Dead layer of skin	Tinea versicolor	*Malassezia*	1+
	Epidermis, hair, nails	Dermatophytosis (ringworm)	*Microsporum, Trichophyton, Epidermophyton*	2+
Subcutaneous	Subcutis	Sporotrichosis	*Sporothrix*	2+
		Mycetoma	Several genera	2+
Systemic	Internal organs	Coccidioidomycosis	*Coccidioides*	4+
		Histoplasmosis	*Histoplasma*	4+
		Blastomycosis	*Blastomyces*	4+
		Paracoccidioidomycosis	*Paracoccidioides*	4+
Opportunistic	Internal organs	Cryptococcosis	*Cryptococcus*	4+
		Candidiasis	*Candida*	2+ to 4+
		Aspergillosis	*Aspergillus*	4+
		Mucormycosis	*Mucor, Rhizopus*	4+

1+, not serious, treatment may or may not be given; 2+, moderately serious, treatment often given; 4+, serious, treatment given especially in disseminated disease.

a thorn, it causes a local pustule or ulcer with nodules along the draining lymphatics. There is little systemic illness. Lesions may be chronic. Sporotrichosis occurs most often in **gardeners, especially those who prune roses,** because they may be stuck by a rose thorn.

In the clinical laboratory, round or cigar-shaped budding yeasts are seen in tissue specimens. In culture, hyphae occur bearing oval conidia in clusters at the tip of slender conidiophores (resembling a daisy). The drug of choice for skin lesions is itraconazole. It can be prevented by protecting skin when touching plants, moss, and wood.

Chromomycosis

This is a slowly progressive granulomatous infection that is caused by several soil fungi (*Fonsecaea, Phialophora, Cladosporium,* etc) when introduced into the skin through trauma. These fungi are collectively called **dematiaceous** fungi, so named because their conidia or hyphae are dark-colored, either gray or black. Wartlike lesions with crusting abscesses extend along the lymphatics. The disease occurs mainly in the tropics and is found on bare feet and legs. In the clinical laboratory, dark brown, round fungal cells are seen in leukocytes or giant cells. The disease is treated with oral flucytosine or thiabendazole, plus local surgery.

Mycetoma

Soil organisms (*Petriellidium, Madurella*) enter through wounds on the feet, hands, or back and cause abscesses, with pus discharged through sinuses. The pus contains compact colored granules. Actinomycetes such as *Nocardia* can cause similar lesions (actinomycotic mycetoma). Sulfonamides may help the actinomycotic form. There is no effective drug against the fungal form; surgical excision is recommended.

SUMMARIES OF ORGANISMS

Brief summaries of the organisms described in this chapter begin on page 503. Please consult these summaries for a rapid review of the essential material.

PRACTICE QUESTIONS: USMLE & COURSE EXAMINATIONS

Questions on the topics discussed in this chapter can be found in the Mycology section of Part XI: USMLE (National Board) Practice Questions starting on page 556. Also see Part XII: USMLE (National Board) Practice Examination starting on page 583.

Systemic Mycoses

These infections result from **inhalation** of the spores of **dimorphic** fungi that have their **mold** forms in the **soil.** Within the **lungs,** the spores differentiate into **yeasts** or other specialized forms. Most lung infections are asymptomatic and self-limited. However, in some persons, disseminated disease develops in which the organisms grow in other organs, cause destructive lesions, and may result in death. Infected persons do *not* communicate these diseases to others.

COCCIDIOIDES

Disease

Coccidioides immitis causes coccidioidomycosis.

Properties

C. immitis is a **dimorphic** fungus that exists as a **mold** in soil and as a **spherule** in tissue (Figure 49–1).

Transmission & Epidemiology

The fungus is **endemic** in arid regions of the **southwestern United States** and **Latin America.** People who live in Central and Southern California, Arizona, New Mexico, Western Texas, and Northern Mexico, a geographic region called the Lower Sonoran Life Zone, are often infected. In soil, it forms hyphae with alternating **arthrospores** and empty cells. Arthrospores are very light and are carried by the wind. They can be **inhaled** and infect the lungs.

Pathogenesis

In the lungs, arthrospores form spherules that are large (30 μm in diameter), have a thick, doubly refractive wall, and are filled with **endospores.** Upon rupture of the wall, endospores are released and differentiate to form new spherules. The organism can spread within a person by direct extension or via the bloodstream. Granulomatous lesions can occur in virtually any organ but are found primarily in bones and the central nervous system (meningitis).

Dissemination from the lungs to other organs occurs in people who have a defect in cell-mediated immunity.

Most people who are infected by *C. immitis* develop a cell-mediated (delayed hypersensitivity) immune response that restricts the growth of the organism. One way to determine whether a person has produced adequate cell-mediated immunity to the organism is to do a skin test (see below). In general, a person who has a positive skin test reaction has developed sufficient immunity to prevent disseminated disease from occurring. If, at a later time, a person's cellular immunity is suppressed by drugs or disease, disseminated disease can occur.

Clinical Findings

Infection of the lungs is often asymptomatic and is evident only by a positive skin test and the presence of antibodies. Some infected persons have an influenzalike illness with fever and cough. About 50% have changes in the lungs (infiltrates, adenopathy, or effusions) as seen on chest x-ray, and 10% develop erythema nodosum (see below) or arthralgias. This syndrome is called "valley fever" (in the San Joaquin Valley of California) or "desert rheumatism" (in Arizona); it tends to subside spontaneously.

Disseminated disease can occur in almost any organ; the meninges, bone, and skin are important sites. The overall incidence of dissemination in persons infected with *C. immitis* is 1%, although the incidence in Filipinos and African Americans is 10 times higher. Women in the third trimester of pregnancy also have a markedly increased incidence of dissemination.

Erythema nodosum (EN) manifests as red, tender nodules ("desert bumps") on extensor surfaces such as the shins. It is a delayed (cell-mediated) hypersensitivity response to fungal antigens and thus is an indicator of a good prognosis. There are no organisms in these lesions; they are not a sign of disseminated disease. EN is not specific for coccidioidomycosis; it occurs in other granulomatous diseases, eg, histoplasmosis, tuberculosis, and leprosy.

In infected persons, **skin tests** with fungal extracts (coccidioidin or spherulin) cause at least a 5-mm induration 48 hours after injection (delayed hypersensitivity reaction). Skin tests become positive within 2–4 weeks of infection and remain so for years but are often negative (anergy) in patients with disseminated disease.

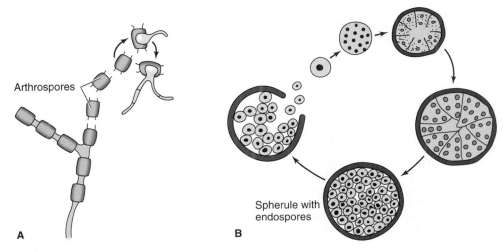

Figure 49–1. Stages of *Coccidioides immitis*. **A:** Arthrospores form at the ends of hyphae in the soil. They germinate in the soil to form new hyphae. If inhaled, the arthrospores differentiate into spherules. **B:** Endospores form within spherules in tissue. When spherules rupture, endospores disseminate and form new spherules. (Modified and reproduced, with permission, from Brooks GF et al: *Medical Microbiology,* 20th ed. Originally published by Appleton & Lange. Copyright © 1995 by The McGraw-Hill Companies, Inc.)

Laboratory Diagnosis

In tissue specimens, spherules are seen microscopically. Cultures on Sabouraud's agar incubated at 25°C show hyphae with arthrospores. (*Caution:* Cultures are highly infectious; precautions against inhaling arthrospores must be taken.) In serologic tests, IgM and IgG precipitins appear within 2–4 weeks of infection and then decline in subsequent months. Complement-fixing antibodies occur at low titer initially, but the titer rises greatly if dissemination occurs.

Treatment & Prevention

No treatment is needed in asymptomatic or mild primary infection. Amphotericin B (Fungizone) or itraconazole is used for persisting lung lesions or disseminated disease. Ketoconazole is also effective in lung disease. If meningitis occurs, fluconazole is the drug of choice. Intrathecal amphotericin B may be required and may induce remission, but long-term results are often poor. There are no means of prevention except avoiding travel to endemic areas.

HISTOPLASMA

Disease

Histoplasma capsulatum causes histoplasmosis.

Properties

H. capsulatum is a **dimorphic** fungus that exists as a **mold** in soil and as a **yeast** in tissue. It forms two types

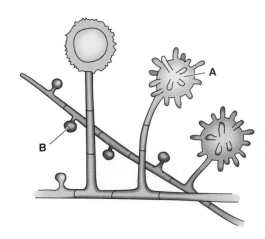

Figure 49–2. Asexual spores of *Histoplasma capsulatum*. **A:** Tuberculate macroconidia. **B:** Microconidia. (Reproduced, with permission, from Brooks GF et al: *Medical Microbiology,* 19th ed. Originally published by Appleton & Lange. Copyright © 1991 by The McGraw-Hill Companies, Inc.)

of asexual spores (Figure 49–2): (1) **tuberculate macroconidia**, with typical thick walls and fingerlike projections that are important in laboratory identification, and (2) **microconidia**, which are smaller, thin, smooth-walled spores that, if inhaled, transmit the infection.

Transmission & Epidemiology

This fungus occurs in many parts of the world. In the United States it is **endemic** in central and eastern states, especially in the **Ohio and Mississippi River valleys**. It grows in soil, particularly if the soil is heavily contaminated with **bird droppings**, especially from starlings. Although the birds are not infected, bats can be infected and can excrete the organism in their guano. In areas of endemic infection, excavation of the soil during construction or exploration of bat-infested caves has resulted in a significant number of infected individuals.

In several tropical African countries, histoplasmosis is caused by *Histoplasma duboisii*. The clinical picture is different from that caused by *H. capsulatum*. A description of the differences between African histoplasmosis and that seen in the United States is beyond the scope of this book.

Pathogenesis & Clinical Findings

Inhaled spores are engulfed by **macrophages** and develop into yeast forms. In tissues, *H. capsulatum* occurs as an **oval budding yeast inside macrophages** (Figure 49–3). The yeasts survive within the phagolysosome of the macrophage by producing alkaline substances, such as bicarbonate and ammonia, that raise the pH and thereby inactivate the degradative enzymes of the phagolysosome.

The organisms spread widely throughout the body, especially to the liver and spleen, but most infections remain asymptomatic, and the small granulomatous

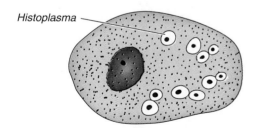

Figure 49–3. *Histoplasma capsulatum.* Yeasts are located within the macrophage. (Reproduced, with permission, from Brooks GF et al: *Medical Microbiology,* 19th ed. Originally published by Appleton & Lange. Copyright © 1991 by The McGraw-Hill Companies, Inc.)

foci heal by calcification. With intense exposure (eg, in a chicken house or bat-infested cave), pneumonia may become clinically manifest. Severe disseminated histoplasmosis develops in a small minority of infected persons, especially infants and individuals with reduced cell-mediated immunity, such as AIDS patients. In AIDS patients, ulcerated lesions on the tongue are typical of disseminated histoplasmosis. In immunocompetent people, EN can occur (see description of EN in *Coccidioides* above). EN is a sign that cell-mediated immunity is active and the organism will probably be contained.

A skin test using histoplasmin (a mycelial extract) becomes positive, ie, shows at least 5 mm of induration, within 2–3 weeks after infection and remains positive for many years. However, because there are many false-positive reactions (due to cross-reactivity) and many false-negative reactions (in disseminated disease), the skin test is not useful for diagnosis. Furthermore, the skin test can stimulate an antibody response and confuse the serologic tests. The skin test is useful for epidemiologic studies, and up to 90% of individuals have positive results in areas of endemic infection.

Laboratory Diagnosis

In tissue biopsy specimens or bone marrow aspirates, oval **yeast cells within macrophages** are seen microscopically. Cultures on Sabouraud's agar show hyphae with tuberculate macroconidia when grown at low temperature, eg, 25°C and yeasts when grown at 37°C. Tests that detect *Histoplasma* antigens by radioimmunoassay and *Histoplasma* RNA with DNA probes are also useful. In immunocompromised patients with disseminated disease, tests for antigens in the urine are especially useful because antibody tests may be negative.

Two serologic tests are useful for diagnosis: complement fixation (CF) and immunodiffusion (ID). An antibody titer of 1:32 in the CF test with yeast phase antigens is considered to be diagnostic. However, cross-reactions with other fungi, especially *Blastomyces*, occur. CF titers fall when the disease becomes inactive and rise in disseminated disease. The ID test detects precipitating antibodies (precipitins) by forming two bands, M and H, in an agar-gel diffusion assay. The ID test is more specific but less sensitive than the CF test.

Treatment & Prevention

No therapy is needed in asymptomatic or mild primary infections. With progressive lung lesions, oral itraconazole is beneficial. In disseminated disease, amphotericin B is the treatment of choice. In meningitis, fluconazole is often used because it penetrates the spinal fluid well. Oral itraconazole is used to treat pulmonary or disseminated disease, as well as for chronic suppression in patients with AIDS. There are no means of prevention except avoiding exposure in areas of endemic infection.

BLASTOMYCES

Disease

Blastomyces dermatitidis causes blastomycosis, also known as North American blastomycosis.

Properties

B. dermatitidis is a **dimorphic** fungus that exists as a mold in soil and as a yeast in tissue. The yeast is round with a doubly refractive wall and a single **broad-based bud** (Figure 49–4). Note that this organism forms a broad-based bud, whereas *Cryptococcus neoformans* is a yeast that forms a narrow-based bud.

Transmission & Epidemiology

This fungus is **endemic** primarily in eastern North America, especially in the region bordering the Ohio, Mississippi, and St. Lawrence rivers, and the Great Lakes region. Less commonly, blastomycosis has also occurred in Central and South America, Africa, and the Middle East. It grows in moist soil rich in organic material, forming hyphae with small pear-shaped conidia. Inhalation of the conidia causes human infection.

Pathogenesis & Clinical Findings

Infection occurs mainly via the respiratory tract. Asymptomatic or mild cases are rarely recognized. Dissemination may result in ulcerated granulomas of skin, bone, or other sites.

Laboratory Diagnosis

In tissue biopsy specimens, thick-walled yeast cells with single broad-based buds are seen microscopically. Hyphae with small pear-shaped conidia are visible on culture. The skin test lacks specificity and has little value. Serologic tests have little value.

Treatment & Prevention

Itraconazole is the drug of choice for most patients, but amphotericin B should be used to treat severe disease. Surgical excision may be helpful. There are no means of prevention.

PARACOCCIDIOIDES

Disease

Paracoccidioides brasiliensis causes paracoccidioidomycosis, also known as South American blastomycosis.

Properties

P. brasiliensis is a **dimorphic** fungus that exists as a mold in soil and as a yeast in tissue. The yeast is thick-

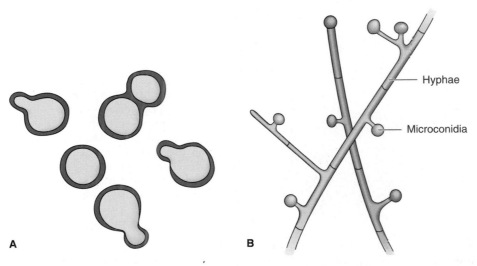

Figure 49–4. *Blastomyces dermatitidis.* **A:** Yeast with a broad-based bud at 37°C. **B:** Mold with microconidia at 20°C. (Reproduced, with permission, from Brooks GF et al: *Medical Microbiology,* 19th ed. Originally published by Appleton & Lange. Copyright © 1991 by The McGraw-Hill Companies, Inc.)

walled with **multiple buds**, in contrast to *B. dermatitidis,* which has a single bud (Figure 49–5).

Transmission & Epidemiology

This fungus grows in the soil and is endemic in rural Latin America. Disease occurs only in that region.

Pathogenesis & Clinical Findings

The spores are **inhaled**, and early lesions occur in the lungs. Asymptomatic infection is common. Alternatively, oral mucous membrane lesions, lymph node enlargement, and sometimes dissemination to many organs develop.

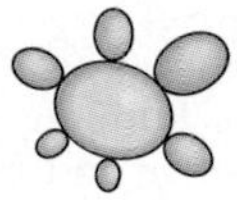

Figure 49–5. *Paracoccidioides brasiliensis.* Note the multiple buds of the yeast form of *Paracoccidioides,* in contrast to the single bud of *Blastomyces.*

Laboratory Diagnosis

In pus or tissues, yeast cells with multiple buds are seen microscopically. A specimen cultured for 2–4 weeks may grow typical organisms. Skin tests are rarely helpful. Serologic testing shows that when significant antibody titers (by immunodiffusion or complement fixation) are found, active disease is present.

Treatment & Prevention

The drug of choice is itraconazole taken orally for several months. There are no means of prevention.

SUMMARIES OF ORGANISMS

Brief summaries of the organisms described in this chapter begin on page 503. Please consult these summaries for a rapid review of the essential material.

PRACTICE QUESTIONS: USMLE & COURSE EXAMINATIONS

Questions on the topics discussed in this chapter can be found in the Mycology section of Part XI: USMLE (National Board) Practice Questions starting on page 556. Also see Part XII: USMLE (National Board) Practice Examination starting on page 583.

Opportunistic Mycoses

Opportunistic fungi fail to induce disease in most immunocompetent persons but can do so in those with **impaired** host defenses.

CANDIDA

Diseases

Candida albicans, the most important species of *Candida,* causes thrush, vaginitis, and chronic mucocutaneous candidiasis, as well as other diseases.

Properties

C. albicans is an **oval yeast with a single bud.** It is part of the **normal flora** of mucous membranes of the upper respiratory, gastrointestinal, and female genital tracts. In tissues it may appear as yeasts or as **pseudohyphae** (Figure 50–1). Pseudohyphae are elongated yeasts that visually resemble hyphae but are not true hyphae. Carbohydrate fermentation reactions differentiate it from other species, eg, *Candida tropicalis, Candida parapsilosis, Candida krusei,* and *Candida glabrata.*

Transmission

As a member of the normal flora, it is already present on the skin and mucous membranes. It is, therefore, not transmitted.

Pathogenesis & Clinical Findings

When local or systemic host defenses are impaired, disease may result. Overgrowth of *C. albicans* in the mouth produces white patches called thrush. (Note that thrush is a "pseudomembrane," a term that is defined in Chapter 7 on page 38.) Vulvovaginitis with itching and discharge is favored by high pH, diabetes, or use of antibiotics. Skin invasion occurs in warm, moist areas, which become red and weeping. Fingers and nails become involved when repeatedly immersed in water; persons employed as dishwashers in restaurants and institutions are commonly affected. Thickening or loss of the nail can occur.

In immunosuppressed individuals, *Candida* may disseminate to many organs or cause chronic mucocutaneous candidiasis. Intravenous drug abuse, indwelling intravenous catheters, and hyperalimentation also predispose to disseminated candidiasis, especially right-sided endocarditis. *Candida* esophagitis, often accompanied by involvement of the stomach and small intestine, is seen in patients with leukemia and lymphoma. Subcutaneous nodules are often seen in neutropenic patients with disseminated disease. *C. albicans* is the most common species to cause disseminated disease in these patients, but *C. tropicalis* and *C. parapsilosis* are important pathogens also.

Laboratory Diagnosis

In exudates or tissues, budding yeasts and pseudohyphae appear gram-positive and can be visualized using calcofluor-white staining. In culture, typical yeast colonies are formed that resemble large staphylococcal colonies. **Germ tubes** form in serum at 37°C, which serves to distinguish *C. albicans* from most other *Candida* species (see Figure 50–1). **Chlamydospores** are typically formed by *C. albicans* but not by other species of *Candida.* Serologic testing is rarely helpful.

Skin tests with *Candida* antigens are uniformly positive in immunocompetent adults and are used as an indicator that the person can mount a cellular immune response. A person who does not respond to *Candida* antigens in the skin test is presumed to have deficient cell-mediated immunity. Such a person is **anergic,** and other skin tests cannot be interpreted. Thus, if a person has a negative *Candida* skin test, a negative PPD skin test for tuberculosis could be a false-negative result.

Treatment & Prevention

The drug of choice for oropharyngeal or esophageal thrush is fluconazole. Caspofungin or micafungin can also be used for esophageal candidiasis. Treatment of skin infections consists of topical antifungal drugs, eg, clotrimazole or nystatin. Mucocutaneous candidiasis can be controlled by ketoconazole.

Treatment of disseminated candidiasis consists of either amphotericin B or fluconazole. These two drugs can be used with or without flucytosine. Treatment of candidal infections with antifungal drugs should be supplemented by reduction of predisposing factors.

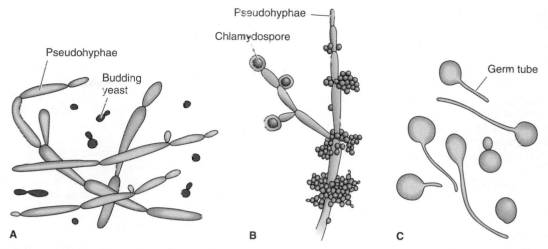

Figure 50–1. *Candida albicans.* **A:** Budding yeasts and pseudohyphae in tissues or exudate. **B:** Pseudohyphae and chlamydospores in culture at 20°C. **C:** Germ tubes at 37°C. (Reproduced, with permission, from Brooks GF et al: *Medical Microbiology*, 20th ed. Originally published by Appleton & Lange. Copyright © 1995 by The McGraw-Hill Companies, Inc.)

Certain candidal infections, eg, thrush, can be prevented by oral clotrimazole troches or nystatin "swish and swallow." Fluconazole is useful in preventing candidal infections in high-risk patients, such as those undergoing bone marrow transplantation and premature infants. Micafungin can also be used. There is no vaccine.

CRYPTOCOCCUS

Disease

Cryptococcus neoformans causes cryptococcosis, especially cryptococcal meningitis. Cryptococcosis is the most common life-threatening fungal disease in AIDS patients.

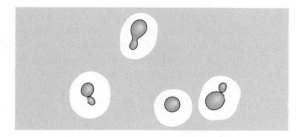

Figure 50–2. *Cryptococcus neoformans.* India ink preparation shows budding yeasts with a wide capsule. India ink forms a dark background; it does not stain the yeast itself. (Reproduced, with permission, from Brooks GF et al: *Medical Microbiology*, 20th ed. Originally published by Appleton & Lange. Copyright © 1995 by The McGraw-Hill Companies, Inc.)

Properties

C. neoformans is an **oval, budding yeast** surrounded by a wide **polysaccharide capsule** (Figure 50–2). It is not dimorphic. Note that this organism forms a narrow-based bud, whereas the yeast form of *Blastomyces dermatitidis* forms a broad-based bud.

Transmission

This yeast occurs widely in nature and grows abundantly in **soil containing bird (especially pigeon) droppings.** The birds are not infected. Human infection results from **inhalation** of the organism. There is no human-to-human transmission.

Pathogenesis & Clinical Findings

Lung infection is often asymptomatic or may produce pneumonia. Disease occurs mainly in patients with reduced cell-mediated immunity, especially AIDS patients, in whom the organism disseminates to the central nervous system (meningitis) and other organs. Subcutaneous nodules are often seen in disseminated disease. Note, however, that roughly half the patients with cryptococcal meningitis fail to show evidence of immunosuppression.

Laboratory Diagnosis

In spinal fluid mixed with **India ink,** the yeast cell is seen microscopically surrounded by a wide, unstained capsule. Appearance of the organism in Gram stain is unreliable, but stains such as methenamine-silver, periodic acid–Schiff, and mucicarmine will allow the organism to be visualized. The organism can be cultured from spinal fluid and other specimens. The colonies are highly mucoid, a reflection of the large amount of capsular polysaccharide produced by the organism.

Serologic tests can be done for both antibody and antigen. In infected spinal fluid, **capsular antigen** occurs in high titer and can be detected by the **latex particle agglutination test.** This test is called the cryptococcal antigen test, often abbreviated as "crag."

Treatment & Prevention

Combined treatment with amphotericin B and flucytosine is used in meningitis and other disseminated disease. There are no specific means of prevention. Fluconazole is used in AIDS patients for long-term suppression of cryptococcal meningitis.

ASPERGILLUS

Disease

Aspergillus species, especially *Aspergillus fumigatus,* cause infections of the skin, eyes, ears, and other organs; "fungus ball" in the lungs; and allergic bronchopulmonary aspergillosis.

Properties

Aspergillus species exist **only as molds;** they are not dimorphic. They have **septate hyphae** that form V-shaped (dichotomous) branches (Figure 50–3). The walls are more or less parallel, in contrast to *Mucor* and *Rhizopus* walls, which are irregular (Figure 50–3; also see below). The conidia of *Aspergillus* form radiating chains, in contrast to those of *Mucor* and *Rhizopus,* which are enclosed within a sporangium (Figure 50–4; also see below).

Transmission

These molds are widely distributed in nature. They grow on decaying vegetation, producing chains of conidia. Transmission is by **airborne conidia.**

Pathogenesis & Clinical Findings

A. fumigatus can colonize and later invade abraded skin, wounds, burns, the cornea, the external ear, or paranasal sinuses. It is the most common cause of fungal sinusitis. In immunocompromised persons, especially those with neutropenia, it can invade the lungs and other organs, producing hemoptysis and granulomas. Aspergilli are well known for their ability to grow in cavities within the lungs, especially cavities caused by tuberculosis. Within the cavities, they produce an aspergilloma (**fungus ball**), which can be seen on chest x-ray as a radiopaque structure that changes its position when the patient is moved from an erect to a supine position.

Allergic bronchopulmonary aspergillosis (ABPA) is an infection of the bronchi by *Aspergillus* species. Patients with ABPA have asthmatic symptoms and a high IgE titer against *Aspergillus* antigens, and they expectorate brownish bronchial plugs containing hyphae. Asthma caused by the inhalation of airborne conidia, especially in certain occupational settings, also occurs. *Aspergillus flavus* growing on cereals or nuts produces aflatoxins that may be carcinogenic or acutely toxic.

Laboratory Diagnosis

Biopsy specimens show **septate, branching hyphae** invading tissue (see Figure 50–3). Cultures show colonies with characteristic radiating chains of conidia (see Figure 50–4). However, positive cultures do not prove disease because colonization is common. In persons with invasive aspergillosis, there may be high titers of galactomannan antigen in serum. Patients with ABPA have high levels of IgE specific for *Aspergillus* antigens and prominent eosinophilia. IgG precipitins are also present.

Treatment & Prevention

Invasive aspergillosis is treated with amphotericin B, but results may be poor. Caspofungin may be effective in cases of invasive aspergillosis that do not respond to amphotericin B. A fungus ball growing in a sinus or in a pulmonary cavity can be surgically removed. Patients with ABPA can be treated with steroids and antifungal agents. There are no specific means of prevention.

MUCOR & RHIZOPUS

Mucormycosis (zygomycosis, phycomycosis) is a disease caused by saprophytic **molds** (eg, *Mucor, Rhizopus,* and *Absidia*) found widely in the environment. They are not dimorphic. These organisms are transmitted by airborne asexual spores and invade tissues of patients with

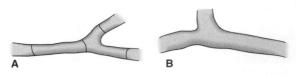

Figure 50–3. *Aspergillus* and *Mucor* in tissue. **A:** *Aspergillus* has septate hyphae with V-shaped branching. **B:** *Mucor* has nonseptate hyphae with right-angle branching.

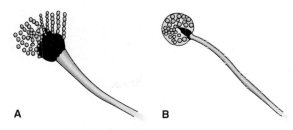

Figure 50–4. *Aspergillus* and *Mucor* in culture. **A:** *Aspergillus* spores form in radiating columns. **B:** *Mucor* spores are contained within a sporangium.

reduced host defenses. They proliferate in the walls of blood vessels, particularly of the paranasal sinuses, lungs, or gut, and cause infarction and necrosis of tissue distal to the blocked vessel. Patients with **diabetic ketoacidosis,** burns, or leukemia are particularly susceptible. One species, *Rhizopus oryzae,* causes about 60% of cases of mucormycosis.

In biopsy specimens, organisms are seen microscopically as **nonseptate hyphae** with broad, irregular walls and branches that form more or less at right angles. Cultures show colonies with spores contained within a sporangium. These organisms are difficult to culture because they are a single, very long cell and damage to any part of the cell can limit its ability to grow. If diagnosis is made early, treatment of the underlying disorder, plus administration of amphotericin B and surgical removal of necrotic infected tissue, has resulted in some remissions and cures.

PNEUMOCYSTIS

Pneumocystis carinii is classified as a yeast on the basis of molecular analysis, but medically many still think of it as a protozoan or as an "unclassified" organism. It is therefore discussed in Chapter 52 with the blood and tissue protozoa.

In 2002, taxonomists renamed the human species of *Pneumocystis* as *P. jiroveci* and recommended that *P. carinii* be used only to describe the rat species of *Pneumocystis.* There is some controversy surrounding this change of names.

FUNGI OF MINOR IMPORTANCE

PENICILLIUM MARNEFFEI

P. marneffei is a dimorphic fungus that causes tuberculosis-like disease in AIDS patients, particularly in south-

east Asian countries such as Thailand. It grows as a mold that produces a rose-colored pigment at 25°C but at 37°C grows as a small yeast that resembles *Histoplasma capsulatum.* Bamboo rats are the only other known hosts. The diagnosis is made either by growing the organism in culture or by using fluorescent-antibody staining of affected tissue. The treatment of choice consists of amphotericin B for 2 weeks followed by oral itraconazole for 10 weeks. Relapses can be prevented with prolonged administration of oral itraconazole.

PSEUDALLESCHERIA BOYDII

P. boydii is a mold that causes disease primarily in immunocompromised patients. The clinical findings and the microscopic appearance of the septate hyphae in tissue closely resemble those of *Aspergillus.* In culture, the appearance of the conidia (pear-shaped) and the color of the mycelium (brownish-gray) of *P. boydii* are different from those of *Aspergillus.* The drug of choice is either ketoconazole or itraconazole because the response to amphotericin B is poor. Debridement of necrotic tissue is important as well.

FUSARIUM SOLANI

F. solani is a mold that causes disease primarily in neutropenic patients. Fever and skin lesions are the most common clinical features. The organism is similar to *Aspergillus* in that it is a mold with septate hyphae that tends to invade blood vessels. Blood cultures are often positive in disseminated disease. In culture, banana-shaped conidia are seen. Liposomal amphotericin B is the drug of choice. Indwelling catheters should be removed or replaced.

SUMMARIES OF ORGANISMS

Brief summaries of the organisms described in this chapter begin on page 504. Please consult these summaries for a rapid review of the essential material.

PRACTICE QUESTIONS: USMLE & COURSE EXAMINATIONS

Questions on the topics discussed in this chapter can be found in the Mycology section of Part XI: USMLE (National Board) Practice Questions starting on page 556. Also see Part XII: USMLE (National Board) Practice Examination starting on page 583.

PART VI
Parasitology

Parasites occur in two distinct forms: single-celled **proto-zoa** and multicellular metazoa called **helminths** or worms. For medical purposes, protozoa can be subdivided into four groups: Sarcodina (amebas), Sporozoa (sporozoans), Mastigophora (flagellates), and Ciliata (ciliates). Metazoa are subdivided into two phyla: the Platy-helminthes (flatworms) and the Nemathelminthes (roundworms, nematodes). The phylum Platyhelminthes contains two medically important classes: Cestoda (tapeworms) and Trematoda (flukes). This classification is diagrammed in Figure VI-1.

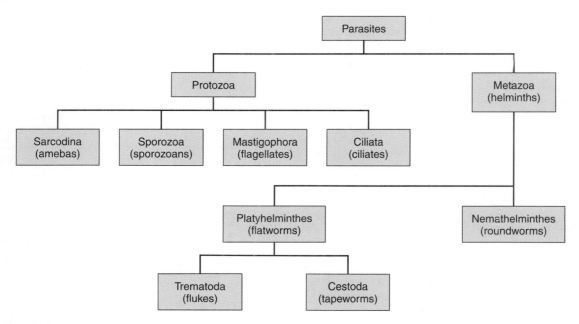

Figure VI–1. Relationships of the medically important parasites.

Intestinal & Urogenital Protozoa

51

In this book, the major protozoan pathogens are grouped according to the location in the body where they most frequently cause disease. The intestinal and urogenital protozoa are described in this chapter, and the blood and tissue protozoa are described in Chapter 52.

(1) Within the intestinal tract, three organisms—the ameba *Entamoeba histolytica,* the flagellate *Giardia lamblia,* and the sporozoan *Cryptosporidium* species—are the most important.

(2) In the urogenital tract, the flagellate *Trichomonas vaginalis* is the important pathogen.

(3) The blood and tissue protozoa are a varied group consisting of the flagellates *Trypanosoma* and *Leishmania* and the sporozoans *Plasmodium* and *Toxoplasma.* The important opportunistic lung pathogen *Pneumocystis* will be discussed in this group, although there is molecular evidence that it should be classified as a fungus.

The major and minor pathogenic protozoa are listed in Table 51–1.

Although immigrants and Americans returning from abroad can present to physicians in the United States with any parasitic disease, certain parasites are much more likely to occur outside the United States. The features of the medically important protozoa, including their occurrence in the United States, are described in Table 51–2.

The medically important stages in the life cycle of the intestinal protozoa are described in Table 51–3.

■ INTESTINAL PROTOZOA

ENTAMOEBA

Diseases

Entamoeba histolytica causes amebic dysentery and liver abscess.

Important Properties

The life cycle of *E. histolytica* has two stages: the motile ameba (**trophozoite**) and the nonmotile **cyst** (Figure 51–1A and B). The trophozoite is found within the intestinal and extraintestinal lesions and in diarrheal stools. The cyst predominates in nondiarrheal stools. These cysts are not highly resistant and are readily killed by boiling but not by chlorination of water supplies. They are removed by filtration of water.

The cyst has **four nuclei,** an important diagnostic criterion. Upon excystation in the intestinal tract, an ameba with four nuclei emerges and then divides to form eight trophozoites. The mature trophozoite has a single nucleus with an even lining of peripheral chromatin and a prominent central nucleolus (karyosome).

Antibodies are formed against trophozoite antigens in invasive amebiasis, but they are not protective; previous infection does not prevent reinfection. The antibodies are useful, however, for serologic diagnosis.

Pathogenesis & Epidemiology

The organism is acquired by ingestion of cysts that are transmitted primarily by the **fecal-oral** route in contaminated food and water. Anal-oral transmission, eg, among male homosexuals, also occurs. There is **no animal reservoir.** The ingested cysts differentiate into trophozoites in the ileum but tend to colonize the cecum and colon.

The trophozoites invade the colonic epithelium and secrete enzymes that cause localized necrosis. Little inflammation occurs at the site. As the lesion reaches the muscularis layer, a typical "flask-shaped" ulcer forms that can undermine and destroy large areas of the intestinal epithelium. Progression into the submucosa leads to invasion of the portal circulation by the trophozoites. By far the most frequent site of systemic disease is the liver, where abscesses containing trophozoites form.

Infection by *E. histolytica* is found worldwide but occurs most frequently in tropical countries, especially in areas with poor sanitation. About 1–2% of people in the United States are affected. The disease is widely prevalent among male homosexuals.

Table 51–1. Major and minor pathogenic protozoa.

Type and Location	Species	Disease
Major protozoa		
Intestinal tract	*Entamoeba histolytica*	Amebiasis
	Giardia lamblia	Giardiasis
	Cryptosporidium parvum	Cryptosporidiosis
Urogenital tract	*Trichomonas vaginalis*	Trichomoniasis
Blood and tissue	*Plasmodium* species	Malaria
	Toxoplasma gondii	Toxoplasmosis
	Pneumocystis carinii	Pneumonia
	Trypanosoma species	Trypanosomiasis
	T. cruzi	Chagas' disease
	T. gambiense[1]	Sleeping sickness
	T. rhodesiense[1]	Sleeping sickness
	Leishmania species	Leishmaniasis
	L. donovani	Kala-azar
	L. tropica	Cutaneous leishmaniasis[2]
	L. mexicana	Cutaneous leishmaniasis[2]
	L. braziliensis	Mucocutaneous leishmaniasis
Minor protozoa		
Intestinal tract	*Balantidium coli*	Dysentery
	Isospora belli	Isosporosis
	Enterocytozoon bienusi	Microsporidiosis
	Septata intestinalis	Microsporidiosis
	Cyclospora cayetanensis	Cyclosporiasis
Blood and tissue	*Naegleria* species	Meningitis
	Acanthamoeba species	Meningitis
	Babesia microti	Babesiosis

[1]Also known as *T. brucei gambiense* and *T. brucei rhodesiense,* respectively.
[2]*L. tropica* and *L. mexicana* cause Old World and New World cutaneous leishmaniasis, respectively.

Clinical Findings

Acute intestinal amebiasis presents as **dysentery** (ie, bloody, mucus-containing diarrhea) accompanied by lower abdominal discomfort, flatulence, and tenesmus. Chronic amebiasis with low-grade symptoms such as occasional diarrhea, weight loss, and fatigue also occurs. Roughly 90% of those infected have asymptomatic infections, but they may be carriers, whose feces contain cysts that can be transmitted to others. In some patients, a granulomatous lesion called an **ameboma** may form in the cecal or rectosigmoid areas of the colon. These lesions can resemble an adenocarcinoma of the colon and must be distinguished from them.

Amebic abscess of the liver is characterized by right-upper-quadrant pain, weight loss, fever, and a tender, enlarged liver. Right-lobe abscesses can penetrate the diaphragm and cause lung disease. Most cases of amebic liver abscess occur in patients who have not had overt intestinal amebiasis. Aspiration of the liver abscess yields brownish-yellow pus with the consistency of **anchovy-paste.**

Laboratory Diagnosis

Diagnosis of intestinal amebiasis rests on finding either trophozoites in diarrheal stools or cysts in formed stools. Diarrheal stools should be examined within 1 hour of collection to see the ameboid motility of the trophozoite. Trophozoites characteristically contain ingested red blood cells. The most common error is to mistake fecal leukocytes for trophozoites. Because cysts are passed intermittently, at least three specimens should be examined. About half of the patients with extraintestinal amebiasis have negative stool examinations.

Table 51–2. Features of medically important protozoa.

Organism	Mode of Transmission	Occurrence in United States	Diagnosis	Treatment
I. Intestinal and Urogenital Protozoa				
Entamoeba	Ingestion of cysts in food	Yes	Trophozoites or cysts in stool; serology	Metronidazole or tinidazole
Giardia	Ingestion of cysts in food	Yes	Trophozoites or cysts in stools	Metronidazole
Cryptosporidium	Ingestion of cysts in food	Yes	Cysts on acid-fast stain	Paromomycin may be useful
Trichomonas	Sexual	Yes	Trophozoites in wet mount	Metronidazole
II. Blood and Tissue Protozoa				
Trypanosoma T. cruzi	Reduviid bug	Rare	Blood smear, bone marrow, xenodiagnosis	Nifurtimox
T. gambiense, T. rhodesiense	Tsetse fly	No	Blood smear	Suramin[1]
Leishmania L. donovani	Sandfly	No	Bone marrow, spleen, or lymph node	Stibogluconate
L. tropica, L. mexicana, L. braziliensis	Sandfly	No	Fluid from lesion	Stibogluconate
Plasmodium P. vivax, P. ovale, P. malariae	Anopheles mosquito	Rare	Blood smear	Chloroquine if sensitive; also primaquine for P. vivax and P. ovale
P. falciparum	Anopheles mosquito	No	Blood smear	Chloroquine if sensitive; mefloquine or quinine plus doxycycline if resistant
Toxoplasma	Ingestion of cysts in raw meat; contact with cat feces	Yes	Serology; microscopic examination of tissue; mouse inoculation	Sulfonamide and pyrimethamine for congenital disease and immunocompromised patients
Pneumocystis	Inhalation	Yes	Lung biopsy or lavage	Trimethoprim-sulfamethoxazole. Also pentamidine or atovaquone

[1]Melarsoprol is used if the central nervous system is involved.

E. histolytica can be distinguished from other amebas by two major criteria. (1) The first is the nature of the **nucleus** of the trophozoite. The *E. histolytica* nucleus has a small central nucleolus and fine chromatin granules along the border of the nuclear membrane. The nuclei of other amebas are quite different. (2) The second is **cyst size and number of its nuclei**. Mature cysts of *E. histolytica* are smaller than those of

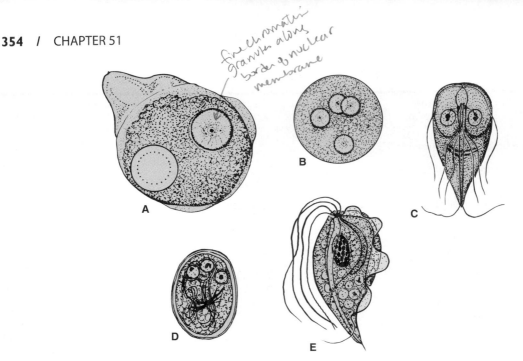

fine chromatin granules along border of nuclear membrane

Figure 51–1. **A:** *Entamoeba histolytica* trophozoite with one ingested red blood cell and one nucleus (circle with inner dotted line represents a red blood cell). **B:** *Entamoeba histolytica* cyst with four nuclei. **C:** *Giardia lamblia* trophozoite. **D:** *Giardia lamblia* cyst. **E:** *Trichomonas vaginalis* trophozoite. 1200 ×.

Entamoeba coli and contain four nuclei, whereas *E. coli* cysts have eight nuclei. The trophozoites of *Entamoeba dispar,* a nonpathogenic species of *Entamoeba,* are morphologically indistinguishable from those of *E. histolytica;* therefore, a person who has trophozoites in the stool is only treated if symptoms warrant it. Two tests are highly specific for *E. histolytica* in the stool: one detects *E. histolytica* antigen and the other detects nucleic acids of the organism in a PCR-based assay.

A complete examination for cysts includes a wet mount in saline, an iodine-stained wet mount, and a fixed, trichrome-stained preparation, each of which brings out different aspects of cyst morphology. These preparations are also helpful in distinguishing amebic from bacillary dysentery. In the latter, many inflammatory cells such as polymorphonuclear leukocytes are seen, whereas in amebic dysentery they are not.

Serologic testing is useful for the diagnosis of invasive amebiasis. The indirect hemagglutination test is usually positive in patients with invasive disease but is frequently negative in asymptomatic individuals who are passing cysts.

Treatment

The treatment of choice for symptomatic intestinal amebiasis or hepatic abscesses is metronidazole (Flagyl) or tinidazole. Hepatic abscesses need not be drained.

Asymptomatic cyst carriers should be treated with iodoquinol or paromomycin.

Prevention

Prevention involves avoiding fecal contamination of food and water and observing good personal hygiene such as hand washing. Purification of municipal water supplies is usually effective, but outbreaks of amebiasis in city dwellers still occur when contamination is heavy. The use of "night soil" (human feces) for fertilization of crops should be prohibited. In areas of endemic infection, vegetables should be cooked.

GIARDIA

Disease

Giardia lamblia causes giardiasis.

Important Properties

The life cycle consists of two stages, the **trophozoite** and the **cyst** (Figure 51–1C and D). The trophozoite is pear-shaped with two nuclei, four pairs of flagella, and a suction disk with which it attaches to the intestinal wall. The oval cyst is thick-walled with four nuclei and several internal fibers. Each cyst gives rise to two trophozoites during excystation in the intestinal tract.

Table 51–3. Medically important stages in life cycle of intestinal protozoa.

Organism	Insect Vector	Stage That Infects Humans	Stage(s) in Humans Most Associated with Disease	Important Stage(s) Outside of Humans
Entamoeba	None	Cyst	Trophozoites cause bloody diarrhea and liver abscess	Cyst
Giardia	None	Cyst	Trophozoites cause watery diarrhea	Cyst
Cryptosporidium	None	Cyst	Trophozoites cause watery diarrhea	Cyst
Trichomonas	None	Trophozoite	Trophozoites cause vaginal discharge	None

Pathogenesis & Epidemiology

Transmission occurs by ingestion of the cyst in **fecally contaminated** food and water. Excystation takes place in the duodenum, where the trophozoite attaches to the gut wall but does *not* invade. The trophozoite causes inflammation of the duodenal mucosa, leading to **malabsorption** of protein and fat.

The organism is found worldwide; about 5% of stool specimens in the United States contain *Giardia* cysts. Approximately half of those infected are asymptomatic carriers who continue to excrete the cysts for years. IgA deficiency greatly predisposes to symptomatic infection.

In addition to being endemic, giardiasis occurs in outbreaks related to contaminated water supplies. Chlorination does not kill the cysts, but filtration removes them. Hikers who drink untreated stream water are frequently infected. Many species of mammals as well as humans act as the reservoirs. They pass cysts in the stool, which then contaminates water sources. Giardiasis is common in male homosexuals as a result of oral-anal contact. The incidence is high among children in day-care centers and among patients in mental hospitals.

Clinical Findings

Watery (**nonbloody**), **foul-smelling diarrhea** is accompanied by nausea, anorexia, flatulence, and abdominal cramps persisting for weeks or months. There is no fever.

Laboratory Diagnosis

Diagnosis is made by finding trophozoites or cysts or both in diarrheal stools. In formed stools, eg, in asymptomatic carriers, only cysts are seen. An ELISA test that detects a *Giardia* cyst wall antigen in the stool is also very useful.

If microscopic examination of the stool is negative, the **string test**, which consists of swallowing a weighted piece of string until it reaches the duodenum, should be performed. The trophozoites adhere to the string and can be visualized after withdrawal of the string. No serologic test is available.

Treatment

The treatment of choice is metronidazole (Flagyl) or quinacrine hydrochloride.

Prevention

Prevention involves drinking boiled, filtered, or iodine-treated water in endemic areas and while hiking. No prophylactic drug or vaccine is available.

CRYPTOSPORIDIUM

Disease

Cryptosporidium parvum causes cryptosporidiosis, the main symptom of which is diarrhea. The diarrhea is most severe in **immunocompromised** patients, eg, those with AIDS.

Important Properties

Some aspects of the life cycle remain uncertain, but the following stages have been identified. Oocysts release sporozoites, which form trophozoites. Several stages ensue, involving the formation of schizonts and merozoites. Eventually microgametes and macrogametes form; these unite to produce a zygote, which differentiates into an oocyst. This cycle has several features in common with other sporozoa, eg, *Isospora*. Taxonomically, *Cryptosporidium* is in the subclass Coccidia.

Pathogenesis & Epidemiology

The organism is acquired by **fecal-oral** transmission of oocysts from either human or animal sources. The oocysts excyst in the small intestine, where the trophozoites (and other forms) attach to the gut wall. Invasion does not occur. The jejunum is the site most heavily infested. The pathogenesis of the diarrhea is unknown; no toxin has been identified.

Cryptosporidia cause diarrhea worldwide. Large outbreaks of diarrhea caused by cryptosporidia in several cities in the United States are attributed to inadequate purification of drinking water.

Clinical Findings

The disease in immunocompromised patients presents primarily as a watery, nonbloody **diarrhea** causing large fluid loss. Symptoms persist for long periods in immunocompromised patients, whereas they are self-limited in immunocompetent patients. Although immunocompromised patients usually do not die of cryptosporidiosis, the fluid loss and malnutrition are severely debilitating.

Laboratory Diagnosis

Diagnosis is made by finding oocysts in fecal smears when using a modified Kinyoun acid-fast stain. Serologic tests are not available.

Treatment & Prevention

There is no effective drug therapy for immunocompromised patients, but paromomycin may be useful in reducing diarrhea. Nitazoxanide is approved for the treatment of diarrhea caused by *C. parvum* in children ages 1 to 11 years.

Symptoms are self-limited in immunocompetent patients. There is no vaccine or other specific means of prevention. Purification of the water supply, including filtration to remove the cysts, which are resistant to the chlorine used for disinfection, can prevent cryptosporidiosis.

■ UROGENITAL PROTOZOA

TRICHOMONAS
Disease

Trichomonas vaginalis causes trichomoniasis.

Important Properties

T. vaginalis is a pear-shaped organism with a central nucleus and four anterior flagella (Figure 51–1E). It has an undulating membrane that extends about two-thirds of its length. It exists **only as a trophozoite**; there is no cyst form.

Pathogenesis & Epidemiology

The organism is transmitted by sexual contact, and hence there is no need for a durable cyst form. The primary locations of the organism are the vagina and the prostate.

Trichomoniasis is one of the most common infections worldwide. Roughly 25–50% of women in the United States harbor the organism. The frequency of symptomatic disease is highest among sexually active women in their 30s and lowest in postmenopausal women.

Clinical Findings

In women, a watery, foul-smelling, greenish vaginal discharge accompanied by itching and burning occurs. Infection in men is usually asymptomatic, but about 10% of infected men have urethritis.

Laboratory Diagnosis

In a wet mount of vaginal (or prostatic) secretions, the pear-shaped trophozoites have a typical jerky motion. There is no serologic test.

Treatment & Prevention

The drug of choice is metronidazole (Flagyl) for both partners to prevent reinfection. Maintenance of the low pH of the vagina is helpful. Condoms limit transmission. No prophylactic drug or vaccine is available.

SUMMARIES OF ORGANISMS

Brief summaries of the organisms described in this chapter begin on page 506. Please consult these summaries for a rapid review of the essential material.

PRACTICE QUESTIONS: USMLE & COURSE EXAMINATIONS

Questions on the topics discussed in this chapter can be found in the Parasitology section of Part XI: USMLE (National Board) Practice Questions starting on page 559. Also see Part XII: USMLE (National Board) Practice Examination starting on page 583.

Blood & Tissue Protozoa

The medically important organisms in this category of protozoa consist of the sporozoans *Plasmodium* and *Toxoplasma* and the flagellates *Trypanosoma* and *Leishmania*. *Pneumocystis* is discussed in this book as a protozoan because it is considered as such from a medical point of view. However, molecular data indicate that it is related to yeasts such as *Saccharomyces cerevisiae*. Table 51–2 summarizes several important features of these blood and tissue protozoa.

The medically important stages in the life cycle of the blood and tissue protozoa are described in Table 52–1.

PLASMODIUM

Disease

Malaria is caused by four plasmodia: *Plasmodium vivax*, *Plasmodium ovale*, *Plasmodium malariae*, and *Plasmodium falciparum*. *P. vivax* and *P. falciparum* are more common causes of malaria than are *P. ovale* and *P. malariae*. Worldwide, malaria is one of the most common infectious diseases and a leading cause of death.

Important Properties

The vector and definitive host for plasmodia is the **female *Anopheles* mosquito** (only the female takes a blood meal). There are two phases in the life cycle: the sexual cycle, which occurs primarily in mosquitoes, and the asexual cycle, which occurs in humans, the intermediate hosts.[1]

The sexual cycle is called **sporogony** because sporozoites are produced, and the asexual cycle is called **schizogony** because schizonts are made.

The life cycle in humans begins with the introduction of sporozoites into the blood from the saliva of the biting mosquito. The sporozoites are taken up by hepatocytes within 30 minutes. This "exoerythrocytic" phase consists of cell multiplication and differentiation into **merozoites**. *P. vivax* and *P. ovale* produce a latent form (**hypnozoite**) in the liver; this form is the cause of relapses seen with vivax and ovale malaria.

Merozoites are released from the liver cells and infect red blood cells. During the erythrocytic phase, the organism differentiates into a ring-shaped trophozoite (Figure 52–1A–F). The ring form grows into an ameboid form and then differentiates into a schizont filled with merozoites. After release, the merozoites infect other erythrocytes. This cycle in the red blood cell repeats at regular intervals typical for each species. The periodic release of merozoites causes the typical recurrent symptoms of chills, fever, and sweats seen in malaria patients.

The sexual cycle begins in the human red blood cells when some merozoites develop into male and others into female gametocytes. The gametocyte-containing red blood cells are ingested by the female *Anopheles* mosquito and, within her gut, produce a female macrogamete and eight spermlike male microgametes. After fertilization, the diploid zygote differentiates into a motile ookinete that burrows into the gut wall, where it grows into an oocyst within which many haploid sporozoites are produced. The sporozoites are released and migrate to the salivary glands, ready to complete the cycle when the mosquito takes her next blood meal.

Pathogenesis & Epidemiology

Most of the pathologic findings of malaria result from the **destruction of red blood cells**. Red cells are destroyed both by the release of the merozoites and by the action of the spleen to first sequester the infected red cells and then to lyse them. The enlarged spleen characteristic of malaria is due to congestion of sinusoids with erythrocytes, coupled with hyperplasia of lymphocytes and macrophages.

Malaria caused by *P. falciparum* is **more severe** than that caused by other plasmodia. It is characterized by infection of far more red cells than the other malarial species and by occlusion of the capillaries with aggregates of parasitized red cells. This leads to life-threatening hemorrhage and necrosis, particularly in the brain (cerebral malaria). Furthermore, extensive hemolysis and kidney damage occur, with resulting hemoglobinuria. The dark color of the patient's urine has given rise

---

[1] The sexual cycle is initiated in humans with the formation of gametocytes within red blood cells (gametogony) and completed in mosquitoes with the fusion of the male and female gametes, oocyst formation, and production of many sporozoites (sporogony).

Table 52–1. Medically important stages in life cycle of blood and tissue protozoa.

Organism	Insect Vector	Stage That Infects Humans	Stage(s) in Humans Most Associated with Disease	Important Stage(s) Outside of Humans
Plasmodium	Female mosquito (*Anopheles*)	Sporozoite in mosquito saliva	Trophozoites and merozoites in red blood cells	Mosquito ingests gametocytes→ fuse to form zygote→ ookinete→ sporozoites
Toxoplasma	None	Tissue cyst (pseudocysts) in undercooked meat or oocyst in cat feces	Rapidly multiplying trophozoites (tachyzoites) within various cell types; tachyzoites can pass placenta and infect fetus; slowly multiplying trophozoites (bradyzoites) in tissue cysts	Cat ingests tissue cysts containing bradyzoites→ gametes→ ookinete→ oocysts in feces
Pneumocystis	None	Uncertain; probably cyst	Cysts	None known
Trypanosoma cruzi	Reduviid bug (*Triatoma*)	Trypomastigote in bug feces	Amastigotes in cardiac muscle and neurons	Bug ingests trypomastigote in human blood → epimastigote → trypomastigote
Trypanosoma gambiense and *T. rhodesiense*	Tsetse fly (*Glossina*)	Trypomastigote in fly saliva	Trypomastigotes in blood and brain	Fly ingests trypomastigote in human blood → epimastigote → trypomastigote
Leishmania donovani	Sandfly (*Phlebotomus* and *Lutzomyia*)	Promastigotes in fly saliva	Amastigotes in macrophages in spleen, liver, and bone marrow	Fly ingests macrophages containing amastigotes → promastigotes
Leishmania tropica and others	Sandfly (*Phlebotomus* and *Lutzomyia*)	Promastigotes in fly saliva	Amastigotes in macrophages in skin	Fly ingests macrophages containing amastigotes → promastigotes

to the term "blackwater fever." The hemoglobinuria can lead to acute renal failure.

The timing of the fever cycle is 72 hours for *P. malariae* and 48 hours for the other plasmodia. Disease caused by *P. malariae* is called quartan malaria because it recurs every fourth day, whereas malaria caused by the others is called tertian malaria because it recurs every third day. Tertian malaria is subdivided into malignant malaria, caused by *P. falciparum*, and benign malaria, caused by *P. vivax* and *P. ovale*.

P. falciparum causes a high level of parasitemia, because it can infect red cells of all ages. In contrast, *P. vivax* infects only reticulocytes and *P. malariae* infects only mature red cells; therefore, they produce much lower levels of parasites in the blood. Individuals with sickle cell trait (heterozygotes) are protected against malaria because their red cells have too little ATPase activity and cannot produce sufficient energy to support the growth of the parasite. People with homozygous sickle cell anemia are also protected but rarely live long enough to obtain much benefit.

The receptor for *P. vivax* is the Duffy blood group antigen. People who are homozygous recessive for the genes that encode this protein are resistant to infection

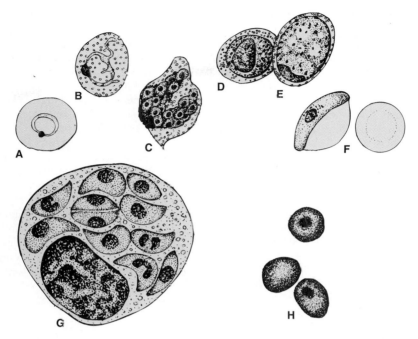

Figure 52–1. **A:** *Plasmodium vivax* signet-ring trophozoite within a red blood cell. **B:** *Plasmodium vivax* ameboid trophozoite within a red blood cell, showing Schüffner's dots. **C:** *Plasmodium vivax* mature schizont with merozoites inside. **D:** *Plasmodium vivax* microgametocyte. **E:** *Plasmodium vivax* macrogametocyte. **F:** *Plasmodium falciparum* "banana-shaped" gametocyte with attached red cell ghost. **G:** *Toxoplasma gondii* trophozoites within macrophage. **H:** *Pneumocystis carinii* cysts. A–G, 1200 ×; H, 800 ×.

by *P. vivax.* More than 90% of black West Africans and many of their American descendants do not produce the Duffy antigen and are thereby resistant to vivax malaria. People with glucose-6-phosphate dehydrogenase (G6PD) deficiency are also protected against the severe effects of falciparum malaria. G6PD deficiency is an X-linked hemoglobinopathy found in high frequency in tropical areas where malaria is endemic. Both male and female carriers of the mutated gene are protected against malaria.

Malaria is transmitted primarily by mosquito bites, but transmission across the placenta, in blood transfusions, and by intravenous drug abuse also occurs.

Partial immunity based on humoral antibodies that block merozoites from invading the red cells occurs in infected individuals. A low level of parasitemia and low-grade symptoms result; this condition is known as **premunition.** In contrast, a nonimmune person, such as a first-time traveler to an area where falciparum malaria is endemic, is at risk of severe, life-threatening disease.

More than 200 million people worldwide have malaria, and more than 1 million die of it each year, making it the most common lethal infectious disease. It occurs primarily in tropical and subtropical areas, espe-

cially in Asia, Africa, and Central and South America. Malaria in the United States is seen in Americans who travel to areas of endemic infection without adequate chemoprophylaxis and in immigrants from areas of endemic infection. It is not endemic in the United States. Certain regions in Southeast Asia, South America, and east Africa are particularly affected by chloroquine-resistant strains of *P. falciparum.* People who have lived or traveled in areas where malaria occurs should seek medical attention for febrile illnesses up to 3 years after leaving the malarious area.

Clinical Findings

Malaria presents with abrupt onset of fever and chills, accompanied by headache, myalgias, and arthralgias, about 2 weeks after the mosquito bite. Fever may be continuous early in the disease; the typical periodic cycle does not develop for several days after onset. The fever spike, which can reach 41°C, is frequently accompanied by shaking chills, nausea, vomiting, and abdominal pain. The fever is followed by drenching sweats. Patients usually feel well between the febrile episodes. Splenomegaly is seen in most patients, and hepatomegaly occurs in roughly one-third. Anemia is prominent.

Untreated malaria caused by *P. falciparum* is potentially life-threatening as a result of extensive brain (cerebral malaria) and kidney (blackwater fever) damage. Malaria caused by the other three plasmodia is usually self-limited, with a low mortality rate. However, relapses of *P. vivax* and *P. ovale* malaria can occur up to several years after the initial illness as a result of hypnozoites latent in the liver.

Laboratory Diagnosis

Diagnosis rests on microscopic examination of blood, using both **thick** and **thin** Giemsa-stained smears. The thick smear is used to screen for the presence of organisms, and the thin smear is used for species identification. It is important to identify the species, because the treatment of different species can differ. Ring-shaped trophozoites can be seen within infected red blood cells. The gametocytes of *P. falciparum* are **crescent-shaped** ("banana-shaped"), whereas those of the other plasmodia are spherical (Figure 52–1F). If more than 5% of red blood cells are parasitized, the diagnosis is usually *P. falciparum* malaria.

If blood smears do not reveal the diagnosis, then a PCR-based test for *Plasmodium* nucleic acids or an ELISA test for a protein specific for *P. falciparum* can be useful.

Treatment

Chloroquine is the drug of choice for acute malaria caused by sensitive strains. Chloroquine kills the merozoites, thereby reducing the parasitemia, but does not affect the hypnozoites of *P. vivax* and *P. ovale* in the liver. These are killed by primaquine, which must be used to prevent relapses. Primaquine may induce severe hemolysis in those with G6PD deficiency, so testing for this enzyme should be done before the drug is given.

For chloroquine-resistant strains of *P. falciparum*, either mefloquine or a combination of quinine and doxycycline is used. A combination of atovaquone and proguanil (Malarone), in a fixed dose, is available for the treatment of malaria caused by chloroquine-resistant *P. falciparum*. Strains of *P. falciparum* resistant to both chloroquine and mefloquine have emerged in some countries, eg, Thailand. In severe cases, parenteral quinidine or quinine is used. Note that in the United States, quinidine is available but quinine is not.

Prevention

Chemoprophylaxis of malaria for travelers to areas where chloroquine-resistant *P. falciparum* is endemic consists of mefloquine or doxycycline. A combination of atovaquone and proguanil (Malarone), in a fixed dose, can also be used. Chloroquine should be used in areas where *P. falciparum* is sensitive to that drug. Travelers to areas where the other plasmodia are found should take chloroquine starting 2 weeks before arrival and continuing for 6 weeks after departure. This should be followed by a 2-week course of primaquine if exposure was high. Primaquine will kill the hypnozoites of *P. vivax* and *P. ovale*.

Other preventive measures include the use of mosquito netting, window screens, protective clothing, and insect repellents. The mosquitoes feed from dusk to dawn, so protection is particularly important during the night. Communal preventive measures are directed against reducing the mosquito population. Many insecticide sprays, such as DDT, are no longer effective because the mosquitoes have developed resistance. Drainage of stagnant water in swamps and ditches reduces the breeding areas. There is no vaccine.

TOXOPLASMA

Disease

Toxoplasma gondii causes toxoplasmosis, including congenital toxoplasmosis.

Important Properties

The definitive host is the **domestic cat** and other felines; humans and other mammals are intermediate hosts. Infection of humans begins with the **ingestion of cysts** in undercooked meat or from contact with cat feces. In the small intestine, the cysts rupture and release forms that invade the gut wall, where they are ingested by macrophages and differentiate into rapidly multiplying trophozoites (**tachyzoites**), which kill the cells and infect other cells (Figure 52–1G). Cell-mediated immunity usually limits the spread of tachyzoites, and the parasites enter host cells in the brain, muscle, and other tissues, where they develop into cysts in which the parasites multiply slowly. These forms are called **bradyzoites**. These tissue cysts are both an important diagnostic feature and a source of organisms when the tissue cyst breaks in an immunocompromised patient.

The cycle within the cat begins with the ingestion of cysts in raw meat, eg, mice. Bradyzoites are released from the cysts in the small intestine, infect the mucosal cells, and differentiate into male and female gametocytes, whose gametes fuse to form oocysts that are excreted in cat feces. The cycle is completed when soil contaminated with cat feces is accidentally ingested. Human infection usually occurs from eating undercooked meat, eg, lamb and pork, from animals that grazed in soil contaminated with infected cat feces.

Pathogenesis & Epidemiology

T. gondii is usually acquired by **ingestion** of cysts in uncooked meat or cat feces.

Transplacental transmission from an infected mother to the fetus occurs also. Human-to-human transmission, other than transplacental transmission, does not occur. After infection of the intestinal epithelium, the organisms spread to other organs, especially the brain, lungs, liver, and eyes. Progression of the infection is usually limited by a competent immune system. **Cell-mediated immunity** plays the major role, but circulating antibody enhances killing of the organism. Most initial infections are asymptomatic. When contained, the organisms persist as cysts within tissues. There is no inflammation, and the individual remains well unless immunosuppression allows activation of organisms in the cysts.

Congenital infection of the fetus occurs *only* when the mother is infected during pregnancy. If she is infected before the pregnancy, the organism will be in the cyst form and there will be no trophozoites to pass through the placenta. The mother who is reinfected during pregnancy but who has immunity from a previous infection will not transmit the organism to her child. Roughly one-third of mothers infected during pregnancy give birth to infected infants, but only 10% of these infants are symptomatic.

Infection by *T. gondii* occurs worldwide. Serologic surveys reveal that in the United States antibodies are found in 5–50% of people in various regions. Infection is usually sporadic, but outbreaks associated with ingestion of raw meat or contaminated water occur. Approximately 1% of domestic cats in the United States shed *Toxoplasma* cysts.

Clinical Findings

Most primary infections in immunocompetent adults are asymptomatic, but some resemble infectious mononucleosis, except that the heterophil antibody test is negative. Congenital infection can result in abortion, stillbirth, or neonatal disease with encephalitis, **chorioretinitis**, and hepatosplenomegaly. Fever, jaundice, and **intracranial calcifications** are also seen. Most infected newborns are asymptomatic, but chorioretinitis or mental retardation will develop in some children months or years later. Congenital infection with *Toxoplasma* is one of the leading causes of blindness in children. In patients with reduced cell-mediated immunity (eg, AIDS patients), life-threatening disseminated disease, primarily encephalitis, occurs.

Laboratory Diagnosis

For the diagnosis of acute and congenital infections, an immunofluorescence assay for **IgM antibody** is used.

IgM is used to diagnose congenital infection, because IgG can be maternal in origin. Tests of IgG antibody can be used to diagnose acute infections if a significant rise in antibody titer in paired sera is observed.

Microscopic examination of Giemsa-stained preparations shows crescent-shaped trophozoites during acute infections. Cysts may be seen in the tissue. The organism can be grown in cell culture. Inoculation into mice can confirm the diagnosis.

Treatment

Congenital toxoplasmosis, whether symptomatic or asymptomatic, should be treated with a combination of sulfadiazine and pyrimethamine. These drugs also constitute the treatment of choice for disseminated disease in immunocompromised patients. Acute toxoplasmosis in an immunocompetent individual is usually self-limited, but any patient with chorioretinitis should be treated.

Prevention

The most effective means of preventing toxoplasmosis is to cook meat thoroughly to kill the cysts. Pregnant women should be especially careful to avoid undercooked meat and contact with cats. They should refrain from emptying cat litter boxes. Cats should not be fed raw meat.

PNEUMOCYSTIS

Disease

Pneumocystis carinii is an important cause of pneumonia in immunocompromised individuals. In 2002, taxonomists renamed the human species of *Pneumocystis* as *P. jiroveci* and recommended that *P. carinii* be used only to describe the rat species of *Pneumocystis*. There is some controversy surrounding this change of names, and *P. carinii* will be used here.

Important Properties

The classification and life cycle of *Pneumocystis* are unclear. Many aspects of its biochemistry indicate that it is a yeast, but it also has several attributes of a protozoan. An analysis of rRNA sequences published in 1988 indicates that *Pneumocystis* should be classified as a **fungus** related to yeasts such as *Saccharomyces cerevisiae*. Subsequent analysis of mitochondrial DNA and of various enzymes supports the idea that it is a fungus. However, it does not have ergosterol in its membranes as do the fungi. It has cholesterol.

Medically, it is still thought of as a protozoan. In tissue, it appears as a cyst that resembles the cysts of protozoa. The findings that it does not grow on fungal media and that antifungal drugs are ineffective have delayed acceptance of its classification as a fungus.

Pneumocystis species are found in domestic animals such as horses and sheep and in a variety of rodents, but it is thought that these animals are not a reservoir for human infection. Each mammalian species is thought to have its own species of *Pneumocystis.*

Pneumocystis species have a major surface glycoprotein that exhibits significant antigenic variation in a manner similar to that of *Trypanosoma brucei. Pneumocystis* species have multiple genes encoding these surface proteins, but only one is expressed at a time. This process of programmed rearrangements was first observed in *T. brucei.*

Pathogenesis & Epidemiology

Transmission occurs by **inhalation**, and infection is predominantly in the lungs. The presence of cysts in the alveoli induces an inflammatory response consisting primarily of plasma cells, resulting in a frothy exudate that blocks oxygen exchange. (The presence of plasma cells has led to the name "plasma cell pneumonia.") The organism does not invade the lung tissue.

Pneumonia occurs when host defenses, eg, the number of CD4-positive (helper) T cells, are reduced. This accounts for the prominence of *Pneumocystis* pneumonia in patients with AIDS and in premature or debilitated infants. Hospital outbreaks do not occur and patients with *Pneumocystis* pneumonia are not isolated.

P. carinii is distributed worldwide. It is estimated that 70% of people have been infected. Most 5-year-old children in the United States have antibodies to this organism. Asymptomatic infection is therefore quite common. Prior to the advent of immunosuppressive therapy, *Pneumocystis* pneumonia was rarely seen in the United States. Its incidence has paralleled the increase in immunosuppression and the rise in the number of AIDS cases.

Most *Pneumocystis* infections in AIDS patients are new rather than a reactivation of a prior latent infection. This conclusion is based on the finding that *Pneumocystis* recovered from AIDS patients shows resistance to drugs that the patient has not taken.

Clinical Findings

The sudden onset of fever, nonproductive cough, dyspnea, and tachypnea is typical of *Pneumocystis* pneumonia. Bilateral rales and rhonchi are heard, and the chest x-ray shows a diffuse interstitial pneumonia with "ground glass" infiltrates bilaterally. In infants, the disease usually has a more gradual onset. Extrapulmonary *Pneumocystis* infections occur in the late stages of AIDS

and affect primarily the liver, spleen, lymph nodes, and bone marrow. The mortality rate of untreated *Pneumocystis* pneumonia approaches 100%.

Laboratory Diagnosis

Diagnosis is made by finding the typical cysts by microscopic examination of lung tissue or fluids obtained by bronchoscopy, bronchial lavage, or open lung biopsy (Figure 52–1H). Sputum is usually less suitable. The cysts can be visualized with methenamine-silver, Giemsa, or other tissue stains. Fluorescent-antibody staining is also commonly used for diagnosis. The organism stains poorly with Gram stain. There is no serologic test, and the organism has not been grown in culture. PCR-based tests are being developed.

Treatment

The treatment of choice is a combination of trimethoprim and sulfamethoxazole (Bactrim, Septra). Pentamidine and atovaquone are alternative drugs.

Prevention

Trimethoprim-sulfamethoxazole or aerosolized pentamidine should be used as chemoprophylaxis in patients whose CD4 counts are below 200.

TRYPANOSOMA

The genus *Trypanosoma* includes three major pathogens: *Trypanosoma cruzi, Trypanosoma gambiense,* and *Trypanosoma rhodesiense.*[2]

1. *Trypanosoma cruzi*

Disease

T. cruzi is the cause of Chagas' disease (American trypanosomiasis).

Important Properties

The life cycle involves the **reduviid bug** (*Triatoma,* cone-nose or kissing bug) as the vector and both humans and animals as reservoir hosts. The animal reservoirs include domestic cats and dogs and wild species such as the armadillo, raccoon, and rat. The cycle in the reduviid bug begins with ingestion of trypomastigotes in the blood of the reservoir host. In the insect gut, they multiply and differentiate first into epimastigotes and

---

[2] Taxonomically, the last two organisms are morphologically identical species called *T. brucei gambiense* and *T. brucei rhodesiense,* but the shortened names are used here.

then into trypomastigotes. When the bug bites again, the site is contaminated with feces containing trypomastigotes, which enter the blood of the person (or other reservoir) and form nonflagellated amastigotes within host cells. Many cells can be affected, but myocardial, glial, and reticuloendothelial cells are the most frequent sites. To complete the cycle, amastigotes differentiate into trypomastigotes, which enter the blood and are taken up by the reduviid bug (Figure 52–2A–C).

Pathogenesis & Epidemiology

Chagas' disease occurs primarily in rural Central and South America. Acute Chagas' disease occurs rarely in the United States, but the chronic form is seen with increasing frequency in immigrants from Latin America. The disease is seen primarily in rural areas because the reduviid bug lives in the walls of rural huts and feeds at night. It bites preferentially around the mouth or eyes, hence the name "kissing bug."

The amastigotes can kill cells and cause inflammation, consisting mainly of mononuclear cells. **Cardiac muscle** is the most frequently and severely affected tissue. In addition, neuronal damage leads to cardiac arrhythmias and loss of tone in the colon (**megacolon**) and esophagus (**megaesophagus**). During the acute phase, there are both trypomastigotes in the blood and amastigotes intracellularly in the tissues. In the chronic phase, the organism persists in the amastigote form.

Clinical Findings

The acute phase of Chagas' disease consists of facial edema and a nodule (chagoma) near the bite, coupled with fever, lymphadenopathy, and hepatosplenomegaly. The acute phase resolves in about 2 months. Most individuals then remain asymptomatic, but some progress to the chronic form with myocarditis and megacolon. Death from chronic Chagas' disease is usually due to cardiac arrhythmias and failure.

Laboratory Diagnosis

Acute disease is diagnosed by demonstrating the presence of trypomastigotes in thick or thin films of the patient's blood. Both stained and wet preparations should be examined, the latter for motile organisms. Because the trypomastigotes are not numerous in the blood, other diagnostic methods may be required, namely, (1) a stained preparation of a bone marrow aspirate or muscle biopsy specimen (which may reveal amastigotes); (2) culture of the organism on special medium; and (3) **xenodiagnosis**, which consists of allowing an uninfected, laboratory-raised reduviid bug to feed on the patient and, after several weeks, examining the intestinal contents of the bug for the organism.

Serologic tests can be helpful also. The indirect fluorescent-antibody test is the earliest to become positive. Indirect hemagglutination and complement fixation tests are also available. Diagnosis of chronic disease is difficult, because there are few trypomastigotes in the blood. Xenodiagnosis and serologic tests are used.

Treatment

The drug of choice for the acute phase is nifurtimox, which kills trypomastigotes in the blood but is much

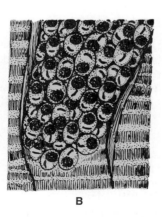
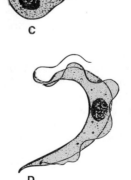
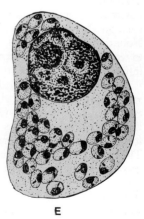

Figure 52–2. **A:** *Trypanosoma cruzi* trypomastigote found in human blood. 1200 ×. **B:** *Trypanosoma cruzi* amastigotes found in cardiac muscle. 850 ×. **C:** *Trypanosoma cruzi* epimastigote found in reduviid bug. 1200 ×. **D:** *Trypanosoma brucei gambiense* or *rhodesiense* trypomastigote found in human blood. 1200 ×. **E:** *Leishmania donovani* amastigotes within splenic macrophages. 1000 ×. (Circle with inner dotted line represents a red blood cell.)

less effective against amastigotes in tissue. Benznidazole is an alternative drug. There is no effective drug against the chronic form.

Prevention

Prevention involves protection from the reduviid bite, improved housing, and insect control. No prophylactic drug or vaccine is available.

2. *Trypanosoma gambiense* & *Trypanosoma rhodesiense*

Disease

These organisms cause sleeping sickness (African trypanosomiasis). They are also known as *Trypanosoma brucei gambiense* and *Trypanosoma brucei rhodesiense.*

Important Properties

The morphology and life cycle of the two species are similar. The vector for both is the **tsetse fly,** *Glossina,* but different species of fly are involved for each. Humans are the reservoir for *T. gambiense,* whereas *T. rhodesiense* has reservoirs in both domestic animals (especially cattle) and wild animals (eg, antelopes).

The 3-week life cycle in the tsetse fly begins with ingestion of trypomastigotes in a blood meal from the reservoir host. They multiply in the insect gut and then migrate to the salivary glands, where they transform into epimastigotes, multiply further, and then form metacyclic trypomastigotes, which are transmitted by the tsetse fly bite. The organisms in the saliva are injected into the skin, where they enter the bloodstream, differentiate into blood-form trypomastigotes, and multiply, thereby completing the cycle (Figure 52–2D). Note that these species are rarely found as amastigotes in tissue, in contrast to *T cruzi* and *Leishmania* species, in which amastigotes are commonly found.

These trypanosomes exhibit remarkable **antigenic variation** of their surface glycoproteins, with hundreds of antigenic types found. One antigenic type will coat the surface of the parasites for approximately 10 days, followed by other types in sequence in the new progeny. This variation is due to sequential movement of the glycoprotein genes to a preferential location on the chromosome, where only that specific gene is transcribed into mRNA. These antigenic variations allow the organism to continually evade the host immune response.

Pathogenesis & Epidemiology

The trypomastigotes spread from the skin through the blood to the lymph nodes and the brain. The typical somnolence (**sleeping sickness**) progresses to coma as a result of a demyelinating encephalitis.

In the acute form, a cyclical fever spike (approximately every 2 weeks) occurs that is related to antigenic variation. As antibody-mediated agglutination and lysis of the trypomastigotes occur, the fever subsides. However, a few antigenic variants survive, multiply, and cause a new fever spike. This cycle repeats itself over a long period. The lytic antibody is directed against the surface glycoprotein.

The disease is endemic in sub-Saharan Africa, the natural habitat of the tsetse fly. Both sexes of fly take blood meals and can transmit the disease. The fly is infectious throughout its 2- to 3-month lifetime. *T. gambiense* is the species that causes the disease along water courses in west Africa, whereas *T. rhodesiense* is found in the arid regions of east Africa. Both species are found in central Africa.

Clinical Findings

Although both species cause sleeping sickness, the progress of the disease differs. *T. gambiense*–induced disease runs a low-grade chronic course over a few years, whereas *T. rhodesiense* causes a more acute, rapidly progressive disease that, if untreated, is usually fatal within several months.

The initial lesion is an indurated skin ulcer ("trypanosomal chancre") at the site of the fly bite. After the organisms enter the blood, intermittent weekly fever and lymphadenopathy develop. Enlargement of the posterior cervical lymph nodes (Winterbottom's sign) is commonly seen. The encephalitis is characterized initially by headache, insomnia, and mood changes, followed by muscle tremors, slurred speech, and apathy that progress to somnolence and coma. Untreated disease is usually fatal as a result of pneumonia.

Laboratory Diagnosis

During the early stages, microscopic examination of the blood (either wet films or thick or thin smears) reveals trypomastigotes. An aspirate of the chancre or enlarged lymph node can also demonstrate the parasites. The presence of trypanosomes in the spinal fluid, coupled with an elevated protein level and pleocytosis, indicates that the patient has entered the late, encephalitic stage. Serologic tests, especially the ELISA for IgM antibody, can be helpful.

Treatment

Treatment must be initiated before the development of encephalitis, because suramin, the most effective drug, does not pass the blood-brain barrier well. Suramin will effect a cure if given early. Pentamidine is an alternative drug. If central nervous system symptoms are present, suramin (to clear the parasitemia) followed by melarsoprol should be given.

Prevention

The most important preventive measure is protection against the fly bite, using netting and protective clothing. Clearing the forest around villages and using insecticides are helpful measures. No vaccine is available.

LEISHMANIA

The genus *Leishmania* includes four major pathogens: *Leishmania donovani, Leishmania tropica, Leishmania mexicana,* and *Leishmania braziliensis.*

1. Leishmania donovani

Disease

L. donovani is the cause of kala-azar (visceral leishmaniasis).

Important Properties

The life cycle involves the **sandfly**[3] as the vector and a variety of mammals such as dogs, foxes, and rodents as reservoirs.

Only female flies are vectors because only they take blood meals (a requirement for egg maturation). When the sandfly sucks blood from an infected host, it ingests **macrophages containing amastigotes.**[4]

After dissolution of the macrophages, the freed amastigotes differentiate into promastigotes in the gut. They multiply and then migrate to the pharynx, where they can be transmitted during the next bite. The cycle in the sandfly takes approximately 10 days.

Shortly after an infected sandfly bites a human, the promastigotes are engulfed by macrophages, where they transform into amastigotes (Figure 52–2E). The infected cells die and release progeny amastigotes that infect other macrophages and reticuloendothelial cells. The cycle is completed when the fly ingests macrophages containing the amastigotes.

Pathogenesis & Epidemiology

In visceral leishmaniasis, the organs of the **reticuloendothelial** system (liver, spleen, and bone marrow) are the most severely affected. Reduced bone marrow activity, coupled with cellular destruction in the spleen, results in anemia, leukopenia, and thrombocytopenia. This leads to secondary infections and a tendency to bleed. The striking **enlargement of the spleen** is due to a combination of proliferating macrophages and sequestered blood cells. The marked increase in IgG is neither specific nor protective.

Kala-azar occurs in three distinct epidemiologic patterns. In one area, which includes the Mediterranean basin, the Middle East, southern Russia, and parts of China, the reservoir hosts are primarily dogs and foxes. In sub-Saharan Africa, rats and small carnivores, eg, civets, are the main reservoirs. A third pattern is seen in India and neighboring countries (and Kenya), in which humans appear to be the only reservoir.

Clinical Findings

Symptoms begin with intermittent fever, weakness, and weight loss. Massive enlargement of the spleen is characteristic. Hyperpigmentation of the skin is seen in light-skinned patients (kala-azar means **black sickness**). The course of the disease runs for months to years. Initially, patients feel reasonably well despite persistent fever. As anemia, leukopenia, and thrombocytopenia become more profound, weakness, infection, and gastrointestinal bleeding occur. Untreated severe disease is nearly always fatal as a result of secondary infection.

Laboratory Diagnosis

Diagnosis is usually made by detecting amastigotes in a bone marrow, spleen, or lymph node biopsy or "touch" preparation. The organisms can also be cultured. Serologic (indirect immunofluorescence) tests are positive in most patients. Although not diagnostic, a very high concentration of IgG is indicative of infection. A skin test using a crude homogenate of promastigotes (leishmanin) as the antigen is available. The skin test is negative during active disease but positive in patients who have recovered.

Treatment

The treatment is sodium stibogluconate, a pentavalent antimony compound. With proper therapy, the mortality rate is reduced to near 5%. Recovery results in permanent immunity.

Prevention

Prevention involves protection from sandfly bites (use of netting, protective clothing, and insect repellents) and insecticide spraying.

---

[3] *Phlebotomus* species in the Old World; *Lutzomyia* species in South America.

[4] Amastigotes are nonflagellated, in contrast to promastigotes, which have a flagellum with a characteristic anterior kinetoplast.

2. *Leishmania tropica, Leishmania mexicana, & Leishmania braziliensis*

Disease

L. tropica and *L. mexicana* both cause cutaneous leishmaniasis; the former organism is found in the Old World, whereas the latter is found only in the Americas. *L. braziliensis* causes mucocutaneous leishmaniasis, which occurs only in Central and South America.

Important Properties

Sandflies are the vectors for these three organisms, as they are for *L. donovani,* and forest rodents are their main reservoirs. The life cycle of these parasites is essentially the same as that of *L. donovani.*

Pathogenesis & Epidemiology

The lesions are confined to the skin in cutaneous leishmaniasis and to the mucous membranes, cartilage, and skin in mucocutaneous leishmaniasis. A granulomatous response occurs, and a necrotic ulcer forms at the bite site. The lesions tend to become superinfected with bacteria.

Old World cutaneous leishmaniasis (Oriental sore, Delhi boil), caused by *L. tropica,* is endemic in the Middle East, Africa, and India. New World cutaneous leishmaniasis (chicle ulcer, bay sore), caused by *L. mexicana,* is found in Central and South America. Mucocutaneous leishmaniasis (espundia), caused by *L. braziliensis,* occurs mostly in Brazil and Central America, primarily in forestry and construction workers.

Clinical Findings

The initial lesion of cutaneous leishmaniasis is a red papule at the bite site, usually on an exposed extremity. This enlarges slowly to form multiple satellite nodules that coalesce and ulcerate. There is usually a single lesion that heals spontaneously in patients with a competent immune system. However, in certain individuals, if cell-mediated immunity does not develop, the lesions can spread to involve large areas of skin and contain enormous numbers of organisms. (Compare tuberculoid and lepromatous leprosy, Chapter 21.)

Mucocutaneous leishmaniasis begins with a papule at the bite site, but then metastatic lesions form, usually at the mucocutaneous junction of the nose and mouth. Disfiguring granulomatous, ulcerating lesions destroy nasal cartilage but not adjacent bone. These lesions heal slowly, if at all. Death can occur from secondary infection.

Laboratory Diagnosis

Diagnosis is usually made microscopically by demonstrating the presence of **amastigotes** in a smear taken from the skin lesion. The leishmanin skin test becomes positive when the skin ulcer appears and can be used to diagnose cases outside the area of endemic infection.

Treatment

The drug of choice is sodium stibogluconate, but the results are frequently unsatisfactory.

Prevention

Prevention involves protection from sandfly bites by using netting, window screens, protective clothing, and insect repellents.

SUMMARIES OF ORGANISMS

Brief summaries of the organisms described in this chapter begin on page 507. Please consult these summaries for a rapid review of the essential material.

PRACTICE QUESTIONS: USMLE & COURSE EXAMINATIONS

Questions on the topics discussed in this chapter can be found in the Parasitology section of Part XI: USMLE (National Board) Practice Questions starting on page 559. Also see Part XII: USMLE (National Board) Practice Examination starting on page 583.

Minor Protozoan Pathogens

53

The medically important stages in the life cycle of certain minor protozoa are described in Table 53–1.

ACANTHAMOEBA & NAEGLERIA

Acanthamoeba castellanii and *Naegleria fowleri* are free-living **amebas** that cause **meningoencephalitis.** The organisms are found in warm freshwater lakes and in soil. Their life cycle involves trophozoite and cyst stages. Cysts are quite resistant and are not killed by chlorination.

Naegleria trophozoites usually enter the body through mucous membranes while an individual is **swimming.** They can penetrate the nasal mucosa and cribriform plate to produce a purulent meningitis and encephalitis that are usually rapidly fatal. *Acanthamoeba* is carried into the skin or eyes during trauma. *Acanthamoeba* infections occur primarily in immunocompromised individuals, whereas *Naegleria* infections occur in otherwise healthy persons, usually children. In the United States, these rare infections occur mainly in the southern states and California.

Diagnosis is made by finding amebas in the spinal fluid. The prognosis is poor even in treated cases. Amphotericin B may be effective in *Naegleria* infections. Pentamidine, ketoconazole, or flucytosine may be effective in *Acanthamoeba* infections.

Acanthamoeba also causes **keratitis,** an inflammation of the cornea that occurs primarily in those who wear contact lenses. With increasing use of contact lenses, keratitis has become the most common disease associated with *Acanthamoeba* infection. The amebas have been recovered from contact lenses, lens cases, and lens disinfectant solutions. Tap water contaminated with amebas is the source of infection for lens users.

BABESIA

Babesia microti causes babesiosis, a zoonosis acquired chiefly in the coastal areas and islands off the northeastern coast of the United States, eg, Nantucket Island. The sporozoan organism is endemic in rodents and is transmitted by the bite of the **tick** *Ixodes dammini* (renamed *I. scapularis*), the same species of tick that transmits *Borrelia burgdorferi,* the agent of Lyme disease. *Babesia* infects red blood cells, causing them to lyse, but unlike plasmodia, it has no exoerythrocytic phase. Asplenic patients are affected more severely.

The influenzalike symptoms begin gradually and may last for several weeks. Hepatosplenomegaly and anemia occur. Diagnosis is made by seeing intraerythrocytic ring-shaped parasites on Giemsa-stained blood smears. The intraerythrocytic ring-shaped trophozoites are often in tetrads in the form of a **Maltese cross.** Unlike the case with plasmodia, there is no pigment in the erythrocytes. Combined therapy with quinine and clindamycin may be effective. Prevention involves protection from tick bites and, if a person is bitten, prompt removal of the tick.

BALANTIDIUM

Balantidium coli is the **only ciliated protozoan** that causes human disease, ie, **diarrhea.** It is found worldwide but only infrequently in the United States. Domestic animals, especially pigs, are the main reservoir for the organism, and humans are infected after ingesting the cysts in food or water contaminated with animal or human feces. The trophozoites excyst in the small intestine, travel to the colon, and, by burrowing into the wall, cause an ulcer similar to that of *Entamoeba histolytica.* However, unlike the case with *E. histolytica,* extraintestinal lesions do not occur.

Most infected individuals are asymptomatic; diarrhea rarely occurs. Diagnosis is made by finding large ciliated trophozoites or large cysts with a characteristic V-shaped nucleus in the stool. There are no serologic tests. The treatment of choice is tetracycline. Prevention consists of avoiding contamination of food and water by domestic-animal feces.

CYCLOSPORA

Cyclospora cayetanensis is an intestinal protozoan that causes watery diarrhea in both immunocompetent and immunocompromised individuals. It is classified as a member of the Coccidia.[1]

---

[1] Coccidia is a subclass of Sporozoa.

367

Table 53–1. Medically important stages in life cycle of certain minor protozoa.

Organism	Insect Vector	Stage That Infects Humans	Stage(s) in Humans Most Associated with Disease	Important Stage(s) Outside of Humans
Acanthamoeba and *Naegleria*	None	Trophozoite	Trophozoites in meninges	Cyst
Babesia	Tick (*Ixodes*)	Sporozoite in tick saliva	Trophozoites and merozoites in red blood cells	None

The organism is acquired by fecal-oral transmission, especially via contaminated water supplies. One outbreak in the United States was attributed to the ingestion of contaminated raspberries. There is no evidence for an animal reservoir.

The diarrhea can be prolonged and relapsing, especially in immunocompromised patients. Infection occurs worldwide. The diagnosis is made microscopically by observing the spherical oocysts in a modified acid-fast stain of a stool sample. There are no serologic tests. The treatment of choice is trimethoprim-sulfamethoxazole.

ISOSPORA

Isospora belli is an intestinal protozoan that causes **diarrhea,** especially in **immunocompromised patients,** eg, those with AIDS. Its life cycle parallels that of other members of the Coccidia. The organism is acquired by fecal-oral transmission of oocysts from either human or animal sources. The oocysts excyst in the upper small intestine and invade the mucosa, causing destruction of the brush border.

The disease in immunocompromised patients presents as a chronic, profuse, watery diarrhea. The pathogenesis of the diarrhea is unknown. Diagnosis is made by finding the typical oocysts in fecal specimens. Serologic tests are not available. The treatment of choice is trimethoprim-sulfamethoxazole.

MICROSPORIDIA

Microsporidia are a group of protozoa characterized by obligate intracellular replication and spore formation.

As the name implies, the spores are quite small, approximately 1 to 3 μ, about the size of *Escherichia coli.* One unique feature of these spores is a "polar tube," which is coiled within the spore and extrudes to attach to the human cells upon infection. The protoplasm of the spore then enters the human cell via the polar tube.

Enterocytozoon bieneusi and *Encephalitozoon intestinalis* are two important microsporidial species that cause severe, persistent, watery diarrhea in AIDS patients. The organisms are transmitted from human to human by the fecal-oral route. Microsporidia are also implicated in infections of the central nervous system, the genitourinary tract, and the eye. It is uncertain whether an animal reservoir exists. Diagnosis is made by visualization of spores in stool samples or intestinal biopsy samples. The treatment of choice is albendazole.

SUMMARIES OF ORGANISMS

Brief summaries of the organisms described in this chapter begin on page 508. Please consult these summaries for a rapid review of the essential material.

PRACTICE QUESTIONS: USMLE & COURSE EXAMINATIONS

Questions on the topics discussed in this chapter can be found in the Parasitology section of Part XI: USMLE (National Board) Practice Questions starting on page 559. Also see Part XII: USMLE (National Board) Practice Examination starting on page 583.

Cestodes

Platyhelminthes (platy means flat; helminth means worm) are divided into two classes: Cestoda (tapeworms) and Trematoda (flukes). The Trematodes are described in Chapter 55.

Tapeworms consist of two main parts: a rounded head called a **scolex** and a flat body of multiple segments called **proglottids.** The scolex has specialized means of attaching to the intestinal wall, namely, suckers, hooks, or sucking grooves. The worm grows by adding new proglottids from its germinal center next to the scolex. The oldest proglottids at the distal end are gravid and produce many eggs, which are excreted in the feces and transmitted to various intermediate hosts such as cattle, pigs, and fish.

Humans usually acquire the infection when undercooked flesh containing the larvae is ingested. However, in two important human diseases, cysticercosis and hydatid disease, it is the eggs that are ingested and the resulting larvae cause the disease.

There are four medically important cestodes: *Taenia solium, Taenia saginata, Diphyllobothrium latum,* and *Echinococcus granulosus.* Their features are summarized in Table 54–1, and the medically important stages in the life cycle of these organisms are described in Table 54–2. Three cestodes of lesser importance, *Echinococcus multilocularis, Hymenolepis nana,* and *Dipylidium caninum,* are described at the end of this chapter.

TAENIA

There are two important human pathogens in the genus *Taenia: T. solium* (the pork tapeworm) and *T. saginata* (the beef tapeworm).

1. Taenia solium

Disease

The adult form of *T. solium* causes taeniasis. *T. solium* larvae cause cysticercosis.

Important Properties

T. solium can be identified by its scolex, which has **four suckers and circle of hooks,** and by its gravid proglottids, which have 5–10 primary uterine branches (Figure 54–1A and B). The eggs appear the same microscopically as those of *T. saginata* and *Echinococcus* species (Figure 54–2A).

In taeniasis, the adult tapeworm is located in the human intestine. This occurs when humans are infected by eating raw or undercooked **pork** containing the larvae, called **cysticerci.** (A cysticercus consists of a pea-sized fluid-filled bladder with an invaginated scolex.) In the small intestine, the larvae attach to the gut wall and take about 3 months to grow into adult worms measuring up to 5 m. The gravid terminal proglottids containing many eggs detach daily, are passed in the feces, and are accidentally eaten by pigs. Note that pigs are infected by the worm eggs; therefore, it is the larvae (cysticerci) that are found in the pig. A six-hooked embryo (oncosphere) emerges from each egg in the pig's intestine. The embryos burrow into a blood vessel and are carried to skeletal muscle. They develop into cysticerci in the muscle, where they remain until eaten by a human. Humans are the definitive hosts, and pigs are the intermediate hosts.

In cysticercosis, a more dangerous sequence occurs when a person **ingests the worm eggs** in food or water that has been contaminated with human feces. Note that in cysticercosis, humans are infected by eggs excreted in human feces, *not* by ingesting undercooked pork. Also pigs do not have the adult worm in their intestine, so they are not the source of the eggs that cause human cysticercosis. The eggs hatch in the small intestine, and the oncospheres burrow through the wall into a blood vessel. They can disseminate to many organs, especially the eyes and brain, where they encyst to form cysticerci.

Pathogenesis & Epidemiology

The adult tapeworm attached to the intestinal wall causes little damage. The **cysticerci,** on the other hand, can become very large, especially in the **brain,** where they manifest as a **space-occupying lesion.** Living cysticerci do not cause inflammation, but when they die they can release substances that provoke an inflammatory response. Eventually, the cysticerci calcify.

The epidemiology of taeniasis and cysticercosis is related to the access of pigs to human feces and to consumption of raw or undercooked pork. The disease oc-

Table 54–1. Features of medically important cestodes (tapeworms).

Cestode	Mode of Transmission	Intermediate Host(s)	Main Sites Affected in Human Body	Diagnosis	Treatment
Taenia solium	(A) Ingest larvae in undercooked pork	Pigs	Intestine	Proglottids in stool	Praziquantel
	(B) Ingest eggs in food or water contaminated with human feces		Brain and eyes (cysticerci)	Biopsy, CT scan	Praziquantel or surgical removal of cysticerci
Taenia saginata	Ingest larvae in undercooked beef	Cattle	Intestine	Proglottids in stool	Praziquantel
Diphyllobothrium latum	Ingest larvae in undercooked fish	Copepods and fish	Intestine	Operculated eggs in stool	Praziquantel
Echinococcus granulosus	Ingest eggs in food contaminated with dog feces	Sheep	Liver, lungs, and brain (hydatid cysts)	Biopsy, CT scan, serology	Albendazole or surgical removal of cyst

curs worldwide but is endemic in areas of Asia, South America, and eastern Europe. Most cases in the United States are imported.

Clinical Findings

Most patients with adult tapeworms are asymptomatic, but anorexia and diarrhea can occur. Some may notice proglottids in the stools. Cysticercosis in the brain causes headache, vomiting, and seizures. Cysticercosis in the eyes can appear as uveitis or retinitis, or the larvae can be visualized floating in the vitreous. Subcutaneous nodules containing cysticerci commonly occur.

Laboratory Diagnosis

Identification of *T. solium* consists of finding gravid proglottids with 5–10 primary uterine branches in the stools. In contrast, *T. saginata* proglottids have 15–20 primary uterine branches. Eggs are found in the stools less often than are proglottids. Diagnosis of cysticercosis depends on demonstrating the presence of the cyst in tissue, usually by surgical removal or computed tomography (CT) scan. Serologic tests, eg, ELISA, that detect antibodies to *T. solium* antigens are available, but they may be negative in neurocysticercosis.

Treatment

The treatment of choice for the intestinal worms is praziquantel. The treatment for cysticercosis is either praziquantel or albendazole, but surgical excision may be necessary.

Prevention

Prevention of taeniasis involves cooking pork adequately and disposing of waste properly so that pigs cannot ingest human feces. Prevention of cysticercosis consists of treatment of patients to prevent autoinfection plus observation of proper hygiene, including hand washing, to prevent contamination of food with the eggs.

2. *Taenia saginata*

Disease

T. saginata causes taeniasis. *T. saginata* larvae do not cause cysticercosis.

Important Properties

T. saginata has a scolex with four suckers but, in contrast to *T. solium*, **no hooklets.** Its gravid proglottids have 15–25 primary uterine branches, in contrast to *T. solium* proglottids, which have 5–10 (Figure 54–1C and D). The eggs are morphologically indistinguishable from those of *T. solium*.

Humans are infected by eating raw or undercooked **beef** containing larvae (cysticerci). In the small intestine, the larvae attach to the gut wall and take about 3

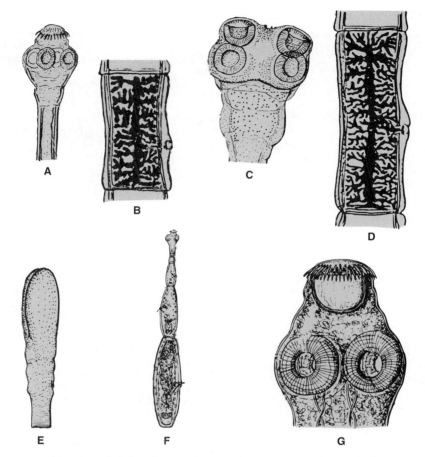

Figure 54–1. **A:** *Taenia solium* scolex with suckers and hooks. 10 ×. **B:** *Taenia solium* gravid proglottid. This has fewer uterine branches than does the proglottid of *Taenia saginata* (see panel D). 2 ×. **C:** *Taenia saginata* scolex with suckers. 10 ×. **D:** *Taenia saginata* gravid proglottid. 2 ×. **E:** *Diphyllobothrium latum* scolex with sucking grooves. 7 ×. **F:** Entire adult worm of *Echinococcus granulosus*. 7 ×. **G:** *Echinococcus granulosus* adult scolex. 70 ×.

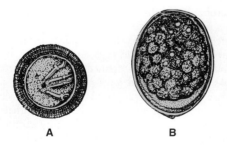

Figure 54–2. **A:** *Taenia solium* egg containing oncosphere embryo. Four hooklets are visible. *Taenia saginata* and *Echinococcus granulosus* eggs are very similar to the *Taenia solium* egg but do not have hooklets. **B:** *Diphyllobothrium latum* operculated egg. 300 ×.

months to grow into adult worms measuring up to 10 m. The gravid proglottids detach, are passed in the feces, and are eaten by cattle. The embryos (**oncospheres**) emerge from the eggs in the cow's intestine and burrow into a blood vessel, where they are carried to skeletal muscle. In the muscle, they develop into cysticerci. The cycle is completed when the cysticerci are ingested. Humans are the definitive hosts and cattle the intermediate hosts. Unlike *T. solium*, *T. saginata* **does not cause cysticercosis** in humans.

Pathogenesis & Epidemiology

Little damage results from the presence of the adult worm in the small intestine. The epidemiology of taeniasis caused by *T. saginata* is related to the access of cattle to human feces and to the consumption of raw or

Table 54–2. Medically important stages in life cycle of cestodes (tapeworms).

Organism	Insect Vector	Stage That Infects Humans	Stage(s) in Humans Most Associated with Disease	Important Stage(s) Outside of Humans
Taenia solium	None	1. Larvae in undercooked pork	Adult tapeworm in intestine	Larvae in muscle of pig
		2. Eggs in food or water contaminated with human feces	Cysticercus, especially in brain	None
Taenia saginata	None	Larvae in undercooked beef	Adult tapeworm in intestine	Larvae in muscle of pig
Diphyllobothrium latum	None	Larvae in undercooked fish	Adult tapeworm in intestine can cause vitamin B_{12} deficiency	Larvae in muscle of freshwater fish
Echinococcus granulosus	None	Eggs in food or water contaminated with dog feces	Hydatid cysts, especially in liver and lung	Adult tapeworm in dog intestine produces eggs

undercooked beef. The disease occurs worldwide but is endemic in Africa, South America, and eastern Europe. In the United States, most cases are imported.

Clinical Findings

Most patients with adult tapeworms are asymptomatic, but malaise and mild cramps can occur. In some, proglottids appear in the stools and may even protrude from the anus.

Laboratory Diagnosis

Identification of *T. saginata* consists of finding gravid proglottids with 15–20 uterine branches in the stools. Eggs are found in the stools less often than are the proglottids.

Treatment

The treatment of choice is praziquantel.

Prevention

Prevention involves cooking beef adequately and disposing of waste properly so that cattle cannot consume human feces.

DIPHYLLOBOTHRIUM

Disease

Diphyllobothrium latum, the fish tapeworm, causes diphyllobothriasis.

Important Properties

In contrast to the other cestodes, which have suckers, the scolex of *D. latum* has two elongated **sucking grooves** by which the worm attaches to the intestinal wall (Figure 54–1E). The scolex has no hooks, unlike *T. solium* and *Echinococcus*. The proglottids are wider than they are long, and the gravid uterus is in the form of a rosette. Unlike other tapeworm eggs, which are round, *D. latum* eggs are oval and have a lidlike opening (**operculum**) at one end (Figure 54–2B). *D. latum* is the longest of the tapeworms, measuring up to 13 m.

Humans are infected by ingesting raw or undercooked **fish** containing larvae (called plerocercoid or sparganum larvae). In the small intestine, the larvae attach to the gut wall and develop into adult worms. Gravid proglottids release fertilized eggs through a genital pore, and the eggs are then passed in the stools. The immature eggs must be deposited in fresh water for the life cycle to continue. The embryos emerge from the eggs and are eaten by tiny copepod crustacea (first intermediate hosts). There, the embryos differentiate and form procercoid larvae in the body cavity. When the copepod is eaten by freshwater fish, eg, pike, trout, and perch, the larvae differentiate into plerocercoids in the muscle of the fish (second intermediate host). The cycle is completed when raw or undercooked fish is eaten by humans (definitive hosts).

Pathogenesis & Epidemiology

Infection by *D. latum* causes little damage in the small intestine. In some individuals, megaloblastic anemia occurs as a result of vitamin B_{12} deficiency caused by preferential uptake of the vitamin by the worm.

The epidemiology of *D. latum* infection is related to the ingestion of raw or inadequately cooked fish and to contamination of bodies of fresh water with human feces. The disease is found worldwide but is endemic in areas where eating raw fish is the custom, such as Scandinavia, northern Russia, Japan, Canada, and certain north-central states of the United States.

Clinical Findings

Most patients are asymptomatic, but abdominal discomfort and diarrhea can occur.

Laboratory Diagnosis

Diagnosis depends on finding the typical eggs, ie, oval, yellow-brown eggs with an operculum at one end, in the stools. There is no serologic test.

Treatment

The treatment of choice is praziquantel.

Prevention

Prevention involves adequate cooking of fish and proper disposal of human feces.

ECHINOCOCCUS

Disease

The larva of *Echinococcus granulosus* (dog tapeworm) causes unilocular hydatid cyst disease. Multilocular hydatid disease is caused by *E. multilocularis*, which is a minor pathogen and is discussed below.

Important Properties

E. granulosus is composed of a scolex and only three proglottids, making it **one of the smallest tapeworms** (Figure 54–1F and G). The scolex has a circle of hooks and four suckers similar to *T. solium*. **Dogs** are the most important definitive hosts. The intermediate hosts are usually **sheep**. Humans are almost always dead-end intermediate hosts.

In the typical life cycle, worms in the dog's intestine liberate thousands of eggs, which are ingested by sheep (or humans). The oncosphere embryos emerge in the small intestine and migrate primarily to the liver but also to the lungs, bones, and brain. The embryos develop into large fluid-filled **hydatid cysts**, the inner germinal layer of which generates many protoscoleces within "brood capsules." The life cycle is completed when the entrails (eg, liver containing hydatid cysts) of slaughtered sheep are eaten by dogs.

Pathogenesis & Epidemiology

E. granulosus usually forms one large fluid-filled cyst (unilocular) that contains thousands of individual scoleces as well as many daughter cysts within the large cyst. Individual scoleces lying at the bottom of the large cyst are called "hydatid sand." The cyst acts as a space-occupying lesion, putting pressure on adjacent tissue. The outer layer of the cyst is thick, fibrous tissue produced by the host. The cyst fluid contains parasite antigens, which can sensitize the host. Later, if the cyst ruptures spontaneously or during trauma or surgical removal, life-threatening **anaphylaxis** can occur. Rupture of a cyst can also spread protoscoleces widely.

The disease is found primarily in shepherds living in the Mediterranean region, the Middle East, and Australia. In the United States, the western states report the largest number of cases.

Clinical Findings

Many individuals with hydatid cysts are asymptomatic, but **liver cysts** may cause hepatic dysfunction. Cysts in the lungs can erode into a bronchus, causing bloody sputum, and cerebral cysts can cause headache and focal neurologic signs. Rupture of the cyst can cause fatal anaphylactic shock.

Laboratory Diagnosis

Diagnosis is based either on microscopic examination demonstrating the presence of brood capsules containing multiple protoscoleces or on serologic tests, eg, the indirect hemagglutination test.

Treatment

Treatment involves albendazole with or without surgical removal of the cyst. Extreme care must be exercised to prevent release of the protoscoleces during surgery. A protoscolicidal agent, eg, hypertonic saline, should be injected into the cyst to kill the organisms and prevent accidental dissemination.

Prevention

Prevention of human disease involves not feeding the entrails of slaughtered sheep to dogs.

CESTODES OF MINOR IMPORTANCE

Echinococcus multilocularis

Many of the features of this organism are the same as those of *E. granulosus*, but the definitive hosts are mainly foxes and the intermediate hosts are various rodents. Humans are infected by accidental ingestion of food contaminated with fox feces. The disease occurs primarily in hunters and trappers and is endemic in northern Europe, Siberia, and the western provinces of Canada. In the United States, it occurs in North and South Dakota, Minnesota, and Alaska.

Within the human liver, the larvae form multiloculated cysts with few protoscoleces. No outer fibrous capsule forms, so the cysts continue to proliferate, producing a honeycomb effect of hundreds of small vesicles. The clinical picture usually involves jaundice and weight loss. The prognosis is poor. Albendazole treatment may be successful in some cases. Surgical removal may be feasible.

Hymenolepis nana

H. nana (dwarf tapeworm) is the **most frequently** found tapeworm in the United States. It is only 3–5 cm long and is different from other tapeworms because its eggs are **directly infectious** for humans; ie, ingested eggs can develop into adult worms without an intermediate host. Within the duodenum, the eggs hatch and differentiate into cysticercoid larvae and then into adult worms. Gravid proglottids detach, disintegrate, and release fertilized eggs. The eggs either pass in the stool or can reinfect the small intestine (autoinfection). In contrast to infection by other tapeworms, where only one adult worm is present, many *H. nana* worms (sometimes hundreds) are found.

Infection causes little damage, and most patients are asymptomatic. The organism is found worldwide, commonly in the tropics. In the United States, it is most prevalent in the southeastern states, usually in children. Diagnosis is based on finding eggs in stools. The char-

acteristic feature of *H. nana* eggs is the 8–10 polar filaments lying between the membrane of the six-hooked larva and the outer shell. The treatment is praziquantel. Prevention consists of good personal hygiene and avoidance of fecal contamination of food and water.

Dipylidium caninum

D. caninum is the most common tapeworm of dogs and cats. It occasionally infects humans, usually young children, while playing with their pets. Human infection occurs when dog or cat fleas carrying cysticerci are ingested. The cysticerci develop into adult tapeworms in the small intestine. Most human infections are asymptomatic, but diarrhea and pruritus ani can occur. The diagnosis in animals and humans is made by observing the typical "barrel-shaped" proglottids in the stool or diapers. Niclosamide is the drug of choice.

SUMMARIES OF ORGANISMS

Brief summaries of the organisms described in this chapter begin on page 509. Please consult these summaries for a rapid review of the essential material.

PRACTICE QUESTIONS: USMLE & COURSE EXAMINATIONS

Questions on the topics discussed in this chapter can be found in the Parasitology section of Part XI: USMLE (National Board) Practice Questions starting on page 559. Also see Part XII: USMLE (National Board) Practice Examination starting on page 583.

Trematodes

55

Trematoda (flukes) and Cestoda (tapeworms) are the two large classes of parasites in the phylum Platyhelminthes. The most important trematodes are *Schistosoma* species (blood flukes), *Clonorchis sinensis* (liver fluke), and *Paragonimus westermani* (lung fluke). Schistosomes have by far the greatest impact in terms of the number of people infected, morbidity, and mortality. Features of the medically important trematodes are summarized in Table 55–1, and the medically important stages in the life cycle of these organisms are described in Table 55–2. Three trematodes of lesser importance, *Fasciola hepatica, Fasciolopsis buski,* and *Heterophyes heterophyes,* are described at the end of this chapter.

The life cycle of the medically important trematodes involves a sexual cycle in humans and asexual reproduction in **freshwater snails** (intermediate hosts). Transmission to humans takes place either via penetration of the skin by the **free-swimming cercariae** of the schistosomes or via **ingestion of cysts** in undercooked (raw) fish or crabs in *Clonorchis* and *Paragonimus* infection, respectively.

Trematodes that cause human disease are not endemic in the United States. However, immigrants from tropical areas, especially Southeast Asia, are frequently infected.

SCHISTOSOMA

Disease

Schistosoma causes schistosomiasis. *Schistosoma mansoni* and *Schistosoma japonicum* affect the gastrointestinal tract,[1] whereas *Schistosoma haematobium* affects the urinary tract.

Important Properties

In contrast to the other trematodes, which are hermaphrodites, adult schistosomes exist as **separate sexes** but live attached to each other. The female resides in a groove in the male, the gynecophoric canal ("schist"), where he continuously fertilizes her eggs (Figure

55–1A). The three species can be distinguished by the appearance of their eggs in the microscope: *S. mansoni* eggs have a **prominent lateral spine**, whereas *S. japonicum* eggs have a very small lateral spine and *S. haematobium* eggs have a terminal spine (Figure 55–2A and B). *S. mansoni* and *S. japonicum* adults live in the **mesenteric veins**, whereas *S. haematobium* lives in the veins draining the urinary bladder. Schistosomes are therefore known as **blood flukes.**

Humans are infected when the free-swimming, fork-tailed **cercariae** penetrate the skin (Figure 55–1D). They differentiate to larvae (schistosomula), enter the blood, and are carried via the veins into the arterial circulation. Those that enter the superior mesenteric artery pass into the portal circulation and reach the liver, where they mature into adult flukes. *S. mansoni* and *S. japonicum* adults migrate against the portal flow to reside in the mesenteric venules. *S. haematobium* adults reach the bladder veins through the venous plexus between the rectum and the bladder.

In their definitive venous site, the female lays fertilized eggs, which penetrate the vascular endothelium and enter the gut or bladder lumen, respectively. The eggs are excreted in the stools or urine and must enter fresh water to hatch. Once hatched, the ciliated larvae (miracidia) penetrate **snails** and undergo further development and multiplication to produce many cercariae. (The three schistosomes use different species of snails as intermediate hosts.) Cercariae leave the snails, enter fresh water, and complete the cycle by penetrating human skin.

Pathogenesis & Epidemiology

Most of the pathologic findings are caused by the presence of eggs in the liver, spleen, or wall of the gut or bladder. Eggs in the liver induce granulomas, which lead to fibrosis, hepatomegaly, and portal hypertension. The granulomas are formed in response to antigens secreted by the eggs. Hepatocytes are usually undamaged, and liver function tests remain normal. Portal hypertension leads to **splenomegaly.**

S. mansoni eggs damage the wall of the distal colon (inferior mesenteric venules), whereas *S. japonicum* eggs damage the walls of both the small and large intestines

---

[1] As does *Schistosoma mekongi.*

Table 55–1. Features of medically important trematodes (flukes).

Trematode	Mode of Transmission	Main Sites Affected	Intermediate Host(s)	Diagnostic Features of Eggs	Endemic Area(s)	Treatment
Schistosoma mansoni	Penetrate skin	Veins of colon	Snail	Large lateral spine	Africa, Latin America (Caribbean)	Praziquantel
Schistosoma japonicum	Penetrate skin	Veins of small intestine, liver	Snail	Small lateral spine	Asia	Praziquantel
Schistosoma haematobium	Penetrate skin	Veins of urinary bladder	Snail	Large terminal spine	Africa, Middle East	Praziquantel
Clonorchis sinensis	Ingested with raw fish	Liver	Snail and fish	Operculated	Asia	Praziquantel
Paragonimus westermani	Ingested with raw crab	Lung	Snail and crab	Operculated	Asia, India	Praziquantel

(superior and inferior mesenteric venules). The damage is due both to digestion of tissue by proteolytic enzymes produced by the egg and to the host inflammatory response that forms granulomas in the venules. The eggs of *S. haematobium* in the wall of the bladder induce granulomas and fibrosis, which can lead to **carcinoma of the bladder.**

Schistosomes have evolved a remarkable process for **evading the host defenses.** There is evidence that their surface becomes coated with host antigens, thereby limiting the ability of the immune system to recognize them as foreign.

The epidemiology of schistosomiasis depends on the presence of the specific freshwater snails that serve as intermediate hosts. *S. mansoni* is found in Africa and Latin America (including Puerto Rico), whereas *S. haematobium* is found in Africa and the Middle East. *S. japonicum* is found only in Asia and is the only one for which domestic animals, eg, water buffalo and pigs, act as important reservoirs. More than 150 million people in the tropical areas of Africa, Asia, and Latin America are affected.

Clinical Findings

Most patients are asymptomatic, but chronic infections may become symptomatic. The acute stage, which begins shortly after cercarial penetration, consists of itching and dermatitis followed 2–3 weeks later by fever, chills, diarrhea, lymphadenopathy, and hepatosplenomegaly. Eosinophilia is seen in response to the migrating larvae. This stage usually resolves spontaneously.

Table 55–2. Medically important stages in life cycle of trematodes (flukes).

Organism	Insect Vector	Stage That Infects Humans	Stage(s) in Humans Most Associated with Disease	Important Stage(s) Outside of Humans
Schistosoma mansoni, S. hematobium, S. japonicum	None	Cercariae penetrate skin	Adult flukes living in mesenteric or bladder veins lay eggs that cause granulomas	Miracidium (ciliated larvae) infect snails→ cercariae infect humans
Clonorchis	None	Larvae in undercooked fish	Adult flukes live in biliary ducts	Eggs ingested by snails→ cercariae infect fish
Paragonimus	None	Larvae in undercooked crab	Adult flukes live in lung	Eggs ingested by snails→ cercariae infect crab

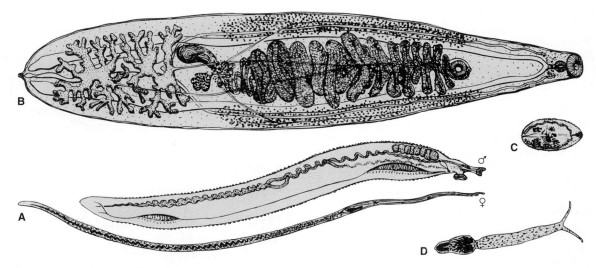

Figure 55–1. **A:** Male and female *Schistosoma mansoni* adults. The female lives in the male's schist, shown as a ventral opening. 6 ×. **B:** *Clonorchis sinensis* adult. 6 ×. **C:** *Paragonimus westermani* adult. 0.6 ×. **D:** *Schistosoma mansoni* cercaria. 300 ×.

The chronic stage can cause significant morbidity and mortality. In patients with *S. mansoni* or *S. japonicum* infection, gastrointestinal hemorrhage, hepatomegaly, and massive splenomegaly can develop. The most common cause of death is exsanguination from ruptured esophageal varices. Patients infected with *S. haematobium* have hematuria as their chief early complaint. Superimposed bacterial urinary tract infections occur frequently.

"Swimmer's itch," which consists of pruritic papules, is a frequent problem in many lakes in the United States. The papules are an immunologic reac-

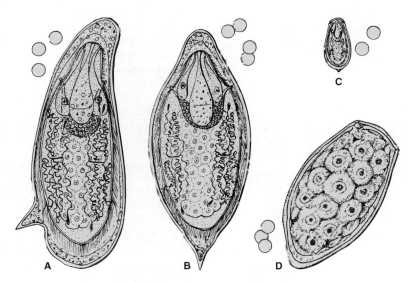

Figure 55–2. **A:** *Schistosoma mansoni* ovum with lateral spine. **B:** *Schistosoma haematobium* ovum with terminal spine. **C:** *Clonorchis sinensis* ovum with operculum. **D:** *Paragonimus westermani* ovum with operculum. 300 ×. (Circles represent red blood cells.)

tion to the presence in the skin of the cercariae of nonhuman schistosomes. These nonhuman schistosomes are incapable of replicating in humans and do not cause disseminated disease.

Laboratory Diagnosis

Diagnosis depends on finding the characteristic ova in the feces or urine. The large lateral spine of *S. mansoni* and the rudimentary spine of *S. japonicum* are typical, as is the large terminal spine of *S. haematobium* (Figure 55–2A and B). Serologic tests are not useful. Moderate eosinophilia occurs.

Treatment

Praziquantel is the treatment of choice for all three species.

Prevention

Prevention involves proper disposal of human waste and eradication of the snail host when possible. Swimming in areas of endemic infection should be avoided.

CLONORCHIS

Disease

Clonorchis sinensis causes clonorchiasis (Asian liver fluke infection).

Important Properties

Humans are infected by eating raw or undercooked **fish** containing the encysted larvae (metacercariae). After excystation in the duodenum, immature flukes enter the **biliary ducts** and differentiate into adults (Figure 55–1B). The hermaphroditic adults produce eggs, which are excreted in the feces (Figure 55–2C). Upon reaching fresh water, the eggs are ingested by snails, which are the first intermediate hosts. The eggs hatch within the gut and differentiate first into larvae (rediae) and then into many free-swimming cercariae. Cercariae encyst under the scales of certain freshwater fish (second intermediate hosts), which are then eaten by humans.

Pathogenesis & Epidemiology

In some infections, the inflammatory response can cause hyperplasia and fibrosis of the biliary tract, but often there are no lesions. Clonorchiasis is endemic in China, Japan, Korea, and Indochina, where it affects about 20 million people. It is seen in the United States among immigrants from these areas.

Clinical Findings

Most infections are asymptomatic. In patients with a heavy worm burden, upper abdominal pain, anorexia, hepatomegaly, and eosinophilia can occur.

Laboratory Diagnosis

Diagnosis is made by finding the typical small, brownish, operculated eggs in the stool (Figure 55–2C). Serologic tests are not useful.

Treatment

Praziquantel is an effective drug.

Prevention

Prevention centers on adequate cooking of fish and proper disposal of human waste.

PARAGONIMUS

Disease

Paragonimus westermani, the lung fluke, causes paragonimiasis.

Important Properties

Humans are infected by eating raw or undercooked **crab meat** (or crayfish) containing the encysted larvae (metacercariae). After excystation in the small intestine, immature flukes penetrate the intestinal wall and migrate through the diaphragm into the **lung** parenchyma. They differentiate into hermaphroditic adults (Figure 55–1C) and produce eggs that enter the bronchioles and are coughed up or swallowed (Figure 55–2D). Eggs in either sputum or feces that reach fresh water hatch into miracidia, which enter snails (first intermediate hosts). There, they differentiate first into larvae (rediae) and then into many free-swimming cercariae. The cercariae infect and encyst in freshwater crabs (second intermediate hosts). The cycle is completed when undercooked infected crabs are eaten by humans.

Pathogenesis & Epidemiology

Within the lung, the worms exist in a fibrous capsule that communicates with a bronchiole. Secondary bacterial infection frequently occurs, resulting in bloody sputum. Paragonimiasis is endemic in Asia and India. In the United States, it occurs in immigrants from these areas.

Clinical Findings

The main symptom is a chronic cough with bloody sputum. Dyspnea, pleuritic chest pain, and recurrent attacks of bacterial pneumonia occur. The disease can resemble tuberculosis.

Laboratory Diagnosis

Diagnosis is made by finding the typical operculated eggs in sputum or feces (Figure 55–2D). Serologic tests are not useful.

Treatment

Praziquantel is the treatment of choice.

Prevention

Cooking crabs properly is the best method of prevention.

TREMATODES OF MINOR IMPORTANCE

Fasciola

Fasciola hepatica, the sheep liver fluke, causes disease primarily in sheep and other domestic animals in Latin America, Africa, Europe, and China. Humans are infected by **eating watercress** (or other aquatic plants) contaminated by larvae (metacercariae) that excyst in the duodenum, penetrate the gut wall, and reach the liver, where they mature into adults. Hermaphroditic adults in the bile ducts produce eggs, which are excreted in the feces. The eggs hatch in fresh water, and miracidia enter the snails. Miracidia develop into cercariae, which then encyst on aquatic vegetation. Sheep and humans eat the plants, thus completing the life cycle.

Symptoms are due primarily to the presence of the adult worm in the biliary tract. In early infection, right-upper-quadrant pain, fever, and hepatomegaly can occur, but most infections are asymptomatic. Months or years later, obstructive jaundice can occur. Halzoun is a painful pharyngitis caused by the presence of adult flukes on the posterior pharyngeal wall. The adult flukes are acquired by eating raw sheep liver.

Diagnosis is made by identification of eggs in the feces. There is no serologic test. Praziquantel and bithionol are effective drugs. Adult flukes in the pharynx and larynx can be removed surgically. Prevention involves not eating wild aquatic vegetables or raw sheep liver.

Fasciolopsis

Fasciolopsis buski is an intestinal parasite of humans and pigs that is endemic to Asia and India. Humans are in-fected by **eating aquatic vegetation** that carries the cysts. After excysting in the small intestine, the parasites attach to the mucosa and differentiate into adults. Eggs are passed in the feces; on reaching fresh water, they differentiate into miracidia. The ciliated miracidia penetrate snails and, after several stages, develop into cercariae that encyst on aquatic vegetation. The cycle is completed when plants carrying the cysts are eaten.

Pathologic findings are due to damage of the intestinal mucosa by the adult fluke. Most infections are asymptomatic, but ulceration, abscess formation, and hemorrhage can occur. Diagnosis is based on finding typical eggs in the feces. Praziquantel is the treatment of choice. Prevention consists of proper disposal of human sewage.

Heterophyes

Heterophyes heterophyes is an intestinal parasite of people living in Africa, the Middle East, and Asia who are infected by **eating raw fish** containing cysts. Larvae excyst in the small intestine, attach to the mucosa, and develop into adults. Eggs are passed in the feces and, on reaching brackish water, are ingested by snails. After several developmental stages, cercariae are produced that encyst under the scales of certain fish. The cycle is completed when fish carrying the infectious cysts are eaten.

Pathologic findings are due to inflammation of the intestinal epithelium as a result of the presence of the adult flukes. Most infections are asymptomatic, but abdominal pain and nonbloody diarrhea can occur. Diagnosis is based on finding the typical eggs in the feces. Praziquantel is the treatment of choice. Prevention consists of proper disposal of human sewage.

SUMMARIES OF ORGANISMS

Brief summaries of the organisms described in this chapter begin on page 510. Please consult these summaries for a rapid review of the essential material.

PRACTICE QUESTIONS: USMLE & COURSE EXAMINATIONS

Questions on the topics discussed in this chapter can be found in the Parasitology section of Part XI: USMLE (National Board) Practice Questions starting on page 559. Also see Part XII: USMLE (National Board) Practice Examination starting on page 583.

Nematodes

Nematodes (also known as Nemathelminthes) are roundworms with a cylindrical body and a complete digestive tract, including a mouth and an anus. The body is covered with a noncellular, highly resistant coating called a cuticle. Nematodes have separate sexes; the female is usually larger than the male. The male typically has a coiled tail.

The medically important nematodes can be divided into two categories according to their primary location in the body, namely, **intestinal** and **tissue** nematodes.

(1) The intestinal nematodes include *Enterobius* (pinworm), *Trichuris* (whipworm), *Ascaris* (giant roundworm), *Necator* and *Ancylostoma* (the two hookworms), *Strongyloides* (small roundworm), and *Trichinella. Enterobius, Trichuris,* and *Ascaris* are transmitted by ingestion of eggs; the others are transmitted as larvae. There are two larval forms: the first- and second-stage (**rhabditiform**) larvae are noninfectious, feeding forms; the third-stage (**filariform**) larvae are the infectious, nonfeeding forms. As adults, these nematodes live within the human body, except for *Strongyloides,* which can also exist in the soil.

(2) The important tissue nematodes *Wuchereria, Onchocerca,* and *Loa* are called the "filarial worms," because they produce motile embryos called **microfilariae** in blood and tissue fluids. These organisms are transmitted from person to person by bloodsucking mosquitoes or flies. A fourth species is the guinea worm, *Dracunculus,* whose larvae inhabit tiny crustaceans (copepods) and are ingested in drinking water.

The nematodes described above cause disease as a result of the presence of adult worms within the body. In addition, several species cannot mature to adults in human tissue, but their larvae can cause disease. The most serious of these diseases is visceral larva migrans, caused primarily by the larvae of the dog ascarid, *Toxocara canis.* Cutaneous larva migrans, caused mainly by the larvae of the dog and cat hookworm, *Ancylostoma caninum,* is less serious. A third disease, anisakiasis, is caused by the ingestion of *Anisakis* larvae in raw seafood.

In infections caused by certain nematodes that migrate through tissue, eg, *Strongyloides, Trichinella, Ascaris,* and the two hookworms *Ancylostoma* and *Necator,* a striking increase in the number of eosinophils (**eosinophilia**) occurs. Eosinophils do not ingest the organisms; rather, they attach to the surface of the parasite via IgE and secrete cytotoxic enzymes contained within their eosinophilic granules. Host defenses against helminths are stimulated by interleukins synthesized by the Th-2 subset of helper T cells; eg, the production of IgE is increased by interleukin-4, and the number of eosinophils is increased by interleukin-5 (see Chapter 58). Cysteine proteases produced by the worms to facilitate their migration through tissue are the stimuli for IL-5 production.

Features of the medically important nematodes are summarized in Table 56–1. The medically important stages in the life cycle of the intestinal nematodes are described in Table 56–2 and those of the tissue nematodes are described in Table 56–3.

■ INTESTINAL NEMATODES

ENTEROBIUS

Disease

Enterobius vermicularis causes pinworm infection (enterobiasis).

Important Properties

The life cycle is **confined to humans.** The infection is acquired by ingesting the worm eggs. The eggs hatch in the small intestine, where the larvae differentiate into adults and migrate to the colon. The adult male and female worms live in the colon, where mating occurs (Figure 56–1A). At night, the female migrates from the anus and releases thousands of fertilized eggs on the perianal skin and into the environment. Within 6 hours, the eggs develop into larvae and become infectious. Reinfection can occur if they are carried to the mouth by fingers after scratching the itching skin.

Pathogenesis & Clinical Findings

Perianal pruritus is the most prominent symptom. Pruritus is thought to be an allergic reaction to the

Table 56-1. Features of medically important nematodes.

Primary Location	Species	Common Name or Disease	Mode of Transmission	Endemic Areas	Diagnosis	Treatment
Intestines	Enterobius	Pinworm	Ingestion of eggs	Worldwide	Eggs on skin	Mebendazole or pyrantel pamoate
	Trichuris	Whipworm	Ingestion of eggs	Worldwide, especially tropics	Eggs in stools	Mebendazole
	Ascaris	Ascariasis	Ingestion of eggs	Worldwide, especially tropics	Eggs in stools	Mebendazole or pyrantel pamoate
	Ancylostoma and Necator	Hookworm	Larval penetration of skin	Worldwide, especially tropics (Ancylostoma), United States (Necator)	Eggs in stools	Mebendazole or pyrantel pamoate
	Strongyloides	Strongyloidiasis	Larval penetration of skin, also autoinfection	Tropics primarily	Larvae in stools	Ivermectin
	Trichinella	Trichinosis	Larvae in undercooked meat	Worldwide	Larvae encysted in muscle; serology	Thiabendazole against adult worm
	Anisakis	Anisakiasis	Larvae in undercooked seafood	Japan, United States, Netherlands	Clinical	No drug available
Tissue	Wuchereria	Filariasis	Mosquito bite	Tropics primarily	Blood smear	Diethylcarbamazine
	Onchocerca	Onchocerciasis (river blindness)	Blackfly bite	Africa, Central America	Skin biopsy	Ivermectin
	Loa	Loiasis	Deer fly bite	Tropical Africa	Blood smear	Diethylcarbamazine
	Dracunculus	Guinea worm	Ingestion of copepods in water	Tropical Africa and Asia	Clinical	Thiabendazole prior to extracting worm
	Toxocara larvae	Visceral larva migrans	Ingestion of eggs	Worldwide	Clinical and serologic	Albendazole or mebendazole
	Ancylostoma larvae	Cutaneous larva migrans	Penetration of skin	Worldwide	Clinical	Thiabendazole

Table 56–2. Medically important stages in life cycle of intestinal nematodes (roundworms).

Organism	Insect Vector	Stage That Infects Humans	Stage(s) in Humans Most Associated with Disease	Important Stage(s) Outside of Humans
Enterobius	None	Eggs	Female worm migrates out anus and lays eggs on perianal skin, causing itching	None
Trichuris	None	Eggs	Worms in colon may cause rectal prolapse	Eggs survive in environment
Ascaris	None	Eggs	Larvae migrate to lung, causing pneumonia	Eggs survive in environment
Ancylostoma and Necator	None	Filariform larvae enter skin	Worms in colon cause blood loss (anemia)	Egg → rhabditiform larva → filariform larvae
Strongyloides	None	Filariform larvae enter skin	Worms disseminate to various tissues in immunocompromised (autoinfection)	Egg → rhabditiform larva → filariform larvae; also "free-living" cycle in soil
Trichinella	None	Larvae in meat ingested	Larvae encyst in muscle causing myalgia	Larvae in muscle of pig, bear, and other animals
Anisakis	None	Larvae in fish ingested	Larvae in submucosa of GI tract	Larvae in muscle of fish

Table 56–3. Medically important stages in life cycle of tissue nematodes (roundworms).

Organism	Insect Vector	Stage That Infects Humans	Stage(s) in Humans Most Associated with Disease	Important Stage(s) Outside of Humans
Wuchereria	Mosquito	Larvae	Adult worms in lymphatics (elephantiasis)	Mosquito ingests microfilariae in human blood → larvae
Onchocerca	Blackfly	Larvae	Adult worms in skin; microfilariae in eye (blindness)	Blackfly ingests microfilariae in human skin → larvae
Loa	Deer fly (mango fly)	Larvae	Adult worms in tissue (skin, conjunctivae)	Deer fly ingests microfilariae → larvae
Dracunculus	None	Larvae in copepods are swallowed in drinking water	Female worms cause skin blister; see head of worm	Copepods ingest larvae
Toxocara canis	None	Eggs in dog feces	Larvae in internal organs	Adult worms in dog intestine→ eggs
Ancylostoma caninum	None	Filariform larvae penetrate skin	Larvae in subcutaneous tissue	Adult worms in dog intestine→ eggs → larvae

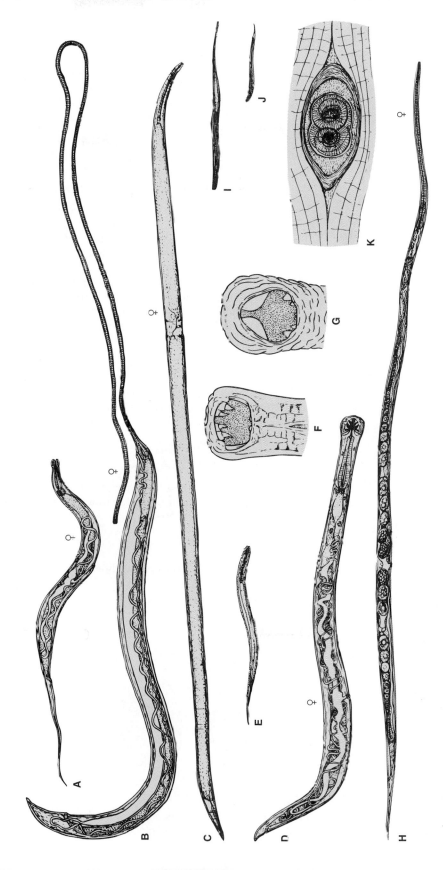

Figure 56–1. **A:** *Enterobius vermicularis* female adult. 6 ×. **B:** *Trichuris trichiura* female adult. Note the thin anterior (whiplike) end. 6 ×. **C:** *Ascaris lumbricoides* female adult. 0.6 ×. **D:** *Ancylostoma duodenale* female adult. 6 ×. **E:** *Ancylostoma duodenale* filariform larva. 60 ×. **F:** *Ancylostoma duodenale* head with teeth. 25 ×. **G:** *Necator americanus* head with cutting plates. 25 ×. **H:** *Strongyloides stercoralis* female adult. 60 ×. **I:** *Strongyloides stercoralis* filariform larva. 60 ×. **J:** *Strongyloides stercoralis* rhabditiform larva. 60 ×. **K:** *Trichinella spiralis* cyst containing two larvae in muscle. 60 ×.

presence of either the adult female or the eggs. Scratching predisposes to secondary bacterial infection.

Epidemiology

Enterobius is found worldwide and is the **most common** helminth in the United States. Children younger than 12 years of age are the most commonly affected group.

Laboratory Diagnosis

The eggs are recovered from perianal skin by using the **Scotch tape** technique and can be observed microscopically (Figure 56–2A). Unlike those of other intestinal nematodes, these **eggs are not found in the stools.** The small, whitish adult worms can be found in the stools or near the anus of diapered children. No serologic tests are available.

Treatment

Either mebendazole or pyrantel pamoate is effective. They kill the adult worms in the colon but not the eggs, so that retreatment in 2 weeks is suggested. Reinfection is very common.

Prevention

There are no means of prevention.

TRICHURIS

Disease

Trichuris trichiura causes whipworm infection (trichuriasis).

Important Properties

Humans are **infected by** ingesting worm eggs in food or water contaminated with human feces. The eggs hatch in the small intestine, where the larvae differentiate into immature adults. These forms migrate to the colon, where they mature, mate, and produce thousands of fertilized eggs daily, which are passed in the feces. Eggs deposited in warm, moist soil form embryos. When the embryonated eggs are ingested, the cycle is completed. Figure 56–1B illustrates the characteristic "whiplike" appearance of the adult worm.

Pathogenesis & Clinical Findings

Although adult *Trichuris* worms burrow their hairlike anterior ends into the intestinal mucosa, they do not cause significant anemia, unlike the hookworms. *Trichuris* may cause diarrhea, but most infections are asymptomatic.

Trichuris may also cause **rectal prolapse** in children with heavy infection. Prolapse results from increased peristalsis that occurs in an effort to expel the worms. The whitish worms may be seen on the prolapsed mucosa.

Epidemiology

Whipworm infection occurs worldwide, especially in the tropics; more than 500 million people are affected. In the United States, it occurs mainly in the southern states.

Laboratory Diagnosis

Diagnosis is based on finding the typical eggs, ie, barrel-shaped (lemon-shaped) with a plug at each end, in the stool (Figure 56–2B).

Treatment

Mebendazole is the drug of choice.

Prevention

Proper disposal of feces prevents transmission.

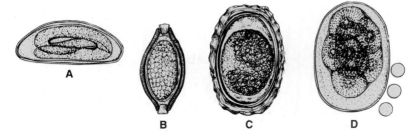

Figure 56–2. **A:** *Enterobius vermicularis* ovum. **B:** *Trichuris trichiura* ovum. **C:** *Ascaris lumbricoides* ovum. **D:** *Ancylostoma duodenale* or *Necator americanus* ovum. 300 ×. (Circles represent red blood cells.)

ASCARIS

Disease

Ascaris lumbricoides causes ascariasis.

Important Properties

Humans are **infected by** ingesting worm eggs in food or water contaminated with human feces. The eggs hatch in the small intestine, and the larvae migrate through the gut wall into the bloodstream and then to the lungs. They enter the alveoli, pass up the bronchi and trachea, and are swallowed. Within the small intestine, they become adults (Figure 56–1C). They live in the lumen, do not attach to the wall, and derive their sustenance from ingested food. The adults are the **largest intestinal nematodes,** often growing to 25 cm or more. Thousands of eggs are laid daily, are passed in the feces, and form embryos in warm, moist soil (Figure 56–2C). Ingestion of the embryonated eggs completes the cycle.

Pathogenesis & Clinical Findings

The major damage occurs during larval migration rather than from the presence of the adult worm in the intestine. The principal sites of tissue reaction are the **lungs,** where inflammation with an **eosinophilic exudate** occurs in response to larval antigens. Because the adults derive their nourishment from ingested food, a heavy worm burden may contribute to malnutrition, especially in children in developing countries.

Most infections are asymptomatic. *Ascaris* **pneumonia** with fever, cough, and eosinophilia can occur with a heavy larval burden. Abdominal pain and even obstruction can result from the presence of adult worms in the intestine.

Epidemiology

Ascaris infection is very common, especially in the tropics; hundreds of millions of people are infected. In the United States, most cases occur in the southern states.

Laboratory Diagnosis

Diagnosis is usually made microscopically by detecting eggs in the stools. The egg is oval with an irregular surface (Figure 56–2C). Occasionally, the patient sees adult worms in the stools.

Treatment

Both mebendazole and pyrantel pamoate are effective.

Prevention

Proper disposal of feces can prevent ascariasis.

ANCYLOSTOMA & NECATOR

Disease

Ancylostoma duodenale (Old World hookworm) and *Necator americanus* (New World hookworm) cause hookworm infection.

Important Properties

Humans are infected when **filariform larvae in moist soil penetrate the skin,** usually of the feet or legs (Figure 56–1E). They are carried by the blood to the lungs, migrate into the alveoli and up the bronchi and trachea, and then are swallowed. They develop into adults in the small intestine, attaching to the wall with either cutting plates (*Necator*) or teeth (*Ancylostoma*) (Figure 56–1D, F, and G). They feed on blood from the capillaries of the intestinal villi. Thousands of eggs per day are passed in the feces (Figure 56–2D). Eggs develop first into noninfectious, feeding (rhabditiform) larvae and then into third-stage, infectious, nonfeeding (filariform) larvae (Figure 56–1E), which penetrate the skin to complete the cycle.

Pathogenesis & Clinical Findings

The major damage is due to the **loss of blood** at the site of attachment in the small intestine. Up to 0.1–0.3 mL per worm can be lost per day. Blood is consumed by the worm and oozes from the site in response to an anticoagulant made by the worm. Weakness and pallor accompany the microcytic anemia caused by blood loss. These symptoms occur in patients whose nutrition cannot compensate for the blood loss. "Ground itch," a pruritic papule or vesicle, can occur at the site of entry of the larvae into the skin. Pneumonia with eosinophilia can be seen during larval migration through the lungs.

Epidemiology

Hookworm is found worldwide, especially in tropical areas. In the United States, *Necator* is endemic in the rural southern states. Walking barefooted on soil predisposes to infection. An important public health measure was requiring children to wear shoes to school.

Laboratory Diagnosis

Diagnosis is made microscopically by observing the eggs in the stools (Figure 56–2D). Occult blood in the stools is frequent. Eosinophilia is typical.

Treatment

Both mebendazole and pyrantel pamoate are effective.

Prevention

Disposing of sewage properly and wearing shoes are effective means of prevention.

STRONGYLOIDES

Disease

Strongyloides stercoralis causes strongyloidiasis.

Important Properties

S. stercoralis has **two distinct life cycles,** one within the human body and the other free-living in the soil. The life cycle in the human body begins with the **penetration of the skin,** usually of the feet, by **infectious (filariform) larvae** (Figure 56–1I) and their migration to the lungs. They enter the alveoli, pass up the bronchi and trachea, and then are swallowed. In the small intestine, the larvae molt into adults (Figure 56–1H) that enter the mucosa and produce eggs.

The eggs usually hatch within the mucosa, forming rhabditiform larvae (Figure 56–1J) that are passed in the feces. Some larvae molt to form filarial larvae, which penetrate the intestinal wall directly without leaving the host and migrate to the lungs (**autoinfection**). In immunocompetent patients, this is an infrequent, clinically unimportant event, but in T cell–deficient, eg, AIDS, or malnourished patients, it can lead to **massive reinfection,** with larvae passing to many organs and with severe, sometimes fatal consequences.

If larvae are passed in the feces and enter warm, moist soil, they molt through successive stages to form adult male and female worms. After mating, the entire life cycle of egg, larva, and adult can occur in the soil. After several free-living cycles, filarial larvae are formed. When they contact skin, they penetrate and again initiate the parasitic cycle within humans.

Pathogenesis & Clinical Findings

Most patients are asymptomatic, especially those with a low worm burden. Adult female worms in the wall of the small intestine can cause inflammation, resulting in watery diarrhea. In autoinfection, the penetrating larvae may cause sufficient damage to the intestinal mucosa that sepsis caused by enteric bacteria can occur. Larvae in the lungs can produce a pneumonitis similar to that caused by *Ascaris.* Pruritus (ground itch) can occur at the site of larval penetration of the skin, as with hookworm.

Epidemiology

Strongyloidiasis occurs primarily in the tropics, especially in Southeast Asia. Its geographic pattern is similar to that of hookworm because the same type of soil is required. In the United States, *Strongyloides* is endemic in the southeastern states.

Laboratory Diagnosis

Diagnosis depends on finding larvae in the stool. As with all migratory nematode infections, **eosinophilia can be striking.** Serologic tests are useful when the larvae are not visualized. An enzyme immunoassay that detects antibody to larval antigens is available through the CDC in Atlanta.

Treatment

Ivermectin is the drug of choice. Thiabendazole is an alternative drug.

Prevention

Prevention involves disposing of sewage properly and wearing shoes.

TRICHINELLA

Disease

Trichinella spiralis causes trichinosis.

Important Properties

Any mammal can be infected, but **pigs** are the most important reservoirs of human disease in the United States (except in Alaska, where bears constitute the reservoir). Humans are infected by **eating raw** or **undercooked meat** containing larvae encysted in the muscle (Figure 56–1K). The larvae excyst and mature into adults within the mucosa of the small intestine. Eggs hatch within the adult females, and larvae are released and distributed via the bloodstream to many organs; however, they develop only in **striated muscle cells.** Within these "nurse cells," they encyst within a fibrous capsule and can remain viable for several years but eventually calcify.

The parasite is maintained in nature by cycles within reservoir hosts, primarily swine and rats. Humans are **end-stage hosts,** because the infected flesh is not consumed by other animals.

Pathogenesis & Clinical Findings

A few days after eating undercooked meat, usually pork, the patient experiences diarrhea followed 1–2 weeks later by **fever, muscle pain, periorbital edema,** and **eosinophilia.** Subconjunctival hemorrhages are an important diagnostic criterion. Signs of cardiac and central nervous system disease are frequent, because the larvae migrate to these tissues as well. Death, which is rare, is usually due to congestive heart failure or respiratory paralysis.

Epidemiology

Trichinosis occurs worldwide, especially in eastern Europe and west Africa. In the United States, it is related to eating home-prepared sausage, usually on farms where the pigs are fed uncooked garbage. Bear and seal meat also are sources. In many countries, the disease occurs primarily in hunters who eat undercooked wild game.

Laboratory Diagnosis

Muscle biopsy reveals **larvae within striated muscle** (Figure 56–1K). Serologic tests, especially the bentonite flocculation test, become positive 3 weeks after infection.

Treatment

There is no treatment for trichinosis, but for patients with severe symptoms, steroids plus mebendazole can be tried. Thiabendazole is effective against the adult intestinal worms early in infection.

Prevention

The disease can be prevented by properly cooking pork and by feeding pigs only cooked garbage.

■ TISSUE NEMATODES

WUCHERERIA

Disease

Wuchereria bancrofti causes filariasis.[1] Elephantiasis is a striking feature of this disease. Tropical pulmonary eosinophilia is an immediate hypersensitivity reaction to *W. bancrofti* in the lung.

Important Properties

Humans are infected when the **female mosquito** (especially *Anopheles* and *Culex* species) deposits infective larvae on the skin while biting. The larvae penetrate the skin, enter a lymph node, and, after 1 year, mature to adults that produce **microfilariae** (Figure 56–3A). These circulate in the blood, chiefly at night, and are ingested by biting mosquitoes. Within the mosquito, the microfilariae produce infective larvae that are transferred with the next bite. Humans are the only definitive hosts.

---

[1] *Brugia malayi* causes filariasis in Malaysia.

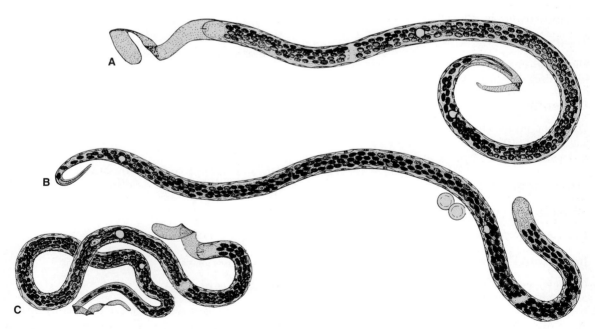

Figure 56–3. **A:** *Wuchereria bancrofti* microfilaria in blood. Note that the pointed tail is free of nuclei. 225–300 × 8–10 μm. **B:** *Onchocerca volvulus* microfilaria in skin (rare in blood). 300–350 × 5–9 μm. **C:** *Loa loa* microfilaria in blood. Note that the pointed tail contains nuclei. 250–300 × 6–9 μm. (Circles represent red blood cells.)

Pathogenesis & Clinical Findings

Adult worms in the lymph nodes cause inflammation that eventually obstructs the lymphatic vessels, causing edema. Massive edema of the legs is called **elephantiasis**. Note that microfilariae do *not* cause symptoms.

Early infections are asymptomatic. Later, fever, lymphangitis, and cellulitis develop. Gradually, the obstruction leads to edema and fibrosis of the legs and genitalia, especially the scrotum. Elephantiasis occurs mainly in patients who have been repeatedly infected over a long period. Tourists, who typically are infected only once, do *not* get elephantiasis.

Tropical pulmonary eosinophilia is characterized by coughing and wheezing, especially at night. These symptoms are caused by microfilariae in the lung that elicit an immediate hypersensitivity reaction characterized by a high immunoglobulin E (IgE) concentration and eosinophilia.

Epidemiology

This disease occurs in the tropical areas of Africa, Asia, and Latin America. The species of mosquito that acts as the vector varies from area to area. Altogether, 200–300 million people are infected.

Laboratory Diagnosis

Thick blood smears taken from the patient at night reveal the microfilariae. Serologic tests are not useful.

Treatment

Diethylcarbamazine is effective only against microfilariae; no drug therapy for adult worms is available.

Prevention

Prevention involves mosquito control with insecticides and the use of protective clothing, mosquito netting, and repellents.

ONCHOCERCA

Disease

Onchocerca volvulus causes onchocerciasis.

Important Properties

Humans are infected when the **female blackfly,** *Simulium,* deposits infective larvae while biting. The larvae enter the wound and migrate into the subcutaneous tissue, where they differentiate into adults, usually within **dermal nodules.** The female produces microfilariae (Figure 56–3B) that are ingested when another blackfly bites. The microfilariae develop into infective larvae in the fly to complete the cycle. Humans are the only definitive hosts.

Pathogenesis & Clinical Findings

Inflammation occurs in subcutaneous tissue, and pruritic papules and nodules form in response to the adult worm proteins. Microfilariae migrate through subcutaneous tissue, ultimately concentrating in the eyes. There they cause lesions that can lead to blindness. Loss of subcutaneous elastic fibers leads to wrinkled skin, which is called "hanging groin" when it occurs in the inguinal region. Thickening, scaling, and dryness of the skin accompanied by severe itching are the manifestations of a dermatitis often called "lizard skin."

Epidemiology

Millions of people are affected in Africa and Central America. The disease is a major cause of blindness. It is called **river blindness,** because the blackflies develop in rivers and people who live along those rivers are affected. Infection rates are often greater than 80% in areas of endemic infection.

Laboratory Diagnosis

Biopsy of the affected skin reveals microfilariae (Figure 56–3B). Examination of the blood is not useful, because microfilariae do not circulate in the blood. Serologic tests are also not helpful.

Treatment

Ivermectin is effective against microfilariae but not adults. Suramin kills adult worms but is quite toxic and is used particularly in those with eye disease. Skin nodules can be removed surgically, but new nodules can develop; therefore, a surgical cure is unlikely in areas of endemic infection.

Prevention

Prevention involves control of the blackfly with insecticides. Ivermectin prevents the disease.

LOA

Disease

Loa loa causes loiasis.

Important Properties

Humans are infected by the bite of the **deer fly** (mango fly), *Chrysops,* which deposits infective larvae on the skin. The larvae enter the bite wound, wander in the body, and develop into adults. The females release microfilariae (Figure 56–3C) that enter the blood, particularly during the day. The microfilariae are taken up by the fly during a blood meal and differentiate into infective larvae, which continue the cycle when the fly bites the next person.

Pathogenesis & Clinical Findings

There is no inflammatory response to the microfilariae or adults, but a hypersensitivity reaction causes transient, localized, nonerythematous, subcutaneous edema (Calabar swellings). The most dramatic finding is an adult worm **crawling across the conjunctiva** of the eye, a harmless but disconcerting event.

Epidemiology

The disease is found only in tropical central and west Africa, the habitat of the vector *Chrysops*.

Laboratory Diagnosis

Diagnosis is made by visualization of the microfilariae in a blood smear (Figure 56–3C). There are no useful serologic tests.

Treatment

Diethylcarbamazine eliminates the microfilariae and may kill the adults. Worms in the eyes may require surgical excision.

Prevention

Control of the fly by insecticides can prevent the disease.

DRACUNCULUS

Disease

Dracunculus medinensis (guinea fire worm) causes dracunculiasis.

Important Properties

Humans are infected when tiny **crustaceans (copepods)** containing infective larvae are **swallowed in drinking water.** The larvae are released in the small intestine and migrate into the body, where they develop into adults. Meter-long adult females cause the skin to ulcerate and then release motile larvae into fresh water. Copepods eat the larvae, which molt to form infective larvae. The cycle is completed when these are ingested in the water.

Pathogenesis & Clinical Findings

The adult female produces a substance that causes inflammation, blistering, and ulceration of the skin, usually of the lower extremities. The inflamed papule

burns and itches, and the ulcer can become secondarily infected. Diagnosis is usually made clinically by finding the **head of the worm in the skin ulcer.**

Epidemiology

The disease occurs over large areas of tropical Africa, the Middle East, and India. Tens of millions of people are infected.

Laboratory Diagnosis

The laboratory usually does not play a role in diagnosis.

Treatment

The time-honored treatment consists of gradually extracting the worm by winding it up on a stick over a period of days. Thiabendazole or metronidazole makes the worm easier to extract.

Prevention

Prevention consists of filtering or boiling drinking water.

■ NEMATODES WHOSE LARVAE CAUSE DISEASE

TOXOCARA

Disease

Toxocara canis is the major cause of visceral larva migrans. *T. cati* and several other related nematodes also cause this disease.

Important Properties

The definitive host for *T. canis* is the dog. The adult *T. canis* female in the dog intestine produces eggs that are passed in the feces into the soil. Humans ingest soil containing the eggs, which hatch into larvae in the small intestine. The larvae migrate to many organs, especially the liver, brain, and eyes. The larvae eventually are encapsulated and die. The life cycle is not completed in humans; humans are therefore accidental, dead-end hosts.

Pathogenesis & Clinical Findings

Pathology is related to the granulomas that form around the dead larvae as a result of a delayed hypersensitivity response to larval proteins. The most serious clinical finding is blindness associated with retinal involvement. Fever, hepatomegaly, and eosinophilia are common.

Epidemiology

Young children are primarily affected, because they are likely to ingest soil containing the eggs. *T. canis* is a common parasite of dogs in the United States.

Laboratory Diagnosis

Serologic tests are commonly used, but the definitive diagnosis depends on visualizing the larvae in tissue. The presence of hypergammaglobulinemia and eosinophilia supports the diagnosis.

Treatment

The treatment of choice is either albendazole or mebendazole, but there is no proven effective treatment. Many patients recover without treatment.

Prevention

Dogs should be dewormed, and children should be prevented from eating soil.

ANCYLOSTOMA

Cutaneous larva migrans is caused by the filariform larvae of *Ancylostoma caninum* (dog hookworm) and *Ancylostoma braziliense* (cat hookworm), as well as other nematodes. The organism cannot complete its life cycle in humans. The larvae penetrate the skin and **migrate through subcutaneous tissue,** causing an inflammatory response. The lesions ("creeping eruption") are extremely pruritic. The disease occurs primarily in the southern United States, in children and construction workers who are exposed to infected soil. The diagnosis is made clinically; the laboratory is of little value. Oral or topical thiabendazole is usually effective.

ANGIOSTRONGYLUS

The larvae of the rat lung nematode *Angiostrongylus cantonensis* cause eosinophilic meningitis, ie, a meningitis characterized by many eosinophils in the spinal fluid and in the blood. Usually at least 10% of the white cells are eosinophils. The larvae are typically ingested in undercooked seafood, such as crabs, prawns, and snails. Infection by this organism most often occurs in Asian countries. The diagnosis is made primarily on clinical grounds, but occasionally, the laboratory will find a larva in the spinal fluid. There is no treatment. Most patients recover spontaneously without major sequelae.

Eosinophilic meningitis is also caused by the larvae of two additional nematodes. *Gnathostoma spinigerum,* an intestinal nematode of cats and dogs, is acquired by eating undercooked fish and *Baylisascaris procyonis,* a raccoon roundworm, is acquired by accidentally ingesting raccoon feces. These organisms cause more severe disease than *Angiostrongylus,* and fatalities occur. Albendazole may be effective against *Gnathostoma,* but there is no treatment for *Baylisascaris.*

ANISAKIS

Anisakiasis is caused by the larvae of the nematode, *Anisakis simplex.* The larvae are **ingested in raw seafood** and can penetrate the submucosa of the stomach or intestine. The adult worms live in the intestines of marine mammals such as whales, dolphins, and seals. The eggs produced by the adults are eaten by crustaceans, which are then eaten by marine fish such as salmon, mackerel, and herring. Gastroenteritis, abdominal pain, eosinophilia, and occult blood in the stool typically occur. Acute infection can resemble appendicitis, and chronic infection can resemble gastrointestinal cancer.

Most cases in the United States have been traced to eating sushi and sashimi (especially salmon and red snapper) in Japanese restaurants. The diagnosis is typically made endoscopically or on laparotomy. Microbiologic and serologic tests are not helpful in the diagnosis. There are no effective drugs. Surgical removal may be necessary. Prevention consists of cooking seafood adequately or freezing it for 24 hours before eating.

Another member of the Anisakid family of nematodes is *Pseudoterranova decepiens,* whose larvae cause a noninvasive form of anisakiasis. The larvae are acquired by eating undercooked fish and cause vomiting and abdominal pain. The diagnosis is made by finding the larvae in the intestinal tract or in the vomitus. There is no drug treatment. The larvae can be removed during endoscopy.

SUMMARIES OF ORGANISMS

Brief summaries of the organisms described in this chapter begin on page 511. Please consult these summaries for a rapid review of the essential material.

PRACTICE QUESTIONS: USMLE & COURSE EXAMINATIONS

Questions on the topics discussed in this chapter can be found in the Parasitology section of Part XI: USMLE (National Board) Practice Questions starting on page 559. Also see Part XII: USMLE (National Board) Practice Examination starting on page 583.

PART VII
Immunology

Immunity

INTRODUCTION

The main function of the immune system is to **prevent or limit infections** by microorganisms such as bacteria, viruses, fungi, and parasites. The first line of defense against microorganisms is the **intact skin and mucous membranes**. If microorganisms breach this line and enter the body, then the **innate arm** of the immune system (second line of defense) is available to destroy the invaders. Because the components of the innate arm (Table 57–1) are preformed and fully active, they can function immediately upon entry of the microorganisms. The ability of the innate arm to kill microorganisms is not specific. For example, a neutrophil can ingest and destroy many different kinds of bacteria.

Highly specific protection is provided by the acquired (adaptive) arm of the immune system (third line of defense), but it takes several days for this arm to become fully functional. The two components of the acquired arm are **cell-mediated immunity** and **antibody-mediated (humoral) immunity**. An overview of the functions and interactions between many of the important members of the innate and acquired arms of the immune response is provided in Figure 57–1. (The features of the innate and the acquired arms of the immune system are contrasted in Table 57–2.)

The cell-mediated arm consists primarily of **T lymphocytes** (eg, helper T cells and cytotoxic T cells), whereas the antibody-mediated arm consists of antibodies (immunoglobulins) and **B lymphocytes** (and plasma cells). Some of the major functions of T cells and B cells are shown in Table 57–3. The main functions of antibodies are (1) to **neutralize toxins and viruses** and (2) to **opsonize bacteria**, making them easier

to phagocytize. Opsonization is the process by which immunoglobulin G (IgG) antibody and the C3b component of complement enhance phagocytosis (see Figure 8–3). Cell-mediated immunity, on the other hand, inhibits organisms such as fungi, parasites, and certain intracellular bacteria such as *Mycobacterium tuberculosis;* it also kills **virus-infected cells** and **tumor cells.**

Both the cell-mediated and antibody-mediated responses are characterized by three important features: (1) they exhibit remarkable **diversity** (ie, they can respond to millions of different antigens); (2) they have a long **memory** (ie, they can respond many years after the initial exposure because memory T cells and memory B cells are produced); and (3) they exhibit exquisite **specificity** (ie, their actions are specifically directed against the antigen that initiated the response).

The combined effects of certain cells (eg, T cells, B cells, macrophages, and neutrophils) and certain proteins (eg, antibodies and complement) produce an **inflammatory response,** one of the body's main defense mechanisms. The process by which these components interact to cause inflammation is described in Chapter 8.

Macrophages and certain other phagocytic cells such as dendritic cells participate in both the innate and acquired arms of the immune response. They are, in effect, a bridge between the two arms. As part of the innate arm, they ingest and kill various microbes. They also present antigen to helper T cells, which is the essential first step in the activation of the acquired arm (see below). It is interesting to note that neutrophils, which are also phagocytes and have excellent microbicidal abilities, do *not* present antigen to helper T cells and therefore function in innate but not acquired immunity.

Table 57–1. Main components of innate and acquired immunity that contribute to humoral (antibody-mediated) immunity and cell-mediated immunity.

	Humoral Immunity	Cell-Mediated Immunity
Innate	Complement Neutrophils	Macrophages Natural killer cells
Acquired	B cells Antibodies (made by plasma cells)	Helper T cells Cytotoxic T cells

SPECIFICITY OF THE IMMUNE RESPONSE

Cell-mediated immunity and antibody are both highly specific for the invading organism. How do these spe-

cific protective mechanisms originate? The process by which these host defenses originate can be summarized by three actions: the **recognition** of the foreign organism by specific immune cells, the **activation** of these immune cells to produce a specific response (eg, antibodies), and the **response** that specifically targets the organism for destruction. The following examples briefly describe how specific immunity to microorganisms occurs. An overview of these processes with a viral infection as the model is shown in Figure 57–2. A detailed description is presented in Chapter 58.

1. Cell-Mediated Immunity

In the following example, a bacterium, eg, *Mycobacterium tuberculosis,* enters the body and is ingested by a macrophage. The bacterium is broken down, and fragments of it called **antigens** or **epitopes** appear on the surface of the macrophage in association with **class II major histocompatibility complex (MHC)** proteins.

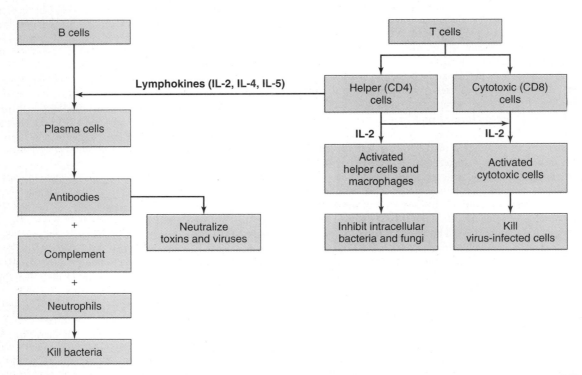

Figure 57–1. Introduction to the interactions and functions of the major components of the immune system. **Left:** Antibody-mediated (humoral) immunity. This is our main defense against extracellular, encapsulated, pyogenic bacteria such as staphylococci and streptococci. Antibodies also neutralize toxins, such as tetanus toxin, as well as viruses, such as hepatitis B virus. **Right:** Cell-mediated immunity. There are two distinct components. (1) Helper T cells and macrophages are our main defense against intracellular bacteria, such as *Mycobacterium tuberculosis,* and fungi, such as *Histoplasma capsulatum.* (2) Cytotoxic T cells are an important defense against viruses and act by destroying virus-infected cells.

Table 57–2. Important features of innate and acquired immunity.

Type of Immunity	Specificity	Effective Immediately After Exposure to Microbe	Improves After Exposure	Has Memory
Innate	Nonspecific	Yes—acts within minutes	No	No
Acquired	Highly specific	No—requires several days before becoming effective	Yes	Yes

The antigen–class II MHC protein complex interacts with an antigen-specific receptor on the surface of a **helper T lymphocyte.** Activation and clonal proliferation of this antigen-specific helper T cell occur as a result of the production of **interleukins,** the most important of which are interleukin-1 (produced by macrophages) and interleukin-2 (produced by lymphocytes). These activated helper T cells, aided by activated macrophages, mediate one important component of cellular immunity, ie, a **delayed hypersensitivity reaction** specifically against *M. tuberculosis.*

Cytotoxic (cytolytic) T lymphocytes are also specific effectors of the cellular immune response, particularly against virus-infected cells. In this example, a virus, eg, influenza virus, is inhaled and infects a cell of the respiratory tract. Viral envelope glycoproteins appear on the surface of the infected cell in association with **class I MHC** proteins. A cytotoxic T cell binds via its antigen-specific receptor to the viral antigen–class I MHC protein complex and is stimulated to grow into a clone of cells by interleukin-2 produced by helper T cells. These cytotoxic T cells specifically kill influenza virus–infected cells (and not cells infected by other viruses) by recognizing viral antigen–class I MHC protein complexes on the cell surface and releasing perforins that destroy the membrane of the infected cell.

2. Antibody-Mediated Immunity

Antibody synthesis typically involves the cooperation of three cells: **macrophages, helper T cells,** and **B cells.** After processing by a macrophage, fragments of antigen appear on the surface of the macrophage in association with **class II MHC** proteins. The antigen–class II MHC protein complex binds to specific receptors on the surface of a helper T cell, which then produces interleukins such as interleukin-2 (T-cell growth factor), interleukin-4 (B-cell growth factor), and interleukin-5 (B-cell differentiation factor). These factors activate the B cell capable of producing antibodies specific for that antigen. (Note that the interleukins are nonspecific; the specificity lies in the T cells and B cells and is mediated by the antigen receptors on the surface of these cells.) The activated B cell proliferates and differentiates to form many plasma cells that secrete large amounts of **immunoglobulins** (antibodies).

Although antibody formation usually involves helper T cells, certain antigens, eg, bacterial polysaccharides, can activate B cells directly, without the help of T cells, and are called **T-cell-independent antigens.** In this T-cell-independent response, **only IgM is produced** by B cells because it requires interleukins 4 and 5 made by the helper T cell for the B cell to "class switch" to produce IgG, IgA, and IgE. See Chapter 59 for a discussion of "class switching," the process by which the B cell switches the antibody it produces from IgM to one of the other classes.

Figure 57–3 summarizes the human host defenses against virus-infected cells and illustrates the close interaction of various cells in mounting a coordinated attack against the pathogen. The specificity of the response is provided by the antigen receptor (T-cell receptor [TCR]) on the surface of both the CD4-positive T cell and the CD8-positive T cell and by the antigen receptor (IgM) on the surface of the B cell. The interleukins, on the other hand, are **not specific.**

As depicted in Figure 57–3, B cells can perform two important functions during the induction process: (1) they **recognize antigens** with their surface IgM that acts as an antigen receptor and (2) they **present epitopes** to helper T cells in association with class II MHC proteins. Note that the IgM antigen receptor on the B cell can recognize not only foreign proteins but also carbohydrates, lipids, DNA, RNA, and other types of molecules. The class II MHC proteins of the B cell, however, can only present peptide fragments to the helper T cells. This distinction will become important when haptens are discussed later in this chapter. It is this remarkable ability of the IgM antigen receptor on the B cell to bind to an incredibly broad range of molecules that activates B cells to produce **antibodies against virtually every molecule known.** How the B cell generates such a diverse array of antibodies is described on page 426.

INNATE & ACQUIRED IMMUNITY

Our immune host defenses can be divided into two major categories: **innate (natural)** and **acquired (adap-**

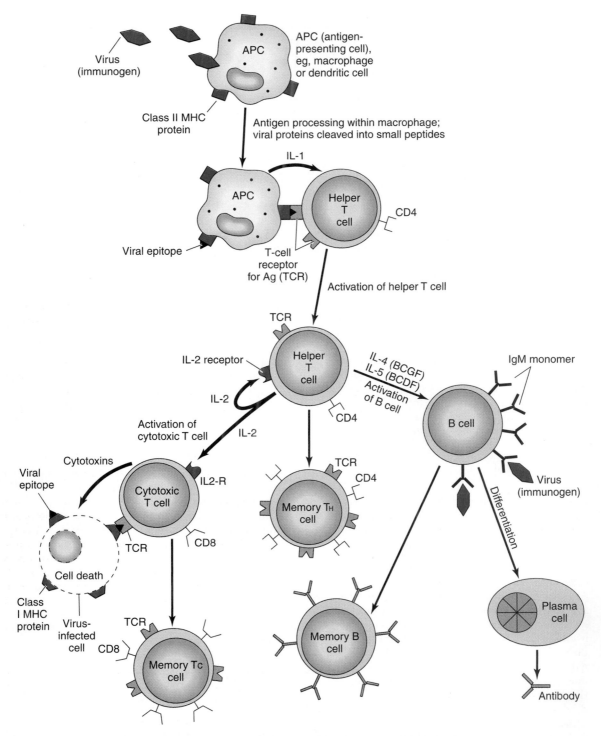

Figure 57–2. Overview of the process by which cell-mediated immunity and antibody-mediated immunity are induced by exposure to a virus. (Modified and reproduced, with permission, from Stites D, Terr A, Parslow T [editors]: *Basic & Clinical Immunology,* 9th ed. Originally published by Appleton & Lange. Copyright © 1997 by The McGraw-Hill Companies, Inc.)

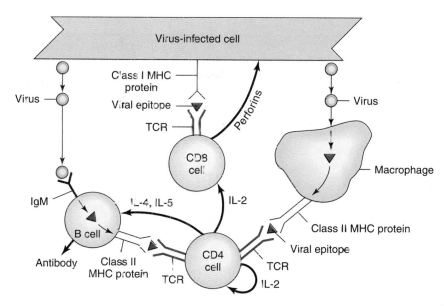

Figure 57–3. Induction of cell-mediated immunity and antibody against a viral infection. **Right:** Virus released by an infected cell is ingested and processed by an antigen-presenting cell (APC), eg, a macrophage. The viral epitope is presented in association with a class II MHC protein to the virus-specific T-cell receptor (TCR) on the CD4 cell. The macrophage makes IL-1, which helps activate the CD4 cell. The activated CD4 cell makes interleukins (eg, IL-2, which activates the CD8 cell to attack the virus-infected cell, and IL-4 and IL-5, which activate the B cell to produce antibody). The specificity of the cytotoxic response mounted by the CD8 cell is provided by its TCR, which recognizes the viral epitope presented by the virus-infected cell in association with a class I MHC protein. **Left:** Virus released by an infected cell interacts with the antigen receptor (IgM monomer) specific for that virus located on the surface of a B cell. The virus is internalized, and the viral proteins are broken down into small peptides. B cells (as well as macrophages) can present viral epitopes in association with class II MHC proteins and activate CD4 cells. The CD4-positive helper cell produces IL-4 and IL-5, which induce the B cell to differentiate into a plasma cell that produces antibody specifically against this virus.

tive). The features of these two important components of our host defenses are compared in Table 57–3.

1. Innate Immunity

Innate immunity is resistance that exists **prior to exposure** to the microbe (antigen). It is **nonspecific** and includes host defenses such as barriers to infectious agents (eg, skin and mucous membranes), certain cells (eg, natural killer cells), certain proteins (eg, the complement cascade and interferons), and involves processes such as phagocytosis and inflammation (Table 57–4). Innate immunity **does not improve after exposure** to the organism, in contrast to acquired immunity, which

Table 57–3. Major functions of T cells and B cells.

Antibody-Mediated Immunity (B Cells)	Cell-Mediated Immunity (T Cells)
1. Host defense against infection (opsonize bacteria, neutralize toxins and viruses)	1. Host defense against infection (especially *M. tuberculosis*, fungi, and virus-infected cells)
2. Allergy (hypersensitivity), eg, hay fever, anaphylactic shock	2. Allergy (hypersensitivity), eg, poison oak
3. Autoimmunity	3. Graft and tumor rejection
	4. Regulation of antibody response (help and suppression)

Table 57–4. Important components of innate immunity.

Factor	Mode of Action
I. Factors that limit entry of microorganisms into the body	
Keratin layer of intact skin	Acts as mechanical barrier
Lysozyme in tears and other secretions	Degrades peptidoglycan in bacteria cell wall
Respiratory cilia	Elevate mucus-containing trapped organisms
Low pH in stomach and vagina; fatty acids in skin	Retards growth of microbes
Surface phagocytes (eg, alveolar macrophages)	Ingest and destroy microbes
Defensins (cationic peptides)	Create pores in microbial membrane
Normal flora of throat, colon, and vagina	Occupy receptors, which prevents colonization by pathogens
II. Factors that limit growth of microorganisms within the body	
Natural killer cells	Kill virus-infected cells
Neutrophils	Ingest and destroy microbes
Macrophages and dendritic cells	Ingest and destroy microbes, and present antigen to helper T cells
Interferons	Inhibit viral replication
Complement	C3b is an opsonin; membrane attack complex creates holes in bacterial membranes
Transferrin and lactoferrin	Sequester iron required for bacterial growth
Fever	Elevated temperature retards bacterial growth
Inflammatory response	Limits spread of microbes
APOBEC3G (apolipoprotein B RNA-editing enzyme)	Causes hypermutation in retroviral DNA and mRNA

does. In addition, **innate immune processes have no memory,** whereas acquired immunity is characterized by long-term memory.

Note that the innate arm of our host defenses performs two major functions: **killing invading microbes and activating acquired (adaptive) immune processes.** Some components of the innate arm, such as neutrophils, only kill microbes, whereas others, such as macrophages and dendritic cells, perform both functions, ie, they kill microbes and present antigen to helper T cells, which activates acquired immune processes.

Although innate immunity is often successful in eliminating microbes and preventing infectious diseases, it is, in the long run, *not* sufficient for human survival. This conclusion is based on the observation that children with severe combined immunodeficiency disease (SCID), who have intact innate immunity but

no acquired immunity, suffer from repeated, life-threatening infections.

Several components of the innate arm recognize what is foreign by detecting certain carbohydrates or lipids on the surface of microorganisms that are different from those on human cells. Components of the innate arm have receptors called **pattern-recognition receptors** that recognize a molecular pattern present on the surface of many microbes and—very importantly—that is not present on human cells. By using this strategy, these components of the innate arm do not have to have a highly specific receptor for every different microbe but can still distinguish between what is foreign and what is self.

Note that the type of host defense mounted by the body differs depending on the type of organism. For example, a humoral (antibody-mediated) response is produced against one type of bacteria, but a cell-mediated response occurs in response to a different type of bacteria. The process that determines the type of response depends on the cytokines produced by the macrophages, and this in turn depends on which "pattern-recognition receptor" is activated by the organism, as described in the next paragraph.

Two important examples of this pattern recognition are:

(1) Endotoxin is a lipopolysaccharide (LPS) found on the surface of most gram-negative bacteria (but not on human cells). The lipid A portion of LPS is the most important cause of septic shock and death in hospitalized patients. When released from the bacterial surface, LPS combines with LPS-binding protein, a normal component of plasma. This binding protein transfers LPS to a receptor on the surface of macrophages called CD14. LPS stimulates a pattern-recognition receptor called **toll-like receptor 4 (TLR4),** which transmits a signal, via several intermediates, to the nucleus of the cell. This induces the production of cytokines, such as IL-1, IL-6, IL-8, and tumor necrosis factor (TNF), and induces the costimulator protein, B7, which is required to activate helper T cells and to produce antibodies. Note that a different toll-like receptor, TLR2, signals the presence of gram-positive bacteria and yeasts because they have a different molecular pattern on their surface. Drugs that modify the action of these toll-like receptors may become important in preventing endotoxin-mediated septic shock, a leading cause of death in hospitalized patients.

(2) Many bacteria and yeasts have a polysaccharide called mannan on their surface that is not present on human cells. (Mannan is a polymer of the sugar, mannose.) A pattern-recognition receptor called **mannan-binding lectin (MBL)** (also known as mannose-binding protein) binds to the mannan on the surface of the microbes, which then activates complement (see Chapter 63), resulting in death of the microbe. MBL also enhances phagocytosis (acts as an opsonin) via receptors to which it binds on the surface of phagocytes, such as macrophages. MBL is a normal serum protein whose concentration in the plasma is greatly increased during the acute-phase response.

The **acute-phase response,** which consists of an increase in the levels of various plasma proteins, eg, C-reactive protein and mannose-binding protein, is also part of innate immunity. These proteins are synthesized by the liver and are nonspecific responses to microorganisms and other forms of tissue injury. The liver synthesizes these proteins in response to certain cytokines, namely, IL-1, IL-6, and TNF, produced by the macrophage after exposure to microorganisms. These cytokines, IL-1, IL-6, and TNF, are often called the **proinflammatory cytokines,** meaning that they enhance the inflammatory response.

Some acute-phase proteins bind to the surface of bacteria and activate complement, which can kill the bacteria. For example, C-reactive protein binds to a carbohydrate in the cell wall of *Streptococcus pneumoniae* and, as mentioned above, MBL binds to mannan (mannose) on the surface of many bacteria.

Defensins are another important component of innate immunity. Defensins are highly positively charged (ie, cationic) peptides that create pores in the membranes of bacteria and thereby kill them. How they distinguish between microbes and our cells is unknown. Defensins are located primarily in the gastrointestinal and lower respiratory tracts. Neutrophils and Paneth cells in the intestinal crypts contain one type of defensin (α-defensins), whereas the respiratory tract produces different defensins called β-defensins.

α-Defensins also have antiviral activity. They interfere with human immunodeficiency virus (HIV) binding to the CXCR4 receptor and block entry of the virus into the cell. The production of α-defensins may explain why some HIV-infected individuals are long-term "nonprogressors."

APOBEC3G (apolipoprotein B RNA-editing enzyme) is an important member of the innate host defenses against retroviral infection, especially against HIV. APOBEC3G is an enzyme that causes hypermutation in retroviral DNA by deaminating cytosines in both mRNA and retroviral DNA, thereby inactivating these molecules and reducing infectivity. HIV defends itself against this innate host defense by producing Vif (viral infectivity protein), which counteracts APOBEC3G, thereby preventing hypermutation from occurring.

2. Adaptive (Acquired) Immunity

Adaptive immunity occurs **after exposure** to an agent, **improves upon repeated exposure,** and is **specific.** It is mediated by antibody produced by B lymphocytes and by two types of T lymphocytes, namely, helper T cells and cytotoxic T cells. The cells responsible for acquired immunity have **long-term memory** for a specific antigen. Acquired immunity can be active or passive. Chapter 58 describes how the specificity and memory of acquired immunity is produced.

Macrophages and other antigen-presenting cells such as dendritic cells play an important role in both the innate and the acquired arms of the immune system (Figure 57–4). When they phagocytose and kill microbes, they function as part of the innate arm, but when they present antigen to a helper T lymphocyte, they activate the acquired arm that leads to the production of antibody and of cells such as cytotoxic T lymphocytes. Note that the acquired arm can be activated only after the innate arm has recognized the microbe.

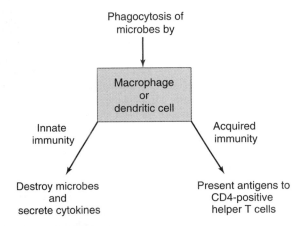

Figure 57–4. Macrophages and other antigen-presenting cells, such as dendritic cells, participate in both the innate arm and the acquired arm of the immune system. These cells are considered part of the innate arm because they phagocytose and kill many types of microbes and also produce cytokines that cause inflammation. They are also part of the acquired arm because they present antigen in association with class II MHC proteins to CD4-positive helper T cells. (In common with all other nucleated cells, they also can present antigen in association with class I MHC proteins to CD8-positive cytotoxic T cells.)

ACTIVE & PASSIVE IMMUNITY

Active immunity is resistance induced after **contact** with foreign antigens, eg, microorganisms. This contact may consist of clinical or subclinical infection, immunization with live or killed infectious agents or their antigens, or exposure to microbial products (eg, toxins and toxoids). In all these instances, the host actively produces an immune response consisting of antibodies and activated helper and cytotoxic T lymphocytes.

The main advantage of active immunity is that resistance is **long-term** (Table 57–5). Its major disadvantage is its **slow onset,** especially the primary response (see Chapter 60).

Passive immunity is resistance based on antibodies **preformed** in another host. Administration of antibody against diphtheria, tetanus, botulism, etc, makes large amounts of antitoxin immediately available to neutralize the toxins. Likewise, preformed antibodies to certain viruses (eg, rabies and hepatitis A and B viruses) can be injected during the incubation period to limit viral multiplication. Other forms of passive immunity are IgG passed from mother to fetus during pregnancy and IgA passed from mother to newborn during breast feeding.

The main advantage of passive immunization is the **prompt availability** of large amounts of antibody; disadvantages are the **short life span** of these antibodies and possible hypersensitivity reactions if globulins from another species are used. (See serum sickness in Chapter 65.)

Passive-active immunity involves giving both preformed antibodies (immune globulins) to provide immediate protection and a vaccine to provide long-term protection. These preparations should be given at different sites in the body to prevent the antibodies from neutralizing the immunogens in the vaccine. This approach is used in the prevention of tetanus (see Chapters 12 and 17), rabies (see Chapters 36 and 39), and hepatitis B (see Chapters 36 and 41).

ANTIGENS

Antigens are molecules that react with antibodies, whereas immunogens are molecules that induce an immune response. In most cases, antigens are immunogens, and the terms are used interchangeably. However, there are certain important exceptions, eg, haptens. A **hapten** is a molecule that is not immunogenic by itself but can react with specific antibody. Haptens are usually small molecules, but some high-molecular-weight nucleic acids are haptens as well. Many drugs, eg, penicillins, are haptens, and the catechol in the plant oil that causes poison oak and poison ivy is a hapten.

Haptens are not immunogenic because they cannot activate helper T cells. The failure of haptens to activate is due to their inability to bind to MHC proteins; they cannot bind because they are not polypeptides and only polypeptides can be presented by MHC proteins. Furthermore, haptens are univalent and therefore cannot

Table 57–5. Characteristics of active and passive immunity.

	Mediators	Advantages	Disadvantages
Active immunity	Antibody and T cells	Long duration (years)	Slow onset
Passive immunity	Antibody only	Immediate availability	Short duration (months)

activate B cells by themselves. (Compare to the T-independent response of multivalent antigens in Chapter 58.) Although haptens cannot stimulate a primary or secondary response by themselves, they can do so when covalently bound to a "carrier" protein (Figure 57–5). In this process, the hapten interacts with an IgM receptor on the B cell and the hapten-carrier protein complex is internalized. A peptide of the carrier protein is presented in association with class II MHC protein to the helper T cells. The activated helper T cell then produces interleukins, which stimulate the B cells to produce antibody to the hapten (see Chapter 58, page 401, for additional information).

Two additional ideas are needed to understand how haptens interact with our immune system. The first is that many haptens, such as drugs (eg, penicillin) and poison oak oil, bind to our normal proteins, to which we are tolerant. The hapten-protein combination now becomes immunogenic; ie, the hapten modifies the protein sufficiently such that when the hapten-peptide combination is presented by the MHC protein, it is recognized as foreign.

The second idea is that although most haptens are univalent, type I hypersensitivity reactions such as anaphylaxis (see Chapter 65) require cross-linking of adjacent IgEs to trigger the release of the mediators. By itself, a univalent hapten cannot cross-link, but when many hapten molecules are bound to the carrier protein, they are arranged in such a way that cross-linking can occur. This is how a univalent hapten, such as penicillin, causes anaphylaxis. Sufficient penicillin binds to one of our proteins to cross-link IgE. An excellent example of this is penicilloyl polylysine, which is used in skin tests to determine whether a patient is allergic to penicillin. Each lysine in the polylysine has a penicillin molecule attached to it. These univalent penicillin molecules form a "multivalent" array and can cross-link adjacent IgEs on the surface of mast cells. The consequent release of mediators causes a "wheal and flare" reaction in the skin of the penicillin-allergic patient.

The interaction of antigen and antibody is highly specific, and this characteristic is frequently used in the diagnostic laboratory to identify microorganisms. Antigen and antibody bind by **weak forces** such as hydrogen bonds and van der Waals' forces rather than by covalent bonds. The strength of the binding (the affinity) is proportionate to the fit of the antigen with its antibody-combining site, ie, its ability to form more of these bonds. The affinity of antibodies increases with successive exposures to the specific antigen (see Chapter 60). Another term, avidity, is also used to express certain aspects of binding. It need not concern us here.

The features of molecules that determine **immunogenicity** are as follows.

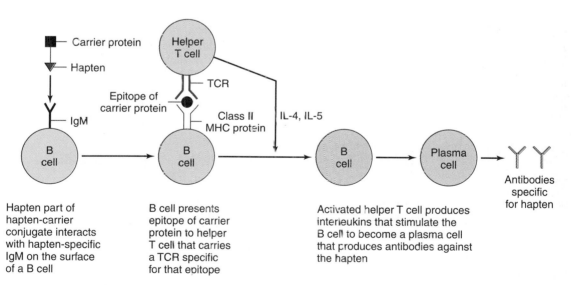

Figure 57–5. Hapten-carrier conjugate induces antibody against the hapten. A hapten covalently bound to a carrier protein can induce antibody to a hapten by the mechanism depicted in the figure. A hapten alone cannot induce antibody, because the helper T cells are not activated by the hapten. Although the hapten alone (without the carrier protein) can bind to the IgM receptor on the B-cell surface, the interleukins essential for the B cell to become a plasma cell are not made.

A. Foreignness

In general, molecules recognized as "self" are not immunogenic; ie, we are tolerant to those self-molecules (see Chapter 66). To be immunogenic, molecules must be recognized as "nonself," ie, foreign.

B. Molecular Size

The most potent immunogens are proteins with high molecular weights, ie, above 100,000. Generally, molecules with molecular weight below 10,000 are weakly immunogenic, and very small ones, eg, an amino acid, are nonimmunogenic. Certain small molecules, eg, haptens, become immunogenic only when linked to a carrier protein.

C. Chemical-Structural Complexity

A certain amount of chemical complexity is required; eg, amino acid homopolymers are less immunogenic than heteropolymers containing two or three different amino acids.

D. Antigenic Determinants (Epitopes)

Epitopes are small chemical groups on the antigen molecule that can elicit and react with antibody. An antigen can have one or more determinants (epitopes). Most antigens have many determinants; ie, they are multivalent. In general, a determinant is roughly five amino acids or sugars in size. The overall three-dimensional structure is the main criterion of antigenic specificity.

E. Dosage, Route, and Timing of Antigen Administration

These factors also affect immunogenicity. In addition, the genetic constitution of the host (HLA genes) determines whether a molecule is immunogenic. Different strains of the same species of animal may respond differently to the same antigen.

Adjuvants enhance the immune response to an immunogen. They are chemically unrelated to the immunogen and differ from a carrier protein because the adjuvant is not covalently bound to the immunogen, whereas the carrier protein is. Adjuvants can act in a variety of ways: cause slow release of immunogen, thereby prolonging the stimulus; enhance uptake of immunogen by antigen-presenting cells; and induce costimulatory molecules ("second signals"). (See Chapter 58 regarding costimulators.) Some human vaccines contain adjuvants such as aluminum hydroxide or lipids.

AGE & THE IMMUNE RESPONSE

Immunity is **less than optimal** at both ends of life, ie, in the **newborn** and the **elderly.** The reason for the relatively poor immune response in newborns is unclear, but newborns appear to have less effective T-cell function than do adults. In newborns, antibodies are provided primarily by the transfer of maternal IgG across the placenta. Because maternal antibody decays over time (little remains by 3–6 months of age), the risk of infection in the child is high. Colostrum also contains antibodies, especially secretory IgA, which can protect the newborn against various respiratory and intestinal infections.

The fetus can mount an IgM response to certain (probably T-cell-independent) antigens, eg, to *Treponema pallidum,* the cause of syphilis, which can be acquired congenitally. IgG and IgA begin to be made shortly after birth. The response to protein antigens is usually good; hence hepatitis B vaccine can be given at birth and poliovirus immunization can begin at 2 months of age. However, young children respond poorly to polysaccharide antigens unless they are conjugated to a carrier protein. For example, the pneumococcal vaccine containing the unconjugated polysaccharides does not induce protective immunity when given prior to 18 months of age, but the pneumococcal vaccine containing the polysaccharides conjugated to a carrier protein is effective when given as early as 2 months of age.

In the elderly, immunity generally declines. There is a reduced IgG response to certain antigens, fewer T cells, and a reduced delayed hypersensitivity response. As in the very young, the frequency and severity of infections are high. The frequency of autoimmune diseases is also high in the elderly, possibly because of a decline in the number of regulatory T cells, which allows autoreactive T cells to proliferate and cause disease.

PRACTICE QUESTIONS: USMLE & COURSE EXAMINATIONS

Questions on the topics discussed in this chapter can be found in the Immunology section of Part XI: USMLE (National Board) Practice Questions starting on page 562. Also see Part XII: USMLE (National Board) Practice Examinations starting on page 583.

Cellular Basis of the Immune Response

58

ORIGIN OF IMMUNE CELLS

The capability of responding to immunologic stimuli rests mainly with lymphoid cells. During embryonic development, blood cell precursors originate mainly in the fetal liver and yolk sac; in postnatal life, the stem cells reside in the bone marrow. Stem cells differentiate into cells of the erythroid, myeloid, or lymphoid series. The latter evolve into two main lymphocyte populations: **T cells** and **B cells** (Figure 58–1 and Table 58–1). The ratio of T cells to B cells is approximately 3:1. Figure 58–1 describes the origin of B cells and the two types of T cells: helper T cells and cytotoxic T cells. Table 58–1 compares various important features of B cells and T cells. These features will be described in detail later in the chapter.

T-cell precursors differentiate into immunocompetent T cells within the thymus. Prior to entering the thymus, stem cells lack antigen receptors and lack CD3, CD4, and CD8 proteins on their surface. During passage through the thymus they differentiate into T cells that can express both antigen receptors and the various CD proteins. The stem cells, which initially express neither CD4 nor CD8 (double-negatives), first differentiate to express both CD4 and CD8 (double-positives) and then proceed to express either CD4 or CD8. A double-positive cell will differentiate into a CD4-positive cell if it contacts a cell bearing class II MHC proteins but will differentiate into a CD8-positive cell if it contacts a cell bearing class I MHC proteins. (Mutant mice that do not make class II MHC proteins will not make CD4-positive cells, indicating that this interaction is required for differentiation into single-positive cells to occur.) The double-negative cells and the double-positive cells are located in the cortex of the thymus, whereas the single-positive cells are located in the medulla, from which they migrate out of the thymus into the blood and extrathymic tissue.

Within the thymus, two very important processes called **thymic education** occur.

(1) CD4-positive, CD8-positive cells bearing antigen receptors for "self" proteins are killed (**clonal deletion**) by a process of "programmed cell death" called **apoptosis** (Figure 58–2). The removal of these self-reactive cells, a process called **negative selection,** results in **tolerance** to our own proteins, ie, self-tolerance, and prevents autoimmune reactions (see Chapter 66).

(2) CD4-positive, CD8-positive cells bearing antigen receptors that do not react with self MHC proteins (see the section on activation, page 405) are also killed. This results in a **positive selection** for T cells that react well with self MHC proteins.

These two processes produce T cells that are selected for their ability to react both with foreign antigens via their antigen receptors and with self MHC proteins. Both of these features are required for an effective immune response by T cells.

Note that MHC proteins perform two essential functions in the immune response; one is the **positive selection** of T cells in the thymus, as just mentioned, and the other, which is described below, is the **presentation of antigens** to T cells, the initial step required to activate those cells. MHC proteins are also the most important antigens recognized in the graft rejection process (see Chapter 62).

During their passage through the thymus, each double-positive T cell synthesizes a different, highly specific antigen receptor called the **T-cell receptor (TCR).** The rearrangement of the variable, diversity, and joining genes (see Chapter 59) that encode the receptor occurs early in T-cell differentiation and accounts for the remarkable ability of T cells to recognize millions of different antigens.

Some T lymphocytes, perhaps as much as 40% of the total, do not develop in the thymus but rather in the "gut-associated lymphoid tissue" (GALT). These intraepithelial lymphocytes (IELs) are thought to provide protection against intestinal pathogens. Their antigen receptors and surface proteins are different from those of thymus-derived lymphocytes. IELs cannot substitute for thymus-derived lymphocytes because patients with DiGeorge's syndrome who lack a thymus (see Chapter 68) are profoundly immunodeficient and have multiple infections.

The thymus involutes in adults, yet T cells continue to be made. Two explanations have been offered for this

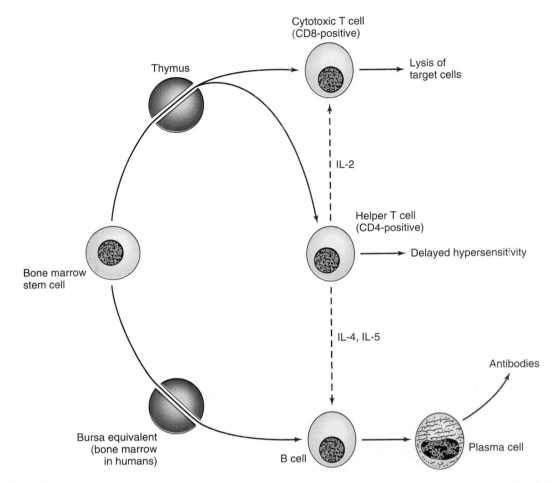

Figure 58–1. Origin of T and B cells. Stem cells in the bone marrow (or fetal liver) are the precursors of both T and B lymphocytes. Stem cells differentiate into T cells in the thymus, whereas they differentiate into B cells in the bone marrow. Within the thymus, T cells become either CD4-positive (helper) cells or CD8-positive (cytotoxic) cells. B cells can differentiate into plasma cells that produce large amounts of antibodies (immunoglobulins). Dotted lines indicate interactions mediated by interleukins. (Modified and reproduced, with permission, from Brooks GF et al: *Medical Microbiology*, 20th ed. Originally published by Appleton & Lange. Copyright © 1995 by The McGraw-Hill Companies, Inc.)

apparent paradox. One is that a remnant of the thymus remains functional throughout life and the other is that an extrathymic site takes over for the involuted thymus. Individuals who have had their thymus removed still make T cells, which supports the latter explanation.

B-cell precursors differentiate into immunocompetent B cells in the bone marrow; they do not pass through the thymus. B cells also undergo clonal deletion of those cells bearing antigen receptors for self proteins, a process that induces tolerance and reduces the occurrence of autoimmune diseases (see Chapter 66). The site of clonal deletion of B cells is uncertain, but it is not the thymus.

Natural killer (NK) cells are large granular lymphocytes that do not pass through the thymus, do not have an antigen receptor, and do not bear CD4 or CD8 proteins. They recognize and kill target cells, such as virus-infected cells and tumor cells, without the requirement that the antigens be presented in association with class I or class II MHC proteins. Rather, NK cells target those cells to be killed by detecting that they do *not* display class I MHC proteins on the cell surface. This detection process is effective because many cells lose their ability to synthesize class I MHC proteins after they have been infected by a virus (see page 416).

In contrast to T cells, B cells, and NK cells, which dif-

Table 58–1. Comparison of T cells and B cells.

Feature	T Cells	B Cells
Antigen receptors on surface	Yes	Yes
Antigen receptor recognizes only processed peptides in association with MHC protein	Yes	No
Antigen receptor recognizes whole, unprocessed proteins and has no requirement for presentation by MHC protein	No	Yes
IgM on surface	No	Yes
CD3 proteins on surface	Yes	No
Clonal expansion after contact with specific antigen	Yes	Yes
Immunoglobulin synthesis	No	Yes
Regulator of antibody synthesis	Yes	No
IL-2, IL-4, IL-5, and gamma interferon synthesis	Yes	No
Effector of cell-mediated immunity	Yes	No
Maturation in thymus	Yes	No
Maturation in bursa or its equivalent	No	Yes

ferentiate from lymphoid stem cells, macrophages arise from myeloid precursors. Macrophages have two important functions, namely, phagocytosis and antigen presentation. They do not pass through the thymus and do not have an antigen receptor. On their surface, they display class II MHC proteins, which play an essential role in antigen presentation to helper T cells. Macrophages also display class I MHC proteins, as do all nucleated cells. The cell surface proteins that play an important role in the immune response are listed in Table 58–2.

T CELLS

T cells perform several important functions, which can be divided into two main categories, namely, **regulatory** and **effector**. The regulatory functions are mediated primarily by **helper** (CD4-positive) T cells, which produce **interleukins** (Table 58–3). For example, helper T cells make (1) interleukin-4 (IL-4) and IL-5, which help B cells produce antibodies; (2) IL-2, which activates CD4 and CD8 cells; and (3) gamma interferon, which activates macrophages, the main mediators of delayed hypersensitivity against intracellular organisms such as *Mycobacterium tuberculosis*. (Suppressor T cells are postulated to downregulate the immune response, but the precise action of these cells is uncertain.) The effector functions are carried out primarily by cytotoxic (CD8-positive) T cells, which kill virus-infected cells, tumor cells, and allografts.

CD4 & CD8 Types of T Cells

Within the thymus, perhaps within the outer cortical epithelial cells (nurse cells), T-cell progenitors differentiate under the influence of thymic hormones (thymosins and thymopoietins) into T-cell subpopulations. These cells are characterized by certain surface glycoproteins, eg, CD3, CD4, and CD8. **All T cells have CD3** proteins on their surface in association with antigen receptors (T-cell receptor, TCR [see below]). The CD3 complex of five transmembrane proteins is involved with transmitting, from the outside of the cell to the inside, the information that the **antigen receptor is occupied**. One of the CD3 transmembrane proteins, the zeta chain, is linked to a tyrosine kinase called *fyn*, which is involved with signal transduction. The signal is transmitted via several second messengers, which are described in the section on activation (see below). CD4 is a single transmembrane polypeptide, whereas CD8 consists of two transmembrane polypeptides. They may signal via tyrosine kinase (the *lck* kinase) also.

T cells are subdivided into two major categories on the basis of whether they have CD4 or CD8 proteins on their surface. Mature T cells have either CD4 or CD8 proteins but not both.

CD4 lymphocytes perform the following **helper** functions: (1) they help B cells develop into antibody-producing plasma cells; (2) they help CD8 T cells to become activated cytotoxic T cells; and (3) they help macrophages effect delayed hypersensitivity (eg, limit infection by *M.*

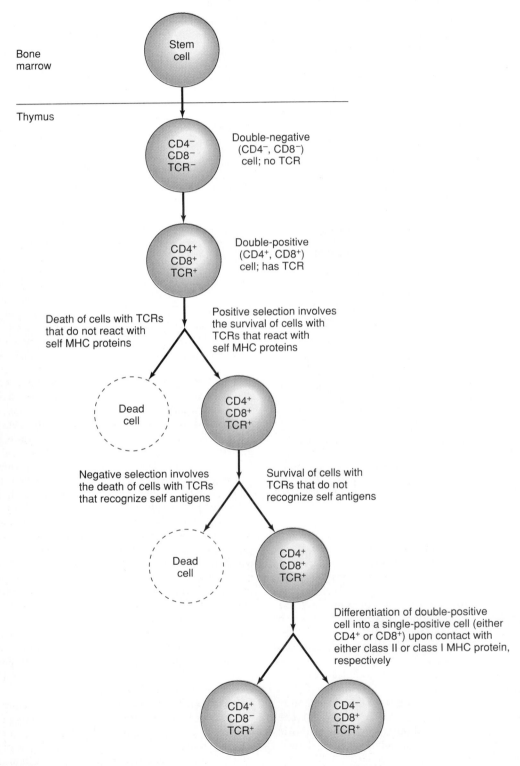

Figure 58–2. Development of T cells. Note the positive and negative selection that occurs in the thymus.

Table 58–2. Cell surface proteins that play an important role in the immune response.[1]

Type of Cells	Surface Proteins
Helper T cells	CD4, TCR,[2] CD28
Cytotoxic T cells	CD8, TCR
B cells	IgM, B7
Macrophages[3]	Class II MHC
Natural killer cells	Receptors for class I MHC
All cells other than mature red cells[4]	Class I MHC

[1]There are many other cell surface proteins that play a role in the immune response, but the proteins listed in this table are the most important for understanding the fundamental aspects of this response.
[2]TCR, T-cell antigen receptor.
[3]Macrophages and other "antigen-presenting cells."
[4]Mature red blood cells do not synthesize class I MHC proteins because they do not have a functioning nucleus.

tuberculosis). These functions are performed by two subpopulations of CD4 cells: **Th-1 cells** help activate cytotoxic T cells by producing IL-2 and help initiate the delayed hypersensitivity response by producing primarily IL-2 and gamma interferon, whereas **Th-2 cells** perform the B-cell helper function by producing primarily IL-4 and IL-5 (Figure 58–3). One important regulator of the balance between Th-1 cells and Th-2 cells is interleukin-12 (IL-12), which is produced by macrophages. IL-12 increases the number of Th-1 cells, thereby enhancing host defenses against organisms that are controlled by a delayed hypersensitivity response (Table 58–4). Another important regulator is gamma interferon, which inhibits the production of Th-2 cells. CD4 cells make up about 65% of peripheral T cells and predominate in the thymic medulla, tonsils, and blood.

To mount a protective immune response against a specific microbe requires that the appropriate subpopulation, ie, either Th-1 or Th-2 cells, play a dominant role in the response. For example, if an individual is infected with *M. tuberculosis* and Th-2 cells are the major responders, then humoral immunity will be stimulated rather than cell-mediated immunity. Humoral immunity is not protective against *M. tuberculosis* and the patient will suffer severe tuberculosis. Similarly, if an individual is infected with *Streptococcus pneumoniae* and Th-1 cells are the major responders, then humoral immunity will be not be stimulated and the patient will have severe pneumococcal disease. Precisely what component of a microbe activates either Th-1 or Th-2 cells is unknown.

How the appropriate response is stimulated is known for one medically important organism, namely, *M. tuberculosis.* A lipoprotein of that bacterium interacts with a specific "toll-like receptor" on the surface of the macrophage, which induces the production of IL-12 by the macrophage. IL-12 drives the differentiation of naïve helper T cells to form the Th-1 type of helper T cells that are required to mount a cell-mediated (delayed hypersensitivity) response against the organism.

CD8 lymphocytes perform cytotoxic functions; that is, they kill virus-infected, tumor, and allograft cells. They kill by either of two mechanisms, namely, the release of perforins, which destroy cell membranes, or the induction of programmed cell death (apoptosis). CD8 cells predominate in human bone marrow and gut lymphoid tissue and constitute about 35% of peripheral T cells.

Activation of T Cells

The activation of **helper T cells** requires that their TCR recognize a complex on the surface of antigen-presenting cells (APCs), eg, macrophages and dendritic cells,[1] consisting of **both the antigen and a class II MHC protein.**

What follows is a description of this activation process beginning with the ingestion of the foreign protein (or microbe) into the APC. Within the cytoplasm of the macrophage, the foreign protein is cleaved into small peptides that associate with the class II MHC proteins. The complex is transported to the surface of the macrophage, where the antigen, in association with a class II MHC protein, is presented to the receptor on

Table 58–3. Main functions of helper T cells.

Main Functions	Cytokine That Mediates That Function
Activates the antigen-specific helper T cell to produce a clone of these cells	IL-2
Activates cytotoxic T cells	IL-2
Activates B cells	IL-4 and IL-5
Activates macrophages	Gamma interferon

---

[1] Macrophages and dendritic cells are the most important antigen-presenting cells, but B cells and Langerhans' cells on the skin also present antigen, ie, have class II proteins on their surface. An essential first step for certain antigen-presenting cells, eg, Langerhans' cells in the skin, is migration from the site of the skin infection to the local lymphoid tissue, where helper T cells are encountered.

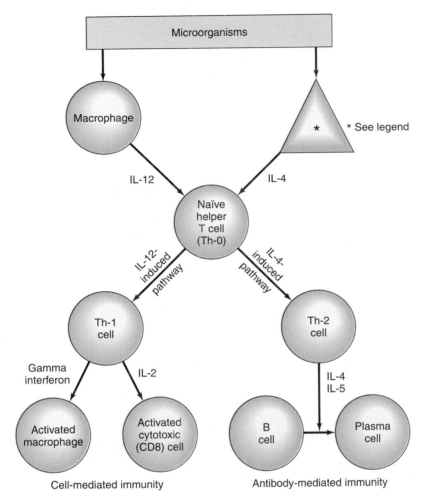

Figure 58–3. The origin of Th-1 and Th-2 cells. On the **left** side, the origin of Th-1 cells is depicted. Microorganisms are ingested by macrophages and IL-12 is produced. IL-12 induces naïve Th-0 cells to become Th-1 cells that produce gamma interferon and IL-2. These interleukins activate macrophages and cytotoxic T cells, respectively, and cell-mediated immunity occurs. On the **right** side, the origin of Th-2 cells is depicted. Microorganisms are ingested by an unknown type of cell (see footnote below) and IL-4 is produced. IL-4 induces naïve Th-0 cells to become Th-2 cells that produce IL-4 and IL-5. These interleukins activate B cells to become plasma cells and antibodies are produced. Not shown in the figure is an important regulatory step, namely, that IL-10 produced by Th-2 cells inhibits IL-12 production by macrophages and drives the system toward an antibody response and away from a cell-mediated response.

* The human cell that produces the IL-4, which induces naïve helper T cells to become Th-2 cells, has not been identified.

the CD4-positive helper cell. Similar events occur within a virus-infected cell, except that the cleaved viral peptide associates with a **class I** rather than a class II MHC protein. The complex is transported to the surface, where the viral antigen is presented to the receptor on a **CD8-positive cytotoxic cell.** Remember the rule of eight: CD4 cells interact with class II (4 × 2 = 8), and CD8 cells interact with class I (8 × 1 = 8).

There are many different alleles within the class I and class II MHC genes; hence, there are many different MHC proteins. These various MHC proteins bind to different peptide fragments. The polymorphism of the MHC genes and the proteins they encode are a means of presenting many different antigens to the T-cell receptor. Note that class I and class II MHC proteins can *only* present peptides; other types of molecules

Table 58–4. Comparison of Th-1 cells and Th-2 cells.

Property	Th-1 Cells	Th-2 Cells
Produces IL-2 and gamma interferon	Yes	No
Produces IL-4, IL-5, IL-6, and IL-10	No	Yes
Enhances cell-mediated immunity and delayed hypersensitivity primarily	Yes	No
Enhances antibody production primarily	No	Yes
Stimulated by IL-12	Yes	No
Stimulated by IL-4	No	Yes

do not bind and therefore cannot be presented. Note also that MHC proteins present peptides derived from self proteins as well as from foreign proteins; therefore whether an immune response occurs is determined by whether a T cell bearing a receptor specific for that peptide has survived the positive and negative selection processes in the thymus.

Two signals are required to activate T cells. The first signal in the activation process is the interaction of the antigen and the MHC protein with the T-cell receptor specific for that antigen (Figure 58–4). IL-1 produced by the macrophage is also necessary for efficient helper T-cell activation. Note that when the T-cell receptor interacts with the antigen-MHC protein complex, the CD4 protein on the surface of the helper T cell also interacts with the class II MHC protein. In addition to the binding of the CD4 protein with the MHC class II protein, other proteins interact to help

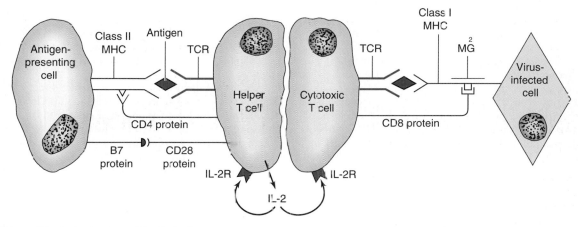

Figure 58–4. Activation of T cells. **Left:** An antigen-presenting cell (APC) presents processed antigen in association with a class II MHC protein. The antigen is recognized by the T-cell receptor (TCR) specific for that antigen, and the helper T cell is activated to produce interleukin-2 (IL-2). IL-2 binds to its receptor on the helper T cell and further activates it. Note that CD4 protein on the helper T cell binds to the MHC class II protein on the APC, which stabilizes the interaction between the two cells, and that B7 on the APC must interact with CD28 on the helper T cell for full activation of helper T cells to occur. **Right:** A virus-infected cell presents viral antigen in association with class I MHC protein. The viral antigen is recognized by the TCR specific for that antigen and, in conjunction with IL-2 produced by the helper T cell, the cytotoxic T cell is activated to kill the virus-infected cell. The CD8 protein on the cytotoxic T cell binds to the class I protein on the virus-infected cell, which stabilizes the interaction between the two cells. Note that the class II MHC protein consists of two polypeptides, both of which are encoded by genes in the HLA locus. The class I protein, in contrast, consists of one polypeptide encoded by the HLA locus and β_2-microglobulin (β_2 MG), which is encoded elsewhere.

stabilize the contact between the T cell and the APC; eg, LFA-1 protein[2] on T cells (both CD4-positive and CD8-positive) binds to ICAM-1 protein[2] on APCs.

A second **costimulatory signal** is also required; that is, B7 protein on the APC must interact with CD28 protein on the helper T cell (Figure 58–4). If the co-stimulatory signal occurs, IL-2 is made by the helper T cell, and it is this step that is crucial to producing a helper T cell capable of performing its regulatory, effector, and memory functions. If, on the other hand, the T-cell receptor interacts with its antigen (epitope) and the costimulatory signal does not occur, a state of unre-sponsiveness called **anergy** ensues (see Chapter 66). The anergic state is specific for that epitope, since other helper T cells specific for other epitopes are not af-fected. Production of the costimulatory protein de-pends on activation of the "toll-like receptor" on the APC surface. Foreign antigens, such as bacterial pro-teins, induce B7 protein, whereas self antigens do not.

After the T cell has been activated, a different pro-tein called CTLA-4 appears on the T-cell surface and binds to B7 by displacing CD28. The **interaction of B7 with CTLA-4 inhibits T-cell activation** by block-ing IL-2 synthesis. This restores the activated T cell to a quiescent state and thereby plays an important role in T-cell homeostasis. Mutant T cells that lack CTLA-4 and therefore cannot be deactivated participate with in-creased frequency in autoimmune reactions. Further-more, administration of CTLA-4 reduced the rejection of organ transplants in experimental animals.

T cells recognize *only* polypeptide antigens. Fur-thermore, they recognize those polypeptides only when they are presented in association with MHC proteins. Helper T cells recognize antigen in association with class II MHC proteins, whereas cytotoxic T cells recog-nize antigen in association with class I MHC proteins. This is called **MHC restriction;** ie, the two types of T cells (CD4 helper and CD8 cytotoxic) are "restricted" because they are able to recognize antigen *only* when the antigen is presented with the proper class of MHC protein. This restriction is mediated by specific binding sites primarily on the T-cell receptor, but also on the CD4 and CD8 proteins that bind to specific regions on the class II and class I MHC proteins, respectively.

Generally speaking, class I MHC proteins present **endogenously synthesized** antigens, eg, viral proteins, whereas class II MHC proteins present the antigens of

extracellular microorganisms that have been phagocy-tized, eg, bacterial proteins. One important conse-quence of these observations is that killed viral vaccines do not activate the cytotoxic (CD8-positive) T cells, because the virus does not replicate within cells and therefore viral epitopes are not presented in association with class I MHC proteins. Class I and class II proteins are described in more detail in Chapter 62.

This distinction between endogenously synthesized and extracellularly acquired proteins is achieved by pro-cessing the proteins in different compartments within the cytoplasm. The endogenously synthesized proteins, eg, viral proteins, are cleaved by a proteasome, and the peptide fragments associate with a "TAP transporter" that transports the fragment into the rough endoplas-mic reticulum, where it associates with the class I MHC protein. The complex of peptide fragment and class I MHC protein then migrates via the Golgi appa-ratus to the cell surface. In contrast, the extracellularly acquired proteins are cleaved to peptide fragments within an endosome, where the fragment associates with class II MHC proteins. This complex then mi-grates to the cell surface.

An additional protection that prevents endoge-nously synthesized proteins from associating with class II MHC proteins is the presence of an "invariant chain" that is attached to the class II MHC proteins when these proteins are outside of the endosome. The invariant chain is degraded by proteases within the endosome, allowing the peptide fragment to attach to the class II MHC proteins only within that compart-ment.

B cells, on the other hand, can interact directly with antigens via their surface immunoglobulins (IgM and IgD). Antigens do not have to be presented to B cells in association with class II MHC proteins, unlike T cells. Note that B cells can then present the antigen, after in-ternalization and processing, to helper T cells in associ-ation with class II MHC proteins located on the sur-face of the B cells (see the section on B cells, below). Unlike the antigen receptor on T cells, which recog-nizes only peptides, the antigen receptors on B cells (IgM and IgD) recognize many different types of mole-cules, such as peptides, polysaccharides, nucleic acids, and small molecules, eg, drugs such as penicillin.

These differences between T cells and B cells explain the hapten-carrier relationship described in Chapter 57. To stimulate hapten-specific antibody, the hapten must be covalently bound to the carrier protein. The hapten binds to the IgM receptor on the B-cell surface. That IgM is specific for the hapten, not the carrier pro-tein. The hapten-carrier conjugate is internalized and the carrier protein processed into small peptides that are presented in association with class II MHC proteins to a helper T cell bearing a receptor for that peptide.

---

[2] LFA proteins belong to a family of cell surface proteins called integrins, which mediate adhesion to other cells. Integrin proteins are embedded in the surface membrane and have both extracellular and intracellular domains. Hence they interact with other cells externally and with the cytoplasm internally. Abbreviations: LFA, lymphocyte function-associated antigen; ICAM, intercellular adhe-sion molecule.

The helper T cell then secretes lymphokines that activate the B cell to produce antibodies to the hapten.

When the antigen-MHC protein complex on the APC interacts with the T-cell receptor, a signal is transmitted by the CD3 protein complex through several pathways that eventually lead to a large influx of calcium into the cell. (The details of the signal transduction pathway are beyond the scope of this book, but it is known that stimulation of the T-cell receptor activates a series of phosphokinases, which then activate phospholipase C, which cleaves phosphoinositide to produce inositol triphosphate, which opens the calcium channels.) Calcium activates calcineurin, a serine phosphatase. Calcineurin moves to the nucleus and is involved in the activation of the genes for IL-2 and the IL-2 receptor. (Calcineurin function is blocked by cyclosporine, one of the most effective drugs used to prevent rejection of organ transplants [see Chapter 62].)

The end result of this series of events is the activation of the helper T cell to produce various lymphokines, eg, **IL-2**, as well as the **IL-2 receptor**. IL-2, also known as T-cell growth factor, stimulates the helper T cell to multiply into a clone of antigen-specific helper T cells. Most cells of this clone perform effector and regulatory functions, but some become **memory cells** (see below), which are capable of being rapidly activated upon exposure to antigen at a later time. (Cytotoxic T cells and B cells also form memory cells.) Note that IL-2 stimulates CD8 cytotoxic T cells as well as CD4 helper T cells. Activated CD4-positive T cells also produce another lymphokine called **gamma interferon**, which increases the expression of class II MHC proteins on APCs. This enhances the ability of APCs to present antigen to T cells and upregulates the immune response. (Gamma interferon also enhances the microbicidal activity of macrophages.)

The process of activating T cells does not function as a simple "on-off" switch. The binding of an epitope to the T-cell receptor can result in either full activation, partial activation in which only certain lymphokines are made, or no activation, depending on which of the signal transduction pathways is stimulated by that particular epitope. This important observation may have profound implications for our understanding of how helper T cells shape our response to infectious agents.

There are three genes at the class I locus (A, B, and C) and three genes at the class II locus (DP, DQ, and DR). We inherit one set of class I and one set of class II genes from each parent. Therefore, our cells can express as many as six different class I and six different class II proteins (see Chapter 62). Furthermore, there are multiple alleles at each gene locus. Each of these MHC proteins can present peptides with a different amino acid sequence. This explains, in part, our ability to respond to many different antigens.

Memory T Cells

Memory T (and B) cells, as the name implies, endow our host defenses with the ability to respond rapidly and vigorously for many years after the initial exposure to a microbe or other foreign material. This memory response to a specific antigen is due to several features: (1) many memory cells are produced, so that the secondary response is greater than the primary response, in which very few cells respond; (2) memory cells live for many years or have the capacity to reproduce themselves; (3) memory cells are activated by smaller amounts of antigen and require less costimulation than do naïve, unactivated T cells; and (4) activated memory cells produce greater amounts of interleukins than do naïve T cells when they are first activated.

T-Cell Receptor

The T-cell receptor (TCR) for antigen consists of two polypeptides, alpha and beta,[3] which are associated with CD3 proteins.

TCR polypeptides are similar to immunoglobulin heavy chains in that (1) the genes that code for them are formed by rearrangement of multiple regions of DNA (see Chapter 59); (2) there are V (variable), D (diversity), J (joining), and C (constant) segments that rearrange to provide diversity, giving rise to an estimated number of more than 10^7 different receptor proteins; (3) the variable regions have hypervariable domains; and (4) the two genes (RAG-1 and RAG-2) that encode the recombinase enzymes that catalyze these gene rearrangements are similar in T cells and B cells.

Note that each T cell has a unique T-cell receptor on its surface, which means that hundreds of millions of different T cells exist in each person. Activated T cells, like activated B cells, clonally expand to yield large numbers of cells specific for that antigen.

Although TCRs and immunoglobulins (antibodies) are analogous in that they both interact with antigen in a highly specific manner, the T-cell receptor is different in two important ways: (1) it has two chains rather than four; and (2) it recognizes antigen only in conjunction with MHC proteins, whereas immunoglobulins recognize free antigen. Note that the receptor on the surface of B cells (either IgM or IgG) recognizes antigen directly without the need for presentation by MHC proteins. Also TCR proteins are always anchored into the outer membrane of T cells. There is no circu-

---

[3] Some TCRs have a different set of polypeptides called gamma and delta. These TCRs are unusual because they do not require that antigen be presented in association with MHC proteins. Gamma/delta T cells constitute approximately 10% of all T cells. Some of the T cells bearing these TCRs are involved in cell-mediated immunity against *M. tuberculosis*.

lating form as there is with certain antibodies (eg, monomeric IgM is in the B-cell membrane, but pentameric IgM circulates in the plasma).

Effect of Superantigens on T Cells

Certain proteins, particularly staphylococcal enterotoxins and toxic shock syndrome toxin, act as "superantigens" (Figure 58–5). In contrast to the typical (non-super) antigen, which activates one (or a few) helper T cell, superantigens are "super" because they activate a large number of helper T cells. For example, toxic shock syndrome toxin binds directly to class II MHC proteins without internal processing of the toxin. This complex interacts with the variable portion of the beta chain (Vβ) of the T-cell receptor of many T cells.[4]

This activates the T cells, causing the release of IL-2 from the T cells and IL-1 and TNF from macrophages. These interleukins account for many of the findings seen in toxin-mediated staphylococcal diseases. Certain viral proteins, eg, those of mouse mammary tumor virus (a retrovirus), also possess superantigen activity.

Features of T Cells

T cells constitute 65–80% of the recirculating pool of small lymphocytes. Within lymph nodes, they are located in the inner, subcortical region, not in the germinal centers. (B cells make up most of the remainder of the pool of small lymphocytes and are found primarily in the germinal centers of lymph nodes.) The life span of T cells is long: months or years. They can be stimulated to divide when exposed to certain mitogens, eg, phytohemagglutinin or concanavalin A (endotoxin, a lipopolysaccharide found on the surface of gram-negative bacteria, is a mitogen for B cells but not T cells). Most human T cells have receptors for sheep erythrocytes on their surface and can form "rosettes" with them; this finding serves as a means of identifying T cells in a mixed population of cells.

Effector Functions of T Cells

There are two important components of host defenses mediated by T cells: delayed hypersensitivity and cytotoxicity.

A. Delayed Hypersensitivity

Delayed hypersensitivity reactions are produced particularly against antigens of **intracellular microorganisms** including certain fungi, eg, *Histoplasma* and *Coccidioides*,

and certain intracellular bacteria, eg, *M. tuberculosis*. Delayed hypersensitivity is mediated by **macrophages** and **CD4 cells**, in particular by the Th-1 subset of CD4 cells. Important interleukins for these reactions include gamma interferon, macrophage activation factor, and macrophage migration inhibition factor. CD4 cells pro-

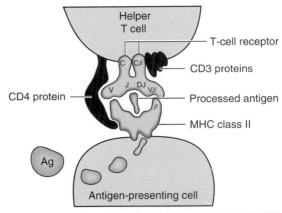

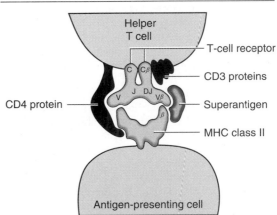

Figure 58–5. Activation of helper T cells by superantigen. **Top:** The helper T cell is activated by the presentation of processed antigen in association with class II MHC protein to the antigen-specific portion of the T-cell receptor. Note that superantigen is not involved and that only one or a small number of helper T cells specific for the antigen are activated. **Bottom:** The helper T cell is activated by the binding of superantigen to the Vβ portion of the T-cell receptor outside of its antigen-specific site without being processed by the antigen-presenting cell. Because it bypasses the antigen-specific site, superantigen can activate many helper T cells. (Modified and reproduced, with permission, from Pantaleo G et al: *N Engl J Med* 1993;328:327.)

---

[4] Each superantigen, eg, the different staphylococcal enterotoxins, interacts with different Vβ chains. This explains why many but not all helper T cells are activated by the various superantigens.

duce the interleukins, and macrophages are the ultimate effectors of delayed hypersensitivity. A deficiency of cell-mediated immunity manifests itself as a marked susceptibility to infection by such microorganisms.

In the case of *M. tuberculosis,* a lipoprotein of the bacterium stimulates a specific "toll-like receptor" on the macrophage, which signals the cell to synthesize IL-12. IL-12 then induces naïve helper T cells to differentiate into the Th-1 type of helper T cells that participates in the cell-mediated (delayed hypersensitivity) response.

Th-1 cells produced gamma interferon, which activates macrophages, thereby enhancing their ability to kill *M. tuberculosis.* This "IL-12–gamma interferon axis" is very important in the ability of our host defenses to control infections by intracellular pathogens, such as *M. tuberculosis* and *Listeria monocytogenes.*

B. Cytotoxicity

The **cytotoxic response** is concerned primarily with destroying **virus-infected cells** and **tumor cells** but also plays an important role in **graft rejection.** In response to virus-infected cells, the CD8 lymphocytes must recognize both viral antigens and class I molecules on the surface of infected cells. To kill the virus-infected cell, the cytotoxic T cell must be activated by IL-2 produced by a helper (CD-4-positive) T cell. To become activated to produce IL-2, helper T cells recognize viral antigens bound to class II molecules on an APC, eg, a macrophage. The activated helper T cells secrete cytokines such as IL-2, which stimulates the virus-specific cytotoxic T cell to form a clone of activated cytotoxic T cells. These cytotoxic T cells kill the virus-infected cells by inserting **perforins** and degradative enzymes called **granzymes** into the infected cell. Perforins form a channel through the membrane, the cell contents are lost, and the cell dies. Granzymes are proteases that degrade proteins in the cell membrane, which also leads to the loss of cell contents. They also activate caspases that initiate apoptosis, resulting in cell death. After killing the virus-infected cell, the cytotoxic T cell itself is not damaged and can continue to kill other cells infected with the same virus. Cytotoxic T cells have no effect on free virus, only on virus-infected cells.

A third mechanism by which cytotoxic T cells kill target cells is the **Fas-Fas ligand (FasL)** interaction. Fas is a protein displayed on the surface of many cells. When a cytotoxic T-cell receptor recognizes an epitope on the surface of a target cell, FasL is induced in the cytotoxic T cell. When Fas and FasL interact, apoptosis (death) of the target cell occurs. NK cells can also kill target cells by Fas-FasL-induced apoptosis.

In addition to direct killing by cytotoxic T cells, virus-infected cells can be destroyed by a combination of IgG and phagocytic cells. In this process, called **anti-body-dependent cellular cytotoxicity (ADCC)**, antibody bound to the surface of the infected cell is recognized by IgG receptors on the surface of phagocytic cells, eg, macrophages or NK cells, and the infected cell is killed. The ADCC process can also kill helminths (worms). In this case, IgE is the antibody involved and eosinophils are the effector cells. IgE binds to surface proteins on the worm, and the surface of eosinophils displays receptors for the epsilon heavy chain. The major basic protein located in the granules of the eosinophils is released and damages the surface of the worm.

Many tumor cells develop new antigens on their surface. These antigens bound to class I proteins are recognized by cytotoxic T cells, which are stimulated to proliferate by IL-2. The resultant clone of cytotoxic T cells can kill the tumor cells, a phenomenon called **immune surveillance.**

In response to allografts, cytotoxic (CD8) cells recognize the class I MHC molecules on the surface of the foreign cells. Helper (CD4) cells recognize the foreign class II molecules on certain cells in the graft, eg, macrophages and lymphocytes. The activated helper cells secrete IL-2, which stimulates the cytotoxic cell to form a clone of cells. These cytotoxic cells kill the cells in the allograft.

Regulatory Functions of T Cells

T cells play a central role in regulating both the humoral (antibody) and cell-mediated arms of the immune system.

A. Antibody Production

Antibody production by B cells usually requires the participation of helper T cells (**T-cell-dependent response**), but antibodies to some antigens, eg, polymerized (multivalent) macromolecules such as bacterial capsular polysaccharide, are **T-cell-independent.** These polysaccharides are long chains consisting of repeated subunits of several sugars. The **repeated subunits act as a multivalent antigen** that cross-links the IgM antigen receptors on the B cell and activates it in the absence of help from CD4 cells. Other macromolecules, such as DNA, RNA, and many lipids, also elicit a T-cell-independent response.

In the following example illustrating the T-cell-dependent response, B cells are used as the APC, although macrophages commonly perform this function. In this instance, antigen binds to surface IgM or IgD, is internalized within the B cell, and is fragmented. Some of the fragments return to the surface in association with class II MHC molecules (Figure 58–6A).[5] These

---

[5] Note that one important difference between B cells and T cells is that B cells recognize antigen itself, whereas T cells recognize antigen only in association with MHC proteins.

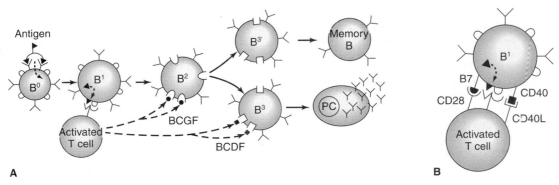

Figure 58–6. **A:** B-cell activation by helper T cells. B⁰ is a resting B cell to which a multivalent antigen (⨸) is attaching to monomer IgM receptors (Y). The antigen is internalized, and a fragment (▲) is returned to the surface in conjunction with a class II molecule (∩). A receptor on an activated T cell recognizes the complex on the B-cell surface, and the T cell produces B-cell growth factor (BCGF, IL-4; ●) and B-cell differentiation factor (BCDF, IL-5; ■). These factors cause the progression of the B¹ cell to form B² and B³ cells, which differentiate into antibody-producing (eg, pentamer IgM) plasma cells (PC). Memory B cells are also produced. **B:** Inducible protein B7 (▶) on the B cell must interact with CD28 protein on the helper T cell in order for the helper T cell to be fully activated, and CD40L (CD40 ligand) on the helper T cell must interact with CD40 on the B cell for the B cell to be activated and synthesize the full range of antibodies. (Modified and reproduced, with permission, from Stites DP, Terr A [editors]: *Basic & Clinical Immunology*, 7th ed. Originally published by Appleton & Lange. Copyright © 1991 by The McGraw-Hill Companies, Inc.)

interact with the receptor on the helper T cell, and, if the costimulatory signal is given by the B7 protein on the B cell interacting with CD28 protein on the helper T cell, the helper T cell is then stimulated to produce lymphokines, eg, IL-2, B-cell growth factor (IL-4), and B-cell differentiation factor (IL-5). IL-4 and IL-5 induce "class switching" from IgM, which is the first class of immunoglobulins produced, to other classes, namely, IgG, IgA, and IgE (see the end of Chapter 59). These factors stimulate the B cell to divide and differentiate into many antibody-producing plasma cells.

Note that interleukins alone are *not* sufficient to activate B cells. A membrane protein on activated helper T cells, called CD40 ligand (CD40L), must interact with a protein called CD40 on the surface of the resting B cells to stimulate the differentiation of B cells into antibody-producing plasma cells (Figure 58–6B). Furthermore, other proteins on the surface of these cells serve to strengthen the interaction between the helper T cell and the antigen-presenting B cell; eg, CD28 on the T cell interacts with B7 on the B cell, and LFA-1 on the T cell interacts with ICAM-1 on the B cell. (There are also ICAM proteins on the T cell that interact with LFA proteins on the B cell.)

In the T-cell-dependent response, all classes of antibody are made (IgG, IgM, IgA, etc), whereas in the **T-cell-independent response, primarily IgM is made.** This indicates that lymphokines produced by the helper T cell

are needed for class switching. The T-cell-dependent response generates memory B cells, whereas the T-cell-independent response does not; therefore, a secondary antibody response (see Chapter 60) does not occur in the latter. The T-cell-independent response is the main response to bacterial capsular polysaccharides, because these molecules are not effectively processed and presented by APCs and hence do not activate helper T cells. The most likely reason for this is that polysaccharides do not bind to class II MHC proteins, whereas peptide antigens do.

B. CELL-MEDIATED IMMUNITY

In the cell-mediated response, the initial events are similar to those described above for antibody production. The antigen is processed by macrophages, is fragmented, and is presented in conjunction with class II MHC molecules on the surface. These interact with the receptor on the helper T cell, which is then stimulated to produce lymphokines such as IL-2 (T-cell growth factor), which stimulates the specific helper and cytotoxic T cells to grow.

C. SUPPRESSION OF CERTAIN IMMUNE RESPONSES

A subset of T cells called regulatory T cells (TR) has been shown to inhibit several immune-mediated diseases, especially autoimmune diseases, in animals. (These cells are also called suppressor T cells.) TR cells are 5% to 10% of the CD4-positive cells and are characterized by possessing the CD25 marker. Interleukin-6 produced by activated dendritic cells can block the inhibitory action of TR cells and allow effector T cells to function properly in defense against pathogenic microbes. It is not known how regulatory cells reduce/ suppress the immune response.

When there is an imbalance in numbers or activity between CD4 and CD8 cells, cellular immune mechanisms are greatly impaired. For example, in lepromatous leprosy there is unrestrained multiplication of *Mycobacterium leprae,* a lack of delayed hypersensitivity to *M. leprae* antigens, a lack of cellular immunity to that organism, and an excess of CD8 cells in lesions. Removal of some CD8 cells can restore cellular immunity in such patients and limit *M. leprae* multiplication. In acquired immunodeficiency syndrome (AIDS), the normal ratio of CD4:CD8 cells (> 1.5) is greatly reduced. Many CD4 cells are destroyed by the human immunodeficiency virus (HIV), and the number of CD8 cells increases. This imbalance, ie, a loss of helper activity and an increase in suppressor activity results in a susceptibility to opportunistic infections and certain tumors.

One important part of the host response to infection is the increased expression of class I and class II MHC proteins induced by various cytokines, especially interferons such as gamma interferon. The increased amount of MHC proteins leads to increased antigen presentation and a more vigorous immune response. However, certain viruses can suppress the increase in MHC protein expression, thereby enhancing their survival. For example, hepatitis B virus, adenovirus, and cytomegalovirus can prevent an increase in class I MHC protein expression, thereby reducing the cytotoxic T-cell response against cells infected by these viruses.

B CELLS

B cells perform two important functions: (1) They differentiate into plasma cells and produce antibodies, and (2) they can present antigen to helper T cells.

Origin

During embryogenesis, B-cell precursors are recognized first in the fetal liver. From there they migrate to the **bone marrow,** which is their main location during adult life. Unlike T cells, they **do not require the thymus for maturation.** Pre-B cells lack surface immunoglobulins and light chains but do have μ heavy chains in the cytoplasm. The maturation of B cells has two phases: the antigen-independent phase consists of stem cells, pre-B cells, and B cells, whereas the antigen-dependent phase consists of the cells that arise subsequent to the interaction of antigen with the B cells, eg, activated B cells and plasma cells (Figure 58–7). B cells display surface IgM, which serves as a receptor for antigens. This surface IgM is a monomer, in contrast to circulating IgM, which is a pentamer. The monomeric IgM on the surface has an extra transmembrane domain that anchors the protein in the cell membrane that is not present in the circulating pentameric form of IgM. Surface IgD on some B cells may also be an antigen receptor. Pre-B cells are found in the bone marrow, whereas B cells circulate in the bloodstream.

B cells constitute about 30% of the recirculating pool of small lymphocytes, and their life span is short, ie, days or weeks. Approximately 10^9 B cells are produced each day. Within lymph nodes, they are located in germinal centers; within the spleen, they are found in the white pulp. They are also found in the gut-associated lymphoid tissue, eg, Peyer's patches.

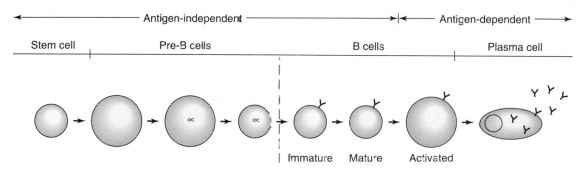

Figure 58–7. Maturation of B cells. B cells arise from stem cells and differentiate into pre-B cells expressing μ heavy chains in the cytoplasm and then into B cells expressing monomer IgM on the surface. This occurs independent of antigen. Activation of B cells and differentiation into plasma cells is dependent on antigen. Cells to the left of the vertical dotted line do not have IgM on their surface, whereas B cells, to the right of the vertical line, do. μ, mu heavy chains in cytoplasm; Y, IgM. (Modified and reproduced, with permission, from Stites DP, Terr A [editors]: *Basic & Clinical Immunology,* 7th ed. Originally published by Appleton & Lange. Copyright © 1991 by The McGraw-Hill Companies, Inc.)

Clonal Selection

How do antibodies arise? Does the antigen "instruct" the B cell to make an antibody, or does the antigen "select" a B cell endowed with the preexisting capacity to make the antibody?

It appears that the latter alternative, ie, **clonal selection,** accounts for antibody formation. Each individual has a large pool of B lymphocytes (about 10^7). Each immunologically responsive B cell bears a surface receptor (either IgM or IgD) that can react with one antigen (or closely related group of antigens); ie, there are about 10^7 different specificities. An antigen interacts with the B lymphocyte that shows the best "fit" with its immunoglobulin surface receptor. After the antigen binds, the B cell is stimulated to proliferate and form a clone of cells. These selected B cells soon become plasma cells and secrete antibody specific for the antigen. Plasma cells synthesize the immunoglobulins with the same antigenic specificity (ie, they have the same heavy chain and the same light chain) as those carried by the selected B cell. Antigenic specificity does *not* change when heavy-chain class switching occurs (see Chapter 59).

Note that clonal selection also occurs with T cells. The antigen interacts with a specific receptor located on the surface of either a CD4-positive or a CD8-positive T cell. This "selects" this cell and activates it to expand into a clone of cells with the same specificity.

Activation of B Cells

In the following example, the B cell is the APC. Multivalent antigen binds to surface IgM (or IgD) and cross-links adjacent immunoglobulin molecules. The immunoglobulins aggregate to form "patches" and eventually migrate to one pole of the cell to form a cap. Endocytosis of the capped material follows, the antigen is processed, and epitopes appear on the surface in conjunction with class II MHC proteins. This complex is recognized by a helper T cell with a receptor for the antigen on its surface.[6] The T cell now produces various interleukins (IL-2, IL-4, and IL-5) that stimulate the growth and differentiation of the B cell.

The activation of B cells to produce the full range of antibodies requires two other interactions in addition to recognition of the epitope by the T-cell antigen receptor and the production of IL-4 and IL-5 by the helper T cell. These costimulatory interactions, which occur between surface proteins on the T and B cells, are as follows: (1) CD28 on the T cell must interact with B7 on the B cell, and (2) CD40L on the T cell must interact with CD40 on the B cell. The CD28-B7 interaction is required for activation of the T cell to produce IL-2, and the CD40L-CD40 interaction is required for class switching from IgM to IgG and other immunoglobulin classes to occur.

Effector Functions of B Cells/Plasma Cells

The end result of the activation process is the production of many **plasma cells** that produce large amounts of immunoglobulins specific for the epitope. Plasma cells secrete thousands of antibody molecules per second for a few days and then die. Some activated B cells form **memory cells,** which can remain quiescent for long periods but are capable of being activated rapidly upon reexposure to antigen. Most memory B cells have surface IgG that serves as the antigen receptor, but some have IgM. Memory T cells secrete interleukins that enhance antibody production by the memory B cells. The presence of these cells explains the rapid appearance of antibody in the secondary response (see Chapter 60).

ANTIGEN-PRESENTING CELLS

1. Macrophages

Macrophages have three main functions: phagocytosis, antigen presentation, and cytokine production (Table 58–5).

(1) **Phagocytosis.** Macrophages ingest bacteria, viruses, and other foreign particles. They have surface Fc receptors that interact with the Fc portion of IgG, thereby enhancing the uptake of opsonized organisms. Macrophages also have receptors for C3b, another important opsonin. After ingestion, the phagosome containing the microbe fuses with a lysosome. The microbe is killed within this phagolysosome by reactive oxygen and reactive nitrogen compounds and by lysosomal enzymes.

(2) **Antigen presentation.** Foreign material is ingested and degraded, and fragments of antigen are presented on the macrophage cell surface (in conjunction with class II MHC proteins) for interaction with the TCR of CD4-positive helper T cells. Degradation of the foreign protein stops when the fragment associates with the class II MHC protein in the cytoplasm. The complex is then transported to the cell surface by specialized "transporter" proteins.

---

[6] Macrophages bearing antigen bound to class II MHC proteins can also present antigen to the T cell, resulting in antibody formation. In general, B cells are poor activators of "virgin" T cells in the primary response because B cells do not make IL-1. B cells are, however, very good activators of memory T cells because little, if any, IL-1 is needed.

Table 58–5. Important features of macrophages.

Functions	Mechanisms
Phagocytosis	Ingestion and killing of microbes in phagolysosomes. Killing caused by reactive oxygen intermediates such as superoxides, reactive nitrogen intermediates such as nitric oxide, and lysosomal enzymes such as proteases, nucleases, and lysozyme.
Antigen presentation	Presentation of antigen in association with class II MHC proteins to CD4-positive helper T cells. Also displays B7 protein, which acts as a costimulator of helper T cells.
Cytokine production	Synthesis and release of cytokines such as IL-1 and TNF, and chemokines such as IL-8.

(3) **Cytokine production.** Macrophages produce several cytokines (macrokines, monokines), the most important of which are IL-1 and TNF. IL-1 (endogenous pyrogen) plays a role in the activation of helper T cells, and TNF is an important inflammatory mediator (see page 419). In addition, macrophages produce interleukin-8 (IL-8), an important chemokine that attracts neutrophils and T cells to the site of infection.

These three functions are greatly enhanced when a process called **macrophage activation** occurs. Macrophages are activated initially by substances such as bacterial lipopolysaccharide (LPS, endotoxin), by bacterial peptidoglycan, and by bacterial DNA. (Human DNA is methylated, whereas bacterial DNA is unmethylated and therefore is perceived as foreign.) These substances interact with "toll-like receptors" on the macrophage surface and signal the cell to produce certain cytokines. Macrophages are also activated by gamma interferon produced by helper T cells. Gamma interferon increases the synthesis of class II MHC proteins, which enhances antigen presentation and increases the microbicidal activity of macrophages.

Macrophages are derived from bone marrow histiocytes and exist both free, eg, monocytes, and fixed in tissues, eg, Kupffer cells of the liver. Macrophages migrate to the site of inflammation, attracted by certain mediators, especially C5a, an anaphylatoxin released in the complement cascade.

2. Dendritic Cells

Dendritic cells are a third type of cell that function as "professional" antigen-presenting cells (macrophages and B cells are the other two); ie, they express class II MHC proteins and present antigen to CD4-positive T cells. They are particularly important because they are the main inducers of the primary antibody response. The name "dendritic" describes their many long, narrow processes (that resemble neuronal dendrites), which make them very efficient at making contact with foreign material. Dendritic cells are primarily located

under the skin and the mucosa, eg, Langerhans' cells in the skin. Dendritic cells migrate from their peripheral location under the skin and mucosa to local lymph nodes, where they present antigen to helper T cells.

SUMMARY OF THE INTERACTION OF ANTIGEN-PRESENTING CELLS, T CELLS, & B CELLS

The interactive process is initiated by the ingestion of a microbe by an antigen-presenting cell, for example, the ingestion of a bacterium by a dendritic cell in the skin. The dendritic cell migrates to the lymph node via lymph vessels, attracted there by chemokines. In the lymph node, the dendritic cell presents antigen to the T cell bearing a receptor specific for that antigen. While this process is occurring, fragments of the microbe circulate to the lymph node and bind directly to the B cell antigen receptor (membrane IgM). The antigen is internalized, processed, and presented to helper T cells with the correct receptor. Various chemokines and chemokine receptors (such as CCR7) facilitate the migration of these cells to a junctional area in the lymph node where they have a high probability of interacting with each other. The proximity of the B cell to the helper T cell allows interleukins produced by the helper T cell to efficiently activate antibody synthesis by the B cell.

FOLLICULAR DENDRITIC CELLS

These cells have a similar appearance to the dendritic cells mentioned above but are quite different from them in their location and function. Follicular dendritic cells (FDCs) are located in the B-cell-containing germinal centers of the follicles in the spleen and lymph nodes. They do not present antigen to helper T cells because they do not produce class II MHC proteins. Rather, they capture antigen-antibody complexes via Fc receptors located on their surface. The antigen-antibody complexes are then detected by activated B cells. The antibody produced by these B cells undergoes affinity maturation. (Affinity maturation is the improvement in the affinity of an antibody for the antigen that occurs upon repeated exposure to the antigen.) Affinity maturation is described in Chapter 60. In addition, FDCs produce chemokines that attract B cells to the follicles in the spleen and lymph nodes.

NATURAL KILLER CELLS

NK cells play an important role in the innate host defenses (Table 58–6). They specialize in killing virus-infected cells and tumor cells by secreting cytotoxins (perforins and granzymes) similar to those of cytotoxic T lymphocytes and by participating in Fas-Fas ligand-mediated apoptosis. They are called "natural" killer cells because they are active without prior exposure to the virus, are not enhanced by exposure, and are not specific for any virus. They can kill without antibody, but antibody (IgG) enhances their effectiveness, a process called antibody-dependent cellular cytotoxicity (ADCC) (see the section on effector functions of T cells [above]). IL-12 and gamma interferon are potent activators of NK cells. Approximately 5% to 10% of peripheral lymphocytes are NK cells.

NK cells are lymphocytes with some T-cell markers, but they do not have to pass through the thymus in order to mature. They have no immunologic memory and, unlike cytotoxic T cells, have no T-cell receptor; also, killing does not require recognition of MHC pro-teins. In fact, NK cells have receptors that detect the presence of class I MHC proteins on the cell surface. If a cell displays sufficient class I MHC proteins, that cell is *not* killed by the NK cell. Many virus-infected cells and tumor cells display a significantly reduced amount of class I MHC proteins, and it is those cells that are recognized and killed by the NK cells. Humans who lack NK cells are predisposed to life-threatening infections with varicella-zoster virus and cytomegalovirus.

NK cells detect the presence of cancer cells by recognizing a protein called MICA that is found on the surface of many cancer cells but not normal cells. Interaction of MICA with a receptor on NK cells triggers the production of cytotoxins by the NK cell and death of the tumor cell.

POLYMORPHONUCLEAR NEUTROPHILS

Neutrophils are a very important component of our innate host defenses, and severe bacterial infections occur if they are too few in number (neutropenia) or are deficient in function, as in chronic granulomatous disease. They have cytoplasmic granules that stain a pale pink (neutral) color with blood stains such as Wright stain, in contrast to eosinophils and basophils whose granules stain red and blue, respectively. These granules are lysosomes, which contain a variety of degradative enzymes that are important in the **bactericidal** action of these cells. The process of phagocytosis and the bactericidal action of neutrophils is described in detail in Chapter 8.

Table 58–6. Important features of natural killer (NK) cells.

I. Nature of NK Cells
• Large granular lymphocytes
• Lack T-cell receptor, CD3 proteins, and surface IgM and IgD
• Thymus not required for development
• Normal numbers in Severe Combined Immunodeficiency Disease (SCID) patients
• Activity not enhanced by prior exposure
II. Function of NK Cells
• Kill virus-infected cells and cancer cells
• Killing is nonspecific, ie, not specific for viral or cancer antigens
• Killing is not dependent on foreign antigen presentation by class I or II MHC proteins
• Killing is activated by the failure of a cell to present self antigen in association with class I MHC proteins or by a reduction in the number of class I MHC proteins on the cell surface
• Kill by producing perforins and granzymes, which cause apoptosis of target cell

Note that neutrophils do not display class II MHC proteins on their surface and therefore do not present antigen to helper T cells. This is in contrast to macrophages that are also phagocytes but do present antigen to helper T cells.

Neutrophils can be thought of as a "two-edged" sword. The positive edge of the sword is their powerful microbicidal activity, but the negative edge is the tissue damage caused by the release of degradative enzymes. An excellent example of the latter is the damage to the glomeruli in acute post-streptococcal glomerulonephritis. The damage is caused by enzymes released by neutrophils attracted to the glomeruli by C5a activated by the antigen-antibody complexes deposited on the glomerular membrane.

EOSINOPHILS

Eosinophils are white blood cells with cytoplasmic granules that appear red when stained with Wright stain. The red color is caused by the negatively charged eosin dye binding to the positively charged major basic protein in the granules. The eosinophil count is elevated in two medically important types of diseases: **parasitic diseases**, especially those caused by nematodes (see Chapter 56), and **hypersensitivity diseases**, such as asthma and serum sickness (see Chapter 65). Diseases caused by protozoa are typically not characterized by eosinophilia.

The function of eosinophils has not been clearly established. It seems likely that their main function is to defend against the migratory larvae of nematodes, such as *Strongyloides* and *Trichinella*. They attach to the surface of the larvae and discharge the contents of their granules, which in turn damages the cuticle of the larvae. Attachment to the larvae is mediated by receptors on the eosinophil surface for the Fc portion of the heavy chain of IgG and IgE.

Another function of eosinophils may be to mitigate the effects of immediate hypersensitivity reactions because the granules of eosinophils contain histaminase, an enzyme that degrades histamine, which is an important mediator of immediate reactions. However, the granules of the eosinophils also contain leukotrienes and peroxidases, which can damage tissue and cause inflammation. The granules also contain major basic protein that damages respiratory epithelium and contributes to the pathogenesis of asthma.

Eosinophils can phagocytose bacteria but they do so weakly and are not sufficient to protect against pyogenic bacterial infections in neutropenic patients. Although they can phagocytose, they do not present antigen to helper T cells. The growth and differentiation of eosinophils is stimulated by interleukin-5.

BASOPHILS & MAST CELLS

Basophils are white blood cells with cytoplasmic granules that appear blue when stained with Wright stain. The blue color is caused by the positively charged methylene blue dye binding to several negatively charged molecules in the granules. Basophils circulate in the bloodstream, whereas mast cells, which are similar to basophils in many ways, are fixed in tissue, especially under the skin and in the mucosa of the respiratory and gastrointestinal tracts.

Basophils and mast cells have receptors on their surface for the Fc portion of the heavy chain of IgE. When adjacent IgE molecules are cross-linked by antigen, immunologically active mediators, such as histamine, and enzymes, such as peroxidases and hydrolases, are released. These cause inflammation and, when produced in large amounts, cause **severe immediate hypersensitivity reactions such as systemic anaphylaxis.** Mast cells also play a role in the inflammatory changes seen in the joints in rheumatoid arthritis. They produce both inflammatory cytokines and enzymes that degrade cartilage in the joints.

IMPORTANT CYTOKINES

The important functions of the main cytokines are described in Table 58–7.

Mediators Affecting Lymphocytes

(1) **IL-1** is a protein produced mainly by macrophages. It activates a wide variety of target cells, eg, T and B lymphocytes, neutrophils, epithelial cells, and fibroblasts, to grow, differentiate, or synthesize specific products. For example, it stimulates helper T cells to differentiate and produce IL-2 (see below). In addition, IL-1 is **endogenous pyrogen,** which acts on the hypothalamus to cause the fever associated with infections and other inflammatory reactions. (Exogenous pyrogen is endotoxin, a lipopolysaccharide found in the cell wall of gram-negative bacteria [see Chapter 7].)

(2) **IL-2** is a protein produced mainly by helper T cells that **stimulates both helper and cytotoxic T cells to grow. IL-2 is T-cell growth factor.** Resting T cells are stimulated by antigen (or other stimulators) both to produce IL-2 and to form IL-2 receptors on their surface, thereby acquiring the capacity to respond to IL-2. Interaction of IL-2 with its receptor stimulates DNA synthesis. IL-2 acts synergistically with IL-4 (see below) to stimulate the growth of B cells.

(3) **IL-4 and IL-5** are proteins produced by helper T cells; they promote the growth and differentiation of B cells, respectively. IL-4 enhances humoral immunity by increasing the number of Th-2 cells, the subset of helper

Table 58–7. Important functions of the main cytokines.

Cytokine	Major Source	Important Functions
Interleukin-1	Macrophages	Activates helper T cells. Causes fever.
Interleukin-2	Th-1 subset of helper T cells	Activates helper and cytotoxic T cells. Also activates B cells.
Interleukin-4	Th-2 subset of helper T cells	Stimulates B-cell growth. Increases isotype switching and IgE. Increases Th-2 subset of helper T cells.
Interleukin-5	Th-2 subset of helper T cells	Stimulates B-cell differentiation. Increases eosinophils and IgA.
Gamma interferon	Th-1 subset of helper T cells	Stimulates phagocytosis and killing by macrophages and NK cells. Increases class I and II MHC protein expression.
Tumor necrosis factor	Macrophages	Low concentration: activates neutrophils and increases their adhesion to endothelial cells. High concentration: mediates septic shock, acts as cachectin, causes necrosis of tumors.

T cells that produces IL-4 and IL-5 (Figure 58–3). IL-4 is required for class (isotype) switching, ie, the switching from one class of antibody to another, within the antibody-producing cell (see Chapter 59). It also enhances the synthesis of IgE and hence may predispose to type I (immediate) hypersensitivity. IL-5 enhances the synthesis of IgA and stimulates the production and activation of eosinophils. Eosinophils are an important host defense against many helminths (worms), eg, *Strongyloides* (see Chapter 56), and are increased in immediate hypersensitivity (allergic) reactions (see Chapter 65).

(4) Other interleukins, such as IL-6, IL-10, IL-12, and IL-13, also affect lymphocytes. IL-6 is produced by helper T cells and macrophages. It stimulates B cells to differentiate, induces fever by affecting the hypothalamus, and induces the production of acute-phase proteins by the liver. Acute-phase proteins are described on page 397.

IL-10 and IL-12 regulate the production of Th-1 cells, the cells that mediate delayed hypersensitivity (Figure 58–3). IL-12 is produced by macrophages and promotes the development of Th-1 cells, whereas IL-10 is produced by Th-2 cells and inhibits the development of Th-1 cells by limiting gamma interferon production. (Gamma interferon is described below.) The relative amounts of IL-4, IL-10, and IL-12 drive the differentiation of Th-1 and Th-2 cells and therefore enhance either cell-mediated or humoral immunity, respectively. This is likely to have important medical consequences because the main host defense against certain infections is either cell-mediated or humoral immunity. For example, *Leishmania* infections in mice are lethal if a humoral response predominates but are controlled if a vigorous cell-mediated response occurs.

The **IL-12–gamma interferon axis** is very important in the ability of our host defenses to control infections by intracellular pathogens, such as *M. tuberculosis* and *L. monocytogenes*. IL-12 increases the number of Th-1 cells, and Th-1 cells produce the gamma interferon that activates the macrophages that phagocytose and kill the intracellular bacterial pathogens mentioned above.

IL-13 is implicated as the mediator of allergic airway disease (asthma). IL-13 is made by Th-2 cells and binds to a receptor that shares a chain with the IL-4 receptor. In animals, IL-13 was shown to be necessary and sufficient to cause asthma. IL-13 is involved in producing the airway hyperresponsiveness seen in asthma but not in increasing the amount of IgE.

(5) The main function of transforming growth factor-β (TGF-β) is to **inhibit** the growth and activities of T cells. It is viewed as an "anti-cytokine" because, in addition to its action on T cells, it can inhibit many functions of macrophages, B cells, neutrophils, and natural killer cells by counteracting the action of other activating factors. Although it is a "negative regulator" of the immune response, it stimulates wound healing by enhancing the synthesis of collagen. It is produced by many types of cells, including T cells, B cells, and macrophages. In summary, the role of TGF-β is to dampen or suppress the immune response when it is no longer needed after an infection and to promote the healing process.

Mediators Affecting Macrophages & Monocytes

Chemokines are a group of cytokines that can attract either macrophages or neutrophils to the site of infection. The term "chemokine" is a contraction of **chemo**tactic and cyto**kine**. Chemokines are produced by various cells in the infected area, such as endothelial cells and resident macrophages. The circulating neutrophils and macrophages (monocytes) are attracted to the site by an increasing gradient of chemokines, then bind to selectins on the endothelial cell surface. Chemokines also activate integrins on the surface of the neutrophils and macrophages that bind to ICAM proteins on the endothelial cell surface. The interaction between integrin and ICAM facilitates the movement of the white cells into the tissue to reach the infected area.

Approximately 50 chemokines have been identified; they are small polypeptides ranging in size from 68 to 120 amino acids. The alpha-chemokines have two adjacent cysteines separated by another amino acid (Cys-X-Cys), whereas the beta-chemokines have two adjacent cysteines (Cys-Cys) (Table 58–8). The alpha-chemokines attract neutrophils and are produced by activated mononuclear cells. IL-8 is a very important member of this group. The beta-chemokines attract macrophages and monocytes and are produced by activated T cells. RANTES and MCAF are important beta-chemokines.

There are specific receptors for chemokines on the surface of cells, such as neutrophils and monocytes. Interaction of the chemokine with its receptor results in changes in cell surface proteins that allow the cell to adhere to and migrate through the endothelium to the site of infection.

Mediators Affecting Polymorphonuclear Leukocytes

(1) TNF activates the phagocytic and killing activities of neutrophils and increases the synthesis of adhesion molecules by endothelial cells. The adhesion molecules mediate the attachment of neutrophils at the site of infection.

(2) Chemotactic factors for neutrophils, basophils, and eosinophils selectively attract each cell type. Interleukin-8 and complement component C5a are important attractants for neutrophils. (See the discussion of chemokines [above] and Table 58–8.)

(3) Leukocyte-inhibitory factor inhibits migration of neutrophils, analogous to migration-inhibitory factor (below). Its function is to retain the cells at the site of infection.

Mediators Affecting Stem Cells

IL-3 is made by activated helper T cells and supports the growth and differentiation of bone marrow stem cells. Granulocyte-macrophage colony-stimulating factor (GM-CSF, sargramostim) is made by T lymphocytes and macrophages. It stimulates the growth of granulocytes and macrophages and enhances the antimicrobial activity of macrophages. It is used clinically to improve regeneration of these cells after bone marrow transplantation. Granulocyte colony-stimulating factor (G-CSF, filgrastim) is made by various cells, eg, macrophages, fibroblasts, and endothelial cells. It enhances the development of neutrophils from stem cells and is used clinically to prevent infections in patients who have received cancer chemotherapy. The stimulation of neutrophil production by G-CSF and GM-CSF results in the increased number of these cells in the peripheral blood after infection.

Mediators Produced by Macrophages That Affect Other Cells

(1) TNF-α is an **inflammatory mediator** released primarily by macrophages. It has many important effects that differ depending on the concentration. At low concentrations, it increases the synthesis of adhesion molecules by endothelial cells, which allows neutrophils to adhere to blood vessel walls at the site of infection. It also activates the respiratory burst within neutrophils, thereby enhancing the killing power of these phagocytes. It increases lymphokine synthesis by helper T cells and stimulates the growth of B cells. At high concentrations, it is an important mediator of **endotoxin-induced septic shock**; antibody to TNF-α prevents the action of endotoxin. (The action of endotoxin is described in Chapter 7.) TNF-α is also known as **cachectin** because it inhibits lipoprotein lipase in adipose tissue, thereby reducing the utilization of fatty acids. This results in cachexia. TNF-α, as its name implies, causes the **death and necrosis of certain tumors** in experimental animals. It may do this by promoting intravascular coagulation that causes infarction of the tumor tissue. Note the similarity of this intravascular coagulation with the DIC of septic shock, both of which are caused by TNF-α.

Table 58–8. Chemokines of medical importance.

Class	Chemistry	Attracts	Produced by	Examples
Alpha	C-X-C	Neutrophils	Activated mononuclear cells	Interleukin-8
Beta	C-C	Monocytes	Activated T cells	RANTES,[1] MCAF[2]

[1]RANTES is an abbreviation for regulated upon activation, normal T expressed and secreted.
[2]MCAF is an abbreviation for macrophage chemoattractant and activating factor.

(2) **Nitric oxide** (NO) is an important mediator made by macrophages in response to the presence of endotoxin, a lipopolysaccharide found in the cell wall of gram-negative bacteria. NO causes vasodilation, which contributes to the hypotension seen in septic shock. Inhibitors of NO synthase, the enzyme that catalyzes the synthesis of NO from arginine, can prevent the hypotension associated with septic shock.

(3) **Macrophage migration inhibitory factor** (MIF) is another important mediator made by macrophages in response to endotoxin. The function of MIF is to retain the macrophages at the site of infection. Recent studies have shown that MIF plays a major role in the induction of septic shock. Antibody against MIF can prevent septic shock in animals genetically incapable of producing TNF. The mechanism of action of MIF in septic shock is unclear at this time.

Mediators With Other Effects

(1) **Interferons** are glycoproteins that block virus replication and exert many immunomodulating functions. Alpha interferon (from leukocytes) and beta interferon (from fibroblasts) are induced by viruses (or dou-ble-stranded RNA) and have antiviral activity (see Chapter 33). **Gamma interferon** is a lymphokine produced primarily by the Th-1 subset of helper T cells. It is one of the most potent activators of the phagocytic activity of macrophages, NK cells, and neutrophils, thereby enhancing their ability to kill microorganisms and tumor cells. For example, it greatly increases the killing of intracellular bacteria, such as *M. tuberculosis,* by macrophages. It also increases the synthesis of class I and II MHC proteins in a variety of cell types. This enhances antigen presentation by these cells.

(2) **Lymphotoxin** (also known as TNF-β) is made by activated T lymphocytes and causes effects similar to those of TNF-α. It binds to the same receptor as TNF-α and hence has the same effects as TNF-α.

PRACTICE QUESTIONS: USMLE & COURSE EXAMINATIONS

Questions on the topics discussed in this chapter can be found in the Immunology section of Part XI: USMLE (National Board) Practice Questions starting on page 562. Also see Part XII: USMLE (National Board) Practice Examination starting on page 583.

Antibodies are globulin proteins (immunoglobulins) that react specifically with the antigen that stimulated their production. They make up about 20% of the protein in blood plasma. Blood contains three types of globulins, alpha, beta, and gamma, based on their electrophoretic migration rate. Antibodies are gamma globulins. There are five classes of antibodies: IgG, IgM, IgA, IgD, and IgE. Antibodies are subdivided into these five classes based on differences in their heavy chains.

The most important functions of antibodies are to **neutralize toxins and viruses,** to **opsonize microbes** so they are more easily phagocytosed, to **activate complement,** and to **prevent the attachment** of microbes to mucosal surfaces. The specific antibody classes that mediate these functions are described in Table 59–1. In addition to these functions, antibodies have a **catalytic (enzymatic) capability** that is described in a separate section at the end of this chapter.

MONOCLONAL ANTIBODIES

Antibodies that arise in an animal in response to typical antigens are heterogeneous, because they are formed by several different clones of plasma cells; ie, they are **polyclonal.** Antibodies that arise from a single clone of cells, eg, in a plasma cell tumor (myeloma),[1] are homogeneous; ie, they are **monoclonal.**

Monoclonal antibodies also can be made in the laboratory by fusing a myeloma cell with an antibody-producing cell (Figure 59–1; also see Box). Such **hybridomas** produce virtually unlimited quantities of monoclonal antibodies that are useful in diagnostic tests and in research (see Box on page 423).

IMMUNOGLOBULIN STRUCTURE

Immunoglobulins are glycoproteins made up of **light** (L) and **heavy** (H) polypeptide chains. The terms "light" and "heavy" refer to molecular weight; light

chains have a molecular weight of about 25,000, whereas heavy chains have a molecular weight of 50,000–70,000. The simplest antibody molecule has a Y shape (Figure 59–2) and consists of four polypeptide chains: two H chains and two L chains. The four chains are linked by disulfide bonds. An individual antibody molecule always consists of **identical** H chains and **identical** L chains. This is primarily the result of two phenomena: allelic exclusion (see page 429) and regulation within the B cell, which ensure the synthesis of either kappa (κ) or lambda (λ) L chains but not both.

L and H chains are subdivided into **variable** and **constant** regions. The regions are composed of three-dimensionally folded, repeating segments called domains. An L chain consists of one variable (V_L) and one constant (C_L) domain. Most H chains consist of one variable (V_H) and three constant (C_H) domains. (IgG and IgA have three C_H domains, whereas IgM and IgE have four.) Each domain is approximately 110 amino acids long. The **variable** regions of both the light and heavy chain are responsible for **antigen-binding,** whereas the **constant** region of the heavy chain is responsible for **various biologic functions,** eg, complement activation and binding to cell surface receptors. The complement binding site is in the C_H2 domain. The constant region of the light chain has no known biologic function.

The variable regions of both L and H chains have three extremely variable (**hypervariable**) amino acid sequences at the amino-terminal end that form the antigen-binding site (Figure 59–3). Only 5–10 amino acids in each hypervariable region form the antigen-binding site. Antigen-antibody binding involves electrostatic and van der Waals' forces and hydrogen and hydrophobic bonds rather than covalent bonds. The remarkable specificity of antibodies is due to these hypervariable regions (see the discussion of idiotypes on page 426).

L chains belong to one of two types, κ (**kappa**) or λ (**lambda**), on the basis of amino acid differences in their constant regions. Both types occur in all classes of immunoglobulins (IgG, IgM, etc), but any one immunoglobulin molecule contains only one type of L chain.[2]

The amino-terminal portion of each L chain participates in the antigen-binding site. H chains are distinct

---

[1] Multiple myeloma is a malignant disease characterized by an overproduction of plasma cells (B cells). All the myeloma cells in a patient produce the same type of immunoglobulin molecule, which indicates that all the cells arose from a single progenitor. Excess κ or λ L chains are synthesized and appear as dimers in the urine. These are known as Bence Jones proteins and have the unusual attribute of precipitating at 50–60 °C but dissolving when the temperature is raised to the boiling point.

[2] In humans, the ratio of immunoglobulins containing κ chains to those containing λ chains is approximately 2:1.

Table 59–1. Properties of human immunoglobulins.

Property	IgG	IgA	IgM	IgD	IgE
Percentage of total immunoglobulin in serum (approx)	75	15	9	0.2	0.004
Serum concentration (mg/dL) (approx)	1000	200	120	3	0.05
Sedimentation coefficient	7S	7S or 11S[1]	19S	7S	8S
Molecular weight ($\times 1000$)	150	170 or 400[1]	900	180	190
Structure	Monomer	Monomer or dimer	Monomer or pentamer	Monomer	Monomer
H-chain symbol	γ	α	μ	δ	ε
Complement fixation	+	–	+	–	–
Transplacental passage	+	–	–	–	–
Mediation of allergic responses	–	–	–	–	+
Found in secretions	–	+	–	–	–
Opsonization	+	–	–[2]	–	–
Antigen receptor on B cell	–	–	+	?	–
Polymeric form contains J chain	–	+	+	–	–

[1]The 11S form is found in secretions (eg, saliva, milk, and tears) and fluids of the respiratory, intestinal, and genital tracts.
[2] IgM opsonizes indirectly by activating complement. This produces C3b, which is an opsonin.

for each of the five immunoglobulin classes and are designated γ, α, μ, ε, and δ (Table 59–2). The amino-terminal portion of each H chain participates in the antigen-binding site; the carboxy terminal forms the Fc fragment, which has the biologic activities described above and in Table 59–2.

If an antibody molecule is treated with a proteolytic enzyme such as papain, peptide bonds in the "hinge" region are broken, producing two identical **Fab fragments,** which carry the antigen-binding sites, and one **Fc fragment,** which is involved in placental transfer, complement fixation, attachment site for various cells, and other biologic activities (Figure 59–2).

IMMUNOGLOBULIN CLASSES

IgG

Each IgG molecule consists of two L chains and two H chains linked by disulfide bonds (molecular formula H2L2). Because it has two identical antigen-binding sites, it is said to be **divalent.** There are four subclasses, IgG1–IgG4, based on antigenic differences in the H chains and on the number and location of disulfide bonds. IgG1 makes up most (65%) of the total IgG. IgG2 anti-

body is directed against polysaccharide antigens and is an important host defense against encapsulated bacteria.

IgG is the predominant antibody in the **secondary response** and constitutes an important defense against bacteria and viruses (Table 59–1). IgG is the only antibody to **cross the placenta;** only its Fc portion binds to receptors on the surface of placental cells. It is therefore the **most abundant immunoglobulin in newborns.** IgG is one of the two immunoglobulins that can activate complement; IgM is the other (see Chapter 63).

IgG is the immunoglobulin that **opsonizes.** It can opsonize, ie, enhance phagocytosis, because there are receptors for the γH chain on the surface of phagocytes. IgM does not opsonize directly, because there are no receptors on the phagocyte surface for the μH chain. However, IgM activates complement, and the resulting C3b can opsonize because there are binding sites for C3b on the surface of phagocytes.

IgA

IgA is the main immunoglobulin in **secretions** such as colostrum, saliva, tears, and respiratory, intestinal, and genital tract secretions. It prevents attachment of microorganisms, eg, bacteria and viruses, to mucous

HYBRIDOMAS & MONOCLONAL ANTIBODIES

One of the most important scientific advances of this century is the hybridoma cell, which has the remarkable ability to produce large quantities of a single molecular species of immunoglobulin. These immunoglobulins, which are known as monoclonal antibodies, are called "monoclonal" because they are made by a clone of cells that arose from a single cell. Note, however, that this single cell is, in fact, formed by the fusion of two different cells; ie, it is a hybrid, hence the term "hybridoma."

Hybridoma cells are made in the following manner: (1) An animal, eg, a mouse, is immunized with the antigen of interest. (2) Spleen cells from this animal are grown in a culture dish in the presence of mouse myeloma cells. The myeloma cells have two important attributes: they grow indefinitely in culture, and they do not produce immunoglobulins. (3) Fusion of the cells is encouraged by adding certain chemicals, eg, polyethylene glycol. (4) The cells are grown in a special culture medium (HAT medium) that supports the growth of the fused, hybrid cells but not of the "parental" cells. (5) The resulting clones of cells are screened for the production of antibody to the antigen of interest.

Chimeric monoclonal antibodies consisting of mouse variable regions and human constant regions are being made for use in treating human diseases such as leukemia. The advantages of the human constant chain are that human complement is activated (whereas it is not if the constant region is mouse-derived) and that antibodies against the monoclonal antibody are not formed (whereas antibodies are formed if the constant region is mouse-derived). The advantage of the mouse variable region is that it is much easier to obtain monoclonal antibodies against, for example, a human tumor antigen by inoculating a mouse with the tumor cells. Chimeric antibodies can kill tumor cells either by complement-mediated cytotoxicity or by delivering toxins, eg, diphtheria toxin, specifically to the tumor cell.

Monoclonal antibodies are now used in a variety of clinical situations, such as immunosuppression related to organ transplants, treatment of autoimmune disease, treatment of cancer, and the prevention of infectious disease. Table 62–2 describes these monoclonal antibodies, their cellular targets, and their clinical use.

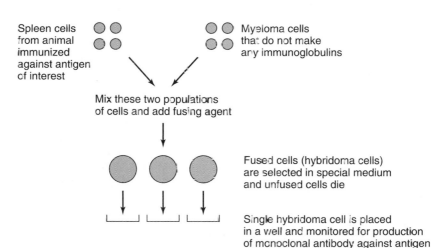

Figure 59–1. Production of monoclonal antibodies.

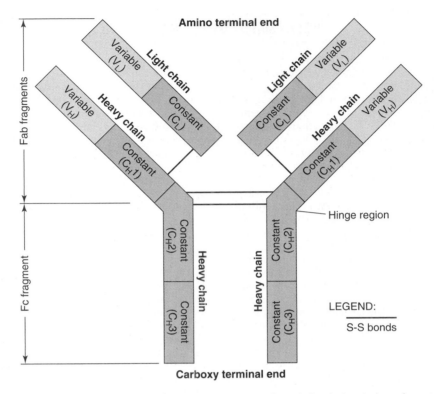

Figure 59–2. Structure of IgG. The Y-shaped IgG molecule consists of two light chains and two heavy chains. Each light chain consists of a variable region and a constant region. Each heavy chain consists of a variable region and a constant region that is divided into three domains: C_H1, C_H2, and C_H3. The C_H2 domain contains the complement-binding site, and the C_H3 domain is the site of attachment of IgG to receptors on neutrophils and macrophages. The antigen-binding site is formed by the variable regions of both the light and heavy chains. The specificity of the antigen-binding site is a function of the amino acid sequence of the hypervariable regions (see Figure 59–3). (Modified and reproduced, with permission, from Brooks GF et al: *Medical Microbiology*, 20th ed. Originally published by Appleton & Lange. Copyright © 1995 by The McGraw-Hill Companies, Inc.)

membranes. Each secretory IgA molecule consists of two H2L2 units plus one molecule each of J (joining) chain[3] and secretory component (Figure 59–4). The two heavy chains in IgA are α heavy chains.

The secretory component is a polypeptide synthesized by epithelial cells that provides for IgA passage to the mucosal surface. It also protects IgA from being degraded in the intestinal tract. In serum, some IgA exists as monomeric H2L2.

IgM

IgM is the main immunoglobulin produced early in the **primary response.** It is present as a monomer on the surface of virtually all B cells, where it functions as an antigen-binding receptor.[4] In serum, it is a **pentamer** composed of five H2L2 units plus one molecule of J (joining) chain (Figure 59–4). IgM has a μ heavy chain. Because the pentamer has 10 antigen-binding

---

[3] Only IgA and IgM have J chains. Only these immunoglobulins exist as multimers (dimers and pentamers, respectively). The J chain initiates the polymerization process, and the multimers are held together by disulfide bonds between their Fc regions.

[4] The surface monomer IgM and the serum IgM both have μ heavy chains, but the heavy chain of the surface IgM has a hydrophobic sequence that mediates binding within the cell membrane, whereas the serum IgM does not.

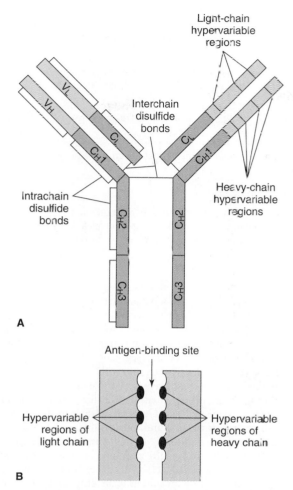

Figure 59–3. The antigen-binding site is formed by the hypervariable regions. **A:** Hypervariable regions on IgG. **B:** Magnified view of antigen-binding site. (Modified and reproduced, with permission, from Stites DP, Terr A, Parslow T [editors]: *Basic & Clinical Immunology,* 8th ed. Originally published by Appleton & Lange. Copyright © 1994 by The McGraw-Hill Companies, Inc.)

sites, it is the **most efficient** immunoglobulin in agglutination, complement fixation (activation), and other antibody reactions and is important in defense against bacteria and viruses. It can be produced by the fetus in certain infections. It has the **highest avidity** of the immunoglobulins; its interaction with antigen can involve all 10 of its binding sites.

IgD

This immunoglobulin has no known antibody function but may function as an antigen receptor; it is present on the surface of many B lymphocytes. It is present in small amounts in serum.

IgE

IgE is medically important for two reasons: (1) it mediates immediate (anaphylactic) hypersensitivity (see Chapter 65), and (2) it participates in host defenses against certain parasites, eg, helminths (worms) (see Chapter 56). The Fc region of IgE binds to the surface of mast cells and basophils. Bound IgE serves as a receptor for antigen (allergen). When the antigen-binding sites of adjacent IgEs are cross-linked by allergens, several mediators are released by the cells and immediate (anaphylactic) hypersensitivity reactions occur (see Figure 65–1). Although IgE is present in **trace** amounts in normal serum (approximately 0.004%), persons with allergic reactivity have greatly increased amounts, and IgE may appear in external secretions. IgE does not fix complement and does not cross the placenta.

IgE is the main host defense against certain important helminth (worm) infections, such as *Strongyloides, Trichinella, Ascaris,* and the hookworms *Necator* and *Ancylostoma.* The serum IgE level is usually increased in these infections. Because worms are too large to be ingested by phagocytes, they are killed by eosinophils that release worm-destroying enzymes. IgE specific for worm proteins binds to receptors on eosinophils, triggering the antibody-dependent cellular cytotoxicity (ADCC) response.

ISOTYPES, ALLOTYPES, & IDIOTYPES

Because immunoglobulins are proteins, they are antigenic, and that property allows them to be subdivided into isotypes, allotypes, and idiotypes.

(1) **Isotypes** are defined by antigenic (amino acid) differences in their constant regions. Although different antigenically, all isotypes are found in all normal humans. For example, IgG and IgM are different isotypes; the constant region of their H chains (γ and μ) is different antigenically (the five immunoglobulin classes—IgG, IgM, IgA, IgD, and IgE—are different isotypes; their H chains are antigenically different). The IgG isotype is subdivided into four subtypes, IgG1, IgG2, IgG3, and IgG4, based on antigenic differences of their heavy chains. Similarly, IgA1 and IgA2 are different isotypes (the antigenicity of the constant region of their H chains is different), and κ and λ chains are different isotypes (their constant regions also differ antigenically).

(2) **Allotypes,** on the other hand, are additional antigenic features of immunoglobulins that vary among individuals. They vary because the genes that code for the L and H chains are polymorphic, and individuals can have different alleles. For example, the γ H chain

Table 59–2. Important functions of immunoglobulins.

Immunoglobulin	Major Functions
IgG	Main antibody in the secondary response. Opsonizes bacteria, making them easier to phagocytize. Fixes complement, which enhances bacterial killing. Neutralizes bacterial toxins and viruses. Crosses the placenta.
IgA	Secretory IgA prevents attachment of bacteria and viruses to mucous membranes. Does not fix complement.
IgM	Produced in the primary response to an antigen. Fixes complement. Does not cross the placenta. Antigen receptor on the surface of B cells.
IgD	Uncertain. Found on the surface of many B cells as well as in serum.
IgE	Mediates immediate hypersensitivity by causing release of mediators from mast cells and basophils upon exposure to antigen (allergen). Defends against worm infections by causing release of enzymes from eosinophils. Does not fix complement. Main host defense against helminth infections.

contains an allotype called Gm, which is due to a one- or two-amino-acid difference that provides a different antigenicity to the molecule. Each individual inherits different allelic genes that code for one or another amino acid at the Gm site.[5]

(3) **Idiotypes** are the antigenic determinants formed by the specific amino acids in the hypervariable region.[6] Each idiotype is unique for the immunoglobulin produced by a specific clone of antibody-producing cells. Anti-idiotype antibody reacts only with the hypervariable region of the specific immunoglobulin molecule that induced it.

IMMUNOGLOBULIN GENES

To produce the very large number of different immunoglobulin molecules (10^6–10^9) without requiring excessive numbers of genes, special genetic mechanisms, eg, **DNA rearrangement** and **RNA splicing**, are used. The DNA rearrangements are performed by **recombinases**. Two important genes that encode recombinases are RAG-1 and RAG-2 (recombination-activating genes). Mutations in these genes arrest the development of lymphocytes and result in severe combined immunodeficiency (see page 472).

Each of the four immunoglobulin chains consists of two distinct regions: a variable (V) and a constant (C) region. For each type of immunoglobulin chain, ie, kappa light chain (κL), lambda light chain (λL), and the five heavy chains (γH, αH, μH, εH, and δH), there is a separate pool of gene segments located on different chromosomes.[7] Each pool contains a set of different V gene segments widely separated from the D (diversity, seen only in H chains), J (joining), and C gene segments (Figure 59–5). In the synthesis of an H chain, for example, a particular V region is translocated to lie close to a D segment, several J segments, and a C region. These genes are transcribed into mRNA, and all but one of the J segments are removed by splicing the RNA. During B-cell differentiation the first translocation brings a V_H gene near a $C\mu$ gene, leading to the formation of IgM as the first antibody produced in a primary response. Note that the J (joining) gene does *not* encode the J chain found in IgM and IgA. Note also that the DNA of the unused V, H, and J genes is discarded so a particular B cell is committed to making antibody with only one specificity.

The V region of each L chain is encoded by two gene segments (V + J). The V region of each H chain is encoded by three gene segments (V + D + J). These various segments are united into one functional V gene by DNA rearrangement. Each of these assembled V genes is then transcribed with the appropriate C genes and spliced to produce an mRNA that codes for the complete peptide chain. L and H chains are synthesized separately on polysomes and then assembled in the cytoplasm by means of disulfide bonds to form H2L2 units. Finally, an oligosaccharide is added to the constant region of the heavy chain and the immunoglobulin molecule is released from the cell.

The gene organization mechanism outlined above permits the assembly of a very large number of different molecules. Antibody **diversity** depends on (1) mul-

---

[5] Allotypes related to γ H chains are called Gm (an abbreviation of gamma); allotypes related to κ L chains are called Inv (an abbreviation of a patient's name).

[6] Any one of these antigen determinants is called an idiotope.

[7] The genes for κL, λL, and the five heavy chains are on chromosomes 2, 22, and 14, respectively.

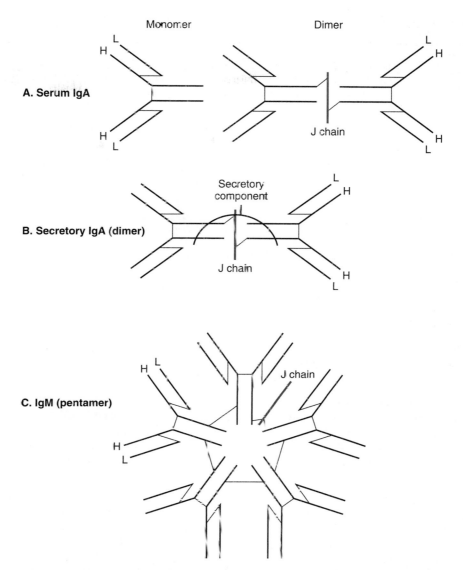

Figure 59–4. Structure of serum IgA (**A**), secretory IgA (**B**), and IgM (**C**). Note that both IgA and IgM have a J chain but that only secretory IgA has a secretory component. (Reproduced, with permission, from Stites D, Terr A, Parslow T [editors]: *Basic & Clinical Immunology*, 8th ed. Originally published by Appleton & Lange. Copyright © 1994 by The McGraw-Hill Companies, Inc.)

tiple gene segments, (2) their rearrangement into different sequences, (3) the combining of different L and H chains in the assembly of immunoglobulin molecules, and (4) mutations. A fifth mechanism called junctional diversity applies primarily to the antibody heavy chain. Junctional diversity occurs by the addition of new nucleotides at the splice junctions between the V-D and D-J gene segments.

The diversity of the T-cell antigen receptor is also dependent on the joining of V, D, and J gene segments and the combining of different alpha and beta polypeptide chains. However, unlike antibodies, mutations do *not* play a significant role in the diversity of the T-cell receptor.

Several lymphoid cancers manifest chromosomal translocations involving the VDJ region and a cellular oncogene. For example, in Burkitt's lymphoma, the *c-myc* oncogene on chromosome 8 is translocated to a

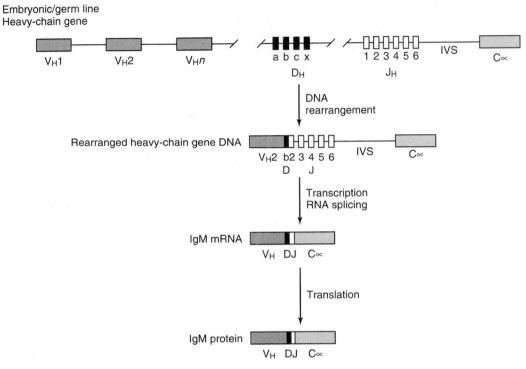

Figure 59–5. Gene rearrangement to produce a μ H chain. The antigen-binding site is formed by randomly choosing one of the V_H genes, one of the D_H genes, and one of the J_H genes. After transcription and RNA splicing, the mRNA is translated to produce an IgM heavy chain. V, variable regions; D, diversity segments; J, joining segments; C, constant region; IVS, intervening sequence. (Modified and reproduced, with permission, from Stites DP, Terr A, Parslow T [editors]: *Basic & Clinical Immunology*, 8th ed. Originally published by Appleton & Lange. Copyright © 1994 by The McGraw-Hill Companies, Inc.)

position adjacent to the VDJ region of a heavy-chain gene. The active promoter of the heavy-chain gene increases transcription of the *c-myc* oncogene, which predisposes to malignancy.

IMMUNOGLOBULIN CLASS SWITCHING (ISOTYPE SWITCHING)

Initially, all B cells carry IgM specific for an antigen and produce IgM antibody in response to exposure to that antigen. Later, gene rearrangement permits the elaboration of antibodies of the same antigenic specificity but of different immunoglobulin classes (Figure 59–6). Note that the antigenic specificity **remains the same** for the lifetime of the B cell and plasma cell because the specificity is determined by the variable region genes (V, D, and J genes on the heavy chain and V and J genes on the light chain) no matter which heavy-chain constant region is being utilized.

In **class switching**, the same assembled V_H gene can sequentially associate with different C_H genes so that the immunoglobulins produced later (IgG, IgA, or IgE) are specific for the same antigen as the original IgM but have different biologic characteristics. This is illustrated in the "class switch" section of Figure 59–6. A different molecular mechanism is involved in the switching from IgM to IgD. In this case, a single mRNA consisting of VDJ CμCδ is initially transcribed and is then spliced into separate VDJ Cμ and VDJ Cδ mRNAs. Mature B cells can, in this manner, express both IgM and IgD (see Figure 59–6, alternative RNA splicing). Note that once a B cell has "class" switched past a certain H-chain gene, it can no longer make that class of H chain because the intervening DNA is excised and discarded. Class switching occurs only with heavy chains; light chains do not undergo class switching. "Switch recombinase" is the enzyme that catalyzes the rearrangement of the VDJ genes during class switching.

The control of class switching is dependent on at

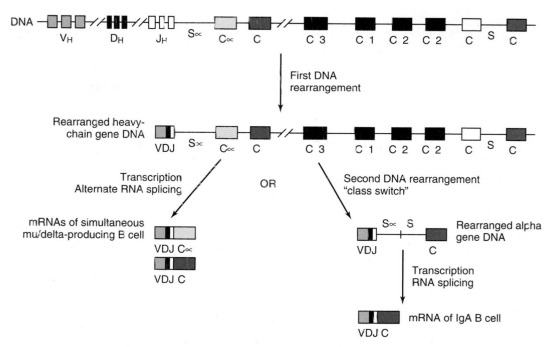

Figure 59–6. Gene rearrangement to produce different immunoglobulin classes. IgM is formed first because the μ constant region is closest to the VDJ DNA. Later the μ constant region can be switched with a γ, ε, or α constant region to form the heavy chain of IgG, IgE, or IgA, respectively. Note that the antigenic specificity of the B cell remains the same because the VDJ DNA remains the same. V, variable regions; D, diversity segments; J, joining segments; C, constant regions; S, switch sites. (Modified and reproduced, with permission, from Stites DP, Terr A, Parslow T [editors]: *Basic & Clinical Immunology,* 8th ed. Originally published by Appleton & Lange. Copyright © 1994 by The McGraw-Hill Companies, Inc.)

least two factors. One is the concentration of various interleukins. For example, IL-4 enhances the production of IgE, whereas IL-5 increases IgA (see Table 58–7). The other is the interaction of the CD40 protein on the B cell with CD40 ligand protein on the helper T cell. In hyper-IgM syndrome, the failure to interact properly results in an inability of the B cell to switch to the production of IgG, IgA, or IgE. Therefore, only IgM is made (see Chapter 68).

ALLELIC EXCLUSION

A single B cell expresses only one L-chain gene (either κ or λ) and one H-chain gene. In theory, a B cell could express two sets of immunoglobulin genes, a maternal set and a paternal set. But this is *not* what happens. Only one set of genes is expressed, either maternal or paternal, and the other set is silent; ie, it is excluded. This is called **allelic exclusion.** Each individual contains a mixture of B cells, some expressing the paternal genes and others the maternal ones. The mechanism of this exclusion is unknown.

CATALYTIC ANTIBODY

Antibody can act as an enzyme to catalyze the synthesis of ozone (O_3) that has microbicidal activity. Antibody can take the singlet oxygen produced by neutrophils and react it with water to produce hydrogen peroxide and O_3. The O_3 generated can kill *Escherichia coli.* The catalytic function of antibodies is independent of their antigen specificity and of the requirement to bind to any antigen. The importance of these observations to our host defenses remains to be determined.

PRACTICE QUESTIONS: USMLE & COURSE EXAMINATIONS

Questions on the topics discussed in this chapter can be found in the Immunology section of Part XI: USMLE (National Board) Practice Questions starting on page 562. Also see Part XII: USMLE (National Board) Practice Examination starting on page 583.

Humoral Immunity

Humoral (antibody-mediated) immunity is directed primarily against (1) exotoxin-mediated diseases such as tetanus and diphtheria, (2) infections in which virulence is related to polysaccharide capsules (eg, pneumococci, meningococci, *Haemophilus influenzae*), and (3) certain viral infections. In this chapter the kinetics of antibody synthesis, ie, the primary and secondary responses, are described. The functions of the various immunoglobulins are summarized in this chapter and described in detail in Chapter 59.

THE PRIMARY RESPONSE

When an antigen is first encountered, antibodies are detectable in the serum after a **longer lag period** than occurs in the secondary response. The lag period is typically **7–10 days** but can be longer depending on the nature and dose of the antigen and the route of administration (eg, parenteral or oral). A small clone of B cells and plasma cells specific for the antigen is formed. The serum antibody concentration continues to rise for several weeks, then declines and may drop to very low levels (Figure 60–1). The **first** antibodies to appear are **IgM**, followed by IgG or IgA. IgM levels decline earlier than IgG levels.

THE SECONDARY RESPONSE

When there is a second encounter with the same antigen or a closely related (or cross-reacting) one, months or years after the primary response, there is a **rapid** antibody response (the lag period is typically only **3–5 days**) to **higher** levels than the primary response. This is attributed to the persistence of antigen-specific "memory cells" after the first contact. These memory cells proliferate to form a large clone of specific B cells and plasma cells, which mediate the secondary antibody response.

During the secondary response, the amount of IgM produced is similar to that after the first contact with antigen. However, a much **larger** amount of **IgG** antibody is produced and the levels tend to persist much **longer** than in the primary response.

With each succeeding exposure to the antigen, the antibodies tend to bind antigen more firmly. Antibody binding improves because mutations occur in the DNA that encodes the antigen-binding site, a process called **somatic hypermutation.** Some mutations result in the insertion of different amino acids in the hypervariable region that result in a better fit and cause the antigen to be bound more strongly. The subset of plasma cells with these improved hypervariable regions are more strongly (and more frequently) selected by antigen and therefore constitute an increasingly larger part of the population of antibody-producing cells. This process is called **affinity maturation.** One important effect of booster doses of vaccines is to improve antibody binding by enhancing the affinity maturation process.

Affinity maturation occurs in the germinal centers of the follicles in the spleen and lymph nodes. Follicle dendritic cells capture antigen-antibody complexes on their surface via Fc receptors. The complexes interact with an activated B cell bearing the immunoglobulin that best fits the antigen, and it is that B cell that is stimulated to form a clone of many B cells capable of synthesizing the improved antibody.

RESPONSE TO MULTIPLE ANTIGENS ADMINISTERED SIMULTANEOUSLY

When two or more antigens are administered at the same time, the host reacts by producing antibodies to all of them. Competition of antigens for antibody-producing mechanisms occurs experimentally but appears to be of little significance in medicine. Combined immunization is widely used, eg, the diphtheria, tetanus, and pertussis (DTP) vaccine or the measles, mumps, rubella (MMR) vaccine.

FUNCTION OF ANTIBODIES

The primary function of antibodies is to protect against infectious agents or their products (see Table 59–2). Antibodies provide protection because they can (1) **neutralize** toxins and viruses and (2) **opsonize** microorganisms. Opsonization is the process by which antibodies make microorganisms more easily ingested by phagocytic cells. This occurs by either of two reactions:

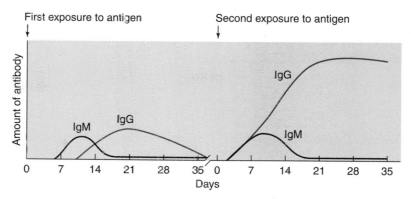

Figure 60–1. Antibody synthesis in the primary and secondary responses. In the primary response, IgM is the first type of antibody to appear. In the secondary response, IgG appears earlier and shows a more rapid rise and a higher final concentration than in the primary response. If at the time of the second exposure to the antigen (Ag1), a second, non-cross-reacting antigen (Ag2) was injected, a primary response to Ag2 would occur while a secondary response to Ag1 was occurring.

(1) The Fc portion of IgG interacts with its receptors on the phagocyte surface to facilitate ingestion; or (2) IgG or IgM activates complement to yield C3b, which interacts with its receptors on the surface of the phagocyte.

Antibodies can be induced **actively** in the host or acquired **passively** and are thus immediately available for defense. In medicine, passive immunity is used in the neutralization of the toxins of diphtheria, tetanus, and botulism by antitoxins and in the inhibition of such viruses as rabies and hepatitis A and B viruses early in the incubation period.

ANTIBODIES IN THE FETUS

IgM is the antibody made in greatest amounts by the fetus. Small amounts of fetal IgG and IgA are made also. Note, however, that the fetus has more total IgG than IgM because maternal IgG passes the placenta in large amounts.

TESTS FOR EVALUATION OF HUMORAL IMMUNITY

Evaluation of humoral immunity consists primarily of measuring the amount of each of the three important immunoglobulins, ie, IgG, IgM, and IgA, in the patient's serum. This is usually done by radial immunodiffusion. Immunoelectrophoresis can also provide valuable information. These techniques are described in Chapter 64.

PRACTICE QUESTIONS: USMLE & COURSE EXAMINATIONS

Questions on the topics discussed in this chapter can be found in the Immunology section of Part XI: USMLE (National Board) Practice Questions starting on page 562. Also see Part XII: USMLE (National Board) Practice Examination starting on page 583.

Cell-Mediated Immunity

Although humoral (antibody-mediated immunity) is an important host defense against many bacterial and viral diseases, in many other bacterial infections (especially intracellular infections such as tuberculosis) and viral infections, it is primarily the cell-mediated arm that imparts resistance and aids in recovery. Furthermore, cell-mediated immunity is important in defense against fungi, parasites, and tumors and in the rejection of organ transplants. The strongest evidence for the importance of cell-mediated immunity comes from clinical situations in which its suppression (by immunosuppressive drugs or disease, eg, AIDS) results in overwhelming infections or tumors.

The constituents of the cell-mediated immune system include several cell types: (1) **macrophages,** which present the antigen to T cells; (2) **helper T cells,** which participate in antigen recognition and in regulation (helper and suppressor) functions (see Chapter 58); (3) **natural killer (NK) cells,** which can inactivate pathogens; and (4) **cytotoxic T cells,** which can kill virus-infected cells with or without antibody. Macrophages and helper T cells produce cytokines that activate helper and cytotoxic T cells, leading to the killing of the pathogen or tumor cell.

Infection with some viruses, namely, measles virus and cytomegalovirus, can suppress cell-mediated immunity against other microorganisms. In particular, measles virus infection in people infected with *Mycobacterium tuberculosis* can result in a loss of PPD skin test reactivity, reactivation of dormant organisms, and clinical disease. A proposed explanation for these findings is that when measles virus binds to its receptor on the surface of human macrophages, the production of IL-12 by the macrophages, which is necessary for cell-mediated immunity to occur, is suppressed.

The terms primary and secondary response are associated primarily with antibody formation as described in Chapter 60, but the timing of the T-cell response also follows the same pattern. After the initial exposure to the antigen, the specific T cell proliferates to form a small clone of cells; ie, a primary response occurs. Then, on subsequent exposure to the antigen, the small clone expands and many more specific T cells are formed. These cells constitute the secondary response.

Although the interactions between various cells and various cytokines are complex, the result is relatively simple: In the person with competent cellular immunity, opportunistic pathogens rarely or never cause disease, and the spread of other agents—for example, certain viruses (eg, herpesviruses) or tumors (eg, Kaposi's sarcoma)—is limited. The assessment of the competence of cell-mediated immunity is therefore important.

TESTS FOR EVALUATION OF CELL-MEDIATED IMMUNITY

Evaluation of the immunocompetence of persons depends either on the demonstration of delayed-type hypersensitivity to commonly present antigens (equating the ability to respond with the competence of cell-mediated immunity) or on laboratory assessments of T cells.

In Vivo Tests for Lymphoid Cell Competence (Skin Tests)

A. SKIN TESTS FOR THE PRESENCE OF DELAYED-TYPE HYPERSENSITIVITY

Most normal persons respond with delayed-type reactions to skin test antigens of *Candida,* streptokinase-streptodornase, or mumps virus because of past exposure to these antigens. Absence of reactions to several of these skin tests suggests impairment of cell-mediated immunity.

B. SKIN TESTS FOR THE ABILITY TO DEVELOP DELAYED-TYPE HYPERSENSITIVITY

Most normal persons readily develop reactivity to simple chemicals (eg, dinitrochlorobenzene [DNCB]) applied to their skin in lipid solvents. When the same chemical is applied to the same area 7–14 days later, they respond with a delayed-type skin reaction. Immunocompromised persons with incompetent cell-mediated immunity fail to develop such delayed-type hypersensitivity.

In Vitro Tests for Lymphoid Cell Competence

A. LYMPHOCYTE BLAST TRANSFORMATION

When sensitized T lymphocytes are exposed to the specific antigen, they transform into large blast cells with greatly increased DNA synthesis, as measured by incorporation of tritiated thymidine. This *specific* effect involves relatively few cells. A larger number of T cells undergo *nonspecific* blast transformation when exposed to certain mitogens. The mitogens phytohemagglutinin and concanavalin A are plant extracts that stimulate T cells specifically. (Bacterial endotoxin, a lipopolysaccharide, stimulates B cells specifically.)

B. MACROPHAGE MIGRATION INHIBITORY FACTOR

Macrophage migration inhibitory factor is elaborated by cultured T cells when exposed to the antigen to which they are sensitized. Its effect can be measured by observing the reduced migration of macrophages in the presence of the factor compared with the level in controls.

C. ENUMERATION OF T CELLS, B CELLS, AND SUBPOPULATIONS

The number of each type of cell can be counted by use of a machine called a fluorescence-activated cell sorter (FACS) (see Chapter 64). In this approach, cells are labeled with monoclonal antibody tagged with a fluorescent dye, such as fluorescein or rhodamine. Single cells are passed through a laser light beam, and the number of cells that fluoresce is registered.

B cells (and plasma cells) making different classes of antibodies can be detected by using monoclonal antibodies against the various heavy chains. The total number of B cells can be counted by using fluorescein-labeled antibody against all immunoglobulin classes. Specific monoclonal antibodies directed against T-cell markers permit the enumeration of T-cells, CD4 helper cells, CD8 suppressor cells, and others. The normal ratio of CD4 to CD8 cells is 1.5 or greater, whereas in some immunodeficiencies (eg, AIDS) it is less than 1.

ROLE OF ADJUVANTS & LIPIDS IN ESTABLISHING CELL-MEDIATED REACTIVITY

Weak antigens or simple chemicals tend not to elicit cell-mediated hypersensitivity when administered alone, but they do so when given as a mixture with an adjuvant. The role of the **adjuvant** is to enhance the uptake of the antigen by antigen-presenting cells, eg, macrophages, to stimulate the expression of costimulators, such as B7, and to enhance the production of cytokines, such as IL-12, that promotes the development of Th-1 cells. A common experimental adjuvant is a mixture of mineral oil, lanolin, and killed mycobacteria (Freund's adjuvant), which stimulates the formation of local granulomas. It is prohibited for human use.

PRACTICE QUESTIONS: USMLE & COURSE EXAMINATIONS

Questions on the topics discussed in this chapter can be found in the Immunology section of Part XI: USMLE (National Board) Practice Questions starting on page 562. Also see Part XII: USMLE (National Board) Practice Examination starting on page 583.

Major Histocompatibility Complex & Transplantation

The success of tissue and organ transplants depends on the donor's and recipient's **human leukocyte antigens** (HLA) encoded by the HLA genes. These proteins are alloantigens; ie, they differ among members of the same species. If the HLA proteins on the donor's cells differ from those on the recipient's cells, an immune response occurs in the recipient. The genes for the HLA proteins are clustered in the major histocompatibility complex (MHC), located on the short arm of chromosome 6. Three of these genes (HLA-A, HLA-B, and HLA-C) code for the class I MHC proteins. Several HLA-D loci determine the class II MHC proteins, ie, DP, DQ, and DR (Figure 62–1). The features of class I and class II MHC proteins are compared in Table 62–1.

Each person has two **haplotypes,** ie, two sets of these genes, one on the paternal and the other on the maternal chromosome 6. These genes are very diverse (**polymorphic**) (ie, there are many alleles of the class I and class II genes). For example, there are at least 47 HLA-A genes, 88 HLA-B genes, 29 HLA-C genes, and more than 300 HLA-D genes, but any individual inherits only a single allele at each locus from each parent and thus can make no more than 2 class I and II proteins at each gene locus. Expression of these genes is **codominant;** ie, the proteins encoded by *both* the paternal and maternal genes are produced. Each person can make as many as 12 different HLA proteins: 3 at class I loci and 3 at class II loci, from both chromosomes. A person can make less than 12 different HLA proteins if the person is homozygous at any of the 6 loci, ie, if both parents have the same HLA allele.

In addition to the major antigens encoded by the HLA genes, there are an unknown number of **minor** antigens encoded by genes at sites other than the HLA locus. These minor antigens can induce a weak immune response that can result in slow rejection of a graft. The cumulative effect of several minor antigens can lead to a more rapid rejection response. These minor antigens are various normal body proteins that have one or more amino acid differences from one person to another; ie, they are "allelic variants." Because these proteins have an amino acid difference, they are immunogenic when introduced as part of the donor graft tissue. There are no laboratory tests for minor antigens.

Between the class I and class II gene loci is a third locus (Figure 62–1), sometimes called class III. This lo-

cus contains several immunologically important genes, encoding two cytokines (tumor necrosis factor and lymphotoxin) and two complement components (C2 and C4), but it does not have any genes that encode histocompatibility antigens.

MHC PROTEINS

Class I MHC Proteins

These are glycoproteins found on the **surface of virtually all nucleated cells.** There are approximately 20 different proteins encoded by the allelic genes at the A locus, 40 at the B locus, and 8 at the C locus. The complete class I protein is composed of a 45,000-molecular-weight heavy chain noncovalently bound to a β_2-microglobulin. The heavy chain is highly polymorphic and is similar to an immunoglobulin molecule; it has hypervariable regions in its N-terminal region. The **polymorphism** of these molecules is important in the **recognition of self** and **nonself.** Stated another way, if these molecules were more similar, our ability to accept foreign grafts would be correspondingly improved. The heavy chain also has a constant region where the CD8 protein of the cytotoxic T cell binds.

Class II MHC Proteins

These are glycoproteins found on the surface of certain cells, including macrophages, B cells, dendritic cells of the spleen, and Langerhans' cells of the skin. They are highly polymorphic glycoproteins composed of two polypeptides (MW 33,000 and 28,000) that are noncovalently bound. Like class I proteins, they have hypervariable regions that provide much of the polymorphism. Unlike class I proteins, which have only one chain encoded by the MHC locus (β_2-microglobulin is encoded on chromosome 15), both chains of the class II proteins are encoded by the MHC locus. The two peptides also have a constant region where the CD4 proteins of the helper T cells bind.

BIOLOGIC IMPORTANCE OF MHC

The ability of T cells to recognize antigen is dependent on association of the antigen with either class I or class II proteins. For example, cytotoxic T cells respond to anti-

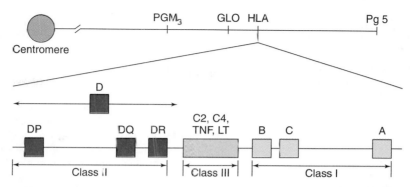

Figure 62–1. The human leukocyte antigen (HLA)-gene complex. A, B, and C are class I loci. DP, DQ, and DR are class II loci. C2 and C4 are complement loci. TNF is tumor necrosis factor; LT is lymphotoxin. PGM$_3$, GLO, and Pg 5 are adjacent, unrelated genes. (Reproduced, with permission, from Stites DP, Terr A, Parslow T [editors]: *Basic & Clinical Immunology*, 9th ed. Originally published by Appleton & Lange. Copyright © 1997 by The McGraw-Hill Companies, Inc.)

gen in association with class I MHC proteins. Thus, a cytotoxic T cell that kills a virus-infected cell will not kill a cell infected with the same virus if the cell does not also express the appropriate class I proteins. This finding was determined by mixing cytotoxic T cells bearing certain class I MHC proteins with virus-infected cells bearing different class I MHC proteins and observing that no killing of the virus-infected cells occurred. Helper T cells recognize class II proteins. Helper-cell activity depends in general on *both* the recognition of the antigen on antigen-presenting cells *and* the presence on these cells of "self" class II MHC proteins. This requirement to recognize antigen in association with a "self" MHC protein is called

MHC restriction. Note that T cells recognize antigens only when the antigens are presented on the surface of cells (in association with either class I or II MHC proteins), whereas B cells do not have that requirement and can recognize soluble antigens in plasma with their surface monomer IgM acting as the antigen receptor.

MHC genes and proteins are also important in two other medical contexts. One is that many autoimmune diseases occur in people who carry certain MHC genes (see Chapter 66), and the other is that the success of organ transplants is, in large part, determined by the compatibility of the MHC genes of the donor and recipient (see below).

Table 62–1. Comparison of class I and class II MHC proteins.

Feature	Class I MHC Proteins	Class II MHC Proteins
Present antigen to CD4-positive cells	No	Yes
Present antigen to CD8-positive cells	Yes	No
Found on surface of all nucleated cells	Yes	No
Found on surface of "professional" antigen-presenting cells, such as dendritic cells, macrophages, and B cells	Yes[1]	Yes
Encoded by genes in the HLA locus	Yes	Yes
Expression of genes is codominant	Yes	Yes
Multiple alleles at each gene locus	Yes	Yes
Composed of two peptides encoded in the HLA locus	No	Yes
Composed of one peptide encoded in the HLA locus and a β$_2$-microglobulin	Yes	No

[1]Note that class I MHC proteins are found on the surface of all nucleated cells, including those that have class II MHC proteins on their surface. Mature red blood cells are non-nucleated; therefore, they do synthesize class I MHC proteins.

TRANSPLANTATION

An **autograft** (transfer of an individual's own tissue to another site in the body) is always permanently accepted, ie, it always "takes." A **syngeneic graft**[1] is a transfer of tissue between genetically identical individuals, ie, identical twins, and almost always "takes" permanently. A **xenograft,**[1] a transfer of tissue between different species, is always rejected by an immunocompetent recipient.

An **allograft**[1] is a graft between genetically different members of the same species, eg, from one human to another. Allografts are usually rejected unless the recipient is given immunosuppressive drugs. The severity and rapidity of the rejection will vary depending on the degree of the differences between the donor and the recipient at the MHC loci.

Allograft Rejection

Unless immunosuppressive measures are taken, allografts are rejected by a process called the **allograft reaction.** In an acute allograft reaction, vascularization of the graft is normal initially, but in 11–14 days, marked reduction in circulation and mononuclear cell infiltration occurs, with eventual necrosis. This is called a **primary (first-set)** reaction. A **T-cell-mediated reaction is the main cause of rejection** of many types of grafts, eg, skin, but antibodies contribute to the rejection of certain transplants, especially bone marrow. In experimental animals, rejection of most types of grafts can be transferred by cells, not serum. Also, T-cell-deficient animals do not reject grafts but B-cell-deficient animals do. The role of cytotoxic T cells in allograft rejection is described on page 411.

If a second allograft from the same donor is applied to a sensitized recipient, it is rejected in 5–6 days. This **accelerated (second-set)** reaction is caused primarily by presensitized cytotoxic T cells.

The acceptance or rejection of a transplant is determined, in large part, by the class I and class II MHC proteins on the donor cells, with **class II** playing the **major** role. The proteins encoded by the DR locus are especially important. These alloantigens activate T cells, both helper and cytotoxic, which bear T-cell receptors specific for the alloantigens. The activated T cells proliferate and then react against the alloantigens on the donor cells. **CD8-positive cytotoxic T cells do most of the killing** of the allograft cells.

Foreign MHC proteins typically activate many more T cells (ie, they elicit a much stronger reaction) than do foreign proteins that are not MHC proteins. The strength of the response to foreign MHC proteins can be explained by the observation that there are three processes by which the recipient's immune response is stimulated. These processes are (1) antigen-presenting cells (eg, macrophages and dendritic cells) in the graft can present self (the donor's) proteins in association with their class I and class II MHC proteins and activate the recipient's immune response; (2) antigen-presenting cells in the graft can present the recipient's proteins and activate the recipient's immune response (because the recipient's proteins are recognized as foreign when presented by a foreign MHC protein); and (3) the donor's self proteins and class I and class II MHC proteins can be shed and subsequently processed by the recipient's antigen-presenting cells, which activates the recipient's immune response.

A graft that survives an acute allograft reaction can nevertheless become nonfunctional as a result of **chronic rejection.** This can occur months to years after engraftment. The main pathologic finding in grafts undergoing chronic rejection is atherosclerosis of the vascular endothelium. The immunologic cause of chronic rejection is unclear, but incompatibility of minor histocompatibility antigens and side effects of immunosuppressive drugs are likely to play a role.

In addition to acute and chronic rejection, a third type called **hyperacute rejection** can occur. Hyperacute rejection typically occurs within minutes of engraftment and is due to the reaction of **preformed** anti-ABO antibodies in the recipient with ABO antigens on the surface of the endothelium of the graft. Hyperacute rejection is often called the "white graft" reaction, because the graft turns white as a result of the loss of blood supply caused by spasm and occlusion of the vessels serving the graft. In view of this severe rejection reaction, the ABO blood group of donors and recipients must be matched and a crossmatching test (see below) must be done.

HLA Typing in the Laboratory

Prior to transplantation surgery, laboratory tests, commonly called **HLA-typing** or **tissue-typing,** are performed to determine the closest MHC match between the donor and the recipient.

There are two methods commonly used in the laboratory to determine the haplotype (ie, the class I and class II alleles on both chromosomes) of both the potential donors and the recipient. One method is **DNA sequencing** using polymerase chain reaction (PCR) amplification and specific probes to detect the different alleles. This method is highly specific and sensitive, and is the method of choice when available. The other method is **serologic assays,** in which cells from the donor and recipient are reacted with a battery of antibodies, each one of which is specific for a different class I and class II protein. Complement is then added, and any cell bearing an MHC protein homologous to the

---

[1] Previously used synonyms for these terms include isograft (syngeneic graft), heterograft (xenograft), and homograft (allograft).

known antibody will lyse. This method is satisfactory in most instances but has failed to identify certain alleles that have been detected by DNA sequencing.

If sufficient data cannot be obtained by DNA sequencing or serologic assays, then additional information regarding the compatibility of the class II MHC proteins can be determined by using the **mixed lymphocyte culture (MLC)** technique. This test is also known as the **mixed lymphocyte reaction (MLR)**. In this test, "stimulator" lymphocytes from a potential donor are first killed by irradiation and then mixed with live "responder" lymphocytes from the recipient; the mixture is incubated in cell culture to permit DNA synthesis, which is measured by incorporation of tritiated thymidine. The greater the amount of DNA synthesis in the responder cells, the more foreign are the class II MHC proteins of the donor cells. A large amount of DNA synthesis indicates an unsatisfactory "match"; ie, donor and recipient class II (HLA-D) MHC proteins are *not* similar, and the graft is likely to be rejected. The best donor is, therefore, the person whose cells stimulated the incorporation of the **least** amount of tritiated thymidine in the recipient cells.

In addition to the tests used for matching, preformed cytotoxic antibodies in the recipient's serum reactive against the graft are detected by observing the lysis of donor lymphocytes by the recipient's serum plus complement. This is called **crossmatching** and is done to prevent hyperacute rejections from occurring. (The donor and recipient are also matched for the compatibility of their ABO blood groups.)

Among siblings in a single family, there is a 25% chance for both haplotypes to be shared, a 50% chance for one haplotype to be shared, and a 25% chance for no haplotypes to be shared. For example, if the father is haplotype AB, the mother is CD, and the recipient child is AC, there is a 25% chance for a sibling to be AC, ie, a two-haplotype match; a 50% chance for a sibling to be either BC or AD, ie, a one-haplotype match; and a 25% chance for a sibling to be BD, ie, a zero-haplotype match.

The Fetus Is an Allograft That Is Not Rejected

A fetus has MHC genes inherited from the father that are foreign to the mother, yet allograft rejection of the fetus does not occur. This is true despite many pregnancies from the same mother-father combination that produce offspring with the same MHC haplotypes. The reason that the mother fails to reject the fetus is unclear. The mother forms antibodies against the foreign paternal MHC proteins; therefore, the reason is not that the mother is not exposed to fetal antigens. One possible explanation is that the trophoblast layer of the placenta does not allow maternal T cells to enter the fetus.

Results of Organ Transplants

If the donor and recipient are well matched by mixed-lymphocyte culture and histocompatibility antigen-typing, the long-term survival of a transplanted organ or tissue is greatly enhanced. In 1986, the 5-year survival rate of two-haplotype-matched kidney transplants from related donors was near 95%, that of one-haplotype-matched kidney transplants was near 80%, and that of transplant of kidneys from cadaver donors was near 60%. The survival rate of the last category was higher if the graft recipient had had several previous blood transfusions. The reason for this is unknown (but may be associated with tolerance). The heart transplant survival rate for 5 years is near 50–60%; the liver transplant rate is lower. Corneas are easily grafted because they are avascular and the lymphatic supply of the eye prevents many antigens from triggering an immune response; consequently, the proportion of "takes" is very high. Because corneal transplants elicit a weak rejection response, immunosuppression is usually necessary for only a year. In contrast, most other transplants require lifelong immunosuppression, although the dose of immunosuppressive drugs typically decreases with time and in some recipients a state of tolerance ensues and the drugs can be stopped.

Graft-versus-Host Reaction

Well-matched transplants of bone marrow may establish themselves initially in 85% of recipients, but subsequently a **graft-versus-host (GVH)** reaction develops in about two-thirds of them.[2]

This reaction occurs because grafted immunocompetent T cells proliferate in the irradiated, immunocompromised host and reject cells with "foreign" proteins, resulting in severe organ dysfunction. The donor's cytotoxic T cells play a major role in destroying the recipient's cells. Among the main symptoms are maculopapular rash, jaundice, hepatosplenomegaly, and diarrhea. Many GVH reactions end in overwhelming infections and death.

There are three requirements for a GVH reaction to occur: (1) the graft must contain immunocompetent T cells; (2) the host must be immunocompromised; and (3) the recipient must express antigens (eg, MHC proteins) foreign to the donor; ie, the donor T cells recognize the recipient cells as foreign. Note that even when donor and recipient have identical class I and class II MHC proteins, ie, identical haplotypes, a GVH reaction can occur because it can be elicited by differences

---

[2] GVH reactions can also occur in immunodeficient patients given a blood transfusion, because there are immunocompetent T cells in the donor's blood that react against the recipient's cells.

in minor antigens. The GVH reaction can be reduced by treating the donor tissue with antithymocyte globulin or monoclonal antibodies before grafting; this eliminates mature T cells from the graft. Cyclosporine (see below) is also used to reduce the GVH reaction.

EFFECT OF IMMUNOSUPPRESSION ON GRAFT REJECTION

To reduce the chance of rejection of transplanted tissue, immunosuppressive measures, eg, cyclosporine, tacrolimus (FK506, Prograf), sirolimus (rapamycin, Rapamune), corticosteroids, azathioprine, monoclonal antibodies, and radiation, are used. Cyclosporine prevents the activation of T lymphocytes by inhibiting the synthesis of IL-2 and IL-2 receptor. It does so by inhibiting calcineurin, a protein (a serine phosphatase) involved in the activation of transcription of the genes for IL-2 and the IL-2 receptor. Cyclosporine is well-tolerated and is remarkably successful in preventing the rejection of transplants. Cyclosporine and tacrolimus have the same mode of action; tacrolimus is more immunosuppressive but causes more side effects. Rapamycin also inhibits signal transduction but at a site different from that of cyclosporine and tacrolimus.

Corticosteroids act primarily by inhibiting cytokine (eg, IL-1 and tumor necrosis factor) production by macrophages and by lysing certain types of T cells. Corticosteroids inhibit cytokine production by blocking transcription factors, such as NFkB and AP-1, which prevents the mRNA for these cytokines from being synthesized. Azathioprine is an inhibitor of DNA synthesis and blocks the growth of T cells. Mycophenolate mofetil also inhibits DNA synthesis and has fewer side effects than azathioprine.

Monoclonal antibodies are used in immunosuppressive regimens, both to prevent rejection and to treat rejection episodes. Muromonab (OKT3) is a monoclonal antibody against CD3, and basiliximab and daclizumab are monoclonal antibodies against the IL-2 receptor. Table 62–2 describes these monoclonal antibodies as well as others in clinical use.

Unfortunately, immunosuppression greatly enhances the recipient's susceptibility to opportunistic infections and neoplasms. For example, some patients undergoing treatment for multiple sclerosis with the monoclonal antibody, natalizumab, developed progressive multifocal leukoencephalopathy (see Chapter 44 for a description of this viral disease). The incidence of cancer is increased as much as 100-fold in transplant recipients. Immunosuppressive drugs, eg, cyclosporine, also reduce GVH reactions.

Note that although these drugs suppress the allograft reaction, tolerance to the graft tissue does not ensue. Therefore, most patients must take these drugs during their entire lives.

PRACTICE QUESTIONS: USMLE & COURSE EXAMINATIONS

Questions on the topics discussed in this chapter can be found in the Immunology section of Part XI: USMLE (National Board) Practice Questions starting on page 562. Also see Part XII: USMLE (National Board) Practice Examination starting on page 583.

Table 62–2. Monoclonal antibodies in clinical use.

Clinical Function	Name of the Monoclonal Antibody[1]	Target of Antibody	Specific Clinical Use
Transplant-related immunosuppression	1. Basiliximab, daclizumab 2. Muromonab (OKT3)	IL-2 receptor CD3 on T cells	Prevent or treat allograft rejection and graft-versus-host reaction
Treatment of autoimmune disease	1. Infliximab 2. Adalimumab	Tumor necrosis factor-α	Treat rheumatoid arthritis and Crohn's disease (regional ileitis)
	3. Natalizumab	α-integrin	Treatment of multiple sclerosis and Crohn's disease
Prevention of infectious disease	Palivizumab	Fusion protein of respiratory syncytial virus	Prevent pneumonia in susceptible neonates
Treatment of cancer	1. Rituximab	CD20 protein on B cells	Treat non-Hodgkins lymphoma
	2. Trastuzumab	Epidermal growth factor receptor	Treat breast cancer

[1] Note that most of the names end in "mab," which is an abbreviation for monoclonal antibodies.

Complement

The complement system consists of approximately 20 proteins that are present in normal human (and other animal) serum. The term "complement" refers to the ability of these proteins to complement, ie, augment, the effects of other components of the immune system, eg, antibody. Complement is an important component of our innate host defenses.

There are three main effects of complement: (1) **lysis** of cells such as bacteria, allografts, and tumor cells; (2) **generation of mediators** that participate in inflammation and attract neutrophils; and (3) **opsonization,** ie, enhancement of phagocytosis. Complement proteins are synthesized mainly by the liver. Complement is heat-labile; ie, it is inactivated by heating serum at 56°C for 30 minutes. Immunoglobulins are not inactivated at this temperature.

ACTIVATION OF COMPLEMENT

Several complement components are proenzymes, which must be cleaved to form active enzymes. Activation of the complement system can be initiated either by antigen-antibody complexes or by a variety of nonimmunologic molecules, eg, endotoxin.

Sequential activation of complement components (Figure 63–1) occurs via one of three pathways: the classic pathway, the lectin pathway, and the alternative pathway (see below). Of these pathways, the **lectin and the alternative pathways are more important the first time** we are infected by a microorganism because the antibody required to trigger the classic pathway is not present. The lectin pathway and the alternative pathway are, therefore, participants in the innate arm of the immune system.

All three pathways lead to the production of **C3b, the central molecule** of the complement cascade. The presence of C3b on the surface of a microbe marks it as foreign and targets it for destruction. C3b has two important functions: (1) It combines with other complement components to generate C5 convertase, the enzyme that leads to the production of the membrane attack complex; and (2) it opsonizes bacteria because phagocytes have receptors for C3b on their surface.

(1) In the **classic** pathway, antigen-antibody complexes[1] activate C1[2] to form a protease, which cleaves C2 and C4 to form a C4b,2b complex. The latter is C3 convertase, which cleaves C3 molecules into two fragments, C3a and C3b. C3a, an **anaphylatoxin,** is discussed below. C3b forms a complex with C4b,2b, producing a new enzyme, C5 convertase (C4b,2b,3b), which cleaves C5 to form C5a and C5b. C5a is an anaphylatoxin and a chemotactic factor (see below). C5b binds to C6 and C7 to form a complex that interacts with C8 and C9 to produce the **membrane attack** complex (C5b,6,7,8,9), which causes cytolysis. Note that the "b" fragment continues in the main pathway, whereas the "a" fragment is split off and has other activities.

(2) In the **lectin** pathway, mannan-binding lectin (MBL) (also known as mannose-binding protein) binds to the surface of microbes bearing mannan (a polymer of the sugar, mannose). This activates proteases associated with MBL that cleave C2 and C4 components of complement and activate the classic pathway. Note that this process bypasses the antibody-requiring step and so is protective early in infection before antibody is formed.

(3) In the **alternative** pathway, many unrelated cell surface substances, eg, bacterial lipopolysaccharides (endotoxin), fungal cell walls, and viral envelopes, can initiate the process by binding $C3(H_2O)$ and factor B. This complex is cleaved by a protease, factor D, to produce C3b,Bb. This acts as a C3 convertase to generate more C3b.

---

[1] Only IgM and IgG fix complement. One molecule of IgM can activate complement; however, activation by IgG requires two cross-linked IgG molecules. C1 is bound to a site located in the Fc region of the heavy chain. Of the IgGs, only IgG1, IgG2, and IgG3 subclasses fix complement; IgG4 does not.

[2] C1 is composed of three proteins, C1q, C1r, and C1s. C1q is an aggregate of 18 polypeptides that binds to the Fc portion of IgG and IgM. It is multivalent and can cross-link several immunoglobulin molecules. C1s is a proenzyme that is cleaved to form an active protease. Calcium is required for the activation of C1.

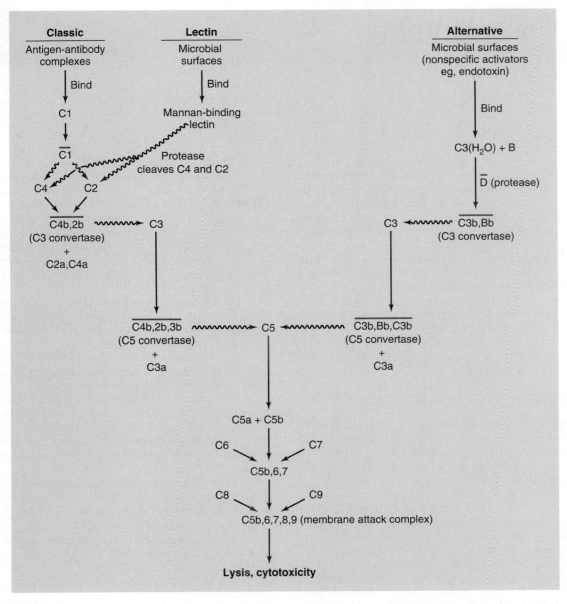

Figure 63–1. The classic and alternative pathways of the complement system. ∿➤ indicates that proteolytic cleavage of the molecule at the tip of the arrow has occurred; a line over a complex indicates that it is enzymatically active. Note that the nomenclature of the cleavage products of C2 is undecided. Some call the large fragment C2a and others call it C2b. In this book, all small fragments are labeled "a," and all large fragments are labeled "b." Hence, the C3 convertase is depicted as C4b,2b. Note that proteases associated with the mannose-binding lectin cleave C4 as well as C2.

REGULATION OF THE COMPLEMENT SYSTEM

The first regulatory step in the classic pathway is at the level of the antibody itself. The complement-binding site on the heavy chain of IgM and IgG is unavailable to the C1 component of complement if antigen is not bound to these antibodies. This means that complement is not activated by IgM and IgG despite being present in the blood at all times. However, when antigen binds to its specific antibody, a conformational shift occurs and the C1 component can bind and initiate the cascade.

Several serum proteins regulate the complement system at different stages.

(1) C1 inhibitor is an important regulator of the classic pathway. It inactivates the protease activity of C1. Activation of the classic pathway proceeds past this point by generating sufficient C1 to overwhelm the inhibitor.

(2) Regulation of the alternative pathway is mediated by the binding of factor H to C3b and cleavage of this complex by factor I, a protease. This reduces the amount of C5 convertase available. The alternative pathway can proceed past this regulatory point if sufficient C3b attaches to cell membranes. Attachment of C3b to cell membranes protects it from degradation by factors H and I. Another component that enhances activation of the alternative pathway is properdin, which protects C3b and stabilizes the C3 convertase.

(3) Protection of human cells from lysis by the membrane attack complex of complement is mediated by **decay-accelerating factor** (DAF), a glycoprotein located on the surface of human cells. DAF acts by destabilizing C3 convertase and C5 convertase. This prevents the formation of the membrane attack complex.

BIOLOGIC EFFECTS OF COMPLEMENT

Opsonization

Microbes, such as bacteria and viruses are phagocytized much better in the presence of C3b because there are C3b receptors on the surface of many phagocytes.

Chemotaxis

C5a and the C5, 6, 7 complex attract neutrophils. They migrate especially well toward C5a. C5a also enhances the adhesiveness of neutrophils to the endothelium.

Anaphylatoxin

C3a, C4a, and C5a cause degranulation of mast cells with release of mediators, eg, histamine, leading to increased vascular permeability and smooth muscle contraction, especially contraction of the bronchioles leading to bronchospasm. Anaphylatoxins can also bind directly to smooth muscle cells of the bronchioles and cause bronchospasm. C5a is, by far, the most potent of these anaphylatoxins. Anaphylaxis caused by these complement components is less common than anaphy-

laxis caused by type I (IgE-mediated) hypersensitivity (see Chapter 65).

Cytolysis

Insertion of the C5b,6,7,8,9 complex into the cell membrane leads to killing or lysis of many types of cells including erythrocytes, bacteria, and tumor cells. Cytolysis is not an enzymatic process; rather, it appears that insertion of the complex results in disruption of the membrane and the entry of water and electrolytes into the cell.

Enhancement of Antibody Production

The binding of C3b to its receptors on the surface of activated B cells greatly enhances antibody production compared with that by B cells that are activated by antigen alone. The clinical importance of this is that patients who are deficient in C3b produce significantly less antibody than do those with normal amounts of C3b. The low concentration of both antibody and C3b significantly impairs host defenses, resulting in multiple, severe pyogenic infections.

CLINICAL ASPECTS OF COMPLEMENT

(1) Inherited (or acquired) deficiency of some complement components, especially C5–C8, greatly enhances susceptibility to *Neisseria* **bacteremia** and other infections. A deficiency of MBL also predisposes to severe *Neisseria* infections. A deficiency of C3 leads to severe, recurrent pyogenic sinus and respiratory tract infections.

(2) Inherited deficiency of C1 esterase inhibitor results in **angioedema.** When the amount of inhibitor is reduced, an overproduction of esterase occurs. This leads to an increase in anaphylatoxins, which cause capillary permeability and edema.

(3) Acquired deficiency of decay-accelerating factor on the surface of cells results in an increase in complement-mediated hemolysis. Clinically, this appears as the disorder paroxysmal nocturnal hemoglobinuria (see Chapter 68).

(4) In transfusion mismatches, eg, when type A blood is given by mistake to a person who has type B blood, antibody to the A antigen in the recipient binds to A antigen on the donor red cells, complement is activated, and large amounts of anaphylatoxins and membrane attack complexes are generated. The anaphylatoxins cause shock, and the membrane attack complexes cause red cell hemolysis.

(5) Immune complexes bind complement, and thus complement levels are low in immune complex diseases, eg, acute glomerulonephritis and systemic lupus erythe-

matosus. Binding (activating) complement attracts polymorphonuclear leukocytes, which release enzymes that damage tissue.

(6) Patients with severe liver disease, eg, alcoholic cirrhosis or chronic hepatitis B, who have lost significant liver function and therefore cannot synthesize sufficient complement proteins, are predisposed to infections caused by pyogenic bacteria.

PRACTICE QUESTIONS: USMLE & COURSE EXAMINATIONS

Questions on the topics discussed in this chapter can be found in the Immunology section of Part XI: USMLE (National Board) Practice Questions starting on page 562. Also see Part XII: USMLE (National Board) Practice Examination starting on page 583.

Antigen-Antibody Reactions in the Laboratory

Reactions of antigens and antibodies are highly specific. An antigen will react only with antibodies elicited by itself or by a closely related antigen. Because of the great specificity, reactions between antigens and antibodies are suitable for identifying one by using the other. This is the basis of serologic reactions. However, cross-reactions between related antigens can occur, and these can limit the usefulness of the test. The results of many immunologic tests are expressed as a **titer**, which is defined as the highest dilution of the specimen, eg, serum, that gives a positive reaction in the test. Note that a patient's serum with an antibody titer of, for example, 1/64 contains **more** antibodies, ie, is a higher titer, than a serum with a titer of, for example, 1/4.

Table 64–1 describes the medical importance of serologic (antibody-based) tests. Their major uses are in the diagnosis of infectious diseases, in the diagnosis of autoimmune diseases, and in the typing of blood and tissues prior to transplantation.

Microorganisms and other cells possess a variety of antigens and thus induce antisera containing many different antibodies; ie, the antisera are polyclonal. Monoclonal antibodies excel in the identification of antigens because cross-reacting antibodies are absent; ie, monoclonal antibodies are highly specific.

TYPES OF DIAGNOSTIC TESTS

Many types of diagnostic tests are performed in the immunology laboratory. Most of these tests can be designed to determine the presence of either antigen or antibody. To do this, one of the components, either antigen or antibody, is known and the other is unknown. For example, with a known antigen such as influenza virus, a test can determine whether antibody to the virus is present in the patient's serum. Alternatively, with a known antibody, such as antibody to herpes simplex virus, a test can determine whether viral antigens are present in cells taken from the patient's lesions.

Agglutination

In this test, the antigen is **particulate** (eg, bacteria and red blood cells)[1] or is an inert particle (latex beads) coated with an antigen. Antibody, because it is divalent or multivalent, cross-links the antigenically multivalent particles and forms a latticework, and clumping (agglutination) can be seen. This reaction can be done in a small cup or tube or with a drop on a slide. One very commonly used agglutination test is the test that determines a person's ABO blood group (Figure 64–1; see the section on blood groups at the end of this chapter).

Precipitation (Precipitin)

In this test, the antigen is **in solution.** The antibody cross-links antigen molecules in variable proportions, and aggregates (precipitates) form. In the **zone of equivalence,** optimal proportions of antigen and antibody combine; the maximal amount of precipitates forms, and the supernatant contains neither an excess of antibody nor an excess of antigen (Figure 64–2). In the **zone of antibody excess,** there is too much antibody for efficient lattice formation, and precipitation is less than maximal.[2] In the **zone of antigen excess,** all antibody has combined, but precipitation is reduced because many antigen-antibody complexes are too small to precipitate; ie, they are "soluble."

Precipitin tests can be done in solution or in semisolid medium (agar).

A. PRECIPITATION IN SOLUTION

This reaction can be made quantitative; ie, antigen or antibody can be measured in terms of micrograms of nitrogen present. It is used primarily in research.

---

[1] When red cells are used, the reaction is called hemagglutination.
[2] The term "prozone" refers to the failure of a precipitate or flocculate to form because too much antibody is present. For example, a false-negative serologic test for syphilis (VDRL) is occasionally reported because the antibody titer is too high. Dilution of the serum yields a positive result.

Table 64–1. Major uses of serologic (antibody-based) tests.

I. Diagnosis of infectious diseases
• When the organism cannot be cultured, eg, syphilis and hepatitis A, B, and C.
• When the organism is too dangerous to culture, eg, rickettsial diseases.
• When culture techniques are not readily available, eg, HIV, EBV.
• When the organism takes too long to grow, eg, *Mycoplasma*.
One problem with this approach is that it takes time for antibodies to form, eg, 7–10 days in the primary response. For this reason, acute and convalescent serum samples are taken and a 4-fold or greater rise in antibody titer is required to make a diagnosis. By this time the patient has often recovered and the diagnosis becomes a retrospective one. If a test is available that can detect IgM antibody in the patient's serum, it can be used to make a diagnosis of current infection. In certain infectious diseases, an arbitrary IgG antibody titer of sufficient magnitude is used to make a diagnosis.
II. Diagnosis of autoimmune diseases
• Antibodies against various normal body components are used, eg, antibody against DNA in systemic lupus erythematosus, antibody against human IgG (rheumatoid factor) in rheumatoid arthritis.
III. Determination of blood type and HLA type
• Known antibodies are used to determine ABO and Rh blood types.
• Known antibodies are used to determine class I and class II HLA proteins prior to transplantation, although DNA sequencing is also being used.

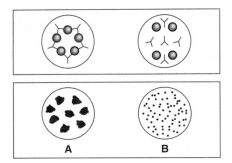

Figure 64–1. Agglutination test to determine ABO blood type. On the slide at the bottom of the figure, a drop of the patient's blood was mixed with antiserum against either type A (**left**) or type B (**right**) blood cells. Agglutination (clumping) has occurred in the drop on the left containing the type A antiserum but not in the drop containing the type B antiserum, indicating that the patient is type A, ie, has A antigen on the red cells. The slide at the top shows that the red cells (circles) are cross-linked by the antibodies (Y-shapes) in the drop on the left but not in the drop on the right. If agglutination had occurred in the right side as well, it would indicate that the patient was producing B antigen as well as A and was type AB.

B. Precipitation in Agar

This is done as either single or double diffusion. It can also be done in the presence of an electric field.

1. Single diffusion—In single diffusion, antibody is incorporated into agar and antigen is measured into a well. As the antigen diffuses with time, precipitation rings form depending on the antigen concentration. The greater the amount of antigen in the well, the farther the ring will be from the well. By calibrating the method, such **radial immunodiffusion** is used to measure IgG, IgM, complement components, and other substances in serum. (IgE cannot be measured because its concentration is too low.)

2. Double diffusion—In double diffusion, antigen and antibody are placed in different wells in agar and allowed to diffuse and form concentration gradients. Where optimal proportions (see zone of equivalence, above) occur, lines of precipitate form (Figure 64–3). This method (Ouchterlony) indicates whether antigens are identical, related but not identical, or not related (Figure 64–4).

C. Precipitation in Agar With an Electric Field

1. Immunoelectrophoresis—A serum sample is placed in a well in agar on a glass slide (Figure 64–5). A current is passed through the agar, and the proteins move in the electric field according to their charge and size. Then a

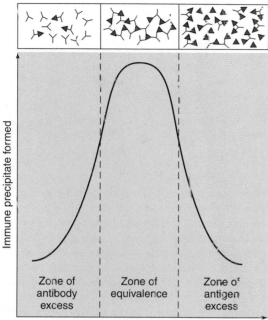

Figure 64–2. Precipitin curve. In the presence of a constant amount of antibody, the amount of immune precipitate formed is plotted as a function of increasing amounts of antigen. In the top part of the figure, the binding of antigen (▲) and antibody (Y) in the three zones is depicted. In the zones of antibody excess and antigen excess, a lattice is not formed and precipitation does not occur, whereas in the equivalence zone, a lattice forms and precipitation is maximal. (Modified and reproduced, with permission, from Stites D, Terr A, Parslow T [editors]: *Basic & Clinical Immunology,* 9th ed. Originally published by Appleton & Lange. Copyright © 1997 by The McGraw-Hill Companies.)

trough is cut into the agar and filled with antibody. As the antigen and antibody diffuse toward each other, they form a series of arcs of precipitate. This permits the serum proteins to be characterized in terms of their presence, absence, or unusual pattern (eg, human myeloma protein).

2. Counter-immunoelectrophoresis—This method relies on movement of antigen toward the cathode and of antibody toward the anode during the passage of electric current through agar. The meeting of the antigen and antibody is greatly accelerated by this method and is made visible in 30–60 minutes. This has been applied to the detection of bacterial and fungal polysaccharide antigens in cerebrospinal fluid.

Radioimmunoassay (RIA)

This method is used for the quantitation of antigens or haptens that can be radioactively labeled. It is based on the competition for specific antibody between the labeled (known) and the unlabeled (unknown) concentration of material. The complexes that form between the antigen and antibody can then be separated and the amount of radioactivity measured. The more unlabeled antigen is present, the less radioactivity there is in the complex. The concentration of the unknown (unlabeled) antigen or hapten is determined by comparison with the effect of standards. RIA is a highly sensitive method and is commonly used to assay hormones or drugs in serum. The radioallergosorbent test (RAST) is a specialized RIA that is used to measure the amount of serum IgE antibody that reacts with a known allergen (antigen).

Enzyme-Linked Immunosorbent Assay (ELISA)

This method can be used for the quantitation of either antigens or antibodies in patient specimens. It is based

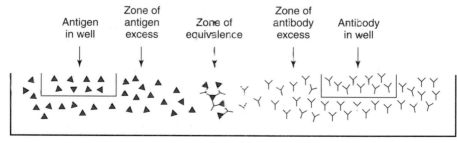

Figure 64–3. Double diffusion in agar. Antigen is placed in the well on the left, and antibody is placed in the well on the right. The antigen and antibody diffuse through the agar and form a precipitate in the zone of equivalence. Close to the antigen-containing well is the zone of antigen excess, and close to the antibody-containing well is the zone of antibody excess. No precipitate forms in the zones of antigen and antibody excess.

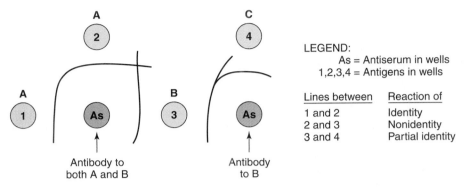

Figure 64–4. Double-diffusion (Ouchterlony) precipitin reactions. In these Ouchterlony reactions, wells are cut into an agar plate and various antigens and antisera are placed in the wells. The antigens and antibodies diffuse toward each other within the agar, and a line of precipitate forms in the zone of equivalence. Close to the antigen-containing well, a zone of antigen excess exists and no precipitate forms; close to the antibody-containing well, a zone of antibody excess exists and no precipitate forms. A and B are unrelated antigens; ie, they have no epitopes in common. B and C are related antigens; ie, they have some epitopes in common but some that are different. For example, chicken lysozyme (well B) and duck lysozyme (well C) share some epitopes because they are both lysozymes but have unique epitopes as well because they are from different species. The line of identity between B and C is caused by the reaction of the anti-B antibody with the shared epitopes on antigens B and C. The spur pointing toward well 4 is caused by the reaction of some of the anti-B antibody with the unique epitopes on antigen B in well 3. These lines of partial identity occur because antibody to B (chicken lysozyme) is polyclonal and has some immunoglobulins that react with the epitopes common to chicken and duck lysozyme and other immunoglobulins that react only with the epitopes unique to chicken lysozyme. (Modified and reproduced, with permission, from Brooks GF et al: *Medical Microbiology,* 19th ed. Originally published by Appleton & Lange. Copyright © 1991 by The McGraw-Hill Companies, Inc.)

on covalently linking an enzyme to a known antigen or antibody, reacting the enzyme-linked material with the patient's specimen, and then assaying for enzyme activity by adding the substrate of the enzyme. The method is nearly as sensitive as RIA yet requires no special equipment or radioactive labels (Figure 64–6).

For measurement of antibody, known antigens are fixed to a surface (eg, the bottom of small wells on a plastic plate), incubated with dilutions of the patient's serum, washed, and then reincubated with antibody to human IgG labeled with an enzyme, eg, horseradish peroxidase. Enzyme activity is measured by adding the substrate for the enzyme and estimating the color reaction in a spectrophotometer. The amount of antibody bound is proportional to the enzyme activity. The titer of antibody in the patient's serum is the highest dilution of serum that gives a positive color reaction.

Immunofluorescence (Fluorescent Antibody)

Fluorescent dyes, eg, fluorescein and rhodamine, can be covalently attached to antibody molecules and made visible by UV light in the fluorescence microscope. Such "labeled" antibody can be used to identify anti-

gens, eg, on the surface of bacteria (such as streptococci and treponemes), in cells in histologic section, or in other specimens (Figure 64–7). The immunofluorescence reaction is **direct** when known labeled antibody interacts directly with unknown antigen and **indirect** when a two-stage process is used. For example, known antigen is attached to a slide, the patient's serum (unlabeled) is added, and the preparation is washed; if the patient's serum contains antibody against the antigen, it will remain fixed to it on the slide and can be detected on addition of a fluorescent dye–labeled antibody to human IgG and examination by UV microscopy. The indirect test is often more sensitive than direct immunofluorescence, because more labeled antibody adheres per antigenic site. Furthermore, the labeled antiglobulin becomes a "universal reagent"; ie, it is independent of the nature of the antigen used because the antibody to IgG is reactive with all human IgG.

Complement Fixation

The complement system consists of 20 or more plasma proteins that interact with one another and with cell membranes. Each protein component must be activated sequentially under appropriate conditions for the reac-

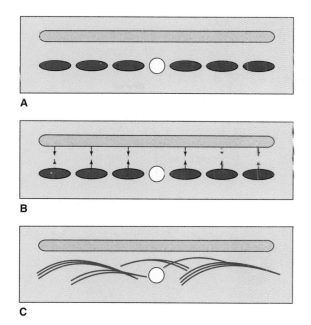

Figure 64–5. Immunoelectrophoresis. **A:** Human serum placed in the central well is electrophoresed, and the proteins migrate to different regions (orange ellipses). Antiserum to human serum is then placed in the elongated trough (gray areas). **B:** Human serum proteins and antibodies diffuse into agar. **C:** Precipitate arcs (orange lines) form in the agar. (Modified and reproduced, with permission, from Stites D, Terr A, Parslow T [editors]: *Basic & Clinical Immunology*, 9th ed. Originally published by Appleton & Lange. Copyright © 1997 by The McGraw-Hill Companies, Inc.)

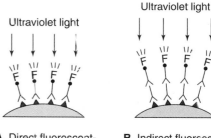

A. Direct fluorescent-antibody test   **B.** Indirect fluorescent-antibody test

Figure 64–7. Fluorescent-antibody test. **A:** In the direct fluorescent-antibody test, the fluorescent dye is attached directly to the antibody that is interacting with the antigen (dark triangles) on the surface of the cell. **B:** In the indirect fluorescent-antibody test, the fluorescent dye is attached to antibody made against human IgG.

tion to progress. Antigen-antibody complexes are among the activators, and the complement fixation test can be used to identify one of them if the other is known.

The reaction consists of the following two steps (Figure 64–8): (1) Antigen and antibody (one known and the other unknown; eg, use a known antigen and determine whether a patient's serum contains antibodies to that antigen) are mixed, and a measured amount of complement (usually from guinea pig) is added. If the antigen and antibody match, they will combine and use up ("fix") the complement. (2) An indicator system, consisting of "sensitized" red blood cells (ie, red blood cells plus anti–red blood cell antibody), is added. If the antibody matched the antigen in the first step, complement was fixed and less (or none) is available to attach to the sensitized red blood cells. The red blood cells remain **unhemolyzed**; ie, the test is **positive**, because the

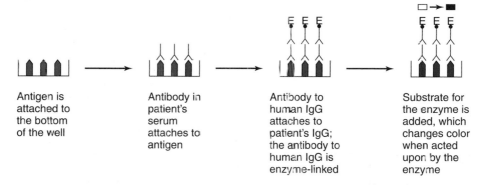

Antigen is attached to the bottom of the well

Antibody in patient's serum attaches to antigen

Antibody to human IgG attaches to patient's IgG; the antibody to human IgG is enzyme-linked

Substrate for the enzyme is added, which changes color when acted upon by the enzyme

Figure 64–6. Enzyme-linked immunosorbent assay (ELISA).

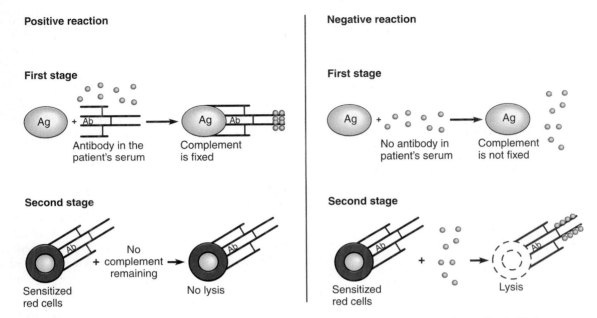

Positive reaction

First stage

Ag + Ab
Antibody in the patient's serum
→
Ag Ab
Complement is fixed

Second stage

Sensitized red cells
+ No complement remaining
→
No lysis

Negative reaction

First stage

Ag +
No antibody in patient's serum
→
Ag
Complement is not fixed

Second stage

Sensitized red cells
+
→
Lysis

Figure 64–8. Complement fixation. **Left:** Positive reaction; ie, the patient's serum contains antibody. If a known antigen is mixed with the patient's serum containing antibody against that antigen, then complement (solid circles) will be fixed. Because no complement is left over, the sensitized red cells are *not* lysed. **Right:** Negative reaction. If a known antigen is mixed with the patient's serum that does *not* contain antibody against that antigen, complement (solid circles) is *not* fixed. Complement is left over and the sensitized red cells are lysed.

patient's serum had antibodies to that antigen. If the antibody did *not* match the antigen in the first step, complement is free to attach to the sensitized red blood cells and they are **lysed**; ie, the test is **negative.**

Complement must be carefully standardized, and the patient's serum must be heated to 56°C for 30 minutes to inactivate any human complement activity. The antigen must be quantitated. The result is expressed as the highest dilution of serum that gives positive results. Controls to determine whether antigen or antibody alone fixes complement are needed to make the test results valid. If antigen or antibody alone fixes complement, it is said to be anticomplementary.

Neutralization Tests

These use the ability of antibodies to block the effect of toxins or the infectivity of viruses. They can be used in cell culture (eg, inhibition of cytopathic effect and plaque-reduction assays) or in host animals (eg, mouse protection tests).

Immune Complexes

Immune complexes in tissue can be stained with fluorescent complement. Immune complexes in serum can be detected by binding to C1q or by attachment to certain (eg, Raji lymphoblastoid) cells in culture.

Hemagglutination Tests

Many viruses clump red blood cells from one species or another (active hemagglutination). This can be inhibited by antibody specifically directed against the virus (hemagglutination inhibition) and can be used to measure the titer of such antibody. Red blood cells also can absorb many antigens and, when mixed with matching antibodies, will clump (this is known as passive hemagglutination, because the red cells are passive carriers of the antigen).

Antiglobulin (Coombs) Test

Some patients with certain diseases, eg, hemolytic disease of the newborn (Rh incompatibility) and drug-related hemolytic anemias, become sensitized but do not exhibit symptoms of disease. In these patients, antibodies against the red cells are formed and bind to the red cell surface but do not cause hemolysis. These cell-bound antibodies can be detected by the direct antiglobulin (Coombs) test, in which antiserum against human immunoglobulin is used to agglutinate the patient's red cells. In some cases, antibody against the red cells is not bound to the red cells but is in the serum and the indirect antiglobulin test for antibodies in the patient's serum should be performed. In the indirect Coombs test, the patient's serum is mixed with normal red cells and antiserum to human immunoglobulins is added. If antibodies are present in the patient's serum, agglutination occurs.

Western Blot

This test is typically used to determine whether a positive result in a screening immunologic test is a true-positive or a false-positive result. For example, patients who are positive in the screening ELISA for HIV infection or for Lyme disease should have a Western blot test performed. Figure 64–9 illustrates a Western blot test for the presence of HIV antibodies in the patient's serum. In this test, HIV proteins are separated electrophoretically in a gel, resulting in discrete bands of viral protein. These proteins are then transferred from the gel, ie, blotted, onto filter paper, and the person's serum is added. If antibodies are present, they bind to the viral proteins (primarily gp41 and p24) and can be detected by adding antibody to human IgG labeled with either radioactivity or an enzyme such as horseradish peroxidase, which produces a visible color change when the enzyme substrate is added.

Fluorescence-Activated Cell Sorting (Flow Cytometry)

This test is commonly used to measure the number of the various types of immunologically active blood cells

(Figure 64–10). For example, it is used in HIV-infected patients to determine the number of CD4-positive T cells. In this test, the patient's cells are labeled with monoclonal antibody to the protein specific to the cell of interest, eg, CD4 protein if the number of helper T cells is to be determined. The monoclonal antibody is tagged with a fluorescent dye, such as fluorescein or rhodamine. Single cells are passed through a laser light beam, and the number of cells that fluoresce is counted by use of a machine called a fluorescence-activated cell sorter (FACS).

ANTIGEN-ANTIBODY REACTIONS INVOLVING RED BLOOD CELL ANTIGENS

Many different blood group systems exist in humans. Each system consists of a gene locus specifying antigens on the erythrocyte surface. The two most important blood groupings, ABO and Rh, are described below.

The ABO Blood Groups & Transfusion Reactions

All human erythrocytes contain alloantigens (ie, antigens that vary among individual members of a species) of the ABO group. This is an important system, which is the basis for blood-typing and transfusions. The A and B genes encode enzymes that add specific sugars to the end of a polysaccharide chain on the surface of many cells, including red cells (Figure 64–11). People

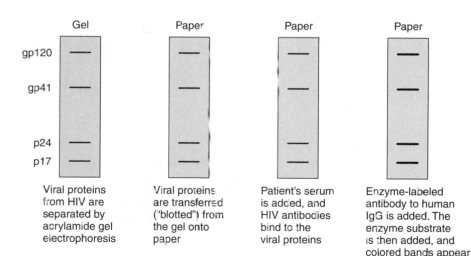

Figure 64–9. Western blot.

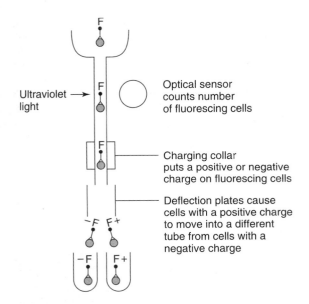

Figure 64–10. Flow cytometry. At the top of the figure, a cell has interacted with monoclonal antibody labeled with a fluorescent dye. As the cell passes down the tube, ultraviolet light causes the dye to fluoresce and a sensor counts the cell. Farther down the tube, an electrical charge can be put on the cell, which allows it to be deflected into a test tube and subjected to additional analysis.

Ultraviolet light →

Optical sensor counts number of fluorescing cells

Charging collar puts a positive or negative charge on fluorescing cells

Deflection plates cause cells with a positive charge to move into a different tube from cells with a negative charge

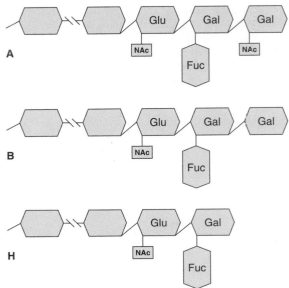

Figure 64–11. ABO blood groups. Structures of the terminal sugars that determine ABO blood groups are shown. Blood group O cells have H antigen on their surface; blood group A cells have *N*-acetylgalactosamine added to the end of the H antigen; and blood group B cells have galactosamine added to the end of the H antigen. (Reproduced, with permission, from Stites DP, Stobo JD, Wells JV [editors]: *Basic & Clinical Immunology,* 6th ed. Originally published by Appleton & Lange. Copyright © 1987 by The McGraw-Hill Companies, Inc.)

who inherit neither gene are type O. The genes are codominant, so people who inherit both genes are type AB. People who are either homozygous AA or heterozygous AO are type A, and, similarly, people who are either homozygous BB or heterozygous BO are type B.

The A and B antigens are carbohydrates that differ by a single sugar. Despite this small difference, A and B antigens do not cross-react. Erythrocytes have three terminal sugars in common on their surface: *N*-acetylglucosamine, galactose, and fucose. These three sugars form the H antigen (Figure 64–11). People who are blood group O have only the H antigen on the surface of their red cells. People who are blood group A have *N*-acetylgalactosamine added to the galactose of the H antigen, whereas people who are blood group B have galactose added to the galactose of the H antigen.

There are four combinations of the A and B antigens called A, B, AB, and O (Table 64–2). A person's blood group is determined by mixing the person's blood with antiserum against A antigen on one area on a slide and with antiserum against B antigen on another area (Figure 64–1). If agglutination occurs only with A antiserum, the blood group is A; if it occurs

only with B antiserum, the blood group is B; if it occurs with both A and B antisera, the blood group is AB; and if it occurs with neither A nor B antisera, the blood group is O.

The plasma contains antibody against the absent antigens; ie, people with blood group A have antibodies

Table 64–2. ABO blood groups.

Group	Antigen on Red Cell	Antibody in Plasma
A	A	Anti-B
B	B	Anti-A
AB	A and B	No anti-A or anti-B
O	No A or B	Anti-A and anti-B

to B in their plasma. These antibodies are formed against cross-reacting bacterial or food antigens, are first detectable at 3–6 months of age, and are of the IgM class. Individuals are tolerant to their own blood group antigens, so that a person with blood group A does not form antibodies to A antigen. The end result is that antigen and corresponding antibody do *not* coexist in the same person's blood. Transfusion reactions occur when incompatible donor red blood cells are transfused, eg, if group A blood were transfused into a group B person (because anti-A antibody is present). The red cell–antibody complex activates complement, and a reaction consisting of shock caused by large amounts of C3a and C5a (anaphylatoxins) and hemolysis caused by C5, C6, C7, C8, and C9 (membrane attack complex) occurs.

To avoid antigen-antibody reactions that would result in transfusion reactions, all blood for transfusions must be carefully **matched**; ie, erythrocytes are typed for their surface antigens by specific sera. As shown in Table 64–2, persons with group O blood have no A or B antigens on their red cells and so are **universal donors**; ie, they can give blood to people in all four groups (Table 64–3). Note that type O blood has A and B antibodies. Therefore when type O blood is given to a person with type A, B, or AB blood, you might expect a reaction to occur. A clinically detectable reaction does not occur because the donor antibody is rapidly diluted below a significant level. Persons with group AB blood have neither A nor B antibody and thus are **universal recipients.**

In addition to red blood cells, the A and B antigens appear on the cells of many tissues. Furthermore, these antigens can be secreted in saliva and other body fluids. Secretion is controlled by a secretor gene. Approximately 85% of people carry the dominant form of the gene, which allows secretion to occur.

ABO blood group differences can lead to neonatal jaundice and anemia, but the effects on the fetus are usually less severe than those seen in Rh incompatibility (see below). For example, mothers with blood group O have antibodies against both A and B antigens. These IgG antibodies can pass the placenta and, if the fetus is blood group A or B, cause lysis of fetal red cells. Mothers with either blood group A or B have a lower risk of having a neonate with jaundice because these mothers produce antibodies to either B or A antigens, respectively, that are primarily IgM, and IgM does not pass the placenta.

Rh Blood Type & Hemolytic Disease of the Newborn

About 85% of humans have erythrocytes that express the Rh(D) antigen, ie, are Rh(D)$^+$. When an Rh(D)$^-$ person is transfused with Rh(D)$^+$ blood or when an Rh(D)$^-$ woman has an Rh(D)$^+$ fetus (the D gene being inherited from the father), the Rh(D) antigen will stimulate the development of antibodies (Table 64–4). This occurs most often when the Rh(D)$^+$ erythrocytes of the fetus leak into the maternal circulation during delivery of the first Rh(D)$^+$ child. Subsequent Rh(D)$^+$ pregnancies are likely to be affected by the mother's anti-D antibody, and hemolytic disease of the newborn (**erythroblastosis fetalis**) often results. This disease results from the passage of maternal IgG anti-Rh(D) antibodies through the placenta to the fetus, with subsequent lysis of the fetal erythrocytes. The direct antiglobulin (Coombs) test is typically positive (see above for a de-

Table 64–3. Compatibility of blood transfusions between ABO blood groups.[1]

Donor	Recipient			
	O	A	B	AB
O	Yes	Yes	Yes	Yes
A (AA or AO)	No	Yes	No	Yes
B (BB or BO)	No	No	Yes	Yes
AB	No	No	No	Yes

[1]Yes indicates that a blood transfusion from a donor with that blood group to a recipient with that blood group is compatible, ie, that no hemolysis will occur. No indicates that the transfusion is incompatible and that hemolysis of the donor's cells will occur.

Table 64–4. Rh status and hemolytic disease of the newborn.

Rh Status			
Father	Mother	Child	Hemolysis[1]
+	+	+ or −	No
+	−	+	No (1st child) Yes (2nd child and subsequent children)
+	−	−	No
−	+	+ or −	No
−	−	−	No

[1]No indicates that hemolysis of the newborn's red cells will not occur and that hemolytic disease will therefore not occur. Yes indicates that hemolysis of the newborn's red cells is likely to occur and that symptoms of hemolytic disease will therefore probably occur.

scription of the Coombs test). The problem can be prevented by administration of **high-titer Rh(D) immune globulins (Rho-Gam)** to an Rh(D)⁻ mother at 28 weeks of gestation and immediately upon the delivery of an Rh(D)⁺ child. These antibodies promptly attach to Rh(D)⁺ erythrocytes and prevent their acting as sensitizing antigen. This prophylaxis is widely practiced and effective.

PRACTICE QUESTIONS: USMLE & COURSE EXAMINATIONS

Questions on the topics discussed in this chapter can be found in the Immunology section of Part XI: USMLE (National Board) Practice Questions starting on page 562. Also see Part XII: USMLE (National Board) Practice Examination starting on page 583.

Hypersensitivity (Allergy)

Hypersensitivity is the term used when an immune response results in exaggerated or inappropriate reactions harmful to the host. The term "allergy" is often equated with hypersensitivity but more accurately should be limited to the IgE-mediated reactions discussed below in the section Type I: Immediate (Anaphylactic) Hypersensitivity.

The clinical manifestations of these reactions are typical in a given individual and occur on contact with the specific antigen to which the individual is hypersensitive. The first contact of the individual with the antigen sensitizes, ie, induces the antibody, and the subsequent contacts elicit the allergic response.

Hypersensitivity reactions can be subdivided into four main types. Types I, II, and III are **antibody-mediated**, whereas type IV is **cell-mediated** (Table 65–1). Type I reactions are mediated by IgE, whereas types II and III are mediated by IgG.

TYPE I: IMMEDIATE (ANAPHYLACTIC) HYPERSENSITIVITY

An immediate hypersensitivity reaction occurs when an antigen (allergen) binds to IgE on the surface of mast cells with the consequent release of several mediators (see list of mediators below) (Figure 65–1). The process begins when an antigen induces the formation of **IgE antibody**, which binds firmly by its Fc portion to receptors on the surface of basophils and mast cells. Reexposure to the same antigen results in cross-linking of the cell-bound IgE, degranulation, and release of pharmacologically active mediators within minutes (**immediate phase**). Cyclic nucleotides and calcium play essential roles in release of the mediators.[1] Symptoms such as edema and erythema ("wheal and flare") and itching appear rapidly because these mediators, eg, histamine, are preformed.

The **late phase** of IgE-mediated inflammation occurs approximately 6 hours after exposure to the antigen and is due to mediators, eg, leukotrienes (SRS-A),

that are synthesized after the cell degranulates. These mediators cause an influx of inflammatory cells, such as neutrophils and eosinophils, and symptoms such as erythema and induration occur. Complement is not involved with either the immediate or late reactions because IgE does not activate complement.

Note that the allergens involved in hypersensitivity reactions are substances, such as pollens, animal danders, foods (nuts, shellfish), and various drugs, to which most people do *not* exhibit clinical symptoms. However, some individuals respond to those substances by producing large amounts of IgE and, as a result, manifest various allergic symptoms. The increased IgE is the result of increased class switching to IgE in B cells caused by large amounts of IL-4 produced by Th-2 cells. Nonallergic individuals respond to the same antigen by producing IgG, which does not cause the release of mediators from mast cells and basophils. (There are no receptors for IgG on those cells.) There is a genetic predisposition to immediate hypersensitivity reactions, which is discussed in the Atopy section below.

The clinical manifestations of type I hypersensitivity can appear in various forms, eg, urticaria (also known as hives), eczema, rhinitis and conjunctivitis (also known as hay fever), and asthma. Which clinical manifestation occurs depends in large part on the route of entry of the allergen and on the location of the mast cells bearing the IgE specific for the allergen. For example, some individuals exposed to pollens in the air get hay fever, whereas others who ingest allergens in food get diarrhea. Furthermore, people who respond to an allergen with urticaria have the allergen-specific IgE on mast cells in the skin, whereas those who respond with rhinitis have the allergen-specific mast cells in the nose.

The most severe form of type I hypersensitivity is **systemic anaphylaxis**, in which severe bronchoconstriction and hypotension (shock) can be life-threatening. The most common causes of anaphylaxis are foods, such as peanuts and shellfish, bee venom, and drugs. Of particular interest to medical personnel are type I hypersensitivity reactions to the wearing of latex rubber gloves, which include urticaria, asthma, and even systemic anaphylaxis. Table 65–2 summarizes some of the important clinical aspects of immediate hypersensitivities.

---

[1] An increase in cyclic GMP within these cells increases mediator release, whereas an increase in cyclic AMP decreases the release. Therefore, drugs that increase intracellular cyclic AMP, such as epinephrine, are used to treat type I reactions. Epinephrine also has sympathomimetic activity, which is useful in treating type I reactions.

Table 65–1. Hypersensitivity reactions.

Mediator	Type	Reaction
Antibody (IgE)	I (immediate, anaphylactic)	IgE antibody is induced by allergen and binds to mast cells and basophils. When exposed to the allergen again, the allergen cross-links the bound IgE, which induces degranulation and release of mediators, eg, histamine.
Antibody (IgG)	II (cytotoxic)	Antigens on a cell surface combine with antibody; this leads to complement-mediated lysis, eg, tranfusion or Rh reactions, or autoimmune hemolytic anemia.
Antibody (IgG)	III (immune complex)	Antigen-antibody immune complexes are deposited in tissues, complement is activated, and polymorphonuclear cells are attracted to the site. They release lysosomal enzymes, causing tissue damage.
Cell	IV (delayed)	Helper T lymphocytes sensitized by an antigen release lymphokines upon second contact with the same antigen. The lymphokines induce inflammation and activate macrophages, which, in turn, release various mediators.

No single mediator accounts for all the manifestations of type I hypersensitivity reactions. Some important mediators and their effects are as follows:

(1) **Histamine** occurs in granules of tissue mast cells and basophils in a preformed state. Its release causes vasodilation, increased capillary permeability, and smooth-muscle contraction. Clinically, disorders such as allergic rhinitis (hay fever), urticaria, and angioedema can occur. The bronchospasm so prominent in acute anaphylaxis results, in part, from histamine release. Antihistamine drugs block histamine receptor sites and can be relatively effective in allergic rhinitis but not in asthma (see below).

(2) **Slow-reacting substance of anaphylaxis (SRS-A)** consists of several **leukotrienes**, which do not exist in a preformed state but are produced during anaphylactic reactions. This accounts for the slow onset of the effect of SRS-A. Leukotrienes are formed from arachidonic acid by the lipoxygenase pathway and cause increased vascular permeability and smooth-muscle contraction. They are the principal mediators in the bronchoconstriction of asthma and are not influenced by antihistamines.

(3) **Eosinophil chemotactic factor of anaphylaxis (ECF-A)** is a tetrapeptide that exists preformed in mast cell granules. When released during anaphylaxis, it attracts eosinophils that are prominent in immediate allergic reactions. The role of eosinophils in type I hypersensitivity reactions is uncertain, but they do release histaminase and arylsulfatase, which degrade two important mediators, histamine and SRS-A, respec-

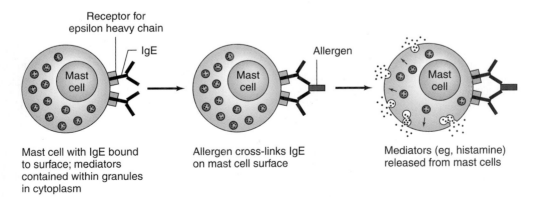

Mast cell with IgE bound to surface; mediators contained within granules in cytoplasm

Allergen cross-links IgE on mast cell surface

Mediators (eg, histamine) released from mast cells

Figure 65–1. Immediate (anaphylactic) hypersensitivity.

Table 65–2. Important clinical aspects of immediate hypersensitivities.

Main Organ Affected	Disease	Main Symptoms	Typical Allergens	Route of Acquisition
Lung	Asthma	Wheezing, dyspnea, tachypnea	Pollens, house dust (feces of dust mite), animal danders, many occupational airborne allergens	Inhalation
Nose and eyes	Rhinitis, conjunctivitis, "hay fever"	Runny nose, redness and itching of eyes	Pollens	Contact with mucous membranes
Skin	1. Eczema (atopic dermatitis)	Pruritic, vesicular lesions	Uncertain	Uncertain
	2. Urticaria (hives)	Pruritic, bullous lesions	1. Various foods 2. Drugs	Ingestion Various
Intestinal tract	Allergic gastroenteropathy	Vomiting, diarrhea	Various foods	Ingestion
Systemic	Anaphylaxis	Shock, hypotension, wheezing	1. Insect venom eg, bee venom 2. Drugs, eg, penicillin 3. Foods, eg, peanuts	Sting Various Ingestion

tively. Eosinophils may therefore reduce the severity of the type I response.

(4) **Serotonin** (hydroxytryptamine) is preformed in mast cells and blood platelets. When released during anaphylaxis, it causes capillary dilation, increased vascular permeability, and smooth-muscle contraction but is of minor importance in human anaphylaxis.

(5) **Prostaglandins and thromboxanes** are related to leukotrienes. They are derived from arachidonic acid via the cyclooxygenase pathway. Prostaglandins cause dilation and increased permeability of capillaries and bronchoconstriction. Thromboxanes aggregate platelets.

The above-mentioned mediators are active only for a few minutes after release; they are enzymatically inactivated and resynthesized slowly. Manifestations of anaphylaxis vary among species, because mediators are released at different rates in different amounts and tissues vary in their sensitivity to them. For example, the respiratory tract (bronchospasm, laryngeal edema) is a principal shock organ in humans, but the liver (hepatic veins) plays that role in dogs.

In allergic airway disease (asthma), the airway hyperactivity appears to be caused by IL-13. IL-13 is made by Th-2 cells and binds to a receptor that shares a chain with the IL-4 receptor. IL-13 does not increase the amount of IgE.

In contrast to anaphylactic reactions, which are IgE-mediated, **anaphylactoid** reactions, which appear clinically similar to anaphylactic ones, are not IgE-medi-ated. In anaphylactoid reactions, the inciting agents, usually drugs or iodinated contrast media, directly induce the mast cells and basophils to release their mediators without the involvement of IgE.

Atopy

Atopic disorders, such as hay fever, asthma, eczema, and urticaria, are immediate-hypersensitivity reactions that exhibit a strong **familial predisposition** and are associated with **elevated IgE levels.** Several processes seem likely to play a role in atopy, for example, failure of regulation at the T-cell level (eg, increased production of interleukin-4 leads to increased IgE synthesis), enhanced uptake and presentation of environmental antigens, and hyperreactivity of target tissues. Target tissues often contain large numbers of **Th-2 cells,** and these are thought to play a major role in the pathogenesis of atopic reactions.

It is estimated that up to 40% of people in the United States have experienced an atopic disorder at some time in their lives. The incidence of allergic diseases, such as asthma, is increasing markedly in the developed countries of North America and Europe. One hypothesis that might explain this increase is that the parasite burden is low in those countries. IgE evolved as a host defense against parasites. In regions where the parasite burden is high, IgE is used for host defense against those organisms. But in developed regions where the parasite burden is low, IgE is available to cause allergic diseases. This is called the "hygiene" hypothesis, which states that people who live in countries with a high parasite burden have fewer allergic diseases, whereas those who live in countries with a low parasite burden have more allergic diseases.

The symptoms of these atopic disorders are induced by exposure to the specific allergens. These antigens are typically found in the environment (eg, pollens released by plants and dust mite feces often found in bedding and carpet) or in foods (eg, shellfish and nuts). Exposure of nonatopic individuals to these substances does not elicit an allergic reaction. Many sufferers give immediate-type reactions to skin tests (injection, patch, or scratch) containing the offending antigen.

Atopic hypersensitivity is transferable by serum (ie, it is antibody-mediated), not by lymphoid cells. In the past, this observation was used for diagnosis in the passive cutaneous anaphylaxis (Prausnitz-Küstner) reaction, which consists of taking serum from the patient and injecting it into the skin of a normal person. Some hours later the test antigen, injected into the "sensitized" site, will yield an immediate wheal-and-flare reaction. This test is now impractical because of the danger of transmitting certain viral infections. Radioallergosorbent tests (RAST) permit the identification of specific IgE against potentially offending allergens if suitable specific antigens for in vitro tests are available.

Several genes associated with atopy have been identified. Mutations in the gene encoding the alpha chain of the IL-4 receptor strongly predispose to atopy. These mutations enhance the effectiveness of IL-4, resulting in an increased amount of IgE synthesis by B cells. Other genes identified include the gene for IL-4 itself, the gene for the receptor for the epsilon heavy chain, and several class II MHC genes.

Drug Hypersensitivity

Drugs, particularly antimicrobial agents such as penicillin, are now among the most common causes of hypersensitivity reactions. Usually it is not the intact drug that induces antibody formation. Rather, a metabolic product of the drug, which acts as a hapten and binds to a body protein, does so. The resulting antibody can react with the hapten or the intact drug to give rise to type I hypersensitivity.[2]

When reexposed to the drug, the person may exhibit rashes, fevers, or local or systemic anaphylaxis of variable severity. Reactions to very small amounts of the drug can occur, eg, in a skin test with the hapten. A clinically useful example is the skin test using penicilloyl-polylysine to reveal an allergy to penicillin.

Desensitization

Major manifestations of anaphylaxis occur when large amounts of mediators are suddenly released as a result of a massive dose of antigen abruptly combining with IgE on many mast cells. This is systemic anaphylaxis, which is potentially fatal. Desensitization can prevent systemic anaphylaxis.

Acute desensitization involves the administration of very small amounts of antigen at 15-minute intervals. Antigen-IgE complexes form on a small scale, and not enough mediator is released to produce a major reaction. This permits the administration of a drug or foreign protein to a hypersensitive person, but the hypersensitive state returns because IgE continues to be made.

Chronic desensitization involves the long-term weekly administration of the antigen to which the person is hypersensitive. This stimulates the production of IgA- and IgG-blocking antibodies, which can prevent subsequent antigen from reaching IgE on mast cells, thus preventing a reaction.

Treatment & Prevention

Treatment of anaphylactic reactions includes drugs to counteract the action of mediators, maintenance of an airway, and support of respiratory and cardiac function. Epinephrine, antihistamines, corticosteroids, or cromolyn sodium, either singly or in combination, should be given. Cromolyn sodium prevents release of mediators, eg, histamine, from mast cell granules. Prevention relies on identification of the allergen by a skin test and avoidance of that allergen.

There are several approaches to the treatment of asthma. Inhaled β-adrenergic bronchodilators, such as albuterol, are commonly used. Corticosteroids, such as prednisone, are also effective. Aminophylline, a bronchodilator, is effective but not commonly used. A monoclonal anti-IgE antibody (omalizumab, Xolair) is indicated for patients with severe asthma whose symptoms are not controlled by corticosteroids. For the prevention of asthma, leukotriene receptor inhibitors, such as montelukast (Singulair), and cromolyn sodium are effective.

The treatment of allergic rhinitis typically involves antihistamines along with nasal decongestants. For allergic conjunctivitis, eye drops containing antihistamines or vasoconstrictors are effective. Avoidance of the inciting allergens, such as pollens, is helpful in prophylaxis. Desensitization can also be helpful.

TYPE II: CYTOTOXIC HYPERSENSITIVITY

Cytotoxic hypersensitivity occurs when antibody directed at antigens of the **cell membrane** activates complement (Figure 65–2). This generates a membrane at-

---

[2] Some drugs are involved in cytotoxic hypersensitivity reactions (type II) and in serum sickness (type III).

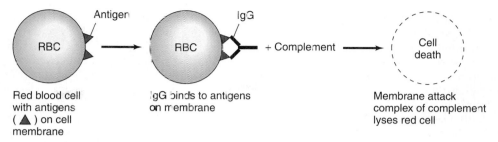

Figure 65–2. Cytotoxic hypersensitivity.

tack complex (see Chapter 63), which damages the cell membrane. The antibody (IgG or IgM) attaches to the antigen via its Fab region and acts as a bridge to complement via its Fc region. As a result, there is complement-mediated lysis as in hemolytic anemias, ABO transfusion reactions, or Rh hemolytic disease. In addition to causing lysis, complement activation attracts phagocytes to the site, with consequent release of enzymes that damage cell membranes.

Drugs (eg, penicillins, phenacetin, quinidine) can attach to surface proteins on red blood cells and initiate antibody formation. Such autoimmune antibodies (IgG) then interact with the red blood cell surface and result in hemolysis. The direct antiglobulin (Coombs) test is typically positive (see Chapter 64). Other drugs (eg, quinine) can attach to platelets and induce autoantibodies that lyse the platelets, producing thrombocytopenia and, as a consequence, a bleeding tendency. Others (eg, hydralazine) may modify host tissue and induce the production of autoantibodies directed at cell

DNA. As a result, disease manifestations resembling those of systemic lupus erythematosus occur. Certain infections, eg, *Mycoplasma pneumoniae* infection, can induce antibodies that cross-react with red cell antigens, resulting in hemolytic anemia. In rheumatic fever, antibodies against the group A streptococci cross-react with cardiac tissue. In Goodpasture's syndrome, antibody to basement membranes of the kidneys and lungs bind to those membranes and activate complement. Severe damage to the membranes is caused by proteases released from leukocytes attracted to the site by complement component C5a (see page 467).

TYPE III: IMMUNE-COMPLEX HYPERSENSITIVITY

Immune-complex hypersensitivity occurs when antigen-antibody complexes induce an inflammatory response in tissues (Figure 65–3). Normally, immune complexes are promptly removed by the reticuloen-

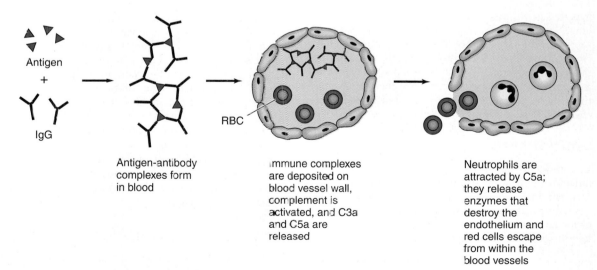

Figure 65–3. Immune-complex hypersensitivity.

dothelial system, but occasionally they persist and are **deposited in tissues,** resulting in several disorders. In persistent microbial or viral infections, immune complexes may be deposited in organs, eg, the kidneys, resulting in damage. In autoimmune disorders, "self" antigens may elicit antibodies that bind to organ antigens or deposit in organs as complexes, especially in joints (arthritis), kidneys (nephritis), or blood vessels (vasculitis).

Wherever immune complexes are deposited, they activate the complement system. Polymorphonuclear cells are attracted to the site, and inflammation and tissue injury occur. Two typical type III hypersensitivity reactions are the Arthus reaction and serum sickness.

Arthus Reaction

Arthus reaction is the name given to the inflammation caused by the deposition of immune complexes at a localized site. It is named for Dr. Arthus, who first described the inflammatory response that occurs under the following conditions. If animals are given an antigen repeatedly until they have high levels of IgG antibody[3] and that antigen is then injected subcutaneously or intradermally, intense edema and hemorrhage develop, reaching a peak in 3–6 hours.

Antigen, antibody, and complement are deposited in vessel walls; polymorphonuclear cell infiltration and intravascular clumping of platelets then occur. These reactions can lead to vascular occlusion and necrosis.

A clinical manifestation of the Arthus reaction is hypersensitivity pneumonitis (allergic alveolitis) associated with the inhalation of thermophilic actinomycetes ("farmer's lung") growing in plant material such as hay. There are many other occupation-related examples of hypersensitivity pneumonitis, such as "cheese-workers lung," "woodworker's lung," and "wheat-millers lung." Most of these are caused by the inhalation of some microorganism, either bacterium or fungus, growing on the starting material. An Arthus reaction can also occur at the site of tetanus immunizations if they are given at the same site with too short an interval between immunizations. (The minimum interval is usually 5 years.)

Serum Sickness

In contrast to the Arthus reaction, which is localized inflammation, serum sickness is a systemic inflammatory response to the presence of immune complexes deposited in many areas of the body. After the injection of foreign serum (or, more commonly these days, certain drugs), the antigen is excreted slowly. During this time, antibody production starts. The simultaneous presence of antigen and antibody leads to the formation of immune complexes, which may circulate or be deposited at various sites. Typical serum sickness results in fever, urticaria, arthralgia, lymphadenopathy, splenomegaly, and eosinophilia a few days to 2 weeks after injection of the foreign serum or drug. Although it takes several days for symptoms to appear, serum sickness is classified as an immediate reaction because symptoms occur promptly after immune complexes form. Symptoms improve as the immune system removes the antigen and subside when the antigen is eliminated. Nowadays, serum sickness is caused more commonly by drugs, eg, penicillin, than by foreign serum because foreign serum is used so infrequently.

Immune-Complex Diseases

Many clinical disorders associated with immune complexes have been described, although the antigen that initiates the disease is often in doubt. Several representative examples are described below.

A. Glomerulonephritis

Acute poststreptococcal glomerulonephritis is a well-accepted immune-complex disease. Its onset follows several weeks after a group A beta-hemolytic streptococcal infection, particularly of the skin, and often with nephritogenic serotypes of *Streptococcus pyogenes*. Typically, the complement level is low, suggesting an antigen-antibody reaction. Lumpy deposits of immunoglobulin and C3 are seen along glomerular basement membranes by immunofluorescence, suggesting the presence of antigen-antibody complexes. It is assumed that streptococcal antigen-antibody complexes, after being deposited on glomeruli, fix complement and attract neutrophils, which start the inflammatory process.

Similar lesions with "lumpy" deposits containing immunoglobulin and C3 occur in infective endocarditis, serum sickness, and certain viral infections, eg, hepatitis B and dengue hemorrhagic fever. Lesions containing immune complexes also occur in autoimmune diseases, eg, the nephritis of systemic lupus erythematosus, in which the "lumpy" deposits contain DNA as the antigen (see below and page 466).

IgA nephropathy is one of the most common forms of immune-complex glomerulonephritis worldwide. This disease is characterized by deposits of IgA on the glomeruli. The cause is unknown; no infectious agent has been associated with this disease. The course of the disease varies widely. Some patients are asymptomatic, some have mild symptoms, and others progress rapidly to kidney failure. Diagnosis is made by doing renal biopsy and demonstrating IgA deposits by immunohistologic testing.

---

[3] Much more antibody is typically needed to elicit an Arthus reaction than an anaphylactic reaction.

B. RHEUMATOID ARTHRITIS

Rheumatoid arthritis is a chronic inflammatory autoimmune disease of the joints seen commonly in young women. It is a systemic disease involving not only the joints but other organs as well, most often the lung and pericardium. Serum and synovial fluid of patients contain "rheumatoid factor," ie, IgM and IgG antibodies that bind to the Fc fragment of normal human IgG. Deposits of immune complexes (containing the normal IgG and rheumatoid factor) on synovial membranes and in blood vessels activate complement and attract polymorphonuclear cells, causing inflammation. Patients have high titers of rheumatoid factor and low titers of complement in serum especially during periods when their disease is most active (see page 467).

C. SYSTEMIC LUPUS ERYTHEMATOSUS

Systemic lupus erythematosus is a chronic inflammatory autoimmune disease that affects several organs, especially the skin of the face, the joints, and the kidneys. Antibodies are formed against DNA and other components of the nucleus of cells. These antibodies form immune complexes that activate complement. Complement activation produces C5a, which attracts neutrophils that release enzymes, thereby damaging tissue (see page 466).

TYPE IV: DELAYED (CELL-MEDIATED) HYPERSENSITIVITY

Delayed hypersensitivity is a function of T **lymphocytes, not antibody** (Figure 65–4). It can be transferred by immunologically committed (sensitized) T cells, not by serum. The response is "delayed"; ie, it starts hours (or days) after contact with the antigen and often lasts for days.

In certain contact hypersensitivities, such as poison oak, the pruritic, vesicular skin rash is caused by CD8-positive cytotoxic T cells that attack skin cells that display the plant oil as a foreign antigen. In the tuberculin skin test, the indurated skin rash is caused by CD4-positive helper T cells and macrophages that are attracted to the injection site. Table 65–3 describes some of the important clinical aspects of delayed hypersensitivities.

Clinically Important Delayed Hypersensitivity Reactions

A. CONTACT HYPERSENSITIVITY

This manifestation of cell-mediated hypersensitivity occurs after sensitization with simple chemicals (eg, nickel, formaldehyde), plant materials (eg, poison ivy, poison oak), topically applied drugs (eg, sulfonamides, neomycin), some cosmetics, soaps, and other substances. In all cases, the small molecules acting as haptens enter the skin, attach to body proteins, and become complete antigens. It is thought that these normal skin proteins to which the immune system is tolerant now can act as a carrier protein, because the hapten alters the protein enough that the immune system recognizes it as foreign. Cell-mediated hypersensitivity is induced, particularly in the skin. Upon a later skin contact with the offending agent, the sensitized person develops erythema, itching, vesicles, eczema, or necrosis of skin within 12–48 hours caused by the attack of cytotoxic T cells. Patch testing on a small area of skin can sometimes identify the offending antigen. Subsequent avoidance of the material will prevent recurrences.

B. TUBERCULIN-TYPE HYPERSENSITIVITY

Delayed hypersensitivity to antigens of microorganisms occurs in many infectious diseases and has been used as an aid in diagnosis. It is typified by the tuberculin reaction. When a patient previously exposed to *Mycobac-*

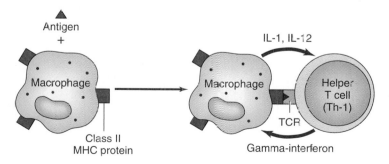

Figure 65–4. Delayed (cell-mediated) hypersensitivity. The macrophage ingests the antigen, processes it, and presents an epitope on its surface in association with class II MHC protein. The helper T (Th-1) cell is activated and produces gamma interferon, which activates macrophages. These two types of cells mediate delayed hypersensitivity.

Table 65–3. Important clinical aspects of delayed hypersensitivities.

Main Immune Cells Involved	Important Disease or Skin Test	Pathologic or Clinical Feature	Common Inducing Agents
CD4 (helper) T cells and macrophages	1. Tuberculosis, coccidioidomycosis	Granuloma	Constituents of bacterium or fungus
	2. Tuberculin or coccidioidin (or spherulin) skin tests	Induration	PPD (purified protein derivative) or coccidioidin (or spherulin)
CD8 (cytotoxic) T cells	Contact dermatitis	Pruritic, vesicular rash	Oil of poison oak or poison ivy, topical drugs, soaps, heavy metals (in jewelry)

terium tuberculosis is injected with a small amount of tuberculin (PPD) intradermally, there is little reaction in the first few hours. Gradually, however, induration and redness develop and reach a peak in 48–72 hours. A positive skin test indicates that the person **has been infected** with the agent, but it does *not* confirm the presence of current disease. However, if the skin test converts from negative to positive, it suggests that the patient has been recently infected. Infected persons do not always have a positive skin test, because overwhelming infection, disorders that suppress cell-mediated immunity (eg, uremia, measles, sarcoidosis, lymphoma, and AIDS), or the administration of immunosuppressive drugs (eg, corticosteroids, antineoplastics) may cause anergy.

A positive skin test response assists in diagnosis and provides support for chemoprophylaxis or chemotherapy. In leprosy, a positive lepromin test indicates the presence of tuberculoid leprosy with competent cell-mediated immunity, whereas a negative lepromin test suggests the presence of lepromatous leprosy with impaired cell-mediated immunity. In systemic mycotic infections (eg, coccidioidomycosis and histoplasmosis), a positive skin test with the specific antigen indicates exposure to the organism. Cell-mediated hypersensitivity develops in many viral infections; however, serologic tests are more specific than skin tests both for diagnosis and for assessment of immunity. In protozoan and helminthic infections, skin tests may be positive, but they are generally not as useful as specific serologic tests.

PRACTICE QUESTIONS: USMLE & COURSE EXAMINATIONS

Questions on the topics discussed in this chapter can be found in the Immunology section of Part XI: USMLE (National Board) Practice Questions starting on page 562. Also see Part XII: USMLE (National Board) Practice Examination starting on page 583.

Tolerance & Autoimmune Disease

TOLERANCE

Tolerance is **specific immunologic unresponsiveness**; ie, an immune response to a certain antigen (or epitope) does not occur, although the immune system is otherwise functioning normally. In general, antigens that are present during embryonic life are considered "self" and **do not stimulate** an immunologic response, ie, we are tolerant to those antigens. The lack of an immune response in the fetus is caused by the **deletion of self-reactive T-cell precursors** in the thymus (Figure 66–1). On the other hand, antigens that are not present during the process of maturation, ie, that are encountered first when the body is immunologically mature, are considered "nonself" and usually elicit an immunologic response. Although both B cells and T cells participate in tolerance, it is **T-cell tolerance** that plays the primary role.

T-Cell Tolerance

The main process by which T lymphocytes acquire the ability to distinguish self from nonself occurs in the fetal thymus (see Chapter 58). This process, called **clonal deletion**, involves the killing of T cells ("negative selection") that react against antigens (primarily self MHC proteins) present in the fetus at that time. (Note that exogenous substances injected into the fetus early in development are treated as self.) The self-reactive cells die by a process of programmed cell death called **apoptosis.** Tolerance to self acquired within the thymus is called **central tolerance,** whereas tolerance acquired outside the thymus is called **peripheral tolerance.**

Peripheral tolerance is necessary because some antigens do not reach the thymus and therefore some self-reactive T cells are not killed in the thymus. There are several mechanisms involved in peripheral tolerance: some self-reactive T cells are killed, some are not activated, and others are suppressed by regulatory T cells producing inhibitory cytokines. **Clonal anergy** is the term used to describe self-reactive T cells that are not activated because proper costimulation does not occur (Figure 66–2). **Clonal ignorance** refers to self-reactive T cells that ignore self antigens. These self-reactive T cells are either kept ignorant by physical separation from the target antigens, eg, the blood-brain barrier, or ignore self antigens because the antigens are present in such small amounts.

Although T cells that are clonally anergic cells are nonfunctional, they can become functional and initiate an autoimmune disease if conditions change later in life. The mechanism of clonal anergy involves the inappropriate presentation of antigen, leading to a failure of interleukin-2 (IL-2) production. Inappropriate presentation is due to a failure of "costimulatory signals"; eg, sufficient amounts of IL-1 might not be made, or cell surface proteins, such as CD28 on the T cell and B7 on the B cell, might not interact properly, leading to a failure of signal transduction by *ras* proteins. For example, the inhibitory protein CTL-4 on the surface of the T cells may displace CD28 and interact with B7, resulting in a failure of T-cell activation. Furthermore, B7 is an inducible protein, and failure to induce it in sufficient amounts can lead to anergy. In addition, the costimulatory proteins, CD40 on the B cell and CD40L on the helper T cell, may fail to interact properly.

The failure of costimulatory signals most often occurs when there is an insufficient inflammatory response at the site of infection. The presence of microbes typically stimulates the production of proinflammatory cytokines such as TNF and IL-1. However, if the inflammatory response is insufficient, ie, if the adjuvant effect of the cytokines is inadequate, the T cells will die instead of being activated.

B-Cell Tolerance

B cells also become tolerant to self by two mechanisms: (1) clonal deletion, probably while the B-cell precursors are in the bone marrow, and (2) clonal anergy of B cells in the periphery. However, tolerance in B cells is less complete than in T cells, an observation supported by the finding that most autoimmune diseases are mediated by antibodies.

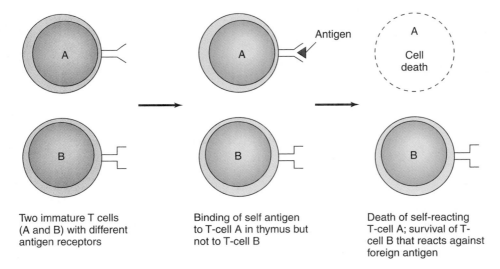

Figure 66–1. Production of T-cell tolerance in the thymus.

INDUCTION OF TOLERANCE

Whether an antigen will induce tolerance rather than an immunologic response is largely determined by the following:

(1) The immunologic **maturity** of the host; eg, neonatal animals are immunologically immature and do not respond well to foreign antigens (for instance, neonates will accept allografts that would be rejected by mature animals).

(2) The **structure** and **dose** of the antigen; eg, a very simple molecule induces tolerance more readily than a complex one, and very high or very low doses of antigen may result in tolerance instead of an immune response.

Purified polysaccharides or amino acid copolymers injected in very large doses result in "immune paralysis"—a lack of response.

Other aspects of the induction or maintenance of tolerance are as follows:

(1) T cells become tolerant more readily and remain tolerant longer than B cells.

(2) Administration of a cross-reacting antigen tends to terminate tolerance.

(3) Administration of immunosuppressive drugs enhances tolerance, eg, in patients who have received organ transplants.

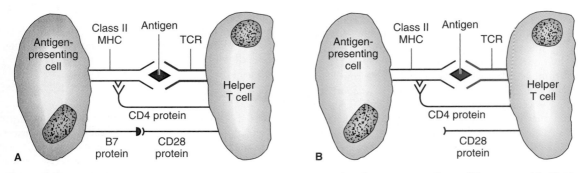

Figure 66–2. Clonal anergy outside the thymus. **A:** B7 protein on the antigen-presenting cell interacts with CD28 on the helper T cell, and full activation of the helper T cell occurs. **B:** B7 protein on the antigen-presenting cell is not produced; therefore, CD28 on the helper T cell does not give a costimulatory signal. Anergy of the helper T cell occurs despite interaction of the T-cell receptor (TCR) with the epitope.

(4) Tolerance is maintained best if the antigen to which the immune system is tolerant continues to be present.

AUTOIMMUNE DISEASES

The adult host usually exhibits tolerance to tissue antigens present during fetal life that are recognized as "self." However, in certain circumstances tolerance may be lost and immune reactions to host antigens may develop, resulting in autoimmune diseases. The most important step in the production of autoimmune disease is the **activation of self-reactive helper (CD4) T cells**. These self-reactive Th-1 or Th-2 cells can induce either cell-mediated or antibody-mediated autoimmune reactions, respectively. As described in Table 66–1, **most autoimmune diseases are antibody-mediated**.

Genetic Factors

Many autoimmune diseases exhibit a marked familial incidence, which suggests a **genetic predisposition** to these disorders. There is a strong association of some diseases with certain human leukocyte antigen (HLA)

specificities, especially the class II genes. For example, rheumatoid arthritis occurs predominantly in individuals carrying the HLA-DR4 gene. Ankylosing spondylitis is 100 times more likely to occur in people who carry HLA-B27, a class I gene, than in those who do not carry that gene.

There are two hypotheses offered to explain the relationship between certain HLA genes and autoimmune diseases. One is that those genes encode class I or class II MHC proteins that present autoantigens with greater efficiency than do the MHC proteins that are not associated with autoimmune diseases. The other hypothesis is that autoreactive T cells escape negative selection in the thymus because they bind poorly to those class I or class II MHC proteins on the surface of the thymic epithelium.

It should be noted, however, that whether a person develops an autoimmune disease or not is clearly multifactorial, because people with HLA genes known to predispose to certain autoimmune diseases nevertheless do not develop the disease; eg, many people carrying the HLA-DR4 gene do not develop rheumatoid arthritis. That is to say, HLA genes appear to be necessary

Table 66–1. Important autoimmune diseases.

Type of Immune Response	Autoimmune Disease	Target of the Immune Response
Antibody to receptors	Myasthenia gravis	Acetylcholine receptor
	Graves' disease	TSH[1] receptor
	Insulin-resistant diabetes	Insulin receptor
	Lambert-Eaton myasthenia	Calcium channel receptor
Antibody to cell components other than receptors	Systemic lupus erythematosus	dsDNA, histones
	Rheumatoid arthritis[2]	IgG in joints
	Rheumatic fever	Heart and joint tissue
	Hemolytic anemia	RBC membrane
	Idiopathic thrombocytopenic purpura	Platelet membranes
	Goodpasture's syndrome	Basement membrane of kidney and lung
	Pernicious anemia	Intrinsic factor and parietal cells
	Hashimoto's thyroiditis[2]	Thyroglobulin
	Insulin-dependent diabetes mellitus[2]	Islet cells
	Addison's disease	Adrenal cortex
	Acute glomerulonephritis	Glomerular basement membrane
	Periarteritis nodosa	Small and medium-sized arteries
	Guillain-Barré syndrome	Myelin protein
	Wegener's granulomatosis	Cytoplasmic enzymes of neutrophils
	Pemphigus	Desmoglein in tight junctions of skin
	IgA nephropathy	Glomerulus
Cell-mediated	Allergic encephalomyelitis and multiple sclerosis	Reaction to myelin protein causes demyelination of brain neurons
	Celiac disease	Enterocytes

[1]TSH, thyroid-stimulating hormone.
[2]These diseases involve a significant cell-mediated as well as antibody-mediated response.

but not sufficient to cause autoimmune diseases. In general, class II MHC-related diseases, eg, rheumatoid arthritis, Graves' disease (hyperthyroidism), and systemic lupus erythematosus, occur more commonly in women, whereas class I MHC-related diseases, eg, ankylosing spondylitis and Reiter's syndrome, occur more commonly in men.

Hormonal Factors

Approximately **90% of all autoimmune diseases occur in women.** Although the explanation for this markedly unequal gender ratio is unclear, there is some evidence from animal models that estrogen can alter the B-cell repertoire and enhance the formation of antibody to DNA. Clinically, the observation that systemic lupus erythematosus either appears or exacerbates during pregnancy (or immediately postpartum) supports the idea that hormones play an important role in predisposing women to autoimmune diseases.

Environmental Factors

There are several environmental agents that trigger autoimmune diseases, most of which are either bacteria or viruses. For example, pharyngitis caused by *Streptococcus pyogenes* predisposes to rheumatic fever. Other examples are described in Table 66–2. It is speculative at this time, but members of the normal flora of the bowel are thought to play a role in the genesis of inflammatory bowel diseases, such as Crohn's disease and ulcerative colitis.

Certain infections cause autoimmune diseases in animals, eg, coxsackievirus infection in mice causes type I diabetes, but have not been established as a cause in humans. Other environmental triggers include certain drugs such as procainamide, which causes systemic lupus erythematosus, and certain heavy metals such as gold and mercury, which cause autoimmune diseases in experimental animals.

There are two main mechanisms by which environmental factors could trigger autoimmune diseases. One is molecular mimicry, which proposes that infectious agents possess antigens that elicit an immune response that cross-reacts with components of human cells. The other is that tissue injury releases intracellular (sequestered) antigens that elicit an immune response. These mechanisms are described in more detail in the next section.

In summary, the current model is that autoimmune diseases occur in people (1) with a genetic predisposition that is determined by their MHC genes and (2) who are exposed to an environmental agent that triggers a cross-reacting immune response against some component of normal tissue. Furthermore, because au-

Table 66–2. Microbial infections associated with autoimmune diseases.

Microbe	Autoimmune Disease
1. Bacteria	
Streptococcus pyogenes	Rheumatic fever
Campylobacter jejuni	Guillain-Barré syndrome
Escherichia coli	Primary biliary cirrhosis
Chlamydia trachomatis	Reiter's syndrome
Shigella species	Reiter's syndrome
Yersinia enterocolitica	Graves' disease
Borrelia burgdorferi	Lyme arthritis
2. Viruses	
Hepatitis B virus[1]	Multiple sclerosis
Hepatitis C virus	Mixed cryoglobulinemia
Measles virus	Allergic encephalitis
Coxsackievirus B3[2]	Myocarditis
Coxsackievirus B4[3]	Type 1 diabetes mellitus
Cytomegalovirus	Scleroderma
Human T-cell leukemia virus	HTLV-associated myelopathy

[1]Other viruses, such as Epstein-Barr virus, human herpes virus-6, influenza A virus, and measles virus are also implicated as the possible cause of multiple sclerosis. No virus has definitely been shown to be the environmental trigger at this time.
[2]Coxsackievirus infects and kills cardiac myocytes causing the acute symptoms, but the late phase is caused by the attack of cytotoxic T cells on the myocytes.
[3]Causes diabetes mellitus in mice, but it is uncertain whether it is a cause in humans.

toimmune diseases increase in number with advancing age, another possible factor is a decline in the number of regulatory T cells, which allows any surviving autoreactive T cells to proliferate and cause disease.

Mechanisms

The following main mechanisms for autoimmunity have been proposed.

A. Molecular Mimicry

Various bacteria and viruses are implicated as the source of cross-reacting antigens that trigger the activation of autoreactive T cells or B cells. For example, Reiter's syndrome occurs following infections with *Shigella* or *Chlamydia,* and Guillain-Barré syndrome occurs following infections with *Campylobacter.* The concept of **molecular mimicry** is used to explain these phenomena; ie, the environmental trigger resembles (mimics) a component of the body sufficiently that an immune attack is directed against the cross-reacting body component. One of the best-characterized examples of molecular mimicry is the relationship between the M protein of *S. pyogenes* and the myosin of cardiac muscle. Antibodies against certain M proteins cross-react with cardiac myosin, leading to rheumatic fever.

Additional evidence supporting the molecular mimicry hypothesis includes the finding that there are identical amino acid sequences in certain viral proteins and certain human proteins. For example, there is an identical six–amino acid sequence in the hepatitis B viral polymerase and the human myelin basic protein.

B. ALTERATION OF NORMAL PROTEINS

Drugs can bind to normal proteins and make them immunogenic. Procainamide-induced systemic lupus erythematosus is an example of this mechanism.

C. RELEASE OF SEQUESTERED ANTIGENS

Certain tissues, eg, sperm, central nervous system, and the lens and uveal tract of the eye, are sequestered so that their antigens are **not exposed** to the immune system. These are known as **immunologically privileged sites.** When such antigens enter the circulation accidentally, eg, after damage, they elicit both humoral and cellular responses, producing aspermatogenesis, encephalitis, or endophthalmitis, respectively. Sperm, in particular, must be in a sequestered, immunologically privileged site, because they develop after immunologic maturity has been reached and yet are normally not subject to immune attack.

Intracellular antigens, such as DNA, histones, and mitochondrial enzymes, are normally sequestered from the immune system. However, bacterial or viral infection may damage cells and cause the release of these sequestered antigens, which then elicit an immune response. Once autoantibodies are formed, subsequent release of sequestered antigens results in the formation of immune complexes and the symptoms of the autoimmune disease. In addition to infection, radiation and chemicals can also damage cells and release sequestered intracellular components. For example, sunlight is known to exacerbate the skin rash in patients with systemic lupus erythematosus. It is thought that UV radiation damages cells, which releases the normally sequestered DNA and histones that are the major antigens in this disease.

D. EPITOPE SPREADING

Epitope spreading is the term used to describe the new exposure of sequestered autoantigens as a result of damage to cells caused by viral infection. These newly exposed autoantigens stimulate autoreactive T cells, and autoimmune disease results. In an animal model, a multiple sclerosis–like disease was caused by infection with an encephalomyelitis virus. Note that the self-reactive T cells were directed against cellular antigens rather than the antigens of the virus.

Diseases

Table 66–1 describes several important autoimmune diseases according to the type of immune response causing the disease and the target affected by the autoimmune response. Some examples of autoimmune disease are described in more detail below.

A. DISEASES INVOLVING PRIMARILY ONE TYPE OF CELL OR ORGAN

1. Allergic encephalitis—A clinically important example of allergic encephalitis occurs when people are injected with rabies vaccine made in rabbit brains. The immune response against the foreign myelin protein in the vaccine cross-reacts with human myelin, leading to inflammation of the brain. Although rare, this is a serious disease, and rabies vaccine made in rabbit brain is no longer used in the United States (see Chapter 39). Allergic encephalitis can also occur following certain viral infections, eg, measles or influenza, or following immunizations against these infections. These reactions are rare, and the basis for the autoimmune reaction is uncertain. Allergic encephalitis can be reproduced in the laboratory by injecting myelin basic protein into a rodent's brain, which initiates a cell-mediated response leading to demyelination.

2. Multiple sclerosis—In this disease, autoreactive T cells and activated macrophages cause demyelination of the white matter of the brain. The trigger that stimulates the autoreactive T cells is thought to be a viral infection. There is molecular evidence that the polymerase of Epstein-Barr virus may be the trigger. The findings in multiple sclerosis typically wax and wane and affect both sensory and motor functions. MRI of the brain reveals plaques in the white matter. Oligoclonal bands of IgG are found in the spinal fluid of most patients. Immunosuppressive drugs, eg, prednisone, methotrexate, or beta interferon, are effective in reducing the severity of some of the symptoms.

3. Chronic thyroiditis—When animals are injected with thyroid gland material, they develop humoral and cell-mediated immunity against thyroid antigens and chronic thyroiditis. Humans with Hashimoto's chronic thyroiditis have antibodies to thyroglobulin, suggesting that these antibodies may provoke an inflammatory process that leads to fibrosis of the gland.

4. Hemolytic anemias, thrombocytopenias, and granulocytopenias—Various forms of these disorders have been attributed to the attachment of autoantibodies to cell surfaces and subsequent cell destruction. Pernicious anemia is caused by antibodies to intrinsic factor, a protein secreted by parietal cells of the stomach that facilitates the absorption of vitamin B_{12}. Idiopathic thrombocytopenic purpura is caused by antibodies directed against platelets. Platelets coated with antibody are either destroyed in the spleen or lysed by the membrane attack complex of complement.

Several drugs, acting as haptens, bind to the platelet membrane and form a "neoantigen" that induces the cytotoxic antibody that results in platelet destruction. Penicillins, cephalothin, tetracyclines, sulfonamides, isoniazid, and rifampin as well as drugs that are not antimicrobials can have this effect. Autoimmune hemolytic anemia caused by penicillins and cephalosporins is due to the same mechanism.

5. Insulin-dependent diabetes mellitus (IDDM)—In this disease, autoreactive T cells destroy the islet cells of the pancreas. The main antigen against which the T-cell attack is directed is the islet cell enzyme, glutamic acid decarboxylase. Infection with coxsackievirus B4 has been shown to be a trigger of IDDM in mice, but it has yet to be established as a cause in human diabetes. There is a six–amino acid sequence in common between a coxsackievirus protein and glutamic acid decarboxylase. Antibodies against various antigens of the beta cells also are produced, but the major damage is T-cell mediated.

6. Insulin-resistant diabetes, myasthenia gravis, and hyperthyroidism (Graves' disease)—In these diseases, antibodies to receptors play a pathogenic role. In insulin-resistant diabetes, antibodies to insulin receptors have been demonstrated that interfere with insulin binding. In myasthenia gravis, which is characterized by severe muscular weakness, antibodies to acetylcholine receptors of neuromuscular junctions are found in the serum. Muscular weakness also occurs in Lambert-Eaton syndrome, in which antibodies form against the proteins in calcium channels. Some patients with Graves' disease have circulating antibodies to thyrotropin receptors, which, when they bind to the receptors, resemble thyrotropin in activity and stimulate the thyroid to produce more thyroxine.

7. Guillain-Barré syndrome—This disease is the most common cause of acute paralysis in the United States. It follows a variety of infectious diseases such as viral illnesses (eg, upper respiratory tract infections, HIV infection, and mononucleosis caused by Epstein-Barr virus and cytomegalovirus) and diarrhea caused by *Campylobacter jejuni*. Antibodies against myelin protein are formed and result in a demyelinating polyneuropathy. The main symptoms are those of a rapidly progressing ascending paralysis. The treatment involves either intravenous immunoglobulins or plasmapheresis.

8. Pemphigus—Pemphigus is a skin disease characterized by bullae (blisters). It is caused by autoantibodies against desmoglein, a protein in the desmosomes that forms the tight junctions between epithelial cells in the skin. When the tight junctions are disrupted, fluid fills the spaces between cells and forms the bullae. One form of pemphigus, pemphigus foliaceus, is endemic in rural areas of South America, which lends support to the idea that infection with an endemic pathogen is the environmental trigger for this disease.

9. Reactive arthritis—Reactive arthritis is an acute inflammation of the joints that follows infection with various bacteria, but the joints are sterile; ie, the inflammation is a "reaction" to the presence of bacterial antigen elsewhere in the body. Reactive arthritis is associated with enteric infections caused by *Shigella, Campylobacter, Salmonella,* and *Yersinia* and with urethritis caused by *Chlamydia trachomatis.* The arthritis is usually oligoarticular and asymmetric. The bacterial infection precedes the arthritis by a few weeks. People who are HLA-B27-positive are at higher risk for reactive arthritis. Antibiotics directed against the organism have no effect. Anti-inflammatory agents are typically used. (Reiter's syndrome includes a reactive arthritis, but the syndrome affects multiple organs and is described in the next section.)

10. Celiac disease—Celiac disease (also known as celiac sprue and gluten enteropathy) is characterized by diarrhea, painful abdominal distention, fatty stools, and failure to thrive. Symptoms are induced by ingestion of gliadin, a protein found primarily in wheat, barley, and rye grains. Gliadin is the antigen that stimulates a cytotoxic T-cell attack on enterocytes, resulting in villous atrophy. A gluten-free diet typically results in marked improvement.

11. IgA Nephropathy—This disease is one of the most common types of glomerulonephritis and is characterized primarily by hematuria, but proteinuria and progression to end-stage renal disease can occur. Immune complexes containing IgA are found lining the glomeruli. Symptoms are temporally related to viral infections, especially pharyngitis, but no specific virus has been identified. No treatment regimen is clearly effective. Fish oil has been tried, with variable results.

B. DISEASES INVOLVING MULTIPLE ORGANS (SYSTEMIC DISEASES)

1. Systemic lupus erythematosus—In this disease, autoantibodies are formed against DNA, histones, nucleolar proteins, and other components of the cell nucleus. Antibodies against double-stranded DNA are the hallmark of systemic lupus erythematosus. The disease affects primarily women between the ages of 20 and 60 years. Individuals with HLA-DR2 or -DR3 genes are predisposed to systemic lupus erythematosus. The agent that induces these autoantibodies in most patients is unknown. However, two drugs, procainamide and hydralazine, are known to cause systemic lupus erythematosus.

Most of the clinical findings are caused by immune complexes that activate complement and, as a consequence, damage tissue. For example, the characteristic rash on the cheeks is the result of a vasculitis caused by immune complex deposition. The arthritis and glomerulonephritis commonly seen in systemic lupus erythematosus are also caused by immune complexes. The immune complexes found on the glomerulus contain antibodies (IgG, IgM, or IgA) and the C3 component of complement but not fibrinogen. However, the anemia, leukopenia, and thrombocytopenia are caused by cytotoxic antibodies rather than immune complexes.

The diagnosis of systemic lupus erythematosus is supported by detecting antinuclear antibodies (ANA) with fluorescent antibody tests and anti-double-stranded DNA antibodies with ELISA. Antibodies to several other nuclear components are also detected, as is a reduced level of complement. Treatment of systemic lupus erythematosus varies depending upon the severity of the disease and the organs affected. Aspirin, nonsteroidal anti-inflammatory drugs, or corticosteroids are commonly used.

2. Rheumatoid arthritis—In this disease, autoantibodies are formed against IgG. These autoantibodies are called rheumatoid factors and are of the IgM class. Rheumatoid arthritis affects primarily women between the ages of 30 and 50 years. People with HLA-DR4 genes are predisposed to rheumatoid arthritis. The agent that induces these autoantibodies is unknown. Within the inflamed joints, the synovial membrane is infiltrated with T cells, plasma cells, and macrophages, and the synovial fluid contains high levels of macrophage-produced inflammatory cytokines such as tumor necrosis factor (TNF), IL-1, and IL-8.

The main clinical finding is inflammation of the small joints of the hands and feet. Other organs, such as the pleura, pericardium, and skin, can also be involved. Most of the clinical findings are caused by immune complexes that activate complement and, as a consequence, damage tissue. The diagnosis of rheumatoid arthritis is supported by detecting rheumatoid factors in the serum. Detection of antibody to citrullinated peptide in the serum also supports the diagnosis.

Treatment of rheumatoid arthritis typically involves aspirin, nonsteroidal anti-inflammatory drugs, immunosuppressive drugs, or corticosteroids. Anticytokine therapy consisting of a fusion protein of TNF receptor and the Fc fragment of human IgG (etaner-

cept, Enbrel) is also available. The soluble TNF receptor neutralizes TNF, which is an important inflammatory mediator in rheumatoid arthritis. Etanercept is particularly effective in combination with methotrexate in reducing the severity of joint inflammation in patients with persistently active rheumatoid arthritis. The monoclonal antibodies infliximab (Remicade) and adalimumab (Humira) are useful for the treatment of rheumatoid arthritis. These antibodies neutralize TNF, thereby decreasing the joint inflammation. Table 62–1 describes infliximab and other monoclonal antibodies that have different clinical uses.

3. Rheumatic fever—Group A streptococcal infections regularly precede the development of rheumatic fever. Antibodies against the M protein of group A streptococci that cross-react with myosin in cardiac muscle and proteins in joint and brain tissue are involved in the pathogenesis of rheumatic fever.

4. Reiter's syndrome—This syndrome is characterized by the triad of arthritis, conjunctivitis, and urethritis. Cultures of the affected areas do not reveal a causative agent. Infection by one of the intestinal pathogens, eg, *Shigella, Salmonella, Yersinia,* and *Campylobacter,* as well as other organisms such as *Chlamydia* predisposes to the disease. Most patients are men who are HLA-B27-positive. The pathogenesis of the disease is unclear, but immune complexes may play a role.

5. Goodpasture's syndrome—In this syndrome, autoantibodies are formed against the collagen in basement membranes of the kidneys and lungs. Goodpasture's syndrome (GS) affects primarily young men, and those with HLA-DR2 genes are at risk for this disease. The agent that induces these autoantibodies is unknown, but GS often follows a viral infection.

The main clinical findings are hematuria, proteinuria, and pulmonary hemorrhage. The clinical findings are caused by cytotoxic antibodies that activate complement. As a consequence, C5a is produced, neutrophils are attracted to the site, and enzymes are released by the neutrophils that damage the kidney and lung tissue. The diagnosis of GS is supported by detecting antibody and complement bound to basement membranes in fluorescent-antibody test. Because this is a rapidly progressive, often fatal disease, treatment, including plasma exchange to remove the antibodies and the use of immunosuppressive drugs, must be instituted promptly.

6. Wegener's granulomatosis—The main pathologic finding in this disease is a necrotizing granulomatous vasculitis that primarily affects the upper and lower respiratory tracts and the kidneys. Common clinical findings include sinusitis, otitis media, cough, sputum production, and arthritis. Glomerulonephritis is one of the main features of this disease. The diagnosis is supported by finding antineutrophil cytoplasmic antibodies (ANCA) in the patient's serum. Immunosuppressive therapy with cyclophosphamide and prednisone is effective.

7. Other collagen vascular diseases—Other diseases in this category include ankylosing spondylitis, which is very common in people carrying the HLA-B27 gene, polymyositis-dermatomyositis, scleroderma, periarteritis nodosa, and Sjögren's syndrome.

Treatment

The conceptual basis for the treatment of autoimmune diseases is to reduce the patient's immune response sufficiently to eliminate the symptoms. Corticosteroids, such as prednisone, are the mainstay of treatment, to which antimetabolites, such as azathioprine and methotrexate, can be added. The latter are nucleoside analogues that inhibit DNA synthesis in the immune cells. Immunosuppressive therapy must be given cautiously because of the risk of opportunistic infections.

Two approaches to therapy that do not involve systemic suppression of the immune system include antibody to TNF and soluble receptor for TNF that acts as a decoy. Both infliximab and adalimumab (antibody to TNF) as well as etanercept (TNF receptor) have been shown to ameliorate the joint inflammation of rheumatoid arthritis.

Certain antibody-mediated autoimmune diseases, such as Guillain-Barré syndrome and myasthenia gravis, can be treated either with plasmapheresis, which removes autoimmune antibodies, or with high doses of IgG pooled from healthy donors. One hypothesis regarding the mode of action of high-dose intravenous IgG is that it binds to Fc receptors on the surface of neutrophils and blocks the attachment of immune complexes that activate the neutrophils. Another hypothesis is that excess IgG saturates the FcRn receptor on the surface of vascular endothelial cells, which accelerates the catabolism of IgG, thereby reducing the level of autoimmune antibodies.

PRACTICE QUESTIONS: USMLE & COURSE EXAMINATIONS

Questions on the topics discussed in this chapter can be found in the Immunology section of Part XI: USMLE (National Board) Practice Questions starting on page 562. Also see Part XII: USMLE (National Board) Practice Examination starting on page 583.

Tumor Immunity

TUMOR-ASSOCIATED ANTIGENS

Animals carrying a chemically or virally induced malignant tumor can develop an immune response to that tumor and cause its **regression**. In the course of neoplastic transformation, **new antigens**, called **tumor-associated antigens (TAA)**, develop at the cell surface and the host recognizes such cells as "nonself." An immune response then causes the tumor to regress.

In chemically induced tumors in experimental animals, TAAs are highly specific; ie, cells of one tumor will have different TAAs from those on cells of another tumor even when they arise within the same animal. In contrast, virally induced tumors possess TAAs that cross-react with one another if induced by the same virus. TAAs on tumor cells induced by different viruses do not cross-react.

MECHANISM OF TUMOR IMMUNITY

Cell-mediated reactions attack these "nonself" tumor cells and limit their proliferation. Such immune responses probably act as a **surveillance** system to detect and eliminate newly arising clones of neoplastic cells. In general, the immune response against tumor cells is weak and can be overcome experimentally by a large dose of tumor cells. Some tumor cells can escape surveillance by "modulation," ie, internalizing the surface antigen so that it no longer presents a target for immune attack.

The cell-mediated immune responses that affect tumor cells in vitro include natural killer (NK) cells, which act without antibody; killer (K) cells, which mediate antibody-dependent cytolysis (antibody-dependent cellular cytotoxicity); cytotoxic T cells; and activated macrophages. Whether these immune responses function to prevent or control tumors in vivo is unknown.

Tumor antigens can stimulate the development of specific antibodies as well. Some of these antibodies are cytotoxic, but others, called blocking antibodies, enhance tumor growth, perhaps by blocking recognition of tumor antigens by the host. Spontaneously arising human tumors may have new cell surface antigens against which the host develops both cytotoxic anti-

bodies and cell-mediated immune responses. Enhancement of these responses can contain the growth of some tumors. For example, the administration of BCG vaccine (bacillus Calmette-Guérin, a bovine mycobacterium) into surface melanomas can lead to their partial regression. Immunomodulators, such as interleukins and interferons, are also being tested in such settings. One interleukin, tumor necrosis factor-α (cachectin), is experimentally effective against a variety of solid tumors (see Chapter 58). In addition, lymphocytes activated by interleukin-2 (lymphokine-activated killer [LAK] cells) may be useful in cancer immunotherapy.

Another approach to cancer immunotherapy involves the use of tumor-infiltrating lymphocytes (TIL). The basis for this approach is the observation that some cancers are infiltrated by lymphocytes (NK cells and cytotoxic T cells) that seem likely to be trying to destroy the cancer cells. These lymphocytes are recovered from the surgically removed cancer, grown in cell culture until large numbers of cells are obtained, activated with interleukin-2, and returned to the patient in the expectation that the TIL will "home in" specifically on the cancer cells and kill them.

CARCINOEMBRYONIC ANTIGEN & ALPHA FETOPROTEIN

Some human tumors contain antigens that normally occur in fetal but not in adult human cells.

(1) **Carcinoembryonic antigen** circulates at elevated levels in the serum of many patients with carcinoma of the colon, pancreas, breast, or liver. It is found in fetal gut, liver, and pancreas and in very small amounts in normal sera. Detection of this antigen (by radioimmunoassay) is not helpful in diagnosis but may be helpful in the management of such tumors. If the level declines after surgery, it suggests that the tumor is not spreading. Conversely, a rise in the level of carcinoembryonic antigen in patients with resected carcinoma of the colon suggests recurrence or spread of the tumor.

(2) **Alpha fetoprotein** is present at elevated levels in the sera of hepatoma patients and is used as a marker for this disease. It is produced by fetal liver and is found in small amounts in some normal sera. It is, however, non-

specific; it occurs in several other malignant and non-malignant diseases.

Monoclonal antibodies directed against new surface antigens on malignant cells (eg, B-cell lymphomas) can be useful in diagnosis. Monoclonal antibodies coupled to toxins, such as diphtheria toxin or ricin, a product of the *Ricinus* plant, can kill tumor cells in vitro and someday may be useful for cancer therapy.

PRACTICE QUESTIONS: USMLE & COURSE EXAMINATIONS

Questions on the topics discussed in this chapter can be found in the Immunology section of Part XI: USMLE (National Board) Practice Questions starting on page 562. Also see Part XII: USMLE (National Board) Practice Examination starting on page 583.

Immunodeficiency

Immunodeficiency can occur in any of the four major components of the immune system: (1) B cells (antibody), (2) T cells, (3) complement, and (4) phagocytes. The deficiencies can be either congenital or acquired (Table 68–1). Clinically, recurrent or opportunistic infections are commonly seen. **Recurrent infections with pyogenic bacteria, eg, staphylococci, indicate a B-cell deficiency, whereas recurrent infections with certain fungi, viruses, or protozoa indicate a T-cell deficiency.**

CONGENITAL IMMUNODEFICIENCIES

B-Cell Deficiencies

A. X-Linked Hypogammaglobulinemia (Bruton's Agammaglobulinemia)

Very low levels of all immunoglobulins (IgG, IgA, IgM, IgD, and IgE) and a virtual **absence of B cells** are found in young **boys;** female carriers are immunologically normal. Pre-B cells are present, but they fail to differentiate into B cells. This failure is caused by a mutation in the gene encoding tyrosine kinase, an important signal transduction protein. Cell-mediated immunity is relatively normal. Clinically, recurrent pyogenic bacterial infections, eg, otitis media, sinusitis, and pneumonia caused by *Streptococcus pneumoniae* and *Haemophilus influenzae,* occur in infants at about 6 months of age, when maternal antibody is no longer present in sufficient amount to be protective. Treatment with pooled gamma globulin reduces the number of infections.

B. Selective Immunoglobulin Deficiencies

IgA deficiency is the **most common** of these; IgG and IgM deficiencies are rarer. Patients with a deficiency of IgA typically have recurrent sinus and lung infections. (However, some individuals with IgA deficiency do not have frequent infections, possibly because their IgG and IgM levels confer protection.) The cause of IgA deficiency may be a failure of heavy-chain gene switching, because the amounts of IgG and IgM are normal. Patients with a deficiency of IgA should not be treated with gamma globulin preparations, because these patients may form antibodies against the foreign IgA and, by cross-reaction, deplete their already low level of IgA.

Patients with selective IgM deficiency or deficiency of one or more of the IgG subclasses also have recurrent sinopulmonary infections caused by pyogenic bacteria such as *S. pneumoniae, H. influenzae,* or *Staphylococcus aureus.*

T-Cell Deficiencies

A. Thymic Aplasia (DiGeorge's Syndrome)

Severe viral, fungal, or protozoal infections occur in affected infants early in life as a result of a profound **deficit of T cells.** Pneumonia caused by *Pneumocystis carinii* and thrush caused by *Candida albicans* are two common infections in these patients. Antibody production may be decreased or normal. If decreased, severe pyogenic bacterial infections can occur.

Both the **thymus and the parathyroids fail to develop properly** as a result of a defect in the third and fourth pharyngeal pouches. The most common presenting symptom is **tetany due to hypocalcemia** caused by hypoparathyroidism. Other congenital abnormalities are common. A transplant of fetal thymus may reconstitute T-cell immunity. A thymus from a child older than 14 weeks should not be used, because a graft-versus-host reaction may occur.

B. Chronic Mucocutaneous Candidiasis

In this disease, the skin and mucous membranes of children are infected with *C. albicans,* which in immunocompetent individuals is a nonpathogenic member of the normal flora. These children have a T-cell deficiency **specifically** for this organism; other T-cell and B-cell functions are normal. Treatment consists primarily of antifungal drugs.

C. Hyper-IgM Syndrome

In this syndrome, severe, recurrent pyogenic bacterial infections resembling those seen in X-linked hypogammaglobulinemia begin early in life. Patients have a high concentration of IgM but very little IgG, IgA, and IgE. They have normal numbers of T cells and B cells. Although the main manifestations of this syndrome are alterations in antibodies, the mutation is in the gene encoding the CD40 ligand in the CD4-positive helper

Table 68–1. Important congenital immunodeficiencies.

Deficient Component and Name of Disease	Specific Deficiency	Molecular Defect	Clinical Features
B cell			
X-linked (Bruton's)	Absence of B cells; very low Ig levels.	Mutant tyrosine kinase.	Pyogenic infections.
Selective IgA	Very low IgA levels.	Failure of heavy-chain gene switching.	Sinus and lung infections.
T cell			
Thymic aplasia (DiGeorge's)	Absence of T cells.	Defective development of pharyngeal pouches; not a genetic disease.	Viral, fungal, and protozoal infections; tetany.
Chronic mucocutaneous candidiasis	Deficient T-cell response to *Candida*.	Unknown.	Skin and mucous membrane infections with *Candida*.
Combined B and T cell			
Severe combined immunodeficiency (SCID)	Deficiency of both B-cell and T-cell function.	Either defective IL-2 receptor, defective recombinases, defective kinases, absence of class II MHC proteins, or ADA or PNP deficiency.	Bacterial, viral, fungal, and protozoal infections.
Complement			
Hereditary angioedema	Deficiency of C1 protease inhibitor.	Too much C3a, C4a, and C5a generated.	Edema, especially laryngeal edema.
C3b	Insufficient C3.	Unknown.	Pyogenic infections, especially with *S. aureus*.
C6,7,8	Insufficient C6,7,8.	Unknown.	*Neisseria* infections.
Phagocytes			
Chronic granulomatous disease	Defective bactericidal activity because no oxidative burst.	Deficient NADPH oxidase activity.	Pyogenic infections, especially with *S. aureus*.

T cells. As a result, the helper T cells have a defect in the surface protein (CD40 ligand) that interacts with CD40 on the B-cell surface. The failure to properly interact with CD40 results in an inability of the B cell to switch from the production of IgM to the other classes of antibodies. Treatment with pooled gamma globulin results in fewer infections.

D. Interleukin-12 Receptor Deficiency

Patients with a deficiency of IL-12 receptor have disseminated mycobacterial infections. The absence of the receptor prevents IL-12 from initiating a Th-1 response, which is required to limit mycobacterial infections.

Combined B-Cell & T-Cell Deficiencies

A. Severe Combined Immunodeficiency Disease (SCID)

Recurrent infections caused by bacteria, viruses, fungi, and protozoa occur in early infancy (3 months of age), because **both B cells and T cells** are defective. In some children, the B and T cells are absent; in others, the number of cells is normal but they do not function properly. Immunoglobulin levels are very low and tonsils and lymph nodes are absent. *Pneumocystis* pneumonia is the most common presenting infection in these infants. Infections caused by *C. albicans* and viruses such as varicella-zoster virus, cytomegalovirus, and respiratory syncytial virus are common and often fatal.

This is a group of inherited diseases, all of which are due to a defect in the differentiation of an early stem cell. There are two types: X-linked and autosomal; the X-linked form constitutes about 75% of cases. Some patients with X-linked SCID have a defect in the IL-2 receptor on T cells. They lack the γ chain of the IL-2 receptor that is essential for the development of T cells. This is the most common form of SCID in the United States. Some patients with the autosomal form have a mutation in the gene encoding a tyrosine kinase called ZAP-70 that plays a role in signal transduction in T cells. Another autosomal form has mutations in the gene for a different kinase called Janus kinase 3. Other SCID patients with the autosomal form have a mutation in the RAG-1 or RAG-2 genes that encode the recombinase enzymes that catalyze the recombination of the DNA required to generate the T-cell antigen receptor and the IgM monomer on the B cell that acts as the antigen receptor.

Because immunity is so profoundly depressed, these children must be protected from exposure to microorganisms, usually by being enclosed in a plastic "bubble." Live, attenuated viral vaccines should *not* be given. Bone marrow transplantation may restore immunity. It is interesting that because infants with SCID do not reject allografts, bone marrow transplants do not require immunosuppressive drugs.

Patients with a hereditary absence of **adenosine deaminase (ADA) and purine nucleoside phosphorylase (PNP)** can have a severe deficiency of B cells and T cells, causing SCID, although some have only mild dysfunction. The absence of these enzymes results in an accumulation of dATP, an inhibitor of ribonucleotide reductase, and a consequent decrease in the deoxynucleoside triphosphate precursors of DNA. This reduces the formation of B-cell and T-cell precursors in the bone marrow. Bone marrow transplantation can be helpful. Injections of ADA conjugated to polyethylene glycol reduce the number and severity of infections. Several patients with ADA deficiency have benefited from gene therapy. A retroviral vector carrying a normal copy of the ADA gene was allowed to infect the patient's bone marrow cells. The ADA gene functioned within some of these cells, and the patient's immune status improved.

Patients with **bare lymphocyte syndrome** exhibit the signs and symptoms of a severe combined immunodeficiency and are especially susceptible to viral infections. These patients have defective class I or class II MHC proteins or both. Mutations resulting in the inability to synthesize a transcription factor required for the synthesis of the mRNA for class II MHC proteins are an important cause of the failure to produce those proteins. Mutations in the gene encoding the TAP protein have been identified as one cause of the inability to display antigens on class I MHC proteins. (The TAP transporter protein is described on page 408.)

B. WISKOTT-ALDRICH SYNDROME

Recurrent pyogenic infections, eczema, and bleeding caused by thrombocytopenia characterize this syndrome. These symptoms typically appear during the first year of life. It is an X-linked disease and thus occurs only in male infants. The most important defect is the inability to mount an IgM response to the capsular polysaccharides of bacteria, such as pneumococci. IgG levels and IgA levels are normal, but cell-mediated immunity is variable. The defect appears to be in the ability of T cells to provide help to B cells. The mutant gene encodes a protein involved in actin filament assembly. Bone marrow transplantation may be helpful.

C. ATAXIA-TELANGIECTASIA

In this disease, ataxia (staggering), telangiectasia (enlarged small blood vessels of the conjunctivas and skin), and recurrent infections appear by 2 years of age. It is an autosomal recessive disease caused by mutations in the genes that encode DNA repair enzymes. Lymphopenia and IgA deficiency commonly occur. Treatment designed to correct the immunodeficiency has not been successful.

Complement Deficiencies

A. HEREDITARY ANGIOEDEMA

This is an uncommon autosomal dominant disease caused by a deficiency of C1 inhibitor. In the absence of inhibitor, C1 continues to act on C4 to generate C4a and subsequently additional vasoactive components such as C3a and C5a. This leads to capillary permeability and edema in several organs. Laryngeal edema can be fatal. Steroid drugs, such as oxymetholone and danazol, can be useful in increasing the concentration of C1 inhibitor.

B. RECURRENT INFECTIONS

Patients with deficiencies in C1, C3, or C5 or the later components C6, C7, or C8 have an increased susceptibility to bacterial infections. Patients with C3 deficiency are particularly susceptible to sepsis with pyogenic bacteria such as *S. aureus*. Those with reduced levels of C6, C7, or C8 are especially prone to bacteremia with *Neisseria meningitidis* or *Neisseria gonorrhoeae*.

C. AUTOIMMUNE DISEASES

Patients with C2 and C4 deficiencies have diseases resembling systemic lupus erythematosus or other autoimmune diseases. C2 deficiency is the most common complement defect and is frequently asymptomatic.

D. Paroxysmal Nocturnal Hemoglobinuria

This rare disease is characterized by episodes of brownish urine (hemoglobinuria), particularly upon arising. The hemoglobinuria is due to complement-mediated hemolysis. This occurs especially at night because the lower oxygen concentration in the blood during sleep increases the susceptibility of the red cells to lyse. Hemolysis occurs because there is a deficiency of decay-accelerating factor (DAF) on the surface of blood cell precursors, leading to an increased activation of complement (see Chapter 63). These patients have a defect in the gene for the molecules that anchor DAF and other proteins to the cell membrane. There is no specific treatment. Iron can be given for the anemia, and prednisone can be helpful.

Phagocyte Deficiencies

A. Chronic Granulomatous Disease (CGD)

Patients with this disease are very susceptible to opportunistic infections with certain bacteria and fungi, eg, *S. aureus,* enteric gram-negative rods, especially *Serratia* and *Burkholderia,* and *Aspergillus fumigatus.* Recurrent infections with catalase-positive bacteria, such as staphylococci, are common in these patients; whereas infections with catalase-negative bacteria, such as streptococci, are rare. Viral, mycobacterial, and protozoal infections are not a major concern. In 60% to 80% of cases, this is an X-linked disease that appears by the age of 2 years. (In the remaining patients, the disease is autosomal.)

CGD is due to a defect in the intracellular microbicidal activity of neutrophils as a result of a **lack of NADPH oxidase** activity (or similar enzymes). As a result, no hydrogen peroxide or superoxides are produced (ie, no oxidative burst occurs), and the organisms, although ingested, are not killed. B-cell and T-cell functions are usually normal. In the laboratory, diagnosis can be confirmed by the **nitroblue tetrazolium** dye reduction test or by the dichlorofluorescein (DCF) test. The DCF test is the more informative of the two because the analysis is done by flow cytometry, which provides information regarding the oxidative ability of single cells. For example, in the mothers of boys with CGD who are carriers, half of their neutrophils show normal oxidative activity because the X-chromosome carrying the mutant gene has been inactivated, whereas the other half show no oxidative activity because the X-chromosome carrying the normal gene has been inactivated.

Prompt, aggressive treatment of infection with the appropriate antibiotics is important. Chemoprophylaxis using trimethoprim-sulfamethoxazole can reduce the number of infections. Gamma interferon significantly reduces the frequency of recurrent infections, probably because it increases phagocytosis by macrophages.

The name chronic granulomatous disease arises from the widespread granulomas seen in these patients, even in the absence of clinically apparent infection. These granulomas can become large enough to cause obstruction of the stomach, esophagus, or bladder. The cause of these granulomas is unknown.

B. Chédiak-Higashi Syndrome

In this autosomal recessive disease, recurrent pyogenic infections, caused primarily by staphylococci and streptococci, occur. This is due to the failure of the **lysosomes** of neutrophils to fuse with phagosomes. The degradative enzymes in the lysosomes are, therefore, not available to kill the ingested organisms. Large granular inclusions composed of abnormal lysosomes are seen. In addition, the neutrophils do not function correctly during chemotaxis as a result of faulty microtubules. The mutant gene in this disease encodes a cytoplasmic protein involved in protein transport. Peroxide and superoxide formation is normal, as are B-cell and T-cell functions. Treatment involves antimicrobial drugs. There is no useful therapy for the phagocyte defect.

C. Job's Syndrome (Hyper-IgE Syndrome)

Patients with this syndrome have recurrent "cold"[1] staphylococcal abscesses, eczema, skeletal effects, and high levels of IgE.

The main immunologic defect is a failure to produce gamma interferon by helper T cells, which reduces the ability of macrophages to kill bacteria. This leads to an increase in Th-2 cells and, as a consequence, a high IgE level. The increased IgE causes histamine release, which blocks certain aspects of the inflammatory response, hence the "cold" abscesses. Histamine also inhibits neutrophil chemotaxis, another feature of this syndrome. Treatment consists of antimicrobial drugs.

D. Leukocyte Adhesion Deficiency Syndrome

Patients with this syndrome have severe pyogenic infections early in life because they have defective adhesion (LFA-1) proteins on the surface of their phagocytes. This is an autosomal recessive disease in which there is a mutation in the gene encoding the β chain of an integrin that mediates adhesion. As a result, neutrophils adhere poorly to endothelial cell surfaces and phagocytosis of the bacteria is inadequate.

E. Cyclic Neutropenia

In this autosomal dominant disease, patients have a very low neutrophil count (less than 200/μL) for 3 to 6

---

[1] "Cold" refers to the absence of inflammation of the lesions; ie, the lesions are not warm and red.

days of a 21-day cycle. During the neutropenic stage, patients are susceptible to life-threatening bacterial infections, but when neutrophil counts are normal, patients are not susceptible. Mutations in the gene encoding neutrophil elastase have been identified in these patients, but it is unclear how these contribute to the cyclic nature of the disease. It is hypothesized that irregular production of granulocyte colony-stimulating factor may play a role in the cyclic aspect of the disease.

F. MYELOPEROXIDASE DEFICIENCY

Deficiency of myeloperoxidase (either reduced amount or reduced function) is quite common but has little clinical importance. Surprisingly, most patients with this deficiency do not have a significant increase in infectious diseases. Myeloperoxidase catalyzes the production of hypochlorite, an important microbicidal agent, so an increase in infections would be expected. However, other intracellular killing mechanisms are intact and must be sufficient to kill the ingested microbes.

G. INTERFERON-GAMMA RECEPTOR DEFICIENCY

Patients with this deficiency have severe infections with atypical mycobacteria or with bacillus Calmette-Guérin (BCG), the attenuated mycobacterium in the BCG vaccine. They have a mutation in the gene encoding either the ligand-binding portion or the signal-transducing portion of the receptor for interferon-gamma. As a result, macrophages are not activated and severe mycobacterial infections occur. Defects in the production of interleukin-12 or in the receptor for interleukin-12 cause the same clinical picture.

ACQUIRED IMMUNODEFICIENCIES

B-Cell Deficiencies

A. COMMON VARIABLE HYPOGAMMAGLOBULINEMIA

Patients present with recurrent infections caused by pyogenic bacteria, eg, sinusitis and pneumonia caused by pyogenic bacteria such as *S. pneumoniae* and *H. influenzae*. The infections usually occur in persons between the ages of 15 and 35 years. The number of B cells is usually normal, but the ability to synthesize IgG (and other immunoglobulins) is greatly reduced. Cell-mediated immunity is usually normal. The cause of the failure to produce IgG is unknown but appears to be due to defective T-cell signaling. Intravenous gamma globulin given monthly reduces the number of infections.

B. MALNUTRITION

Severe malnutrition can reduce the supply of amino acids and thereby reduce the synthesis of IgG. This predisposes to infection by pyogenic bacteria.

T-Cell Deficiencies

A. ACQUIRED IMMUNODEFICIENCY SYNDROME

Patients with acquired immunodeficiency syndrome (AIDS) present with opportunistic infections caused by certain bacteria, viruses, fungi, and protozoa (eg, *Mycobacterium avium-intracellulare*, herpesviruses, *C. albicans*, and *P. carinii*). This is due to greatly reduced helper T-cell numbers caused by infection with the retrovirus human immunodeficiency virus (HIV; see Chapter 45). This virus specifically infects and kills cells bearing the CD4 protein as a surface receptor. The response to specific immunizations is poor; this is attributed to the loss of helper T-cell activity. AIDS patients also have a high incidence of tumors such as lymphomas, which may be the result of a failure of immune surveillance. See Chapter 45 for information on treatment and prevention.

B. MEASLES

Patients with measles have a transient suppression of delayed hypersensitivity as manifested by a loss of PPD skin test reactivity. Quiescent tuberculosis can become active. In these patients, T-cell function is altered but immunoglobulins are normal.

Complement Deficiencies

A. LIVER FAILURE

Liver failure caused by alcoholic cirrhosis or by chronic hepatitis B or hepatitis C can reduce the synthesis of complement proteins by the liver to a level that severe pyogenic infections can occur.

B. MALNUTRITION

Severe malnutrition can reduce the supply of amino acids and thereby reduce the synthesis of complement proteins by the liver. This predisposes to infection by pyogenic bacteria.

Phagocyte Deficiencies

A. NEUTROPENIA

Patients with neutropenia present with severe infections caused by pyogenic bacteria such as *S. aureus* and *S. pneumoniae* and enteric gram-negative rods. Neutrophil counts below 500/μL predispose to these infections. Common causes of neutropenia include cytotoxic drugs, such as those used in cancer chemotherapy; leukemia, in which the bone marrow is "crowded out" by leukemic cells; and autoimmune destruction of the neutrophils. Ciprofloxacin is used to try to prevent infections in neutropenic patients.

Chronic Fatigue Syndrome (Chronic Fatigue Immune Dysfunction Syndrome)

The predominant finding in patients with chronic fatigue syndrome (CFS) is persistent, debilitating fatigue that has lasted for at least 6 months and is not relieved by bed rest. Because fatigue is a nonspecific symptom, all other causes of fatigue, including physical (eg, cancer, autoimmune disease, and infection) and psychiatric (eg, depression and neurosis), as well as prolonged use of drugs (eg, tranquilizers), must be ruled out. The cause of CFS is unknown; attempts to isolate a causative organism from these patients have failed. A proposed relationship between CFS and chronic Epstein-Barr virus infection remains unsubstantiated.

There is a similarity between the symptoms of CFS and the symptoms that occur when alpha interferon or interleukin-2 is administered to patients. Abnormalities in various components of the immune system have been reported, eg, loss of delayed hypersensitivity reactivity in skin tests and increased levels of cytotoxic T cells, but no definitive findings have emerged. There is no specific laboratory test for CFS. The approach to therapy involves treating the symptoms. Treatment with various antimicrobial drugs, such as acyclovir, ketoconazole, and gamma globulin, had no effect.

PRACTICE QUESTIONS: USMLE & COURSE EXAMINATIONS

Questions on the topics discussed in this chapter can be found in the Immunology section of Part XI: USMLE (National Board) Practice Questions starting on page 562. Also see Part XII: USMLE (National Board) Practice Examination starting on page 583.

PART VIII

Brief Summaries of Medically Important Organisms

SUMMARIES OF MEDICALLY IMPORTANT BACTERIA

GRAM-POSITIVE COCCI (CHAPTER 15)

Staphylococcus aureus

Diseases—Abscesses of many organs, endocarditis, gastroenteritis (food poisoning), toxic shock syndrome, hospital-acquired pneumonia, surgical wound infections, and sepsis. It is one of the most common causes of human infections.

Characteristics—Gram-positive cocci in clusters. Coagulase-positive. Catalase-positive. Most isolates produce β-lactamase.

Habitat and Transmission—Main habitat is human nose; also found on human skin. Transmission is via the hands.

Pathogenesis—Abscess containing pus is the most common lesion. Three exotoxins are also made. Toxic shock syndrome toxin is a superantigen and causes toxic shock syndrome by stimulating many helper T cells to release large amounts of lymphokines, especially IL-2. Enterotoxin, which causes food poisoning, is also a superantigen. Food poisoning has a short incubation period because it is preformed in food. Scalded skin syndrome toxin is a protease that cleaves desmoglein in tight junctions in the skin. Protein A is an important virulence factor because it binds to the heavy chain of IgG and prevents the activation of complement. Predisposing factors to infection include breaks in the skin, foreign bodies such as sutures, neutrophil levels below 500/μL, intravenous drug use (predisposes to right-sided endocarditis), and tampon use (predisposes to toxic shock syndrome).

Laboratory Diagnosis—Gram-stained smear and culture. Yellow or gold colonies on blood agar. *Staphylococcus aureus* is coagulase-positive; *Staphylococcus epidermidis* is coagulase-negative. Serologic tests not useful.

Treatment—Penicillin G for sensitive isolates; β-lactamase-resistant penicillins such as nafcillin for resistant isolates; vancomycin for isolates resistant to nafcillin. About 85% are resistant to penicillin G. Plasmid-encoded β-lactamase mediates most resistance. Resistance to nafcillin is caused by changes in binding proteins. Some isolates are tolerant to penicillin. Rare vancomycin-resistant strains have emerged.

Prevention—Cefazolin is used to prevent surgical wound infections. No vaccine is available. Hand washing reduces spread.

Staphylococcus epidermidis

Diseases—Endocarditis on prosthetic heart valves, prosthetic hip infection, intravascular catheter infection, cerebrospinal fluid shunt infection, neonatal sepsis.

Characteristics—Gram-positive cocci in clusters. Coagulase-negative. Catalase-positive.

Habitat and Transmission—Normal flora of the human skin and mucous membranes. It is probably the patient's own strains that cause infection, but transmission from person to person via hands may occur.

Pathogenesis—Glycocalyx-producing strains adhere well to foreign bodies such as prosthetic implants and catheters. It is a low-virulence organism that causes disease primarily in immunocompromised patients and in those with implants. It is a major cause of hospital-

477

acquired infections. Unlike *S. aureus,* no exotoxins have been identified.

Laboratory Diagnosis—Gram-stained smear and culture. Whitish, non-hemolytic colonies on blood agar. It is coagulase-negative. *S. epidermidis* is sensitive to novobiocin, whereas the other coagulase-negative staphylococcus, *S. saprophyticus,* is resistant. Serologic tests are not useful.

Treatment—Vancomycin plus either rifampin or an aminoglycoside. It produces β-lactamases and is resistant to many antibiotics.

Prevention—There is no drug or vaccine.

Staphylococcus saprophyticus

Gram-positive cocci in clusters. Coagulase-negative. Resistant to novobiocin in contrast to *S. epidermidis,* which is sensitive. Causes community-acquired urinary tract infections in young women (but *Escherichia coli* is a much more common cause).

Streptococcus pyogenes (Group A Streptococcus)

Diseases—Suppurative (pus-producing) diseases, eg, pharyngitis and cellulitis; nonsuppurative (immunologic) diseases, eg, rheumatic fever and acute glomerulonephritis.

Characteristics—Gram-positive cocci in chains. Beta-hemolytic. Catalase-negative. Bacitracin-sensitive. Beta-hemolytic streptococci are subdivided into group A, B, etc, by differences in the antigenicity of their cell wall carbohydrate.

Habitat and Transmission—Habitat is the human throat and skin. Transmission is via respiratory droplets.

Pathogenesis—For suppurative infections, hyaluronidase ("spreading factor") mediates subcutaneous spread seen in cellulitis; erythrogenic toxin (a superantigen) causes the rash of scarlet fever; M protein impedes phagocytosis. For nonsuppurative (immunologic) diseases, rheumatic fever is caused by immunologic cross-reaction between bacterial antigen and human heart and joint tissue (ie, antibody against streptococcal M protein reacts with myosin in cardiac muscle), and acute glomerulonephritis is caused by immune complexes formed between streptococcal antigens and antibody to those antigens. The immune complexes are trapped by glomeruli, complement is activated, neutrophils are attracted to the site by C5a, and proteases produced by neutrophils damage glomeruli.

Laboratory Diagnosis—The diagnosis of suppurative infections, eg, cellulitis, differs from immunologic diseases, eg, rheumatic fever. For suppurative infections, use Gram-stained smear and culture. Beta-hemolytic colonies on blood agar. (Hemolysis due to streptolysins O and S.) If isolate is sensitive to bacitracin, it is identified as *Streptococcus pyogenes.* Rapid ELISA tests for group A streptococcal antigens in throat swabs are available. Assay for antibody in patient's serum is not done for suppurative infections. If rheumatic fever is suspected, patient's antistreptolysin O (ASO) antibody titer is tested to determine whether previous exposure to *S. pyogenes* has occurred. If acute glomerulonephritis is suspected, antibody to streptococcal DNase B is used as evidence of a previous skin infection by *S. pyogenes.*

Treatment—Penicillin G (no significant resistance).

Prevention—Penicillin is used in patients with rheumatic fever to prevent recurrent *S. pyogenes* pharyngitis. This prevents additional damage to heart valves. There is no vaccine.

Streptococcus agalactiae (Group B Streptococcus)

Diseases—Neonatal meningitis and sepsis.

Characteristics—Gram-positive cocci in chains. Beta-hemolytic. Catalase-negative. Bacitracin-resistant. Beta-hemolytic streptococci are subdivided into group A, B, etc, by differences in the antigenicity of their cell wall carbohydrate.

Habitat and Transmission—Main habitat is the human vagina. Transmission occurs during birth.

Pathogenesis—Pyogenic organism. No exotoxins identified. Predisposing factors to neonatal infection include rupture of membranes more than 18 hours before delivery, labor prior to 37 weeks (infant is premature), absence of maternal antibody, and heavy colonization of the genital tract by the organism.

Laboratory Diagnosis—Gram-stained smear and culture. Beta-hemolytic (narrow zone) colonies on blood agar that are resistant to bacitracin. Organisms hydrolyze hippurate and are CAMP test–positive.

Treatment—Penicillin G.

Prevention—No vaccine. Ampicillin should be given to mothers if prolonged rupture of membranes occurs, if mother has a fever, or if the neonate is premature.

Enterococcus faecalis

Diseases—Urinary tract and biliary tract infections are most frequent. Endocarditis rare but life-threatening.

Characteristics—Gram-positive cocci in chains. Catalase-negative.

Habitat and Transmission—Habitat is the human colon; urethra and female genital tract can be colonized. May enter bloodstream during gastrointestinal (GI) or genitourinary tract procedures. May infect other sites, eg, endocarditis.

Pathogenesis—No exotoxins or virulence factors identified.

Laboratory Diagnosis—Gram-stained smear and culture. Alpha-, beta-, or nonhemolytic colonies on blood agar. Grows in 6.5% NaCl and hydrolyzes esculin in the presence of 40% bile. Serologic tests not useful.

Treatment—Penicillin or vancomycin plus an aminoglycoside such as gentamicin is bactericidal. Organism is resistant to either drug given individually, but given together they have a synergistic effect. Aminoglycoside alone is ineffective because it cannot penetrate. Penicillin or vancomycin weakens the cell wall, allowing the aminoglycoside to penetrate. Vancomycin-resistant enterococci (VRE) are important causes of nosocomial (hospital-acquired) infections. Linezolid can be used to treat VRE.

Prevention—Penicillin and gentamicin should be given to patients with damaged heart valves prior to intestinal or urinary tract procedures. No vaccine is available.

Streptococcus pneumoniae (Pneumococcus)

Diseases—The most common diseases are pneumonia and meningitis in adults and otitis media and sinusitis in children.

Characteristics—Gram-positive "lancet-shaped" cocci in pairs (diplococci) or short chains. Alpha-hemolytic. Catalase-negative. Sensitive to bile and optochin in contrast to viridans streptococci, which are resistant. Prominent polysaccharide capsule. 85 serotypes based on antigenicity of polysaccharide capsule. One of the three classical encapsulated pyogenic bacteria (*Neisseria meningitidis* and *Haemophilus influenzae* are the other two).

Habitat and Transmission—Habitat is the human upper respiratory tract. Transmission is via respiratory droplets.

Pathogenesis—Induces inflammatory response. No known exotoxins. Polysaccharide capsule retards phagocytosis. Antipolysaccharide antibody opsonizes the organism and provides type-specific immunity. IgA protease degrades secretory IgA on respiratory mucosa, allowing colonization. Viral respiratory infection predisposes to pneumococcal pneumonia by damaging mucociliary elevator; splenectomy predisposes to sepsis. Skull fracture with spinal fluid leakage from nose predisposes to meningitis.

Laboratory Diagnosis—Gram-stained smear and culture. Alpha-hemolytic colonies on blood agar. Growth inhibited by bile and optochin. Quellung reaction occurs (swelling of capsule with type-specific antiserum). Serologic tests for antibody not useful. Latex agglutination test for capsular antigen in spinal fluid can be diagnostic.

Treatment—Penicillin G. Low-level and high-level resistance is caused by alterations in penicillin-binding proteins. No β-lactamase is made.

Prevention—Two vaccines are available. The one used in adults contains capsular polysaccharide of the 23 serotypes that cause bacteremia most frequently. The other, which is used primarily in children under the age of 2 years, contains capsular polysaccharide of 7 serotypes coupled to carrier protein (diphtheria toxoid). Oral penicillin is used in immunocompromised children.

Viridans Group Streptococci (eg, *S. sanguis, S. mutans*)

Diseases—Endocarditis is the most important. Also brain abscess, especially in mixed infections with mouth anaerobes. *S. mutans* implicated in dental caries.

Characteristics—Gram-positive cocci in chains. Alpha-hemolytic. Catalase-negative. Resistant to bile and optochin in contrast to pneumococci, which are sensitive.

Habitat and Transmission—Habitat is the human oropharynx. Organism enters bloodstream during dental procedures.

Pathogenesis—Bacteremia from dental procedures spreads organism to damaged heart valves. Organism is protected from host defenses within vegetations. No known toxins. Glycocalyx composed of polysaccharide enhances adhesion to heart valves.

Laboratory Diagnosis—Gram-stained smear and culture. Alpha-hemolytic colonies on blood agar. Growth not inhibited by bile or optochin, in contrast to pneumococci. Viridans streptococci are classified into species by using various biochemical tests. Serologic tests not useful.

Treatment—Penicillin G with or without an aminoglycoside.

Prevention—Penicillin to prevent endocarditis in patients with damaged or prosthetic heart valves who undergo dental procedures.

GRAM-NEGATIVE COCCI (CHAPTER 16)
Neisseria meningitidis (Meningococcus)

Diseases—Meningitis and meningococcemia.

Characteristics—Gram-negative "kidney-bean" diplococci. Oxidase-positive. Large polysaccharide capsule. One of the three classic encapsulated pyogenic bacteria (*Streptococcus pneumoniae* and *Haemophilus influenzae* are the other two).

Habitat and Transmission—Habitat is the human upper respiratory tract; transmission is via respiratory droplets.

Pathogenesis—After colonizing the upper respiratory tract, the organism reaches the meninges via the bloodstream. Endotoxin in cell wall causes symptoms of septic shock seen in meningococcemia. No known exotoxins; IgA protease produced. Capsule is antiphagocytic. Deficiency in late complement components predisposes to recurrent meningococcal infections.

Laboratory Diagnosis—Gram-stained smear and culture. Oxidase-positive colonies on chocolate agar. Ferments maltose in contrast to gonococci, which do not. Serologic tests not useful.

Treatment—Penicillin G (no significant resistance).

Prevention—Vaccine contains capsular polysaccharide of strains A, C, Y, and W-135. One form of the vaccine contains the polysaccharides coupled to a carrier protein (diphtheria toxoid) and one contains only the polysaccharides. Rifampin or ciprofloxacin given to close contacts to decrease oropharyngeal carriage.

Neisseria gonorrhoeae (Gonococcus)

Disease—Gonorrhea. Also neonatal conjunctivitis and pelvic inflammatory disease.

Characteristics—Gram-negative "kidney-bean" diplococci. Oxidase-positive. Insignificant capsule.

Habitat and Transmission—Habitat is the human genital tract. Transmission in adults is by sexual contact. Transmission to neonates is during birth.

Pathogenesis—Organism invades mucous membranes and causes inflammation. Endotoxin present but weaker than that of meningococcus, so less severe disease when bacteremia occurs. No exotoxins identified. IgA protease and pili are virulence factors.

Laboratory Diagnosis—Gram-stained smear and culture. Organism visible intracellularly within neutrophils in urethral exudate. Oxidase-positive colonies on Thayer-Martin medium. Gonococci do not ferment maltose, whereas meningococci do. Serologic tests not useful.

Treatment—Ceftriaxone for uncomplicated cases. Tetracycline added for urethritis caused by *Chlamydia trachomatis.* High-level resistance to penicillin is caused by plasmid-encoded penicillinase. Low-level resistance to penicillin is caused by reduced permeability and altered binding proteins.

Prevention—No drug or vaccine. Condoms offer protection. Trace contacts and treat to interrupt transmission. Treat eyes of newborns with erythromycin ointment or silver nitrate to prevent conjunctivitis.

GRAM-POSITIVE RODS (CHAPTER 17)

Bacillus anthracis

Disease—Anthrax.

Characteristics—Aerobic, gram-positive, spore-forming rods. Capsule composed of poly-D-glutamate. *B. anthracis* is the only medically important organism that has a capsule composed of amino acids rather than polysaccharides.

Habitat and Transmission—Habitat is soil. Transmission is by contact with infected animals or inhalation of spores from animal hair and wool.

Pathogenesis—Anthrax toxin consists of three proteins: edema factor, which is an adenylate cyclase; lethal factor, which kills cells by inhibiting a signal transduction protein involved in cell division; and protective antigen, which mediates the entry of the other two components into the cell. The capsule is antiphagocytic.

Laboratory Diagnosis—Gram-stained smear plus aerobic culture on blood agar. *B. anthracis* is nonmotile, in contrast to other *Bacillus* species. Rise in antibody titer in indirect hemagglutination test is diagnostic.

Treatment—Penicillin G (no significant resistance).

Prevention—Vaccine consisting of protective antigen is given to individuals in high-risk occupations.

Bacillus cereus

Disease—Food poisoning.

Characteristics—Aerobic, gram-positive, spore-forming rod.

Habitat and Transmission—Habitat is grains, such as rice. Spores survive boiling during preparation of rice, then germinate when rice held at warm temperature.

Pathogenesis—Two enterotoxins are produced: one acts like cholera toxin, ie, cyclic AMP is increased within enterocytes; the other acts like staphylococcal enterotoxin, ie, it is a superantigen.

Laboratory Diagnosis—Not done.

Treatment—Symptomatic only.

Prevention—No vaccine.

Clostridium tetani

Disease—Tetanus.

Characteristics—Anaerobic, gram-positive, spore-forming rods. Spore is at one end ("terminal spore") so organism looks like a "tennis racket."

Habitat and Transmission—Habitat is the soil. Organism enters through traumatic breaks in the skin.

Pathogenesis—Spores germinate under anaerobic conditions in the wound. Organism produces exotoxin, which blocks release of inhibitory neurotransmitters (glycine and GABA) from spinal neurons. Excitatory neurons are unopposed, and extreme muscle spasm (tetanus, spastic paralysis) results. "Lockjaw" and "risus sardonicus" are two examples of the muscle spasms. Tetanus toxin (tetanospasmin) is a protease that cleaves proteins involved in the release of neurotransmitters.

Laboratory Diagnosis—Primarily a clinical diagnosis. Organism is rarely isolated. Serologic tests not useful.

Treatment—Hyperimmune human globulin to neutralize toxin. Also penicillin G and spasmolytic drugs (eg, Valium). No significant resistance to penicillin.

Prevention—Toxoid vaccine (toxoid is formaldehyde-treated toxin). Usually given to children in combination with diphtheria toxoid and pertussis vaccine (DTaP). If patient is injured and has not been immunized, give hyperimmune globulin plus toxoid (passive-active immunization). Debride wound. Give tetanus toxoid booster every 10 years.

Clostridium botulinum

Disease—Botulism.

Characteristics—Anaerobic, gram-positive, spore-forming rods.

Habitat and Transmission—Habitat is the soil. Organism and botulinum toxin transmitted in improperly preserved food.

Pathogenesis—Botulinum toxin is a protease that cleaves proteins involved in the release of acetylcholine at the myoneural junction, causing flaccid paralysis. Failure to sterilize food during preservation allows spores to survive. Spores germinate in anaerobic environment and produce toxin. The toxin is heat-labile; therefore, foods eaten without proper cooking are usually implicated.

Laboratory Diagnosis—Presence of toxin in patient's serum or stool or in food. Detection of toxin involves either antitoxin in serologic tests or production of the disease in mice. Serologic tests for antibody in the patient are not useful.

Treatment—Antitoxin to types A, B, and E made in horses. Respiratory support may be required.

Prevention—Observing proper food preservation techniques, cooking all home-canned food, and discarding bulging cans.

Clostridium perfringens

Diseases—Gas gangrene (myonecrosis) and food poisoning.

Characteristics—Anaerobic, gram-positive, spore-forming rods.

Habitat and Transmission—Habitat is soil and human colon. Myonecrosis results from contamination of wound with soil or feces. Food poisoning is transmitted by ingestion of contaminated food.

Pathogenesis—Gas gangrene in wounds is caused by germination of spores under anaerobic conditions and the production of several cytotoxic factors, especially alpha toxin, a lecithinase that cleaves cell membranes. Gas in tissue (CO_2 and H_2) is produced by organism's anaerobic metabolism. Food poisoning is caused by production of enterotoxin within the gut. Enterotoxin acts as a superantigen, similar to that of *S. aureus*.

Laboratory Diagnosis—Gram-stained smear plus anaerobic culture. Spores not usually seen in clinical specimens; the organism is growing, and nutrients are not restricted. Production of lecithinase is detected on egg yolk agar and identified by enzyme inhibition with specific antiserum. Serologic tests not useful.

Treatment—Penicillin G plus debridement of the wound in gas gangrene (no significant resistance to penicillin). Only symptomatic treatment needed in food poisoning.

Prevention—Extensive debridement of the wound plus administration of penicillin decreases probability of gas gangrene. There is no vaccine.

Clostridium difficile

Disease—Pseudomembranous colitis.

Characteristics—Anaerobic, gram-positive, spore-forming rods.

Habitat and Transmission—Habitat is the human colon. Transmission is fecal-oral.

Pathogenesis—Antibiotics suppress normal flora of colon, allowing *C. difficile* to overgrow and produce large amounts of exotoxins. Exotoxins A and B inhibit GTPases, causing inhibition of signal transduction and depolymerization of actin filaments. This leads to apoptosis and death of enterocytes. The pseudomembranes seen in the colon are the visual result of the death of enterocytes.

Laboratory Diagnosis—Exotoxin in stool detected by cytopathic effect on cultured cells. Identified by neutralization of cytopathic effect with antibody. Exotoxin in the stool can also be detected by using an ELISA test.

Treatment—Metronidazole. Vancomycin, although effective, should not be used because it may select for vancomycin-resistant enterococci.

Prevention—No vaccine or drug is available.

Corynebacterium diphtheriae

Disease—Diphtheria.

Characteristics—Club-shaped gram-positive rods arranged in V or L shape. Granules stain metachromatically. Aerobic, non-spore-forming organism.

Habitat and Transmission—Habitat is the human throat. Transmission is via respiratory droplets.

Pathogenesis—Organism secretes an exotoxin that inhibits protein synthesis by adding ADP-ribose to elongation factor-2 (EF-2). Toxin has two components: subunit A, which has the ADP-ribosylating activity, and subunit B, which binds the toxin to cell surface receptors. Pseudomembrane in throat caused by death of mucosal epithelial cells.

Laboratory Diagnosis—Gram-stained smear and culture. Black colonies on tellurite plate. Document toxin production with precipitin test or by disease produced in laboratory animals. Serologic tests not useful.

Treatment—Antitoxin made in horses neutralizes the toxin. Penicillin G kills the organism. No significant resistance to penicillin.

Prevention—Toxoid vaccine (toxoid is formaldehyde-treated toxin), usually given to children in combination with tetanus toxoid and pertussis vaccine (DTaP).

Listeria monocytogenes

Diseases—Meningitis and sepsis in newborns and immunocompromised adults. Gastroenteritis.

Characteristics—Small gram-positive rods. Aerobic, non-spore-forming organism.

Habitat and Transmission—Organism colonizes the GI and female genital tracts; in nature it is widespread in animals, plants, and soil. Transmission is across the placenta or by contact during delivery. Outbreaks of sepsis in neonates and gastroenteritis in the general population are related to ingestion of unpasteurized milk products, eg, cheese.

Pathogenesis—Listeriolysin is an exotoxin that degrades cell membranes. Reduced cell-mediated immunity and immunologic immaturity as in neonates pre-

dispose to disease. Intracellular pathogen that moves from cell-to-cell via "actin rockets."

Laboratory Diagnosis—Gram-stained smear and culture. Small, beta-hemolytic colonies on blood agar. Tumbling motility. Serologic tests not useful.

Treatment—Ampicillin with or without gentamicin.

Prevention—Pregnant women and immunocompromised patients should not ingest unpasteurized milk products or raw vegetables. Trimethoprim-sulfamethoxazole given to immunocompromised patients to prevent *Pneumocystis* pneumonia also can prevent listeriosis. No vaccine is available.

GRAM-NEGATIVE RODS RELATED TO THE ENTERIC TRACT (CHAPTER 18)

Escherichia coli

Diseases—Urinary tract infection (UTI), sepsis, neonatal meningitis, and "traveler's diarrhea" are the most common.

Characteristics—Facultative gram-negative rods; ferment lactose.

Habitat and Transmission—Habitat is the human colon; it colonizes the vagina and urethra. From the urethra, it ascends and causes UTI. Acquired during birth in neonatal meningitis and by the fecal-oral route in diarrhea.

Pathogenesis—Endotoxin in cell wall causes septic shock. Two enterotoxins are produced. The heat-labile toxin (LT) stimulates adenylate cyclase by ADP-ribosylation. Increased cyclic AMP causes outflow of chloride ions and water, resulting in diarrhea. The heat-stable toxin (ST) causes diarrhea, perhaps by stimulating guanylate cyclase. Virulence factors include pili for attachment to mucosal surfaces and a capsule that impedes phagocytosis. Verotoxin (Shiga-like toxin) is an enterotoxin produced by *E. coli* strains with the O157:H7 serotype. It causes bloody diarrhea and hemolytic-uremic syndrome associated with eating undercooked meat. Verotoxin inhibits protein synthesis by removing adenine from the 28S rRNA of human ribosomes.

Predisposing factors to UTI in women include the proximity of the anus to the vagina and urethra, as well as a short urethra. This leads to colonization of the urethra and vagina by the fecal flora. Abnormalities, eg, strictures, valves, and stones, predispose as well. Indwelling urinary catheters and intravenous lines predispose to UTI and sepsis, respectively. Colonization of the vagina leads to neonatal meningitis acquired during birth.

Laboratory Diagnosis—Gram-stained smear and culture. Lactose-fermenting colonies on EMB or Mac-

Conkey's agar. Green sheen on EMB agar. TSI agar shows acid slant and acid butt with gas out no H$_2$S. Differentiate from other lactose-positive organisms by biochemical reactions. For epidemiologic studies, type organism by O and H antigens by using known antisera. Serologic tests for antibodies in patient's serum not useful.

Treatment—Ampicillin or sulfonamides for urinary tract infections. Third-generation cephalosporins for meningitis and sepsis. Rehydration is effective in traveler's diarrhea; trimethoprim-sulfamethoxazole may shorten duration of symptoms. Antibiotic resistance mediated by plasmid-encoded enzymes, eg, β-lactamase and aminoglycoside-modifying enzymes.

Prevention—Prevention of UTI involves limiting the frequency and duration of urinary catheterization. Prevention of sepsis involves promptly removing or switching sites of intravenous lines. Traveler's diarrhea is prevented by eating only cooked food and drinking boiled water in certain countries. Prophylactic doxycycline or Pepto-Bismol may prevent traveler's diarrhea. There is no vaccine that prevents any of the diseases caused by *E. coli*.

Salmonella typhi

Disease—Typhoid fever.

Characteristics—Facultative gram-negative rods. Non-lactose-fermenting. Produces H$_2$S.

Habitat and Transmission—Habitat is the human colon only, in contrast to other salmonellae, which are found in the colon of animals as well. Transmission is by the fecal-oral route.

Pathogenesis—Infects the cells of the reticuloendothelial system, especially in the liver and spleen. Endotoxin in cell wall causes fever. Capsule (Vi antigen) is a virulence factor. No exotoxins known. Decreased stomach acid resulting from ingestion of antacids or gastrectomy predisposes to *Salmonella* infections. Chronic carrier state established in gallbladder. Organism excreted in bile results in fecal-oral spread to others.

Laboratory Diagnosis—Gram-stained smear and culture. Non-lactose-fermenting colonies on EMB or MacConkey's agar. TSI agar shows alkaline slant and acid butt, with no gas and a small amount of H$_2$S. Biochemical and serologic reactions used to identify species. Identity can be determined by using known antisera against O, H, and Vi antigens in agglutination test. Widal test detects agglutinating antibodies to O and H antigens in patient's serum, but its use is limited.

Treatment—Most effective drug is ceftriaxone. Ampicillin and trimethoprim-sulfamethoxazole can be used

in patients who are not severely ill. Resistance to chloramphenicol and ampicillin is mediated by plasmid-encoded acetylating enzymes and β-lactamase, respectively.

Prevention—Public health measures, eg, sewage disposal, chlorination of the water supply, stool cultures for food handlers, and hand washing prior to food handling. Two vaccines are in common use; one vaccine contains purified Vi polysaccharide capsule as the immunogen and the other contains live, attenuated *S. typhi* as the immunogen.

Salmonella enteritidis (also known as Salmonella enterica)

Diseases—Enterocolitis. Sepsis with metastatic abscesses occasionally.

Characteristics—Facultative gram-negative rods. Non-lactose-fermenting. Produces H$_2$S. Motile, in contrast to *Shigella*. More than 1500 serotypes.

Habitat and Transmission—Habitat is the enteric tract of humans and animals, eg, chickens and domestic livestock. Transmission is by the fecal-oral route.

Pathogenesis—Invades the mucosa of the small and large intestines. Can enter blood, causing sepsis. Infectious dose is at least 10^5 organisms, much greater than the infectious dose of *Shigella*. Infectious dose is high because organism is inactivated by stomach acid. Endotoxin in cell wall; no exotoxin. Predisposing factors include lowered stomach acidity from either antacids or gastrectomy. Sickle cell anemia predisposes to *Salmonella* osteomyelitis.

Laboratory Diagnosis—Gram-stained smear and culture. Non-lactose-fermenting colonies on EMB or MacConkey's agar. TSI agar shows alkaline slant and acid butt, with gas and H$_2$S. Biochemical and serologic reactions used to identify species. Can identify the organism by using known antisera in agglutination assay. Widal test detects antibodies in patient's serum to the O and H antigens of the organism but is not widely used.

Treatment—Antibiotics usually not recommended for uncomplicated enterocolitis. Ceftriaxone or other drugs are used for sepsis depending on sensitivity tests. Resistance to ampicillin and chloramphenicol is mediated by plasmid-encoded β-lactamases and acetylating enzymes, respectively.

Prevention—Public health measures, eg, sewage disposal, chlorination of the water supply, stool cultures for food handlers, and hand washing prior to food handling. Do not eat raw eggs or meat. No vaccine is available.

Shigella species (eg, S. dysenteriae, S. sonnei)

Disease—Enterocolitis (dysentery).

Characteristics—Facultative gram-negative rods. Non-lactose-fermenting. Nonmotile, in contrast to *Salmonella*.

Habitat and Transmission—Habitat is the human colon only; unlike *Salmonella*, there are no animal carriers for *Shigella*. Transmission is by the fecal-oral route.

Pathogenesis—Invades the mucosa of the ileum and colon but does not penetrate farther; therefore, sepsis is rare. Endotoxin in cell wall. Infectious dose is much lower (1–10 organisms) than that of *Salmonella*. The infectious dose of *Shigella* is low because it is resistant to stomach acid. Children in mental institutions and day-care centers experience outbreaks of shigellosis. No chronic carrier state.

Laboratory Diagnosis—Gram-stained smear and culture. Non-lactose-fermenting colonies on EMB or MacConkey's agar. TSI agar shows an alkaline slant with an acid butt and no gas or H_2S. Identified by biochemical reactions or by serology with anti-O antibody in agglutination test. Serologic tests for antibodies in the patient's serum are not done.

Treatment—In most cases, fluid and electrolyte replacement only. In severe cases, ciprofloxacin. Resistance is mediated by plasmid-encoded enzymes, eg, β-lactamase, which degrades ampicillin, and a mutant pteroate synthetase, which reduces sensitivity to sulfonamides.

Prevention—Public health measures, eg, sewage disposal, chlorination of the water supply, stool cultures for food handlers, and hand washing prior to food handling. Prophylactic drugs not used. No vaccine is available.

Vibrio cholerae

Disease—Cholera.

Characteristics—Comma-shaped gram-negative rods. Oxidase-positive, which distinguishes them from Enterobacteriaceae.

Habitat and Transmission—Habitat is the human colon. Transmission is by the fecal-oral route.

Pathogenesis—Massive, watery diarrhea caused by enterotoxin that activates adenylate cyclase by adding ADP-ribose to the stimulatory G protein. Increase in cyclic AMP causes outflow of chloride ions and water. Toxin has two components: subunit A, which has the ADP-ribosylating activity; and subunit B, which binds the toxin to cell surface receptors. Organism produces mucinase, which enhances attachment to the intestinal mucosa. Role of endotoxin is unclear. Infectious dose is high (> 10^7 organisms). Carrier state rare.

Laboratory Diagnosis—Gram-stained smear and culture. (During epidemics, cultures not necessary.) Agglutination of the isolate with known antisera confirms the identification.

Treatment—Treatment of choice is fluid and electrolyte replacement. Tetracycline is not necessary but shortens duration and reduces carriage.

Prevention—Public health measures, eg, sewage disposal, chlorination of the water supply, stool cultures for food handlers, and hand washing prior to food handling. Vaccine containing killed cells has limited effectiveness. Tetracycline used for close contacts.

Vibrio parahemolyticus

Comma-shaped gram-negative rod found in warm sea water. Causes watery diarrhea. Acquired by eating contaminated raw seafood. Outbreaks have occurred on cruise ships in Caribbean. Diarrhea is mediated by enterotoxin similar to cholera toxin.

Vibrio vulnificus

Comma-shaped gram-negative rod found in warm sea water. Causes cellulitis and life-threatening sepsis with hemorrhagic bullae. Acquired either by trauma to skin, especially in shellfish handlers, or by ingestion of raw shellfish, especially in patients who are immunocompromised or have liver damage.

Campylobacter jejuni

Disease—Enterocolitis.

Characteristics—Comma-shaped gram-negative rods. Microaerophilic. Grows well at 42°C.

Habitat and Transmission—Habitat is human and animal feces. Transmission is by the fecal-oral route.

Pathogenesis—Invades mucosa of the colon but does not penetrate; therefore, sepsis rarely occurs. No enterotoxin known.

Laboratory Diagnosis—Gram-stained smear plus culture on special agar, eg, Skirrow's agar, at 42°C in high-CO_2, low-O_2 atmosphere. Serologic tests not useful.

Treatment—Usually symptomatic treatment only; erythromycin for severe disease.

Prevention—Public health measures, eg, sewage disposal, chlorination of the water supply, stool cultures for food handlers, and hand washing prior to food handling. No preventive vaccine or drug is available.

Helicobacter pylori

Disease—Gastritis and peptic ulcer. Risk factor for gastric carcinoma.

Characteristics—Curved gram-negative rod.

Habitat and Transmission—Habitat is the human stomach. Transmission is by ingestion.

Pathogenesis—Organisms synthesize urease, which produces ammonia that damages gastric mucosa. Ammonia also neutralizes acid pH in stomach, which allows the organism to live in gastric mucosa.

Laboratory Diagnosis—Gram stain and culture. Urease-positive. Serologic tests for antibody and the "urea breath" test are useful.

Treatment—Amoxicillin, metronidazole, and bismuth (Pepto-Bismol).

Prevention—No vaccine or drug is available.

Klebsiella pneumoniae

Diseases—Pneumonia, UTI, and sepsis.

Characteristics—Facultative gram-negative rods with large polysaccharide capsule.

Habitat and Transmission—Habitat is the human upper respiratory and enteric tracts. Organism is transmitted to the lungs by aspiration from upper respiratory tract and by inhalation of respiratory droplets. It is transmitted to the urinary tract by ascending spread of fecal flora.

Pathogenesis—Endotoxin causes fever and shock associated with sepsis. No exotoxin known. Organism has large capsule, which impedes phagocytosis. Chronic pulmonary disease predisposes to pneumonia; catheterization predisposes to UTI.

Laboratory Diagnosis—Gram-stained smear and culture. Characteristic mucoid colonies are a consequence of the organism's abundant polysaccharide capsule. Lactose-fermenting colonies on MacConkey's agar. Differentiated from *Enterobacter* and *Serratia* by biochemical reactions.

Treatment—Cephalosporins alone or with aminoglycosides, but antibiotic sensitivity testing must be done. Resistance is mediated by plasmid-encoded enzymes.

Prevention—No vaccine or drug is available. Urinary and intravenous catheters should be removed promptly.

Enterobacter cloacae

Enteric gram-negative rod similar to *K. pneumoniae*. Causes hospital-acquired pneumonia, UTI, and sepsis. Highly antibiotic-resistant.

Serratia marcescens

Enteric gram-negative rod similar to *K. pneumoniae*. Causes hospital-acquired pneumonia, UTI, and sepsis. Red-pigmented colonies. Highly antibiotic-resistant.

Proteus species (eg, P. vulgaris, P. mirabilis)

Diseases—UTI and sepsis.

Characteristics—Facultative gram-negative rods. Non-lactose-fermenting. Highly motile. Produce urease, as do *Morganella* and *Providencia* species (see below). Antigens of OX strains of *P. vulgaris* cross-react with many rickettsiae.

Habitat and Transmission—Habitat is the human colon and the environment (soil and water). Transmission to urinary tract is by ascending spread of fecal flora.

Pathogenesis—Endotoxin causes fever and shock associated with sepsis. No exotoxins known. Urease is a virulence factor because it degrades urea to produce ammonia, which raises the pH. This leads to "struvite" stones, which can obstruct urine flow, damage urinary epithelium, and serve as a nidus for recurrent infection by trapping bacteria within the stone. Organism is highly motile, which may facilitate entry into the bladder. Predisposing factors are colonization of the vagina, urinary catheters, and abnormalities of the urinary tract such as strictures, valves, and stones.

Laboratory Diagnosis—Gram-stained smear and culture. "Swarming" (spreading) effect over blood agar plate as a consequence of the organism's active motility. Non-lactose-fermenting colonies on EMB or MacConkey's agar. TSI agar shows an alkaline slant and acid butt with H_2S. Organism produces urease, whereas *Salmonella*, which can appear similar on TSI agar, does not. Serologic tests not useful. *P. mirabilis* is indole-negative, whereas *P. vulgaris*, *M. morganii*, and *Providencia* species are indole-positive.

Treatment—Trimethoprim-sulfamethoxazole or ampicillin is often used for uncomplicated UTIs, but a third-generation cephalosporin should be used for serious infections. The indole-negative species *P. mirabilis* is more likely to be sensitive to antibiotics such as ampicillin than are the indole-positive species. Antibiotic sensitivities should be tested. Resistance is mediated by plasmid-encoded enzymes.

Prevention—No vaccine or drug is available. Prompt removal of urinary catheters helps prevent urinary tract infections.

Morganella morganii

Enteric gram-negative rod similar to *Proteus* species. Causes UTIs and sepsis. Highly motile and produces urease. Indole-positive and more resistant to antibiotics than *P. mirabilis.*

Providencia rettgeri

Enteric gram-negative rod similar to *Proteus* species. Causes UTIs and sepsis. Highly motile and produces urease. Indole-positive and more resistant to antibiotics than *P. mirabilis.*

Pseudomonas aeruginosa

Diseases—Wound infection, UTI, pneumonia, and sepsis. One of the most important causes of nosocomial infections, especially in burn patients and those with cystic fibrosis. Causes endocarditis in intravenous drug users.

Characteristics—Aerobic gram-negative rods. Non-lactose-fermenting. Pyocyanin (blue-green) pigment produced. Oxidase-positive, which distinguishes it from members of the Enterobacteriaceae family.

Habitat and Transmission—Habitat is environmental water sources, eg, in hospital respirators and humidifiers. Also inhabits the skin, upper respiratory tract, and colon of about 10% of people. Transmission is via water aerosols, aspiration, and fecal contamination.

Pathogenesis—Endotoxin is responsible for fever and shock associated with sepsis. Produces exotoxin A, which acts like diphtheria toxin (inactivates EF-2). Pili and capsule are virulence factors that mediate attachment and inhibit phagocytosis, respectively. Glycocalyx-producing strains predominate in chronic infections in cystic fibrosis patients. Strains with type III secretion systems are more virulent than those without. Severe burns and neutropenia are important predisposing factors.

Laboratory Diagnosis—Gram-stained smear and culture. Non-lactose-fermenting colonies on EMB or MacConkey's agar. TSI agar shows an alkaline slant and an alkaline butt because the sugars are not fermented. Oxidase-positive. Serologic tests not useful.

Treatment—Antibiotics must be chosen on the basis of antibiotic sensitivities because resistance is common. Antipseudomonal penicillin and aminoglycoside are often used. Resistance is mediated by a variety of plasmid-encoded enzymes, eg, β-lactamases and acetylating enzymes.

Prevention—Disinfection of water-related equipment in the hospital, hand washing, and prompt removal of urinary and intravenous catheters. There is no vaccine.

Burkholderia cepacia

Gram-negative rod resembling *P. aeruginosa.* Important cause of chronic infections in patients with cystic fibrosis. Formerly called *Pseudomonas cepacia.*

Stenotrophomonas maltophilia

Gram-negative rod resembling *P. aeruginosa.* Important cause of chronic infections in patients with cystic fibrosis. Formerly called *Pseudomonas maltophilia.*

Bacteroides fragilis

Diseases—Sepsis, peritonitis, and abdominal abscess.

Characteristics—Anaerobic, gram-negative rods.

Habitat and Transmission—Habitat is the human colon, where it is the predominant anaerobe. Transmission occurs by spread from the colon to the blood or peritoneum.

Pathogenesis—Lipopolysaccharide in cell wall is chemically different from and less potent than typical endotoxin. No exotoxins known. Capsule is antiphagocytic. Predisposing factors to infection include bowel surgery and penetrating abdominal wounds.

Laboratory Diagnosis—Gram-stained smear plus anaerobic culture. Identification based on biochemical reactions and gas chromatography. Serologic tests not useful.

Treatment—Metronidazole, clindamycin, and cefoxitin are all effective. Abscesses should be surgically drained. Resistance to penicillin G, some cephalosporins, and aminoglycosides is common. Plasmid-encoded β-lactamase mediates resistance to penicillin.

Prevention—In bowel surgery, perioperative cefoxitin can reduce the frequency of postoperative infections. No vaccine is available.

Prevotella melaninogenica

Anaerobic gram-negative rod resembling *B. fragilis.* Member of normal flora found primarily above the diaphragm (eg, mouth) in contrast to *B. fragilis,* which is found below (eg, colon). Often involved in brain and lung abscesses. Formerly called *Bacteroides melaninogenicus.*

GRAM-NEGATIVE RODS RELATED TO THE RESPIRATORY TRACT (CHAPTER 19)

Haemophilus influenzae

Diseases—Sinusitis, otitis media, and pneumonia are common. Epiglottitis is uncommon, but *H. influenzae* is the most important cause. *H. influenzae* used to be a leading cause of meningitis, but the vaccine has greatly reduced the number of cases.

Characteristics—Small gram-negative (coccobacillary) rods. Requires factors X (hemin) and V (NAD) for growth. Of the six capsular polysaccharide types, type b causes 95% of invasive disease. Type b capsule is polyribitol phosphate.

Habitat and Transmission—Habitat is the upper respiratory tract. Transmission is via respiratory droplets.

Pathogenesis—Polysaccharide capsule is the most important determinant of virulence. Unencapsulated ("untypeable") strains cause mucosal infections but not invasive infections. IgA protease is produced. Most cases of meningitis occur in children younger than 2 years of age, because maternal antibody has waned and the immune response of the child to capsular polysaccharides can be inadequate. No exotoxins identified.

Laboratory Diagnosis—Gram-stained smear plus culture on chocolate agar. Growth requires both factors X and V. Determine serotype by using antiserum in various tests, eg, latex agglutination. Capsular antigen can be detected in serum or cerebrospinal fluid. Serologic test for antibodies in patient's serum not useful.

Treatment—Ceftriaxone is the treatment of choice for meningitis. Approximately 25% of strains produce β-lactamase.

Prevention—Vaccine containing the type b capsular polysaccharide conjugated to diphtheria toxoid or other protein is given between 2 and 18 months of age. Rifampin can prevent meningitis in close contacts.

Bordetella pertussis

Disease—Whooping cough (pertussis).

Characteristics—Small gram-negative rods.

Habitat and Transmission—Habitat is the human respiratory tract. Transmission is via respiratory droplets.

Pathogenesis—Pertussis toxin stimulates adenylate cyclase by adding ADP-ribose onto the inhibitory G protein. Toxin has two components: subunit A, which has the ADP-ribosylating activity, and subunit B, which binds the toxin to cell surface receptors. Pertussis toxin causes lymphocytosis in the blood by inhibiting chemokine receptors. Inhibition of these receptors prevents lymphocytes from entering tissue, resulting in large numbers being retained in the blood. Inhibition of chemokine receptors occurs because pertussis toxin ADP-ribosylates the inhibitory G protein which prevents signal transduction within the cell. In addition, extracellular adenylate cyclase is produced, which can inhibit killing by phagocytes. Tracheal cytotoxin damages ciliated epithelium of respiratory tract.

Laboratory Diagnosis—Gram-stained smear plus culture on Bordet-Gengou agar. Identified by biochemical reactions and slide agglutination with known antisera. PCR tests, if available, are both sensitive and specific. Serologic tests for antibody in patient's serum not useful.

Treatment—Erythromycin.

Prevention—The acellular vaccine containing pertussis toxoid and four other purified proteins is recommended rather than the killed vaccine, which contains whole organisms. Usually given to children in combination with diphtheria and tetanus toxoids (DTaP).

Legionella pneumophila

Disease—Legionnaires' disease ("atypical" pneumonia).

Characteristics—Gram-negative rods, but stain poorly with standard Gram stain. Require increased iron and cysteine for growth in culture.

Habitat and Transmission—Habitat is environmental water sources. Transmission is via aerosol from the water source. Person-to-person transmission does not occur.

Pathogenesis—Aside from endotoxin, no toxins, enzymes, or virulence factors are known. Predisposing factors include being older than 55 years of age, smoking, and having a high alcohol intake. Immunosuppressed patients, eg, renal transplant recipients, are highly susceptible. The organism replicates intracellularly, therefore cell-mediated immunity is an important host defense. Smoking damages alveolar macrophages, which explains why it predisposes to pneumonia.

Laboratory Diagnosis—Microscopy with silver impregnation stain or fluorescent antibody. Culture on charcoal yeast extract agar containing increased amounts of iron and cysteine. Urinary antigen provides rapid diagnosis. Diagnosis can be made serologically by detecting rise in antibody titer in patient's serum.

Treatment—Azithromycin or erythromycin. Rifampin can be added in severe cases.

Prevention—No vaccine or prophylactic drug is available.

GRAM-NEGATIVE RODS RELATED TO ANIMAL SOURCES (ZOONOTIC ORGANISMS) (CHAPTER 20)

Brucella species (eg, B. abortus, B. suis, B. melitensis)

Disease—Brucellosis (undulant fever).

Characteristics—Small gram-negative rods.

Habitat and Transmission—Reservoir is domestic livestock. Transmission is via unpasteurized milk and cheese or direct contact with the infected animal.

Pathogenesis—Organisms localize in reticuloendothelial cells, especially the liver and spleen. Able to survive and replicate intracellularly. No exotoxins. Predisposing factors include consuming unpasteurized dairy products and working in an abattoir.

Laboratory Diagnosis—Gram-stained smear plus culture on blood agar plate. Identified by biochemical reactions and by agglutination with known antiserum. Diagnosis may be made serologically by detecting antibodies in patient's serum.

Treatment—Tetracycline plus rifampin.

Prevention—Pasteurize milk; vaccinate cattle. No human vaccine is available.

Francisella tularensis

Disease—Tularemia.

Characteristics—Small gram-negative rods.

Habitat and Transmission—Reservoir is many species of wild animals, especially rabbits, deer, and rodents. Transmission is by ticks (eg, *Dermacentor*), aerosols, contact, and ingestion.

Pathogenesis—Organisms localize in reticuloendothelial cells. No exotoxins.

Laboratory Diagnosis—Culture is rarely done, because special media are required and there is a high risk of infection of laboratory personnel. Diagnosis is usually made by serologic tests that detect antibodies in patient's serum.

Treatment—Streptomycin.

Prevention—Live, attenuated vaccine for persons in high-risk occupations. Protect against tick bites.

Pasteurella multocida

Disease—Wound infection, eg, cellulitis.

Characteristics—Small gram-negative rods.

Habitat and Transmission—Reservoir is the mouth of many animals, especially cats and dogs. Transmission is by animal bites.

Pathogenesis—Spreads rapidly in skin and subcutaneous tissue. No exotoxins.

Laboratory Diagnosis—Gram-stained smear and culture.

Treatment—Penicillin G.

Prevention—Ampicillin should be given to individuals with cat bites. There is no vaccine.

Yersinia pestis

Disease—Bubonic and pneumonic plague.

Characteristics—Small gram-negative rods with bipolar ("safety pin") staining. One of the most virulent organisms, ie, very low ID_{50}.

Habitat and Transmission—Reservoir is wild rodents, eg, rats, prairie dogs, and squirrels. Transmission is by flea bite.

Pathogenesis—Virulence factors include endotoxin, an exotoxin, two antigens (V and W), and an envelope (capsular) antigen that protects against phagocytosis. V and W proteins allow organism to grow within cells. Bubo is a swollen inflamed lymph node, usually located in the region of the flea bite.

Laboratory Diagnosis—Gram-stained smear. Other stains, eg, Wayson's, show typical "safety-pin" appearance more clearly. Cultures are hazardous and should be done only in specially equipped laboratories. Organism is identified by immunofluorescence. Diagnosis can be made by serologic tests that detect antibody in patient's serum.

Treatment—Streptomycin either alone or in combination with tetracycline. Strict quarantine for 72 hours.

Prevention—Control rodent population and avoid contact with dead rodents. Killed vaccine is available for persons in high-risk occupations. Close contacts should be given tetracycline.

MYCOBACTERIA (CHAPTER 21)

Mycobacterium tuberculosis

Diseases—Tuberculosis.

Characteristics—Aerobic, acid-fast rods. High lipid content of cell wall, which prevents dyes used in Gram stain from staining organism. Lipids include mycolic acids and wax D. Grows very slowly, which requires that drugs be present for long periods (months). Produces catalase, which is required to activate isoniazid to the active drug.

Habitat and Transmission—Habitat is the human lungs. Transmission is via respiratory droplets produced by coughing.

Pathogenesis—Granulomas and caseation mediated by cellular immunity, ie, macrophages and CD4-positive T cells (delayed hypersensitivity). Cord factor (trehalose mycolate) correlates with virulence. No exotoxins or endotoxin. Immunosuppression increases risk of reactivation and dissemination.

Laboratory Diagnosis—Acid-fast rods seen with Ziehl-Neelsen (or Kinyoun) stain. Slow-growing (3–6 weeks) colony on Löwenstein-Jensen medium. Organisms produce niacin and are catalase-positive. Serologic tests for antibody in patient's serum not useful.

Skin Test—PPD skin test is positive if induration measuring 10 mm or more appears 48 hours after inoculation. Induration is caused by a delayed hypersensitivity response. Positive skin test indicates that the person has been infected but not necessarily that the person has the disease tuberculosis.

Treatment—Long-term therapy (6–9 months) with three drugs, isoniazid, rifampin, and pyrazinamide. A fourth drug, ethambutol, is used in severe cases (eg, meningitis), in immunocompromised patients (eg, those with AIDS), and where the chance of isoniazid-resistant organisms is high, as in Southeast Asians. Most patients become noninfectious within 2 weeks of adequate therapy. Treatment of latent (asymptomatic) infections consists of isoniazid taken for 6–9 months. Multidrug-resistant (MDR) strains have emerged and require other drug combinations.

Prevention—BCG vaccine containing live, attenuated *Mycobacterium bovis* organisms may prevent or limit extent of disease but does not prevent infection with *M. tuberculosis*. Vaccine used rarely in the United States but widely used in parts of Europe and Asia.

Atypical Mycobacteria

These mycobacteria are called atypical because they differ from *M. tuberculosis* in various ways. The most important difference is that the atypicals are found in the environment, whereas *M. tuberculosis* is found only in humans. The atypicals are also called "Mycobacteria other than *M. tuberculosis*," or MOTTS.

The atypicals are subdivided into slow growers and rapid growers based on whether they form colonies in more than or less than 7 days. (Pigment production by the slow growers need not concern us here.)

The important slow growers are:

1. *Mycobacterium avium-intracellulare* complex (MAC) causes tuberculosis-like disease, especially in immunocompromised patients, such as those with AIDS. It is highly antibiotic-resistant.

2. *Mycobacterium kansasii* also causes tuberculosis-like disease but is less antibiotic-resistant than MAC.

3. *Mycobacterium marinum* causes "swimming pool granuloma or fish tank granuloma," which is a skin lesion at the site of an abrasion acquired in a swimming pool or an aquarium.

4. *Mycobacterium scrofulaceum* causes scrofula, which manifests as swollen, nontender cervical lymph nodes (cervical adenitis).

The important rapid grower is *Mycobacterium fortuitum-chelonei* complex, which causes infections of prosthetic joints and indwelling catheters. It also causes skin and soft tissue infections at the site of puncture wounds. The organisms are usually resistant to most antituberculosis drugs.

Mycobacterium leprae

Disease—Leprosy.

Characteristics—Aerobic, acid-fast rods. Cannot be cultured in vitro. Optimal growth at less than body temperature, so lesions are on cooler parts of the body, such as skin, nose, and superficial nerves.

Habitat and Transmission—Humans are the reservoir. Also found in armadillos, but it's uncertain whether they are a source of infections for humans. Most important mode of transmission is probably nasal secretions of patients with the lepromatous form. Patients with the lepromatous form are more likely to transmit than those with the tuberculoid form because they have much higher numbers of organisms than those with tuberculoid leprosy. Prolonged exposure is usually necessary.

Pathogenesis—Lesions usually occur in the cooler parts of the body, eg, skin and peripheral nerves. In tuberculoid leprosy, destructive lesions are due to the cell-mediated response to the organism. Damage to fingers is due to burns and other trauma, because nerve damage causes loss of sensation. In lepromatous leprosy, the cell-mediated response to *M. leprae* is lost and large numbers of organisms appear in the lesions and blood. No toxins or virulence factors are known.

Laboratory Diagnosis—Acid-fast rods are abundant in lepromatous leprosy, but few are found in the tuberculoid form. Cultures and serologic tests not done. Lepromin skin test is positive in the tuberculoid but not in the lepromatous form.

Treatment—Dapsone plus rifampin for the tuberculoid form. Clofazamine is added to that regimen for the lepromatous form or if the organism is resistant to dapsone. Treatment is for at least 2 years.

Prevention—Dapsone for close family contacts. No vaccine is available.

ACTINOMYCETES (CHAPTER 22)

Actinomyces israelii

Disease—Actinomycosis (abscesses with draining sinus tracts).

Characteristics—Anaerobic, gram-positive filamentous, branching rods.

Habitat and Transmission—Habitat is human mouth, especially anaerobic crevices around the teeth. Transmission into tissues occurs during dental disease or trauma. Organism also aspirated into lungs, causing thoracic actinomycosis. Retained intrauterine device (IUD) predisposes to pelvic actinomycosis.

Pathogenesis—No toxins or virulence factors known. Organism forms sinus tracts that open onto skin and contain "sulfur granules," which are mats of intertwined filaments of bacteria.

Laboratory Diagnosis—Gram-stained smear plus anaerobic culture on blood agar plate. "Sulfur granules" visible in the pus. No serologic tests.

Treatment—Penicillin G and surgical drainage.

Prevention—No vaccine or drug is available.

Nocardia asteroides

Disease—Nocardiosis (especially lung and brain abscesses).

Characteristics—Aerobic, gram-positive filamentous, branching rods. Weakly acid-fast.

Habitat and Transmission—Habitat is the soil. Transmission is via airborne particles, which are inhaled into the lungs.

Pathogenesis—No toxins or virulence factors known. Immunosuppression and cancer predispose to infection.

Laboratory Diagnosis—Gram-stained smear and modified Ziehl-Neelsen stain. Aerobic culture on blood agar plate. No serologic tests.

Treatment—Sulfonamides.

Prevention—No vaccine or drug is available.

MYCOPLASMAS (CHAPTER 23)
Mycoplasma pneumoniae

Disease—"Atypical" pneumonia.

Characteristics—Smallest free-living organisms. Not seen on Gram-stained smear because they have no cell wall, so dyes are not retained. The only bacteria with cholesterol in cell membrane. Can be cultured in vitro.

Habitat and Transmission—Habitat is the human respiratory tract. Transmission is via respiratory droplets.

Pathogenesis—No exotoxins produced. No endotoxin because there is no cell wall. Produces hydrogen peroxide, which may damage the respiratory tract.

Laboratory Diagnosis—Gram stain not useful. Can be cultured on special bacteriologic media but takes at least 10 days to grow, which is too long to be clinically

useful. Positive cold-agglutinin test is presumptive evidence. Complement fixation test for antibodies to *Mycoplasma pneumoniae* is more specific.

Treatment—Erythromycin or tetracycline.

Prevention—No vaccine or drug is available.

SPIROCHETES (CHAPTER 24)
Treponema pallidum

Disease—Syphilis.

Characteristics—Spirochetes. Not seen on Gram-stained smear because organism is too thin. Not cultured in vitro.

Habitat and Transmission—Habitat is the human genital tract. Transmission is by sexual contact and from mother to fetus across the placenta.

Pathogenesis—Organism multiplies at site of inoculation and then spreads widely via the bloodstream. Many features of syphilis are attributed to blood vessel involvement causing vasculitis. Primary (chancre) and secondary lesions heal spontaneously. Tertiary lesions consist of gummas (granulomas in bone, muscle, and skin), aortitis, or central nervous system inflammation. No toxins or virulence factors known.

Laboratory Diagnosis—Seen by dark-field microscopy or immunofluorescence. Serologic tests important: VDRL (or RPR) is nontreponemal (nonspecific) test used for screening; FTA-ABS is the most widely used specific test for *Treponema pallidum*. Antigen in VDRL is beef heart cardiolipin; antigen in FTA-ABS is killed *T. pallidum*. VDRL declines with treatment, whereas FTA-ABS remains positive for life.

Treatment—Penicillin is effective in the treatment of all stages of syphilis. In primary and secondary syphilis, use benzathine penicillin G (a depot preparation) because *T. pallidum* grows slowly, so drug must be present for a long time. There is no resistance.

Prevention—Benzathine penicillin given to contacts. No vaccine is available.

Borrelia burgdorferi

Disease—Lyme disease.

Characteristics—Spirochetes. Gram stain not useful. Can be cultured in vitro, but not usually done.

Habitat and Transmission—The main reservoir is the white-footed mouse. Transmitted by the bite of ixodid ticks, especially in three areas in the United States: Northeast (eg, Connecticut), Midwest (eg, Wisconsin), and West Coast (eg, California). Eighty percent of cases are in the Northeastern states of Connecticut, New

York, and New Jersey. Very small nymph stage of ixodid tick (deer tick) is most common vector. Tick must feed for at least 24 hours to deliver an infectious dose of *B. burgdorferi*.

Pathogenesis—Organism invades skin, causing a rash called erythema migrans. It then spreads via the bloodstream to involve primarily the heart, joints, and central nervous system. No toxins or virulence factors identified.

Laboratory Diagnosis—Diagnosis usually made serologically, ie, by detecting IgM antibody. Confirm positive serologic test with Western blot assay.

Treatment—Doxycycline for early stages; penicillin G for late stages.

Prevention—Vaccine containing outer membrane protein of the organism was available but has been withdrawn. Avoid tick bite. Can give doxycycline or amoxicillin to people who are bitten by a tick in endemic areas.

Leptospira interrogans

Disease—Leptospirosis.

Characteristics—Spirochetes that can be seen on darkfield microscopy but not light microscopy. Can be cultured in vitro.

Habitat and Transmission—Habitat is wild and domestic animals. Transmission is via animal urine. In the United States, transmission is chiefly via dog, livestock, and rat urine.

Pathogenesis—Two phases: an initial bacteremic phase and a subsequent immunopathologic phase with meningitis. No toxins or virulence factors known.

Laboratory Diagnosis—Dark-field microscopy and culture in vitro are available but not usually done. Diagnosis usually made by serologic testing for antibodies in patient's serum.

Treatment—Penicillin G. There is no significant antibiotic resistance.

Prevention—Doxycycline effective for short-term exposure. Vaccination of domestic livestock and pets. Rat control.

Borrelia recurrentis

Causes relapsing fever. Transmitted by human body louse. Organism well known for its rapid antigenic changes, which account for the relapsing nature of disease. Antigenic changes are due to programmed rearrangements of bacterial DNA encoding surface proteins.

CHLAMYDIAE (CHAPTER 25)
Chlamydia trachomatis

Diseases—Nongonococcal urethritis, cervicitis, inclusion conjunctivitis, lymphogranuloma venereum, and trachoma. Also pneumonia in infants.

Characteristics—Obligate intracellular parasites. Not seen on Gram-stained smear. Exists as inactive elementary body extracellularly and as metabolically active, dividing reticulate body intracellularly.

Habitat and Transmission—Habitat is the human genital tract and eyes. Transmission is by sexual contact and during passage of neonate through birth canal. Transmission in trachoma is chiefly by hand-to-eye contact.

Pathogenesis—No toxins or virulence factors known.

Laboratory Diagnosis—Cytoplasmic inclusions seen on Giemsa-stained or fluorescent-antibody-stained smear. Glycogen-filled cytoplasmic inclusions can be visualized with iodine. Organism grows in cell culture and embryonated eggs, but these are not often used. PCR-based assay and an ELISA using patient's urine are available.

Treatment—A tetracycline (such as doxycycline) or a macrolide (such as azithromycin).

Prevention—Erythromycin effective in infected mother to prevent neonatal disease. No vaccine is available.

Chlamydia pneumoniae

Disease—Atypical pneumonia.

Characteristics—Same as *C. trachomatis*.

Habitat and Transmission—Habitat is human respiratory tract. Transmission is by respiratory aerosol.

Pathogenesis—No toxins or virulence factors known.

Laboratory Diagnosis—Serologic tests for antibody in patient's serum.

Treatment—A tetracycline, such as doxycycline.

Prevention—No vaccine or drug is available.

Chlamydia psittaci

Disease—Psittacosis.

Characteristics—Same as *C. trachomatis*.

Habitat and Transmission—Habitat is birds, both psittacine and others. Transmission is via aerosol of dried bird feces.

Pathogenesis—No toxins or virulence factors known.

Laboratory Diagnosis—Diagnosis usually made by testing for antibodies in patient's serum. Cytoplasmic inclusion seen by Giemsa or fluorescent-antibody staining. Organism can be isolated from sputum, but this is rarely done.

Treatment—Tetracycline.

Prevention—No vaccine or drug is available.

RICKETTSIAE (CHAPTER 26)
Rickettsia rickettsii

Disease—Rocky Mountain spotted fever.

Characteristics—Obligate intracellular parasites. Not seen well on Gram-stained smear. Antigens cross-react with OX strains of *Proteus vulgaris* (Weil-Felix reaction).

Habitat and Transmission—*Dermacentor* (dog) ticks are both the vector and the main reservoir. Transmission is via tick bite. Dogs and rodents can be reservoirs as well.

Pathogenesis—Organism invades endothelial lining of capillaries, causing vasculitis. No toxins or virulence factors identified.

Laboratory Diagnosis—Diagnosis made by detecting antibody in serologic tests such as the ELISA test. Weil-Felix test is no longer used. Stain and culture rarely done.

Treatment—Tetracycline.

Prevention—Protective clothing and prompt removal of ticks. Tetracycline effective in exposed persons. No vaccine is available.

Rickettsia prowazekii

Disease—Typhus.

Characteristics—Same as *R. rickettsii.*

Habitat and Transmission—Humans are the reservoir, and transmission is via the bite of the human body louse.

Pathogenesis—No toxins or virulence factors known.

Laboratory Diagnosis—Serologic tests for antibody in patient's serum.

Treatment—A tetracycline, such as doxycycline.

Prevention—A killed vaccine is used in the military but is not available for civilian use.

Coxiella burnetii

Disease—Q fever.

Characteristics—Obligate intracellular parasites. Not seen well on Gram-stained smear.

Habitat and Transmission—Habitat is domestic livestock. Transmission is by inhalation of aerosols of urine, feces, amniotic fluid, or placental tissue. The only rickettsia not transmitted to humans by an arthropod.

Pathogenesis—No toxins or virulence factors known.

Laboratory Diagnosis—Diagnosis usually made by serologic tests. Weil-Felix test is negative. Stain and culture rarely done.

Treatment—Tetracycline.

Prevention—Killed vaccine for persons in high-risk occupations. No drug is available.

MINOR BACTERIAL PATHOGENS (CHAPTER 27)

Only the more important of the minor bacterial pathogens are summarized in this section.

Bartonella henselae

Gram-negative rod. Causes cat-scratch fever in immunocompetent individuals and bacillary angiomatosis in immunocompromised, especially AIDS, patients. Found as normal flora in the mouth of cats. Transmitted to humans by cat bite or scratch and from cat to cat by fleas.

Ehrlichia chaffeensis

Member of rickettsia family. Causes human monocytic ehrlichiosis. Transmitted from dog reservoir to humans by ticks, especially *Dermacentor,* the dog tick. Endemic in southern states, eg, Arkansas. Forms morulae in cytoplasm of monocytes. (A morula is a "mulberry-shaped" inclusion body composed of many *E. chaffeensis* cells.)

Fusobacterium nucleatum

Anaerobic gram-negative rod with pointed ends. Member of the normal human flora in mouth, colon, and female genital tract. Causes brain, lung, abdominal, and pelvic abscesses, typically in combination with other anaerobes and facultative bacteria.

Gardnerella vaginalis

Facultative gram-variable rod. Involved in bacterial vaginosis, along with *Mobiluncus* species, which are anaerobic. See "clue cells," which are vaginal epithelial cells covered with *G. vaginalis* cells. Positive "whiff" test found in bacterial vaginosis.

Haemophilus ducreyi

Small gram-negative rod. Causes chancroid. Sexually transmitted disease with painful ulcer on genitals (in contrast to syphilis, which is painless). To grow in culture, it requires factor X (heme) but not factor V (in contrast to *H. influenzae*, which requires both).

Moraxella catarrhalis

Small coccobacillary gram-negative rod that resembles the cocci of the genus *Neisseria*. Causes otitis media and sinusitis primarily in children. Also causes bronchitis and pneumonia, primarily in older people with chronic obstructive pulmonary disease. It is found only in humans and is transmitted by respiratory aerosol.

Yersinia enterocolitica

Gram-negative rods. Causes enterocolitis similar to that caused by *Shigella* and *Salmonella*. Also causes mesenteric adenitis, which can mimic appendicitis. Found in domestic animals and transmitted to humans by fecal contamination of food.

SUMMARIES OF MEDICALLY IMPORTANT VIRUSES

DNA ENVELOPED VIRUSES (CHAPTER 37)

Herpes Simplex Virus Type 1

Diseases—Herpes labialis (fever blisters or cold sores), keratitis, encephalitis.

Characteristics—Enveloped virus with icosahedral nucleocapsid and linear double-stranded DNA. No virion polymerase. One serotype; cross-reaction with HSV-2 occurs. No herpes group–specific antigen.

Transmission—By saliva or direct contact with virus from the vesicle.

Pathogenesis—Initial vesicular lesions occur in the mouth or on the face. The virus then travels up the axon and becomes latent in sensory (trigeminal) ganglia. Recurrences occur in skin innervated by affected sensory nerve and are induced by fever, sunlight, stress, etc. Dissemination to internal organs occurs in patients with depressed cell-mediated immunity with life-threatening consequences. HSV-1 encephalitis often affects the temporal lobe.

Laboratory Diagnosis—Virus causes cytopathic effect (CPE) in cell culture. It is identified by antibody neutralization or fluorescent-antibody test. Tzanck smear of cells from the base of the vesicle reveals multinucleated giant cells with intranuclear inclusions. These giant cells are not specific for HSV-1; they are seen in the vesicular lesions caused by HSV-2 and varicella-zoster virus as well. A rise in antibody titer can be used to diagnose a primary infection but not recurrences. HSV encephalitis can be diagnosed using a PCR assay to detect HSV-1 DNA in spinal fluid.

Treatment—Acyclovir for encephalitis and disseminated disease. Acyclovir has no effect on the latent state of the virus. Trifluorothymidine for keratitis. Primary infections and localized recurrences are self-limited.

Prevention—Recurrences can be prevented by avoiding the specific inciting agent such as intense sunlight. Acyclovir can reduce recurrences. No vaccine is available.

Herpes Simplex Virus Type 2

Diseases—Herpes genitalis, aseptic meningitis, and neonatal infection.

Characteristics—Enveloped virus with icosahedral nucleocapsid and linear double-stranded DNA. No virion polymerase. One serotype; cross-reaction with HSV-1 occurs. No herpes group–specific antigen.

Transmission—Sexual contact in adults and during passage through the birth canal in neonates.

Pathogenesis—Initial vesicular lesions occur on genitals. The virus then travels up the axon and becomes latent in sensory (lumbar or sacral) ganglion cells. Recurrences are less severe than the primary infection. HSV-2 infections in neonate can be life-threatening because neonates have reduced cell-mediated immunity. Asymptomatic shedding of HSV-2 in the female genital tract is an important contributing factor to neonatal infections.

Laboratory Diagnosis—Virus causes CPE in cell culture. Identify by antibody neutralization or fluorescent-antibody test. Tzanck smear reveals multinucleated giant cells but is not specific for HSV-2. A rise in antibody titer can be used to diagnose a primary infection but not recurrences.

Treatment—Acyclovir is useful in the treatment of primary and recurrent genital infections as well as neonatal infections. It has no effect on the latent state.

Prevention—Primary disease can be prevented by protection from exposure to vesicular lesions. Recurrences can be reduced by the long-term use of oral acyclovir. Neonatal infection can be prevented by delivering the child by cesarean section if the mother has visible vesicular lesions in the birth canal. There is no vaccine.

Varicella-Zoster Virus

Diseases—Varicella (chickenpox) in children and zoster (shingles) in adults.

Characteristics—Enveloped virus with icosahedral nucleocapsid and linear double-stranded DNA. No virion polymerase. One serotype.

Transmission—Varicella is transmitted primarily by respiratory droplets. Zoster is not transmitted; it is caused by a reactivation of latent virus.

Pathogenesis—Initial infection is in the oropharynx. It spreads via the blood to the internal organs such as the liver and then to the skin. After the acute episode of varicella, the virus remains latent in the sensory ganglia and can reactivate to cause zoster years later, especially in older and immunocompromised individuals.

Laboratory Diagnosis—Virus causes CPE in cell culture and can be identified by fluorescent-antibody test. Multinucleated giant cells seen in smears from the base of the vesicle. Intranuclear inclusions seen in infected cells. A 4-fold or greater rise in antibody titer in convalescent-phase serum is diagnostic.

Treatment—No antiviral therapy is indicated for varicella or zoster in the immunocompetent patient. In the immunocompromised patient, acyclovir can prevent dissemination.

Prevention—Vaccine contains live, attenuated virus. Immunocompromised patients exposed to the virus should receive passive immunization with varicella-zoster immune globulin (VZIG) and acyclovir to prevent disseminated disease.

Cytomegalovirus

Diseases—Most common cause of congenital abnormalities in the United States. Cytomegalic inclusion body disease in infants. Mononucleosis in transfusion recipients. Pneumonia and hepatitis in immunocompromised patients. Retinitis and enteritis, especially in AIDS patients.

Characteristics—Enveloped virus with icosahedral nucleocapsid and linear double-stranded DNA. No virion polymerase. One serotype.

Transmission—Virus is found in many human body fluids, including blood, saliva, semen, cervical mucus, breast milk, and urine. It is transmitted via these fluids, across the placenta, or by organ transplantation.

Pathogenesis—Initial infection usually in the oropharynx. In fetal infections, the virus spreads to many organs, eg, central nervous system and kidneys. In adults, lymphocytes are frequently involved. A latent state occurs in leukocytes. Disseminated infection in immuno-

compromised patients can result from either a primary infection or reactivation of a latent infection.

Laboratory Diagnosis—The virus causes CPE in cell culture and can be identified by fluorescent-antibody test. "Owl's eye" nuclear inclusions are seen. A 4-fold or greater rise in antibody titer in convalescent-phase serum is diagnostic.

Treatment—Ganciclovir is beneficial in treating pneumonia and retinitis. Acyclovir is ineffective.

Prevention—No vaccine is available. Ganciclovir suppresses retinitis. Do not transfuse CMV antibody-positive blood into newborns or antibody-negative immunocompromised patients.

Epstein-Barr Virus

Diseases—Infectious mononucleosis; associated with Burkitt's lymphoma in East African children.

Characteristics—Enveloped virus with icosahedral nucleocapsid and linear double-stranded DNA. No virion polymerase. One serotype.

Transmission—Virus found in human oropharynx and B lymphocytes. It is transmitted primarily by saliva.

Pathogenesis—Infection begins in the pharyngeal epithelium, spreads to the cervical lymph nodes, then travels via the blood to the liver and spleen. EBV establishes latency in B lymphocytes.

Laboratory Diagnosis—The virus is rarely isolated. Lymphocytosis, including atypical lymphocytes, occurs. Heterophil antibody is typically positive (Monospot test). Heterophil antibody agglutinates sheep or horse red blood cells. A significant rise in EBV-specific antibody to viral capsid antigen is diagnostic.

Treatment—No effective drug is available.

Prevention—There is no drug or vaccine.

Human Herpesvirus 8

Causes Kaposi's sarcoma, especially in AIDS patients. Transmitted sexually. Diagnosis made by pathologic examination of lesion biopsy. See spindle cells and extravasated red blood cells. Purple color of lesions due to collections of red cells. No specific antiviral treatment and no vaccine.

Smallpox Virus

Disease—Smallpox. The disease smallpox has been eradicated by use of the vaccine. The last known case was in 1977 in Somalia.

Characteristics—Poxviruses are the largest viruses. Enveloped virus with linear double-stranded DNA. DNA-dependent RNA polymerase in virion. One serologic type.

Transmission—By respiratory droplets or direct contact with the virus from skin lesions.

Pathogenesis—The virus infects the mucosal cells of the upper respiratory tract, then spreads to the local lymph nodes and by viremia to the liver and spleen and later the skin. Skin lesions progress in the following order: macule, papule, vesicle, pustule, crust.

Laboratory Diagnosis—Virus identified by CPE in cell culture or "pocks" on chorioallantoic membrane. Electron microscopy reveals typical particles; cytoplasmic inclusions seen in light microscopy. Viral antigens in the vesicle fluid can be detected by precipitin tests. A 4-fold or greater rise in antibody titer in the convalescent-phase serum is diagnostic.

Treatment—None.

Prevention—Vaccine contains live, attenuated vaccinia virus. Vaccine is no longer used except by the military, because the disease has been eradicated.

Molluscum Contagiosum Virus

Causes molluscum contagiosum. See pinkish, papular skin lesions with an umbilicated center. Lesions usually on the face, especially around the eyes. Transmitted by direct contact. Diagnosis made clinically; laboratory is not involved. There is no established antiviral therapy and no vaccine. Cidofovir may be useful in the treatment of the extensive lesions that occur in immunocompromised patients.

DNA NONENVELOPED VIRUSES (CHAPTER 38)

Adenovirus

Diseases—Upper and lower tract respiratory disease, especially pharyngitis and pneumonia. Enteric strains cause diarrhea. Some strains cause sarcomas in certain animals but not humans.

Characteristics—Nonenveloped virus with icosahedral nucleocapsid and linear double-stranded DNA. No virion polymerase. There are 41 serotypes, some associated with specific diseases.

Transmission—Respiratory droplet primarily; iatrogenic transmission in eye disease; fecal-oral transmission with enteric strains.

Pathogenesis—Virus preferentially infects epithelium of respiratory tract and eyes. After acute infection, persistent, low-grade virus production without symptoms can occur in the pharynx.

Laboratory Diagnosis—Virus causes CPE in cell culture and can be identified by fluorescent-antibody or complement fixation test. Antibody titer rise in convalescent-phase serum is diagnostic.

Treatment—None.

Prevention—Live vaccine against types 3, 4, and 7 is used in the military to prevent pneumonia.

Human Papillomavirus

Diseases—Papillomas (warts); condylomata acuminata (genital warts); associated with carcinoma of the cervix and penis.

Characteristics—Nonenveloped virus with icosahedral nucleocapsid and circular double-stranded DNA. No virion polymerase. There are at least 60 types, which are determined by DNA sequence not by antigenicity. Many types infect the epithelium and cause papillomas at specific body sites.

Transmission—Direct contact of skin or genital lesions.

Pathogenesis—Two early viral genes, E6 and E7, encode proteins that inhibit the activity of proteins encoded by tumor suppressor genes, eg, the p53 gene and the retinoblastoma gene, respectively.

Laboratory Diagnosis—Diagnosis is made clinically by finding koilocytes in the lesions. DNA hybridization tests are available. Virus isolation and serologic tests are not done.

Treatment—Podophyllin or liquid nitrogen are most commonly used. Alpha interferon is also available.

Prevention—There is no drug or vaccine.

Parvovirus B19

Diseases—Slapped cheek syndrome (erythema infectiosum), aplastic anemia, arthritis, and hydrops fetalis.

Characteristics—Nonenveloped virus with icosahedral symmetry and single-stranded DNA genome. Virion contains no polymerase. There is one serotype.

Transmission—Respiratory droplets and transplacental.

Pathogenesis—Virus preferentially infects erythroblasts, causing aplastic anemia in patients with hereditary anemias; immune complexes cause rash and arthritis. Virus can infect fetus and cause severe anemia, leading to congestive heart failure and edema (hydrops fetalis).

Laboratory Diagnosis—Serologic tests.

Treatment—None.

Prevention—There is no drug or vaccine.

RNA ENVELOPED VIRUSES (CHAPTER 39)

Influenza Virus

Disease—Influenza. Influenza A virus is the main cause of worldwide epidemics (pandemics).

Characteristics—Enveloped virus with a helical nucleocapsid and segmented, single-stranded RNA of negative polarity. RNA polymerase in virion. The two major antigens are the hemagglutinin (HA) and the neuraminidase (NA) on separate surface spikes. Antigenic shift in these proteins as a result of reassortment of RNA segments accounts for the epidemics of influenza caused by influenza A virus. Influenza A viruses of animals are the source of the new RNA segments. Antigenic drift due to mutations also contributes. The virus has many serotypes because of these antigenic shifts and drifts. The antigenicity of the internal nucleocapsid protein determines whether the virus is an A, B, or C influenza virus.

Transmission—Respiratory droplets.

Pathogenesis—Infection is limited primarily to the epithelium of the respiratory tract.

Laboratory Diagnosis—Virus grows in cell culture and embryonated eggs and can be detected by hemadsorption or hemagglutination. It is identified by hemagglutination inhibition or complement fixation. A 4-fold or greater antibody titer rise in convalescent-phase serum is diagnostic.

Treatment—Amantadine or rimantadine can be used. The neuraminidase inhibitors zanamivir and oseltamivir are also available.

Prevention— Two vaccines available: a killed (subunit) vaccine containing HA and NA and one containing a live, temperature-sensitive mutant of influenza virus. Live vaccine replicates in cool nasal passages where it induces secretory IgA, but not in warm lower respiratory tract. Both vaccines contain the strains of influenza A and B virus currently causing disease. The killed vaccine is not a good immunogen and must be given annually. Recommended for people older than age 65 years and for those with chronic diseases, especially of the heart and lungs. Amantadine, rimantadine, zanamivir, or oseltamivir can be used for prophylaxis in unimmunized people who have been exposed.

Measles Virus

Disease—Measles. Subacute sclerosing panencephalitis is a rare late complication.

Characteristics—Enveloped virus with a helical nucleocapsid and one piece of single-stranded, negative-polarity RNA. RNA polymerase in virion. It has a single serotype.

Transmission—Respiratory droplets.

Pathogenesis—Initial site of infection is the upper respiratory tract. Virus spreads to local lymph nodes and then via the blood to other organs, including the skin. Giant cell pneumonia and encephalitis can occur. The maculopapular rash is due to cell-mediated immune attack by cytotoxic T cells on virus-infected vascular endothelial cells in the skin.

Laboratory Diagnosis—The virus is rarely isolated. Serologic tests are used if necessary.

Treatment—No antiviral therapy is available.

Prevention—Vaccine contains live, attenuated virus. Usually given in combination with mumps and rubella vaccines.

Mumps Virus

Disease—Mumps. Sterility due to bilateral orchitis is a rare complication.

Characteristics—Enveloped virus with a helical nucleocapsid and one piece of single-stranded, negative-polarity RNA. RNA polymerase in virion. It has a single serotype.

Transmission—Respiratory droplets.

Pathogenesis—The initial site of infection is the upper respiratory tract. The virus spreads to local lymph nodes and then via the bloodstream to other organs, especially the parotid glands, testes, ovaries, meninges, and pancreas.

Laboratory Diagnosis—The virus can be isolated in cell culture and detected by hemadsorption. Diagnosis can also be made serologically.

Treatment—No antiviral therapy is available.

Prevention—Vaccine contains live, attenuated virus. Usually given in combination with measles and rubella vaccines.

Rubella Virus

Disease—Rubella. Congenital rubella syndrome is characterized by congenital malformations, especially affecting the cardiovascular and central nervous systems, and by prolonged virus excretion. The incidence of congenital rubella has been greatly reduced by the widespread use of the vaccine.

Characteristics—Enveloped virus with an icosahedral nucleocapsid and one piece of single-stranded positive-polarity RNA. No polymerase in virion. It has a single serotype.

Transmission—Respiratory droplets and across the placenta from mother to fetus.

Pathogenesis—The initial site of infection is the nasopharynx, from which it spreads to local lymph nodes. It then disseminates to the skin via the bloodstream. The rash is attributed to both viral replication and immune injury. During maternal infection, the virus replicates in the placenta and then spreads to fetal tissue. If infection occurs during the first trimester, a high frequency of congenital malformations occurs.

Laboratory Diagnosis—Virus growth in cell culture is detected by interference with plaque formation by coxsackievirus; rubella virus does not cause CPE. To determine whether an adult woman is immune, a single serum specimen to detect IgG antibody in the hemagglutination inhibition test is used. To detect whether recent infection has occurred, either a single serum specimen for IgM antibody or a set of acute- and convalescent-phase sera for IgG antibody can be used.

Treatment—No antiviral therapy is available.

Prevention—Vaccine contains live, attenuated virus. Usually given in combination with measles and mumps vaccine.

Parainfluenza Virus

Disease—Bronchiolitis in infants, croup in young children, and the common cold in adults.

Characteristics—Enveloped virus with helical nucleocapsid and one piece of single-stranded, negative-polarity RNA. RNA polymerase in virion. Unlike influenza viruses, the antigenicity of its hemagglutinin and neuraminidase is stable. There are four serotypes.

Transmission—Respiratory droplets.

Pathogenesis—Infection and death of respiratory epithelium without systemic spread of the virus. Multinucleated giant cells caused by the viral fusion protein are a hallmark.

Laboratory Diagnosis—Isolation of the virus in cell culture is detected by hemadsorption. Immunofluorescence is used for identification. A 4-fold or greater rise in antibody titer can also be used for diagnosis

Treatment—None.

Prevention—No vaccine or drug is available.

Respiratory Syncytial Virus

Diseases—Most important cause of bronchiolitis and pneumonia in infants. Also causes otitis media in older children.

Characteristics—Enveloped virus with a helical nucleocapsid and one piece of single-stranded, negative-polarity RNA. RNA polymerase in virion. Unlike other paramyxoviruses, it has only a fusion protein in its surface spikes. It has no hemagglutinin. It has a single serotype.

Transmission—Respiratory droplets.

Pathogenesis—Infection involves primarily the lower respiratory tract in infants without systemic spread. Immune response probably contributes to pathogenesis.

Laboratory Diagnosis—Isolation in cell culture. Multinucleated giant cells visible. Immunofluorescence is used for identification. Serology is not useful for diagnosis in infants.

Treatment—Aerosolized ribavirin for very sick infants.

Prevention—Passive immunization with palivizumab (monoclonal antibody) or immune globulins in infants who have been exposed may be effective. Hand washing and the use of gloves may prevent nosocomial outbreaks in the newborn nursery.

Coronavirus

Disease—Common cold and SARS (severe acute respiratory syndrome).

Characteristics—Enveloped virus with helical nucleocapsid and one piece of single-stranded, positive-polarity RNA. No virion polymerase. There are two serotypes.

Transmission—Respiratory droplets. Animal coronaviruses may be the source of human infection.

Pathogenesis—Infection is typically limited to the mucosal cells of the respiratory tract. At least 50% of infections are asymptomatic. Immunity is brief and reinfection occurs.

Laboratory Diagnosis—The diagnosis primarily a clinical one. Antibody-based and PCR-based test are available but not often done.

Treatment—None.

Prevention—No vaccine or drug available.

Rabies Virus

Disease—Rabies. (Rabies is an encephalitis.)

Characteristics—Bullet-shaped enveloped virus with a helical nucleocapsid and one piece of single-stranded, negative-polarity RNA. RNA polymerase in virion. The virus has a single serotype.

Transmission—Main reservoir is wild animals such as skunks, raccoons, and bats. Transmission to humans is usually by animal bite, but the virus is also transmitted by aerosols of bat saliva. In the United States, dogs are infrequently involved because canine immunization is so common, but in developing countries they are often involved.

Pathogenesis—Viral receptor is the acetylcholine receptor. Replication of virus at the site of the bite, followed by axonal transport up the nerve to the central nervous system. After replicating in the brain, the virus migrates peripherally to the salivary glands, where it enters the saliva. When the animal is in the agitated state as a result of encephalitis, virus in the saliva can be transmitted via a bite.

Laboratory Diagnosis—Tissue can be stained with fluorescent antibody or with various dyes to detect cytoplasmic inclusions called Negri bodies. The virus can be grown in cell culture, but the process takes too long to be useful in determining whether a person should receive the vaccine. Serologic testing is useful only to make the diagnosis in the clinically ill patient. Antibody does not form quickly enough to help in the decision whether or not to immunize the person who has been bitten. Serologic testing is also used to evaluate the antibody response to the vaccine given before exposure to those in high-risk occupations.

Treatment—No antiviral therapy is available.

Prevention—Preexposure prevention of rabies consists of the vaccine only. Postexposure prevention consists of (1) washing the wound; (2) giving rabies immune globulins (passive immunization), mostly into the wound; and (3) giving the inactivated vaccine (active immunization) made in human cell culture. The decision to give the immune serum and the vaccine depends on the circumstances. Prevention of rabies in dogs and cats by using a killed vaccine has reduced human rabies significantly.

RNA NONENVELOPED VIRUSES (CHAPTER 40)

Poliovirus

Diseases—Paralytic poliomyelitis and aseptic meningitis. Poliomyelitis has been eradicated in the Western Hemisphere and in many other countries.

Characteristics—Naked nucleocapsid with single-stranded, positive-polarity RNA. Genome RNA acts as mRNA and is translated into one large polypeptide, which is cleaved by virus-encoded protease to form functional viral proteins. No virion polymerase. There are three serotypes.

Transmission—Fecal-oral route. Humans are the natural reservoir.

Pathogenesis—The virus replicates in the pharynx and the GI tract. It can spread to the local lymph nodes and then through the bloodstream to the central nervous system. Most infections are asymptomatic or very mild. Aseptic meningitis is more frequent than paralytic polio. Paralysis is the result of death of motor neurons, especially anterior horn cells in the spinal cord. Pathogenesis of postpolio syndrome is unknown.

Laboratory Diagnosis—Recovery of the virus from spinal fluid indicates infection of the central nervous system. Isolation of the virus from stools indicates infection but not necessarily disease. It can be found in the GI tract of asymptomatic carriers. The virus can be detected in cell culture by CPE and identified by neutralization with type-specific antiserum. A significant rise in antibody titer in convalescent-phase serum is also diagnostic.

Treatment—No antiviral therapy is available.

Prevention—Disease can be prevented by both the inactivated (Salk) vaccine and the live, attenuated (Sabin) vaccine; both induce humoral antibody that neutralizes the virus in the bloodstream. However, only the oral vaccine induces intestinal IgA, which interrupts the chain of transmission by preventing GI tract infection. For that reason and because it induces immunity of longer duration and is orally administered rather than injected, the Sabin vaccine has been the preferred vaccine for many years. However, there have been a few vaccine-associated cases of paralytic polio caused by poliovirus in the vaccine that reverted to virulence. In view of this, the current recommendation in the United States is to use the killed vaccine.

Coxsackieviruses

Diseases—Aseptic meningitis, herpangina, pleurodynia, myocarditis, and pericarditis are the most important diseases. Also coxsackievirus B4 may cause juvenile diabetes, since it will do so in mice.

Characteristics—Naked nucleocapsid with single-stranded, positive-polarity RNA. No virion polymerase. Group A and B viruses are defined by their different pathogenicity in mice. There are multiple serotypes in each group.

Transmission—Fecal-oral route.

Pathogenesis—The initial site of infection is the oropharynx, but the main site is the GI tract. The virus spreads through the bloodstream to various organs.

Laboratory Diagnosis—The virus can be detected by CPE in cell culture and identified by neutralization. A significant rise in antibody titer in convalescent-phase serum is diagnostic.

Treatment—No antiviral therapy is available.

Prevention—No vaccine is available.

Rhinoviruses

Disease—Common cold.

Characteristics—Naked nucleocapsid viruses with single-stranded, positive-polarity RNA. No virion polymerase. There are more than 100 serotypes, which explains why the common cold is so common. Rhinoviruses are destroyed by stomach acid and therefore do not replicate in the GI tract, in contrast to other picornaviruses such as poliovirus, coxsackievirus, and echovirus, which are resistant to stomach acid.

Transmission—Aerosol droplets and hand-to-nose contact.

Pathogenesis—Infection is limited to the mucosa of the upper respiratory tract and conjunctiva. The virus replicates best at the low temperatures of the nose and less well at 37°C, which explains its failure to infect the lower respiratory tract.

Laboratory Diagnosis—Laboratory tests are rarely used clinically. The virus can be recovered from nose or throat washings by growth in cell culture. Serologic tests are not useful.

Treatment—No antiviral therapy is available.

Prevention—No vaccine is available because there are too many serotypes.

Norwalk Virus (Norovirus)

Disease—Gastroenteritis (watery diarrhea).

Characteristics—Nonenveloped virus with icosahedral nucleocapsid and one piece of single-stranded, positive-polarity RNA. No virion polymerase. The number of serotypes is uncertain.

Transmission—Fecal-oral route.

Pathogenesis—Infection is typically limited to the mucosal cells of the intestinal tract. Many infections are asymptomatic. Immunity is brief and reinfection occurs.

Laboratory Diagnosis—The diagnosis primarily a clinical one. A PCR-based test is available but not often done.

Treatment—No antiviral drugs available. Treat diarrhea with fluid and electrolytes.

Prevention—No vaccine or drug available.

Rotavirus

Disease—Rotavirus causes gastroenteritis (diarrhea), especially in young children.

Characteristics—Naked double-layered capsid with 10 or 11 segments of double-stranded RNA. RNA polymerase in virion. Rotavirus is resistant to stomach acid and hence can reach the small intestine. There are at least six serotypes.

Transmission—Rotavirus is transmitted by the fecal-oral route.

Pathogenesis—Rotavirus infection is limited to the GI tract, especially the small intestine.

Laboratory Diagnosis—Detection of rotavirus in the stool by ELISA. Isolation of the virus is not done from clinical specimens.

Treatment—No antiviral drug is available.

Prevention—A vaccine containing live, attenuated virus was available but has been withdrawn because of side effects.

HEPATITIS VIRUSES (CHAPTER 41)

Hepatitis A Virus

Disease—Hepatitis A.

Characteristics—Naked nucleocapsid virus with a single-stranded, positive-polarity RNA. No virion polymerase. Virus has a single serotype.

Transmission—Fecal-oral route. In contrast to HBV and HCV, blood-borne transmission of HAV is uncommon because viremia is brief and of low titer.

Pathogenesis—The virus replicates in the GI tract and then spreads to the liver during a brief viremic period. The virus is not cytopathic for the hepatocyte. Hepatocellular injury is caused by immune attack by cytotoxic T cells.

Laboratory Diagnosis—The most useful test to diagnose acute infection is IgM antibody. Isolation of the virus from clinical specimens is not done.

Treatment—No antiviral drug is available.

Prevention—Vaccine contains killed virus. Administration of immune globulin during the incubation period can mitigate the disease.

Hepatitis B Virus

Diseases—Hepatitis B; implicated as a cause of hepatocellular carcinoma.

Characteristics—Enveloped virus with incomplete circular double-stranded DNA; ie, one strand has about one-third missing and the other strand is "nicked" (not covalently bonded). DNA polymerase in virion. HBV-encoded polymerase acts as a reverse transcriptase by using viral mRNA as the template for the synthesis of progeny genome DNA. There are three important antigens: the surface antigen, the core antigen, and the e antigen, which is located in the core. In the patient's serum, long rods and spherical forms composed solely of HBsAg predominate. HBV has one serotype based on the surface antigen.

Transmission—Transmitted by blood, during birth, and by sexual intercourse.

Pathogenesis—Hepatocellular injury due to immune attack by cytotoxic (CD8) T cells. Antigen-antibody complexes cause arthritis, rash, and glomerulonephritis. About 5% of HBV infections result in a chronic carrier state. Chronic hepatitis, cirrhosis, and hepatocellular carcinoma can occur. Hepatocellular carcinoma may be related to the integration of part of the viral DNA into hepatocyte DNA.

Laboratory Diagnosis—HBV has not been grown in cell culture. Three serologic tests are commonly used: surface antigen (HBsAg), surface antibody (HBsAb), and core antibody (HBcAb). Detection of HbsAg for more than 6 months indicates a chronic carrier state. The presence of e antigen indicates a chronic carrier who is making infectious virus. An HBV-infected person who has neither detectable HBs antigen nor HBs antibody is said to be in the "window" phase. Diagnosis of this patient is made by detecting HB core antibody. See Chapter 41 for a discussion of the results of these tests.

Treatment—Alpha interferon and lamivudine, a reverse transcriptase inhibitor, can reduce the inflammation associated with chronic hepatitis B but does not cure the carrier state.

Prevention—There are three main approaches: (1) vaccine that contains HBsAg as the immunogen; (2) hyperimmune serum globulins obtained from donors with high titers of HBsAb; and (3) education of chronic carriers regarding precautions.

Hepatitis C Virus

Disease—Hepatitis C; associated with hepatocellular carcinoma. HCV is the most prevalent blood-borne pathogen in the United States.

Characteristics—Enveloped virus with one piece of single-stranded, positive-polarity RNA. No polymerase in virion. HCV has multiple serotypes.

Transmission—Most transmission is via blood. Sexual transmission and transmission from mother to child probably occurs as well.

Pathogenesis—Hepatocellular injury probably caused by cytotoxic T cells. HCV replication itself does not kill cells, ie, does not cause a cytopathic effect. More than 50% of infections result in the chronic carrier state. The chronic carrier state predisposes to chronic hepatitis and to hepatocellular carcinoma.

Laboratory Diagnosis—Serologic testing detects antibody to HCV. A PCR-based assay for "viral load" can be used to evaluate whether active infection is present.

Treatment—Alpha interferon plus ribavirin mitigates chronic hepatitis but does not eradicate the carrier state.

Prevention—Posttransfusion hepatitis can be prevented by detection of antibodies in donated blood. There is no vaccine, and hyperimmune globulins are not available.

Hepatitis D Virus

Disease—Hepatitis D (hepatitis delta).

Characteristics—Defective virus that uses hepatitis B surface antigen as its protein coat. HDV can replicate only in cells already infected with HBV; ie, HBV is a helper virus for HDV. Genome is one piece of single-stranded, negative-polarity, circular RNA. No polymerase in virion. HDV has one serotype (because HBV has only one serotype).

Transmission—Transmitted by blood, sexually, and from mother to child.

Pathogenesis—Hepatocellular injury probably caused by cytotoxic T cells. Chronic hepatitis and chronic carrier state occur.

Laboratory Diagnosis—Serologic testing detects either delta antigen or antibody to delta antigen.

Treatment—Alpha interferon mitigates symptoms but does not eradicate the carrier state.

Prevention—Prevention of HBV infection by using the HBV vaccine and the HBV hyperimmune globulins will prevent HDV infection also.

Hepatitis E Virus

Member of calicivirus family. Causes outbreaks of hepatitis, primarily in developing countries. Similar to hepatitis A virus in the following ways: transmitted by fecal-oral route, no chronic carrier state, no cirrhosis, and no hepatocellular carcinoma. No antiviral therapy and no vaccine.

ARBOVIRUSES (CHAPTER 42)

All arboviruses are transmitted by arthropods (*arthropod-borne*) such as mosquitoes and ticks from the wild animal reservoir to humans.

Eastern Equine Encephalitis Virus

Member of the togavirus family. Causes encephalitis along the East Coast of the United States. Encephalitis is severe but uncommon. Transmitted to humans (and horses) by mosquitoes from small wild birds, such as sparrows. Humans and horses are "dead-end" hosts because viremia is low. There is no antiviral therapy and no vaccine for humans.

Western Equine Encephalitis Virus, St. Louis Encephalitis Virus, California Encephalitis Virus, and West Nile Virus

The transmission of these encephalitis viruses are similar, ie, they are transmitted to humans by mosquitoes from small wild birds. However, they differ in details; ie, they belong to different virus families and cause disease in different geographic areas. Please consult Chapter 42 in the text for specific information.

Yellow Fever Virus

Member of the flavivirus family. Causes yellow fever in the tropical areas of Africa and South America. "Jungle" yellow fever is transmitted from monkeys to humans by mosquitoes. "Urban" yellow fever is transmitted from human to human by *Aedes* mosquitoes, ie, humans are the reservoir in the urban form. Humans are not a "dead-end" host because viremia is high. There is no antiviral therapy. There is a live, attenuated vaccine for humans.

Dengue Virus

Member of the flavivirus family. Causes dengue fever in the Caribbean region and other tropical areas. Transmitted by *Aedes* mosquitoes from one human to another. A monkey reservoir is suspected. Second episodes may result in dengue hemorrhagic fever, a life-threatening complication. There is no antiviral therapy and no vaccine for humans.

TUMOR VIRUSES (CHAPTER 43)

Human T-Cell Lymphotropic Virus (HTLV)

Diseases—Adult T-cell leukemia/lymphoma and HTLV-associated myelopathy (also known as tropical spastic paraparesis or chronic progressive myelopathy).

Characteristics—HTLV is a member of the retrovirus family. It causes malignant transformation of CD4-positive T cells (in contrast to HIV, which kills those cells). HTLV has three structural genes common to all retroviruses, namely, *gag*, *pol*, and *env*, plus two regulatory genes, *tax* and *rex*. The Tax protein is required for malignant transformation. It activates the synthesis of IL-2 (which is T-cell growth factor) and of the IL-2 receptor. IL-2 promotes rapid T-cell growth, which predisposes to malignant transformation.

Transmission—HTLV is transmitted primarily by intravenous drug use, sexually, and by breast feeding. Transmission by donated blood has greatly decreased in the United States because donated blood that has antibodies to HTLV is discarded. HTLV infection is endemic in certain geographic areas, namely, the Caribbean region including southern Florida; eastern South America; western Africa; and southern Japan.

Pathogenesis—HTLV induces malignant transformation of CD4-positive T lymphocytes by activating IL-2 synthesis as described above. It also causes HTLV-associated myelopathy (HAM), which is a demyelinating disease of the brain and spinal cord caused either by an autoimmune cross-reaction in which the immune response against HTLV damages the neurons or by cytotoxic T cells that kill HTLV-infected neurons.

Laboratory Diagnosis—Detect anti-HTLV antibodies in the patient's serum using the ELISA test. Western blot assay is used to confirm a positive ELISA result. PCR assay can detect the presence of HTLV RNA or DNA within infected cells.

Treatment and Prevention—No specific antiviral treatment for HTLV infection and no antiviral drug will cure latent infections by HTLV. No vaccine against HTLV. Preventive measures include discarding donated blood if anti-HTLV antibodies are present, using condoms to prevent sexual transmission, and encouraging women with HTLV antibodies to refrain from breast feeding.

Human Papillomavirus

See summary in section on DNA Nonenveloped Viruses (page 495).

SLOW VIRUSES & PRIONS (CHAPTER 44)

JC Virus

Member of the papovavirus family. Causes progressive multifocal leukoencephalopathy (PML). Infection with JC virus is widespread, but PML occurs only in immunocompromised patients such as those with AIDS. Invariably fatal. No antiviral therapy and no vaccine.

Prions

Diseases—Creutzfeldt-Jakob disease (CJD), variant CJD, and kuru. These are transmissible spongiform encephalopathies. There is a hereditary form of CJD called Gerstmann-Sträussler-Scheinker (GSS) syndrome.

Characteristics—Prions are composed of protein only. They have no detectable nucleic acid and are highly resistant to UV light, formaldehyde, and heat. They are encoded by a cellular gene. The pathogenic form increases in amount by inducing conformational change in normal form. Normal conformation is alpha helix; abnormal is beta-pleated sheet. In GSS syndrome, a mutation occurs that enhances the probability of the conformational change to the beta-pleated sheet form.

Transmission—In most cases of CJD, mode of transmission is unknown. CJD has been transmitted by pituitary extracts, brain electrodes, and corneal transplants. Kuru was transmitted by ingestion or inoculation of human brain tissue. Variant CJD probably is transmitted by ingestion of cow brain tissue in undercooked food.

Pathogenesis—Aggregation of prion filaments within neurons occurs; vacuoles within neurons cause spongiform changes in brain; no inflammation or immune response occurs.

Laboratory Diagnosis—Brain biopsy shows spongiform changes. No serologic tests. Prions cannot be grown in culture.

Treatment—None.

Prevention—There is no drug or vaccine.

HUMAN IMMUNODEFICIENCY VIRUS (CHAPTER 45)

Disease—Acquired immunodeficiency syndrome (AIDS).

Characteristics—Enveloped virus with two copies (diploid) of a single-stranded, positive-polarity RNA genome. RNA-dependent DNA polymerase (reverse transcriptase) makes a DNA copy of the genome, which integrates into host cell DNA. Precursor polypeptides must be cleaved by virus-encoded protease to produce functional viral proteins. The *tat* gene encodes a protein that activates viral transcription. Antigenicity of the gp120 protein changes rapidly; therefore, there are many serotypes.

Transmission—Transfer of body fluids, eg, blood and semen. Also transplacental and perinatal transmission.

Pathogenesis—Two receptors are required for HIV to enter cells. One receptor is CD4 protein found primarily on helper T cells. HIV infects and kills helper T cells, which predisposes to opportunistic infections. Other cells bearing CD4 proteins on the surface, eg, astrocytes, are infected also. The other receptor for HIV is a chemokine receptor such as CCR5. The NEF protein is an important virulence factor. It reduces class I MHC protein synthesis, thereby reducing the ability of cytotoxic T cells to kill HIV-infected cells. Cytotoxic T cells are the main host defense against HIV.

Laboratory Diagnosis—HIV can be isolated from blood or semen, but this procedure is not routinely available. Diagnosis is usually made by detecting antibody with ELISA as screening test and Western blot as confirmatory test. Determine the "viral load," ie, the amount of HIV RNA in the plasma, using PCR-based assays. A high viral load predicts a more rapid progression to AIDS than a low viral load. PCR-based assays can also detect viral RNA in infected cells, which is useful to detect early infections before antibody is detectable.

Treatment—Nucleoside analogues, such as zidovudine (AZT), lamivudine (3TC), stavudine (d4T), didanosine (ddI), and zalcitabine (ddC), inhibit HIV replication by inhibiting reverse transcriptase. Non-nucleoside inhibitors of reverse transcriptase, such as nevirapine and efavirenz, are used also. Protease inhibitors, eg, indinavir, ritonavir, and saquinavir, prevent cleavage of precursor polypeptides. Highly active anti-retroviral therapy (HAART) consists of two nucleoside inhibitors and one protease inhibitor. Clinical improvement occurs, but the virus persists. Treatment of the opportunistic infection depends on the organism.

Prevention—Screening of blood prior to transfusion for the presence of antibody. "Safe sex," including the use of condoms. AZT with or without a protease inhibitor should be given to HIV-infected mothers and their newborns. Zidovudine (AZT), lamivudine (3TC), and a protease inhibitor should be given after a needle-stick injury. There is no vaccine.

MINOR VIRAL PATHOGENS (CHAPTER 46)

Only the more important of the minor viral pathogens are summarized in this section.

Ebola Virus

Member of the filovirus family. Causes Ebola hemorrhagic fever, which has a very high mortality rate. Animal reservoir and mode of transmission to humans are unknown. Human-to-human transmission, especially in hospital setting, is by blood and other body fluids. Diagnosis is usually a clinical one, but serologic tests are available. In electron microscope, see long "threadlike" viruses. Culturing the virus is very dangerous and should be done only in special laboratories. There is no antiviral therapy and no vaccine.

Hantavirus (Sin Nombe Virus)

Member of the bunyavirus family. Causes hantavirus pulmonary syndrome. Sin Nombre virus (SNV) is a robovirus, ie, it is *rodent-borne*. Deer mice are the reservoir, and the virus is acquired by inhalation of dried urine and feces. Diagnosis made by detecting viral RNA in lung tissue or by serologic tests. No antiviral therapy and no vaccine.

Japanese Encephalitis Virus

Member of the flavivirus family. Causes outbreaks of encephalitis in Asian countries. Transmitted to humans by mosquitoes from the reservoir hosts, birds and pigs. No antiviral therapy. An inactivated vaccine is available.

SUMMARIES OF MEDICALLY IMPORTANT FUNGI

FUNGI CAUSING CUTANEOUS & SUBCUTANEOUS MYCOSES (CHAPTER 48)

Dermatophytes (eg, *Trichophyton, Microsporum, Epidermophyton* species)

Diseases—Dermatophytoses, eg, tinea capitis, tinea cruris, and tinea pedis.

Characteristics—These fungi are molds that use keratin as a nutritional source. Not dimorphic. Habitat of most dermatophytes that cause human disease is human skin, with the exception of *Microsporum canis,* which infects dogs and cats also.

Transmission—Direct contact with skin scales.

Pathogenesis—These fungi grow only in the superficial keratinized layer of the skin. They do not invade underlying tissue. The lesions are due to the inflammatory response to the fungi. Frequency of infection is enhanced by moisture and warmth, eg, inside shoes. An important host defense is provided by the fatty acids produced by sebaceous glands. The "id" reaction is a hypersensitivity response in one skin location, eg, fingers, to the presence of the organism in another, eg, feet.

Laboratory Diagnosis—Skin scales should be examined microscopically in a KOH preparation for the presence of hyphae. The organism is identified by the appearance of its mycelium and its asexual spores on Sabouraud's agar. Serologic tests are not useful.

Skin Test—Trichophytin antigen can be used to determine the competence of a patient's cell-mediated immunity. Not used for diagnosis of tinea.

Treatment—Topical agents, such as miconazole, clotrimazole, or tolnaftate, are used. Undecylenic acid is effective against tinea pedis. Griseofulvin is the treatment of choice for tinea unguium and tinea capitis.

Prevention—Skin should be kept dry and cool.

Sporothrix schenckii

Disease—Sporotrichosis.

Characteristics—Thermally dimorphic. Mold in the soil, yeast in the body at 37°C. Habitat is soil or vegetation.

Transmission—Mold spores enter skin in puncture wounds caused by rose thorns and other sharp objects in the garden.

Pathogenesis—Local abscess or ulcer with nodules in draining lymphatics.

Laboratory Diagnosis—Cigar-shaped budding yeasts visible in pus. Culture on Sabouraud's agar shows typical morphology.

Skin Test—None.

Treatment—Itraconazole.

Prevention—Skin should be protected when gardening.

FUNGI CAUSING SYSTEMIC MYCOSES (CHAPTER 49)

Histoplasma capsulatum

Disease—Histoplasmosis.

Characteristics—Thermally dimorphic, ie, a yeast at body temperature and a mold in the soil at ambient temperature. The mold grows preferentially in soil enriched with bird droppings. Endemic in Ohio and Mississippi River valley areas.

Transmission—Inhalation of airborne asexual spores (microconidia).

Pathogenesis—Microconidia enter the lung and differentiate into yeast cells. The yeast cells are ingested by alveolar macrophages and multiply within them. An immune response is mounted, and granulomas form. Most infections are contained at this level, but suppression of cell-mediated immunity can lead to disseminated disease.

Laboratory Diagnosis—Sputum or tissue can be examined microscopically and cultured on Sabouraud's agar. Yeasts visible within macrophages. The presence of tuberculate chlamydospores in culture at 25°C is diagnostic. A rise in antibody titer is useful for diagnosis, but cross-reaction with other fungi (eg, *Coccidioides*) occurs.

Skin Test—Histoplasmin, a mycelial extract, is the antigen. Useful for epidemiologic purposes to determine the incidence of infection. A positive result indicates only that infection has occurred; it cannot be used to diagnose active disease. Because skin testing can induce antibodies, serologic tests must be done first.

Treatment—Amphotericin B for disseminated disease; itraconazole for pulmonary disease.

Prevention—No vaccine is available. Itraconazole can be used for chronic suppression in AIDS patients.

Coccidioides immitis

Disease—Coccidioidomycosis.

Characteristics—Thermally dimorphic. At 37°C in the body, it forms spherules containing endospores. At 25°C, either in the soil or on agar in the laboratory, it grows as a mold. The cells at the tip of the hyphae differentiate into asexual spores (arthrospores). Natural habitat is the soil of arid regions, eg, San Joaquin valley in California and parts of Arizona and New Mexico.

Transmission—Inhalation of airborne arthrospores.

Pathogenesis—Arthrospores differentiate into spherules in the lungs. Spherules rupture, releasing endospores that form new spherules, thereby disseminating the infection within the body. A cell-mediated immune response contains the infection in most people, but those who are immunocompromised are at high risk for disseminated disease.

Laboratory Diagnosis—Sputum or tissue should be examined microscopically for spherules and cultured on Sabouraud's agar. A rise in IgM (using precipitin test) antibodies indicates recent infection. A rising titer of IgG antibodies (using complement-fixation test) indicates dissemination; a decreasing titer indicates a response to therapy.

Skin Test—Either coccidioidin, a mycelial extract, or spherulin, an extract of spherules, is the antigen. Useful in determining whether the patient has been infected. A positive test indicates prior infection but not necessarily active disease.

Treatment—Amphotericin B or itraconazole for disseminated disease; ketoconazole for limited pulmonary disease.

Prevention—No vaccine or prophylactic drug is available.

Blastomyces dermatitidis

Disease—Blastomycosis.

Characteristics—Thermally dimorphic. Mold in the soil, yeast in the body at 37°C. The yeast form has a single, broad-based bud and a thick, refractile wall. Natural habitat is rich soil (eg, near beaver dams), especially in the upper midwestern region of the United States.

Transmission—Inhalation of airborne spores (conidia).

Pathogenesis—Inhaled conidia differentiate into yeasts, which initially cause abscesses followed by formation of granulomas. Dissemination is rare, but when it occurs, skin and bone are most commonly involved.

Laboratory Diagnosis—Sputum or skin lesions examined microscopically for yeasts with a broad-based bud. Culture on Sabouraud's agar also. Serologic tests are not useful.

Skin Test—Little value.

Treatment—Itraconazole is the drug of choice.

Prevention—No vaccine or prophylactic drug is available.

Paracoccidioides brasiliensis

Disease—Paracoccidioidomycosis.

Characteristics—Thermally dimorphic. Mold in the soil, yeast in the body at 37°C. The yeast form has multiple buds (resembles the steering wheel of a ship).

Transmission—Inhalation of airborne conidia.

Pathogenesis—Inhaled conidia differentiate to the yeast form in lungs. Can disseminate to many organs.

Laboratory Diagnosis—Yeasts with multiple buds visible in pus or tissues. Culture on Sabouraud's agar shows typical morphology.

Skin Test—Not useful.

Treatment—Itraconazole.

Prevention—No vaccine or prophylactic drug is available.

FUNGI CAUSING OPPORTUNISTIC MYCOSES (CHAPTER 50)

Candida albicans

Diseases—Thrush, disseminated candidiasis, and chronic mucocutaneous candidiasis.

Characteristics—*Candida albicans* is a yeast when part of the normal flora of mucous membranes but forms pseudohyphae and hyphae when it invades tissue. The yeast form produces germ tubes when incubated in serum at 37°C. Not thermally dimorphic.

Transmission—Part of the normal flora of skin, mucous membranes, and GI tract. No person-to-person transmission.

Pathogenesis—Opportunistic pathogen. Predisposing factors include reduced cell-mediated immunity, altered skin and mucous membrane, suppression of normal flora, and presence of foreign bodies. Thrush is most common in infants, immunosuppressed patients, and persons receiving antibiotic therapy. Skin lesions occur frequently on moisture-damaged skin. Disseminated infections, such as endocarditis and endophthalmitis, occur in immunosuppressed patients and intravenous drug users. Chronic mucocutaneous candidiasis occurs in children with a T-cell defect in immunity to *Candida*.

Laboratory Diagnosis—Microscopic examination of tissue reveals yeasts and pseudohyphae. If only yeasts are found, colonization is suggested. The yeast is gram-positive. Forms colonies of yeasts on Sabouraud's agar. Germ tube formation and production of chlamydospores distinguish *C. albicans* from virtually all other species of *Candida*. Serologic tests not useful.

Skin Test—Used to determine competency of cell-mediated immunity rather than to diagnose candidal disease.

Treatment—Skin and mucous membrane disease can be treated with oral or topical antifungal agents such as nystatin or miconazole. Disseminated disease requires amphotericin B. Chronic mucocutaneous candidiasis is treatable with ketoconazole.

Prevention—Predisposing factors should be reduced or eliminated. Oral thrush can be prevented by using clotrimazole troches or nystatin "swish and swallow." There is no vaccine.

Cryptococcus neoformans

Disease—Cryptococcosis, especially cryptococcal meningitis.

Characteristics—Heavily encapsulated yeast. Not dimorphic. Habitat is soil, especially where enriched by pigeon droppings.

Transmission—Inhalation of airborne yeast cells.

Pathogenesis—Organisms cause influenzalike syndrome or pneumonia. They spread via the bloodstream to the meninges. Reduced cell-mediated immunity predisposes to severe disease, but some cases of cryptococcal meningitis occur in immunocompetent people.

Laboratory Diagnosis—Visualization of the encapsulated yeast in India ink preparations of spinal fluid. Culture of sputum or spinal fluid on Sabouraud's agar produces colonies of yeasts. Latex agglutination test detects polysaccharide capsular antigen in spinal fluid.

Skin Test—Not available.

Treatment—Amphotericin B plus flucytosine for meningitis.

Prevention—Cryptococcal meningitis can be prevented in AIDS patients by using oral fluconazole. There is no vaccine.

Aspergillus fumigatus

Diseases—Invasive aspergillosis is the major disease. Allergic bronchopulmonary aspergillosis and aspergilloma (fungus ball) are important also.

Characteristics—Mold with septate hyphae that branch at a V-shaped angle (low-angle branching). Not dimorphic. Habitat is the soil.

Transmission—Inhalation of airborne spores (conidia).

Pathogenesis—Opportunistic pathogen. In immunocompromised patients, invasive disease occurs. The organism invades blood vessels, causing thrombosis and infarction. A person with a lung cavity, eg, from tuberculosis, may develop a "fungal ball" (aspergilloma). An allergic person, eg, one with asthma, can develop allergic bronchopulmonary aspergillosis mediated by IgE antibody.

Laboratory Diagnosis—Septate hyphae invading tissue are visible microscopically. Invasion distinguishes disease from colonization. Forms characteristic mycelium when cultured on Sabouraud's agar. See chains of conidia radiating from a central stalk. Serologic tests detect IgG precipitins in patients with aspergillomas and IgE antibodies in patients with allergic bronchopulmonary aspergillosis.

Skin Test—None available.

Treatment—Amphotericin B for invasive aspergillosis. Some lesions (eg, fungus balls) can be surgically removed. Steroid therapy is recommended for allergic bronchopulmonary aspergillosis.

Prevention—No vaccine or prophylactic drug is available.

Mucor & Rhizopus Species

Disease—Mucormycosis.

Characteristics—Molds with nonseptate hyphae that typically branch at a 90-degree angle (wide-angle branching). Not dimorphic. Habitat is the soil.

Transmission—Inhalation of airborne spores.

Pathogenesis—Opportunistic pathogens. They cause disease primarily in ketoacidotic diabetic and leukemic patients. The sinuses and surrounding tissue are typically involved. Hyphae invade the mucosa and progress into underlying tissue and vessels, leading to necrosis and infarction.

Laboratory Diagnosis—Microscopic examination of tissue for the presence of non-septate hyphae that branch at wide angles. Forms characteristic mycelium when cultured on Sabouraud's agar. See spores contained within a sac called a sporangium. Serologic tests are not available.

Skin Test—None.

Treatment—Amphotericin B and surgical debridement.

Prevention—No vaccine or prophylactic drug is available. Control of underlying disease, eg, diabetes, tends to prevent mucormycosis.

Pneumocystis carinii

Although there is molecular evidence that *Pneumocystis carinii* is a fungus, it is described in this book in the section on protozoa that cause blood and tissue infections (see page 507).

SUMMARIES OF MEDICALLY IMPORTANT PARASITES

PROTOZOA CAUSING INTESTINAL & UROGENITAL INFECTIONS (CHAPTER 51)

Entamoeba histolytica

Diseases—Amebic dysentery and liver abscess.

Characteristics—Intestinal protozoan. Motile ameba (trophozoite); forms cysts with four nuclei. Life cycle: Humans ingest cysts, which form trophozoites in small intestine. Trophozoites pass to the colon and multiply. Cysts form in the colon, which then pass in the feces.

Transmission and Epidemiology—Fecal-oral transmission of cysts. Human reservoir. Occurs worldwide, especially in tropics.

Pathogenesis—Trophozoites invade colon epithelium and produce flask-shaped ulcer. Can spread to liver and cause amebic abscess.

Laboratory Diagnosis—Trophozoites or cysts visible in stool. Serologic testing (indirect hemagglutination test) positive with invasive (eg, liver) disease.

Treatment—Metronidazole or tinidazole for symptomatic disease. Iodoquinol or paromomycin for asymptomatic cyst carriers.

Prevention—Proper disposal of human waste. Water purification. Hand washing.

Giardia lamblia

Disease—Giardiasis, especially diarrhea.

Characteristics—Intestinal protozoan. Pear-shaped, flagellated trophozoite, forms cyst with four nuclei. Life cycle: Humans ingest cysts, which form trophozoites in duodenum. Trophozoites encyst and are passed in feces.

Transmission and Epidemiology—Fecal-oral transmission of cysts. Human and animal reservoir. Occurs worldwide.

Pathogenesis—Trophozoites attach to wall but do not invade. They interfere with absorption of fat and protein.

Laboratory Diagnosis—Trophozoites or cysts visible in stool. String test used if necessary.

Treatment—Metronidazole.

Prevention—Water purification. Hand washing.

Cryptosporidium parvum

Disease—Cryptosporidiosis, especially diarrhea.

Characteristics—Intestinal protozoan. Life cycle: Oocysts release sporozoites; they form trophozoites. After schizonts and merozoites form, microgametes and macrogametes are produced; they unite to form a zygote and then an oocyst.

Transmission and Epidemiology—Fecal-oral transmission of cysts. Human and animal reservoir. Occurs worldwide.

Pathogenesis—Trophozoites attach to wall of small intestine but do not invade.

Laboratory Diagnosis—Oocysts visible in stool with acid-fast stain.

Treatment—No effective therapy; however, paromomycin may reduce symptoms.

Prevention—None.

Trichomonas vaginalis

Disease—Trichomoniasis.

Characteristics—Urogenital protozoan. Pear-shaped, flagellated trophozoites. No cysts or other forms.

Transmission and Epidemiology—Transmitted sexually. Human reservoir. Occurs worldwide.

Pathogenesis—Trophozoites attach to wall of vagina and cause inflammation and discharge.

Laboratory Diagnosis—Trophozoites visible in secretions.

Treatment—Metronidazole for both sexual partners.

Prevention—Condoms limit transmission.

PROTOZOA CAUSING BLOOD & TISSUE INFECTIONS (CHAPTER 52)

Plasmodium species (P. vivax, P. ovale, P. malariae, & P. falciparum)

Disease—Malaria.

Characteristics—Protozoan that infects red blood cells and tissue, eg, liver, kidney, and brain. Life cycle: Sexual cycle consists of gametogony (production of gametes) in humans and sporogony (production of sporozoites) in mosquitoes; asexual cycle (schizogony) occurs in humans. Sporozoites in saliva of female *Anopheles* mosquito enter the human bloodstream and rapidly invade hepatocytes (exoerythrocytic phase). There they multiply and form merozoites (*Plasmodium vivax* and *Plasmodium ovale* also form hypnozoites, a latent form). Merozoites leave the hepatocytes and infect red cells (erythrocytic phase). There they form schizonts that release more merozoites, which infect other red cells in a synchronous pattern (3 days for *Plasmodium malariae*; 2 days for the others). Some merozoites become male and female gametocytes, which, when ingested by female *Anopheles*, release male and female gametes. These unite to produce a zygote, which forms an oocyst containing many sporozoites. These are released and migrate to salivary glands.

Transmission and Epidemiology—Transmitted by female *Anopheles* mosquitoes. Occurs primarily in the tropical areas of Asia, Africa, and Latin America.

Pathogenesis—Merozoites destroy red cells, resulting in anemia. Cyclic fever pattern is due to periodic release of merozoites. *Plasmodium falciparum* can infect red cells of all ages and cause aggregates of red cells that occlude capillaries. This can cause tissue anoxia, especially in the brain (cerebral malaria) and the kidney (blackwater fever). Hypnozoites can cause relapses.

Laboratory Diagnosis—Organisms visible in blood smear. Thick smear is used to detect presence of organism and thin smear to speciate.

Treatment—Chloroquine if sensitive. For chloroquine-resistant *P. falciparum*, use mefloquine or quinine plus doxycycline. Primaquine for hypnozoites of *P. vivax* and *P. ovale*. In severe cases, use parenteral quinidine or quinine.

Prevention—Chloroquine in areas where organisms are sensitive. For those in areas with a high risk of chloroquine resistance, mefloquine or doxycycline. Primaquine to prevent relapses. Protection from bites. Control mosquitoes by using insecticides and by draining water from breeding areas.

Toxoplasma gondii

Disease—Toxoplasmosis, including congenital toxoplasmosis.

Characteristics—Tissue protozoan. Life cycle: Cysts in cat feces or in meat are ingested by humans and differentiate in the gut into forms that invade the gut wall. They infect macrophages and form trophozoites (tachyzoites) that multiply rapidly, kill cells, and infect other cells. Cysts containing bradyzoites form later. Cat ingests cysts in raw meat, and bradyzoites excyst, multiply, and form male and female gametocytes. These fuse to form oocysts in cat gut, which are excreted in cat feces.

Transmission and Epidemiology—Transmitted by ingestion of cysts in raw meat and in food contaminated with cat feces. Also by passage of trophozoites transplacentally from mother to fetus. Infection of fetus occurs only when mother is infected during pregnancy and when she is infected for the first time, ie, she has no protective antibody. Cat is definitive host; humans and other mammals are intermediate hosts. Occurs worldwide.

Pathogenesis—Trophozoites infect many organs, especially brain, eyes, and liver. Cysts persist in tissue, enlarge, and cause symptoms. Severe disease in patients with deficient cell-mediated immunity, eg, encephalitis in AIDS patients.

Laboratory Diagnosis—Serologic tests for IgM and IgG antibodies are usually used. Trophozoites or cysts visible in tissue.

Treatment—Sulfadiazine plus pyrimethamine for congenital or disseminated disease.

Prevention—Meat should be cooked. Pregnant women should not handle cats, cat litter boxes, or raw meat.

Pneumocystis carinii

Disease—Pneumonia.

Characteristics—Respiratory pathogen. Reclassified in 1988 as a yeast based on molecular evidence but medically has several attributes of a protozoan. Life cycle: uncertain.

Transmission and Epidemiology—Transmitted by inhalation. Humans are reservoir. Occurs worldwide. Most infections asymptomatic.

Pathogenesis—Organisms in alveoli cause inflammation. Immunosuppression predisposes to disease.

Laboratory Diagnosis—Organisms visible in silver stain of lung tissue or lavage fluid.

Treatment—Trimethoprim-sulfamethoxazole, pentamidine.

Prevention—Trimethoprim-sulfamethoxazole or aerosolized pentamidine in immunosuppressed individuals.

Trypanosoma cruzi

Disease—Chagas' disease.

Characteristics—Blood and tissue protozoan. Life cycle: Trypomastigotes in blood of reservoir host are ingested by reduviid bug and form epimastigotes and then trypomastigotes in the gut. When the bug bites, it defecates and feces containing trypomastigotes contaminate the wound. Organisms enter the blood and form amastigotes within cells; these then become trypomastigotes.

Transmission and Epidemiology—Transmitted by reduviid bugs. Humans and many animals are reservoirs. Occurs in rural Latin America.

Pathogenesis—Amastigotes kill cells, especially cardiac muscle leading to myocarditis. Also neuronal damage leading to megacolon and megaesophagus.

Laboratory Diagnosis—Trypomastigotes visible in blood, but bone marrow biopsy, culture in vitro, xenodiagnosis, or serologic tests may be required.

Treatment—Nifurtimox or benznidazole for acute disease. No effective drug for chronic disease.

Prevention—Protection from bite. Insect control.

Trypanosoma gambiense & Trypanosoma rhodesiense

Disease—Sleeping sickness (African trypanosomiasis).

Characteristics—Blood and tissue protozoan. Life cycle: Trypomastigotes in blood of human or animal reservoir are ingested by tsetse fly. They differentiate in the gut to form epimastigotes and then metacyclic trypomastigotes in salivary glands. When fly bites, trypomastigotes enter the blood. Repeated variation of surface antigen occurs, which allows the organism to evade the immune response.

Transmission and Epidemiology—Transmitted by tsetse flies. *Trypanosoma gambiense* has a human reservoir and occurs primarily in west Africa. *Trypanosoma rhodesiense* has an animal reservoir (especially wild antelope) and occurs primarily in east Africa.

Pathogenesis—Trypomastigotes infect brain, causing encephalitis.

Laboratory Diagnosis—Trypomastigotes visible in blood in early stages and in cerebrospinal fluid in late stages. Serologic tests useful.

Treatment—Suramin in early disease. Suramin plus melarsoprol if central nervous system symptoms exist.

Prevention—Protection from bite. Insect control.

Leishmania donovani

Disease—Kala-azar (visceral leishmaniasis).

Characteristics—Blood and tissue protozoan. Life cycle: Human macrophages containing amastigotes are ingested by sandfly. Amastigotes differentiate in fly gut to promastigotes, which migrate to pharynx. When fly bites, promastigotes enter blood macrophages and form amastigotes. These can infect other reticuloendothelial cells, especially in spleen and liver.

Transmission and Epidemiology—Transmitted by sandflies (*Phlebotomus* or *Lutzomyia*). Animal reservoir (chiefly dogs, small carnivores, and rodents) in Africa, Middle East, and parts of China. Human reservoir in India.

Pathogenesis—Amastigotes kill reticuloendothelial cells, especially in liver, spleen, and bone marrow.

Laboratory Diagnosis—Amastigotes visible in bone marrow smear. Serologic tests useful. Skin test indicates prior infection.

Treatment—Sodium stibogluconate.

Prevention—Protection from bite. Insect control.

Leishmania tropica, Leishmania mexicana, and Leishmania braziliensis

L. tropica and *L. mexicana* cause cutaneous leishmaniasis; *L. braziliensis* causes mucocutaneous leishmaniasis. *L. tropica* occurs primarily in the Middle East, Asia, and India, whereas *L. mexicana* and *L. braziliensis* occur in Central and South America. All are transmitted by sandflies. Forest rodents are the main reservoir. Diagnosis is made by observing amastigotes in smear of skin lesion. Treatment is sodium stibogluconate. No specific means of prevention.

MINOR PROTOZOAN PATHOGENS (CHAPTER 53)

Acanthamoeba castellanii

Ameba that causes meningoencephalitis. Also causes keratitis in contact lens wearers. Life cycle includes trophozoite and cyst stages. Found in freshwater lakes and soil. Transmitted via trauma to skin or eyes. Disease occurs primarily in immunocompromised patients. Diagnosis made by finding ameba in spinal fluid. Treatment with pentamidine, ketoconazole, or flucytosine may be effective. No specific means of prevention.

Naegleria fowleri

Ameba that causes meningoencephalitis. Found in freshwater lakes and soil. Life cycle includes trophozoite and cyst stages. Transmitted while swimming or diving in contaminated lake. Disease occurs primarily in healthy individuals. Diagnosis made by finding ameba in spinal fluid. Treatment with amphotericin B may be effective. No specific means of prevention.

Babesia microti

Sporozoa that causes babesiosis. Endemic in rodents along the northeast coast of the United States. Transmitted by *Ixodes* ticks to humans. Infects red blood cells, causing them to lyse, and anemia results. Asplenic patients have severe disease. Diagnosis is made by observing organism in red blood cells. Treat with combination of quinine and clindamycin. No specific means of prevention.

Balantidium coli

Only ciliated protozoan to cause human disease. Causes diarrhea. Acquired by fecal-oral transmission from domestic animals, especially pigs. Diagnosis is made by finding trophozoites or cysts in feces. Treat with tetracycline. No specific means of prevention.

Cyclospora cayetanensis

Coccidian protozoan. Causes diarrhea, especially in immunocompromised (eg, AIDS) patients. Acquired by fecal-oral transmission. No evidence for animal reservoir. Diagnosis is made by finding oocytes in acid-fast stain of feces. Treat with trimethoprim-sulfamethoxazole. No specific means of prevention.

Isospora belli

Coccidian protozoan. Causes diarrhea, especially in immunocompromised (eg, AIDS) patients. Acquired by fecal-oral transmission from either human or animal sources. Diagnosis is made by finding oocytes in acid-fast stain of feces. Treat with trimethoprim-sulfamethoxazole. No specific means of prevention.

Microsporidia

Group of spore-forming, obligate intracellular protozoa. Two important species are *Enterocytozoon bieneusi* and *Septata intestinalis*. Cause diarrhea, especially in immunocompromised, eg, AIDS, patients. Acquired by fecal-oral transmission from human sources. Diagnosis is made by finding spores within cells in feces or intestinal biopsy specimens. Treat with albendazole. No specific means of prevention.

CESTODES (CHAPTER 54)

Diphyllobothrium latum

Disease—Diphyllobothriasis.

Characteristics—Cestode (fish tapeworm). Scolex has two elongated sucking grooves; no circular suckers or hooks. Gravid uterus forms a rosette. Oval eggs have an operculum at one end. Life cycle: Humans ingest undercooked fish containing sparganum larvae. Larvae attach to gut wall and become adults containing gravid proglottids. Eggs are passed in feces. In fresh water, eggs hatch and the embryos are eaten by copepods. When these are eaten by freshwater fish, larvae form in the fish muscle.

Transmission and Epidemiology—Transmitted by eating raw or undercooked freshwater fish. Humans are definitive hosts; copepods are the first and fish the second intermediate hosts, respectively. Occurs worldwide but endemic in Scandinavia, Japan, and north-central United States.

Pathogenesis—Tapeworm in gut causes little damage.

Laboratory Diagnosis—Eggs visible in stool.

Treatment—Praziquantel.

Prevention—Adequate cooking of fish. Proper disposal of human waste.

Echinococcus granulosus

Disease—Hydatid cyst disease.

Characteristics—Cestode (dog tapeworm). Scolex has four suckers and a double circle of hooks. Adult worm has only three proglottids. Life cycle: Dogs are infected when they ingest the entrails of sheep, eg, liver, containing hydatid cysts. The adult worms develop in the gut, and eggs are passed in the feces. Eggs are ingested by sheep (and humans) and hatch hexacanth larvae in the gut that migrate in the blood to various organs, especially the liver and brain. Larvae form large, unilocular hydatid cysts containing many protoscoleces and daughter cysts.

Transmission and Epidemiology—Transmitted by ingestion of eggs in food contaminated with dog feces. Dogs are main definitive hosts; sheep are intermediate hosts; humans are dead-end hosts. Endemic in sheep-raising areas, eg, Mediterranean, Middle East, some western states of the United States.

Pathogenesis—Hydatid cyst is a space-occupying lesion. Also, if cyst ruptures, antigens in fluid can cause anaphylaxis.

Laboratory Diagnosis—Serologic tests, eg, indirect hemagglutination. Pathologic examination of excised cyst.

Treatment—Albendazole or surgical removal of cyst.

Prevention—Sheep entrails should not be fed to dogs.

Taenia saginata

Disease—Taeniasis.

Characteristics—Cestode (beef tapeworm). Scolex has four suckers but no hooks. Gravid proglottids have 15–20 uterine branches. Life cycle: Humans ingest undercooked beef containing cysticerci. Larvae attach to gut wall and become adult worms with gravid proglottids. Terminal proglottids detach, pass in feces, and are eaten by cattle. In the gut, oncosphere embryos hatch, burrow into blood vessels, and migrate to skeletal muscles, where they develop into cysticerci.

Transmission and Epidemiology—Transmitted by eating raw or undercooked beef. Humans are definitive hosts; cattle are intermediate hosts. Occurs worldwide but endemic in areas of Asia, Latin America, and eastern Europe.

Pathogenesis—Tapeworm in gut causes little damage. In contrast to *Taenia solium,* cysticercosis does not occur.

Laboratory Diagnosis—Gravid proglottids visible in stool. Eggs seen less frequently.

Treatment—Praziquantel.

Prevention—Adequate cooking of beef. Proper disposal of human waste.

Taenia solium

Diseases—Taeniasis and cysticercosis.

Characteristics—Cestode (pork tapeworm). Scolex has four suckers and a circle of hooks. Gravid proglottids have 5–10 uterine branches. Life cycle: Humans ingest undercooked pork containing cysticerci. Larvae attach to gut wall and develop into adult worms with gravid proglottids. Terminal proglottids detach, pass in feces, and are eaten by pigs. In gut, oncosphere (hexacanth) embryos burrow into blood vessels and migrate to skeletal muscle, where they develop into cysticerci. If humans eat *T. solium* eggs in food contaminated with human feces, the oncospheres burrow into blood vessels and disseminate to organs (eg, brain, eyes), where they encyst to form cysticerci.

Transmission and Epidemiology—Taeniasis acquired by eating raw or undercooked pork. Cysticercosis acquired only by ingesting eggs in fecally contaminated food or water. Humans are definitive hosts; pigs or humans are intermediate hosts. Occurs worldwide but endemic in areas of Asia, Latin America, and southern Europe.

Pathogenesis—Tapeworm in gut causes little damage. Cysticerci can expand and cause symptoms of mass lesions, especially in brain.

Laboratory Diagnosis—Gravid proglottids visible in stool. Eggs seen less frequently.

Treatment—Praziquantel for intestinal worms and for cerebral cysticercosis.

Prevention—Adequate cooking of pork. Proper disposal of human waste.

Hymenolepsis nana

H. nana infection is the most common tapeworm in the United States. Infection is usually asymptomatic. It is endemic in the southeastern states, mostly in children. It is called the dwarf tapeworm because of its small size. It is also different from other tapeworms because the eggs are directly infectious for humans without the need for an intermediate animal host. Diagnosis is made by finding eggs in feces. Treat with praziquantel. No specific means of prevention.

TREMATODES (CHAPTER 55)

Schistosoma (S. mansoni, S. japonicum, & S. haematobium)

Disease—Schistosomiasis.

Characteristics—Trematode (blood fluke). Adults exist as two sexes but are attached to each other. Eggs are distinguished by spines: *Schistosoma mansoni* has large lateral spine; *Schistosoma japonicum* has small lateral spine; *Schistosoma haematobium* has terminal spine. Life cycle: Humans are infected by cercariae penetrating skin. Cercariae form larvae that penetrate blood vessels and are carried to the liver, where they become adults. The flukes migrate retrograde in the portal vein to reach the mesenteric venules (*S. mansoni* and *S. japonicum*) or urinary bladder venules (*S. haematobium*). Eggs penetrate the gut or bladder wall, are excreted, and hatch in fresh water. The ciliated larvae (miracidia) penetrate snails and multiply through generations to produce many free-swimming cercariae.

Transmission and Epidemiology—Transmitted by penetration of skin by cercariae. Humans are definitive hosts; snails are intermediate hosts. Endemic in tropical areas: *S. mansoni* in Africa and Latin America, *S. haematobium* in Africa and Middle East, *S. japonicum* in Asia.

Pathogenesis—Eggs in tissue induce inflammation, granulomas, fibrosis, and obstruction, especially in liver and spleen. *S. mansoni* damages the colon (inferior mesenteric venules), *S. japonicum* damages the small intestine (superior mesenteric venules), and *S. haematobium* damages the bladder. Bladder damage predisposes to carcinoma.

Laboratory Diagnosis—Eggs visible in feces or urine. Eosinophilia occurs.

Treatment—Praziquantel.

Prevention—Proper disposal of human waste. Swimming in endemic areas should be avoided.

Clonorchis sinensis

Disease—Clonorchiasis.

Characteristics—Trematode (liver fluke). Life cycle: Humans ingest undercooked fish containing encysted larvae (metacercariae). In duodenum, immature flukes enter biliary duct, become adults, and release eggs that are passed in feces. Eggs are eaten by snails; the eggs hatch and form miracidia. These multiply through generations (rediae) and then produce many free-swimming cercariae, which encyst under scales of fish and are eaten by humans.

Transmission and Epidemiology—Transmitted by eating raw or undercooked freshwater fish. Humans are definitive hosts; snails and fish are first and second intermediate hosts, respectively. Endemic in Asia.

Pathogenesis—Inflammation of biliary tract.

Laboratory Diagnosis—Eggs visible in feces.

Treatment—Praziquantel.

Prevention—Adequate cooking of fish. Proper disposal of human waste.

Paragonimus westermani

Disease—Paragonimiasis.

Characteristics—Trematode (lung fluke). Life cycle: Humans ingest undercooked freshwater crab meat containing encysted larvae (metacercariae). In gut, immature flukes enter peritoneal cavity, burrow through diaphragm into lung parenchyma, and become adults. Eggs enter bronchioles and are coughed up or swallowed. In fresh water, eggs hatch, releasing miracidia that enter snails, multiply through generations (rediae), and then form many cercariae that infect and encyst in crabs.

Transmission and Epidemiology—Transmitted by eating raw or undercooked crab meat. Humans are definitive hosts; snails and crabs are first and second intermediate hosts, respectively. Endemic in Asia and India.

Pathogenesis—Inflammation and secondary bacterial infection of lung.

Laboratory Diagnosis—Eggs visible in sputum or feces.

Treatment—Praziquantel.

Prevention—Adequate cooking of crabs. Proper disposal of human waste.

NEMATODES (CHAPTER 56)

1. Intestinal Infection

Ancylostoma duodenale & Necator americanus

Disease—Hookworm.

Characteristics—Intestinal nematode. Life cycle: Larvae penetrate skin, enter the blood, and migrate to the lungs. They enter alveoli, pass up the trachea, then are swallowed. They become adults in small intestine and attach to walls via teeth (*Ancylostoma*) or cutting plates (*Necator*). Eggs are passed in feces and form noninfectious rhabditiform larvae and then infectious filariform larvae.

Transmission and Epidemiology—Filariform larvae in soil penetrate skin of feet. Humans are the only hosts. Endemic in the tropics.

Pathogenesis—Anemia due to blood loss from GI tract.

Laboratory Diagnosis—Eggs visible in feces. Eosinophilia occurs.

Treatment—Mebendazole or pyrantel pamoate.

Prevention—Use of footwear. Proper disposal of human waste.

Ascaris lumbricoides

Disease—Ascariasis.

Characteristics—Intestinal nematode. Life cycle: Humans ingest eggs, which form larvae in gut. Larvae migrate through the blood to the lungs, where they enter the alveoli, pass up the trachea, and are swallowed. In the gut, they become adults and lay eggs that are passed in the feces. They embryonate, ie, become infective in soil.

Transmission and Epidemiology—Transmitted by food contaminated with soil containing eggs. Humans are the only hosts. Endemic in the tropics.

Pathogenesis—Larvae in lung can cause pneumonia. Heavy worm burden can cause intestinal obstruction or malnutrition.

Laboratory Diagnosis—Eggs visible in feces. Eosinophilia occurs.

Treatment—Mebendazole or pyrantel pamoate.

Prevention—Proper disposal of human waste.

Enterobius vermicularis

Disease—Pinworm infection.

Characteristics—Intestinal nematode. Life cycle: Humans ingest eggs, which develop into adults in gut. At night, females migrate from the anus and lay many eggs on skin and in environment. Embryo within egg becomes an infective larva within 4–6 hours. Reinfection is common.

Transmission and Epidemiology—Transmitted by ingesting eggs. Humans are the only hosts. Occurs worldwide.

Pathogenesis—Worms and eggs cause perianal pruritus.

Laboratory Diagnosis—Eggs visible by "Scotch tape" technique. Adult worms found in diapers.

Treatment—Mebendazole or pyrantel pamoate.

Prevention—None.

Strongyloides stercoralis

Disease—Strongyloidiasis.

Characteristics—Intestinal nematode. Life cycle: Larvae penetrate skin, enter the blood, and migrate to the lungs. They move into alveoli and up the trachea and are swallowed. They become adults and enter the mucosa, where females produce eggs that hatch in the colon into noninfectious, rhabditiform larvae that are usually passed in feces. Occasionally, rhabditiform larvae molt in the gut to form infectious, filariform larvae that can enter the blood and migrate to the lung (autoinfection). The noninfectious larvae passed in feces form infectious filariform larvae in the soil. These larvae can either penetrate the skin or form adults. Adults in soil can undergo several entire life cycles there. This free-living cycle can be interrupted when filariform larvae contact the skin.

Transmission and Epidemiology—Filariform larvae in soil penetrate skin. Endemic in the tropics.

Pathogenesis—Little effect in immunocompetent persons. In immunocompromised persons, massive superinfection can occur accompanied by secondary bacterial infections.

Laboratory Diagnosis—Larvae visible in stool. Eosinophilia occurs.

Treatment—Ivermectin is the drug of choice. Thiabendazole is an alternative.

Prevention—Proper disposal of human waste.

Trichinella spiralis

Disease—Trichinosis.

Characteristics—Intestinal nematode that encysts in tissue. Life cycle: Humans ingest undercooked meat containing encysted larvae, which mature into adults in small intestine. Female worms release larvae that enter blood and migrate to skeletal muscle or brain, where they encyst.

Transmission and Epidemiology—Transmitted by ingestion of raw or undercooked meat, usually pork. Reservoir hosts are primarily pigs and rats. Humans are dead-end hosts. Occurs worldwide but endemic in eastern Europe and west Africa.

Pathogenesis—Larvae encyst within striated muscle cells called "nurse cells," causing inflammation of muscle.

Laboratory Diagnosis—Encysted larvae visible in muscle biopsy. Eosinophilia occurs. Serologic tests positive.

Treatment—Thiabendazole effective early against adult worms. For severe symptoms, steroids plus mebendazole can be tried.

Prevention—Adequate cooking of pork.

Trichuris trichiura

Disease—Whipworm infection.

Characteristics—Intestinal nematode. Life cycle: Humans ingest eggs, which develop into adults in gut. Eggs are passed in feces into soil, where they embryonate, ie, become infectious.

Transmission and Epidemiology—Transmitted by food or water contaminated with soil containing eggs. Humans are the only hosts. Occurs worldwide, especially in the tropics.

Pathogenesis—Worm in gut usually causes little damage.

Laboratory Diagnosis—Eggs visible in feces.

Treatment—Mebendazole.

Prevention—Proper disposal of human waste.

2. Tissue Infection

Dracunculus medinensis

Disease—Dracunculiasis.

Characteristics—Tissue nematode. Life cycle: Humans ingest copepods containing infective larvae in drinking water. Larvae are released in gut, migrate to body cavity, mature, and mate. Fertilized female migrates to subcutaneous tissue and forms a papule, which ulcerates. Motile larvae are released into water, where they are eaten by copepods and form infective larvae.

Transmission and Epidemiology—Transmitted by copepods in drinking water. Humans are major definitive hosts. Many domestic animals are reservoir hosts. Endemic in tropical Africa, Middle East, and India.

Pathogenesis—Adult worms in skin cause inflammation and ulceration.

Laboratory Diagnosis—Not useful.

Treatment—Thiabendazole or metronidazole. Extraction of worm from skin ulcer.

Prevention—Purification of drinking water.

Loa loa

Disease—Loiasis.

Characteristics—Tissue nematode. Life cycle: Bite of deer fly (mango fly) deposits infective larvae, which crawl into the skin and develop into adults that migrate subcutaneously. Females produce microfilariae, which enter the blood. These are ingested by deer flies, in which the infective larvae are formed.

Transmission and Epidemiology—Transmitted by deer flies. Humans are the only definitive hosts. No animal reservoir. Endemic in central and west Africa.

Pathogenesis—Hypersensitivity to adult worms causes "swelling" in skin. Adult worm seen crawling across conjunctivas.

Laboratory Diagnosis—Microfilariae visible on blood smear.

Treatment—Diethylcarbamazine.

Prevention—Deer fly control.

Onchocerca volvulus

Disease—Onchocerciasis (river blindness).

Characteristics—Tissue nematodes. Life cycle: Bite of female blackfly deposits larvae in subcutaneous tissue, where they mature into adult worms within skin nodules. Females produce microfilariae, which migrate in interstitial fluids and are ingested by blackflies, in which the infective larvae are formed.

Transmission and Epidemiology—Transmitted by female blackflies. Humans are the only definitive hosts. No animal reservoir. Endemic along rivers of tropical Africa and Central America.

Pathogenesis—Microfilariae in eye ultimately can cause blindness ("river blindness"). Adult worms induce inflammatory nodules in skin. See scaly dermatitis called "lizard skin." Also loss of subcutaneous tissue called "hanging groin."

Laboratory Diagnosis—Microfilariae visible in skin biopsy, not in blood.

Treatment—Ivermectin affects microfilariae, not adult worms. Suramin for adult worms.

Prevention—Blackfly control and ivermectin.

Wuchereria bancrofti

Disease—Filariasis.

Characteristics—Tissue nematodes. Life cycle: Bite of female mosquito deposits infective larvae that penetrate bite wound, form adults, and produce microfilariae. These circulate in the blood, chiefly at night, and are ingested by mosquitoes, in which the infective larvae are formed.

Transmission and Epidemiology—Transmitted by female mosquitoes of several genera, especially *Anopheles* and *Culex,* depending on geography. Humans are the only definitive hosts. Endemic in many tropical areas.

Pathogenesis—Adult worms cause inflammation that blocks lymphatic vessels (elephantiasis). Chronic, repeated infection required for symptoms to occur.

Laboratory Diagnosis—Microfilariae visible on blood smear.

Treatment—Diethylcarbamazine affects microfilariae. No treatment for adult worms.

Prevention—Mosquito control.

3. Nematodes Whose Larvae Cause Disease

Toxocara canis

Disease—Visceral larva migrans.

Characteristics—Nematode larvae cause disease. Life cycle in humans: *Toxocara* eggs are passed in dog feces and ingested by humans. They hatch into larvae in small intestine; larvae enter the blood and migrate to organs, especially liver, brain, and eyes, where they are trapped and die.

Transmission and Epidemiology—Transmitted by ingestion of eggs in food or water contaminated with dog feces. Dogs are definitive hosts. Humans are dead-end hosts.

Pathogenesis—Granulomas form around dead larvae. Granulomas in the retina can cause blindness.

Laboratory Diagnosis—Larvae visible in tissue. Serologic tests useful.

Treatment—Albendazole or mebendazole.

Prevention—Dogs should be dewormed.

Ancylostoma caninum & Ancylostoma braziliense

The filariform larvae of *A. caninum* (dog hookworm) and *A. braziliense* (cat hookworm) cause cutaneous larva migrans. The larvae in the soil burrow through the skin, then migrate within the subcutaneous tissue, causing a pruritic rash called "creeping eruption." These organisms cannot complete their life cycle in humans. The diagnosis is made clinically. Thiabendazole is effective.

Anisakis simplex

The larvae of *A. simplex* cause anisakiasis. They are ingested in raw seafood, such as sashimi and sushi, and migrate into the submucosa of the intestinal tract. Acute infection resembles appendicitis. Diagnosis is not dependent on the clinical laboratory. There is no effective drug therapy. Prevention consists of not eating raw fish.

PART IX
Clinical Cases

These brief clinical case vignettes are typical presentations of common infectious diseases. Learning the most likely causative organisms of these classic cases will help you answer the USMLE questions and improve your diagnostic skills. These cases are presented in random order similar to the way they are on the USMLE. The important features of the case are written in **boldface**.

CASE 1

A 22-year-old woman has a severe sore throat. Findings on physical exam include an inflamed throat, swollen cervical lymph nodes, and an enlarged spleen. **Her heterophile agglutinin test (Monospot test) is positive.**

DIAGNOSIS: Infectious mononucleosis caused by Epstein-Barr virus. Other viruses and bacteria, especially *Streptococcus pyogenes,* can cause pharyngitis and cervical lymphadenopathy, but an enlarged spleen and a positive Monospot test make infectious mononucleosis the most likely diagnosis. See page 257 for additional information.

CASE 2

A 5-year-old boy with diabetic ketoacidosis has ptosis of his right eyelid, periorbital swelling, and a black, necrotic skin lesion under his eye. Biopsy of the skin lesion shows **nonseptate hyphae with wide-angle branching.**

DIAGNOSIS: Mucormycosis caused by *Mucor* or *Rhizopus* species. Diabetic ketoacidosis and renal acidosis predispose to mucormycosis. Fungal spores are inhaled into the sinuses, resulting in lesions on the face. See page 348 for additional information.

CASE 3

A 40-year-old man complains of watery, foul-smelling diarrhea and flatulence for the past 2 weeks. He drank untreated water on a camping trip about a month ago. See **pear-shaped flagellated trophozoites** in stool.

DIAGNOSIS: Giardiasis caused by *Giardia lamblia.* Of the protozoa that are common causes of diarrhea, *Giardia* and *Cryptosporidium* cause watery diarrhea, whereas *Entamoeba* causes bloody diarrhea. See page 354 for additional information on *Giardia,* page 355 for additional information on *Cryptosporidium,* and page 351 for additional information on *Entamoeba.*

CASE 4

A 35-year-old man who is HIV-antibody-positive has had a persistent headache and a low-grade fever (temperature, 100°F) for the past 2 weeks. See **budding yeasts with a wide capsule in India ink preparation** of spinal fluid.

DIAGNOSIS: Meningitis caused by *Cryptococcus neoformans*. The latex agglutination test, which detects the capsular polysaccharide antigen of *Cryptococcus* in the spinal fluid, is a more sensitive and specific test than is the test with India ink. See page 347 for additional information. If **acid-fast rods** are seen in spinal fluid, think *Mycobacterium tuberculosis*. See page 161 for additional information.

CASE 5

A 12-year-old boy has a painful arm that he thought he had injured while pitching in a Little League baseball game. The pain has gotten worse over a 2-week period and he now has a temperature of 100°F. X-ray of the humerus reveals raised periosteum. Aspirate of lesion reveals **gram-positive cocci in clusters.**

DIAGNOSIS: Osteomyelitis caused by *Staphylococcus aureus*. This organism is the **most common cause of osteomyelitis in children.** Osteomyelitis in prosthetic joints is often caused by *Staphylococcus epidermidis*. See page 106 for additional information on staphylococci.

CASE 6

A 50-year-old woman receiving chemotherapy via a subclavian catheter for acute leukemia has the sudden onset of blindness in her right eye. Her total WBC = 120/μL. Blood cultures grew **budding yeasts that formed germ tubes.**

DIAGNOSIS: Endophthalmitis (infection inside the eye) caused by *Candida albicans*. A catheter-related infection gave rise to an embolus containing the organism, which traveled through the bloodstream to reach the eye. *C. albicans* is a member of the normal flora of the skin and enters through a break in the skin at the catheter site. See page 346 for additional information.

If the blood culture grew colonies of gram-positive cocci in clusters that were coagulase-negative, think *Staphylococcus epidermidis,* another member of the skin flora that is also a common cause of catheter-associated infections. See page 106 for additional information.

CASE 7

A 60-year-old man has had a nonproductive cough and fever (temperature, 101°F) for 1 week. He received a kidney transplant 6 weeks ago and has had one episode of rejection that required increased prednisone. There was no response to erythromycin, indicating that *Legionella* and *Mycoplasma* are unlikely causes. See **owl's-eye inclusion bodies within the nucleus** of infected cells in bronchoalveolar lavage fluid.

DIAGNOSIS: Cytomegalovirus pneumonia. These intranuclear inclusions are typical findings in CMV infections. Immunosuppression predisposes to disseminated CMV infections. See page 256 for additional information.

CASE 8

A 45-year-old woman complains that her right arm has become increasingly weak during the past few days. This morning, she had a generalized seizure. She recently finished a course of cancer chemotherapy. MRI of the brain reveals a lesion resembling an abscess. Brain biopsy shows **gram-positive rods in long filaments.** Organism is **weakly acid-fast.**

DIAGNOSIS: Brain abscess caused by *Nocardia asteroides*. *N. asteroides* initially infects the lung, where it may or may not cause symptoms in immunocompetent people. Dissemination to the brain is common in immunocompromised patients. See page 169 for additional information.

CASE 9

A 20-year-old man has a severe headache and vomiting that began yesterday. He is now confused. On exam, his temperature is 39°C and his neck is stiff. Spinal fluid reveals no bacteria on Gram stain, 25 lymphs, normal protein, and normal glucose. Culture of the spinal fluid on blood agar shows no bacterial colonies.

DIAGNOSIS: **Viral meningitis, which is most often caused by coxsackievirus.** Can isolate the virus from spinal fluid. See page 286 for additional information.

CASE 10

A 60-year-old man with a history of tuberculosis now has a cough productive of bloody sputum. Chest x-ray reveals a round opaque mass within a cavity in his left upper lobe. Culture of the sputum grew an organism with **septate hyphae that had straight, parallel walls.** The hyphae exhibited **low-angle branching.**

DIAGNOSIS: "Fungus ball" caused by *Aspergillus fumigatus.* Fungal spores are inhaled into the lung, where they grow within a preexisting cavity caused by infection with *Mycobacterium tuberculosis.* See page 348 for additional information.

CASE 11

A 3-month-old girl has watery, nonbloody diarrhea. Stool culture reveals only normal enteric flora.

DIAGNOSIS: Think **rotavirus, the most common cause of diarrhea in infants.** The ELISA test for rotavirus antigen in the stool is positive, which confirms the diagnosis. See page 289 for additional information.

CASE 12

A 30-year-old woman has a painless ulcer on her tongue. She is HIV-antibody-positive and has a CD4 count of 25. Her serum is nonreactive in the VDRL test. Biopsy of the lesion revealed **yeasts within macrophages.**

DIAGNOSIS: Disseminated histoplasmosis caused by *Histoplasma capsulatum.* Patients with a low CD4 count have severely reduced cell-mediated immunity, which predisposes to disseminated disease caused by this dimorphic fungus. A negative VDRL test indicates the ulcer was not caused by *Treponema pallidum.* See page 342 for additional information on *Histoplasma.*

CASE 13

A 20-year-old man has a swollen, red, hot, tender ankle, accompanied by a temperature of 100°F for the past 2 days. There is no history of trauma. See **gram-negative diplococci** in joint fluid aspirate. Organism is **oxidase-positive.**

DIAGNOSIS: Arthritis caused by *Neisseria gonorrhoeae,* the **most common cause of infectious arthritis in sexually active adults.** Sugar fermentation tests were used to identify the organism as *N. gonorrhoeae.* See page 121 for additional information.

CASE 14

A 40-year-old woman has blurred vision and slurred speech. She is afebrile. She is famous in her neighborhood for her home-canned vegetables and fruits.

DIAGNOSIS: Botulism caused by *Clostridium botulinum.* Botulinum toxin causes a descending paralysis that starts with the cranial nerves, typically appearing initially as diplopia. The toxin is a **protease that cleaves the proteins involved in the release of acetylcholine** at the neuromuscular junction. Treat with antiserum immediately. **Confirm diagnosis with mouse protection test** using a sample of food suspected of containing the toxin. See page 127 for additional information.

Wound botulism occurs in heroin users (eg, users of black tar heroin), especially in those who "skin pop." Bacterial spores in the heroin germinate in the anaerobic conditions in necrotic skin tissue.

CASE 15

A neonate was born with a small head (microcephaly), jaundice, and hepatosplenomegaly. Urine contained **multinucleated giant cells with intranuclear inclusions.**

DIAGNOSIS: Cytomegalovirus infection acquired in utero. Cytomegalovirus is the **leading cause of congenital abnormalities.** For fetal infection to occur, the mother must be infected for the first time during pregnancy. She therefore would have no preexisting antibodies to neutralize the virus prior to its infecting the placenta and the fetus. See page 256 for additional information.

CASE 16

A 14-year-old girl has a rapidly spreading, painful, erythematous rash on her leg. The rash is warm and tender, and her temperature is 38°C. **Gram-positive cocci in chains** were seen in an aspirate from the lesion. Culture of the aspirate on blood agar grew colonies surrounded by **clear (beta) hemolysis.** Growth of the organism was **inhibited by bacitracin.**

DIAGNOSIS: Cellulitis caused by *Streptococcus pyogenes.* The rapid spread of cellulitis caused by *S. pyogenes* is due to hyaluronidase (spreading factor) that degrades hyaluronic acid in subcutaneous tissue. **Acute glomerulonephritis (AGN)** can follow skin infections caused by *S. pyogenes.* AGN is an immunologic disease caused by **antigen-antibody complexes.** See page 110 for additional information.

CASE 17

A 4-year-old boy wakes up at night because his anal area is itching. See **worm eggs in "Scotch tape" preparation.**

DIAGNOSIS: Pinworm infection (enterobiasis) caused by *Enterobius vermicularis.* Pinworm infection is the most common helminth disease in the United States. See page 380 for additional information.

CASE 18

A 25-year-old woman has a painful, inflamed swollen hand. She was bitten by a cat about 8 hours ago. See **small gram-negative rods** in the exudate from lesion.

DIAGNOSIS: Cellulitis caused by *Pasteurella multocida.* Organism is **normal flora in cat's mouth.** See page 160 for additional information.

CASE 19

A 7-year-old girl has bloody diarrhea and fever (temperature, 38°C), but no nausea or vomiting. Only lactose-fermenting colonies are seen on EMB agar.

DIAGNOSIS: Think *Campylobacter jejuni* or enterohemorrhagic strains of *Escherichia coli* (*E. coli* O157:H7). If *Campylobacter* is the cause, see colonies on *Campylobacter* agar containing **curved gram-negative rods,** and the colonies on EMB agar are likely to be nonpathogenic *E. coli.* If *E. coli* O157:H7 is the cause, the organism in the lactose-fermenting colonies on EMB agar is **unable to ferment sorbitol.** The absence of non-lactose-fermenting colonies indicates that *Shigella* and *Salmonella* are not the cause. See page 145 for additional information on *Campylobacter* and page 138 for additional information on *E. coli* O157:H7.

CASE 20

A 15-year-old girl has had a nonproductive cough and temperature of 100°F for the past 5 days. The symptoms came on gradually. Lung exam shows few scattered rales. Chest x-ray shows patchy infiltrate in left lower lobe but no consolidation. **Cold agglutinin test is positive.**

DIAGNOSIS: Atypical pneumonia caused by *Mycoplasma pneumoniae.* This organism is the most common cause of atypical pneumonia in teenagers and young adults. In the cold agglutinin test, antibodies in the patient's serum agglutinate human red blood cells in the cold (4°C). These antibodies do not react with *Mycoplasma.* See page 171 for additional information.

CASE 21

A 45-year-old man sustained a skull fracture in an automobile accident. The following day, he noted clear fluid dripping from his nose, but he did not notify the hospital personnel. The following day he spiked a fever to

39°C and complained of a severe headache. Nuchal rigidity was found on physical exam. Spinal fluid analysis revealed 5200 WBC/µL, 90% of which were neutrophils. Gram stain showed gram-positive diplococci.

DIAGNOSIS: Meningitis caused by *Streptococcus pneumoniae*. Patients with a **fracture of the cribriform plate who leak spinal fluid into the nose** are predisposed to meningitis by this organism. Pneumococci can colonize the nasal mucosa and enter the subarachnoid space through the fractured cribriform plate. See page 116 for additional information.

CASE 22

A 7-year-old girl was well until about 3 weeks ago, when she began complaining of being "tired all the time." On exam, her temperature is 38°C and there is tenderness below the right knee. Hemoglobin: 10.2; WBC: 9600 with increased neutrophils. A sickle cell prep shows a moderate sickling tendency. **Gram-negative rods** grew in the blood culture.

DIAGNOSIS: Osteomyelitis caused by *Salmonella* species. **Sickle cell anemia predisposes to osteomyelitis caused by *Salmonella* species.** The abnormally shaped sickle cells are trapped in the small capillaries of the bone and cause micro-infarcts. These micro-infarcts enhance the likelihood of infection by *Salmonella*. See page 140 for additional information.

CASE 23

A 3-month-old boy has a persistent cough and severe wheezing for the past 2 days. On physical exam, his temperature is 39°C and coarse rhonchi are heard bilaterally. Chest x-ray shows interstitial infiltrates bilaterally. Diagnosis was made by **ELISA that detected viral antigen in nasal washings.**

DIAGNOSIS: Think pneumonia caused by respiratory syncytial virus, the **most common cause of pneumonia and bronchiolitis in infants.** RSV causes **giant cells (syncytia)** that can be seen in respiratory secretions and in cell culture. See page 274 for additional information.

CASE 24

A 34-year-old man was in his usual state of health until last night, when he felt feverish, had a shaking chill, and became short of breath at rest. T 39°C, BP 110/60, P 104, R 18. Scattered rales were heard in both bases. A new murmur consistent with tricuspid insufficiency was heard. Needle tracks were seen on both forearms. **Gram-positive cocci in clusters** grew in blood culture.

DIAGNOSIS: Acute endocarditis caused by *Staphylococcus aureus*. This organism is the most common cause of acute endocarditis in intravenous drug users. The valves on the right side of the heart are often involved. See page 106 for additional information.

CASE 25

A 2-week-old infant was well on discharge from the hospital 10 days ago and remained so until last night, when he appeared drowsy and flushed. His skin felt hot to the touch. On physical exam, the infant was very difficult to arouse, but there were no other positive findings. His temperature was 40°C. Blood culture grew **gram-positive cocci in chains.** A narrow zone of **clear (beta) hemolysis** was seen around the colonies. **Hippurate hydrolysis** test was positive.

DIAGNOSIS: Neonatal sepsis caused by *Streptococcus agalactiae* (group B streptococci). Group B streptococci are the most common cause of neonatal sepsis. Think *Escherichia coli* if gram-negative rods are seen or *Listeria monocytogenes* if gram-positive rods are seen. See page 114 for additional information on group B streptococci, page 136 for additional information on *Escherichia coli,* and page 131 for additional information on *Listeria monocytogenes*.

CASE 26

A 70-year-old woman had a hip replacement because of severe degenerative joint disease. She did well until a year later, when a fall resulted in a fracture of the femur and the prosthesis had to be replaced. Three weeks later, bloody fluid began draining from the wound site. The patient was afebrile and the physical examination was otherwise unremarkable. Two days later, because of increasing drainage, the wound was debrided and pus was obtained. Gram stain of the pus was negative, but an **acid-fast stain revealed red rods.**

DIAGNOSIS: Prosthetic joint infection caused by *Mycobacterium fortuitum-chelonei* complex. Think *Staphylococcus epidermidis* if gram-positive cocci in clusters are seen. See page 166 for additional information on *Mycobacterium fortuitum-chelonei* complex and page 109 for additional information on *Staphylococcus epidermidis.*

CASE 27

An 80-year-old man complains of a painful rash on his left forehead. The rash is vesicular and only on that side. He is being treated with chemotherapy for leukemia. Smear of material from the base of the vesicle reveals **multinucleated giant cells with intranuclear inclusions.**

DIAGNOSIS: Herpes zoster (shingles) caused by varicella-zoster virus. The rash of zoster follows the dermatome of the neuron that was latently infected. Herpes simplex type 1 virus can cause a similar picture. Can distinguish these viruses using fluorescent antibody assay. See page 255 for additional information.

CASE 28

A 55-year-old woman has an inflamed ulcer on her right hand and several tender nodules on the inner aspect of her right arm. She is an avid gardener and especially enjoys pruning her roses. Biopsy of the lesion reveals budding yeasts.

DIAGNOSIS: Sporotrichosis caused by *Sporothrix schenckii.* The organism is a mold in the soil and a yeast in the body, ie, it is **dimorphic.** Infection occurs when spores produced by the mold form are introduced into the skin by a penetrating injury. See page 339 for additional information.

CASE 29

A 15-year-old boy sustained a broken tooth in a fist fight several weeks ago. He now has an inflamed area on the skin over the broken tooth, in the center of which is a draining sinus tract. Gram stain of the drainage fluid reveals **filamentous gram-positive rods.**

DIAGNOSIS: Actinomycosis caused by *Actinomyces israelii.* See "**sulfur granules**" in the sinus tract. These granules are particles composed of interwoven filaments of bacteria. See page 169 for additional information.

CASE 30

A 24-year-old woman experienced the sudden onset of high fever, myalgias, vomiting, and diarrhea. Her vital signs were T 40°C, BP 70/30, P 140, R 30. A sunburn-like rash appeared over most of her body. Blood cultures and stool cultures are negative. She is recovering from a surgical procedure on her maxillary sinus and the bleeding was being staunched with nasal tampons. Gram-positive cocci in clusters were seen in blood adherent to the nasal tampon.

DIAGNOSIS: Toxic shock syndrome caused by *Staphylococcus aureus.* Toxic shock syndrome toxin is a **superantigen that stimulates the release of large amounts of cytokines from many helper T cells.** See page 109 for additional information.

CASE 31

An 8-year-old girl has a pruritic rash on her chest. Lesions are round or oval with an inflamed border and central clearing. The lesions contain both papules and vesicles. See **hyphae in KOH prep** of scrapings from the lesion.

DIAGNOSIS: Tinea corporis (ringworm) caused by one of the dermatophytes, especially species of *Microsporum, Trichophyton,* or *Epidermophyton.* Dermatophytes utilize **keratin** as a nutrient source, so lesions are limited to the skin. See page 339 for additional information.

CASE 32

A 25-year-old woman has a papular rash on her trunk, arms, and palms. She says the rash does not itch. Vaginal exam reveals two flat, moist, slightly raised lesions on the labia. Material from a labial lesion examined in a **darkfield microscope revealed spirochetes.**

DIAGNOSIS: Secondary syphilis caused by *Treponema pallidum*. The rash on the palms coupled with the vaginal lesions (condylomata lata) are compatible with secondary syphilis. **Serologic tests, such as the nonspecific test (VDRL) and the specific test (FTA-ABS), were positive.** See page 173 for additional information.

CASE 33

A 5-year-old girl complains of an earache for the past 2 days. On examination, she has a temperature of 39°C, the right external canal contained dried blood, the drum was perforated, and a small amount of purulent fluid was seen. Gram stain of the pus revealed **gram-positive diplococci.** Colonies formed **green (alpha) hemolysis on blood agar.** Growth was inhibited by **optochin.**

DIAGNOSIS: Otitis media caused by *Streptococcus pneumoniae*. Think *Haemophilus influenzae* if small gram-negative rods are seen. These organisms colonize the oropharynx and enter the middle ear via the eustachian tube. See page 116 for additional information on *Streptococcus pneumoniae* and page 152 for additional information on *Haemophilus influenzae*.

CASE 34

A 25-year-old woman was well until the sudden onset of high fever (temperature, 40°C) accompanied by several purple skin lesions (ecchymoses, purpura). The lesions are scattered over the body, are irregularly shaped, and are not raised. Her blood pressure is 60/10 and her pulse rate is 140. Blood culture grew **gram-negative diplococci.**

DIAGNOSIS: Meningococcemia caused by *Neisseria meningitidis*. The endotoxin (lipopolysaccharide, or LPS) of the organism triggers release of interleukin-1, tumor necrosis factor, and nitric oxide from macrophages. These cause the high fever and low blood pressure. The purpuric lesions are a manifestation of **disseminated intravascular coagulation (DIC).** Endotoxin activates the coagulation cascade, causing DIC. **Lipid A** is the toxic part of LPS. See page 119 for additional information.

CASE 35

A 40-year-old woman was well until 2 days ago, when she experienced the sudden onset of fever, shaking chills, and profuse sweating. Today, she also complains of headache and abdominal pain but no nausea, vomiting, or diarrhea. She does not have a stiff neck, rash, or altered mental status. Travel history reveals she returned from an extended trip to several countries in Central Africa 1 week ago. Blood smear reveals **ring-shaped trophozoites within red blood cells.**

DIAGNOSIS: Malaria caused by *Plasmodium* species. If **banana-shaped gametocytes** seen in the blood smear, think *Plasmodium falciparum*. *P. falciparum* is the species that causes the life-threatening complications of malaria, such as cerebral malaria. The fever and chills experienced by the patient coincide with the release of merozoites from infected red blood cells and occur in either a tertian or quartan pattern. See page 357 for additional information.

CASE 36

A 35-year-old man is seen in the emergency room complaining of severe headache and vomiting that began last night. His temperature is 40°C. While in the ER, he is increasingly combative and has a grand-mal seizure. He is "foaming at the mouth" and cannot drink any liquids. Analysis of his spinal fluid reveals no abnormality, and no organisms are seen in the Gram stain. Two days later, despite supportive measures, he died. Pathologic examination of the brain revealed **eosinophilic inclusion bodies in the cytoplasm of neurons.**

DIAGNOSIS: Rabies (an encephalitis) caused by rabies virus. The inclusions are **Negri bodies.** Diagnosis can be confirmed by using fluorescent-antibody assays. The patient was a farm worker who was **bitten by a bat** about a month prior to the onset of symptoms. Note the long incubation period, which can be as long as 6 months. People bitten by a bat (or any wild animal) should receive rabies immunization consisting of the inactivated vaccine plus rabies immune globulins (passive-active immunization). See page 278 for additional information.

CASE 37

A 70-year-old man was admitted to the hospital after suffering extensive third-degree burns. Three days later, he spiked a fever, and there was pus on the dressing that had a **blue-green color.** Gram stain of the pus revealed **gram-negative rods.**

DIAGNOSIS: Wound (burn) infection caused by *Pseudomonas aeruginosa.* The blue-green color is caused by **pyocyanin,** a pigment produced by the organism. See page 149 for additional information.

CASE 38

A 65-year-old woman reports that she has had several episodes of confusion and memory loss during the past few weeks. On examination, she is afebrile but has a staggering gait and myoclonus can be elicited. Over the next several months, her condition deteriorates and death ensues. On autopsy, microscopic examination of the brain reveals **many vacuoles** but no viral inclusion bodies.

DIAGNOSIS: Creutzfeldt-Jakob disease caused by prions. CJD is a **spongiform encephalopathy.** The vacuoles give the brain a sponge-like appearance. See page 317 for additional information.

CASE 39

A 20-year-old man complains of several episodes of blood in his urine. He has no dysuria or urethral discharge. He is not sexually active. He is a college student but was born and raised in Egypt. Physical exam reveals no penile lesions. Urinalysis shows many red cells, no white cells, and several large **eggs with terminal spines.**

DIAGNOSIS: Schistosomiasis caused by *Schistosoma haematobium.* Schistosome eggs in venules of the bladder damage the bladder epithelium and cause bleeding. The eggs are excreted in the urine. See page 375 for additional information.

CASE 40

A 35-year-old man complains of night sweats, chills, and fatigue at varying intervals during the past 2 months. These episodes began while he was traveling in Latin America. When questioned, he says that cheeses, especially the unpasteurized varieties, are some of his favorite foods. On examination, his temperature is 39°C, and his liver and spleen are palpable. His hematocrit is 30% and his white blood count is 5000. Blood culture grew **small gram-negative rods.**

DIAGNOSIS: Brucellosis caused by *Brucella* species. **Domestic animals** such as cows and goats are the main reservoir for *Brucella,* and it is often transmitted in **unpasteurized dairy products.** This patient could also have typhoid fever caused by *Salmonella typhi,* but *S. typhi* is only a human pathogen, ie, there is no animal reservoir. See page 157 for additional information on *Brucella* species and page 140 for additional information on *Salmonella typhi.*

CASE 41

A 6-year-old girl has a rash on her face that appeared yesterday. The rash is **erythematous and located over the malar eminences** bilaterally. The rash is macular; there are no papules, vesicles, or pustules. A few days prior to the appearance of the rash, she had a runny nose and anorexia.

DIAGNOSIS: Slapped cheek syndrome caused by parvovirus B19. This virus also causes **aplastic anemia because it preferentially infects and kills erythroblasts.** It also **infects the fetus, causing hydrops fetalis,** and causes an immune complex–mediated **arthritis,** especially in adult women. See page 264 for additional information.

CASE 42

A 20-year-old man fell off his motorcycle and suffered a compound fracture of the femur. The fracture was surgically reduced and the wound debrided. Forty-eight hours later, he spiked a fever (temperature, 40°C) and the wound area became necrotic. Crepitus was felt, and a foul-smelling odor was perceived originating from the wound. Marked anemia and a white blood count of 22,800 were found. Gram stain of the exudate showed **large gram-positive rods.** Colonies grew on blood agar incubated **anaerobically** but not aerobically.

DIAGNOSIS: Gas gangrene (myonecrosis) caused by *Clostridium perfringens*. The main virulence factor produced by this organism is an **exotoxin that is a lecithinase.** It causes necrosis of tissue and lysis of red blood cells (causing hemolytic anemia). The spores of the organism are in the soil and enter at the wound site. A foul-smelling exudate is characteristic of infections caused by anaerobic bacteria. See page 128 for additional information.

CASE 43

A 30-year-old woman complains of a burning feeling in her mouth and pain on swallowing. Sexual history reveals she is a commercial sex worker and has had unprotected vaginal, oral, and anal intercourse with multiple partners. On examination, whitish lesions are seen on the tongue, palate, and pharynx. No vesicles are seen. The test for HIV antibody is positive and her CD4 count is 65. Gram stain of material from the lesions reveals **budding yeasts and pseudohyphae.**

DIAGNOSIS: Thrush caused by *Candida albicans*. This organism forms pseudohyphae when it invades tissue. The absence of vesicles indicates that her symptoms are not caused by herpes simplex virus type 2. See page 346 for additional information.

CASE 44

You're a physician at a refugee camp in sub-Saharan Africa, when an outbreak of diarrhea occurs. Massive amounts of watery stool, without blood, are produced by the patients. **Curved gram-negative rods** are seen in a Gram stain of the stool.

DIAGNOSIS: Cholera caused by *Vibrio cholerae*. There are three genera of curved gram-negative rods: *Vibrio, Campylobacter,* and *Helicobacter*. *Vibrio cholerae* causes watery, nonbloody diarrhea, whereas *Campylobacter jejuni* typically causes bloody diarrhea. *Helicobacter pylori* causes gastritis and peptic ulcer, not diarrhea.

Enterotoxigenic *Escherichia coli* causes watery diarrhea by producing an exotoxin that has the same mode of action as does the exotoxin produced by *V. cholerae*. However, *E. coli* is a straight gram-negative rod, not a curved one. If an outbreak of bloody diarrhea had occurred in the refugee camp, then *Shigella dysenteriae* would be the most likely cause. See the following pages for additional information: *Vibrio*, page 143; *Campylobacter*, page 145; *Helicobacter*, page 146; *Escherichia*, page 136; and *Shigella*, page 142.

CASE 45

A 40-year-old man with low-grade fever and night sweats for the past 4 weeks now has increasing fatigue and shortness of breath. He says he has difficulty climbing the one flight of stairs to his apartment. Pertinent past history includes rheumatic fever when he was 15 years old and the extraction of two wisdom teeth about 3 weeks before his symptoms began. No chemoprophylaxis was given at the time of the extractions. There is no history of intravenous drug use. His temperature is 38.5°C, and a loud holosystolic murmur can be heard over the precordium. His spleen is palpable. He is anemic and his white blood count is 13,500. Blood cultures grow **gram-positive cocci in chains that produce green (alpha) hemolysis on blood agar.** Growth is **not inhibited by optochin.**

DIAGNOSIS: Subacute bacterial endocarditis caused by one of the viridans group streptococci, such as *Streptococcus sanguis*. The laboratory findings are also compatible with *Enterococcus faecalis*, but the history of dental surgery makes the viridans group streptococci more likely to be the cause. Endocarditis caused by *E. fae-*

calis is associated with GI or GU tract surgery. See page 112 for additional information on both viridans group streptococci and *E. faecalis.*

CASE 46

A 60-year-old woman is asymptomatic but has a lung nodule seen on chest x-ray. Pertinent past history includes her cigarette smoking (2 packs per day for 40 years) and her occupation as an archaeologist, digging primarily in Arizona and New Mexico. Because of concern that the nodule may be malignant, it was surgically removed. Pathologic examination revealed **large (25 μ) round structures with thick walls and many round spores inside.** No malignant cells were seen.

DIAGNOSIS: Coccidioidomycosis caused by *Coccidiodes immitis.* These structures are **spherules,** which are pathognomonic for this disease. The mold form of the organism is found in the soil of the Southwestern United States, and the organism is acquired by inhalation of arthrospores produced by the mold. The inhaled arthrospores form spherules in the lung. *C. immitis* is dimorphic and forms spherules at 37°C. See page 341 for additional information.

CASE 47

A 20-year-old woman in her 30th week of pregnancy had an ultrasound examination that revealed a growth-retarded fetus with a large head (indicating hydrocephalus) and calcifications within the brain. Umbilical blood was cultured and **crescent-shaped trophozoites** were grown.

DIAGNOSIS: Toxoplasmosis caused by *Toxoplasma gondii.* Detection of IgM antibody in the Sabin-Feldman dye test can also be used to make a diagnosis. The main reservoir is domestic cats. Domestic farm animals, such as cattle, acquire the organism by accidentally eating cat feces. Pregnant women should **not be exposed to cat litter or eat undercooked meat.** See page 360 for additional information.

CASE 48

A 10-day-old neonate has several vesicles on the scalp and around the eyes. The child is otherwise well, afebrile and feeding normally. A Giemsa-stained smear of material from the base of a vesicle revealed **multinucleated giant cells with intranuclear inclusions.**

DIAGNOSIS: Neonatal infection caused by herpes simplex virus type 2. Infection is acquired during passage through the birth canal. Life-threatening encephalitis and disseminated infection of the neonate also occur. See page 251 for additional information.

CASE 49

A 40-year-old woman has just had a grand-mal seizure. There is a history of headaches for the past week and one episode of vertigo but no previous seizures. She is afebrile. She is a native of Honduras but has lived in the United States for the past 5 years. MRI reveals a mass in the parietal lobe. Surgical removal of the mass reveals a **larva within a cyst-like sac.**

DIAGNOSIS: Cysticercosis caused by the larva of *Taenia solium.* Infection is acquired by ingesting the tapeworm eggs, *not* by ingesting undercooked pork. This clinical picture can also be caused by a brain abscess, a granuloma such as a tuberculoma, or a brain tumor. See page 369 for additional information.

CASE 50

A 1-week-old neonate has a yellowish exudate in the corners of both eyes. The child is otherwise well, afebrile and feeding normally. Gram stain of the exudate reveals no gram-negative diplococci. A Giemsa-stained smear of the exudate reveals **a large cytoplasmic inclusion.**

DIAGNOSIS: Conjunctivitis caused by *Chlamydia trachomatis.* Confirm the diagnosis with direct fluorescent antibody test. Infection is acquired during passage through the birth canal. The inclusion contains large numbers of the **intracellular replicating forms called reticulate bodies.** See page 179 for additional information.

PART X
Pearls for the USMLE

Many questions on the USMLE can be answered by knowing the meaning of the epidemiological information provided in the case description. In order to do this, the student should know the reservoir of the organism, its mode of transmission, and the meaning of factors such as travel, occupation, and exposure to pets, farm animals, or wild animals. Knowledge of the microbes that typically cause disease in individuals with specific immunodeficiencies will also be helpful.

In addition to being useful for the USMLE, this information will prove valuable to make the diagnosis of infectious diseases on the wards and in your clinical practice.

The "Pearls" are presented in tables entitled:

Table X-1. Farm animals and household pets as reservoirs of medically important organisms.

Table X-2. Wild animals as reservoirs of medically important organisms.

Table X-3. Insects as vectors of medically important organisms.

Table X-4. Environmental sources of medically important organisms.

Table X-5. Main geographical location of medically important organisms.

Table X-6. Occupations and avocations that increase exposure to medically important organisms.

Table X-7. Hospital-related events that predispose to infection by medically important organisms.

Table X-8. Organisms that commonly cause disease in patients with immunodeficiencies or reduced host defenses.

Table X–1. Farm animals and household pets as reservoirs of medically important organisms.

Animal	Mode of Transmission	Important Organisms	Disease
Cattle/cows	1. Ingestion of meat[1]	1. *Escherichia coli* O157	Enterocolitis and hemolytic-uremic syndrome
		2. *Salmonella enterica*	Enterocolitis
		3. Prions	Variant CJD
		4. *Taenia saginata*	Taeniasis (intestinal tapeworm)
		5. *Toxoplasma gondii*	Toxoplasmosis
	2. Ingestion of milk products[2]	1. *Listeria monocytogenes*	Neonatal sepsis
		2. *Brucella* species	Brucellosis
		3. *Mycobacterium bovis*	Intestinal tuberculosis
	3. Contact with animal hides	*Bacillus anthracis*	Anthrax
Sheep	Inhalation of amniotic fluid	*Coxiella burnetii*	Q fever
Goats	Ingestion of milk products[2]	*Brucella* species	Brucellosis
Pigs	Ingestion of meat[1]	1. *Taenia solium*	Taeniasis (intestinal tapeworm)[3]
		2. *Trichinella spiralis*	Trichinosis
Poultry (chickens; turkeys)	Ingestion of meat or eggs[1]	1. *Salmonella enterica*	Enterocolitis
		2. *Campylobacter jejuni*	Enterocolitis
Dogs	1. Ingestion of dog feces	1. *Echinococcus granulosus*	Echinococcosis
		2. *Toxocara canis*	Visceral larva migrans
	2. Ingestion of dog urine	*Leptospira interrogans*	Leptospirosis
	3. Dog bite	Rabies virus	Rabies
Cats	1. Ingestion of cat feces	*Toxoplasma gondii*	Toxoplasmosis
	2. Cat bite/scratch	1. *Pasteurella multocida*	Cellulitis
		2. *Bartonella henselae*	Cat-scratch fever; bacillary angiomatosis
		3. Rabies virus	Rabies

[1]Raw or undercooked.
[2]Unpasteurized.
[3]Ingestion of eggs in human feces, not ingestion of pork, results in cysticercosis.

Table X–2. Wild animals as reservoirs of medically important organisms.

Animal	Mode of Transmission	Important Organisms	Disease
Rats	1. Flea bite 2. Ingestion of urine	*Yersinia pestis* *Leptospira interrogans*	Plague Leptospirosis
Mice	1. Tick bite 2. Inhale aerosol of droppings	*Borrelia burgdorferi* Hantavirus	Lyme disease Hantavirus Pulmonary syndrome
Bats, skunks, raccoons, and foxes	Bite	Rabies virus	Rabies
Rabbits	Contact	*Francisella tularensis*	Tularemia
Civet cat	Inhale aerosol	Coronavirus—SARS	Pneumonia
Monkeys	Mosquito bite	Yellow fever virus	Yellow fever
Birds 1. Psittacine birds (eg, parrots) 2. Chickens 3. Pigeons 4. Starlings 5. Sparrows	Inhale aerosol Inhale aerosol Inhale aerosol Inhale aerosol Mosquito bite	*Chlamydia psittaci* Influenzavirus *Cryptococcus neoformans* *Histoplasma capsulatum* Encephalitis viruses (eg, West Nile virus)	Psittacosis Influenza Meningitis, pneumonia Histoplasmosis Encephalitis
Snakes, turtles	Fecal-oral	*Salmonella enterica*	Enterocolitis
Fish	Ingestion of fish[1]	*Anisakis simplex* *Diphyllobothrium latum*	Anisakiasis Diphyllobothriasis

[1]Raw or undercooked.

Table X–3. Insects as vectors of medically important organisms.

Insects	Important Organisms	Reservoir	Disease
Ticks			
1. *Ixodes* (deer tick)	1. *Borrelia burgdorferi*	Mice	Lyme disease
	2. *Babesia microti*	Mice	Babesiosis
2. *Dermacentor* (dog tick)	1. *Rickettsia rickettsii*	Rodents, dogs	Rocky Mountain spotted fever
	2. *Ehrlichia chaffeensis*	Dogs	Ehrlichiosis
Lice	*Rickettsia prowazekii*	Humans	Typhus
Mosquitos			
1. *Anopheles*	*Plasmodium falciparum,* *P. vivax, P. ovale, P. malariae*	Humans	Malaria
2. *Aedes*	Yellow fever virus	Humans and monkeys	Yellow fever
3. *Aedes*	Dengue virus	Humans	Dengue
4. *Culex*	Encephalitis viruses, such as West Nile virus	Birds	Encephalitis
5. *Anopheles* and *Culex*	*Wuchereria bancrofti*	Humans	Filariasis, especially elephantiasis
Fleas			
Rat flea	*Yersinia pestis*	Rats	Plague
Flies			
1. Sandfly	*Leishmania donovani*	Various animals	Leishmaniasis
2. Tse-tse fly	*Trypanosoma brucei*	Humans and various animals	Sleeping sickness
3. Blackfly	*Onchocerca volvulus*	Humans	River blindness
Bugs			
Reduviid bug	*Trypanosoma cruzi*	Various animals	Chagas' disease

Table X–4. Environmental sources of medically important organisms.

Environmental Source	Important Organisms	Mode of Transmission	Disease
Water	1. *Legionella pneumophila*	Inhale aerosol	Pneumonia
	2. *Pseudomonas aeruginosa*	Inhale aerosol or direct contact	Pneumonia, burn and wound infections
	3. *Mycobacterium marinum*	Skin abrasion	Swimming pool granuloma
	4. *Vibrio vulnificus*	Skin abrasion	Cellulitis
	5. *Schistosoma mansoni, S. hematobium*	Cercariae enter skin	Schistosomiasis
	6. *Naegleria fowleri*	Ameba enter nose while swimming	Meningoencephalitis
Soil	1. *Clostridium tetani*	Spores in soil enter wound	Tetanus
	2. *Clostridium botulinum*	Spores in soil contaminate food that is improperly canned	Botulism
	3. *Clostridium perfringens*	Spores in soil enter wound	Gas gangrene
	4. *Bacillus anthracis*	Spores in soil enter wound	Anthrax
	5. Atypical mycobacteria (eg, *M. avium-intracellulare*)	Inhale aerosol	Tuberculosis-like disease
	6. *Nocardia asteroides*	Inhale aerosol	Nocardiosis
	7. *Cryptococcus neoformans*	Inhale yeast in aerosol associated with pigeons	Meningitis, pneumonia
	8. *Histoplasma capsulatum*	Inhale spores in aerosol associated with starlings	Histoplasmosis
	9. *Coccidioides immitis*	Inhale spores in aerosol of soil dust	Coccidioidomycosis
	10. *Sporothrix schenckii*	Spores on thorns enter wound	Sporotrichosis
	11. *Ancylostoma duodenale* and *Necator americanus*	Filariform larvae enter skin	Hookworm, especially anemia
	12. *Strongyloides stercoralis*	Filariform larvae enter skin	Strongyloidiasis
	13. *Ancylostoma caninum*	Filariform larvae enter skin	Cutaneous larva migrans

Table X–5. Main geographical location of medically important organisms.

Main Geographical Location	Important Organism	Disease
Within the United States		
1. South central states (eg, North Carolina and Virginia)	*Rickettsia rickettsii*	Rocky Mountain spotted fever
2. Northeastern states (eg, Connecticut, New York, and New Jersey)	*Borrelia burgdorferi*	Lyme disease
3. Midwestern states in the Ohio and Mississippi River valleys (eg, Missouri and Illinois)	*Histoplasma capsulatum*	Histoplasmosis
4. Southwestern states (eg, California and Arizona)	*Coccidioides immitis*	Coccidioidomycosis
Outside the United States		
1. Tropical areas of Africa, Asia, and South America	*Plasmodium* species	Malaria
2. Central America	*Trypanosoma cruzi*	Chagas' disease
3. Caribbean Islands and Africa	Dengue virus	Dengue fever
4. West Africa	Ebola virus	Ebola hemorrhagic fever
5. Tropical areas of Africa and South America	Yellow fever virus	Yellow fever
6. Sub-Saharan Africa	*Neisseria meningitidis*	Meningococcal meningitis

Table X–6. Occupations and avocations that increase exposure to medically important organisms.

Occupation/Avocation	Predisposing Factor	Important Organism	Disease
Hiking/camping	Tick exposure	*Borrelia burgdorferi*	Lyme disease
Rancher/farm worker	Skin wound contaminated with soil	*Bacillus anthracis*	Anthrax
Sewer worker	Exposure to rat urine	*Leptospira interrogans*	Leptospirosis
Cave explorer (spelunker) in bat-infested caves	Exposure to aerosol of bat saliva	Rabies virus	Rabies
Cave explorer (spelunker) or construction worker	Exposure to aerosol of bat guano	*Histoplasma capsulatum*	Histoplasmosis
Archaeologist or construction worker digging in soil	Exposure to soil dust containing spores	*Coccidioides immitis*	Coccidioidomycosis
Pigeon fancier	Exposure to aerosol of bird guano	*Cryptococcus neoformans*	Cryptococcosis
Bear hunter in Alaska	Ingestion of bear meat	*Trichinella spiralis*	Trichinosis

Table X–7. Hospital-related events that predispose to infection by medically important organisms.

Hospital-Related Event	Important Organism	Disease
Surgery	*Staphylococcus aureus*	Wound infection
Urinary catheter	1. *Escherichia coli* primarily, but also other enteric gram-negative rods (eg, *Proteus, Serratia,* and *Pseudomonas*) 2. *Enterococcus faecalis*	Urinary tract infection Urinary tract infection
Prosthetic device (eg, hip or heart valve)	1. *Staphylococcus epidermidis* 2. *Mycobacterium fortuitum-cheloni*	Osteomyelitis or endocarditis Osteomyelitis
Respiratory therapy	*Pseudomonas aeruginosa*	Pneumonia
Burn therapy	*Pseudomonas aeruginosa*	Wound infection
Intracerebral electrodes	Prion	Creutzfeldt-Jakob disease
Needlestick	1. HBV, HCV 2. HIV	Hepatitis B or C AIDS
Premature nursery	Respiratory syncytial virus	Bronchiolitis or pneumonia

Table X–8. Organisms that commonly cause disease in patients with immunodeficiencies or reduced host defenses.

Immunodeficiency or Reduced Host Defense	Organisms
Reduced antibodies (eg, agammaglobulinem a and IgA deficiency)	Encapsulated bacteria (eg, *Streptococcus pneumoniae, Haemophilus influenzae* type b)
Reduced phagocytosis (eg, chronic granulomatous disease, cancer chemotherapy [neutropenia])	*Staphylococcus aureus, Pseudomonas aeruginosa, Aspergillus fumigatus*
Reduced complement 1. C3b 2. C678&9 (membrane attack complex)	*Streptococcus pneumoniae, Haemophilus influenzae* type b, *Staphylococcus aureus* *Neisseria meningitidis*
Reduced cell-mediated immunity 1. Thymic aplasia (DiGeorge's syndrome) 2. HIV infection (AIDS), corticosteroids	*Candida albicans, Pneumocystis carinii* Intracellular bacteria (eg, *Mycobacterium tuberculosis,* MAI,[1] *Listeria, Salmonella*) Opportunistic fungi (eg, *Candida, Cryptococcus*) Herpesviruses (eg, herpes simplex virus, varice la-zoster virus, cytomegalovirus) Protozoa (eg, *Toxoplasma, Cryptosporidium*) *Pneumocystis*
Disrupted epithelial surface (eg, burns)	*Pseudomonas aeruginosa*
Splenectomy	*Streptococcus pneumoniae*
Diabetes mellitus	*Staphylococcus aureus*

[1]MAI, *Mycobacterium avium-intracellulare* complex.

PART XI

USMLE (National Board) Practice Questions

These practice questions are presented in the format used by the United States Medical Licensing Examination (USMLE) Step 1. Note that in the computerized version of the USMLE, all questions are of the "ONE-BEST-ANSWER" type. There are no questions of the "EXCEPT" or "LEAST ACCURATE" type in which you are asked to determine the one wrong answer. Nevertheless, for studying purposes, the EXCEPT or LEAST ACCURATE type of questions are excellent learning tools because they provide you with several correct statements and only one incorrect statement rather than several incorrect ones. In view of this learning advantage, many practice questions in Part X of this book are of the EXCEPT or LEAST ACCURATE type. However, in Part XI, the questions in the

USMLE Practice Examination are presented in the ONE-BEST-ANSWER format and no EXCEPT type questions are used.

After the questions regarding the specific content areas, ie, bacteriology, virology, mycology, parasitology, and immunology, there are two additional sections, one containing questions in an extended matching format and the other containing questions based on infectious disease cases. The questions in the computerized version of the USMLE have 4–10 answer choices. Although the format of the questions in the extended matching section of this book is different from the format used in the USMLE, the questions in this section are designed to be a highly time-effective way of transmitting the important information.

Basic Bacteriology

DIRECTIONS (Questions 1–39): Select the ONE lettered answer that is BEST in each question.

1. Each of the following statements concerning the surface structures of bacteria is correct EXCEPT:
   (A) Pili mediate the interaction of bacteria with mucosal epithelium
   (B) Polysaccharide capsules retard phagocytosis
   (C) Both gram-negative rods and cocci have lipopolysaccharide ("endotoxin") in their cell wall
   (D) Bacterial flagella are nonantigenic in humans because they closely resemble human flagella in chemical composition

2. Each of the following statements concerning peptidoglycan is correct EXCEPT:
   (A) It has a backbone composed of alternating units of muramic acid and acetylglucosamine
   (B) Cross-links between the tetrapeptides involve D-alanine
   (C) It is thinner in gram-positive than in gram-negative cells
   (D) It can be degraded by lysozyme

3. Each of the following statements concerning bacterial spores is correct EXCEPT:
   (A) Their survival ability is based on their enhanced metabolic activity

(B) They are formed by gram-positive rods

(C) They can be killed by being heated to 121°C for 15 minutes

(D) They contain much less water than bacterial cells

4. Which one of the statements is the MOST accurate comparison of human, bacterial, and fungal cells?

(A) Human cells undergo mitosis, whereas neither bacteria nor fungi do

(B) Human and fungal cells have a similar cell wall, in contrast to bacteria, whose cell wall contains peptidoglycan

(C) Human and bacterial cells have plasmids, whereas fungal cells do not

(D) Human and fungal cells have similar ribosomes, whereas bacterial ribosomes are different

5. Which statement is MOST accurate regarding the drug depicted in the diagram?

(A) It inhibits DNA synthesis

(B) It is bacteriostatic

(C) It binds to 30S ribosomes

(D) It prevents formation of folic acid

6. Each of the following statements regarding the selective action of antibiotics on bacteria is correct EXCEPT:

(A) Chloramphenicol affects the large subunit of the bacterial ribosome, which is different from the large subunit of the human ribosome

(B) Isoniazid affects the DNA polymerase of bacteria but not that of human cells

(C) Sulfonamides affect folic acid synthesis in bacteria, a pathway that does not occur in human cells

(D) Penicillins affect bacteria rather than human cells because bacteria have a cell wall, whereas human cells do not

7. Each of the following statements concerning endotoxins is correct EXCEPT:

(A) They are less potent (ie, less active on a weight basis) than exotoxins

(B) They are more stable on heating than exotoxins

(C) They bind to specific cell receptors, whereas exotoxins do not

(D) They are part of the bacterial cell wall, whereas exotoxins are not

8. The MAIN host defense against bacterial exotoxins is

(A) Activated macrophages secreting proteases

(B) IgG and IgM antibodies

(C) Helper T cells

(D) Modulation of host cell receptors in response to the toxin

9. Each of the following events involves recombination of DNA EXCEPT:

(A) Transduction of a chromosomal gene

(B) Transposition of a mobile genetic element

(C) Integration of a temperate bacteriophage

(D) Conjugation, eg, transfer of an R (resistance) factor

10. Each of the following statements concerning the normal flora is correct EXCEPT:

(A) The most common organism found on the skin is *Staphylococcus epidermidis*

(B) *Escherichia coli* is a prominent member of the normal flora of the throat

(C) The major site where *Bacteroides fragilis* is found is the colon

(D) One of the most common sites where *Staphylococcus aureus* is found is the nose

11. Each of the following statements concerning the mechanism of action of antimicrobial drugs is correct EXCEPT:

(A) Vancomycin acts by inhibiting peptidoglycan synthesis

(B) Quinolones, such as ciprofloxacin, act by inhibiting the DNA gyrase of bacteria

(C) Erythromycin is a bactericidal drug that disrupts cell membranes by a detergentlike action

(D) Aminoglycosides such as streptomycin are bactericidal drugs that inhibit protein synthesis

12. Each of the following statements concerning the resistance of bacteria to antimicrobial drugs is correct EXCEPT:

(A) Resistance to chloramphenicol is known to be due to an enzyme that acetylates the drug

(B) Resistance to penicillin is known to be due to reduced affinity of transpeptidases

(C) Resistance to penicillin is known to be due to cleavage by β-lactamase

(D) Resistance to tetracycline is known to be due to an enzyme that hydrolyzes the ester linkage

13. Of the following choices, the MOST important function of antibody in host defenses against bacteria is
    (A) Activation of lysozyme that degrades the cell wall
    (B) Acceleration of proteolysis of exotoxins
    (C) Facilitation of phagocytosis
    (D) Inhibition of bacterial protein synthesis

14. Which of the following events is MOST likely to be due to bacterial conjugation?
    (A) A strain of *Corynebacterium diphtheriae* produces a toxin encoded by a prophage *transd.*
    (B) A strain of *Pseudomonas aeruginosa* produces β-lactamase encoded by a plasmid similar to a plasmid of another gram-negative organism
    (C) An encapsulated strain of *Streptococcus pneumoniae* acquires the gene for capsule formation from an extract of DNA from another encapsulated strain *transf.*
    (D) A gene encoding resistance to gentamicin in the *Escherichia coli* chromosome appears in the genome of a virulent bacteriophage that has infected *E. coli* *transd.*

15. Which one of the following BEST describes the mode of action of endotoxin?
    (A) Degrades lecithin in cell membranes *exotoxins*
    (B) Inactivates elongation factor 2
    (C) Blocks release of acetylcholine
    (D) Causes the release of tumor necrosis factor *IL-1*

16. The identification of bacteria by serologic tests is based on the presence of specific antigens. Which one of the following bacterial components is LEAST likely to contain useful antigens?
    (A) Capsule *K*
    (B) Flagella *H*
    (C) Cell wall *O*
    (D) Ribosomes

17. Each of the following statements concerning bacterial spores is correct EXCEPT:
    (A) Spores are formed under adverse environmental conditions such as the absence of a carbon source
    (B) Spores are resistant to boiling
    (C) Spores are metabolically inactive and contain dipicolinic acid, a calcium chelator
    (D) Spores are formed primarily by organisms of the genus *Neisseria*

18. Each of the following statements concerning the mechanism of action of antibacterial drugs is correct EXCEPT:

(A) Cephalosporins are bactericidal drugs that inhibit the transpeptidase reaction and prevent cell wall synthesis

(B) Tetracyclines are bacteriostatic drugs that inhibit protein synthesis by blocking tRNA binding

(C) Aminoglycosides are bacteriostatic drugs that inhibit protein synthesis by activating ribonuclease, which degrades mRNA

(D) Erythromycin is a bacteriostatic drug that inhibits protein synthesis by blocking translocation of the polypeptide

19. Each of the following is a typical property of obligate anaerobes EXCEPT:
    (A) They generate energy by using the cytochrome system
    (B) They grow best in the absence of air
    (C) They lack superoxide dismutase
    (D) They lack catalase

20. Each of the following statements concerning the Gram stain is correct EXCEPT:
    (A) *Escherichia coli* stains pink because it has a thin peptidoglycan layer
    (B) *Streptococcus pyogenes* stains blue because it has a thick peptidoglycan layer
    (C) *Mycobacterium tuberculosis* stains blue because it has a thick lipid layer
    (D) *Mycoplasma pneumoniae* isn't visible in the Gram stain because it doesn't have a cell wall

21. Each of the following statements concerning the killing of bacteria is correct EXCEPT:
    (A) Lysozyme in tears can hydrolyze bacterial cell walls
    (B) Silver nitrate can inactivate bacterial enzymes
    (C) Detergents can disrupt bacterial cell membranes
    (D) Ultraviolet light can degrade bacterial capsules

22. In the Gram stain, the decolorization of gram-negative bacteria by alcohol is MOST closely related to
    (A) Proteins encoded by F plasmids
    (B) Lipids in the cell wall
    (C) 70S ribosomes
    (D) Branched polysaccharides in the capsule

23. Chemical modification of benzylpenicillin (penicillin G) has resulted in several beneficial changes in the clinical use of this drug. Which one of the following is NOT one of those beneficial changes?
    (A) Lowered frequency of anaphylaxis
    (B) Increased activity against gram-negative rods
    (C) Increased resistance to stomach acid
    (D) Reduced cleavage by penicillinase

24. Each of the following statements concerning resistance to antibiotics is correct EXCEPT:

(A) Resistance to aminoglycosides can be due to phosphorylating enzymes encoded by R plasmids

(B) Resistance to sulfonamides can be due to enzymes that hydrolyze the five-membered ring structure

(C) Resistance to penicillins can be due to alterations in binding proteins in the cell membrane

(D) Resistance to cephalosporins can be due to cleavage of the β-lactam ring

25. The effects of endotoxin include each of the following EXCEPT:
(A) Opsonization
(B) Fever
(C) Activation of the coagulation cascade
(D) Hypotension

26. Bacterial surface structures that show antigenic diversity include each of the following EXCEPT:
(A) Pili
(B) Capsules
(C) Flagella
(D) Peptidoglycan

27. The effects of antibody on bacteria include each of the following EXCEPT:
(A) Lysis of gram-negative bacteria in conjunction with complement
(B) Augmentation of phagocytosis
(C) Increase in the frequency of lysogeny
(D) Inhibition of adherence of bacteria to mucosal surfaces

28. Each of the following statements concerning exotoxins is correct EXCEPT:
(A) When treated chemically, some exotoxins lose their toxicity and can be used as immunogens in vaccines
(B) Some exotoxins are capable of causing disease in purified form, free of any bacteria
(C) Some exotoxins act in the gastrointestinal tract to cause diarrhea
(D) Some exotoxins contain lipopolysaccharides as the toxic component

29. Each of the following statements concerning bacterial and human cells is correct EXCEPT:
(A) Bacteria are prokaryotic (ie, they have one molecule of DNA, are haploid, and have no nuclear membrane), whereas human cells are eukaryotic (ie, they have multiple chromosomes, are diploid, and have a nuclear membrane)
(B) Bacteria derive their energy by oxidative phosphorylation within mitochondria in a manner similar to human cells
(C) Bacterial and human ribosomes are of different sizes and chemical compositions
(D) Bacterial cells possess peptidoglycan, whereas human cells do not

30. Each of the following statements concerning penicillin is correct EXCEPT:
(A) An intact β-lactam ring of penicillin is required for its activity
(B) The structure of penicillin resembles that of a dipeptide of alanine, which is a component of peptidoglycan
(C) Penicillin is a bacteriostatic drug because autolytic enzymes are not activated
(D) Penicillin inhibits transpeptidases, which are required for cross-linking peptidoglycan

31. Each of the following statements concerning the mechanisms of resistance to antimicrobial drugs is correct EXCEPT:
(A) R factors are plasmids that carry the genes for enzymes which modify one or more drugs
(B) Resistance to some drugs is due to a chromosomal mutation that alters the receptor for the drug
(C) Resistance to some drugs is due to transposon genes that code for enzymes which inactivate the drugs
(D) Resistance genes are rarely transferred by conjugation

32. Each of the following statements concerning endotoxins is correct EXCEPT:
(A) The toxicity of endotoxins is due to the lipid portion of the molecule
(B) Endotoxins are found in most gram-positive bacteria
(C) Endotoxins are located in the cell wall
(D) The antigenicity of somatic (O) antigen is due to repeating oligosaccharides

33. Each of the following statements concerning exotoxins is correct EXCEPT:
(A) Exotoxins are polypeptides
(B) Exotoxins are more easily inactivated by heat than are endotoxins
(C) Exotoxins are less toxic than the same amount of endotoxins
(D) Exotoxins can be converted to toxoids

34. Each of the following statements concerning the killing of bacteria is correct EXCEPT:
(A) A 70% solution of ethanol kills more effectively than absolute (100%) ethanol
(B) An autoclave uses steam under pressure to reach the killing temperature of 121°C
(C) The pasteurization of milk kills pathogens but allows many organisms and spores to survive
(D) Iodine kills by causing the formation of thymine dimers in bacterial DNA

35. Each of the following statements concerning the drug depicted in the diagram is correct EXCEPT:

(A) The drug is bacteriostatic
(B) The drug inhibits cell wall synthesis
(C) The drug is made by a fungus
(D) The portion of the molecule required for activity is labeled B

36. Each of the following statements concerning the normal flora is correct EXCEPT:
   (A) The normal flora of the colon consists predominantly of anaerobic bacteria
   (B) The presence of the normal flora prevents certain pathogens from colonizing the upper respiratory tract
   (C) Fungi, eg, yeasts, are not members of the normal flora
   (D) Organisms of the normal flora are permanent residents of the body surfaces

37. Each of the following statements concerning the structure and chemical composition of bacteria is correct EXCEPT:
   (A) Some gram-positive cocci contain a layer of teichoic acid external to the peptidoglycan
   (B) Some gram-positive rods contain dipicolinic acid in their spores
   (C) Some gram-negative rods contain lipid A in their cell wall
   (D) Some mycoplasmas contain pentaglycine in their peptidoglycan

38. Each of the following statements concerning the normal flora is correct EXCEPT:
   (A) *Streptococcus mutans* is found in the mouth and contributes to the formation of dental caries
   (B) The predominant organisms in the alveoli are viridans streptococci
   (C) *Bacteroides fragilis* is found in greater numbers than *Escherichia coli* in the colon
   (D) *Candida albicans* is part of the normal flora of both men and women

39. Each of the following statements concerning cholera toxin is correct EXCEPT:
   (A) Cholera toxin inhibits elongation factor 2 in the mucosal epithelium
   (B) Binding of cholera toxin to the mucosal epithelium occurs via interaction of the B subunit of the toxin with a ganglioside in the cell membrane

(C) Cholera toxin acts by adding ADP-ribose to a G protein
(D) Cholera toxin activates the enzyme adenylate cyclase in the mucosal epithelium

Answers (Questions 1–39):

1 (D)	9 (D)	17 (D)	25 (A)	33 (C)
2 (C)	10 (B)	18 (C)	26 (D)	34 (D)
3 (A)	11 (C)	19 (A)	27 (C)	35 (A)
4 (D)	12 (D)	20 (C)	28 (D)	36 (C)
5 (C)	13 (C)	21 (D)	29 (B)	37 (D)
6 (B)	14 (B)	22 (B)	30 (C)	38 (B)
7 (C)	15 (D)	23 (A)	31 (D)	39 (A)
8 (B)	16 (D)	24 (B)	32 (B)	

DIRECTIONS (Questions 40–51): Select the ONE lettered option that is MOST closely associated with the numbered items. Each lettered option may be selected once, more than once, or not at all.

Questions 40–43

   (A) Penicillins
   (B) Aminoglycosides
   (C) Chloramphenicol
   (D) Rifampin
   (E) Sulfonamides

40. Inhibit(s) bacterial RNA polymerase
41. Inhibit(s) cross-linking of peptidoglycan
42. Inhibit(s) protein synthesis by binding to the 30S ribosomal subunit
43. Inhibit(s) folic acid synthesis

Questions 44–46

   (A) Transduction
   (B) Conjugation
   (C) DNA transformation
   (D) Transposition

44. During an outbreak of gastrointestinal disease caused by an *Escherichia coli* strain sensitive to ampicillin, tetracycline, and chloramphenicol, a stool sample from one patient yields *E. coli* with the same serotype resistant to the three antibiotics *Conjugation*

45. A mutant cell line lacking a functional thymidine kinase gene was exposed to a preparation of DNA from normal cells; under appropriate growth conditions, a colony of cells was isolated that makes thymidine kinase *DNA trans*

46. A retrovirus without an oncogene does not induce leukemia in mice; after repeated passages through mice, viruses recovered from a tumor were highly oncogenic and contained a new gene *trans*

Questions 47–51

(A) Diphtheria toxin
(B) Tetanus toxin
(C) Botulinum toxin
(D) Toxic shock syndrome toxin
(E) Cholera toxin

47. Causes paralysis by blocking release of acetylcholine

48. Inhibits protein synthesis by blocking elongation factor 2

49. Stimulates T cells to produce cytokines

50. Stimulates the production of cyclic AMP by adding ADP-ribose to a G protein

51. Inhibits the release of inhibitory neurotransmitters causing muscle spasms

Answers (Questions 40–51)

40 (D)	43 (E)	46 (A)	48 (A)	50 (E)
41 (A)	44 (B)	47 (C)	49 (D)	51 (B)
42 (B)	45 (C)			

Clinical Bacteriology

DIRECTIONS (Questions 52–136): Select the ONE lettered answer that is BEST in each question.

52. An outbreak of sepsis caused by *Staphylococcus aureus* has occurred in the newborn nursery. You are called upon to investigate. According to your knowledge of the normal flora, what is the MOST likely source of the organism?
   (A) Colon
   (B) Nose
   (C) Throat
   (D) Vagina

53. Each of the statements about the classification of streptococci is correct EXCEPT:
   (A) Pneumococci (*Streptococcus pneumoniae*) are alpha-hemolytic and can be serotyped on the basis of their polysaccharide capsules
   (B) Enterococci are group D streptococci and can be classified by their ability to grow in 6.5% sodium chloride
   (C) Although pneumococci and the viridans streptococci are alpha-hemolytic, they can be differentiated by the bile solubility test and their susceptibility to optochin
   (D) Viridans streptococci are identified by Lancefield grouping, which is based on the C carbohydrate in the cell wall

54. Each of the following agents is a recognized cause of diarrhea EXCEPT:
   (A) *Clostridium perfringens*
   (B) *Enterococcus faecalis* UTI

(C) *Escherichia coli*
(D) *Vibrio cholerae*

55. Each of the following organisms is an important cause of urinary tract infections EXCEPT:
   (A) *Escherichia coli*
   (B) *Proteus mirabilis*
   (C) *Klebsiella pneumoniae* UTI & pneumonia
   (D) *Bacteroides fragilis* peritonitis, GU/GI abscess

56. Your patient is a 30-year-old woman with non-bloody diarrhea for the past 14 hours. Which one of the following organisms is LEAST likely to cause this illness?
   (A) *Clostridium difficile*
   (B) *Streptococcus pyogenes*
   (C) *Shigella dysenteriae*
   (D) *Salmonella enteritidis*

57. Each of the following statements concerning *Mycobacterium tuberculosis* is correct EXCEPT:
   (A) After being stained with carbolfuchsin, *M. tuberculosis* resists decolorization with acid alcohol
   (B) *M. tuberculosis* has a large amount of mycolic acid in its cell wall
   (C) *M. tuberculosis* appears as a red rod in Gram-stained specimens
   (D) *M. tuberculosis* appears as a red rod in acid-fast stained specimens

58. A 50-year-old homeless alcoholic has a fever and is coughing up 1 cup of green, foul-smelling sputum per day. You suspect that he may have a lung

abscess. Which one of the following pairs of organisms is MOST likely to be the cause?
(A) *Listeria monocytogenes* and *Legionella pneumophila*
(B) *Nocardia asteroides* and *Mycoplasma pneumoniae*
(C) *Fusobacterium nucleatum* and *Peptostreptococcus intermedius*
(D) *Clostridium perfringens* and *Chlamydia psittaci*

59. Which one of the following diseases is BEST diagnosed by serologic means?
(A) Q fever
(B) Pulmonary tuberculosis
(C) Gonorrhea
(D) Actinomycosis

60. Your patient has subacute bacterial endocarditis caused by a member of the viridans group of streptococci. Which one of the following sites is MOST likely to be the source of the organism?
(A) Skin
(B) Colon
(C) Oropharynx
(D) Urethra

61. A culture of skin lesions from a patient with pyoderma (impetigo) shows numerous colonies surrounded by a zone of beta hemolysis on a blood agar plate. A Gram-stained smear shows gram-positive cocci. If you found the catalase test to be negative, which one of the following organisms would you MOST probably have isolated?
(A) *Streptococcus pyogenes*
(B) *Staphylococcus aureus*
(C) *Staphylococcus epidermidis*
(D) *Streptococcus pneumoniae*

62. The coagulase test, in which the bacteria cause plasma to clot, is used to distinguish
(A) *Streptococcus pyogenes* from *Enterococcus faecalis*
(B) *Streptococcus pyogenes* from *Staphylococcus aureus*
(C) *Staphylococcus aureus* from *Staphylococcus epidermidis*
(D) *Staphylococcus epidermidis* from *Neisseria meningitidis*

63. Which one of the following is considered a virulence factor for *Staphylococcus aureus*?
(A) A heat-labile toxin that inhibits glycine release at the internuncial neuron
(B) An oxygen-labile hemolysin
(C) Resistance to novobiocin
(D) Protein A that binds to the Fc portion of IgG

64. Which one of the following host defense mechanisms is the MOST important for preventing dysentery caused by *Salmonella?*
(A) Gastric acid
(B) Salivary enzymes

(C) Normal flora of the mouth
(D) Alpha interferon

65. The MOST important protective function of the antibody stimulated by tetanus immunization is
(A) To opsonize the pathogen (*Clostridium tetani*)
(B) To prevent growth of the pathogen
(C) To prevent adherence of the pathogen
(D) To neutralize the toxin of the pathogen

66. Five hours after eating fried rice at a restaurant, a 24-year-old woman and her husband both developed nausea, vomiting, and diarrhea. Which one of the following organisms is the MOST likely to be involved?
(A) *Clostridium perfringens*
(B) Enterotoxigenic *Escherichia coli*
(C) *Bacillus cereus*
(D) *Salmonella typhi*

67. Which one of the following bacteria has the LOWEST 50% infective dose (ID_{50})?
(A) *Shigella sonnei*
(B) *Vibrio cholerae*
(C) *Salmonella typhi*
(D) *Campylobacter jejuni*

68. For which one of the following enteric illnesses is a chronic carrier state MOST likely to develop?
(A) *Campylobacter* enterocolitis
(B) *Shigella* enterocolitis
(C) Cholera
(D) Typhoid fever

69. Which one of the following zoonotic illnesses has NO arthropod vector?
(A) Plague
(B) Lyme disease
(C) Brucellosis
(D) Epidemic typhus

70. Which one of the following organisms principally infects vascular endothelial cells?
(A) *Salmonella typhi*
(B) *Rickettsia typhi*
(C) *Haemophilus influenzae*
(D) *Coxiella burnetii*

71. Which one of the following statements MOST accurately depicts the ability of the organism to be cultured in the laboratory?
(A) *Treponema pallidum* from a chancre can be grown on a special artificial medium supplemented with cholesterol
(B) *Mycobacterium leprae* can be grown in the armadillo and the mouse footpad but not on any artificial media
(C) *Mycobacterium tuberculosis* can be grown on enriched artificial media and produces visible colonies in 48–96 hours
(D) Atypical mycobacteria are found widely in soil and water but cannot be cultured on artificial media in the laboratory

72. Each of the following statements concerning chlamydiae is correct EXCEPT:
    (A) Chlamydiae are strict intracellular parasites because they cannot synthesize sufficient ATP
    (B) Chlamydiae possess both DNA and RNA and are bounded by a cell wall
    (C) C. trachomatis has multiple serotypes, but C. psittaci has only one serotype
    (D) Most chlamydiae are transmitted by arthropods

73. For which one of the following bacterial vaccines are toxic side effects an important concern?
    (A) The vaccine containing pneumococcal polysaccharide
    (B) The vaccine containing killed Bordetella pertussis
    (C) The vaccine containing tetanus toxoid
    (D) The vaccine containing diphtheria toxoid

74. Each of the following statements concerning Staphylococcus aureus is correct EXCEPT:
    (A) Gram-positive cocci in grapelike clusters are seen on Gram-stained smear
    (B) The coagulase test is positive
    (C) Treatment should include a β-lactamase-resistant penicillin
    (D) Endotoxin is an important pathogenetic factor

75. Your patient is a 70-year-old man who underwent bowel surgery for colon cancer 3 days ago. He now has a fever and abdominal pain. You are concerned that he may have peritonitis. Which one of the following pairs of organisms is MOST likely to be the cause?
    (A) Bacteroides fragilis and Klebsiella pneumoniae
    (B) Bordetella pertussis and Salmonella enteritidis
    (C) Actinomyces israelii and Campylobacter jejuni
    (D) Clostridium botulinum and Shigella dysenteriae

76. A 65-year-old man develops dysuria and hematuria. A Gram stain of a urine sample shows gram-negative rods. Culture of the urine on EMB agar reveals lactose-negative colonies without evidence of swarming motility. Which one of the following organisms is MOST likely to be the cause of his urinary tract infection?
    (A) Enterococcus faecalis
    (B) Pseudomonas aeruginosa
    (C) Proteus vulgaris
    (D) Escherichia coli

77. A 25-year-old man complains of a urethral discharge. You perform a Gram stain on a specimen of the discharge and see neutrophils but no bacteria. Of the organisms listed, the one MOST likely to cause the discharge is

(A) Treponema pallidum
(B) Chlamydia trachomatis
(C) Candida albicans
(D) Coxiella burnetii

78. Two hours after a delicious Thanksgiving dinner of barley soup, roast turkey, stuffing, sweet potato, green beans, cranberry sauce, and pumpkin pie topped with whipped cream, the Smith family of four experience vomiting and diarrhea. Which one of the following organisms is MOST likely to cause these symptoms?
    (A) Shigella flexneri
    (B) Campylobacter jejuni
    (C) Staphylococcus aureus
    (D) Salmonella enteritidis

79. Your patient has a brain abscess that was detected 1 month after a dental extraction. Which one of the following organisms is MOST likely to be involved?
    (A) Anaerobic streptococci
    (B) Mycobacterium smegmatis
    (C) Lactobacillus acidophilus
    (D) Mycoplasma pneumoniae

80. The MOST important contribution of the capsule of Streptococcus pneumoniae to virulence is
    (A) To prevent dehydration of the organisms on mucosal surfaces
    (B) To retard phagocytosis by polymorphonuclear leukocytes
    (C) To inhibit polymorphonuclear leukocyte chemotaxis
    (D) To accelerate tissue invasion by its collagenaselike activity

81. The MOST important way the host circumvents the function of the pneumococcal polysaccharide capsule is via
    (A) T lymphocytes sensitized to polysaccharide antigens
    (B) Polysaccharide-degrading enzymes
    (C) Anticapsular antibody
    (D) Activated macrophages

82. The pathogenesis of which one of the following organisms is MOST likely to involve invasion of the intestinal mucosa?
    (A) Vibrio cholerae
    (B) Shigella sonnei
    (C) Enterotoxigenic Escherichia coli
    (D) Clostridium botulinum

83. Which one of the following organisms that infects the gastrointestinal tract is the MOST frequent cause of bacteremia?
    (A) Shigella flexneri
    (B) Campylobacter jejuni
    (C) Vibrio cholerae
    (D) Salmonella typhi

84. A 30-year-old woman with systemic lupus erythematosus is found to have a positive serologic test for syphilis (VDRL test). She denies having had sexual contact with a partner who had symptoms of a venereal disease. The next best step would be to
    (A) Reassure her that the test is a false-positive reaction related to her autoimmune disorder
    (B) Trace her sexual contacts for serologic testing
    (C) Treat her with penicillin
    (D) Perform a fluorescent treponemal antibody-absorbed (FTA-ABS) test on a specimen of her serum

85. Each of the following statements concerning *Treponema* is correct EXCEPT:
    (A) *T. pallidum* produces an exotoxin that stimulates adenylate cyclase
    (B) *T. pallidum* cannot be grown on conventional laboratory media
    (C) Treponemes are members of the normal flora of the human oropharynx
    (D) Patients infected with *T. pallidum* produce antibodies that react with beef heart cardiolipin

86. Each of the following statements concerning clostridia is correct EXCEPT:
    (A) Pathogenic clostridia are found both in the soil and in the normal flora of the colon
    (B) Antibiotic-associated (pseudomembranous) colitis is due to a toxin produced by *Clostridium difficile*
    (C) Anaerobic conditions at the wound site are not required to cause tetanus, because spores will form in the presence of oxygen
    (D) Botulism, which is caused by ingesting preformed toxin, can be prevented by boiling food prior to eating

87. Each of the following statements concerning *Bacteroides fragilis* is correct EXCEPT:
    (A) *B. fragilis* is a gram-negative rod that is part of the normal flora of the colon
    (B) *B. fragilis* forms endospores, which allow it to survive in the soil
    (C) The capsule of *B. fragilis* is an important virulence factor
    (D) *B. fragilis* infections are characterized by foul-smelling pus

88. Each of the following statements concerning staphylococci is correct EXCEPT:
    (A) *S. aureus* is differentiated from *S. epidermidis* by the production of coagulase
    (B) *S. aureus* infections are often associated with abscess formation
    (C) The majority of clinical isolates of *S. aureus* elaborate penicillinase; therefore, presumptive antibiotic therapy for *S. aureus* infections should not consist of penicillin G
    (D) Scalded skin syndrome caused by *S. aureus* is due to enzymatic degradation of epidermal desmosomes by catalase

89. Acute glomerulonephritis is a nonsuppurative complication that follows infection by which one of the following organisms?
    (A) *Enterococcus faecalis*
    (B) *Streptococcus pyogenes*
    (C) *Streptococcus pneumoniae*
    (D) *Streptococcus agalactiae*

90. Each of the following statements concerning gram-negative rods is correct EXCEPT:
    (A) *Escherichia coli* is part of the normal flora of the colon; therefore, it does not cause diarrhea
    (B) *E. coli* ferments lactose, whereas the enteric pathogens *Shigella* and *Salmonella* do not
    (C) *Klebsiella pneumoniae*, although a cause of pneumonia, is part of the normal flora of the colon
    (D) *Proteus* species are highly motile organisms that are found in the human colon and cause urinary tract infections

91. A 70-year-old man is found to have a hard mass in his prostate, which is suspected to be a carcinoma. Twenty-four hours after surgical removal of the mass, he develops fever to 39°C and has several shaking chills. Of the organisms listed, which one is LEAST likely to be involved?
    (A) *Escherichia coli*
    (B) *Enterococcus faecalis*
    (C) *Klebsiella pneumoniae*
    (D) *Legionella pneumophila*

92. Five days ago a 65-year-old woman with a lower urinary tract infection began taking ampicillin. She now has a fever and severe diarrhea. Of the organisms listed, which one is MOST likely to be the cause of the diarrhea?
    (A) *Clostridium difficile*
    (B) *Bacteroides fragilis*
    (C) *Proteus mirabilis*
    (D) *Bordetella pertussis*

93. The pathogenesis of which one of the following diseases does NOT involve an exotoxin?
    (A) Scarlet fever
    (B) Typhoid fever
    (C) Toxic shock syndrome
    (D) Botulism

94. Regarding the effect of benzylpenicillin (penicillin G) on bacteria, which one of the following organisms is LEAST likely to be resistant?
    (A) *Staphylococcus aureus*
    (B) *Enterococcus faecalis*

(C) *Streptococcus pyogenes*
(D) *Neisseria gonorrhoeae*

95. Which one of the following organisms is MOST likely to be the cause of pneumonia in an immunocompetent patient?
(A) *Nocardia asteroides*
(B) *Serratia marcescens*
(C) *Mycoplasma pneumoniae* walking pneumonia
(D) *Legionella pneumophila*

96. Each of the following statements concerning chlamydial genital tract infections is correct EXCEPT:
(A) Infection can be diagnosed by finding antichlamydial antibody in a serum specimen
(B) Infection can persist after administration of penicillin
(C) Symptomatic infections can be associated with urethral or cervical discharge containing many polymorphonuclear leukocytes
(D) There is no vaccine against these infections

97. Which one of the following illnesses is NOT a zoonosis?
(A) Typhoid fever
(B) Q fever
(C) Tularemia
(D) Rocky Mountain spotted fever

98. Which one of the following is NOT a characteristic of the staphylococcus associated with toxic shock syndrome?
(A) Elaboration of enterotoxin F
(B) Coagulase production
(C) Appearance of the organism in grapelike clusters on Gram-stained smear
(D) Catalase-negative reaction

99. Which one of the following is NOT an important characteristic of either *Neisseria gonorrhoeae* or *Neisseria meningitidis*?
(A) Polysaccharide capsule
(B) IgA protease
(C) M protein
(D) Pili

100. Which one of the following is NOT an important characteristic of *Streptococcus pyogenes*?
(A) Protein A
(B) M protein
(C) Beta-hemolysin
(D) Polysaccharide group-specific substance

101. Each of the following is associated with the Lancefield group B streptococci (*S. agalactiae*) EXCEPT:
(A) Pyoderma (impetigo)
(B) Vaginal carriage in 5–25% of normal women of childbearing age
(C) Neonatal sepsis and meningitis
(D) Beta-hemolysis

102. Three organisms, *Streptococcus pneumoniae*, *Neisseria meningitidis*, and *Haemophilus influenzae*, cause the vast majority of cases of bacterial meningitis. What is the MOST important pathogenic component they share?
(A) Protein A
(B) Capsule
(C) Endotoxin
(D) β-Lactamase

103. Diarrhea caused by which one of the following agents is characterized by the presence of fecal leukocytes?
(A) *Campylobacter jejuni*
(B) Rotavirus
(C) *Clostridium perfringens*
(D) Enterotoxigenic *Escherichia coli*

104. Each of the following statements concerning *Chlamydia trachomatis* is correct EXCEPT:
(A) It is an important cause of nongonococcal urethritis
(B) It is the cause of lymphogranuloma venereum
(C) It is an important cause of subacute bacterial endocarditis
(D) It is an important cause of conjunctivitis

105. Each of the following statements concerning *Actinomyces* and *Nocardia* is correct EXCEPT:
(A) *A. israelii* is an anaerobic rod found as part of the normal flora in the mouth
(B) Both *Actinomyces* and *Nocardia* are branching, filamentous rods
(C) *N. asteroides* causes infections primarily in immunocompromised patients
(D) Infections are usually diagnosed by detecting a significant rise in antibody titer

106. Which one of the following types of organisms is NOT an obligate intracellular parasite and therefore can replicate on bacteriologic media?
(A) *Chlamydia*
(B) *Mycoplasma*
(C) Adenovirus
(D) *Rickettsia*

107. Tissue-degrading enzymes play an important role in the pathogenesis of several bacteria. Which one of the following is NOT involved in tissue or cell damage?
(A) Lecithinase of *Clostridium perfringens*
(B) Hyaluronidase of *Streptococcus pyogenes*
(C) M protein of *Streptococcus pneumoniae*
(D) Leukocidin of *Staphylococcus aureus*

108. The soil is the natural habitat for certain microorganisms of medical importance. Which one of the following is LEAST likely to reside there?
(A) *Clostridium tetani*
(B) *Mycobacterium intracellulare*

(C) *Bacillus anthracis*

(D) *Chlamydia trachomatis*

109. Of the organisms listed below, which one is the MOST frequent bacterial cause of pharyngitis?

(A) *Staphylococcus aureus*

(B) *Streptococcus pneumoniae*

(C) *Streptococcus pyogenes*

(D) *Neisseria meningitidis*

110. Several pathogens are transmitted either during gestation or at birth. Which one of the following is LEAST likely to be transmitted at these times?

(A) *Haemophilus influenzae*

(B) *Treponema pallidum*

(C) *Neisseria gonorrhoeae*

(D) *Chlamydia trachomatis*

111. Each of the following statements concerning exotoxins is correct EXCEPT:

(A) Some strains of *Escherichia coli* produce an enterotoxin that causes diarrhea

(B) Cholera toxin acts by stimulating adenylate cyclase

(C) Diphtheria is caused by an exotoxin that inhibits protein synthesis by inactivating an elongation factor

(D) Botulism is caused by a toxin that hydrolyzes lecithin (lecithinase), thereby destroying nerve cells

112. Each of the following statements concerning the VDRL test for syphilis is correct EXCEPT:

(A) The antigen is composed of inactivated *Treponema pallidum*

(B) The test is usually positive in secondary syphilis

(C) False-positive results are more frequent than with the FTA-ABS test

(D) The antibody titer declines with adequate therapy

113. Each of the following statements concerning the fluorescent treponemal antibody-absorbed (FTA-ABS) test for syphilis is correct EXCEPT:

(A) The test is specific for *Treponema pallidum*

(B) The patient's serum is absorbed with saprophytic treponemes

(C) Once positive, the test remains so despite adequate therapy

(D) The test is rarely positive in primary syphilis

114. Each of the following statements concerning *Corynebacterium diphtheriae* is correct EXCEPT:

(A) *C. diphtheriae* is a gram-positive rod that does not form spores

(B) Toxin production is dependent on the organism's being lysogenized by a bacteriophage

(C) Diphtheria toxoid should not be given to children under the age of 3 years because the incidence of complications is too high

(D) Antitoxin should be used to treat patients with diphtheria

115. Each of the following statements concerning certain gram-negative rods is correct EXCEPT:

(A) *Pseudomonas aeruginosa* causes wound infections that are characterized by blue-green pus as a result of pyocyanin production

(B) Invasive disease caused by *Haemophilus influenzae* is most often due to strains possessing a type b polysaccharide capsule

(C) *Legionella pneumophila* infection is acquired by inhalation of aerosols from environmental water sources

(D) Whooping cough, which is caused by *Bordetella pertussis,* is on the rise because changing antigenicity has made the vaccine relatively ineffective

116. Each of the following statements concerning enterotoxins is correct EXCEPT:

(A) Enterotoxins typically cause bloody diarrhea with leukocytes in the stool

(B) *Staphylococcus aureus* produces an enterotoxin that causes vomiting and diarrhea

(C) *Vibrio cholerae* causes cholera by producing an enterotoxin that activates adenylate cyclase

(D) *Escherichia coli* enterotoxin mediates ADP-ribosylation of a G protein

117. Each of the following statements concerning plague is correct EXCEPT:

(A) Plague is caused by a gram-negative rod that can be cultured on blood agar

(B) Plague is transmitted to humans by flea bite

(C) The main reservoirs in nature are small rodents

(D) Plague is of concern in many underdeveloped countries but has not occurred in the United States since 1968

118. Which one of the following statements concerning the organisms that cause brucellosis is CORRECT?

(A) Brucellae are transmitted primarily by tick bite

(B) The principal reservoirs of brucellae are small rodents

(C) Brucellae are found in reticuloendothelial cells and often cause granulomatous lesions

(D) Brucellae are obligate intracellular parasites that are usually identified by growth in human cell culture

119. Each of the following statements concerning epidemic typhus is correct EXCEPT:

(A) The disease is characterized by a rash

(B) The Weil-Felix test can aid in diagnosis of the disease

(C) The disease is caused by a rickettsia

(D) The causative organism is transmitted from rodents to humans by a tick

120. Which one of the following organisms causes diarrhea by producing an enterotoxin that activates adenylate cyclase?
    (A) *Escherichia coli*
    (B) *Bacteroides fragilis*
    (C) *Staphylococcus aureus*
    (D) *Enterococcus faecalis*

121. Each of the following statements concerning Rocky Mountain spotted fever is correct EXCEPT:
    (A) The causative organism can be identified in blood agar culture
    (B) Headache, fever, and rash are characteristic features of the disease
    (C) The disease occurs primarily east of the Mississippi
    (D) The disease is caused by a rickettsia

122. Each of the following statements concerning *Clostridium perfringens* is correct EXCEPT:
    (A) It causes gas gangrene
    (B) It causes food poisoning
    (C) It produces an exotoxin that degrades lecithin and causes necrosis and hemolysis
    (D) It is a gram-negative rod that does not ferment lactose

123. Each of the following statements concerning *Clostridium tetani* is correct EXCEPT:
    (A) It is a gram-positive, spore-forming rod
    (B) Pathogenesis is due to the production of an exotoxin that blocks inhibitory neurotransmitters
    (C) It is a facultative organism; it will grow on a blood agar plate in the presence of room air
    (D) Its natural habitat is primarily the soil

124. Each of the following statements concerning spirochetes is correct EXCEPT:
    (A) Species of *Treponema* are part of the normal flora of the mouth
    (B) Species of *Borrelia* cause a tick-borne disease called relapsing fever
    (C) The species of *Leptospira* that cause leptospirosis grow primarily in humans and are usually transmitted by human-to-human contact
    (D) Species of *Treponema* cause syphilis and yaws

125. Each of the following statements concerning gonorrhea is correct EXCEPT:
    (A) Infection in men is more frequently symptomatic than in women
    (B) A presumptive diagnosis can be made by finding gram-negative kidney-bean-shaped diplococci within neutrophils in a urethral discharge

    (C) The definitive diagnosis can be made by detecting at least a 4-fold rise in antibody titer to *Neisseria gonorrhoeae*
    (D) Gonococcal conjunctivitis of the newborn rarely occurs in the United States, because silver nitrate or erythromycin is commonly used as prophylaxis

126. Each of the following statements concerning *Mycobacterium tuberculosis* is correct EXCEPT:
    (A) Some strains isolated from individuals with previously untreated cases of tuberculosis are resistant to isoniazid
    (B) *M. tuberculosis* contains a small amount of lipid in its cell wall and therefore stains poorly with the Gram stain
    (C) The organism grows slowly, often requiring 3–6 weeks before colonies appear
    (D) The antigen in the skin test is a protein extracted from the organism

127. Which one of the following statements concerning immunization against diseases caused by clostridia is CORRECT?
    (A) Antitoxin against tetanus protects against botulism as well, because the two toxins share antigenic sites
    (B) Vaccines containing alpha toxin (lecithinase) are effective in protecting against gas gangrene
    (C) The toxoid vaccine against *Clostridium difficile* infection should be administered to immunocompromised patients
    (D) Immunization with tetanus toxoid induces effective protection against tetanus toxin

128. Each of the following statements concerning neisseriae is correct EXCEPT:
    (A) They are gram-negative diplococci
    (B) They produce IgA protease as a virulence factor
    (C) They are oxidase-positive
    (D) They grow best under anaerobic conditions

129. Which one of the following statements concerning *Legionella pneumophila* is CORRECT?
    (A) It is part of the normal flora of the colon
    (B) It cannot be grown on laboratory media
    (C) It does not have a cell wall
    (D) It is an important cause of pneumonia in renal transplant patients

130. Each of the following statements concerning wound infections caused by *Clostridium perfringens* is correct EXCEPT:
    (A) An exotoxin plays a role in pathogenesis
    (B) Gram-positive rods are found in the exudate
    (C) The organism grows only in human cell culture
    (D) Anaerobic culture of the wound site should be ordered

131. Each of the following statements concerning infection with *Chlamydia psittaci* is correct EXCEPT:
  - **(A)** *C. psittaci* can be isolated by growth in cell culture and will not grow in blood agar
  - **(B)** The organism appears purple in Gram-stained smears of sputum
  - **(C)** The infection is more readily diagnosed by serologic tests than by isolation of the organism
  - **(D)** The infection is more commonly acquired from a nonhuman source than from another human

132. Ticks are vectors for the transmission of each of the following diseases EXCEPT:
  - **(A)** Rocky Mountain spotted fever
  - **(B)** epidemic typhus
  - **(C)** tularemia
  - **(D)** Lyme disease

133. Each of the following statements concerning pneumonia caused by *Mycoplasma pneumoniae* is correct EXCEPT:
  - **(A)** The disease is associated with a rise in the titer of cold agglutinins
  - **(B)** The disease occurs primarily in immunocompetent individuals
  - **(C)** The disease is one of the "atypical" pneumonias
  - **(D)** The organism cannot be cultured in vitro because it has no cell wall

134. Each of the following statements concerning *Neisseria meningitidis* is correct EXCEPT:
  - **(A)** It is an oxidase-positive, gram-negative diplococcus
  - **(B)** It contains endotoxin in its cell wall
  - **(C)** It produces an exotoxin that stimulates adenylate cyclase
  - **(D)** It has a polysaccharide capsule that is antiphagocytic

135. Each of the following statements concerning Q fever is correct EXCEPT:
  - **(A)** Rash is a prominent feature *no arth. vector*
  - **(B)** It is transmitted by respiratory aerosol
  - **(C)** Farm animals are an important reservoir
  - **(D)** It is caused by *Coxiella burnetii*

136. Each of the following statements concerning *Mycobacterium leprae* is correct EXCEPT:
  - **(A)** In lepromatous leprosy, large numbers of organisms are usually seen in acid-fast-stained smears
  - **(B)** The organism will grow on bacteriologic media in 3–6 weeks *mouse pad & armadillo*
  - **(C)** Prolonged therapy (9 months or longer) is required to prevent recurrence
  - **(D)** Skin tests for delayed hypersensitivity are useful diagnostically

Answers (Questions 52–136)

52 (B)	69 (C)	86 (C)	103 (A)	120 (A)
53 (D)	70 (B)	87 (B)	104 (C)	121 (A)
54 (B)	71 (B)	88 (D)	105 (D)	122 (D)
55 (D)	72 (D)	89 (B)	106 (B)	123 (C)
56 (B)	73 (B)	90 (A)	107 (C)	124 (C)
57 (C)	74 (D)	91 (D)	108 (D)	125 (C)
58 (C)	75 (A)	92 (A)	109 (C)	126 (B)
59 (A)	76 (B)	93 (B)	110 (A)	127 (D)
60 (C)	77 (B)	94 (C)	111 (D)	128 (D)
61 (A)	78 (C)	95 (C)	112 (A)	129 (D)
62 (C)	79 (A)	96 (A)	113 (D)	130 (C)
63 (D)	80 (B)	97 (A)	114 (C)	131 (B)
64 (A)	81 (C)	98 (D)	115 (D)	132 (B)
65 (D)	82 (B)	99 (C)	116 (A)	133 (D)
66 (C)	83 (D)	100 (A)	117 (D)	134 (C)
67 (A)	84 (D)	101 (A)	118 (C)	135 (A)
68 (D)	85 (A)	102 (B)	119 (D)	136 (B)

DIRECTIONS (Questions 137–158): Select the ONE lettered option that is MOST closely associated with the numbered items. Each lettered option may be selected once, more than once, or not at all.

Questions 137–140
  - **(A)** *Mycobacterium avium-intracellulare*
  - **(B)** *Treponema pallidum*
  - **(C)** *Rickettsia prowazekii*
  - **(D)** *Mycoplasma pneumoniae*

137. Is an obligate intracellular parasite
138. Is found primarily in the soil
139. Has no cell wall
140. Is an acid-fast rod

Questions 141–143
  - **(A)** *Borrelia burgdorferi*
  - **(B)** *Helicobacter pylori*
  - **(C)** *Pasteurella multocida*
  - **(D)** *Brucella melitensis*

141. Peptic ulcer in a 45-year-old salesman
142. Cellulitis of the hand following a cat bite
143. Migratory skin rash followed by arthritis in a 6-year-old boy after a camping trip

Questions 144–147
  - **(A)** *Corynebacterium diphtheriae*
  - **(B)** *Listeria monocytogenes*
  - **(C)** *Bacillus anthracis*
  - **(D)** *Clostridium botulinum*

144. Causes both skin lesions and a severe pneumonia
145. Causes flaccid paralysis

146. Lysogeny with a prophage is required for production of a toxin that inhibits protein synthesis

147. Causes meningitis in neonates and the immunosuppressed

Questions 148–150

(A) *Escherichia coli*
(B) *Klebsiella pneumoniae*
(C) *Salmonella enteritidis*
(D) *Proteus mirabilis*

148. Is frequently implicated in nosocomial infections and is an important cause of community-acquired pneumonia in adults

149. Is the most common cause of urinary tract infections

150. Pathogenicity associated primarily with urinary tract infections; produces urease

Questions 151–154

(A) *Staphylococcus aureus*
(B) *Streptococcus pyogenes*
(C) *Enterococcus faecalis*
(D) *Streptococcus pneumoniae*

151. Grows in 6.5% sodium chloride

152. Is bile soluble

153. Produces enterotoxin

154. Is associated with rheumatic fever

Questions 155–158

(A) *Bacteroides fragilis*
(B) *Haemophilus influenzae*
(C) *Pseudomonas aeruginosa*
(D) *Chlamydia pneumoniae*

155. Coccobacillary gram-negative rod that is an important cause of meningitis in young children

156. Oxidase-positive gram-negative rod that is an important cause of wound and burn infections

157. Causes atypical pneumonia in immunocompetent adults

158. Anaerobic gram-negative rod that is an important cause of peritonitis

Answers (Questions 137–158)

137 (C)	142 (C)	147 (B)	151 (C)	155 (B)
138 (A)	143 (A)	148 (B)	152 (D)	156 (C)
139 (D)	144 (C)	149 (A)	153 (A)	157 (D)
140 (A)	145 (D)	150 (D)	154 (B)	158 (A)
141 (B)	146 (A)			

Basic Virology

DIRECTIONS (Questions 159–192): Select the ONE lettered answer that is BEST in each question.

159. Viruses enter cells by adsorbing to specific sites on the outer membrane of cells. Each of the following statements regarding this event is correct EXCEPT:

(A) The interaction determines the specific target organs for infection
(B) The interaction determines whether the purified genome of a virus is infectious
(C) The interaction can be prevented by neutralizing antibody
(D) If the sites are occupied, interference with virus infection occurs

160. Many viruses mature by budding through the outer membrane of the host cell. Each of the following statements regarding these viruses is correct EXCEPT:

(A) Some of these viruses cause multinucleated giant cell formation
(B) Some new viral antigens appear on the surface of the host cell
(C) Some of these viruses contain host cell lipids
(D) Some of these viruses do not have an envelope

161. Biochemical analysis of a virus reveals the genome to be composed of eight unequally sized pieces of single-stranded RNA, each of which is complementary to viral mRNA in infected cells. Which one of the following statements is UNLIKELY to be correct?

(A) Different proteins are encoded by each segment of the viral genome
(B) The virus particle contains a virus-encoded enzyme that can copy the genome into its complement
(C) Purified RNA extracted from the virus particle is infectious
(D) The virus can undergo high-frequency recombination via reassortment of its RNA segments

162. Latency is an outcome particularly characteristic of which one of the following virus groups?
(A) Polioviruses

(B) Herpesviruses

(C) Rhinoviruses

(D) Influenza viruses

163. Each of the following statements concerning viral serotypes is correct EXCEPT:

(A) In naked nucleocapsid viruses, the serotype is usually determined by the outer capsid proteins

(B) In enveloped viruses, the serotype is usually determined by the outer envelope proteins, especially the spike proteins

(C) Some viruses have multiple serotypes

(D) Some viruses have an RNA polymerase that determines the serotype

164. The ability of a virus to produce disease can result from a variety of mechanisms. Which one of the following mechanisms is LEAST likely?

(A) Cytopathic effect in infected cells

(B) Malignant transformation of infected cells

(C) Immune response to virus-induced antigens on the surface of infected cells

(D) Production of an exotoxin that activates adenylate cyclase

165. Which one of the following forms of immunity to viruses would be LEAST likely to be lifelong?

(A) Passive immunity

(B) Passive-active immunity

(C) Active immunity

(D) Cell-mediated immunity

166. Which one of the following statements concerning interferons is LEAST accurate?

(A) Interferons are proteins that influence host defenses in many ways, one of which is the induction of an antiviral state

(B) Interferons are synthesized only by virus-infected cells

(C) Interferons inhibit a broad range of viruses, not just the virus that induced the interferon

(D) Synthesis of several host enzymes is induced by interferon in target cells

167. You have isolated a virus from the stool of a patient with diarrhea and shown that its genome is composed of multiple pieces of double-stranded RNA. Which one of the following is UNLIKELY to be true?

(A) Each piece of RNA encodes a different protein

(B) The virus encodes an RNA-directed RNA polymerase

(C) The virion contains an RNA polymerase

(D) The genome integrates into the host chromosome

168. A temperate bacteriophage has been induced from a new pathogenic strain of *Escherichia coli* that produces a toxin. Which one of the follow-

ing is the MOST convincing way to show that the phage encodes the toxin?

(A) Carry out conjugation of the pathogenic strain with a nonpathogenic strain

(B) Infect an experimental animal with the phage

(C) Lysogenize a nonpathogenic strain with the phage

(D) Look for transposable elements in the phage DNA

169. Each of the following statements concerning retroviruses is correct EXCEPT:

(A) The virus particle carries an RNA-directed DNA polymerase encoded by the viral genome

(B) The viral genome consists of three segments of double-stranded RNA

(C) The virion is enveloped and enters cells via an interaction with specific receptors on the host cell

(D) During infection, the virus synthesizes a DNA copy of its RNA, and this DNA becomes covalently integrated into host cell DNA

170. A stock of virus particles has been found by electron microscopy to contain 10^8 particles/mL, but a plaque assay reveals only 10^5 plaque-forming units/mL. The BEST interpretation of these results is that

(A) Only one particle in 1000 is infectious

(B) A nonpermissive cell line was used for the plaque assay

(C) Several kinds of viruses were present in the stock

(D) The virus is a temperature-sensitive mutant

171. Reasonable mechanisms for viral persistence in infected individuals include all of the following EXCEPT:

(A) Generation of defective-interfering particles

(B) Virus-mediated inhibition of host DNA synthesis

(C) Integration of a provirus into the genome of the host

(D) Host tolerance to viral antigens

172. Each of the following statements concerning viral surface proteins is correct EXCEPT:

(A) They elicit antibody that neutralizes infectivity of the virus

(B) They determine the species specificity of the virus-cell interaction

(C) They participate in active transport of nutrients across the viral envelope membrane

(D) They protect the genetic material against nucleases

173. Each of the following statements concerning viral vaccines is correct EXCEPT:

(A) In live, attenuated vaccines, the virus has lost its ability to cause disease but has retained its ability to induce neutralizing antibody

(B) In live, attenuated vaccines, the possibility of reversion to virulence is of concern

(C) With inactivated vaccines, IgA mucosal immunity is usually induced

(D) With inactivated vaccines, protective immunity is due mainly to the production of IgG

174. The major barrier to the control of rhinovirus upper respiratory infections by immunization is

(A) The poor local and systemic immune response to these viruses

(B) The number and antigenic diversity of the viruses

(C) The side effects of the vaccine

(D) The inability to grow the viruses in cell culture

175. The feature of the influenza virus genome that contributes MOST to the antigenic variation of the virus is

(A) A high G + C content, which augments binding to nucleoproteins

(B) Inverted repeat regions, which create "sticky ends"

(C) Segmented nucleic acid

(D) Unique methylated bases

176. What is the BEST explanation for the selective action of acyclovir (acycloguanosine) in herpes simplex virus–infected cells?

(A) Acyclovir binds specifically to herpesvirus receptors on the infected cell surface

(B) Viral phosphokinase phosphorylates acyclovir more effectively than does the host cell phosphokinase

(C) Acyclovir inhibits the RNA polymerase in the virus particle

(D) Acyclovir blocks the matrix protein of the virus, thereby preventing release by budding

177. Each of the following statements concerning interferon is correct EXCEPT:

(A) Interferon inhibits the growth of both DNA and RNA viruses

(B) Interferon is induced by double-stranded RNA

(C) Interferon made by cells of one species acts more effectively in the cells of that species than in the cells of other species

(D) Interferon acts by preventing viruses from entering the cell

178. Each of the following statements concerning the viruses that infect humans is correct EXCEPT:

(A) The ratio of physical particles to infectious particles is less than 1

(B) The purified nucleic acid of some viruses is infectious, but at a lower efficiency than the intact virions

(C) Some viruses contain lipoprotein envelopes derived from the plasma membrane of the host cell

(D) The nucleic acid of some viruses is single-stranded DNA and that of others is double-stranded RNA

179. Which one of the following statements about virion structure and assembly is CORRECT?

(A) Most viruses acquire surface glycoproteins by budding through the nuclear membrane

(B) Helical nucleocapsids are found primarily in DNA viruses

(C) The symmetry of virus particles prevents inclusion of any nonstructural proteins, such as enzymes

(D) Enveloped viruses use a matrix protein to mediate interactions between viral glycoproteins in the plasma membrane and structural proteins in the nucleocapsid

180. Each of the following statements concerning viruses is correct EXCEPT:

(A) Viruses can reproduce only within cells

(B) The proteins on the surface of the virus mediate the entry of the virus into host cells

(C) Neutralizing antibody is directed against proteins on the surface of the virus

(D) Viruses replicate by binary fission

181. Viruses are obligate intracellular parasites. Each of the following statements concerning this fact is correct EXCEPT:

(A) Viruses cannot generate energy outside of cells

(B) Viruses cannot synthesize proteins outside of cells

(C) Viruses must degrade host cell DNA in order to obtain nucleotides

(D) Enveloped viruses require host cell membranes to obtain their envelopes

182. Each of the following statements concerning lysogeny is correct EXCEPT:

(A) Viral genes replicate independently of bacterial genes

(B) Viral genes responsible for lysis are repressed

(C) Viral DNA is integrated into bacterial DNA

(D) Some lysogenic bacteriophage encode toxins that cause human disease

183. Each of the following viruses possesses an outer envelope of lipoprotein EXCEPT:

(A) Varicella-zoster virus

(B) Papillomavirus

(C) Influenza virus

(D) Human immunodeficiency virus

184. Which one of the following viruses possesses a genome of single-stranded RNA that is infectious when purified?

(A) Influenza virus
(B) Rotavirus
(C) Measles virus
(D) Poliovirus

185. Each of the following viruses possesses an RNA polymerase in the virion EXCEPT:
(A) Hepatitis A virus
(B) Smallpox virus
(C) Mumps virus
(D) Rotavirus

186. Each of the following viruses possesses a DNA polymerase in the virion EXCEPT:
(A) Human immunodeficiency virus
(B) Human T-cell lymphotropic virus
(C) Epstein-Barr virus
(D) Hepatitis B virus

187. Each of the following viruses possesses double-stranded nucleic acid as its genome EXCEPT:
(A) Coxsackievirus
(B) Herpes simplex virus
(C) Rotavirus
(D) Adenovirus

188. Viroids
(A) Are defective viruses that are missing the DNA coding for the matrix protein
(B) Consist of RNA without a protein or lipoprotein outer coat
(C) Cause tumors in experimental animals
(D) Require an RNA polymerase in the particle for replication to occur

189. Each of the following statements about both measles virus and rubella virus is correct EXCEPT:
(A) They are RNA enveloped viruses
(B) Their virions contain an RNA polymerase
(C) They have a single antigenic type
(D) They are transmitted by respiratory aerosol

190. Each of the following statements about both influenza virus and rabies virus is correct EXCEPT:
(A) They are enveloped RNA viruses
(B) Their virions contain an RNA polymerase
(C) A killed vaccine is available for both viruses
(D) They each have a single antigenic type

191. Each of the following statements about both poliovirus and rhinoviruses is correct EXCEPT:
(A) They are nonenveloped RNA viruses
(B) They have multiple antigenic types
(C) Their virions contain an RNA polymerase
(D) They do not integrate their genome into host cell DNA

192. Each of the following statements about human immunodeficiency virus (HIV) is correct EXCEPT:
(A) HIV is an enveloped RNA virus

(B) The virion contains an RNA-dependent DNA polymerase
(C) A DNA copy of the HIV genome integrates into host cell DNA
(D) Acyclovir inhibits HIV replication

Answers (Questions 159–192)

159 (B)	166 (B)	173 (C)	180 (D)	187 (A)
160 (D)	167 (D)	174 (B)	181 (C)	188 (B)
161 (C)	168 (C)	175 (C)	182 (A)	189 (B)
162 (B)	169 (B)	176 (B)	183 (B)	190 (D)
163 (D)	170 (A)	177 (D)	184 (D)	191 (C)
164 (D)	171 (B)	178 (A)	185 (A)	192 (D)
165 (A)	172 (C)	179 (D)	186 (C)	

DIRECTIONS (Questions 193–211): Select the one lettered option that is MOST CLOSELY associated with the numbered items. Each lettered option may be selected once, more than once, or not at all.

Questions 193–196

(A) DNA enveloped virus
(B) DNA nonenveloped virus
(C) RNA enveloped virus
(D) RNA nonenveloped virus
(E) Viroid

193. Herpes simplex virus
194. Human T-cell lymphotropic virus
195. Human papillomavirus
196. Rotavirus

Questions 197–201

(A) Attachment and penetration of virion
(B) Viral mRNA synthesis
(C) Viral protein synthesis
(D) Viral genome DNA synthesis
(E) Assembly and release of progeny virus

197. Main site of action of acyclovir
198. Main site of action of amantadine
199. Function of virion polymerase of influenza virus
200. Main site of action of antiviral antibody
201. Step at which budding occurs

Questions 202–206

(A) Poliovirus
(B) Epstein-Barr virus
(C) Agent of scrapie and kuru
(D) Hepatitis B virus
(E) Respiratory syncytial virus

202. Part of the genome DNA is synthesized by the virion polymerase
203. The translation product of viral mRNA is a polyprotein that is cleaved to form virion structural proteins

204. It is remarkably resistant to ultraviolet light

205. It causes latent infection of B cells

206. It carries a fusion protein on the surface of the virion envelope

Questions 207–211

    (A) Hepatitis A virus
    (B) Hepatitis B virus
    (C) Hepatitis C virus
    (D) Hepatitis D virus

207. Enveloped DNA virus that is transmitted by blood

208. Enveloped RNA virus that has the surface antigen of another virus

209. Enveloped RNA virus that is the most common cause of non-A, non-B hepatitis

210. Nonenveloped RNA virus that is transmitted by the fecal-oral route

211. Purified surface protein of this virus is the immunogen in a vaccine

Answers (Questions 193–211)

193 (A)	197 (D)	201 (E)	205 (B)	209 (C)
194 (C)	198 (A)	202 (D)	206 (E)	210 (A)
195 (B)	199 (B)	203 (A)	207 (B)	211 (B)
196 (D)	200 (A)	204 (C)	208 (D)	

Clinical Virology

DIRECTIONS (Questions 212–275): Select the ONE lettered answer that is BEST in each question.

212. Which one of the following outcomes is MOST common following a primary herpes simplex virus infection?

    (A) Complete eradication of virus and virus-infected cells
    (B) Persistent asymptomatic viremia
    (C) Establishment of latent infection
    (D) Persistent cytopathic effect in infected cells

213. Each of the following pathogens is likely to establish chronic or latent infection EXCEPT:

    (A) Cytomegalovirus
    (B) Hepatitis A virus
    (C) Hepatitis B virus
    (D) Herpes simplex virus

214. Each of the following statements regarding poliovirus and its vaccine is correct EXCEPT:

    (A) Poliovirus is transmitted by the fecal-oral route
    (B) Pathogenesis by poliovirus primarily involves the death of sensory neurons
    (C) The live, attenuated vaccine contains all three serotypes of poliovirus
    (D) An unimmunized adult traveling to underdeveloped countries should receive the inactivated vaccine

215. Which one of the following strategies is MOST likely to induce lasting intestinal mucosal immunity to poliovirus?

    (A) Parenteral (intramuscular) vaccination with inactivated vaccine
    (B) Oral administration of poliovirus immune globulin
    (C) Parenteral vaccination with live vaccine
    (D) Oral vaccination with live vaccine

216. Each of the following clinical syndromes is associated with infection by picornaviruses EXCEPT:

    (A) Myocarditis/pericarditis
    (B) Hepatitis
    (C) Mononucleosis
    (D) Meningitis

217. Each of the following statements concerning rubella vaccine is correct EXCEPT:

    (A) The vaccine prevents reinfection, thereby limiting the spread of virulent virus
    (B) The immunogen in the vaccine is killed rubella virus
    (C) The vaccine induces antibodies that prevent dissemination of the virus by neutralizing it during the viremic stage
    (D) The incidence of both childhood rubella and congenital rubella syndrome has decreased significantly since the advent of the vaccine

218. Each of the following statements concerning the rabies vaccine for use in humans is correct EXCEPT:

    (A) The vaccine contains live, attenuated rabies virus
    (B) If your patient is bitten by a wild animal, eg, a skunk, the rabies vaccine should be given
    (C) When the vaccine is used for postexposure prophylaxis, rabies immune globulin should also be given

(D) The virus in the vaccine is grown in human cell cultures, thus decreasing the risk of allergic encephalomyelitis

219. Each of the following statements concerning influenza is correct EXCEPT:
(A) Major epidemics of the disease are caused by influenza A viruses rather than influenza B and C viruses
(B) Likely sources of new antigens for influenza A viruses are the viruses that cause influenza in animals
(C) Major antigenic changes (shifts) of viral surface proteins are seen primarily in influenza A viruses rather than in influenza B and C viruses
(D) The antigenic changes that occur with antigenic drift are due to reassortment of the multiple pieces of the influenza virus genome

220. Each of the following statements concerning the prevention and treatment of influenza is correct EXCEPT:
(A) As with all live vaccines, the influenza vaccine should not be given to pregnant women
(B) Booster doses of the vaccine are recommended because the duration of immunity is only a year
(C) Amantadine is an effective prophylactic drug only against influenza A viruses
(D) The major antigen in the vaccine is the hemagglutinin

221. A 6-month-old child develops a persistent cough and a fever. Physical examination and chest x-ray suggest pneumonia. Which one of the following organisms is LEAST likely to cause this infection?
(A) Respiratory syncytial virus
(B) Adenovirus
(C) Parainfluenza virus
(D) Rotavirus

222. A 45-year-old man was attacked by a bobcat and bitten repeatedly about the face and neck. The animal was shot by a companion and brought back to the public health authorities. Once you decide to immunize against rabies virus, how would you proceed?
(A) Use hyperimmune serum only
(B) Use active immunization only
(C) Use hyperimmune serum and active immunization
(D) Use active immunization and follow this with hyperimmune serum if adequate antibody titers are not obtained in the patient's serum

223. Each of the following statements concerning mumps is correct EXCEPT:
(A) Mumps virus is a paramyxovirus and hence has a single-stranded RNA genome

(B) Meningitis is a recognized complication of mumps
(C) Mumps orchitis in children prior to puberty often causes sterility
(D) During mumps, the virus spreads through the bloodstream (viremia) to various internal organs

224. Each of the following statements concerning respiratory syncytial virus (RSV) is correct EXCEPT:
(A) RSV has a single-stranded RNA genome
(B) RSV induces the formation of multinucleated giant cells
(C) RSV causes pneumonia primarily in children
(D) RSV infections can be effectively treated with acyclovir

225. The principal reservoir for the antigenic shift variants of influenza virus appears to be
(A) People in isolated communities such as the Arctic
(B) Animals, specifically pigs, horses, and fowl
(C) Soil, especially in the tropics
(D) Sewage

226. The role of an infectious agent in the pathogenesis of kuru was BEST demonstrated by which one of the following observations?
(A) A 16-fold rise in antibody titer to the agent was observed
(B) The viral genome was isolated from infected neurons
(C) Electron micrographs of the brains of infected individuals demonstrated intracellular structures resembling paramyxovirus nucleocapsids
(D) The disease was serially transmitted to experimental animals

227. A 64-year-old man with chronic lymphatic leukemia develops progressive deterioration of mental and neuromuscular function. At autopsy the brain shows enlarged oligodendrocytes whose nuclei contain naked, icosahedral virus particles. The MOST likely diagnosis is
(A) Herpes encephalitis
(B) Creutzfeldt-Jakob disease
(C) Subacute sclerosing panencephalitis
(D) Progressive multifocal leukoencephalopathy
(E) Rabies

228. A 20-year-old man, who for many years had received daily injections of growth hormone prepared from human pituitary glands, develops ataxia, slurred speech, and dementia. At autopsy the brain shows widespread neuronal degeneration, a spongy appearance due to many vacuoles between the cells, no inflammation, and no evidence of virus particles. Mice injected with ho-

mogenized brain tissue develop a similar disease after 6 months. The MOST likely diagnosis is
- (A) Herpes encephalitis
- (B) Creutzfeldt-Jakob disease
- (C) Subacute sclerosing panencephalitis
- (D) Progressive multifocal leukoencephalopathy
- (E) Rabies

229. A 24-year-old woman has had fever and a sore throat for the past week. Moderately severe pharyngitis and bilateral cervical lymphadenopathy are seen on physical examination. Which one of the following viruses is LEAST likely to cause this picture?
- (A) Varicella-zoster virus
- (B) Adenovirus
- (C) Coxsackievirus
- (D) Epstein-Barr virus

230. Scrapie and kuru possess all of the following characteristics EXCEPT:
- (A) A histologic picture of spongiform encephalopathy
- (B) Transmissibility to animals associated with a long incubation period
- (C) Slowly progressive deterioration of brain function
- (D) Prominent intranuclear inclusions in oligodendrocytes

231. Each of the following statements concerning subacute sclerosing panencephalitis is correct EXCEPT:
- (A) Immunosuppression is a frequent predisposing factor
- (B) Aggregates of helical nucleocapsids are found in infected cells
- (C) High titers of measles antibody are found in cerebrospinal fluid
- (D) Slowly progressive deterioration of brain function occurs

232. The slow virus disease that MOST clearly has immunosuppression as an important factor in its pathogenesis is
- (A) progressive multifocal leukoencephalopathy
- (B) subacute sclerosing panencephalitis
- (C) Creutzfeldt-Jakob disease
- (D) scrapie

233. A 30-year-old man develops fever and jaundice. He consults a physician, who finds that blood tests for HBs antigen and anti-HBs antibody are negative. Which one of the following additional tests is MOST useful to establish that the hepatitis was indeed due to hepatitis B virus?
- (A) HBe antigen
- (B) Anti-HBc antibody
- (C) Anti-HBe antibody
- (D) Delta antigen

234. Which one of the following is the MOST reasonable explanation for the ability of hepatitis B virus to cause chronic infection?
- (A) Infection does not elicit the production of antibody
- (B) The liver is an "immunologically sheltered" site
- (C) Viral DNA can persist within the host cell
- (D) Many humans are immunologically tolerant to HBs antigen

235. The routine screening of transfused blood for HBs antigen has not eliminated the problem of posttransfusion hepatitis. For which one of the following viruses has screening eliminated a large number of cases of posttransfusion hepatitis?
- (A) Hepatitis A virus
- (B) Hepatitis C virus
- (C) Cytomegalovirus
- (D) Epstein-Barr virus

236. A 35-year-old man addicted to intravenous drugs has been a carrier of HBs antigen for 10 years. He suddenly develops acute fulminant hepatitis and dies within 10 days. Which one of the following laboratory tests would contribute MOST to a diagnosis?
- (A) Anti-HBs antibody
- (B) HBe antigen
- (C) Anti-HBc antibody
- (D) Anti-delta virus antibody

237. Which one of the following is the BEST evidence on which to base a decisive diagnosis of acute mumps disease?
- (A) A positive skin test
- (B) A 4-fold rise in antibody titer to mumps surface antigen
- (C) A history of exposure to a child with mumps
- (D) Orchitis in young adult male

238. Varicella-zoster virus and herpes simplex virus share many characteristics. Which one of the following characteristics is NOT shared?
- (A) Inapparent disease, manifested only by virus shedding
- (B) Persistence of latent virus after recovery from acute disease
- (C) Vesicular rash
- (D) Linear, double-stranded DNA genome

239. Herpes simplex virus and cytomegalovirus share many features. Which one of the following features is LEAST likely to be shared?
- (A) Important cause of morbidity and mortality in the newborn
- (B) Congenital abnormalities due to transplacental passage
- (C) Important cause of serious disease in immunosuppressed individuals
- (D) Mild or inapparent infection

240. The eradication of smallpox was facilitated by several features of the virus. Which one of the following contributed LEAST to eradication?
    (A) It has one antigenic type
    (B) Inapparent infection is rare
    (C) Administration of live vaccine reliably induces immunity
    (D) It multiplies in the cytoplasm of infected cells

241. Which one of the following statements concerning infectious mononucleosis is the MOST accurate?
    (A) Multinucleated giant cells are found in the skin lesions
    (B) Infected T lymphocytes are abundant in peripheral blood
    (C) Isolation of virus is necessary to confirm the diagnosis
    (D) Infectious mononucleosis is transmitted by virus in saliva

242. Which one of the following statements about genital herpes is LEAST accurate?
    (A) Acyclovir reduces the number of recurrent disease episodes by eradicating latently infected cells
    (B) Genital herpes can be transmitted in the absence of apparent lesions
    (C) Multinucleated giant cells with intranuclear inclusions are found in the lesions
    (D) Initial disease episodes are generally more severe than recurrent episodes

243. The influenza vaccine currently in use in the United States is
    (A) An inactivated vaccine consisting of formaldehyde-treated influenza virions, which primarily induce antibody to hemagglutinin
    (B) A live, attenuated vaccine prepared from a variant of equine influenza virus
    (C) A vaccine consisting of purified peptide fragments of the hemagglutinin and neuraminidase glycoproteins
    (D) A live, attenuated vaccine composed of the current influenza A, B, and C isolates

244. Which of the following is the MOST common lower respiratory pathogen in infants?
    (A) Respiratory syncytial virus
    (B) Adenovirus
    (C) Rhinovirus
    (D) Coxsackievirus

245. Which of the following conditions is LEAST likely to be caused by adenoviruses?
    (A) Conjunctivitis
    (B) Pneumonia
    (C) Pharyngitis
    (D) Glomerulonephritis

246. Regarding the serologic diagnosis of infectious mononucleosis, which one of the following is CORRECT?

(A) A heterophil antibody is formed that reacts with a capsid protein of Epstein-Barr virus
(B) A heterophil antibody is formed that agglutinates sheep or horse red blood cells
(C) A heterophil antigen occurs that cross-reacts with *Proteus* OX19 strains
(D) A heterophil antigen occurs following infection with cytomegalovirus

247. Herpes simplex virus type 1 (HSV-1) is distinct from HSV-2 in several different ways. Which one of the following is the LEAST accurate statement?
    (A) HSV-1 causes lesions above the umbilicus more frequently than HSV-2 does
    (B) Infection by HSV-1 is not associated with any tumors in humans
    (C) Antiserum to HSV-1 neutralizes HSV-1 much more effectively than HSV-2
    (D) HSV-1 causes frequent recurrences, whereas HSV-2 infection rarely recurs

248. Which one of the following statements about the *src* gene and *src* protein of Rous sarcoma virus is INCORRECT?
    (A) The *src* gene encodes a protein with epidermal growth factor activity
    (B) The *src* protein catalyzes phosphotransfer from ATP to tyrosine residues in protein
    (C) The *src* protein is required to maintain neoplastic transformation of infected cells
    (D) The viral *src* gene is derived from a cellular gene found in all vertebrate species

249. Each of the following statements supports the idea that cellular proto-oncogenes participate in human carcinogenesis EXCEPT:
    (A) The c-*abl* gene is rearranged on the Philadelphia chromosome in myeloid leukemias and encodes a protein with heightened tyrosine kinase activity
    (B) The N-*myc* gene is amplified as much as 100-fold in many advanced cases of neuroblastoma
    (C) The receptor for platelet-derived growth factor is a transmembrane protein that exhibits tyrosine kinase activity
    (D) The c-Ha-*ras* gene is mutated at specific codons in several types of human cancer

250. Each of the following statements concerning human immunodeficiency virus (HIV) is correct EXCEPT:
    (A) Screening tests for antibodies are useful to prevent transmission of HIV through transfused blood
    (B) The opportunistic infections seen in AIDS are primarily the result of a loss of cell-mediated immunity

(C) Zidovudine (azidothymidine) inhibits the RNA-dependent DNA polymerase

(D) The presence of circulating antibodies that neutralize HIV is evidence that an individual is protected against HIV-induced disease

251. Which one of the following statements concerning viral meningitis and viral encephalitis is CORRECT?

(A) Herpes simplex virus type 2 is the leading cause of viral meningitis

(B) Herpes simplex virus type 1 is an important cause of viral encephalitis

(C) The spinal fluid protein is usually decreased in viral meningitis

(D) The diagnosis of viral meningitis can be made by using the India ink stain on a sample of spinal fluid

252. Each of the following statements is correct EXCEPT:

(A) Coxsackieviruses are enteroviruses and can replicate in both the respiratory and gastrointestinal tracts

(B) Influenza viruses have multiple serotypes based on hemagglutinin and neuraminidase proteins located on the envelope surface

(C) Flaviviruses are RNA enveloped viruses that replicate in animals as well as humans

(D) Adenoviruses are RNA enveloped viruses that are an important cause of sexually transmitted disease

253. Which one of the following statements concerning the prevention of viral disease is CORRECT?

(A) Adenovirus vaccine contains purified penton fibers and is usually given to children in conjunction with polio vaccine

(B) Coxsackievirus vaccine contains live virus that induces IgA, which prevents reinfection by homologous serotypes

(C) Flavivirus immunization consists of hyperimmune serum plus a vaccine consisting of subunits containing the surface glycoprotein

(D) Influenza virus vaccine contains killed virus that induces neutralizing antibody directed against the hemagglutinin

254. Each of the following statements concerning hepatitis C virus (HCV) and hepatitis D virus (HDV) is correct EXCEPT:

(A) HCV is an important cause of posttransfusion hepatitis

(B) Delta virus is a defective virus with an RNA genome and a capsid composed of hepatitis B surface antigen

(C) HDV is transmitted primarily by the fecal-oral route

(D) People infected with HCV commonly become chronic carriers of HCV and are predisposed to hepatocellular carcinoma

255. Each of the following statements concerning measles virus is correct EXCEPT:

(A) Measles virus is an enveloped virus with a single-stranded RNA genome

(B) One of the important complications of measles is encephalitis

(C) The initial site of measles virus replication is the upper respiratory tract, from which it spreads via the blood to the skin

(D) Latent infection by measles virus can be explained by the integration of provirus into the host cell DNA

256. Each of the following statements concerning measles vaccine is correct EXCEPT:

(A) The vaccine contains live, attenuated virus

(B) The vaccine should not be given in conjunction with other viral vaccines because interference can occur

(C) Virus in the vaccine contains only one serotype

(D) The vaccine should not be given prior to 15 months of age because maternal antibodies can prevent an immune response

257. Each of the following statements concerning rubella is correct EXCEPT:

(A) Congenital abnormalities occur primarily when a pregnant woman is infected during the first trimester

(B) Women who say that they have never had rubella can, nevertheless, have neutralizing antibody in their serum

(C) In a 6-year-old child, rubella is a mild, self-limited disease with few complications

(D) Acyclovir is effective in the treatment of congenital rubella syndrome

258. Each of the following statements concerning rabies and rabies virus is correct EXCEPT:

(A) The virus has a lipoprotein envelope and single-stranded RNA as its genome

(B) The virus has a single antigenic type (serotype)

(C) In the United States, dogs are the most common reservoir

(D) The incubation period is usually long (several weeks) rather than short (several days)

259. Each of the following statements concerning arboviruses is correct EXCEPT:

(A) The pathogenesis of dengue hemorrhagic shock syndrome is associated with the heterotypic anamnestic response

(B) Wild birds are the reservoir for encephalitis viruses but not for yellow fever virus

554 / PART XI

(C) Ticks are the main mode of transmission for both encephalitis viruses and yellow fever virus

(D) There is a live, attenuated vaccine that effectively prevents yellow fever

260. Each of the following statements concerning rhinoviruses is correct EXCEPT:

(A) Rhinoviruses are picornaviruses, ie, small, nonenveloped viruses with an RNA genome

(B) Rhinoviruses are an important cause of lower respiratory tract infections, especially in patients with chronic obstructive pulmonary disease

(C) Rhinoviruses do not infect the gastrointestinal tract because they are inactivated by the acid pH in the stomach

(D) There is no vaccine against rhinoviruses because they have too many antigenic types

261. Each of the following statements concerning herpes simplex virus type 2 (HSV-2) is correct EXCEPT:

(A) Natural infection with HSV-2 confers only partial immunity against a second primary infection

(B) HSV-2 causes vesicular lesions, typically in the genital area

(C) HSV-2 can cause virus-specific alterations of the cell membrane, leading to cell fusion and the formation of multinucleated giant cells

(D) Recurrent disease episodes due to reactivation of latent HSV-2 are usually more severe than the primary episode

262. Each of the following statements concerning Epstein-Barr virus is correct EXCEPT:

(A) Many infections are mild or inapparent

(B) The earlier in life primary infection is acquired, the more likely the typical picture of infectious mononucleosis will be manifest

(C) Latently infected lymphocytes regularly persist following an acute episode of infection

(D) Infection confers immunity against second episodes of infectious mononucleosis

263. Each of the following statements regarding rotaviruses is correct EXCEPT:

(A) The rotavirus vaccine contains recombinant RNA polymerase as the immunogen

(B) Rotaviruses are a leading cause of diarrhea in young children

(C) Rotaviruses are transmitted primarily by the fecal-oral route

(D) Rotaviruses belong to the reovirus family, which have a double-stranded, segmented RNA genome

264. Each of the following statements concerning the antigenicity of influenza A virus is correct EXCEPT:

(A) Antigenic shifts, which represent major changes in antigenicity, occur infrequently and are due to the recombination (reassortment) of segments of the viral genome

(B) Antigenic shifts affect both the hemagglutinin and the neuraminidase

(C) The worldwide epidemics caused by influenza A virus are due to antigenic shifts

(D) The protein involved in antigenic drift is primarily the internal ribonucleoprotein

265. Each of the following statements concerning adenoviruses is correct EXCEPT:

(A) Adenoviruses are composed of a double-stranded DNA genome and a capsid without an envelope

(B) Adenoviruses cause both sore throat and pneumonia

(C) Adenoviruses have only one serologic type

(D) Adenoviruses are implicated as a cause of tumors in animals but not humans

266. Each of the following statements concerning the prevention of viral respiratory tract disease is correct EXCEPT:

(A) To prevent disease caused by adenoviruses, a live enteric-coated vaccine that causes asymptomatic enteric infection is used in the military

(B) To prevent disease caused by influenza A virus, an inactivated vaccine is available for the civilian population

(C) There is no vaccine available against respiratory syncytial virus

(D) To prevent disease caused by rhinoviruses, a vaccine containing purified capsid proteins is used

267. Each of the following statements concerning herpesvirus latency is correct EXCEPT:

(A) Exogenous stimuli can cause reactivation of latent infection, with induction of symptomatic disease

(B) During latency, antiviral antibody is not demonstrable in the sera of infected individuals

(C) Episodes of herpesvirus reactivation are more frequent and more severe in patients with impaired cell-mediated immunity

(D) Virus can be recovered from latently infected cells by cocultivation with susceptible cells

268. Each of the following statements concerning rhinoviruses is correct EXCEPT:

(A) Rhinoviruses are one of the most frequent causes of the common cold

(B) Rhinoviruses grow better at 33°C than at 37°C; hence, they tend to cause disease in the upper respiratory tract rather than the lower respiratory tract

(C) Rhinoviruses are members of the picor-naviruses family and hence resemble poliovirus in their structure and replication

(D) The immunity provided by the rhinovirus vaccine is excellent because there is only one serotype

269. Which one of the following statements concerning poliovirus infection is CORRECT?

(A) Congenital infection of the fetus is an important complication

(B) The virus replicates extensively in the gastrointestinal tract

(C) A skin test is available to determine prior exposure to the virus

(D) Amantadine is an effective preventive agent

270. Each of the following statements concerning yellow fever is correct EXCEPT:

(A) Yellow fever virus is transmitted by the *Aedes aegypti* mosquito in the urban form of yellow fever

(B) Infection by yellow fever virus causes significant damage to hepatocytes

(C) Nonhuman primates in the jungle are a major reservoir of yellow fever virus

(D) Acyclovir is an effective treatment for yellow fever

271. Which one of the following statements concerning mumps is CORRECT?

(A) Although the salivary glands are the most obvious sites of infection, the testes, ovaries, and pancreas can be involved as well

(B) Because there is no vaccine against mumps, passive immunization is the only means of preventing the disease

(C) The diagnosis of mumps is made on clinical grounds because the virus cannot be grown in cell culture and serologic tests are inaccurate

(D) Second episodes of mumps can occur because there are two serotypes of the virus and protection is type-specific

272. Many of the oncogenic retroviruses carry oncogenes closely related to normal cellular genes, called proto-oncogenes. Which one of the following statements concerning proto-oncogenes is INCORRECT?

(A) Several proto-oncogenes have been found in mutant form in human cancers that lack evidence for viral etiology

(B) Several viral oncogenes and their progenitor proto-oncogenes encode protein kinases specific for tyrosine

(C) Some proto-oncogenes encode cellular growth factors and receptors for growth factors

(D) Proto-oncogenes are closely related to transposons found in bacteria

273. Each of the following statements concerning human immunodeficiency virus is correct EXCEPT:

(A) The CD4 protein on the T-cell surface is the receptor for the virus

(B) There is appreciable antigenic diversity in the envelope glycoprotein of the virus

(C) One of the viral genes codes for a protein that augments the activity of the viral transcriptional promoter

(D) A major problem with testing for antibody to the virus is its cross-reactivity with human T-cell lymphoma virus type I

274. Each of the following statements concerning human immunodeficiency virus is correct EXCEPT:

(A) Patients infected with HIV typically form antibodies against both the envelope glycoproteins (gp120 and gp41) and the internal group-specific antigen (p24)

(B) HIV probably arose as an endogenous virus of humans because HIV proviral DNA is found in the DNA of certain normal human cells

(C) Transmission of HIV occurs primarily by the transfer of blood or semen in adults, and neonates can be infected at the time of delivery

(D) The Western blot test is more specific for HIV infection than the ELISA is

275. Each of the following statements concerning hepatitis A virus is correct EXCEPT:

(A) The initial site of viral replication is the gastrointestinal tract

(B) Hepatitis A virus commonly causes asymptomatic infection in children

(C) The diagnosis is usually made by isolating the virus in cell culture

(D) Gamma globulin is used to prevent the disease in exposed persons

Answers (Questions 212–275)

212 (C)	225 (B)	238 (A)	251 (B)	264 (D)
213 (B)	226 (D)	239 (B)	252 (D)	265 (C)
214 (B)	227 (D)	240 (D)	253 (D)	266 (D)
215 (D)	228 (B)	241 (D)	254 (C)	267 (B)
216 (C)	229 (A)	242 (A)	255 (D)	268 (D)
217 (B)	230 (D)	243 (A)	256 (B)	269 (B)
218 (A)	231 (A)	244 (A)	257 (D)	270 (D)
219 (D)	232 (A)	245 (D)	258 (C)	271 (A)
220 (A)	233 (B)	246 (B)	259 (C)	272 (D)
221 (D)	234 (C)	247 (D)	260 (B)	273 (D)
222 (C)	235 (B)	248 (A)	261 (D)	274 (B)
223 (C)	236 (D)	249 (C)	262 (B)	275 (C)
224 (D)	237 (B)	250 (D)	263 (A)	

DIRECTIONS (Questions 276–294): Select the ONE lettered option that is MOST closely associated with the numbered items. Each lettered option may be selected once, more than once, or not at all.

Questions 276–279

    (A) Yellow fever virus
    (B) Rabies virus
    (C) Rotavirus
    (D) Rubella virus
    (E) Rhinovirus
276. Diarrhea
277. Jaundice
278. Congenital abnormalities
279. Encephalitis

Questions 280–284

    (A) Bronchiolitis
    (B) Meningitis
    (C) Pharyngitis
    (D) Shingles
    (E) Subacute sclerosing panencephalitis
280. Adenovirus
281. Measles virus
282. Respiratory syncytial virus
283. Coxsackievirus
284. Varicella-zoster virus

Questions 285–289

    (A) Adenovirus
    (B) Parainfluenza virus

    (C) Rhinovirus
    (D) Coxsackievirus
    (E) Epstein-Barr virus
285. Causes myocarditis and pleurodynia
286. Grows better at 33°C than 37°C
287. Causes tumors in laboratory rodents
288. Causes croup in young children
289. Causes infectious mononucleosis

Questions 290–294

    (A) Hepatitis C virus
    (B) Cytomegalovirus
    (C) Human papillomavirus
    (D) Dengue virus
    (E) St. Louis encephalitis virus
290. It is implicated as the cause of carcinoma of the cervix
291. Wild birds are an important reservoir
292. It is an important cause of pneumonia in immunocompromised patients
293. Donated blood containing antibody to this RNA virus should not be used for transfusion
294. It causes a hemorrhagic fever that can be life-threatening

Answers (Questions 276–294)

276 (C)	280 (C)	284 (D)	288 (B)	292 (B)
277 (A)	281 (E)	285 (D)	289 (E)	293 (A)
278 (D)	282 (A)	286 (C)	290 (C)	294 (D)
279 (B)	283 (B)	287 (A)	291 (E)	

Mycology

DIRECTIONS (Questions 295–317): Select the ONE lettered answer that is BEST in each question.

295. Which one of the following fungi is MOST likely to be found within reticuloendothelial cells?
    (A) *Histoplasma capsulatum*
    (B) *Candida albicans*
    (C) *Cryptococcus neoformans*
    (D) *Sporothrix schenckii*

296. Your patient is a woman with a vaginal discharge. You suspect, on clinical grounds, that it may be due to *Candida albicans*. Which one of the following statements is LEAST accurate or appropriate?
    (A) A Gram stain of the discharge should reveal budding yeasts

    (B) Culture of the discharge on Sabouraud's agar should produce a white mycelium with aerial conidia
    (C) To identify the organism, you should determine whether germ tubes are produced
    (D) You should ask her whether she is taking antibiotics

297. You have made a clinical diagnosis of meningitis in a 50-year-old immunocompromised woman. A latex agglutination test on the spinal fluid for capsular polysaccharide antigen is positive. Of the following organisms, which one is the MOST likely cause?
    (A) *Histoplasma capsulatum*
    (B) *Cryptococcus neoformans*

(C) *Aspergillus fumigatus*

(D) *Candida albicans*

298. Fungi often colonize lesions due to other causes. Which one of the following is LEAST likely to be present as a colonizer?
   (A) *Aspergillus*
   (B) *Mucor*
   (C) *Sporothrix*
   (D) *Candida*

299. Your patient complains of an "itching rash" on her abdomen. On examination, you find that the lesions are red, circular, with a vesiculated border and a healing central area. You suspect tinea corporis. Of the following choices, the MOST appropriate laboratory procedure to make the diagnosis is a
   (A) Potassium hydroxide mount of skin scrapings
   (B) Giemsa stain for multinucleated giant cells
   (C) Fluorescent-antibody stain of the vesicle fluid
   (D) 4-fold rise in antibody titer against the organism

300. Each of the following statements concerning *Cryptococcus neoformans* is correct EXCEPT:
   (A) Its natural habitat is the soil, especially associated with pigeon feces
   (B) Pathogenesis is related primarily to the production of exotoxin A
   (C) Budding yeasts are found in the lesions
   (D) The initial site of infection is usually the lung

301. A woman who pricked her finger while pruning some rose bushes develops a local pustule that progresses to an ulcer. Several nodules then develop along the local lymphatic drainage. The MOST likely agent is
   (A) *Cryptococcus neoformans*
   (B) *Candida albicans*
   (C) *Sporothrix schenckii*
   (D) *Aspergillus fumigatus*

302. Several fungi are associated with disease in immunocompromised patients. Which one of the following is the LEAST frequently associated?
   (A) *Cryptococcus neoformans*
   (B) *Aspergillus fumigatus*
   (C) *Malassezia furfur*
   (D) *Mucor* species

303. Fungal cells that reproduce by budding are seen in the infected tissues of patients with
   (A) Candidiasis, cryptococcosis, and sporotrichosis
   (B) Mycetoma, candidiasis, and mucormycosis
   (C) Tinea corporis, tinea unguium, and tinea versicolor
   (D) Sporotrichosis, mycetoma, and aspergillosis

304. Infection by a dermatophyte is MOST often associated with
   (A) Intravenous drug abuse

(B) Inhalation of the organism from contaminated bird feces

(C) Adherence of the organism to perspiration-moist skin

(D) Fecal-oral transmission

305. Aspergillosis is recognized in tissue by the presence of
   (A) Budding cells
   (B) Septate hyphae
   (C) Metachromatic granules
   (D) Pseudohyphae - *Candida*

306. Which one of the following is NOT a characteristic of histoplasmosis?
   (A) Person-to-person transmission
   (B) Specific geographic distribution
   (C) Yeasts in the tissue
   (D) Mycelial phase in the soil

307. Each of the following statements concerning mucormycosis is correct EXCEPT:
   (A) The fungi that cause mucormycosis are transmitted by airborne asexual spores
   (B) Tissue sections from a patient with mucormycosis show budding yeasts - mold only
   (C) Hyphae typically grow in blood vessels and cause necrosis of tissue
   (D) Ketoacidosis in diabetic patients is a predisposing factor to mucormycosis

308. Each of the following statements concerning fungi is correct EXCEPT:
   (A) Yeasts are fungi that reproduce by budding
   (B) Molds are fungi that have elongated filaments called hyphae
   (C) Thermally dimorphic fungi exist as yeasts at 37°C and as molds at 25°C
   (D) Both yeasts and molds have a cell wall made of peptidoglycan

309. Each of the following statements concerning yeasts is correct EXCEPT:
   (A) Yeasts have chitin in their cell walls and ergosterol in their cell membranes
   (B) Yeasts form ascospores when they invade tissue
   (C) Yeasts have eukaryotic nuclei and contain mitochondria in their cytoplasm
   (D) Yeasts produce neither endotoxin nor exotoxins

310. Each of the following statements concerning fungi and protozoa is correct EXCEPT:
   (A) Both fungi and protozoa are eukaryotic organisms
   (B) Fungi possess a cell wall, whereas protozoa do not
   (C) Both fungi and protozoa use flagella as their organ of motility
   (D) Both fungi and protozoa generate energy in mitochondria

311. You suspect that your patient's disease may be caused by *Cryptococcus neoformans*. Which one of the following findings would be MOST useful in establishing the diagnosis?
  (A) A positive heterophil agglutination test for the presence of antigen
  (B) A history of recent travel in the Mississippi River valley area
  (C) The finding of encapsulated budding cells in spinal fluid
  (D) Recovery of an acid-fast organism from the patient's sputum

312. Each of the following statements concerning *Candida albicans* is correct EXCEPT:
  (A) *C. albicans* is a budding yeast that forms pseudohyphae when it invades tissue
  (B) *C. albicans* is transmitted primarily by respiratory aerosol
  (C) *C. albicans* causes thrush
  (D) Impaired cell-mediated immunity is an important predisposing factor to disease

313. Each of the following statements concerning *Coccidioides immitis* is correct EXCEPT:
  (A) The mycelial phase of the organism grows primarily in the soil, which is its natural habitat
  (B) In the body, spherules containing endospores are formed
  (C) A rising titer of complement-fixing antibody indicates disseminated disease
  (D) Most infections are symptomatic and require treatment with amphotericin B

314. Each of the following statements concerning *Histoplasma capsulatum* is correct EXCEPT:
  (A) The natural habitat of *H. capsulatum* is the soil, where it grows as a mold
  (B) *H. capsulatum* is transmitted by airborne conidia, and its initial site of infection is the lung
  (C) Within the body, *H. capsulatum* grows primarily intracellularly within macrophages
  (D) Infection does not elicit a cell-mediated immune response, and no skin test is available

315. Each of the following statements concerning infection caused by *Coccidioides immitis* is correct EXCEPT:
  (A) *C. immitis* is a dimorphic fungus
  (B) *C. immitis* is acquired by inhalation of arthrospores
  (C) Resistance to amphotericin B is plasmid-mediated
  (D) Infection occurs primarily in the southwestern states and California

316. Each of the following statements concerning *Blastomyces dermatitidis* is correct EXCEPT:

  (A) *B. dermatitidis* grows as a mold in the soil in North America
  (B) *B. dermatitidis* is a dimorphic fungus that forms yeast cells in tissue
  (C) *B. dermatitidis* infection is commonly diagnosed by serologic tests because it does not grow in culture
  (D) *B. dermatitidis* causes granulomatous skin lesions

317. *Aspergillus fumigatus* can be involved in a variety of clinical conditions. Which one of the following is LEAST likely to occur?
  (A) Tissue invasion in immunocompromised host
  (B) Allergy following inhalation of airborne particles of the fungus
  (C) Colonization of tuberculous cavities in the lung
  (D) Thrush

Answers (Questions 295–317)

295 (A)	300 (B)	305 (B)	310 (C)	314 (D)
296 (B)	301 (C)	306 (A)	311 (C)	315 (C)
297 (B)	302 (C)	307 (B)	312 (B)	316 (C)
298 (C)	303 (A)	308 (D)	313 (D)	317 (D)
299 (A)	304 (C)	309 (B)		

DIRECTIONS (Questions 318–325): Select the ONE lettered option that is MOST closely associated with the numbered items. Each lettered option may be selected once, more than once, or not at all.

Questions 318–321

  (A) *Histoplasma capsulatum*
  (B) *Candida albicans*
  (C) *Aspergillus fumigatus*
  (D) *Sporothrix schenckii*

318. A budding yeast that is a member of the normal flora of the vagina

319. A dimorphic organism that is transmitted by trauma to the skin

320. A dimorphic fungus that typically is acquired by inhalation of asexual spores

321. A mold that causes pneumonia in immunocompromised patients

Questions 322–325

  (A) *Coccidioides immitis*
  (B) *Rhizopus nigricans*
  (C) *Blastomyces dermatitidis*
  (D) *Cryptococcus neoformans*

322. A yeast acquired by inhalation that causes meningitis primarily in immunocompromised patients

323. A mold that invades blood vessels primarily in patients with diabetic ketoacidosis

324. A dimorphic fungus that is acquired by inhalation by people living in certain areas of the southwestern states in the United States

325. A dimorphic fungus that causes granulomatous skin lesions in people living throughout North America

Parasitology

DIRECTIONS (Questions 326–352): Select the ONE lettered answer that is BEST in each question.

326. Children at day-care centers in the United States have a high rate of infection with which one of the following?
(A) *Ascaris lumbricoides*
(B) *Entamoeba histolytica*
(C) *Enterobius vermicularis*
(D) *Necator americanus*

327. The anatomic location of inflammation caused by *Schistosoma mansoni* is primarily
(A) Lung alveoli
(B) Intestinal venules
(C) Renal tubules
(D) Bone marrow

328. In malaria, the form of plasmodia that is transmitted from mosquito to human is the
(A) Sporozoite
(B) Gametocyte
(C) Merozoite
(D) Hypnozoite

329. Which one of the following protozoa primarily infects macrophages?
(A) *Plasmodium vivax*
(B) *Leishmania donovani*
(C) *Trypanosoma cruzi*
(D) *Trichomonas vaginalis*

330. Each of the following parasites has an intermediate host as part of its life cycle EXCEPT:
(A) *Trichomonas vaginalis*
(B) *Taenia solium*
(C) *Echinococcus granulosus*
(D) *Toxoplasma gondii*

331. Each of the following parasites passes through the lung during human infection EXCEPT:
(A) *Strongyloides stercoralis*
(B) *Necator americanus*
(C) *Wuchereria bancrofti*
(D) *Ascaris lumbricoides*

332. Each of the following parasites is transmitted by flies EXCEPT:
(A) *Schistosoma mansoni*
(B) *Onchocerca volvulus*
(C) *Trypanosoma gambiense*
(D) *Loa loa*

333. Each of the following parasites is transmitted by mosquitoes EXCEPT:
(A) *Leishmania donovani*
(B) *Wuchereria bancrofti*
(C) *Plasmodium vivax*
(D) *Plasmodium falciparum*

334. Pigs or dogs are the source of human infection by each of the following parasites EXCEPT:
(A) *Echinococcus granulosus*
(B) *Taenia solium*
(C) *Ascaris lumbricoides*
(D) *Trichinella spiralis*

335. Each of the following parasites is transmitted by eating inadequately cooked fish or seafood EXCEPT:
(A) *Diphyllobothrium latum*
(B) *Ancylostoma duodenale*
(C) *Paragonimus westermani*
(D) *Clonorchis sinensis*

336. Laboratory diagnosis of a patient with a suspected liver abscess due to *Entamoeba histolytica* should include
(A) Stool examination and indirect hemagglutination test
(B) Stool examination and blood smear
(C) Indirect hemagglutination test and skin test
(D) Xenodiagnosis and string test

337. Each of the following statements concerning *Toxoplasma gondii* is correct EXCEPT:
(A) *T. gondii* can be transmitted across the placenta to the fetus
(B) *T. gondii* can be transmitted by cat feces
(C) *T. gondii* can cause encephalitis in immunocompromised patients
(D) *T. gondii* can be diagnosed by finding trophozoites in the stool

338. Each of the following statements concerning *Giardia lamblia* is correct EXCEPT:

(A) *G. lamblia* has both a trophozoite and a cyst stage in its life cycle

(B) *G. lamblia* is transmitted by the fecal-oral route from both human and animal sources

(C) *G. lamblia* causes hemolytic anemia

(D) *G. lamblia* can be diagnosed by the string test

339. Each of the following statements concerning malaria is correct EXCEPT:

(A) The female *Anopheles* mosquito is the vector

(B) Early in infection, sporozoites enter hepatocytes

(C) Release of merozoites from red blood cells causes periodic fever and chills

(D) The principal site of gametocyte formation is the human gastrointestinal tract

340. Each of the following statements concerning *Trichomonas vaginalis* is correct EXCEPT:

(A) *T. vaginalis* is transmitted sexually

(B) *T. vaginalis* can be diagnosed by visualizing the trophozoite

(C) *T. vaginalis* can be treated effectively with metronidazole

(D) *T. vaginalis* causes bloody diarrhea

341. Which one of the following agents is used to prevent malaria?

(A) Mebendazole

(B) Chloroquine

(C) Inactivated vaccine

(D) Praziquantel

342. Each of the following statements concerning *Pneumocystis carinii* is correct EXCEPT:

(A) *P. carinii* infections primarily involve the respiratory tract

(B) *P. carinii* can be diagnosed by seeing cysts in tissue

(C) *P. carinii* infections are symptomatic primarily in immunocompromised patients

(D) *P. carinii* symptomatic infections can be prevented by administering penicillin orally

343. Each of the following statements concerning *Trypanosoma cruzi* is correct EXCEPT:

(A) *T. cruzi* is transmitted by the reduviid bug

(B) *T. cruzi* occurs primarily in tropical Africa

(C) *T. cruzi* can be diagnosed by seeing trypomastigotes in a blood smear

(D) *T. cruzi* typically affects heart muscle, leading to cardiac failure

344. Each of the following statements concerning sleeping sickness is correct EXCEPT:

(A) Sleeping sickness is caused by a trypanosome

(B) Sleeping sickness is transmitted by tsetse flies

(C) Sleeping sickness can be diagnosed by finding eggs in the stool

(D) Sleeping sickness occurs primarily in tropical Africa

345. Each of the following statements concerning kala-azar is correct EXCEPT:

(A) Kala-azar is caused by *Leishmania donovani*

(B) Kala-azar is transmitted by the bite of sandflies

(C) Kala-azar occurs primarily in rural Latin America

(D) Kala-azar can be diagnosed by finding amastigotes in bone marrow

346. Each of the following statements concerning *Diphyllobothrium latum* is correct EXCEPT:

(A) *D. latum* is transmitted by undercooked fish

(B) *D. latum* has operculated eggs

(C) Crustaceans (copepods) are intermediate hosts for *D. latum*

(D) *D. latum* has a scolex with a circle of hooks

347. Each of the following statements concerning hydatid cyst disease is correct EXCEPT:

(A) The disease is caused by *Echinococcus granulosus*

(B) The cysts occur primarily in the liver

(C) The disease is caused by a parasite whose adult form lives in dogs' intestines

(D) The disease occurs primarily in tropical Africa

348. Each of the following statements concerning *Schistosoma haematobium* is correct EXCEPT:

(A) *S. haematobium* is acquired by humans when cercariae penetrate the skin

(B) Snails are intermediate hosts of *S. haematobium*

(C) *S. haematobium* eggs have no spine

(D) *S. haematobium* infection predisposes to bladder carcinoma

349. Each of the following statements concerning hookworm infection is correct EXCEPT:

(A) Hookworm infection can cause anemia

(B) Hookworm infection is acquired by humans when filariform larvae penetrate the skin

(C) Hookworm infection is caused by *Necator americanus*

(D) Hookworm infection can be diagnosed by finding the trophozoite in the stool

350. Each of the following statements concerning *Ascaris lumbricoides* is correct EXCEPT:

(A) *A. lumbricoides* is one of the largest nematodes

(B) *A. lumbricoides* is transmitted by ingestion of eggs

(C) Both dogs and cats are intermediate hosts of *A. lumbricoides*

(D) *A. lumbricoides* can cause pneumonia

351. Each of the following statements concerning *Strongyloides stercoralis* is correct EXCEPT:

(A) *S. stercoralis* is acquired by ingestion of eggs

(B) *S. stercoralis* undergoes a free-living life cycle in soil

(C) *S. stercoralis* causes a marked eosinophilia

(D) *S. stercoralis* produces filariform larvae

352. Each of the following statements concerning trichinosis is correct EXCEPT:

(A) Trichinosis is acquired by eating under-cooked pork

(B) Trichinosis is caused by a protozoan that has both a trophozoite and a cyst stage in its life cycle

(C) Trichinosis can be diagnosed by seeing cysts in muscle biopsy specimens

(D) Eosinophilia is a prominent finding

Answers (Questions 326–352)

326 (C)	332 (A)	338 (C)	343 (B)	348 (C)
327 (B)	333 (A)	339 (D)	344 (C)	349 (D)
328 (A)	334 (C)	340 (D)	345 (C)	350 (C)
329 (B)	335 (B)	341 (B)	346 (D)	351 (A)
330 (A)	336 (A)	342 (D)	347 (D)	352 (B)
331 (C)	337 (D)			

DIRECTIONS (Questions 353–386): Select the ONE lettered option that is MOST closely associated with the numbered items. Each lettered option may be selected once, more than once, or not at all.

Questions 353–360

(A) *Dracunculus medinensis*

(B) *Loa loa*

(C) *Onchocerca volvulus*

(D) *Wuchereria bancrofti*

(E) *Toxocara canis*

353. Causes river blindness

354. Transmitted by mosquito

355. Acquired by drinking contaminated water

356. Treated by extracting worm from skin ulcer

357. Transmitted by deer fly or mango fly

358. Causes visceral larva migrans

359. Causes filariasis

360. Acquired by ingestion of worm eggs

Questions 361–372

(A) *Giardia lamblia*

(B) *Plasmodium vivax*

(C) *Taenia saginata*

(D) *Clonorchis sinensis*

(E) *Enterobius vermicularis*

361. A trematode (fluke) acquired by eating under-cooked fish

362. A cestode (tapeworm) acquired by eating under-cooked beef

363. A nematode (roundworm) transmitted primarily from child to child

364. A protozoan transmitted by mosquito

365. A protozoan transmitted by the fecal-oral route

366. Primarily affects the biliary ducts

367. Causes diarrhea as the most prominent symptom

368. Causes perianal itching as the most prominent symptom

369. Causes fever, chills, and anemia

370. Can be treated with metronidazole

371. Can be treated with mebendazole or pyrantel pamoate

372. Can be treated with chloroquine and primaquine

Questions 373–386

(A) *Entamoeba histolytica*

(B) *Plasmodium falciparum*

(C) *Taenia solium*

(D) *Paragonimus westermani*

(E) *Strongyloides stercoralis*

373. A cestode (tapeworm) acquired by eating under-cooked pork

374. A nematode (roundworm) acquired when filariform larvae penetrate the skin

375. A protozoan transmitted by the fecal-oral route

376. A trematode (fluke) acquired by eating under-cooked crab meat

377. A protozoan that infects red blood cells

378. Laboratory diagnosis based on finding eggs in sputum

379. Causes cysticercosis in humans

380. Chloroquine-resistant strains occur

381. Autoinfection within humans, especially in immunocompromised patients

382. Causes blackwater fever

383. Causes bloody diarrhea and liver abscesses

384. Produces "banana-shaped" gametocytes

385. Produces cysts with four nuclei

386. Has a scolex with suckers and a circle of hooks

Answers (Questions 353–386)

353 (C)	360 (E)	367 (A)	374 (E)	381 (E)
354 (D)	361 (D)	368 (E)	375 (A)	382 (B)
355 (A)	362 (C)	369 (B)	376 (D)	383 (A)
356 (A)	363 (E)	370 (A)	377 (B)	384 (B)
357 (B)	364 (B)	371 (E)	378 (D)	385 (A)
358 (E)	365 (A)	372 (B)	379 (C)	386 (C)
359 (D)	366 (D)	373 (C)	380 (B)	

Immunology

DIRECTIONS (Questions 387–474): Select the ONE lettered answer that is BEST in each question.

387. Which category of hypersensitivity BEST describes hemolytic disease of the newborn caused by Rh incompatibility?
(A) Atopic or anaphylactic
(B) Cytotoxic
(C) Immune complex
(D) Delayed

388. The principal difference between cytotoxic (type II) and immune complex (type III) hypersensitivity is
(A) The class (isotype) of antibody
(B) The site where antigen-antibody complexes are formed
(C) The participation of complement
(D) The participation of T cells

389. A child stung by a bee experiences respiratory distress within minutes and lapses into unconsciousness. This reaction is probably mediated by
(A) IgE antibody
(B) IgG antibody
(C) sensitized T cells
(D) complement
(E) IgM antibody

390. A patient with rheumatic fever develops a sore throat from which beta-hemolytic streptococci are cultured. The patient is started on treatment with penicillin, and the sore throat resolves within several days. However, 7 days after initiation of penicillin therapy the patient develops a fever of 103°F, a generalized rash, and proteinuria. This MOST probably resulted from
(A) Recurrence of the rheumatic fever
(B) A different infectious disease
(C) An IgE response to penicillin
(D) An IgG-IgM response to penicillin
(E) A delayed hypersensitivity reaction to penicillin

391. A kidney biopsy specimen taken from a patient with acute glomerulonephritis and stained with fluorescein-conjugated anti-human IgG antibody would probably show
(A) No fluorescence
(B) Uniform fluorescence of the glomerular basement membrane
(C) Patchy, irregular fluorescence of the glomerular basement membrane

(D) Fluorescent B cells
(E) Fluorescent macrophages

392. A patient with severe asthma gets no relief from antihistamines. The symptoms are MOST likely to be caused by
(A) Interleukin-2
(B) Slow-reacting substance A (leukotrienes)
(C) Serotonin
(D) Bradykinin

393. Hypersensitivity to penicillin and hypersensitivity to poison oak are both
(A) Mediated by IgE antibody
(B) Mediated by IgG and IgM antibody
(C) Initiated by haptens
(D) Initiated by Th-2 cells

394. A recipient of a 2-haplotype MHC-matched kidney from a relative still needs immunosuppression to prevent graft rejection because
(A) Graft-versus-host disease is a problem
(B) Class II MHC antigens will not be matched
(C) Minor histocompatibility antigens will not be matched
(D) Complement components will not be matched

395. Bone marrow transplantation in immunocompromised patients presents which major problem?
(A) Potentially lethal graft-versus-host disease
(B) High risk of T-cell leukemia
(C) Inability to use a live donor
(D) Delayed hypersensitivity

396. What is the role of class II MHC proteins on donor cells in graft rejection?
(A) They are the receptors for interleukin-2, which is produced by macrophages when they attack the donor cells
(B) They are recognized by helper T cells, which then activate cytotoxic T cells to kill the donor cells
(C) They induce the production of blocking antibodies that protect the graft
(D) They induce IgE which mediates graft rejection

397. Grafts between genetically identical individuals (ie, identical twins)
(A) Are rejected slowly as a result of minor histocompatibility antigens
(B) Are subject to hyperacute rejection

(C) Are not rejected, even without immunosuppression

(D) Are not rejected if a kidney is grafted, but skin grafts are rejected

398. Penicillin is a hapten in both humans and mice. To explore the hapten-carrier relationship, a mouse was injected with penicillin covalently bound to bovine serum albumin and, at the same time, with egg albumin to which no penicillin was bound. Of the following, which one will induce a secondary response to penicillin when injected into the mouse 1 month later?

(A) Penicillin

(B) Penicillin bound to egg albumin

(C) Egg albumin

(D) Bovine serum albumin

399. AIDS is caused by a human retrovirus that kills

(A) B lymphocytes

(B) Lymphocyte stem cells

(C) CD4-positive T lymphocytes

(D) CD8-positive T lymphocytes

400. Chemically induced tumors have tumor-associated transplantation antigens that

(A) Are always the same for a given carcinogen

(B) Are different for two tumors of different histologic type even if induced by the same carcinogen

(C) Are very strong antigens

(D) Do not induce an immune response

401. Polyomavirus (a DNA virus) causes tumors in "nude mice" (nude mice do not have a thymus because of a genetic defect) but not in normal mice. The BEST interpretation is that

(A) Macrophages are required to reject polyomavirus-induced tumors

(B) Natural killer cells can reject polyomavirus-induced tumors without help from T lymphocytes

(C) T lymphocytes play an important role in the rejection of polyomavirus-induced tumors

(D) B lymphocytes play no role in rejection of polyomavirus-induced tumors

402. C3 is cleaved to form C3a and C3b by C3 convertase. C3b is involved in all of the following EXCEPT:

(A) Altering vascular permeability

(B) Promoting phagocytosis

(C) Forming alternative-pathway C3 convertase

(D) Forming C5 convertase

403. After binding to its specific antigen, a B lymphocyte may switch its

(A) Immunoglobulin light-chain isotype

(B) Immunoglobulin heavy-chain class

(C) Variable region of the immunoglobulin heavy chain

(D) Constant region of the immunoglobulin light chain

404. Diversity is an important feature of the immune system. Which one of the following statements about it is INCORRECT?

(A) Humans can make antibodies with about 10^8 different $V_H \times V_L$ combinations

(B) A single cell can synthesize IgM antibody then switch to IgA antibody

(C) The hematopoietic stem cell carries the genetic potential to create more than 10^4 immunoglobulin genes

(D) A single B lymphocyte can produce antibodies of many different specificities, but a plasma cell is monospecific

405. C3a and C5a can cause

(A) Bacterial lysis

(B) Vascular permeability

(C) Phagocytosis of IgE-coated bacteria

(D) Aggregation of C4 and C2

406. Neutrophils are attracted to an infected area by

(A) IgM

(B) C1

(C) C5a

(D) C8

407. Complement fixation refers to

(A) The ingestion of C3b-coated bacteria by macrophages

(B) The destruction of complement in serum by heating at 56°C for 30 minutes

(C) The binding of complement components by antigen-antibody complexes

(D) The interaction of C3b with mast cells

408. The classic complement pathway is initiated by interaction of C1 with

(A) Antigen

(B) Factor B

(C) Antigen-IgG complexes

(D) Bacterial lipopolysaccharides

409. Patients with severely reduced C3 levels tend to have

(A) Increased numbers of severe viral infections

(B) Increased numbers of severe bacterial infections

(C) Low gamma globulin levels

(D) Frequent episodes of hemolytic anemia

410. Individuals with a genetic deficiency of C6 have

(A) Decreased resistance to viral infections

(B) Increased hypersensitivity reactions

(C) Increased frequency of cancer

(D) Decreased resistance to *Neisseria* bacteremia

411. Natural killer cells are

(A) B cells that can kill without complement

(B) Cytotoxic T cells

(C) Increased by immunization

(D) Able to kill virus-infected cells without prior sensitization

412. A positive tuberculin skin test (a delayed hypersensitivity reaction) indicates that

(A) A humoral immune response has occurred
(B) A cell-mediated immune response has occurred
(C) Both the T- and B-cell systems are functional
(D) Only the B-cell system is functional

413. Reaction to poison ivy or poison oak is
(A) An IgG-mediated response
(B) An IgE-mediated response
(C) A cell-mediated response
(D) An Arthus reaction

414. A child disturbs a wasp nest, is stung repeatedly, and goes into shock within minutes, manifesting respiratory failure and vascular collapse. This is MOST likely to be due to
(A) Systemic anaphylaxis
(B) Serum sickness
(C) An Arthus reaction
(D) Cytotoxic hypersensitivity

415. "Isotype switching" of immunoglobulin classes by B cells involves
(A) Simultaneous insertion of V_H genes adjacent to each C_H gene
(B) Successive insertion of a single V_H gene adjacent to different C_H genes
(C) Activation of homologous genes on chromosome 6
(D) Switching of light-chain types (kappa and lambda)

416. Which one of the following pairs of genes is linked on a single chromosome?
(A) V gene for lambda chain and C gene for kappa chain
(B) C gene for gamma chain and C gene for kappa chain
(C) V gene for lambda chain and V gene for heavy chain
(D) C gene for gamma chain and C gene for alpha chain

417. Idiotypic determinants are located within
(A) Hypervariable regions of heavy and light chains
(B) Constant regions of light chains
(C) Constant regions of heavy chains
(D) The hinge region

418. A primary immune response in an adult human requires approximately how much time to produce detectable antibody levels in the blood?
(A) 12 hours
(B) 3 days
(C) 1 week
(D) 3 weeks

419. The membrane IgM and IgD on the surface of an individual B cell
(A) Have identical heavy chains but different light chains

(B) Are identical except for their C_H regions
(C) Are identical except for their V_H regions
(D) Have different V_H and V_L regions

420. During the maturation of a B lymphocyte, the first immunoglobulin heavy chain synthesized is the
(A) Mu chain
(B) Gamma chain
(C) Epsilon chain
(D) Alpha chain

421. In the immune response to a hapten-protein conjugate, in order to get anti-hapten antibodies it is essential that
(A) The hapten be recognized by helper T cells
(B) The protein be recognized by helper T cells
(C) The protein be recognized by B cells
(D) The hapten be recognized by suppressor T cells

422. In the determination of serum insulin levels by radioimmunoassay, which one of the following is NOT needed?
(A) Isotope-labeled insulin
(B) Anti-insulin antibody made in goats
(C) Anti-goat gamma globulin made in rabbits
(D) Isotope-labeled anti-insulin antibody made in goats

423. Which one of the following sequences is appropriate for testing a patient for antibody against the AIDS virus with the ELISA procedure? (The assay is carried out in a plastic plate with an incubation and a wash step after each addition except the final one.)
(A) Patient's serum/enzyme substrate/HIV antigen/enzyme-labeled antibody against HIV
(B) HIV antigen/patient's serum/enzyme-labeled antibody against human gamma globulin/enzyme substrate
(C) Enzyme-labeled antibody against human gamma globulin/patient's serum/HIV antigen/enzyme substrate
(D) Enzyme-labeled antibody against HIV/HIV antigen/patient's serum/enzyme substrate

424. The BEST method to demonstrate IgG on the glomerular basement membrane in a kidney tissue section is the
(A) Precipitin test
(B) Complement fixation test
(C) Agglutination test
(D) Indirect fluorescent-antibody test

425. A woman had a high fever, hypotension, and a diffuse macular rash. When all cultures showed no bacterial growth, a diagnosis of toxic shock syndrome was made. Regarding the mechanism by which the toxin causes this disease, which one of the following is LEAST accurate?

(A) The toxin is not processed within the macrophage

(B) The toxin binds to both the class II MHC protein and the T-cell receptor

(C) The toxin activates many CD4-positive T cells, and large amounts of interleukins are released

(D) The toxin has an A-B subunit structure—the B subunit binds to a receptor, and the A subunit enters the cells and activates them.

426. A patient with a central nervous system disorder is maintained on the drug methyldopa. Hemolytic anemia develops, which resolves shortly after the drug is withdrawn. This is MOST probably an example of

(A) Atopic hypersensitivity

(B) Cytotoxic hypersensitivity

(C) Immune-complex hypersensitivity

(D) Cell-mediated hypersensitivity

427. Which one of the following substances is NOT released by activated helper T cells?

(A) Alpha interferon

(B) Gamma interferon

(C) Interleukin-2

(D) Interleukin-4

428. A delayed hypersensitivity reaction is characterized by

(A) Edema without a cellular infiltrate

(B) An infiltrate composed of neutrophils

(C) An infiltrate composed of helper T cells and macrophages

(D) An infiltrate composed of eosinophils

429. Two dissimilar inbred strains of mice, A and B, are crossed to yield an F_1 hybrid strain, AB. If a large dose of spleen cells from an adult A mouse is injected into an adult AB mouse, which one of the following is MOST likely to occur? An explanation of the answer to this question is given on page 571.

(A) The spleen cells will be destroyed

(B) The spleen cells will survive and will have no effect in the recipient

(C) The spleen cells will induce a graft-versus-host reaction in the recipient

(D) The spleen cells will survive and induce tolerance of strain A grafts in the recipient

430. This question is based on the same strains of mice described in the previous question. If adult AB spleen cells are injected into a newborn B mouse, which one of the following is MOST likely to occur? An explanation of the answer to this question is given on page 571.

(A) The spleen cells will be destroyed

(B) The spleen cells will survive without any effect on the recipient

(C) The spleen cells will induce a graft-versus-host reaction in the recipient

(D) The spleen cells will survive and induce tolerance of strain A grafts in the recipient

431. The minor histocompatibility antigens on cells

(A) Are detected by reaction with antibodies and complement

(B) Are controlled by several genes in the major histocompatibility complex

(C) Are unimportant in human transplantation

(D) Induce reactions that can cumulatively lead to a strong rejection response

432. Which one of the following is NOT true of class I MHC antigens?

(A) They can be assayed by a cytotoxic test that uses antibody and complement

(B) They can usually be identified in the laboratory in a few hours

(C) They are controlled by at least three gene loci in the major histocompatibility complex

(D) They are found mainly on B cells, macrophages, and activated T cells

433. An antigen found in relatively high concentration in the plasma of normal fetuses and a high proportion of patients with progressive carcinoma of the colon is

(A) Viral antigen

(B) Carcinoembryonic antigen

(C) Alpha-fetoprotein

(D) Heterophil antigen

434. An antibody directed against the idiotypic determinants of a human IgG antibody would react with

(A) The Fc part of the IgG

(B) An IgM antibody produced by the same plasma cell that produced the IgG

(C) All human kappa chains

(D) All human gamma chains

435. Which one of the following is NOT true of the gene segments that combine to make up a heavy-chain gene?

(A) Many V region segments are available

(B) Several J segments and several D segments are available

(C) V, D, and J segments combine to encode the antigen-binding site

(D) A V segment and a J segment are preselected by an antigen to make up the variable-region portion of the gene

436. When immune complexes from the serum are deposited on glomerular basement membrane, damage to the membrane is caused mainly by

(A) Gamma interferon

(B) Phagocytosis

(C) Cytotoxic T cells

(D) Enzymes released by polymorphonuclear cells

437. If an individual was genetically unable to make J chains, which immunoglobulin(s) would be affected?
    (A) IgG
    (B) IgM
    (C) IgA
    (D) IgG and IgM
    (E) IgM and IgA

438. The antibody-binding site is formed primarily by
    (A) The constant regions of H and L chains
    (B) The hypervariable regions of H and L chains
    (C) The hypervariable regions of H chains
    (D) The variable regions of H chains
    (E) The variable regions of L chains

439. The class of immunoglobulin present in highest concentration in the blood of a human newborn is
    (A) IgG
    (B) IgM
    (C) IgA
    (D) IgD
    (E) IgE

440. Individuals of blood group type AB
    (A) Are Rh(D)-negative
    (B) Are "universal recipients" of transfusions
    (C) Have circulating anti-A and anti-B antibodies
    (D) Have the same haplotype

441. Cytotoxic T cells induced by infection with virus A will kill target cells
    (A) From the same host infected with any virus
    (B) Infected by virus A and identical at class I MHC loci of the cytotoxic T cells
    (C) Infected by virus A and identical at class II MHC loci of the cytotoxic T cells
    (D) Infected with a different virus and identical at class I MHC loci of the cytotoxic cells
    (E) Infected with a different virus and identical at class II MHC loci of the cytotoxic cells

442. Antigen-presenting cells that activate helper T cells must express which one of the following on their surfaces?
    (A) IgE
    (B) Gamma interferon
    (C) Class I MHC antigens
    (D) Class II MHC antigens

443. Which one of the following does NOT contain C3b?
    (A) Classic-pathway C5 convertase
    (B) Alternative-pathway C5 convertase
    (C) Classic-pathway C3 convertase
    (D) Alternative-pathway C3 convertase

444. Which one of the following is NOT true regarding the alternative complement pathway?
    (A) It can be triggered by infectious agents in absence of antibody
    (B) It does not require C1, C2, or C4

    (C) It cannot be initiated unless C3b fragments are already present
    (D) It has the same terminal sequence of events as the classic pathway

445. In setting up a complement fixation test for antibody, the reactants should be added in what sequence? (Ag = antigen; Ab = antibody; C = complement; EA = antibody-coated indicator erythrocytes.)
    (A) Ag + EA + C/wait/ + patient's serum
    (B) C + patient's serum + EA/wait/ + Ag
    (C) Ag + patient's serum + EA/wait/ + C
    (D) Ag + patient's serum + C/wait/ + EA

446. Proteins from two samples of animal blood, A and B, were tested by the double-diffusion (Ouchterlony) test in agar against antibody to bovine albumin. Which sample(s) contain horse blood? An explanation of the answer to this question is given on page 571.

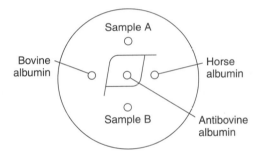

    (A) Sample A
    (B) Sample B
    (C) Both samples
    (D) Neither sample

447. Complement lyses cells by
    (A) Enzymatic digestion of the cell membrane
    (B) Activation of adenylate cyclase
    (C) Insertion of complement proteins into the cell membrane
    (D) Inhibition of elongation factor 2

448. Graft and tumor rejection are mediated primarily by
    (A) Non-complement-fixing antibodies
    (B) Phagocytic cells
    (C) Helper T cells
    (D) Cytotoxic T cells

449. Which one of the following properties of antibodies is NOT dependent on the structure of the heavy-chain constant region?
    (A) Ability to cross the placenta
    (B) Isotype (class)
    (C) Ability to fix complement
    (D) Affinity for antigen

450. In which one of the following situations would a graft-versus-host reaction be MOST likely to occur? (Mouse strains A and B are highly inbred; AB is an F_1 hybrid between strain A and strain B.)
  (A) Newborn strain A spleen cells injected into a strain B adult
  (B) X-irradiated adult strain A spleen cells injected into a strain B adult
  (C) Adult strain A spleen cells injected into an x-irradiated strain AB adult
  (D) Adult strain AB spleen cells injected into a strain A newborn

451. In a mixed-lymphocyte culture, lymphocytes from person X, who is homozygous for the HLA-Dw7 allele, are irradiated and then cultured with lymphocytes from person Z. It is found that DNA synthesis is NOT stimulated. The proper conclusion to be drawn is that
  (A) Person Z is homozygous for HLA-Dw7
  (B) Person Z is homozygous or heterozygous for HLA-Dw7
  (C) Person Z is heterozygous for HLA-Dw7
  (D) Person Z does not carry the HLA-Dw7 allele

452. A patient skin-tested with purified protein derivative (PPD) to determine previous exposure to *Mycobacterium tuberculosis* develops induration at the skin test site 48 hours later. Histologically, the reaction site would MOST probably show
  (A) Eosinophils
  (B) Neutrophils
  (C) Helper T cells and macrophages
  (D) B cells

453. Hemolytic disease of the newborn caused by Rh blood group incompatibility requires maternal antibody to enter the fetal bloodstream. Therefore, the mediator of this disease is
  (A) IgE antibody
  (B) IgG antibody
  (C) IgM antibody
  (D) IgA antibody

454. An Rh-negative woman married to a heterozygous Rh-positive man has three children. The probability that all three of their children are Rh-positive is
  (A) 1:2
  (B) 1:4
  (C) 1:8
  (D) zero

455. Which one of the following statements BEST explains the relationship between inflammation of the heart (carditis) and infection with group A beta-hemolytic streptococci?
  (A) Streptococcal antigens induce antibodies cross-reactive with heart tissue
  (B) Streptococci are polyclonal activators of B cells

  (C) Streptococcal antigens bind to IgE on the surface of heart tissue and histamine is released
  (D) Streptococci are ingested by neutrophils that release proteases that damage heart tissue

456. Your patient became ill 10 days ago with a viral disease. Laboratory examination reveals that the patient's antibodies against this virus have a high ratio of IgM to IgG. What is your conclusion?
  (A) It is unlikely that the patient has encountered this organism previously
  (B) The patient is predisposed to IgE-mediated hypersensitivity reactions
  (C) The information given is irrelevant to previous antigen exposure
  (D) It is likely that the patient has an autoimmune disease

457. If you measure the ability of cytotoxic T cells from an HLA-B27 person to kill virus X–infected target cells, which one of the following statements is CORRECT?
  (A) Any virus X–infected target cell will be killed
  (B) Only virus X–infected cells of HLA-B27 type will be killed
  (C) Any HLA-B27 cell will be killed
  (D) No HLA-B27 cell will be killed

458. You have a patient who makes autoantibodies against his own red blood cells, leading to hemolysis. Which one of the following mechanisms is MOST likely to explain the hemolysis?
  (A) Perforins from cytotoxic T cells lyse the red cells
  (B) Neutrophils release proteases that lyse the red cells
  (C) Interleukin-2 binds to its receptor on the red cells, which results in lysis of the red cells
  (D) Complement is activated, and membrane attack complexes lyse the red cells

459. Your patient is a child who has no detectable T or B cells. This immunodeficiency is most probably the result of a defect in
  (A) The thymus
  (B) The bursal equivalent
  (C) T cell–B cell interaction
  (D) Stem cells originating in the bone marrow

460. The role of the macrophage during an antibody response is to
  (A) Make antibody
  (B) Lyse virus-infected target cells
  (C) Activate cytotoxic T cells
  (D) Process antigen and present it

461. The structural basis of blood group A and B antigen specificity is
  (A) A single terminal sugar residue
  (B) A single terminal amino acid

(C) Multiple differences in the carbohydrate portion

(D) Multiple differences in the protein portion

462. Complement can enhance phagocytosis because of the presence on macrophages and neutrophils of receptors for

(A) factor D

(B) C3b

(C) C6

(D) properdin

463. The main advantage of passive immunization over active immunization is that

(A) It can be administered orally

(B) It provides antibody more rapidly

(C) Antibody persists for a longer period

(D) It contains primarily IgM

464. On January 15, a patient developed an illness suggestive of influenza, which lasted 1 week. On February 20, she had a similar illness. She had no influenza immunization during this period. Her hemagglutination inhibition titer to influenza A virus was 10 on January 18, 40 on January 30, and 320 on February 20. Which one of the following is the MOST appropriate interpretation?

(A) The patient was ill with influenza A on January 15

(B) The patient was ill with influenza A on February 20

(C) The patient was not infected with influenza virus

(D) The patient has an autoimmune disease

465. An individual who is heterozygous for Gm allotypes contains two allelic forms of IgG in serum, but individual lymphocytes produce only one of the two forms. This phenomenon, known as "allelic exclusion," is consistent with

(A) A rearrangement of a heavy-chain gene on only one chromosome in a lymphocyte

(B) Rearrangements of heavy-chain genes on both chromosomes in a lymphocyte

(C) A rearrangement of a light-chain gene on only one chromosome in a lymphocyte

(D) Rearrangements of light-chain genes on both chromosomes in a lymphocyte

466. Each of the following statements concerning class I MHC proteins is correct EXCEPT:

(A) They are cell surface proteins on virtually all cells

(B) They are recognition elements for cytotoxic T cells

(C) They are codominantly expressed

(D) They are important in the skin test response to *Mycobacterium tuberculosis*

467. Which one of the following is the BEST method of reducing the effect of graft-versus-host disease in a bone marrow recipient?

(A) Matching the complement components of donor and recipient

(B) Administering alpha interferon

(C) Removing mature T cells from the graft

(D) Removing pre-B cells from the graft

468. Regarding Th-1 and Th-2 cells, which one of the following is LEAST accurate?

(A) Th-1 cells produce gamma interferon and promote cell-mediated immunity

(B) Th-2 cells produce interleukin-4 and -5 and promote antibody-mediated immunity

(C) Both Th-1 and Th-2 cells have both CD3 and CD4 proteins on their outer cell membrane

(D) Before naive Th cells differentiate into Th-1 or Th-2 cells, they are double-positives; ie, they produce both gamma interferon and interleukin-4

469. Each of the following statements concerning the variable regions of heavy chains and the variable regions of light chains in a given antibody molecule is correct EXCEPT:

(A) They have the same amino acid sequence

(B) They define the specificity for antigen

(C) They are encoded on different chromosomes

(D) They contain the hypervariable regions

470. Each of the following statements concerning class II MHC proteins is correct EXCEPT:

(A) They are found on the surface of both B and T cells

(B) They have a high degree of polymorphism

(C) They are involved in the presentation of antigen by macrophages

(D) They have a binding site for CD4 proteins

471. Which one of the following statements concerning immunoglobulin allotypes is CORRECT?

(A) Allotypes are found only on heavy chains

(B) Allotypes are determined by class I MHC genes

(C) Allotypes are confined to the variable regions

(D) Allotypes are due to genetic polymorphism within a species

472. Each of the following statements concerning immunologic tolerance is correct EXCEPT:

(A) Tolerance is not antigen-specific; ie, paralysis of the immune cells results in a failure to produce a response against many antigens

(B) Tolerance is more easily induced in T cells than in B cells

(C) Tolerance is more easily induced in neonates than in adults

(D) Tolerance is more easily induced by simple molecules than by complex ones

473. Each of the following statements concerning a hybridoma cell is correct EXCEPT:

(A) The spleen cell component provides the ability to form antibody

(B) The myeloma cell component provides the ability to grow indefinitely

(C) The antibody produced by a hybridoma cell is IgM, because heavy-chain switching does not occur

(D) The antibody produced by a hybridoma cell is homogeneous; ie, it is directed against a single epitope

474. Each of the following statements concerning haptens is correct EXCEPT:

(A) A hapten can combine with (bind to) an antibody

(B) A hapten cannot induce an antibody by itself; rather, it must be bound to a carrier protein to be able to induce antibody

(C) In both penicillin-induced anaphylaxis and poison ivy, the allergens are haptens

(D) Haptens must be processed by CD8+ cells to become immunogenic

Answers (Questions 387–474)

387 (B)	405 (B)	423 (B)	441 (B)	458 (D)
388 (B)	406 (C)	424 (D)	442 (D)	459 (D)
389 (A)	407 (C)	425 (D)	443 (C)	460 (D)
390 (D)	408 (C)	426 (B)	444 (C)	461 (A)
391 (C)	409 (B)	427 (A)	445 (D)	462 (B)
392 (B)	410 (D)	428 (C)	446 (B)	463 (B)
393 (C)	411 (D)	429 (C)	447 (C)	464 (A)
394 (C)	412 (B)	430 (D)	448 (D)	465 (A)
395 (A)	413 (C)	431 (D)	449 (D)	466 (D)
396 (B)	414 (A)	432 (D)	450 (C)	467 (C)
397 (C)	415 (B)	433 (B)	451 (B)	468 (D)
398 (D)	416 (D)	434 (B)	452 (C)	469 (A)
399 (C)	417 (A)	435 (D)	453 (B)	470 (A)
400 (B)	418 (C)	436 (D)	454 (C)	471 (D)
401 (C)	419 (B)	437 (E)	455 (A)	472 (A)
402 (A)	420 (A)	438 (B)	456 (A)	473 (C)
403 (B)	421 (B)	439 (A)	457 (B)	474 (D)
404 (D)	422 (D)	440 (B)		

DIRECTIONS (Questions 475–535): Select the ONE lettered option that is MOST closely associated with the numbered items. Each lettered option may be selected once, more than once, or not at all.

Questions 475–480

(A) T cells
(B) B cells
(C) Macrophages
(D) B cells and macrophages
(E) T cells, B cells, and macrophages

475. Major source of interleukin-1
476. Acted on by interleukin-1
477. Major source of interleukin-2
478. Express class I MHC markers
479. Express class II MHC markers
480. Express surface immunoglobulin

Questions 481–484

(A) Primary antibody response
(B) Secondary antibody response

481. Appears more quickly and persists longer
482. Relatively richer in IgG
483. Relatively richer in IgM
484. Typically takes 7–10 days for antibody to appear

Questions 485–488

(A) Blood group A
(B) Blood group O
(C) Blood groups A and O
(D) Blood group AB

485. People with this type have circulating anti-A antibodies
486. People with this type have circulating anti-B antibodies
487. People with this type are called "universal donors"
488. People with this type are called "universal recipients"

Questions 489–494

(A) Variable region of light chain
(B) Variable region of heavy chain
(C) Variable regions of light and heavy chains
(D) Constant region of heavy chain
(E) Constant regions of light and heavy chains

489. Determines immunoglobulin class
490. Determines allotypes
491. Determines idiotypes
492. Binding of IgG to macrophages
493. Fixation of complement by IgG
494. Antigen-binding site

Questions 495–498

The following double-immunodiffusion plate contains antibody prepared against whole human serum in the center well. Identify the contents of each peripheral well from the following list (each well to be used once). An explanation of the answer to this question is given on page 571.

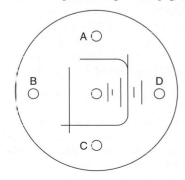

495. Whole human serum
496. Human IgG
497. Baboon IgG
498. Human transferrin

Questions 499–501

   (A) Immediate hypersensitivity
   (B) Cytotoxic hypersensitivity
   (C) Immune-complex hypersensitivity
   (D) Delayed hypersensitivity

499. Irregular deposition of IgG along glomerular basement membrane
500. Involves mast cells and basophils
501. Mediated by lymphokines

Questions 502–505

   (A) IgM
   (B) IgG
   (C) IgA
   (D) IgE

502. Crosses the placenta
503. Can contain a polypeptide chain not synthesized by a B lymphocyte
504. Found in the milk of lactating women
505. Binds firmly to mast cells and triggers anaphylaxis

Questions 506–509

   (A) Agglutination
   (B) Precipitin test
   (C) Immunofluorescence
   (D) Enzyme immunoassay

506. Concentration of IgG in serum
507. Surface IgM on cells in a bone marrow smear
508. Growth hormone in serum
509. Type A blood group antigen on erythrocytes

Questions 510–513

   (A) IgA
   (B) IgE
   (C) IgG
   (D) IgM

510. Present in highest concentration in serum
511. Present in highest concentration in secretions
512. Present in lowest concentration in serum
513. Contains 10 heavy and 10 light chains

Questions 514–517

In this double-diffusion (Ouchterlony) assay, the center well contains antibody against whole human serum. The peripheral (numbered) wells each contain one of the following proteins:

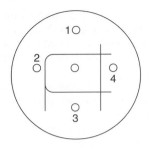

   (A) Human serum albumin at low concentration
   (B) Human serum albumin at high concentration
   (C) Human serum transferrin
   (D) Sheep serum albumin

514. Which protein is present in well No. 1?
515. Which protein is present in well No. 2?
516. Which protein is present in well No. 3?
517. Which protein is present in well No. 4?

An explanation of the answer to this question is given on page 571.

Questions 518–521

   (A) Class I MHC proteins
   (B) Class II MHC proteins

518. Involved in the presentation of antigen to CD4-positive cells
519. Involved in the presentation of antigen to CD8-positive cells
520. Involved in antibody responses to T-dependent antigens
521. Involved in target cell recognition by cytotoxic T cells

Questions 522–525

   (A) Fab fragment of IgG
   (B) Fc fragment of IgG

522. Contains an antigen-combining site
523. Contains hypervariable regions
524. Contains a complement-binding site
525. Is crystallizable

Questions 526–530

   (A) Severe combined immunodeficiency disease (SCID)
   (B) X-linked hypogammaglobulinemia
   (C) Thymic aplasia
   (D) Chronic granulomatous disease
   (E) Hereditary angioedema

526. Caused by a defect in the ability of neutrophils to kill microorganisms
527. Caused by a development defect that results in a profound loss of T cells

528. Caused by a deficiency in an inhibitor of the C1 component of complement

529. Caused by a marked deficiency of B cells

530. Caused by a virtual absence of both B and T cells

Questions 531–535

    (A) Systemic lupus erythematosus
    (B) Rheumatoid arthritis
    (C) Rheumatic fever
    (D) Graves' disease
    (E) Myasthenia gravis

531. Associated with antibody to the thyroid-stimulating hormone (TSH) receptor

532. Associated with antibody to IgG

533. Associated with antibody to the acetylcholine receptor

534. Associated with antibody to DNA

535. Associated with antibody to streptococci

Answers (Questions 475–535)

475 (C)	488 (D)	501 (D)	513 (D)	525 (B)
476 (A)	489 (D)	502 (B)	514 (B)	526 (D)
477 (A)	490 (E)	503 (C)	515 (A)	527 (C)
478 (E)	491 (C)	504 (C)	516 (D)	528 (E)
479 (D)	492 (D)	505 (D)	517 (C)	529 (B)
480 (B)	493 (D)	506 (D)	518 (B)	530 (A)
481 (B)	494 (C)	507 (C)	519 (A)	531 (D)
482 (B)	495 (D)	508 (D)	520 (B)	532 (B)
483 (A)	496 (C)	509 (A)	521 (A)	533 (E)
484 (A)	497 (A)	510 (C)	522 (A)	534 (A)
485 (B)	498 (B)	511 (A)	523 (A)	535 (C)
486 (C)	499 (C)	512 (B)	524 (B)	
487 (B)	500 (A)			

Explanation of question 429: Spleen cells from the adult donor A will recognize the B antigen on the recipient's cells as foreign. Spleen cells from the adult donor will contain mature CD4 and CD8 cells that will attack the recipient cells, causing a graft-versus-host reaction; therefore, answer C is correct. Because the recipient is tolerant to antigen A, the donor A spleen cells will not be destroyed; therefore, answer A is incorrect. Answer B is incorrect because, although the donor cells will survive, they will have an effect on the recipient. Answer D is incorrect because the recipient is already tolerant to antigen A.

Explanation of question 430: Because the donor AB spleen cells will not see any foreign antigen in the recipient, no graft-versus-host reaction will occur; therefore, answer C is incorrect. The immune cells of the newborn mouse do not have the capability to kill the donor cells; therefore, answer A is incorrect. Answer D is more correct than answer B because the donor cells will survive and induce tolerance to antigen A in the newborn recipient.

Explanation of question 446: There is a line of identity between sample A and bovine albumin; therefore, sample A is bovine albumin. There is a line of identity between sample B and horse albumin; therefore, sample B is horse albumin. The answer to the question is therefore B. Note that there is a spur formed between the wells containing sample A and horse albumin and between the wells containing sample B and bovine albumin. The spur indicates partial identity between the two proteins. Partial identity means that there are epitopes shared between the two albumins but that, because they are from different species, there are epitopes unique to each protein, also. A spur is formed by the interaction of the subset of antibodies in the anti-bovine serum with the unique epitopes in bovine albumin. The other lines are formed by the interaction of the subset of antibodies in the anti-bovine serum with the epitopes shared by the two albumins.

Explanation of questions 495–498: The center well contains antibody against whole human serum; therefore, well D must contain whole human serum because there are multiple lines representing some of the many proteins in whole human serum. There is a line of identity between well C and a protein in whole human serum and a line of partial identity with that same protein and well A. This indicates that well C contains human IgG and well A contains baboon IgG. The concept of partial identity is explained above in the discussion of question 446. There is a line of nonidentity between wells B and C; therefore, well B contains human transferrin, a protein immunologically distinct from human IgG.

Explanation of questions 514–517: There is a line of identity between wells 1 and 2; therefore, they contain human serum albumin (HSA). Note that the line of immunoprecipitate is very close to well 2. This line would not form if well 2 contained the high concentration of HSA because it would be a zone of antigen excess and the line only forms in a zone of equivalence. Therefore, well 2 contains the low concentration and well 1 contains the high concentration of HSA. There is a line of partial identity between wells 2 and 3; therefore, well 3 contains sheep serum albumin (SSA). There is a line of nonidentity between wells 1 and 4 and wells 3 and 4, therefore well 4 contains human transferrin, which is immunologically distinct from HSA and SSA.

Extended Matching Questions

DIRECTIONS (Questions 536–593): Each set of matching questions in this section consists of a list of lettered options followed by several numbered items. For each numbered item, select the ONE lettered option that is MOST closely associated with it. Each lettered option may be selected once, more than once, or not at all.

(A) Capsule
(B) Periplasmic space
(C) Peptidoglycan
(D) Lipid A
(E) 30S ribosomal subunit
(F) G protein
(G) Pilus
(H) ADP-ribosylating enzyme
(I) Mesosome
(J) Flagellum
(K) Transposon

536. Is the site of action of lysozyme
537. Mediates adherence of bacteria to mucous membranes
538. Is the toxic component of endotoxin

(A) Skin
(B) Colon
(C) Nose
(D) Stomach
(E) Vagina
(F) Mouth
(G) Outer third of urethra
(H) Gingival crevice
(I) Pharynx

539. Anatomic location where *Bacteroides fragilis* is most commonly found
540. Anatomic location where *Actinomyces israelii* is most commonly found

(A) Toxic shock syndrome toxin
(B) Tetanus toxin
(C) Diphtheria toxin
(D) Cholera toxin
(E) Coagulase
(F) Botulinum toxin
(G) Alpha toxin of *C. perfringens*
(H) M protein
(I) Endotoxin
(J) Verotoxin

541. Blocks release of acetylcholine
542. Its lipid component causes fever and shock by inducing TNF

543. Causes fever and shock by binding to the T cell receptor
544. Inhibits protein synthesis by ADP-ribosylation of elongation factor 2
545. Increases cyclic AMP by ADP-ribosylation of a G protein

(A) Ampicillin
(B) Nafcillin
(C) Clindamycin
(D) Gentamicin
(E) Tetracycline
(F) Amphotericin B
(G) Ciprofloxacin
(H) Rifampin
(I) Sulfonamide
(J) Erythromycin
(K) Metronidazole
(L) Isoniazid

546. Inhibits protein synthesis by blocking formation of the initiation complex so that no polysomes form
547. Inhibits DNA gyrase
548. Inhibits folic acid synthesis; analogue of para-aminobenzoic acid
549. Inhibits peptidoglycan synthesis; resistant to β-lactamase
550. Inhibits RNA polymerase

(A) *Streptococcus pneumoniae*
(B) *Streptococcus pyogenes*
(C) *Haemophilus influenzae*
(D) *Salmonella typhi*
(E) *Staphylococcus aureus*
(F) *Enterococcus faecalis*
(G) *Clostridium tetani*
(H) *Bordetella pertussis*
(I) *Escherichia coli*
(J) *Streptococcus agalactiae*
(K) *Staphylococcus epidermidis*
(L) *Streptococcus mutans*

551. Immunogen in the vaccine is one capsular polysaccharide coupled to a protein carrier
552. Immunogen in the vaccine is a toxoid
553. Causes acute glomerulonephritis; is beta-hemolytic
554. Causes urinary tract infections; grows in 6.5% NaCl
555. Causes neonatal meningitis; is bacitracin-resistant
556. Causes meningitis in adults; is alpha-hemolytic and optochin-sensitive

557. Causes food poisoning; is coagulase-positive
- **(A)** *Escherichia coli*
- **(B)** *Shigella sonnei*
- **(C)** *Salmonella typhi*
- **(D)** *Salmonella enteritidis*
- **(E)** *Proteus mirabilis*
- **(F)** *Pseudomonas aeruginosa*
- **(G)** *Vibrio cholerae*
- **(H)** *Campylobacter jejuni*
- **(I)** *Helicobacter pylori*
- **(J)** *Bacteroides fragilis*

558. Causes of gastritis and peptic ulcer; produces urease

559. Causes bloody diarrhea; does not ferment lactose and does not produce H_2S

560. Causes peritonitis; is an obligate anaerobe

561. Causes wound infections with blue-green pus; is oxidase-positive

562. Comma-shaped rod; causes high-volume watery diarrhea
- **(A)** *Legionella pneumophila*
- **(B)** *Yersinia pestis*
- **(C)** *Haemophilus influenzae*
- **(D)** *Corynebacterium diphtheriae*
- **(E)** *Pasteurella multocida*
- **(F)** *Bordetella pertussis*
- **(G)** *Brucella melitensis*
- **(H)** *Listeria monocytogenes*
- **(I)** *Clostridium perfringens*
- **(J)** *Neisseria gonorrhoeae*

563. Gram-positive spore-forming rod that causes myonecrosis

564. Gram-negative rod that is transmitted by cat bite

565. Gram-negative rod that causes cough and lymphocytosis
- **(A)** *Mycobacterium tuberculosis*
- **(B)** *Borrelia burgdorferi*
- **(C)** *Nocardia asteroides*
- **(D)** *Treponema pallidum*
- **(E)** *Coxiella burnetii*
- **(F)** *Mycoplasma pneumoniae*
- **(G)** *Mycobacterium leprae*
- **(H)** *Chlamydia trachomatis*
- **(I)** *Rickettsia rickettsii*
- **(J)** *Leptospira interrogans*

566. Spirochete that does not have an animal reservoir

567. Obligate intracellular parasite that forms elementary bodies

568. Respiratory pathogen without a cell wall
- **(A)** Influenza virus
- **(B)** Adenovirus
- **(C)** Hepatitis A virus
- **(D)** Hepatitis B virus
- **(E)** Herpes simplex virus
- **(F)** Measles virus
- **(G)** Human immunodeficiency virus
- **(H)** Rabies virus
- **(I)** Rotavirus

569. Nonenveloped virus with single-stranded, positive-polarity RNA

570. Enveloped virus with two identical strands of positive-polarity RNA

571. Enveloped virus with double-stranded DNA and DNA polymerase in the virion

572. Enveloped virus with segmented, negative-polarity, single-stranded RNA

573. Nonenveloped virus with segmented double-stranded RNA
- **(A)** Herpes simplex virus type 1
- **(B)** Rabies virus
- **(C)** Varicella-zoster virus
- **(D)** Measles virus
- **(E)** Epstein-Barr virus
- **(F)** Influenza virus
- **(G)** Rubella virus
- **(H)** Herpes simplex virus type 2
- **(I)** Mumps virus
- **(J)** Cytomegalovirus
- **(K)** Parainfluenza virus
- **(L)** Respiratory syncytial virus

574. Leading cause of congenital malformations; no vaccine available

575. Causes a painful vesicular rash along the course of a thoracic nerve

576. Causes encephalitis; killed vaccine available

577. Causes pharyngitis, lymphadenopathy, and a positive heterophil test

578. Causes retinitis and pneumonia in patients deficient in helper T cells

579. Causes encephalitis, especially in the temporal lobe

580. Causes pneumonia primarily in infants; induces giant cells

581. Causes orchitis that can result in sterility
- **(A)** Human papillomavirus
- **(B)** Hepatitis A virus
- **(C)** Rotavirus
- **(D)** Adenovirus
- **(E)** Hepatitis delta virus
- **(F)** Parvovirus B19
- **(G)** Human immunodeficiency virus
- **(H)** Hepatitis B virus
- **(I)** Muerto Canyon virus (Hantavirus)
- **(J)** Human T-cell lymphotropic virus
- **(K)** Prion
- **(L)** Hepatitis C virus

582. Most important cause of diarrhea in infants

583. A vaccine containing purified viral protein is available

584. Defective virus with an RNA genome

(A) *Coccidioides immitis*
(B) *Cryptococcus neoformans*
(C) *Blastomyces dermatitidis*
(D) *Sporothrix schenckii*
(E) *Aspergillus fumigatus*
(F) *Candida albicans*
(G) *Histoplasma capsulatum*
(H) *Mucor* species
(I) *Microsporum canis*

585. Dimorphic fungus that enters the body through puncture wounds in the skin
586. Nonseptate mold that invades tissue, especially in acidotic patients
587. Yeast that forms pseudohyphae when it invades tissue

(A) *Giardia lamblia*
(B) *Plasmodium vivax*
(C) *Leishmania donovani*
(D) *Entamoeba histolytica*
(E) *Toxoplasma gondii*
(F) *Trypanosoma cruzi*
(G) *Pneumocystis carinii*
(H) *Plasmodium falciparum*
(I) *Naegleria* species
(J) *Trichomonas vaginalis*

588. Acquired while swimming; causes meningitis
589. Transmitted by reduviid bug and invades cardiac muscle

590. Amastigotes found within macrophages
(A) *Echinococcus granulosus*
(B) *Clonorchis sinensis*
(C) *Strongyloides stercoralis*
(D) *Taenia solium*
(E) *Necator americanus*
(F) *Enterobius vermicularis*
(G) *Schistosoma haematobium*
(H) *Wuchereria bancrofti*
(I) *Trichinella spiralis*
(J) *Taenia saginata*

591. Infection predisposes to bladder carcinoma
592. Ingestion of larvae can cause cysticercosis
593. Acquired by penetration of feet by larvae; causes anemia

Answers (Questions 536–593)

536 (C)	548 (I)	560 (J)	572 (A)	583 (H)
537 (G)	549 (B)	561 (F)	573 (I)	584 (E)
538 (D)	550 (H)	562 (G)	574 (J)	585 (D)
539 (B)	551 (C)	563 (I)	575 (C)	586 (H)
540 (H)	552 (G)	564 (E)	576 (B)	587 (F)
541 (F)	553 (B)	565 (F)	577 (E)	588 (I)
542 (I)	554 (F)	566 (D)	578 (J)	589 (F)
543 (A)	555 (J)	567 (H)	579 (A)	590 (C)
544 (C)	556 (A)	568 (F)	580 (L)	591 (G)
545 (D)	557 (E)	569 (C)	581 (I)	592 (D)
546 (D)	558 (I)	570 (G)	582 (C)	593 (E)
547 (G)	559 (B)	571 (D)		

Clinical Case Questions

DIRECTIONS (Questions 594–654): Select the ONE lettered answer that is BEST in each question.

CASE 1. Your patient is a 20-year-old woman with the sudden onset of fever to 104°F and a severe headache. Physical examination reveals nuchal rigidity. You suspect meningitis and do a spinal tap. Gram stain of the spinal fluid reveals many neutrophils and many gram-negative diplococci.

594. Of the following bacteria, which one is MOST likely to be the cause?
(A) *Haemophilus influenzae*
(B) *Neisseria meningitidis*
(C) *Streptococcus pneumoniae*
(D) *Pseudomonas aeruginosa*

595. Additional history reveals that she has had several serious infections with this organism previously.

On the basis of this, which one of the following is the MOST likely predisposing factor?
(A) She is HIV antibody–positive
(B) She is deficient in CD8-positive T cells
(C) She is deficient in one of the late-acting complement components
(D) She is deficient in antigen presentation by her macrophages

CASE 2. Your patient is a 70-year-old man with a long history of smoking who now has a fever and a cough productive of greenish sputum. You suspect pneumonia, and a chest x-ray confirms your suspicion.

596. If a Gram stain of the sputum reveals very small gram-negative rods and there is no growth on a blood agar but colonies do grow on chocolate agar supplemented with NAD and heme, which one of the following bacteria is the MOST likely cause?

(A) *Chlamydia pneumoniae*
(B) *Legionella pneumophila*
(C) *Mycoplasma pneumoniae*
(D) *Haemophilus influenzae*

CASE 3. Your patient is a 50-year-old woman who returned yesterday from a vacation in Peru, where there is an epidemic of cholera. She now has multiple episodes of diarrhea.

597. Of the following, which one is MOST compatible with cholera?

(A) Watery diarrhea without blood, no polys in the stool, and growth of curved gram-negative rods in the blood culture
(B) Watery diarrhea without blood, no polys in the stool, and no organisms in the blood culture
(C) Bloody diarrhea, polys in the stool, and growth of curved gram-negative rods in the blood culture
(D) Bloody diarrhea, polys in the stool, and no organisms in the blood culture

CASE 4. Your patient is a 55-year-old man who is coughing up greenish blood-streaked sputum. For the past 2 weeks, he has had fever and night sweats. He thinks he has lost about 10 pounds. On physical examination, there are crackles in the apex of the right lung, and a chest x-ray shows a cavity in that location.

598. Of the following, which one is the LEAST likely finding?

(A) Gram stain of the sputum shows no predominant organism
(B) Culture of the sputum on blood agar shows no predominant organism
(C) Culture of the sputum on Löwenstein-Jensen medium shows tan colonies after incubation for 4 weeks
(D) Rapid plasma reagin test reveals the causative organism

CASE 5. Your patient is a 5-year-old girl with bloody diarrhea and no vomiting. There is no history of travel outside of San Francisco. Stool culture grows both lactose-positive and lactose-negative colonies on EMB agar.

599. Of the following organisms, which one is MOST likely to be the cause?

(A) *Shigella sonnei*
(B) *Salmonella typhi*
(C) *Campylobacter jejuni*
(D) *Helicobacter pylori*

CASE 6. Your patient is a 25-year-old woman with acute onset of pain in her left lower quadrant. On pelvic examination, there is a cervical exudate and tenderness in the left adnexa. You conclude that she has pelvic inflammatory disease (PID) and order laboratory tests.

600. Of the following, which one is the LEAST informative laboratory result?

(A) Gram stain of the cervical exudate shows gram-negative diplococci within polys
(B) Culture of the cervical exudate on Thayer-Martin agar shows oxidase-positive colonies
(C) Fluorescent-antibody test shows cytoplasmic inclusions
(D) Complement fixation test shows a rise in antibody titer

CASE 7. Your patient is a 22-year-old man with fever, fatigue, and a new diastolic murmur. You suspect endocarditis and do a blood culture.

601. Which of the following statements is LEAST accurate?

(A) If he had dental surgery recently, one of the most likely organisms to grow would be a viridans group streptococcus
(B) If he is an intravenous drug user, one of the most likely organisms to grow would be *Candida albicans*
(C) If he had colon surgery recently, one of the most likely organisms to grow would be *Enterococcus faecalis*
(D) If he has a prosthetic aortic valve, one of the most likely organisms to grow would be *Streptococcus agalactiae*

In fact, none of the above organisms grew in the blood culture. What did grow was a gram-positive coccus arranged in clusters. When subcultured on blood agar, the colonies were surrounded by a zone of clear hemolysis, and a coagulase test was positive.

602. In view of this, which one of the following is MOST accurate?

(A) He is probably an intravenous drug user
(B) He probably lives on a farm and has had contact with pregnant sheep
(C) He probably has a common sexually transmitted disease
(D) He probably has been camping and was bitten by a tick

CASE 8. Your patient is a 70-year-old woman who had a hysterectomy for carcinoma of the uterus 3 days ago. She has an indwelling urinary catheter in place and now has a fever to 39°C, and the urine in the collection bottle is cloudy. A Gram stain of the urine specimen shows many neutrophils and gram-positive cocci in chains. You also do a urine culture.

603. Which one of the following is the MOST likely set of findings on the urine culture?

(A) Beta-hemolytic colonies that are bacitracin-sensitive

(B) Alpha-hemolytic colonies that are optochin-sensitive

(C) Nonhemolytic colonies that grow in 6.5% sodium chloride

(D) Nonhemolytic colonies that grow only anaerobically

CASE 9. Your patient is a 27-year-old woman who was treated with oral ampicillin for cellulitis caused by *Streptococcus pyogenes.* Several days later, she developed bloody diarrhea. You suspect that she may have pseudomembranous colitis.

604. Regarding the causative organism of pseudomembranous colitis, which one of the following is the MOST accurate?

(A) It is an anaerobic gram-positive rod that produces exotoxins

(B) It is a comma-shaped gram-negative rod that grows best at 41°C

(C) It is an obligate intracellular parasite that grows in cell culture but not on blood agar

(D) It is a yeast that forms germ tubes when incubated in human serum at 37°C

CASE 10. Your patient is a 10-year-old girl who has had pain in her left arm for the past 5 days. On physical examination, her temperature is 38°C and there is tenderness of the humerus near her deltoid. On x-ray of the humerus, an area of raised periosteum and erosion of bone is seen. You do a blood culture.

605. Which one of the following is the MOST likely set of findings?

(A) Gram-negative rods that grow on EMB agar, forming purple colonies and a green sheen

(B) Gram-positive cocci that grow on blood agar, causing a clear zone of hemolysis, and are coagulase-positive

(C) Gram-positive rods that grow only anaerobically and form a double zone of hemolysis on blood agar

(D) Gram-negative diplococci that grow on blood agar, are oxidase-positive, and ferment maltose

CASE 11. Your patient is a 30-year-old man who is HIV antibody–positive and has a history of *Pneumocystis* pneumonia 2 years ago. He now has an ulcerating lesion on the side of his tongue. A Giemsa stain of the biopsy specimen reveals budding yeasts within macrophages. A culture of the specimen grows an organism that is a budding yeast at 37°C but produces hyphae at 25°C.

606. Of the following, which one is the MOST likely organism to cause this infection?

(A) *Coccidioides immitis*

(B) *Aspergillus fumigatus*

(C) *Histoplasma capsulatum*

(D) *Cryptococcus neoformans*

CASE 12. Your patient is a 10-year-old boy who is receiving chemotherapy for acute leukemia. He develops fever, headache, and a stiff neck, and you make a presumptive diagnosis of meningitis and do a lumbar puncture. A Gram stain reveals a small gram-positive rod, and culture of the spinal fluid grows a beta-hemolytic colony on blood agar.

607. Regarding this organism, which one of the following is MOST accurate?

(A) It has more than 100 serologic types

(B) It produces an exotoxin that inhibits elongation factor 2

(C) It is commonly acquired by eating unpasteurized dairy products

(D) There is a toxoid vaccine available against this organism

CASE 13. Ms. Jones calls to say that she, her husband, and their child have had nausea and vomiting for the past hour or so. Also, they have had some nonbloody diarrhea. You ask when their last meal together was, and she says they had a picnic lunch in the park about 3 hours ago. They have no fever.

608. Which one of the following is the MOST likely finding?

(A) Gram stain of the leftover food would show many gram-positive cocci in clusters

(B) Gram stain of the stool would show many gram-negative diplococci

(C) KOH prep of the leftover food would show many budding yeasts

(D) Acid-fast stain of the stool would show many acid-fast rods

CASE 14. Your patient is a 9-year-old boy who was sent home from school because his teacher thought he was acting strangely. This morning, he had a seizure and was rushed to the hospital. On physical examination, his temperature is 40°C and he has no nuchal rigidity. A CT scan is normal. A lumbar puncture is done, and the spinal fluid protein and glucose are normal. A Gram stain of the spinal fluid reveals no organisms and no polys. He is treated with various antibiotics but becomes comatose and dies 2 days later. The blood culture and spinal fluid culture grow no bacteria or fungi. On autopsy of the brain, eosinophilic inclusion bodies are seen in the cytoplasm of neurons.

609. Of the following, which one is the MOST likely cause?

(A) Prions

(B) JC virus

(C) Rabies virus

(D) Herpes simplex virus type 1

CASE 15. Your patient is a 20-year-old man who was in a fist fight and suffered a broken jaw and lost two teeth. Several weeks later, he developed an abscess at the site of the trauma that drained to the surface of the skin, and yellowish granules were seen in the pus.

610. Regarding this disease, which one of the following is MOST accurate?

    (A) The causative organism is a gram-positive rod that forms long filaments

    (B) The causative organism is a comma-shaped gram-negative rod that produces an exotoxin which increases cyclic AMP

    (C) The causative organism cannot be seen in the Gram stain but can be seen in an acid-fast stain

    (D) A combination of gram-negative cocci and spirochetes cause this disease

CASE 16. Your patient is a 25-year-old man who is HIV antibody–positive and has a CD4 count of 120 cells (normal, 1000–1500). He has had a mild headache for the past week and vomited once yesterday. On physical examination, he has a temperature of 38°C and mild nuchal rigidity but no papilledema. The rest of the physical examination is negative.

611. Of the following, which one is the MOST likely to be found on examination of the spinal fluid?

    (A) Lymphs and gram-positive cocci resembling *Streptococcus pneumoniae*

    (B) Lymphs and budding yeasts resembling *Cryptococcus neoformans*

    (C) Polys and anaerobic gram-negative rods resembling *Bacteroides fragilis*

    (D) Polys and septate hyphae resembling *Aspergillus fumigatus*

CASE 17. Your patient is a 25-year-old woman with a sore throat since yesterday. On physical examination, her throat is red but no exudate is seen. Two enlarged, tender cervical lymph nodes are palpable. Her temperature is 101°F. A throat culture reveals no beta-hemolytic colonies. After receiving this result, you do another physical examination, which reveals an enlarged spleen. A heterophil antibody test finds that sheep red blood cells are agglutinated by the patient's serum.

612. Which one of the following is the MOST likely cause of this disease?

    (A) *Streptococcus pyogenes*

    (B) *Corynebacterium diphtheriae*

    (C) Epstein-Barr virus

    (D) Influenza virus

CASE 18. Your patient is a 15-year-old boy with migratory polyarthritis, fever, and a new, loud cardiac murmur. You make a clinical diagnosis of rheumatic fever.

613. Which one of the following laboratory results is MOST compatible with this diagnosis?

    (A) A blood culture is positive for *Streptococcus pyogenes* at this time

    (B) A throat culture is positive for *Streptococcus pyogenes* at this time

    (C) A Gram stain of the joint fluid shows gram-positive cocci in chains at this time

    (D) An anti-streptolysin O assay is positive at this time

614. Which one of the following modes of pathogenesis is MOST compatible with this diagnosis?

    (A) Bacteria attach to joint and heart tissue via pili, invade, and cause inflammation

    (B) Bacteria secrete exotoxins that circulate via the blood to the joints and heart

    (C) Bacterial antigens induce antibodies that cross-react with joint and heart tissue

    (D) Bacterial endotoxin induces interleukin-1 and tumor necrosis factor, which cause inflammation in joint and heart tissue

615. Which one of the following approaches is MOST likely to prevent endocarditis in patients with rheumatic fever?

    (A) They should take the streptococcal polysaccharide vaccine

    (B) They should take penicillin if they have dental surgery

    (C) They should take the toxoid vaccine every 5 years

    (D) They should take rifampin if they have abdominal surgery

CASE 19. Your patient is a 10-year-old girl who has leukemia and is receiving chemotherapy through an indwelling venous catheter. She now has a fever of 39°C but is otherwise asymptomatic. You do a blood culture, and the laboratory reports growth of *Staphylococcus epidermidis*.

616. Which one of the following results is LEAST likely to be found by the clinical laboratory?

    (A) Gram-positive cocci in clusters were seen on Gram stain of the blood culture

    (B) Subculture of the blood culture onto blood agar revealed nonhemolytic colonies

    (C) A coagulase test on the colonies was negative

    (D) A catalase test on the colonies was negative

CASE 20. Your patient is a 25-year-old woman with several purpuric areas indicative of bleeding into the skin. Her vital signs are as follows: temperature, 38°C; blood pressure, 70/40; pulse, 140; respiratory rate, 24. You think she has septic shock and do a blood culture.

617. Which one of the following organisms is LEAST likely to be the cause of her septic shock?
(A) *Corynebacterium diphtheriae*
(B) *Neisseria meningitidis*
(C) *Clostridium perfringens*
(D) *Escherichia coli*

618. Of the following mechanisms, which one is LEAST likely to be involved with the pathogenesis of her septic shock?
(A) Increased amount of interleukin-1
(B) Activation of the alternate pathway of complement
(C) Increased amount of tumor necrosis factor
(D) Increased amount of antigen-antibody complexes

CASE 21. Your patient is a 55-year-old man with severe cellulitis of the right leg, high fever, and a teeth-chattering chill. He is a fisherman who was working on his boat in the waters off the Texas coast yesterday.

619. Which one of the following organisms is MOST likely to be the cause of his disease?
(A) *Yersinia pestis*
(B) *Vibrio vulnificus*
(C) *Pasteurella multocida*
(D) *Brucella melitensis*

CASE 22. Your patient is a 30-year-old woman with facial nerve paralysis. She also has fever and headache but does not have a stiff neck. On physical examination, she has a circular, erythematous, macular rash on the back of her thigh. You suspect that she has Lyme disease.

620. Of the following tests, which one is the MOST appropriate to order to confirm a diagnosis of Lyme disease?
(A) Blood culture to grow the organism
(B) Stain for inclusion bodies within cells involved in the rash
(C) Test for serum antibody against the organism
(D) Dark-field microscopy

CASE 23. Your patient is a 60-year-old man with confusion for 2 months. He has no history of fever or stiff neck. On physical examination, he was ataxic and his coordination was abnormal. A diagnosis of tertiary syphilis was made by the laboratory.

621. Of the following tests, which one is the MOST appropriate to make a diagnosis of tertiary syphilis?
(A) Spinal fluid culture to grow the organism
(B) Stain for inclusion bodies in the lymphocytes in the spinal fluid
(C) Test for antibody in the spinal fluid that reacts with cardiolipin
(D) ELISA for the antigen in the spinal fluid

CASE 24. Your patient is a 65-year-old man who had an adenocarcinoma of the pancreas that was surgically removed. Several blood transfusions were given, and he did well until 2 weeks later, when fever, vomiting, and diarrhea began. Blood and stool cultures were negative, and the tests for *Clostridium difficile* and hepatitis B surface antigen were negative. A liver biopsy revealed intranuclear inclusion bodies.

622. Of the following, which one is the MOST likely cause?
(A) Adenovirus
(B) Cytomegalovirus
(C) Hepatitis A virus
(D) Rotavirus

CASE 25. Your patient is a 3-year-old girl with fever and pain in her right ear. On physical examination, the drum is found to be perforated and a bloody exudate is seen. A Gram stain of the exudate reveals gram-positive diplococci.

623. Of the following, which one is the MOST likely cause?
(A) *Streptococcus pyogenes*
(B) *Staphylococcus aureus*
(C) *Corynebacterium diphtheriae*
(D) *Streptococcus pneumoniae*

CASE 26. Your patient is a 70-year-old man with a fever of 40°C and a very painful cellulitis of the right buttock. The skin appears necrotic, and there are several fluid-filled bullae. Crepitus can be felt, indicating gas in the tissue. A Gram stain of the exudate reveals large gram-positive rods.

624. Of the following, which one is the MOST likely cause?
(A) *Clostridium perfringens*
(B) *Bacillus anthracis*
(C) *Corynebacterium diphtheriae*
(D) *Actinomyces israelii*

CASE 27. Your patient is a 45-year-old woman with a cadaveric renal transplant that is being rejected despite immunosuppressive therapy. She is now in renal failure with a blood pH of 7.32. This morning, she awoke with a pain near her right eye. On physical examination, her temperature is 38°C and the skin near her eye is necrotic. A biopsy specimen of the lesion contains nonseptate hyphae invading the blood vessels.

625. Of the following, which one is the MOST likely cause?
(A) *Histoplasma capsulatum*
(B) *Aspergillus fumigatus*
(C) *Cryptococcus neoformans*
(D) *Mucor* species

CASE 28. Your patient is a 35-year-old man who is HIV antibody–positive and has a CD4 count of 35 cells. He recently had a seizure, and an MRI scan indicates a lesion in the temporal lobe. A brain biopsy specimen reveals multinucleated giant cells with intranuclear inclusions.

626. Of the following, which one is the MOST likely cause?

    (A) Herpes simplex virus
    (B) Parvovirus B19
    (C) Coxsackievirus
    (D) Western equine encephalitis virus

CASE 29. Your patient is a 40-year-old woman with a severe attack of diarrhea that began on the airplane while she was returning from a vacation in the Middle East. She had had multiple episodes of watery, non-bloody diarrhea and little vomiting. She is afebrile. A stool culture reveals only lactose-fermenting colonies on EMB agar.

627. Of the following, which one is the MOST likely cause?

    (A) *Shigella sonnei*
    (B) *Helicobacter pylori*
    (C) *Escherichia coli*
    (D) *Pseudomonas aeruginosa*

CASE 30. Your patient is a 20-year-old man with a sore throat for the past 3 days. On physical examination, his temperature is 38°C, the pharynx is red, and several tender submaxillary nodes are palpable.

628. Of the following, which one is the MOST likely organism to cause this infection?

    (A) *Streptococcus agalactiae* (group B streptococcus)
    (B) *Streptococcus sanguis* (a viridans group streptococcus)
    (C) Parvovirus B19
    (D) Epstein-Barr virus

You do a throat culture, and many small, translucent colonies that are beta-hemolytic grow on blood agar. Gram stain of one of these colonies reveals gram-positive cocci in chains.

629. Of the following, which one is the MOST likely organism to cause this infection?

    (A) *Streptococcus pneumoniae*
    (B) *Streptococcus pyogenes*
    (C) *Streptococcus agalactiae* (group B streptococcus)
    (D) *Peptostreptococcus* species

CASE 31. Your patient is a 55-year-old woman with a lymphoma who is receiving chemotherapy via intravenous catheter. She suddenly develops fever, shaking chills, and hypotension.

630. Of the following, which one is the LEAST likely organism to cause this infection?

    (A) *Streptococcus pneumoniae*
    (B) *Klebsiella pneumoniae*
    (C) *Mycoplasma pneumoniae*
    (D) *Proteus mirabilis*

631. If a blood culture grows a gram-negative rod, which one of the following is the LEAST likely organism to cause this infection?

    (A) *Bordetella pertussis*
    (B) *Escherichia coli*
    (C) *Pseudomonas aeruginosa*
    (D) *Serratia marcescens*

632. Of the following virulence factors, which one is the MOST likely to cause the fever and hypotension?

    (A) Pilus
    (B) Capsule
    (C) Lecithinase
    (D) Lipopolysaccharide

CASE 32. Your patient is a 30-year-old woman who was part of a tour group visiting a Central American country. The day before leaving, several members of the group developed fever, abdominal cramps, and bloody diarrhea.

633. Of the following, which one is the LEAST likely organism to cause this infection?

    (A) *Shigella dysenteriae*
    (B) *Salmonella enteritidis*
    (C) *Vibrio cholerae*
    (D) *Campylobacter jejuni*

A stool culture reveals no lactose-negative colonies on the EMB agar.

634. Which one of the following is the MOST likely organism to cause this infection?

    (A) *Shigella dysenteriae*
    (B) *Salmonella enteritidis*
    (C) *Vibrio cholerae*
    (D) *Campylobacter jejuni*

CASE 33. Your patient is a 78-year-old man who had an episode of acute urinary retention and had to be catheterized. He then underwent cystoscopy to determine the cause of the retention. Two days later, he developed fever and suprapubic pain. Urinalysis revealed 50 WBC and 10 RBC per high-power field. Culture of the urine revealed a thin film of bacterial growth over the entire blood agar plate, and the urease test was positive.

635. Which one of the following is the MOST likely organism to cause this infection?

    (A) *Escherichia coli*
    (B) *Proteus mirabilis*
    (C) *Streptococcus faecalis*
    (D) *Branhamella (Moraxella) catarrhalis*

CASE 34. Your patient is a 40-year-old man with a depigmented lesion on his chest that appeared about a month ago. The skin of the lesion is thickened and has lost sensation. He has lived most of his life in rural Louisiana.

636. Of the following tests, which one is the MOST appropriate to do to reveal the cause of this disease?
- **(A)** Perform a biopsy of the lesion and do an acid-fast stain
- **(B)** Culture on Sabouraud's agar and look for germ tubes
- **(C)** Culture on blood agar anaerobically and do a Gram stain
- **(D)** Obtain serum for a Weil-Felix agglutination test

CASE 35. Your patient is a 28-year-old man with third-degree burns over a large area of his back and left leg. This morning, he spiked a fever to 40°C and had two teeth-chattering chills. A blood culture grows a gram-negative rod that is oxidase-positive and produces a blue-green pigment.

637. Of the following, which one is the MOST likely organism to cause this infection?
- **(A)** *Bacteroides melaninogenicus*
- **(B)** *Pseudomonas aeruginosa*
- **(C)** *Proteus mirabilis*
- **(D)** *Haemophilus influenzae*

CASE 36. Your patient is a 32-year-old moving-van driver who lives in St. Louis. He arrived in San Francisco about 10 days ago after picking up furniture in Little Rock, Dallas, Albuquerque, and Phoenix. He now has a persistent cough and fever to 101°F, and he feels poorly. On physical examination, crackles are heard in the left lower lobe, and chest x-ray reveals an infiltrate in that area.

638. Of the following, which one is the LEAST accurate statement?
- **(A)** He probably has spherules containing endospores in his lung
- **(B)** If dissemination to the bone occurs, this indicates a failure of his cell-mediated immunity
- **(C)** He probably acquired this disease by inhaling arthrospores
- **(D)** The causative organism of this disease exists as a yeast in the soil

CASE 37. Your patient is a 25-year-old man with an ulcerated lesion on his penis that is not painful. You suspect that it may be a chancre.

639. Which one of the following tests is the MOST appropriate to do with the material from the lesion?

- **(A)** Darkfield microscopy
- **(B)** Gram stain
- **(C)** Acid-fast stain
- **(D)** Culture on Thayer-Martin agar

640. Which one of the following tests is the MOST appropriate to do with the patient's blood?
- **(A)** Culture on blood agar
- **(B)** Assay for antibodies that react with cardiolipin
- **(C)** Assay for neutralizing antibody in human cell culture
- **(D)** Heterophil antibody test

CASE 38. Your patient is a 6-year-old boy with papular and pustular skin lesions on his face. A serous, "honey-colored" fluid exudes from the lesions. You suspect impetigo. A Gram stain of the pus reveals many neutrophils and gram-positive cocci in chains.

641. If you cultured the pus on blood agar, which one of the following would you be MOST likely to see?
- **(A)** Small beta-hemolytic colonies containing bacteria that are bacitracin-sensitive
- **(B)** Small alpha-hemolytic colonies containing bacteria that are resistant to optochin
- **(C)** Large nonhemolytic colonies containing bacteria that are oxidase-positive
- **(D)** Small nonhemolytic colonies containing bacteria that grow in 6.5% NaCl

CASE 39. Your patient is a 66-year-old woman being treated with chemotherapy for lymphoma. She develops fever to 38°C and a nonproductive cough. A chest x-ray reveals an infiltrate. You treat her empirically with an appropriate antibiotic. The following day, several vesicles appear on her chest.

642. Which one of the following viruses is the MOST likely cause of her disease?
- **(A)** Measles virus
- **(B)** Respiratory syncytial virus
- **(C)** Varicella-zoster virus
- **(D)** Rubella virus

CASE 40. Your patient is a 40-year-old woman with systemic lupus erythematosus who is being treated with high-dose prednisone during a flare of her disease. She develops a fever to 38°C and a cough productive of a small amount of greenish sputum. On physical examination, you hear coarse breath sounds in the left lower lobe. Chest x-ray reveals an infiltrate in that region. Gram stain of the sputum reveals long filaments of gram-positive rods.

643. Which one of the following organisms is the MOST likely cause of this disease?
- **(A)** *Mycobacterium kansasii*
- **(B)** *Listeria monocytogenes*

(C) *Nocardia asteroides*
(D) *Mycoplasma pneumoniae*

CASE 41. Your patient is a 10-year-old girl with acute leukemia who responded well to her first round of chemotherapy but not to the most recent one. In view of this, she had a bone marrow transplant and is on an immunosuppressive regimen. She is markedly granulocytopenic. Ten days after the transplant, she spikes a fever and coughs up bloody, purulent sputum. Chest x-ray shows pneumonia. A wet mount of the sputum shows septate hyphae with dichotomous (Y-shape) branching.

644. Which one of the following organisms is the MOST likely cause of this disease?

(A) *Histoplasma capsulatum*
(B) *Aspergillus fumigatus*
(C) *Rhizopus nigricans*
(D) *Candida albicans*

CASE 42. Your patient is a 30-year-old man with acute onset of fever to 40°C and a swollen, very tender right femoral node. His blood pressure is 90/50, and his pulse is 110. As you examine him, he has a teeth-chattering shaking chill. He returned from a camping trip in the Southern California desert 2 days ago.

645. Regarding this disease, which one of the following is MOST accurate?

(A) An aspirate of the node will reveal a small gram-negative rod
(B) The organism was probably acquired by eating food contaminated with rodent excrement
(C) The aspirate of the node should be cultured on Löwenstein-Jensen agar and an acid-fast stain performed
(D) The organism causes disease primarily in people with impaired cell-mediated immunity

CASE 43. Your patient is a 62-year-old woman with a history of carcinoma of the sigmoid colon that was removed 5 days ago. The surgery was complicated by the escape of bowel contents into the peritoneal cavity. She now has fever and pain in the perineum and left buttock. On physical examination, her temperature is 39°C and myonecrosis with a foul-smelling discharge is found. A Gram stain of the exudate reveals gram-negative rods.

646. Of the following, which one is the MOST likely organism to cause this infection?

(A) *Helicobacter pylori*
(B) *Bacteroides fragilis*
(C) *Salmonella typhi*
(D) *Vibrio parahaemolyticus*

CASE 44. Your patient is an 18-year-old woman with a swollen left ankle. Two days ago, when the ankle began

to swell, she thought she had twisted it playing soccer. However, today she has a fever to 38°C and the ankle has become noticeably more swollen, warm, and red. Her other joints are asymptomatic. You aspirate fluid from the joint.

647. Using the joint fluid, which one of the following procedures is MOST likely to provide diagnostic information?

(A) Acid-fast stain and culture on Löwenstein-Jensen medium
(B) Gram stain and culture on chocolate agar
(C) Darkfield microscopy and the VDRL test
(D) India ink stain and culture on Sabouraud's agar

CASE 45. Your patient is a 6-year-old boy with a history of several episodes of pneumonia. A sweat test revealed an increased amount of chloride, indicating that he has cystic fibrosis. He now has a fever and is coughing up a thick, greenish sputum. A Gram stain of the sputum reveals gram-negative rods.

648. Of the following, which one is the MOST likely organism to cause this infection?

(A) *Pseudomonas aeruginosa*
(B) *Haemophilus influenzae*
(C) *Legionella pneumophila*
(D) *Bordetella pertussis*

CASE 46. Your patient is a 7-year-old boy with fever, two episodes of vomiting, and a severe headache that began this morning. He has no diarrhea. On physical examination, his temperature is 39°C and nuchal rigidity is found. Examination of the spinal fluid revealed a white cell count of 800, of which 90% were lymphs, and a normal concentration of both protein and glucose. A Gram stain of the spinal fluid revealed no bacteria.

649. Of the following, which one is the MOST likely to cause this infection?

(A) *Chlamydia trachomatis*
(B) *Mycobacterium avium-intracellulare*
(C) Coxsackievirus
(D) Adenovirus

CASE 47. Your patient is a 22-year-old man who has been on a low-budget trip to India, where he ate many of the local foods. He has had a low-grade fever, anorexia, and mild abdominal pain for about a month. You suspect that he may have typhoid fever.

650. If he does have typhoid fever, which one of the following is the LEAST likely laboratory finding?

(A) Culture of the blood reveals gram-negative rods
(B) Culture of the stool grows lactose-negative colonies in EMB agar

(C) His serum contains antibodies that agglutinate *Salmonella typhi*

(D) His serum contains antibodies that cause a positive Weil-Felix reaction

CASE 48. Your patient is a 30-year-old man who is HIV antibody–positive and has had two episodes of *Pneumocystis pneumonia*. He now complains of pain in his mouth and difficulty swallowing. On physical examination, you find several whitish plaques on his oropharyngeal mucosa.

651. Regarding the most likely causative organism, which one of the following statements is MOST accurate?

(A) It is a filamentous gram-positive rod that is part of the normal flora in the mouth

(B) It is an anaerobic gram-negative rod that is part of the normal flora in the colon

(C) It is a yeast that forms pseudohyphae when it invades tissue

(D) It is a spirochete that grows only in cell culture

CASE 49. Your patient is a 20-year-old woman with a rash that began this morning. She has been feeling feverish and anorexic for the past few days. On physical examination, there is a papular rash bilaterally over the chest, abdomen, and upper extremities including the hands. There are no vesicles. Cervical and axillary lymph nodes were palpable. Her temperature was 38°C. White blood count was 9000 with a normal differential.

652. Of the following organisms, which one is the MOST likely cause of her disease?

(A) *Histoplasma capsulatum*

(B) *Coxiella burnetii*

(C) *Neisseria meningitidis*

(D) *Treponema pallidum*

CASE 50. Your patient is a 10-year-old boy who fell, abraded the skin of his thigh, and developed cellulitis; ie, the skin was red, hot, and tender. Several days later, the infection was treated with a topical antibiotic ointment and the cellulitis gradually healed. However, 2 weeks later, he told his mother that his urine was cloudy and reddish, and she noted that his face was swollen. You suspect acute glomerulonephritis.

653. Regarding the causative organism, what is the MOST likely appearance of a Gram stain of the exudate from the skin infection?

(A) Gram-positive cocci in grapelike clusters

(B) Gram-positive cocci in chains

(C) Gram-positive diplococci

(D) Gram-negative diplococci

654. What is the pathogenesis of the cloudy urine and facial swelling?

(A) Toxin-mediated

(B) Direct invasion by the bacteria

(C) Immune complex–mediated

(D) Cell-mediated immunity (delayed hypersensitivity)

Answers (Questions 594–654)

594 (B)	607 (C)	619 (B)	631 (A)	643 (C)
595 (C)	608 (A)	620 (C)	632 (D)	644 (B)
596 (D)	609 (C)	621 (C)	633 (C)	645 (A)
597 (B)	610 (A)	622 (B)	634 (D)	646 (B)
598 (D)	611 (B)	623 (D)	635 (B)	647 (B)
599 (A)	612 (C)	624 (A)	636 (A)	648 (A)
600 (D)	613 (D)	625 (D)	637 (B)	649 (C)
601 (D)	614 (C)	626 (A)	638 (D)	650 (D)
602 (A)	615 (B)	627 (C)	639 (A)	651 (C)
603 (C)	616 (D)	628 (D)	640 (B)	652 (D)
604 (A)	617 (A)	629 (B)	641 (A)	653 (B)
605 (B)	618 (D)	630 (C)	642 (C)	654 (C)
606 (C)				

PART XII

USMLE (National Board) Practice Examination

This practice examination consists of two blocks, each containing 40 microbiology and immunology questions. You should be able to complete each block in 50 minutes. The proportion of the questions devoted to bacteriology, virology, mycology, parasitology, and immunology is approximately that of the USMLE. As in the USMLE, the questions are randomly assorted; ie, they are not grouped according to subject matter.

All of the questions have between 4 and 10 answer choices. Each question has a single "BEST" answer; there are no "EXCEPT" type questions. The answer choices are listed either in alphabetical order or in order of the length of the answer. The answer key is located at the end of each block.

QUESTIONS

BLOCK ONE

Directions (Questions 1–40)—Select the ONE lettered answer that is BEST in each question.

1. A 9-year-old girl was playing soccer when she began to limp. She has a pain in her leg and points to her upper thigh when asked where it hurts. Her temperature is 101°F. X-ray of the femur reveals that the periosteum is eroded. You order a blood culture. Which one of the following would be the MOST likely blood culture findings?
    - **(A)** Gram-negative rods that grow on EMB agar, forming purple colonies and a green sheen
    - **(B)** Gram-positive cocci that grow on blood agar, causing a clear zone of hemolysis, and are coagulase-positive
    - **(C)** Gram-positive rods that grow only anaerobically and form a double zone of hemolysis on blood agar
    - **(D)** Gram-negative diplococci that grow on chocolate agar, are oxidase-positive, and ferment maltose
    - **(E)** Gram-positive cocci that grow on blood agar, causing a green zone of hemolysis, and are not inhibited by optochin and bile

2. Your summer research project is to study the viruses that cause upper respiratory tract infections. You have isolated a virus from a patient's throat and find that its genome is RNA. Furthermore, you find that the genome is the complement of viral mRNA within the infected cell. Of the following, which one is the MOST appropriate conclusion you could draw?
    - **(A)** The virion contains a polymerase
    - **(B)** The genome RNA is infectious
    - **(C)** The genome RNA is segmented
    - **(D)** A single-stranded DNA is synthesized during replication
    - **(E)** The genome RNA encodes a precursor polypeptide which must be cleaved by a protease.

3. A 25-year-old man has a history of four episodes of boils in the last year. Boils are abscesses caused by *Staphylococcus aureus*. Which one of the following is MOST likely to be the underlying immunologic factor that predisposes him to multiple episodes of boils?
    - **(A)** A deficient amount of the C8 component of complement in his plasma
    - **(B)** An inability of his macrophages to present antigen in association with class I MHC proteins

(C) A failure to release granzymes from his cytotoxic T cells

(D) An insufficient amount of IgG in his plasma

4. You are reading an article that says that otitis media is commonly caused by nonencapsulated strains of *Haemophilus influenzae*. You are surprised that nonencapsulated strains can cause this disease. Which one of the following BEST explains why your surprise is justified?

(A) Nonencapsulated strains would not have endotoxin

(B) Nonencapsulated strains cannot secrete exotoxin A

(C) Nonencapsulated strains should be easily phagocytosed

(D) Nonencapsulated strains should be rapidly killed by ultraviolet light

(E) Nonencapsulated strains should be susceptible to killing by cytotoxic T cells

5. A 35-year-old man is HIV antibody–positive and has a CD4 count of 50/μL (normal, 1000–1500). He has had a fever of 101°F for a few weeks and "feels tired all the time." He has no other symptoms, and findings on physical examination are normal. Complete blood cell count, urinalysis, and chest x-ray are normal. Blood, stool, and urine cultures show no growth. A bone marrow biopsy reveals granulomas, and a culture grows an organism that is a budding yeast at 37°C but produces hyphae at 25°C. Of the following, which one is the MOST likely cause?

(A) *Aspergillus fumigatus*

(B) *Cryptococcus neoformans*

(C) *Mucor* species

(D) *Histoplasma capsulatum*

(E) *Coccidioides immitis*

6. A 70-year-old woman has sustained third-degree burns over a significant area of her body. Despite appropriate burn care in the hospital, she spiked a fever to 39°C, and the nurse reports blue-green pus on the dressing covering the burned area. Gram stain of the pus reveals gram-negative rods, and antibiotic sensitivity tests show resistance to most antibiotics. Which one of the following organisms is MOST likely to cause this disease?

(A) *Nocardia asteroides*

(B) *Vibrio vulnificus*

(C) *Bacteroides fragilis*

(D) *Haemophilus influenzae*

(E) *Pseudomonas aeruginosa*

7. A 20-year-old woman has had several episodes of high fever, shaking chills, and a severe headache. She has a hematocrit of 30%. She has recently returned from Africa, where she was a Peace Corps volunteer. Which one of the following is MOST likely to be seen in the blood smear sample from this patient?

(A) Acid-fast rods

(B) Banana-shaped gametocytes

(C) Nonseptate hyphae

(D) Spherules

(E) Tachyzoites

8. Certain microorganisms, such as the protozoan *Trypanosoma* and the bacterium *Neisseria gonorrhoeae*, can change their surface antigens quite frequently. This allows the organisms to evade our host defenses. Which one of the following BEST explains how this frequent change in antigenicity occurs?

(A) It is due to the transposition of existing genes into an active expression site

(B) It is due to the acquisition of new fertility plasmids by transduction

(C) It is due to conjugation, during which the recipient obtains new chromosomal genes

(D) It is due to new mutations that occur at "hot spots" in the genome

9. A 60-year-old woman had an adenocarcinoma of the colon that was surgically removed. Several blood transfusions were given and she did well until 3 weeks after surgery, when fever, vomiting, and diarrhea began. Blood and stool cultures were negative for bacteria, and the tests for *Clostridium difficile* and hepatitis B surface antigen were negative. A liver biopsy revealed intranuclear inclusion bodies. Which one of the following is the MOST likely cause?

(A) Cytomegalovirus

(B) Dengue virus

(C) Hepatitis A virus

(D) Rotavirus

(E) Yellow fever virus

10. Which one of the immunoglobulins BEST fits the following description: It is found in plasma as a dimer with a J chain. As it passes through mucosal cells, it acquires a secretory piece that protects it from degradation by proteases.

(A) IgM

(B) IgG

(C) IgA

(D) IgD

(E) IgE

11. *Mycobacterium tuberculosis* (MTB) and *Mycobacterium avium-complex* (MAC) are important causes of disease, especially in immunocompromised patients. (MAC is also known as *Mycobacterium avium-intracellulare*.) Regarding MTB and MAC, which one of the following statements is the MOST accurate?

(A) Cell-mediated immunity is the most important host defense mechanism against MTB, whereas antibody-mediated immunity is the most important host defense mechanism against MAC

(B) In the clinical laboratory, MAC can be distinguished from MTB by the fact that MAC forms colonies in 7 days, whereas MTB does not

(C) Multidrug-resistant strains of MAC are much less common than multidrug-resistant strains of MTB

(D) MAC is found in the environment and is not transmitted from person-to-person, whereas MTB is found in humans and is transmitted from person to person

12. In the lab, a virologist was studying the properties of HIV. She infected the same cell with both HIV and rabies virus. (HIV can infect only human CD4-positive cells, whereas rabies virus can infect both human cells and dog cells.) Some of the progeny virions were able to infect dog cells, within which she found HIV-specific RNA. Which one of the following is the BEST term to describe the ability of the progeny virions to infect dog cells?

(A) Complementation
(B) Phenotypic mixing
(C) Reassortment
(D) Recombination

13. Your patient has been treated for endocarditis with penicillin G for the past 2 weeks. She now has a fever and maculopapular erythematous rash over her chest and abdomen. A urinalysis shows significant protein in the urine. If the fever, rash, and proteinuria are immunologic in origin, which one of the following is MOST likely to be involved?

(A) IgG and complement
(B) IgE and histamine
(C) IL-2 and cytotoxic T cells
(D) Gamma interferon and macrophages

14. Endotoxin is an important underlying cause of septic shock and death, especially in hospitalized patients. Regarding endotoxin, which one of the following is the MOST accurate?

(A) It acts by phosphorylating the G stimulating protein
(B) It is a polypeptide with an A-B subunit configuration
(C) It induces the synthesis of tumor necrosis factor
(D) It is found primarily in gram-positive rods
(E) It can be treated with formaldehyde to form an effective toxoid vaccine

15. A 12-year-old girl had a seizure this morning and was rushed to the hospital. On examination, her

temperature was 40°C and she had no nuchal rigidity. CT scan revealed no abnormality. A spinal tap was done and the protein and glucose were normal. Gram stain of the spinal fluid showed no organisms and no polys. She was treated with various antibiotics but became comatose and died 2 days later. The routine blood culture and spinal fluid culture grew no organism. On autopsy of the brain, eosinophilic inclusion bodies were seen in the cytoplasm of neurons. Of the following, which one is the MOST likely cause?

(A) Prions
(B) J-C virus
(C) Rabies virus
(D) Parvovirus B19
(E) Herpes simplex virus type 1

16. A 70-year-old woman has the rapid onset of fever to 39°C and a cough productive of greenish sputum. She is not hospitalized and not immunocompromised. A chest x-ray reveals a left lower lobe infiltrate. Of the following, which set of findings describes the MOST likely causative organism found in the sputum culture?

(A) Gram-positive diplococci that form an alpha-hemolytic colony
(B) Gram-negative diplococci that form an oxidase-positive colony
(C) Gram-positive rods that form a beta-hemolytic colony
(D) Gram-negative rods that form an oxidase-positive colony
(E) Gram-negative cocci that grow only anaerobically

17. Regarding the function of chemokines in host defenses, which one of the following is the MOST accurate?

(A) Chemokines bind to the T-cell receptor outside of the antigen-binding site and activate many T cells
(B) Chemokines induce gene switching in B cells that increases the amount of IgE synthesized, thereby predisposing to allergies
(C) Chemokines penetrate the membranes of target cells during attack by cytotoxic T cells
(D) Chemokines attract neutrophils to the site of bacterial infection, thereby playing a role in the inflammatory response

18. Which one of the following answer choices consists of bacteria, BOTH of which produce exotoxins that act by ADP-ribosylation?

(A) *Salmonella typhi* and *Vibrio cholerae*
(B) *Vibrio cholerae* and *Corynebacterium diphtheriae*
(C) *Salmonella typhi* and *Clostridium perfringens*

(D) *Corynebacterium diphtheriae* and *Staphylococcus aureus*

(E) *Clostridium perfringens* and *Streptococcus pyogenes*

19. Regarding hepatitis C virus (HCV) and hepatitis D virus (HDV), which one of the following is MOST accurate?
    (A) HCV is transmitted by blood, but HDV is not
    (B) Both HCV and HDV can establish a chronic carrier state
    (C) There is an effective vaccine against HCV but not against HDV
    (D) Both HCV and HDV are defective RNA viruses and require concurrent HBV infection to replicate

20. Which one of the following is MOST likely to induce an IgM antibody response without the participation of helper T cells?
    (A) Bacterial capsular polysaccharide
    (B) Toxic shock syndrome toxin
    (C) Penicillin-bovine serum albumin (BSA) complex
    (D) Tetanus toxoid

21. A 25-year-old pregnant woman in the third trimester comes to the emergency room saying that about 12 hours ago she began to feel feverish and weak. On examination, she has a temperature of 40°C but no other pertinent findings. A blood culture grows small gram-positive rods that cause beta-hemolysis on a blood agar plate incubated in room air. Which one of the following bacteria is the MOST likely cause?
    (A) *Clostridium perfringens*
    (B) *Streptococcus pyogenes*
    (C) *Bacillus cereus*
    (D) *Listeria monocytogenes*
    (E) *Brucella abortus*

22. Regarding the mode of action of antiviral drugs, which one of the following is MOST accurate?
    (A) Amantadine inhibits influenza A virus by inhibiting the RNA polymerase carried by the virion
    (B) Foscarnet inhibits varicella-zoster virus by inhibiting the RNA polymerase carried by the virion
    (C) Acyclovir action is greater in herpesvirus-infected cells than in uninfected cells because herpesvirus-infected cells contain an enzyme that phosphorylates acyclovir very efficiently
    (D) Azidothymidine inhibits human immunodeficiency virus (HIV) by inhibiting viral mRNA synthesis more efficiently than cellular mRNA synthesis
    (E) Indinavir blocks HIV replication by inhibiting the protease required for the envelope

protein gp120 to bind to the CD8 protein on the surface of the T cell

23. Which one of the following diseases is MOST likely to be caused by a delayed hypersensitivity reaction?
    (A) Serum sickness
    (B) Poststreptococcal glomerulonephritis
    (C) Systemic lupus erythematosus
    (D) Hemolytic disease of the newborn
    (E) Contact dermatitis

24. Members of the genus *Mycobacterium* stain better with the acid-fast stain than with the Gram stain. Which one of the following is the BEST explanation for this finding?
    (A) They lack a cell wall; therefore, they cannot adsorb the crystal violet
    (B) They have a very thin cell wall that does not retain the crystal violet
    (C) They have a thick polysaccharide capsule that prevents entry of the iodine solution
    (D) They have a large amount of lipid in their cell wall that prevents entry of the crystal violet

25. A 50-year-old man with a cadaveric renal transplant is rejecting the transplant despite immunosuppressive drugs. He is now in renal failure with a blood pH of 7.31. Yesterday, he developed a pain near his left eye that has become progressively more severe. On examination, his temperature is 37.5°C and the skin near his eye is swollen and necrotic. Microscopic examination of a biopsy of the lesion reveals nonseptate hyphae with right-angle branching. Which one of the following organisms is the MOST likely cause?
    (A) *Candida albicans*
    (B) *Coccidioides immitis*
    (C) *Cryptococcus neoformans*
    (D) *Histoplasma capsulatum*
    (E) *Mucor* species

26. A 60-year-old woman had surgery for ovarian carcinoma 4 days ago and has an indwelling urinary catheter in place. She now spikes a fever to 39°C and has cloudy urine in the collection bottle. Gram stain of the urine shows many polys and gram-positive cocci in chains. Which one of the following would be the MOST likely findings in the urine culture?
    (A) Alpha-hemolytic colonies on the blood agar plate that are optochin-sensitive
    (B) Beta-hemolytic colonies on the blood agar plate that are bacitracin-sensitive
    (C) Nonhemolytic colonies on the blood agar plate that hydrolyze hippurate
    (D) Nonhemolytic colonies on the blood agar plate that grow in 6.5% sodium chloride

27. Your patient is a 40-year-old man with a history of confusion for the past 2 days and a grand-mal seizure that occurred this morning. He is HIV antibody–positive and has a CD4 count of 100/µL. On examination, his temperature is 37.5°C and the findings of the remainder of the examination are within normal limits. An MRI reveals several "ring-enhancing" cavitary brain lesions. He has not traveled outside of the United States, is employed as the manager of a supermarket, is a strict vegetarian, and has several household pets, namely, a dog, a cat, a parrot, and a turtle. Which one of the following organisms is the MOST likely cause?
    (A) *Toxocara canis*
    (B) *Toxoplasma gondii*
    (C) *Taenia saginata*
    (D) *Trichinella spiralis*
    (E) *Trypanosoma cruzi*

28. The emergence of antibiotic-resistant bacteria, especially in enteric gram-negative rods, is an extremely important phenomenon. The acquisition of resistance most commonly occurs by a process that involves a sex pilus and the subsequent transfer of plasmids carrying one or more transposons. Which one of the following is the name that BEST describes this process?
    (A) Conjugation
    (B) Combination
    (C) Transformation
    (D) Transduction
    (E) Translocation

29. Regarding the diagnosis, treatment, and prevention of HIV, which one of the following is the MOST accurate?
    (A) The drug zidovudine (AZT) is a "chain terminating" drug; that is, it inhibits the growing polypeptide chain by causing misreading of the viral mRNA
    (B) The drug lamivudine (3TC) acts by binding to the integrase, which prevents integration of the viral DNA into cellular DNA
    (C) In the screening test for HIV infection, the ELISA test detects the presence of antibody to the p24 protein of HIV
    (D) A major limitation to our ability to produce a vaccine against HIV is that there are many serologic types of the viral p24 protein

30. Regarding haptens, which one of the following statements is the MOST accurate?
    (A) They are typically polypeptides that are resistant to proteolytic cleavage within the antigen-presenting cell
    (B) They bind to class II MHC proteins but not to class I MHC proteins

(C) They cannot induce antibodies unless they are bound to a carrier protein
(D) They activate complement by binding to the Fc part of the heavy chain of IgG

31. Your patient is a 20-year-old man with a urethral discharge. Gram stain of the pus reveals many neutrophils but no bacteria. Which one of the following organisms is the MOST likely cause?
    (A) *Treponema pallidum*
    (B) *Haemophilus ducreyi*
    (C) *Mycobacterium marinum*
    (D) *Candida albicans*
    (E) *Chlamydia trachomatis*

32. Regarding host defenses against viruses, which one of the following is MOST accurate?
    (A) IgA exerts its main antiviral effect by enhancing the cytopathic effect of natural killer cells, a process called antibody-dependent cellular cytotoxicity
    (B) IgG plays a major role in neutralizing virus infectivity during the primary infection
    (C) Complexes of virus and IgE are the cause of the inflammatory arthritis seen in several viral infections, such as hepatitis B and rubella
    (D) Interferons exert their antiviral action by inducing a ribonuclease that degrades viral mRNA but not cellular mRNA
    (E) Interferons exert their antiviral effect against viruses with RNA genomes but not against those with DNA genomes

33. Allergic rhinitis is characterized by sneezing, rhinorrhea, nasal congestion, and itching of the eyes and nose. Persons with allergic rhinitis have "X" that bind to high-affinity receptors on "Y." On nasal reexposure to antigen, the Y of patients with allergic rhinitis degranulate, releasing "Z" and other mediators. Which one of the following sets BEST describes X, Y, and Z?
    (A) X is IgE, Y is macrophages, and Z is tumor necrosis factor
    (B) X is IgE, Y is basophils, and Z is histamine
    (C) X is IgG, Y is eosinophils, and Z is histamine
    (D) X is IgG, Y is neutrophils, and Z is tumor necrosis factor
    (E) X is IgA, Y is eosinophils, and Z is interleukin-5

34. An outbreak of postsurgical wound infections caused by *Staphylococcus aureus* has occurred. The infection control team was asked to determine whether the organism could be carried by one of the operating room personnel. Using your knowledge of normal flora, which one of the following body sites is the MOST likely location for this organism?
    (A) Colon

(B) Gingival crevice
(C) Nose
(D) Throat
(E) Vagina

35. A 35-year-old man who is HIV antibody–positive and has a CD4 count of 30 says "I can't remember the simplest things." You are concerned about dementia. An MRI indicates several widely scattered lesions in the brain. Over the next 4 months, he develops visual field defects, becomes paralyzed, and dies. Autopsy reveals that many neurons of the brain have lost myelin and contain intranuclear inclusions. Electron microscopy reveals the inclusions contain nonenveloped viruses. Which one of the following viruses is the MOST likely cause?
(A) Adenovirus
(B) Cytomegalovirus
(C) Herpes simplex virus
(D) JC virus
(E) Coxsackievirus

36. A 75-year-old man with substernal chest pain was found to have angina pectoris caused by syphilitic aortitis that affected his coronary arteries. Of the following, which one is the MOST likely way that the diagnosis of syphilis was made?
(A) Blood culture
(B) Culture on Thayer-Martin medium (chocolate agar with antibiotics)
(C) Detecting antibodies to cardiolipin in his blood
(D) Detecting treponemal antigen in his blood
(E) Western blot assay

37. A 22-year-old woman has an erythematous rash on the malar eminences of her face that gets worse when she is out in the sun. She has lost about 10 lb and feels tired much of the time. She took her temperature a few times and it was 99°F. Physical examination was normal except for the rash. Laboratory tests revealed a hemoglobin of 11 and a white blood cell count of 5500. Urinalysis showed albumin in the urine but no red cells, white cells, or bacteria. Which one of the following is the MOST likely laboratory finding in this disease?
(A) Decreased number of helper (CD4-positive) T cells
(B) High level of antibodies to double-stranded DNA
(C) Increased number of cytotoxic (CD8-positive) T cells
(D) Low level of C1 inhibitor
(E) Low microbicidal activity of neutrophils

38. Regarding antimicrobial drugs that act by inhibiting nucleic acid synthesis in bacteria, which one of the following is the MOST accurate?
(A) Quinolones, such as ciprofloxacin, inhibit the RNA polymerase in bacteria by acting as nucleic acid analogues
(B) Rifampin inhibits the RNA polymerase in bacteria by binding to the enzyme and inhibiting messenger RNA synthesis
(C) Sulfonamides inhibit the DNA polymerase in bacteria by causing chain termination of the elongating strand
(D) Trimethoprim inhibits the DNA polymerase in bacteria by preventing the unwinding of double-stranded DNA

39. Regarding parvovirus B19, which one of the following is the MOST accurate?
(A) Parvovirus B19 has a double-stranded DNA genome but requires a DNA polymerase in the virion because it replicates in the cytoplasm
(B) Parvovirus B19 is transmitted primarily by sexual intercourse
(C) Parvovirus B19 causes severe anemia because it preferentially infects erythrocyte precursors
(D) Patients infected by parvovirus B19 can be diagnosed in the laboratory using the cold agglutinin test
(E) Patients with disseminated disease caused by parvovirus B19 should be treated with acyclovir

40. Which one of the following laboratory tests would be the BEST to order to determine the number of CD4-positive cells in a patient infected with HIV?
(A) Agglutination
(B) Enzyme-linked immunosorbent assay (ELISA)
(C) Flow cytometry
(D) Immunoelectrophoresis
(E) Ouchterlony gel assay

ANSWERS TO BLOCK ONE

1 (B)	9 (A)	17 (D)	25 (E)	33 (B)
2 (A)	10 (C)	18 (B)	26 (D)	34 (C)
3 (D)	11 (D)	19 (B)	27 (B)	35 (D)
4 (C)	12 (B)	20 (A)	28 (A)	36 (C)
5 (D)	13 (A)	21 (D)	29 (C)	37 (B)
6 (E)	14 (C)	22 (C)	30 (C)	38 (B)
7 (B)	15 (C)	23 (E)	31 (E)	39 (C)
8 (A)	16 (A)	24 (D)	32 (D)	40 (C)

BLOCK TWO

1. A 4-year-old girl has papular and pustular lesions on her face. The lesions are exuding a honey-colored serous fluid. You make a clinical diagnosis of impetigo. A Gram stain of the exudate reveals gram-positive cocci in chains and a culture reveals beta-hemolytic colonies on blood agar. For which one of the following sequelae is she MOST at risk?
   (A) Bloody diarrhea
   (B) Blurred vision
   (C) Paralysis of the facial nerve (Bell's palsy)
   (D) Red blood cells and albumin in her urine
   (E) Rusty-colored sputum

2. The purified genome of certain RNA viruses can enter a cell and elicit the production of progeny viruses; ie, the genome is infectious. Regarding these viruses, which one of the following statements is MOST accurate?
   (A) They have a segmented genome
   (B) They have a polymerase in the virion
   (C) Their genome RNA is double-stranded
   (D) They encode a protease that cleaves a precursor polypeptide
   (E) Their genome RNA has the same base sequence as mRNA

3. A 77-year-old man with enterococcal endocarditis needed to be treated with penicillin G but had a history of a severe penicillin reaction. He was therefore skin tested using penicilloyl-polylysine as the antigen. Which one of the following is MOST likely to occur in a positive skin test?
   (A) The antigen forms immune complexes with IgG
   (B) The antigen activates CD4-positive T cells and macrophages
   (C) The antigen activates the alternative pathway of complement
   (D) The antigen activates CD8-positive T cells by binding to class MHC proteins
   (E) The antigen cross-links IgE on the mast cells and causes the release of histamine

4. Regarding the Gram stain, which one of the following is the MOST accurate?
   (A) After adding crystal violet and Gram's iodine, both gram-positive bacteria and gram-negative bacteria will appear blue
   (B) If you forget to stain with the red dye (safranin or basic fuchsin), both gram-positive bacteria and gram-negative bacteria will appear blue
   (C) If you forget to heat-fix, both gram-positive bacteria and gram-negative bacteria will appear blue

   (D) One reason why bacteria have a different color in this stain is because the gram-positive bacteria have lipid in their membrane, whereas gram-negative bacteria do not

5. A 35-year-old man with a CD4 count of 50 presents with a skin nodule on his chest. The nodule is about 3 cm in diameter and not red, hot, or tender. He says it has been slowly growing bigger for the past 3 weeks. You biopsy the nodule, and the pathologist calls to say that the patient has disseminated cryptococcosis. Which one of the following is the BEST description of what the pathologist saw in the biopsy specimen?
   (A) Spherules
   (B) Nonseptate hyphae
   (C) Germ tubes
   (D) Budding yeasts with a thick capsule
   (E) Septate hyphae with low-angle branching

6. A 22-year-old woman complains of a persistent nonproductive cough and a fever of 101°F that came on slowly over the last 4 days. Physical examination reveals some rales in the left lung base. A patchy infiltrate is seen on chest x-ray. She works as a secretary in a law office and has not traveled recently. She is not immunocompromised and has not been hospitalized recently. A sample of her serum agglutinates red blood cells at 4°C but not at 37°C. Which one of the following BEST describes the organism that is the MOST likely cause of her disease?
   (A) A very small bacterium that has no cell wall
   (B) A gram-negative diplococcus with a large capsule
   (C) An acid-fast rod that forms colonies within 7 days
   (D) A filamentous gram-positive rod that is weakly acid-fast
   (E) A gram-positive rod that is an obligate intracellular parasite

7. The mother of a 4-year-old child notes that her child is sleeping poorly and scratching his anal area. You suspect the child may have pinworms. Which one of the following is the BEST method to make that diagnosis?
   (A) Examine the stool for the presence of cysts
   (B) Examine the stool for the presence of trophozoites
   (C) Examine a blood smear for the presence of microfilaria
   (D) Determine the titer of IgE antibody against the organism
   (E) Examine transparent adhesive tape for the presence of eggs

8. Regarding bacterial spores, which one of the following is the MOST accurate?

(A) One spore germinates to form one bacterium

(B) They are produced primarily within human red blood cells

(C) They are killed by boiling at sea level but not at high altitude

(D) They are produced by anaerobes only in the presence of oxygen

(E) They contain endotoxin, which accounts for their ability to cause disease

9. A 22-year-old woman had fever to 100°F and anorexia for the past 2 days, and this morning she appears jaundiced. On examination, her liver is enlarged and tender. She has a total bilirubin of 5 mg/dL (normal, < 1) and elevated transaminases. She received the complete course of the hepatitis B vaccine 2 years ago but has not had the hepatitis A vaccine. The results of her hepatitis serologies are as follows: HAV-IgM-negative, HAV-IgG-positive, HBsAg-negative, HBsAb-positive, HBcAb-negative, HCV-Ab-positive. Of the following, which one is the MOST accurate?

(A) She probably has hepatitis A now, probably has not been infected with HBV, and probably had hepatitis C in the past

(B) She probably has hepatitis A now, probably has been infected with HBV in the past, and probably had hepatitis C in the past

(C) She has been infected with HAV in the past, probably has not been infected with HBV, and probably has hepatitis C now

(D) She has been infected with HAV in the past, probably has hepatitis B now, and probably had hepatitis C in the past

10. Regarding the function of the different classes of antibodies, which one of the following statements is the MOST accurate?

(A) IgA acts as an antigen receptor on the surface of B cells

(B) IgG activates the alternative pathway of complement, resulting in the production of C3a that degrades the bacterial cell wall

(C) IgG binds to the bacterial surface and makes the bacteria more easily ingested by phagocytes

(D) IgM defends against worm parasites, such as hookworms

(E) IgE blocks the binding of viruses to the gut mucosa

11. A 6-year-old boy fell and sustained a deep wound from a rusty nail that penetrated his thigh. His mother removed the nail and cleaned the wound with soap and water. The next morning, he had a temperature of 102°F, and his thigh was very painful and swollen. In the emergency room, crepitus (gas in the tissue) was noted. A Gram stain of exudate from the wound area revealed large gram-positive rods. Which one of the following is the MOST likely cause?

(A) *Actinomyces israelii*

(B) *Clostridium perfringens*

(C) *Clostridium tetani*

(D) *Listeria monocytogenes*

(E) *Mycobacterium fortuitum-chelonei* complex

(F) *Nocardia asteroides*

(G) *Pseudomonas aeruginosa*

12. The two most common types of viral vaccines are killed vaccines and live, attenuated vaccines. Regarding these vaccines, which one of the following statements is the MOST accurate?

(A) Killed vaccines induce a longer-lasting response than do live, attenuated vaccines

(B) Killed vaccines are no longer used in this country because they do not induce secretory IgA

(C) Killed vaccines induce a broader range of immune responses than do live, attenuated vaccines

(D) Killed vaccines are safer to give to immunocompromised patients than are live, attenuated vaccines

13. Regarding anaphylactic (type I) and immune complex (type III) hypersensitivities, which one of the following is the MOST accurate?

(A) IgE is involved in both anaphylactic and immune complex hypersensitivities

(B) Complement is involved in both anaphylactic and immune complex hypersensitivities

(C) Less antigen is typically needed to trigger an anaphylactic reaction than an immune complex reaction

(D) Neutrophils play a more important role in anaphylactic reactions than in immune complex reactions

14. Disease caused by which one of the following bacteria can be prevented by a toxoid vaccine?

(A) *Actinomyces israelii*

(B) *Bacteroides fragilis*

(C) *Borrelia burgdorferi*

(D) *Corynebacterium diphtheriae*

(E) *Haemophilus influenzae*

(F) *Listeria monocytogenes*

(G) *Neisseria meningitidis*

(H) *Salmonella typhi*

(I) *Streptococcus pneumoniae*

(J) *Yersinia pestis*

15. A 50-year-old woman has had a gradual onset of headaches that have become increasingly more severe during the past 3 weeks. On examination, she is confused as to time, place, and person, and she is febrile to 39°C. Her spinal fluid reveals a

normal glucose, normal protein, and 17 cells, all of which were lymphocytes. Gram stain of the spinal fluid shows no organism. An MRI reveals a 2-cm radiolucent lesion in the temporal lobe. A biopsy of the brain lesion was performed. A Giemsa stain of the tissue shows multinucleated giant cells with intranuclear inclusion bodies. Which one of the following is the MOST likely causative organism?

(A) Adenovirus
(B) Coxsackievirus
(C) Cytomegalovirus
(D) Herpes simplex virus type 1
(E) Influenza virus
(F) Measles virus
(G) Parvovirus B19
(H) Poliovirus
(I) Prion
(J) Rabies virus

16. An 80-year-old man had a carcinoma of the colon removed 3 days ago. He was doing well until this morning, when he spiked a fever to 39°C and complained of severe abdominal pain. Examination revealed a "boardlike" abdomen indicative of peritonitis. He was taken to the operating room, where it was discovered that his anastomosis had broken down and bowel contents had spilled into the peritoneal cavity. A foul-smelling exudate was observed. A Gram stain of the peritoneal exudate revealed many gram-negative rods. Which one of the following sets of bacteria is the MOST likely cause of this infection?

(A) *Escherichia coli* and *Brucella melitensis*
(B) *Enterobacter cloacae* and *Salmonella enteritidis*
(C) *Fusobacterium nucleatum* and *Bacteroides fragilis*
(D) *Haemophilus influenzae* and *Actinomyces israelii*
(E) *Shigella dysenteriae* and *Serratia marcescens*

17. Regarding the primary and secondary anamnestic immune responses, which one of the following statements is MOST accurate?

(A) The IgM made in the primary response is made primarily by memory B cells
(B) The lag phase is shorter in the primary response than in the secondary response
(C) In the primary response, memory B cells are produced, but memory T cells are not
(D) Antigen must be processed and presented in the primary response but not in the secondary response
(E) The amount of IgG made in the secondary response is greater than the amount made in the primary response

18. A 70-year-old man who is receiving chemotherapy for leukemia develops a fever to 40°C, has two episodes of teeth-chattering chills, and his blood pressure drops to 80/20 mmHg. Of the following factors, which one is MOST likely to be the cause of his fever, chills, and hypotension?

(A) Coagulase
(B) Dipicolinic acid
(C) Glycocalyx
(D) Lipid A
(E) Mycolic acid
(F) Pili
(G) Polysaccharide capsule

19. A 22-year-old woman presents with "the worst sore throat I've ever had." She also complains of fatigue and anorexia. She is not immunocompromised and has not been hospitalized recently. On examination, she is febrile to 38°C, the pharynx is inflamed, and there are a few tender cervical nodes bilaterally. There are no white lesions on the tongue or pharynx. A throat culture grows alpha-hemolytic colonies on blood agar that are optochin-resistant. Of the following, which one is the MOST likely cause?

(A) *Candida albicans*
(B) Epstein-Barr virus
(C) Parvovirus B19
(D) *Pneumocystis carinii*
(E) Poliovirus
(F) *Serratia marcescens*
(G) *Streptococcus mutans*
(H) *Streptococcus pneumoniae*
(I) *Streptococcus pyogenes*
(J) *Strongyloides stercoralis*

20. Regarding the complement pathway, which one of the following is MOST accurate?

(A) C5a mediates chemotaxis and attracts neutrophils to the site of infection
(B) C5b plays an important role in the opsonization of gram-negative bacteria
(C) C3a is a decay-accelerating factor that causes the rapid decay and death of bacteria
(D) C1 binds to the surface of gram-positive bacteria, which initiates the classic pathway
(E) The membrane attack complex is produced in the classic pathway but not in the alternative pathway

21. A 65-year-old woman had symptoms of dementia. An MRI revealed significant cortical atrophy. It was determined that her intraventricular pressure was very high, and a ventriculoperitoneal shunt (from the brain, tunneling under the skin into the peritoneal cavity) was placed to relieve the pressure. Three weeks later she developed a fever to 38°C, malaise, and anorexia but no other symptoms. Of the following, which one BEST describes the MOST likely organism causing her current symptoms?

(A) A gram-positive coccus that does not clot plasma

(B) A curved gram-negative rod that produces urease

(C) An acid-fast rod that does not grow on bacteriologic media

(D) An obligate intracellular parasite that forms a cytoplasmic inclusion body

(E) A spirochete that induces an antibody that agglutinates a lipid from a cow's heart

22. Two mutants of poliovirus, one mutated at gene X and the other mutated at gene Y, have been isolated. If a cell is infected with each mutant alone, no virus is produced. If a cell is infected with both mutants, which one of the following is MOST likely to occur?

(A) Complementation between the mutant gene products may occur, and, if so, both X and Y progeny viruses will be made

(B) Phenotypic mixing may occur, and, if so, both X and Y progeny viruses will be made

(C) Reassortment of the genome segments may occur, and, if so, both X and Y progeny viruses will be made

(D) The genome may be transcribed into DNA, and, if so, both X and Y viruses will be made

23. A 40-year-old woman has a history of chronic inflammation of the small joints of the hands bilaterally. You suspect rheumatoid arthritis. Which one of the following is the MOST accurate regarding the pathogenesis of this disease?

(A) It is caused by sensitized CD4-positive T lymphocytes and macrophages invading the joints

(B) It is caused by antibody against human IgG-forming immune complexes within the joints

(C) It is caused by the release of mediators from mast cells when environmental agents cross-link adjacent IgEs within the joints

(D) It is caused by superantigens inducing the release of large amounts of lymphokines from helper T cells within the joints

24. Listed below are five bacteria paired with a mode of transmission. Which one of the pairings is MOST accurate?

(A) Borrelia burgdorferi—mosquito bite

(B) Coxiella burnetii—bat guano

(C) Haemophilus influenzae—water aerosols

(D) Rickettsia rickettsii—contaminated food

(E) Yersinia pestis—flea bite

25. A 70-year-old man with leukemia initially responded to chemotherapy but now is refractory. He therefore underwent a bone marrow transplant and is now receiving large doses of cyclosporine A and prednisone. Three weeks after the transplant, he became febrile to 39°C and began coughing up purulent sputum. A chest x-ray revealed pneumonia. A Gram stain of the sputum did not reveal a predominant organism, but a KOH prep of the sputum revealed septate hyphae with parallel walls and low-angle branching. Of the following organisms, which one is MOST likely to be the cause of this pneumonia?

(A) Aspergillus fumigatus

(B) Candida albicans

(C) Coccidioides immitis

(D) Cryptococcus neoformans

(E) Rhizopus nigricans

26. Your patient is a 20-year-old woman with severe diarrhea that began yesterday. She has just returned from a 3-week trip to Peru, where she ate some raw shellfish at the farewell party. She now has watery diarrhea, perhaps 20 bowel movements a day, and is feeling quite weak and dizzy. Her stool is guaiac-negative, a test that determines whether there is blood in the stool. A Gram stain of the stool reveals curved gram-negative rods. Of the following organisms, which one is MOST likely to be the cause of her diarrhea?

(A) Bacteroides fragilis

(B) Campylobacter jejuni

(C) Entamoeba histolytica

(D) Helicobacter pylori

(E) Shigella dysenteriae

(F) Vibrio cholerae

(G) Yersinia enterocolitica

27. A 50-year-old man has had low-grade, persistent headaches for several months. In the last few days, nausea, vomiting, and blurred vision have occurred. An MRI reveals several cystlike lesions in the brain parenchyma. The patient lived for many years on one of the small Caribbean islands. On the basis of a positive serologic test, a diagnosis of neurocysticercosis was made. Of the following, which one is the MOST likely mode by which this disease was acquired?

(A) Sandfly bite

(B) Mosquito bite

(C) Sexual intercourse

(D) Ingestion of the larvae of the organism in raw fish

(E) Ingestion of the eggs of the organism in contaminated food

(F) Penetration of the skin by the organism while walking bare-footed

(G) Penetration of the skin by the organism while bathing in fresh water

28. A 30-year-old woman with a previous history of rheumatic fever now has a fever for the past 2

weeks. Physical examination reveals a new heart murmur. You suspect endocarditis and do a blood culture, which grows a viridans group streptococcus later identified as *Streptococcus sanguis*. Of the following body sites, which one is the MOST likely source of this organism?

(A) Colon
(B) Mouth
(C) Skin
(D) Stomach
(E) Vagina

29. Regarding poliovirus, which one of the following is MOST accurate?

(A) Poliovirus remains latent within sensory ganglia, and reactivation occurs primarily in immunocompromised patients
(B) When the live, attenuated virus in the oral vaccine replicates, revertant mutants can occur that can cause paralytic polio
(C) The widespread use of the killed vaccine in the countries of North and South America has led to the virtual elimination of paralytic polio in those areas
(D) The current recommendation is to give the live, attenuated vaccine for the first 3 immunizations to prevent the child from acting as a reservoir, followed by boosters using the killed vaccine

30. Regarding ABO and Rh blood types, which one of the following is the MOST accurate?

(A) People with type O are called universal recipients because they have antibodies against H substance but not against A and B antigens
(B) If the father is Rh-positive and the mother is Rh-negative, hemolytic disease of the newborn only occurs when the child is Rh-negative
(C) People who are Rh-negative usually have antibodies to the Rh antigen because they are exposed to cross-reacting antigen located on bacteria in the colon
(D) If type A blood is transfused into a person with type B blood, complement will be activated and the membrane attack complex will cause lysis of the type A red cells

31. A 25-year-old man was in a motorcycle accident 3 days ago, in which he sustained severe head trauma. He has had spinal fluid leaking from his nose since the accident and now develops a severe headache. His temperature is 39°C, and on examination you find nuchal rigidity. You do a lumbar puncture and find that the spinal fluid is cloudy and contains 5000 WBC/µL, 90% of which are polys. Of the following, which one is the MOST likely result observed in the laboratory analysis of the spinal fluid?

(A) Gram-negative rods that grew only anaerobically
(B) A motile spirochete that formed beta-hemolytic colonies on blood agar
(C) Gram-positive cocci that formed alpha-hemolytic colonies on blood agar
(D) Gram-positive cocci that grew only in the presence of 6.5% sodium chloride
(E) Gram-positive rods that grew only on chocolate agar supplemented with X and V factors
(F) No organism was seen using Gram stain, but tissue stains revealed cytoplasmic inclusion bodies

32. Regarding prions and prion-caused diseases, which one of the following is MOST accurate?

(A) Prions are highly resistant to both ultraviolet light and to boiling but are inactivated by hypochlorite
(B) Prions are protein-containing particles surrounded by a lipoprotein envelope with a DNA polymerase in the envelope
(C) The diagnosis of prion-caused diseases such as Creutzfeldt-Jakob disease is typically made by observing cytopathic effect in cell culture
(D) Creutzfeldt-Jakob disease occurs primarily in children younger than the age of 2 years because they cannot mount an adequate immune response to the prion protein

33. A 2-year-old boy has had several infections of the sinuses and lungs and is being evaluated to determine whether he has chronic granulomatous disease. Regarding this disease, which one of the following is the MOST accurate?

(A) There is a deficiency in NADPH oxidase activity
(B) The defect is primarily in antigen-presenting cells such as macrophages
(C) *Pneumocystis carinii* infections are common in patients with this disease
(D) The diagnosis is primarily made by ELISA, in which antibody against the affected cell component is detected

34. Regarding *Chlamydiae,* which one of the following is MOST accurate?

(A) They are gram-positive rods that do not form spores
(B) They exhibit swarming motility on a blood agar plate
(C) Their life cycle consists of a metabolically inactive particle in the extracellular phase
(D) They can replicate only within cells because they lack the ability to produce certain essential mRNAs
(E) They replicate in the nucleus of infected cells, where they form inclusions that are useful diagnostically

35. Regarding human papillomavirus (HPV), which one of the following is MOST accurate?
    (A) Blood and blood products are an important mode of transmission of HPV
    (B) HPV is an enveloped virus with a genome composed of double-stranded RNA
    (C) Amantadine is a chain-terminating drug that inhibits HPV replication by blocking DNA synthesis
    (D) HPV induces the formation of koilocytes in the skin that are an important diagnostic feature of HPV infection
    (E) The P2 capsid protein of HPV activates the c-*sarc* oncogene in human cells, which is the process by which HPV predisposes to malignancy

36. Regarding Lyme disease, which one of the following is MOST accurate?
    (A) The causative organism is a small gram-positive rod
    (B) Mice are the main reservoir of the causative organism
    (C) There is no vaccine available to protect people against this disease
    (D) Fleas are the principal mode of transmission of the causative organism
    (E) The diagnosis in the clinical laboratory is typically made by culturing the organism on chocolate agar

37. Regarding Bruton's agammaglobulinemia, which one of the following is the MOST accurate?
    (A) VDJ gene switching does not occur
    (B) There is very little IgG, but IgM and IgA levels are normal
    (C) The number of B cells is normal, but they cannot differentiate into plasma cells
    (D) There is a defect in a tyrosine kinase, one of the enzymes in the signal transduction pathway
    (E) Viral infections are more common in patients with this disease than are pyogenic bacterial infections

38. A 20-year-old woman presents with a history of vaginal discharge for the past 3 days. On pelvic examination, you see a mucopurulent exudate at the cervical os and there is tenderness on palpation of the right fallopian tube. You do a Gram stain and culture on the cervical discharge. The culture is done on Thayer-Martin medium, which is a chocolate agar that contains antibiotics that inhibit the growth of normal flora. Of the following, which findings are the MOST likely to be found?
    (A) A Gram stain reveals many neutrophils and spirochetes, and culture on Thayer-Martin medium reveals no colonies
    (B) A Gram stain reveals many neutrophils and gram-variable rods, and culture on Thayer-Martin medium reveals beta-hemolytic colonies
    (C) A Gram stain reveals many neutrophils and gram-negative diplococci, and culture on Thayer-Martin medium reveals oxidase-positive colonies
    (D) A Gram stain reveals many neutrophils but no gram-negative diplococci are seen, and culture on Thayer-Martin medium reveals coagulase-positive colonies

39. Regarding human immunodeficiency virus (HIV), which one of the following is MOST accurate?
    (A) The term "viral load" refers to the concentration of HIV RNA in the patient's blood plasma
    (B) Both didanosine (ddI) and zalcitabine (ddC) block HIV replication by inhibiting cleavage of the precursor polypeptide by the virion-encoded protease
    (C) The antigenicity of the GAG protein of HIV is highly variable, which is a significant impediment to the development of a vaccine against HIV
    (D) A person whose serum is positive for antibodies to HIV in the screening Western blot test should have an ELISA test to confirm that they have actually been infected by HIV

40. Regarding Th-1 and Th-2 cells, which one of the following is MOST accurate?
    (A) Th-1 cells produce gamma interferon and promote cell-mediated immunity
    (B) Th-2 cells produce interleukin-12, which enhances the formation of Th-1 cells
    (C) Both Th-1 and Th-2 cells have class II MHC proteins on their outer cell membrane
    (D) Before they differentiate into Th-1 or Th-2 cells, naïve Th cells are double-positives; ie, they produce both gamma interferon and interleukins-4 and -5

ANSWERS TO BLOCK TWO

1 (D)	9 (C)	17 (E)	25 (A)	33 (A)
2 (E)	10 (C)	18 (D)	26 (F)	34 (C)
3 (E)	11 (B)	19 (B)	27 (E)	35 (D)
4 (A)	12 (D)	20 (A)	28 (B)	36 (B)
5 (D)	13 (C)	21 (A)	29 (B)	37 (D)
6 (A)	14 (D)	22 (A)	30 (D)	38 (C)
7 (E)	15 (D)	23 (B)	31 (C)	39 (A)
8 (A)	16 (C)	24 (E)	32 (A)	40 (A)

Index

Note: Page numbers followed by *f* and *t* indicate figures and tables, respectively. Those followed by *b* and *n* indicate boxes and notes, respectively. Page numbers followed by *s* indicate summary; those in **boldface** indicate main discussion.

mechanism of action, 237*t*
in pregnancy, 329
New Guinea, Fore tribes of, kuru, 318
New World hookworm, 385
Newborn infants. *See* Neonates
Niacin, *Mycobacterium tuberculosis* production, 164
Niclosamide, for *Dipylidium caninum* infection, 374
Nicotinamide adenine dinucleotide, in *H. influenzae* culture, 65
Nifurtimox, for trypanosomiasis, 353*t*, 363
Nipah virus, 331*t*, 332–333
Nitazoxanide, for diarrhea, *Cryptosporium parvum,* 356
Nitrate reduction, by Enterobacteriaceae, 133
Nitric oxide, 47*t*, **420**
as microbicidal agent, 56
Nitric oxide synthase, 56
Nitroblue tetrazolium dye reduction test, for chronic granulomatous disease, 474
Nitrofurantoin, for urinary tract infection chemoprophylaxis, 140
Nitrogen, liquid, for skin warts, 264
NNTRIs. *See* Non-nucleoside reverse transcriptase inhibitors
Nocardia spp., 24*t*
Gram stain, 103*t*
Nocardia asteroides, 169–170, 490*s*, 529*t*
acid-fast, 169
brain abscess, 170*t*
case history of, 516
characteristics, 490*s*
growth, 170*t*
habitat, 169
Nocardia brasiliensis, 169
Nocardiosis, 24*t*, 170*t*, 529*t*
clinical findings, 169
laboratory diagnosis, 169–170
pathogenesis, 169
sulfonamides for, 77, 170*t*
treatment, 170
Non-A, non-B hepatitis, 297. *See also* Hepatitis C
Noncapsid viral protein 00, 283
Nonchromogens, 165, 166
Nonenveloped (naked) viruses
DNA, 216, 217*t*, 248, **262–265**, 331*t*, 495*s*
RNA, 249–250, **283–290**, 331*t*
Nongonococcal urethritis
Chlamydia trachomatis, 181
Ureaplasma, 172
Nonhemolytic streptococci, 112
Non-Hodgkin's lymphoma, monoclonal antibodies for, 438*t*
Nonhomologous recombination, 21
Non-nucleoside reverse transcriptase inhibitors
for HIV infection, 239, 328
mechanism of action, 239
Nonparalytic poliomyelitis, 284

Nonpermissive cells, 310
Nonseptate hyphae, 334
of *Mucor,* 348*f*, 349, 515
Nonspecific immunity. *See* Innate (natural) immunity
Nonsteroid anti-inflammatory drugs
for rheumatoid arthritis, 467
for systemic lupus erythematosus, 467
Norfloxacin, 78
for urinary tract infection, 110
Normal flora, 25–28, 31
anatomic locations, 25*t*
in cat's mouth, 518
clindamycin suppression of, 27
in colon, 25, 25*t*, 27*t*, 28, 128, 396*t*
colonization resistance, 26, 28, 60
in debilitated individuals, 26
in disease, 26
in genitourinary tract, 28
in immunocompromised individuals, 26
in oropharynx, 25, 25*t*, 28
respiratory tract, 27
in skin, 25, 25*t*, 26–27, 26*t*, 28
Staphylococcal epidermidis in, 107*t*
suppression, 27, 60
throat, 395*t*
vagina, 25, 25*t*, 28–29, 128, 396*t*
Norovirus. *See* Norwalk virus(es)
North American blastomycosis, 344
Norvir. *See* Ritonavir
Norwalk virus (Norovirus), 250, **288**, 499*s*
characteristics, 213*t*, 499*s*
in intestinal tract, 284*t*
transmission, 35*t*
Nose
normal flora in, 25*t*, 28
persistent colonization of *Staphylococcus aureus,* 110
as portal of bacterial entry, 35*t*
Nosocomial (hospital-acquired) infection
antibiotic-resistant, 85
Escherichia coli, 139
Klebsiella-Enterobacter-Serratia, 147
Proteus-Providencia-Serratia-Morganella, 143
Pseudomonas aeruginosa, 149
respiratory syncytial virus, in infants, 274
Staphylococcus aureus, 106
Nramp gene, 163
Nuclear antigen, Epstein-Barr virus, 257
Nuclease(s)
in phagocytosis, 57
Staphylococcus aureus production, 109
Nucleic acid(s), 2*t*
bacterial, antimicrobial drugs inhibiting synthesis of, 77–79
infectious, 200
in microorganisms, 1, 2, 2*t*
modification, 99–100
synthesis, inhibition of, 70*t*
viral, 192, 193, 195*f*
antiviral drugs inhibiting synthesis of, **236**, 237*t*, **238–239**
infectious, 199, 199*f*

Nucleic acid–based methods of diagnosis, 67
Nucleocapsid, 193
helical, 193
icosahedral, 193
Nucleoid, of prokaryotic cells, 2, 5*f*, 6*t*, **10**
Nucleoside inhibitors
for autoimmune diseases, 468
for hepatitis, 296
for herpesviruses, **236, 238–239**
for HIV, 239, 328
for retroviruses, **236, 238–239**
Nucleotides, cyclic, in immediate (anaphylactic) hypersensitivity reactions, 453
Nucleus, eukaryotic cell, 2
Nurse cells, 386
Nystatin
candidiasis, 79, 347
mechanism of action, 70*t*, 79
toxicity, 79

O

O antigen, 10, 13
of Enterobacteriaceae, 134
of *Escherichia coli,* 137
of *Proteus,* 148
of *Salmonella,* 140
of *Shigella,* 142
of *Vibrio,* 143
O antigens (blood group), **449–451**, 450*f*, 450*t*
Obligate aerobes, 104*t*
Obligate anaerobes, 104*t*
Obligate intracellular parasites, 23, 24*t*, 30, 36
bacterial, 30
chlamydiae, 179
rickettsiae, 182
viruses, 192
Ofloxacin, 78
Ogawa serotype, of *Vibrio,* 143
OKT3, 438*t*
Old World hookworm, 380, 381*t*, 382*t*, 385, 390
Omalizumab, for asthma, 456
Onchocerca spp., 381*t*
life cycle, 382*t*
Onchocerca volvulus, 388, 513*s*, 528*t*
characteristics, 513*s*
disease (*See* Onchocerciasis)
microfilaria, 387*f*
Onchocerciasis (river blindness), **388**, 528*t*
treatment, 381*t*, 388
Oncogene(s), **308–309**, 309*t*
amplification and, 309
cancer and, **308–309**
cellular, 308
cytoplasmic proteins, 308
G proteins, 308
growth factor, 308
identification, 308
insertion of DNA copy near, 309
overexpression, 308, 309